Fodor's 99

Italy

The complete guide, thoroughly up-to-date

Packed with details that will make your trip

The must-see sights, off and on the beaten path

What to see, what to skip

Mix-and-match vacation itineraries

City strolls, countryside adventures

Smart lodging and dining options

Essential local do's and taboos

Transportation tips, distances and directions

Key contacts, savvy travel tips

When to go, what to pack

Clear, accurate, easy-to-use maps

Books to read, videos to watch, background essays:

Fodor's Travel Publications, Inc.
New York • Toronto • London • Sydney • Auckland
www.fodors.com

Fodor's Italy

EDITOR: Caragh Rockwood

Editorial Contributors: Barbara Walsh Angelillo, Barbara Lazear Ascher, David Brown, Sheila Brownlee, Nancy Coons, Fionn Davenport, Jon Eldan, Valerie Hamilton, Nancy Hart, Carla Lionello, Patricia Rucidlo, Helayne Schiff, M. T. Schwartzman (Gold Guide editor)

Editorial Production: Melissa Klurman

Maps: David Lindroth, *cartographer*; Steven K. Amsterdam, *map editor*

Design: Fabrizio La Rocca, *creative director*; Guido Caroti, *associate art director*; Jolie Novak, *photo editor*

Production/Manufacturing: Mike Costa

Cover Photograph: Angelo Lomeo

Copyright

Special Sales

Fodor's Travel Publications are available at special discounts for bulk purchases for sales promotions or premiums. Special editions, including personalized covers, excerpts of existing guides, and corporate imprints, can be created in large quantities for special needs. For more information, contact your local bookseller or write to Special Markets, Fodor's Travel Publications, 201 East 50th Street, New York, NY 10022. Inquiries from Canada should be directed to your local Canadian bookseller or sent to Random House of Canada, Ltd., Marketing Department, 2775 Matheson Boulevard East, Mississauga, Ontario L4W 4P7. Inquiries from the United Kingdom should be sent to Fodor's Travel Publications, 20 Vauxhall Bridge Road, London SW1V 2SA, England.

PRINTED IN THE UNITED STATES OF AMERICA

10 9 8 7 6 5 4 3 2 1

CONTENTS

ON THE ROAD WITH FODOR'S

WHEN I PLAN A VACATION, the first thing I do is cast around among my friends and colleagues to find someone who's just been where I'm going. That's because there's no substitute for a recommendation from a good friend who knows your tastes, your budget, and your circumstances, someone who's just been there. Unfortunately, such friends are few and far between. So it's nice to know that there's *Fodor's Italy*.

In the first place, this book won't stay home when you hit the road. It will accompany you every step of the way, steering you away from wrong turns and wrong choices and never expecting a thing in return. *Fodor's Italy 99* includes a wonderful, full-color map from Rand McNally, the world's largest commercial mapmaker. Most important of all, it's written and assiduously updated by the kind of people you *would* hit up for travel tips if you knew them. They're as choosy as your pickiest friend, except they've probably seen a lot more of Italy. In these pages, they don't send you chasing down every town and sight in Italy but have instead selected the best ones, the ones that are worthy of your time and money. Just tear out the map at the perforation, and join us on the road in Italy.

About Our Writers

Our success in helping to make your trip the best of all possible vacations is a credit to the hard work of our extraordinary writers. We'd also like to thank Alitalia for its ever-superb service and generosity, plus the Trentino APT for an eye-opening trip.

After living and working in Italy for six years, **Rob Andrews** decided he was getting too comfortable and retreated to the rougher pastures of England. But he's convinced his quarter-Italian blood is concentrated in his stomach, as he can't help extolling the Mediterranean diet. He returns every year to get his fill.

The first time veteran Fodorite **Barbara Walsh Angelillo** arrived in Rome, she was traveling on a tight schedule; still, she had time to fall in love with both the city and a dark-eyed Italian—simultaneously. Within a year, Barbara said *arrivederci* to her native New York City to settle, marry, and raise three children in Italy. Barbara unwinds in what she calls "two of Italy's most special places," Umbria and the Amalfi Coast.

Based in her 300-year-old farmhouse in Lorraine, **Nancy Coons** divides her time in Italy among churches, museums, and the kitchens of native friends. In addition to the filling research for the essay, "The Artless Art of Italian Cooking," she has tasted many a fondue, Luxembourg ham, and quiche for her work in northeastern France for Fodor's.

Irish-born freelance writer and editor **Fionn Davenport** has spent most of his summers enjoying the delights of the Italian peninsula, a luxury of having an Italian mother. A former editor of *Fodor's Italy,* he has left the Fodor's New York offices in the dust to explore the nooks and crannies of his beloved Italia firsthand.

Jon Eldan studied European history in Berkeley, California, before packing his bags in 1994 to see the real thing. He now lives and bakes bread in Rome, and goes back to visit the old country from time to time. **Carla Lionello** grew up in Venice. Seven years ago she traded Piazza San Marco for the Spanish Steps and moved to Rome. Although she still hasn't learned to drive, it doesn't stop her from traveling all over Italy in search of endangered pastry.

After a decade's long-distance love affair with Rome, **Valerie Hamilton** recently settled in the city permanently, working in television—covering topics from wine making to heli-rescue dogs—in between stints for Fodor's. While classic Italian specialties have charmed her since adolescence, it is Italy's subtle side that has captured her heart: the creative yet calculated twist of a *tortello*, or the gentle curve of an Italian shoe.

Nancy Hart, a former U.S. newspaper and television feature reporter, came to Italy in 1991, expecting to stay the proverbial one year, but failed. Based in Rome, she now travels in the Third World and creates documentary videos (among other things) dealing with developmental issues. Her time spent writing the Chianti chapter was interrupted by travels to Ouagadougou, Abidjan, and Gangtok—interesting places to visit, but the wine isn't nearly as good.

Patricia Rucidlo lives in Florence with her dog, Tillie, who occasionally accompanies her on the Tuscan art history and food beat. Though she has master's degrees in Italian Renaissance history and art history, Patti's true love is Italian food (as is Tillie's). Patti has also taught Italian cooking classes and ran her own catering business in the United States.

New This Year

In *Fodor's Italy 99,* we've expanded coverage of both Tuscany (chapter 4) and Umbria (chapter 12), adding more towns for you to discover during your countryside rambles. Since we know how much you love Venice, we've listed more of our favorite hotels for you to choose from. We've also added some fun "Close-Up" features to give you more background info—they highlight Rome's Jubilee in 2000 (chapter 2); the restoration of Venice (chapter 5); the fashion scene in Milan (chapter 9); and tasty pizza from Naples (chapter 13). Check them out.

Connections

We're pleased that the American Society of Travel Agents continues to endorse Fodor's as its guidebook of choice. ASTA is the world's largest and most influential travel trade association, operating in more than 170 countries, with 27,000 members pledged to adhere to a strict code of ethics reflecting the Society's motto, "Integrity in Travel." ASTA shares Fodor's devotion to providing smart, honest travel information and advice to travelers, and we've long recommended that our readers—even those who have guidebooks and traveling friends—consult ASTA member agents for the experience and professionalism they bring to your vacation planning.

On Fodor's Web site (www.fodors.com), check out the new Resource Center, an online companion to the Gold Guide chapter of this book, complete with useful hot links to related sites. In our forums, you can also get lively advice from other travelers and more great tips from Fodor's experts worldwide.

How to Use This Book

Organization

Up front is the **Gold Guide,** an easy-to-use section arranged alphabetically by topic. Under each listing you'll find tips and information that will help you accomplish what you need to in Italy. You'll also find addresses and telephone numbers of organizations and companies that offer destination-related services and detailed information and publications.

The first chapter in the guide, Destination: Italy helps get you in the mood for your trip. New and Noteworthy cues you in on trends and happenings, What's Where gets you oriented, Pleasures and Pastimes describes the activities and sights that make Italy unique, Great Itineraries lays out a selection of complete trips, Fodor's Choice showcases our top picks, and Festivals and Seasonal Events alerts you to special events you'll want to seek out.

Chapters in *Fodor's Italy 99* are arranged from north to south, with the exception of Rome and Florence which come first. Each city chapter begins with Exploring information, which is divided into neighborhood sections; each recommends a walking or driving tour and lists sights in alphabetical order. Each regional chapter is divided by geographical area; within each area, towns are covered in logical geographical order, and attractive stretches of road and minor points of interest between them are indicated by the designation *En Route.* And within town sections, all restaurants and lodgings are grouped.

To help you decide what to visit in the time you have, all chapters begin with our recommended itineraries. The A to Z section that ends all chapters covers getting there and getting around. It also provides helpful contacts and resources.

At the end of the book you'll find Portraits, wonderful essays about Italian art and regional Italian food, followed by suggestions for pretrip research, from recommended reading to movies on tape that use Italy as a backdrop.

Icons and Symbols

★ Our special recommendations
✕ Restaurant
🏠 Lodging establishment
✕🏠 Lodging establishment whose restaurant warrants a special trip
🐥 Good for kids (rubber duck)
☞ Sends you to another section of the guide for more information
✉ Address
☎ Telephone number
🕐 Opening and closing times
💷 Admission prices (those we give apply to adults; substantially reduced fees are almost always available for children, students, and senior citizens)

Numbers in white and black circles ③ ❸ that appear on the maps, in the margins, and within the tours correspond to one another.

Dining and Lodging

The restaurants and lodgings we list are the cream of the crop in each price range. Price charts appear in the Pleasures and Pastimes section that follows each regional chapter introduction; in city chapters, price charts are in the dining and lodging sections, right before the reviews.

Hotel Facilities

We always list the facilities that are available—but we don't specify whether you'll be charged extra to use them: When pricing accommodations, always ask what's included. In addition, assume that all rooms have private baths unless noted otherwise. In addition, when you book a room, be sure to mention if you have a disability or are traveling with children, if you prefer a private bath or a certain type of bed, or if you have specific dietary needs or other concerns.

Assume that hotels in Italy operate on the **European Plan** (EP, with no meals) or **Continental Plan** (CP, with a Continental breakfast daily), **Modified American Plan** (MAP, with breakfast and dinner daily), or the **Full American Plan** (FAP, with all meals). Such plans are noted in some, but not all, chapters.

Restaurant Reservations and Dress Codes

Reservations are always a good idea; we mention them only when they're essential or are not accepted. Book as far ahead as you can, and reconfirm as soon as you arrive. Unless otherwise noted, the restaurants listed are open daily for lunch and dinner. We mention dress only when men are required to wear a jacket or a jacket and tie. Look for an overview of local dining-out habits in the Gold Guide.

Credit Cards

The following abbreviations are used: **AE**, American Express; **D**, Discover; **DC**, Diners Club; **MC**, MasterCard; and **V**, Visa.

Don't Forget to Write

You can use this book in the confidence that all prices and opening times are based on information supplied to us at press time; Fodor's cannot accept responsibility for any errors. Time inevitably brings changes, so always confirm information when it matters—especially if you're making a detour to visit a specific place.

Were the restaurants we recommended as described? Did our hotel picks exceed your expectations? Did you find a museum we recommended a waste of time? Keeping a travel guide fresh and up-to-date is a big job, and we welcome your feedback, positive *and* negative. If you have complaints, we'll look into them and revise our entries when the facts warrant it. If you've discovered a special place that we haven't included, we'll pass the information along to our correspondents and have them check it out. So send us your thoughts via e-mail at editors@fodors.com (specifying the name of the book on the subject line) or on paper in care of the Italy editor at Fodor's, 201 East 50th Street, New York, New York 10022. In the meantime, have a wonderful trip!

Karen Cure

Karen Cure
Editorial Director

Italy

Europe

SMART TRAVEL TIPS A TO Z

Basic Information on Traveling in Italy, Savvy Tips to Make Your Trip a Breeze, and Companies and Organizations to Contact

AIR TRAVEL

BOOKING YOUR FLIGHT

Price is just one factor to consider when booking a flight: frequency of service and even a carrier's safety record are often just as important. Major airlines offer the greatest number of departures. Smaller airlines—including regional and no-frills airlines—usually have a limited number of flights daily. On the other hand, so-called low-cost airlines usually are cheaper, and their fares impose fewer restrictions, such as advance-purchase requirements. Safety-wise, low-cost carriers as a group have a good history—about equal to that of major carriers.

When you book, **look for nonstop flights** and **remember that "direct" flights stop at least once.** Try to **avoid connecting flights,** which require a change of plane. Two airlines may jointly operate a connecting flight, so ask if your airline operates every segment—you may find that your preferred carrier flies you only part of the way. International flights on a country's flag carrier are almost always nonstop; U.S. airlines often fly direct.

CARRIERS

When flying internationally, you must usually choose between a domestic carrier, the national flag carrier of the country you are visiting, and a foreign carrier from a third country. You may, for example, choose to fly Alitalia to Italy. National flag carriers have the greatest number of nonstops. Domestic carriers may have better connections to your home town and serve a greater number of gateway cities. Third-party carriers may have a price advantage.

Alitalia—in addition to other major European airlines and smaller, privately run companies such as Meridi-

ana and Air One—complete an extensive network of internal flights in Italy. Ask your domestic or Italian travel agent about discounts, which include a 50% family reduction and up to 30% off certain night flights.

Many carriers have prohibited smoking on all of their international flights; others allow smoking only on certain routes or certain departures, so **contact your carrier regarding its smoking policy.**

➤ MAJOR AIRLINES: **Alitalia** (☎ 800/223–5730) to Rome, Milan, and Venice. **American Airlines** (☎ 800/433–7300) to Milan. **Continental Airlines** (☎ 800/231–0856) to Rome and Milan. **Delta Air Lines** (☎ 800/241–4141) to Rome and Milan. **Northwest Airlines** (☎ 800/225–2525) to Milan. **TWA** (☎ 800/892–4141) to Rome and Milan. **United Airlines** (☎ 800/538–2929) to Milan. **US Airways** (☎ 800/428–4322) to Rome.

➤ FROM THE U.K.: Direct service from Heathrow is provided by **Alitalia** (☎ 0171/602–7111 or 0990/448–259) and **British Airways** (☎ 0345/222–111). From Manchester there are one or two direct flights daily to Milan, and at least three weekly to Rome. Privately run **Meridiana** (☎ 0171/839–2222) has direct flights between London and Olbia on Sardinia on Tuesday and Saturday in summer, and daily flights to Cagliari via Florence throughout the year. Lower-priced charter flights to a range of Italian destinations are available throughout the year.

➤ WITHIN ITALY: **Alitalia** (☎ 06/65621 or 06/65643 for main Rome office; 02/62811 for main Milan office). **Meridiana** (☎ 0789/4745057 for main Olbia office). **Air One** (☎ 1478/48880 for reservations and information.

CHARTERS

Charters usually have the lowest fares but are the least dependable. Departures are infrequent and seldom on time, flights can be delayed for up to 48 hours or can be canceled for any reason up to 10 days before you're scheduled to leave. Itineraries and prices can change after you've booked your flight.

In the U.S., the Department of Transportation's Aviation Consumer Protection Division has jurisdiction over charters and provides a certain degree of protection. The DOT requires that money paid to charter operators be held in escrow, so if you can't pay with a credit card, **always make your check payable to a charter carrier's escrow account.** The name of the bank should be in the charter contract. If you have any problems with a charter operator, contact the DOT (☞ Airline Complaints, *below*). If you buy a charter package that includes both air and land arrangements, remember that the escrow requirement applies only to the air component.

CONSOLIDATORS

Consolidators buy tickets for scheduled international flights at reduced rates from the airlines, then sell them at prices that beat the best fare available directly from the airlines, usually without restrictions. Sometimes you can even get your money back if you need to return the ticket. Carefully read the fine print detailing penalties for changes and cancellations, and **confirm your consolidator reservation with the airline.**

➤ CONSOLIDATORS: **Cheap Tickets** (☎ 800/377–1000). **Up & Away Travel** (☎ 212/889–2345). **Discount Travel Network** (☎ 800/576–1600). **Unitravel** (☎ 800/325–2222). **World Travel Network** (☎ 800/409–6753).

COURIERS

When you fly as a courier, you trade your checked-luggage space for a ticket deeply subsidized by a courier service. It's all perfectly legitimate, but there are restrictions: You can usually book your flight only a week or two in advance, your length of stay may be set for a certain number of days, and you probably won't be able to book a companion on the same flight.

CUTTING COSTS

The least-expensive airfares to Italy are priced for round-trip travel and usually must be purchased in advance. It's smart to **call a number of airlines, and when you are quoted a good price, book it on the spot**—the same fare may not be available the next day. Airlines generally allow you to change your return date for a fee. If you don't use your ticket, you can apply the cost toward the purchase of a new ticket, again for a small charge. However, most low-fare tickets are nonrefundable. To get the lowest airfare, **check different routings.** Compare prices of flights to and from different airports if your destination or home city has more than one gateway. Also price off-peak flights, which may be significantly less expensive.

Travel agents, especially those who specialize in finding the lowest fares (☞ Discounts & Deals, *below*), can be especially helpful when booking a plane ticket. When you're quoted a price, **ask your agent if the price is likely to get any lower.** Good agents know the seasonal fluctuations of airfares and can usually anticipate a sale or fare war. However, waiting can be risky: The fare could go *up* as seats become scarce, and you may wait so long that your preferred flight sells out. A wait-and-see strategy works best if your plans are flexible. If you must arrive and depart on certain dates, don't delay.

CHECK IN & BOARDING

Airlines routinely overbook planes, assuming that not everyone with a ticket will show up, but sometimes everyone does. When that happens, airlines ask for volunteers to give up their seats. In return these volunteers usually get a certificate for a free flight and are rebooked on the next flight out. If there are not enough volunteers, the airline must choose who will be denied boarding. The first to get bumped are passengers who checked in late and those flying on discounted tickets, so **get to the gate and check in as early as possible,** especially during peak periods.

THE GOLD GUIDE / SMART TRAVEL TIPS

SMART TRAVEL TIPS / THE GOLD GUIDE

Although the trend on international flights is to drop reconfirmation requirements, many airlines still ask you to reconfirm each leg of your international itinerary. Failure to do so may result in your reservation being canceled.

Always **bring a government-issued photo ID to the airport.** You may be asked to show it before you are allowed to check in.

FLYING TIMES

Flying time is 8½ hours from New York, 10–11 hours from Chicago, and 12–13 hours from Los Angeles.

HOW TO COMPLAIN

If your baggage goes astray or your flight goes awry, complain right away. Most carriers require that you **file a claim immediately.**

➤ AIRLINE COMPLAINTS: U.S. Department of Transportation **Aviation Consumer Protection Division** (⊠ C-75, Room 4107, Washington, DC 20590, ☎ 202/366–2220). **Federal Aviation Administration Consumer Hotline** (☎ 800/322–7873).

AIRPORTS

The major gateways to Italy include Rome's **Aeroporto Leonardo da Vinci,** better known as **Fiumicino,** and Milan's **Aeroporto Malpensa.** If you are going directly to Florence and landing at Rome's Fiumicino, you can make connections at the airport for a flight to Florence; you can also take the FS airport train to Rome's Termini Station, where fast trains for Florence are frequent during the day. Smaller, minor gateways (☞ *below*) are served by domestic and some international flights).

➤ MAJOR AIRPORTS: Rome's **Aeroporto Leonardo da Vinci or Fiumicino** (⊠ 30 km/19 mi southeast of Rome, ☎ 06/65953640). Milan's **Aerporto Malpensa** (☎ 02/38011172).

➤ MINOR AIRPORTS: Milan's **Linate** (⊠ 10 km/ 6 mi east of Milan, ☎ 02/74852200). Venice's **Marco Polo** airport (⊠ Tessera, about 10 km/6 mi north of Venice, ☎ 041/2609260). Florence's **Aerporto A. Vespucci,** called Peretola (⊠ 10 km/6 mi northwest of Florence, ☎ 055/333498) and

Aeroporto Galileo Galilei (⊠ Pisa, 80 km/50 mi west of Florence, ☎ 050/500707). Bologna's **Guglielmo Marconi** (⊠ Borgo Panigale, 7 km/4½ mi from Bologna, ☎ 051/6479615). Naples's **Aeroporto Capodichino** (⊠ 8 km/5 mi north of Naples, ☎ 081/7896111). Palermo's **Aeroporto Punta Raisi** (⊠ 32 km/20 mi west of Palermo, ☎ 091/591698).

BIKES IN FLIGHT

Most airlines will accommodate bikes as luggage, provided they are dismantled and put into a box. Call to see if your airline sells bike boxes (about $5; bike bags are at least $100) although you can often pick them up free at bike shops. International travelers can sometimes substitute a bike for a piece of checked luggage for free; otherwise, it will cost about $100. Domestic and Canadian airlines charge a $25–$50 fee.

BOAT & FERRY TRAVEL

Ferries connect the mainland with all major islands. There is frequent daily ferry and hydrofoil service between towns and lakes in the lake district. Car ferries operate to Sicily, Sardinia, Elba, Ponza, Capri, Ischia, the Lido near Venice, and other islands.

➤ FERRY LINES: **Tirrenia** (☎ 06/4814779 in Rome, 010/258041 in Genoa, 081/7613688 in Naples) operates ferries to Sicily and Sardinia. **SNAV** (☎ 081/7612348) operates high-speed ferries between Naples and Palermo. **Lauro** (☎ 081/5522838) has hydrofoils and car ferries to Capri and Ischia. **Adriatica** (☎ 06/4818341) connects Italy with Greece. **FS** (☎ 0766/23273) ferries sail from Civitavecchia to Golfo Aranci, near Olbia. **Navarma** (⊠ Piazzale Premuda, Elba, ☎ 0565/225211), **Elba Ferries** (⊠ Viale Regina Margherita, Elba, ☎ 0565/220956), and **Toremar** (⊠ Piazzale Premuda 13, Elba, ☎ 0565/31100) serve Elba from Piombino. For the lake district contact **Navigazione Laghi** (⊠ Via Ariosto 21, Milan, ☎ 02/4812086).

BUS TRAVEL

Italy's bus network is extensive, although not as attractive as those in other European countries, partly because of the low cost of train travel.

Schedules are often drawn up with commuters and students in mind and may be sketchy on weekends. Regional bus companies often provide the only means of getting to out-of-the-way places. Even when this is not the case, buses can be faster and more direct than local trains, so it's a good idea to **compare bus and train schedules.**

Local bus companies operate in many regions (☞ Getting Around by Bus *in* individual chapters). In the hillier parts of Italy, particularly in the Alpine north, they take over when the gradients become too steep for train travel. A village shop or café will sometimes double as the ticket office and bus stop. You should **buy your ticket before you board.**

Most of the major cities have urban bus services, usually operating on a system involving the purchase of tickets before you board (from a machine, newsstand, or tobacco store) and stamping the ticket in the machine on the bus. These buses are inexpensive, but they can become unbearably jammed at rush hours. Remember that there are also lunchtime rush hours in the hotter periods, particularly in the south, when people go home for a siesta.

➤ Bus Lines: **SITA** (✉ Viale Cadorna 105, Florence, ☎ 055/278611) operates throughout the country. **Autostradale** (✉ Piazzale Castello 1, Milan, ☎ 02/801161) serves much of northern Italy. **Lazzi** (✉ Via Mercadante 2, Florence, ☎ 055/363041) operates in Tuscany and central Italy. Bus information is available at local tourist offices and travel agencies.

FROM THE U.K.

If you're traveling by bus from the United Kingdom, **bring a few French francs to spend en route.** And be sure to consider the train (☞ Train Travel, *below*), as bus fares are quite high, especially when you take the long and tiring overnight journey into account. Eurolines runs a weekly bus service to Rome that increases to three times a week between June and September.

➤ Information: **Eurolines** (✉ 52 Grosvenor Gardens, London SW1W 0AU, ☎ 0171/730–8235 or 0171/ 730–3499; or contact any National Express agent).

BUSINESS HOURS

Banks are open weekdays 8:30–1:30 and 2:45–3:45. Most churches are open from early morning until noon or 12:30, when they close for two hours or more; they open again in the afternoon, closing about 7 PM or later. Major cathedrals and basilicas, such as St. Peter's, are open all day. Note that sightseeing in churches during religious rites is usually discouraged.

Museum hours vary and may change with the seasons. Many important national museums are closed one day a week, often on Monday. Always check locally. Most shops are open from 9:30 to 1 and from 3:30 or 4 to 7 or 7:30, but they may stay open until 10 according to a new national ordinance. In all but resorts and small towns, shops close on Sunday and one half day during the week. Some tourist-oriented shops in places such as Rome and Venice are open all day, also on Sunday, as are some department stores and supermarkets.

Post offices are open 8–2; central and main district post offices stay open until 6 or 8 PM for some operations. The main post office in major cities is open on Sunday 8:30–7. Barbers and hairdressers, with some exceptions, are closed Sunday and Monday.

CAMERAS & COMPUTERS

EQUIPMENT PRECAUTIONS

Always **keep your film, tape, or computer disks out of the sun.** Carry an extra supply of batteries, and **be prepared to turn on your camera, camcorder, or laptop** to prove to security personnel that the device is real. Always **ask for hand inspection of film,** which becomes clouded after successive exposure to airport X-ray machines, and **keep videotapes and computer disks away from metal detectors.**

ONLINE ON THE ROAD

➤ Internet Cafés: **Internet Café** (✉ Via Marruccini 12, ☎ 06/445–4953. **Internet Centre** (✉ Via delle Fosse di Castello 8, ☎ 06/686–1464).

➤ Photo Help: **Kodak Information Center** (☎ 800/242–2424). *Kodak*

Guide to Shooting Great Travel Pictures, available in bookstores or from Fodor's Travel Publications (☎ 800/533–6478; $16.50 plus $4 shipping).

CAR RENTALS

Rates in Rome begin at $49 a day and $167 a week for an economy car with air-conditioning, a manual transmission, and unlimited mileage. This does not include the 19% tax on car rentals. Note that Italian legislation now permits certain rental wholesalers, such as Auto Europe, to drop the VAT (☞ Taxes, *below*). Many companies impose mandatory theft insurance on all rentals; coverage costs $12–$18 a day.

➤ MAJOR AGENCIES: **Avis** (☎ 800/331–1084, 800/879–2847 in Canada, 008/225–533 in Australia). **Budget** (☎ 800/527–0700, 0800/181181 in the U.K.). **Dollar** (☎ 800/800–4000; 0990/565656 in the U.K., where it is known as Eurodollar). **Hertz** (☎ 800/654–3001, 800/263–0600 in Canada, 0345/555888 in the U.K., 03/9222–2523 in Australia, 03/358–6777 in New Zealand). **National InterRent** (☎ 800/227–3876; 0345/222525 in the U.K., where it is known as Europcar InterRent).

CUTTING COSTS

➤ RENTAL WHOLESALERS: **Auto Europe** (☎ 207/842–2000 or 800/223–5555, FAX 800–235–6321). **Europe by Car** (☎ 212/581–3040 or 800/223–1516, FAX 212/246–1458). **DER Travel Services** (✉ 9501 W. Devon Ave., Rosemont, IL 60018, ☎ 800/782–2424, FAX 800/282–7474 for information or 800/860–9944 for brochures). **Kemwel Holiday Autos** (☎ 914/835–5555 or 800/678–0678, FAX 914/835–5126).

INSURANCE

When driving a rented car you are generally responsible for any damage to or loss of the vehicle. Before you rent, **see what coverage you already have** under the terms of your personal auto-insurance policy and credit cards.

Collision policies that car-rental companies sell for European rentals typically do not cover stolen vehicles.

Before you buy additional coverage for theft, check with your credit-card company and personal auto insurance—you may already be covered. All car-rental companies operating in Italy require that you buy theft-protection policies.

REQUIREMENTS

In Italy your own driver's license is acceptable. An International Driver's Permit is a good idea; it's available from the American or Canadian automobile association, and, in the United Kingdom, from the Automobile Association or Royal Automobile Club. These international permits are universally recognized, and having one in your wallet may save you a problem with the local authorities.

SURCHARGES

Before you pick up a car in one city and leave it in another, **ask about drop-off charges or one-way service fees,** which can be substantial. Note, too, that some rental agencies charge extra if you return the car before the time specified in your contract. To avoid a hefty refueling fee, **fill the tank just before you turn in the car,** but be aware that gas stations near the rental outlet may overcharge.

CAR TRAVEL

There is an extensive network of *autostrade* (toll highways), complemented by equally well-maintained but free *superstrade* (expressways). All are clearly signposted and numbered. The ticket you are issued upon entering an autostrada must be returned when you exit and pay the toll; on some shorter autostrade, mainly connecting highways, the toll is paid upon entering. Viacard cards, on sale at many autostrada locations, make paying tolls easier and faster. A *raccordo* is a connecting expressway. *Strade statali* (state highways, denoted by *S* or *SS* numbers) may be single-lane roads, as are all secondary roads; directions and turnoffs are not always clearly marked.

AUTO CLUBS

➤ INFORMATION: **Australian Automobile Association** (☎ 06/247–7311). **Canadian Automobile**

Association (CAA, ☎ 613/247–0117). **New Zealand Automobile Association** (☎ 09/377–4660). (In the U.K.)**Automobile Association** (AA, ☎ 0990/500–600); **Royal Automobile Club** (RAC, ☎ 0990/722–722 for membership, 0345/121–345 for insurance). **American Automobile Association** (☎ 800/564–6222).

➤ BREAKDOWNS: **ACI Emergency Service** (✉ Servizio Soccorso Stradale, Via Solferino 32, 00185 Roma, ☎ 06/44595) offers 24-hour road service. Dial 116 from any phone, 24 hours a day, to reach the nearest ACI service station.

GASOLINE

Only a few gas stations are open on Sunday, and most close for a couple of hours at lunchtime and at 7 PM for the night. Self-service pumps may be few and far between outside major cities. Gas stations on autostrade are open 24 hours. Gas costs about 2,500 lire per liter.

PARKING

In most cities, parking space is at a premium; historic town centers are closed to most traffic, and peripheral parking areas are usually full. Parking in an area signposted ZONA DISCO is allowed for limited periods (from 30 minutes to two hours or more—the limit is posted); if you don't have the cardboard disk to show what time you parked, you can use a piece of paper. The *parcometro,* the Italian version of metered parking, has been introduced in some cities such as Rome. It's advisable to **leave your car only in guarded parking areas.** Unofficial parking attendants can help you find a space but offer no guarantees. In major cities your car may be towed away if illegally parked.

ROAD CONDITIONS

Autostrade are well maintained, as are most interregional highways. The condition of provincial (county) roads varies, but road maintenance at this level is generally good in Italy. Italians drive fast and are impatient with those who don't. Traffic is heaviest around cities in morning and late afternoon commuter hours, and on weekends.

RULES OF THE ROAD

Driving is on the right, as in the United States. Regulations are largely as in Britain and the United States, except that the police have the power to levy on-the-spot fines. In most Italian towns the use of the horn is forbidden in certain, if not all, areas; a large sign, ZONA DI SILENZIO, indicates where. Speed limits are 130 kph (80 mph) on autostrade and 110 kph (70 mph) on state and provincial roads, unless otherwise marked. Fines for driving after drinking are heavy, with the additional possibility of six months' imprisonment.

CHILDREN & TRAVEL

CHILDREN IN ITALY

Although Italians love children and are generally very tolerant and patient with them, they provide few amenities for them. In restaurants and trattorias you may find a high chair or a cushion for the child to sit on, but rarely do they offer a children's menu. Order a *mezza porzione* (half-portion) of any dish, or ask the waiter for a *porzione da bambino* (child's portion).

Discounts do exist. Always ask about a *sconto bambino* (child's discount) before purchasing tickets. Children under a certain height ride free on municipal buses and trams. Children under 18 who are EU citizens are admitted free to state-run museums and galleries, and there are similar privileges in many municipal or private museums.

FLYING

If your children are two or older, **ask about children's airfares.** As a general rule, infants under two not occupying a seat fly at greatly reduced fares or even for free.

In general the adult baggage allowance applies to children paying half or more of the adult fare. When booking, **ask about carry-on allowances for those traveling with infants.** In general, for babies charged 10% of the adult fare you are allowed one carry-on bag and a collapsible stroller, which may have to be checked; you may be limited to less if the flight is full.

Experts agree that it's a good idea to use safety seats aloft for children weighing less than 40 pounds. Airlines, however, can set their own policies: U.S. carriers allow FAA-approved models but usually require that you buy a ticket, even if your child would otherwise ride free, since the seats must be strapped into regular seats. Airline rules vary, so it's important to **check your airline's policy about using safety seats during takeoff and landing.** Safety seats cannot obstruct the movement of other passengers in the row, so get an appropriate seat assignment as early as possible.

When making your reservation, **request children's meals or a free-standing bassinet** if you need them; the latter are available only to those seated at the bulkhead, where there's enough legroom. Remember, however, that bulkhead seats may not have their own overhead bins, and there's no storage space in front of you—a major inconvenience.

GROUP TRAVEL

When planning to take your kids on a tour, look for companies that specialize in family travel.

➤ FAMILY-FRIENDLY TOUR OPERATORS: **Grandtravel** (✉ 6900 Wisconsin Ave., Suite 706, Chevy Chase, MD 20815, ☎ 301/986–0790 or 800/247–7651) for people traveling with grandchildren ages 7–17. **Families Welcome!** (✉ 92 N. Main St., Ashland, OR 97520, ☎ 541/482–6121 or 800/326–0724, FAX 541/482–0660). **Rascals in Paradise** (✉ 650 5th St., Suite 505, San Francisco, CA 94107, ☎ 415/978–9800 or 800/872–7225, FAX 415/442–0289).

HOTELS

Most hotels in Italy allow children under a certain age to stay in their parents' room at no extra charge, but others charge them as extra adults; be sure to **ask about the cutoff age for children's discounts.**

The Luxury Collection of ITT-Sheraton Hotels has more than 20 properties in Italy, all of which welcome families. Notable are the two on the Lido in Venice, which are right on the beach and have a parklike area for children to enjoy. Club Med has a "Mini Club" (for ages 4–9) and a "Kids Club" (for ages 10 and 11) at its ski village in Sestriere; there are also kids' programs at summer resort villages in Metaponto (Basilicata) and on the islands of Sicily and Sardinia, marketed mainly to Europeans. Some of the Valtur vacation villages also have special facilities and activities for children.

➤ BEST CHOICES: **ITT-Sheraton Hotels** (☎ 800/221–2340). **Club Med** (✉ 40 W. 57th St., New York, NY 10019, ☎ 800/258–2633). **Valtur** (✉ Via Milano 42, Roma, ☎ 06/4821000, FAX 06/4706334).

CONSUMER PROTECTION

Whenever possible, **pay with a major credit card** so you can cancel payment or get reimbursed if there's a problem, provided that you can provide documentation. This is the best way to pay, whether you're buying travel arrangements before your trip or shopping at your destination.

Finally, if you're buying a package or tour, always **consider travel insurance** that includes default coverage (☞ Insurance, *below*).

➤ LOCAL BBBs: **Council of Better Business Bureaus** (✉ 4200 Wilson Blvd., Suite 800, Arlington, VA 22203, ☎ 703/276–0100, FAX 703/525–8277).

CUSTOMS & DUTIES

When shopping, **keep receipts** for all of your purchases. Upon reentering the country, **be ready to show customs officials what you've bought.** If you feel a duty is incorrect, appeal the assessment. If you object to the way your clearance was handled, get the inspector's badge number. In either case, first ask to see a supervisor, then write to the appropriate authorities, beginning with the port director at your point of entry.

IN ITALY

Of goods obtained anywhere outside the EU or goods purchased in a duty-free shop within an EU country, the allowances are: (1) 200 cigarettes or 100 cigarillos or 50 cigars or 250 grams of tobacco; (2) 2 liters of still table wine or 1 liter of spirits over

22% volume or 2 liters of spirits under 22% volume or 2 liters of fortified and sparkling wines; and (3) 50 milliliters of perfume and 250 milliliters of toilet water.

Of goods obtained (duty and tax paid) within another EU country, the allowances are: (1) 800 cigarettes or 400 cigarillos or 400 cigars or 1 kilogram of tobacco; (2) 90 liters of still table wine plus (3) 10 liters of spirits over 22% volume plus 20 liters of spirits under 22% volume plus 60 liters of sparkling wines plus 110 liters of beer.

IN AUSTRALIA

Australia residents who are 18 or older may bring back $A400 worth of souvenirs and gifts (including jewelry), 250 cigarettes or 250 grams of tobacco, and 1,125 ml of alcohol (including wine, beer, and spirits). Residents under 18 may bring back $A200 worth of goods.

➤ INFORMATION: **Australian Customs Service** (Regional Director, ✉ Box 8, Sydney, NSW 2001, ☎ 02/9213–2000, ℻ 02/9213–4000).

IN CANADA

Canadian residents who have been out of Canada for at least seven days may bring in C$500 worth of goods duty-free. If you've been away less than seven days but more than 48 hours, the duty-free allowance drops to C$200; if your trip lasts 24–48 hours, the allowance is C$50. You may not pool allowances with family members. Goods claimed under the C$500 exemption may follow you by mail; those claimed under the lesser exemptions must accompany you. Alcohol and tobacco products may be included in the seven-day and 48-hour exemptions but not in the 24-hour exemption. If you meet the age requirements of the province or territory through which you reenter Canada, you may bring in, duty-free, 1.14 liters (40 imperial ounces) of wine or liquor *or* 24 12-ounce cans or bottles of beer or ale. If you are 16 or older you may bring in, duty-free, 200 cigarettes and 50 cigars.

You may send an unlimited number of gifts worth up to C$60 each duty-free to Canada. Label the package UNSOLICITED GIFT—VALUE UNDER $60. Alcohol and tobacco are excluded.

➤ INFORMATION: **Revenue Canada** (✉ 2265 St. Laurent Blvd. S, Ottawa, Ontario K1G 4K3, ☎ 613/993–0534, 800/461–9999 in Canada).

IN NEW ZEALAND

Although greeted with a "Haere Mai" ("Welcome to New Zealand"), homeward-bound residents with goods to declare must present themselves for inspection. If you're 17 or older, you may bring back $700 worth of souvenirs and gifts. Your duty-free allowance also includes 4.5 liters of wine or beer; one 1,125-ml bottle of spirits; and either 200 cigarettes, 250 grams of tobacco, 50 cigars, or a combo of all three up to 250 grams.

➤ INFORMATION: **New Zealand Customs** (✉ Custom House, ✉ 50 Anzac Ave., Box 29, Auckland, New Zealand, ☎ 09/359–6655, ☎ 09/309–2978).

IN THE U.K.

If you are a U.K. resident and your journey was wholly within the European Union (EU), you won't have to pass through customs when you return to the United Kingdom. If you plan to bring back large quantities of alcohol or tobacco, check EU limits beforehand.

➤ INFORMATION: **HM Customs and Excise** (✉ Dorset House, ✉ Stamford St., London SE1 9NG, ☎ 0171/202–4227).

IN THE U.S.

U.S. residents may bring home $400 worth of foreign goods duty-free if they've been out of the country for at least 48 hours (and if they haven't used the $400 allowance or any part of it in the past 30 days).

U.S. residents 21 and older may bring back 1 liter of alcohol duty-free. In addition, regardless of your age, you are allowed 200 cigarettes and 100 non-Cuban cigars. Antiques, which the U.S. Customs Service defines as objects more than 100 years old, enter duty-free, as do original works of art done entirely by hand, including paintings, drawings, and sculptures.

You may also send packages home duty-free: up to $200 worth of goods for personal use, with a limit of one parcel per addressee per day (and no alcohol or tobacco products or perfume worth more than $5); label the package PERSONAL USE, and attach a list of its contents and their retail value. Do not label the package UNSOLICITED GIFT, or your duty-free exemption will drop to $100. Mailed items do not affect your duty-free allowance on your return.

➤ INFORMATION: **U.S. Customs Service** (Inquiries, ✉ Box 7407, Washington, DC 20044, ☎ 202/927–6724; complaints, Office of Regulations and Rulings, ✉ 1301 Constitution Ave. NW, Washington, DC 20229; registration of equipment, Resource Management, ✉ 1301 Constitution Ave. NW, Washington, DC 20229, ☎ 202/927–0540).

DISABILITIES & ACCESSIBILITY

ACCESS IN ITALY

Italy has only recently begun to provide facilities such as ramps, telephones, and rest rooms for people with disabilities; such things are still the exception, not the rule. Travelers' wheelchairs must be transported free of charge, according to Italian law, but the logistics of getting a wheelchair on and off trains and buses can make this requirement irrelevant. Seats are reserved for people with disabilities on public transportation, but few buses have lifts for wheelchairs. High, narrow steps for boarding trains create additional problems. In many monuments and museums, even in some hotels and restaurants, architectural barriers make it difficult, if not impossible, for those with disabilities to gain access. In Rome, however, the Basilica di San Pietro, the Cappella Sistina, and the Musei Vaticani are all accessible by wheelchair, as is the Uffizi in Florence.

Contact the nearest Italian consulate regarding bringing a Seeing Eye dog into Italy; this requires an import license, a current certificate detailing the dog's inoculations, and a letter from your veterinarian certifying the dog's health.

➤ LOCAL RESOURCES: The **Italian Government Travel Office** (ENIT; Visitor Information, *below*) can provide a list of hotels that provide access and addresses of Italian associations for travelers with disabilities.

MAKING RESERVATIONS

When discussing accessibility with an operator or reservations agent, **ask hard questions.** Are there any stairs, inside *or* out? Are there grab bars next to the toilet *and* in the shower/tub? How wide is the doorway to the room? To the bathroom? For the most extensive facilities meeting the latest legal specifications, **opt for newer accommodations,** which are more likely to have been designed with access in mind. Older buildings or ships may have more limited facilities. Be sure to **discuss your needs before booking.**

➤ COMPLAINTS: **Disability Rights Section** (✉ U.S. Department of Justice, Civil Rights Division, ✉ Box 66738, Washington, DC 20035–6738, ☎ 202/514–0301 or 800/514–0301, TTY 202/514–0383 or 800/514–0383, FAX 202/307–1198) for general complaints. **Aviation Consumer Protection Division** (☞ Air Travel, *above*) for airline-related problems. **Civil Rights Office** (✉ U.S. Department of Transportation, Departmental Office of Civil Rights, S-30, ✉ 400 7th St. SW, Room 10215, Washington, DC, 20590, ☎ 202/366–4648, FAX 202/366–9371) for problems with surface transportation.

TRAVEL AGENCIES & TOUR OPERATORS

As a whole, the travel industry has become more aware of the needs of travelers with disabilities. In the U.S., the Americans with Disabilities Act requires that travel firms serve the needs of all travelers. Note, though, that some agencies and operators specialize in making travel arrangements for individuals and groups with disabilities.

➤ TRAVELERS WITH MOBILITY PROBLEMS: **Access Adventures** (✉ 206 Chestnut Ridge Rd., Rochester, NY 14624, ☎ 716/889–9096), run by a former physical-rehabilitation counselor. **Accessible Journeys** (✉ 35 W.

Sellers Ave., Ridley Park, PA 19078, ☎ 610/521–0339 or 800/846–4537, ℻ 610/521–6959), for escorted tours exclusively for travelers with mobility impairments. **CareVacations** (✉ 5019 49th Ave., Suite 102, Leduc, Alberta T9E 6T5, ☎ 403/986–6404, 800/648–1116 in Canada) has group tours and is especially helpful with cruise vacations. **Flying Wheels Travel** (✉ 143 W. Bridge St., Box 382, Owatonna, MN 55060, ☎ 507/451–5005 or 800/535–6790, ℻ 507/451–1685), a travel agency specializing in customized tours and itineraries worldwide. **Hinsdale Travel Service** (✉ 201 E. Ogden Ave., Suite 100, Hinsdale, IL 60521, ☎ 630/325–1335), a travel agency that benefits from the advice of wheelchair traveler Janice Perkins.

DISCOUNTS & DEALS

Be a smart shopper and **compare all your options** before making any choice. A plane ticket bought with a promotional coupon may not be cheaper than the least expensive fare from a discount ticket agency. For high-price travel purchases, such as packages or tours, keep in mind that what you get is just as important as what you save. Just because something is cheap doesn't mean it's a bargain.

CREDIT-CARD BENEFITS

When you use your credit card to make travel purchases you may get free travel-accident insurance, collision-damage insurance, and medical or legal assistance, depending on the card and the bank that issued it. American Express, MasterCard, and Visa provide one or more of these services, so **get a copy of your credit card's travel-benefits policy.** If you are a member of an auto club, always **ask hotel and car-rental reservations agents about auto-club discounts.** Some clubs offer additional discounts on tours, cruises, and admission to attractions.

PACKAGE DEALS

Packages and guided tours can save you money, but don't confuse the two. When you buy a package, your travel remains independent, just as though you had planned and booked

the trip yourself. Fly/drive packages, which combine airfare and car rental, are often a good deal. If you **buy a rail/drive pass,** you'll save on train tickets and car rentals. All Eurail- and Europass holders get a discount on Eurostar fares through the Channel Tunnel.

ELECTRICITY

To use your U.S.-purchased electric-powered equipment, **bring a converter and adapter.** The electrical current in Italy is 220 volts, 50 cycles alternating current (AC); wall outlets take Continental-type plugs, with two round prongs.

If your appliances are dual-voltage, you'll need only an adapter. Don't use 110-volt outlets, marked FOR SHAVERS ONLY, for high-wattage appliances such as blow-dryers. Most laptops operate equally well on 110 and 220 volts and so require only an adapter.

EMERGENCIES

➤ EMERGENCIES: **Carabinieri** (militarized police; ☎ 112). **Fire** (☎ 115). **Italian Automobile Club** (☎ 116). **Medical emergency and ambulance** (☎ 118; not yet operational in all areas; alternatively call ☎ 113). **Police** (☎ 113).

GAY & LESBIAN TRAVEL

➤ GAY- AND LESBIAN-FRIENDLY TOUR OPERATORS: **Hanns Ebensten Travel** (✉ 513 Fleming St., Key West, FL 33040, ☎ 305/294–8174, ℻ 305/292–9665), one of the oldest operators in the gay market.

➤ GAY- AND LESBIAN-FRIENDLY TRAVEL AGENCIES: **Corniche Travel** (✉ 8721 Sunset Blvd., Suite 200, West Hollywood, CA 90069, ☎ 310/854–6000 or 800/429–8747, ℻ 310/659–7441). **Islanders Kennedy Travel** (✉ 183 W. 10th St., New York, NY 10014, ☎ 212/242–3222 or 800/988–1181, ℻ 212/929–8530). **Now Voyager** (✉ 4406 18th St., San Francisco, CA 94114, ☎ 415/626–1169 or 800/255–6951, ℻ 415/626–8626). **Yellowbrick Road** (✉ 1500 W. Balmoral Ave., Chicago, IL 60640, ☎ 773/561–1800 or 800/642–2488, ℻ 773/561–4497). **Skylink Travel and Tour** (✉ 3577 Moorland Ave., Santa Rosa, CA 95407, ☎ 707/585–

8355 or 800/225–5759, FAX 707/584–5637), serving lesbian travelers.

HEALTH

The Centers for Disease Control and Prevention (CDC) in Atlanta caution that most of Southern Europe is in the "intermediate" range for risk of contacting traveler's diarrhea. Part of this risk may be attributed to an increased consumption of olive oil and wine, which can have a laxative effect on stomachs used to a different diet. The CDC also advises all international travelers to swim only in chlorinated swimming pools, unless they are absolutely certain the local beaches and freshwater lakes are not contaminated.

MEDICAL PLANS

No one plans to get sick while traveling, but it happens, so **consider signing up with a medical-assistance company.** Members get doctor referrals, emergency evacuation or repatriation, 24-hour telephone hot lines for medical consultation, cash for emergencies, and other personal and legal assistance. Coverage varies by plan, so **review the benefits of each carefully.**

➤ MEDICAL-ASSISTANCE COMPANIES: **International SOS Assistance** (✉ 8 Neshaminy Interplex, Suite 207, Trevose, PA 19053, ☎ 215/245–4707 or 800/523–6586, FAX 215/244–9617; ✉ 12 Chemin Riantbosson, 1217 Meyrin 1, Geneva, Switzerland, ☎ 4122/785–6464, FAX 4122/785–6424; ✉ 10 Anson Rd., 14-07/08 International Plaza, Singapore, 079903, ☎ 65/226–3936, FAX 65/226–3937).

HOLIDAYS

National holidays include January 1 (New Year's Day); January 6 (Epiphany); April 4 and 5 (Easter Sunday and Monday); April 25 (Liberation Day); May 1 (Labor Day or May Day); August 15 (Assumption of Mary, also known as Ferragosto); November 1 (All Saints' Day); December 8 (Immaculate Conception); December 25 and 26 (Christmas Day and Boxing Day).

The feast days of patron saints are observed locally. Many businesses and shops may be closed in Florence, Genoa, and Turin on June 24 (St. John the Baptist); in Rome on June 29 (Sts. Peter and Paul); in Palermo on July 15 (Santa Rosalia); in Naples on September 19 (San Gennaro); in Bologna on October 4 (San Petronio); in Trieste on November 3 (San Giusto); and in Milan on December 7 (St. Ambrose). Venice's feast of St. Mark is April 25, the same as Liberation Day. (*See also* Festivals and Seasonal Events *in* Chapter 1.)

INSURANCE

Travel insurance is the best way to **protect yourself against financial loss.** The most useful plan is a comprehensive policy that includes coverage for trip cancellation and interruption, default, trip delay, and medical expenses (with a waiver for preexisting conditions).

Without insurance, you will lose all or most of your money if you cancel your trip, regardless of the reason. Default insurance covers you if your tour operator, airline, or cruise line goes out of business. Trip-delay covers unforeseen expenses that you may incur due to bad weather or mechanical delays. It's important to compare the fine print regarding trip-delay coverage when comparing policies.

For overseas travel, one of the most important components of travel insurance is its medical coverage. Supplemental health insurance will pick up the cost of your medical bills should you get sick or injured while traveling. U.S. residents should note that Medicare generally does not cover health-care costs outside the United States, nor do many privately issued policies. Residents of the United Kingdom can buy an annual travel-insurance policy valid for most vacations taken during the year in which the coverage is purchased. If you are pregnant or have a preexisting condition, make sure you're covered. British citizens should buy extra medical coverage when traveling overseas, according to the Association of British Insurers. Australian travelers should buy travel insurance, including extra medical coverage, whenever they go abroad, according to the Insurance Council of Australia.

Always **buy travel insurance directly from the insurance company**; if you buy it from a cruise line, airline, or tour operator that goes out of business you probably will not be covered for the agency or operator's default, a major risk. Before you make any purchase, **review your existing health and home-owner's policies** to find out whether they cover expenses incurred while traveling.

➤ TRAVEL INSURERS: In the U.S., **Access America** (✉ 6600 W. Broad St., Richmond, VA 23230, ☎ 804/285–3300 or 800/284–8300). **Travel Guard International** (✉ 1145 Clark St., Stevens Point, WI 54481, ☎ 715/345–0505 or 800/826–1300). In Canada, **Mutual of Omaha** (✉ Travel Division, ✉ 500 University Ave., Toronto, Ontario M5G 1V8, ☎ 416/598–4083, 800/268–8825 in Canada).

➤ INSURANCE INFORMATION: In the U.K., **Association of British Insurers** (✉ 51 Gresham St., London EC2V 7HQ, ☎ 0171/600–3333). In Australia, the **Insurance Council of Australia** (☎ 613/9614–1077, FAX 613/9614–7924).

LANGUAGE

In the main tourist cities, language is not a big problem. You can always find someone who speaks at least a little English; remember that the Italian language is pronounced exactly as it is written (many Italians try to speak English by enunciating every syllable, with disconcerting results). You may run into a language barrier in the countryside, but a phrase book and close attention to the Italians' astonishing use of pantomime and expressive gestures will go a long way. Try to **master a few phrases for daily use,** (☞ Italian Vocabulary, at the back of this book) and familiarize yourself with the terms you'll need to decipher signs and museum labels.

LANGUAGES FOR TRAVELERS

A phrase book and language tape set can help get you started.

➤ PHRASE BOOKS AND LANGUAGE-TAPE SETS: *Fodor's Italian for Travelers* (☎ 800/733–3000, 800/668–4247 in Canada, FAX 212/5722–6045 interna-

tional orders; audio set $16.95 [$23.50 in Canada]).

LODGING

Options are numerous, from hotels to camping grounds to short-term rentals in city or country.

APARTMENT & VILLA RENTALS

If you want a home base that's roomy enough for a family and comes with cooking facilities, **consider a furnished rental.** These can save you money, especially if you're traveling with a large group of people. Home-exchange directories list rentals (often second homes owned by prospective house swappers), and some services search for a house or apartment for you (even a castle if that's your fancy) and handle the paperwork. Some send an illustrated catalog; others send photographs only of specific properties, sometimes at a charge. Up-front registration fees may apply.

➤ RENTAL AGENTS: **At Home Abroad** (✉ 405 E. 56th St., Suite 6H, New York, NY 10022, ☎ 212/421–9165, FAX 212/752–1591). **Drawbridge to Europe** (✉ 5456 Adams Rd., Talent, OR 97540, ☎ 541/512–8927 or 888/268–1148, FAX 541/512–0978).**Europa-Let/Tropical Inn-Let** (✉ 92 N. Main St., Ashland, OR 97520, ☎ 541/482–5806 or 800/462–4486, FAX 541/482–0660). **Hometours International** (✉ Box 11503, Knoxville, TN 37939, ☎ 423/690–8484 or 800/367–4668). **Interhome** (✉ 124 Little Falls Rd., Fairfield, NJ 07004, ☎ 973/882–6864 or 800/882–6864, FAX 973/808–1742). **Property Rentals International** (✉ 1008 Mansfield Crossing Rd., Richmond, VA 23236, ☎ 804/378–6054 or 800/220–3332, FAX 804/379–2073). **Rental Directories International** (✉ 2044 Rittenhouse Sq., Philadelphia, PA 19103, ☎ 215/985–4001, FAX 215/985–0323). **Rent-a-Home International** (✉ 7200 34th Ave. NW, Seattle, WA 98117, ☎ 206/789–9377 or 800/488–7368, FAX 206/789–9379). **Vacation Home Rentals Worldwide** (✉ 235 Kensington Ave., Norwood, NJ 07648, ☎ 201/767–9393 or 800/633–3284, FAX 201/767–5510). **Villas and Apartments Abroad** (✉ 420 Madison Ave., Suite 1003, New York,

NY 10017, ☎ 212/759–1025 or 800/433–3020, ℻ 212/755–8316). **Villas International** (✉ 950 Northgate Dr., Suite 206, San Rafael, CA 94903, ☎ 415/499–9490 or 800/221–2260, ℻ 415/499–9491). **Hideaways International** (✉ 767 Islington St., Portsmouth, NH 03801, ☎ 603/430–4433 or 800/843–4433, ℻ 603/430–4444; membership $99) is a club for travelers who arrange rentals among themselves.

➤ ITALY-ONLY AGENCIES: **Cuendet USA** (✉ 165 Chestnut St., Allendale, NJ 07041, ☎ 201/327–2333; ✉ Suzanne T. Pidduck, c/o Rentals in Italy, 1742 Calle Corva, Camarillo, CA 93010, ☎ 800/726–6702). **Vacanze in Italia** (✉ 22 Railroad St., Great Barrington, MA 01230, ☎ 413/528–6610 or 800/533–5405).

➤ IN THE U.K.: **CV Travel** (✉ 43 Cadogan St., London SW3 2PR, England, ☎ 0171/581–0851). **Magic of Italy** (✉ 227 Shepherds Bush Rd., London W6 7AS, England, ☎ 0181/748–7575).

CAMPING

Camping is a good way to find accommodations in otherwise overcrowded resorts, and camper rental agencies operate throughout Italy; contact your travel agent for details. Make sure you **stay only on authorized campsites** (camping on private land is frowned upon), and **get an international camping** *carnet* **(permit)** from your local camping association before you leave home. The Touring Club Italiano publishes a multilingual *Guida Camping d'Italia* (Guide to the Camping in Italy), available in bookstores in Italy for about 30,000 lire, with more detailed information on sites. Camp rates for two people, with car and tent, average about 50,000 lire a day.

➤ DIRECTORY OF CAMPGROUNDS: Write to the **Federazione Italiana del Campeggio e del Caravanning** (✉ Federcampeggio, Casella Postale 23, 50041 Calenzano, Firenze, ℻ 055/8825918) and request *Campeggiare in Italia*; send three international reply coupons to cover mailing. It's also available through the ENIT office in the United States and at tourist information offices in Italy (☞ Visitor Information, *below* and *in* individual chapters).

FARM HOLIDAYS & AGRITOURISM

Rural accommodations in the Agritourism category are increasingly popular with both Italians and tourists.

➤ AGENCIES: **Italy Farm Holidays** (✉ 547 Martling Ave., Tarrytown, NY 10591, ☎ 914/631–7880, ℻ 914/631–8831). **Essentially Tuscany** (✉ 30 York St., Nantucket, MA 02554, ☎ ℻ 508/2282514). **Agriturist** (✉ Corso Vittorio 101, 00186 Roma, ☎ 06/6852342). **Terra Nostra** (✉ Via XXIV Maggio 43, 00187 Roma, ☎ 06/46821). **Turismo Verde** (✉ Via Flaminia 56, 00196 Roma, ☎ 06/3611051).

HOME EXCHANGES

If you would like to exchange your home for someone else's, **join a home-exchange organization,** which will send you its updated listings of available exchanges for a year and will include your own listing in at least one of them. It's up to you to make specific arrangements.

➤ EXCHANGE CLUBS: **HomeLink International** (✉ Box 650, Key West, FL 33041, ☎ 305/294–7766 or 800/638–3841, ℻ 305/294–1148; $83 per year).

HOSTELS

No matter what your age, you can **save on lodging costs by staying at hostels.** In some 5,000 locations in more than 70 countries around the world, Hostelling International (HI), the umbrella group for a number of national youth hostel associations, offers single-sex, dorm-style beds and, at many hostels, "couples" rooms and family accommodations. Membership in any HI national hostel association, open to travelers of all ages, allows you to stay in HI-affiliated hostels at member rates (one-year membership is about $25 for adults; hostels run about $10–$25 per night). Members also have priority if the hostel is full; they're eligible for discounts around the world, even on rail and bus travel in some countries.

➤ HOSTEL ORGANIZATIONS: **Hostelling International—American Youth Hostels** (✉ 733 15th St. NW, Suite 840, Washington, DC 20005, ☎ 202/783–6161, FAX 202/783–6171). **Hostelling International—Canada** (✉ 400-205 Catherine St., Ottawa, Ontario K2P 1C3, ☎ 613/237–7884, FAX 613/237–7868). **Youth Hostel Association of England and Wales** (✉ Trevelyan House, ✉ 8 St. Stephen's Hill, St. Albans, Hertfordshire AL1 2DY, ☎ 01727/855215 or 01727/845047, FAX 01727/844126; membership in the U.S. $25, in Canada C$26.75, in the U.K. £9.30).

HOTELS

Italian hotels are classified from five-star (deluxe) to one-star (very basic hotels and small inns). Stars are assigned according to standards set by regional boards (there are 20 in Italy), but rates are set by each hotel. During slack periods, or when a hotel is not full, it is often possible to negotiate a discounted rate. In the major cities, room rates are on a par with other European capitals: Deluxe and four-star rates can be downright extravagant. In those categories, **ask for one of the better rooms,** since less desirable rooms—and there usually are some—don't give you what you're paying for. Except in deluxe and some four-star hotels, rooms may be very small compared to U.S standards.

In all hotels there is a rate card inside the door of your room, or inside the closet door; it tells you exactly what you will pay for that particular room (rates in the same hotel may vary according to the location and type of room). On this card, breakfast and any other optionals must be listed separately. Any discrepancy between the basic room rate and that charged on your bill is cause for complaint to the manager and to the local tourist office.

Although, by law, breakfast is supposed to be optional, most hotels quote room rates including breakfast. When you book a room, specifically **ask whether the rate includes breakfast** (*colazione*). You are under no obligation to take breakfast at your hotel, but in practice most hotels expect you to do so. It is encouraging to note that many of the hotels we recommend are offering generous buffet breakfasts instead of simple, even skimpy "continental breakfasts." Remember, if the latter is the case, you can **eat for less at the nearest coffee bar.**

Hotels that we list as ($$) and ($)—moderate to inexpensively priced accommodations—may charge extra for optional air-conditioning. In older hotels the quality of the rooms may be very uneven; if you don't like the room you're given, request another. This applies to noise, too. Front rooms may be larger and have a view, but they also may have a lot of street noise. If you're a light sleeper, **request a quiet room when making reservations.** Rooms in lodgings listed in this guide have a shower and/or bath, unless noted otherwise. Remember **to specify whether you care to have a bath or shower** since not all rooms, especially lodgings outside major cities, have both.

Major cities, such as Rome and Milan, have no official off-season as far as hotel rates go, though some hotels will reduce rates during the slack season upon request. Always **inquire about special rates.** You can save considerably on hotel rooms in Venice and Florence and in such resorts as Sorrento and Capri during their off-seasons. Major cities have hotel-reservation service booths in train stations.

➤ BEST-KNOWN CHAINS: **ITT-Sheraton/The Luxury Collection** (✉ 745 5th Ave., New York, NY 10151, ☎ 800/221–2340, 1678/835035 toll-free in Italy, FAX 212/421–5929) has more than 20 Italian properties, almost all five-star deluxe. **Jolly** (☎ 800/247–1277 in New York state, 800/221–2626 elsewhere, 800/237–0319 in Canada, 1670/17703 toll-free in Italy) has 32 four-star hotels in Italy. **Atahotels** (✉ Via Lampedusa 11/A, 20141 Milano, ☎ 02/895261, 1678/23013 toll-free in Italy, FAX 02/8465568; some bookable through E&M Associates, ☎ 212/599–8280 or 800/223–9832) has 20 mostly four- and five-star hotels. **Starhotels** (✉ Via Belfiore 27, 50144 Firenze; ☎ 055/36921, 1678/

SMART TRAVEL TIPS

THE GOLD GUIDE /

60200 toll-free in Italy, 800/448–8355 for bookings, FAX 055/36924) has with 14 mainly four-star hotels. **Space Hotels** (☎ 1678/13013 toll-free in Italy). Book through **Suprana-tional** (☎ 416/927–1133 or 800/843–3311), which about 50 independently owned four- and five-star (some three-star) hotels. **Italhotels** (☎ 1678/01004 toll-free in Italy) also has about 50 independently owned four- and five-star hotels.

AGIP Motels (☎ 06/4440183 reservations in Italy) is a chain of about 50, mostly four-star motels on main highways; the motels are commercial, functional digs for traveling salesmen and tourists needing 40 winks, but they—and the Jolly hotels—can be the best choice in many out-of-the-way places. The Forte group has taken over some top-of-the-line AGIP properties throughout Italy. **Best Western** (☎ 800/528–1234 for reservations), an international association of independently owned hotels, has some 75 mainly three- and four-star hotels in Italy; call to request the *Europe and Middle East Atlas* that lists them.

Family Hotels (✉ Via Faenza 77, 50123 Firenze, ☎ 055/217975, FAX 055/2381905; for information, not booking), which groups about 75 independently owned, family-run two- and three-star hotels (some one-star), offers good value. A spin-off of this group, the **Sun Rays Pool** (☎ 055/4620080) comprises three- and four-star hotels.

MAIL

The Italian mail system can be notoriously erratic and slow. Until a trend toward greater efficiency is confirmed, allow up to 15 days for mail to and from the United States and Canada, almost as much to and from the United Kingdom, and much longer for postcards.

POSTAL RATES

Airmail letters (lightweight stationery) to the United States and Canada cost 1,300 lire for the first 19 grams and an additional 600 lire for every additional unit of 20 grams. Airmail postcards cost 1,100 lire if the message is limited to a few words and a signature; otherwise, you pay the letter rate. Airmail letters to the United Kingdom cost 800 lire; postcards, 650 lire. You can buy stamps at tobacconists.

RECEIVING MAIL

Correspondence can be addressed to you care of the Italian post office. Letters should be addressed to your name, "c/o Ufficio Postale Centrale," followed by "Fermo Posta" on the next line, and the name of the city (preceded by its postal code) on the next. You can **collect it at the central post office** by showing your passport or photo-bearing ID and paying a small fee. American Express also has a general-delivery service. There's no charge for cardholders, holders of American Express Traveler's checks, or anyone who booked a vacation with American Express.

MONEY

COSTS

Italy's prices are in line with those in the rest of Europe, with costs in its main cities comparable to those in other major capitals, such as Paris and London. The days when the country's high-quality attractions came with a comparatively low Mediterranean price tag are long gone. With the cost of labor and social benefits rising and an economy weighed down by the public debt, Italy is therefore not a bargain, but there is an effort to hold the line on hotel and restaurant prices that had become inordinately expensive by U.S. standards. Depending on season and occupancy, you may be able to obtain unadvertised lower rates in hotels; always inquire. Among major cities, Venice and Milan are the most expensive; resorts such as the Costa Smeralda, Portofino, and Cortina d'Ampezzo cater to the rich and famous and charge top prices. Though Capri is generally considered a millionaire's playground, it can accommodate the less affluent. Everywhere in Italy, if you want the luxury of four- and five-star hotels, be prepared to pay top rates.

As in most countries, prices vary from region to region and are a bit lower in the countryside than in the cities.

Good value for the money can be had in the scenic Trentino–Alto Adige region and in the Dolomites, in Umbria and the Marches, and on the Amalfi Coast. With a few exceptions, southern Italy, Sicily, and Sardinia also offer good values, but hotels are not always up to par.

When you make hotel reservations, ask explicitly whether breakfast is included in the rate. By law, breakfast is optional, but some hotels pressure guests to eat breakfast on the premises—and then charge a whopping amount for it. Find out what breakfast will cost at the time you book, or at least when you check in, and if it seems high, avoid misunderstanding by clearly stating that you want a room without breakfast.

Admission to the Musei Vaticani is 15,000 lire; to the Galleria degli Uffizi, 12,000 lire. The cheapest seat at Rome's Teatro dell'Opera runs 25,000 lire; a movie ticket is 12,000 lire. Going to a Milan nightclub will set you back about 35,000 lire. A daily English-language newspaper is 2,500 lire. A Rome taxi ride (1⅓ km, or 1 mi) costs 10,000 lire. An inexpensive hotel room for two, including breakfast, in Rome is about 190,000 lire; an inexpensive Rome dinner is 40,000 lire, and a ½ liter carafe of house wine, 6,000 lire. A simple pasta item on the menu runs about 13,000 lire, a cup of coffee 1,200–1,400 lire, and a rosticceria lunch, about 15,000 lire. A Coca-Cola (standing) at a café is 2,200 lire and a pint of beer is 7,000 lire.

CREDIT & DEBIT CARDS

Should you use a credit card or a debit card when traveling? Both have benefits. A credit card allows you to delay payment and gives you certain rights as a consumer (☞ Consumer Protection, *above*). A debit card, also known as a check card, deducts funds directly from your checking account and helps you stay within your budget. When you want to rent a car, though, you may still need an old-fashioned credit card. Although you can always *pay* for your car with a debit card, some agencies will not allow you to *reserve* a car with a debit card.

Otherwise, the two types of plastic are virtually the same. Both will get you cash advances at ATMs worldwide if your card is properly programmed with your personal identification number (PIN). (For use in Italy, your PIN must be four digits long.) Both offer excellent, wholesale exchange rates, and both protect you against unauthorized use if the card is lost or stolen. Your liability is limited to $50, as long as you report the card missing.

➤ ATM LOCATIONS: **Cirrus** (☎ 800/424–7787). **Plus** (☎ 800/843–7587) for locations in the U.S. and Canada, or visit your local bank.

➤ REPORTING LOST CARDS: **American Express** (☎ 800/554–2639 toll-free or 312/935–3602 collect). **Diners Club** (☎ 0357/5333 or 303/779–1504 collect). **Mastercard** (☎ 1678/70866 toll-free or 314/542–7111 collect). **Visa** (☎ 1678/77232 toll-free or 410/581–3836 collect).

CURRENCY

The unit of currency in Italy is the lira. There are bills of 500,000 (practically impossible to change outside of banks), 100,000, 50,000, 10,000, 5,000, 2,000, and 1,000 lire. Coins are 500, 200, 100 and 50 lire. At press time, the exchange rate was about 1,780 lire to the U.S. dollar, 1,210 lire to the Canadian dollar, and 2,900 lire to the pound sterling. In 1999 the Euro unit of currency will exist alongside the lire, but everyday business will still be conducted in lire.

EXCHANGING MONEY

For the most favorable rates, **change money through banks.** Although fees charged for ATM transactions may be higher abroad than at home, Cirrus and Plus exchange rates are excellent, because they are based on wholesale rates offered only by major banks. You won't do as well at exchange booths in airports or rail and bus stations, in hotels, in restaurants, or in stores, although you may find their hours more convenient. To avoid lines at airport exchange booths, **get a bit of local currency before you leave home.**

➤ EXCHANGE SERVICES: **Chase *Currency To Go*** (☎ 800/935–9935;

935–9935 in NY, NJ, and CT). **International Currency Express** (☎ 888/842–0880 on the East Coast, 888/278–6628 on the West Coast). **Thomas Cook Currency Services** (☎ 800/287–7362 for telephone orders and retail locations).

TRAVELER'S CHECKS

Do you need traveler's checks? It depends on where you're headed. If you're going to rural areas and small towns, go with cash; traveler's checks are best used in cities. Lost or stolen checks can usually be replaced within 24 hours. To ensure a speedy refund, buy your own traveler's checks— don't let someone else pay for them: irregularities like this can cause delays. The person who bought the checks should make the call to request a refund.

OUTDOOR ACTIVITIES & SPORTS

Italians are sports lovers, and there are several daily newspapers devoted solely to sports. *Calcio* (soccer) is fiercely popular in Italy, and if you make the effort to get tickets to a match, you won't be denied fancy footwork and raving fans. The climate makes it almost impossible to resist the temptation to try a cannonball serve on the red-clay tennis courts, sink a birdie putt on a scenic green, or just hike up a hill to savor the fresh air and views. Come winter, skiers take to the resorts and slopes of the Apennines and the Alps for world-class conditions (☞ Regional chapters for recommended resorts).

PARTICIPANT SPORTS

➤ CANOEING: **Federazione Italiana Canoa e Kayak** (⊠ Viale Tiziano 70, 00196 Roma, ☎ 06/36858525).

➤ GOLF: **Federazione Italiana Golf** (⊠ Viale Tiziano 74, 00196 Roma, ☎ 06/36858108).

➤ HORSEBACK RIDING: **Associazione Nazionale per il Turismo Equestre** (⊠ Via Ponte Castel Giubileo 27, 00188 Roma, ☎ 06/3328063).

➤ SAILING: **Federazione Italiana Vela** (⊠ Viale Brigata Bisagno 2, 16129 Genoa, ☎ 010/589431).

SPECTATOR SPORTS

➤ BASKETBALL: **Federazione Italiana Pallacanestro** (⊠ Via Vitorchiano 113, 00189 Roma, ☎ 06/36856514).

➤ SOCCER: **Federazione Italiana Giuoco Calcio** (⊠ Via Gregorio Allegri 14, 00198 Roma, ☎ 06/84911).

➤ TENNIS: **Italian Tennis Federation** (⊠ Viale Tiziano 74, 00196 Roma, ☎ 06/36858510).

PACKING

LUGGAGE

How many carry-on bags you can bring with you is up to the airline. Most allow two, but the limit is often reduced to one on certain flights. Gate agents will take excess baggage—including bags they deem oversize—from you as you board and add it to checked luggage. To avoid this situation, make sure that everything you carry aboard will fit under your seat. Also, get to the gate early, and request a seat at the back of the plane; you'll probably board first, while the overhead bins are still empty. Since big, bulky baggage attracts the attention of gate agents and flight attendants on a busy flight, make sure your carry-on is really a carry-on. Finally, a carry-on that's long and narrow is more likely to remain unnoticed than one that's wide and squarish.

If you are flying internationally, note that baggage allowances may be determined not by piece but by weight—generally 88 pounds (40 kilograms) in first class, 66 pounds (30 kilograms) in business class, and 44 pounds (20 kilograms) in economy.

Airline liability for baggage is limited to $1,250 per person on flights within the United States. On international flights it amounts to $9.07 per pound or $20 per kilogram for checked baggage (roughly $640 per 70-pound bag) and $400 per passenger for unchecked baggage. You can buy additional coverage at check-in for about $10 per $1,000 of coverage, but it excludes a rather extensive list of items, shown on your airline ticket.

Before departure, **itemize your bags' contents** and their worth, and label the bags with your name, address, and phone number. (If you use your home address, cover it so that potential thieves can't see it readily.) Inside each bag, **pack a copy of your itinerary.** At check-in, **make sure that each bag is correctly tagged** with the destination airport's three-letter code. If your bags arrive damaged or fail to arrive at all, file a written report with the airline before leaving the airport.

PACKING LIST

The weather is considerably milder in Italy than in the north and central United States or Great Britain. In summer, stick with clothing that is as light as possible, although a sweater may be necessary for cool evenings, especially in the mountains even during the hot months. Brief summer afternoon thunderstorms are common in Rome and inland cities, so an umbrella will come in handy. In winter bring a medium-weight coat and a raincoat for Rome and farther south; northern Italy calls for heavier clothes, gloves, hats, and boots. Even in Rome and other milder areas, central heating may not be up to your standards, and interiors can be cold and damp; take wools or flannel rather than sheer fabrics. Bring sturdy shoes for winter, and comfortable walking shoes in any season.

Italians dress exceptionally well. They do not usually wear shorts in the city, unless longish Bermudas happen to be in fashion. Men aren't required to wear ties or jackets anywhere, except in some of the grander hotel dining rooms and top-level restaurants, but are expected to look reasonably sharp—and they do. Formal wear is the exception rather than the rule at the opera nowadays, though people in expensive seats usually do get dressed up.

Dress codes are strict for visits to churches—especially the Basilica di San Pietro in Rome and the Basilica di San Marco in Venice—and to the Musei Vaticani. Women must cover bare shoulders and arms but no longer need cover their heads. Shorts are taboo for both men and women. For the huge general papal audiences, no rules of dress apply other than those of common sense. For other types of audience, the Vatican Information Office will give requirements.

For sightseeing, **pack a pair of binoculars;** they will help you get a good look at painted ceilings and domes. If you stay in budget hotels, **take your own soap;** many such hotels do not provide it or give guests only one tiny bar per room.

In your carry-on luggage **bring an extra pair of eyeglasses or contact lenses** and **enough of any medication you take** to last the entire trip. You may also want your doctor to write a spare prescription using the drug's generic name, since brand names may vary from country to country. **Never put prescription drugs or valuables in luggage to be checked.** To avoid customs delays, carry medications in their original packaging. And don't forget to copy down and carry addresses of offices that handle refunds of lost traveler's checks.

PASSPORTS & VISAS

When traveling internationally, **carry a passport even if you don't need one** (it's always the best form of I.D.), and make **two photocopies of the data page** (one for someone at home and another for you, carried separately from your passport). If you lose your passport, promptly call the nearest embassy or consulate and the local police.

ENTERING ITALY

U.S. CITIZENS

All U.S. citizens, even infants, need only a valid passport to enter Italy for stays of up to 90 days.

CANADIAN CITIZENS

You need only a valid passport to enter Italy for stays of up to 90 days.

U.K. CITIZENS

Citizens of the United Kingdom need only a valid passport to enter Italy for stays of up to 90 days.

AUSTRALIAN CITIZENS

Citizens of Australia need only a valid passport to enter Italy for stays of up to 90 days.

THE GOLD GUIDE / SMART TRAVEL TIPS

NEW ZEALAND CITIZENS

Citizens of New Zealand need only a valid passport to enter Italy for stays of up to 90 days.

PASSPORT OFFICES

➤ AUSTRALIAN CITIZENS: **Australian Passport Office** (☎ 131–232).

➤ CANADIAN CITIZENS: **Passport Office** (☎ 819/994–3500 or 800/567–6868).

➤ NEW ZEALAND CITIZENS: **New Zealand Passport Office** (☎ 04/494–0700 for information on how to apply, 0800/727–776 for information on applications already submitted).

➤ U.K. CITIZENS: **London Passport Office** (☎ 0990/21010), for fees and documentation requirements and to request an emergency passport.

➤ U.S. CITIZENS: **National Passport Information Center** (☎ 900/225–5674; calls are charged at 35¢ per minute for automated service, $1.05 per minute for operator service).

SAFETY

The best way to **protect yourself against purse snatchers and pickpockets** is to wear a money belt or a pouch on a string around your neck, both concealed. If you carry a bag or camera, be absolutely sure it has straps; you should sling it across your body bandolier-style. Always be astutely aware of stealthy pickpockets, especially when in jam-packed big-city buses and subways, when making your way through train corridors, and in busy piazzas.

SENIOR-CITIZEN TRAVEL

EU citizens over 60 are entitled to free admission to state museums, as well as to many other museums—always ask at the ticket office. Older travelers may be eligible for special fares on Alitalia. When renting a car, **ask about promotional car-rental discounts,** which can be cheaper than senior-citizen rates.

To qualify for age-related discounts, **mention your senior-citizen status up front** when booking hotel reservations (not when checking out) and before you're seated in restaurants (not when paying the bill). Note that discounts

may be limited to certain menus, days, or hours. When renting a car, **ask about promotional car-rental discounts,** which can be cheaper than senior-citizen rates.

➤ ADVENTURES: **Overseas Adventure Travel** (✉ Grand Circle Corporation, ✉ 625 Mt. Auburn St., Cambridge, MA 02138, ☎ 617/876–0533 or 800/221–0814, ℻ 617/876–0455).

➤ EDUCATIONAL PROGRAMS: **Elderhostel** (✉ 75 Federal St., 3rd floor, Boston, MA 02110, ☎ 617/426–8056). **Interhostel** (✉ University of New Hampshire, ✉ 6 Garrison Ave., Durham, NH 03824, ☎ 603/862–1147 or 800/733–9753, ℻ 603/862–1113). **Folkways Institute** (✉ 14600 Southeast Aldridge Rd., Portland, OR 97236-6518, ☎ 503/658–6600 or 800/225–4666, ℻ 503/658–8672).

SHOPPING

The notice PREZZI FISSI (fixed prices) means just that; in shops displaying this sign it's a waste of time to bargain unless you're buying a sizable quantity of goods or a particularly costly object. Always try to bargain, however, at outdoor markets (except food markets) and when buying from street vendors. For information on VAT refunds, *see* Taxes, *below.*

STUDENT TRAVEL

Italy is a popular student destination, and in the major art cities there are plenty of facilities (information, lodging) geared to students' needs. A students with identification cards may obtain discounts at museums, galleries, exhibitions, entertainment venues, and on some transportation.

LOCAL RESOURCES

The Centro Turistico Studentesco (CTS; ☞ Travel Agencies, *below*) is a student and youth travel agency with offices in major Italian cities; CTS helps its clients find low-cost accommodations and bargain fares for travel in Italy and elsewhere. CTS is also the Rome representative for EuroTrain International.

TRAVEL AGENCIES

To save money, **look into deals available through student-oriented travel**

agencies. To qualify you'll need a bona fide student I.D. card. Members of international student groups are also eligible.

➤ STUDENT I.D.s & SERVICES: **Centro Turistico Studentesco** (CTS; ✉ Via Genova 16, Roma, ☎ 06/4679271). **Council on International Educational Exchange** (✉ CIEE, ✉ 205 E. 42nd St., 14th floor, New York, NY 10017, ☎ 212/822–2600 or 888/268–6245, 𝐅𝐀𝐗 212/822–2699), for mail orders only, in the United States. **Travel Cuts** (✉ 187 College St., Toronto, Ontario M5T 1P7, ☎ 416/979–2406 or 800/ 667–2887) in Canada.

➤ STUDENT TOURS: **Contiki Holidays** (✉ 300 Plaza Alicante, Suite 900, Garden Grove, CA 92840, ☎ 714/ 740–0808 or 800/266–8454, 𝐅𝐀𝐗 714/740–2034). **AESU Travel** (✉ 2 Hamill Rd., Suite 248, Baltimore, MD 21210-1807, ☎ 410/323–4416 or 800/638–7640, 𝐅𝐀𝐗 410/323– 4498).

TAXES

HOTEL

The service charge and the 9% IVA, or VAT tax, are included in the rate except in five-star deluxe hotels, where the IVA (12% on luxury hotels) may be a separate item added to the bill at departure.

RESTAURANT

A service charge of approximately 15% is added to all restaurant bills; in some cases the menu may state that the service charge is already included in the menu prices.

VALUE-ADDED TAX (V.A.T.)

Value-added tax (IVA or VAT) is 19% on clothing, and luxury goods. On most consumer goods, it is already included in the amount shown on the price tag, whereas on services, it may not be.

To **get an IVA refund,** when you are leaving Italy take the goods and the invoice to the customs office at the airport or other point of departure and have the invoice stamped. (If you return to the United States or Canada directly from Italy, go through the procedure at Italian customs; if your return is, say, via Britain, take the

Italian goods and invoice to British customs.) Under Italy's IVA-refund system, a non-EU resident can obtain a refund of tax paid after spending a total of 300,000 lire in one store (before tax—and note that price tags and prices quoted, unless otherwise stated, include IVA). Shop with your passport and ask the store for an invoice itemizing the article(s), price(s), and the amount of tax. Once back home—and within 90 days of the date of purchase—mail the stamped invoice to the store, which will send the IVA rebate to you. A growing number of stores in Italy (and Europe) are members of the Tax-Free Shopping System, which expedites things by providing an invoice that is actually a Tax-Free Cheque in the amount of the refund. Once stamped, it can be cashed at the Tax-Free Cash refund window at major airports and border crossings, you can also opt to have the refund credited to your credit card or bank account, or sent directly home. To save a step at the airport or border, you can send the Cheque to a Tax-Free Shopping address.

TELEPHONES

COUNTRY CODES

The country code for Italy is 39. Here are area codes for major cities: Bologna, 051; Brindisi, 0831; Florence, 055; Genoa, 010; Milan, 02; Naples, 081; Palermo, 091; Perugia, 075; Pisa, 050; Rome, 06; Siena, 0577; Turin, 011; Venice, 041; Verona, 045. When calling from abroad, the initial 0 from the local area code should be left out. For example, a call from New York City to Rome would be dialed as 011 + 39 + 6 + phone number.

DIRECTORY & OPERATOR INFORMATION

For general information in English, dial 176. To place international telephone calls via operator-assisted service, dial 170 or long-distance access numbers ☞ International Calls *below*).

INTERNATIONAL CALLS

Since hotels tend to overcharge, sometimes exorbitantly, for long-distance and international calls, it is best to make such calls from public phones, using telephone cards. At Telefoni offices, operators sell international telephone cards and will help you place your call. There are Telefoni offices, designated TELECOM, in all cities and towns, usually in major train stations and in the center business districts. You can **make collect calls from any phone by dialing 172–1011,** which will get you an English-speaking operator. Rates to the United States are lowest 'round the clock on Sunday and 10 PM–8 AM (Italian time) on weekdays.

From major Italian cities, you can place a direct call to the United States by reversing the charges or using your phone credit card number. When calling from pay telephones, insert a 200-lire coin that will be returned upon completion of your call. You automatically reach an operator in the country of destination and thereby avoid all language difficulties.

AT&T, MCI, and Sprint international access codes make calling the United States relatively convenient, but you may find the local access number blocked in many hotel rooms. First ask the hotel operator to connect you. If the hotel operator balks, ask for an international operator, or dial the international operator yourself. One way to improve your odds of getting connected to your long-distance carrier is to travel with more than one company's calling card (a hotel may block Sprint, for example, but not MCI). If all else fails, call from a pay phone in the hotel lobby.

➤ ACCESS CODES: **AT&T USADirect** (☎ 172–1011). **MCI Call USA** (☎ 172–1022). **Sprint Express** (☎ 172–1877).

LOCAL AND LONG-DISTANCE CALLS WITHIN ITALY

For all calls within Italy—local and long distance—you must dial the area code (*prefisso*), which begins with a 0, as 06 for Rome, 041 for Venice. If you are calling from a public phone you must deposit a coin or use a calling card to get a dial tone.

PUBLIC PHONES

Pay phones accept a 200-lire coin, two 100-lire coins, or a 500-lire coin, but **consider buying a** *carta telefonica* **(prepaid calling card).** Scheda phones are becoming common everywhere. You buy the card (values vary—5,000 lire, 10,000 lire, etc.) at Telefoni offices, post offices, and tobacconists. Tear off the corner of the card, and insert it in the slot. When you dial, its value appears in the window. After you hang up, the card is returned so you can use it until its value runs out.

TIPPING

The following guidelines apply in major cities, but Italians tip smaller amounts in smaller cities and towns. In restaurants a service charge of about 15% usually appears as a separate item on your check. A few restaurants state on the menu that cover and service charge are included. Either way, it's customary to leave an additional 5%–10% tip for the waiter, depending on the service. Tip checkroom attendants 500 lire per person, rest room attendants 200 lire (more in expensive hotels and restaurants). Tip 100 lire for whatever you drink standing up at a coffee bar, 500 lire or more for table service in cafés. At a hotel bar tip 1,000 lire and up for a round or two of cocktails.

From Rome south, tip taxi drivers 5%–10% of the meter amount. Railway and airport porters charge a fixed rate per bag. Tip an additional 500 lire per person, but more if the porter is very helpful. Theater ushers expect 500 lire per person, and more for very expensive seats. Give a barber 2,000–3,000 lire and a hairdresser's assistant 3,000–8,000 lire for a shampoo or cut, depending on the type of establishment.

On sightseeing tours, tip guides about 2,000 lire per person for a half-day group tour, more if they are very good. In museums and other places of interest where admission is free, a contribution is expected (500–1,000 lire). Service station attendants are tipped only for special services, for example, 1,000 lire for checking your tires.

In hotels, give the *portiere* (concierge) about 15% of his bill for services, or 5,000–10,000 lire if he has been generally helpful. For two people in a double room, leave the chambermaid about 1,000 lire per day, or about 4,000–5,000 a week, in a moderately priced hotel; tip a minimum of 1,000 lire for valet or room service. Double amounts in a very expensive hotel. In very expensive hotels, tip doormen 1,000 lire for calling a cab and 2,000 lire for carrying bags to the check-in desk, bellhops 3,000–5,000 lire for carrying your bags to the room and 3,000–5,000 lire for room service.

TOUR OPERATORS

Buying a prepackaged tour or independent vacation can make your trip to Italy less expensive and more hassle-free. Because everything is prearranged, you'll spend less time planning.

Operators that handle several hundred thousand travelers per year can use their purchasing power to give you a good price. Their high volume may also indicate financial stability. But some small companies provide more personalized service; because they tend to specialize, they may also be more knowledgeable about a given area.

BOOKING WITH AN AGENT

Travel agents are excellent resources. In fact, large operators accept bookings made only through travel agents. But it's a good idea to **collect brochures from several agencies,** because some agents' suggestions may be influenced by relationships with tour and package firms that reward them for volume sales. If you have a special interest, **find an agent with expertise in that area**; ASTA (☞ Travel Agencies, *below*) has a database of specialists worldwide.

Make sure your travel agent knows the accommodations and other services. Ask about the hotel's location, room size, beds, and whether it has a pool, room service, or programs for children, if you care about these. Has your agent been there in person or sent others you can contact?

Do some homework on your own, too: Local tourism boards can provide information about lesser-known and small-niche operators, some of which may sell only direct.

BUYER BEWARE

Each year consumers are stranded or lose their money when tour operators—even very large ones with excellent reputations—go out of business. So **check out the operator.** Find out how long the company has been in business, and ask several travel agents about its reputation. If the package or tour you are considering is priced lower than in your wildest dreams, **be skeptical.** Try to **book with a company that has a consumer-protection program.** If the operator has such a program, you'll find information about it in the company's brochure. If the operator you are considering does not offer some kind of consumer protection, then ask for references from satisfied customers.

In the U.S., members of the National Tour Association and United States Tour Operators Association are required to set aside funds to cover your payments and travel arrangements in case the company defaults. It's also a good idea to choose a company that participates in the American Society of Travel Agent's Tour Operator Program (TOP). This gives you a forum if there are any disputes between you and your tour operator; ASTA will act as mediator.

➤ TOUR-OPERATOR RECOMMENDATIONS: **American Society of Travel Agents** (☞ Travel Agencies, *below*). **National Tour Association** (✉ NTA, ✉ 546 E. Main St., Lexington, KY 40508, ☎ 606/226–4444 or 800/755–8687). **United States Tour Operators Association** (✉ USTOA, ✉ 342 Madison Ave., Suite 1522, New York, NY 10173, ☎ 212/599–6599 or 800/468–7862, FAX 212/599–6744).

COSTS

The more your package or tour includes, the better you can predict the ultimate cost of your vacation. Make sure you know exactly what is covered, and **beware of hidden costs.** Are taxes, tips, and service charges included? Transfers and baggage handling? Entertainment and excursions? These can add up.

Prices for packages and tours are usually quoted per person, based on two sharing a room. If traveling solo, you may be required to pay the full double-occupancy rate. Some operators eliminate this surcharge if you agree to be matched with a roommate of the same sex, even if one is not found by departure time.

GROUP TOURS

Among companies that sell tours to Italy, the following have a proven reputation and offer plenty of options. The classifications used below represent different price categories, and you'll probably encounter these terms when talking to a travel agent or tour operator. The key difference is usually in accommodations, which run from budget to better, and better-yet to best.

➤ SUPER-DELUXE: **Abercrombie & Kent** (⊠ 1520 Kensington Rd., Oak Brook, IL 60521-2141, ☎ 630/954–2944 or 800/323–7308, FAX 630/954–3324). **Travcoa** (⊠ Box 2630, 2350 S.E. Bristol St., Newport Beach, CA 92660, ☎ 714/476–2800 or 800/992–2003, FAX 714/476–2538).

➤ DELUXE: **Central Holidays** (⊠ 206 Central Ave., Jersey City, NJ 07307, ☎ 201/798–5777 or 800/935–5000). **Donna Franca Tours** (⊠ 470 Commonwealth Ave., Boston, MA 02215, ☎ 617/375–9400 or 800/225–6290). **Globus** (⊠ 5301 S. Federal Circle, Littleton, CO 80123-2980, ☎ 303/797–2800 or 800/221–0090, FAX 303/347–2080). **Maupintour** (⊠ 1515 St. Andrews Dr., Lawrence, KS 66047, ☎ 913/843–1211 or 800/255–4266, FAX 913/843–8351). **Perillo Tours** (⊠ 577 Chestnut Ridge Rd., Woodcliff Lake, NJ 07675, ☎ 201/307–1234 or 800/431–1515). **Tauck Tours** (⊠ Box 5027, 276 Post Rd. W, Westport, CT 06881-5027, ☎ 203/226–6911 or 800/468–2825, FAX 203/221–6866).

➤ FIRST-CLASS: **Brendan Tours** (⊠ 15137 Califa St., Van Nuys, CA 91411, ☎ 818/785–9696 or 800/421–8446, FAX 818/902–9876). **Caravan Tours** (⊠ 401 N. Michigan Ave., Chicago, IL 60611, ☎ 312/321–9800 or 800/227–2826, FAX 312/321–9845). **Collette Tours** (⊠ 162 Middle St., Pawtucket, RI 02860, ☎ 401/728–3805 or 800/832–4656, FAX 401/728–1380). **DER Tours** (⊠ 9501 W. Devon St., Rosemont, IL

60018, ☎ 800/937–1235, FAX 847/692–4141 or 800/282–7474, 800/860–9944 for brochures). **Gadabout Tours** (⊠ 700 E. Tahquitz Canyon Way, Palm Springs, CA 92262-6767, ☎ 619/325–5556). **Insight International Tours** (⊠ 745 Atlantic Ave., #720, Boston, MA 02111, ☎ 617/482–2000 or 800/582–8380, FAX 617/482–2884 or 800/622–5015). **Trafalgar Tours** (⊠ 11 E. 26th St., New York, NY 10010, ☎ 212/689–8977 or 800/854–0103, FAX 800/457–6644). **TWA Getaway Vacations** (☎ 800/438–2929).

➤ BUDGET: **Cosmos** (☞ Globus, *above*). **Trafalgar** (☞ *above*).

PACKAGES

Like group tours, independent vacation packages are available from major tour operators and airlines. The companies listed below offer vacation packages in a broad price range.

➤ AIR/HOTEL: **Continental Vacations** (☎ 800/634–5555). **DER Tours** (☞ Group Tours, *above*). **4th Dimension Tours** (⊠ 7101 S.W. 99th Ave., #105, Miami, FL 33173, ☎ 305/279–0014 or 800/644–0438, FAX 305/273–9777). **US Airways Vacations** (☎ 800/455–0123).

➤ FROM THE U.K.: **British Airways Holidays** (⊠ Astral Towers, Betts Way, London Rd., Crawley, West Sussex RH10 2XA, ☎ 01293/722–727, FAX 01293/722–624). **Italian Escapades** (⊠ 227 Shepherds Bush Rd., London W6 7AS, ☎ 0181/748–2661). **Page and Moy Holidays** (⊠ 136–140 London Rd., Leicester, LE2 1EN, ☎ 0116/250–7676). **Carefree Italy** (⊠ Allied Dunbar House, East Park, Crawley, West Sussex RH10 6AJ, ☎ 01293/552277) offers accommodations in apartments, castles, and farmhouses.

THEME TRIPS

Travel Contacts (⊠ Box 173, Camberley, GU15 1YE, England, ☎ 01276/677217, FAX 01276/63477) represents over 150 tour operators in Europe.

➤ ADVENTURE: **Adventure Center** (⊠ 1311 63rd St., #200, Emeryville, CA 94608, ☎ 510/654–1879 or 800/

227–8747, FAX 510/654–4200).
Mountain Travel-Sobek (✉ 6420
Fairmount Ave., El Cerrito, CA
94530, ☎ 510/527–8100 or 888/
687–6235, FAX 510/525–7710).

➤ ART & ARCHITECTURE: **Amelia
Tours International** (✉ 28 Old Country Rd., Hicksville, NY 11801, ☎
516/433–0696 or 800/742–4591, FAX
516/822–6220). **Archeological Tours**
(✉ 271 Madison Ave., Ste. 904, New
York, NY 10016, ☎ 212/986–3054,
FAX 212/370–1561). **Endless Beginnings Tours** (✉ 9285 Dowdy Dr., San
Diego, CA 92126, ☎ 619/566–4166
or 800/822–7855, FAX 619/544–
9655).

➤ BALLOONING: **Buddy Bombard
European Balloon Adventures** (✉
855 Donald Ross Rd., Juno Beach,
FL 33408, ☎ 561/837–6610 or 800/
862–8537, FAX 561/837–6623).

➤ BICYCLING: **Backroads** (✉ 801
Cedar St., Berkeley, CA 94710-1800,
☎ 510/527–1555 or 800/462–2848,
FAX 510-527–1444). **Bike Riders** (✉
Box 254, Boston, MA 02113, ☎ 617/
723–2354 or 800/473–7040, FAX
617/723–2355). **Butterfield &
Robinson** (✉ 70 Bond St., Toronto,
Ontario, Canada M5B 1X3, ☎ 416/
864–1354 or 800/678–1147, FAX
416/864–0541). **Ciclismo Classico**
(✉ 13 Marathon St., Arlington, MA
02174, ☎ 781/646–3377 or 800/
866–7314, FAX 781/641–1512).
Classic Adventures (✉ Box 153,
Hamlin, NY 14464-0153, ☎ 716/
964–8488 or 800/777–8090, FAX
716/964–7297). **Euro-Bike Tours** (✉
Box 990, De Kalb, IL 60115, ☎ 800/
321–6060, FAX 815/758–8851).
Europeds (✉ 761 Lighthouse Ave.,
Monterey, CA 93940, ☎ 800/321–
9552, FAX 408/655–4501). **Himalayan
Travel** (✉ 110 Prospect St., Stamford,
CT 06901, ☎ 203/359–3711 or 800/
225–2380, FAX 203/359–3669).
Progressive Travels (✉ 224 W. Galer
Ave., Ste. C, Seattle, WA 98119,
☎ 206/285–1987 or 800/245–2229,
FAX 206/285–1988). **Rocky Mountain
Worldwide Cycle Tours** (✉ 333
Baker St., Nelson, BC, Canada V1L
4H6, ☎ 250/354–1241 or 800/661–
2453, FAX 250/354–2058). **Uniquely
Europe** (✉ 2819 1st Ave., Ste. 280,
Seattle, WA 98121-1113, ☎ 206/

441–8682 or 800/426–3615,
FAX 206/441–8862).

➤ CRUISING: **Annemarie Victory
Organization** (✉ 136 E. 64th St.,
New York, NY 10021, ☎ 212/486–
0353, FAX 212/751–3149). **Euro-
Cruises** (✉ 303 W. 13th St., New
York, NY 10014-1207, ☎ 800/688–
3876, FAX 212/366–4747).

➤ FOOD & WINE: **Amelia Tours** (☞
Art and Architecture, *above*). **An-
nemarie Victory Organization** (☞
Cruising, *above*). **Cuisine Interna-
tional** (✉ Box 25228, Dallas, TX
75225, ☎ 214/373–1161 or FAX 214/
373–1162). **Donna Franca Tours** (☞
Group Tours, *above*). **Hazan Classic
Enterprises** (✉ Box 285, Circleville,
NY 10919, ☎ 914/692–7104,
FAX 914/692–2659).

➤ HOMES & GARDENS: **Coopersmith's
England** (✉ Box 900, Inverness, CA
94937, ☎ 415/669–1914, FAX 415/
669–1942). **Endless Beginnings Tours**
(☞ Art and Architecture, *above*).
Esplanade Tours (✉ 581 Boylston St.,
Boston, MA 02116, ☎ 617/266–
7465 or 800/426–5492, FAX 617/
262–9829). **Expo Garden Tours** (✉
70 Great Oak, Redding, CT 06896,
☎ 203/938–0410 or 800/448–2685,
FAX 203/938–0427).

➤ HORSEBACK RIDING: **Cross Country
International Equestrian Vacations**
(✉ Box 1170, Millbrook, NY 12545,
☎ 800/828–8768, FAX 914/677–
6077). **Equitour FITS Equestrian**
(✉ Box 807, Dubois, WY 82513,
☎ 307/455–3363 or 800/545–0019,
FAX 307/455–2354).

➤ LEARNING: **Earthwatch** (✉ Box
9104, 680 Mount Auburn St., Water-
town, MA 02272, ☎ 617/926–8200
or 800/776–0188, FAX 617/926–
8532) organizes research expeditions.
IST Cultural Tours (✉ 225 W. 34th
St., New York, NY 10122-0913,
☎ 212/563–1202 or 800/833–2111,
FAX 212/594–6953). **Naturequest** (✉
934 Acapulco St., Laguna Beach, CA
92651, ☎ 714/499–9561 or 800/
369–3033, FAX 714/499–0812).
**Smithsonian Study Tours and
Seminars** (✉ 1100 Jefferson Dr. SW,
Room 3045, MRC 702, Washington,
DC 20560, ☎ 202/357–4700,
FAX 202/633–9250).

➤ MOTORCYCLE: **Beach's Motorcycle Adventures** (✉ 2763 W. River Pkwy., Grand Island, NY 14072-2053, ☎ 716/773–4960, FAX 716/773–5227).

➤ MUSIC: **Dailey-Thorp Travel** (✉ 330 W. 58th St., #610, New York, NY 10019-1817, ☎ 212/307–1555 or 800/998–4677, FAX 212/974–1420).

➤ PILGRIMAGES: **Pilgrimage Tours and Travel** (✉ 39 Beechwood Ave., Manhasset, NY 11030, ☎ 516/627–2636 or 800/669–0757, FAX 516/365–1667).

➤ SPAS: **Great Spas of the World** (✉ 55 John St., New York, NY 10038, ☎ 212/267–5500 or 800/772–8463, FAX 212/571–0510). **Spa-Finders** (✉ 91 5th Ave., #301, New York, NY 10003-3039, ☎ 212/924–6800 or 800/255–7727). **Spa Trek Travel** (✉ 475 Park Ave. S., New York, NY 10016, ☎ 212/779–3480 or 800/ 272–3480, FAX 212/779–3471).

➤ TENNIS: **Championship Tennis Tours** (✉ 8040 E. Morgan Trail #12, Scottsdale, AZ 85258, ☎ 602/443– 9499 or 800/468–3664, FAX 602/ 443–8982). **Steve Furgal's International Tennis Tours** (✉ 11828 Rancho Bernardo Rd., #123-305, San Diego, CA 92128, ☎ 619/675–3555 or 800/258–3664).

➤ VILLA RENTALS: **Eurovillas** (✉ 1398 55th St., Emeryville, CA 94608, ☎ FAX 707/648–2066). **Rentals in Italy** (✉ 1742 Calle Corva, Camarillo, CA 93010-8428, ☎ 805/987–5278 or 800/726–6702, FAX 805/482–7976). (Also ☞ Lodging, *above*).

➤ WALKING/HIKING: **Abercrombie & Kent** (☞ Group Tours, *above*). **Above the Clouds Trekking** (✉ Box 398, Worcester, MA 01602-0398, ☎ 508/ 799–4499 or 800/233–4499, FAX 508/ 797–4779). **Backroads** (☞ Bicycling, *above*). **Butterfield & Robinson** (☞ Bicycling, *above*). **Ciclismo Classico** (☞ Bicycling, *above*). **Country Walkers** (✉ Box 180, Waterbury, VT 05676-0180, ☎ 802/244–1387 or 800/464–9255, FAX 802/244–5661). **Euro-Bike Tours** (☞ Bicycling, *above*). **Mountain Travel-Sobek** (☞ Adventure, *above*). **Progressive Travels** (☞ Bicycling, *above*). **Uniquely Europe** (☞ Bicycling, *above*). **Walking the World** (✉ Box 1186, Fort Collins, CO 80522, ☎ 970/498–0500 or 800/ 340–9255, FAX 970/498–9100) specializes in tours for ages 50 and older. **Wilderness Travel** (✉ 1102 Ninth St., Berkeley, CA 94710, ☎ 510/558– 2488 or 800/368–2794).

➤ YACHT CHARTERS: **Huntley Yacht Vacations** (✉ 210 Preston Rd., Wernersville, PA 19565, ☎ 610/678–2628 or 800/322–9224, FAX 610/670– 1767). **Lynn Jachney Charters** (✉ Box 302, Marblehead, MA 01945, ☎ 617/ 639–0787 or 800/223–2050, FAX 617/ 639–0216). **Ocean Voyages** (✉ 1709 Bridgeway, Sausalito, CA 94965, ☎ 415/332–4681 or 800/299–4444, FAX 415/332–7460).

TRAIN TRAVEL

All Italian trains have first and second classes. On local trains the higher first-class fare gets you little more than a clean doily on the headrest of your seat, but on long-distance trains you get wider seats and more legroom and better ventilation and lighting. At peak travel times, first-class train travel is worth the difference. Remember to **always make seat reservations in advance,** for either class.

The fastest trains on the Ferrovie dello Stato (FS), the Italian State Railways, are the Eurostar trains, operating on several main lines, including Rome–Milan, via Florence and Bologna; seat reservations and supplement are included in the fare. Some of these (the ETR 460 trains) have little aisle and luggage space (though there is a space near the door where you can put large bags). To avoid having to squeeze through narrow aisles, board only at your car (look for the number on the reservation ticket). Car numbers are displayed on their exterior. Next-fastest trains are the Intercity (IC) trains, for which you pay a supplement and for which seat reservations may be required and **are always advisable.** *Interregionale* trains usually make more stops and are a little slower. *Regionale* and *locale* trains are the slowest; many serve commuters.

To avoid long lines at station windows, **buy tickets and make seat reservations up to two months in advance** at travel agencies displaying the FS emblem. Agencies cannot make same-day seat reservations, but can sell tickets for the same day. If you have to reserve at the last minute, reservation offices at the station accept reservations up to three hours before departure. You may be able to get a seat assignment just before boarding the train; look for the conductor on the platform. Trains can be very crowded on weekends and during holiday and vacation seasons; reserve seats in advance or, if the train originates where you get on, get to the station early to find a seat. A card just outside the compartment or over the seat indicates whether it has been reserved. Carry compact bags for easy overhead storage.

All **tickets must be date-stamped in the small yellow or red machines near the tracks before you board.** Once stamped, your ticket is valid for six hours if your destination is within 200 km (124 mi), for 24 hours for destinations beyond that. You can get on and off at will at stops in between for the duration of the ticket's validity. If you don't stamp your ticket in the machine, you must actively seek out a conductor to validate the ticket on the train, paying 10,000 lire extra for the service. If you merely wait in your seat for him to collect your ticket, you must pay a 30,000 lire fine in addition. You also pay a hefty penalty if you purchase your ticket on board the train. You can buy train tickets for destinations within a 100-km (62-mi) range at tobacconists and at ticket machines in stations.

Note that in some Italian cities (including Milan, Turin, Genoa, Naples, and Rome) there are two or more main-line stations, although one is usually the principal terminal or through-station. Be sure of the name of the station at which your train will arrive, or from which it will depart.

There is refreshment service on all long-distance trains, with mobile carts and a cafeteria or dining car. Tap water on trains is not drinkable.

To save money, **look into rail passes.** But be aware that if you don't plan to cover many miles, you may come out ahead by buying individual tickets.

➤ FROM THE U.K.: British Rail (☎ 0171/834–2345). **French Railways** (☎ 0891/515–477); calls charged at 49p a minute peak rate, 39p all other times.

DISCOUNT PASSES

If Italy is your only destination in Europe, **consider purchasing an Italian Railpass,** which allows unlimited travel on the entire Italian Rail network. Prices begin at $135 for four days of travel in second class within a one-month period and $194 in first class. Passes that are good for longer periods of time are also available, as are Flexipasses, which allow a limited amount of train travel within a certain period, and the Italian Kilometric Ticket, which is valid for two months and can be used by as many as five people to travel a total of 3,000 km (1,800 mi).

Once in Italy, **inquire about the Carta Verde if you're under 26** (40,000 lire for one year), which entitles the holder to a 20% discount on all first- and second-class tickets. Those under 26 should also inquire about discount travel fares under the Billet International Jeune (BIJ) scheme. The special one-trip tickets are sold by EuroTrain International at its offices in various European cities and by travel agents, mainline rail stations, and youth travel specialists.

You can **purchase the Carta d'Argento if you're over 60** (40,000 lire for one year), good for a 20% discount on all first- and second-class tickets, except for travel June 26–August 14 and December 18–28.

Italy is one of 17 countries in which you can **use EurailPasses,** which provide unlimited first-class rail travel, in all of the participating countries, for the duration of the pass. If you plan to rack up the miles, get a standard pass. These are available for 15 days ($522), 21 days ($678), one month ($838), two months ($1,188), and three months ($1,468). If your plans call for only limited train travel, **look into a EuroPass,** which costs less money than a EurailPass. Unlike EurailPasses, however, you get a limited number of travel days, in a limited number of countries, during a specified time period. For example, a two-month pass ($316) allows five days of rail travel (additional days $42 each) and is good only in France, Germany, Italy, Spain, and Switzerland; rail travel to Austria, Hungary, Portugal, Greece, Holland, Luxembourg, and Belgium can be added to the pass for additional fees.

In addition to standard EurailPasses, **ask about special rail-pass plans.** Among these are the Eurail Youthpass (for those under age 26), the Eurail Saverpass (which gives a discount for two or more people traveling together), a Eurail Flexipass (which allows a certain number of travel days within a set period), the Euraildrive Pass and the Europass Drive (which combines travel by train and rental car).

Whichever pass you choose, remember that you must **purchase your EurailPass or EuroPass before you leave** for Europe.

Many travelers assume that rail passes guarantee them seats on the trains they wish to ride. Not so. You need to **book seats ahead even if you are using a rail pass**; seat reservations are required on some European trains, particularly high-speed trains, and are a good idea on trains that may be crowded—particularly in summer on popular routes. You will also need a reservation if you purchase sleeping accommodations.

➤ INFORMATION AND PASSES: Eurail- and EuroPasses are available through travel agents and **Rail Europe** (✉ 226-230 Westchester Ave., White Plains, NY 10604, ☎ 914/682–5172 or 800/438–7245; ✉ 2087 Dundas E., Suite 105, Mississauga, Ontario L4X 1M2, ☎ 416/602–4195). **DER Tours** (✉ Box 1606, Des Plaines, IL 60017, ☎ 800/782–2424, 𝖥𝖠𝖷 800/282–7474). **CIT Tours Corp.** (✉ 342 Madison Ave., Suite 207, New York, NY 10173, ☎ 212/697–2100, 800/248–8687, 800/248–7245 in western U.S.). Italian rail passes can be purchased through DER Tours or CIT Tours as well.

➤ UNIQUE GUIDEBOOK: *Italy by Train* by Tim Jepson (Fodor's Travel Publications, ☎ 800/533–6478 or from bookstores); $16.

TRANSPORTATION

Public transportation is the fastest mode of travel among Italy's cities. It is also relatively inexpensive in comparison to the costs of renting a car and paying for gas and tolls. Italy's cities are served by an extensive state railway system (FS, ☞ Train Travel, *above*), with fast service on main lines (Milan–Venice–Florence–Rome–Naples) that in some cases beats plane travel in time and cost. The state system and some private lines radiate to smaller towns, but service can be sporadic.

Buses (☞ Bus Travel, *above*), somewhat less comfortable than trains and slightly less expensive, offer more frequent service to certain smaller cities and towns that are served only by secondary train lines, Siena included. Buses are also better relied upon in more rugged areas: the Dolomites, Liguria, Tuscany, and the Amalfi Coast, for instance. Ferries and hydrofoils ply among the islands; some islands, such as Capri and Ischia, have helicopter service, a more expensive alternative.

Getting around in Italy by plane (☞ Air Travel, *above*) is an expensive but viable option, and it is the fastest means of traveling long distances, as in to Sicily and Sardinia. Look for special bargain rates that can defray costs. Train and bus connections between airports and city centers are usually smooth.

Italy has an intricate network of autostrade routes, good highways, and secondary roads, making renting a car (☞ Car Rentals, *above*) for travel among most cities a feasible but expensive alternative to public transportation (not to mention complaints of white-knuckle driving by those inexperienced with autostrade speeds). A car can be a good investment if you are interested in carefree countryside rambles, offering time to explore more remote towns. Having a car in major cities, however, often leads to parking and traffic headaches, plus additional expense in the form of garage and parking fees.

TRAVEL AGENCIES

A good travel agent puts your needs first. Look for an agency that has been in business at least five years, emphasizes customer service, and has someone on staff who specializes in your destination. In addition, **make sure the agency belongs to a professional trade organization,** such as ASTA in the United States. If your travel agency is also acting as your tour operator, ☞ Buyer Beware *in* Tour Operators, *above*).

➤ LOCAL AGENT REFERRALS: **American Society of Travel Agents** (ASTA, ☎ 800/965–2782 24-hr hot line, FAX 703/684–8319). **Association of Canadian Travel Agents** (✉ Suite 201, 1729 Bank St., Ottawa, Ontario K1V 7Z5, ☎ 613/521–0474, FAX 613/521–0805). **Association of British Travel Agents** (✉ 55–57 Newman St., London W1P 4AH, ☎ 0171/637–2444, FAX 0171/637–0713). **Australian Federation of Travel Agents** (☎ 02/9264–3299). **Travel Agents' Association of New Zealand** (☎ 04/499–0104).

VISITOR INFORMATION

TOURIST INFORMATION

➤ AT HOME: **Italian Government Tourist Board** (ENIT; ✉ 630 5th Ave., New York, NY 10111, ☎ 212/245–4822, FAX 212/586–9249; ✉ 401 N. Michigan Ave., Chicago, IL 60611, ☎ 312/644–0990, FAX 312/644–3019; ✉ 12400 Wilshire Blvd., Suite 550, Los Angeles, CA 90025, ☎ 310/820–0098, FAX 310/820–6357; ✉ 1 Pl. Ville Marie, Ste 1914, Montréal, Québec H3B 3M9, ☎ 514/866–7667, FAX 514/392–1429; ✉ 1 Princes St., London W1R 8AY, ☎ 0171/408–1254, FAX 0171/493–6695).

➤ TOURIST OFFICES IN ITALY: **Rome** (✉ Via Parigi 5, 00185, ☎ 06/48899255). **Florence** (✉ Via Cavour 1/r, next to Palazzo Medici–Riccardi, 50100, ☎ 055/290832). **Venice** (✉ Palazzetto Selva, off Piazza San Marco, 30124, ☎ 041/5226356). **Milan** (✉ Via Marconi 1, 20121, ☎ 02/72524301). **Naples** (✉ Piazza dei Martiri 58, 80100, ☎ 081/405311). **Palermo** (✉ Piazza Castelnuovo 35, 90141, ☎ 091/583847).

U.S. GOVERNMENT

➤ ADVISORIES: **U.S. Department of State** (✉ Overseas Citizens Services Office, ✉ Room 4811 N.S., Washington, DC, 20520; ☎ 202/647–5225 or FAX 202/647–3000 for interactive hot line; ☎ 301/946–4400 for computer bulletin board); enclose a self-addressed, stamped, business-size envelope.

WEB SITES

Do check out the World Wide Web when you're planning. You'll find everything from up-to-date weather forecasts to virtual tours of famous cities. Fodor's Web site, www.fodors.com, is a great place to start your on-line travels.

➤ SUGGESTED WEB SITES: For more information specifically on Italy, visit: http://www.initaly.com and http://www.wel.it.

WHEN TO GO

The main tourist season runs from April to mid-October. For serious sightseers the best months are from fall to early spring. The so-called low season may be cooler and inevitably rainier, but it has its rewards: less time waiting on lines and closer-up, unhurried views of what you want to see.

Tourists crowd the major art cities at Easter, when Italians flock to resorts and to the country. From March through May, busloads of eager schoolchildren on excursions take cities of artistic and historical interest by storm.

CLIMATE

Weatherwise, the best months for sightseeing are April, May, June, September, and October—generally pleasant and not too hot. The hottest months are July and August, when brief afternoon thunderstorms are common in inland areas. Winters are relatively mild in most places on the main tourist circuit but always include some rainy spells. In general, the northern half of the peninsula and the entire Adriatic Coast, with the exception of Apulia, are rainier than the rest of Italy.

If you can avoid it, don't travel at all in Italy in August, when much of the population is on the move, especially around Ferragosto, the August 15 national holiday, when cities such as Rome and Milan are deserted and many restaurants and shops are closed. (Of course, with residents away on vacation, this makes crowds less of a bother for tourists.) Except for a few year-round resorts, such as Taormina and some towns on the Italian Riviera, coastal resorts usually close up tight from October or November to April; they're at their best in June and September, when everything is open but uncrowded.

MILAN

Jan.	40F	5C	May	74F	23C	Sept.	75F	24C
	32	0		57	14		61	16
Feb.	46F	8C	June	80F	27C	Oct.	63F	17C
	35	2		63	17		52	11
Mar.	56F	13C	July	84F	29C	Nov.	51F	10C
	43	6		67	20		43	6
Apr.	65F	18C	Aug.	82F	28C	Dec.	43F	6C
	49	10		66	19		35	2

ROME

Jan.	52F	11C	May	74F	23C	Sept.	79F	26C
	40	5		56	13		62	17
Feb.	55F	13C	June	82F	28C	Oct.	71F	22C
	42	6		63	17		55	13
Mar.	59F	15C	July	87F	30C	Nov.	61F	16C
	45	7		67	20		49	10
Apr.	66F	19C	Aug.	86F	30C	Dec.	55F	13C
	50	10		67	20		44	6

VENICE

Jan.	42F	6C	May	70F	21C	Sept.	75F	24C
	33	1		56	13		61	16
Feb.	46F	8C	June	76F	25C	Oct.	65F	19C
	35	2		63	17		53	12
Mar.	53F	12C	July	81F	27C	Nov.	53F	12C
	41	5		66	19		44	7
Apr.	62F	17C	Aug.	80F	27C	Dec.	46F	8C
	49	10		65	19		37	3

➤ FORECASTS: **Weather Channel Connection** (☎ 900/932–8437), 95¢ per minute from a Touch-Tone phone.

1 Destination: Italy

UNDER THE SPELL OF ITALY

THEY CAME FOR THE LIGHT, they came for culture, they came for inspiration. Above all, they came to discover something that was missing in themselves. Passion, perhaps. A heightened sense of awareness. They came not simply to find themselves but to become their best selves.

Keats, Shelley, Byron, James, Goethe, Wagner, Prendergast, Renoir, Monet, and centuries of tourists who did not record their inspiration for the ages, but who, like Miss Lavish in E. M. Forster's *Room with a View,* knew that "one doesn't come to Italy for niceness . . . one comes for life."

And how is this life delivered unto one? If you ask the traveler of this decade, the answers will be various. For some it is the layers of history, physically present to walk upon, the reassuring sense of place and continuity that comes from a casual coexistence with antiquity. Twentieth-century businessmen and -women stroll through the Roman Forum, swinging their briefcases and chatting of today's deals as they pass between the 5th-century-BC Corinthian columns of the Temple of Castor and Pollux.

It is as if one could hold out a hand and feel the touch of Pliny the Elder, Livy, or Catullus. A young woman, fresh from college Latin, made the mistake of visiting the Forum at high noon in August, suffered heat stroke, and was certain she heard Cicero speak before she fainted. There are those who would tell you that it wasn't the heat—Cicero *had* spoken.

Another woman, seven months pregnant when she and her husband traveled to Ravenna, swears that as she beheld the dazzling gold and lapis lazuli of San Vitale's 5th-century mosaics her unborn child leapt for joy. There is no guarding against it; life will fill you to brimming as Italy has its way with you.

For the sybarite, the palate is awakened by the clear, true flavors of wine and food that taste faintly of the earth and sea from which they came. Buckwheat pasta in Bormio; polenta, black with squid ink, in Venice; creamy gelato at Giolitti in Rome; or the perfectly comforting bowl of risotto in Siena, served by a family in their nameless restaurant. You will hear, on the other side of the Atlantic, the longings of travelers returned home, who, as the light begins to change in early September, yearn for *gamberetti,* Venetian shrimp the size of a baby's fingertip. Summer causes them to recall the simple delight of sitting beneath large shade trees on the banks of Lake Como, drinking cool wine from earthenware pitchers. Winter's winds bring memories of Alpine chills chased by a fiery draft of grappa.

It is the dream that takes you back, just as it was the dream that enveloped you while you were there. You will notice that those who travel in Italy seem to do so in a state of reverie. Perhaps it is the diaphanous gauze of light that softens physical outlines and blurs the distinction between past and present. A light conducive to daydreams. A light that both intensifies life and makes it gentler to the touch.

Of course, there are those who have been rudely awakened from the dream by a revved-up 1990s state-of-the-art motorcycle outside their 19th-century Roman hotel. They will grumpily tell of the shocking presence of 20th-century blight in a land that seemed impervious to such intrusion. In the heat of disillusion, they will complain of the "real" Italy, of Roman traffic jams, thefts in Naples, Venice as Disneyland, a highway system around Milan as attractive as the New Jersey Turnpike. They will warn that you, a woman, must not be persuaded by the charms of an Italian gentleman who commits his heart and future within a three-minute walk across a piazza.

There is truth in what they say, but the generosity of the Italians and the striking physical beauty of their land make it possible to live in the dream alongside the blight. You cannot arrive in Venice without driving through the gray air of Mestre, polluted by oil refineries. But once your water taxi is negotiating the Grand Canal, you lose yourself in time and space. And that is what Italy is about . . . losing and finding yourself in time and space. By morning, as the rudely awakened dreamer stands on the Palatine Hill and smells the wild fennel just as Horace did, all is forgiven.

It is the natural as well as the man-made wonders that entrance. In the Valtellina Valley you will sit in grottoes where the Caesars sat to soak in hot mineral springs, and you will feel the curing effects of waters that were said to ease the pain of gout, arthritis, and politics. You can indulge in the mindless delights of the Amalfi Coast exactly as 19th-century English travelers did when they came to rest their minds, weary from the obligatory acquisition of culture in the north. Here, where rocky cliffs are caught in a perpetual dive to the sea, nothing seems more important than tonight's dinner or lovemaking.

Italy may be the most sensual of countries. Perhaps it is the basic simplicity that returns one to the simplest human emotions: the organic nature of all that surrounds you, each century seeming to grow from the land. Or perhaps it is the heightened sense of romance that comes from the constant reminders of the very best of that of which people are capable—the serenity of Bellini's altarpiece in San Zaccaria, the compassion of Michelangelo's *Pietà* in St. Peter's, the symmetry of a Palladian villa rising from the earth of the Veneto. Or it could be living among people for whom life's pleasures are celebrated rather than guiltily indulged.

Whatever it is, to experience Italy one needs time, not necessarily in days but in solitude. It is in the silent times that Italy will be revealed to you. Early morning, watching the light shine on the Pantheon, while strong Italian coffee wakens your senses. Dawn on the Grand Canal as dark green water is sprayed with gold and the only sound is a gondolier's oar breaking the silent surface. Midnight in the Forum, Daisy Miller's undoing and Byron's inspiration. Sunrise in Stelvio National Park, where eagles soar overhead and you are knee-deep in wildflowers.

And one must believe in that elusive commodity, happiness. This is a country that, through the ages, in fact and fiction, has promised that possibility. Goethe, having fled the restrictive court life of Weimar, wrote from Rome in September 1788: "I can honestly say I have never been so happy in my life as now." And in *Room with a View,* Forster observed that when his young provincial heroine, Lucy, finally dared forfeit her Baedeker for experience, "then the pernicious charm of Italy worked on her, and, instead of acquiring information, she began to be happy."

You, too, should relinquish this book from time to time and observe with an uninstructed eye, drift into the dream, and allow yourself to be charmed.

— Barbara Lazear Ascher

NEW AND NOTEWORTHY

During 1999 in Rome the rush to finish public works and infrastructure planned for the **Jubilee Year of 2000** will be evident in road works in progress and in the number of public buildings still covered with shrouds of scaffolding for restoration. The cleaning of the facade of the Basilica di San Pietro itself will be concluded in 1999. Among the Vatican facilities being constructed to handle the millions of pilgrims who will arrive for the Jubilee is an entirely new entrance to the Vatican Museums, which will be near the former one on Viale Vaticano. Since you are to be channeled on a one-way route, exiting from what was formerly the entrance, your itineraries will be altered slightly. On the edge of the Vatican, work continues for the construction of a huge underground garage for tour buses within a bastion of the Vatican walls. For more Jubilee details, ☞ Close-Up: Jubilee 2000 *in* Chapter 2.

For museum goers, the most welcome news has been the **extension of opening hours** of a number of major museums throughout Italy, which are now open roughly from 9 AM to 10 PM on weekdays (except for one day closed) and from 9 to 8 or so on Sunday. It is expected that the hours will alleviate overcrowding and long waits for entrance at the major galleries. In Rome, the list includes the newly refurbished and highly popular Galleria Borghese, as well as the recently opened Palazzo Massimo alle Terme and Palazzo Altemps, which contain marvelous antiquities, and the Galleria Nazionale d'Arte Antica in Palazzo Barberini. You don't even have to appreciate art to enjoy an evening visit to Castel Sant'Angelo, where terraces afford spectacular views of Rome by night. Also open late, the Galleria d'Arte Moderna in Rome now has a terrace café-restaurant that has become a chic rendezvous.

The Pinacoteca Brera in Milan (where Da Vinci's *Last Supper* also is on view until 10 PM), the Galleria dell'Accademia in Venice, and, of course, the Galleria degli Uffizi in Florence are also open late. You can visit Michelangelo's *David* in Florence's Galleria dell'Accademia until 10, and linger in the Galleria Palatina in Palazzo Pitti. In Naples, where the early (2 PM) closing of the Museo Nazionale Archeologico has always irked museum goers, the museum is finally accessible all day long, until 10, as is the Museo di Capodimonte. In a number of smaller cities and towns, such gems as Palazzo Ducale in Mantua and the Reggia in Caserta are now open until 10, but on Sunday only.

The **telephone dialing system** in Italy has changed. Even for local calls, you must dial the area code: for example, within Rome you have to dial 06 (the area code) before the number you are calling. The system of calling Italy from outside the country will also change; to call Rome you now dial 39-06-(plus the local number). No area code is required for emergency numbers such as 112 (carabinieri) or 118 (ambulance or emergency).

Plans to recruit business sponsors to foot the bills for the extensive restoration work needed at **Pompeii,** Italy's most-visited site, should make exploring the ruins a more pleasant and satisfying experience. The lack of maintenance and information at Pompeii has long been lamented by visitors. A long-term restoration project should be underway in 1999.

Rome loses one obelisk and gains another: The **Obelisk of Axum,** a victory trophy brought from Ethiopia by Mussolini and placed near the Circo Massimo, has been returned to that country as a gesture of reconciliation. U.S. architect Richard Meier is putting up a new obelisk as part of his refurbishing of **Piazza dell'Augusteo** and the building containing the **Ara Pacis.** Many of Rome's piazzas, large and small, central or not, have been done over

as part of a beautification project focused on Jubilee Year 2000.

You now have to pay a small entrance fee to visit 13 of **Venice**'s most interesting churches. At 12 of the churches, including the Redentore, San Giorgio dei Greci, and San Stae, admission is 2,000 lire; Chiesa dei Frari is 3,000 lire. Admission to San Marco is still free. Daily tickets valid for entrance to six churches cost 10,000 lire; a three-month ticket for all 13 churches is 26,000 lire. The churches are open Monday–Saturday 10–6 and Sunday 3–6.

Thanks to the new *Sicilia Jet* ferry service, it is easy to make a quick excursion from Naples to Sicily. The ferry, which takes cars, leaves from Naples at convenient times of the day, and reaches Palermo in only four hours. It is run by SNAV (☎ 167/254138 toll-free, ℻ 081/7612141); you can call direct or get details from travel agents.

Several small airlines have elbowed in on the former Alitalia monopoly of air routes in Italy and Europe. Among them are Virgin, Debonair, and Air Europe. They offer competitive rates and often use airports that are closer to the city centers than the big hub airports.

WHAT'S WHERE

Like a Santa Claus stocking, the boot of Italy overflows with unsurpassable sights—from top to toe. Here is a sampling of the infinite variety of the country's many regions and attractions.

Rome

Latium's holy claim to fame, Rome is split on its west side by the zigzagged Tiber River, which is a mere 25 km (16 mi) from its mouth at the Tyrrhenian Sea. Antique, Renaissance, Baroque—and always papal—the Eternal City allows you a walk around where Nero fiddled, a visit to the Forum in which the Romans crowded to hear Mark Antony's eulogy, and a lunch in the vicinity of Charlemagne's coronation site. Rome possesses a veritable Grand Canyon of culture, built up with stratified layers of pagan, medieval, and modern. But it's also about a walk through the cobblestone alleys of Trastevere—Rome's Greenwich Village; a Campari break in a timeless piazza; an hour stolen alongside a splashing fountain, blessed by the balm of Roman sunshine. From here you are a cool 190 km (117 mi) northwest of Naples, the gateway to the splendorous south.

Florence

Florence, the "Athens of Italy" and the key to the Renaissance, hugs the banks of the Arno River where it lies folded among the emerald cypress-studded hills of north-central Tuscany. Elegant and somewhat aloof, as if set apart by its past greatness, this historic center of European civilization still shares with Rome the honor of first place among Italian cities for the magnitude of its artistic works, among them Botticelli's goddess and Michelangelo's powerful *David*. Down every street and *vicolo* (alley) and in every piazza you'll make new discoveries of Romanesque, Gothic, or Renaissance architecture; sheltered within these churches, cloisters, and towers are masterful painting and sculpture of the Quattrocento and Cinquecento periods. Equally as splendid are the magnificent chapels and palaces of the Medici—whose patronage rocketed Florence to the forefront of the Renaissance—which stand unabashed amid the city's vibrant modern pulse.

Tuscany

Without a doubt, Nature outdid herself in Tuscany, the region on the Ligurian and Tyrrhenian seas that beholds Florence. Punctuated by thickly wooded hills, snowcapped peaks, sun-warmed vineyards, olive groves, and dramatic hill towns, Tuscany's milk-and-honey vistas have changed little since Renaissance artists first beheld them. Not surprisingly, you'll find some of Italy's greatest art treasures here, including the 13th-century Leaning Tower of Pisa and Piero della Francesca's *Legend of the True Cross* frescoes in Arezzo. The time traveler will be entranced by medieval Siena, "the Pompeii of the Middle Ages," as it was called by the philosopher Taine. Perched dramatically above a fertile valley, San Gimignano—with its Manhattanlike skyline of medieval towers—may jettison you into a Who-turned-back-the-clock? sensation of Mark Twain's Connecticut Yankee when he arrived in King Arthur's court. With a glass of Vernaccia di San Gimignano in hand, you'll feel like lingering long.

Venice

Rising from the waters of the Venetian lagoons like a mirage, the city of canals is unlike any other. A romantic maze of alleys, waterways, and tiny squares and bridges playing hide-and-seek with each other, Venice is a magical world apart. In this city of Marco Polo, Titian, and Vivaldi, a vaporetto ride down the Grand Canal—Venice's own Fifth Avenue—is a fairy-tale-like journey past the city's shimmering, slightly decaying palaces, the Ca' Rezzonico, the Palazzo Pésaro, and the Ca' d'Oro. "Venice is like eating an entire box of chocolate liqueurs in one go," Truman Capote once remarked, and he's right: the city is stuffed with the most spectacular Bellini, Veronese, and Tiepolo paintings. During February's Carnivale, you'll find even the pigeons are pressed for space in Piazza San Marco, the city's heart. The best time to catch Venice is during the Historic Regatta (the first week of September) when the 18th-century canvases of Canaletto seem to come to life.

Venetian Arc

The green plains of the mainland stretching beyond the Venetian lagoon harbor some of Italy's smaller art cities, individual artistic variations on the overall Venetian theme. Elegant Vicenza, which bears the signature of the great 16th-century architect Andrea Palladio, blends rustic beauty with a jigger of 18th-century Venetian chic. Here, the wealthy citizenry devised ways to make la vita all the more dolce at noble villas (many of which are now museums): Palladio's La Rotonda, Villa Pisani in Stra, and the Villa Barbaro in Maser. Farther west, Verona is famed for the Tombs of the Della Scala lords, the romantic settings associated with Shakespeare's *Romeo and Juliet*, and an ancient Roman arena (still packing in the crowds for thrilling opera performances). Art lovers head for Padua to catch Giotto's Scrovegni Chapel and Donatello's powerful statue of the *condottiere* (mercenary general) Gattamelata. To truly unwind, head for Asolo, the City with a Hundred Horizons: it's a magical hill town replete with villas and gardens, but there's not a single souvenir shop or espresso bar.

Italian Riviera

The Italians perfected *il dolce far niente*—the sweet art of idleness—and they must have done it right here in Liguria, site of the Italian rivieras. Called "the island," the province is enclosed by mountain ranges that create an ideal climate for the narrow coastal strip (you can sip coffee outdoors in winter and linger under palm trees at Christmastime). Here, in patinated jet-set resorts and quaint fishing villages, tourists recover from vacation overload. The Riviera di Ponente (Western Riviera) runs from the French border to Genoa and is best known for San Remo, Monte Carlo's less expensive cousin. The eastern counterpart, the Riviera di Levante, is made up of Camogli, Rapallo, Levanto, Cinque Terre, Portovenere, San Fruttuoso, glowing like pearls on a string. Of these, Portofino—the Palm Beach of Italy—is the beauty-contest winner. The Crusaders, who once used Portofino for its refueling resources, have been replaced by today's top-of-the-heap who arrive in their yachts to sun and soak. When doing nothing becomes too exhausting, there is always Genoa—the region's thriving metropolis—for stimulation.

Piedmont/Valle d'Aosta

Piedmont and the grand Valle d'Aosta in the northwest corner of Italy come as delightful surprises in a land of continuous natural splendor. The characteristics of neighboring France and Switzerland blend harmoniously with the region's Italian heritage. Geographically, the area combines the lure of the highest Alpine peaks—such as Monte Bianco and Monte Cervino (the Matterhorn)—in ranges that fan out along the south, west, and north boundaries and the broad flatlands of the plain. Here, at Breuil-Cervinia, Courmayeur, and Sestriere, skiing is at its best. Alpine valleys harboring 14th- and 15th-century castles—witnesses to turbulent days of old—are anchored by Turin, the "Italian Detroit," home of the Fiat empire. The city's other well-known imports—Borsalino hats, vermouth, and Asti Spumante—mark it as a great cosmopolitan center.

Milan, Lombardy, and the Lakes

Lombardy stretches south from the Alps to the River Po, and not far from the modern metropolis of Milan are the dreamlike resort lakes of Como, Maggiore, and Garda, whose 19th-century summer palaces, exotic formal gardens, and Alpine vistas give them some of the most stunning settings in Italy. Milan's cultural identity is as diverse as its changeable weather: international fashion capital, industrial and banking center, crucible of modern design. The must-see's here include Teatro alla Scala—the equivalent of paradise to opera performers and fans; the gigantic Gothic Duomo; Leonardo da Vinci's *The Last Supper;* and, of course, stopping and shopping at Versace, Valentino, and Armani. Farther south, tour the great Renaissance cities of the plain: Pavia, Cremona, and Mantua, home to the palaces of the Gonzaga. On the edge of the Alps, Bergamo awaits with its hilltop *città alta,* a charming medieval center. For those who believe holidays are fantasies, the apricot-color villages, palaces, and gardens of the lakes region cannot be bettered. Lake Como has gorgeous villas, many around the beguiling town of Bellagio; along Lake Garda is the Brescian Riviera, and on Lake Maggiore you'll find the storybook Borromean Islands and glowing Stresa. Here you may not find great art treasures or encounter the long-lost pagan past, but, if you are in search of it, you will certainly find peace.

The Dolomites

Northwest Italy's Dolomite Mountains—Nature's skyscrapers—draw scenery-hungry tourists by the thousands. Many come in hot pursuit of the charming meadows and valleys; the crystal clear lakes; the stupefying cliffs, curiously shaped peaks, and splintered crags whose resplendent hues range from pale rose at dawn to declamatory purple at dusk. (Leonardo da Vinci depicted these peaks in the haunting background of his *Mona Lisa.*) For other visitors this region is the ultimate year-round sports playground—with the seeing just as important as the skiing in jet-set Cortina d'Ampezzo. Take the Strada del Vino (Wine Route) from Bolzano to Trento, where there is a famous cathedral and the moated Castello del Buonconsiglio; enjoy the "grape cure" at Merano; zip along the 48 hairpin turns of the Stelvio Pass; absorb the vistas of the Grande Strada delle Dolomiti (Great Dolomites Road); and top it all off with a skydiving stop at the historic town of Bressanone, where Gothic and Baroque art blend harmoniously.

Emilia-Romagna

Gourmets the world over argue that Emilia-Romagna's greatest contribution to mankind has been gastronomic. In the birthplace of fettucine, prosciutto, tortellini, and lasagna, you need never worry about any of the restaurants you walk into. The region on the Adriatic between Tuscany and Lombardy also contains an abundance of cultural riches—the legacies of the Farnese family in Piacenza and Parma, the Este family in Modena and Ferrara, the Malatesta in Rimini, and the Bentivoglio in Bologna. Bologna—*dotta e grassa* (learned and fat)—is home to Italy's oldest university as well as to the spirits of Copernicus, Galileo, and Dante. The area between Piacenza and Parma is opera country—Verdi's villa of Sant'Agata is in Busseto. The polished city of Parma nourished two of Italy's greatest painters, Parmigianino and Correggio. For a breather, head along the Adriatic coast to the principal summer resort of Rimini and the Byzantine beauty of mosaic-rich Ravenna, glittering as brightly as it did 1,500 years ago.

Umbria and the Marches

Legends linger here in the evergreen land of the saints, the birthplace of St. Francis and St. Claire (Assisi), St. Benedict (Norcia), and St. Rita (Cascia). The strange, bluish haze that tints the landscape has inspired writers to characterize the region as mystical and ethereal. Here, medieval enclaves wear their ancient histories lightly, and majestic valleys refuse to pose for tourists' cameras. Umbria, the region surrounded by Latium, Tuscany, and the Marches, bears a rich artistic inheritance that includes the frescoes of Giotto and Pietro Lorenzetti in Assisi's Basilica of St. Francis, the brooding Palazzo dei Consoli in Gubbio, and the Gothic glory of Orvieto's cathedral. For a "deep, delicious bath of medievalism," as Henry James wrote, a visit to Assisi is an imperative; the spirit of St. Francis gently permeates the hillside town. For more urbane pleasures, head for Spoleto's celebrated Festival of Two Worlds or Perugia's popular jazz concerts. Eastward, in the off-the-beaten-track region of the Marches on the Adriatic, is Urbino, where the Renaissance first came to full flower. It is full of treasures by such illustrious artists as Bramante, Raphael, and Piero della Francesca. A visit to its Ducal Palace reveals more about the wealth and artistic

energy of the Renaissance than a shelf of history books.

Campania

Magnetic, magical, and magnificent, Campania is the Italy many travelers dream about. Emperors and kings, popes and artists, musicians and writers have made its sea-wreathed resorts and starlit isles their homes for more than 2,000 years—and well they might, for this is a compressed realm of undiluted beauty. Naples—the most operatic of cities—rules over the unequaled panorama of its bay. Once ancient Romans led the carefree life at nearby Pompeii; today, travelers soak up the 24-karat sun on Capri—a pint-size island paradise that is as intoxicating as its delicious wines. Down the shoreline along Amalfi Drive is shockingly beautiful Ravello, where just about the bluest view on tap takes in the Gulf of Salerno. From here, take a day trip to Paestum's ancient temples. Head back to Sorrento, Positano, and Amalfi, famed as places of play and pleasure.

Apulia

Misguided tourists think that after a visit to Naples and a drive around the Amalfi Coast to Salerno (maybe as far afield as Paestum) they have seen Italy's south. The truth is they have barely entered the gate. Italy's far south is composed of the ancient provinces of Apulia (Puglia), Lucania (Basilicata), and Calabria—the heel, instep, and arch, respectively, of Italy's boot. Often overlooked Apulia is steeped in ancient history and rich with tantalizing sights that are only now coming to the surface. The region invites aimless exploration: seek out its whitewashed ports, imposing castles, and strange igloo-shape dwellings called *trulli*. The cities of Brindisi, Bari, and Lecce hold many fascinations, and the coastline is full of seductions—unspoiled coves, bougainvillea-draped vistas, and seas that shimmer like sheets of turquoise.

Sicily

On this fabled island, you may ski down a snow-muffled volcano, walk through palm and orange groves, and swim within sight of flowering almond trees—all in the same day. Many visitors first head for Taormina, a town whose natural beauties are so great that even the overdevelopment of the past 50 years has not spoiled its grandeur. The city's views of the sea and

Mt. Etna come close to panoramic perfection. In summer, Taormina hosts an arts festival, with many of its events held in its spectacular 3rd-century-BC Greek Theater. Sicily's main metropolis, Palermo, has always been at the crossroads of civilization: Phoenician colony, Carthaginian town, capital of an Arab emirate, commercial hub of Europe and Asia under Norman rule, center of learning under Frederick II. Nearby is Sicily's most important art treasure, the cathedral of Monreale, with its glorious medieval mosaics. On the southwestern coast lies Agrigento, with its stellar relic from antiquity, the Valley of the Temples. Among the ancient Greek buildings here, the Temple of Concord is the best preserved in the world after that of Theseus in Athens.

Sardinia

Too distant from imperial and papal Rome to be influenced by the character of the mainland, Sardinia is as unique as its weather-worn landscape. Visitors arrive at this diamond-in-the-rough landscape by air or sea at Cagliari in the south, Olbia in the northeast, or Alghero in the northwest. Although the indigenous culture is one of Italy's most interesting, many travelers opt to explore the high-profile Costa Smeralda. This chic resort was developed by the Aga Khan, who discovered its charms when his yacht took shelter from a storm. "Secret paradise" of tycoons and actresses in years past, the Costa is now an open, upscale vacationland. Sardinia's most expensive hotels are here, and the current scions of the House of Savoy—modern Italy's one royal dynasty—return annually in their yachts. Intrepid travelers head for the *nuraghi,* cyclopean stones that are among prehistory's enigmas. Severely beautiful Sardinia remains a prime destination for those in search of a vacation getaway.

PLEASURES AND PASTIMES

The Art of Enjoying Art

Travel veterans will tell you that the endless series of masterpieces in Italy's churches, palaces, and museums can cause first-time visitors—eyes glazed over from a heavy downpour of images, dates, and names—to lean, Pisa-like, on their companions for support. After a surfeit of Botticellis and Bronzinos and the 14th Raphael, even the miracle of the High Renaissance may begin to pall. The secret, of course, is to act like a turtle—not a hare—and take your sweet time. Instead of trotting after briskly efficient tour guides, allow the splendors of the age to unfold—slowly. Get out and explore the actual settings—medieval chapels, Rococo palaces, and Romanesque town squares—for which these marvelous examples of Italy's art and sculpture were conceived centuries ago and where many of them may still be seen in situ.

Museums are only the most obvious places to view art; there are always the trompe l'oeil renderings of Assumptions that float across Baroque church ceilings and piazza scenes that might be Renaissance paintings brought to life. Instead of studying a Gothic statue in Florence's Bargello, spend an hour in the medieval cloisters of the nearby convent of San Marco; by all means, take in Michelangelo's *David* and *Slaves* in Florence's Accademia, but then meander down the 15th-century street, a short bus ride away, where he was born. You'll find that after three days trotting through museums, a walk through a quiet neighborhood will act as a much-needed restorative of perspective.

Of course, there may be many art treasures that will not quicken your pulse, but one morning you may see a Caravaggio so perfect, so beautiful, that your knees will buckle.

Il Dolce Far Niente

The idea of vacation was probably invented by some hardworking Roman emperor and, ever since, the Italians have been fine-tuning what they call il dolce far niente—the sweet art of idleness. Today, even relaxing can feel like a chore, but thanks to Italy's opulent villas, picture-perfect coastal resorts, and dreamy hill towns, you can idle here more successfully than anywhere else. But it takes more than trading in a silk tie for a T-shirt; you have to adjust to the deeper, subtler rhythms of leisure, Italian style. Hours spent over a Campari in a sun-splashed café; days spent soaking up the sun on the Amalfi Coast; an afternoon spent painting a watercolor on the shores of Lake Como: You may be pleasantly surprised to find that such pursuits prove more beneficial than forced marches through the obligatory sights. The luxury is often in the lingering.

Dining

In Italy, cookery is civilization. In the days of the Roman legions, pundits used to say, *"Ubi Roma ibi allium"* (Where there are Romans, there is garlic). Ever since the days of the Caesars—when emperors quickly learned the wisdom of *"Stomaco pieno, anima consolata"* (Full stomach, satisfied soul)—Italian chefs have taken one of life's sensory pleasures and made it into an art, and today you can feast on an incredible array of culinary delights. Of course, Italian food has come a long way since the days when Horace, the great poet of ancient Rome, feasted on lamprey boiled in five-year-old wine, the liver of a goose fattened on figs, and apples picked by the light of the waning moon. But you can still enter restaurants in Bologna, enjoy a dish of tortellini, and be told, *"Anche Dante le ha mangiate cósi"* (Dante also ate them this way). In fact, the newest trend in Italian cooking is to serve up the old—the simple, rustic, time-honored forms of cucina *simpatica, rustica,* and *trattoria*—with a nouvelle flair.

You have a choice of eating places, ranging from a *ristorante* (restaurant) to a trattoria, *tavola calda,* or *rosticceria.* The line separating ristoranti from trattorie have blurred of late, but a trattoria is usually a family-run place, simpler in decor, menu, and service than a ristorante, and slightly less expensive. Some rustic-looking spots call themselves *osterie* but are really restaurants. (A true osteria is a basic, down-to-earth tavern.) At a tavola calda or rosticceria, prepared food is sold to be consumed on the spot or taken out; you choose what you want at the counter, and pay at the cashier. An *enoteca* is a wine bar where you can order wine by the glass or bottle; most have tables, and many serve savory, light meals and nibbles. A *caffè* (coffee bar) serves those beloved coffee drinks replicated abroad, plus sandwiches, pastries, and other snacks. Tell the cashier what you want, pay for it, and then take the stub to the counter, where you restate your order, and then drink and eat standing at the counter. Remember that table service is extra, almost double; don't sit at a table unless you want to be served.

Shopping

"Made in Italy" has become synonymous with style, quality, and craftsmanship whether it refers to high fashion or Maserati automobiles. The best buys are leather goods of all kinds—from gloves to bags to jackets—silk goods, knitwear, gold jewelry, ceramics, and local handicrafts. The most important thing to keep in mind when shopping in Italy is that every region has its specialties. Venice is known for glassware, lace, and velvet; Milan and Como for silk; the Dolomites and the mountainous regions of Calabria and Sicily for hand-carved wooden objects; Florence for straw goods, gold jewelry, leather, and paper products; Naples for coral and cameos; Assisi for embroidery; and Deruta, Gubbio, Vietri, and many towns in Apulia and Sicily for ceramics. Unless your purchases are too bulky, avoid having them shipped home; if the shop appears to be reliable about shipping, get a written statement of what will be sent, when, and how.

GREAT ITINERARY

Classical Highlights

Well colonized by the ancient Greeks, then epicenter of the Roman Empire, Italy has a wealth of classical sites, many of them quite well preserved, thanks in part to the Italian appreciation for history and heritage. Rome was, of course, the glorious capital of the Roman Empire, and a number of ancient sites remain there today, seemingly plunked down in the middle of the bustling modern metropolis. It is quite an experience to turn a corner and see a famous building, such as the Colosseum, across the street, with Fiats and Vespas buzzing blithely past its crumbling arches. Campania, too, has a number of important classical landmarks, from both the Roman and the Greek eras. Below the volcanic cone of Mt. Vesuvius, the buried ruins of Pompeii are the most famous, but even better-preserved relics are still being unearthed from the lava at nearby Herculaneum. Farther down the coast is Paestum, the remains of an ancient town with remarkably well-preserved Greek temples; some classicists enjoy uncrowded Paestum more than either Pompeii or Herculaneum.

Those with more time or a more intense interest in ancient times will want to follow this itinerary all the way to Sicily, the large island just off the toe of Italy's boot. Heavily colonized by the Greeks, Sicily was a center of trade and culture in the Hellenic world, and it still is richly endowed with remarkable sites, most notably Agrigento and Siracusa.

Duration

7–17 days

Getting Around

BY CAR➤ On the A2 autostrada, it takes about three hours to drive from Rome to Naples. Most of the classical sites in Campania can be seen on day trips from Naples; the farthest away is Paestum, 99 km (60 mi) down the coast on S18. If you choose to continue on to Sicily, take either the overnight car ferry from Naples to Palermo, Sicily, or drive down the A3 autostrada (488 km/302 mi) to Villa San Giovanni in Calabria, where frequent ferry service crosses the strait in a half hour to Messina, Sicily, 235 km (145 mi) east of Palermo. Sicily's main sites are spread out to every corner of the large island, so you will have to stop overnight near each site. It's a 128-km (80-mi) drive south from Palermo to Agrigento, on the island's southwest coast; Selinunte is up the coast from Agrigento, along S115 about 100 km (60 mi). Agrigento is 212 km (132 mi) from Siracusa.

PUBLIC TRANSPORTATION➤ Train service between Rome and Naples is fast and frequent, taking less than two hours on express trains. The Circumvesuviana train line can take you conveniently from Naples to Pompeii and Herculaneum. There is an FS train station right in Paestum. There is a ferry from Naples to Palermo, Sicily, and a main train line runs from Palermo to Siracusa. Other sites on Sicily are better reached by bus than by the unreliable local train service.

The Main Route

2–3 NIGHTS: ROME➤ Spend at least a day exploring Ancient Rome—the Colle Capitolino, the Foro Romano, the Circo Massimo, the Colosseo, the Pantheon—and on subsequent days, venture out to the Via Appia and the catacombs, or study classical sculptures in the Musei Vaticani and antiquities in the Museo Nazionale.

3–5 NIGHTS: NAPLES AND CAMPANIA➤ After arriving from Rome, spend the afternoon at the Museo Archeologico Nazionale. Herculaneum and Pompeii can be visited in one day from Naples, but it would be a very full day, and it is best to break it into two separate excursions. On another day, enjoy an excursion down the Amalfi Coast or take the A3 autostrada to Paestum, with its well-preserved Greek temples. An optional day can be spent touring the area just west of Naples, taking in the Roman amphitheater at Pozzuoli, spooky Lake Avernus, the Roman resort town at Baia with its excavated baths, and the Sibyl's Cave at Cumae, perhaps the oldest Greek colony in Italy.

1 NIGHT: FERRY TO SICILY

1 Night: Palermo➤ VISIT THE NATIONAL ARCHAEOLOGICAL MUSEUM AND NEARBY SEGESTA, WITH ITS FINE DORIC GREEK TEMPLE.

1–2 NIGHTS: AGRIGENTO➤ Explore the Valley of the Temples, an extensive Greek site, and if you have time, make your way up the coast to see the Greek temple complex at Selinunte.

1–2 NIGHTS: SIRACUSA➤ Visit the Parco Archeologico in town, the splendid Museo Archeologico, and, if there's time, take an excursion to see the mosaics at the Imperial Roman Villa at Casale, just north of Piazza Amerina.

1 NIGHT (OPTIONAL): TAORMINA➤ Get a fine view of Mt. Etna and see the town's Greek theater, still used for the summer arts festival.

1 Night: Ferry to Naples

1 Night: Return to Rome

Information

For information, *see* chapters 2, 13, and 15.

FODOR'S CHOICE

No two people agree on what makes a perfect vacation, but it's fun and helpful to know what others think. Here's a compendium drawn from the must-see lists of hundreds of Italian tourists. For detailed information about these memories-in-the-making, refer to the appropriate chapters in this book.

Quintessential Italy

★ **Bellagio, Lake Como.** Once called "Italy's prettiest town," it still seems to be more of an operetta set than a resort. Surrounded by sumptuous villas and gardens, the town has long played host to honeymooners, kings, and celebrated visitors who love its faded millionaires' gentility.

★ **Piazza del Campo, Siena.** This shell-shape piazza delimited by the austere Palazzo Civico symbolizes the grace and power of a proud medieval city where an age-old rivalry with Florence still fires the tongues and souls of the Senesi. During the Palio, the square explodes in a frenzy of medieval pageantry and passion with the dizzying horse race.

★ **Lecce, Apulia.** Extravagant Baroque churches—a flowering of golden stone—are the showpieces of this city in Italy's deep south, stomping ground of the ancient Greeks, bold Crusaders, and a landed aristocracy. All left their marks.

★ **San Gimignano, Tuscany.** In this quintessential Tuscan town, stand on the steps of the Collegiata church at sunset as the swallows swoop in and out of the famous medieval towers, twittering softly as they coast on the air.

Lodging and Dining Gems

★ **Bellevue Syrene, Sorrento.** Luxuriate in the lavish charm of this clifftop palace, close to the energy of Sorrento, but wholly restful within. The views over the Bay of Naples are spellbinding. $$$$

★ **Gualtiero Marchesi, Erbusco, Lago d'Iseo.** Spectacular flights of fantasy grounded with classic Lombardian finesse are masterminded by the restaurant's namesake chef, the founder of *la cucina nuova*. No creative fancy is spared—from Far East touches to the whimsy of origami to caviar garnishes. $$$$

★ **Villa Las Tronas, Alghero, Sardinia.** Turn-of-century gentility pervades this royal mansion on a rocky bluff above the sea. Plush gardens shelter you regally, amid modern comforts and expansive views. $$$–$$$$

★ **Cibrèo, Florence.** In one of Florence's best restaurants, chef Fabrio Picci reinterprets Tuscan classics, served in Tuscan

surroundings gone upscale. It's off the beaten path, but its location next to a marketplace promises the freshest of ingredients—and imagination. $$$

★ **Accademia, Venice.** Just beyond the hotel's iron gate, a secret garden awaits, complete with mini Palladian-style villa, canal parterre, and verdant trees. It's both enchanting and cheery, but no secret. $$

★ **Teatro di Pompeo, Rome.** You truly feel the heart of Old Rome here, with an ancient Roman brick-vaulted breakfast room and typical Old Rome beamed ceilings in the bedrooms. $$

★ **La Tazza d'Oro, Rome.** Those who claim that the national coffee habit is the key to the Italian disposition find conclusive proof here in Italy's best cup of coffee. Do as the Romans do: order a glass of water as a chaser. $

Special Memories

★ **Piazza del Duomo Spoleto, Umbria.** Descending the stairs toward Spoleto's medieval cathedral, you see the broad piazza, flanked by low medieval buildings, fan out as it spills down toward the pale stone sanctuary, studded with rose-colored windows and mosaics set against the verdant green backdrop of Umbria's hills.

★ **Passeggiata, Taormina.** For perfect people-watching in an unforgettable seaside setting, head for Corso Umberto at dusk and witness the pageantry. All turn out for the promenade, pausing for *gelato* or *caffè* and casting a vigilant eye toward hovering Mt. Etna.

★ **Procession of San Efisio, Cagliari.** Tradition isn't just a cliché in Sardinia's tourist-trade lexicon, and none of the island's other time-honored festivals has the exuberance of Cagliari's annual binge.

★ **Sunset Gondola Ride, Grand Canal, Venice.** For a truly magic moment, ply along the surrealistic waterway, lined with fairytale-like palazzi, veiled in silvery mists.

★ **Sunset at Porto Ponente, Vulcano (Aeolian Islands).** Memorable sunsets in the Aeolian Islands are no rare thing, but that magic moment when the peach sun melts into the tangerine sea in between the *faraglioni*—soaring spires of rock—will live with you forever.

Where Art Comes First

⭐ **Cappelle Medicee, San Lorenzo, Florence.** This grandiose complex is a Michelangelan tour de force: the earthy marble slabs in the Cappella dei Principi resonate in architectural equilibrium; the allegorical sculptural figures in the New Sacristy have such an impact, his contemporaries invented a word for the phenomenon—*terribilità* (dreadfulness).

⭐ **Ducal Palace, Urbino.** If the Renaissance was, in ideal form, a celebration of the nobility of man and his works, of the light and purity of the soul, then in no other palace in Italy are these tenets better illustrated.

⭐ **Giotto Fresco Cycle, Cappella degli Scrovegni, Padua.** The realism depicted in these frescoes—executed from 1303 to 1305—which includes the first blue skies in Western painting, was revolutionary.

⭐ **I Frari, Venice.** In this great Venetian Gothic church, you'll find two of Titian's most spectacular altarpieces; their blazing colors and luminosity cast 20th-century electricity into shadow.

⭐ **La Rotonda, Vicenza.** Italy's most famous Palladian villa was the inspiration for Thomas Jefferson's Monticello. If you run into the delightfully friendly owner, Count Ludovico di Valmarana, he'll direct you to the unequaled Tiepolo frescoes at his family's Villa of the Dwarfs down the road.

⭐ **Valley of the Temples, Agrigento, Sicily.** More than 20 centuries of silence and solitude greet you at this famous archaeological site, where more than 100 evocative structures built before the year 1 AD have been preserved.

FESTIVALS AND SEASONAL EVENTS

Italy's top seasonal events are listed below, and any one of them could provide the stuff of lasting memories. Contact the **Italian Government Travel Office** (☞ Visitor Information *in* the Gold Guide) for exact dates and further information.

WINTER

EARLY DEC.➤ The **Feast of St. Ambrose,** in Milan, officially opens La Scala's opera season.

DEC.–JUNE➤ The **Opera Season** is in full swing at La Scala in Milan and elsewhere, notably in Turin, Rome, Naples, Parma, Venice, and Genoa.

DEC. 31➤ Rome stages a rousing **New Year's Eve** celebration, with fireworks, in Piazza del Popolo.

JAN. 5–6➤ **Epiphany Celebrations.** Roman Catholic Epiphany celebrations and decorations are evident throughout Italy. Notable is the Epiphany Fair at Piazza Navona in Rome.

EARLY FEB.➤ **Almond Blossom Festival** in Agrigento. A week of folk music and dancing, with groups from many countries, in the Valley of the Temples.

FEB. 4–16➤ **Carnival in Venice.** A big do in the 18th century, revived in the last half of the 20th century, this includes plays, masked balls, fireworks, and indoor and outdoor happenings of every sort. During **Carnival in Viareggio,** masked pageants, fireworks, a flower show, and parades are among the festivities on the Tuscan Riviera.

FEB.➤ The **Carnival in Ivrea,** near Turin, includes three days of folklore, costumes, and parades, culminating in the Battle of the Oranges, with real fruit flying through the air.

SPRING

MAR. 28➤ In Rome, a torchlit nighttime **Good Friday Procession** led by the pope winds from the Colosseum past the Foro Romano and up the Colle Palatino.

APR. 4➤ The Easter Sunday **Scoppio del Carro,** or "Explosion of the Cart," in Florence, is the eruption of a cartful of fireworks in the Piazza del Duomo, set off by a mechanical dove released from the altar during High Mass.

LATE APR.–EARLY JULY➤ The **Florence May Music Festival** is the oldest and most prestigious Italian festival of the performing arts.

MAY 1➤ The **Feast of Sant'Efisio** in Cagliari sees a procession of marchers and others in splendid Sardinian costume.

MID-MAY➤ During the **Race of the Candles,** the procession of bearers, in local costume, carrying towering wooden pillars, leads to the top of Mt. Ingino in Gubbio.

MAY 20➤ **Sardinian Cavalcade.** A traditional procession of more than 3,000 people in Sardinian costumes makes its way through Sassari.

LATE MAY➤ The **Palio of the Archers** is a medieval crossbow contest in Gubbio.

SUMMER

EARLY JUNE➤ The **Battle of the Bridge,** in Pisa, is a medieval parade and contest. The **Flower Festival,** in Genzano (Rome), is a religious procession along streets carpeted with flowers in splendid designs. The **Regatta of the Great Maritime Republics** sees keen competition among the four former maritime republics—Amalfi, Genoa, Pisa, and Venice.

LATE JUNE➤ **Soccer Games in 16th-Century Costume,** in Florence, commemorate a match played in 1530. Festivities include fireworks displays.

LATE JUNE–EARLY JULY➤ The **Festival of Two Worlds,** in Spoleto, is a famous performing-arts festival.

JUNE AND JULY➤ The **Summer Operetta Festival** is held in Trieste.

EARLY JULY AND MID-AUG.➤ The **Palio Horse Race,** in Siena, is a colorful bareback horse race with participants competing for the *palio* (banner).

MID-JULY➤ The **Feast of the Redeemer** is a procession of gondolas and other craft, commemorating the end of the epidemic of 1575 in Venice. The fireworks over the lagoon are spectacular.

EARLY JULY–LATE AUG.➤ The **Arena of Verona Outdoor Opera Season** heralds spectacular productions in the 22,000-seat Roman amphitheater of Verona.

EARLY AUG.➤ The **Joust of the Quintana** is a historical pageant in Ascoli Piceno.

LATE AUG.–EARLY SEPT.➤ The **Siena Music Week** features opera, concerts, and chamber music. The **Venice Film Festival,** oldest of the international film festivals, takes place mostly on the Lido.

LATE AUG.–MID-SEPT.➤ The **Stresa Musical Weeks** comprise a series of concerts and recitals in Stresa.

AUTUMN

EARLY SEPT.➤ The **Historic Regatta** includes a tradi-

tional competition between two-oar gondolas in Venice. The **Joust of the Saracen** is a tilting contest with knights in 13th-century armor in Arezzo.

MID-SEPT.➤ The **Joust of the Quintana** is a 17th-century-style joust and historical procession in Foligno.

EARLY OCT.➤ Alba's **100 Towers Tournament** features costumes and races and is held simultaneously with the **Truffle Fair,** a food fair centered on the white truffle.

OCT. 4➤ The **Feast of St. Francis** is celebrated in Assisi, his birthplace.

2 Rome

In the Eternal City Nero fiddled, Mark Anthony praised Caesar, and Charlemagne was crowned. Today you can marvel at the venerated Renaissance and Baroque treasures in their footsteps while sipping a caffè, *exploring swank boutiques, and dodging speeding Vespas. In no other city will you find such a heady mix of elegance, earthiness, and energy.*

Updated by
Barbara Walsh
Angelillo

HOWEVER YOU ARRIVE in Rome, by autostrada, or train or plane, you can tell by the traffic that you are entering a grand nexus: All paths lead to Rome. As you enter the city proper, edifices, icons, and images to match your expectations take shape: a bridge with heroic statues along its parapets; a towering cake of ornate marble decorated with allegorical figures in extravagant poses; a piazza and an obelisk under an umbrella of pine trees; a massive marble arena, even bigger than you imagined, that you realize with awe is the fabled Colosseo.

More than Florence, more than Venice, Rome is Italy's treasure trove, packed as it is with masterpieces from more than two millennia of artistic achievement—for this is where Republican Rome once bustled around the extravagant buildings of the Roman Forum, centuries later Michelangelo Buonarroti painted the ceiling in the Cappella Sistina, and in modern times, Federico Fellini filmed *La Dolce Vita* and *8½* at Cinecittà Studios.

Rome is like a big layer cake, and your job, as a visitor, is to pry it open and get a feel for each of the layers. You'll find pieces of Ancient Rome casually strewn about, topped by Medieval and Renaissance Rome, topped by Fascist Rome and finally today's Rome, where decades of political apathy are giving way to a revitalized city. Ancient Romans, Vandals, Popes and the Borgias, Michelangelo and Gianlorenzo Bernini, Napoléon, and Mussolini all left their physical and spiritual marks on the city. Today Rome's formidable legacy is upheld by its people, history knit into the fabric of their everyday life. Students walk dogs in the park that was once the mausoleum of the family of the Emperor Augustus; Raphaelesque madonnas line up for buses on busy corners; a priest in flowing robes walks through a medieval piazza talking on a cell phone. Modern Rome has one foot in the past, one in the present—a delightful stance that allows you to have an espresso in a square designed by Bernini, then take the Metro back to your hotel room in a renovated Renaissance palace. "When you first come here you assume that you must burrow about in ruins and prowl in museums to get back to the days of Numa Pompilius or Mark Anthony," Maud Howe observes in her book, *Roma Beata*. "It is not necessary; you only have to live, and the common happenings of daily life—yes, even the trolley car and your bicycle—carry you back in turn to the Dark Ages, to the early Christians, even to prehistoric Rome."

Pleasures and Pastimes

Dining

Rome is a city distinguished more by its good attitude toward eating out than by a multitude of outstanding restaurants. Don't look for star chefs here, nor the latest trends—with a few notable exceptions, the city's food scene is a bit like its historical sites, well worn but still standing. But food lovers nonetheless have much to look forward to. Romans have been known since ancient times for great feasts and banquets, and though the days of the triclinium and the saturnalia are long past, dining out is still all the nightlife most Romans need. In fact, a lingering meal alfresco is one of Rome's great pleasures. Lunch is served from noon to 3, dinner from 8 until about 10:30 or 11, but some restaurants stay open later, especially in summer, when patrons linger at sidewalk tables to enjoy the *ponentino* (evening breeze).

Lodging

Rome has the range of accommodations you would expect of any great city, from the squalid *alberghetti* (little hotels) and pensione around the railway station to the grand monuments to luxury and elegance on Via Vittorio Veneto. Appearances can be misleading here: Many crumbling stucco facades may promise little from the outside, but they often hide interiors of considerable elegance.

EXPLORING ROME

Rome presents a particular challenge for you: Just as you begin to feel hopelessly smitten by the spell of the city, you realize you don't have the time to see more than a fraction of its treasures. It's wise to start out knowing this, and to have a focused but flexible itinerary. A ramble through a picturesque quarter of Old Rome can be just as enlightening as seeking a chapel redolent of spicy incense or a trek through marbled miles of museum corridors.

Though large, Rome invites walking; the bus system is also an option for weary legs. Plan your day to take into account the varying hours places are open—which usually means mixing the ancient, classical, and Baroque, museums and parks, the center and the environs. Most churches are usually open from 8 or 9 until noon or 12:30, and from 3 or 4 until about 7. Major basilicas are open all day in season. You may take refuge in the age-old adage, Rome wasn't built in a day; be Nero-esque in your rambles and fiddle while you roam with frequent gelato breaks. The Italian author Silvio Negro said it best: *"Roma, non basta una vita"* (Rome, a lifetime is not enough).

Numbers in the text correspond to numbers in the margin and on the Rome and Old Rome maps.

Great Itineraries

IF YOU HAVE 3 DAYS

Begin your first day at Piazza Venezia and survey Rome from atop the Colle Capitolino. Next, explore the Foro Romano and see the Colle Palatino and the Colosseo. In the afternoon, combine sightseeing with shopping and make your way through the neighborhood around the Scalinata di Spagna and the Fontana di Trevi. The following morning, visit the Basilica di San Pietro and the Cappella Sistina (during weekdays in certain months, the last admission into the Vatican Museums is 4 PM, so you have the option to visit St. Peter's Basilica on the afternoon of your first day during these times, stamina permitting; ☞ The Vatican: Rome of the Popes, *below*). After lunch, walk through Baroque Rome, exploring its splendor. Take it easy on your third morning: Explore a museum or site of interest and then relax at a café and watch the passing parade. Spend your final afternoon and evening exploring the picturesque Ghetto and Trastevere neighborhoods.

IF YOU HAVE 5 DAYS

On the morning of the fourth day wander through Villa Borghese and see the Canova and Bernini sculptures in the Galleria Borghese. On the fifth day, make an excursion either along Via Appia Antica or to Ostia Antica (☞ Side Trips, *below*), an ancient city comparable to Pompeii for interest and atmosphere. After a sustaining lunch, see some of Rome's most historic churches, with Michelangelo's *Moses* in San Pietro in Vincoli a highlight.

IF YOU HAVE 7 DAYS

Devote more time to the museums and galleries that interest you most. Explore a neighborhood you have not seen yet, or return to one you

liked best, allowing plenty of time for poking into odd corners and courtyards and churches, and for café-sitting. Make a couple of excursions
outside Rome, to Tivoli or perhaps to Tarquinia and Cerveteri.

Ancient Rome: Glories of the Caesars

A walk through the very core of Roman antiquity, through what was
once the epicenter of the known world—the Foro Romano—gives you
a look at how Michelangelo transformed the Colle Capitolino, the seat
of ancient Rome's government, into a Renaissance showcase. The rub-
blescape of marble fragments scattered over the area of the Forum makes
all but students of archaeology ask: Is this the grandeur that was
Rome? Just consider that much of the history fed to students the world
over happened right here. This square—occasionally an enormous
banquet hall where imperial Rome could be simultaneously enter-
tained (as our times have observed thanks to such Hollywood epics as
Quo Vadis, Ben-Hur, and *Cleopatra*)—was the birthplace of much of
Western civilization. Roman law and powerful armies were created here,
banishing the barbarian world for a millennium. Here, all Rome
shouted as one, "Caesar has been murdered," and crowded to hear Mark
Anthony's eulogy for the fallen leader. Legend has it that St. Paul tra-
versed the Forum en route to his audience with Nero. After a more-
than-27-centuries-long parade of pageantry, it is not surprising that
Shelley and Gibbon reflected on the sense of *sic transit gloria mundi*
(so passes away the glory of the world) on these same grounds.

*Numbers in the text correspond to numbers in the margin and on the
Rome map.*

A Good Walk

Rome, as everyone knows, was built on seven hills (Colle Capitolino,
Colle Palatino, Monte Esquilino, Monte Viminale, Monte Celio,
Monte Quirinale, and Colle Aventino). Begin your walk on the **Colle
Capitolino** ①—the site of Michelangelo's spectacular piazza and Rome's
city hall, Palazzo Senatorio, which was built over the Tabularium, the
ancient hall of records. Flanking the palazzo are both halves of Rome's
most noteworthy museum complex, the **Musei Capitolini** ②, made up
of the Museo Capitolino and the Palazzo dei Conservatori, which contain works of art gathered by Pope Sixtus V (1520–90), one of the
earliest papal patrons of the arts. Off to the side of the Colle Capitolino, at the head of its formidable flight of steep steps, stands the
ancient redbrick church of **Santa Maria d'Aracoeli** ③. Below the gardens to the left of the Palazzo Senatorio are the **Foro di Cesare** and
the forum named after the Emperor Trajan, separated by Via dei Fori
Imperiali; the latter contains the **Colonna di Traiano** ④. Descend Via
San Pietro in Carcere, actually a flight of stairs, to the gloomy **Carcere
Mamertino** ⑤ and the **Foro Romano** ⑥, continuing along the ancient
Via Sacra where, on the right, you will come across the **Colle Palatino** ⑦, site of Rome's earliest settlement. Leaving the Colle Palatino
by way of the San Gregorio exit, you'll come upon the imposing **Arco
di Costantino** ⑧ and, beyond it, the **Colosseo** ⑨, one of antiquity's most
famous monuments. Don't forget to check out the view from the
park laid out over the ruins of Nero's **Domus Aurea** ⑩, his sumptuous palace, behind the Colosseo.

TIMING
It takes about 30 minutes to walk the route, plus two hours to visit
the Musei Capitolini, from two to three hours to explore the Foro Romano and the Colle Palatino, and from 20 minutes to an hour to see
the Colosseo.

Sights to See

8 **Arco di Costantino** (Arch of Constantine). This imposing arch was erected in AD 315 to celebrate Constantine's (280–337) victory over Maxentius (died 312). Not only is it the best preserved of Rome's triumphal arches, it is also the largest (69 ft high, 85 ft wide, and 23 ft deep) and one of the last great monuments of ancient Rome. It once stood at the head of the Via Sacra, but now stands in glorious isolation alongside the Colosseo.

OFF THE BEATEN PATH **CIMITERO ACCATTOLICO** – Behind the Piramide, a stone pyramid built in 12 BC at the order of the Roman *praetor* (senior magistrate) who was buried there, is a cemetery reminiscent of a country churchyard that was for non-Catholics. You'll find Keats's tomb and the place where Shelley's heart was buried. It's about a 20-minute walk south from the Arco di Costantino along Via San Gregorio and Viale Aventino. ⊠ *Via Caio Cestio 6,* ☎ *06/5741141 (ring bell for custodian).* ☞ *Offering of 500 lire–1,000 lire.* ☉ *Daily 8–11:30 and 3:20–5:30.*

5 **Carcere Mamertino** (Mamertine Prison). This series of gloomy, subterranean cells under a 17th-century church is where Rome's vanquished enemies were finished off. Some historians believe that St. Peter was held prisoner here, and legend has it that he miraculously brought forth a spring of water to baptize his jailers. ⊠ *Via San Pietro in Carcere.* ☞ *Donation requested.* ☉ *Daily 9–12:30 and 2–7:30.*

★ **1** **Colle Capitolino** (Capitoline Hill). Though most of the buildings on Michelangelo's piazza date from the Renaissance, the hill was once the epicenter of the Roman Empire, the place where the city's first and holiest temples stood, including its most sacred, the Temple of Jupiter. The city's archives were kept in the Tabularium (hall of records), the tall, gray-stone structure that forms the foundation of today's city hall, **Palazzo Senatorio.** By the Middle Ages, the Campidoglio (the Capitol), as the hill was already called then, had fallen into ruin. In 1537, Pope Paul III decided to restore its grandeur for the triumphal entry into the city of Charles V, the Holy Roman Emperor, and called upon Michelangelo to create the staircase ramp; the buildings and facades on three sides of the Campidoglio; the slightly convex pavement and its decoration; and the pedestal for the bronze equestrian statue of Marcus Aurelius. A work from the 2nd century AD, the statue stood here from the 16th century until 1981. The statue—the most celebrated equestrian bronze to survive from classical antiquity—was mistakenly believed to represent the Christian emperor Constantine rather than the pagan Marcus Aurelius, hence its survival through the centuries. A legend foretells that some day the statue's original gold patina will return, heralding the end of the world. To forestall destiny, the city fathers had it restored and placed in the Museo Capitolino, saving not only what was left of the gold, but also the statue's bronze, once seriously menaced by air pollution. A copy was set up on the original pedestal in 1997. As Michelangelo's preeminent urban set piece, the piazza sums up all the majesty of High-Renaissance Rome.

7 **Colle Palatino** (Palatine Hill). A lane known as the Clivus Palatinus, whose worn paving stones were once trod by emperors and their slaves, climbs from the Forum area to a site that historians identify with Rome's earliest settlement. About a century ago, illustrious archaeologist Rodolfo Lanciani excavated a site on Palatine Hill and found evidence testifying to Romulus's historical presence, thereby contradicting early critics who deemed Romulus to be a myth. The story goes that the twins Romulus and Remus were abandoned as infants but were suckled by a she wolf on the banks of the Tiber and adopted by a shep-

herd. Encouraged by the gods to build a city, the twins chose a site in 735 BC, fortifying it with a wall that Lanciani identified by digging on the Palatine Hill. During the building of the city, the brothers quarreled, and in a fit of anger Romulus killed Remus.

Despite its location overlooking the Forum with its extreme traffic congestion and attendant noise, the Palatine Hill was the most coveted address for ancient Rome's rich and famous. More than a few of the 12 Caesars called the Palatine Hill home—including Caligula, who met his premature end in the Cryptoporticus tunnel, which today still stands and remains unnerving. The palace of Tiberius was the first to be built here; others followed, most notably the gigantic extravaganza constructed for emperor Domitian. ⊠ *Entrance at the Arco di Tito in the Foro Romano,* ☎ *06/6990110.* 🎟 *12,000 lire.* ☉ *Mon.–Sat. 9– 2 hrs before sunset. Possible evening opening during summer.*

In the **Circo Massimo** (Circus Maximus), the giant arena laid out between Palatine and Aventine hills, more than 300,000 spectators watched chariot races while the emperor surveyed the scene from his palace on the Palatine Hill.

❹ **Colonna di Traiano** (Trajan's Column). Trajan's (53–117) ashes were buried inside the base of this column, which stands in what was once the **Foro di Traiano** (Trajan's Forum), with its huge semicircular market building, adjacent to the ruins of the **Foro di Augusto** (Forum of Augustus [63 BC–AD 14]). ⊠ *Piazza Santa Maria di Loreto.*

★ ❾ **Colosseo** (Colosseum). Massive and majestic, ancient Rome's most famous monument was begun by the Flavian emperor Vespasian in AD 72, and inaugurated eight years later with a program of games and shows lasting 100 days. More than 50,000 spectators could sit within the arena's 573-yard circumference, which was faced with marble, accented with hundreds of statues, and had the velarium—an ingenious system of sail-like awnings rigged on ropes manned by imperial sailors—to protect the audience from the sun and rain. Before the imperial box, gladiators would salute the emperor and cry, *"Ave, imperator, morituri te salutant"* (Hail, emperor, men soon to die salute thee); it is said that when one day they heard the emperor Claudius respond, "or maybe not," they became so offended that they called a strike.

Originally known as the Anfiteatro Flavio (Flavian Amphitheater), it was called the Colosseum, as reported by the Venerable Bede in 730, after a truly colossal gilded bronze statue of Nero in the vicinity that stood until the end of the 6th century. The arena later served as a quarry from which materials were filched to build Renaissance-era churches and palaces. Finally, it was declared sacred by the Vatican in memory of the many Christians believed martyred there (scholars now maintain that no Christians met their death in the Colosseum, but rather in Rome's imperial circuses). During the 19th century, romantic poets lauded the glories of the amphitheater when viewed by moonlight. Now its arches glow at night with mellow golden spotlights—less romantic, perhaps, but still impressive. Portions of the arena will be closed during ongoing restoration. ⊠ *Piazza del Colosseo,* ☎ *06/7004261.* 🎟 *10,000 lire.* ☉ *Mon.–Sat. 9–2 hrs before sunset, Sun. 9–1.*

❿ **Domus Aurea.** On the Colle Oppio (Oppian Hill), a ridge of the Monte Esquilino (Esquiline Hill), are faint traces of Nero's sumptuous palace— later buried under Terme di Traiano (Baths of Trajan)—which was built after the great fire of AD 64 destroyed much of the city. (Incidentally, historians now believe Nero to be blameless in this event.) Also known as the Domus Aureus (Golden House), it was a structure so huge it evoked the complaint, "All Rome has become a villa."

Foro di Cesare (Caesar's Forum). This is the oldest of the Imperial Fora, those built by the emperors as opposed to those built during the earlier, Republican period (6th–1st centuries BC) as part of the original Roman Forum.

⑥ Foro Romano (Roman Forum). In what was once a marshy valley between the Capitoline and Palatine hills, this was the civic heart of Republican Rome, the austere enclave that preceded the hedonistic society that grew up under the emperors in the 1st to the 4th century AD. Today it seems no more than a baffling series of ruins, marble fragments, isolated columns, a few worn arches, and occasional paving stones. Yet it once was filled with stately and extravagant buildings—temples, palaces, shops—and crowded with people from all corners of the world. What you see today are the ruins not of one period, but of almost 900 years, from about 500 BC to AD 400. Making sense of these scarred and pitted stones is not easy; you may want just to wander along, letting your imagination dwell on Cicero (106–43 BC), Julius Caesar (100–44 BC), and Mark Anthony (circa 81–30 BC), who delivered the funeral address in Caesar's honor from the rostrum just left of the **Arco di Settimio Severo** (Arch of Septimius Severus).

One of the grandest of all antiquity, this arch was built in AD 203 to celebrate the emperor Severus's victory over the Parthians, and was topped by a bronze equestrian statuary group with no fewer than six horses. Most visitors also explore the large brick senate hall, the **Curia**, which survives as it was in the era of Diocletian in the late 3rd century AD; the three Corinthian columns (a favorite of 19th-century poets), all that remains of the **Tempio di Vespasiano** (Temple of Vespasian); the circular **Tempio di Vesta** (Temple of Vesta), where the highly privileged vestal virgins kept the sacred flame alive; and the **Arco di Tito** (Arch of Titus), which stands in a slightly elevated position on a spur of Palatine Hill. The view of the Colosseum from the arch is superb and reminds us that it was the emperor Titus who helped finish the vast amphitheater, begun earlier by his father, Vespasian. Now cleaned and restored, the arch was erected in AD 81 to celebrate the sack of Jerusalem 10 years earlier, after the great Jewish revolt. A famous relief shows the captured contents of Herod's Temple—including its huge seven-branched menorah—being carried in triumph down Rome's Via Sacra. ⊠ *Entrances to the Via Sacra: Via dei Fori Imperiali, Piazza del Colosseo, Via San Teodoro,* ☏ *06/6990110.* ☐ *Free. Audio guide available at bookshop/ticket office at Via dei Fori Imperiali entrance.* ☉ *Mon.–Sat. 9–2 hrs before sunset, Sun. 9–1. Possible evening opening in summer.*

② Musei Capitolini (Capitoline Museums). The collections in the twin Museo Capitolino and Palazzo dei Conservatori were assembled in the 15th century by Pope Sixtus V, one of the earliest of the great papal patrons of the arts. Although parts of the collection may excite only archaeologists and art historians, others contain some of the most famous—and not to be missed—pieces of classical sculpture, such as the poignant *Dying Gaul,* the regal *Capitoline Venus* (recently identified as another Mediterranean beauty, Cleopatra herself), and the delicate *Marble Faun* that inspired 19th-century novelist Nathaniel Hawthorne's novel of the same name. Remember that many of the works here and in Rome's other museums were copied from Greek originals. For hundreds of years, craftsmen of ancient Rome prospered by producing copies of Greek statues, using a process called "pointing," by which exact replicas could be created to order.

Portraiture, however, was one area in which the Romans outstripped the Greeks. The hundreds of Roman portrait busts in the Sala degli

Imperatori and Sala dei Filosofi of the **Museo Capitolino** constitute an ancient *Who's Who*. Within these serried ranks are 48 of the Roman emperors, ranging from Augustus to Theodosius (346–395). Many of them were eminently forgettable, but some were men of genius; a few added nothing to the Roman way of life except new ways of dying. On one console, you'll see the handsomely austere Augustus, who "found Rome a city of brick and left it one of marble." On another rests Claudius "the stutterer," an indefatigable builder brought vividly to life in Robert Graves's *I, Claudius*. In this company is also Nero, most notorious of the emperors—though by no means the worst—who built for himself the fabled Domus Aurea (☞ *above*). And, of course, the baddies: cruel Caligula and Caracalla, and the dissolute, eerily modern boy-emperor, Heliogabalus.

Unlike the Greeks, whose portraits are idealized and usually beautiful, the Romans belonged to the "warts and all" school of representation. Many of the busts that have come down to us, seen clearly in that of Commodus, the emperor-gladiator (found in a gallery on the upper level of the museum), are nearly savage in the relentlessness of their portrayals. As you leave the museum, be sure to stop in the courtyard at the gigantic, reclining figure of Oceanus, found in the Roman Forum and later dubbed Marforio, one of Rome's famous "talking statues" to which citizens from the 1500s up to the 20th century affixed anonymous notes of political protest and satirical verses.

The **Palazzo dei Conservatori** is a trove of ancient and Baroque treasures. Lining the courtyard are the colossal fragments of a head, leg, foot, and hand—all that remains of the famous statue of the emperor Constantine the Great, who believed that Rome's future in the 3rd century AD lay with Christianity. These immense effigies were much in vogue in the later days of the Roman empire. The resplendent Salone dei Orazi e Curiazi on the first floor is a ceremonial hall with a magnificent gilt ceiling, carved wooden doors, and 16th-century frescoes. At either end of the hall reign statues of the Baroque Age's most charismatic popes, Bernini's (1598–1680) marble effigy of Urban VIII and his rival Algardi's (1595–1654) bronze statue of Innocent X (1574–1655). The world-renowned symbol of Rome, the *Capitoline Wolf*, a 6th-century-BC Etruscan bronze, holds a place of honor in the museum; the suckling twins were added during the Renaissance to adapt the statue to the legend of Romulus and Remus (☞ Colle Palatino, *above*). ⊠ *Museo Capitolino and Palazzo dei Conservatori, Piazza del Campidoglio,* ☎ *06/67102071.* 🎟 *10,000 lire, free last Sun. of month.* 🕐 *Tues.–Sat. 9–7, Sun. 9–6:45.*

❸ **Santa Maria d'Aracoeli.** This stark, redbrick church is one of the first Christian churches in Rome. Legend recounts that it was on this spot that the Sybil predicted to Augustus the coming of a Redeemer. The emperor responded by erecting the Ara Coeli, the Altar of Heaven. The Aracoeli is best known for Pinturicchio's (1454–1513) 15th-century frescoes in the first chapel on the right. ⊠ *Piazza d'Aracoeli.* 🕐 *Oct.– May, daily 7–noon and 4–6; June–Sept., daily 7–noon and 4–6:30.*

The Vatican: Rome of the Popes

You might go to the Vatican to behold a work of art—Michelangelo's frescoes, rare archaeological marbles, or Bernini's statues. Others make the pilgrimage to find their souls in the most overwhelming architectural achievement of the Renaissance, the Basilica di San Pietro. In between these two extremes lies an awe-inspiring landscape with a sight for every taste and inclination. Museum rooms decorated by Raphael, antique sculptures like the *Apollo Belvedere* and the *Laocoön,* walls

JUBILEE 2000

THE HOLY YEAR, OR IL GIUBILEO (Jubilee), in 2000 will bring an estimated 35 million pilgrims to Rome to visit the major basilicas, see the pope, and pay homage to the tomb of St. Peter. Both the city of Rome and the Vatican—which, you must remember, are two separate entities—are working together to see that these record crowds can be welcomed, housed, fed, and moved about more or less efficiently.

While the Vatican has been quietly going ahead with its plans, cleaning up the front of the Basilica di San Pietro, installing a new entrance-exit system for the Musei Vaticani, and organizing the practical aspects of the Holy Year program, Rome's administrators have had to cope with glitches. A projected underpass that would have sped traffic past a perennial bottleneck at Castel Sant'Angelo and a new Metro line in the city center are among the public works that have been scrapped (archaeological risk and delays the main culprits). On the bright side, part of the funds for these projects will instead be spent on improving tourist services for getting hotels and information. More welcome fallout are the extended hours at several major city museums and promises to revamp public transportation lines.

The city has pledged to do what it calls a "restyling" of the areas around the basilicas and will enlarge the Termini Metro station. Even before 1998, city sprucing-up projects have seen many monuments and churches shrouded for restoration and several museums undergoing refurbishment. On the eastern outskirts of Rome at Tor Tre Teste, where many non-pilgrims will not venture, an important new church is being built as a symbol of the Jubilee. Designed by Richard Meier, it, too, was started behind schedule, so heavenly intervention may be required to get it finished on time.

Opening ceremonies begin before midnight on December 24, 1999, when the pope strikes the Holy Door with a silver hammer, symbolically opening it. The door will remain open for 54 weeks. Special prayer vigils will be held in the basilica on December 31, 1999 and December 31, 2000; on both occasions, the bells of the world's Roman Catholic churches will be rung at midnight. The Holy Doors at the other patriarchal churches will also be opened: San Giovanni in Laterano and Santa Maria Maggiore on December 25, 1999, and San Paolo fuori le Mura January 18, 1999. St. Peter's feast day on June 29 is sure to be a major celebration, with up to 250,000 people packed into Piazza San Pietro for a papal mass. August 19–20, the culmination of the weeklong Youth Jubilee, will draw some two million young people for a mega-prayer meeting at a site on the city's outskirts. The Holy Year will end with the closing of the Holy Door by the pope on January 6, 2001, in the Basilica di San Pietro. Closing ceremonies at the three other major basilicas in Rome will be held the preceding day, January 5.

The pope should be in Rome most of the year, with the exception of his much-heralded visit to the Holy Land. Every evening throughout the Holy Year, the pope will appear at a window of the Palazzo Vaticano to pray with and bless pilgrims in the square. For up-to-date Jubilee information, contact the **Vatican Information Office** (⌧ Piazza San Pietro, ☎ 06/69884466).

daubed by Fra Angelico, paintings by Giotto and Leonardo, and chief among revered *non plus ultras,* the ceiling of the Cappella Sistina: For the lover of beauty, few places are as historically important as this epitome of faith and grandeur. What gave all this impetus was a new force that emerged as the emperors of ancient Rome presided over their declining empire: Christianity came to Rome, and the seat of the popes was established over the tomb of St. Peter, thereby making the Vatican the spiritual core of the Roman Catholic Church. Note that dress rules must be adhered to in St. Peter's and the Vatican (☞ Basilica di San Pietro, *below*).

A Good Walk

Start your walk at the **Castel Sant'Angelo** ⑪, the fortress that stands sentinel over the Vatican, and take in the beauty of the Ponte Sant'Angelo before turning right onto Via della Conciliazione (or taking the more picturesque route west along Borgo Pio) to the Vatican. Once inside **Piazza San Pietro** ⑫, sumptuous architectural detail awaits at **Basilica di San Pietro** ⑬, the largest church of Christendom. To the right as you enter is Michelangelo's stunning *Pietà;* of the many treasures to be seen, be sure not to miss the Museo Storico in the Sacristy. Below the church, visit the Grotte Vaticane, the last repose of many of the popes, and, if you have time, arrange to explore the excavations below the church and the Giardini Vaticani.

TIMING

Allow two hours for a visit to Castel Sant'Angelo. You'll need an hour to see the Basilica di San Pietro, plus 30 minutes for the Museo Storico, 15 minutes for the Grotte Vaticane, 30 minutes to visit the roof, and an hour to climb to the lantern. To avoid the crowds, get to the Basilica di San Pietro early in the morning, at lunchtime, or in the late afternoon. Note that free one-hour English-language tours of the basilica are offered Monday–Saturday at 10 and 3, Sunday at 2:30 (sign up at the little desk under the portico).

Sights to See

★ ⑬　**Basilica di San Pietro** (St. Peter's Basilica). The physical statistics of Rome's sublime sanctuary are staggering: It covers about 18,100 square yards, extends 212 yards in length, and carries a dome that rises 435 ft and measures 138 ft across its base. Its history is equally impressive: No fewer than five of Italy's greatest artists—Bramante (1444–1514), Raphael (1483–1520), Peruzzi, Antonio Sangallo the Younger, and Michelangelo (1475–1564)—died during the course of construction of this new St. Peter's. The history of the original St. Peter's goes back to the year AD 319, when the emperor Constantine built a basilica over the site of the tomb of St. Peter. This early church stood for more than 1,000 years, undergoing a number of restorations, until it was on the verge of collapse. Reconstruction began in 1452, but was abandoned due to a lack of funds. In 1506 Pope Julius II instructed the architect Donato Bramante to raze the existing structure and build a new and greater basilica, but it wasn't until 1626 that the new church was completed and dedicated. In 1546 Pope Paul III persuaded the aging Michelangelo to take on the job of completing the building. Returning to Bramante's ground plan, Michelangelo designed the dome to cover the crossing, but his plans, too, were modified after his death. The cupola, one of the most beautiful in the world, was completed by Della Porta and Fontana. Under the portico, Filarete's 15th-century bronze doors, salvaged from the old basilica, are in the central portal. Off the entry portico, Bernini's famous *Scala Regia,* the ceremonial entryway to the Palazzo Vaticano and one of the most magnificent staircases in the world, is graced with Bernini's dramatic statue of Constantine the Great.

The cherubs over the holy-water fonts will give you an idea of just how huge St. Peter's is: The sole of the cherub's foot is as long as the distance from your fingers to your elbow. It is because the proportions of this giant building are in such perfect harmony that its vastness may escape you at first. But in its megascale—inspired by the spatial volumes of ancient Roman ruins—it reflects Roman *grandiosità* in all its majesty.

Over an altar in a side chapel is Michelangelo's **Pietà**. It is difficult to determine whether this moving work, sculpted when he was only 22, owes more to the man's art than to his faith. As we contemplate this masterpiece we are able to understand a little better that art and faith sometimes partake of the same impulse.

Four massive piers support the dome at the crossing, where the mighty Bernini **baldacchino** (canopy) rises high above the papal altar. "What the barbarians didn't do, the Barberini did," 17th-century wags quipped when Barberini Pope Urban VIII had the bronze stripped from the Pantheon's portico and melted down to make the baldacchino (using what was left over for cannonballs). The pope celebrates mass here, over the grottoes holding the tombs of many of his predecessors. Deep in the excavations under the foundations of the original basilica is what is believed to be the tomb of St. Peter. The bronze throne above the main altar in the apse, the Cathedra Petri, is Bernini's work (1656) and it covers a wooden and ivory chair that St. Peter himself is said to have used. However, scholars tell us that this throne probably dates only from the Middle Ages. See how the adoration of a million lips has completely worn down the bronze on the right foot of the statue of St. Peter.

The scale of the aisles and decoration and the vast sweep of the dome over the ceremonial entrance to the crypt, which is surrounded by votive lamps, bring home the point that St. Peter's is much more than a church; it was intended to function as the glorious setting for all the pomp and panoply of ecclesiastical ceremony. Indeed, only when it serves as the brightly lit background for a great gathering do its vast dimensions find their full expression. *Note: Ushers at the entrance of St. Peter's Church will not allow entry to persons wearing shorts, miniskirts, sleeveless T-shirts, or other revealing clothing (it's advisable for women to carry a scarf to cover bare shoulders and upper arms). This dress code pertains to the entire Vatican, including the Cappella Sistina and the museums.*

A small but rich collection of Vatican treasures is housed in the **Museo Storico** (Historical Museum) in the *Sagrestia* (Sacristy), among them precious antique chalices and the massive 15th-century sculptured bronze tomb of Pope Sixtus V by Antonio Pollaiuolo (1429–98). ▣ *8,000 lire.* ☉ *Apr.–Sept., daily 9–6; Oct.–Mar., daily 9–5.*

The entrance to the **Grotte Vaticane** (Vatican Grottoes), which hold the tombs of many popes, is at the crossing. The only exit from the grottoes leads outside St. Peter's, to the courtyard that holds the entrance to the roof and dome. ▣ *Free.* ☉ *Apr.–Sept., daily 7–6; Oct.–Mar., daily 7–5.*

The roof of the church, reached by elevator or stairs, is a landscape of domes and towers. A short interior staircase leads to the base of the dome for a dove's-eye view of the interior of St. Peter's Basilica. Then, only if you are stout of heart and sound of lung should you attempt the very taxing and claustrophobic climb up the narrow stairs—there's no turning back!—to the balcony of the lantern, where the view embraces the Giardini Vaticani and all of Rome. ▣ *Elevator 6,000 lire, stairs 5,000 lire.* ☉ *Apr.–Sept., daily 8–6; Oct.–Mar., daily 8–5.*

OFF THE
BEATEN PATH

TOMBA DI SAN PIETRO E NECROPOLI PRECOSTANTINIANA – Visit St. Peter's Tombs and the Pre-Constantine Necropolis under St. Peter's for a fascinating glimpse of the underpinnings of the great basilica, which was built over the cemetery where archaeologists say they have found St. Peter's tomb. Apply a few days in advance (or try in the morning for the same day) to the Ufficio Scavi (Excavations Office), on the right beyond the Arco delle Campane entrance to the Vatican, which is left of the basilica. Tell the Swiss guard you want the Ufficio Scavi, and he will let you by. ☎ *06/69885318.* ▣ *Guide 10,000 lire, audiotape tour 6,000 lire if available.* ☉ *Ufficio Scavi: Mon.–Sat. 9–5.*

🕊 ⑪ **Castel Sant'Angelo** (Castle of the Holy Angel). For hundreds of years this fortress guarded the Vatican, to which it is linked by the Passetto, an arcaded passageway. According to legend, Castel Sant'Angelo got its name during the plague of 590, when Pope Gregory the Great, passing by in a religious procession, had a vision of an angel sheathing its sword atop the stone ramparts. Though it may look like a stronghold, Castel Sant'Angelo was in fact built as a tomb for the emperor Hadrian (76–138) in AD 135. By the 6th century, it had been transformed into a fortress, and it remained a refuge for the popes for almost 1,000 years. It has dungeons, battlements, cannons and cannonballs, and a collection of antique weaponry and armor.

The upper terrace, below the massive bronze angel commemorating Gregory's vision, evokes memories of Tosca, Puccini's poignant heroine in the opera of the same name, who threw herself off these ramparts with the cry, *"Scarpia, avanti a Dio!"* ("Scarpia, we meet before God!"). One of Rome's most beautiful bridges, **Ponte Sant'Angelo** spans the Tiber in front of the fortress and is studded with graceful angels designed by Gianlorenzo Bernini.

The lower levels formed the base of Hadrian's mausoleum; ancient ramps and narrow staircases climb through the castle's core to courtyards and frescoed halls and rooms holding a collection of antique arms and armor. Off the loggia is a café. ✉ *Lungotevere Castello 50,* ☎ *06/6875036.* ▣ *8,000 lire.* ☉ *Mon.–Sat. 9–10, Sun. 10–6; closed 2nd and 4th Tues. of month.*

Giardini Vaticani (Vatican Gardens). A tour offers a two-hour jaunt through the pope's backyard, half by bus and half on foot, with a guide. Tickets are available at the Vatican Information Office (✉ Piazza San Pietro, ☎ 06/69884466). Make reservations two or three days in advance. ▣ *18,000 lire.* ☉ *Apr.–Oct., Mon., Tues., Thurs.–Sat. at 10; Nov.–Mar., Sat. at 10, weekdays on request for groups.*

Papal Audience. John Paul II, 264th pope of the Roman Catholic Church, holds mass audiences on Wednesday mornings at 11, in a large modern audience hall or in St. Peter's Square in summer. You must apply for tickets in advance; there are several sources (☞ *below*), but if you are pressed for time, it may be easier to arrange for them through a travel agency. You can avoid the formalities by seeing the pope when he makes his weekly appearance at the window of the Palazzo Vaticano, every Sunday at noon when he is in Rome, to bless the crowd. On summer Sundays he may give the blessing at his summer residence at Castel Gandolfo. For audience tickets, apply in writing well in advance to the Papal Prefecture (Prefettura della Casa Pontificia, ✉ 00120 Vatican City, ☎ 06/69883865, ℻ 06/69885863), indicating the date you prefer, the language you speak, and the hotel where you will be staying. Or go to the prefecture, through the bronze door in the right-hand colonnade; the office is open Monday and Tuesday 9–1 for the Wednesday audience, although last-minute tickets may be available.

You also may be able to pick up free tickets at **Santa Susanna American Church** (✉ Piazza San Bernardo, ☎ 06/4827510). For a fee, travel agencies make arrangements that include transportation (☞ Guided Tours *in* Rome A to Z, *below*).

⑫ **Piazza San Pietro** (St. Peter's Square). As you enter the square you are entering Vatican territory. This square (actually an oval) is one of Bernini's most spectacular masterpieces. Completed in 1667, after 11 years' work—a relatively short time in those days, considering the vastness of the task—the square can hold 400,000 people. It is surrounded by a curving pair of quadruple colonnades, which are topped by a balustrade and statues of 140 saints. Look for the two stone disks set into the pavement on either side of the obelisk. If you stand on one disk, a trick of perspective makes the colonnades seem to consist of a single row of columns. Bernini had an even grander visual effect in mind when he designed the square. By opening up this immense, airy, and luminous space in a neighborhood of narrow, shadowy streets, he created a contrast that would surprise and impress anyone who emerged from the darkness into the light, in a characteristically Baroque metaphor. But in the 1930s, Mussolini ruined it all. To celebrate the "conciliation" between the Vatican and the Italian government under the Lateran Pact of 1929, he conceived of Via della Conciliazione, the broad, rather soulless avenue that now forms the main approach to St. Peter's and gives the eye time to adjust to the enormous dimensions of the square and church, nullifying Bernini's grand Baroque effect.

Musei Vaticani: Beyond the Sistine Ceiling

The Palazzo Vaticano has been the residence of popes since 1377. Actually, it represents a collection of buildings that cover more than 13 acres, containing an estimated (no one has bothered to count them) 1,400 rooms, chapels, and galleries. Other than the pope and his papal court, the occupants are some of the most famous art masterpieces in the world. The main entrance to the museums, on Viale Vaticano, is a long walk from Piazza San Pietro, but there is bus service between the Vatican Information Office (✉ Piazza San Pietro, ☎ 06/69884466) and a secondary museum entrance. The bus goes through the Vatican gardens and costs 2,000 lire, and although it deposits you at a side entrance, it saves a lot of walking and allows a glimpse of some of the Città del Vaticano that would be off-limits otherwise. Some city buses stop near the museums' main entrance on Viale Vaticano: Bus 49 from Piazza Cavour stops right in front; Bus 80 and Tram 19 stop at Piazza Risorgimento, halfway between St. Peter's and the museums. The Ottaviano–S. Pietro stop on Metro A also is in the vicinity. Be aware that dress rules must be adhered to in St. Peter's and the Vatican (☞ Musei Vaticani, *below*).

A Good Tour

Beyond the **Cappella Sistina**, many sections of the **Musei Vaticani** ⑭ are not to be overlooked: the **Museo Egiziano**; the **Chiaramonti** and **Museo Pio Clementino**, which are given over to classical sculptures (among them some of the best-known statues in the world—the *Laocoön,* the *Belvedere Torso,* and the *Apollo Belvedere*—works that, with their vibrant humanism, had a tremendous impact on Renaissance art); and the **Museo Etrusco**. Finally, you should make sure to visit the **Stanze di Raffaello**, and see Raphael's paintings in the **Pinacoteca**.

TIMING

The shortest itinerary takes approximately 90 minutes; others range from three to 4½ hours. To avoid the crowds, get there before opening time, or go at lunchtime or in the last few hours before closing.

Sights to See

★ ⑭ **Musei Vaticani** (Vatican Museums). The immense collections housed here are so rich that unless you are an art history buff, you will probably want to just skim the surface, concentrating on pieces that strike your fancy. The Cappella Sistina is a must, of course, and that's why you may have to wait in line to see it; after all, every tourist in Rome has the same idea. Pick up a leaflet at the main entrance to the museums to see the overall layout. Special posters at the entrance and throughout the museums plot a choice of four color-coded itineraries. The Cappella Sistina is at the far end of the complex, and the leaflet charts two abbreviated itineraries through other collections to reach it. You can rent a taped commentary in English for the Cappella Sistina and the Stanze di Raffaello.

The **Galleria delle Carte Geografiche** (Gallery of Maps) is intriguing; the **Appartamento di S. Pio V** (Apartment of Pope Pius V) a little less so. The **Stanze di Raffaello** (Raphael Rooms), are second only to the Cappella Sistina in artistic interest. In 1508, Pope Julius II employed Raphael Sanzio, on the recommendation of Bramante, to decorate the rooms with biblical scenes. The result was a Renaissance tour de force. Of the four rooms, the second and third were decorated mainly by Raphael. The others were decorated by Giulio Romano and other assistants of Raphael; the first room is known as the Incendio Room, with frescoes painted by Romano.

It's hard to overstate the importance of the **Stanza della Segnatura** (Room of the Signature); here papal bulls were signed. When people talk about the High Renaissance—thought by many to be the pinnacle of Western art—these frescoes often come up. The theme of the room— which may broadly be said to be "enlightenment"—reflects the fact that this was Julius's private library. Theology triumphs in the fresco known as the *Disputa,* or *Debate on the Holy Sacrament.* The *School of Athens* glorifies some of philosophy's greatest exponents, including Plato and Socrates at the fresco's center. The pensive figure on the stairs is sometimes thought to be modeled on Michelangelo, who was painting the Sistine Ceiling at the same time Raphael was working here. All the revolutionary characteristics of High Renaissance paintings are here: naturalism (Raphael's figures lack the awkwardness that pictures painted only a few years earlier still contained); humanism (the idea that man is the most noble and admirable of God's creatures); and a profound interest in the ancient world, the result of the 15th-century rediscovery of archaeology and classical antiquity. There's a tendency to go into something of a stupor when confronted with "great art" of this kind. The fact remains that the frescoes in this room virtually dared its occupants to aspire to the highest ideas of law and learning—an amazing feat for an artist not yet 30.

The tiny **Cappella di Nicholas V** (Chapel of Nicholas V) is aglow with frescoes by Fra Angelico (1387–1455), the Florentine monk whose sensitive paintings were guiding lights for the Renaissance. The **Appartamento Borgia** is worth seeing for the elaborately painted ceilings, designed and partially executed by Pinturicchio, but the rooms have been given over to the Vatican's large, but not particularly impressive, collection of modern religious art.

In 1508, while Raphael was put to work on his series of rooms, the redoubtable Pope Julius II commissioned Michelangelo to fresco the more than 10,000 square ft of the **Cappella Sistina** (Sistine Chapel) ceiling singlehandedly. The task took four years of mental and physical anguish. It's said that for years afterward Michelangelo couldn't read anything without holding it up over his head. The result, however, was the masterpiece that you can now see, its colors cool and brilliant after restoration. Bring a pair of binoculars to get a better look at this incredible work (unfortunately, you're not allowed to lie down on the floor to study the frescoes above, the viewing position of choice in decades past; by the time you leave the chapel, your neck may feel like Michelangelo's, so you may also want to study it—to take a cue from 19th-century visitors—with the aid of a pocket mirror).

The ceiling is literally a painted Bible: Michelangelo's subject was the story of humanity before the coming of Christ, seen through Augustinian tenets of faith popular in early 16th-century theological circles. While some of the frescoed panels are veritable stews of figures, others—especially the depiction of God's outstretched hand giving Adam the spark of life in the *Creation of Adam*—are forcefully simple, revealing how much Michelangelo imparted on the school of painting from the discipline of sculpture. In 1541, some 30 years after completing the ceiling, Michelangelo was commissioned to paint the *Last Judgment* on the wall over the altar. If the artist's ceiling may be taken as an expression of the optimism of the High Renaissance, the *Last Judgment,* by contrast, is a veritable guided tour through Hell. This is not surprising, since in the intervening years Rome had been sacked and pillaged by the French (who had used the Sistine Chapel to stable their horses).

In the interim, the grim Counter-Reformation movement had been adopted by the Church, and the papal court was now so offended by the nakedness of Michelangelo's *Last Judgment* figures that they hired artist Daniele da Volterra—forever after known as *il braghettone* (the breeches-maker)—to paint loincloths over the offending parts. The aged and embittered artist painted his own face on the wrinkled human skin in the hand of St. Bartholomew, below and to the right of the figure of Christ, which he clearly modeled on the *Apollo Belvedere* (now on exhibit in the Vatican galleries). Like the ceiling, the *Last Judgment* has been cleaned, surprising viewers with its clarity and color after restorers unveiled their work in April 1994. Was Michelangelo a master of vibrant color? Or is the "new" Sistine a travesty of Michelangelo's intentions? Opinions remain divided, but most art historians believe the restoration is true to Michelangelo's original vision.

The exhibition halls of the **Biblioteca Vaticana** (Vatican Library) are bright with frescoes and contain a sampling of the library's rich collections of precious manuscripts. Room X, Room of the Aldobrandini Marriage, holds a beautiful Roman fresco of a nuptial rite. More classical statues are on view in the new wing. At the Quattro Cancelli, a cafeteria offers a well-earned break. The **Pinacoteca** (Picture Gallery) displays mainly religious paintings by such artists as Giotto, Fra Angelico, and Filippo Lippi, and Raphael's exceptional *Transfiguration, Coronation,* and *Foligno Madonna.*

In the **Museo Profano** (Pagan Antiquities Museum), modern display techniques enhance another collection of Greek and Roman sculptures. The **Museo Pio Cristiano** (Christian Antiquities Museum) has early Christian and medieval art (its most famous piece is the 3rd-century AD statue, the *Good Shepherd*). The **Museo Missionario-Etnologico** (Ethnological Museum) exhibits art and artifacts from exotic places throughout the world; it's open Wednesday and Saturday only. The complete itinerary ends with the **Museo della Storia** (Historical Museum), whose collection of carriages, uniforms, and arms can be opened by a custodian on request.

In all, the Vatican Museums offer a staggering foray into the realms of art and history; it's foolhardy to try to see all the collections in one day. ✉ *Viale Vaticano,* ☎ *06/69883041.* 🎫 *15,000 lire; free last Sun. of month.* ⏱ *Easter wk and mid-Mar.–Oct., weekdays 8:45–3:45, Sat. 8:45–12:45; Nov.–mid-Mar. (except Easter), Mon.–Sat. 8:45–12:45; last Sun. of every month 8:45–12:45; closed religious holidays (Jan. 1 and 6, Feb. 11, Mar. 19, Easter Sun. and Mon., May 1, Ascension Thurs., Corpus Christi, June 29, Aug. 15 and 16, Nov. 1, Dec. 8, Dec. 25 and 26) and Sun., excepting last Sun. of month. Visitors wearing shorts, miniskirts, sleeveless T-shirts, and tank tops (revealing bare arms or shoulders) will be refused admission.*

NEED A BREAK?   Neighborhood trattorias that are far better and far less popular with tourists than those opposite the Vatican Museums entrance include **Hostaria Dino e Toni** (✉ Via Leone IV 60), where you can dine on typical Roman fare at moderate, even inexpensive prices; **La Caravella** (✉ Via degli Scipioni 32 at Via Vespasiano, off Piazza Risorgimento) serves Roman specialties, including pizza during lunch, every day but Thursday, when it's closed.

Old Rome: Gold and Grandeur

The neighborhood known as Vecchia Roma (Old Rome) is one of Rome's most beautiful districts, thick with narrow streets with curious names, airy Baroque piazzas, and picturesque courtyards. Occupying the horn of land that pushes the Tiber westward toward the Vatican, it has been an integral part of the city since ancient times, and its position between the Vatican and the Lateran palaces, both seats of papal rule, puts it in the mainstream of Rome's development from the Middle Ages onward. It includes such world-famous sights as the Pantheon, but it is mainly an excursion into the 16th and 17th centuries, when Baroque art triumphed. Some of Rome's most coveted residential addresses are here.

The most important clue to the Romans is their Baroque art—not its artistic technicalities, but its spirit. When you understand that, you will no longer be a stranger in Rome. Flagrantly emotional, heavily expressive, and sensuously visual, the 17th-century artistic movement known as the Baroque was born in Rome, the creation of three geniuses, the sculptor and architect Gianlorenzo Bernini and the painters Annibale Carracci (1560–1609) and Caravaggio (1573–1610). From the austere drama found in Caravaggio's painted altarpieces to the jewel-laden, gold-on-gold detail of 17th-century Roman palaces, Baroque style was intended to both shock and delight by upsetting the placid, "correct" rules of the Renaissance. By appealing to the emotions, it became a powerful weapon in the hands of the Counter-Reformation.

Numbers in the text correspond to numbers in the margin and on the Old Rome map.

A Good Walk

Start on Via del Plebiscito, near Piazza Venezia, at the huge church of **Il Gesù** ⑮, the grandmother of all Baroque churches. Walk north to Piazza della Minerva, where in the church of **Santa Maria sopra Minerva** ⑯ you will find the tomb of Fra Angelico. Turn down Via della Minerva to reach the **Pantheon** ⑰. From Piazza della Rotonda in front of the Pantheon, take Via Giustiniani onto Via della Dogana Vecchia to the church of **San Luigi dei Francesi** ⑱, a pilgrimage spot for art lovers everywhere. Just north on Via della Dogana is the church of **Sant'Agostino** ⑲, in the piazza of the same name. Check out historic **Palazzo Altemps** ⑳, off

Piazza Sant'Apollinare, before arriving at **Piazza Navona** ㉑, one of Rome's showpiece piazzas, home to Bernini's Fontana dei Quattro Fiumi and the church of Sant'Agnese in Agone, the quintessence of Baroque architecture. Take Via Tor Millina west to Via della Pace and follow it north to Piazza della Pace, where a semicircular portico stands in front of the 15th-century church of **Santa Maria della Pace** ㉒. Explore the byways on the north side of Corso Vittorio Emanuele II before crossing over one of Rome's great thoroughfares and take a side street south to aristocratic **Via Giulia** east to **Palazzo Falconieri** ㉓, and, just east, **Palazzo Farnese** ㉔, perhaps the most beautiful Renaissance palace in Rome. On your way back to Corso Vittorio Emanuele II along Via Farnese, go through **Campo dei Fiori** ㉕ before coming to the **Museo Baracco** ㉖. Across the way, note one of the outstanding architectural monuments of Renaissance Rome, the **Palazzo Massimo alle Colonne** ㉗, and, two blocks east along the bustling street, the huge, 17th-century church of **Sant'Andrea della Valle** ㉘. Finally, head down Corso del Rinascimento to No. 40, the church of **Sant'Ivo alla Sapienza** ㉙, with a golden lantern atop the dome in the shape of a spiral.

TIMING

Allow about three hours for this walk, plus 10 or 15 minutes to see each church along the way.

Sights to See

㉕ **Campo dei Fiori.** The best time to visit this square, literally the Field of Flowers, is in the morning, when the bustling outdoor food market is in full swing. It was once the scene of public executions, including that of philosopher-monk Giordano Bruno (1548–1600), his statue brooding in the square center. ☉ *Market: Mon.–Sat. 7–1:30.*

⑮ **Il Gesù.** Grandmother of all Baroque churches, this huge structure was designed by Giacomo da Vignola (1507–73). The church is the tangible symbol of the power of the Jesuits, who were a major force in the Counter-Reformation in Europe. It remained undecorated for about 100 years, but when it finally was decorated, no expense was spared. Its interior drips with gold and lapis lazuli, gold and precious marbles, gold and more gold—all covered by a fantastically painted ceiling by Baciccia (1639–1709) that seems to swirl down to merge with the painted stucco figures at its base. ⊠ *Piazza del Gesù.*

㉖ **Museo Baracco.** Housed in a little Renaissance town house, this museum features a varied collection of sculptures from ancient Mediterranean civilizations. ⊠ *Via dei Baullari 1,* ☎ *06/68806848.* ▭ *3,750 lire.* ☉ *Tues.–Sat. 9–7, Sun. 9–1.*

⑳ **Palazzo Altemps.** Those interested in ancient sculpture should not miss one of Rome's greatest collections of classical antiquities, housed in this 16th-century building. Opened in 1997, it houses the collections of ancient Roman and Egyptian sculpture of the **Museo Nazionale Romano.** Look for the large, intricately sculptured *Ludovisi Sarcophagus,* and the *Galata,* a poignant work portraying a barbarian warrior who chooses death for himself and his wife rather than humiliation by the enemy, also in the famed Ludovisi collection. The palace's stunning courtyard and gorgeously frescoed ceilings and loggia make an impressive setting for the sculptures. ⊠ *Piazza Sant'Apollinare 46,* ☎ *06/6833759.* ▭ *12,000 lire.* ☉ *Tues.–Sat. 9–10, Sun. 9–6.*

㉓ **Palazzo Falconieri.** Francesco Borromini's (1599–1667) masterful work of architecture houses nothing of interest to the visitor, but the building itself makes one of Rome's most elegant attractions. In order to get a good look at this gracefully imposing building, go around the block and view it from along the Tiber embankment. ⊠ *Via Giulia 1.*

Old Rome

㉔ Palazzo Farnese. Michelangelo had a hand in building what is now the French Embassy and perhaps the most beautiful Renaissance palace in Rome. Within is the **Galleria Carracci** (Carracci Gallery) vault painted by Annibale Carracci between 1597 and 1604—the second-greatest ceiling in Rome; write in advance to the embassy (Ambassador, ✉ French Embassy, Piazza Farnese 64, 00186 Rome) for special permission to view it. It depicts the loves of the gods, a supremely pagan theme that the artist painted in a swirling style that announced the birth of Baroque. It's said that Carracci was so dismayed at the miserly fee he received—the Farnese family was extravagantly rich even by the standards of 15th- and 16th-century Rome's extravagantly rich—that he took to drink and died shortly thereafter. Those who sympathize with the poor man's plight will be further dismayed to learn that the French government pays one lira every 99 years as rent for their sumptuous embassy. ✉ *Piazza Farnese.*

㉗ Palazzo Massimo alle Colonne. A graceful columned portico marks this inconspicuous but seminal architectural monument of Renaissance Rome, built by Baldassare Peruzzi in 1527. Via del Paradiso, across Corso Vittorio Emanuele II, affords a better view. ✉ *Corso Vittorio Emanuele II 141.*

⑰ Pantheon. Paradoxically, this is one of Rome's most perfect, well-preserved, and perhaps least-appreciated ancient monuments. Built on the site of an earlier pantheon erected in 27 BC by Augustus's general Agrippa, it was entirely rebuilt by the emperor Hadrian around AD 120. It was actually designed by Hadrian himself. The most striking thing about the Pantheon is not its size, immense though it is (until 1960 the dome was the largest ever built); rather it is the remarkable unity of the building. You don't have to look far to find the reason for this harmony: The diameter of the dome is exactly equal to the height of the walls. The hole in the ceiling is intentional: The oculus at the apex of the dome signifies the "all-seeing eye of heaven." Note the original bronze doors: They have survived more than 1,800 years, centuries more than the interior's rich gold ornamentation, long since plundered by popes and emperors. ✉ *Piazza della Rotonda,* ☎ *06/68300230.* 🎫 *Free.* ☉ *Mon.–Sat. 9–6:30, Sun. 9–1.*

★ ☙ ㉑ Piazza Navona. This famed 17th-century piazza, which mimics the oval form of Emperor Domitian's stadium, is one of Rome's showpiece attractions. It still has the carefree air of the days when it was the scene of Roman circus games, medieval jousts, and 17th-century carnivals. Today, this renowned spot often attracts fashion photographers and Romans out for their evening *passeggiata* (promenade). The Christmas fair held in the piazza from early December through January 6 is lively and fun for children, with rides, games, Santa Claus, and the Befana, the ugly but good witch who brings candy and toys to Italian children on the Epiphany. Bernini's splashing **Fontana dei Quattro Fiumi** (Fountain of the Four Rivers), with an enormous rock squared off by statues representing the four corners of the world, makes a fitting centerpiece. Behind the fountain stands the church of **Sant'Agnese in Agone,** the absolute quintessence of Baroque architecture, built by the Pamphili Pope Innocent X and still owned by his descendants, the Doria Pamphili. The facade—a wonderfully rich mélange of bell towers, concave spaces, and dovetailed stone and marble—is by Carlo Rainaldi and Francesco Borromini, a contemporary and sometime rival of Bernini. One story has it that the Bernini statue nearest the church (which represents the River Plate) has its hand up before his eye because it can't bear to look upon the "inferior" Borromini facade. But the facade wasn't built until after the fountain was installed.

NEED A
BREAK? **Tre Scalini** café (⊠ Piazza Navona 30, closed Wed.) actually invented
the *tartufo,* a luscious chocolate-covered ice-cream specialty.

★ ⑱ **San Luigi dei Francesi.** In the last chapel on the left are three stunningly
dramatic works by Caravaggio, the master of the heightened approach
to light and dark. The inevitable coin machine will light up his *Calling
of St. Matthew, Matthew and the Angel,* and *Matthew's Martyrdom,* seen
from left to right, and Caravaggio's mastery of light takes it from there.
Time has fully vindicated the artist's patron, Cardinal Francesco del Monte,
who commissioned these works and stoutly defended their worth from
the consternation of the clergy of San Luigi, who didn't appreciate the
artist's roistering and unruly lifestyle. ⊠ *Piazza San Luigi dei Francesi.*
⊙ *Fri.–Wed. 7:30–12:30 and 3:30–7, Thurs. 7:30–12:30.*

⑲ **Sant'Agostino.** Caravaggio's celebrated *Madonna of the Pilgrims*—which
scandalized all Rome because it pictured pilgrims with dirt on the soles
of their feet—can be found in this small church, over the first altar on
the left. ⊠ *Piazza di Sant'Agostino.*

㉘ **Sant'Andrea della Valle.** This huge, 17th-century church looms mightily over a busy intersection. Aficionados of Puccini, who set the first
act of his opera *Tosca* here, have been known to hire a horse-drawn
carriage at night for an evocative journey that traces the course of the
opera (from Sant'Andrea up Via Giulia to Palazzo Farnese—Scarpia's
headquarters—to the locale of the opera's climax, Castel Sant'Angelo). ⊠ *Piazza Vidoni 6.*

㉙ **Sant'Ivo alla Sapienza.** Borromini's inspirational church has what
must surely be the most fascinating dome in all Rome—topped by a
golden spiral said to have been inspired by a bee's stinger. ⊠ *Corso
Rinascimento 40.*

㉒ **Santa Maria della Pace.** Hidden away in a corner of Old Rome, grac-
ing Piazza Santa Maria della Pace, are a semicircular portico and 15th-
century church. In 1656, Pietro da Cortona (1596–1669) was
commissioned by Pope Alexander VII to enlarge its tiny piazza (to accommodate the carriages of the church's wealthy parishioners), and
the result was one of Rome's most delightful little architectural stage
sets, complete with bijou-size palaces. Within the church are two Renaissance treasures: Raphael's frescoes of the Sibyls (above the first altar
on the right near the front door) and the cloister designed by Bramante,
the very first expression of High Renaissance style in Rome. It's rarely
open, except for guided visits, but the cloister is used in the summer
for concerts. ⊠ *Piazza Santa Maria della Pace.*

⑯ **Santa Maria sopra Minerva.** Practically the only Gothic-style church
in Rome, the attractions are Michelangelo's *Risen Christ* and the tomb
of the gentle 15th-century artist Fra Angelico. Have some coins handy
for the *luce* (light) boxes that illuminate the **Cappella Carafa** (Carafa
Chapel) in the right transept, where exquisite 15th-century frescoes by
Filippino Lippi (circa 1457–1504) are well worth the small investment
(Lippi's most famous student was Botticelli). In front of the church,
Bernini's charming elephant bearing an Egyptian obelisk has an inscription on the base stating something to the effect that it takes a strong
mind to sustain solid wisdom. ⊠ *Piazza della Minerva.*

Via Giulia. Named after Pope Julius II and having functioned for more
than four centuries as the "salon of Rome," this street is the address
of choice for Roman aristocrats. It is lined with elegant palaces, including
Palazzo Falconieri (☞ *above*), and old churches (one, San Eligio, reputedly designed by Raphael himself). The area around Via Giulia is

a wonderful section to wander through and get the feel of daily life as carried on in a centuries-old setting; this experience is enhanced by the dozens of antiques shops in the neighborhood.

Vistas and Views: From the Scalinata di Spagna to the Fontana di Trevi

Though it has a bustling commercial air, this part of the city also holds some great visual allurements. The most extravagant of all is the elaborate marble confection that is the monument to Vittorio Emanuele II. Among the things to look for are stately palaces, Baroque ballrooms, and the greatest example of portraiture in Rome, Velázquez's incomparable *Innocent X*. Those with a taste for the sumptuous theatricality of Roman ecclesiastical architecture—heroic illusionistic ceiling painting in particular—will find this a rewarding area. The highlights are the Fontana di Trevi and the Scalinata di Spagna, 18th-century Rome's most famous example of city planning.

Numbers in the text correspond to numbers in the margin and on the Rome map.

A Good Walk

Start at the flamboyant **Monumento di Vittorio Emanuele II** ㉚ in Piazza Venezia, a mass of marble studded with statuary. As you look up Via del Corso, to your left is **Palazzo Venezia** ㉛, an art-filled Renaissance palace where Mussolini once addressed the crowds. On Saturday, you can visit the picture gallery known as Galleria Colonna, in the **Palazzo Colonna** ㉜, east of Piazza Venezia. From Piazza Venezia head north on Via del Corso, one of the city's busiest shopping streets, to the **Palazzo Doria Pamphili** ㉝. A quick detour west will bring you to the sumptuous 17th-century church of **Sant'Ignazio** ㉞. If you continue north on Via del Corso you will reach Piazza Colonna and the ancient **Colonna di Marcus Aurelius** ㉟. Continue north on Via del Corso and take a right onto chic Via Condotti, which gives you a head-on view of the Piazza di Spagna and the **Scalinata di Spagna** ㊱; to the right of the steps, at No. 26, is the **Fondazione Keats-Shelley Memorial** ㊲, in which the English Romantic poet Keats lived. If you climb the Spanish Steps you will get a good view of Rome's skyline from the top, and you can take a quick detour onto Via Gregoriana to discover the **Palazzetto Zuccari** ㊳. From the narrow (southern) end of Piazza di Spagna, take Via Propaganda Fide to Sant'Andrea delle Fratte, and take a left onto Via del Nazareno, then cross busy Via del Tritone to Via della Stamperia. This street leads to the **Fontana di Trevi** ㊴, one of Rome's most famous landmarks.

TIMING

The walk takes approximately two to three hours. In the morning the air is cleaner and car and pedestrian traffic is lighter.

Sights to See

㉟ **Colonna di Marcus Aurelius.** This ancient column is an extraordinary stone history book. Its detailed reliefs spiraling up to the top illustrate the emperor Marcus Aurelius's (121–180) victorious campaigns against the barbarians. ⊠ *Piazza Colonna.*

㊲ **Fondazione Keats-Shelley Memorial** (Keats and Shelley Memorial House). English Romantic poet John Keats (1795–1821) lived in what is now a museum dedicated to him and his great contemporary and friend, Percy Bysshe Shelley (1792–1822). You can visit his tiny rooms, preserved as they were when he died here in 1821. ⊠ *Piazza di Spagna 26, next to the Spanish Steps,* ☎ *06/6784235.* ☞ *5,000 lire.* ☉ *June–Sept., weekdays 9–1 and 3–6; Oct.–May, weekdays 9–1 and 2:30–5:30.*

★ ③ **Fontana di Trevi** (Trevi Fountain). Tucked away off Via del Tritone in a minuscule piazza, the fountain, designed by Nicola Salvi (1697–1751), is a spectacular fantasy of mythical sea creatures amidst cascades of splashing waters. It was featured in the 1954 film *Three Coins in the Fountain* and, of course, was the scene of Anita Ekberg's aquatic frolic in Fellini's *La Dolce Vita*. The fountain is the world's most spectacular wishing well: Legend has it that you can ensure your return to Rome by tossing a coin into the fountain. At night, the spotlit piazza takes on the festive air of a crowded outdoor party.

NEED A BREAK? — You can get your supreme gelato fix at **Il Gelato di San Crispino** (✉ Via della Panetteria 54, near the Trevi Fountain, ☎ 06/70450412), closed Tuesday; devoted fans addicted to exquisite and unusual flavors single it out as one of Rome's best.

③⓪ **Monumento di Vittorio Emanuele II.** The huge bronze sculpture group atop this vast marble monument is visible from many parts of the city, making this modern Rome's most flamboyant landmark. It was erected in the late 19th century to honor Italy's first king, Vittorio Emanuele II, and the unification of Italy. Sometimes said to resemble a typewriter in the Victorian style, it houses the **Tomba del Milite Ignoto** (Tomb of the Unknown Soldier), with its eternal flame. Although the monument has been closed to the public for many years, plans are in the works to reopen it. The views from the top of the steps are among Rome's best. Opposite the monument, note the enclosed wooden veranda fronting the palace on the corner of Via del Plebiscito and Via Corso. For the many years that she lived in Rome, Napoléon's mother had a fine view from here of the local goings-on. ✉ *Piazza Venezia*.

✋ ③⑧ **Palazzetto Zuccari.** Near the top of the Scalinata di Spagna stands what many consider the most amusing house in all of Italy, with a facade designed to look like a grimacing stone monster. The entrance is through the monster's mouth; the eyes are the house's windows. It was designed in 1591 by the Mannerist painter Federico Zuccari (1540–1609), whose home this was. Zuccari sank all his money into this bizarre creation, dying in debt before his curious memorial, as it turned out to be, was completed. It is now the property of the **Biblioteca Hertziana**, Rome's prestigious fine arts library. ✉ *Via Gregoriana 30*.

③② **Palazzo Colonna.** Rome's patrician family opens up its fabulous home to the public once a week. The entrance to the picture gallery, **Galleria Colonna**, open only on Saturday morning, is a secondary one, behind a plain, obscure-seeming door. The old masters are lackluster, but the gallery should be on your must-do list because the **Sala Grande** is truly the grandest 17th-century room in Rome. More than 300 ft long, and a bedazzlement of chandeliers, colored marble, and enormous paintings, it is best known today as the site where Audrey Hepburn met the press in *Roman Holiday*. ✉ *Via della Pilotta 17*, ☎ 06/6794362. 💶 10,000 lire. ⏰ Sept.–July, Sat. 9–1.

③③ **Palazzo Doria Pamphili.** The 18th-century facade of this palazzo on Via del Corso is only a small part of a bona-fide patrician palace, still the residence of a princely family, who rent out many of the palazzo's 1,000 rooms. You shouldn't miss seeing the family's incredibly rich art collection in the frescoed **Pinacoteca** and the few salons opened in 1996. Pride of place is given to the famous (and pitiless) 17th-century Diego Velázquez (1599–1660) portrait of the Pamphili Pope *Innocent X*, but don't overlook Caravaggio's poignant *Rest on the Flight to Egypt*—and, time permitting, catch the guided tour of the state apartments, which gives a discreet glimpse of an aristocratic lifestyle. Pundits say most Roman palazzi consist of one bathroom, two bedrooms, and 40 ballrooms, and after this tour, you can understand why. ✉ *Piazza del Collegio Romano 2,* ☎ *06/6797323.* ☜ *Pinacoteca 12,000 lire, private-apartments tour 5,000 lire.* ☉ *Fri.–Wed. 10–5.*

㉛ **Palazzo Venezia.** A blend of medieval solidity and genuine Renaissance grace, this building houses a good collection of paintings, sculptures, and objets d'art in its grand salons, some of which Mussolini (1883–1945) used as his offices. Notice the balcony over the main portal, from which Il Duce addressed huge crowds in **Piazza Venezia** below. Nowadays, the square's most imposing figure is the policeman directing traffic from his little podium in the middle, whose almost comical display of orchestration is a constant source of amusement to passersby. ✉ *Via del Plebiscito 118,* ☎ *06/69994221.* ☜ *8,000 lire.* ☉ *Tues.–Sat. 9–1:30, Sun. 9–12:30.*

㉞ **Sant'Ignazio.** The false interior dome in this sumptuous 17th-century church is a trompe l'oeil oddity among the lavishly frescoed domes of the Eternal City. To get the full effect of the illusionistic ceiling painted by Andrea del Pozzo (1642–1709), stand on the small disk set into the floor of the nave to view his *Glory of St. Ignatius Loyola.* The church contains some of Rome's most splendorous, jewel-encrusted altars. If you're lucky, you might be able to catch an evening concert performed here. The church is the focus of Filippo Raguzzini's 18th-century rococo piazza, where the buildings are arranged almost as in a stage set, reminding us that theatricality was a key element of almost all the best Baroque and rococo art. ✉ *Piazza Sant'Ignazio.*

NEED A BREAK?   The **Antico Caffè Greco** (✉ Via Condotti 86, ☎ 06/6791700, closed Sun.), a 200-year-old institution, ever a haunt of artists and literati, has tiny, marble-top tables and velour settees. Goethe, Byron, and Liszt were habitués; Buffalo Bill stopped in when his Wild West road show hit Rome.

★ **㊱** **Scalinata di Spagna** (Spanish Steps). Both the steps and the **Piazza di Spagna** get their names from the Spanish Embassy and the Holy See (the Vatican), opposite the American Express office, though the staircase was built with French funds in 1723. In an allusion to the Church of Trinità (Trinity) dei Monti at the top of the hill, the staircase is divided by three landings (beautifully banked with blooming azaleas from mid-April to mid-May). For centuries, the Scalinata (as natives refer to the steps) has been the place to see and be seen. This area has always welcomed tourists: 18th-century dukes and duchesses on their Grand Tour, 19th-century artists and writers in search of inspiration—among them, Stendhal, Balzac, Thackeray, and Byron—and today's enthusiastic hordes. Bernini's **Fontana della Barcaccia** (Fountain of the Old Boat) is near the center of the piazza. ✉ *Piazza di Spagna.*

Historic Churches: Heavenly Monuments of Faith

It is hard not to be impressed by the historic and architectural grandeur of Rome's major churches. Three churches are the highlights of this walk, two of them major basilicas with roots in the early centuries of Christianity.

A Good Walk

Not far from Piazza Venezia and the Roman Forum is the church of **San Pietro in Vincoli** ㊵, off Via Cavour. Look for Via San Francesco da Paola, a street staircase that passes under the old Borgia palace and leads to the church. Return to Via Cavour, which veers northeast to **Santa Maria Maggiore** ㊶, and from there go south on Via Merulana, which leads straight to **San Giovanni in Laterano** ㊷. The adjoining

Palazzo Laterano houses the Museo Storico Vaticano; across the street, a small building houses the **Scala Santa** ㊸, or Holy Stairs, supposedly from Pilate's Jerusalem palace. Circle the Palazzo Laterano to see the 6th-century octagonal Battistero di San Giovanni, forerunner of many such buildings throughout Italy.

TIMING

The walk alone takes approximately 90 minutes, plus 15–20 minutes in the churches. Allow at least an hour to explore San Clemente. A visit to the Museo Storico Vaticano will take you about 45 minutes.

Sights to See

㊷ **San Giovanni in Laterano.** Many are surprised when they discover that the cathedral of Rome is not St. Peter's but this church. Dominating the piazza whose name it shares, this immense building is where the present pope still officiates in his capacity as Rome's bishop. The towering facade and Borromini's cool Baroque interior emphasize the majesty of its proportions.

The adjoining **Palazzo Laterano** (Lateran Palace), once the early popes' official residence and still technically part of the Vatican, now houses the offices of the Rome Diocese and the **Museo Storico Vaticano** (Vatican Historical Museum). ⊠ *Piazza San Giovanni in Laterano.* ☎ *6,000 lire.* ☉ *Museum: Sat. and the 1st Sun. of each month 8:45–1.*

OFF THE
BEATEN PATH

SAN CLEMENTE – The remains of ancient Roman dwellings and a 4th-century church below the upper church of San Clemente are among Rome's most intriguing subterranean sights. ⊠ *Via San Giovanni in Laterano,* ☎ *06/70451018.* ☎ *Donation requested.* ☉ *Mon.–Sat. 9–noon and 3:30–6, Sun. 10–noon.*

SANTI QUATTRO CORONATI – The 12th-century Four Crowned Saints church, part of a fortified abbey that provided refuge to early popes and emperors, is in one of the most unusual corners of Rome, a quiet island that has resisted the tide of time and traffic flowing beneath its ramparts. Few places in Rome are as reminiscent of the Middle Ages. Don't miss the cloister with its well-tended gardens and 12th-century fountain. The entrance is the door in the left nave; ring if it's not open. You can also ring at the adjacent convent for the key to the Oratorio di San Silvestro (Oratory of St. Sylvester), with 13th-century frescoes. ⊠ *Largo Santi Quattro Coronati.*

㊵ **San Pietro in Vincoli.** The church houses St. Peter's chains (under the altar) and Michelangelo's *Moses,* a powerful statue almost as famed as his frescoes in the Sistine Chapel. The *Moses* was destined for the tomb of Julius II, but Michelangelo was driven to distraction by the interference of Pope Julius (1443–1513) and his successors, and the tomb was never finished. The statue is a remarkable sculpture but the church is usually jammed with tour groups, and the monument itself fronts a large, ugly souvenir shop. ⊠ *Piazza San Pietro in Vincoli off Via Cavour.*

㊶ **Santa Maria Maggiore.** One of the oldest and most spacious churches in Rome, it was built on the spot where a 3rd-century pope witnessed a miraculous midsummer snowfall. The gleaming mosaics on the arch in front of the main altar date from the 5th century. The apse mosaic dates from the 13th century—an opulently carved wood ceiling believed to have been gilded with the first gold brought from the New World. ⊠ *Piazza Santa Maria Maggiore off Via Cavour.*

㊸ **Scala Santa** (Sacred Stairs). A small building opposite the Lateran Palace (☞ *above*) houses the so-called Holy Stairs, claimed to be the staircase from Pilate's palace in Jerusalem. Behind the palace is the 6th-century octagonal **Battistero di San Giovanni** (St. John's Baptistery), forerunner of many similar buildings throughout Italy, and Rome's oldest and tallest obelisk, brought from Thebes and dating from the 15th century BC. ⊠ *Piazza San Giovanni in Laterano.*

From the Monte Quirinale to the Piazza della Repubblica: Princely Palaces and Romantic Fountains

You'll see ancient Roman sculptures and early Christian churches but concentrate on the 16th and 17th centuries, when Baroque art—and Bernini—triumphed in Rome.

A Good Walk

Begin on **Monte Quirinale** ㊹, the highest of Rome's seven hills. Here you'll find the Palazzo del Quirinale, official residence of the president of Italy. Also of note is the **Palazzo Pallavicini-Rospigliosi** ㊺, a 17th-century palace. Along Via del Quirinale (which becomes Via XX Settembre) is the church of **Sant'Andrea** ㊻, considered by many to be Bernini's finest work, and, at the Quattro Fontane (Four Fountains) crossroads, the church of **San Carlo alle Quattro Fontane** ㊼, designed by Bernini's rival Borromini. Take a left on Via delle Quattro Fontane to reach the imposing **Palazzo Barberini** ㊽, where the Galleria Nazionale d'Arte Antica is home to splendid masterpieces by Raphael and Caravaggio. Down the hill is Piazza Barberini and the **Fontana del Tritone** ㊾, another Bernini design. Cross the piazza and begin your gradual climb up Via Vittorio Veneto, curving past **Santa Maria della Concezione** ㊿ and the U.S. Embassy and turning off onto Via Bissolati. On the corner of Piazza San Bernardo is the church of **Santa Maria della Vittoria** �51, known for Bernini's Baroque decoration. It's not far down Via Orlando to **Piazza della Repubblica** �52, where you will find the pretty Fontana delle Naiadi. On one side of the square is an ancient Roman brick facade, which marks the church of Santa Maria degli Angeli. Beyond, on the near corner of Piazza del Cinquecento, the vast square in front of Stazione Termini, is the last stop on this walk, **Palazzo Massimo alle Terme** �53, which houses part of the Museo Nazionale Romano's collections, highlighting examples of the fine mosaics and masterful paintings that decorated ancient Rome's villas and palaces.

TIMING

The walk takes approximately 90 minutes, plus 10–15 minutes for each church visited, and two hours each for visits to the Galleria Nazionale in Palazzo Barberini and the Palazzo Massimo alle Terme.

Sights to See

㊾ **Fontana del Tritone** (Triton Fountain). Centerpiece of Piazza Barberini is Bernini's graceful fountain, designed in 1637 for the sculptor's munificent patron, Pope Urban VIII (1568–1644), whose Barberini coat of arms, featuring bees, is at the base of the large shell.

㊹ **Monte Quirinale** (Quirinal Hill). This is the highest of ancient Rome's seven hills and the one where ancient Romans and, later, the popes built their residences in order to escape the deadly miasmas and the malaria of the low-lying area around the Forum. Every day at 4 PM the ceremony of the changing of the guards at the portal includes a sprightly miniparade, complete with band. The fountain in the square boasts ancient statues of Castor and Pollux reining in their unruly steeds, and a basin salvaged from the Roman Forum. The **Palazzo del Quirinale**, the largest on Piazza Quirinale, belonged first to the popes, then to Italy's kings, and is now the official residence of the nation's president.

48 Palazzo Barberini. Along with architect Carlo Maderno, Borromini helped make the splendid 17th-century Palazzo Barberini a residence worthy of Rome's leading art patron, Pope Urban VIII, who began this palazzo for his family in 1625. Inside, the **Galleria Nazionale d'Arte Antica** offers some fine works by Raphael (the *Fornarina*) and by Caravaggio. Rome's biggest ballroom is here; its ceiling, painted by Pietro da Cortona, depicts Immortality bestowing a crown upon Divine Providence escorted by—"a bomber squadron," to quote Sir Michael Levey—of mutant bees (bees featured prominently in the heraldic device of the Barberini). ✉ *Via delle Quattro Fontane 13,* ☎ *06/4814591.* ☞ *8,000 lire.* ☼ *Tues.–Sat. 9–10, Sun. 9–6.*

53 Palazzo Massimo alle Terme. This 19th-century palace in early Baroque style holds part of the collections of antiquities belonging to the Museo Nazionale Romano (also exhibited in the Palazzo Altemps; ☞ *above*). Here you can see extraordinary examples of the fine mosaics and masterful paintings that decorated ancient Rome's palaces and villas. Don't miss the fresco—depicting a lush garden in bloom—that came from the villa that Livia, wife of Emperor Augustus, owned outside Rome. ✉ *Largo Villa Peretti 2,* ☎ *06/48903501.* ☞ *12,000 lire (includes Museo delle Terme di Diocleziano,* ☞ *Piazza della Repubblica, below).* ☼ *Tues.– Sat. 9–10, Sun. 9–6.*

45 Palazzo Pallavicini-Rospigliosi. This palace was built in 1605 for Cardinal Scipione Borghese; on the first day of each month, you can view Guido Reni's fresco of *Aurora*—a landmark in Baroque painting—in the palace's park pavilion. ✉ *Via XXIV Maggio 43, just off Piazza del Quirinale,* ☎ *06/4827224.* ☞ *Free.* ☼ *1st day of month 10–noon and 3–5.*

52 Piazza della Repubblica. This piazza has a typical 19th-century layout, but the curving porticoes echo the immense ancient **Terme di Diocleziano** (Baths of Diocletian), which once stood here. Built in the 4th century AD, they were the largest and most impressive of the baths of ancient Rome, and their vast halls, pools, and gardens could accommodate 3,000 people at a time. Also part of the great baths was an **Aula Ottagonale** (Octagonal Hall) that now holds a sampling of ancient sculptures found there, including two beautiful bronzes. ✉ *Via Romita.* ☞ *Free.* ☼ *Daily 10–1 and 3–6.*

Another part of the Baths of Diocletian was later transformed into a monastery and then into the **Museo delle Terme di Diocleziano.** The cloister holds the Museo Nazionale Romano's collection of ancient stone inscriptions. Lining the garden paths are bits and pieces of ancient Rome. ✉ *Viale E. De Nicola 79,* ☎ *06/4880530.* ☞ *12,000 lire (includes Palazzo Massimo alle Terme).* ☼ *Tues.–Sat. 10–2, Sun. 9–1.*

The pretty **Fontana delle Naiadi** (Fountain of the Naiads), a turn-of-the-century addition to the piazza, delights with voluptuous bronze ladies wrestling happily with marine monsters. The curving ancient Roman brick facade on one side of the piazza marks the church of **Santa Maria degli Angeli,** adapted by Michelangelo from the vast central chamber of the colossal baths. The scale of the church's interior gives you an idea of the grandeur of the ancient building.

47 San Carlo alle Quattro Fontane. Borromini's church at the Four Fountains crossroads is an architectural gem. In a space no larger than the base of one of the piers of St. Peter's, Borromini attained geometric perfection. Characteristically, the architect chose a subdued white stucco for the interior decoration, so as not to distract from the form. The exterior of the church is Borromini at his bizarre best, all curves and rippling movement. Outside, four charming fountains frame views in four directions. ⊠ *Via del Quirinale 23*.

50 **Santa Maria della Concezione.** One of the most bizarre sights in Rome is the crypt of this Capuchin church, where you can see—if you like that sort of thing—the skeletons and assorted bones of 4,000 dead monks artistically arranged in four macabre chapels. ⊠ *Via Veneto 27*, ☎ *06/4871185*. 🎫 *Donation requested*. ☉ *Daily 9–noon and 3–6*.

51 **Santa Maria della Vittoria.** This church is known for Bernini's Baroque decoration of the Cappella Cornaro, an exceptional fusion of architecture, painting, and sculpture, in which the *Ecstasy of St. Teresa* is the focal point. Bernini's audacious conceit was to model the chapel as a theater: Members of the Cornaro family—sculpted in white marble—watch from theater boxes as, center stage, St. Teresa, in the throes of mystical rapture, is pierced by a gilded arrow held by an angel. To quote one 18th-century observer, President de Brosses: "If that is divine love, I know what it is." ⊠ *Via XX Settembre*.

46 **Sant'Andrea.** This small but imposing Baroque church was designed and decorated by Bernini, who considered it one of his finest works. ⊠ *Via del Quirinale*.

Amid Sylvan Glades: From the Villa Borghese to the Ara Pacis

Beautiful masterpieces are as common as bricks on this walk, which offers more visual excitement than most cities possess in their entire environs. Along the way, Villa Borghese, Rome's largest park, can alleviate gallery gout by offering an oasis in which to enjoy a picnic under the ilex trees. Just be sure to pick up your foodstuffs in advance, whether ready-to-go from the snack bars or do-it-yourself from *alimentari* (food shops), as you'll find only fast-food carts within the park itself.

A Good Walk

Start at **Porta Pinciana** �io, one of the entrances to Villa Borghese. Follow Viale del Museo Borghese to the **Galleria Borghese** ㊌ and its fabulous art collection in an extraordinary setting. Head to the southwest corner of the park to enjoy the view of Rome from the **Pincio** ㊌ belvedere before descending the ramps to **Piazza del Popolo** ㊌. At the north end of the piazza, next to the 400-year-old city gate, the Porta del Popolo, is the church of **Santa Maria del Popolo** ㊌, with one of the richest art collections of any church in the city. Stroll south along Via di Ripetta to the **Augusteum,** built by Caesar Augustus; next to it is the **Ara Pacis** ㊌, built in 13 BC.

TIMING

The walk takes approximately two hours; allow an additional hour for the Galleria Borghese, and another additional hour for the stroll past the Augusteum and to see the Ara Pacis.

Sights to See

59 **Ara Pacis** (Altar of Augustan Peace). This altar, sheltered in an unattractive modern edifice on the northwest corner of Piazza Augusto Imperatore, was erected in 13 BC to celebrate the era of peace ushered in by Augustus's military victories. The reliefs showing the procession of the Roman imperial family are magnificent and moving. Notice the poignant presence of several forlorn children; historians now believe they attest to the ambition of Augustus's wife, the Empress Livia, who succeeded in having her son, Tiberius, ascend to the throne by dispatching his family rivals with poison. Next to it is the imposing bulk of the marble-clad **Mausoleo di Augusto** (Mausoleum of Augustus) Augus-

tus built for himself and his family. ⊠ *Via Ripetta,* ☎ *06/68806848.*
🎟 *3,750 lire.* 🕐 *Tues.–Sat. 9–7, Sun. 9–1:30.*

★ ⑤⑤ **Galleria Borghese** (Borghese Gallery). Cardinal Scipione Borghese's
(1576–1633) 1613 palace—a place to flaunt his fabulous antiquities
collection and elegant fetes—is today a monument to 18th-century
Roman interior decoration at its most extravagant, dripping with porphyry and alabaster. Throughout the grand salons are ancient Roman
mosaic pavements and statues of various deities, including one officially known as Venus Vincitrix, but there has never been any doubt
as to its real subject: Pauline Bonaparte, Napoléon's sister, who married Prince Camillo Borghese in one of the storied matches of the 19th
century. Sculpted by Canova (1757–1822), the princess reclines on a
chaise lounge, bare-bosomed, her hips swathed in classical drapery, the
very model of haughty detachment and sly come-hither. Pauline is
known to have been shocked that her husband took pleasure in showing off the work to his guests. This coyness seems all the more curious
given the reply she is supposed to have made to a lady who asked her
how she could have posed for the work: "Oh, but the studio was heated."
But then it was exactly the combination of aristocratic disdain and naïveté
that is said to have made her irresistible in the first place.

Other rooms hold important sculptures by Bernini, including the *David*
and *Apollo and Daphne.* The renowned picture collection has splendid works by Titian, Caravaggio, and Raphael, among others. ⊠ *Piazza Scipione Borghese, off Via Pinciana,* ☎ *06/8548577.* 🎟 *12,000
lire.* 🕐 *Booking compulsory, Tues.–Sat. 9–10, Sun. 9–6.*

⑤⑦ **Piazza del Popolo.** Designed by neoclassic architect Giuseppe Valadier
(1762–1839) in the early 1800s, this square is one of the largest in Rome,
and it has a 3,000-year-old **obelisco** (obelisk) in the middle. The book-
end **Baroque churches** at the southern end of the piazza are not, first
appearances to the contrary, twins. At one end of the square is the 400-
year-old **Porta del Popolo,** Rome's northern city gate.

NEED A   **Rosati** (⊠ Piazza del Popolo 5, ☎ 06/3225859) café, with a tearoom
BREAK?   and upstairs dining room, has never gone out of style, forever a ren-
           dezvous of literati, artists, and actors.

🕑 ⑤⑥ **Pincio.** The southwestern corner of **Villa Borghese,** Rome's peaceful
17th-century park built as the pleasure gardens of the powerful Borghese family, occupies the Pincian Hill, one of the seven hills of ancient
Rome. The park and belvedere were laid out by the early 19th-cen-
tury architect Valadier as part of his overall plan for Piazza del Popolo.
Back then, counts and countesses liked to take their evening passeggiata here in the hopes of meeting Pius IX, the last pope to go about
Rome on foot. A Punch and Judy show is staged regularly for tots, and
band concerts are held seasonally on Sunday mornings.

⑤④ **Porta Pinciana** (Pincian Gate). One of the historic city gates in the Au-
relian Walls surrounding Rome, the Porta itself was built in the 6th
century AD, about three centuries after the walls were built to keep out
the barbarians. These days it is one of the entrances to Villa Borghese.

⑤⑧ **Santa Maria del Popolo.** This church next to the Porta del Popolo goes
almost unnoticed, but it has one of the richest collections of art of any
church in Rome. Here you'll find Raphael's High Renaissance masterpiece, the **Cappella Chigi** (Chigi Chapel) as well as two stunning Caravaggios in the **Cappella Cerasi** (Cerasi Chapel), which definitively prove
just how modern 17th-century art can be. Elsewhere in the church, the

great names—Bramante, Bernini, Pinturicchio, Sansovino (1486–1570), Carracci—resound in the silence. ⊠ *Piazza del Popolo.*

Across the Tiber: The Ghetto, Tiberina Island, and Trastevere

This walk takes you through separate communities, each staunchly resisting the tides of change, including the Jewish Ghetto. In picturesque Trastevere you will find a resident colony of foreigners coexisting with "the Romans of Rome": blunt, uninhibited, sharp-eyed, friendly, sincere, often beautiful, and seldom varnished. Despite rampant gentrification, Trastevere remains about the most tightly knit community in Rome, its inhabitants proudly proclaiming their descent—whether real or imagined—from the ancient Romans.

A Good Walk

Begin in the old Ghetto, on Via del Teatro Marcello, which leads to Piazza Campitelli, just north; take Via dei Funari to Piazza Mattei, where one of Rome's loveliest fountains, the 16th-century **Fontana delle Tartarughe** ⑥, is tucked away. Take Via della Reginella into **Via Portico d'Ottavia,** heart of the Jewish Ghetto. On the Tiber is a **synagogue.** The **Teatro di Marcello** ⑥, behind the **Portico d'Ottavia,** was originally a theater designed to hold 20,000 people. Follow Via di Teatro di Marcello south, passing the ruins of two small temples: the **Tempio della Fortuna Virilis** ⑥ and the circular **Tempio di Vesta** ⑥. Across Piazza Santa Maria in Cosmedin is the 12th-century church of Santa Maria in Cosmedin, in **Piazza Bocca della Verità** ⑥, with the marble Bocca della Verità. Retracing your steps, walk upstream along the Tiber, cross Ponte Fabricio over **Isola Tiberina** ⑥, and then head into **Trastevere.**

Begin your exploration of Trastevere at **Piazza in Piscinula** (you will need a good street map to make your way around this intricate maze of winding side streets), take Via dell'Arco dei Tolomei, cross Via dei Salumi, and turn left onto Via dei Genovesi and then right to the piazza in front of **Santa Cecilia in Trastevere** ⑥. Aficionados of the Baroque will want to walk several blocks southwest down Via Anicia to **San Francesco a Ripa** ⑥ to see a famous Bernini sculpture. Follow Via San Francesco a Ripa to the very heart of the *rione,* or district, of Trastevere, to **Piazza di Santa Maria in Trastevere** ⑥, site of the lovely 12th-century church of Santa Maria in Trastevere. With a detailed map, find your way through the narrow byways to Piazza Sant'Egidio and Via della Scala, continuing on to Via della Lungara, where you'll find **Villa Farnesina** ⑥, where you can see frescoes by Raphael. From Trastevere, climb Via Garibaldi to the Janiculum Hill, which offers views spanning the whole city, and where you'll find the church of **San Pietro in Montorio** ⑦, built in 1481.

TIMING

The walk takes approximately three hours, plus 10–15 minutes for each church visited, and about 30 minutes for a visit to Villa Farnesina.

Sights to See

⑥ **Fontana della Tartarughe.** The 16th-century Fountain of the Turtles in Piazza Mattei is one of Rome's loveliest. Designed by Giacomo della Porta in 1581 and sculpted by Taddeo Landini, the piece revolves around four bronze boys, each clutching a dolphin that jets water into marble shells. Several bronze tortoises, a 17th-century addition by Bernini, are held in each of the boys' hands and drink from the fountain's upper basin. The piazza is named for the Mattei family, which built **Palazzo Mattei** on Via Caetani, worth a peek for its sculpture-rich courtyard and staircase.

65 **Isola Tiberina.** Ancient Ponte Fabricio links the Ghetto neighborhood of Trastevere to this island, where a city hospital stands on a site that has been dedicated to healing ever since a temple to Aesculapius was erected here in 291 BC. If you have time, and if the river's not too high, walk down the stairs for a different perspective on the island and the Tiber.

Palazzo Corsini. This elegant palace holds a collection of large, dark, and dull paintings, but stop in to climb the extraordinary 17th-century stone staircase, itself a drama of architectural shadows and sculptural voids. ⊠ *Via della Lungara 10.*

64 **Piazza Bocca della Verità** (Mouth of Truth Square). On the site of the Foro Boario (Forum Boarium), ancient Rome's cattle market, this square was later used for public executions. Its sinister name is derived from the marble **Bocca della Verità**—actually part of an ancient drain cover—set into the entry portico of the 12th-century church of **Santa Maria in Cosmedin.** In the Middle Ages anyone accused of lying would be forced to put his hand into the mouth and warned that if he didn't tell the truth the mouth would close and cut off his hand.

OFF THE
BEATEN PATH

COLLE AVENTINO – One of the seven hills of ancient Rome, Aventine Hill is now a quiet residential neighborhood that most tourists don't see. It has several of the city's oldest and least-visited churches, and some surprises: the view from the keyhole in the gate to the garden of the Knights of Malta (⊠ Piazza Cavalieri di Malta) and another, unusual view of Rome from the walled park next to the church of Santa Sabina, off Via Santa Sabina.

TERME DI CARACALLA – The scale of the towering ruins of ancient Rome's most beautiful and luxurious public baths, the Baths of Caracalla, hints at their past splendor. Inaugurated by Caracalla in 217, the baths were used until the 6th century. An ancient version of a swank athletic club, the baths were open to all, though men and women used them separately; citizens could bathe, socialize, and exercise in huge pools and richly decorated halls and libraries. ⊠ *Via delle Terme di Caracalla.* ☉ *Apr.–Sept., Tues.–Sat. 9–6, Sun.–Mon. 9–1; Oct.–Mar., Tues.–Sat. 9–3, Sun.–Mon. 9–1.*

68 **Piazza di Santa Maria in Trastevere.** The showpiece of this piazza is the 12th-century church of **Santa Maria in Trastevere.** The 13th-century mosaics on the church's facade—which add light and color to the piazza, especially at night when they are spotlit—are believed to represent the Wise and Foolish Virgins. The interior often produces involuntary gasps from unsuspecting viewers: an enormous nave bathed in a mellow glow from medieval mosaics and overhead gilding, the whole framed by a processional of two rows of gigantic columns. There are larger naves in Rome, but none quite so majestic.

67 **San Francesco a Ripa.** This church in Piazza San Francesco d'Assisi is a must for fans of the Baroque. It holds one of Bernini's most hallucinatory sculptures, a dramatically lighted statue of the Blessed Ludovica Albertoni, ecstatic at the prospect of entering heaven as she expires on her deathbed. ⊠ *Piazza San Francesco d'Assisi.*

70 **San Pietro in Montorio.** One of the key Renaissance buildings stands in the cloister of this church, built by order of Ferdinand and Isabella of Spain in 1481 over the spot where St. Peter is said to have been crucified. Bramante's **Tempietto** is an architectural gem and was one of the earliest and most successful attempts to produce an entirely classical building. ⊠ *Via Garibaldi, Gianicolo.* ☉ *Daily 9–noon and 4–6.*

⊙ 🏵 **Santa Cecilia in Trastevere.** Mothers and children love to dally in the delightful little garden in front of this church in Piazza Santa Cecilia, and there's no reason why you shouldn't join them for a bit before you duck inside for a look at the very grand 18th-century interior and the languid statue of St. Cecilia under the altar.

Sinagoga (Synagogue). The large, bronze-roofed synagogue on the Tiber is a Roman landmark. It contains a museum of precious ritual objects and fabrics and other exhibits documenting the history of the Jewish community in Rome. ⊠ *Lungotevere Cenci,* ☎ *06/6840061.* 🎫 *8,000 lire.* ⊙ *Mon.–Thurs. 9– 5, Fri. 9–2, Sun. 9:30–12:30.*

🅖 **Teatro di Marcello.** The Teatro, hardly recognizable as a theater today, was originally designed to hold 20,000 spectators. It was begun by Julius Caesar; today, the apartments carved out in its remains have become one of Rome's most prestigious residential addresses. ⊠ *Via del Teatro di Marcello.* ⊙ *Concerts only.*

🅖 **Tempio della Fortuna Virilis** (Temple of Manly Fortune). This rectangular temple dates from the 2nd century BC and is built in the Greek style, as was the norm in the early years of Rome. For its age, it is remarkably well preserved, in part due to its subsequent consecration as a Christian church. ⊠ *Piazza Bocca della Verità.*

🅖 **Tempio di Vesta.** All but one of the 20 original Corinthian columns in Rome's most evocative small ruin remain intact. Like the Temple of Manly Fortune (☞ *above*), it was built in the 2nd century BC, considerably earlier than the ruins in the Roman Forum. ⊠ *Piazza Bocca dell Verità.*

Trastevere. This area consists of a maze of narrow streets that is still, despite evident gentrification, one of the city's most authentically Roman neighborhoods. Literally translated, Trastevere means "across the Tiber," and indeed the Trasteverini, a breed apart, have always been proud and combative, chagrined at the reputation their quarter has acquired for purse snatching (but it does happen; don't carry a purse and keep your camera out of sight). Among self-consciously picturesque trattorias and trendy tearooms, you also find old shops and dusty artisans' workshops in alleys festooned with laundry hung out to dry. One of the most unaffected parts of Trastevere lies around **Piazza in Piscinula,** where the tiny **San Benedetto,** the smallest medieval church in the city, is opposite the restored medieval Casa dei Mattei. Take a stroll along Via dell'Arco dei Tolomei and Via dei Salumi, shadowy streets showing the patina of the ages.

Via Portico d'Ottavia. Along this street in the heart of the Jewish Ghetto are buildings where medieval inscriptions, ancient friezes, and half-buried classical monuments attest to the venerable history of this neighborhood. The old **Chiesa di Sant'Angelo in Pescheria** was built right into the ruins of the Portico d'Ottavia, which was a monumental area enclosing a temple, library, and other buildings within colonnaded porticoes.

🅖 **Villa Farnesina.** Money was no object to extravagant host Agostino Chigi, a Siena banker who financed many a papal project. His munificence is evident in his elegant villa, built about 1511. When Raphael could steal some precious time from his work on the Vatican Stanze and from his wooing of the Fornarina, he executed some of the frescoes, notably a luminous *Galatea.* Chigi delighted in impressing guests by having his servants clear the table by casting precious dinnerware into the Tiber. Naturally, the guests did not know of the nets he had stretched under the waterline to catch everything. ⊠ *Via della Lungara 230,* ☎ *06/6540565.* 🎫 *Free.* ⊙ *Mon.–Sat. 9–1.*

Quo Vadis? The Catacombs and the Via Appia Antica

An exploration of the beginnings of Christianity in Rome on this tour offers a respite from museums, but requires a long time on your feet. Do it on a sunny day and take along a picnic or have lunch at one of the pleasant restaurants near the catacombs. The Rome EPT office offers a free, informative pamphlet on this itinerary.

A Good Tour

Resist any temptation to undertake the 1½-km (1-mi) walk between Porta San Sebastiano and the catacombs; it is a dull and tiring hike on a heavily trafficked, cobblestone road, with stone walls the only scenery. Instead, hop on Bus 660 from the Colli Albani Metro stop on Line A to the **Via Appia Antica** ⑦. (Bus 218 from San Giovanni in Laterano also passes near the catacombs, but you have to walk about ½ km/¼ mi east from Via Ardeatina to Via Appia Antica.)

TIMING

Allow one hour for this walk, plus one hour for the catacombs.

Sights to See

❼ **Via Appia Antica.** This is "the Queen of Roads," completed in 312 BC by Appius Claudius, who also built Rome's first aqueduct. **San Callisto** is one of the best preserved of the underground catacombs. A friar will guide you through its crypts and galleries. ⊠ *Via Appia Antica 110,* ☎ *06/5136725.* ▣ *8,000 lire.* ⊙ *Apr.–Sept., Thurs.–Tues. 8:30–noon and 2:30–5:30; Oct.–Jan. and Mar., Thurs.–Tues. 8:30–noon and 2:30–5.*

The 4th-century **San Sebastiano** catacomb was named for the saint who was buried here. It burrows underground on four levels. The only one of the catacombs to remain accessible during the Middle Ages, it is the origin of the term "catacomb," for it was in a spot where the road dips into a hollow, a place the Romans called *catacumbas* (near the hollow). Eventually, the Christian cemetery that had existed here since the 2nd century came to be known by the same name, which was applied to all underground cemeteries discovered in Rome in later centuries. ⊠ *Via Appia Antica 136,* ☎ *06/7887035.* ▣ *8,000 lire.* ⊙ *Apr.–Sept., Fri.–Wed. 8:30–noon and 2:30–5:30; Oct. and Dec.–Mar., Fri.–Wed. 8:30–noon and 2:30–5.*

On the east side of Via Appia Antica are the ruins of the **Circo di Massenzio** (Circus of Maxentius), where the obelisk now in Piazza Navona once stood.

The circular **Tomba di Cecilia Metella** (Tomb of Cecilia Metella), mausoleum of a Roman noblewoman who lived at the time of Julius Caesar, was transformed into a fortress in the 14th century. It marks the beginning of the most evocative stretch of Via Appia Antica, lined with tombs and fragments of statuary. Cypresses and umbrella pines stand guard over the ruined sepulchers, and the occasional tracts of ancient paving stones are the same ones trod by triumphant Roman legions.

DINING

Revised by
Carla Lionello
and Jon Eldan

Roman cooking is predominantly simple; dishes rarely have more than a few ingredients. Meat and fish are most often roasted, baked, or grilled. Although many traditional recipes are based on innards, you won't find much of that on the menu in restaurants in the city center, with the exception of *trippa alla romana* (tripe stewed in tomatoes with wild mint).

The typical Roman fresh pasta is fettuccine, golden egg noodles that are at their classic best when laced with *ragú*, a thick, rich tomato and meat sauce. Spaghetti *alla carbonara* is spaghetti tossed with a sauce of egg yolk, chunks of rendered *guanciale* (cured pork cheek) or pancetta (salt-cured bacon), pecorino romano cheese, and lots of freshly ground black pepper. *Pasta all'amatriciana* has a sauce of tomato, guanciale, and onion. Potato gnocchi, served with a tomato sauce and a dusting of Parmesan or pecorino, are a Roman favorite for Thursday dinner. The best meat on the menu is often *abbacchio*, milk-fed lamb. Legs of lamb are usually roasted with rosemary and potatoes, and the chops are grilled *alla scottadito* (literally "burn your finger" for small chops eaten with your fingers hot off the grill). Most Mediterranean fish are light yet flavorful, among them *spigola* (sea bass), *orata* (bream), and *rombo* (turbot or flounder).

Local cheeses are made from sheep's milk; the most well known is the aged, sharp pecorino romano. Fresh ricotta is a treat all on its own, and finds its way into a number of dishes and desserts. Many restaurants make a specialty of the *fritto misto* (literally "mixed fry") with whatever vegetables are in season. Rome is famous for artichokes (the season runs from November to April), traditionally prepared *alla romana* (stuffed with garlic and mint and braised in oil), or *alla giudia* (fried whole, making each petal crisp). A special springtime treat is *vignarola*, a mixture of tender peas, fava beans, and artichokes, cooked with bits of guanciale.

Typical wines of Rome are those of the Castelli Romani, the towns in the hills to the southeast: Frascati, Colli Albani, Marino, and Velletri. Though the water in Rome is good to drink, restaurants will usually have you choose between bottled *gassata* (sparkling) or *liscia* (not sparkling) water.

CATEGORY	COST*
$$$$	over 100,000 lire
$$$	70,000–100,000 lire
$$	40,000–70,000 lire
$	under 40,000 lire

Prices are per person, for a three-course meal, including house wine, service, and tax.

Old Rome

$$$$ ✕ **El Toulà.** Rome's prestigious El Toulà has the warm, welcoming comforts of a 19th-century country house, with white walls, antique furniture in dark wood, heavy silver serving dishes, and spectacular fruit and flower arrangements. There's a cozy bar off the entrance, where you can sip a Prosecco, a Venetian aperitif best paired with the chef's Venetian specialties that are always on offer, along with contemporary interpretations of Italian classics. ⊠ *Via della Lupa 29/b,* ☎ *06/ 6873750. Reservations essential. Jacket and tie. AE, DC, MC, V. Closed Sun. and in Aug. No lunch Sat.*

$$$$ ✕ **Il Convivio.** It's easy to walk right by this small restaurant, hidden behind an unassuming facade on the corner of a narrow street just north of Piazza Navona, with anything-but-anonymous dishes that combine seasonal Italian cooking and innovation. Chef Angelo Troiani's inventions may have long names, but they are tasty and well presented: *rollé di agnello farcito con frittatine alle erbe* (lamb roll stuffed with herb fritters) and *soufflé di crema di mandorle e prugne, profumato di arancia* (almond and prune soufflé, perfumed with orange). Brothers Massimo and Giuseppe manage the dining room and pour wine, chosen from one of the finest cellars in town. ⊠ *Via dell'Orso 44,* ☎ *06/6869432 . Reservations essential. AE, DC, MC, V. Closed Sun.*

$$$$ ✕ **La Rosetta.** In 1992, chef-owner Massimo Riccioli took the nets and
★   fishing gear off the walls of his parents' trattoria to create the place to
go in Rome for first-rate fish, artfully presented. The space is elegant
in its simplicity, with warm woods, fresh flowers, and a stunning display of fish at the entrance. Particularly good dishes are the *vongole
veraci* (sautéed clams), *tonnarelli ai frutti di mare*, (poached fish on
artichokes or potatoes), and sea bass with black truffles. Homemade
desserts are worth saving room for. ⊠ *Via della Rosetta 9,* ☎ *06/
6861002. Dinner reservations essential. AE, DC, MC, V.*

$$$ ✕ **Al Ceppo.** A warm space with antiques and oil paintings in the out-
of-the-way Parioli neighborhood, Al Ceppo has been the Sunday lunch
favorite for a generation of Roman families. Classic dishes prepared
with a creative flair always include a few specialties from the Marche
region—where the owners come from—such as *olive ascolane* (large
green olives stuffed, breaded, and fried). Trademark starters are *polpet-
tine di melanzane al vapore* (steamed eggplant balls) and *fiori di zucca
ripieni e fritti* (fried stuffed zucchini flowers). Pasta is made fresh every
day, and meats, fish, and vegetables are prepared in a fireplace with a
grill. ⊠ *Via Panama 2,* ☎ *06/8419696. AE, DC, MC, V. Closed Mon.
and in Aug.*

$$$ ✕ **Piperno.** An old favorite in the old Jewish Ghetto next to historic
Palazzo Cenci, Piperno is *the* place to go for Rome's extraordinary *car-
ciofi alla giudia* (fried whole artichoke). You eat in three small wood-
paneled dining rooms or at one of a handful of tables outdoors. Try
filetti di baccalà (fillet of cod), *pasta e ceci* (a thick soup of pasta tubes
and chickpeas), and fiori di zucca ripieni e fritti. ⊠ *Monte dei Cenci
9,* ☎ *06/6542772. AE, DC, MC, V. Closed Mon. and Aug. No dinner Sun.*

$$$ ✕ **Sangallo.** An intimate little restaurant not far from the Pantheon,
Sangallo specializes in first-quality fish that is light in presentation, well
cooked, and invitingly presented in dishes such as *tagliolini con po-
modorini, mazzancolle, e scaglie di pecorino* (fresh pasta with cherry
tomatoes, shrimp, and scales of pecorino cheese) and *spigola in crosta
di sale* (sea bass baked in a salt crust). The *menu degustazione* offers
better value than the à la carte offerings. Service can be less than
speedy, so plan on a long meal. ⊠ *Vicolo della Vaccarella 11/a,* ☎ *06/
6865549. AE, DC, MC, V. Closed Sun., 1 wk in Jan., and 2 wks in
Aug. No lunch Mon.*

$$$ ✕ **Vecchia Roma.** Consistent food, sure-handed service, and a great atmo-
sphere make this restaurant still worthy of attention, even if prices are
a bit exaggerated. With tables outside on a relatively quiet, narrow square
close to the Campidoglio, Vecchia Roma is one of the best places in
town to eat alfresco. The tasteful interior proceeds through several small
rooms, some with floral frescoes, others with stucco panel reliefs. Unlike a great many "old Roman restaurants," the menu covers the classics without being stale. ⊠ *Piazza Campitelli 18,* ☎ *06/6864604.
Reservations essential. AE, DC. Closed Wed. and mid-Aug.*

$$–$$$ ✕ **Dal Bolognese.** Long a haunt of the art crowd, this classic restau-
rant on Piazza del Popolo is a trendy choice for a leisurely lunch between sightseeing and shopping. An array of contemporary paintings
decorate the dining room but the real attraction is the lovely piazza—
prime people-watching real estate. As the name of the restaurant
promises, the cooking here adheres to the hearty tradition of Bologna,
with delicious homemade tortellini *in brodo* (filled pasta in broth), fresh
pastas in creamy sauces, and steaming trays of boiled meats. Among
the desserts, try the *dolce della mamma* (a concoction of gelato,
zabaglione, and chocolate sauce) and the fruit-shape gelato. ⊠ *Piazza
del Popolo 1,* ☎ *06/3611426. AE, MC, V. Closed Mon. and in Aug.*

52

Rome Dining

$$ ✕ **Il Cardinale.** In this small, serene restaurant, fanciful, lightened-up versions of traditional Roman fare are beautifully presented on king-size plates. Oil paintings and enlarged old photos of Roman landmarks hang against golden damask wall coverings; chairs and couches are covered in a pretty floral print. The menu—a selection of composed salads, vegetable soups, and pastas—always has a few suggestions from the chef. Try the *vermicelli cacio e pepe* (pasta with pecorino cheese and black pepper) or ravioli *di borragine* (filled with borage leaves), and various vegetable *sformati* (flans). ⊠ *Via delle Carceri 6,* ☎ *06/ 6869336. AE, DC, MC, V. Closed Sun.*

$$ ✕ **Myosotis.** It may look brand new, but the Myosotis is the sequel to
★ a restaurant on the outskirts of town run by the Marsili family. Central location, extensive menu, and great value make Myosotis a place you might want to return to. The menu rides that delicate line between tradition and innovation, focusing more on the freshness and quality of the ingredients than on elaborate presentation. Fresh pasta gets special attention: It's rolled out by hand to order for the *stracci alla delizia di mare* (pasta with seafood). There's a wide choice of fish, meat, and seasonal veggies to choose from. The wine list is ample, the prices honest. ⊠ *Via della Vaccarella 3/5,* ☎ *06/2053943. AE, DC, MC, V. Closed Mon. and 2 wks in Aug.*

$$ ✕ **Otello alla Concordia.** The clientele in this popular spot—it's off a shopping street near Piazza di Spagna—is about evenly divided between tourists and workers in the area. The former like to sit outdoors in the courtyard in any weather; the latter have their regular tables in one of the inside dining rooms. The menu offers classic Roman and Italian dishes, and service is friendly and efficient. Since the regulars won't relinquish their niches, you may have to wait for a table; go early. ⊠ *Via della Croce 81,* ☎ *06/6781454. Reservations not accepted. AE, DC. Closed Sun.*

$$ ✕ **Sora Lella.** What was once a simple trattoria ensconced on the Tiberina Island (great view from the bathroom) is now a monument to the late founder herself, a beloved example of true Roman warmth and personality. Inside, two small dining rooms are lined with wood paneling and bottles of wine. Although prices are much higher than when Sora Lella presided over the cash desk, the cooking is still 100% Roman. Daily specials as well as menu standards are written on the chalkboard, but you'll usually find rigatoni all'amatriciana and *maialino all'antica roma* (suckling pig with prunes and baby onions). Leave room for the quintessential Roman ricotta cake. ⊠ *Via Ponte Quattro Capi 16,* ☎ *06/6861601. AE, DC, MC. Closed Sun. and Aug.*

$ ✕ **Grappolo d'Oro.** This central trattoria off Campo dei Fiori has been a favorite for decades with locals and foreign residents, one of whom wrote it up in the *New Yorker* some years ago. This measure of notoriety has not induced the graying, courteous owners to change their two half-paneled dining rooms or menu, which features pasta all'amatriciana and scallopini any way you want them. ⊠ *Piazza della Cancelleria 80,* ☎ *06/6897080. AE, DC, MC, V. Closed Sun. and Aug.*

$ ✕ **L'Eau Vive.** You're in for a unique Roman dining experience, even if the food isn't Italian. For the last 28 years this restaurant with (very good) classic French food has been run by a society of French missionary nuns. The atmosphere throughout is serene and soothing, though rather plain (of course). Soft devotional music plays as the smiling sisters speedily bring plate after plate. They take a brief pause before dessert to sing "Ave Maria"—you are welcome to join in. The upstairs rooms, reserved for nonsmokers, have beautiful frescoes. ⊠ *Via Monterone 85,* ☎ *06/68801095. AE, DC, MC, V. Closed Sun. and Aug.*

$ ✕ **Orso 80.** The good kind of tourist restaurant, this bright and bustling trattoria near Piazza Navona is well known for its fabulous antipasto table. Try the homemade egg pasta or the *bucatini* (thick, hollow spaghetti) all'amatriciana; there's plenty of seafood on the menu, too. For dessert, the ricotta cake, a genuine Roman specialty, is always good. ⊠ *Via dell'Orso 33,* ☎ *06/6864904. AE, DC, MC, V. Closed Mon. and Aug.*

$ ✕ **Pierluigi.** This is a longtime favorite with foreign residents of Rome and Italians in the entertainment field. On busy evenings it's almost impossible to get a table. Seafood dominates (if you're in the mood to splurge, try the lobster), but traditional Roman dishes are offered, too, including fried zucchini blossoms and simple spaghetti. Eat in the pretty piazza in summer. ⊠ *Piazza dei Ricci 144,* ☎ *06/6868717. Reservations essential. AE, V. Closed Mon. and 2 wks in Aug.*

Veneto

$$$$ ✕ **Le Sans Souci.** All the glitz and glamour of the 1950s dolce vita days lives on in this overdecorated but superb subterranean sanctuary of French and Italian gourmet delights. Impeccably dressed waiters slide over the carpeted floor with unparalleled grace, their gait reminiscent of Swiss walking lessons. An elaborate coffered ceiling, mirrors, and painted ceramics from Perugia decorate the main room. Carved wooden busts of Roman emperors gaze over tables set in the French fashion, where couples share a couch rather than sit opposite one another (so much easier to see the show). Among the delectable dishes are truffled terrine of foie gras and various sweet and savory soufflés. ⊠ *Via Sicilia 20,* ☎ *06/4821814. Reservations essential. Jacket and tie. AE, DC, MC, V. Closed Mon. and in Aug. No lunch.*

$$ ✕ **Colline Emiliane.** Expect a reliable neighborhood trattoria, not far from Piazza Barberini. Behind an opaque glass facade are a couple of plain dining rooms, where you are served light homemade pastas, *tortelli di zucca* (squash-filled ravioli), and meats from *bollito misto* (boiled beef) to *cotoletta alla bolognese* (fried veal cutlet with cheese and prosciutto). Family run, it's quiet and soothing—a good place to rest after a sightseeing stint. Service is cordial and discreet. ⊠ *Via San Nicolò da Tolentino 26,* ☎ *06/4818564. Reservations essential. AE, DC, MC, V. Closed Sun. and Aug.*

$$ ✕ **Papá Baccus.** Italo Cipriani takes his meat as seriously as any Tuscan. He uses real Chianina beef, the prized breed traditionally used for the bistecca alla fiorentina, a house specialty. In this, Rome's best Tuscan restaurant, you can depend on the genuineness of the rest of the dishes, too. Cipriani brings many ingredients from his home town in northern Tuscany. Try the sweet and delicate prosciutto from Pratomagno. The welcome is warm, the service excellent. ⊠ *Via Toscana 36,* ☎ *06/42742808. AE, DC, MC, V. Closed Sun., 2 wks in Aug., and over Christmas. No lunch Sat.*

Near Termini

$ ✕ **Pommidoro.** Mamma's in the kitchen and the rest of the family greets, serves, and keeps you happy and well fed at this popular trattoria near Rome's main university, a short cab ride east of Stazione Termini. The menu—not so well translated—offers especially good grilled meats and game birds, and classic home-style *cucina* (cooking). You can dine outside in warm weather. ⊠ *Via Marmorata 39,* ☎ *06/5742415. No credit cards. Closed Wed.*

Vatican

$$$$ ✕ **La Pergola.** High atop Monte Mario, the Cavalieri Hilton's rooftop
★ La Pergola restaurant offers a commanding view onto the city below.
The dining room is warmly elegant with trompe l'oeil ceilings, handsome wood paneling, and large windows. Amply spaced tables and low
lighting create an intimate atmosphere not matched by other restaurants in town. Celebrated wunder-chef Heinz Beck is a skilled techni-
cian, and brings Rome its finest example of Mediterranean *alta cucina*
(haute cuisine); dishes are balanced and light, and presentation is striking. The wine list and the cheese cart offer ample and interesting
choices from Italy and France. ✉ *Cavalieri Hilton, Via Cadlolo 101,*
☎ *06/3509221. Reservations essential. Jacket and tie. AE, DC, MC,*
V. Closed Sun.–Mon. No lunch.

$$$$ ✕ **La Terrazza dell'Eden.** The Hotel Eden's La Terrazza restaurant un-
furls an unparalleled view of Rome's seven hills before your eyes, un-
fairly distracting you from some of the best food in the city. Modern
yet simple Italian cuisine—high on flavor and herbs and low on butter and cream—is the vision of chef Enrico Derflingher. Always on the
prowl for superior fresh ingredients, he has taken the search to a new
level: How many other restaurants have their own fishing boat, which
reserves the best of the day's catch for the chef? The restaurant is also
open for breakfast (7–10 AM). A piano bar (with jazz from 8:00 PM
to 1 AM) with a small outdoor terrace shares the view. ✉ *Hotel Eden,*
Via Ludovisi 49, ☎ *06/47812552. Dinner reservations essential. Jacket*
and tie. AE, DC, MC, V.

$ ✕ **Dal Toscano.** An open wood-fired grill and classic dishes like *ribol-*
★ *lita* (a thick bread and vegetable soup) and *pici* (fresh thick pasta, served
with a wild hare sauce) are the draw at this great family-run Tuscan
trattoria near the Vatican. The refrigerator opposite the entrance tells
you right away that the house special is the prized *bistecca alla*
fiorentina, a thick, bone-in steak, grilled but rare in the middle. Wash
it all down with a strong Chianti, or a half liter of the Tuscan house
wine. Desserts such as pastry cream tarts, apple strudel, and *castag-*
naccio (a tasty chestnut and pine nut treat) in wintertime are all homemade. Service is friendly and speedy. ✉ *Via Germanico 58,* ☎ *06/*
39725717. DC, MC, V. Closed Mon. and Aug. and 2 wks in Dec.

$ ✕ **Tre Pupazzi.** The "three puppets," after which the trattoria is named,
are the worn stone figures on a fragment of an ancient sarcophagus
that embellishes a building on this byway near the Vatican. The tavern, founded in 1625, wears its centuries lightly, upholding a tradition
of good food, courteous service, and reasonable prices. The menu offers classic Roman and Abruzzese trattoria fare, including fettuccine
and abbacchio, plus pizzas at lunchtime (a rarity in Rome) and well
past midnight. ✉ *Via dei Tre Pupazzi at Borgo Pio,* ☎ *06/6868371.*
AE, MC, V. Closed Sun.

Trastevere/Testaccio

$$$ ✕ **Checchino dal 1887.** Literally carved out of a hillside made of pot-
sherds from Roman times, Checchino turns out the most traditional
Roman cuisine served without fanfare in a clean, austere space. Though
the slaughterhouses of Rome's Testaccio quarter—a short cab ride
from the city center—are long gone, you can still try the variety meats
that make up the soul of Roman cooking: *trippa* (tripe), *testina* (head),
pajata (intestine), *zampa* (trotter), and *coratella* (sweetbreads). There's
also plenty to choose from if you're uninterested in innards: House spe-
cialties include *coda alla vaccinara* (stewed oxtail), a popular Roman
dish the owners claim was invented here, and abbacchio *alla caccia-*
tora (braised milk-fed lamb). Desserts are very good. ✉ *Via di Monte*

Testaccio 30, ☎ 06/5746318. AE, DC, MC, V. Closed Mon., Aug., and over Christmas. No dinner Sun.

$$$ ✕ **Da Checco er Carettiere.** Maybe this is what all Italian restaurants once looked like: an aging doorman, garlic braids hanging from the ceiling, black and white photos in small frames lining the wood-paneled walls. Family-run for three generations, Checco is a great place to soak up genuine Trastevere color and hospitality. All the Roman standards, solidly prepared with first-rate ingredients, plus plenty of local vegetables and an unusually good selection of fish, are true to tradition. You can eat outdoors in summer. ✉ Via Benedetta 10, ☎ 06/5817018. AE, DC, MC, V. Closed Mon. No dinner Sun.

$$–$$$ ✕ **Paris.** On a small square just off Piazza Santa Maria in Trastevere, Paris (named after a former owner) has a reassuring, understated ambience, without the hokey flamboyance of so many eateries in this neighborhood. The menu features the best of classic Roman cuisine: homemade fettuccine, delicate fritto misto and, of course, baccalà (cod). You can also choose from a good wine list. In fair weather opt for tables on the piazza. ✉ Piazza San Callisto 7/a, ☎ 06/5815378. AE, DC, MC, V. Closed Mon. and 3 wks in Aug. No dinner Sun.

$–$$ ✕ **Antico Arco.** Run by three friends with a passion for wine and fine
★ food, the Antico Arco, at the top of the Janiculum Hill, has quickly won the hearts of Roman foodies with innovative dishes and moderate prices. There are always 30 wines to choose from by the glass, plus an excellent list of Italian and French labels. Particularly good are starters like *sformato di finocchi in salsa d'arancia* (fennel flan with orange sauce) and second courses like *petto d'anatra con salsa di lamponi* (duck breast with raspberry sauce). Don't miss dessert. At press time a plan was in the works to open daily for lunch as well. ✉ Piazzale Aurelio 7, ☎ 06/5815274. AE, DC, MC, V. Closed Mon. No lunch Mon.–Sat.

$ ✕ **Perilli.** A bastion of authentic Roman cooking and trattoria atmosphere since 1911 (the decor has changed very little), this is the place to go to try rigatoni *con pajata* (with baby veal's intestines)—if you're into that sort of thing. Otherwise the all'amatriciana and carbonara sauces are classics. The house wine is a golden nectar from the Castelli Romani. ✉ Via Marmorata 39, ☎ 06/5742415. No credit cards. Closed Wed.

Along Via Appia Antica

$$ ✕ **Cecilia Metella.** From the entrance on Via Appia Antica, practically opposite the catacombs, you walk uphill to a low-lying but sprawling construction designed for wedding feasts and banquets. There's a large terrace shaded by vines for outdoor dining. Although obviously geared to larger groups, Cecilia Metella also gives couples and small groups full attention, good service, and traditional Roman cuisine. The specialties are the searing-hot *crespelle* (crepes), served in individual casseroles, and pollo *al Nerone* (chicken à la Nero; flambéed, of course). ✉ Via Appia Antica 125, ☎ 06/5136743. AE, MC, V. Closed Mon. and last 2 wks in Aug.

$$ ✕ **L'Archeologia.** In this farmhouse just beyond the catacombs, you dine indoors beside the fireplace in cool weather or in the garden under age-old vines in the summer. The atmosphere is friendly and intimate, and specialties include homemade pastas, abbacchio scottadito, seafood, and some Greek dishes. ✉ Via Appia Antica 139, ☎ 06/7880494. AE, MC, V. Closed Thurs.

Pizzerias

It may have been invented somewhere else (☞ Close-Up: Disciplined Pizzas *in* Chapter 13), but in Rome it's hard to walk a block without passing pizza in one form or another. Pizza from a bakery is usually made without cheese—*pizza bianca* (just olive oil and salt) or *pizza rossa* (with tomato sauce). Many small shops specialize in pizza *a taglio* (by the cut), priced by the *etto* (100 grams, about a ¼ pound), according to the kind of topping. Both of these make a great snack any time of day. Here are a few good places to find the real McCoy on the go: **Il Forno di Campo dei Fiori** (⊠ Campo dei Fiori), closed Sunday, makes excellent pizza bianca and rossa all day. Just around the corner is **Pizza alla Pala** (⊠ Via del Pellegrino), closed Sunday, and **Zí Fenizia** (⊠ Via Santa Maria del Pianto 64) makes kosher pizza in the old Jewish Ghetto; it's closed sundown Friday, Saturday, and Jewish holidays.

But don't leave Rome without sitting down to a Roman pizza in a pizzeria. Most are open only for dinner, usually from 8 PM to midnight. Look for a place with a *forno a legna* (wood-burning oven), a must for a good thin crust on your plate-size Roman pizza. Standard models are the *margherita* (tomato, mozzarella, and basil) and the *capricciosa* (a little bit of everything, depending upon the "caprices" of the pizza chef: tomato, mozzarella, sausage, olives, artichoke hearts, and prosciutto, even egg), but most pizzerias have a long list of additional options, including tasty mozzarella *di bufala* (buffalo-milk mozzarella).

$$ ✕ **Baffetto.** Down a cobblestone street not far from Piazza Navona, this is Rome's best-known pizzeria and a summer favorite for outside dining. The plainly decorated interior is mostly given over to the ovens, but there's another room with more paper-covered tables. Turnover is fast; this is not the place to linger. ⊠ *Via del Governo Vecchio 114, Centro Storico,* ☎ *06/6861617. Reservations not accepted. No credit cards. Closed Sun. and Aug. No lunch.*

$ ✕ **Dar Poeta.** Romans drive across town for great pizza, a bit cheaper than average, from this neighborhood joint on a small street in Trastevere. Maybe it's the dough—made from a secret blend of flours reputed to be easier to digest than the competition. For dessert, an unusual calzone is baked with Nutella (a chocolate and hazelnut spread) and ricotta. ⊠ *Vicolo del Bologna 45, Trastevere,* ☎ *06/5880516. Reservations not accepted. AE, MC, V. Closed Mon. No lunch.*

$ ✕ **Il Leoncino.** Lines out the door on weekends attest to the popularity of the flourescent-lit pizzeria in the otherwise big-ticket neighborhood around Piazza di Spagna.This is one of the few pizzerias open for lunch as well as dinner. ⊠ *Via Via del Lioncino 28, near the Corso, Centro Storico,* ☎ *06/6876306. Reservations not accepted. No credit cards. Closed Sun. and Aug.*

$ ✕ **La Soffitta.** You pay more, but hey, it's imported. This is Rome's hottest spot for classic Neapolitan pizza (thick, though crusty on the bottom, rather than paper thin and crispy like the Roman kind), and the only pizzeria in town that has been certified by the True Neapolitan Pizza Association. Desserts are brought in daily from Naples, of course. ⊠ *Via dei Villini 1/e, near Stazione Termini,* ☎ *06/4404642. Reservations not accepted. No credit cards. Closed Sun. and Aug. No lunch.*

Enoteche

It was not so long ago that wine in Rome (and other towns) was strictly local; you didn't have to walk far to find an *osteria* (tavern), where you could buy wine straight from the barrel or sit down to drink and nibble a bit, chat, or play cards. The tradition continues today, as many Roman wine shops are also open as *enoteche* (wine bars). The folding chairs and rickety tables have given way to designer interiors and chic ambience. Shelves are lined with hundreds of bottles from all over the country, representing the best in Italian wine making, many available by the glass. Behind the bar you'll find a serious wine enthusiast, maybe even a sommelier. There's usually carefully selected cheeses and cured meats, and a short menu of simple dishes and desserts.

$ ✕ **Enoteca Corsi.** Very convenient to the historic center for lunch (no dinner) or an afternoon break, it looks like this little wine bar missed the revolution; prices and decor are *come una volta* (like once upon a time) when the shop sold—as the sign says—wine (red or white) and oil. The genuinely dated feel of the place has its charm: You can still get wine here by the liter, or choose from a good variety of fairly priced bottles. There are nicely prepared pastas and kind service. ⊠ *Via del Gesù 88, Centro Storico,* ☎ *06/6790821. AE, MC, V. Closed Sun. No dinner.*

$ ✕ **Il Simposio di Costantini.** At the classiest wine bar in town, wrapped in wrought iron vines, wood paneling, and velvet, you can choose from about 30 wines. Food is appropriately fancy: marinated and smoked fish, composed salads, top-quality salami and cured meats (classical and wild), terrines and pâtés, and several gussied-up hot vegetable and meat dishes. It has 80 assorted cheeses, grouped according to origin or type (French, goat, Italian, hard, herb crusted). ⊠ *Via Appia Antica 139, near the Vatican,* ☎ *06/7880494. AE, MC, V. Closed Thurs.*

$ ✕ **La Bottega del Vino di Anacleto Bleve.** This cozy wine shop in the Jewish Ghetto sets out tables and opens up for lunch. Owner Anacleto Bleve and his sons make the rounds, proposing the latest cheese they have procured from the farthest reaches of Italy. Instead of a menu, there's mamma at the counter, chatting up a good selection of mixed salads, smoked fish and sliced meats, as well as a few soups and sformati. You point and she plates it up. There are always wines to drink by the glass, or you can choose from the several hundred bottles on the shelves that surround you. ⊠ *Via Santa Maria del Pianto, Centro Storico,* ☎ *06/7880494. AE, D, MC, V. Closed Thurs.*

$ ✕ **L'Osteria dell'Ingegno.** A perfect stop for a quick lunch or dinner after sightseeing or shopping, with hip modern decor and happening feel, this trendy wine bar seems almost out of place among the ruins of the old town. The short menu changes weekly, with simple dishes that emphasize fine ingredients. Service is fast. ⊠ *Piazza di Pietra 45, Centro Storico,* ☎ *06/6780662. No reservations accepted. AE, D, MC, V. Closed Sun.*

$ ✕ **Trimani Il Winebar.** This is a handy address for diners in a town where most restaurants don't unlock the door before 8 PM. Trimani opens up at 6 PM for snacks and cold plates, at 7:30 for hot food, and stays open until 11:30. The feel is modern and casually reserved. There's always a choice of a soup and a few pasta plates, as well as second courses and *torte salate* (savory tarts). Around the corner is a wine shop, one of the oldest in Rome, of the same name. Call about wine tastings and short courses (in Italian). ⊠ *Via Cernaia 37/b, Near Stazione Termini,* ☎ *06/4469630. AE, D, MC, V. Closed Sun. and 2 wks in Aug. No lunch Sat.*

Caffè

As elsewhere in Italy, there is a *caffè* (café-bar) on nearly every corner in Rome. Locals usually stop in for a quickie at the bar, which is also much less expensive than the same drink taken at table. Pricey **Antico Caffè Greco** (⊠ Via dei Condotti 86, ☎ 06/6791700) is a national landmark; its red-velvet chairs and marble tables have hosted the likes of Byron, Shelley, Keats, Goethe, and Casanova. **Caffè Sant'Eustachio** (⊠ P. Sant'Eustachio 82, ☎ 06/861309), traditionally frequented by Rome's literati, vies with **Tazza d'Oro** (⊠ Via degli Orfani, near the Pantheon, ☎ 06/5835869) for the city's best coffee. If you want your *caffè* (espresso) without sugar, ask for it *amaro*. Other great caffè where you

can sit yourself down and watch the world go by are **Rosati** (⊠ Piazza
del Popolo 5, ☎ 06/3225859), **Antico Caffè della Pace** (⊠ Via della Pace
3, ☎ 06/6861216) near Piazza Navona, and **Caffè Teichner** (⊠ Piazza
Santa Maria in Lucina 17, ☎ 06/6871449) just off the Corso.

Gelaterie and Pasticcerie

Gelato is more a snack for Italians than a serious desert. **Il Gelato di
San Crispino** (⊠ Via della Panetteria 54, near the Trevi Fountain, ☎
06/70450412), closed Tuesday, is perhaps the most celebrated gelato
in all of Italy, made without artificial colors or flavors. It's worth crossing town for—nobody else makes flavors this balanced, ice cream this
real. Other worthwhile addresses for gelato are **Fiocco di Neve** (⊠ Via
del Pantheon 51, no phone), closed Sunday, and **Fonte della Salute** ⊠
(Via Cardinal Marmagi 2, ☎ 06/5897471). The old-fashioned **Creme-
ria Ottaviani** (⊠ Via Leone IV 83/85, ☎ 06/37514774), closed Wednesday, has an excellent *granita di caffè* (coffee ice slush). Romans consider
Giolitti (⊠ Via Uffizi del Vicario 40), near the Pantheon, superlative.

Romans are not known for their sweet tooths, and there are few *pas-
ticcerie* (pastry shops) in town that distinguish themselves with particularly good examples of the few regional desserts. One exception is the
Forno del Ghetto (⊠ Via del Portico díOttavia 20/b, ☎ 06/6878637),
closed Friday after sundown, Saturday, and Jewish holidays. So maybe
you didn't expect a Jewish bakery in Rome? This hole-in-the-wall—no
sign, no tables, just a take-away counter—is an institution, preserving a
tradition of Italian-Jewish sweets that cannot be found anywhere else.
The ricotta cake (with sour cherry jam or chocolate) is unforgettable.
Just down the street is **Dolceroma** (⊠ Via del Portico díOttavia 20/b, ☎
06/6892196), closed Monday and four weeks in July–August, where the
specialties, alas, are not Roman: American pies and Austrian pastries.

Salumerie

There are several hundred *salumerie* (gourmet food shops) in town,
but a few stand out for a particularly ample selection and items of rare,
superior quality. Foodies should head straight for **Franchi** (⊠ Via Cola
di Rienzo 200, ☎ 06/6864576), closed Sunday, which will vacuum-
pack meats and cheeses if you aren't ready to eat them just then. They
also have Rome's best deli-style takeout. Right next door is **Castroni**
(⊠ Via Cola di Rienzo 196, ☎ 06/6864383), closed Sunday, a fine general food shop with lots of imported items. **Volpetti** (⊠ Via Mar-
morata 47, ☎ 06/5742352), closed Thursday afternoon and Sunday,
also keeps the highest quality meats and specializes in aged cheeses from
small producers. The **Antico Forno** (⊠ Via delle Muratte 8, ☎ 06/
6792866), at the Trevi Fountain, is not nearly at the same level, but it
is open on Sunday; it's closed Thursday afternoon in winter, Saturday
afternoon in summer.

Emporiums for the Food Curious

Pricey **C.u.c.i.n.a.** (⊠ Via del Babuino 118A, ☎ 06/6791275), closed
Sunday, is one of the better kitchen supply stores in town. For a food-
history interlude, try the **Museo Nazionale di Paste Alimentari** (⊠ Piazza Scanderbeg 114, ☎ 06/6991120), open Monday–Friday
9:30–12:30 and 4–7, Saturday 9:30–12:30, a showcase of Italy's
most famous culinary item. Small galleries named "The Wheat Room"
and "The Ligurian Room" unfold the compelling saga of pasta and
its present-day production.

LODGING

Palatial surroundings, luxurious comfort, and high standards of service can be taken for granted in the city's five-star ($$$$) establishments, but in other categories, especially $$ and $, standards vary considerably. Fortunately for you, many Rome hotels have upgraded their facilities, readjusting their rates only slightly. The old-fashioned Roman pensione no longer exists as an official category, but, although now graded as inexpensive hotels, some preserve the homey atmosphere that makes you prefer them, especially for longer stays. One disadvantage of staying in the center is noise, because Romans are voluble. Ask for an inside room if you are a light sleeper, but don't be disappointed if it faces a dark courtyard.

Because Rome's religious importance makes it a year-round tourist destination, there is never a period when hotels are predictably empty, so you should always try to make reservations, even if only a few days in advance, by phone or fax. Always inquire about special low rates, often available in both winter and summer if occupancy is low. If you do arrive without reservations, try **HR** (☎ 06/6991000), English-speaking operator available daily 7 AM–10 PM, with desks at Aeroporto Fiumicino and Stazione Termini. **EPT** information offices (☞ Visitor Information in Rome A to Z, *below*) can also help.

CATEGORY	COST*
$$$$	over 600,000 lire
$$$	350,000–450,000 lire
$$	250,000–350,000 lire
$	under 250,000 lire**

*Prices are for a standard double room for two, including tax and service. The top rate is rarely applied; **most hotels in this category charge 120,000–180,000 lire, depending on the season.*

Old Rome

$$$$ 🏨 **Minerva.** The Holiday Inn Crowne Plaza Minerva is the very stylish reincarnation of the hostelry that occupied this 17th-century palazzo for centuries, hosting literati from Stendhal to Sartre and de Beauvoir. Entirely redone, with a stunning stained-glass lobby ceiling designed by renowned architect Paolo Portoghesi, the Minerva has everything a guest could want in the way of comfort, all in an absolutely central location. And from the roof terrace, open for summer dining in fair weather, you can almost touch the immense, flattened dome of Hadrian's Pantheon. ⊠ *Piazza della Minerva 69, 00186,* ☎ *06/69941888,* 𝔽𝔸𝕏 *06/6794165. 118 rooms, 16 suites. Restaurant, bar. AE, DC, MC, V. EP.*

$$$–$$$$ 🏨 **Dei Borgognoni.** This quietly chic hotel near Piazza Colonna is as central as you could want, yet the winding byway stage set gives you a sense of being off the beaten track. The centuries-old building provides spacious lounges, a glassed-in garden, and rooms well arranged to create an illusion of space, though they are actually compact. The hotel has a garage (fee), a rarity in such a central location. ⊠ *Via del Bufalo 126, 00187,* ☎ *06/69941505,* 𝔽𝔸𝕏 *06/69941501. 50 rooms. Parking (fee). AE, DC, MC, V. EP.*

$$$ 🏨 **Albergo del Sole al Pantheon.** This small hotel has been in its central location opposite the Pantheon since the 15th century. It has been tastefully decorated with a blend of modern and antique furnishings. Ceilings are high, floors are tiled in terra-cotta, and there is a charming courtyard for alfresco breakfast in good weather. ⊠ *Piazza della Rotonda 63, 00186,* ☎ *06/6780441,* 𝔽𝔸𝕏 *06/69940689. 25 rooms. Bar. AE, DC, MC, V. CP.*

62

Rome Lodging

$$$ ☷ **Cardinal.** Staying at this hotel is like stepping inside a Renaissance
★ painting—it was built by Bramante and is set on magnificent Via Giu-
lia, whose immutable vistas have scarcely changed since the 15th cen-
tury. Cardinals would feel right at home: The lobby is a riot of red,
while the rooms upstairs are almost ascetic. Serene, severe, and sub-
dued, many of the rooms feature antique engravings and Olympian-
high ceilings. Of course, the interiors don't matter much when Via
Giulia—lined with beautiful palazzi and opulent antiques stores—is
right outside your doorstep. ☒ *Via Giulia 62, 00186,* ☎ *06/68802719,*
℻ *06/6786376. 73 rooms. Bar. AE, DC, MC, V. EP.*

$$ ☷ **Portoghesi.** In the heart of Old Rome, the Portoghesi is a small hotel
with big atmosphere. From a tiny lobby, an equally tiny elevator takes
you to the quiet bedrooms, all decorated with floral prints and reproduction antique furniture. It has a charming roof garden with a view
of the city's domes and rooftops. ☒ *Via dei Portoghesi 1, 00186,* ☎
06/6864231, ℻ *06/6876976. 22 rooms, 6 suites. MC, V. CP.*

$$ ☷ **Teatro di Pompeo.** Where else can you breakfast under the ancient
★ stone vaults of Pompey's Theater, historic site of Julius Caesar's as-
sassination? At this intimate and refined little hotel in the heart of Old
Rome you are part of that history; at night, guests sleep under restored
beamed ceilings that date from the days of Michelangelo. The taste-
fully furnished rooms offer comfort as well as charm. Book well in ad-
vance. ☒ *Largo del Pallaro 8, 00186,* ☎ *06/68300170,* ℻ *06/
68805531. 13 rooms. AE, DC, MC, V. CP.*

$ ☷ **Arenula.** This hotel—with a luminous and cheerful all-white inte-
rior—is one of Rome's best values. Rooms have pale wood furnish-
ings and gleaming bathrooms, as well as double-glazed windows and
air-conditioning (summer only; no help on warm spring or fall days).
Two rooms accommodate four beds. The catch at the four-story
Arenula is that the graceful oval staircase of white marble and wrought
iron is the only way up—there is no elevator. The hotel is on an age-
worn byway off central Via Arenula, on the edge of the Ghetto. ☒ *Via
Santa Maria dei Calderari 47 (Via Arenula), 00186,* ☎ *06/6879454,*
℻ *06/6896188. 50 rooms. DC, MC, V. CP.*

$ ☷ **Campo dei Fiori.** Frescoes, exposed brickwork, and picturesque ef-
fects throughout this little hotel in Old Rome could well be the work
of a set designer. There's an aura of fantasy and romanticism in the
decoration, with the layout cleverly designed to make the most of lim-
ited space. A few rooms are so compact they're almost claustropho-
bic; other rooms are larger, and all have an unusual decorative feature
of some kind to remind you that you are in the heart of Rome. The
hotel has no elevator, but the climb to the roof terrace rewards you
with a marvelous view. Rates for the best rooms exceed parameters in
this price category. ☒ *Via del Biscione 6, 00186,* ☎ *06/68806865,* ℻
06/6876003. 27 rooms, 13 without bath. MC, V. EP.

Spanish Steps

$$$$ ☷ **De La Ville Inter-Continental.** For the well-heeled, this is a finely honed
option just a stone's throw from the top of the Spanish Steps. Guests
often ask for the rooms their great-grandparents favored; regulars are
treated like family here—one reason the place is usually booked solid.
Other lures include a lobby replete with marble and gilt furnishings;
tastefully subdued guest rooms; and a staff high on initiative. Don't
miss the morning meal or Sunday brunch served in La Piazzetta restau-
rant: Adorned with twinkling chandeliers and taffeta-draped French
doors, it has to be the prettiest breakfast in Rome. ☒ *Via Sistina 69,
00187,* ☎ *06/67331,* ℻ *06/6784213. 192 rooms, 23 suites. Restau-
rant, bar, parking (fee). AE, DC, MC, V. CP.*

$$$$ 🏨 **Hassler.** Positioned at the top of the Spanish Steps, the Hassler
★ boasts sweeping views of Rome from its front rooms and rooftop
restaurant; other rooms overlook the gardens of Villa Medici. The hotel
is run by the distinguished Wirth family of hoteliers, which assures a
cordial atmosphere and imperial service from the well-trained staff. The
public rooms have an extravagant 1950s elegance—especially the
clubby winter bar, summer garden bar, and the glass-roofed lounge,
with gold marble walls and a hand-painted tile floor. The comfortable
guest rooms are decorated in a variety of classic styles, some with frescoed walls. The penthouse suite is resplendent with antiques and has
a huge terrace. ⊠ *Piazza Trinità dei Monti 6, 00187,* ☎ *06/699340,*
℻ *06/6789991. 85 rooms, 15 suites. Restaurant, 2 bars, lobby lounge,
beauty salon. AE, DC, MC, V. EP.*

$$ 🏨 **Carriage.** The Carriage's location is what makes it special: It's just
two blocks away from the Spanish Steps, in the heart of Rome. The
stylish decor uses subdued Baroque accents and antique reproduc-
tions to give the hotel a touch of elegance. Though some of the rooms
are pint-size, and a couple open onto an air shaft, several have little
terraces, and all guests can avail of the roof garden. ⊠ *Via delle Car-
rozze 36, 00187,* ☎ *06/6793312,* ℻ *06/6788279. 27 rooms and
suites. AE, DC, MC, V. CP.*

$$ 🏨 **Locarno.** Art aficionados have long appreciated this hotel's fin-de-
siècle charm, intimate feel, and its central location off Piazza del
Popolo. Rooms feature coordinated wallpaper and fabric prints, lac-
quered wrought-iron beds, and some antiques juxtaposed with modern gadgets: electronic safes and air-conditioning. Amenities include
an ample buffet breakfast, bar service on the panoramic roof garden,
and complimentary bicycles. ⊠ *Via della Penna 22, 00186,* ☎ *06/
3610841,* ℻ *06/3215249. 46 rooms, 2 suites. Bar, breakfast room, lobby
lounge. AE, DC, MC, V. CP.*

$$ 🏨 **Scalinata di Spagna.** An old-fashioned pensione loved by genera-
tions of romantics, this tiny hotel is booked solid for months—even
years—ahead. Its location at the top of the Spanish Steps, inconspic-
uous little entrance, and view from the terrace where you breakfast make
it seem like your own special, exclusive inn. And that's why rates for
some rooms go over the top of this category. ⊠ *Piazza Trinità dei Monti
17, 00187,* ☎ *06/6793006,* ℻ *06/69940598. 16 rooms. Parking (fee).
AE, MC, V. CP.*

$ 🏨 **Marcus.** The location, down the street from the Spanish Steps, is
the premier feature of this small hotel occupying a large apartment on
one floor of an 18th-century cardinal's palazzo. Many rooms have an-
tique fireplaces but modern bathrooms. The main living room has com-
fortable armchairs and a crystal chandelier. Double-glazed windows
keep out most of the noise. ⊠ *Via Clementina 94, 00184,* ☎ *06/
68300320,* ℻ *06/68300312. 15 rooms. AE, MC, V. EP.*

$ 🏨 **Margutta.** The lobby and halls in this small hotel are unassuming,
★ but rooms are a pleasant surprise, with a clean and airy look, attrac-
tive wrought-iron bedsteads, and modern baths. Though it's in an old
building, there is an elevator. It's central on a quiet side street between
the Spanish Steps and Piazza del Popolo. ⊠ *Via Laurina 34, 00187,*
☎ *06/3223674,* ℻ *06/3200395. 21 rooms. AE, DC, MC, V. CP.*

Veneto

$$$$ 🏨 **Eden.** A superlative hotel that combines dashing elegance and stun-
★ ning vistas of Rome with the warm charm of Italian hospitality, the
Eden was once the preferred haunt of Hemingway, Ingrid Bergman,
and Fellini, and of many celebrities before them. Precious antiques, sump-
tuous Italian fabrics, linen sheets, and marble baths exude understated

elegance. The views from the rooftop bar and restaurant will take your breath away, and La Terrazza dell'Eden (☞ Dining, *above*) merits raves, too. ⊠ *Via Ludovisi 49, 00187,* ☎ *06/478121,* 𝄜 *06/4821584. 101 rooms, 12 suites. Restaurant, bar, exercise room, free parking. AE, DC, MC, V. EP.*

$$$$ ▥ **Excelsior.** To Romans and many others, the white Victorian cupola of the Excelsior is a symbol of Rome at its most cosmopolitan. The hotel's porte cochere has long sheltered Europe's aristocrats and Hollywood's royalty as they alighted from their Rollses and Ferraris. They entered the polished doors that still open onto a world of luxury lavished with mirrors, carved moldings, Oriental rugs, crystal chandeliers, and huge, Baroque floral arrangements. The theme of gracious living prevails throughout the hotel in splendidly appointed rooms and marble baths. ⊠ *Via Veneto 125, 00187,* ☎ *06/4708,* 𝄜 *06/4826205. 282 rooms, 45 suites. Restaurant, bar, barbershop, beauty salon, free parking. AE, DC, MC, V. EP.*

$$$$ ▥ **Majestic.** In the 19th-century tradition of grand hotels, this establishment on Via Veneto offers sumptuous furnishings and spacious rooms, with up-to-date accessories such as CNN, minibars, strongboxes, and white marble bathrooms. There are authentic antiques in the public rooms, and the excellent restaurant looks like a Victorian conservatory. The Ninfa grill-café on street level is an intimate venue for light meals and drinks. Many suites have whirlpool baths. ⊠ *Via Veneto 50, 00187,* ☎ *06/486841,* 𝄜 *06/4880984. 87 rooms, 8 suites. Restaurant, bar, parking (fee). AE, DC, MC, V. CP.*

$$$ ▥ **Victoria.** A 1950s luxury in the public rooms, solid comfort throughout at reasonable rates, and impeccable management are the main features of this hotel near Via Veneto. Oriental rugs, oil paintings, welcoming armchairs, and fresh flowers add charm to the public spaces, and the rooms are well furnished with armchairs and other amenities ignored by many modern decorators. American businesspeople, who prize the hotel's personalized service and restful atmosphere, are frequent guests. Some upper rooms and the roof terrace overlook the majestic pines of Villa Borghese. ⊠ *Via Campania 41, 00187,* ☎ *06/473931,* 𝄜 *06/ 4871890. 108 rooms. Restaurant, bar. AE, DC, MC, V. CP, FAP, MAP.*

$$ ▥ **La Residenza.** Mainly Americans frequent this hotel in a converted
★ town house near Via Veneto, with first-class comfort and a great atmosphere. The canopied entrance, spacious well-furnished lounges, and the bar and terrace are of the type you would expect to find in a deluxe lodging. Rooms, done out in aquamarine and beige with bentwood furniture, have large closets, color TVs, refrigerator-bars, air-conditioning, and heated towel racks. Rates include a generous American-style buffet breakfast. ⊠ *Via Emilia 22, 00187,* ☎ *06/ 4880789,* 𝄜 *06/485721. 21 rooms, 7 suites. Bar. AE, MC, V. CP.*

$$ ▥ **Marcella.** Known to connoisseurs as one of Rome's best midsize ho-
★ tels, with the feel of a smaller, more intimate establishment, this is 10 minutes from Via Veneto or Stazione Termini. Here you can do your sightseeing from the roof terrace, taking in the view while you breakfast. Rooms are furnished with flair, showing a tasteful use of color, floral prints, and mirrored walls, echoing the elegant winter-garden decor of the lounges and bar. The spacious and flexible suites are ideal for families. ⊠ *Via Flavia 106, 00187,* ☎ *06/4746451,* 𝄜 *06/4815832. 73 rooms, 2 suites. Bar. AE, DC, MC, V. CP.*

Near Termini

$$$$ ▥ **Grand.** A 100-year-old establishment of class and style, this hotel caters to an elite international clientele. It's only a few minutes from Via Veneto. Off the richly decorated, split-level main salon—where afternoon tea is served every day—is an intimate bar, a chic rendezvous. The spacious bedrooms are decorated in gracious Empire style, with smooth fabrics and thick carpets in tones of blue and pale gold. Crystal chandeliers and marble baths add a luxurious note. The Grand also offers one of Italy's most beautiful dining rooms, called simply Le Restaurant. ⊠ *Via Vittorio Emanuele Orlando 3, 00185,* ☎ *06/47091,* FAX *06/4747307. 134 rooms, 36 suites. Restaurant, bar, free parking. AE, DC, MC, V. EP.*

$$$ ★ **Britannia.** This fine small hotel, with frescoed halls and breakfast room, is a very special place, offering superior quality at moderate rates. Its quiet but central location is one attraction; a caring management is another. Guests are coddled with English-language dailies and local weather reports delivered to their rooms each morning, with sybaritic marble bathrooms (some with Jacuzzis) and well-furnished rooms, two with roof terraces. ⊠ *Via Napoli 64, 00184,* ☎ *06/4883153,* FAX *06/4882343. 32 rooms, 1 suite. Breakfast room, free parking. AE, DC, MC, V. CP.*

$$ **Art Deco.** This hotel's name tells all about its glamorous decor, attuned to the elegance and fancy of the 1920s, with whimsical accents in Deco paintings and antiques. Underlying the style is reassuring technology: a fail-safe electrical system, air-conditioning, and whirlpool baths. The hotel is in a residential neighborhood 10 minutes from Stazione Termini and handy to public transport. Book through Best Western or directly for the best rates. ⊠ *Via Palestro 19, 00185,* ☎ *06/4457588,* FAX *06/4441483. 49 rooms. Restaurant, bar, hot tub. AE, DC, MC, V. EP.*

$$ **D'Este.** The fresh-looking decor in this distinguished 19th-century hotel evokes turn-of-the-century comfort, with brass bedsteads and lamps and dark wood period furniture. Rooms are quiet, light, and spacious; many can accommodate family groups. The attentive owner-manager likes to have fresh flowers in the halls and sees that everything works. He encourages inquiries about special rates, particularly during the slack summer months. It's within hailing distance of Santa Maria Maggiore and close to Stazione Termini (you can arrange to be picked up there by the hotel car). ⊠ *Via Carlo Alberto 4/b, 00185,* ☎ *06/4465607,* FAX *06/4465601. 37 rooms. Bar. AE, DC, MC, V. CP.*

$$ **Duca d'Alba.** This elegant hotel has made a stylish contribution to the ongoing gentrification of the Suburra neighborhood, near the Colosseum and the Roman Forum. The tasteful neoclassic decor is in character with ancient Roman motifs with custom-designed furnishings and marble bathrooms. All rooms are entirely soundproofed; a few have tiny terraces. The four-bed suite with kitchenette is a bargain for a family or a group of friends. This well-run establishment offers exceptionally good value: Rates are at the lowest rung in the category. The attentive staff is another plus. ⊠ *Via Leonina 14, 00184,* ☎ *06/484471,* FAX *06/4884840. 27 rooms, 1 suite. AE, DC, MC, V. CP.*

$$ ★ **Morgana.** After enjoying the dashingly marbled lobby, the antique accents in fully carpeted halls, and soundproofed rooms decorated with fine fabrics, you'll agree this is an elegantly conceived hotel. The Morgana offers excellent value and shows the management's attention to comfort and detail. The atmosphere is cordial and the rates are low in this category. It's also convenient to Stazione Termini. ⊠ *Via Filippo Turati 33, 00185,* ☎ *06/4467230,* FAX *06/4469142. 100 rooms, 2 suites. Bar, airport shuttle, parking (fee). AE, DC, MC, V. CP.*

$$ **Siviglia.** You are transported back to a more opulent era in this 19th-century mansion in the quieter residential fringe of the Stazione Termini area. Like the several embassies in the neighborhood, it, too, has bright flags flying at the entrance. Inside, Venetian glass chandeliers and antique reproduction furniture give the lounges considerable char-

acter; rooms are simpler, with a light, airy touch. ✉ *Via Gaeta 12, 00185,* ☎ *06/4441198,* FAX *06/4441195. 42 rooms. Bar. AE, MC, V. CP.*

$ 🏨 **Miami.** Its location in a dignified 19th-century building on Rome's important Via Nazionale puts this hotel in a strategic spot for sightseeing, shopping, and getting around in general; it is on main bus lines and near Stazione Termini and the Metro. Rates are moderate for the category. The marble floors, chrome trim, and dark colors are brightened by the friendly family-style management. Rooms on the courtyard are quieter. ✉ *Via Nazionale 230, 00184,* ☎ *06/4817180,* FAX *06/ 484562. 32 rooms, 2 suites. AE, DC, MC, V. CP.*

$ 🏨 **Montreal.** This is a compact hotel on a central avenue across the square from Santa Maria Maggiore, only three blocks from Stazione Termini, with bus and subway lines close by. On three floors of an older building, it has been totally renovated and offers fresh-looking rooms. The owner-managers are pleasant and helpful, and the neighborhood has plenty of reasonably priced eating places. ✉ *Via Carlo Alberto 4, 00185,* ☎ *06/4457797,* FAX *06/4465522. 20 rooms. Parking (fee). AE, DC, MC, V. CP.*

$ 🏨 **Romae.** In the better part of the Stazione Termini neighborhood, the Romae has the advantages of a strategic location, a very friendly and helpful management, and good-size rooms that are clean and airy. The pictures of Rome in the small lobby and breakfast room, the luminous white walls and light wood furniture in the rooms, and the bright little baths all have a fresh look. Amenities such as satellite TV, safe, and hair dryer in every room make this hotel a very good value. Families benefit from special rates and services. ✉ *Via Palestro 49, 00185,* ☎ *06/ 4463554,* FAX *06/4463914. 20 rooms. Breakfast room. AE, MC, V. CP.*

Vatican

$$$$ 🏨 **Cavalieri Hilton.** Though the Cavalieri is outside the imaginary confines of the city's center, distance has its advantages, one of them being the magnificent view from the hotel's hilltop site (ask for a room facing the city). This hotel is a stylish oasis of quiet and comfort, with good taste and a distinctive Italian flair. If you can tear yourself away from your balcony, the terraces, gardens, and swimming pool, you will find a courtesy shuttle bus leaving for the center of Rome every hour. Don't miss the deservedly acclaimed rooftop restaurant, La Pergola (☞ Dining, *above*). ✉ *Via Cadlolo 101, 00136,* ☎ *06/35091,* FAX *06/ 35092241. 358 rooms, 18 suites. 2 restaurants, bar, indoor and outdoor pools, beauty salon, spa. AE, DC, MC, V. CP.*

$$$ 🏨 **Farnese.** A turn-of-the-century mansion, the Farnese is near the Metro
★ and within walking distance of St. Peter's. Furnished with great attention to detail in art deco style, it has an intimate atmosphere, dazzling modern baths, charming fresco decorations, and a roof garden. ✉ *Via Alessandro Farnese 30, 00192,* ☎ *06/3212553,* FAX *06/3215129. 24 rooms. Bar, free parking. AE, DC, MC, V. EP.*

$$$ 🏨 **Giulio Cesare.** An aristocratic town house with a garden in the residential, but central, Prati district, the Giulio Cesare is a 10-minute walk across the Tiber from Piazza del Popolo. It's beautifully run, with a friendly staff and a quietly luxurious air. The rooms are elegantly furnished, with chandeliers, thick rugs, floor-length drapes, and rich damasks in soft colors. Public rooms have Oriental carpets, old prints and paintings, marble fireplaces, and a grand piano. The buffet breakfast is a veritable banquet. ✉ *Via degli Scipioni 287, 00192,* ☎ *06/ 3210751,* FAX *06/3211736. 90 rooms. Bar. AE, DC, MC, V. CP.*

$$ 🏨 **Sant'Anna.** An example of the gentrification of the picturesque old Borgo neighborhood in the shadow of St. Peter's, this fashionable small hotel has ample, air-conditioned bedrooms in art deco style. The

frescoes in the breakfast room and fountain in the courtyard are typical Roman touches. The spacious attic rooms have tiny terraces. ⊠ *Borgo Pio 134, 00193,* ☎ *06/68801602,* FAX *06/68308717. 20 rooms. Breakfast room, parking (fee). AE, DC, MC, V. CP.*

$ ⊞ **Alimandi.** On a side street a block from the Vatican Museums, this ★ family-operated hotel offers excellent value in a neighborhood with moderately priced shops and restaurants. A spiffy lobby and ample lounges, a tavern for night owls, terraces, and roof gardens are some of the perks. Rooms are spacious, airy, and well furnished; many can accommodate extra beds. Handy public transportation gets you downtown in 10 minutes or so. ⊠ *Via Tunisi 8, 00192,* ☎ *06/39723948,* FAX *06/39723943. 35 rooms. Bar, parking (fee). AE, DC, MC, V. EP.*

$ ⊞ **Amalia.** Handy to St. Peter's, the Vatican, and the Cola di Rienzo shopping district, this small hotel is owned and operated by the Consoli family—Amalia and her brothers. On several floors of a 19th-century building, it has large rooms with functional furnishings, TV sets, minibars, pictures of angels on the walls, and gleaming marble bathrooms (hair dryers included). The Ottaviano stop of Metro A is a block away. ⊠ *Via Germanico 66, 00192,* ☎ *06/39723356,* FAX *06/39723365. 30 rooms, 5 without bath. Minibars, parking (fee). AE, MC, V. CP.*

NIGHTLIFE AND THE ARTS

The Arts

Rome has a varied and vibrant cultural life, with music, dance, theater, film, and socializing opportunities for every taste. Trends and offerings change constantly, so the best way to take stock of the leisure activities at hand is to avail yourself of one of the many local publications devoted entirely to free time. You'll find listings in English in the back of the weekly *Roma c'è* booklet, along with handy bus and metro information. A new issue is on sale at newsstands every Thursday. The monthly *Time Out Roma* gives comprehensive event schedules as well as editor's picks; listings are in Italian but easy to decipher. Schedules of events are also published in daily newspapers: pick up *Trovaroma,* the weekly entertainment guide published every Thursday as a supplement to the daily newspaper *La Repubblica*; the *Guest in Rome* booklet is distributed free at hotels; flyers are available at EPT and city tourist information offices. An English-language biweekly, *Wanted in Rome,* is available at central newsstands and has good listings of events.

Dance

The **Rome Opera Ballet** performs regularly at the Teatro dell'Opera (☞ Opera, *below*), often with leading international guest stars. Rome is regularly visited by classical and modern ballet companies from Russia, the United States, and Europe; performances are at the Teatro dell'Opera, Teatro Olimpico (☞ Music, *below*), or at one of the open-air venues in summer. Small dance companies from Italy and abroad perform in various places; check concert listings for details.

Film

Rome has dozens of movie houses, but the only one to show exclusively English-language films, in English, is the **Pasquino** (⊠ Vicolo del Piede off Piazza Santa Maria in Trastevere, ☎ 06/5803622). The **Quirinetta** (⊠ Via M. Minghetti 4, off Via del Corso, ☎ 06/6790012) shows films in their original language every day, usually English but occasionally Spanish, French, and others. A few other theaters in the center reserve one night a week for original language movies; check listings in *Roma c'è.* Tickets are usually 12,000 lire.

Music

CLASSICAL

Despite the long-standing criticism that Rome doesn't have a central concert hall (a new one is currently under construction), the city hosts a wide variety of classical music concerts at various small venues throughout the city. This can make for memorable performances in smaller halls and churches whose ambience make up for the less grand spaces, particularly at Christmastime, a particularly busy concert season in Rome. Of the larger companies, one principal concert series is organized year-round by the **Accademia di Santa Cecilia** (concert hall and box office: ✉ Via della Conciliazione 4, ☎ 06/68801044). The **Accademia Filarmonica Romana** concerts are performed at the (✉ Teatro Olimpico, Piazza Gentile da Fabriano 17, ☎ 06/3234890). Other reputable companies performing there include **Istituzione Universitaria dei Concerti** (✉ Aula Magna, Piazzale Aldo Moro 5, ☎ 06/3610051), **Gonfalone** (✉ Via del Gonfalone 32, ☎ 06/6875952), and **Concerti all'Orologio** (☎ 06/68308735).

Il Tempietto (☎ 06/4814800) organizes music festivals and concerts throughout the year. Depending on the venue, tickets run from about 15,000 to 50,000 lire. In addition to the formal concert companies, there are also many small concert groups who perform in cultural centers and churches. Many concerts are free, including all those performed in Catholic churches, where a special ruling permits only concerts of religious music. Look for posters outside churches announcing free concerts, particularly at the church of **Sant'Ignazio** (✉ Piazza Sant'Ignazio, near the Pantheon, ☎ 06/6794506), which often hosts concerts in a spectacularly frescoed setting.

ROCK, POP, AND JAZZ

Rock, pop, and jazz concerts are frequent, especially in summer, although even performances by big-name stars may not be well advertised. Most of the bigger-name acts perform outside the center, so it's worth asking about transportation *before* you buy your tickets. Tickets for these performances are usually handled by **Orbis** (✉ Piazza Esquilino 37, ☎ 06/4744776). **Ricordi** music store (✉ Via del Corso 506, ☎ 06/3612331; ✉ Viale Giulio Cesare 88, ☎ 06/3720216) also sells tickets. For smaller venues, ☞ Music Clubs, *below*.

Opera

Rome's opera season runs from November or December to May, and performances are staged in the **Teatro dell'Opera** (✉ Piazza B. Gigli, ☎ 06/48160255; toll-free in Italy 1670/166665). Tickets go on sale two days before a performance, and the box office is open 10–5. Prices range from about 30,000 to 150,000 lire for regular performances; they can go much higher for an opening night or an appearance by an internationally acclaimed guest singer. Standards may not always measure up to those set by Milan's fabled La Scala, but, despite strikes and shortages of funds, most performances are respectable.

After the summer opera season was evicted from the ruins of the ancient **Terme di Caracalla** (☞ Across the Tiber *in* Exploring Rome *above*) and a temporary venue was created in **Villa Borghese,** the debate over a permanent open-air venue continues. The most likely choice is **Villa Pepoli,** a parklike area adjacent to the ruins of the Baths.

Nightlife

La Dolce Vita notwithstanding, Rome's nightlife is not among the world's most exciting, but locals say it is improving, with the proliferation of discos, live-music spots, and quiet late-night bars in recent years. In keeping with the changing times, the "flavor of the month" factor works here, too, and many places fade into oblivion after their five minutes of fame. The best sources for an up-to-date list of late-night spots are the "Night Scene" section of *Roma c'è* and *Metropolitan*, an English-language biweekly sold at many newsstands.

Bars and Pubs

The last few years have brought an inexplicable inundation of English and Irish-style pubs to Rome, and judging from their tremendous popularity among young Italians and foreigners, it looks like Guinness is here to stay. One of the first of the British invasion, **Flann O'Brien** (⊠ Via Napoli 29, ☎ 06/4480418) has the look and atmosphere of a good Irish pub but also serves decent cappuccino. **Trinity College** (⊠ Via del Collegio Romano 6, near Piazza Venezia, ☎ 06/6786472) has two floors of university-style pub trappings (and Italian snacks all day), with an old-school look and convivial music and drinks until 2 AM. The grand-daddy of Rome's authentic Hibernian-style pubs, **Fiddler's Elbow** (⊠ Via dell'Olmata 43, ☎ 06/4872110) encourages singing, and is open from 5 PM–midnight. **Four Green Fields** (⊠ Via Costantino Morin 42, off Via della Giuliana, ☎ 06/3595091) features live music and is open daily from 8:30 PM to 2 AM.

So where do you go for a cocktail? Jacket and tie are in order in the elegant **Blue Bar** of the Hostaria dell'Orso (⊠ Via dei Soldati 25, ☎ 06/6864250) and in **Le Bar** of the Grand Hotel (⊠ Via Vittorio Emanuele Orlando 3, ☎ 06/482931). **Bar della Pace** (⊠ Piazza della Pace, ☎ 06/6861216) is still the people-watching cocktail bar of choice at stylish Piazza Navona. **Bar del Fico** (⊠ Piazza del Fico 26, ☎ 06/6865205), around the corner, is a down-to-earth, authentically Roman alternative, but watch out for huge crowds on weekend and summer nights. **Taverna del Campo** (⊠ Piazza Campo dei Fiori 16, ☎ 06/6874402) at Campo dei Fiori, is the spot of the moment for wine and elegant hors d'oeuvres.

Nightclubs

Most clubs open about 10:30 PM and charge an entrance fee of around 30,000–35,000 lire, which may include the first drink; subsequent drinks cost about 10,000–15,000 lire. Most clubs are closed Monday.

Jackie O' (⊠ Via Boncompagni 11, ☎ 06/4885754) is an upscale favorite with the rich and famous for dinner and disco dancing. At **Gilda** (⊠ Via Mario dei Fiori 97, near Piazza di Spagna, ☎ 06/6784838) you may spot Italian actors and politicians and American celebrities. This sophisticated nightspot has a piano bar, as well as a restaurant, dance floors, and live music. Jackets are required, and it's closed Monday. Newer but just as exclusive is **Bella Blu** (⊠ Via Luciani 21, ☎ 06/3230490), a Parioli club that caters to Rome's thirtysomething elite.

One of Rome's first discos, **Piper** (⊠ Via Tagliamento 9, ☎ 06/8414459) is still hot and a magnet for young movers and shakers. It has disco music, live groups, and pop videos, and Latin nights once a week. Occasionally, there's ballroom dancing for an older crowd, and Sunday afternoons it's open for teenagers. Testaccio's **The Saint** (⊠ Via Galvani 46, ☎ 06/5747945) is a three-level complex with two discos that play everything from house to New Age music and rooms designated "Paradiso" and "Inferno" (Heaven and Hell). The under-25 crowd lets loose to indie rock and weekend live shows at post-industrial **Black Out** (⊠ Via Saturnia 18, ☎ 06/70496791). **Follia** (⊠ Via Ovidio 17, ☎ 06/68308435), a favorite for film parties, lures celebrities and a tony young crowd with disco music and a piano bar.

Rome's Latin dance fad is still going fast and furious, and new Latin-theme clubs seem to open every day. **Caruso** (⊠ Via di Monte Testaccio, ☎ 06/5745019) is one that has proven its staying power; this Testaccio disco offers a Latin alternative to the many rock clubs that line this strip. **M.A.I.S.** (⊠ Via Cesare Beccaria 22, ☎ 06/36251780) is the latest reinvention of one of Rome's storied disco sites, mainly disco with some nights dedicated to Latin music and even cabaret. The **Open Gate** (⊠ Via San Nicola da Tolentino 4, ☎ 06/42000848) is near Via Veneto and swings to a Latin beat, with disco and live music in a splashy tropical setting complemented by Cuban, Brazilian, and Mexican food.

Music Clubs

Jazz, folk, pop, and Latin music clubs are flourishing in Rome, particularly in Trastevere and Testaccio. Jazz clubs are especially popular, and talented local groups may be joined by visiting musicians from other countries. As admission, many clubs require that you buy a membership card for 10,000–20,000 lire. For popular shows or weekend nights, it's a good idea to reserve a table in advance no matter where you're going.

In the Trionfale district near the Vatican, **Alexanderplatz** (⊠ Via Ostia 9, ☎ 06/39742171), Rome's most famous jazz club, has both a bar and a restaurant, and features live jazz and blues played nightly by both local and internationally-known musicians. **Big Mama** (⊠ Vicolo San Francesco a Ripa 18, Trastevere, ☎ 06/5812551) offers live blues, R&B, African, jazz, and rock. Latin rhythms are the specialty at **Berimbau** (⊠ Via dei Fienaroli 30/b, Trastevere, ☎ 06/5813249), a live music club with a Brazilian accent and disco dancing after the show.

In trendy Testaccio, **Four XXXX Pub** (⊠ Via Galvani 29, ☎ 06/5725091) is a combination restaurant–beer hall–jazz club, with live jazz groups and no-smoking sections downstairs. **Il Locale** (⊠ Vicolo del Fico 3, near Piazza Navona, ☎ 06/6879075) pulls in a lively crowd for new rock sounds from both sides of the Atlantic. The **Jazz Club** (⊠ Via Zanardelli 12, ☎ 06/6861990), near Piazza Navona, is a classic watering hole with seating at the bar or in leather-upholstered booths. Light meals are available, and there's live music a few nights a week. Live performances of jazz, soul, funk, and dance music get people moving at **Jam Session** (formerly St. Louis Music City, ⊠ Via del Cardello 13/a, ☎ 06/4745076). There is also a restaurant. It's closed Sunday.

OUTDOOR ACTIVITIES AND SPORTS

Participant Sports

Biking

You can rent a bike at **I Bike Rome** (⊠ Underground parking lot Sector III at Villa Borghese, ☎ 06/3225240). Also try **St. Peter's Motor Rent** (⊠ Via di Porta Castello 43, ☎ 06/6875714).

Golf

Nonmembers are welcome in these clubs, all with 18 holes, but must show the membership cards of their home golf or country clubs. The oldest and most prestigious golf club here is the **Circolo del Golf Roma** (⊠ Via Appia Nuova 716/a, ☎ 06/7803407). Among the newest is **Golf Club Parco de' Medici** (⊠ Viale Parco de' Medici 22, ☎ 06/6553477). You can also get into the swing at **Country Club Castel Gandolfo** (⊠ Via Santo Spirito 13, Castel Gandolfo, ☎ 06/9312301). The **Golf Club Fioranello** (⊠ Viale della Repubblica, ☎ 06/7138080) is at Santa

Maria delle Mole, off Via Appia Antica. Also try **Olgiata Golf Club** (✉ Largo Olgiata 15, Via Cassia, ☎ 06/30889141).

Health Clubs

The **Cavalieri Hilton** (✉ Via Cadlolo 101, ☎ 06/35091) has a running path on its grounds as well as outdoor and indoor pools, two clay tennis courts, and a luxurious spa, fitness, and beauty center, all open to nonguests. The **Sheraton Roma** (✉ Viale del Pattinaggio, ☎ 06/5453) has a heated outdoor pool, tennis court, two squash courts, and a sauna, but no gym. The **Sheraton Golf** (✉ Viale Parco de' Medici 22, ☎ 06/659788) has a fitness center and 18-hole golf course. Two tennis courts and a 25-meter pool are at the **St. Peter's Holiday Inn** (✉ Via Aurelia Antica 415, ☎ 06/6642).

The **Roman Sport Center** (✉ Via del Galoppatoio 33, ☎ 06/3201667) is a vast, full-fledged health club next to the underground parking lot in Villa Borghese; it has two swimming pools, a gym, aerobic workout areas, squash courts, and saunas. It is affiliated with the **American Health Club** (✉ Largo Somalia 60, ☎ 06/86212411).

Horseback Riding

There are several riding clubs in Rome. The most central is the **Associazione Sportiva Villa Borghese** (✉ Via del Galoppatoio 23, ☎ 06/3606797). Try the **Società Ippica Romana** (✉ Via Monti della Farnesina 18, ☎ 06/3240592) and the **Circolo Ippico Olgiata** (✉ Largo Olgiata 15, ☎ 06/30888792), outside the city on Via Cassia.

Running

The best bet for running in the inner city is the **Villa Borghese,** with an approximate ⅔-km (½-mi) circuit of the Pincio, among the marble statuary. A longer run in the park itself might include a loop around **Piazza di Siena,** a grass horse track. Although most traffic is barred from Villa Borghese, government and police cars sometimes speed through. Be careful to stick to the sides of the roads. For a long run away from all traffic, try **Villa Ada** and **Villa Doria Pamphili** on the Janiculum. On the other hand, if you really love history, run at the old **Circus Maximus,** or along **Via delle Terme di Caracalla,** flanked by a park. There is also a path at **Cavalieri Hilton** (☞ Health Clubs, *above*).

Swimming

The outdoor pools of the **Cavalieri Hilton** (✉ Via Cadlolo 101, ☎ 06/35091) and the **Hotel Aldovrandi** (✉ Via Ulisse Aldovrandi 15, ☎ 06/3223993) are lush summer oases open to nonguests. The **Roman Sport Center** (✉ Via del Galoppatoio 33, ☎ 06/3201667) has two swimming pools, and there's another one at the **American Health Club** (✉ Largo Somalia 60, ☎ 06/86212411).

Tennis

A prominent Roman club is the **Tennis Club Parioli** (✉ Largo de Morpurgo 2, Via Salaria, ☎ 06/86200882).

Spectator Sports

Basketball

Games are played at the **Palazzo dello Sport** in the EUR district (✉ Piazzale dello Sport, ☎ 06/5925107).

Horseback Riding

The **International Riding Show,** held in May, draws a stylish crowd to the amphitheater of Piazza di Siena in Villa Borghese. The competition is stiff, and the program features a cavalry charge staged by the dashing mounted corps of the carabinieri. For information, call the **Ital-**

ian Federation of Equestrian Sports (⊠ Viale Tiziano 74, ☎ 06/ 36858528).

Soccer

Italy's favorite spectator sport stirs passionate enthusiasm among partisans. Games are usually held on Saturday afternoons and Wednesday evenings throughout the fall–spring season. Two teams—Roma and Lazio—play their home games in the Olympic Stadium at the extensive **Foro Italico** sports complex (⊠ Viale dei Gladiatori, ☎ 06/ 3336316), built by Mussolini on the banks of the Tiber. Tickets are on sale at the box office before the games; your hotel concierge may be able to help you get tickets in advance.

SHOPPING

Shopping is a must in Italy, no matter what your budget. Don't expect to get bargains on Italian designers that are exported to the United States; prices are about the same on both sides of the Atlantic. Shops are open from 9 or 9:30 to 1 and from 3:30 or 4 to 7 or 7:30. There's a tendency in Rome for shops in central districts to stay open all day, and hours are generally becoming more flexible throughout the city. Remember that most stores are closed Sunday, though this is changing, too. Generally, with the exception of food and technical-supply stores, most stores also close on Monday mornings from September to June and Saturday afternoons in July and August.

Bargains

You can often find good buys in knitwear and silk scarves at stands on the fringes of outdoor food markets. Bargaining is still an art at **Porta Portese** flea market (☞ Markets, *below*) and is routine when purchasing anything from a street vendor. On **Via Cola di Rienzo** there is usually a stand with a range of blown-glass items. The market at **Via Sannio** (San Giovanni in Laterano) features job lots of designer shoes and ranks of stalls selling new and used clothing at bargain prices. It is open weekdays 10–1, Saturday 10–6. The morning market in the piazza at the center of the **Testaccio** neighborhood is also known for stands selling designer shoes. Bargain hunters will also love **Vesti a Stock** (⊠ Via Germanico 170).

Department Stores and Malls

Rinascente (⊠ Near Piazza Colonna, ☎ 06/6797691) sells clothing and accessories only. Another Rinascente (⊠ Piazza Fiume, ☎ 06/8841231) has the same stock, plus furniture and housewares. **Coin** (⊠ Piazzale Appio, near San Giovanni in Laterano, ☎ 06/7080020; ⊠ Cinecittà Due, ☎ 06/7220931) carries housewares, as well as fashions for men and women. The **UPIM** and **Standa** chains offer low- to moderately priced goods ranging from bathing suits to first-aid supplies to while-you-wait shoe-repair service counters.

The mall **Cinecittà Due** (⊠ Piazza di Cinecittà, Viale Palmiro Togliatti, ☎ 06/7220902) was the first of several megamalls, with 100 stores; take Metro A to the Subaugusta stop.

Markets

All outdoor markets are open from early morning to about 2, except Saturday, when they may stay open all day. Beware of pickpockets and don't go if you can't stand crowds. Downtown Rome's most colorful

outdoor food market is at **Campo dei Fiori** (✉ South of Piazza Navona).
The so-called **Trionfale market** (✉ Via Andrea Doria, about a five-minute
walk north of the entrance to the Vatican Museums) is equally big and
bustling. Smaller markets can be found throughout the city. There's
room for bargaining at the flea market on Sunday morning at **Porta
Portese** (✉ Take Via Ippolito Nievo, off Viale Trastevere); it now offers mainly new or secondhand clothing, but there are still a few dealers in old furniture and intriguing junk.

Shopping Districts

The most elegant and expensive shops are concentrated in the Piazza
di Spagna area, especially along **Via Condotti. Via Borgognona** is lined
with designer boutiques. The shops on **Via Frattina** have either trendy
or classic men's and women's fashions, at competitive prices. Art galleries are concentrated on **Via Margutta. Via del Babuino** is the place
to go for antiques. There are several high-fashion designer establishments on **Via Gregoriana.** Well-heeled clotheshorses also head to **Via
Sistina.** Bordering the top-price Piazza di Spagna shopping district is
Via del Corso, lined with shops and boutiques of all kinds with goods
of varying quality and prices. **Via Campo Marzio,** on the cusp of the
Piazza di Spagna area, is also a good bet for classic fashions and com-
petitively priced, high-end boutiques.

Via del Tritone, leading up from Piazza Colonna off Via del Corso, has
some medium-priced, and a few expensive, shops selling everything from
fashion fabrics to books on Rome. On **Via Veneto** you'll find more high-
priced boutiques and shoe stores, as well as newsstands selling English-
language newspapers, magazines, and paperback books. **Via Nazionale**
features shoe stores, moderately priced boutiques, and shops selling
men's and women's fashions. **Via Cola di Rienzo** offers high-quality wares
of all types; for variety and range of goods, it's a good alternative to
the Piazza di Spagna area.

In Old Rome, **Via dei Coronari** has antiques and designer home accessories. **Via Monserrato** also features antiques dealers galore, plus a few
art galleries. **Via Giulia** is also a decorative arts bonanza. In the **Pantheon** area there are many shops selling liturgical objects and vestments. But the place to go for religious souvenirs is the area around **St.
Peter's,** especially Via della Conciliazione and Via di Porta Angelica.

Specialty Stores

Antiques and Prints

For old prints and antiques, **Tanca** (✉ Salita dei Crescenzi 10, near the
Pantheon, ☎ 06/6875272) is a good hunting ground. Early pho-
tographs of Rome and views of Italy from the archives at **Alinari** (✉
Via Aliberti 16/a, ☎ 06/6792923) make memorable souvenirs. **Nardec-
chia** (✉ Piazza Navona 25, ☎ 06/6869318) is reliable for prints.
Stands in **Piazza della Fontanella Borghese** sell prints and old books.

Clothing

All the big names in Italian fashion—Versace, Ferre, Valentino, Armani,
Missoni—have emporiums in the Piazza di Spagna area. **Sorelle Fontane**
(✉ Salita San Sebastianello 6, ☎ 06/6798652), one of the first houses
to put Italy on the fashion map, has a large boutique with an extensive line of ready-to-wear clothing and accessories. **Ermenegildo Zegna**
(✉ Via Borgognona 7/e, ☎ 06/6789143) has the finest in elegant
men's styles and accessories. **Dolce & Gabbana** (✉ Piazza di Spagna
82, ☎ 06/6792294), a spin-off of the top-of-the-line D&G store on

Rome Shopping

Ai Monasteri, **17**
Albertina, **22**
Aston, **26**
Bruno Magli, **24**
Campo dei Fiori, **8**
Cinecittà Due, **34**
Coin, **35**
Di Cori, **33**
Fratelli Bassetti, **13**
Frugoni, **11**

Furla, **21**
Labels-for-Less, **29**
Lavori Artigianali
Femminili, **27**
Le Tartarughe, **14**
Luisa Spagnoli, **23**
Myricae, **18**
Nardecchia, **15**
Nickol's, **30**
Officina Farmaceutica
di Santa Maria
Novella, **16**

Porta Portese, **9**
Rinascente, **19**
Sac Joli, **20**
Tanca, **12**
Testaccio, **10**
Vesti a Stock, **2**
Via Andrea Doria, **1**
Via Cola di Rienzo, **3**
Via della
Conciliazione, **5**

Via del Tritone, **28**
Via di Porta
Angelica, **4**
Via Giulia, **6**
Via Monserrato, **7**
Via Nazionale, **32**
Via Sannio, **36**
Via Veneto, **25**
Volterra, **31**

78

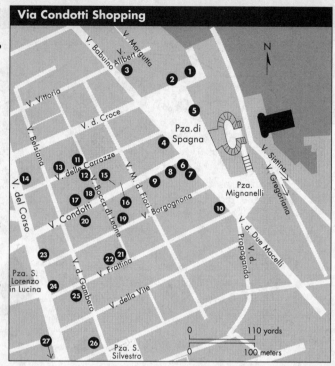

Via Borgognona, shows the trendiest designer fashions in casual wear and accessories for men and women. **Mariselaine** (⌧ Via Condotti 70, ☎ 06/6795817) is a top-quality women's fashion boutique. **Le Tartarughe** (⌧ Via Piè di Marmo 17, ☎ 06/6792240) has understated, versatile, and easy-to-wear garments for women, including packable knits and jerseys. **Mariella Burani** (⌧ Via Bocca di Leone 28, ☎ 06/6790630) is known for elegant and/or trendy boutique fashion for women.

For knitwear, **Luisa Spagnoli** (⌧ Via del Corso 385, ☎ 06/6798169; ⌧ Via Frattina 84/b, ☎ 06/6991706; ⌧ Via Veneto 130, ☎ 06/42011281) is always reliable for good quality at the right price and styles to suit American tastes. **Albertina** (⌧ Via Lazio 20, ☎ 06/4885870) elevates knitwear to the level of high fashion, imparting line and substance to creations that never go out of style.

Crafts and Gifts
For fine pottery, handwoven textiles, and other handicrafts, **Myricae** (⌧ Piazza del Parlamento 38, ☎ 06/6873643) has a good selection. A bottle of liqueur, jar of marmalade, or bar of chocolate handmade by Cistercian monks in several monasteries in Italy makes an unusual, tasty gift to take home; pick from the goodies at **Ai Monasteri** (⌧ Piazza Cinque Lune 2, ☎ 06/68802783). Herbal and floral soaps, lotions, perfumes, and potpourri are easily carried gifts for yourself or others and can be found near Piazza Navona in the Rome branch of Florence's historic apothecary, the **Officina Farmaceutica di Santa Maria Novella** (⌧ Corso Rinascimento 47, ☎ 06/6872446).

Embroidery and Linens
Frette (⌧ Piazza di Spagna 11, ☎ 06/6790673) is a Roman institution for fabulous trousseaux. **Marisa Padovan** (⌧ Via delle Carrozze 81,

☎ 06/6793946) shows exclusive and expensive lingerie. **Venier Colombo** (✉ Via Frattina 42, ☎ 06/6792979) has a selection of exquisite lace goods, including lingerie and linens. **Lavori Artigianali Femminili** (✉ Via Capo le Case 6, ☎ 06/6781100) offers delicately embroidered household linens, infants' and children's clothing, and blouses.

Jewelry and Silver Objects

What Cartier is to Paris, **Bulgari** (✉ Via Condotti 10, ☎ 06/6793876) is to Rome; the shop's elegant display windows hint at what's beyond the guard at the door. **Buccellati** (✉ Via Condotti 31, ☎ 06/6790329) is a tradition-rich Florentine jewelry house renowned for its silver work; it ranks with Bulgari for quality and reliability. You'll find tempting selections of small silver objects at **Fornari** (✉ Via Frattina 133, ☎ 06/6780105) and **Frugoni** (✉ Via Arenula 83, 2nd floor, ☎ 06/68806732). **Bozart** (✉ Via Bocca di Leone 4, ☎ 06/6781026) features dazzling costume jewelry in keeping with the latest fashions.

Shoes and Leather Accessories

The most famous of Rome's leather shops is **Gucci** (✉ Via Condotti 8, ☎ 06/6789340). It has a full assortment of accessories on the first floor, a fashion boutique for men and women and a scarf department on the second floor, and many Japanese customers, who line up to get in on busy days. **Roland's** (✉ Piazza di Spagna 74, ☎ 06/6790391) has an extensive stock of good-quality leather fashions and accessories, as well as stylish casual wear in wool and silk. For the latest styles in handbags and a selection of scarves and costume jewelry at reasonable prices, go to **Furla** (✉ Piazza di Spagna 22, ☎ 06/6878230), which has several stores in downtown Rome. **Sac Joli** (✉ Via Tomacelli 154, ☎ 06/6878431), despite its French name, displays a large collection of fine Italian-made handbags in up-to-the-minute styles. Offbeat and trendy, one-of-a-kind handbags in leather and/or fabrics are made and sold by **Amadei** (✉ Via delle Carrozze 20, ☎ 06/67833452). **Volterra** (✉ Via Barberini 102, ☎ 06/4819315) is well stocked and offers a wide selection of handbags at moderate prices. For gloves as pretty as Holly Golightly's, head to **Sermoneta** (✉ Piazza di Spagna 61, ☎ 06/6791960). **Di Cori** (✉ Piazza di Spagna 53, ☎ 06/6784439) has a spectrum of gloves in every color imaginable. **Merola** (✉ Via del Corso 143, ☎ 06/6791961) carries a line of expensive top-quality gloves and scarves.

For timeless elegance in splendid silk scarves and ties, leather accessories, and fine shoes, **Ferragamo** (✉ Via Condotti 73, ☎ 06/6791565; ✉ Via Condotti 66, ☎ 06/6781130) is one of Rome's best; you pay for quality here, but you can get great buys during the periodic sales. **Nickol's** (✉ Via Barberini 21, ☎ 06/4741648) is in the moderate price range and is one of the few stores in Rome that stocks shoes in American widths. **Charles** (✉ Via del Corso 109, ☎ 06/6792345) has a broad range of shoes, handbags, leather clothing and accessories, and a bilingual sales staff. **Bruno Magli** (✉ Via del Gambero 1, ☎ 06/6793802; ✉ Via Veneto 70, ☎ 06/4884355) is known for well-made shoes and matching handbags at high to moderate prices. **Campanile** (✉ Via Condotti 58, ☎ 06/6790731) has four floors of shoes in the latest—as well as classic—styles and other leather goods.

Silks and Fabrics

Fratelli Bassetti (✉ Corso Vittorio Emanuele II 73, ☎ 06/6892326) has a vast selection of world-famous Italian silks and fashion fabrics in a rambling palazzo. **Aston** (✉ Via Buoncompagni 27, ☎ 06/42871227) stocks couture-level fabrics for men and women. You can find some real bargains when *scampoli* (remnants) are on sale.

SIDE TRIPS

Ostia Antica; Cerveteri and Tarquinia; Tivoli, Palestrina, and Subiaco

One of the easiest excursions from the capital takes you west to the sea, where tall pines stand among the well-preserved ruins of Ostia Antica, the main port of ancient Rome, and an archaeological site that rivals Pompeii. The rolling landscape along the coast northwest of Rome was once Etruscan territory, and at Cerveteri and Tarquinia it holds some intriguing reminders of a people who taught the ancient Romans a thing or two about religion, art, and a pleasurable way of life. East of Rome lie some of the region's star sites, which could be combined along a route that loops through the hills where ancient Romans built their summer resorts. The biggest attraction is Tivoli. Here, Villa Adriana shows you the scale of individual imperial Roman egos, while Villa d'Este demonstrates that Renaissance egos were no smaller. Eastward at Palestrina lies a vast sanctuary famous in ancient times. The monastery where St. Benedict founded the hermitage that gave rise to Western monasticism is farther east in Subiaco.

Ostia Antica

Founded around the 4th century BC, Ostia Antica is reminiscent of Pompeii, but on a smaller scale and in a prettier, parklike setting. Fair weather and good walking shoes are requisites. On hot days, be there when the gates open or go late in the afternoon. A visit to the excavations takes two to three hours, including 15–20 minutes for the museum.

Numbers in the margin correspond to numbers on the Side Trips from Rome map.

❶ Ostia Antica was inhabited by a cosmopolitan population of rich businessmen, wily merchants, sailors, and slaves. The great *horrea* (warehouses) were built in the 2nd century AD to handle huge shipments of grain from Africa; the *insulae* (forerunners of the modern apartment building) provided housing for the growing population. Under the combined assaults of the barbarians and the *Anopheles* mosquito, and after the Tiber changed course, the port was eventually abandoned. Tidal mud and windblown sand covered the city, which lay buried until the beginning of this century. Now it has been extensively excavated and is well maintained. **Porta Romana,** one of the city's three gates, opens onto the **Decumanus Maximus,** the main thoroughfare crossing the city from end to end.

Black-and-white mosaic pavements representing Neptune and Amphitrite decorate the **Terme di Nettuno** (Baths of Neptune). Directly behind the baths is the barracks of the fire department, which played an important role in a town with warehouses full of valuable goods and foodstuffs.

On one side of the Decumanus Maximus is the beautiful **theater,** built by Augustus and completely restored by Septimius Severus in the 2nd century AD. In the vast Piazzale delle Corporazioni, where trade organizations similar to guilds had their offices, is the **Tempio di Cerere** (Temple of Ceres): this is appropriate for a town dealing in grain imports, since Ceres, who gave her name to cereal, was the goddess of agriculture. You can visit the **Casa di Apuleio** (House of Apuleius) built in Pompeiian style—containing fewer windows then, and built lower than those in Ostia. Next to it is the **Mithraeum,** with balconies and a hall decorated with symbols of the cult of Mithras. This men-only religion, imported from Persia, was especially popular with legionnaires.

Side Trips from Rome

N

Orvieto

Lago di
Bolsena

S71

S2

Tiber

Terni

S3

S209

S3

Bomarzo

Narni

S313

Rieti

S79

Marta

Viterbo

Villa Lante

Orte

Caprarola

Lago di
Vico

Civita
Castellana

S4

V. Salaria

S1 bis

Tarquinia

S493

S2

Monterosi

S3

A1

Tiber

Civitavecchia

Lago di
Bracciano

Cassia

Autostrada
Rome-L'Aquila

Mandela

Bracciano

V. Flaminia

Autostrada del Sole

Vicovaro

A24

S1

Cerveteri

A12

V. Aurelia

Rome

V. Tiburtina

Bagni
di Tivoli

S5

Villa d'Este

Subiaco

Villa Adriana

S155

Palestrina

V. Prenestina

V. Casilina

S6

Fiumicino

Ostia Antica

S8

V. del Mare

Lido
di Ostia

A2

Appia

Frascati

S7

S. Cesareo

Autostrada del Sole

S601

S148

Lago di
Albano

Velletri

Ninfa

Sermoneta

Tyrrhenian Sea

S207

Anzio

Latina

TO
SPERLONGA

ITALY

0   10 miles
0   15 km

On Via dei Molini you can see a **mill,** where grain for the warehouses next door was ground with the stones that are still there. Along Via di Diana you come upon a *thermopolium* (bar) with a marble counter and a fresco depicting the fruit and food that were sold here. At the end of Via dei Dipinti is the **Museo Ostiense,** which displays some of the ancient sculptures and mosaics found among the ruins.

The **Foro** holds the monumental remains of the city's most important temple, dedicated to Jupiter, Juno, and Minerva; other ruins of baths; a basilica (in Roman times a basilica served as a secular hall of justice); and smaller temples. **Via Epagathiana** leads toward the Tiber, where there are large warehouses, erected in the 2nd century AD to deal with the enormous amounts of grain imported into Rome during that period, the height of the Empire.

The **Casa di Cupido e Psiche** (House of Cupid and Psyche), a residential house, was named for a statue found there; you can see what remains of a large pool in an enclosed garden decorated with marble and mosaic motifs. It takes little imagination to notice that even in ancient times a premium was placed on water views: The house faces the shore, which would have been only about ⅓ km (¼ mi) away. On Via della Foce are the **Casa del Serapide** (House of Serapis), a 2nd-century multilevel dwelling, and the **Terme dei Sette Sapienti** (Baths of the Seven Wise Men), named for a fresco found there. There is another apartment building on Cardo degli Aurighi.

The **Porta Marina** leads to what used to be the seashore. In the vicinity are the ruins of the **synagogue,** one of the oldest in the Western world. On Via Semita dei Cippi you can see the **Casa di Fortuna Annonaria,** the richly decorated house of a wealthy Ostian. This is another place to marvel at the skill of the mosaic artists and, at the same time, to realize that this really was someone's home. One of the rooms opens onto a secluded garden.

The admission charge to the Ostia Antica excavations includes entrance to the **Museo Ostiense** (Ostiense Museum), which is on the grounds. ✉ *Via dei Romagnoli,* ☎ *06/5650022.* ✍ *8,000 lire.* ☉ *Excavations: daily 9 AM–1 hr before sunset. Museum daily 9–1:30.*

Ostia Antica A to Z

ARRIVING AND DEPARTING

By Car. Follow **Via del Mare** southwest, which leads directly from Rome to Ostia (a 30- to 40-minute trip).

By Train. There is regular train service to the Ostia Antica station from Ostiense train station, near Porta San Paolo; the ride takes about 30 minutes. A long walkway links Ostiense station with the Piramide stop on Metro B; save steps by making connections with the train from Ostiense at the Magliana stop on Metro B. Trains from Ostiense run every half hour. Call 147/888088 for toll-free train information.

Cerveteri and Tarquinia

An excursion northwest of Rome takes you to Etruscan sites on hills near the sea. The Etruscans were an apparently peaceable and pleasure-loving people who held sway over a vast territory north of Rome before the rise of the Roman Republic. They loved life and they were sure that they would enjoy the afterlife, too. The Etruscan necropolis, or "city of the dead," was a cemetery faithfully reproducing the homes and lifestyles of the living. Both of the sites you visit are necropolises.

Beyond Rome's city limits, the countryside is green with pastures and endless fields of artichokes, a premium crop in these parts. You catch glimpses of the sea to the west, where the coast is dotted with suburban developments. Because the beaches in this area are popular with Romans, highways and public transportation can be uncomfortably crowded on weekends from spring to fall. Exploring the Etruscan sites requires some agility in climbing up and down uneven stairs, and you need shoes suitable for walking on rough dirt paths.

At Cerveteri, the principal Etruscan site closest to Rome, in the Etruscan necropolis of the Banditaccia, you walk in a sylvan setting among mossy stones and variously shaped monuments that are memorials to revered ancestors. Tarquinia is close to Civitavecchia, the principal port of Rome. From the highway or train you can see the port installations, which include a fort designed by Michelangelo. The low mountains to the east are the Tolfa range, where the Etruscans mined metals for export to ancient Mediterranean markets.

Cerveteri

The nucleus of the town, in the shadow of a medieval castle, stands on a spur of tufa rock that was the site of the Etruscan city of Caere, a thriving commercial center in the 6th century BC. The necropolis is about a mile on foot or a taxi ride from Cerveteri's main piazza.

In the **Necropoli della Banditaccia** (Banditaccia Necropolis), the Etruscan residents of Caere left a heritage of great historical significance. In this monumental complex of tombs set in parklike grounds, they laid their relatives to rest, some in simple graves, others in burial chambers that are replicas of Etruscan dwellings. In the round tumulus tombs you can recognize the prototypes of Rome's tombs of Augustus and Hadrian (in the Mausoleo di Augusto and Castel Sant'Angelo) and the Tomb of Cecilia Metella on the Via Appia. Look for the **Tomba dei Capitelli**, with carved capitals; the **Tomba dei Rilievi**, its walls carved with reliefs of household objects; and the similar **Tombe degli Scudi e delle Sedie**. The **Tomba Moretti** has a little vestibule with columns. Some tombs have several chambers. ⊠ *Necropoli della Banditaccia.* ☎ *8,000 lire.* ⊗ *Tues.–Sun. 9–1 hr before sunset.*

In Cerveteri's medieval castle, the **Museo Nazionale Cerite** is a small archaeological museum with some of the finds, mostly pottery, from the various Etruscan cemeteries that have been located in the area. ⊠ *Piazza del Castello.* ☎ *Free.* ⊗ *Tues.–Sun. 9–7.*

Tarquinia

Tarquinia sprawls on a hill overlooking the sea. Once a powerful Etruscan city, its medieval core shows that it was a major center in the Middle Ages, too. Though it lacks the harmony of better-preserved medieval towns, Tarquinia offers unexpected visual pleasures, among them views of narrow medieval streets opening onto quaint squares dominated by palaces and churches, and the sight of the majestic, solitary church of Santa Maria di Castello, encircled by medieval walls and towers. To focus on Tarquinia's Etruscan heritage, visit the museum in Palazzo Vitelleschi, and then see the frescoed underground tombs, in the fields east of the city. You can walk to the necropolis from town. From Piazza Matteotti, the town's main square, take Via Porta Tarquinia south past the church of San Francesco; go through the Porta Tarquinia, also known as Porta Clementina, gate and continue south on Via Ripagrotta. At the intersection with Via delle Croci, head east on the main road to reach the necropolis. There is very sketchy bus service from Piazza Cavour to the necropolis, with only a couple of morning and afternoon departures.

The **Museo Nazionale Tarquiniense** (National Museum of Tarquinia), is housed in Palazzo Vitelleschi, a splendid 15th-century building that contains a wealth of Etruscan treasures. Even if pottery vases and end-less ranks of stone sarcophagi leave you cold, what makes a visit here memorable are the horses. A pair of marvelous golden terra-cotta winged horses gleam warmly against the gray stone wall on which they have been mounted in the main hall. They are from a frieze that once decorated an Etruscan temple, and they are strikingly vibrant proof of the degree of artistry attained by the Etruscans in the 4th century BC. The museum and its stately courtyard are crammed with sarcophagi from the underground tombs found under the meadows surrounding the town. The figures of the deceased recline casually on their stone couches, mouths curved in enigmatic smiles. Upstairs are vases and other Etruscan artifacts, together with some of the more precious frescoes from the tombs. The frescoes were removed to keep them from dete-riorating. ⊠ *Piazza Cavour.* 🎫 *8,000 lire.* ☉ *Tues.–Sun. 9–7.*

The entrance to the **Necropoli** (Necropolis), the Etruscan city of the dead, is about 800 m (½ mi) outside the town walls. Frequent, regu-larly scheduled guided tours leave from the ticket office, visiting about 10 of the 100 most interesting tombs, on a rotating basis. The tombs date from the 7th to the 2nd century BC, and they were painted with lively scenes of Etruscan life. The colors are amazingly fresh in some tombs, and the scenes show the vitality and highly civilized lifestyle of this ancient people.

Of the thousands of tombs that exist throughout the territory of Etruria (there are 40,000 in the vicinity of Tarquinia alone), only a small per-centage have been excavated scientifically. Many more have been found and plundered by "experts" called *tombaroli,* who dig illegally, usu-ally at night. The tombs in the Tarquinia necropolis are bare; the only evidence of their original function are the stone platforms on which the sarcophagi rested. The visit takes about 90 minutes. ⊠ *Mon-terozzi, on the Strada Provinciale 1b (Tarquinia–Viterbo).* 🎫 *8,000.* ☉ *9–1 hr before sunset.*

Cerveteri and Tarquinia A to Z

ARRIVING AND DEPARTING

By Bus. COTRAL buses leave for Cerveteri from the Lepanto stop of Metro A, with service every 40 minutes or so during the day. The ride takes about 70 minutes. Also from the Lepanto stop, COTRAL buses de-part for Civitavecchia, where you have to change to another COTRAL bus to Tarquinia. The trip takes about two hours.

By Car. For Cerveteri, take either the **A12** Rome–Civitavecchia toll high-way to the Cerveteri-Ladispoli exit, or take the **Via Aurelia.** The trip takes about 40 minutes. To get to Tarquinia, take the **A12** Rome–Civ-itavecchia highway all the way to the end, where you continue on the Via Aurelia to Tarquinia. The trip takes about 60 minutes.

By Train. From Termini, Ostiense and Trastevere stations in Rome FS and Metropolitana suburban trains take you to the Cerveteri-Ladis-poli station, where you can get a bus for Cerveteri. The train takes 30 minutes; the bus ride takes 15 minutes. To get to Tarquinia, take an FS train (Rome–Genoa line) from Rome or from Cerveteri to the Tar-quinia station, then a local bus from the station up to the hilltop town. The trip takes about 75 minutes.

VISITOR INFORMATION

Cerveteri (⊠ Piazza del Castello, ☎ 06/9941354). **Tarquinia** (☎ Piazza Cavour 1, ☎ 0766/856384).

Tivoli, Palestrina, and Subiaco

East of Rome are two of Lazio's most attractive sights—Villa Adriana and the Villa d'Este in Tivoli—and two less conspicuous attractions, in the mountains farther east. The road from Rome to Tivoli passes through some uninspiring industrial areas and burgeoning suburbs that used to be lush countryside. You'll know you're close to Tivoli when you see vast quarries of travertine marble and smell the sulfurous vapors of the little spa, Bagni di Tivoli. Both sites in Tivoli are outdoors and entail walking.

With a car, you can continue your loop through the mountains east of Rome, taking in two very different sights that are both focused on religion: The ancient pagan sanctuary at Palestrina is set on the slopes of Mt. Ginestro, from which it commands a sweeping view of the green plain and distant mountains. Subiaco, the cradle of Western monasticism, is tucked away in the mountains above Tivoli and Palestrina. If you want to take in all three, unless you start out very early and have lots of energy, plan an overnight stop along the way.

Tivoli

4 **Villa Adriana** (Hadrian's Villa), 3 km (2 mi) south of Tivoli, should be visited first, especially in summer, to take advantage of cool mornings. Hadrian's Villa was an emperor's theme park, an exclusive retreat where the marvels of the classical world were reproduced for a ruler's pleasure. Hadrian, who succeeded Trajan as emperor in AD 117, was a man of genius and intellectual curiosity. Fascinated by the accomplishments of the Hellenistic world, he decided to re-create it for his own enjoyment by building this villa over a vast tract of land below the ancient settlement of Tibur. From AD 118 to 130, architects, laborers, and artists worked on the villa, periodically spurred on by the emperor himself, as he returned from another voyage full of ideas for even more daring constructions. After his death in AD 138, the fortunes of his villa declined. It was sacked by barbarians and Romans alike; by the Renaissance, many of his statues and decorations had ended up in the Villa d'Este. A visit here should take about two hours, more if you like to savor antiquity slowly. ⊠ *Villa Adriana,* ☎ *0774/530203.* ☜ *8,000 lire.* ☉ *Daily 9 AM–90 mins before sunset.*

5 **Villa d'Este** is run-down and bereft of what was once a magical view of the countryside, now blanketed with ugly urban sprawl. Ippolito d'Este, an active figure in the political intrigues of mid-16th-century Italy, was also a cardinal, thanks to his grandfather, Alexander VI, the infamous Borgia pope. To console himself at a time when he saw his political star in decline, Ippolito tore down part of a Franciscan monastery that occupied the hillside site he had chosen for his villa. Then the determined prelate diverted the Aniene River into a channel to run under the town and provide water for the Villa d'Este's fountains. Big, small, noisy, quiet, rushing, and running, the fountains create a late-Renaissance playground. Though time is beginning to take its toll, and the fountains and gardens aren't as well kept as in the cardinal's day, it is easy to see why many travelers of the past considered Villa d'Este one of the most beautiful spots in Italy. Villa d'Este requires a lot of stair climbing and takes about an hour. ⊠ *Villa d'Este.* ☜ *8,000 lire.* ☉ *Tues.–Sun. 9 AM–90 mins before sunset.*

Palestrina

6 Giovanni Pierluigi da Palestrina, born in Palestrina in 1525, was the renowned composer of 105 masses, as well as madrigals, magnificats, and motets. But the town was celebrated long before the composer's lifetime. Ancient Praeneste, modern Palestrina, was founded much earlier than Rome. It was the site of the Temple of Fortuna Primigenia, which dates from the beginning of the 2nd century BC. This was one of the biggest, richest, and most frequented temple complexes in all antiquity. People came from far and wide to consult its famous oracle, yet in modern times, no one had any idea of the extent of the complex until World War II bombings exposed ancient foundations that stretched way out into the plain below the town. It has since become clear that the temple area was larger than the town of Palestrina is today. Now you can make out the four superimposed terraces that formed the main part of the temple; they were built up on great arches and were linked by broad flights of stairs. The whole town sits on top of what was once the main part of the temple.

Large arches and terraces scale the hillside up to the **Palazzo Barberini,** built in the 17th century along the semicircular lines of the original temple. It's now a museum containing material found on the site, some dating back to the 4th century BC. The collection of splendid engraved bronze urns, plundered by thieves in 1991 and later recovered, takes second place to the chief attraction, a 1st-century-BC mosaic representing the Nile in flood. This delightful work—a large-scale composition in which form, color, and innumerable details captivate the eye—is alone worth the trip to Palestrina. But there's more: a model of the temple as it was in ancient times, helps you appreciate the immensity of the original construction. ⊠ *Museo Nazionale Archeologico, Palazzo Barberini,* ☎ *06/9538100.* ⊡ *4,000 lire.* ☉ *Spring and fall, daily 9–6; summer, daily 9–7:30; winter, daily 9–4.*

Subiaco

⑦ Between the town and St. Benedict's hermitage on the mountainside is the **Convento di Santa Scolastica,** the only one of the hermitages founded by St. Benedict to have survived the Lombard invasion of Italy in the 9th century. It has three cloisters; the oldest dates from the 13th century. The library was the site of the first print shop in Italy, set up in 1474. ⊡ *Free.* ☉ *Daily 9–12:30 and 4–7.*

The 6th-century **Monastero di San Benedetto** (Monastery of St. Benedict), a landmark of Western monasticism, was built over the grotto where the saint lived and meditated. Clinging to the cliff on nine great arches, it has resisted the assaults of humans for almost 800 years. Over the little wooden veranda at the entrance, a Latin inscription augurs PEACE TO THOSE WHO ENTER. Every inch of the upper church is covered with frescoes by Umbrian and Sienese artists of the 14th century. In front of the main altar, a stairway leads down to the lower church, carved out of the rock, with yet another stairway down to the grotto where Benedict lived as a hermit for three years. The frescoes here are even earlier than those above; look for the portrait of St. Francis of Assisi, painted from life in 1210, in the Cappella di San Gregorio, and for the oldest fresco in the monastery, in the Shepherd's Grotto. ⊡ *Free.* ☉ *Daily 9–12:30 and 3–6.*

Tivoli, Palestrina, and Subiaco A to Z

ARRIVING AND DEPARTING

By Bus. COTRAL buses (☎ 167431784 toll-free) leave for Tivoli every 15 minutes from the terminal at the Rebbibia stop on Metro B, but not all take the route that passes near Hadrian's Villa. Inquire which bus passes closest to Villa Adriana and tell the driver to let you off there. The ride takes about 60 minutes. From Rome to Palestrina, take the COTRAL bus from the Anagnina stop on Metro A. From Rome to Subiaco, take the COTRAL bus from the Rebbibia stop on Metro B; buses leave every 40 minutes; the circuitous trip takes one hour and 45 minutes.

By Car. For Tivoli, take Via Tiburtina or the Rome–L'Aquila autostrada (**A24**). To get to Palestrina directly from Rome, take either Via Prenestina or Via Casilina or take the Autostrada del Sole (**A2**) to the San Cesareo exit and follow signs for Palestrina; this trip takes about one hour. It's best to drive from Rome to **Subiaco**. Take **S155** east for about 40 km (25 mi) before turning left onto **S411** for the remaining 25 km (15 mi) to Subiaco; the trip takes about 70 minutes.

By Train. FS trains connect Rome's Termini and Tiburtina stations with Tivoli in about 30 minutes; Villa d'Este is about a 20-minute walk from the station in Tivoli. The FS train from Stazione Termini to Palestrina takes about 40 minutes; you can then board a bus from the train station to the center of town.

GETTING AROUND

By Bus. There is local bus service between Tivoli and Palestrina, but check schedules locally.

By Car. From Tivoli to Palestrina, follow signs for Via Prenestina and Palestrina. To get to Subiaco from either Tivoli or Palestrina, take the autostrada for L'Aquila (**A24**) to the Vicovaro–Mandela exit, then follow the local road to Subiaco.

GUIDED TOURS

CIT (☎ 06/47941) has half-day excursions to Villa d'Este in Tivoli. **American Express** (☎ 06/67641), **Appian Line** (☎ 06/4884151), and **Carrani Tours** (☎ 06/4880510) have tours that include Hadrian's Villa.

VISITOR INFORMATION

Palestrina (✉ Piazza Santa Maria degli Angeli, ☎ 06/9573176). **Tivoli** (✉ Largo Garibaldi, ☎ 0774/334522). **Subiaco** (✉ Via Cadorna 59, ☎ 0774/822013).

ROME A TO Z

Arriving and Departing

By Bus

There is no central bus terminal in Rome. **COTRAL** (☎ 167431784 toll-free) is the suburban bus company that connects Rome with outlying areas and other cities in the Lazio region. Long-distance and suburban buses terminate either near Tiburtina Station or near outlying Metro stops such as Rebbibia and Anagnina. The COTRAL terminal at the Lepanto Metro station, for buses to Civitavecchia and towns along the coast northwest of Rome, will be relocated after the 1998 opening of the new extension of Metro A to Circonvallazione Cornelia. For COTRAL bus information, call weekdays 8 AM–8 PM.

By Car

The main access routes from the north are **A1** (Autostrada del Sole) from Milan and Florence or the **A12/E80** highway from Genoa. The principal route to or from points south, including Naples, is the **A2**. All highways connect with the **Grande Raccordo Anulare** (GRA), which channels traffic into the center. Markings on the GRA are confusing: Take time to study the route you need.

By Plane

Most international flights and all domestic flights arrive at **Aeroporto Leonardo da Vinci** (✉ 30 km/19 mi southwest of Rome, ☎ 06/65953640), also known as **Fiumicino**. Some international and charter flights land at **Ciampino** (✉ Via Appia Nuova, 15 km/9 mi southeast of Rome, ☎ 06/794941), a civil and military airport.

BETWEEN THE AIRPORT AND DOWNTOWN

By Car. Follow the signs for Rome on the expressway from the airport, which links with the **GRA**, the beltway around Rome. The direction you take on the GRA depends on where your hotel is, so get directions from the car-rental people at the airport.

By Taxi. A taxi from Fiumicino to the center of town costs about 70,000–80,000 lire, including supplements for airport service and luggage, and the ride takes 30–40 minutes, depending on traffic. Private limousines can be hired at booths in the arrivals hall; they charge a little more than taxis but can take more passengers. Ignore gypsy drivers who approach you inside the terminal; stick to the licensed cabs, yellow or white, that wait by the curb. A booth inside the arrivals hall provides taxi information.

By Train. To get to downtown Rome from Fiumicino Airport, you have a choice of two trains. Inquire at the airport (at EPT or train information counters) as to which takes you closest to your hotel. The nonstop **Airport-Termini express** (marked FS and run by the state railway) takes you directly to Track 22 at Stazione Termini, Rome's main train station, which is well served by taxis and is the hub of Metro and bus lines. The ride to Termini takes 30 minutes; departures are hourly, beginning at 7:50 AM from the airport, with a final departure at 10:05 PM. Tickets cost 13,000 lire. **FM1,** the other airport train, runs from the airport to Rome and beyond, with its terminal in Monterotondo, a suburban town to the east. The main stops in Rome are at Trastevere, Ostiense, and Tiburtina stations; at each you can find taxis and bus and/or Metro connections to other parts of Rome. This train runs from Fiumicino from 6:35 AM to 12:15 AM, with departures every 20 minutes, a little less frequent in off-hours. The ride to Tiburtina takes 40 minutes. Tickets cost 7,000 lire. For either train buy your ticket at automatic vending machines (you need Italian currency). There are ticket counters at some stations (at Termini/Track 22, Trastevere, Tiburtina). Date-stamp the ticket at the gate before you board.

By Train

Stazione Termini is Rome's main train terminal; the **Tiburtina** and **Ostiense** stations serve some long-distance trains, many commuter trains, and the FM1 line to Fiumicino Airport. Some trains for Pisa and Genoa leave Rome from, or pass through, the **Trastevere** Station. For train information, call ☎ 147/888088, 7 AM–9 PM. You can find English-speaking staff at the information office at Stazione Termini, or ask for information at travel agencies. You can purchase tickets up to two months in advance either at the main stations or at travel agencies bearing the FS (Ferrovie dello Stato) emblem (☞ Train Travel *in* The Gold Guide). Lines at station ticket windows may be very long, and electronic ticket machines are complex, though they have instructions in English; you can save time by buying your ticket at a travel agency. Remember that you can reserve a seat up to one day in advance at a travel agency, or up to three hours in advance at a train station. Tickets for train rides within a radius of 100 km (62 mi) of Rome can be purchased at tobacco shops and at some newsstands, as well as at ticket machines on the main concourse. Like all train tickets, they must be date-stamped before you board, at the machine near the track, or you will be fined.

Getting Around

Although most of Rome's sights are in a relatively circumscribed area, the city is too large to be seen solely on foot. Take the Metro (subway),

Rome Metro and Suburban Railway

a bus, or a taxi to the area you plan to visit, and expect to do a lot of walking once you're there. Wear a pair of comfortable, sturdy shoes, preferably with rubber or crepe soles to cushion the impact of the *sampietrini* (cobblestones). Heed our advice on security. Get away from the noise and polluted air of heavily trafficked streets by taking parallel streets whenever possible. You can get free city and transportation-route maps at municipal information booths; the transportation maps are probably more up-to-date than those you can buy at newsstands.

Rome's integrated **Metrebus** transportation system includes buses and trams (ATAC), Metro and suburban trains and buses (COTRAL), and some other suburban trains (FS) run by the state railways. A ticket valid for 75 minutes on any combination of buses and trams and one entrance to the Metro costs 1,500 lire. You are supposed to date-stamp your ticket when you board the first vehicle, stamping it again when boarding for the last time within 75 minutes (the important thing is to stamp it the first time). Tickets are sold at tobacconists, newsstands, some coffee bars, automatic ticket machines positioned in Metro stations and some bus stops, and at ATAC and COTRAL ticket booths (in some Metro stations, on the lower concourse at Stazione Termini, and at a few main bus terminals). A BIG tourist ticket, valid for one day on all public transport, costs 6,000 lire. A weekly ticket (Settimanale, also known as CIS) costs 24,000 lire and can be purchased only at ATAC booths. Try to avoid the rush hours (8–9, 1–2:30, 7–8), and beware of pickpockets, especially when boarding and getting off vehicles, particularly on the Metro and on Buses 64 (Termini–Vatican) and 218 and 660 (Catacombs). When purchasing tickets for excursions outside Rome on COTRAL buses or trains, buy a return ticket, too, to save time at the other end.

By Bicycle

Pedaling through Villa Borghese, along the Tiber, and through the center of the city when traffic is light is a pleasant way to see the sights, but remember: Rome is hilly. (For information on bicycle rentals, ☞ Outdoor Activities and Sports, *above*). **Scala Reale** (⊠ Via Varese 52, 00185 Rome, ☎ 06/44700898) and **Secret Walks** (⊠ Viale Medaglie d'Oro 127, 00136 Rome, ☎ 06/39728728) organize all-day bike tours of Rome for small groups covering major sights and some hidden ones. The same tours are available by moped.

By Bus

ATAC (☎ 167431784 information) city buses and tram lines run from about 6 AM to about midnight, with night buses (indicated N) on some lines. *Remember to board at the back and exit at the middle*. The compact electric buses of Lines 117 and 119 take handy routes through the center of Rome that can save lots of steps.

By Horse-Drawn Carriage

A ride in a horse-drawn carriage can be fun when traffic is light, especially on a Sunday or holiday or during the summer. Come to terms with the driver before starting out. City-regulated rates are about 50,000 lire for a 30-minute ride, and about 85,000 for an hour. Refuse to pay more. You can find carriages at Piazza di Spagna, Piazza Venezia, and on Via del Corso near the Hotel Plaza.

By Metro

This is the easiest and fastest way to get around and there are stops near most of the main tourist attractions. The Metro opens at 5:30 AM, and the last trains leave the farthest station at 11:30 PM (on Saturday night trains run until 12:30 AM). There are two lines—A and B—which intersect at Stazione Termini.

By Moped

You can rent a moped or scooter and mandatory helmet at **Scoot-a-Long** (⊠ Via Cavour 302, ☎ 06/6780206). Also try **St. Peter's Motor Rent** (⊠ Via di Porta Castello 43, ☎ 06/6875714). **Happy Rent** (⊠ Piazza Esquilino 8/h, ☎ 06/4818185) rents scooters, too.

By Taxi

Taxis in Rome do not cruise, but if empty they will stop if you flag them down. Taxis wait at stands and can also be called by phone (☎ 5551, 3570, 4994, or 88177), in which case you're charged a small supplement. The meter starts at 4,500 lire; there are supplements for night service (5,000 lire extra from 10 PM to 7 AM) and on Sunday and holidays, as well as for each piece of baggage. Use only licensed, metered yellow or white cabs, identified by a numbered shield on the side, an illuminated taxi sign on the roof, and a plaque next to the license plate reading SERVIZIO PUBBLICO. Avoid unmarked, unauthorized, unmetered gypsy cabs (numerous at airports and train stations), whose renegade drivers actively solicit your trade and may demand astronomical fares. Some taxis accept some credit cards, but you must specify when calling that you will pay that way.

Being Streetwise in Rome

A (repeat) word of caution: "Gypsy" children, who hang around sights popular with tourists throughout Europe, are rife in Rome and are adept pickpockets. One modus operandi is to approach a tourist and proffer a piece of cardboard with writing on it. While the unsuspecting victim attempts to read the message *on* it, the children's hands are busy *under* it, trying to make off with purses or valuables. If you see such a group (recognizable by their unkempt appearance), do not even allow them near you—they are quick and know more tricks than you do. Also be aware of persons, usually young men, who ride by on motorbikes, grab the shoulder strap of your bag or camera, and step on the gas. Wear or carry your bag on the side away from the street edge of the sidewalk, or, best of all, wear a concealed money belt. Don't carry more money than you need, and don't carry your passport unless you need it to exchange money. A useful expression to ward off pesky panhandlers or vendors is *"Vai via!"* (Go away!).

Contacts and Resources

Car Rentals
Avis (☎ 06/42824728). **Budget** (☎ 06/4820966). **Eurodollar** (☎ 06/167018668). **Hertz** (☎ 06/167808016). **Maggiore** (☎ 06/147867067).

Consulates
U.S. (✉ Via Veneto 121, ☎ 06/46741). **Canada** (✉ Via Zara 30, ☎ 06/445981). **U.K.** (✉ Via Venti Settembre 80A, ☎ 06/4825441).

Doctors and Dentists
Salvator Mundi Hospital (☎ 06/588961). **Rome American Hospital** (☎ 06/22551).

Emergencies
Police (☎ 113). **Ambulance** (☎ 118); **Red Cross** (☎ 06/5510).

English-Language Bookstores
Economy Book and Video Center (✉ Via Torino 136, ☎ 06/4746877). **Anglo-American Bookstore** (✉ Via della Vite 102, ☎ 06/6795222). **Lion Bookshop** (✉ Via dei Greci 33/36, ☎ 06/32654007). **Open Door** (✉ Via della Lungaretta 25, Trastevere, ☎ 06/5896478). **Corner Bookstore** (✉ Via del Moro 48, Trastevere, ☎ 06/5836942).

Guided Tours
BUS TOURS
American Express (✉ Piazza di Spagna 38, ☎ 06/67641). **Appian Line** (☎ 06/4884151). **ATAC** (☎ 167431784). **CIT** (✉ Piazza della Repubblica 64, ☎ 06/47941).

ORIENTATION TOURS
American Express (✉ Piazza di Spagna 38, ☎ 06/67641). **CIT** (✉ Piazza della Repubblica 64, ☎ 06/47941). **EPT** (✉ Via Parigi 5, ☎ 06/48899253).

WALKING TOURS AND BEYOND
Scala Reale (✉ Via Varese 52, 00185 Rome, ☎ 06/44700898; 800/732–2863, ext. 4052, in U.S.). **Secret Walks** (✉ Viale Medaglie d'Oro 127, 00136 Rome, ☎ 06/39728728) .

Late-Night Pharmacies
The following pharmacies have some English-speaking staff. **Farmacia Internazionale Capranica** (✉ Piazza Capranica 96, ☎ 06/6794680). **Farmacia Internazionale Barberini** (✉ Piazza Barberini 49, ☎ 06/4825456). **Farmacia Cola di Rienzo** (✉ Via Cola di Rienzo 213, ☎ 06/3243130). Most are open 8:30–1 and 4–8; some are open all night. Pharmacies take turns opening on Sunday. A schedule is posted in each pharmacy.

Travel Agencies
American Express (✉ Piazza di Spagna 38, ☎ 06/67641). **Appian Line** (✉ Via Barberini 109, ☎ 06/4884151).**Carrani Tours** (✉ Via Vittorio Emanuele Orlando 95, ☎ 06/4880510). **CIT** (✉ Piazza della Repubblica 64, ☎ 06/47941). **CTS** (✉ Via Genova 16, ☎ 06/46791 or 06/4679271).

Villa Rentals

For stays of a week or more, especially for families or groups of friends, an apartment or villa rental may be more convenient than a hotel. Always insist on photos, a map with indication of location, and detailed description of the property. **Property International** (✉ Viale Aventino 79, 00153, ☎ 06/573170, FAX 06/5743182) handles monthly and weekly rentals in Rome and Tuscany. **Homes International** (✉ Via Bissolati 20, 00187, ☎ 064881800, FAX 06/4881808) offers short- and long-term accommodations in Rome.

Visitor Information

EPT (✉ Via Parigi 5, 00185, ☎ 06/48899255; ✉ Stazione Termini, near Track 4, ☎ 06/4871270; ✉ Aeroporto Leonardo da Vinci, ☎ 06/65956074).

3 Florence

Birthplace of the Renaissance, Florence has been a mecca for travelers since the 19th century, when English ladies flocked here to stay in charming pensiones and paint watercolors. They were captivated by a wistful Botticelli smile, impressed by the graceful dignity of Donatello's bronze David, and moved by Michelangelo's provocative Slaves twisting restlessly in their marble prisons.

Updated by
Nancy Hart

FLORENCE IS ONE OF THE PREEMINENT TREASURES of Europe, and it is a time-honored mecca for sightseers from all over the world. But as a city, Florence (Firenze in Italian) can be surprisingly forbidding—at first glance. Its architecture is predominantly Early Renaissance and retains many of the implacable, fortresslike features of pre-Renaissance palazzi, whose facades were mostly meant to keep intruders out rather than to invite sightseers in. With the exception of a very few buildings, the classical dignity of the High Renaissance and the exuberant invention of the Baroque are not to be found here. The typical Florentine exterior gives nothing away, as if obsessively guarding secret treasures within.

The treasures, of course, are very real. And far from being a secret, they are famous the world over. The city is a veritable museum of unique and incomparable proportions. A single historical fact explains the phenomenon: Florence gave birth to the Renaissance. In the early 15th century the study of antiquity—of the glory that was Greece and the grandeur that was Rome—became a Florentine passion, and with it came a new respect for learning and a new creativity in art and architecture. In Florence, that remarkable creativity is everywhere in evidence.

Though there had been a town here since Roman times, it wasn't until the 11th and 12th centuries that Florence started to make its mark. At this time Florentine cloth began to do particularly well in foreign markets, the various trades organized themselves in powerful unions (or *arti*), and the Florentines took over as the most important bankers in Europe, thanks to their florin-based currency. They were perpetually at loggerheads with other Tuscan towns, such as Pisa and Siena, and this is why Florence has such a defensive air, and why its cathedral—the town's symbol—is so huge: It had to be bigger and more splendid than anyone else's. They kept expanding, despite periodic devastating plagues, and equally destructive civil strife. (One of the victims of the internal rift was the great poet Dante, author of the *Divine Comedy,* who happened to be on the losing side; he died in exile, cursing his native town.)

Meanwhile the banking families became more and more powerful, and in the early 15th century one of them, the Medicis, began to outstrip all others. The most famous of them, Lorenzo de' Medici (1449–92), was not only an astute politician, he was also a highly educated man and a great patron of the arts. "Il Magnifico" gathered around him, in the late 15th century, a court of poets, artists, philosophers, architects, and musicians, and organized all kinds of cultural events, festivals, and tournaments. It was Florence's golden period of creativity, when art made great leaps toward a new naturalism through the study of perspective and anatomy, when architects forged a new style based on the techniques used by the ancient Romans. The Renaissance man was born, a man who, like Leonardo da Vinci, could design a canal, paint a fresco, or solve a mathematical problem with equal ease.

Things changed with Lorenzo's death in 1492. First, his successor handed over most of Florence's key territories to the invading French king, Charles VIII, and then the city was sacked by the French army. A "republic" was set up, and one of its most vocal citizens was a charismatic, hellfire-preaching Dominican monk, Girolamo Savonarola (1452–98), who activated a moral cleanup operation to which the Florentines took with fanatical enthusiasm. He himself was accused of heresy and executed, or hanged (his corpse was burned on a pyre in Piazza della Signoria). After a decade or so of internal unrest, the republic fell and the Medicis were recalled to power. But even with the Medicis back, Florence never regained its former prestige. By the 1530s all the major artistic talent had left the city—Michelangelo, for one, had settled in Rome. The now ineffectual Medicis, calling themselves grand dukes, remained nominally in power until the line died out in 1737, and thereafter Florence passed from the Austrians to the French and back again, until the mid-19th-century unification of Italy, when for seven years it was the capital of Italy under King Vittorio Emanuele II.

Florence was "discovered" in the 19th century by the first art historians. It became a mecca for travelers, particularly the Romantics, including Keats and Shelley, who were inspired by the grandeur of its classicism and the elegance of its child, the Renaissance. Today, millions of modern visitors follow in their footsteps. As the sun sets over the Arno and, as Mark Twain described it, "overwhelms Florence with tides of color that make all the sharp lines dim and faint and turn the solid city to a city of dreams," it's hard not to fall under the city's magic spell.

Pleasures and Pastimes

Dining
Florentines are justifiably proud of their robust food, claiming that it became the basis for French cuisine when Catherine de' Medici took a battery of Florentine chefs with her when she reluctantly relocated to become Queen of France in the 16th century. You can sample such specialties as creamy *fagioli al fiasco* (slow-cooked beans) and *ribollita* (a thick soup of white beans, bread, cabbage, and onions) in bustling trattorias where you share long wooden tables set with paper place mats. The casual, convivial atmosphere in these places puts you in the Florentine mode. Like the Florentines, take a break at a *enoteca* (wineshop and/or wine bar) during the day and discover some little-known but excellent types of Chianti.

Lodging
Whether you are in a five-star hotel or a more modest establishment, you may have one of the greatest pleasures of all: a room with a view. Florence has so many famous landmarks that it's not hard to find lodgings with a vista to remember. And the equivalent of the genteel pensiones of yesteryear still exist, though they are now officially classified as hotels. Usually small and intimate, they often have a quaint appeal that fortunately does not preclude modern plumbing.

Shopping
Since the days of the medieval guilds, Florence has been synonymous with fine craftsmanship and good business. Such time-honored Florentine specialties as antiques (and reproductions), bookbinding, jewelry, lace, leather goods, silk, and straw attest to that. More recently, the Pitti fashion shows and the burgeoning textile industry in nearby Prato have added fine clothing to the long list of merchandise available in the shops of Florence. Another medieval feature is the distinct feel of the different shopping areas, a throwback to the days when each district supplied a different product.

EXPLORING FLORENCE

Sightseeing in Florence is space intensive. Everything that you probably want to see is concentrated in the relatively small historic core of the city. But there is so much packed into the area that you may find yourself slogging from one mind-boggling sight to another and feeling overwhelmed. If you are not an inveterate museum enthusiast, take it easy. Don't try to absorb every painting or fresco that comes into view. There is second-rate art even in the Galleria degli Uffizi and the Palazzo Pitti (*especially* the Pitti), so find some favorites and enjoy them at your leisure.

Walking through the streets and alleyways in Florence is a discovery in itself, but to save time and energy (especially on your third or so day in the city), make use of the efficient bus system. Buses also provide the least-fatiguing way to reach Piazzale Michelangelo, San Miniato, and the Fortezza Belvedere. It is easy to make excursions to, say, Fiesole or the Medici villas by city bus. Most churches are usually open from 8 or 9 until noon or 12:30, and from 3 or 4 until about 7. Usually the Duomo in larger towns and cities is open all day throughout the year.

In between your blitzes into the Renaissance and beyond, stop to breathe in the city, the marvelous synergy between history and modern Florentine life. Firenze is a living, bustling metropolis that has managed to preserve its predominantly medieval street plan and mostly Renaissance infrastructure while successfully adapting to the insistent demands of 20th-century life. During the Guelph-Ghibelline conflict of the 13th and 14th centuries, Florence was a forest of towers—more than 200 of them, if the smaller three- and four-story towers are included. Today only a handful survive, but if you look closely you'll find them as you explore the city's core.

Numbers in the text correspond to numbers in the margin and on the Florence map.

Great Itineraries

You can see most of Florence's outstanding sights in three days. Plan your day around the opening hours of museums and churches; to gain a length on the tour groups in high season, go very early in the morning or around closing time. If you can, allow a day to explore each neighborhood.

IF YOU HAVE 3 DAYS

Spend day one exploring the historic core of Florence, which will give you an eyeful of such masterpieces as Ghiberti's renowned bronze doors at the Battistero, Giotto's Campanile, Brunelleschi's cupola hovering atop the Duomo, Botticelli's mystical spring muse at the Galleria degli Uffizi. On day two, wander north of the Duomo and take in the superb treasury of works ranging from Michelangelo's *David* at the Galleria dell'Accademia to the lavish frescoes at the Cappella dei Magi and the Museo di San Marco (don't miss San Lorenzo, and Michelangelo's Biblioteca Laurenziana and the Cappelle Medicee). On this afternoon (or on the afternoon of day three) head southeast to Santa Croce or west to Santa Maria Novella. On the third day, cross the Ponte Vecchio to the Arno's southern bank and explore the Oltrarno district, being sure not miss the Brunelleschi-designed church of Santo Spirito, Masaccio's frescoes in the church of Santa Maria del Carmine, and the effusion of local color.

IF YOU HAVE 5 DAYS

Break down the tours in the above itinerary into shorter ones, adding a few optional sites, such as Piazzale Michelangelo, halfway up a hill on the Arno's southern bank—where the expansive view of the city is yours to savor—and San Miniato, farther up the same hill, or the Cenacolo di Sant'Apollonia, on the northern part of the city center, near the Museo di San Marco. Climb Giotto's Campanile, which rewards with sweeping views of the city and hills beyond. Take Bus 7 from the station or Piazza del Duomo to enchanting Fiesole. Spend more time in the Galleria degli Uffizi and Bargello or one of the smaller museums such as the Museo dell'Opificio delle Pietre Dure, around the corner from the Galleria dell'Accademia, or the excellent Arno-side Museo di Storia della Scienza, and the Museo di Santa Maria Novella.

IF YOU HAVE 8 DAYS

Add an all-day excursion to Siena or a couple of half-day trips to the Medici villas around Florence (☞ Side Trips, *below*). Visit more of Florence's interesting smaller churches, including Oltrarno's Santa Felicita and Santa Maria Maddalena dei Pazzi to see Pontormo and Perugino masterpieces. On the trail of additional and little-known artistic gems, see Andrea del Castagno's fresco of *The Last Supper* in the Cenacolo di Sant'Apollonia, northwest of the Museo di San Marco. There are similar treasures in the Chiostro dello Scalzo, just north of the Museo di San Marco, and the Cenacolo di Santo Spirito, west of Piazza Pitti.

Centro Storico: From the Duomo to the Ponte Vecchio

To say that Florence's historic center, stretching from the Piazza del Duomo in the north to the Giardini Boboli across the Arno to the south, is beautiful could be misconstrued as an understatement. Indeed, this relatively small area is home to some of the most important artistic treasures in the world. This smorgasbord of churches, medieval towers, Renaissance palazzi (palaces), and world-class museums and galleries is not a static testimony to the artistic and architectural genius of the past millennium, but a shrine to some of the most outstanding aesthetic achievements of Western history.

A Good Walk

Start at the **Duomo** ① and **Battistero** ②, climbing the **Campanile** ③ if you wish, then visit the **Museo dell'Opera del Duomo** ④, behind the Duomo. You can go directly south from in front of the Duomo to the Piazza della Signoria by way of Via dei Calzaiuoli (from here you can take a quick detour west on Via Speziali to **Piazza della Repubblica** ⑤), passing **Orsanmichele** ⑥, or go instead directly south from the Museo dell'Opera del Duomo along Via del Proconsolo to the **Bargello** ⑦ (opposite the ancient **Badia Fiorentina** ⑧, built in 1285). From the Bargello head west on Via della Condotta to Via Calzauioli, then south to discover the architectural splendors of the **Piazza della Signoria** ⑨, including the Loggia dei Lanzi and the **Palazzo Vecchio** ⑩. The **Palazzo degli Uffizi** ⑪, Italy's most important art gallery, is off the south side of the piazza. Leave from the piazza's southwest corner along Via Vaccereccia. To the left, at the corner with Via Por Santa Maria (lined with stores), is the **Mercato Nuovo** ⑫. Follow Via Por Santa Maria to the river and Florence's famous bridge, the **Ponte Vecchio** ⑭. From the north side of the Ponte Vecchio, walk east along the Arno to Piazza dei Giudici to see the **Museo di Storia della Scienza** ⑬.

TIMING

Before much of the *centro storico* (historic center) of Florence was closed to traffic, you had to keep dodging passing cars and mopeds as you walked the narrow streets. Now you have to elbow your way through moving masses of fellow tourists, especially in the neighborhood delimited by the Duomo, Piazza Signoria, Uffizi, and Ponte Vecchio. It takes about 40 minutes to walk the route, with 45 minutes to one hour each for the Museo dell'Opera del Duomo and for Palazzo della Signoria; one to 1½ hours for the Bargello, and a minimum of two hours for the Uffizi (reserve tickets in advance to avoid long lines).

A special museum ticket valid for six months at seven city museums, including the Palazzo Vecchio, the Museo di Firenze Com'Era (Museum of Florentine History), and the Museo di Santa Maria Novella, costs 15,000 lire and is a good buy if you're planning to visit some of these museums. Inquire at any city museum.

Sights to See

❽ Badia Fiorentina. This ancient church was built in 1285; its graceful bell tower—best seen from the interior courtyard—is one of the most beautiful in Florence. The interior of the church proper was half-heartedly remodeled in the Baroque style during the 17th century; its best-known work of art is Filippino Lippi's (1457–1504) delicate *Vision of St. Bernard,* on the left as you enter. The painting—one of Lippi's finest—is in superb condition; take a look at the Virgin's hands, perhaps the most beautiful in the city. ⊠ *Via del Proconsolo.*

★ ❼ Bargello. During the Renaissance this building was used as a prison, and the exterior served as a "most wanted" billboard: Effigies of notorious criminals and Medici enemies were painted on its walls. Today, it houses the **Museo Nazionale,** home to what is probably the finest collection of Renaissance sculpture in Italy. Michelangelo (1475–1564), Donatello (circa 1386–1466), and Benvenuto Cellini (1500–71) are the preeminent masters here, and the concentration of masterworks is remarkable, though they stand among an eclectic array of arms, ceramics, and enamels. For Renaissance art lovers, the Bargello is to sculpture what the Uffizi is to painting.

One particular display, easily overlooked, should not be missed. In 1402 Filippo Brunelleschi (1377–1446) and Lorenzo Ghiberti (1378–1455) competed to earn the most prestigious commission of the day: the decoration of the north doors of the baptistery in Piazza del Duomo. For the competition, each designed a bronze bas-relief panel on the theme of the Sacrifice of Isaac; both panels are on display, side by side, in the room devoted to the sculpture of Donatello on the upper floor. The judges chose Ghiberti for the commission; you can decide for yourself whether or not they were right. ⊠ *Via del Proconsolo 4,* ☎ *055/2388606.* 🎟 *8,000 lire.* ☉ *Daily 8:30–1:50. Closed 1st, 3rd, 5th Sun. and 2nd, 4th Mon. of month.*

★ ❷ Battistero (Baptistery). The octagonal baptistery is one of the supreme monuments of the Italian Romanesque and one of Florence's oldest. Local legend has that it was once a Roman temple of Mars; modern excavations, however, suggest its foundation was laid in the 6th or 7th century AD, well after the collapse of the Roman Empire. The round-arched Romanesque decoration on the exterior probably dates from the 11th or 12th century. The interior ceiling mosaics (finished in 1297) are justly famous, but—glitteringly beautiful as they are—they could never outshine the building's most renowned feature: its bronze Renaissance doors decorated with panels crafted by Lorenzo Ghiberti. The doors, on which Ghiberti spent most of his adult life (1403–52), are on the north and east sides of the baptistery—at least copies are—and the Gothic south door panels were designed by Andrea Pisano (1270–circa 1348) in 1330. The originals of the Ghiberti doors were removed to protect them from the effects of pollution and acid rain and have been beautifully restored; some of the panels are now on display in the Museo dell'Opera del Duomo.

Ghiberti's north doors depict scenes from the life of Christ; his later east doors, facing the Duomo facade, render scenes from the Old Testament. They merit close examination, for they are very different in style and illustrate with great clarity the artistic changes that marked the beginning of the Renaissance. Look at the far right panel of the middle row on the earlier north doors (*Jesus Calming the Waters*). Ghiberti here captured the chaos of a storm at sea with great skill and economy, but the artistic conventions he used are basically pre-Renaissance: Jesus is the most important figure, so he is the largest; the disciples are next in size, being next in importance; the ship on which they founder looks like a mere toy.

The panels on the east doors are larger, more expansive, more sweeping, and more convincing. Look at the middle panel on the left-hand door. It tells the story of Jacob and Esau, and the various episodes of the story (the selling of the birthright, Isaac ordering Esau to go hunting, the blessing of Jacob, and so forth) have been merged into a single beautifully realized street scene. A perspective grid is employed to suggest depth, the background architecture looks far more credible than on the north door panels, the figures in the foreground are grouped realistically, and the naturalism and grace of the poses (look at Esau's left leg) have nothing to do with the sacred message being conveyed. Although the religious content remains, man and his place in the natural world are given new prominence and are portrayed with a realism not seen in art since the fall of the Roman Empire, more than a thousand years before.

As a footnote to Ghiberti's panels, one small detail of the east doors is worth a special look. Just to the lower left of the Jacob and Esau panel, Ghiberti placed a tiny self-portrait bust. From either side, the portrait is extremely appealing—Ghiberti looks like everyone's favorite uncle—but the bust is carefully placed so that there is a single spot from which you can make direct eye contact with the tiny head. When that contact is made, the impression of intelligent life—of *modern* intelligent life—is astonishing. It is no wonder that when these doors were completed, they received one of the most famous compliments in the history of art, from a competitor known to be notoriously stingy with praise: Michelangelo himself declared them so beautiful that they could serve as the Gates of Paradise. ⊠ *Piazza del Duomo,* ☎ *055/ 2302885.* ▨ *5,000 lire.* ☉ *Mon.–Sat. 1:30–6:30, Sun. 8:30–1:30.*

❸ **Campanile.** Giotto's (1266–1337) bell tower is a shaft of multicolor marble decorated with reliefs now in the Museo dell'Opera del Duomo. A climb of 414 steps rewards you with a close-up of Brunelleschi's dome and a sweeping view of the city. ⊠ *Piazza del Duomo.* ▨ *10,000 lire.* ☉ *Apr.–Oct., daily 9–7:30; Nov.–Mar., daily 9–5.*

★ ❶ **Duomo** (Cattedrale di Santa Maria del Fiore). In 1296 Arnolfo di Cambio (1245–1302) was commissioned to build "the loftiest, most sumptuous edifice human invention could devise" in the newest Romanesque style on the site of the old church of Santa Reparata. The immense Duomo was not completed until 1436, the year when it was consecrated. The imposing facade dates only from the 19th century; it was added in the neo-Gothic style to complement Giotto's genuine Gothic 14th-century campanile. The real glory of the Duomo, however, is Filippo Brunelleschi's dome, presiding over the cathedral with a dignity and grace that few domes, even to this day, can match.

Brunelleschi's **cupola** was epoch-making as an engineering feat. The space to be enclosed by the dome was so large and so high above the ground that traditional methods of dome construction—wooden centering and scaffolding—were of no use whatever. So Brunelleschi developed entirely new building methods, which he implemented with equipment of his own device (including the modern crane). Beginning work in 1420, he built not one dome but two, one inside the other, and connected them with common ribbing that stretched across the intervening empty space, thereby considerably lessening the crushing weight of the structure. He also employed a new method of bricklay-

100

Florence

Piazza
Mercato
Centrale

V. Panicale

V. dell' Ariento

V. S. Antonio

V. Faenza

V. Canto de Nelli

del Giglio

V. Conti

V. dei Panzani

V. Guelfa

V. S. Gallo

V. Cavour

V. Ricasoli

Cenacolo
di Sant
Apollonia

Chiostro
dello
Scalzo

Piazza
San Marco

Via C. Battisti

Piazza della
SS. Annunziata

Sinagoga/
Museo Ebraico

V. Colonna

V. Laura

Santa Maria
Maddalena
dei Pazzi

Perugino
Crucifixion

V. degli Alfani

V. dei Servi

Piazza
S. Lorenzo

V. Martelli

V. Pucci

V. Cerretani

V. della Pergola

Borgo Pinti

V. Fiesolana

V. dei Pepi

Piazza di
S. Giovanni

Piazza
del Duomo

V. Bufalini

V. S. Egidio

V. Pecori

V. dei Tosinghi

V. d. Studio

V. del Proconsolo

Piazza
della
Repubblica

V. degli
Speziali

Borgo degli Albizi

Piazza
Salvemini

V. Strozzi

V. Vecchietti

V. Anselmi

V. dei Calzaiuoli

V. dei
Tavolini

V. Dante Alighieri

V. dei Pandolfini

AE

V. Porta Rossa

V. Condotta

Piazza
S. Firenze

V. Ghibellina

V. dell' Agnolo

V. Ghibellina

V. delle Terme

V. Por S. Maria

V. Vacchereccia

V. d.
Gondi

V. dei Magazzini

Via Torta

V. Verrazzano

V. della Pinzochere

Borgo
SS. Apostoli

V. Leoni

Borgo dei Greci

Piazza
Santa
Croce

V. di S. Giuseppe

Acciaioli

Ponte Vecchio

Lung. Archibusieri

Piazza
dei
Giudici

V. dei Neri

V. Benci

Borgo S. Croce

Corso Tintori

Arno

Lung. Diaz

Lung. d. Grazie

Piazza
S. Maria
Sopr' Arno

Costa dei Magnoli

Lung. Torrigiani

V. dei Bardi

Ponte alle Grazie

Arno

Lung. Serristori

Piazza
dei Mozzi

V. dei Renai

Via V. di S. Niccolò

Via S. Miniato

V. di Belvedere

S. Giorgio

KEY

i Tourist Information

AE American Express Office

0 ————— 440 yards

0 ————— 400 meters

ing, based on an ancient Roman herringbone pattern, interlocking each new course of bricks with the course below in a way that made the growing structure self-supporting. The result was one of the great engineering breakthroughs of all time: Most of Europe's great domes, including St. Peter's in Rome, were built employing Brunelleschi's methods, and today the Duomo has come to symbolize Florence in the same way that the Eiffel Tower symbolizes Paris. The Florentines are justly proud, and to this day the Florentine phrase for "homesick" is *nostalgia del cupolone* (homesick for the dome).

The interior is a fine example of Italian Gothic. Much of the cathedral's best-known art has been moved to the nearby Museo dell'Opera del Duomo (☞ *below*). Notable among the works that remain, however, are two equestrian frescoes honoring famous soldiers: Andrea del Castagno's (1421–57) *Niccolò da Tolentino,* painted in 1456, and Paolo Uccello's (1397–1475) *Sir John Hawkwood,* painted 20 years earlier; both are on the left-hand wall of the nave. *Niccolò da Tolentino* is particularly impressive: He rides his fine horse with military pride and wears his even finer hat—surely the best in town—with panache. Restorers worked from 1983 to 1995 to repair the structure of Brunelleschi's dome and clean the vast and crowded fresco of the *Last Judgment*—painted by Vasari and Zuccaro—on its interior. Originally, Brunelleschi wanted mosaics to cover the interior of the great ribbed cupola, but by the time the Florentines got around to commissioning the decoration, 150 years later, tastes had changed.

You can explore the upper and lower reaches of the cathedral. Ancient remains have been excavated beneath the nave; the stairway down is near the first pier on the right. The climb to the top of the dome (463 steps) is not for the faint of heart, but the view is superb; the entrance is on the left wall just before the crossing. ⊠ *Piazza del Duomo,* ☎ *055/2302885.* ☉ *Weekdays 10–5, 1st Sat. of month 10–3:30, Sun. 1–5. Excavation:* ▦ *3,000 lire.* ☉ *Mon.–Sat. 10–5. Ascent to dome:* ▦ *10,000 lire.* ☉ *Weekdays 9:30–7 and Sat. 8:30–5 (1st Sat. of month 8:30–3:20).*

⑫ **Mercato Nuovo** (New Market). This open-air loggia was new in 1551. Today it hosts mostly souvenir stands; its main attraction is Pietro Tacca's bronze *Porcellino* (Piglet) fountain on the south side, dating from around 1612 and copied from an earlier Roman work now in the Uffizi. Rubbing its drooling snout is a Florentine tradition, said to bring good luck. ⊠ *Corner of Via Por San Maria and Via Porta Rossa.* ☉ *Tues.–Sat. 8–7, Mon. 1–7.*

★ ❹ **Museo dell'Opera del Duomo** (Cathedral Museum). The major attractions here—other than Ghiberti's original Baptistery door panels and the *cantorie* (choir loft) reliefs by Donatello and Luca della Robbia (1400–82)—are Donatello's *Mary Magdalen* and Michelangelo's *Pietà* (not to be confused with his more famous *Pietà* in St. Peter's). The High Renaissance in sculpture is in part defined by its revolutionary realism, but Donatello's *Magdalen* goes beyond realism: it is suffering incarnate. Michelangelo's heart-wrenching *Pietà* was unfinished at his death; the female figure supporting the body of Christ on the left was added by one Tiberio Calcagni, and never has the difference between competence and genius been manifested so clearly. ⊠ *Piazza del Duomo 9,* ☎ *055/2302885.* ▦ *10,000 lire.* ☉ *Mar.–Oct., Mon.–Sat. 9–7:30; Nov.–Feb., Mon.–Sat. 9–7.*

⑬ **Museo di Storia della Scienza** (Museum of Science History). Though it tends to be obscured by the glamour of the neighboring Uffizi, this science museum has a wealth of interest: Galileo's own instruments, a

collection of antique armillary spheres, some of them real works of art, and a host of other reminders that the Renaissance made not only artistic but also scientific history. ✉ *Piazza dei Giudici 1*, ☎ *055/2398876.* 💳 *10,000 lire.* ⏰ *Tues., Thurs., Sat. 9:30–1; Mon., Wed., Fri. 9:30–1 and 2–5.*

⑥ Orsanmichele. This church, containing a beautifully detailed 14th-century Gothic tabernacle by Andrea Orcagna (1308–68), was originally a granary. The building was transformed in 1336 into a church with 14 exterior niches. Each of the major Florentine trade guilds was assigned its own niche and paid for the sculpture the niche was to contain. The niches soon held works by Florence's most talented sculptors. Unfortunately, the best have been removed and replaced with copies. The originals will eventually be placed in a museum, perhaps even in Orsanmichele. Even so, all the statues are worth examining. One of those removed—Andrea del Verrocchio's (1435–88) *Doubting Thomas* (circa 1470)—was particularly deserving of attention. Were the niche not empty, you would see Christ, like the building's other figures, entirely framed within the niche, and St. Thomas standing on its bottom ledge, with his right foot outside the niche frame. This one detail, the positioning of a single foot, brought the whole composition to life. Appropriately, this is the only niche to be topped with a Renaissance pediment. ✉ *Via dei Calzaiuoli*, ☎ *055/284944.* 💳 *Free.* ⏰ *Daily 9–noon and 4–6. Closed 1st and last Mon. of month.*

★ ⑪ Palazzo degli Uffizi (Uffizi Palace). The **Galleria degli Uffizi** (Uffizi Gallery) occupies the top floor of this U-shape building fronting on the Arno, designed by Giorgio Vasari (1511–74) in 1559 to hold the administrative offices of Medici Grand Duke Cosimo I (1519–74)—*uffizi* means offices in Italian. And here later Medicis installed their art collections, creating what was Europe's first modern museum, open to the public (at first only by request, of course) since 1591. Today the palazzo houses the finest collection of paintings in Italy. If you're a hardcore museum aficionado, you might want to pick up a complete guide to the collections, sold in bookshops and on newsstands.

The collection's highlights include Paolo Uccello's *Battle of San Romano* (its brutal chaos of lances is one of the finest visual metaphors for warfare ever committed to paint); Fra Filippo Lippi's (1406–69) *Madonna and Child with Two Angels* (the foreground angel's bold, impudent eye contact would have been unthinkable prior to the Renaissance); Sandro Botticelli's (1445–1510) ethereal interpretation of the *Birth of Venus* and *Primavera* (its nonrealistic fairy-tale charm exhibits the painter's idiosyncratic genius at its zenith); Leonardo da Vinci's (1452–1519) *Adoration of the Magi* (unfinished and perhaps the best opportunity in Europe to investigate the methods of a great artist at work); Raphael's (1483–1520) *Madonna of the Goldfinch* (darkened by time, but the tenderness with which the figures in the painting touch each other is undimmed); Michelangelo's *Holy Family* (one of the very few easel works in oil he ever painted, clearly reflecting his stated belief that draftsmanship is a necessary ingredient of great painting); Rembrandt's (1606–69) *Self-Portrait as an Old Man*; Titian's (c. 1488–1576) *Venus of Urbino*; and Caravaggio's (1573–1610) *Bacchus* (two very great paintings whose attitudes toward myth and sexuality are—to put it mildly—diametrically opposed). If panic sets in at the prospect of absorbing all this art at one go, bear in mind that the Uffizi is, except on Sunday, open late and isn't usually crowded in the late afternoon. The coffee bar inside the Uffizi has a terrace with a fine close-up view of Palazzo Vecchio. Advance tickets can now be purchased from Consorzio ITA. ✉ *Piazzale degli Uffizi 6*, ☎ *055/23885.*

Advance tickets: ✉ *Consorzio ITA, Viale Gramsca 9a, 50121,* ☎ *055/ 2347941.* 💷 *12,000 lire.* ☉ *Tues.–Sat. 8:30–10, Sun. 8:30–6.*

❿ Palazzo Vecchio (Old Palace). Looming over Piazza della Signoria is Florence's forbidding, fortresslike city hall. The palazzo was begun in 1299 and designed (probably) by Arnolfo di Cambio, and its massive bulk and towering campanile dominate the piazza. It was built as a meeting place for the heads of the seven major guilds that governed the city at the time; over the centuries it has served lesser purposes, but today it is once again the City Hall of Florence. The interior court-yard is a good deal less severe, having been remodeled by Michelozzo (1396–1472) in 1453; the copy of Verrocchio's bronze *puttino* (little putto), topping the central fountain, softens the effect considerably.

The main attraction is on the second floor: two adjoining rooms that supply one of the most startling contrasts in Florence. The first is the vast **Sala dei Cinquecento** (Room of the Five Hundred), named for the 500-member Great Council, the people's assembly established by Savonarola, that met here. The Sala was decorated by Giorgio Vasari, around 1570, with huge—almost grotesquely huge—frescoes cele-brating Florentine history; depictions of battles with nearby cities pre-dominate. Continuing the martial theme, the Sala also contains Michelangelo's *Victory* group, intended for the never-completed tomb of Pope Julius II, plus other sculptures of decidedly lesser quality.

The second room is the little **Studiolo,** to the right of the Sala's entrance. The study of Cosimo de' Medici's son, the melancholy Francesco I (1541–87), it was designed by Vasari and decorated by Vasari and Ag-nolo Bronzino. It is intimate, civilized, and filled with complex, ques-tioning, allegorical art. It makes the vainglorious proclamations next door ring more than a little hollow. ✉ *Piazza della Signoria,* ☎ *055/2768465.* 💷 *10,000 lire.* ☉ *Mon.–Wed. and Fri.–Sat. 9–7, Sun. 8–1.*

❺ Piazza della Repubblica. This square marks the site of the ancient forum that was the core of the original Roman settlement. The street plan in the area around the piazza still reflects the carefully plotted orthogo-nal grid of the Roman military encampment. The Mercato Vecchio (Old Market), located here since the Middle Ages, was demolished at the end of the last century, and the current piazza was constructed between 1890 and 1917 as a neoclassical showpiece. Nominally the center of town, it has yet to earn the love of most Florentines.

★ ❾ Piazza della Signoria. This is by far the most striking square in Flo-rence. It was here, in 1497, that the famous "bonfire of the vanities" took place, when the fanatical monk Savonarola induced his follow-ers to hurl their worldly goods into the flames; it was also here, a year later, that he was hanged as a heretic and, ironically, burned. A bronze plaque in the piazza pavement marks the exact spot of his execution.

The statues in the square and in the 14th-century **Loggia dei Lanzi** on the south side vary in quality. Cellini's famous bronze *Perseus Hold-ing the Head of Medusa* is his masterpiece; even the pedestal is superbly executed. Other works in the loggia include *The Rape of the Sabine Women* and *Hercules and the Centaur,* both late 16th-century works by Giambologna, and, in the back, a row of sober matrons that date from Roman times.

In the square, Bartolomeo Ammannati's (1511–92) Neptune Fountain, dating from 1565, takes something of a booby prize. Even Amman-nati himself considered it a failure, and the Florentines call it *Il Bian-cone,* which may be translated as "the big white man" or "the big white lump," depending on your point of view. Giambologna's equestrian statue, to the left of the fountain, pays tribute to the Medici Grand Duke Cosimo I. Occupying the steps of the Palazzo Vecchio are a copy of Donatello's proud heraldic lion of Florence, known as the *Marzocco* (the original is now in the Bargello); a copy of Donatello's *Judith and Holofernes* (the original is inside the Palazzo Vecchio); a copy of Michelangelo's *David* (the original is now in the Galleria dell'Accademia); and Baccio Bandinelli's *Hercules* (1534).

★ ⑭ **Ponte Vecchio** (Old Bridge). This elegant bridge is to Florence what Tower Bridge is to London. It was built in 1345 to replace an earlier bridge that was swept away by flood, and its shops housed first butchers, then grocers, blacksmiths, and other merchants. But in 1593 the Medici Grand Duke Ferdinando I, whose private corridor linking the Medici palace (Palazzo Pitti) with the Medici offices (the Uffizi) crossed the bridge atop the shops, decided that all this plebeian commerce under his feet was unseemly. So he threw out all the butchers and blacksmiths and installed 41 goldsmiths and eight jewelers. The bridge has been devoted solely to these two trades ever since.

Take a moment to study the **Ponte Santa Trinita,** the next bridge downriver. It was designed by Bartolomeo Ammannati in 1567 (possibly from sketches by Michelangelo), blown up by the retreating Germans during World War II, and painstakingly reconstructed after the war ended. By virtue of its graceful arc and delicate curves, Florentines like to claim it is the most beautiful bridge in the world. Given its simplicity, this may sound like idle Tuscan boasting.

Michelangelo Country: From San Lorenzo to the Accademia

Poet, painter, sculptor, and architect, Michelangelo was a consummate genius. His prodigious energy and virtuoso technique overcame the political and artistic vicissitudes of almost a century to produce some of the greatest sculpture of his—or any—age. The Biblioteca Laurenziana is perhaps his most intuitive work of architecture. The key to understanding Michelangelo's genius is in the magnificent Cappelle Medicee sculptures. The towering and beautiful *David,* his most recognized work, resides in the Galleria dell'Accademia.

A Good Walk

Start at the church of **San Lorenzo** ⑮, visiting the **Biblioteca Laurenziana** ⑯ and its famous anteroom, before circling the church to the northwest and making your way through the San Lorenzo outdoor market on Via del Canto de' Nelli to the entrance of the **Cappelle Medicee** ⑰. Retrace your steps through the market and take Via dei Gori east to Via Cavour and the **Palazzo Medici-Riccardi** ⑱, home to Florence's most important family throughout the Renaissance. Follow Via Cavour two blocks north to Piazza San Marco and the church of the same name, attached to which is the **Museo di San Marco** ⑲, a memorial to the pious and exceptionally talented painter-monk, Fra Angelico. If you have time, go northwest from Piazza San Marco to the Cenacolo di Sant'Apollonia and then north to the Chiostro dello Scalzo. From Piazza San Marco, walk a half block south down Via Ricasoli (which runs back toward the Duomo) to the **Galleria dell'Accademia** ⑳. If you have time to make a detour, return to the east side of Piazza San Marco and take Via Cesare Battisti east into Piazza della Santissima Annunziata, one of Florence's prettiest squares, site of the **Ospedale degli Innocenti** ㉑ and, at the north end of the square, the church of **Santissima Annunziata** ㉒. One block southeast of the entrance to Santissima Annunziata, through the arch and on the left side of Via della Colonna, is the **Museo Archeologico** ㉓.

TIMING

The walk alone takes about one hour, plus 45 minutes for the Cappelle Medicee, 20 minutes for the Palazzo Medici-Riccardi, 40 minutes for the Museo di San Marco, 30 minutes for the Galleria dell'Accademia (*David*), and 40 minutes for the Museo Archeologico. Note that Cappelle Medicee and the Museo di San Marco close at 2. After visiting San Lorenzo, resist the temptation to explore the clothes' market that surrounds the church before going to the Palazzo Medici-Riccardi; you can always come back later, when the churches and museums have closed; the market is open until 7 PM.

Sights to See

⑯ Biblioteca Laurenziana (Laurentian Library). Michelangelo the architect was every bit as original as Michelangelo the sculptor. Unlike Brunelleschi (the architect of San Lorenzo), however, he was not bent on ordered harmony of the spheres in his architecture. He was interested in experimentation and invention and in expressing a personal vision at times highly idiosyncratic.

It was never more idiosyncratic than in the Laurentian Library and its famous **vestibolo** (anteroom). This strangely shaped anteroom has had scholars scratching their heads for centuries. In a space more than two stories high, why did Michelangelo limit his use of columns and pilasters to the upper two-thirds of the wall? Why didn't he rest them on strong pedestals instead of on huge, decorative curlicue scrolls, which rob them of all visual support? Why did he recess them into the wall, which makes them look weaker still? The architectural elements here do not stand firm and strong and tall, as inside the church next door; instead, they seem to be pressed into the wall as if into putty, giving the room a soft, rubbery look that is one of the strangest effects ever achieved by classical architecture. It is almost as if Michelangelo purposely set out to defy his predecessors—intentionally to flout the conventions of the High Renaissance in order to see what kind of bizarre, mannered effect might result. His innovations were tremendously influential and produced a period of architectural experimentation, the Mannerist era, that eventually evolved into the Baroque. As his contemporary Giorgio Vasari put it, "Artisans have been infinitely and perpetually indebted to him because he broke the bonds and chains of a way of working that had become habitual by common usage."

Nobody has ever complained about the anteroom's staircase (best viewed head-on), which emerges from the library with the visual force of an unstoppable lava flow. In its highly sculptural conception and execution, it is quite simply one of the most original and elegant staircases in the world. ⊠ *Piazza San Lorenzo 9, entrance to the left of San Lorenzo,* ☎ *055/213440.* ▣ *Free.* ☉ *Mon.–Sat. 8:30–1.*

★ ⑰ Cappelle Medicee (Medici Chapels). This magnificent complex includes the **Cappella dei Principi,** the Medici chapel and mausoleum that was begun in 1605 and kept marble workers busy for several hundred years, and the **Sagrestia Nuova** (New Sacristy) designed by Michelangelo, so called to distinguish it from Brunelleschi's Sagrestia Vecchia (Old Sacristy).

Michelangelo received the commission for the New Sacristy in 1520 from Cardinal Giulio de' Medici, who later became Pope Clement VII and who wanted a new burial chapel for his father, Giuliano, his uncle Lorenzo the Magnificent, and two recently deceased cousins. The result was a tour de force of architecture and sculpture. Architecturally, Michelangelo was as original and inventive here as ever, but it is—quite properly—the powerful sculptural compositions of the side wall tombs that dominate the room. The scheme is allegorical: On the wall tomb to the right are figures representing day and night, and on the wall tomb to the left are figures representing dawn and dusk; above them are idealized portraits of the two cousins, usually interpreted to represent the active life and the contemplative life. But the allegorical meanings are secondary; what is most important is the intense presence of the sculptural figures, the force with which they hit the viewer. Michelangelo's contemporaries were so awed by the impact of this force (in his sculpture here and elsewhere) that they invented an entirely new word to describe the phenomenon: *terribilità* (dreadfulness). To this day it is used only when describing his work, and it is in evidence here at the peak of its power. During his stormy relations with the Medicis, Michelangelo once hid out in a tiny subterranean room that is accessed from the left of the altar. Ever the artist, he drew some charcoal sketches on the wall. If you want to see them, tell the ticket vendor and pay 1,000 lire extra; guided visit only. ✉ *Piazza di Madonna degli Aldobrandini,* ☎ *055/2388602.* 🎟 *10,000 lire.* ☉ *Daily 8:30–1:50. Closed 1st, 3rd, 5th Mon. of month.*

★ ⓴ **Galleria dell'Accademia** (Accademia Gallery). The collection of Florentine paintings, dating from the 13th to the 18th centuries, is notable, but the statues by Michelangelo are renowned. The unfinished *Slaves,* fighting their way out of their marble prisons, were meant for the tomb of Michelangelo's patron and nemesis Pope Julius II. But the focal point is the original *David,* moved here from Piazza della Signoria in 1873. The *David* was commissioned in 1501 by the Opera del Duomo (Cathedral Works Committee), which gave the 26-year-old sculptor a leftover block of marble that had been ruined by another artist. Michelangelo's success with the block was so dramatic that the city showered him with honors, and the Opera del Duomo voted to build him a house and a studio in which to live and work.

Today the *David* is beset not by Goliath but by tourists, and seeing the statue at all—much less really studying it—can be a trial. After a 1991 attack upon it by a hammer-wielding artist who, luckily, inflicted only a few minor nicks on the toes, the sculpture is surrounded by a Plexiglas barrier. The statue is not quite what it seems. It is so poised and graceful and alert—so miraculously alive—that it is often considered the definitive embodiment of the ideals of the High Renaissance in sculpture. But its true place in the history of art is a bit more complicated.

As Michelangelo well knew, the Renaissance painting and sculpture that preceded his work were deeply concerned with ideal form. Perfection of proportion was the ever-sought Holy Grail; during the Renaissance, ideal proportion was equated with ideal beauty, and ideal beauty was equated with spiritual perfection. But *David,* despite its supremely calm and dignified pose, departs from these ideals. Michelangelo did not give the statue perfect proportions. The head is slightly too large for the body, the arms are too large for the torso, and the hands are dramatically large for the arms. By High Renaissance standards these are defects, but the impact and beauty of the *David* are such that it is the *standards* that must be called into question, not the statue. Michelangelo, revolutionary because he brought a new expressiveness to art, created the "defects" of the *David.* He knew exactly what he was doing, calculating that the perspective of the viewer would be such that, in order for the statue to appear proportioned, the upper body, head, and arms would have to be bigger as they are further away from the viewer's line of vision. But he also did it to express and embody, as powerfully as possible in a single figure, an entire biblical story. David's hands *are* too big, but so was Goliath, and these are the hands that slew him. ✉ *Via Ricasoli 60,* ☎ *055/2388609.* 🎫 *12,000 lire.* ⊙ *Tues.–Sat. 8:30–10, Sun. 8:30–6.*

OFF THE
BEATEN PATH

MUSEO DELL'OPIFICIO DELLE PIETRE DURE – This fascinating small museum is attached to an Opificio, or workshop, established by Ferdinando I de' Medici (1503–1564) to train craftsmen in the art of working with precious and semiprecious stones and marble. It is internationally renowned as a center for the restoration of mosaics and inlays in semi-precious stones. Informative exhibits include some magnificent antique examples of this highly specialized craft. ✉ *Via degli Alfani 78,* ☎ *055/210101.* 🎫 *4,000 lire.* ⊙ *Tues.–Sat. 9–2.*

㉓ **Museo Archeologico** (Archaeological Museum). Of the Etruscan, Egyptian, and Greco-Roman antiquities here, the Etruscan collection is particularly notable—the largest in northern Italy. The famous bronze *Chimera* was discovered (without the tail, a reconstruction) in the 16th century. ✉ *Via della Colonna 36,* ☎ *055/23575.* 🎫 *8,000 lire.* ⊙ *Tues.–Sat. 9–2, Sun. 9–2, 1st, 3rd, and 5th Mon. of month 9–1. Closed 1st, 3rd, and 5th Sun. of month.*

OFF THE
BEATEN PATH

SANTA MARIA MADDALENA DEI PAZZI – One of Florence's hidden treasures, Perugino's cool and composed *Crucifixion*, is in the chapter hall of the monastery adjacent to this church. ✉ *Borgo Pinti 58.* 🎫 *Donation requested.* ⊙ *Daily 9–noon and 5–7.*

CHIOSTRO DELLO SCALZO – Often overlooked, this small, peaceful 16th-century cloister was frescoed in monochrome by Andrea del Sarto (1486–1531) with scenes from the life of St. John the Baptist, Florence's patron saint. ✉ *Via Cavour 69.* 🎫 *Free.* ⊙ *Mon.–Thurs. 9–1.*

TORRE DEI CORBIZI – The tower at the south end of the small Piazza San Pier Maggiore dates from the Middle Ages, when, during the Guelph-Ghibelline conflict of the 13th and 14th centuries, Florence was awash with such towers—more than 200 of them. Today only a handful survive. From the Museo Archeologico, follow Via della Colonna east to Borgo Pinti and turn right, following Borgo Pinti through the arch of San Piero into the piazza. ✉ *Piazza San Pier Maggiore.*

⑲ **Museo di San Marco.** A former Dominican monastery adjacent to the church of San Marco now houses this museum, which is a memorial to Fra Angelico, the Dominican monk famous for his piety as for his painting. When the monastery was built in 1437, he decorated it with his frescoes, which were meant to spur religious contemplation. His paintings are simple and direct and furnish a compelling contrast to the Palazzo Medici-Riccardi chapel. Fra Angelico probably would have considered the glitter of Gozzoli's work there worldly and blasphemous. The entire monastery is worth exploring, for Fra Angelico's paintings are everywhere, including the Chapter House, at the top of the stairs leading to the upper floor (the famous *Annunciation*), in the upper-floor monks' cells, and in the gallery just off the cloister as you enter. The latter room contains, among many other works, his beautiful *Last Judgment;* as usual, the tortures of the damned are far more inventive than the pleasures of the redeemed. ✉ *Piazza San Marco 1,* ☎ *055/2388608.* 🎫 *8,000 lire.* ⊙ *Daily 8:30–1:40. Closed 1st, 3rd, 5th Sun. and 2nd, 4th Mon. of month.*

OFF THE
BEATEN PATH

CENACOLO DI SANT'APOLLONIA – The frescoes of this refectory of a former Benedictine monastery were painted in sinewy style by Andrea del Castagno, a follower of Masaccio (1401–28). The *Last Supper* is a powerful version of this typical refectory theme. From the Cenacolo entrance, walk around the corner to Via San Gallo 25 and take a peek at the lovely 15th-century cloister that belonged to the same monastery but is now part of the University of Florence. ⊠ *Via XXVII Aprile 1.* 🚏 *Free.* ⊙ *Daily 8:30–2. Closed 1st, 3rd, 5th Sun. and 2nd, 4th Mon. of month.*

㉑ Ospedale degli Innocenti. Built by Brunelleschi in 1419 to serve as a foundling hospital, it takes the historical prize as the very first Renaissance building. Brunelleschi designed the building's portico with his usual rigor, building it out of the two shapes he considered mathematically (and therefore philosophically and aesthetically) perfect: the square and the circle. Below the level of the arches, the portico encloses a row of perfect cubes; above the level of the arches, the portico encloses a row of intersecting hemispheres. The whole geometric scheme is articulated with Corinthian columns, capitals, and arches borrowed directly from antiquity. At the time he designed the portico, Brunelleschi was also designing the interior of San Lorenzo, using the same basic ideas. But since the portico was finished before San Lorenzo, the Ospedale degli Innocenti can claim the honor of ushering in Renaissance architecture. The 10 ceramic medallions depicting swaddled infants that decorate the portico are by Andrea della Robbia (1435–1525), done in about 1487. ⊠ *Piazza di Santissima Annunziata 1.*

★ ⑱ Palazzo Medici-Riccardi. The main attraction of this palace, begun in 1444 by Michelozzo for Cosimo de' Medici, is the interior chapel, the so-called **Cappella dei Magi** on the upper floor. Painted on its walls is Benozzo Gozzoli's famous *Procession of the Magi,* finished in 1460 and celebrating both the birth of Christ and the greatness of the Medici family. Like his contemporary Ghirlandaio, Gozzoli was not a revolutionary painter and is today considered less than first rate because of his technique, old-fashioned even for his day. Gozzoli's gift, however, was for entrancing the eye, not challenging the mind, and on those terms his success here is beyond question. The paintings are full of activity yet somehow frozen in time in a way that fails utterly as realism, but succeeds triumphantly as soon as the demand for realism is set aside. Entering the chapel is like walking into the middle of a magnificently illustrated child's storybook, and this beauty makes it one of the most unpretentiously enjoyable rooms in the entire city. ⊠ *Via Cavour 1,* 🕾 *055/2760340.* 🚏 *6,000 lire.* ⊙ *Mon.–Tues. and Thurs.– Sat. 9–1 and 3–6, Sun. 9–1.*

⑮ San Lorenzo. The facade of this church was never finished. Like Santo Spirito on the other side of the Arno, the interior of San Lorenzo was designed by Filippo Brunelleschi in the early 15th century. The two church interiors are similar in design and effect and proclaim with ringing clarity the beginning of the Renaissance in architecture. San Lorenzo possesses one feature that Santo Spirito lacks, however, which considerably heightens the dramatic effect of the interior: the grid of dark, inlaid marble lines on the floor. The grid makes the rigorous regularity with which the interior was designed immediately visible and offers an illuminating lesson on the laws of perspective. If you stand in the middle of the nave at the church entrance, on the line that stretches to the high altar, every element in the church—the grid, the nave columns, the side aisles, the coffered nave ceiling—seems to march inexorably toward a hypothetical vanishing point beyond the high altar, exactly as in a single-point-perspective painting. Brunelleschi's **Sagrestia Vecchia** has stucco decorations by Donatello; it's at the end of the left transept. ⊠ *Piazza San Lorenzo,* 🕾 *055/216634.* ⊙ *Daily 7–noon and 3:30–6:30.*

MERCATO CENTRALE – In this huge, two-story market hall, food is every-where, some of it remarkably exotic. At the Mercato Nuovo (☞ *above*), near the Ponte Vecchio, you will see tourists petting the snout of the bronze piglet for good luck; here you will see Florentines petting the snout of a very real one. There is a coffee bar upstairs among the mountains of vegetables. ⊠ *Piazza del Mercato Centrale.*

㉒ **Santissima Annunziata.** This church was designed in 1447 by Miche-lozzo, who gave it an uncommon (and lovely) entrance cloister. The in-terior is an extreme rarity for Florence: a sumptuous example of the Baroque. But it is not really a fair example, since it is merely 17th-cen-tury Baroque decoration applied willy-nilly to an earlier structure—ex-actly the sort of violent remodeling exercise that has given the Baroque a bad name ever since. The **Tabernacle of the Annunziata**, immediately inside the entrance to the left, illustrates the point. The lower half, with its stately Corinthian columns and carved frieze bearing the Medici arms, was built at the same time as the church; the upper half, with its erupt-ing curves and impish sculpted cherubs, was added 200 years later. Each is effective in its own way, but together they serve only to prove that dignity is rarely comfortable wearing a party hat. ⊠ *Piazza di Santis-sima Annunziata.* ⊙ *Daily 7:30–12:30 and 4–6:30.*

Santa Maria Novella to the Arno

Piazza Santa Maria Novella is near the train station, and like the train stations of most other European cities, it is an area pervaded by a cer-tain squalor, especially at night. Nevertheless, the streets in and around the piazza are an architectural treasure trove, lined with some of Flo-rence's most elegant palazzi.

A Good Walk

Start in the Piazza Santa Maria Novella, its north side dominated by the church of **Santa Maria Novella** ㉔, then take Via delle Belle Donne, which leads from the east side of Piazza Santa Maria Novella to a mi-nuscule square, at the center of which a curious shrine, known as the Croce al Trebbio, stands. Take Via del Trebbio east and turn right onto **Via Tornabuoni,** Florence's finest shopping street. At the intersection of Via Tornabuoni and Via Strozzi is the classical **Palazzo Strozzi** ㉕. If you want a dose of contemporary art, head straight down Via Spada to the **Museo Marino Marini** ㉖. One block west from Via Tornabuoni and Palazzo Strozzi, down Via della Vigna Nuova, is Alberti's High Renaissance–style **Palazzo Rucellai** ㉗. Follow the narrow street opposite the palazzo (Via del Purgatorio) east almost to its end, then zigzag right and left, turning east on Via Parione to reach Piazza di Santa Trinita, where, in the middle, stands the **Colonna della Giustizia,** erected by Cosimo de' Medici in 1537. Halfway down the block to the south (toward the Arno) is the church of **Santa Trinita** ㉘, home to Ghirlandaio's glowing frescoes. Then go east on Borgo Santi Apostoli, a typical me-dieval street flanked by tower houses, to Via Por Santa Maria. Alter-natively, from Piazza Santa Trinita you can cross Ponte Santa Trinita and head into the Oltrarno neighborhood.

TIMING

The walk takes about 30 minutes, plus 30 minutes for Santa Maria Novella and 15 minutes for Santa Trinita. A visit to the Santa Maria Novella museum and cloister takes about 30 minutes.

Sights to See

Croce al Trebbio. This little street shrine was erected in 1308 by the Dominican friars (near Santa Maria Novella is a Dominican church) to commemorate a victory famous locally: It was here that they defeated their avowed enemies, the Patarene heretics, in a bloody street brawl. ⊠ *Via del Trebbio.*

㉖ Museo Marino Marini. The dates of Marino Marini (1901–80) are not a misprint. This is the only museum in Italy dedicated to a contemporary artist. One of Marini's major works, a 21-ft-tall bronze horse and rider, dominates the space of the main gallery. The museum itself is an eruption of contemporary space in a deconsecrated 10th-century church, designed with a series of open stairways, walkways, and balconies that allow you to peer at Marini's work from all angles. In addition to Marini's Etruscanesque sculpture, the museum houses Marini's paintings, drawings, and engravings. ⊠ *Piazza San Pancrazio,* ☎ *055/ 219432.* 🖼 *8,000 lire.* ☉ *Wed.– Mon. 10–5.*

㉗ Palazzo Rucellai. Architect Leon Battista Alberti (1404–72) designed perhaps the very first private residence done in High Renaissance style—which goes a step further than the Palazzo Strozzi. A comparison between the two is illuminating. Evident on the facade of the Palazzo Rucellai is the ordered arrangement of windows and rusticated stonework seen on the Palazzo Strozzi, but Alberti's facade is far less forbidding. Alberti devoted a far larger proportion of his wall space to windows, which soften the facade's appearance, and filled in the remainder with rigorously ordered classical elements borrowed from antiquity. The end result, though still severe, is less fortresslike, and Alberti strove for this effect purposely (he is on record as stating that only tyrants need fortresses). Ironically, the Palazzo Rucellai was built some 30 years *before* the Palazzo Strozzi. Alberti's civilizing ideas here, it turned out, had little influence on the Florentine palazzi that followed. To the Renaissance Florentines, power—in architecture, as in life—was just as impressive as beauty. ⊠ *Via della Vigna Nuova.*

㉕ Palazzo Strozzi. This is the most imposing palazzo on Via Tornabuoni. Designed (probably) by Giuliano da Sangallo around 1489 and modeled after Michelozzo's earlier Palazzo Medici-Riccardi (☞ Michelangelo Country, *above*), the exterior of the palazzo is simple and severe; it is not the use of classical detail but the regularity of its features, the stately march of its windows, that marks it as a product of the early Renaissance. The interior courtyard (entered from the rear of the palazzo) is another matter altogether. It is here that the classical vocabulary—columns, capitals, pilasters, arches, and cornices—is given uninhibited and powerful expression. Unfortunately, the courtyard's effectiveness is all but destroyed by the addition of a severe metal fire escape. Its introduction here is one of the most disgraceful acts of 20th-century vandalism in the entire city. ⊠ *Via Tornabuoni.*

㉔ Santa Maria Novella. The facade of this church looks distinctly clumsy by later Renaissance standards, and with good reason: It is an architectural hybrid. The lower half of the facade was completed mostly in the 14th century; its pointed-arch niches and decorative marble patterns reflect the Gothic style of the day. About a hundred years later (around 1456), architect Leon Battista Alberti was called in to complete the job. The marble decoration of his upper story clearly defers to the already existing work below, but the architectural features he added evince an entirely different style. The central doorway, the four ground-floor half-columns with Corinthian capitals, the triangular pediment atop the second story, the inscribed frieze immediately below the pediment—these are classical features borrowed from antiquity, and they reflect the new Renaissance era in architecture, born some 35 years earlier at the Ospedale degli Innocenti. Alberti's most important addition, however, the S-curve scrolls that surmount the decorative circles on either side of the upper story, had no precedent whatever in antiquity. The problem was to soften the abrupt transition between wide ground floor and narrow upper story. Alberti's solution turned out to be definitive. Once you start to look for them, you will find scrolls such as these (or sculptural variations of them) on churches all over Italy, and every one of them derives from Alberti's example here.

The architecture of the interior is, like the Duomo, a dignified but somber example of Italian Gothic. Exploration is essential, however, because the church's store of art treasures is remarkable. Highlights include the 14th-century stained-glass rose window depicting *The Coronation of the Virgin* (above the central entrance); the Cappella Filippo Strozzi (right of the altar), containing late 15th-century frescoes and stained glass by Filippino Lippi; the chancel (the area around the altar), displaying frescoes by Domenico Ghirlandaio (1485); and the Cappella Gondi (to the left of the altar), containing Filippo Brunelleschi's famous wooden crucifix, carved around 1410 and said to have so stunned the great Donatello when he first saw it that he dropped a basket of eggs.

Of special attention, for it's great historical importance and beauty, is Masaccio's *Holy Trinity with Two Donors,* on the left-hand wall, almost halfway down the nave. Painted around 1425 (at the same time Masaccio was working on his frescoes in Santa Maria del Carmine), it unequivocally announced the arrival of the Renaissance era. The realism of the figure of Christ was revolutionary in itself, but what was probably even more startling to contemporary Florentines was the coffered ceiling in the background. The mathematical rules for employing perspective in painting had just been discovered (probably by Brunelleschi), and this was one of the first paintings to employ them with utterly convincing success. ⊠ *Piazza Santa Maria Novella,* ☎ *055/210113.* ☉ *Sun.–Fri. 7–12:15 and 3–6, Sat. 7–12:15 and 3–5.*

The **Museo di Santa Maria Novella,** to the left of Santa Maria Novella, includes church's cloisters, interesting for the faded fresco cycle by Paolo Uccello depicting tales from Genesis, with a dramatic vision of the Deluge. Earlier and better preserved frescoes painted by Andrea di Firenze in the 1360s are in the chapter hall, or Cappella degli Spagnoli, off the cloisters. ⊠ *Piazza Santa Maria Novella,* ☎ *055/282187.* ✉ *5,000 lire.* ☉ *Mon.–Thurs. and Sat. 9–2, Sun. 8–1.*

28 Santa Trinita. Originally Romanesque in style, the church underwent a Gothic remodeling during the 14th century (remains of the Romanesque construction are visible on the interior front wall). Its major work is the cycle of frescoes and the altarpiece in the Cappella Sassetti, the second to the altar's right, painted by Domenico Ghirlandaio (1449–94), around 1485. Ghirlandaio was a conservative painter for his day, and generally his paintings exhibit little interest in the investigations into the rigorous laws of perspective that had been going on in Florentine painting for more than 50 years. But his work here possesses such graceful decorative appeal it hardly seems to matter. The wall frescoes illustrate the life of St. Francis, and the altarpiece, *The Adoration of the Shepherds,* nearly glows. ⊠ *Piazza Santa Trinita,* ☎ *055/216912.* ☉ *Mon.–Sat. 8–noon and 4–6, Sun. 4–6.*

In the center of Piazza Santa Trinita is a column from Rome's Terme di Caracalla, given to the Medici Grand Duke Cosimo I by Pope Pius IV in 1560. The column was raised here by Cosimo in 1565, to mark the spot where he heard the news, in 1537, that his exiled Ghibelline enemies had been defeated at Montemurlo, near Prato; the victory made his power in Florence unchallengeable and all but absolute. The column is called, with typical Medici self-assurance, the **Colonna della Giustizia,** the Column of Justice.

Oltrarno: Palazzo Pitti, Giardini Boboli, Santo Spirito

A walk through the Oltrarno takes in two very different aspects of Florence: the splendor of the Medicis, manifest in the riches of the mammoth Palazzo Pitti and the gracious Giardini Boboli; and the charm of the Oltrarno, literally "beyond the Arno," a now-gentrified, fiercely proud working-class neighborhood with artisans and antiques shops.

A Good Walk

If you start from Santa Trinita, cross the Arno over Ponte Santa Trinita and continue south down Via Maggio until you reach the crossroads of Sdrucciolo dei Pitti (on the left) and the short Via Michelozzi (on the right). Turn left onto the Sdrucciolo dei Pitti. **Palazzo Pitti** ㉙, Florence's largest architectural monument, lies before you as you emerge onto Piazza Pitti. Behind the palace are the **Giardini Boboli** ㉚. If you have time, walk through the gardens. At the top, the adjacent **Fortezza Belvedere** ㉛ commands a wonderful view and sometimes has art exhibits but is not always open to the public. If you want to see the Pontormo fresco cycle at **Santa Felicita** ㉜, head northeast from Palazzo Pitti on Via Guicciardini back toward the Ponte Vecchio. Return to Via Maggio off of Piazza Pitti, take Via Michelozzi west to Piazza Santo Spirito, dominated at its north end by the unassuming facade of the church of **Santo Spirito** ㉝. After your visit to perhaps Italy's most important architectural interior, and to the Cenacolo di Santo Spirito, next door, take Via Sant'Agostino, diagonally across the square from the church entrance, and follow it west to Via dei Serragli. Cross and follow Via Santa Monaca west through the heart of the Oltrarno neighborhood— the equivalent of Rome's Trastevere—to Piazza del Carmine and the church of **Santa Maria del Carmine** ㉞, where, in the attached Cappella Brancacci, is the Masaccio cycle famous throughout the world. Go to the far end of Piazza del Carmine and turn right onto Borgo San Frediano, then follow Via di Santo Spirito and Borgo San Jacopo east to reach the Ponte Vecchio.

TIMING

The walk alone takes about 45 minutes; allow one hour to visit the Galleria Palatina in Palazzo Pitti, or more if you visit the other galleries. Spend at least 30 minutes to an hour savoring the graceful elegance of the Giardini Boboli. When you reach the crossroads of the Sdrucciolo dei Pitti and Via Michelozzi, you have a choice. If the noon hour approaches, you may want to postpone the next stop temporarily to see the churches of Santo Spirito, Santa Felicita, and Santa Maria del Carmine before they close for the afternoon. Otherwise, proceed to Palazzo Pitti. The churches can be visited in 15 minutes each.

㉛ **Fortezza Belvedere** (Belvedere Fortress). This impressive structure was built in 1429 to help defend the city against siege. But time has effected an ironic transformation, and what was once a first-rate fortification is now a first-rate exhibition venue. Farther up the hill is Piazzale Michelangelo, but, as the natives know, the best views of Florence are right here. To the north, all the city's monuments are spread out in a breathtaking cinemascopic panorama, framed by the rolling Tuscan hills beyond. To the south, the nearby hills furnish a complementary rural view, in its way equally memorable. The fortress, occasionally a setting for art exhibitions, is adjacent to the top of the Giardini Boboli. ⊠ *Porta San Giorgio.* 🎫 *Varies per exhibit.*

㉚ **Giardini Boboli** (Boboli Gardens). The main entrance to these landscaped gardens is in the right wing of Palazzo Pitti. The gardens began to take shape in 1549, when the Pitti family sold the palazzo to Eleanor of Toledo, wife of the Medici Grand Duke Cosimo I. The initial landscaping plans were laid out by Niccolò Pericoli Tribolo. After his death in 1550 development was continued by Bernardo Buontalenti, Giulio, and Alfonso Parigi, and, over the years, many others, who produced the most spectacular backyard in Florence. The Italian gift for landscaping—less formal than the French but still full of sweeping drama—is displayed here at its best. The famous *Bacchino*, near the main entrance, is a copy of the original fountain, showing Pietro Barbino, Cosimo's favorite dwarf, astride a particularly unhappy tortoise. It seems to be illustrating—very graphically, indeed—the perils of too much pasta. ⊠ *Enter through Palazzo Pitti (☞ below),* ☎ *055/213440,* ☎ *4,000 lire.* ⊙ *Daily 9 AM–1 hr before sunset. Closed 1st and last Mon. of each month.*

㉙ Palazzo Pitti. This enormous palace is one of Florence's largest—if not one of its best—architectural set pieces. The original palazzo, built for the Pitti family around 1460, comprised only the middle cube (the width of the middle seven windows on the upper floors) of the present building. In 1549 the property was sold to the Medicis, and Bartolomeo Ammannati was called in to make substantial additions. Although he apparently operated on the principle that more is better, he succeeded only in producing proof that more is just that, more.

Today it houses several museums: the former **Apartamenti Reali** (Royal Apartments), containing furnishings from a remodeling done in the 19th century; the **Museo degli Argenti,** displaying a vast collection of Medici household treasures; the **Galleria del Costume,** a showcase of the fashions of the past 300 years; the **Galleria d'Arte Moderna,** holding a collection of 19th- and 20th-century paintings, mostly Tuscan; and, most famous of all, the **Galleria Palatina,** containing a broad collection of 16th- and 17th-century paintings. The rooms of the latter remain much as the Medici family left them. Their floor-to-ceiling paintings are considered by some as Italy's most egregious exercise in conspicuous consumption, aesthetic overkill, and trumpery. Still, the collection possesses high points, including a number of portraits by Titian and an unparalleled collection of paintings by Raphael, such as the famous *Madonna of the Chair.* ⊠ *Piazza Pitti,* ☎ *055/210323. Museo degli Argenti:* ☎ *8,000 lire (also valid for Galleria del Costume).* ⊙ *Daily 8:30–1:50; closed 2nd, 4th Sun. and 1st, 3rd, 5th Mon. of month. Galleria del Costume:* ☎ *8,000 lire.* ⊙ *Tues.–Sun. 8:30–1:50. Galleria d'Arte Moderna:* ☎ *4,000 lire.* ⊙ *Daily 8:50–1:50; closed 2nd, 4th Sun. and 1st, 3rd, 5th Mon. of month. Galleria Palatina:* ☎ *12,000 lire.* ⊙ *Tues.–Sat. 8:50–10, Sun. 8:50–6.*

㉜ Santa Felicità. This diminutive late Baroque church (its facade was remodeled 1736–39) contains the Mannerist Jacopo Pontormo's (1494–1557) tour de force, the Deposition altarpiece central to his Cappella Capponi fresco cycle (executed 1525–28), regarded as a masterpiece of 16th-century Florentine art. The remote figures, which transcend the realm of Renaissance classical form, are portrayed in an array of tangled shapes and intense pastel colors (well preserved because of the low lights in the church), in space and depth that defy reality. The granite column in the piazza was erected in 1381, and marks a Christian cemetery. ⊠ *Piazza Santa Felicita, Via Guicciardini.* ⊙ *Weekdays 9–6, Sun. 9–11 AM.*

㉞ Santa Maria del Carmine. The **Cappella Brancacci,** at the end of the right transept of this church, houses a masterpiece of Renaissance painting: a fresco cycle that changed the course of art forever. Fire almost destroyed the church in the 18th century; miraculously, the Cappella Brancacci survived almost intact. The cycle is the work of three artists: Masaccio and Masolino, who began it in 1423, and Filippino

Lippi, who finished it, after a long interruption during which the sponsoring Brancacci family was exiled, some 50 years later. It was Masaccio's work that opened a new frontier for painting; tragically, he did not live to experience the revolution his innovations caused, as he died in 1428 at the age of 27.

Masaccio collaborated with Masolino on several of the paintings, but by himself he painted *The Tribute Money* on the upper-left wall; *Peter Baptizing the Neophytes* on the upper altar wall; *The Distribution of the Goods of the Church* on the lower altar wall; and, most famous, *The Expulsion of Adam and Eve* on the chapel's upper-left entrance pier. If you look closely at the latter painting and compare it with some of the chapel's other works, you will see a pronounced difference. The figures of Adam and Eve possess a startling presence primarily due to the dramatic way in which their bodies seem to reflect light. Masaccio here shaded his figures consistently, so as to suggest emphatically a single, strong source of light within the world of the painting but outside its frame. In so doing, he succeeded in imitating with paint the real-world effect of light on mass, and he thereby imparted to his figures a sculptural reality unprecedented in its day.

These matters have to do with technique, but with *The Expulsion of Adam and Eve,* his skill went beyond technical innovation, and if you look hard at the faces of Adam and Eve, you will see more than just finely modeled figures. You will see terrible shame and suffering, and you will see them depicted with a humanity rarely achieved in art. ⊠ *Piazza del Carmine,* ☎ *055/2382195.* ▦ *5,000 lire.* ☉ *Mon. and Wed.–Sat. 10–5, Sun. 1–5.*

❸ **Santo Spirito.** The plain, unfinished facade gives nothing away, but the interior, although it appears chilly (cold, even) compared with later churches, is one of the most important pieces of architecture in all Italy. One of a pair of Florentine church interiors designed by Filippo Brunelleschi in the early 15th century (the other is San Lorenzo), it was here that Brunelleschi supplied definitive solutions to the two main problems of interior Renaissance church design: how to build a cross-shape interior using classical architectural elements borrowed from antiquity and how to reflect in that interior the order and regularity that Renaissance scientists (of which Brunelleschi was one) were at the time discovering in the natural world around them.

Brunelleschi's solution to the first problem was brilliantly simple: turn a Greek temple inside out. To see this clearly, look at one of the stately arch-topped arcades that separate the side aisles from the central nave. Whereas the ancient Greek temples were walled buildings surrounded by classical colonnades, Brunelleschi's churches were classical arcades surrounded by walled buildings. This brilliant architectural idea overthrew the previous era's religious taboo against pagan architecture once and for all, triumphantly reclaiming that architecture for Christian use.

Brunelleschi's solution to the second problem—making the entire interior orderly and regular—was mathematically precise: He designed the ground plan of the church so that all its parts are proportionally related. The transepts and nave have exactly the same width; the side aisles are precisely half as wide as the nave; the little chapels off the side aisles are exactly half as deep as the side aisles; the chancel and transepts are exactly one-eighth the depth of the nave; and so on, with dizzying exactitude. For Brunelleschi, such a design technique would have been far more than a convenience; it would have been a matter of passionate conviction. Like most theoreticians of his day, he believed that mathematical regularity and aesthetic beauty were opposite sides of the same coin, that one was not possible without the other. The conviction stood unchallenged for a hundred years, until Michelangelo turned his hand to architecture and designed the Cappella Medici and the Biblioteca Laurenziana across town, and thereby unleashed a revolution of his own that spelled the end of the Renaissance in architecture and the beginning of the Baroque. In the **Cenacolo di Santo Spirito** adjacent to the church, you can see Andrea Orcagna's fresco of the Crucifixion. *Church: ⊠ Piazza Santo Spirito, ☎ 055/210030. ◷ Thurs.–Tues. 8–noon and 4–6, Wed. 8–noon. Cenacolo: ⊠ Piazza Santo Spirito 29, ☎ 055/287043. ▨ 4,000 lire. ◷ Tues.–Sat. 9–2, Sun. 8–1.*

From Santa Croce to San Miniato al Monte

The Santa Croce neighborhood, on the southwest fringe of the historic center, was built up in the Middle Ages just outside the medieval city walls. The centerpiece of the neighborhood was the church of Santa Croce, which could hold great numbers of worshipers and accommodate the overflow in the vast piazza, which also served as a fairground and playing field for traditional, no-holds-barred football games. A center of leather-working since the Middle Ages, the neighborhood is still packed with leather craftsmen and leather shops.

A Good Walk

Begin your walk at the church of **Santa Croce** ㉟; from here you can take a quick jaunt up Via della Pinzochere to **Casa Buonarroti** ㊱ to see an early Michelangelo work. Return to Santa Croce, and at the southeast end of the piazza go south on Via de' Benci and cross the Arno over Ponte alle Grazie. Turn left onto Lungarno Serristori and continue to Piazza Poggi, where a series of ramps and stairs climbs to **Piazzale Michelangelo** ㊲, where the city lies before you like a painting. From Piazzale Michelangelo, climb the stairs behind La Loggia restaurant to the church of San Salvatore al Monte, and go south on the lane leading to the stairs that climb to **San Miniato al Monte** ㊳, cutting through the fortifications hurriedly built by Michelangelo in 1529 when Florence was threatened by Emperor Charles V's troops. If you prefer, you can avoid the long walk by taking Bus 12 or 13 at the west end of Ponte alle Grazie and get off at the stop after Piazzale Michelangelo. You still have to climb the monumental stairs to San Miniato, but then the rest of your itinerary will be downhill. From San Miniato descend to San Salvatore al Monte and then to Piazzale Michelangelo, where you can get a bus back to town center.

TIMING

The walk alone takes about 1½ hours one way, plus 30 minutes in Santa Croce, 30 minutes in the Museo di Santa Croce, and 30 minutes in San Miniato. Depending on the amount of time you have, you can limit your sightseeing to Santa Croce and Casa Buonarroti or continue on to Piazzale Michelangelo. The walk to Piazzale Michelangelo is a long uphill hike, with the prospect of another climb to San Miniato from there. If you decide to take a bus, remember to buy your ticket before you board. Finally, since you go to Piazzale Michelangelo for the view, skip it if it's a hazy day.

Sights to See

㊱ **Casa Buonarroti.** If you are really enjoying walking in the footsteps of the great genius, you may want to complete the picture by visiting Michelangelo's home. Even though he never actually lived in the house (it was given to his nephew and it was the nephew's son, Michelangelo, who began the process of turning it into a gallery dedicated to his great-uncle), his descendents began the process of filling it with art treasures—some by Michelangelo himself (a marble bas-relief, *The Madonna of the Steps,* carved when he was just a teenager and his earliest known work, and his wooden model for the facade of San Lorenzo) and some by other artists that pay homage to him. ⊠ *Via Ghibellina 70,* ☎ *055/241752.* ▦ *10,000 lire.* ⊘ *Wed.–Mon. 9:30–1:30.*

❸❼ **Piazzale Michelangelo.** From this lookout, you have a marvelous view of Florence and the hills around it, rivaling the vista from the Belvedere Fortress. It has a copy of Michelangelo's *David* and outdoor cafés packed with tourists during the day and with Florentines in the evening. In May, the Giardino dell'Iris (Iris Garden) off the piazza is abloom with more than 2,500 varieties of the flower that has been Florence's symbol since 1251. The Giardino delle Rose (Rose Garden) on the terraces below the piazza is also in full swing May and June.

❸❽ **San Miniato al Monte.** This church, like the Baptistery, is a fine example of Romanesque architecture and one of the oldest churches in Florence, dating from the 11th century. The lively green-and-white marble facade has a 12th-century mosaic topped by a gilded bronze eagle, emblem of San Miniato's sponsors, the Calimala (Wool Merchant's Guild). Inside are a 13th-century inlaid marble floor and apse mosaic. Artist Spinello Aretino covered the walls of the **Sagrestia** with frescoes of the life of St. Benedict. The adjacent **Capella del Cardinale Portoghese** (Chapel of the Portuguese Cardinal) is one of the richest Renaissance works in Florence. Built to hold the tomb of a Portuguese cardinal, Prince James of Lusitania, who died young in Florence in 1459, it has a glorious ceiling by Luca della Robbia, a sculptured tomb by Antonio Rossellini, and inlaid pavement in multicolor marble. ⊠ *Viale Galileo Galilei, Piazzale Michelangelo,* ☎ *055/2342731.* ⊘ *Daily Apr.–Oct., 8–noon and 2–7, Nov.–Mar., 8–noon and 2:30–6.*

★ ❸❺ **Santa Croce.** Like the Duomo, this church is Gothic, but (also like the Duomo) its facade dates only from the 19th century. The interior is most famous for its art and its tombs. As a burial place, the church is a Florentine pantheon and probably contains more Renaissance-celeb skeletons than any church in Italy. Among others, the tomb of Michelangelo is immediately to the right as you enter (he is said to have chosen this spot so that the first thing he would see on Judgment Day, when the graves of the dead fly open, would be Brunelleschi's Duomo dome through Santa Croce's open doors); the tomb of Galileo Galilei (1564–1642), who produced evidence that the earth is not the center of the universe (and who was not granted a Christian burial until 100 years after his death because of it), is on the left wall, opposite Michelangelo; the tomb of Niccolò Machiavelli (1469–1527), the Renaissance political theoretician whose brutally pragmatic philosophy so influenced the Medicis, is halfway down the nave on the right; the grave of Lorenzo Ghiberti, creator of the Gates of Paradise doors to the Baptistery, is halfway down the nave on the left; the tomb of composer Gioacchino Rossini (1792–1868), of "William Tell Overture" fame, is at the end of the nave on the right. The monument to Dante Alighieri (1265–1321), the greatest Italian poet, is a memorial rather than a tomb (he is actually buried in Ravenna); it is on the right wall near the tomb of Michelangelo.

The collection of art within the church and church complex is by far the most important of that in any church in Florence. Historically, the most significant works are probably the Giotto frescoes in the two adjacent chapels immediately to the right of the altar. They illustrate scenes from the lives of St. John the Evangelist and St. John the Baptist (in the right-hand chapel) and scenes from the life of St. Francis (in the left-hand chapel). Time has not been kind to them; over the centuries, wall tombs were introduced into the middle of them, whitewash and plaster covered them, and in the 19th century they underwent a clumsy restoration. But the reality that Giotto introduced into painting can still be seen. He did not paint beautifully stylized symbols of religion, as the Byzantine style that preceded him prescribed; he instead painted drama—St. Francis surrounded by grieving monks at the very moment of his death. This was a radical shift in emphasis, and it changed the course of art. Before him, the role of painting was to symbolize the attributes of God; after him, it was to imitate life. The style of his work is indeed primitive, compared with later painting, but in the proto-Renaissance of the early 14th century, it caused a sensation that was not equaled for another 100 years. He was, for his time, the equal of both Masaccio and Michelangelo.

Among the church's other highlights are Donatello's *Annunciation,* one of the most tender and eloquent expressions of surprise ever sculpted (on the right wall two-thirds of the way down the nave); Taddeo Gaddi's (circa 1330–66) 14th-century frescoes illustrating the life of the Virgin, clearly showing the influence of Giotto (in the chapel at the end of the right transept); and Donatello's *Crucifix,* criticized by Brunelleschi for making Christ look like a peasant (in the chapel at the end of the left transept). Outside the church proper, in the **Museo dell'Opera di Santa Croce** off the cloister, is Giovanni Cimabue's (1240–1302) 13th-century *Triumphal Cross,* badly damaged by the flood of 1966. An epitome of architectural geometry, the **Cappella Pazzi,** at the end of the cloister, is the work of Brunelleschi. ⊠ *Piazza Santa Croce 16,* ☎ *055/244619. Church:* ⊘ *Apr.–Sept., Mon.–Sat. 8–6:30, Sun. 3–5; Oct.–Mar., Mon.–Sat. 8–12:30 and 3–6:30, Sun. 3–5. Cloister and museum:* ✉ *4,000 lire.* ⊘ *Apr.–Sept., Thurs.–Tues. 10–12:30 and 2:30–6:30; Oct.–Mar., Thurs.–Tues. 10–12:30 and 3–5.*

OFF THE
BEATEN PATH

SINAGOGA – The Synagogue was built around 1874–82 in a style best defined as an eclectic interpretation of Byzantine-Moorish motifs. The adjacent **Museo Ebraico** charts the history of Florence's Jewish community. Piazza della Repubblica (☞ *Centro Storico, above*) is the site of the Jewish ghetto, where Jews were forced to live from 1571 until 1848; it was torn down in 1885. The only kosher restaurant in Tuscany is next to the synagogue. **Ruth** (⊠ Via Farini 2, ☎ 055/2480888), closed Friday dinner, and Saturday lunch, offers inexpensive vegetarian and Mediterranean dishes and a large selection of kosher wines. Synagogue and museum: ⊠ *Via Farini 4,* ☎ *055/2346654.* ✉ *6,000 lire.* ⊘ *Apr.–Sept., Sun.–Thurs. 10–1 and 2–5, Fri. 10–1; Oct.–Mar., Sun.–Thurs. 10–1 and 2–4, Fri. 10–1.*

DINING

Revised by
Patricia Rucidlo

A typical Tuscan repast starts with an antipasto of *crostini* (grilled bread spread with various savory toppings) or cured meats such as prosciutto *crudo* (cured ham thinly sliced) and *finocchiona* (salami seasoned with fennel). *Primi piatti* (first courses) can consist of local versions of pasta dishes available throughout Italy. Peculiar to Florence, however, are the vegetable-and-bread soups such as *pappa al pomodoro* (bread and tomato soup), ribollita, or, in the summer, a salad called *panzanella* (tomatoes, onions, vinegar, oil, basil, and bread). Before they are eaten, these are often christened with *un "C" d'olio,* a generous C-shape drizzle of the sumptuous local olive oil.

Unparalleled among the *secondi piatti* (main courses) is *bistecca alla fiorentina*—a thick slab of local Chianina beef, grilled over charcoal, seasoned with olive oil, salt, and pepper, and served rare. *Trippa alla fiorentina* (tripe stewed with tomato sauce) and *arista* (roast loin of pork seasoned with rosemary) are also regional specialties, as are many other roasted meats that go especially well with Chianti. A secondo is usually served with a *contorno* (side dish) of white beans, sautéed greens, or artichokes in season, all of which can be drizzled with more of that wonderful olive oil.

Dining hours are earlier here than in Rome, starting at 1 for the midday meal and at 8 for dinner. Many of Florence's restaurants are small, so reservations are a must.

CATEGORY	COST*
$$$$	over 110,000 lire
$$$	80,000–110,000 lire
$$	35,000–80,000 lire
$	under 35,000 lire

Prices are per person, for a three-course meal, including house wine and taxes.

Centro Storico

$$ ✕ **Buca dell'Orafo.** A Florentine *buca*, meaning hole-in-the-wall, Buca dell'Orafo is set in the cellar of a former goldsmith's shop near the Ponte Vecchio. It's the perfect place to lunch either before or after visiting the Uffizi, as it's just around the corner. The food is typical Tuscan. Here you're paying for the atmosphere and the location; it's a shame the place doesn't take plastic. ⊠ *Via dei Girolami 28,* ☎ *055/213619. No credit cards. Closed Sun.–Mon. and Aug.*

$$ ✕ **Il Latini.** As soon as you spy the primary decoration pieces—innumerable slabs of prosciutto on the bone—you realize you're in hog lover's heaven. This is not the place to come if you are a vegetarian. Portions are big—you'll think you won't be able to eat it all. But you will. This place packs them in, tourists and locals alike, with good reason. Meat dishes don't get much better than this. Reservations are advised. It's around the side of Palazzo Rucellai. ⊠ *Via dei Palchetti 6/r,* ☎ *055/ 210916. AE, DC, MC, V. Closed Mon. and 15 days in Aug.*

$$ ✕ **Osteria n. 1.** "*Osteria,*" nowadays, might be the only pretentious element in this romantic restaurant nestled in the ground floor of an old palazzo in the historic center. The food is expertly handled—try, for example, their delicate artichoke ravioli with olive oil and Parmesan or their *crespelle*, a little package of pasta stuffed with zucchini puree and topped with a subtle walnut sauce, before moving on to any of their grilled specialties. ⊠ *Via del Moro 22,* ☎ *055/284897. AE, DC, MC, V. Closed Sun. and 15 days in Aug. No lunch Mon.*

San Lorenzo and Beyond

$$$ ✕ **Taverna del Bronzino.** Want to have an elegant meal in a 16th-century Renaissance artist's studio? Though it was actually the studio of Santi di Tito, a student of Bronzino, the restaurant—with high ceilings and traces of frescoes on the walls—retains the master's name. The food is classic Tuscan, and superb, the presentation often dramatic; try the *carpaccio di cervo* (cured, thinly sliced venison dribbled with olive oil). The only thing better than the food and outstanding service is the wine list, which has solid, affordable choices. Reservations are advised, especially for eating in the wine cellar's only table. ⊠ *Via delle Ruote 27/r,* ☎ *055/495220. AE, DC, MC, V. Closed Sun. and Aug.*

$$ ✕ **Alfredo.** This place is just on the other side of Piazza della Libertà, which happily puts it somewhat off the beaten tourist path. The decor

is simple—white walls and white tablecloths—and the atmosphere lively. The cooks spin a fine pizza, but even better are the primi and secondi—some are atypical Tuscan and pleasant surprises. There's also plenty on the menu for a vegetarian to eat, and even hard-core meat lovers will rave about the *sformato con tartufo* (a type of soufflé with truffles). You'd be wise to reserve ahead. ⊠ *Viale Don Giovanni Minzoni 3/r,* ☎ *055/578291. AE, DC, MC, V. Closed Mon. and 15 days in Aug.*

$$ ✕ **Toscano.** A small table attractively set in a show window identifies this restaurant, about five minutes from Palazzo Medici-Riccardi. It lives up to its name in ambience and cuisine. The cold-cuts counter at the entrance, terra-cotta tile floors, and beamed ceilings typify a Tuscan trattoria, but the pink tablecloths, arty photos on the walls, and a touch of creative cuisine take it out of the ordinary. The kitchen prides itself on top-quality meat; this is the place to try *tagliata* (thin slivers of rare beef) or *spezzatino peposo* (beef stew with lots of black pepper and a wine sauce). ⊠ *Via Guelfa 70/r,* ☎ *055/215475. AE, DC, MC, V. Closed Tues. and Aug.*

$ ✕ **Mario.** Clean and classic, this family-run trattoria on the corner of Piazza del Mercato near San Lorenzo offers genuine Florentine atmosphere and cooking, with no frills, but under a wooden ceiling dated 1536. It's open for lunch only. ⊠ *Via Rosina 2/r (Piazza del Mercato Centrale,* ☎ *055/218550. Reservations not accepted. No credit cards. Closed Sun. No dinner.*

Santa Maria Novella to the Arno

$$$ ✕ **Harry's Bar.** You don't come to Harry's for the food, but for the swank atmosphere—it's cozy, with a tiny bar, white tablecloths, and plenty of well-heeled customers captured in rosy lighting. Enjoy a Bellini (peach nectar and Prosecco) or, better yet, Harry's absolutely superb Martini before tucking into the menu. The perfectly bilingual staff are more than affable. But don't expect any culinary punches: This is nursery food for the privileged set, and you can eat better elsewhere in Florence. That said, the cheeseburger might be the best on this side of the Atlantic. Reservations are advised. ⊠ *Lungarno Vespucci 22/r,* ☎ *055/2396700. AE, MC, V. Closed Sun. and Dec. 15–Jan. 8.*

$$$ ✕ **Il Cestello.** So named because it is across the Arno from the church of San Frediano in Cestello, the restaurant is part of the Excelsior Hotel. A huge Florentine hearth keynotes the Renaissance tone of the dining room decor, but it's really the only cozy element in an otherwise formal atmosphere. The Tuscan-based menu features delicious risotto and pasta dishes, a rare selection of seafood, and an ever-changing sampling of whatever is fresh from the market. Reservations are advised. ⊠ *Excelsior Hotel, Piazza Ognissanti 3,* ☎ *055/264201. Jacket and tie. AE, DC, MC, V.*

$$ ✕ **Cantinetta Antinori.** Here's the place to lunch after a rough morning of shopping on Via Tornabuoni, Florence's swankiest street. But be prepared to pay: Cantinetta Antinori is the place where Florentine ladies (and men) who lunch come to see and be seen. The food is as elegant as the 15th-century palazzo in which it is served. Try the crostini *di lardo* (toasted bread with hot pork fat) and the *insalata di gamberoni e gamberetti con carciofi freschi* (shrimp salad with raw shaved artichokes). ⊠ *Piazza Antinori 3,* ☎ *055/292234. AE, DC, MC, V. Closed weekends and Aug.*

$$ ✕ **Le Fonticine.** This restaurant is a welcome oasis in a neighborhood
★ near the train station not noted for its fine dining options. Here you dine very well since this place combines the best of two Italian cuisines: Owner Silvano Bruci is from Tuscany and his wife Gianna from Emilia-

Romagna. Start with the mixed vegetable antipasto plate, or the delicately deep-fried cauliflower balls before moving on to their osso buco *alla fiorentina* (veal shanks in a hearty tomato sauce). The interior of the restaurant, filled with the Brucis' painting collection, is as cheery as the food is satisfying. ⊠ *Via Nazionale 79/r,* ☎ *055/282106. AE, DC, MC, V. Closed Sun.–Mon. and July 25–Aug. 25.*

Oltrarno and Santo Spirito

$$ ✕ **Angiolino.** Though some fans have complained recently that standards are slipping here, there's no arguing with their arista served with fresh herbs, or their *acquacotta* (literally cooked water, a delicious Tuscan onion, bread, and tomato peasant soup). This and other good stuff is served in a room with wood-burning stove by a thoroughly wonderful waitstaff. ⊠ *Via Santo Spirito 36/r,* ☎ *055/240 618. AE, DC, MC, V. Closed Mon., and last 3 wks in July. No dinner Sun.*

$$ ✕ **Cammillo.** At this bustling trattoria just on the other side of the Arno, a lot of languages are spoken. The restaurant has been in the capable hands of the Masiero family for three generations, and in its present location since 1945. Their farm in the country supplies the olive oil and wines for the restaurant, which go along nicely with the wide-ranging list of Tuscan specialties. Reservations are advised. ⊠ *Borgo Sant'Jacopo 57/r,* ☎ *055/212427. AE, DC, MC, V. Closed Wed., 15 days in Aug., and 15 days Dec.–Jan.*

$ ✕ **Osteria Antica Mescita San Niccolò.** This bustling osteria is directly next to the church of San Niccolò, and if you sit in the lower part of the restaurant, you will find yourself in what was once a chapel dating from the 11th century. Such subtle but dramatic background plays off nicely with the food, which is simple Tuscan style at its very best. The *pollo con limone* is tasty little pieces of chicken in a fragrant lemon-scented broth. In the winter, try the *spezzatino di cinghiale con aromi* (wild boar stew with herbs). Reservations are advised. ⊠ *Via San Niccolo, 60/r,* ☎ *055/234 2836. No credit cards. Closed Sun.*

Santa Croce

$$$$ ✕ **Enoteca Pinchiorri.** A sumptuous Renaissance palace with high, fres-
★ coed ceilings and bouquets in silver vases is the setting for this restaurant, one of the most expensive in Italy, and also considered one of the best. The enoteca part of the name comes from its former incarnation as a wineshop under owner Giorgio Pinchiorri, who still keeps a stock of vintage bottles in the cellar. A variety of fish, game, and meat dishes are always on the menu, along with splendid pasta combinations like the *ignudi*—ricotta and cheese dumplings with a lobster and coxcomb fricassee. ⊠ *Via Ghibellina 87,* ☎ *055/242777. Reservations essential. Jacket and tie. AE, MC, V. Closed Sun., Aug., and 1 wk in Dec. No lunch Mon. or Wed.*

$$$ ✕ **Alle Murate.** This sophisticated restaurant features creative versions of classic Tuscan dishes—*anatra alle erbe* (duck with herb and orange sauce)—but also southern Italian specialties such as lasagna *con mozzarella e pomodoro fresco* (with mozzarella and fresh tomatoes). The main dining room has a rich, uncluttered look, with warm wood floors and paneling and soft lights. In a smaller adjacent room called the *vineria,* table settings are simpler, the menu more limited. Since the Murate is known for its wine list, this is the place to splurge on a good bottle. ⊠ *Via Ghibellina 52/r,* ☎ *055/240618. AE, DC, MC, V. Closed Mon. No lunch.*

$$$ ✕ **Cibrèo.** The food here is fantastic, from the first bite of seamless,
★ creamy crostini *di fegatini* (savory Tuscan chicken liver spread on crostini) to the last bite of one of the meltingly good desserts. If you

Florence Dining and Lodging

Dining ●

Alfredo, **41**
Alle Murate, **30**
Angiolino, **27**
Baldovino, **31**
Buca dell'Orafo, **24**
Caffè Concerto, **48**
Cammillo, **26**
Cantinetta Antinori, **9**
Cibrèo, **34**
Enoteca Pinchiorri, **33**
Harry's Bar, **4**
Il Cestello, **3**
Il Latini, **6**
La Giostra, **35**
La Maremmana, **32**
Le Fonticine, **15**
Mario, **16**
Maximilian, **38**
Osteria Antica Mescita
San Niccolò, **47**
Osteria de'Benci, **28**
Osteria n. 1, **5**
Pallottino, **29**
Taverna del Bronzino, **42**
Toscano, **17**

Lodging ○

Albergo Firenze, **20**
Alessandra, **22**
Beacci Tornabuoni, **7**
Bellettini, **12**
Bencistà, **45**
Brunelleschi, **19**
Burchianti, **11**
Excelsior, **3**
Grand, **2**
Grand Hotel
Villa Cora, **47**
Hermitage, **23**
J & J, **36**
Kraft, **1**
La Residenza, **8**
Le Vigne, **10**
Loggiato dei Serviti, **40**
Lugarno, **25**
Monna Lisa, **37**
Morandi alla Crocetta, **39**
Nuova Italia, **13**
Pendini, **18**
Plaza Hotel Lucchesi, **49**
Porta Faenza, **14**
Regency, **46**
Ritz, **50**
Torre Guelfa, **21**
Villa Aurora, **43**
Villa San Michele, **44**

thought you'd never try tripe—let alone like it—this is the place to lay any doubts to rest: The *trippa in insalata* (cold tripe salad) with parsley and garlic is an epiphany. So is just about everything else on the menu. It's best to construe the owner Fabio Picchi's adamantly advising his customers on the A to Zs of Italian eating as a manifestation of his enthusiasm about his food—which is warranted as he has created some of the best, most creative food in town. ⊠ *Via A. del Verrocchio 87,* ☎ *055/2341100. Reservations essential. AE, DC, MC, V. Closed Sun.–Mon., July 25–Sept. 5, and Dec. 31–Jan. 7.*

$$ ✕ **Caffè Concerto.** A short taxi ride from city center takes you to this veranda-style restaurant, all glass and polished wood alongside the Arno. The excellent, creative Tuscan cuisine—and equally fine Tuscan wine list—draws visiting celebrities and a steady Florentine clientele. ⊠ *Lungarno Colombo 7,* ☎ *055/677377. Reservations essential. AE, DC, MC, V. Closed Sun.*

$$ ✕ **La Giostra.** The clubby La Giostra, which means "carousel" in Ital-
★ ian, serves unusually good pastas requiring some explanation from Dimitri or Soldano, the owner's good-looking twin sons. In perfect English they'll describe a favorite dish, delicious *gnocchetti alla tibetana* (little potato dumpling morsels with mint and basil pesto). Try the *spianata* (slices of thinly shaved beef baked quickly and served with fresh rosemary and sage). Leave room for dessert: This might be the only show in town with a sublime tiramisu and a wonderfully gooey Sacher torte. ⊠ *Borgo Pinti 12/r,* ☎ *055/241341. AE, DC, MC, V.*

$$ ✕ **Maximilian.** "This is not fast food" appears on the menu outside the door of this intimate trattoria (make reservations) with long narrow tables and white walls. Until recently, Adele, the chef-owner, was the sole employee. Though she has since hired a waitress, the service is still relaxed—slow, in fact. All complaints immediately dissipate with the first bite. The risotto *al tartufo nero* (with black truffle sauce) is a creamy, heavenly perfumed concoction. The menu is rich with vegetarian primi and secondi, a rarity in Florentine restaurants. ⊠ *Via Alfani 10/r,* ☎ *055/2478080. AE, DC, MC, V. Closed Mon. and 3 wks in Aug.*

$$ ✕ **Pallottino.** With its tiled floor, photograph-filled walls, and wooden tables, Pallottino is the quintessential Tuscan trattoria, with hearty, heartwarming classics like pappa al pomodoro and *peposo alla toscana* (a beef stew laced with black pepper). Their lunch special could be, at 13,000 lire, the best bargain in town. ⊠ *Via Isola delle Stinche 1/r,* ☎ *055/289573. AE, DC, MC, V. Closed Mon. and Aug. 1–20.*

$ ✕ **Baldovino.** This lively, brightly hued trattoria across the street from the church of Santa Croce is the brainchild of David Gardner and Catherine Storrar, expat Scots. In addition to turning out fine, thin-crusted pizzas, Baldovino offers some tasty antipasti (try the plate of smoked salmon and tuna) and *insalatone* (big salads). They also serve various pasta dishes and grilled meat til the wee hours. Save room for dessert; they're all winners. If you're pressed for time, duck into their lovely enoteca just across the street for a quick bite to eat and a glass of wine. ⊠ *Via S. Guiseppe, 22/r,* ☎ *055/241 773, AE, DC, MC, V. Closed Mon. and last wk Nov.–1st wk Dec.*

$ ✕ **La Maremmana.** Owners Benedetto Silvanu and Sergio Loria have
★ owned this restaurant for the past 18 years, and their chef has been in place for the same amount of time. It shows. The space is light and cheery—with white walls, tile floor, and pink tablecloths. Dead center is a mixed antipasto table, with a formidable array of choices: cold squid salad, various marinated vegetables, fried whole anchovies, marinated salmon, and more. The spaghetti *alle vongole* (with tiny clams) is a winner, as are their grilled meats. ⊠ *Via dei Macci 77/r,* ☎ *055/241226. DC, MC, V. Closed Sun. and Aug.*

$ ✕ **Osteria de'Benci.** Just a few minutes from Santa Croce, this charming osteria serves some of the most eclectic food in Florence at remarkably low prices. Try the lively spaghetti *degli eretici* (of the heretics), in a fresh tomato sauce laced with fresh herbs and a dash of *peperoncino* (hot chile peppers). When it's warm, you can dine outside with a view of the 13th-century tower belonging to the prestigious Alberti family. The English-speaking staff shouldn't scare you off: Florentines *do* eat here. ✉ *Via de' Benci 11/13/r,* ☎ *055/2344923. AE, DC, MC, V. Closed Sun.*

Pizzerias

Many pizza aficionados believe that the best pizza is town can be found at **Il Pizziauolo** (✉ Via dei Macci 113/r, ☎ 055/241171). In the Oltrarno, **Borgo Antico** (✉ Piazza S. Spirito, 6/r, ☎ 055/210437) serves up a good pizza and other trattoria fare. Others insist that the best pizza in town can be had at **I Tarocchi** (✉ Via de' Renai, 12/14r, ☎ 055/2343912), also in the Oltrarno.

Enoteche

Just a hop, skip, and a jump from Orsanmichele in the heart of the historic center, the little enoteca (wine bar) **I Fratellini** (✉ Via dei Cimatori 38/r, San Giovanni, ☎ 055/2396096) has been around since 1875. It sells wines by the glass and has a list of 27 sandwiches—try the pecorino with sun-dried tomatoes or the spicy wild boar *salame* with goat cheese if you're feeling brave. **Le Volpi e l'Uva** (✉ Piazza de' Rossi 1, Santa Maria Novella, ☎ 055/2398132; closed Sun.), just off Piazza Santa Trinita, is an oenophile's dream: they pour significant wines by the glass and serve equally impressive cheeses and little sandwiches to accompany them.

Caffè

Caffès in Italy serve not only coffee concoctions and pastries, but also sweets, drinks, *panini* (sandwiches), and some offer hot pasta and lunch dishes. They are usually open from early in the morning to late, and closed all day Sunday.

All bars in Italy ought to be like **Caffetteria Piansa** (✉ Borgo Pinti 18/r, Santa Croce, ☎ 055/2342362), great for breakfast, lunch, and drinks at night. After looking at the frescoes in Santissima Annunziata, cross the piazza towards the elegant **Robiglio** (✉ Via dei Servi, 112/r, San Giovanni, ☎ 055/212784). **Gilli** (✉ Piazza della Repubblica 39/r, Centro Storico, ☎ 055/21986; closed Tues.) has been a café, with all the amenities, since 1733. Try any of their chocolates. **Giacosa** (✉ Via Tornabuoni 83/r, Santa Maria Novella, ☎ 055/2396226), in the heart of Florence's ritzy shopping district, serves fancy sandwiches and sweets. The Negroni (a bombshell of a drink: gin, Campari, and sweet vermouth) was supposedly invented here before WWII.

Gelaterie and Pasticcerie

Though the *pasticceria* (bakery) **Dolci e Dolcezze** (✉ Piazza C. Beccaria 8/r, Santa Croce, ☎ 055/2345458; closed Mon.) is somewhat off the beaten path, if you walk down colorful Borgo La Croce, you'll be rewarded with the prettiest and tastiest cakes, sweets, and tarts in town. **Gran Caffe** (✉ Piazza San Marco 11/r, San Giovanni, ☎ 055/215833) is down the street from the Accademia, so it's a perfect stop for a marvelous panino or sweet, while raving about the majesty of Michelangelo's David. Most people seem to think **Vivoli** (✉ Via Isola delle

Stinche 7, Santa Croce, ☎ 055/292334) is the best gelateria in town. What with their *cioccolata con cafe* (chocolate ice cream heavily dosed with coffee), they're probably right.

Salumerie

Salumerie are gourmet food shops strong on fine fresh ingredients, such as meats and cheeses, and are great for picking up the fixings for a picnic lunch. If you find yourself in the Oltrarno and hungry for lunch or a snack, drop into **Azzarri Delicatesse** (⊠ Borgo S. Jacopo, 27/b–27/c, Santo Spirito, ☎ 055/2381714; closed Sun.). They make sandwiches, or you can get the fixings to go. Their list of cheese, some of which comes from France, is rather impressive. Looking for some cheddar cheese to pile in your panino? **Pegna** (⊠ Via dello Studio 8, San Giovanni, ☎ 055/282701, 055/282702; closed Sun. and Sat. afternoon) has been selling Italian food and non-Italian food since 1860. **Perini** (⊠ Mercato Centrale, enter at Via dell'Aretino, near San Lorenzo, San Giovanni, ☎ 055/2398306; closed Sun.) sells everything from prosciutto and mixed meats to sauces for pasta and a wide assortment of antipasti. It's probably the nicest little food shop in all of Florence—bring a lot of money.

LODGING

Florence's importance not only as a tourist city but as a convention center and the site of the Pitti fashion collections throughout the year has guaranteed a variety of accommodations, many in former villas and palazzi. However, these very factors mean that, except during the winter, reservations are a must. If you do find yourself in Florence with no reservations, go to the **Consorzio ITA** office (⊠ Stazione Centrale, ☎ 055/212245, FAX 055/2381226).

CATEGORY	COST*
$$$$	over 450,000 lire
$$$	300,000–450,000 lire
$$	190,000–300,000 lire
$	under 190,000 lire

Prices are for a double room, including service and tax.

Centro Storico

$$$ ☆ 🏨 **Brunelleschi.** Architects united a Byzantine tower, a medieval church, and a later building in a stunning structure in the very heart of Renaissance Florence to make this a truly unique hotel. There's even a museum displaying the ancient Roman foundations and pottery shards found during restoration. Medieval stone walls and brick arches contrast pleasantly with the plush, contemporary decor. The comfortable, soundproof bedrooms are done in coordinated patterns and soft colors; the ample bathrooms feature beige travertine marble. ⊠ *Piazza Sant'Elisabetta (Via dei Calzaiuoli), 50122, ☎ 055/290311, FAX 055/219653. 96 rooms, 7 junior suites. Restaurant, bar, meeting rooms, parking (fee). AE, DC, MC, V. CP.*

$$$ 🏨 **Hermitage.** Comfortable and charming are suitable adjectives for this hotel occupying the top six floors of a palazzo next to Ponte Vecchio and the Uffizi. Bright breakfast rooms, flowered roof terrace, and well-lighted bedrooms have the decor and atmosphere of a well-kept Florentine home. Double glazing and air-conditioning sustain the relaxing ambience. (The hotel has an elevator at the top of a short flight of stairs from the street.) ⊠ *Vicolo Marzio 1 (Piazza del Pesce, Ponte Vecchio), 50122, ☎ 055/287216, FAX 055/212208. 28 rooms. Breakfast room. MC, V. CP.*

$$ ⊞ **Pendini.** The atmosphere of an old-fashioned Florentine pensione is intact at this find in the absolute center of Florence. Public rooms are delightful, complete with a portrait of Signora Pendini, who founded the hotel in 1879, and early 19th-century antiques or reproductions throughout. Most bedrooms have brass or walnut beds, pretty floral wallpaper, and pastel carpeting; baths are modern. Many rooms can accommodate extra beds. Rates are low for the category, and off-season rates are a real bargain. ⊠ *Via Strozzi 2, 50123,* ☎ *055/211170,* ℻ *055/281807. 42 rooms. AE, DC, MC, V. CP.*

$$ ⊞ **Torre Guelfa.** Enter this hidden hotel through an immense wooden door on a narrow street, continue through an iron gate, and up a few steps where an elevator will take you to the third floor of this palazzo where the 12 guest rooms are. A few more steps will take you into the 13th-century Florentine *torre* (tower) itself. Each guest room is different, some with canopied beds, some with balconies. The Torre Guelfa once protected the fabulously wealthy Acciaiuoli family. Now it's one of the best-located small hotels in Florence, where you can have breakfast or sunset drinks on a rooftop that offers unmatched Florentine panoramas. ⊠ *Borgo S.S. Apostoli 8, 50123,* ☎ *055/2396338,* ℻ *055/ 2398577. 12 rooms. Bar, breakfast room. AE, MC, V. CP.*

$ ⊞ **Albergo Firenze.**A block from the Duomo, this hotel is in one of the oldest piazzas in Florence. In fact, it is said that Dante's wife lived in one of the medieval houses in the piazza. The hotel is clean and bright, with a large lobby area and breakfast room. No frills but adequate furnishings are found in the guest rooms, some of which have two bathrooms. ⊠ *Piazza Donati 4, 50122,* ☎ *055/214203,* ℻ *055/212370. 57 rooms. Breakfast room. No credit cards. CP.*

$ ⊞ **Alessandra.** The location, a block from the Ponte Vecchio, and clean, ample rooms make this a good choice. The English-speaking staff is friendly and helpful. ⊠ *Borgo Santi Apostoli 17, 50123,* ☎ *055/ 283438,* ℻ *055/210619. 25 rooms, 9 without bath. AE, MC, V. Closed Dec. 15–26. CP.*

$ ⊞ **Bellettini.** You couldn't ask for anything more central; this small hotel
★ is on three floors (the top floor has two nice rooms with a view) of a palazzo near the Duomo. The cordial family management takes good care of guests, providing a relaxed atmosphere and attractive public rooms with a scattering of antiques. Breakfast, featuring homemade cakes, and air-conditioning are included in the low room rate. The good-size rooms have Venetian or Tuscan provincial decor; bathrooms are bright and modern. ⊠ *Via dei Conti 7, 50123,* ☎ *055/213561,* ℻ *055/ 283551. 28 rooms. Bar, parking (fee). AE, DC, MC, V. CP.*

$ ⊞ **Burchianti.** This hotel is on the first floor of a regal 15th-century palace in the center of Florence, with large, traditionally decorated rooms, many with frescoes and trompe l'oeil images on the walls, and pretty flowers painted on the wooden ceilings. All 12 rooms have showers and sinks, some have complete bathrooms. Some rooms are near busy streets so there is some noise, but this is still a special hotel with a glorious Renaissance feeling if you're looking for a bargain. ⊠ *Via del Giglio 6, 50123,* ☎ *055/212796. 12 rooms. No credit cards. CP.*

San Lorenzo and Beyond

$$ ⊞ **Porta Faenza.** The 12th-century medieval well discovered during renovations has now become a focal point in the lobby. Two small pensiones were combined and a ground floor added to create this new hotel, which offers good value in spacious rooms decorated in Florentine style. The friendly Italian-Canadian owners extend lots of little touches and services, including a no-smoking floor and breakfast room, baby-sitting, new bathrooms, and an E-mail station. ⊠ *Via Faenza 77, 50123,* ☎ *055/ 284119,* FAX *055/210101. 25 rooms. Parking (fee). AE, DC, MC, V. CP.*

Near Piazza San Marco and Beyond

$$–$$$ 🏨 **Loggiato dei Serviti.** This hotel was not designed by Brunelleschi,
★ Florence's architectural genius, but it might as well have been. A mirror image of the architect's famous Ospedale degli Innocenti across the way, the Loggiato is tucked away on one of the city's quietest and loveliest squares. Occupying a 16th-century former monastery, the building was originally a refuge for traveling priests. Vaulted ceilings, tasteful furnishings (some antique), canopy beds, and rich fabrics make this a find if you want to get the feel of Florence in an attractively spare Renaissance building, while enjoying modern creature comforts. ⊠ *Piazza Santissima Annunziata 3, 50122,* ☎ *055/289592,* FAX *055/289595. 29 rooms. Bar, breakfast room, parking (fee). AE, DC, MC, V. CP.*

$$ 🏨 **Morandi alla Crocetta.** Near Piazza Santissima Annunziata, this is
★ a charming and distinguished residence in which guests are made to feel like privileged friends of the family. It is close to the sights but very quiet, in a former monastery, and is furnished comfortably in the classic style of a gracious Florentine home. The Morandi is not only an exceptional hotel but also a good value. It's very small, so try to book well in advance. ⊠ *Via Laura 50, 50121,* ☎ *055/2344747,* FAX *055/ 2480954. 10 rooms. AE, DC, MC, V. CP.*

Santa Maria Novella to the Arno

$$$$ 🏨 **Excelsior.** Traditional old-world charm finds a regal setting at the
★ Excelsior, built as a convent in the 13th century, and once the private residence of Josephine Bonaparte. The neo-Renaissance palace has painted wooden ceilings, stained glass, and acres of Oriental carpets strewn over marble floors in the public rooms. The opulence of 19th-century Florentine antiques and fabrics is set off by charming old prints of the city and long mirrors of the Empire style. ⊠ *Piazza Ognissanti 3, 50123,* ☎ *055/264201,* FAX *055/210278. 168 rooms. Restaurant, piano bar. AE, DC, MC, V. EP.*

$$$$ 🏨 **Grand.** Across the piazza from the Excelsior, this Florentine classic provides all the luxurious amenities of its sister. Here most rooms and public areas are decorated in sumptuous Renaissance style with rich fabrics in distinctive Florentine style. Guests can choose between imperial- or Florentine-style rooms, many with frescoes or canopied beds. Baths are all marble. A few rooms have balconies overlooking the Arno. ⊠ *Piazza Ognissanti 1, 50123,* ☎ *055/288781,* FAX *055/217400. 107 rooms. Restaurant, bar, parking (fee). AE, DC, MC, V. EP.*

$$$ 🏨 **Beacci Tornabuoni.** This is perhaps *the* classic Florentine pensione. Set in a 14th-century palazzo, it has old-fashioned style and just enough modern comfort to keep you happy. The food is good and can be served in the dining room, the garden, or in the rooms, most of which have views of the red-tile roofs in the neighboring downtown area. ⊠ *Via Tornabuoni 3, 50123,* ☎ *055/212645,* FAX *055/283594. 28 rooms. Restaurant, bar. AE, DC, MC, V. CP, MAP.*

$$$ 🏨 **Kraft.** The efficient and comfortable Kraft is modern, but it has many period-style rooms, all with polished wooden floors, some with balconies, and a rooftop terrace café. Its location near the Teatro Comunale (also next to the U.S. consulate) gives it a clientele from the music world. ⊠ *Via Solferino 2, 50123,* ☎ *055/284273,* FAX *055/2398267. 75 rooms, 5 junior suites. Restaurant, bar, pool, parking (fee). AE, DC, MC, V. EP.*

$$ 🏨 **La Residenza.** On Florence's fanciest shopping street, on the upper floors of a restored 15th-century building, La Residenza has character and comfort. The roof garden and adjacent sitting room are added attractions. Paintings and etchings add interest to the rooms, which have soundproofing and satellite TV. ☒ *Via Tornabuoni 8, 50123,* ☎ *055/218684,* 🅵🅰🆇 *055/284197. 24 rooms, 4 without bath. Restaurant, bar, parking (fee). AE, DC, MC, V. CP, MAP.*

$ Le Vigne. At this small hotel on one of Florence's most beautiful and central squares, the new owners have created the warm atmosphere of a private home. Complimentary afternoon tea and homemade breakfast jams and cakes are on offer, in addition to many other amenities such as a play area for children and an Internet connection. The spacious, air-conditioned rooms are furnished in 19th-century Florentine style. The caring management and reasonable rates make this a very special place. ☒ *Piazza Santa Maria Novella 24, 50123,* ☎ *055/294449,* 🅵🅰🆇 *055/2302263. 25 rooms. AE, DC, MC, V. EP.*

$ 🏨 Nuova Italia. Near the train station and within walking distance of the sights, this hotel is run by a genial English-speaking family. It has a homey atmosphere; rooms are clean and simply furnished and have air-conditioning and triple-glazed windows to ensure restful nights. Some rooms can accommodate extra beds. Low bargain rates include breakfast. ☒ *Via Faenza 26, 50123,* ☎ *055/268430,* 🅵🅰🆇 *055/210941. 20 rooms. Parking (fee). AE, DC, MC, V. CP.*

Oltrarno

$$$$ 🏨 Grand Hotel Villa Cora. Built near the Boboli Gardens in 1750, the Villa Cora retains the opulence of the 18th and 19th centuries. The decor of its remarkable public and private rooms runs the gamut from neoclassical to rococo and even Moorish, and reflects the splendor of such former guests as the Empress Eugénie, wife of Napoléon III, and Madame Von Meck, Tchaikovsky's mysterious benefactress. ☒ *Viale Machiavelli 18, 50125,* ☎ *055/2298451,* 🅵🅰🆇 *055/229086. 48 rooms. Restaurant, piano bar, pool, parking (fee). AE, DC, MC, V. CP.*

$$$$ 🏨 Lungarno. During the Florence fashion weeks, this hotel—bought by the fashionable Ferragamo family in 1995—buzzes with fashion industry glitterati. Guest rooms are large, and the blue- and white-trimmed white furnishings (the family colors are blue and white) are crisp and comfortable. Two of the guest rooms are in a medieval tower with exposed stone walls. The lobby bar, filled with oversize white sofas, has one of the most beautiful river views in Florence, and is a lovely place to stop in for a drink, even if you're not a guest. ☒ *Borgo San Jacopo 14, 50125,* ☎ *055/27261,* 🅵🅰🆇 *268437. 61 rooms, 11 suites. Bar, parking (fee). AE, DC, MC, V. CP.*

Santa Croce

$$$$ 🏨 Plaza Hotel Lucchesi. Elegant without being ostentatious, this hotel
★ is right on the Arno near Santa Croce. Front bedrooms have views of the river and hills beyond; rear rooms on the top floor have balconies and knockout views of Santa Croce. Spacious, quiet bedrooms (double glazing throughout) are furnished comfortably in mahogany and pastel fabrics against creamy white walls. The roomy, welcoming lounges and piano bar are favorite meeting places for Florentines. ☒ *Lungarno della Zecca Vecchia 38, 50122,* ☎ *055/26236,* 🅵🅰🆇 *055/2480921. 97 rooms. Restaurant, bar. AE, DC, MC, V. EP.*

$$$$ 🏨 Regency. In this stylish hotel in a residential district near the synagogue, the noise and crowds of Florence seem far away, though you are less than 10 minutes away from the Accademia and Michelangelo's *David*. The rooms are decorated in richly colored and tasteful fabrics and antique-style furniture faithful to the hotel's 19th-century origins as a private mansion. ☒ *Piazza Massimo D'Azeglio 3, 50121,* ☎ *055/*

245247, FAX *055/2346735. 34 rooms. Restaurant, parking (fee). AE, DC, MC, V. CP.*

$$$ ⊞ **J&J.** Away from the crowds, on a quiet street within walking distance of the sights, this unusual hotel is a converted 16th-century monastery. Its large, suitelike rooms are ideal for honeymooners, families, and small groups of friends. Some rooms are on two levels, and all are imaginatively arranged around a central courtyard and decorated with flair. The smaller rooms are more intimate, some opening onto their own little courtyard. The gracious owners chat with guests in the elegant lounge; breakfast is served in a glassed-in Renaissance loggia or in the central courtyard. ⊠ *Via di Mezzo 20, 50121,* ☎ *055/ 2345005,* FAX *055/240282. 20 rooms. Bar. AE, DC, MC, V. CP.*

$$$ ⊞ **Monna Lisa.** Housed in a Renaissance palazzo, the hotel retains its
★ original marble staircase, terra-cotta floors, and painted ceilings. Its rooms still have a rather homey quality, and though on the small side, many have contemplative views of a lovely garden. The ground-floor lounges give you the feel of living in an aristocratic town house. ⊠ *Borgo Pinti 27, 50121,* ☎ *055/2479751,* FAX *055/2479755. 30 rooms. Bar. AE, DC, MC, V. CP.*

$$ ⊞ **Ritz.** Set amidst a row of buildings on the Arno, this old hotel has been given new energy by young owners who have worked to give it a comfortable family feeling. They've decorated to make clients feel as if they are guests in a very pretty 19th-century Florentine home with 20th-century amenities. Almost all the rooms have dramatic views of the river or the domed, red-roofed "skyline" of Florence. ⊠ *Lungarno Zecca Vecchia 24, 50122,* ☎ *055/2340650,* FAX *055/240863. 30 rooms. Bar, breakfast room. AE, DC, MC, V. CP.*

Fiesole

For exploring information, *see* Side Trips, *below.*

$$$$ ⊞ **Villa San Michele.** The setting for this hideaway is so romantic— nestled in a luxuriant garden—that it once attracted Brigitte Bardot for her honeymoon. The villa was originally a monastery whose facade and loggia have been attributed to Michelangelo. Many of the rooms contain sumptuous statuary, paintings, and whirlpool baths. The restaurant is excellent. This is one of Italy's costliest hotels. ⊠ *Via Doccia 4, 50014 Fiesole,* ☎ *055/59451,* FAX *055/598734. 41 rooms. Restaurant, piano bar, pool, exercise room. AE, DC, MC, V. Closed Dec.–mid-Mar. MAP.*

$$$ ⊞ **Villa Aurora.** On the main piazza, this attractive hotel takes advantage of it's hilltop spot, with beautiful views in many of the rooms, some of which are on two levels with beamed ceilings and balconies. ⊠ *Piazza Mino 39, 50014 Fiesole,* ☎ *055/59100,* FAX *055/59587. 25 rooms. Bar, restaurant, meeting rooms. AE, MC, DC, V. EP.*

$$ ⊞ **Bencistà.** Below the luxurious Villa San Michele, this hotel has the same tranquil setting and is even two centuries older. The rooms are furnished with antiques, and dinners are included with the price. ⊠ *Via Benedetto da Maiano 4, 50014 Fiesole,* ☎ *055/59163,* FAX *055/ 59163. 44 rooms, 12 without bath. Dining room. No credit cards. MAP.*

NIGHTLIFE AND THE ARTS

The Arts

Film

You can find movie listings in *La Nazione,* the daily Florence newspaper. English-language films are shown at the **Cinema Astro** (⊠ Piazza San Simone near Santa Croce). There are two shows every evening,

Tuesday through Sunday (closed in July). On Monday, English-language films are offered at the **Odeon** (⊠ Piazza Strozzi) and the **Goldoni** (⊠ Via Serragli). The **Festival del Popolo,** held each December, is devoted to documentaries, and is held in the Fortezza da Basso. An international panel of judges gathers in late spring at the Forte di Belvedere for the **Florence Film Festival** to preside over new releases.

Music

The **Maggio Musicale Fiorentina** series of internationally acclaimed concerts and recitals is held in the Teatro Comunale (⊠ Corso Italia 16, ☎ 055/2779236) from late April through June. From December to early June, there is a concert season of the **Orchestra Regionale Toscana** (⊠ Santo Stefano al Ponte Vecchio church, ☎ 055/210804). **Amici della Musica** organizes concerts at the Teatro della Pergola (⊠ Box office, Via della Pergola 10/r, ☎ 055/2479652).

Opera

Operas are performed in the **Teatro Comunale** (⊠ Corso Italia 16, ☎ 055/2779236 or 055/211158) from December through February.

Nightlife

Unlike the Romans and Milanese, the reserved Florentines do not have a reputation for an active nightlife; however, the following places attract a mixed crowd of Florentines and visitors.

Bars

Rex (⊠ Via Fiesolana 23–25/r, Santa Croce, ☎ 055/2480331) has a hip, trendy atmosphere and an arty clientele. June to September, Rex moves its operations to the courtyard of Le Murate (⊠ Via Ghibellina), a former Renaissance convent and 19th-century prison. **Robin Hood's Tavern** (⊠ Via dell'Oriuolo 58/r, Santa Croce, ☎ 055/244579) is the place to come when you're craving a dose of English beer, English chatter, and formidable plates of Buffalo chicken wings, of all things. **Sant'Ambrogio Caffè** (⊠ Piazza Sant'Ambrogio 7–8/r, Santa Croce, ☎ 055/241035) has outdoor summer seating with a view of an 11th-century church (Sant'Ambrogio) directly across the street. If you're all dressed up and in the center of town, **Hotel Brunelleschi** (⊠ Piazza Santa Elisabetta 3, Centro Storico, ☎ 055/290311) is the place to come for a quiet cocktail. You'll be sitting among the refurbished remains of a tower dating from the 9th century.

Nightclubs

Most clubs are closed either Sunday or Monday. **Yab** (⊠ Via Sassetti 5/r, ☎ 055/282018) is one of the largest clubs, with a young clientele. **Hurricane Roxy** (⊠ Via Il Prato 58/r, ☎ 055/210399) serves up a light lunch during the day, but in the evening there's a deejay, good music, and a welcoming atmosphere. **Space Electronic** (⊠ Via Palazzuolo 37, ☎ 055/293082) has two floors with karaoke upstairs, and enormous disco downstairs. A less frenetic alternative is **Jackie O'** (⊠ Via Erta Canina 24, ☎ 055/2344904).

Full Up (⊠ Via della Vigna Vecchia 21/r, ☎ 055/293006) draws a very young clientele. **Meccanò** (⊠ Viale degli Olmi 1, in Le Cascine park, ☎ 055/331371) is a multimedia experience in a high-tech disco with a late-night restaurant. **River Club** (⊠ Lungarno Corsini 8, ☎ 055/282465) has winter-garden decor and a large dance floor. The accent is on Brazil at **Caffè Voltaire** (⊠ Via della Scala 9/r, ☎ 055/218255), where there's Latin food and music.

OUTDOOR ACTIVITIES AND SPORTS

Participant Sports

Biking

Bikes are a good way of getting out into the hills, but the scope for biking is limited in town center. **Florence by Bike** (⊠ Via della Scala 12/r, ☏ 055/264035) has designed some guided city tours that work quite well. They leave several times a day for one- to three-hour tours of major monuments or for tours with specific themes such as Renaissance Florence or 13th-century Florence. **I Bike Italy** (⊠ Borgo degli Albizi 11, ☏ FAX 055/2342371) offers one-day tours of the Florence countryside. For information on where to rent bicycles, *see* Getting Around *in* Florence A to Z, *below.*

Golf

Golf Club Ugolino (⊠ Via Chiantigiana 3, Impruneta, ☏ 055/2301009) is a hilly 18-hole course in the heart of Chianti country just outside town. It is open to the public.

Health Clubs and Gyms

Palestra Riccardi (⊠ Borgo Pinti 75, ☏ 055/2478444, 055/2478462, ☏ daily 20,000 lire; weekly 50,000 lire) has free weights, stretching, aerobics, and body building. **Centro Sportivo Fiorentino Indoor Club** (⊠ Via Bardazzi 15, ☏ 055/430275, 430703, ☏ daily 30,000 lire, weekly 135,000 lire) has all the usual gym amenities plus sauna and pool. The only drawback is that it's far from the center. **Palestra Gymnasium** (⊠ V. Palazzuolo 49/r, ☏ 055/293308, ☏ daily 20,000 lire) is your basic, run-of-the-mill gym.

Running

Don't even think of running on the skinny city streets, where tour buses and triple-parked Alfa Romeos leave precious little space for pedestrians. Instead, head for **Le Cascine,** the park along the Arno at the western end of the city. You can run to Le Cascine along the Lungarno (stay on the sidewalk), or take Bus 17 from the Duomo. A cinder track lies on the hillside just below **Piazzale Michelangelo,** across the Arno from the city center. The locker rooms are reserved for members, so come ready to run.

Swimming

Bellariva (⊠ Lungarno Colombo 6, ☏ 055/677521). **Circolo Tennis alle Cascine** (⊠ Viale Visarno 1, ☏ 055/356651). **Costoli** (⊠ Viale Paoli, ☏ 055/675744). **Le Pavoniere** (⊠ Viale degli Olmi, ☏ 055/367506).

Tennis

Circolo Tennis alle Cascine (⊠ Viale Visarno 1, ☏ 055/356651). **Tennis Club Rifredi** (⊠ Via Facibeni, ☏ 055/432552). **Il Poggetto** (⊠ Via Mercati 24/b, ☏ 055/460127).

Spectator Sport

Soccer

Italians are passionate about *calcio* (soccer), and the Florentines are no exception; indeed, *tifosi* (fans) of the Fiorentina team are fervent supporters. The team plays its home games at the **Stadio Comunale** (Municipal Stadium, ⊠ Top of Viale Manfredo Fanti, northeast of the center). Tickets for all games except those against their biggest rivals—Juventus of Turin and A. C. Milan—are difficult but not impossible to come by. Try the ticket booth **Chiosco degli Sportivi** (⊠ North side of Piazza della Repubblica, ☏ 055/29236388). Games are usually played on Sunday afternoon, from about late August to May. A medieval version of the game, **Calcio in Costume,** is played on or around June 24, the feast day of St. John the Baptist, each year by teams dressed in costume representing the six Florence neighborhoods.

SHOPPING

Window shopping in Florence is like visiting an enormous contemporary art gallery, for many of today's greatest Italian artists are fashion designers, and most keep shops in Florence. Except during the two sale seasons (Jan. 7–Mar. 7 and July 10–Sept. 10), Florence is a very expensive shopping city. Discerning shoppers may find bargains in the street markets. Shops are generally open 9–1 and 3:30–7:30 but closed Sunday and Monday morning most of the year. Summer (June–September) hours are usually 9–1 and 4–8, and some shops close Saturday afternoon instead of Monday morning. When looking for addresses of shops, you will see two color-coded numbering systems on each street. The red numbers are commercial addresses and are indicated, for example, as 31/r. The blue or black numbers are residential addresses. Most shops take major credit cards and will ship purchases, but due to possible delays it's wiser to take your purchases with you.

Markets

Those with a tight budget or a sense of adventure may want to take a look at the souvenir stands under the loggia of the **Mercato Nuovo** (⊠ Corner of Via Por San Maria and Via Porta Rossa; ☞ Centro Storico *in* Exploring Florence, *above*), or the clothing and leather goods stalls of the **Mercato di San Lorenzo** in the streets next to the San Lorenzo church. The **Mercato Centrale** (⊠ Piazza del Mercato Centrale; ☞ Michelangelo Country *in* Exploring Florence, *above*) is the huge indoor food market in the midst of the San Lorenzo Market. You can find bargains at the **flea market** on Piazza dei Ciompi on the last Sunday of the month. An **open-air market** is held in Le Cascine park every Tuesday morning.

Shopping Districts

Florence's most elegant shops are concentrated in town center. The fanciest designer shops are mainly on **Via Tornabuoni** and **Via della Vigna Nuova.** The city's largest concentration of antiques shops can be found on **Borgo Ognissanti** and Oltrarno's **Via Maggio.** The **Ponte Vecchio** houses reputable jewelry shops, as it has since the 16th century. The area near **Santa Croce** is the heart of the leather merchants' district.

Specialty Stores

Antiques

At **Alberto Pierini** (⊠ Borgo Ognissanti 22/r, ☎ 055/2398138) the rustic Tuscan furniture is all antique, and much of it dates from the days of the Medicis. Specialties at **Paolo Ventura** (⊠ Borgo Ognissanti 61/r, ☎ 055/214397) are antique ceramics from all periods and places of origin. **Galleria Luigi Bellini** (⊠ Lungarno Soderini 5, Oltrarno, ☎ 055/214031) claims to be Italy's oldest antiques dealer, which may be true, since father Mario Bellini was responsible for instituting Florence's international antiques biennial. **Giovanni Pratesi** (⊠ Via Maggio 13/r, ☎ 055/2396568) specializes in Italian antiques, in this case furniture, with some fine paintings, sculpture, and decorative objects turning up from time to time. Vying with Luigi Bellini as one of Florence's oldest antiques dealers, **Guido Bartolozzi** (⊠ Via Maggio 18/r, ☎ 055/215602) deals in predominately period Florentine objects. At **Paolo Paoletti** (⊠

Via Maggio 30/r, ☎ 055/214728) look for Florentine antiques with an emphasis on Medici-era objects from the 15th and 16th centuries.

Books and Paper

Pineider (✉ Piazza della Signoria 14/r and Via Tornabuoni 76/r, ☎ 055/284655) now has shops throughout the world, but it began in Florence and still does all its printing here. Personalized stationery and business cards are the mainstay, but the stores also sell fine desk accessories. **Centro Di** (✉ Piazza dei Mozzi 1, Oltrarno, ☎ 055/2342666) publishes art books and exhibition catalogs for some of the most important organizations in Europe. One of Florence's oldest paper-goods stores, **Giannini** (✉ Piazza Pitti 37/r, Oltrarno, ☎ 055/212621) is *the* place to buy the marbleized stock, which come in a variety of forms, from flat sheets to boxes and even pencils. Long one of Florence's best art bookshops, **Salimbeni** (✉ Via Matteo Palmieri 14/r, ☎ 055/2340904) specializes in publications on Tuscany. **FMR** (✉ Via delle Belle Donne 41/r, ☎ 055/283312), the shop of world famous art book editor and tastemaker Franco Maria Ricci, offers exquisite art books, handmade papers, and small works on paper. **Cozzi Alberto** (✉ Via del Parione 35/r, ☎ 055/294963) stocks an extensive line of Florentine papers and paper products, and the artisans in the shop rebind and restore books and works on paper.

Clothing

The surreal window displays at **Luisa Via Roma** (✉ Via Roma 19, ☎ 055/2381810) hint at the trendy yet elegant clothing that can be found inside this fascinating, *alta moda* boutique featuring the world's top designers as well as Luisa's own line. The sleek, classic **Giorgio Armani** (✉ Via della Vigna Nuova 51/r, ☎ 055/209040) boutique is a centerpiece of the dazzling high-end shops clustered in this part of town. It's sister store, **Emporio Armani** (✉ P. Strozzi 16/r, ☎ 055/284315) offers more-affordable, funky, nightclub-friendly Armani threads. You can take home a custom-made suit or dress from **Giorgio Vannini** (✉ Via Borgo SS Apostoli 43/r, ☎ 055/293037), who has a showroom for his pret-a-porter designs. **Bernardo** (✉ Via Porta Rossa 87/r, ☎ 055/283333) specializes in men's shirts (with details like mother-of-pearl buttons), trousers, and cashmere sweaters.

Jasmine (✉ Borgo San Jacapo 27/r, ☎ 055/213501) is an unpretentious yet sophisticated shop well worth taking a look at in the Oltrarno. If you're looking for something to turn heads in the Florence clubs, try **Metropole** (✉ P. Stazione 24r, ☎ 055/295022). The aristocratic Marchese di Barsento **Emilio Pucci** (✉ Via dei Pucci 6/r; Via della Vigna Nuova, 99/r, ☎ 055/287622) became an international name in the early 1960s, when the stretch ski clothes he designed for himself caught on with the la-dolce-vita crowd—his pseudo-psychedelic prints and "palazzo pajamas" became all the rage. The showroom in the family palazzo and two boutiques still sell the celebrated Pucci prints.

Embroidery and Linens

Signora **Loretta Caponi** (✉ P. Antinori 4/r, ☎ 055/213668) is synonymous with Florentine embroidery, and her luxury lace, linens, and lingerie have earned her worldwide renown. **Valmar** (✉ Via Porta Rossa 53/r, ☎ 055/284493) is filled with tangled spools of cords, ribbons, and fringes, plus an array of buttons, tassels, sachets, and hand-embroidered cushions you can take home—or bring in your own fabric, choose the adornments, and you can have your cushion or table runner made.

Gifts and Housewares

The essence of a Florentine holiday is captured in the sachets of the **Officina Profumo Farmaceutica di Santa Maria Novella** (✉ Via della

Scala 16/r, ☎ 055/216276), an art nouveau emporium of herbal cosmetics and soaps that are made following centuries-old recipes created by monks. For housewares nothing beats **Bartolini** (✉ Via dei Servi 30/r, ☎ 055/211895) for well-designed practical items. **Sbigoli Terrecotte** (✉ Via Sant'Egidio 4/r, ☎ 055/229706) carries traditional Tuscan terra-cotta and ceramic vases, pots, cups, and saucers. If you want to go one step further, you can even shop in the **Sbigoli Laboratorio** (✉ Via di Camaldoli 10/r, ☎ 055/229706), where the artisans are working on their wheels and glazing the pieces. For outstanding contemporary design housewares, check out **Open House** (✉ Via Barbadori 40/r, ☎ 055/212094).

Jewelry

Della Loggia (✉ Ponte Vecchio 52/r, ☎ 055/2396028) combines precious and semiprecious stones and metals in contemporary settings. **Gherardi** (✉ Ponte Vecchio 5/r, ☎ 055/287211), Florence's king of coral, has the city's largest selection of finely crafted pieces, as well as cultured pearls, jade, and turquoise. Antique jewelry, some of which comes from noble families down on their luck, is the specialty at **Lui Lei** (✉ Piazza del Limbo 8/r, corner of Borgo SS Apostoli, ☎ 055/283318), which also collects period furniture and small objets d'art. The venerable **Piccini** (✉ Ponte Vecchio 23/r, ☎ 055/280479) has literally been crowning the heads of Europe for almost a century, and combines its taste for the antique with contemporary designs. One of Florence's oldest jewelers, **Tiffany-Faraone** (✉ Via Tornabuoni 25/r, ☎ 055/215506) has supplied Italian (and other) royalty with finely crafted gems for centuries. Its selection of antique-looking classics has been updated with a choice of contemporary silver. To reach **C. O. I. Wholesale Jewelry** (✉ Via Por S. Maria 8/r, ☎ 055/283970), you must ring the doorbell at the street and take the elevator to the second floor, where the display cases are filled with handsome handmade Florentine designs.

Shoes and Leather Accessories

In the high tourist season, status-conscious shoppers often stand in line outside **Gucci** (✉ Via Tornabuoni 73/r, ☎ 055/264011), ready to buy anything with the famous designer's initials. **Ugolini** (✉ Via Tornabuoni 20/r, ☎ 055/216664) once made gloves for the Italian royal family, but now anyone can have the luxury of its exotic leathers, as well as silk and cashmere ties and scarves. Born near Naples, the late Salvatore **Ferragamo** (✉ Via Tornabuoni 16/r, ☎ 055/292123) made his fortune custom-making shoes for famous feet, especially Hollywood stars. His palace has since passed on to his wife, Wanda, and displays designer clothing and accessories, but elegant footwear still underlies the Ferragamo success.

Giotti (✉ Piazza Ognissanti 3/r) has a full line of leather goods and its own leather clothing. **Leather Guild** (✉ Piazza Santa Croce 20/r, ☎ 055/241932) is one of many such shops that produce inexpensive, antique-looking leather goods of mass appeal, but here you can see the craftspersons at work. **Lily of Florence** (✉ Via Guicciardini 2/r, ☎ 055/294748) offers high quality, classic shoe designs at reasonable prices and in American sizes. **Il Bisonte** (✉ Via del Parione 31/r, just off Via della Vigna Nuova, ☎ 055/215722) is known for its natural-looking leather goods, all stamped with the store's bison symbol. The ultimate fine leathers are crafted into classic shapes at **Casadei** (✉ Via Tornabuoni 33/r, ☎ 055/287240), winding up as women's shoes and bags. **Madova** (✉ Via Guicciardini 1/r, ☎ 055/210244) has a rainbow array of quality leather gloves.

SIDE TRIPS

Fiesole and Gracious Gardens Around Florence

Fiesole

A half-day excursion to Fiesole, set in the hills 8 km (5 mi) above Florence, gives you a pleasant respite from museums and a wonderful vantage point of the city. From here, the view of Brunelleschi's powerful Duomo cupola will give you a new sense of appreciation of what he—and the Renaissance—accomplished. Fiesole began life as an ancient Etruscan and later Roman village that held some power until it succumbed to the barbarian invasions and eventually gave up its independence in exchange for Florence's protection. The medieval cathedral, some other old churches, the ancient Roman amphitheater, and lovely old villas behind garden walls are clustered on a series of hilltops. A walk around Fiesole can take from one to two or three hours, depending on how far you stroll from the main piazza. For information about hotels in Fiesole, *see* Lodging, *above*.

The **Duomo** (✉ Piazza Mino da Fiesole) reveals a stark medieval interior. In the raised presbytery, the **Cappella Salutati** was frescoed by 15th-century artist Cosimo Rosselli, but it was his contemporary, sculptor Mino da Fiesole, who put the town on the artistic map. The Madonna on the altarpiece and the tomb of Bishop Salutati are his work.

The nearby beautifully preserved 2,000-seat **Anfiteatro Romano** (Roman Amphitheater) dates from the 1st century BC and is still used for summer concerts. To the right of the amphitheater are the **Terme Romani** (Roman Baths), where you can see the gymnasium, hot and cold baths, and the rectangular chamber where the water was heated. A beautifully designed **Museo Archeologico**, an intricate series of levels connected by elevators, is built amidst the ruins and contains objects dating from 2000 BC. The nearby **Museo Bandini** is a small venue with a lot to offer. It is filled with the private collection of Canon Angelo Maria Bandini (1726–1803), who fancied 13th- to 15th-century Florentine paintings, terra-cotta pieces, and wood sculpture, which he bequeathed to the Diocese of Fiesole. ✉ *Via San Francesco 3 ,* ☎ *055/ 59477.* 🎫 *10,000 lire (1 ticket provides access to the archaeological park and the museums).* ☉ *May–Oct., Wed.–Sun. 9:30–7; Nov.–Apr., Wed.–Sun. 9:30–5.*

Climb the hill to the church of **San Francesco** for a good view of Florence and the plain below enjoyed from terrace and benches. Halfway up the hill, you'll see sloping steps to the right; they lead to a lovely wooded **park** with trails that loop out and back to the church.

If you really want to stretch your legs, walk 4 km (2½ mi) back toward Florence center along Via Vecchia Fiesolana, a narrow lane, to the church of **San Domenico** (✉ Piazza San Domenico, off Via Giuseppe Mantellini). Sheltered in the church is *Madonna and Child with Saints* by Fra Angelico (1400–55), a.k.a. Fra Giovanni da Fiesole, who was the prior of this church. From the church, it's only a five-minute walk northwest to the **Badia Fiesolana** (✉ Via della Badia dei Roccettini), which was the original cathedral of Fiesole. Bus 7 (☞ Fiesole A to Z, *below*) goes from Florence to Fiesole, and also stops in San Domenico; from here you can walk the rest of the way to Fiesole along the narrow Via Vecchia Fiesolana, followed since the days of the Etruscans.

Nightlife and the Arts

From June through August, **Estate Fiesolana** (✉ Teatro Romano, Fiesole, ☎ 055/599931) is a festival of theater, music, dance, and film that takes place in the churches and the archaeological area of Fiesole.

Fiesole A to Z

ARRIVING AND DEPARTING

The trip from Florence by car or bus takes 20–30 minutes. Take city Bus 7 from the Stazione Centrale di Santa Maria Novella, Piazza San Marco, or the Duomo. There are several possible routes for the two-hour walk from central Florence to Fiesole. One route begins in a residential area of Florence called Salviatino (Via Barbacane, near Piazza Edison, on Bus 7 route), and after a short time it offers glorious peeks over garden walls of beautiful villas, as well as the opportunity to look over your shoulder at the panorama of Florence nestled in the valley.

BIKING TOURS

If you have well-exercised legs and lungs, you can also take a guided half-day bicycle tour from Florence to Fiesole. For bike rental information, *see* Guided Tours *in* Florence A to Z, *below*.

Gracious Gardens Around Florence

Like the Medicis you can get away from Florence's hustle and bustle by heading for the hills. Take a break from city sightseeing to enjoy the gardens and villas set like jewels in the hills around the city. Villa di Castello and Villa La Pietraia, both just northwest of the center in Castello, can be explored in one trip. The Italian garden at Villa Gamberaia is a quick 8-km (5-mi) jaunt east of the center near Settignano.

Villa di Castello

A fortified residence in the Middle Ages, Villa di Castello was rebuilt in the 15th century by the Medicis. The Accademia della Crusca, a 400-year-old institution that is official arbiter of the Italian language, now occupies the palace, which is not open to the public. The gardens are the main attraction. From the villa entrance, walk uphill through the 19th-century park laid out in Romantic style, set above part of the formal garden. You'll reach the terrace, which affords a good view of the geometric layout of the Italian garden below; stairs on either side descend to the parterre.

Though the original garden design has been altered somewhat over the centuries, the allegorical theme of animals devised by Tribolo in the 1540s to the delight of the Medicis is still evident. The artificial cave, Grotta degli Animali (Animal Grotto), displays an imaginative menagerie of sculpted animals by Giambologna and his assistants. Two bronze sculptures by Ammanati, centerpieces of fountains studding the Italian garden, can now be seen indoors in Villa La Pietraia (☞ *below*). Another Ammanati sculpture, a figure of an old man representing the Appenines, is at the center of a pond on the terrace overlooking the Italianate garden. Allow about 45 minutes to visit the gardens; you can easily visit Villa La Pietraia (☞ *below*) from here, making for a four-hour trip in total. ✉ *Via di Castello 47, Castello,* ☎ *055/454791.* ✑ *4,000 lire (includes entrance to Villa La Pietraia).* ☉ *Gardens: daily 9–1 hr before sunset. Closed 1st and 3rd Mon. of month.*

Villa La Pietraia

The Splendidly planted gardens of Villa La Pietraia sit high above the Arno plain on Castello Hill, allowing a sweeping view of Florence. The villa was built around a medieval tower and reconstructed after it was purchased by the Medicis in 1575. Virtually the only trace of the Medicis having lived here is the 17th-century courtyard frescoes depicting glorious episodes of the clan's history. In the 1800s the villa served as a country residence of King Victor Emmanuel II (who kept his mistress here) while Florence was the temporary capital of the newly united Kingdom of Italy.

An Italian-speaking guide will take you through the 19th-century-style salons. The Italian garden—also altered in the 1800s—and the vast park behind the palace suggest a splendid contrast between formal and natural landscapes. Allow 60–90 minutes to explore the park and gardens, plus 30 minutes for the guided tour of the so-called museum, the villa interior. This property is best visited after the Villa di Castello (☞ *above*). ⊠ *Via della Pietraia 40, Castello,* ☎ *050/454791.* ☜ *4,000 lire (includes entrance to Villa di Castello).* ☉ *Tues.–Sun. 9– 1 hr before sunset.*

Villa Gamberaia

Villa Gamberaia, near the village of Settignano on the eastern outskirts of Florence, was the rather modest country home of the Rossellino family, which fostered some great early Renaissance sculptors. In the early 1600s, the villa eventually passed into the hands of the wealthy Capponi family. They spared no expense in rebuilding it and, more importantly, creating the Italian garden, one of the finest near Florence. Festooned with statues and fountains, the garden suffered damage during World War II but has been restored according to the original 17th-century design. This excursion takes about 1½ hours, allowing 45 minutes to visit the garden. ⊠ *Via del Rossellino 72, near Settignano,* ☎ *055/697205.* ☜ *12,000 lire.* ☉ *Gardens: weekdays 9–noon and 1–6, weekends by appointment; villa closed to the public.*

Gracious Gardens Around Florence A to Z

VILLA DI CASTELLO

By car, head northwest from Florence on Via Reginaldo Giuliani (also known as Via Sestese) to Castello, about 6 km (4 mi) northwest of city center in the direction of Sesto Fiorentino; follow signs to Villa di Castello. Or take Bus 28 from city center, and tell the driver you want to get off at Villa di Castello; from the stop, walk north about ½ km (¼ mi) up the tree-lined allée from the main road to the villa.

VILLA LA PIETRAIA

By car, follow directions to Villa di Castello (☞ *above*), but take the right off Via Reginaldo Giuliani, following the sign for Villa La Pietraia. You can walk from Villa di Castello to Villa La Pietraia in about 15 minutes; turn left beyond the gate of Villa di Castello and continue straight along Via di Castello to the imposing Villa Corsini; take Via della Pietraia uphill to the entrance.

VILLA GAMBERAIA

By car, head east on Via Aretina, an extension of Via Gioberti, which is picked up at Piazza Beccaria; follow the sign to the turnoff to the north to Villa Gamberaia, about 8 km (5 mi) from the center. Take Bus 10 to Settignano. From Settignano's main Piazza Tommaseo walk east on Via di San Romano; the second lane on the right is Via del Rossellino, which leads southeast to the entrance of Villa Gamberaia. The walk from the piazza takes about 10 minutes.

FLORENCE A TO Z

Arriving and Departing

By Bus

Long-distance buses offer inexpensive if somewhat claustrophobic service between Florence and other cities in Italy and Europe. One operator is **SITA** (⊠ Via Santa Caterina da Siena 15/r, ☎ 055/483651 weekdays, 055/211487 weekends). Also try **Lazzi Eurolines** (⊠ Via Mercadante 2, ☎ 055/215154).

By Car

Florence is connected to the north and south of Italy by the Autostrada del Sole (**A1**). It takes about an hour via scenic roads to get to Bologna (although heavy truck traffic over the Apennines often makes for slower going) and about three to Rome. The Tyrrhenian Coast is an hour away on **A11** west.

By Plane

Although the Aeroporto A. Vespucci Airport, called **Peretola** (⊠ 10 km/6 mi northwest of Florence, ☎ 055/333498), accommodates flights from Milan, Rome, and some European cities, it is still a relatively minor airport. **Aeroporto Galileo Galilei** (⊠ Pisa, 80 km/50 mi west of Florence, ☎ 050/500707) is used by most international carriers. For flight information, call the **Florence Air Terminal** (⊠ Stazione Centrale di Santa Maria Novella, ☎ 055/216073) or Aeroporto Galileo Galilei.

International travelers flying on Alitalia to Rome's **Aeroporto Leonardo da Vinci** and headed directly for Florence can make connections at the airport for a flight to Florence (the same holds true for Milan's Malpensa), but if the layover is a long one, consider taking the FS airport train to Termini station in Rome, where fast trains for Florence are frequent during the day.

BETWEEN THE AIRPORTS AND DOWNTOWN

By Bus. There is a local bus service from Peretola to Florence. Buy a ticket at the second-floor caffè; the bus shelter is beyond the parking lot. There is no direct bus service from Pisa's airport to Florence. Buses do go to Pisa itself, but then you have to change to a slow train service.

By Car. From Peretola take autostrada **A11** directly into the city. Driving from the airport in Pisa, take **S67**, a direct route to Florence.

By Train. A scheduled service connects the station at Pisa's Aeroporto Galileo Galilei with Florence's Stazione Centrale di Santa Maria Novella, roughly a one-hour trip. Trains start running about 7 AM from the airport, 6 AM from Florence, and continue service every hour until about 11:30 PM from the airport, 8 PM from Florence. You can check in for departing flights at the **air terminal** (⊠ Track 5, Galileo Galilei Airport station, ☎ 055/216073).

By Train

Florence is on the principal Italian train route between most European capitals and Rome and within Italy is served quite frequently from Milan, Venice, and Rome by nonstop Intercity (IC) and Eurostar trains. **Stazione Centrale di Santa Maria Novella** (☎ 1478/88088 toll-free) is the most convenient city-center station. Be sure to avoid trains that stop only at the Campo di Marte or Rifredi stations, which are not convenient to the center.

Getting Around

By Bicycle

Brave souls (cycling in Florence is difficult, at best) may rent bicycles at easy-to-spot locations at Fortezza da Basso, the Stazione Centrale di Santa Maria Novella, and Piazza Pitti. **Motorent** (⊠ Via San Zanobi 9/r, ☎ 055/490113). **Alinari** (⊠ Via Guelfa 85r, ☎ 055/280500).

By Bus

Maps and timetables are available for a small fee at the **ATAF** booth (⊠ Next to the train station; Piazza del Duomo 57/r), or for free at visitor information offices (☞ Contacts and Resources, *below*). Tickets must be bought in advance at tobacco stores, newsstands, from automatic ticket machines near main stops, or at ATAF booths. The ticket must be canceled in the small validation machine immediately upon boarding. Two types of tickets are available, both valid for one or more rides on all lines. One costs 1,500 lire and is valid for one hour from the time it is first canceled; the other costs 2,500 lire and is valid for two hours. A multiple ticket—four tickets each valid for 60 minutes— costs 5,800 lire. A 24-hour tourist ticket costs 6,000 lire. Montly passes are also available.

By Car

In the city, abandon all hope of using a car, since most of the downtown area is a pedestrian zone. For assistance or information, call the **ACI** (Italian Automobile Club, ☎ 055/24861).

By Moped

If you want to go native and rent a noisy Vespa (Italian for "wasp") or other make of motorcycle or moped, you may do so at Motorent (☞ By Bicycle, *above*). Helmets can be rented at either place.

By Taxi

Taxis usually wait at stands throughout the city (such as in front of the train station and in Piazza della Repubblica), or you can call for one (☎ 055/4390 or 055/4798). The meter starts at 4,500 lire, with a 7,000 lire minimum, and extra charges for nights, Sunday, or radio dispatch.

Contacts and Resources

Car Rentals

Eurodollar (⊠ Via Il Prato 72/r–82/r, ☎ 055/2382480). **Hertz Italiana** (⊠ Via Finiguerra 33/r, ☎ 055/239-8205, FAX 055/2302011). **Maggiore-Budget Autonoleggio** (⊠ Via Termine 1, ☎ 055/311256).

Consulates

U.S. (⊠ Lungarno Vespucci 38, ☎ 055/2398276). **U.K.** (⊠ Lungarno Corsini 2, ☎ 055/284133). **Canadians** should contact their consulate in Rome (☞ Chapter 2).

Doctors and Dentists

You can get a list of English-speaking doctors and dentists at the U.S. consulate (☞ *above*). Contact the **Tourist Medical Service** (⊠ Viale Lorenzo Il Magnifico, ☎ 055/475411).

Emergencies

Police (⊠ Via Zara 2, near Piazza della Libertà, ☎ 49/771). **Ambulance** (☎ 118). **Emergencies** (☎ 113). **Misericordia** (Red Cross, ⊠ Piazza del Duomo 20, ☎ 055/212222). If you need hospital treatment, and an interpreter, you can call **AVO** (☎ 055/4250126 or 055/2344567; ☉ Mon., Wed., and Fri. 4–6 PM; Tues. and Thurs. 10–noon), a group of volunteer interpreters.

English-Language Bookstores

Paperback Exchange (⊠ Via Fiesolana 31/r, ☎ 055/2478154). **BM Bookshop** (⊠ Borgo Ognissanti 4/r, ☎ 055/294575). **Seeber** (⊠ Via Tornabuoni 68, ☎ 055/215697).

Guided Tours

BIKING TOURS

See Outdoor Activities and Sports, *above*.

ORIENTATION TOURS

The major bus operators (☞ Arriving and Departing, By Bus, *above*) offer half-day itineraries, all of which use comfortable buses staffed with English-speaking guides. Morning tours begin at 9, when buses pick visitors up at the main hotels. Stops include the cathedral complex, the Galleria dell'Accademia, Piazzale Michelangelo, and the Palazzo Pitti (or, on Monday, the Museo dell'Opera del Duomo). Afternoon tours stop at the main hotels at 2 PM and take in Piazza della Signoria, the Galleria degli Uffizi (or the Palazzo Vecchio on Monday, when the Uffizi is closed), nearby Fiesole, and, on the return, the church of Santa Croce. A half-day tour costs about 48,000 lire, including museum admissions.

Late-Night Pharmacies

The following are open 24 hours a day, seven days a week. For a complete listing, call ☎ 192. **Comunale No. 13** (⊠ Stazione Centrale di Santa Maria Novella, ☎ 055/289435). **Molteni** (⊠ Via Calzaiuoli 7/r, ☎ 055/289490). **Taverna** (⊠ Piazza San Giovanni 20/r, ☎ 055/284013).

Travel Agencies

American Express (⊠ Via Guicciardini 49/r, near Piazza Pitti, ☎ 055/288751; ⊠ Via Dante Alighiere 20/r, ☎ 055/50981) is also represented by **Universalturismo** (⊠ Via Speziali 7/r, off Piazza della Repubblica, ☎ 055/217241). **CIT** (⊠ Via Cavour 56, ☎ 055/294306; ⊠ Piazza Stazione 51, ☎ 055/2396963). **Thomas Cook** is represented by **World Vision** (⊠ Via Cavour 154/r, ☎ 055/579294).

Villa Rentals

Florence and Abroad (⊠ Via S. Zanobi 58, 50100 Florence, ☎ 055/470603). **Chianti e Terre di Toscana** (⊠ Via S. Maria Macerata 23/a, 50020 Montefiridolfi, ☎ 055/8244211, FAX 055/8244382). **Ville e Casali Toscani** (⊠ Via delle Scuole12, 53010 Rosia (Siena), ☎ 0577/344901, FAX 0577/344800).

Visitor Information

Ufficio Informazione Turistiche Commune di Firenze (Florence Tourist Information Office; ⊠ Via Cavour 1/r, next to Palazzo Medici-Riccardi, 50100, ☎ 055/290832; ⊠ Inside Stazione Centrale di Santa Maria Novella, ☎ 055/212245; ⊠ Piazza della Signoria, Chiasso dei Baroncelli 17/r, 50100, ☎ 055/2302124).

4 Tuscany

*Lucca, Siena, Chianti,
and the Hill Towns*

*Punctuated by thickly wooded hills,
sun-warmed vineyards, olive groves,
and dramatic hill towns, Tuscany's
milk-and-honey vistas have changed
little since Renaissance artists first
beheld them. Siena, a maze of steep
cobbled lanes spilling into its fan-shape
piazza, rivals Florence in enchantment.
Grape- and cypress-rich Chianti is the
quintessence of Tuscany.*

Updated by
Jon Eldan,
Nancy Hart,
Carla Lionello,
Patricia Rucidlo

ROME MAY BE THE CAPITAL OF ITALY, but Tuscany is the heart. Stretching from the Apennines to the sea, midway between Milan and Rome, the region is quintessentially Italian, in both its appearance and its history. Its scenic variety is unmatched in Italy; its past has been ignoble—it produced the Guelph-Ghibelline conflict of the Middle Ages—and glorious, for it gave birth to the Renaissance. Its towns are justly famous for their wealth of fine architecture and art, but visitors often go home even more enthusiastic about Tuscany's unspoiled hilly landscapes, about the delicious Chianti wines produced by vineyards on those hills, and about the robust and flavorful Tuscan cooking. Be sure to allot some portion of your time here for leisurely strolls, unhurried meals, and aimless wandering around this peerless countryside, where the true soul of Tuscany is to be found.

Tuscany also produced the Italian language. Thanks to the eminence of their writings, it was the Tuscan dialect of Dante, Petrarch, and Boccaccio, all native sons, that grew to be the national tongue, a fact of which the Tuscans are rightly proud. Today the purest Italian is said to be spoken in the area between Siena and Arezzo, and even visitors with limited textbook Italian can often hear the difference. As they enter the region, the language suddenly becomes much easier to understand and takes on a bell-like clarity and mellifluous beauty unequaled throughout the rest of Italy.

It also takes on a notorious wit. As a common proverb has it, "Tuscans have Paradise in their eyes and the Inferno in their mouths" (a wry reference to Dante), and the sting of their wit is as famous throughout Italy as is the beauty of their speech. Happily, the Tuscans usually reserve their wit for each other and treat visitors with complete and sincere courtesy.

For a long time, the Tuscan hill towns were notorious as well. Even their earliest civilized settlers, the Etruscans, chose their city-sites for defensive purposes (the fortress-town of Fiesole, above Florence, is a fine surviving example). With the end of the Roman Empire, the region fell into disunity, and by the 11th century, Tuscany had evolved into a collection of independent city-states, each city seeking to dominate, and sometimes forcibly overpower, its neighbors. The region then became embroiled in an apparently endless international quarrel between a long succession of popes and Holy Roman Emperors. By the 13th century, Tuscany had become a battleground: The infamous conflict between the Guelphs and the Ghibellines had begun.

The Guelphs and the Ghibellines are the bane of Italian schoolchildren; their infinitely complicated, bloody history is to Italy what the Wars of the Roses are to England. To oversimplify grossly, the Ghibellines were mostly allied with both the Holy Roman Emperor (headquartered over the Alps in Germany) and the local aristocracy (dominated by feudal lords); the Guelphs were mostly allied with both the pope (headquartered in Rome) and the emerging middle class (dominated by the new trade guilds). Florence, flourishing as a trade center, was (most of the time) Guelph; its neighboring city-states Pisa and Siena were (most of the time) Ghibelline. But the bitter struggles that resulted were so Byzantine in their complexity, so full of factional disputes and treachery, that a dizzying series of conflicts within conflicts resulted. (Dante, for instance, was banished from Florence not for being a Ghibelline but for being the wrong brand of Guelph.)

Eventually the Florentine Guelphs emerged victorious, and in the mid-16th century the region was united to become the Grand Duchy of Tuscany under Grand Duke Cosimo I the Great (1519–74). Today the hill towns are no longer fierce, although they retain a uniquely medieval air, and in most of them the citizens walk the same narrow streets and inhabit the same houses that their ancestors did 600 years ago.

Tuscan art, to most people, means Florence, and understandably so. The city is unique and incomparable, and an astonishing percentage of the great artists of the Renaissance lived and worked there. But there is art elsewhere in Tuscany, and too often it is overlooked in favor of another trip to the Uffizi. Siena, particularly, bears its own style of architecture and art quite different from the Florentine variety; the contrast is both surprising and illuminating. And even the smallest of the hill towns can possess hidden treasures, for the artists of the Middle Ages and the Renaissance took their work where they could find it. Piero della Francesca's fresco cycle in the church of San Francesco in Arezzo is perhaps the preeminent hidden treasure. Tucked away in a small church in a small town, and, sadly, faded, the frescoes are artistically the equal of almost everything Florence has to offer and are all the more appealing for their uncrowded setting.

Pleasures and Pastimes

Dining

Just as the ancient Etruscans introduced cypress to the Tuscan landscape, their influence on regional food—in the use of fresh herbs—still persists after more than three millennia. Earthy and austere, Tuscan food evolved from its peasant and noble past, resulting today in a host of fresh vegetables, wonderful peasant soups, and savory meats and game perfumed with sage, rosemary, and thyme. Day-old saltless Tuscan bread is grilled and drizzled with olive oil (*crostini*), or spread with chicken liver (*crostini di fegatini*), or rubbed with garlic, and topped with tomatoes (*bruschetta* or *fettunta*). For their love of beans—particularly *cannellini* (white kidney beans) simmered in olive oil and herbs until creamy—Tuscans have been disparagingly nicknamed *mangiafagioli* (bean eaters) by Italians from other regions. The region's sheep's milk pecorino cheese, delicious with ripe pears, is even seen at the breakfast table.

Grapes have been cultivated here since Etruscan times, and Chianti still rules the wine roost (almost literally when selected by the Gallo Nero Black Rooster label, a symbol of one of the region's most powerful wine-growing consortiums; the other is a putto, or cherub). The robust red wine is still a staple on most tables, and the discerning can select from a multitude of other varieties, including such reds as Brunello di Montalcino and Vino Nobile di Montepulciano, and whites such as Valdinievole and Vergine della Valdichiana. The dessert wine *vin santo* is produced throughout the region and is often sipped with *biscotti di Prato* (hard almond cookies), perfect for dunking.

CATEGORY	COST*
$$$$	over 110,000 lire
$$$	60,000 lire–110,000 lire
$$	35,000 lire–60,000 lire
$	under 35,000 lire

Prices are per person, for a three-course meal, including house wine and taxes.

Lodging

Staying in Tuscany is not a cheap enterprise, especially in well-traveled cities such as Siena, Lucca, San Gimignano, Arezzo, and Cortona.

But wonderful properties abound, including some fine Renaissance and medieval palazzi, where you'll feel more like Lorenzo de Medici than a 20th-century visitor. To keep costs down, overnight in less-visited towns. You might want to consider the now-popular *agriturismo,* staying on a farm and/or vineyard that has opened its rooms or apartments to guests; choices range from rustic to stately (note that some require a minimum stay). Villa rental can also be an economical and enjoyable option for groups.

CATEGORY	COST*
$$$$	over 350,000 lire
$$$	220,000 lire–350,000 lire
$$	100,000 lire–220,000 lire
$	under 100,000 lire

Prices are for a double room, including tax and service.

Exploring Tuscany

It is best to have a car to travel in Tuscany to fully enjoy the region's riches—it's the only way to get to many of the vineyards and estates. If traveling by public transportation, however, plan on traveling by bus service rather than by train. The cities west of Florence—once embroiled in battle with Florence for control of the sea—are easily reached by the A1, which heads east from Florence towards Arezzo. Florence and Siena are connected by a superstrada and also the panoramic S222, which threads through the wine country of Chianti. The hill towns radiating from Siena lie along superstrade and windy local roads—all are well marked, but you should arm yourself with a good map.

Numbers in the text correspond to numbers in the margin and on the Tuscany, Lucca, Pisa, and Siena maps.

Great Itineraries

Although Tuscany is relatively small—no important destination is more than a few hours' drive from Florence—the desire to linger is strong: Can you really get enough of sitting on a hillside *terrazza* (terrace) with a good espresso or a robust Chianti and watching the evening settle over a landscape of soft-edged hills, proud medieval towns, quiet villages, and cypress-ringed villas?

It only takes a few days for the region to leave an indelible mark on your memory, and even your soul. Seven days would allow for leisurely exploration of the main towns and for meandering along country roads to rustic, grand estates and wineries. In five days, you can see the most interesting towns, but you'll need to stick to the main sights and move briskly. If three days is the limit, you can take in all the highlights, if not the small corners.

IF YOU HAVE 3 DAYS

Florence is a practical starting point. See **Lucca** ④–⑩ and the **Torre Pendente** ⑪ in **Pisa** ⑪–⑱, then head for 🏨 **San Gimignano** ㉑ to overnight. The next day, explore the tangle of medieval alleyways in **Siena** ㉔–㉛ for a few hours, then move on to 🏨 **Montepulciano** ㊳ for the night. The following day, see **Arezzo** ㊶ and head back to Florence via the A1 or, if you have time, drive back to Florence through the windy roads of **Chianti** ㉜–㉞ (via S69 west, S408 west, S429 west, and S222 north).

IF YOU HAVE 5 DAYS

From Florence, head for industrial **Prato** ① to see its striking medieval core; historic **Pistoia** ②, site of bitter Guelph-Ghibelline feuding; and, if you enjoy resorts, **Montecatini Terme** ③, one of Europe's most famous spas. Stay over in 🏨 **Lucca** ④–⑩ and spend part of the next day exploring. Head for **Pisa** ⑪–⑱ to see the **Torre Pendente** ⑪, and then move on to the enchanting hilltop town of **San Miniato** ⑲ and either **Volterra** ⑳ or ▦ **San Gimignano** ㉑, the archetypal Tuscan town and a good place to spend your second night. On the third day, either while away the morning driving through ▦ **Chianti** ㉜–㉞ (where you will inevitably want to settle in for a night), or head directly to ▦ **Siena** ㉔–㉛, perhaps Italy's loveliest medieval city. From Siena see the **Abbazia di Monte Oliveto Maggiore** ㉟, **Montalcino** ㊱, the **Abbazia di Sant'Antimo,** and then ▦ **Montepulciano** ㊳, where you should overnight if you don't stay in Siena. On the morning of your fourth day take a tour of **Pienza** ㊲, designed for Pope Pius II to be the perfect Renaissance town. Move on to handsome but underappreciated ▦ **Cortona** ㊵ and **Arezzo** ㊶, stopping at **Chiusi** and **Chianciano** along the way. Spend part of your fifth day in Cortona or Arezzo, or exploring Chianti before returning to Florence.

IF YOU HAVE 7 DAYS

As you approach **Prato** ①, you'll have time to visit the modern collection at the Centro per l'Arte Contemporanea L. Pecci. If you opt to see the resort town of **Montecatini Terme** ③, take a cure in one of the local *terme* (spas) or ride the funicular up to older Montecatini Alto. Extend your ▦ **Pisa** ⑪–⑱ exploration beyond the Piazza del Duomo to include the Renaissance trio in **Piazza dei Cavalieri** ⑰, then stay the night. From Pisa, you have a choice for your next day and overnight: Either explore timeless **San Miniato** ⑲, ▦ **Volterra** ⑳, and/or ▦ **San Gimignano** ㉑ or head east to wine country. Take the S67 east toward Florence, and before entering the city turn south to pick up the meandering S222, the Strada Chiantigiana that runs through the heart of ▦ **Chianti** ㉜–㉞ to ▦ **Siena** ㉔–㉛ through **Castellina in Chianti** ㉞. Stay the night, perhaps in ▦ **Radda in Chianti** ㉝. From your base in Siena, be sure to visit **Monteriggioni** ㉒, a hilltop hamlet between Siena and Colle di Val d'Elsa encircled by formidable 13th-century walls. Don't forget about the possibility of visiting the Tuscan archipelago, including rugged ▦ **Elba** ㉓ and Montecristo, accessible from Livorno, Piombino (by boat), and Pisa (by air).

From Siena head south to discover ▦ **Montepulciano** ㊳, **Pienza** ㊲, and **Montalcino** ㊱. For a moving sight, detour southwest of Siena to the **Abbazia di San Galgano** ㊴. East of Siena and well worth the side trip are ▦ **Cortona** ㊵ and **Arezzo** ㊶, the main hill towns of the Arezzo province. For a taste of a more rugged landscape, don't take the autostrada back to Florence, but detour through the Casentino, a mountainous region blanketed with a vast forest that is a far cry from the pastoral images associated with Tuscany. You'll take the winding S70 (via S71 and S67), called the Consuma, a splendidly scenic road wrought with hairpin turns and blind corners that challenge even the best drivers.

When to Tour Tuscany

In summer, try to arrive in towns early in the morning to avoid crowds and the often oppressive heat. Rising early will not be hard, as Tuscany is not about late nights; most bars close their shutters at midnight. If you plan to visit the frescoes in the Palazzo Pubblico in Siena at midday, be prepared to wait in line and, once inside, to be shuffled along by iron-willed guardians eager to see you in and out in the fastest time possible. If you want to photograph the towers of San Gimignano from a distance, do it in early morning, when the light is good and lines of neon-color, diesel-spewing tour buses snaking up the hill will not ruin a perfect picture.

WESTERN TUSCANY

Set in the shadows of the rugged coastal Alpi Apuane, where Michelangelo quarried his marble, this area isn't as lush as the south and lacks its vineyards and olive groves. The population centers here are sprawling cities, some fringed with industrial areas, but worthy of exploration for their stunning medieval and Renaissance centers.

Prato

❶ *17 km (11 mi) northwest of Florence, 60 km (37 mi) east of Lucca.*

The wool industry in this city, one of the world's largest manufacturers of cloth, was known throughout Europe as early as the 13th century. It was further stimulated in the 14th century by a local cloth merchant, Francesco di Marco Datini, who built his business, according to one of his surviving ledgers, "in the name of God and of profit."

Prato's 11th-century Romanesque **Duomo** is famous for its **Cappella del Sacro Cingolo** (Chapel of the Holy Girdle), to the left of the entrance, which enshrines the sash of the Virgin. It is said that the girdle was given to the apostle Thomas by the Virgin herself when she miraculously appeared after her Assumption. The Duomo also contains 15th-century frescoes by Prato's most famous son, Fra Filippo Lippi (1406–69), who executed scenes from the life of St. Stephen on the left wall and scenes from the life of John the Baptist on the right in the **Cappella Maggiore** (Main Chapel). Bring a flashlight: No illumination is provided. ⊠ *Piazza del Duomo.* ✆ *May–Oct., daily 7–noon and 3:30–7:30; Nov.–Apr., daily 7–noon and 3:30–6:30.*

A sculpture by Donatello that originally adorned the Duomo's exterior pulpit is now on display in the **Museo dell'Opera del Duomo.** ⊠ *Piazza del Duomo 49,* ☎ *0574/29339.* 🎟 *5,000 lire (includes entry to Museo di Pittura Murale;* ☞ *below).* ✆ *Mon. and Wed.–Sat. 9:30–12:30 and 3–6:30, Sun. 9:30–12:30.*

Installed in the **Museo di Pittura Murale** (Museum of Mural Painting) is a fine collection of paintings by Fra Filippo Lippi and other works from the 13th–15th centuries in a special exhibit called "Treasures of the City," on view until 2000. The permanent collection contains frescoes removed from sites in Prato and environs. ⊠ *Piazza San Domenico,* ☎ *0574/29339.* 🎟 *5,000 lire (includes Museo dell'Opera del Duomo).* ✆ *Mon. and Wed.–Sat. 10–1 and 3:30–7:30, Sun. 3:30–7:30.*

Prato's **Centro per l'Arte Contemporanea L. Pecci** (L. Pecci Center of Contemporary Art) has acquired a burgeoning collection of works by Italian and other artists. ⊠ *Viale della Repubblica 277,* ☎ *0574/570620.* 🎟 *10,000 lire.* ✆ *Mon. and Wed.–Sun. 10–7.*

OFF THE BEATEN PATH

POGGIO A CAIANO – For a look at gracious country living, Renaissance style, detour south of Prato to the Medici villa Poggio a Caiano. Lorenzo the Magnificent (1449–92) commissioned Giuliano da Sangallo (circa 1445–1516) to redo the villa, which was lavished with frescoes by important Renaissance painters such as Andrea del Sarto (1486–1530) and Pontormo (1494–1557). You can take a walk around the lovely grounds while waiting for the mandatory group tour to begin. ⊠ *7 km (4½ mi) south of Prato, follow signs,* ☎ *055/877012.* 🎟 *4,000 lire.* ✆ *Apr.–May and Sept., Mon.–Sat. 9–5:30; June–Aug., Mon.–Sat. 9–6:30; Mar. and Oct., Mon.–Sat. 9–4:30; Nov.–Feb., Mon.–Sat. 9–3:30. Guided tours only, hourly on the half hour (9:30–1 hr before closing). Closed 2nd and 3rd Mon. of month. Ticket office closes 1 hr before villa and grounds.*

Tuscany

Dining

$$$ ✗ **Da Delfina.** Veer off the autostrada (after making reservations) to
★   this haven of Tuscan cooking nestled amid vineyards and olive trees
      past Poggio a Caiano in Artimino. Delfina began cooking for hungry
      area hunters, and now she has four comfortably rustic dining rooms
      in a farmhouse where you can enjoy dishes centered around pure in-
      gredients, seasonal vegetables, and savory meats accented with herbs.
      Everything is good: the fegatini; seasonal pasta—always homemade;
      and the *secondi* (second courses) such as *coniglio con olive e pignoli*
      (rabbit sautéed with olives and pine nuts). ⊠ *Via della Chiesa 1, Ar-
      timino,* ☎ *055/8718074. Reservations essential. No credit cards.
      Closed Mon., Jan., and Aug. No dinner Sun.*

$$$ ✗ **Piraña.** Oddly named for the cannibalistic fish swimming in an
      aquarium with a full view of the diners, this sophisticated restaurant,
      decorated in shades of blue with steely accents, is a local favorite. Seafood
      is the specialty and may take the form of ravioli *di branzino in crema
      di scampi* (stuffed with sea bass with a creamy shrimp sauce) and
      rombo al forno (baked turbot). It's a bit out of the way for sightseers
      but handy if you have a car, as it's near the Prato Est autostrada exit.
      ⊠ *Via G. Valentini 110,* ☎ *0574/25746. AE, DC, MC, V. Closed Sun.
      and Aug. No lunch Sat.*

$$ ✗ **Baghino.** In the heart of the historic center, Baghino serves typical
      Tuscan fare as well as atypical Tuscan fare like spaghetti *all'amatri-
      ciana* (with bacon in a spicy tomato sauce) and penne *con vongole e
      curry* (with clams and curry). You can dine in the lovely outdoor ter-
      race in summer. ⊠ *Via dell'Accademia 9,* ☎ *055/27920, AE, DC, MC,
      V. No dinner Sun., no lunch Mon.*

Shopping

Prato's biscotti (literally "twice cooked") have an extra-dense texture,
lending themselves to submersion in your caffè or vin santo. The best
in town are at **Antonio Mattei** (⊠ Via Ricasoli 20/22).

Pistoia

❷   *18 km (11 mi) northwest of Prato, 36 km (22 mi) northwest of Flo-
    rence, 40 km (25 mi) east of Lucca, 108 km (67 mi) north of Siena.*

Pistoia saw the beginning of the bitter Guelph-Ghibelline conflict of
the Middle Ages. Reconstructed after heavy bombing during World War
II, it has preserved some fine Romanesque architecture. The **Cattedrale
di San Zeno** in the main piazza houses the *Dossale di San Jacopo,* a
magnificent silver altar. The two half-figures on its left side were exe-
cuted by Filippo Brunelleschi (1377–1446). ⊠ *Piazza del Duomo.* ☎
0573/25095, 🎟 *Illumination of altarpiece 1,500 lire.* ☉ *Daily 9–
noon and 4–7.*

The **Palazzo del Comune,** begun in 1295, houses the **Museo Civico,**
containing mostly works by local artists from the 14th to 20th cen-
turies. ⊠ *Museo Civico, Piazza del Duomo,* ☎ *0573/371296.* 🎟
5,000 lire; free Sat. 3–7. ☉ *Tues.–Sat. 10–7, Sun. 9–12:30.*

Founded in the 13th century, the **Ospedale del Ceppo** reveals a superb
early 16th-century exterior terra-cotta frieze by the workshop of Santi
and Benedetto Buglioni; it was completed by Giovanni della Robbia
in 1527. ⊠ *Piazza Ospedale, a short way down Via Pacini from Pi-
azza del Duomo.*

In the church of **Sant'Andrea** (⊠ Via Pappe to Via Sant'Andrea), the
fine pulpit (1298–1301) by Giovanni Pisano (1270–circa 1348) de-
picts scenes from the life of Christ.

Ⓒ A 20-minute drive out of town is the **Giardino Zoologico,** a small zoo especially laid out to accommodate the wiles of both animals and children. Take Bus 29 from the train station. ⊠ *Via Pieve a Celle 160/a, Pistoia,* ☎ *0573/911219.* ⊇ *13,000.* ◷ *Apr.–Sept., daily 9–7; Oct.–Mar., daily 9–5.*

Dining

$$ ✕ **Corradossi.** This lovely restaurant is a short walk from Piazza del Duomo, and makes an excellent place to break for lunch or dinner. The food is ornate yet simple, service quick and attentive, and the prices more than reasonable. The menu offers a wide range of options from all over Italy. Start with the *trofie e gamberi,* (corkscrew-shape pasta sauced with perfectly cooked shrimp and sliced baby zucchini), then follow with their *fritte miste* (little sea critters crisply fried). ⊠ *Via Frosini 112,* ☎ *0573/25683. AE, DC, MC, V. Closed Sun.*

$$ ✕ **Rafanelli.** *Maccheroni all'anatra* (pasta with duck sauce) and other game dishes—the specialties here—have been prepared with attention to tradition and quality for more than half a century by the same family. The restaurant is just outside the old city walls in a garden setting with alfresco dining in summer. ⊠ *Via Sant'Agostino 47,* ☎ *0573/532046. AE, DC, MC, V. Closed Mon. and Aug. No dinner Sun.*

$$ ✕ **S. Jacopo.** This charming restaurant, minutes away from the Piazza del Duomo, has white walls, tiled floors, and a gracious host in Bruno Lottini, a native Pistoian fluent in English. The food is as welcoming as he: Bread, flecked with olives, is baked on the premises and arrives hot to the table. The menu has mostly regional favorites, such as the maccheroni S. Jacopo, wide ribbons of house-made pasta with a duck *ragù* (duck sauce), but they can turn out perfectly grilled squid as well. Save room for dessert, especially the apple strudel. ⊠ *Via Crispi 15,* ☎ *0573/27786. AE, DC, MC, V. Closed Mon. No lunch Tues.*

Montecatini Terme

❸ *16 km (10 mi) west of Pistoia, 49 km (30 mi) west of Florence, 55 km (33 mi) northeast of Pisa.*

Immortalized in Fellini's 8½, Montecatini Terme is home to Italy's premier *terme* (spas), reputed for their curative powers and, at least once upon a time, for their great popularity among the wealthy. It is renowned for its mineral springs, which flow from five sources and are used to treat liver and skin disorders. Those "taking the cure" report each morning to one of the town's *stabilimenti termali* (thermal establishments; information: ⊠ Via Verdi 41, ☎ 0572/778451) to drink their prescribed cupful of water, whose curative effects became known in the 1800s. The town's wealth of Art Nouveau buildings went up during its most active period of development, at the beginning of this century. Like most well-heeled resort towns, Montecatini attracts the leisured traveler; aside from taking the waters and people-watching in Piazza del Popolo, there's not a whole lot to do here. Of these structures, the most attractive is the **Terme Tettuccio** (⊠ Viale Verdi 71, ☎ 0572/778501), a neoclassical edifice with colonnades. Here Montecatini's healthful tonic spouts from fountains set up on marble counters, the walls are decorated with bucolic scenes depicted on painted ceramic tiles, and an orchestra plays under a frescoed dome.

The older town of **Montecatini Alto** sits on top of a hill above the spa town and is reached by a funicular from Viale Diaz. A medieval square is lined with restaurants and bars, the air is crisp, and the views of the Nievole, the valley below, are gorgeous.

Lodging

$$$ ⚇ **Croce di Malta.** Taste and sophistication have been the calling cards of this hotel since 1911. It's a short walk on tree-lined streets from town center and it's even closer to the thermal baths. Rooms are spacious, with high ceilings; many have deep bathtubs with water jets. You can enjoy an *aperitivo* (aperitif) in the majestic lobby before dining at the hotel's Tuscan restaurant. ⊠ *Viale IV Novembre 18, 51016,* ☎ *0572/9201,* FAX *0572/767516. 119 rooms, 19 suites. Restaurant, bar, pool, exercise room, convention center. AE, DC, MC, V.*

Lucca

★ *27 km (17 mi) west of Montecatini Terme, 74 km (46 mi) southeast of La Spezia.*

It was in this picturesque fortress town that Caesar, Pompey, and Crassus agreed to rule Rome as a triumvirate in 56 BC; it was later the first town in Tuscany to accept Christianity. Lucca still has a mind of its own, and when most of Tuscany was voting communist as a matter of course, its citizens rarely followed suit. The town is best explored on foot. Within the city's 16th- to 17th-century ramparts, the famous composer Giacomo Puccini (1858–1924) was born; he is celebrated, along with his peers, during the summer Opera Theater of Lucca Festival.

★ ❹ The round-arched facade of the **Duomo** is a fine example of the rigorously ordered Pisan Romanesque style, in this case happily enlivened by an extremely disordered collection of small carved columns. Take a closer look at the decoration of the facade and that of the portico below, making for one of the most entertaining church exteriors in Tuscany. The Gothic interior contains a moving Byzantine crucifix (called the Volto Santo, or Holy Face), brought here in the 8th century, and the masterpiece of the Sienese sculptor Jacopo della Quercia (1374–1438), the marble *Tomb of Ilaria del Caretto* (1406). ⊠ *Piazza del Duomo.* 🎫 *3,000 lire.* ☉ *Apr.–Oct., daily 7–7; Nov.–Mar., daily 7–5.*

❺ Slightly west of town center is the church of **San Michele** (⊠ Piazza San Michele), with a facade even more fanciful than the Duomo's; it was heavily restored in the 19th century, however, and somewhat jarringly displays busts of modern Italian patriots such as Garibaldi (1807–82) and ❻ Cavour (1810–61). The church of **San Frediano** (⊠ Piazza San Frediano, just inside the middle of the north town wall) contains more works by Jacopo della Quercia, and, bizarrely, the lace-clad mummy of the patron saint of domestic servants, Santa Zita. Southeast of the north town ❼ wall is **Piazza del Mercato,** where the **Anfiteatro Romano,** or Roman amphitheater, once stood. The piazza takes its oval shape from the theater, but the tiers disappeared when medieval houses were built on top of them.

❽ The highlights of the **Pinacoteca Nazionale** are the lovely *Portrait of a Youth* by Pontormo and portraits of the Medici painted by Bronzino and others. ⊠ *Palazzo Mansi, Via Galli Tassi 43, near the west walls of the old city,* ☎ *0583/55570.* 🎫 *8,000 lire.* ☉ *Tues.–Sat. 9–7, Sun. 9–2.*

❾ On the eastern end of the historic center, the **Museo Nazionale Guinigi** houses an extensive collection of local Romanesque and Renaissance art. ⊠ *Villa Guinigi, Via della Quarquonia,* ☎ *0583/46033.* 🎫 *4,000 lire.* ☉ *May–Sept., Tues.–Sun. 9–7; Oct.–Apr., Tues.–Sun. 9–2.*

❿ The tower of the medieval **Palazzo Guinigi,** contains one of the city's most curious sights: A grove of ilex trees has grown at the top of the tower, and their roots have grown into the room below. From the top, you will have a magnificent view of the city and the surrounding countryside. ⊠ *Via Guinigi.* 🎫 *4,500 lire.* ☉ *Daily 10–4:30.*

Lucca

Duomo, **4**
Museo Nazionale
Guinigi, **9**
Palazzo Guinigi, **10**
Piazza del Mercato, **7**

Pinacoteca
Nazionale, **8**
San Frediano, **6**
San Michele, **5**

OFF THE
BEATEN PATH

VILLA REALE – Eight kilometers (5 miles) north of Lucca in Marlia, this villa was once the home of Napoléon's sister, Princess Elisa. Restored by the Counts Pecci-Blunt, this estate is celebrated for its spectacular gardens, laid out in the 18th and 19th centuries. Gardening buffs adore the legendary *teatro di verdura*, a theater carved out of hedges and topiaries; concerts are occasionally offered here. One of Tuscany's most popular summer events, the Festival di Marlia, is held in Marlia in July and August; contact the Lucca tourist office (⊠ Piazzale Verdi, ☎ 0583/419689) for details. ⊠ *Villa Reale,* ☎ *0583/30108.* ✆ *8,000 lire.* ☉ *Guided tours July–Sept., Tues.–Sun. at 10, 11, 4, 5, 6; Oct.– Nov. and Mar.–June, Tues.–Sun. at 10, 11, 3, 4, 5. Closed Dec.–Feb.*

FORTE DEI MARMI – Tuscany's most exclusive summer beach resort is a favorite of moneyed Tuscans and Milanese, whose villas are neatly laid out in an extensive pinewood. In summer, a beachcomber's bonanza takes place on Wednesday mornings, when everything from faux designer sunglasses to plastic sandals and terry-cloth towels goes on sale. It's 35 km (22 mi) northwest of Lucca and 65 km (40 mi) northwest of Florence, and also near the marble-producing towns of Carrara (where Michelangelo also quarried his stone), Seravezza, and Pietrasanta.

Dining and Lodging

$$$ ✕ **Solferino.** About 6 km (4 mi) outside town along the road to Viareggio, this restaurant prepares elegant renditions of Tuscan country-style cooking. Amid fine silver, linens, and crystal, you'll be treated to ingredients from the family farm in such dishes as *tagliolini con pernice rossa* (fresh pasta with partridge sauce). Ask for a piece of *buccellato*, Lucca's dessert bread. ⊠ *San Macario in Piano,* ☎ *0583/ 59118. Reservations essential. AE, DC, MC, V. Closed Wed. and Jan. 7–15. No lunch Thurs.*

$$–$$$ ✕ **La Mora.** Detour to this former stagecoach station, now a gracious,
★ rustic country inn 9 km (5½ mi) outside Lucca, for local specialties— from *minestra di farro* (soup made with emmer, a wheat that resembles barley) with beans to homemade *tacconi* (a thin, short, wide pasta) with rabbit sauce and lamb raised in the nearby Garfagnana hills. You might be tempted by the varied crostini and delicious desserts. ⊠ *Via Sesto di Ponte a Moriano 1748,* ☎ *0583/406402,* ℻ *0583/406135. AE, DC, MC, V. Closed Wed. and Oct. 10–30.*

$$ ✕ **Buca di Sant'Antonio.** This restaurant has been around for more than
★ two centuries, and it's easy to see why. The white-walled interior hung with copper pots, expertly prepared food, and an able staff make dining here a real treat. The menu offers something for everyone—from simple pasta meals to such daring dishes as roast *capretto* (kid) with herbs. ⊠ *Via della Cervia 3,* ☎ *0583/55881. AE, DC, MC, V. Closed Mon. and last 3 wks in July. No dinner Sun.*

$$ ✕ **Da Giulio in Pelleria.** A large trattoria that is quintessentially Tuscan in atmosphere, food, and clientele, this tavern is in one of Lucca's characteristic old neighborhoods near the ramparts and Porta San Donato, and handy to the Pinacoteca Nazionale. The menu features Lucca's specialties, including hearty barley or wheat soups and roasted meats—beware, the portions are generous. ⊠ *Via delle Conce 47,* ☎ *0583/555948. AE, DC, MC, V. Closed Sun.–Mon., and Aug.*

$$ ✕ **Il Giglio.** Just off Piazza Napoleone, this restaurant has quiet, turn-of-the-century charm and classic cuisine. It's a place for all seasons, with a big fireplace and an outdoor terrace in summer. Among the local specialties are *farro garfagnino* (a thick soup made with grain and beans), and *coniglio con olive* (rabbit stew with olives). ⊠ *Piazza del Giglio 3,* ☎ *0583/494508. AE, DC, MC, V. Closed Wed. No dinner Tues.*

$$$$ 🏨 **Locanda l'Elisa.** An intimate Relais & Châteaux hotel in a neoclassical villa, this deluxe spin-off of the adjacent Villa La Principessa (☞ *below*) is a notch higher on the scale of style and comfort. ⊠ *Massa Pisana, 55050,* ☎ *0583/379737,* 🗟 *0583/379019. 10 suites. Restaurant, bar, pool. AE, DC, MC, V.*

$$$$ 🏨 **Villa La Principessa.** This exquisitely decorated 19th-century country mansion is found 3 km (2 mi) outside of Lucca. Some rooms have handsome beamed ceilings, and doors are individually decorated; antique furniture and portraits impart an aura of gracious living. The grounds are well manicured, the pool large and inviting. The restaurant is closed Sunday. ⊠ *Massa Pisana, 55050,* ☎ *0583/370037,* 🗟 *0583/379136. 40 rooms and suites. Restaurant, pool. AE, DC, MC, V. Closed Nov.–Mar.*

$$ 🏨 **La Luna.** On a quiet, airy courtyard close to historic Piazza del Mercato, this family-run hotel occupies two renovated wings of an old building. The bathrooms are modern, but some of the rooms still have the atmosphere of Old Lucca. A parking lot for guests is a bonus. ⊠ *Corte Compagni 12 (corner of Via Fillungo), 55100,* ☎ *0583/493634,* 🗟 *0583/490021. 30 rooms. Free parking. AE, DC, MC, V. Closed last 3 wks in Jan.*

$ 🏨 **Piccolo Hotel Puccini.** Steps away from the busy square and church of San Michele, this little hotel is quiet, calm, and handsomely decorated. It also offers parking (which must be reserved in advance) at a reasonable fee, which is a great advantage. ⊠ *Via di Poggio 9, 55100,* ☎ *0583/ 55421,* 🗟 *0583/53487. 14 rooms. Parking (fee). AE, DC, MC, V.*

Nightlife and the Arts

The **Estate Musicale Lucchese,** one of many music festivals throughout Tuscany, runs throughout the summer in Lucca. Contact the Lucca tourist office (⊠ Piazzale Verdi, ☎ 0583/419689) for details. The **Opera Theater of Lucca Festival,** sponsored by the Opera Theater of Lucca and the music college of the University of Cincinnati, runs from mid-June to mid-July; performances are staged in open-air venues. Call the Lucca tourist office or University of Cincinnati, College-Conservatory of Music (☎ 513/566–5662, 🗟 513/566–0202), for information.

Shopping

Lucca's olive oil, available throughout the city, is exported throughout the world. A particularly delicious version of *buccellato*, a sweet, anise-flavored bread with raisins that is a specialty of Lucca, is baked at **Pasticceria Taddeucci** (⊠ Piazza San Michele 34). On the second Sunday of the month, there's a **flea market** in Piazza San Martino.

Pisa

22 km (14 mi) southwest of Lucca, 75 km (47 mi) south of La Spezia, 22 km (14 mi) north of Livorno, 64 km (40 mi) northwest of Volterra, 77 km (48 mi) west of Florence.

If you get beyond the kitschy atmosphere around the Leaning Tower, Pisa has much to offer. Its cathedral-baptistery-tower complex on Piazza del Duomo is among the most dramatic in Italy. Pisa's treasures are more subtle than Florence's, to which it is inevitably compared. Though it sustained heavy damage during World War II, Pisa and its many beautiful Romanesque structures are still preserved and are well worth seeking out. A combination ticket of 10,000 lire allows entry to two sites on the Piazza del Duomo, and a ticket for 15,000 lire allows entry to all four sites.

You'll want to focus your attention to the **Piazza del Duomo,** also known as the Campo dei Miracoli (Field of Miracles), at the city's northwestern edge. On it stand the Duomo, Baptistery, and famous Leaning Tower.

Pisa

⓫ Begun in 1174, the **Torre Pendente** (Leaning Tower) was the last of the three structures to be built, and the lopsided settling began when construction reached the third story. The tower's architects attempted to compensate by making the remaining floors slightly taller on the leaning side, but the extra weight only made the problem worse. The settling has continued, and a few years ago it accelerated to a point that led many to fear it would simply topple over, despite all efforts to prop the structure up. Now it has been firmly anchored to the earth. Legend holds that Galileo conducted an experiment on the nature of gravity by dropping metal balls from the top of the 187-ft-high tower; historians say this legend has no basis in fact (which is not quite to say that it is false). The tower is not open to the public, but you have a great view of its leanings from the outside. ⊠ *Campo dei Miracoli.*

⓬ The **Duomo** was the first building to use the horizontal marble stripe motif (borrowed from Moorish architecture in the 11th century) common to Tuscan cathedrals. It is famous for the Romanesque panels on the transept door facing the tower, which depict the life of Christ, and for its beautifully carved 14th-century pulpit, by Giovanni Pisano. ⊠ *Piazza del Duomo.* ⊞ *2,000 lire (free Oct.–Mar.).* ☉ *Apr.–Sept., Mon.–Sat. 10–7:40, Sun 1–5; Oct.–Mar., daily 10–12:30 and 3–5:30.*

⓭ The lovely Gothic **Battistero,** which stands across from the Duomo's facade, is best known for the pulpit carved by Giovanni's father, Nicola, in 1260. Ask one of the ticket takers if he'll sing for you inside the baptistery. The acoustics are remarkable; a tip of 5,000 lire is appropriate. ⊠ *Piazza del Duomo.* ⊞ *10,000 lire, includes entry to 1 other site.* ☉ *Daily 10–7:40.*

The walled area on the northern side of the Campo dei Miracoli is the ⓮ **Camposanto** (Cemetery), which is filled, according to legend, with earth brought back from the Holy Land during the Crusades. Its galleries contain numerous frescoes, notably *The Drunkenness of Noah,* by Renaissance artist Benozzo Gozzoli, and the disturbing *Triumph of Death* (14th century), whose authorship is disputed, but whose subject matter shows what was on people's minds in a century that saw the ravages of the Black Death. ⊠ *Camposanto,* ☎ *050/560547.* 🖃 *10,000 lire plus entry to 1 other site.* ☉ *Apr.–Oct., daily 8–7:30; Nov.– Mar., daily 9–5:30.*

At the southeast corner of the sprawling Campo dei Miracoli, the
⑮ **Museo dell'Opera del Duomo** holds a wealth of medieval sculptures and the ancient Roman sarcophagi that inspired Nicola Pisano's figures. ⊠ *Via Arcivescovado,* ☎ *050/560547.* 🖃 *10,000 lire plus entry to 1 other site.* ☉ *Apr.–Oct., daily 9–7:30; Nov.–Mar., daily 9–5:30.*

⑯ The well-arranged **Museo delle Sinopie** across the street, on the south side of the square, holds the *sinopie,* or preparatory drawings, for the Camposanto frescoes and is of limited interest to most tourists. ⊠ *Piazza del Duomo,* ☎ *050/560547.* 🖃 *10,000 lire.* 🖃 *Combined admission to Battistero, Camposanto, and museums: 10,000 lire for any 2 sites; 15,000 lire for all 4.* ☉ *Apr.–Oct., daily 8–7:40; Nov.–Mar., daily 9–5:40.*

⑰ In the center of town, **Piazza dei Cavalieri** was laid out by Giorgio Vasari (1511–74) in about 1560 and is central to some fine Renaissance buildings: the **Palazzo dei Cavalieri,** the **Palazzo dell'Orologio,** and the church of **Santo Stefano dei Cavalieri.** Vasari, who was an artist as well as an architect, also wrote *Lives of the Artists* in the mid-sixteenth century and is known as the first art historian.

⑱ Along the northern side of the Arno, the **Museo Nazionale di San Matteo** contains some incisive examples of local Romanesque and Gothic art. ⊠ *Lungarno Mediceo,* ☎ *050/541865.* 🖃 *8,000 lire.* ☉ *Tues.– Sat. 9–7, Sun. 9–1:30.*

Dining and Lodging

$$ ✕ **Bruno.** A pleasant restaurant with beamed ceilings and the look of a country inn, Bruno is just outside Pisa's old city walls, a short walk from the bell tower and cathedral. Dine on classic Tuscan dishes, from *zuppa alla pisana* (a thick vegetable soup) to *baccalà* (cod) with leeks. ⊠ *Via Luigi Bianchi 12,* ☎ *050/560818. AE, DC, MC, V. Closed Tues. No dinner Mon.*

$$ ✕ **La Pergoletta.** On an old town street named for its "beautiful towers," this restaurant in a medieval tower is small and simple, with a shady garden for outdoor dining. The signora who is the owner-cook offers traditional Tuscan minestra di farro and *grigliata* (grilled beef, veal, or lamb). ⊠ *Via delle Belle Torri 36,* ☎ *050/542458. MC, V. Closed Mon. and Aug.*

$$ ✕ **Osteria dei Cavalieri.** This charming white-walled *osteria* (restaurant), a few steps from Piazza dei Cavalieri, is reason enough to come to Pisa. They can do it all here—serve up exquisitely grilled fish dishes, please vegetarians, and prepare *tagliata,* thin slivers of rare beef, four different ways. Three set menus, from the sea, garden, and earth, are put together for you, or you can order à la carte—which can be agonizing because everything sounds so good. And it is. Finish your meal with a lemon sorbet bathed in Prosecco (dry sparkling wine), and walk away feeling like you've eaten like a king at plebeian prices. ⊠ *Via San Frediano 16,* ☎ *055/580858. AE, DC, MC, V. Closed Sun. and July 25–Aug. 25. No lunch Sat.*

$$$ 🏨 **Cavalieri.** Opposite the railway station, in an unremarkable 1950s building, this Jolly Group hotel offers functional, modern comforts in completely soundproof and air-conditioned rooms, all with color TVs

and minibars. The restaurant specializes in homemade pasta and seafood and is open every day. ⊠ *Piazza della Stazione 2, 56100,* ☎ *050/43290,* 𝔽𝔸𝕏 *050/502242. 100 rooms, 3 suites. Restaurant, bar. AE, DC, MC, V.*

$$ 🏨 **Fattoria di Migliarino.** Martino Salviati and his wife Giovanna have turned their working farm (soy, corn, sugar beets) 15 minutes from Pisa into a working inn: Their *fattoria* (farm) is now seven charming, spacious apartments (putting up from 2–8 people), each complete with kitchen, and many with fireplaces. The pool is framed by fields, and the only sound you're likely to hear is the clucking of the hens they keep for eggs. The surrounding woods can be explored by horse or by mountain bike. There is a two-night minimum stay. Migliarino is convenient to Lucca, Florence, and sandy beaches (5-minute drive). ⊠ *Viale dei Pini 289, Migliarino, 56010,* ☎ *050/803046,* 𝔽𝔸𝕏 *050/803170. 7 apartments. Pool, horseback riding. MC, V.*

$$ 🏨 **Royal Victoria.** In a pleasant palazzo facing the Arno, a 10-minute walk from the Campo dei Miracoli, this hotel is about as close as Pisa comes to old-world ambience. It's comfortably furnished, with antiques and reproductions in the lobby and in some rooms, whose style ranges from the 1800s, complete with frescoes, to the 1920s. ⊠ *Lungarno Pacinotti 12, 56100,* ☎ *050/940111,* 𝔽𝔸𝕏 *050/940180. 48 rooms, 8 without bath. AE, DC, MC, V.*

WEST OF SIENA

The reasons to explore San Miniato, Volterra, San Gimignano, and the other enchanting fortified cities west of Siena and south of the A1 are to behold fine art and architecture and striking views, which are particularly stirring in San Miniato, a peaceful hill town with medieval architectural lines and billowy landscape curves in the distance.

San Miniato

★ ⑲   *42 km (26 mi) southeast of Pisa, 43 km (27 mi) southwest of Florence, 66 km (41 mi) northwest of Siena.*

Dating from Etruscan and Roman times, San Miniato was so named when the Lombards erected a church here in the 8th century and consecrated it to San Miniato. The Holy Roman Empire had very strong ties to San Miniato; in fact, the castle was built in 962 under the aegis of Otto I (912–973). Today the pristine, tiny hill town's narrow, cobbled streets are lined with austere 13th–17th century facades, some of them built over already centuries-old buildings. Its artistic treasures are somewhat limited in comparison with Florence, but it's well worth the trip simply because the town is so pretty. St. Francis founded the 1211 **Convento e Chiesa di San Francesco** (Convent and Church of St. Francis), containing two cloisters and an ornate wooden choir. For a dose of monastic living, you can stay overnight (☞ Lodging, *below*). ⊠ *Piazza San Francesco,* ☎ *0571/43051.* ☉ *Daily 9–noon and 3–7 (or ring bell).*

Although the **Museo Diocesano** is small, the modest collection incorporates a number of subtle and pleasant local works of art. Note the rather odd Fra Filippo Lippi *Crucifixion,* Verrocchio's (1435–88) *Il Redentore,* and the small but exquisite *Education of the Virgin* by Tiepolo (1696–1770). ⊠ *Piazza del Castello,* ☎ *0571/418271.* 💷 *2,000 lire.* ☉ *Easter–Jan. 6, daily 9–noon and 2:30–5; Jan. 7–Easter, weekends 9–noon and 2:30–5.*

Lodging

$ 🏨 **Convento San Francesco.** For a complete change of pace, you can stay in this 13th-century monastery in the company of five Franciscan friars. Rooms are simple, bordering on spartan, but clean and quiet. You are given keys, so you're not expected home by a certain time. You can partake in some spiritual activities, or skip them altogether. All rooms have baths, and there are five rooms shared by groups. It's a short 10-minute walk from the center. ⊠ *Piazza San Francesco, 56020,* ☎ *0571/43051,* FAX *0571/4398. 70 rooms. No credit cards.*

Volterra

20 *64 km (40 mi) southwest of Pisa, 50 km (31 mi) west of Siena.*

Unlike other Tuscan hill towns that rise above sprawling vineyards and rolling fields of green, Volterra—recorded by D. H. Lawrence in his *Etruscan Places* as standing "somber and chilly alone on her rock"— is surrounded by bleak terrain marred with industry and mining equipment. The fortress, walls, and gates still stand mightily over Le Balze, a stunning series of gullied hills and valleys to the west that were formed by irregular erosion. The town has long been known for its alabaster, which has been mined since Etruscan times; today the Volterrans use it to make ornaments and souvenirs sold all over town.

Volterra is home to some of Italy's best small museums. The **Museo Etrusco Guarnacci** has a magnificent collection of Etruscan funeral urns found in nearby excavations. ⊠ *Via Don Minzoni 15,* ☎ *0588/ 86347.* 🎟 *12,000 lire for entry to Museo Etrusco, Pinacoteca, and Museo di Arte Sacra.* ☉ *Mid-Mar.–Oct., daily 9–7; Nov.–mid-Mar., 9–2.*

The **Pinacoteca e Museo Civico** houses a highly acclaimed collection of religious art, including Luca Signorelli's *Madonna and Child with Saints* and Rosso Fiorentino's *Deposition.* ⊠ *Via dei Sarti 1,* ☎ *0588/87580.* 🎟 *12,000 lire for entry to Museo Etrusco, Pinacoteca, and Museo di Arte Sacra.* ☉ *Mid-Mar.–Oct., daily 9–7; Nov.–mid-Mar, daily 9–2.*

The impressive facade of medieval **Palazzo dei Priori** (⊠ Piazza dei Priori) is adorned with Florentine medallions and a large five-sided tower. Next to the altar in the town's unfinished **Duomo** are the over-restored 13th-century *Deposition* and Jacopo della Quercia's terra-cotta *Our Lady of Acolytes.* ⊠ *Piazza San Giovanni,* ☎ *0588/86192.* 🎟 *Free.* ☉ *Daily 7–7.*

Original works from the Duomo and adjacent Baptistery are in the **Museo di Arte Sacra.** ⊠ *Via Roma 7,* ☎ *0588/86290.* 🎟 *12,000 lire for entry to Museo Etrusco, Pinacoteca, and Museo di Arte Sacra.* ☉ *Mid-Mar– Oct., daily 9–1 and 3–6; Nov.–mid-Mar., daily 9–1.*

Two of Volterra's best-preserved ancient remains are the **Teatro Romano,** just north of the city gates, open daily 10–5, and the Etruscan **Porta all'Arco,** a 3rd-century arch incorporated into the city walls.

Dining and Lodging

$$ ✗ **Etruria.** Turn-of-the-century frescoes on the walls and outdoor dining in the warm weather denote this restaurant on the town's main square. An array of local game is used in such specialties as *pappardelle alla lepre* (broad noodles in hare sauce) and *cinghiale alla maremmana* (roast boar stewed with olives). ⊠ *Piazza dei Priori 8,* ☎ *0588/ 86064. AE, DC, MC, V. Closed Thurs.*

$$ 🏨 **San Lino.** In a former convent, this hotel has modern comforts and its own regional restaurant. On top of that, it's within the town walls, a 10-minute walk from the main piazza. ⊠ *Via San Lino 26, 56048,* ☎ *0588/85250,* FAX *0588/80620. 43 rooms. Restaurant, pool. AE, DC, MC, V. Closed Nov.*

Shopping

A number of shops in Volterra sell boxes, jewelry, and other objects made of alabaster. The **Cooperativa Artieri Alabastro** (⊠ Piazza dei Priori 5, ☎ 0588/87590) has two large showrooms in a medieval building with an array of alabaster objects. In a former medieval monastery, the **Galleria Agostiniane** showrooms (⊠ Piazza XX Settembre 3, ☎ 0588/86868) craft alabaster objects of all kinds. Visitors can see a free video on how the mineral is quarried and carved. At the **Rossi** (⊠ Via Lungo Mura del Mandorlo, ☎ 0588/86133) you can actually see the craftsmen at work; there are objects for all tastes and budgets.

San Gimignano

★ ㉑ *27 km (17 mi) east of Volterra, 57 km (35 mi) southwest of Florence, 31 km (19 mi) northwest of Siena.*

When you're high on a hill surrounded by crumbling towers in silhouette against the blue sky, it's difficult not to fall under the medieval spell of San Gimignano. Its high walls and narrow streets are typical of Tuscan hill towns, but it is the surviving medieval "skyscrapers" that set the town apart from its neighbors and give the town a uniquely photogenic silhouette. Today 14 towers remain, but at the height of the Guelph-Ghibelline conflict there was a forest of more than 70, and it was possible to cross the town by rooftop rather than road. The towers were built partly for defensive purposes—they were a safe refuge and useful for pouring boiling oil on attacking enemies—and partly to bolster the egos of their owners, who competed with deadly seriousness to build the highest tower in town. When the Black Plague devastated the population in 1348, power and independence faded fast and civic autonomy was ultimately surrendered to Florence.

Today, San Gimignano isn't much more than a gentrified walled city, amply prepared for its booming tourist trade, but still very much worth exploring. Unfortunately, tour groups arrive early and clog the wine-tasting rooms—San Gimignano is famous for its light white Vernaccia wine—and art galleries for the majority of the day, but most sights are open through late afternoon during summer. Escape midday to the uninhabited areas outside the city walls for a hike and a picnic, and return to explore the town in the afternoon and evening, when things quiet down and the long shadows cast by the imposing towers take on fascinating shapes. You can buy a 16,000-lire combination ticket valid for all San Gimignano museums and the Cappella di Santa Fina.

The town's most important medieval buildings are clustered around the central **Piazza del Duomo.** The imposing **Torre Grossa** is the biggest tower in town, with views that are well worth the climb. ⊠ *Piazza del Duomo 1.* 🎫 *8,000 lire.* ☉ *Mar.–Oct., daily 9:30–7:30; Nov.–Feb., Tues.–Sun. 9:30–1 and 2:30–5.*

The **Palazzo del Popolo** houses the **Museo Civico,** featuring Taddeo di Bartolo's celebratory *Bethroned San Gimignano and Stories from His Life.* San Gimignano, a bishop of Modena, was sainted because he drove hordes of barbarians out of the city in the 10th century. Dante visited San Gimignano for only one day in 1300 as a Guelph ambassador, but it was long enough to get a room named after him, which now holds a *Maestà* by Lippo Memmi. A small room contains frescoes by Memmo di Filipuccio (1294–1324) depicting the courtship, shared bath, and wedding of a young, androgynous-looking couple. Recent scholarship indicates that this may actually be the story of a young man's initiation with a prostitute; either way, it's quite an unusual commission for a public palazzo. ⊠ *Palazzo Minucci-Solaini, Via* *dei Sarti 1,* ☎ *0577/87580.* 🎫 *7,000 lire.* ☉ *Mar.–Oct., daily 9:30–7:30; Nov.–Feb., Tues.–Sun. 9:30–1 and 2:30–5.*

The Romanesque **Collegiata** is a treasure trove of fine frescoes, including Bartolo di Fredi's 14th-century *Old Testament Scenes*. Taddeo di Bartolo's otherworldly *Last Judgment,* on the arch just inside the facade, depicts distorted and suffering nudes—avant-garde for such an early work. The New Testament scenes on the opposite wall, mostly done by Barna da Siena just 14 years later, suggest a more reserved, balanced Renaissance manner. The **Cappella di Santa Fina** contains fine frescoes of the story of this local saint by Domenico Ghirlandaio (1449–94). ⊠ *Piazza del Duomo,* ☎ *0577/940316.* 🎫 *3,000 lire.* ☉ *Daily 9:30–12:30 and 3–5:30.*

The **Museo di Criminologia Medievale** (Museum of Medieval Criminology) displays what was on the cutting edge in medieval torture technology, replete with operating instructions and a clear description of the intended effect. The museum was in part created to illustrate the inherent racism and sexism in certain torture devices and to show how they've been updated for current use around the world. ⊠ *Via del Castello,* ☎ *0577/942243.* 🎫 *10,000 lire.* ☉ *Daily 10–1 and 2–7.*

Before leaving San Gimignano, be sure to see its most revered work of art, at the northern end of town, in the church of **Sant'Agostino**: Benozzo Gozzoli's utterly stunning 15th-century fresco cycle depicting the life of St. Augustine. Also try a taste of Vernaccia, the local dry white wine.

Dining and Lodging

$$–$$$ ✕ **Bel Soggiorno.** On the top floor of a 100-year-old inn, this rustic restaurant has a wall of windows from which to view the landscape. Tuscan specialties include *zuppa del granduca* (a medieval soup recipe of mushrooms, grain, and potatoes) and *sorpresa in crosta* (spicy rabbit stew with a bread crust). ⊠ *Via San Giovanni 91,* ☎ *0577/940375. AE, DC, MC, V. Closed Wed. and Jan.–Feb.*

$$–$$$ ✕ **Le Terrazze.** Seasonal Tuscan classics are prepared in this restaurant in a time-honored inn in the heart of San Gimignano. A charming view of rooftops and the countryside and specialties like homemade pasta, a variety of grilled mushrooms, and grilled meats are in store. ⊠ *Piazza della Cisterna 24,* ☎ *0577/940328. AE, DC, MC, V. Closed Tues. and Nov.–Mar. 9. No lunch Wed.*

$$ ✕ **La Mangiatoia.** In this rustic trattoria, near the church of Sant' Agostino, prices are more moderate than at places with a view, and the food is simple Tuscan country cooking. ⊠ *Via Mainardi 5, off Via San Matteo,* ☎ *0577/941528. MC, V. Closed Tues., 3 wks in Nov., and 1 wk in Jan.*

$$$ 🏨 **Santa Chiara.** In a low contemporary building with a plethora of
★ balconies and terraces on a panoramic hillside site just outside San Gimignano's walls, this hotel is an airy and spacious oasis, and an upscale base from which to explore the countryside and hill towns. The hotel has no restaurant but serves an ample buffet breakfast, and light meals in summer. ⊠ *Via Matteotti 15, 53037,* ☎ *0577/940701,* 📠 *0577/942096. 39 rooms and 2 suites. Breakfast room, pool. AE, DC, MC, V. Closed Jan. 10–Feb. 28.*

$$ 🏨 **Pescille.** This rambling farmhouse 4 km (2½ mi) outside San
★ Gimignano has been converted into a handsome hotel, in which restrained contemporary and country classic motifs blend well. ⊠ *Località Pescille, Strada Castel San Gimignano, 53037,* ☎ *0577/940186,* 📠 *0577/943165. 40 rooms. Pool, tennis court. AE, DC, MC, V. Closed Nov.–Feb.*

En Route Pause at Colle Val d'Elsa and take time to make the lengthy detour around Colle Val d'Elsa's workaday lower town to reach the upper town on the ridge, where the medieval center remains practically intact.

Monteriggioni

㉒ *20 km (12 mi) southeast of San Gimignano, 93 km (58 mi) southeast of Pisa, 55 km (33 mi) south of Florence.*

Tiny Monteriggioni makes a nice stop for a quiet walk on the way north to Colle Val d'Elsa, San Gimignano, or Volterra. Its hard to imagine that this little town surrounded by open countryside and poppy fields was ever anything but sleepy. But in the 13th century, Monteriggioni served as Siena's northernmost defense against impending Florentine invasion. The town's formidable walls are in good condition, although the 14 square towers are not as tall as in Dante's time, when the poet likened them to the four giants who guarded the horrifying central pit of hell.

Dining

$$ ✕ **Il Pozzo.** On the village square, this rustic tavern serves hearty Tuscan country cooking and savory wines. The specialties are homemade fresh pasta, main courses of fillet of Tuscan beef with porcini mushrooms and *piccione ripieno* (stuffed squab), and homey desserts. ⊠ *Piazza Roma 2,* ☎ *0577/304127. AE, DC, MC, V. Closed Mon., Jan. 7–Feb. 7, and Aug. 1–7. No dinner Sun.*

Elba

㉓ *Portoferraio: 22 km (14 mi) by sea southwest of Piombino, 183 km (114 mi) southwest of Florence.*

The largest island in the Tuscan archipelago, ringed with pristine beaches and pocked with rugged vegetation, Elba is an hour by ferry or a half hour by Hovercraft from Piombino, or a short hop by air from Pisa. Its main port is Portoferraio, fortified in the 16th century by the Medici Grand Duke Cosimo I. Local wines include Moscato and Aleatico.

Lively **Portoferraio** is the best base for exploring the island. Good beaches can be found at Biodola, Procchio, and Marina di Campo. From Elba, private visits can be arranged to the other islands in the archipelago, including **Montecristo,** which inspired Alexander Dumas's 19th-century best-seller *The Count of Monte Cristo* and is now a wildlife refuge.

Victor Hugo spent his boyhood here, and Napoléon his famous exile in 1814–15, when he built out of two windmills the **Palazzina Napoleonica dei Mulini** and, a few km outside town, the **Villa San Martino.** *Palazzina:* ⊠ *Via del Padiglione, Portoferraio,* ☎ *0565/915846. Villa:* ⊠ *Località San Martino,* ☎ *0565/914688.* ☞ *8,000 lire for both if visited on same day. Both:* ☉ *Apr.–Sept., Mon.–Sat. 9–7, Sun. 9–1; Oct.–Mar., Mon.–Sat. 9–4, Sun. 9–1; possible evening openings in summer.*

You can also visit the **Museo Archeologico,** which reconstructs the island's ancient history through a display of Etruscan and Roman artifacts recovered from shipwrecks. ⊠ *Calata Buccari, Portoferraio,* ☎ *0565/937370.* ☞ *4,000 lire.* ☉ *Apr.–June and Sept., Fri.–Wed. 9:30–12:30 and 4–7; July–Aug., Fri.–Wed. 9:30–12:30 and 6–midnight.*

Dining and Lodging

$$$ ✕ **La Canocchia.** This is in the center of Rio Marina on the eastern shore of Elba, across the street from a public garden. Specialties include fish-

stuffed ravioli with a red shellfish sauce, and *tagliolini* (thin spaghetti) with fresh shrimp. Reservations are essential in summer. ⊠ *Via Palestro 3, Rio Marina,* ☎ *0565/962432. DC, MC, V. Closed Mon. and Nov.–Apr.*

$$$ ✕ **Trattoria da Lido.** In the historic center of Portoferraio, at the beginning of the road heading up to the old Medici walls, this restaurant serves specialties such as *gnocchetti di pesce* (bite-size potato and fish dumplings) with a white cream sauce, and *pesce all'elbana,* fresh white fish baked with vegetables and potatoes. Reservations are encouraged. ⊠ *Salita del Falcone 2, Portoferraio,* ☎ *0565/914650. AE, DC, MC, V. Closed Mon. Nov.–Apr. and Dec. 15–Feb. 15.*

$$$–$$$$ ⚑ **Hermitage.** This hotel, on the most exclusive bay on Elba, 8 km (5 ★ mi) from Portoferraio, is heavenly. It is composed of a central building with rooms and several little cottages, each with six to eight rooms with their own separate entrances. Hotel guests have private access to a white sandy beach, and there are a bar and restaurant on the beach, all part of the hotel. ⊠ *Biodola 57037,* ☎ *0565/936911,* ℻ *0565/ 969984. 110 rooms. Restaurant, bar, 3 pools, 6-hole golf course, 9 tennis courts, soccer, volleyball, meeting rooms. AE, DC, MC, V. Closed Nov.–Apr.*

SIENA

Italy's most enchanting medieval city, Siena is the one trip you should make in Tuscany if you make no other. Florence's great historical rival was founded by Augustus around the time of the birth of Christ, although legend holds that it was founded much earlier by Remus, brother of Romulus, the legendary founder of Rome. During the late Middle Ages, the city was both wealthy and powerful, for it saw the birth of the world's oldest bank, the Monte dei Paschi, still very much in business. It was bitterly envied by Florence, which in 1254 sent forces that besieged the city for over a year, reducing its population by half and laying waste to the countryside. The city was finally absorbed by the Grand Duchy of Tuscany, ruled by Florence, in 1559.

Sienese identity is still very much defined by its 17 medieval *contrade* (neighborhoods), each with its own church, museum, and symbol. Look for streetlights painted in the contrada's colors, plaques displaying its symbol, and statues embodying the spirit of the neighborhood. The various contrade uphold ancestral rivalries during the centuries-old Palio, a yearly horse race through the main square; civic pride rests on the outcome.

Exploring Siena

Practically unchanged since medieval times, Siena is laid out over the slopes of three steep hills, but you will find the most interesting sites in a fairly compact area. Be sure to leave some time to wander off the main streets. Although there are orange electric buses, chances are you will be better off walking between sites. If you only have one day in Siena, see the Piazza del Campo, the Duomo and its Museo dell'Opera del Duomo, and the Palazzo Pubblico. If you are seeing more sights, it will probably be worth buying a cumulative ticket (valid for three days, 8,500 lire), good for entrance to the Duomo's Biblioteca Piccolomini, Battistero, and Museo dell'Opera del Duomo.

From Florence, there are two basic routes to Siena. The speedy modern S2 is good if you're making a day trip from Florence; for a jaunt through Chianti, take the narrower and more meandering S222, known as the Strada Chiantigiana.

A Good Walk

Begin at the **Piazza del Campo** ㉔, one of Italy's finest squares, and visit the **Palazzo Pubblico** ㉕ and its adjacent tower, the **Torre di Mangia,** which you can climb up. Cross the piazza and exit via the stairs on the left to Via di Città, one of Siena's main shopping streets. Up on the left is the enchanting Palazzo Chigi-Saracini, where concerts are often held. Step in to admire the especially well-preserved courtyard. Continue up the hill and take the next street on the right, Via del Capitano, which leads to Piazza del Duomo. The **Duomo** ㉖ is a must-see, along with its **Battistero** ㉗ (around the other side of the Duomo) and **Museo dell'Opera del Duomo** ㉘. Opposite the front of the Duomo is **Santa Maria della Scala** ㉙. Chief among Siena's other gems is the **Pinacoteca Nazionale** ㉚, several blocks straight back down Via del Capitano (becomes Via San Pietro). The church of **San Domenico** ㉛ lies in the other direction; you could take Via della Galluzza to Via della Sapienza.

TIMING

This walk should take a full day, taken at a leisurely pace and allowing some time to relax in the Piazza del Campo. Allow two days to really explore Siena. The *passeggiata* (evening stroll) along the main shopping streets should not be missed. Almost all shops are closed Sunday, and the Pinacoteca is closed Monday.

Sights to See

㉗ **Battistero.** The Duomo's 14th-century Gothic Baptistery was built to prop up one side of the Duomo. There are frescoes throughout, but the highlight is a large bronze 15th-century baptismal font, designed by Jacopo della Quercia (1374–1438) and adorned with bas-reliefs by various artists, including two by Renaissance masters: Lorenzo Ghiberti (1378–1455, *The Baptism of Christ*) and Donatello (circa 1386–1466, *Herod Presented with the Head of St. John*). ⊠ *Piazza San Giovanni.* 🎫 *3,000 lire, combination ticket 8,500 lire.* ⊙ *Mid-Mar.–Sept., daily 9–7:30; Nov.–mid-Mar., daily 10–1 and 2:30–5.*

NEED A
BREAK?

Not far from the Duomo and the Pinacoteca, Siena's **Orto Botanico** (Botanical Gardens; ⊠ V. Pier Andrea Mattioli 4, ☎ 0577/298874) is a great place to relax and enjoy views onto the countryside below. It's open Monday–Friday 8–5:30, Saturday 8–noon.

㉖ **Duomo.** Several blocks west of Piazza del Campo, Siena's Duomo is beyond question one of the finest Gothic cathedrals in Italy. The facade, with its multicolor marbles and painted decoration, is typical of the Italian approach to Gothic architecture, lighter and much less austere than the French. The cathedral as it now stands was completed in the 14th century, but at the time the Sienese had even bigger plans. They had decided to enlarge the building by using the existing church as a transept for a new church, with a new nave running toward the southeast. But in 1348 the Black Death decimated Siena's population, the city fell into decline, funds dried up, and the plans were never carried out. The beginnings of the new nave can be seen from the steps outside the Duomo's right transept.

The Duomo's interior, with its fine coffered and gilded dome, is simply striking. It is most famous for its unique and magnificent inlaid marble floors, which took almost 200 years to complete (beginning around 1370); more than 40 artists contributed to the work, made up of 56 separate compositions depicting biblical scenes, allegories, religious symbols, and civic emblems. The Duomo's carousel pulpit, also much-appreciated, was carved by Nicola Pisano around 1265; the life of Christ is depicted on the rostrum frieze. In the **Biblioteca Piccolo-**

mini, a room painted by Pinturicchio (1454–1513) in 1509, frescoes depict events from the life of native son Aeneas Sylvius Piccolomini, who became Pope Pius II in 1458. The frescoes are in excellent condition and reveal a freshness rarely seen in work so old. ⊠ *Piazza del Duomo,* ☎ *0577/283048.* 🎟 *Biblioteca Piccolomini: 2,000 lire; combination ticket 8,500 lire.* ⊘ *Mid-Mar.–Oct., daily 9–7:30; Nov.–mid-Mar., daily 10–1 and 2:30–5.*

28 **Museo dell'Opera del Duomo.** Built into part of the unfinished new cathedral's nave, the museum contains a small collection of Sienese art and the cathedral treasury. Its masterpiece is unquestionably Duccio's (circa 1255–1318) *Maestà,* painted around 1310 and magnificently displayed in a room devoted entirely to the artist's work. There is a fine view from the tower inside the museum. ⊠ *Piazza del Duomo, next to the Duomo,* ☎ *0577/283048.* 🎟 *6,000 lire, combination ticket 8,500 lire.* ⊘ *Mid-Mar.–Sept., daily 9–7:30; Oct., daily 9–6:30; Nov.–mid-Mar., daily 9–1:30.*

25 **Palazzo Pubblico.** The focal point of Piazza del Campo, the Gothic Palazzo Pubblico has served as Siena's town hall since the 1300s. It now also contains the **Museo Civico,** its walls covered with pre-Renaissance frescoes, including Simone Martini's early 14th-century *Maestà* and *Portrait of Guidoriccio da Fogliano.* The nine governors of Siena once met in the *Sala della Pace,* famous for the most important medieval frescoes in Italy, Ambrogio Lorenzetti's *Allegories of Good and Bad Government,* painted from 1327 to 1329 to demonstrate the dangers of tyranny. The good government side depicts a utopia, showing first the virtuous ruling council surrounded by angels and then scenes of a perfectly running city and countryside. Conversely, the bad government fresco tells a tale straight out of Dante. The evil ruler and his advisors have horns and fondle strange animals, while the town scene depicts the seven mortal sins in action. Interestingly, the bad government fresco is severely damaged, while the good government fresco is in terrific condition. The original bas-reliefs of the Jacopo della Quercia fountain, moved to protect them from the elements, are also on display. The **Torre di Mangia,** the palazzo's famous bell tower, is named after one of the tower's first bell ringers, Giovanni di Duccio (called Mangiaguadagni, or earnings eater). The climb up to the top is long and steep, but the superb view makes it worth every step. ⊠ *Piazza del Campo,* ☎ *0577/292263.* ☞ *6,000 lire includes all sights.* ☉ *Torre di Mangia: daily 10–1 hr before sunset. Museo Civico: Mar.–Oct., Mon.–Sat. 9:30–6:30; Nov.–early Jan., Mon.–Sat. 9:30–1:30.*

㉔ **Piazza del Campo.** Known simply as Il Campo (The Field), this fan-shape piazza is one of the finest in Italy. Built in the 14th century on a market area unclaimed by any contrada, it is still very much the heart of town. The bricks of the Campo are patterned in nine different sections—one for each of the medieval Government of Nine. At the top of the Campo is the **Fonte Gaia,** decorated in the early 15th century by Siena's greatest sculptor, Jacopo della Quercia, with 13 sculptures of biblical events and virtues. The sculptures now lining the rectangular fountain are 19th-century copies; the originals are in the Museo Civico. On Palio days (July 2 and August 16), Il Campo and all its surrounding buildings are packed with cheering, frenzied locals and tourists craning their necks to take it all in.

㉚ **Pinacoteca Nazionale.** The national picture gallery contains a superb collection of Sienese art, including Ambrogio Lorenzetti's 14th-century depiction of a castle that is generally considered the first nonreligious painting—the first pure landscape—of the Christian era. ⊠ *Via San Pietro 29,* ☎ *0577/281161.* ☞ *8,000 lire.* ☉ *Tues.–Sat. 9–7, Mon. 8:30–1:30, Sun. 8–1.*

㉛ **San Domenico.** In the church of San Domenico is the **Cappella di Santa Caterina,** with frescoes by Il Sodoma portraying scenes from the life of St. Catherine. Catherine was a much-respected diplomat, noted for ending the Great Schism by convincing the pope to return to Rome from Avignon. ⊠ *Costa di Sant'Antonio,* ☎ *0577/280330.* ☞ *Free.* ☉ *Daily 9–12:30 and 3:30–6.*

㉙ **Santa Maria della Scala.** In what was a former hospital, built in the 9th–11th centuries, is now an exhibition space and restoration center, with a fine frescoed hall. ⊠ *Piazza del Duomo, opposite the front of the cathedral,* ☎ *0577/586410.* ☞ *5,000 lire.* ☉ *Mid-Apr.–mid-Sept., daily 10:30–6; mid-Sept.–mid-Apr., Mon.–Sat. 11–5.*

Dining and Lodging

Not far from the church of San Domenico, the **Enoteca Italica** (⊠ Fortezza Medicea, Viale Maccari, ☎ 0577/288497) is a fantastically stocked wine cellar in the bastions of the Medici fortress. Here you can taste wines from all over Italy and have a snack, too. It's open from noon to 1 AM.

$$$–$$$$ ✕ **Antica Trattoria Botteganova.** Just outside the city walls, along the
★   road that leads north to Chianti, the Botteganova is arguably the best restaurant in Siena. Contemporary Italian food is rarely this successful; chef Michele Sonentino's cooking is all about clean flavors, balanced combinations, and inviting presentation. The interior, with high vaulting, is relaxed yet classy, and the service is first rate. There is a small room for nonsmokers. ⊠ *Strada Chiantigiana (S222) 29, 2 km (1 mi) north of Siena,* ☎ *0577/284230. AE, DC, MC, V. Closed Mon.*

$$ ✕ **Le Logge.** Near Piazza del Campo, this classic Sienese trattoria has
★ rustic dining rooms on two levels and tables outdoors from June to
October. Tuscan dishes are the draw, such as *malfatti all'osteria* (ri-
cotta and spinach dumplings in a cream sauce) and *anatra al finocchio*
(roast duck with fennel). ⊠ *Via del Porrione 33,* ☎ *0577/48013. AE,
DC, MC, V. Closed Sun. and 2 wks in June and Nov.*

$$ ✕ **Osteria Castelvecchio.** The menu at this cheerful little restaurant with
modern decor, set in an old stall near the Pinacoteca, is an intriguing
mix of rare dishes not seen for centuries and updated Sienese standards.
The choice of dishes is not ample, as chef Mauro prefers a change. He
has chosen a solid selection of wines from Tuscany. ⊠ *Via Castelvecchio 65,* ☎ *0577/49586. AE, MC, V. Closed Tues.*

$$ ✕ **Tullio Tre Cristi.** This is a typical and historic neighborhood trattoria,
still reliable and trammeled by loyal customers. The paintings on the walls
were executed by famous local artists of the 1920s, but the culinary tra-
dition here goes back even further. Try spaghetti *alle briciole,* a poor-
man's dish of pasta with bread crumbs, tomato, and garlic, or veal
escalopes (cutlets) subtly flavored with *dragoncello* (tarragon). You can
eat outdoors in summer. ⊠ *Vicolo di Provenzano 1, take Via dei Rossi
from Via Banchi di Sopra,* ☎ *0577/280608. MC, V. Closed Tues.*

$ ✕ **Enoteca I Terzi.** Near the Campo and the main shopping streets, this
enoteca (wine bar) is hard to beat for a good glass of wine from a list
of several hundred and a little snack or a full meal. Fast but "passionate"
service, very good value, and long opening hours (you can have lunch
as early as 10:30 AM and dinner as late as 1 AM) gained the young own-
ers a dedicated following among locals. The room at the back is for
nonsmokers. ⊠ *Via dei Termini 7,* ☎ *0577/44329. AE, DC, MC, V.
Closed Sun.*

$$$$ ▦ **Certosa di Maggiano.** A former 14th-century monastery converted
★ into an exquisite Relais & Châteaux country hotel, this haven of gra-
cious living is a little more than about 1½ km (1 mi) from the center
of Siena, near the Porta Romana gate. The atmosphere is that of an
exclusive retreat in which a select number of guests enjoy the style and
comfort of an aristocratic villa. In warm weather, breakfast is served
on the patio next to the garden aburst with roses, zinnias, and other
blessed friends. Prices are also heavenly. ⊠ *Via Certosa 82 (take the
Siena Sud exit off superstrada), 53100,* ☎ *0577/288180,* ℻ *0577/
288189. 5 rooms, 12 suites. Restaurant, pool, tennis court, horseback
riding, helipad. AE, DC, MC, V.*

$$$$ ▦ **La Suvera.** This luxurious estate in the lovely valley of the River Elsa,
★ 28 km (17 mi) west of Siena and 56 km (33 mi) south of Florence, was
once owned by Pope Julius II. The papal villa and adjacent building ac-
commodate guests in magnificently furnished rooms and suites ap-
pointed with antiques and modern comforts. With excellent facilities such
as drawing rooms, a library, Italian garden, park, and the Oliviera restau-
rant (serving estate wines), guests find it hard to tear themselves away,
though there is plenty to see in the vicinity. ⊠ *Pievescola (Casola d'Elsa),
off S541, 53030,* ☎ *0577/960300,* ℻ *0577/960220. 19 rooms, 13
suites. Restaurant, bar, pool, sauna, tennis court, horseback riding, li-
brary, meeting rooms, helipad. AE, DC, MC, V. Closed Nov.–Easter.*

$$$$ ▦ **Park.** Set among olive groves and gardens on a hillside just outside
the city walls, this handsome hotel offers solid comfort and spacious dou-
ble rooms with views of the grounds, which also includes a nine-hole
practice golf course. Public rooms in the historic medieval villa lend an
easy elegance and patrician antique charm. Comfortable guest rooms might
seem familiar, with their bold, dark fabrics, mirrors, and modern ap-
pointments. The Olivo restaurant serves fine regional cuisine. ⊠ *Via Mar-
ciano 18, 53100,* ☎ *0577/44803,* ℻ *0577/49020. 63 rooms. Restaurant,
bar, pool, 9-hole golf course, 2 tennis courts. AE, DC, MC, V.*

$$ 🏨 **Antica Torre.** A restored 17th-century tower within the town walls in the southeast corner of Siena, Antica Torre is a 10-minute walk from Piazza del Campo. It is the work of a cordial couple who have created the atmosphere of a private home, furnished simply but tastefully and with only eight guest rooms. The old stone staircase, wooden beams, and original brick vaults here and there are reminders of the building's august age. ⊠ *Via Fieravecchia 7, 53100,* ☎ FAX *0577/222255. 8 rooms. AE, MC, V.*

$$ 🏨 **Chiusarelli.** In a well-kept neoclassic villa, built in the early 1900s complete with caryatids, this hotel has functional rooms that are airy and reasonably quiet. A handy location—near the long-distance bus terminal and a parking area and only a 10-minute walk from the main sites—is the big plus here. The small garden invites reading; a down-stairs restaurant caters to tour groups. ⊠ *Viale Curtatone 9, 53100,* ☎ *0577/280562,* FAX *0577/271177. 50 rooms. Restaurant. MC, V.*

$$ 🏨 **Duomo.** Occupying the top floor of a 300-year-old building near Piazza del Campo, this quiet hotel is furnished in a neat contemporary style, with traces of the past showing in the artfully exposed brickwork in the breakfast room. Many bedrooms have superb views of the city's towers and the hilly countryside. Two rooms have balconies. ⊠ *Via Stalloreggi 38, 53100,* ☎ *0577/289088,* FAX *0577/43043. 23 rooms. Breakfast room. AE, DC, MC, V.*

$$ 🏨 **Pensione Ravizza.** Don't let the "pensione" name confuse you, the Ravizza is a particularly elegant hotel. Rooms are large and furnished with antiques, and those in the back have great views over the garden and countryside. Just a few minutes' walk from Piazza del Campo, this is the best choice in town for location, and the free parking is also a great plus. ⊠ *Pian dei Mantellini 34, 53100,* ☎ *0577/280462,* FAX *0577/ 221597. 30 rooms, 4 suites. Free parking. AE, DC, MC, V.*

$$ 🏨 **Piccolo Hotel Oliveta.** This little hotel in a rejuvenated 18th-century brick farmhouse has lots of atmosphere. Just outside Porta Romana and only 10 minutes from Piazza del Campo on foot, it has simply fur-nished rooms and a garden overlooking olive groves and verdant hills. A Palio-time option includes tickets to the race. ⊠ *Via Piccolomini 35, 53100,* ☎ *0577/283930,* FAX *0577/870009. 16 rooms. Free parking. AE, MC, V.*

$$ 🏨 **Santa Caterina.** Just outside Porta Romana—10 minutes' walk to the Campo— the Santa Caterina is an extremely pleasant, well-run hotel. The rooms are nicely decorated with Tuscan country furniture and tapestries; half overlook the garden. Breakfast is served in a sunny room or out in the garden. ⊠ *Via E. S. Piccolomini 7, 53100,* ☎ *0577/221105,* FAX *0577/271087. 19 rooms. Breakfast room. AE, DC, MC, V.*

Nightlife and the Arts

Music
In late July and August, Siena hosts the **Settimane Musicali Senesi,** a series of concerts held in churches and courtyards with performances of local and other music.

Outdoor Activities and Sports

Siena's **Palio** horse race takes place every year on July 2 and August 16, but its spirit lives all year long. Three laps around a makeshift track in Piazza del Campo earn participants of the Palio the respect or scorn of the other 16 contrade. The event is so important to the Sienese that bribery, brutality, and kidnapping of the jockeys are commonplace—sabotaging a horse's reins is the only thing that remains taboo. A horse doesn't even need its rider to be considered a valid winner. Festivities kick off three days prior to the main event, with trial races, banquets lining the streets, and late-night celebrations. As the Palio approaches, residents don scarves with their contrada's colors and march through city streets in medieval costumes. Tickets are usually sold out eight months in advance of the events; call the tourist office (✉ Piazza del Campo 56, ☎ 0577/280551) for info. It is possible you might luck out and get an unclaimed seat or two; of course, the center of the piazza is free to all on a first-come, first-served basis, until just moments before the start.

Shopping

The city is known for a variety of cakes and cookies, their recipes of medieval origin—*cavallucci* (sweet spice biscuits), *panforte* (traditional Sienese Christmas fruitcake with honey, hazelnuts, almonds, and spices), and *ricciarelli* (almond-paste cookies)—as well as for its ceramics.

CHIANTI

Directly south of Florence is the Chianti district, Italy's most famous wine-producing area; its hill towns, olive groves, and vineyards comprise the quintessential Tuscany. Many British and northern Europeans have relocated here, drawn by the unhurried life, balmy climate, and picturesque villages; there are so many Britons, in fact, that the area has been nicknamed Chiantishire. Still, it remains strongly Tuscan in character, and you'll be drawn to the vistas framing vine-quilted rolling hills and stout cypress.

The sinuous S222, known as the Strada Chiantigiana, runs from Florence through the heart of Chianti. Its most scenic section connects Strada in Chianti, 16 km (10 mi) south of Florence, and Greve in Chianti, whose triangular central piazza is surrounded by restaurants and vintners offering *degustazioni* (wine tastings), 11 km (7 mi) farther south.

Greve in Chianti

③ *27 km (17 mi) south of Florence, 40 km (25 mi) north of Siena.*

If there is a capital of Chianti, it is Greve, a friendly market town with no shortage of cafés, enoteche, and crafts shops along its pedestrian street. The sloping, asymmetrical **Piazza Matteotti** is attractively arcaded and has a statue of Giovanni da Verrazzano (circa 1485–1528), the explorer who discovered New York harbor, in the center. At the small end of the piazza is the **Chiesa di Santa Croce,** with works from the school of Fra Angelico (1387–1455). Just 2 km (1 mi) west, in the tiny hilltop hamlet **Montefioralle,** you'll find the ancestral home of Amerigo Vespucci (1454–1512), the navigator and mapmaker who named America and whose niece Simonetta was the model of Sandro Botticelli's (1445–1510) *Venus*. Chianti's annual mid-September wine festival **Rassegna del Chianti Classico** takes place here.

Dining and Lodging

$$$ ✕ **Trattoria del Montagliari.** Typical home-style cooking is a big draw for locals, who eat around a wood-burning fireplace in the winter and in the garden in the summer. Ravioli in walnut sauce and fragrant apple pie await. ✉ *Via Montagliari 29,* ☎ *055/852184. MC, V. Closed Mon. and mid-Aug.*

$$ ▦ **Castello Vicchiomaggio.** This castle, now a prestigious wine estate with a tasting facility you can visit, can be traced to 956, and was rebuilt during the Renaissance. Throughout the seven apartments and two farmhouses is wonderful heavy wooden furniture, in keeping with the estate's history. The restaurant serves homemade pastas and spe-

cialties such as *stracotto*, meat cooked in the farm's own prize-winning Chianti Classico. The restaurant is closed weekdays April–November. ⊠ *Via Vicchiomaggio 4, 50022, ☎ 055/854079, ℻ 055/853911. 9 apartments. Restaurant, pool. DC, MC, V.*

$$ ⊞ **Il Cenobio/Villa Vignamaggio.** This historic estate has guest rooms and apartments in the villa as well as two small houses and a cottage on the grounds. The villa, surrounded by manicured classical Italian gardens, dates from the 14th century, but was restored in the 16th. It's reputedly the birthplace of Leonardo da Vinci's *Mona Lisa*, and was the setting for Kenneth Branagh's film *Much Ado About Nothing.* ⊠ *50022 Greve in Chianti, ☎ 055/8544840, ℻ 055/8544468. 10 apartments, 2 rooms. Pool, tennis court. AE, DC, MC, V.*

Radda in Chianti

③③ *33 km (20 mi) south of Greve, 31 km (19 mi) north of Siena, 52 km (32 mi) south of Florence.*

Radda in Chianti sits on a hill that separates Val di Pesa from Val d'Arbia. It's one of many tiny Chianti villages that invites you to stroll through its steep streets and to follow the signs that point you toward the *camminamento*, a covered medieval road that circles part of the city inside the walls. In Piazza Ferrucci, you'll find **Il Palazzo del Podesta,** or Palazzo Comunale, the city hall that has served the people of Radda for more than four centuries and has 51 coats of arms imbedded in the facade.

OFF THE
BEATEN PATH

VOLPAIA – Atop a hill 10 km (6 mi) north of Radda is this fairy-tale hamlet, a military outpost from the 10th–16th centuries and once shelter for religious pilgrims. Every July, for the Festa di San Lorenzo, people come to Volpaia to watch for falling stars and a traditional fireworks display put on by the family that owns the surrounding Castello di Volpaia (⊠ Piazza della Cisterna 1, 53017, ☎ 0577/738066) wine estate and agritourist lodging. The 16th-century farmhouse of Podere Terreno (⊠ Via Della Volpaia, 53017, ☎ ℻ 0577/738312), with seven well-sought-after agritourist rooms, was photographed by Helmut Newton for Pirelli tires.

Lodging

$$$ ⊞ **Relais Fattoria Vignale.** Unadorned farmhouse on the main road on the outside, English-country-house comfortable on the inside—with terracotta floors, sitting rooms, and nice stone- and woodwork—best sums up Fattoria Vignale. White rooms with exposed brick and wood beams, contain simple wooden bed frames and furniture, lovely rugs and prints, a bedside candle to promote relaxation, and modern white-tile bathrooms. The grounds, lined with vineyards and plum and olive trees, are equally as inviting, with various lawns, terraces, and a pool. The cavernous and rustic Ristorante Vignale serves excellent wines and various cold and warm Tuscan plates; it's perfect for a sampling of savory meats, pâtés, and cheeses anytime. ⊠ *53017 Radda in Chianti, ☎ 0577/738300, ℻ 0577/738592. 34 rooms. Restaurant, breakfast room, wine shop, pool, library. AE, MC, V. Closed early Dec.–Dec. 25 and early Jan.–late Mar.*

$$–$$$$ ⊞ **Vescine.** Set on what was once an Etruscan settlement is this secluded complex of low-slung medieval stone buildings connected by cobbled paths, punctuated by cypress trees. Unfussy white rooms have terracotta tile floors, attractive woodwork, and comfortable furnishings typical to Tuscany. ⊠ *53017 Radda in Chianti, ☎ 0577/741144, ℻ 0577/740263. 20 rooms, 5 suites. Restaurant, bar, breakfast room, wine shop, pool, tennis court, library. AE, D, MC, V. Closed Dec. (except over Christmas)–Feb.*

Castellina in Chianti

③④ *14 km (8 mi) west of Radda, 50 km (31 mi) south of Florence, 21 km (13 mi) north of Siena.*

Castellina in Chianti, or simply Castellina, is on a ridge above the Val di Pesa, Val d'Arbia, and Val d'Elsa, and the panorama is bucolic no matter which direction you look. The strong 15th-century medieval walls and fortified town gate give a hint of the history of this village, which was an outpost during the continuing wars between Florence and Siena.

Lodging

$$ 🏨 **Hotel Belvedere di San Leonino.** There are wonderful gardens for strolling around this restored country complex that dates from the 14th century. The guest rooms are in two country houses that look out upon vineyards to the north and upon Siena to the south. Homey rooms have antique furniture and exposed beams. There is a restaurant with a fixed menu, and in the summer, the guests can eat dinner in the garden by the pool. ⊠ *Località San Leonino, 53011 Castellina in Chianti,* ☎ *0577/740240,* 🖷 *0577/740998. 28 rooms. Restaurant, pool. AE, MC, V. Closed Nov. 10–Mar. 15.*

ENCLAVES AND WINE TOWNS SOUTH

Along the roads leading south from Siena, soft green olive groves give way to a blanket of oak and rich dark green cypress forests and reddish brown earth; here and there throughout this area are the vineyards that produce excellent wines, among them Brunello di Montalcino. Here, the towns are the size of the roads—small—and as old as the hills.

Abbazia di Monte Oliveto Maggiore

③⑤ *37 km (23 mi) southeast of Siena.*

This Benedictine abbey, Tuscany's most visited, is an oasis of olive and cypress trees amid the harsh landscape of a zone known as the Crete, where erosion has sculpted the hills starkly, laying open gashes of barren rock in lush farmland. Secluded amid thick woodlands in the deepcut hills south of Siena, it is accessible by car but not easily by bus.

Olivetans, or "White Benedictines," founded the abbey in 1313; this breakaway group sought to return to the simple ideals of the early Benedictines. The monastery's mellow brick buildings, restored in the last century and set in one of Tuscany's most striking landscapes, protect a treasure or two. Only the **main cloister** and portions of the **park** are open to the public. The wooden choir in the church, with exquisite inlay designs, is an understated work of art that dates from 1503. In the main cloister of the abbey, the frescoes by Luca Signorelli and Il Sodoma on the walls of the portico relate the life of St. Benedict with earthy realism, a quality that came naturally to Il Sodoma, described by Vasari as "a merry and licentious man . . . of scant chastity." ⊠ *S451 south of Asciano.* 🎫 *Free.* ☉ *Daily 9:15–noon and 3:15–5:45.*

Dining

$–$$ ✕ **La Torre.** This pleasant restaurant and café in the massive tower at the abbey's entrance provides more than adequate sustenance to visitors. The local specialties—served in a cozy dining room in winter or on an attractive terrace under tall cypresses in good weather—include *pici ai funghi* (thick, short spaghetti with mushroom sauce) or *zuppa di funghi* (mushroom soup). The wine list is remarkably good, and the tourist menu is a good value. ☎ *0577/707022. AE, DC, MC, V. Closed Tues.*

Montalcino

㊱ *25 km (15 mi) south of the Abbey of Monte Oliveto Maggiore, 24 km (15 mi) west of Pienza, 41 km (25 mi) south of Siena.*

Another medieval hill town with a special claim to fame, Montalcino is home to Brunello di Montalcino, one of Italy's finest red wines. You can sample it in wine cellars in town or visit a nearby winery for a free guided tour and tasting; you must call ahead for reservations. One such winery is Fattoria dei Barbi e del Casato (☞ *below*).

Dining

$$$ ✕ **Poggio Antico.** One of Italy's renowned gourmet chefs, Roberto Minnetti, abandoned his highly successful restaurant in Rome a few years ago and moved to the country just outside Montalcino. Now he and his wife, Patrizia—who is also Poggio Antico's hostess—serve fine Tuscan cuisine, masterfully interpreted by Roberto, in a relaxed but regal dining room replete with arches and beamed ceilings. The seasonal menu might suggest ravioli *di castagne al burro e salvia* (with chestnut stuffing) or venison in a sweet-and-sour sauce. ⊠ *Località I Poggi, 4 km (2½ mi) outside Montalcino on road to Grossetto,* ☎ *0577/849200. V. Closed Mon. and 20 days in Jan. No dinner Sun.*

$$ ✕🏨 **Fattoria dei Barbi e del Casato.** A meal at the taverna, set among
★ vineyards and mellow brick buildings on a family-owned winery estate, may well be a highlight of your journey through this part of Tuscany. The estate-produced Brunello is excellent. The rustic dining room features a beamed ceiling, huge stone fireplace, and arched windows. The estate farm produces many of the ingredients used in such traditional specialties as *stracotto nel brunello* (braised veal cooked with beans, in Brunello wine); big ravioli pillows filled with ricotta, swathed in butter, and dusted with Parmesan and herbs; and a dessert called ricotta *montata* (farm-fresh ricotta whipped with vin santo, sugar, and vanilla). Two comfortable, traditionally furnished agritourist apartments right next to the taverna and above the cantina—where you can take a tour and buy the fattoria's different labels (call ahead)—each sleep three. Reservations for a meal or a stay are essential. ⊠ *Località Podernuovi, 53024 Podernovaccio. Taverna* ☎ *0577/849357; fattoria* ☎ *0577/849421,* ℻ *0577/849356. 2 apartments. AE, DC, MC, V. Taverna closed Wed., last 2 wks Jan., and 1st 2 wks July.*

$$ 🏨 **La Crociona.** Quiet and serene family owned farm in the middle of a small vineyard with glorious views and all the comforts of home, including antique iron beds and 17th-century wardrobes in the rooms. There's a big terrace and you are invited to hang out around the pool and use the family barbecue as well as to sample the owner's own wine supply. ⊠ *Località Croce di Mezzo, 53024 Montalcino,,* ☎ ℻ *0577/ 848007. 6 apartments. Pool, mountain bikes. AE, DC, MC, V.*

Pienza

㊲ *10 km (6 mi) northeast of the Abbey of Sant'Antimo.*

Pienza owes its visage to Pope Pius II, who had grand plans to transform his home village of Corsignano—the town's former name—into a model Renaissance town. The man entrusted with the transformation was Bernardo Rossellini, a protégé of the great Renaissance architectural theorist Leon Battista Alberti. His mandate was to create a cathedral, a papal palace, and a town hall (plus miscellaneous buildings) that adhered to the vainglorious pope's principles. Gothic and Renaissance styles were fused, and the buildings were decorated with Sienese and Florentine paintings. The net result was a project that expressed Renaissance ideals of art, architecture, and civilized good living in a single scheme: It stands as an exquisite example of the architectural canons that Alberti formulated in the early Renaissance and which were utilized by later architects, including Michelangelo, in designing many of Italy's finest buildings and piazzas. Today the cool nobility of Pienza's center seems almost surreal in this otherwise unpretentious village, known locally for *pienzino*, also called *cacio*, a smooth sheep's-milk cheese. Visit the **Palazzo Piccolomini,** the seat of Pius II's papal court, and the **Duomo** (⌧ *Piazza Pio II.* ☎ *Free.* ☉ *June–Oct., Tues.–Sun. 10–12:30 and 4–7; Nov.–May, Tues.–Sun. 10–12:30 and 3–6*).

Dining

$ ✕ **La Chiocciola.** This restaurant offers typical Pienza fare, including homemade local pici (thick, short spaghetti) with hare or boar sauce, and baked pienzino cheese. It has a nice summer garden. ⌧ *Via dell'Acero 2,* ☎ *0578/748063. No credit cards. Closed Wed. and for about 10 days in mid-Nov.*

Montepulciano

③⑧   *12 km (7 mi) east of Pienza, 13 km (8 mi) west of the A1, 65 km (40 mi) south of Florence.*

Perched high on a hilltop, Montepulciano is made up of a pyramid of redbrick buildings set within a circle of cypress trees. At an altitude of almost 2,000 ft, it is cool in summer and chilled in winter by biting winds that sweep its spiraling streets. The town has an unusually harmonious look, the result of the work of three architects, Sangallo Il Vecchio, Vignola, and Michelozzo, who endowed it with fine palaces and churches in an attempt to impose Renaissance architectural ideals on an ancient Tuscan hill town —the pièce de résistance is the beautiful **Piazza Grande.** On the hillside below the town walls is the church of **San Biagio,** designed by Sangallo, a paragon of Renaissance architectural perfection considered his masterpiece.

Dining and Lodging

$$$$ ✕▥ **Locanda dell'Amorosa.** A medieval hamlet set in Tuscan farmland ★ in Sinalunga has become a rustic retreat for city folk for a meal or weekend in the country, only a half hour by car from Siena or Arezzo and even less from Montepulciano, Cortona, and Monte Oliveto Maggiore. The stone and brick buildings have been tastefully adapted to accommodate guests, and the restaurant serves regional dishes that seem to taste even better in such apt surroundings. You can take home estate-produced wines and preserves as a souvenir of your stay. ⌧ *Località Amorosa, Sinalunga, 10 km (6 mi) off the Valdichiana exit of A1, 53048,* ☎ *0577/679497,* ☒ *0577/632001. 13 rooms, 4 suites. 2 restaurants, wine bar. AE, DC, MC, V.*

$$ ▥ **Il Marzocco.** A 16th-century building within the town walls, this hotel is furnished circa 19th century, complete with dignified, old-fashioned parlors and a billiard room. Furnished in heavy turn-of-the-century style or in spindly white wood, many bedrooms have large terraces overlooking the countryside. Many rooms are large enough to accommodate extra beds. No breakfast is served. ⌧ *Piazza Savonarola 18, 53045,* ☎ *0578/757262,* ☒ *0578/757530. 16 rooms, 1 without bath. Restaurant. AE, DC, MC, V. Closed Jan. 20–Feb. 10.*

$$ ▥ **La Bandita.** This attractive old farmhouse possesses great charm, with terra-cotta floors throughout, lace curtains and antiques in the bedrooms, and a fireplace and 19th-century Tuscan provincial furniture in a large, brick-vaulted living room. Some rooms can accommodate an extra bed. A garden and meals are available to guests. The restaurant is closed Tuesday. ⌧ *Via Bandita 72, Bettolle, 1 km (½ mi) from*

Valdichiana exit of A1 autostrada, 53048, ☎ 0577/624649, ℻ 0577/624649. 7 rooms. Restaurant. AE, DC, MC, V.

Nightlife and the Arts

The **Cantiere Internazionale d'Arte,** held in July and August, is a multifaceted festival of figurative art, music, and theater, ending with a major theatrical production in Piazza Grande. Contact the Montepulciano tourist office (✉ Via Ricci 9, ☎ 0578/758687) for info.

Chianciano Terme

9 km (5½ mi) south of Montepulciano.

This small medieval town, surrounded by walls, has billboards proclaiming that Chianciano's restorative waters are indispensable for a *fegato sano* (healthy liver). Outside the old walls is a well-attended, top-of-the-line modern spa with neat parks and a host of hotels. The spa has grabbed attention away from the old city center, which nevertheless is worth a visit, mainly for its castle.

Chiusi

11 km (7 mi) east of Chianciano, 2½ km (1½ mi) east of the A1, 126 km (78 mi) south of Florence.

Known for the frescoed tombs that date from the 5th century BC in its necropolis, Chiusi was one of the most powerful of the 12 ancient cities in the Etruscan federation. It's a transportation hub accessible from either the main north–south rail line or by car or bus from the A1 autostrada.

Abbazia di San Galgano

🚳 *33 km (20 mi) southwest of Siena, 70 km (43 mi) northwest of Montalcino.*

This Gothic cathedral missing its rooftop is truly a hauntingly beautiful sight to behold. The church was built in the 13th century by Cistercian monks, who designed it after churches built by their order in France. But starting in the 15th century it fell into ruins, declining gradually over centuries. Grass has grown through the floor, and the roof and windows are gone. What's left of its facade and walls makes a grandiose and desolate picture. Behind it, a short climb up a hill brings you to the charming little **Chiesa di San Galgano,** with frescoes by 14th-century painter Ambrogio Lorenzetti (1290–1348), and a sword in stone. Legend has it that Galgano, a medieval warrior, was struck by a revelation on this spot to give up fighting. He thrust his sword into stone, where it remains to this day.

AREZZO AND CORTONA

Cortona

🚳 *46 km (28½ mi) northeast of Chiusi.*

Magnificently situated, with olive trees and vineyards creeping up to its walls, one of Tuscany's prettiest villages commands sweeping views over Lake Trasimeno and the plain of the Valdichiana. Its two fine galleries and scattering of churches are rarely visited; its delightful medieval streets are a pleasure to wander for their own sake.

Cortona may be one of Italy's oldest towns—"Mother of Troy and Grandmother of Rome," in popular speech. Tradition claims that it was founded by Dardanus, the founder of Troy (after whom the Dardanelles are named). He was fighting a local tribe, so the story goes, when he lost his helmet (*corythos* in Greek) on Cortona's hill. In time a town grew up that took its name (Corito) from the missing headgear. By the 4th century BC the Etruscans had built the first set of town walls, whose cyclopean traces can still be seen in the 3-km (2-mi) sweep of the present fortifications. As a member of the Etruscans' 12-city Dodecapolis, it became one of the federation's leading northern cities. An important consular road, the Via Cassia, which passed the foot of its hill, maintained the town's importance under the Romans. Medieval fortunes waned, however, as the plain below reverted to marsh. After holding out against neighbors like Perugia, Arezzo, and Siena, the *comune* was captured by King Ladislas of Naples in 1409 and sold to the Florentines two years later.

The heart of Cortona is formed by **Piazza della Repubblica** and the adjacent **Piazza Signorelli.** Wander into the courtyard of the picturesque 13th-century **Palazzo Pretorio,** and, if you want to see a representative collection of Etruscan bronzes, climb its centuries-old stone staircase to the **Museo dell'Accademia Etrusca** (Gallery of Etruscan Art). ⊠ *Piazza Signorelli 9,* ☎ *0575/630415.* ⊒ *8,000 lire.* ☉ *Apr.–Sept., Tues.–Sun. 10–1 and 4–7; Oct.–Mar., Tues.–Sun. 9–1 and 3–5.*

The **Museo Diocesano** (Diocesan Museum) houses an impressive number of large and splendid paintings by native son Luca Signorelli, as well as a beautiful *Annunciation* by Fra Angelico, a delightful surprise to find in this small, eclectic town. ⊠ *Piazza del Duomo 1,* ☎ *0575/ 62830.* ⊒ *8,000 lire.* ☉ *Apr.–Sept., Tues.–Sun. 9:30–1 and 3:30–7; Oct.–Mar., Tues.–Sun. 10–1 and 3–5.*

Dining and Lodging

$$ ✕ **La Loggetta.** Above Cortona's main medieval square, this attractive restaurant is housed in a 16th-century wine cellar. In good weather you can eat outdoors, overlooking the 13th-century town hall, dining on regional dishes and such specialties as ravioli *gnudi,* "naked ravioli," made with spinach and ricotta but without pasta, and tagliata. The owners pride themselves on their selection of Tuscan wines. ⊠ *Piazza Pescheria 3,* ☎ *0575/630575. AE, DC, MC, V. Closed Nov. 5–20 and Mon. Sept.–June.*

$$ ✕ **Tonino.** It must be host Tonino's own *antipastissimo*— an incredible variety of delectables—that make this large modern establishment noisy and crowded at times. But it is very satisfactory indeed when not, when you can enjoy the view of the Chiana valley and savor Chianina steak. ⊠ *Piazza Garibaldi,* ☎ *0575/630500. AE, DC, MC, V. Closed Tues.*

$$$ ✕⊡ **Il Falconiere.** A charming old villa less than 3½ km (2 mi) outside Cortona, this once belonged to an early 19th-century poet and has been lovingly restored and impeccably furnished in the local style as an upscale inn. The winter garden and terrace have been transformed into a restaurant that features Tuscan dishes and seasonal specialties. The restaurant is closed Monday from November to March. ⊠ *Località San Martino, 52044,* ☎ *0575/612679,* FAX *0575/612927. 12 rooms. Restaurant, bar, pool. AE, DC, MC, V. Closed 1st 3 wks in Nov.*

Arezzo

🐠 *29 km (18 mi) north of Cortona, 81 km (50 mi) southeast of Florence.*

The birthplace of the poet Petrarch; of the Renaissance artist and art historian Giorgio Vasari; and of Guido d'Arezzo, the inventor of musical notation, Arezzo is today best known for the magnificent, but very ★ faint, Piero della Francesca (1420–92) frescoes in the church of **San**

Francesco (✉ Via Cavour in town center). Painted between 1452 and 1466, they depict *The Legend of the True Cross* on three walls of the choir. What Sir Kenneth Clark called "the most perfect morning light in all Renaissance painting" may be seen in the lowest section of the right wall, where the troops of the Emperor Maxentius flee before the sign of the cross. Unfortunately, part of the frescoes may be hidden from view while restoration work takes place.

With its irregular shape and sloping brick pavement, framed by buildings of assorted centuries, Arezzo's **Piazza Grande** echoes Siena's Piazza del Campo. Though not so grand, it is lively enough during the outdoor antiques fair every first Sunday of the month and when the **Joust of the Saracen,** featuring medieval costumes and competition, is held there on the first Sunday of September. The curving, tiered apse on Piazza Grande belongs to **Santa Maria della Pieve,** one of Tuscany's finest Romanesque churches, built in the 12th century. And Arezzo's medieval **Duomo** (✉ At the top of the hill) contains an eye-level fresco of a tender Magdalen by Piero della Francesca; look for it next to the large marble tomb near the organ. ✉ *Piazza Grande.*

The church of **San Domenico** (✉ Piazza Fossombroni, north of Piazza Grande) just inside the walls, houses a 13th-century crucifix by Cimabue (1240–circa 1302).

Casa di Giorgio Vasari (Giorgio Vasari house) was designed and decorated by the region's leading Mannerist artist in 1540 for his own use. ✉ *Via XX Settembre 55,* ☎ *0575/300301.* ▨ *Free.* ☼ *Mon.–Sat. 9–7, Sun. 9–1.*

The **Museo Archeologico** exhibits a fine collection of Etruscan bronzes. ✉ *Via Margaritone 10,* ☎ *0575/20882.* ▨ *8,000 lire.* ☼ *Mon.–Sat. 9–2.*

Dining and Lodging

$$ ✕ **Buca di San Francesco.** A frescoed cellar restaurant in a historic building next to the church of San Francesco, this *buca* (literally "hole," figuratively "cellar") has a medieval atmosphere and serves straightforward local specialties, including *ribollita* (a thick soup of white beans, bread, cabbage, and onions). Meat eaters will find the lean Chianina beef and the *saporita di Bonconte* (a selection of several meats) succulent treats. The owner says he'll give a free gift to those who come with this guide in hand. ✉ *Piazza San Francesco 1,* ☎ *0575/23271. AE, DC, MC, V. Closed Tues. and 2 wks in July. No dinner Mon.*

$$ ✕ **Tastevin.** Tastevin has introduced creative cooking—penne Tastevin (with cream of truffles) and seafood or meat carpaccio—to Arezzo, but also remains true to tradition. Two of the dining rooms are done out in a warm Tuscan provincial style, one in more sophisticated bistro style. At the small bar the talented owner plays and sings Sinatra and show tunes, for which a 15% cover charge will appear on the *conto* (bill). ✉ *Via dei Cenci 9, close to San Francesco and the central Piazza Guido Monaco,* ☎ *0575/28304. AE, MC, V. Closed Sun., except the 1st Sun. of every month, and Aug. 1–20.*

$ ✕ **L'Agania.** The main reason for coming to this central osteria, with plain wood paneling and rather cheap furniture, is the good food for less. Its specialties include boar meat, both as a second course and in a savory sauce with pasta. Also try the tasty *griffi,* which is actually veal cheek, with tomatoes and spices. ✉ *Via Mazzini 10,* ☎ *0575/295381. AE, DC, MC, V. Closed Mon. and 2nd wk June.*

$$ ▥ **Castello di Gargonza.** Enchantment reigns at this tiny 13th-century hamlet in the countryside near Monte San Savino, part of the fiefdom of the aristocratic Florentine Guicciardinis restored by the modern Count

Roberto Guicciardini as a way to rescue a dying village. A castle, church, and the cobbled streets set the stage. Rooms can be had for a minimum of three nights. Cottages and apartments are for rent by the week; they have one to six rooms each, sleep two to seven people, and have as many as four baths. La Torre restaurant (closed Tuesday) serves local fare. ✉ *Monte San Savino, 52100,* ☎ *0575/847021,* ℻ *0575/847054. 7 rooms, 25 cottages and apartments. Restaurant, pool. AE, DC, MC, V. Closed Jan. 10–31 and Nov.*

$$ 🏨 **Continental.** Centrally located near the train station and within walking distance of all major sights, the Continental has been a reliable and convenient place to stay since it opened in the 1950s. Bright white furnishings with yellow accents are throughout; gleaming bathrooms complete with hair dryers, air-conditioning in most rooms, and a pleasant roof garden are welcome pluses. Breakfast is extra. ✉ *Piazza Guido Monaco 7, 52100,* ☎ *0575/20251,* ℻ *0575/350485. 74 rooms. AE, DC, MC, V.*

Outdoor Activities and Sports

HORSEBACK RIDING

A well-reputed outfit is **Etruria Ippo Trekking** (✉ Via Michelangelo da Caravaggio 34–36, just behind Piazza Giotto, ☎ 0575/300417).

Shopping

FLEA MARKET

The first Sunday of each month, a colorful flea market selling antiques and not-so-antiques takes place in the **Piazza Grande.**

GOLD

Gold production here is on an industrial scale. **Uno-A-Erre** is the biggest of several factories. Big-time baubles can be purchased on a small scale in town center. For gold jewelry set with precious or semiprecious stones, try **Il Diamante** (✉ Via Guido Monaco 69), **Borghini** (✉ Corso Italia 126), **Prosperi** (✉ Corso Italia 76), or **Aurea Monilia** (✉ Piazza San Francesco 15).

KNITWEAR

A cottage knitwear industry is burgeoning in Arezzo. For sweaters, try **Maglierie** (✉ Piazza Grande).

TUSCANY A TO Z

Arriving and Departing

By Car

The Autostrada del Sole (**A1**) connects Florence with Bologna, 105 km (65 mi) north, and Rome, 277 km (172 mi) south, and passes close to Arezzo.

By Plane

The largest airports in the region are Pisa's **Aeroporto Galileo Galilei** (✉ Pisa, 80 km/50 mi west of Florence, ☎ 050/500707) and Florence's Aeroporto A. Vespucci, called **Peretola** (✉ 10 km/6 mi northwest of Florence, ☎ 055/333498).

By Train

The coastal line from Rome to Genoa passes through Pisa and all the beach resorts. The main line from Rome to Bologna passes through Arezzo, Florence, and Prato. Call ☎ 147/888088 for toll-free information.

Getting Around

By Bike

I Bike Italy (⊠ Borgo degli Albizi 11, ☎ FAX 055/2342371) offers one-day tours of the Florence countryside. **Bike Riders Tours** (⊠ Box 130254, Boston, MA, ☎ 800/473–7040) runs six-day tours of Southern Tuscany (and other areas in Italy, including Umbria, Sicily and the Aeolian Islands, and the Veneto).

By Boat

Boat services link the islands of Tuscany's archipelago with the mainland; passenger and car ferries leave from Piombino and Livorno for Elba.

Navarma (⊠ Piazzale Premuda, 57025 Piombino, ☎ 0565/225211; ⊠ Via Ninci 1, Portoferraio, ☎ 0565/918901). **Elba Ferries** (⊠ Viale Regina Margherita, 57025 Piombino, ☎ 0565/220956; ⊠ Nuova Stazione Marittima Calata Carrara, 57100 Livorno, ☎ 0586/898979, FAX 0586/896103; ⊠ 57037 Portoferraio, ☎ 0565/930676). **Toremar** (⊠ Porto Mediceo, 57025 Piombino, ☎ 0565/31100; ⊠ Porto Mediceo, 57123 Livorno, ☎ 0586/896113, 0586/886273; ⊠ Piazzale A. Candi, 58019 Porto Santo Stefano, ☎ 0564/818506).

By Bus

Tuscany is crisscrossed by bus lines that connect the smaller towns and cities on the autostrade and superhighways. They are a good mode of transport for touring the hill towns around Siena, such as San Gimignano; you can then take a Tra-In or Lazzi bus from Siena to Arezzo and get back onto the main Rome–Florence train line. From Chiusi on the main train line you can get a bus to Montepulciano. Buses connect Florence and Siena with Volterra.

By Car

The best way to see Tuscany, making it possible to explore the tiny towns and country restaurants that are so much a part of the region's charm, is by car. Drivers should be prepared to navigate through bewildering suburban sprawls around Tuscan cities; to reach the historic sections where most of the sights are, look for the CENTRO STORICO signs. In many small towns you must park outside the walls.

A11 leads west from Florence and meets the coastal **A12** between Viareggio and Livorno. The **A1** autostrada links Florence with Arezzo and Chiusi (where you turn off for Montepulciano). A toll-free superstrada links Florence with Siena. For Chianti wine country scenery, take the **S222** south of Florence through the undulating hills between Strada in Chianti and Greve in Chianti.

By Train

Italy's main rail line, which runs from Milan to Calabria, links Florence and Arezzo in Tuscany and runs past Chiusi and Cortona on its way south. Another main line connects Florence with Pisa by way of Prato, Pistoia, and Lucca. There are a few other local lines. Call ☎ 147/888088 for toll-free information.

Contacts and Resources

Agritourist Agencies

Agriturist (⊠ Piazza San Firenze 3, 50122 Florence, ☎ 055/295163).
Terranostra (⊠ Via dei Magazzini 2, 50122 Florence, ☎ 055/280539).
Turismo Verde (⊠ Via Verdi 5, 50127 Florence, ☎ 055/2344925).

Car Rentals

AREZZO
Avis (⊠ Piazza della Repubblica 1/a, ☎ 0575/354232).

LUCCA
Avis (⊠ Via Luporini 1411/a, ☎ 0583/513614).

PISA
Hertz (⊠ Aeroporto Galileo Galilei, ☎ 050/49187).

PRATO
Hertz (⊠ Via Valentini 60, ☎ 0574/611287).

SIENA
Avis (⊠ Via Simone Martini 36, ☎ 0577/270305; Hertz, ⊠ Viale Sardegna 37, ☎ 0577/45085).

Emergencies

Police, fire (☎ 113). **Ambulance,** medical emergency (☎ 118).

Guided Tours

From Florence, **American Express** (⊠ Via Guicciardini 49/r, ☎ 055/288751) operates one-day excursions to Siena and San Gimignano and can arrange for cars, drivers, and guides for special-interest tours in Tuscany. **CIT** (⊠ Via Cavour 56, ☎ 055/294306) has a three-day Carosello bus tour from Rome to Florence, Siena, and San Gimignano, as well as a five-day tour that also takes in Venice.

Horseback Riding

Rifugio Prategiano (⊠ Montieri, Grosseto, ☎ 0566/997703) is a hotel that offers horseback riding daily. Also try **Le Cannelle** (⊠ Parco dell'Uccellina, Talamone, Grosseto, ☎ 0564/887020).

Sailing

Charters in Tuscany are available through the **Centro Nautico Italiano** (⊠ Piazza della Signoria 31/r, Florence, ☎ 055/287419).

Travel Agencies

In Florence: **American Express** (⊠ Via Guicciardini 49/r, ☎ 055/288751). **CIT** (⊠ Via Cavour 56, ☎ 055/294306). **Thomas Cook** (⊠ c/o World Vision, Via Cavour 154/r, ☎ 055/579294).

Visitor Information

Arezzo (⊠ Piazza della Repubblica 22, ☎ 0575/377678). **Castellina in Chianti** (⊠ Piazza del Comune 1, ☎ 055/740201). **Cortona** (⊠ Via Nazionale 42, ☎ 0575/630352). **Elba** (⊠ Calata Italia 26, Portoferraio, ☎ 0565/914671). **Greve in Chianti** (⊠ Via Luca Cini 1, Palazzo della Torre, ☎ 055/8545243). **Lucca** (⊠ Piazzale Verdi, ☎ 0583/419689). **Montalcino** (⊠ Costa del Municipio 8, ☎ 0577/849331). **Montecatini Terme** (⊠ Viale Verdi 66, 51016, ☎ 0572/772244). **Montepulciano** (⊠ Via Ricci 9, ☎ 0578/758687). **Monteriggioni** (⊠ Strada Cassia 4, Località Colonna). **Pienza** (⊠ Palazzo Pubblico, Piazza Pio II, ☎ 0578/749071). **Pisa** (⊠ Piazza del Duomo 8, ☎ 050/560464). **Pistoia** (⊠ Palazzo dei Vescovi, Via Roma 1, ☎ 0573/21622). **Prato** (⊠ Via Cairoli 48, ☎ 0574/24112). **Radda in Chianti** (⊠ Piazza Ferrucci 1, ☎ 0577/738494; ☉ Mar.–Oct. only). **San Gimignano** (⊠ Piazza del Duomo 1, ☎ 0577/940008). **San Miniato** (⊠ Piazza del Popolo, ☎ 0571/42745). **Siena** (⊠ Piazza del Campo 56, ☎ 0577/280551). **Volterra** (⊠ Via Turazza 2, ☎ 0588/86150).

5 Venice

It's easy to forgive Venice for its eternal preoccupation with its own beauty. All the picture books in the world won't prepare you for the city's exotic landmarks, such as the Basilica di San Marco and the Palazzo Ducale, rising like mirages from the lagoons. With sumptuous palaces and romantic waterways, Venice is straight out of an 18th-century Canaletto masterpiece.

Updated by
Carla Lionello
and Jon Eldan

T IS CALLED LA SERENISSI
this name is ungainly:
"Serene Republic" mo
strous power and majesty of this city that
valed mistress of trade between Europe and the
bulwark of Christendom against the tides of Turkish
gests, too, the extraordinary beauty of the city—and su
the most beautiful city in the world (although the Florentin
surely disagree)—and its lavishness and fantasy, the result not ju
its remarkable buildings but of the very fact that Venice is a city built
on water, a city created more than 1,000 years ago by men who dared
defy the sea, implanting their splendid palaces and churches on mud
banks in a swampy and treacherous lagoon.

No matter how many times you have seen it in movies or TV com-
mercials, the real thing is more surreal and dreamlike than you ever
imagined. Its landmarks, the Basilica di San Marco and the Palazzo
Ducale, seem hardly Italian: Delightfully idiosyncratic, they are exotic
mélanges of Byzantine, Gothic, and Renaissance styles. Sunlight shim-
mers and silvery mist softens every perspective here, a city renowned
in the Renaissance for its artists' rendering of color. It is full of secrets,
ineffably romantic, and—at times—given over entirely to pleasure.

Founded on the marshes by the Roman Veneti escaping from the barbarians, Venice rose from the waters to dominate the Adriatic and hold
the gorgeous East in fee. Early in its history the city called in Byzantine
artists to decorate its churches with brilliant mosaics, still glittering today.
Then the influence of Lombard-Romanesque architecture from the
11th to 13th centuries gave rise to the characteristic type of palace, typically built on two floors with a porticoed entrance at water level and
a loggia on the first floor, for which Venice is famous the world over.
Many of the sumptuous palaces along the Grand Canal were built at
that time, strong reminders of Venice's control of the major trade routes
to the East. Subsequently, Gothic styles from elsewhere in Europe were
adapted to create a new kind of Venetian Gothic art and architecture.

Venice attained a peak of power and prosperity in the 15th and 16th
centuries. It extended its domain inland to include all of what is now
known as the Veneto region and even beyond. In the last half of the
15th century, the Renaissance arrived in Venice, and the city's greatest artists—Giovanni and Gentile Bellini and Carpaccio in the late 15th
century; Giorgione, Titian, Veronese, and Tintoretto in the 16th century—played a decisive role in the development of Western art, and
their work still covers walls and ceilings and altars all over the city today.

The decline of Venice came slowly. For 400 years the powerful maritime city-republic had held sway. After the 16th century the tide
changed. The Ottoman Empire blocked Venice's Mediterranean trade
routes, and newly emerging sea powers, such as Britain and the Netherlands, broke Venice's monopoly by opening oceanic trading routes. Like
its steadily dwindling fortunes, Venice's art and culture began a pro-
longed decline, leaving only the splendid monuments to recall a fabled
past, with the luminous paintings of Canaletto (1697–1768) and the
beautiful frescoes of Giambattista Tiepolo striking a glorious swan song.

You must walk everywhere in Venice (Venezia in Italian) and where
you cannot walk, you go by water. Occasionally, from fall to spring,
you have to walk *in* water, when extraordinarily high tides known as
acqua alta invade the lower parts of the city, flooding Piazza San
Marco for a few hours. The problem of protecting Venice and its la-

goon from dangerously high tides has generated extravagant plans and so many committee reports (☞ Close-Up: Save La Serenissima, *below*), that the city may sink as much under the weight of paper as under water. Progress is being made, however. For centuries Venice's canals were regularly dredged to keep them clean and navigable. After nearly 30 years' neglect, the dredging of canals was finally resumed in 1993. It is hoped that waterless and malodorous canals (caused by *acqua bassa*—exceptionally low tides) will soon be a thing of the past. Today, Venetians are being encouraged by state subsidies to renovate their homes, rather than leave the city to live and work on the mainland—a trend that over the last three decades has drastically reduced Venice's resident population.

In spite of these problems, Venetians have mastered the art of living well in their singular city. You'll see them going about their daily affairs in *vaporetti* (water buses), crowded aboard the *traghetti* (traditional gondola ferries) that ply between the banks of the Grand Canal, in the *campi* (squares), and along the *calli* (narrow Venetian streets). They are nothing if not skilled—and remarkably tolerant—in dealing with the veritable armies of tourists from all over the world that at peak times inundate the city.

Pleasures and Pastimes

Carnevale

" . . . All the world repaire to Venice to see the folly and madnesse of the Carnevall . . .'tis impossible to recount the universal madnesses of this place during this time of licence," commented traveler John Evelyn in 1646. Indeed, Carnevale (Carnival) was once an excuse for all manner of carnal indulgence. In its 18th-century heyday, festivities began on December 26 and lasted two months; the festival has since traded some of its more outlandish flavor for vast commercialization and lasts only for the 10 days preceding Ash Wednesday.

Dining

The general standard of Venetian restaurants has suffered from the onslaught of mass tourism, but it is still possible to eat well in Venice at moderate prices. A great Venetian tradition revolves around *bacari,* the local name for the little watering holes—called *osterie* elsewhere in Italy—where locals have gone for centuries to have a glass of wine, *cicchetti* (little savory snacks), and a chat. Venetian fish specialties include *sarde in saor* (layers of fried sardines, onions, pine nuts, and raisins), *baccalà mantecato* (dried cod with milk and olive oil) and *moeche* (softshell crabs), and *seppie in umido* (cuttlefish braised in tomato sauce).

Lodging

Most of Venice's hotels are in renovated palaces, but space is at a premium—and it comes for a price—with all Venice lodging. The most exclusive hotels are indeed palatial, although even they may have some small, dowdy Cinderella-type rooms. In lower categories, some rooms may be cramped, and not all hotels have lounging areas. Because of preservation laws, some hotels are not allowed to have elevators. Air-conditioning can be essential if you suffer in summer heat; some hotels charge a supplement for it. Although the city has no cars, it does have boats plying the canals and pedestrians chattering in the streets, even late at night, so ask for a quiet room if noise bothers you. During the summer months, don't leave your room lights on at night *and* your window wide open: Mosquitoes can descend en masse.

EXPLORING VENICE

Piazza San Marco is unquestionably the heart of Venice. Although the smaller canals (a canal is called a *rio*) are spanned by frequent bridges, the Grand Canal can only be crossed on foot at three points—Ponte degli Scalzi (near the train station), at the Ponte di Rialto, and at the Ponte dell'Accademia—which decidedly complicates matters. It's supremely maddening to find yourself on the wrong bank of a canal with no bridge in sight.

A street is called a *calle,* but a street that runs alongside a canal is called either a *riva* or a *fondamenta.* The closed-in streetscapes of Venice make it hard to see any reference point, such as the spire of the Campanile, above the rooftops, and the narrow backstreets often take unpredictable turns that confuse your sense of direction. Streets and canals may look deceptively familiar, only to make sudden dead ends. To get around Venice, you should use the vaporetti, which circulate through the city on set routes. A map of vaporetto routes, available at the train station, is always helpful.

A group of 13 Venetian churches selected for their artistic merit have begun charging admission (2,000 or 3,000 lire) for visitors during fixed hours that do not interfere with church services. At these times there should always be someone to provide information there and a free leaflet (available in English). Postcards and booklets about these important sights are on sale. If you plan to visit more than a few, consider the cumulative ticket (one-day ticket for six churches, 10,000 lire; three-month ticket for all churches, 26,000 lire). New lighting systems have been installed in many sites; all take 500-lire coins.

Numbers in the text correspond to numbers in the margin and on the Venice map.

Great Itineraries

IF YOU HAVE 2 DAYS

Spend your first day visiting the sights in and around that most famous of squares, Piazza San Marco, including the Basilica di San Marco. Explore the adjoining neighborhoods San Zaccaria, the Mercerie (shopping district), and Sant'Angelo–San Stefano central quarters if you want to catch a glimpse of Venetian life. Make an early start the following day to explore the Rialto fish and produce market, then spend the rest of the morning cruising down the Grand Canal, stopping to visit the Galleria dell'Accademia and the Ca' Rezzonico. Don't forget to walk over the Ponte di Rialto to the surrounding markets. End your day with a visit to San Stae, near Ca'Pesaro and the Chiesa di San Stae, a neighborhood particularly characteristic of Venice.

IF YOU HAVE 4 DAYS

Follow the itinerary above for the first two days. On the third day, visit the Campo dei Santi Giovanni e Paolo, northwest of the Castello, and the Campo dell'Arsenale, only a short walk from your next stop, the Museo Storico Navale, in the Castello. Return to Piazza San Marco and take the 52 or 82 vaporetto line from San Zaccaria for a look at the impressive churches of San Giorgio Maggiore (on the island of San Giorgio Maggiore) and Redentore (on the Giudecca), both particularly beautiful at sunset. On your final day visit the islands of the lagoon: Be sure not to miss Murano and its glass museums, along with the islands of Burano and Torcello.

IF YOU HAVE 6 DAYS

Start at Piazza San Marco, ending your day on the Ponte dei Sospiri next door. The next day cruise the Grand Canal, stopping at Santa Maria della Salute and the nearby Collezione Peggy Guggenheim, before visiting the Galleria dell'Accademia. Next visit the Ca' Rezzonico and explore the Ponte di Rialto area. Spend the late afternoon walking through the neighborhood of San Stae. On the third day, visit Santa Maria dei Miracoli, Campo dei Santi Giovanni e Paolo, the Campo dell'Arsenale, and finally the Museo Storico Navale. If you have time, try to visit San Pietro di Castello before returning to Piazza San Marco via the Scuola di San Giorgio degli Schiavoni. On the fourth day, take the 52 or 82 vaporetto line from San Zaccaria to explore San Giorgio Maggiore and the Giudecca. Head directly across from the Giudecca to the Zattere, a lively Dorsoduro promenade with lots of pizzerias. Spend the fifth day exploring Titian's works: Start in Campo Santo Stefano and then head for the Scuola dei Carmini and the Chiesa di San Sebastiano. A must is the Frari, home of some of Titian's best. Next, visit the Scuola Grande di San Rocco, with delightful paintings by Tintoretto. On your final day explore the islands of the lagoon. If you can, squeeze in a visit to the cemetery island, Cimitero San Michele.

Piazza San Marco, the Heart of Venice

The most evocative square in the world, Piazza San Marco is the heart of Venice, a vast open square enclosed by an orderly procession of arcades marching toward the fairy-tale cupolas and marble lacework of the Basilica di San Marco. Perpetually animated during the day when it's filled with people and crowds of fluttering pigeons, it can be magical at night, especially in the winter, when melancholy mists swirl around the lampposts and bell tower.

A Good Walk

Start your day in the **Piazza San Marco** ① with a morning visit to the **Basilica di San Marco** ②, home of the Pala d'Oro and the Museo di San Marco. Next, get a bird's-eye view of the piazza and city from the **Campanile** ③. Move on to the smaller **Piazzetta San Marco** for a visit to the glorious **Palazzo Ducale** ④ and a look at the Ponte dei Sospiri at the east wing of the palace. Return to Piazza San Marco where directly opposite the facade of the basilica you will find the **Museo Correr** ⑤ in the Ala Napoleonica.

TIMING

You'll need a full day to visit each sight thoroughly. If you have limited time, you will need to discipline yourself from straying too far from the Piazza San Marco; a half day should be enough to see the essential sights, but do not miss the Pala d'Oro in the basilica, the Palazzo Ducale, and, of course, the piazza itself. If you come in summer, like the Venetians, you will have to adapt to the crowds, visiting at odd hours to avoid tour groups.

Sights to See

★ ❷ **Basilica di San Marco.** An opulent synthesis of Byzantine and Romanesque styles, Venice's gem is laid out in a Greek cross topped off with five plump domes. The basilica did not actually become the cathedral of Venice until as late as 1807, but its role as the church of the doge gave it immense power and wealth. It was begun in 1063, and inaugurated in 1094, to house the remains of St. Mark the Evangelist, which were filched from Alexandria two centuries earlier by two agents of the doge. The story goes that they stole the saint's remains and hid them in a barrel under layers of pickled pork to get them past the Muslim guards. The escapade is illustrated in a mosaic in the semicircular lunette over the farthest left of the front doors. This 13th-century mosaic is the earliest one on this heavily decorated facade; look at it closely to see a picture of the church as it appeared at that time.

Over the years this church stood as a symbol of Venetian wealth and power, and it was endowed with all the riches the Republic's admirals and merchants could carry off from the Orient, earning it the nickname Chiesa d'Oro (Golden Church). The four bronze horses that prance and snort over the central doorway (copies only, but the originals are on view indoors in the Museo di San Marco [☞ *below*]) were classical sculptures that victorious Venetians took away from Constantinople in 1204, along with a lot of other loot on display here. Just inside the central front doors in the church porch, look for a medallion of red porphyry set in the floor to mark the spot of another of Venice's political coups: the reconciliation between Barbarossa, the Holy Roman Emperor, and Pope Alexander III, brought about by Doge Sebastiano Ziani in 1177.

One of the innovations of this church was a roof of brick vaulting, rather than wood, which enabled the ceiling to be decorated with mosaics. As you enter the basilica, you'll find it surprisingly dark inside, compared to the soaring light-filled Gothic cathedrals of northern Europe. This is because many of the original windows were filled in and covered with even more mosaics. In the mysterious dusk, candles flicker and the gold tiles of mosaics glitter softly, sensuously. (The tiles were laid on at slight angles to achieve precisely this effect.) The earliest mosaics are from the 11th and 12th centuries; later ones were done as late as the 16th century, such as the *Last Judgment* on the arch between the porch and the nave, said to be based on drawings by Tintoretto (1518–94). The dim light, the galleries high above the naves—they served as the *matroneum* (women's gallery)—the massive altar screen, or iconostasis, the single massive Byzantine chandelier, even the Greek cross ground plan, give San Marco an exotic feel quite unlike that of most Christian churches. The effect is remarkable. Here the pomp and mystery of Oriental magnificence are wedded to Christian belief, creating an intensely awesome impression.

To the right, just off the porch, is the **Cappella Zen** (Zen Chapel), named after a local cardinal rather than any form of Buddhism, to see some earlier (13th-century) mosaics, telling the story of the life of St. Mark. Next to it, the **Battistero** (Baptistery) contains a bronze font cover by Jacopo Sansovino (1486–1570) and the tomb of Doge Andrea Dandolo (1307–54), a friend of Petrarch (1304–74) and a writer in his own right. Several of the earlier doges were buried here, while later ones were interred in the Chiesa dei Santi Giovanni e Paolo (☞ *below*).

Two more chapels, both in the left transept, are worth a special look: the **Cappella della Madonna di Nicopeia** (Chapel of the Madonna of Nicopeia), which holds a precious icon (part of the loot from Constantinople) that many consider Venice's most powerful protector. Nearby is the **Cappella della Madonna dei Mascoli**, where the Virgin Mary was worshiped by a male confraternity (*mascoli*), with fine 15th-century mosaics depicting her life, possibly based on drawings by Jacopo Bellini (1400–70).

The **Sanctuario** (Sanctuary) in the Basilica of San Marco is well worth the modest admission fee. The main altar, with its green marble canopy lifted high on carved alabaster columns, covers the tomb of St. Mark. Behind this is the real attraction: the extraordinarily sumptuous **Pala d'Oro** (Golden Altarpiece), a dazzling gilded silver screen encrusted with 1,927 precious gems and 255 enameled panels. It was originally made in Constantinople in the 11th century, and then continually embellished over the next three centuries by Byzantine and Venetian master craftsmen. The bronze door leading from the sanctuary back into the sacristy is another work by Sansovino; check out the top left corner,

Sacca
della
Misericordia

Canale delle Navi

CIMITERO

Cimitero
San
Michele

33 36

0 ————— 440 yards
0 ————— 400 meters

ITALY

C. Racchetta
Rio S. Caterina
Fondamenta
FOND. NUOVE

32

R. d. Gesuiti Nuove

Rio della Panada

C.d. Savero

OSPEDALE
CIVILE

Strada
Nuova

D'ORO
Campo d.
Pescheria

Rio d' Santi Apostoli

Rio della Panada

C. d'Testa

dei Mendicanti

Campo Santi
Giovanni e Paolo

16

17 18

Calle delle Tole

R. d. S.
Giustina

CELESTIA

Erberia
del Vin
Ponte di
Rialto

9

ALTO

del Carbon

Rio d. S. Marina

R. d. Barbaria

Ruga
Giuffa

R. d. S. Severo

R. d. S. Lorenzo

19

R. d. S.
Francesco

Canale d. Galeazze

Merceria

C. d. Bande

Sal. di S. Lio

15

C. Lion

23

C. d.
Furlani

R. d. Pietà

R. d. Greci

R. di Scudi

R. d. Gorne

Darsena
Grande

Rio d. Vergini

Rio d. S. Daniele

di S. Pietro

22

Campo
Manin

Fobbri

Frezzaria

S. Moisè

R. d.

5 1 3

2

4

R. d. Palazzo

SAN
ZACCARIA

Ponte dei
Sospiri

Molo

Riva degli

CASTELLO

Fond.
Osmarin

20

R. d. Arsenale

Riva della Tana

V. Garibaldi

Rio d. S. Anna

Schiavoni

RIVA DEGLI
SCHIAVONI

S. ZACCARIA

CAMPO
DELLA
TANA

21

ARSENALE

Riva dei Sette Martiri

R. d. S. Giuseppe

Piazza
San Marco

S. MARCO
GIARDINETTI

S. MARCO
VALLARESSA

SALUTE

Canale di S. Marco

S. GIORGIO

37

S. Giorgio
Maggiore

GIARDINI

Rio dei Giardini

ZITELLE

Fond.
delle Zitelle

DEL
TORE

Calle
Michelangelo

LIDO

KEY

ℹ Tourist Information
▲ Boat stop

where the artist included a self-portrait and, above that, a picture of his friend and fellow artist Titian (circa 1488–1576). Tickets for the Sanctuary also include admission into the **Tesoro** (Treasury), entered from the right transept. Many of the exquisite pieces are exotic treasures borne away from Constantinople and other vanquished places.

From the atrium, climb the steep stairway to the **Galleria** and the **Museo di San Marco** for a look at the interior of the church from the organ gallery and a sweeping view of Piazza San Marco and the Piazzetta dei Leoncini from the outdoor gallery. The highlight of the museum is the close-up of the four magnificent gilded bronze horses that once stood outside on the gallery. The originals were probably cast in Imperial Rome, and later transported to the New Rome, Constantinople. Napoléon hauled them off to Paris after he conquered Venice in 1797, but they were returned after the fall of the French Empire.

Be warned: Guards at the door turn away any visitors, male or female, wearing shorts, short skirts, tank tops, and other attire considered inappropriate. If you want to take a free guided tour in English in summer (with less certainty in winter, since the guides are volunteers), wait on the left in the porch for a group to form. ⊠ *Piazza San Marco,* ☎ *041/5225205. Basilica:* 🎫 *Free.* ☉ *Mon.–Sat. 9:45–5:30 (Oct.–Apr. until 5), Sun. 2–5:30 (Oct.–Apr. until 5). Sanctuary, Pala d'Oro, and Treasury:* 🎫 *3,000 lire.* ☉ *Same as basilica, last entry 30 mins before closing. Gallery and Museum:* ☎ *041/5225205.* 🎫 *3,000 lire.* ☉ *Same as basilica, last entry 30 mins before closing. Tours from left porch:* 🎫 *Free.* ☉ *June–Aug., Mon.–Sat. several tours daily.*

★ ❸ **Campanile.** The brick Bell Tower is a reconstruction of the original, which stood for 1,000 years before it collapsed one morning in 1912, practically without warning (miraculously none of the surrounding buildings suffered serious damage, and the only victim was a cat). In the 15th century, clerics found guilty of immoral behavior were suspended in wooden cages from the tower, sometimes to subsist on bread and water for as long as a year, other times to starve to death. The pretty marble loggia (covered gallery) at its base was built in the early 16th century by Jacopo Sansovino. The view from the tower on a clear day—the Lido, the lagoon, and the mainland as far as the Alps—oddly doesn't include the myriad canals that snake through the 117 islets on which Venice is built. ⊠ *Piazza San Marco,* ☎ *041/5224064.* 🎫 *8,000 lire.* ☉ *June–Sept., daily 9:30–7, Oct.–May, daily 9:30–3:45. Closed 2 wks in Jan.*

❺ **Museo Correr.** In 1830 the aristocrat Teodoro Correr donated his private collection—a fascinating, diverse mix of historical items and old master paintings—to the city. Exhibits range from the absurdly high-soled shoes worn by 16th-century Venetian ladies (who had to be supported by a servant on each side to walk on these precarious perches) to fine art by the talented Bellini family of Renaissance painters. ⊠ *Piazza San Marco, Ala Napoleonica,* ☎ *041/5225625.* 🎫 *14,000 lire includes entrance to Palazzo Ducale (☞ below).* ☉ *Apr.–Oct., daily 9–7; Nov.–Mar., daily 9–5; last entry 1 hr before closing.*

★ ❹ **Palazzo Ducale** (Doge's Palace). This Gothic-Renaissance fantasia of pink-and-white marble, a majestic expression of the prosperity and power attained by Venice during its most glorious period, rises above Piazzetta San Marco. Its top-heavy design (the dense upper floors rest on the graceful ground-floor colonnade) has always confounded architectural purists, who insist that proper architecture be set out the other way around. The building was much more than just a palace—rather it was a sort of combination White House, Senate, torture chamber, and prison rolled into one. Venice's government, set up sometime in the 7th century as a participatory democracy, provided for an elected ruler, the doge, to serve for life, but in practice he was simply a figurehead. Power really rested with the Great Council, originally an elected body but, from the 13th century on, an aristocratic stronghold, with members inheriting their seats from their noble ancestors. Laws were passed by the Senate, a group of 200 elected from the Great Council (which could have as many as 1,700 members). Executive powers belonged to the College, a committee of 25 leaders. In the 14th century, the Council of Ten was formed to deal with emergency situations; though it was often more powerful than the Senate, its members could only serve for limited terms.

A fortress for the doge existed on this spot in the early 9th century; the building you see today was a product of the 12th century, although, like the basilica next door, it was continually added to and transformed throughout the centuries. You enter the palace at the ornate Gothic **Porta della Carta** (Gate of the Paper), where official decrees were traditionally posted; it opens onto an immense courtyard. Ahead is the **Scala dei Giganti** (Stairway of the Giants), guarded by huge statues of Mars and Neptune by Jacopo Sansovino. Ordinary mortals do not get to climb these stairs, however; after paying your fee, walk along the arcade to reach the central interior staircase. Its upper flight is called the **Scala d'Oro** (Golden Staircase), also designed by Sansovino, with its lavish gilded decoration. Although it may seem odd that the government's main council rooms and reception halls would be so far upstairs, imagine how effectively foreign emissaries must have been intimidated by this arduous climb.

Visitors must have also been overwhelmed by the sumptuous decoration of these apartments, their walls and ceilings covered with works by Venice's greatest artists. Among the grand rooms you can visit are the **Anticollegio,** a waiting room outside the Collegio's chamber with two fine paintings, Tintoretto's *Bacchus and Ariadne Crowned by Venus* and Veronese's (1528–88) *Rape of Europa;* the **Sala del Collegio** (College Chamber), its ceiling magnificently painted by Veronese; and the **Sala del Senato** (Senate Chamber), with Tintoretto's *Triumph of Venice* on the ceiling. The huge *Paradise* on the end wall of the **Sala del Maggior Consiglio** (Great Council Hall) is by Jacopo Tintoretto; it is a dark, dynamic masterpiece. This is the world's largest oil painting (23 × 75 ft), a vast work commissioned for a vast hall. The massive carved and gilded ceiling is breathtaking, even dizzying, as you wheel around searching for the best vantage point from which to admire Veronese's majestic *Apotheosis of Venice* filling one of the center panels. Look at the frieze of portraits of the first 76 doges around the upper part of the walls. One portrait is missing: a black painted curtain near the left-hand corner of the wall opposite Tintoretto's painting marks the spot where the portrait of doge Marin Falier should be. A Latin inscription bluntly explains that Falier was executed for treason in 1355. The Republic never forgave him.

A guided tour of the palace's secret rooms takes you to the doge's private apartments, up into the attic and Piombi prison, and through hidden passageways to the torture chambers, where prisoners were interrogated. The 18th-century writer and libertine, Casanova, a native of Venice, was imprisoned here in 1755, having somehow offended someone in power (the official accusation was of being a Freemason); he made a daring escape 15 months later and fled to France, where he continued his career of intrigue and scandal. From the east wing of the Doge's Palace, the enclosed marble **Ponte dei Sospiri** (Bridge of Sighs) arches over a narrow canal to the cramped, gloomy cell blocks of the so-called Nuova Prigione (New Prison). During the age of Romanticism, the bridge's tragic and melancholic history made it one of the prize sights for 19th-century tourists. The bridge's name comes from the sighs of those being led to execution. Take a look out its windows to see the last earthly view many of these prisoners had. ⊠ *Palazzo Ducale, Piazzetta San Marco,* ☎ *041/ 5224951.* 🎫 *14,000 lire includes entrance to Museo Correr (☞ above).* ☉ *Apr.–Oct., daily 9–7; Nov.–Mar., daily 9–5 (last entry 1½ hrs before closing). "Secret Itineraries" tour:* 🎫 *24,000 lire.* ☉ *English tours usually daily at 10:30, but call that morning to confirm. Reservations not accepted.*

★ ❶ **Piazza San Marco.** If you stand at the far end of the piazza, facing the basilica, you'll notice that rather than being a strict rectangle, it opens wider at the basilica end, enhancing the perspective and creating the illusion of being even larger than it is. On your left, the long arcaded building is the **Procuratie Vecchie,** built in the early 16th century as offices and residences for the powerful Procurators of San Marco. Across the piazza, on your right-hand side, is the **Procuratie Nuove,** built half a century later in a more grandiose classical style. The Procuratie Nuove has impeccable architectural lineage: It was originally planned by perhaps Venice's greatest Renaissance architect, Jacopo Sansovino of Florence, to carry on the look of his **Libreria Vecchia,** where the **Biblioteca Nazionale Marciana** (Marciana National Library) is now housed (open occasionally for special exhibits), though Sansovino died before the building was begun. The actual designer was Vincenzo Scamozzi (circa 1552–1616), a pupil of Andrea Palladio (1508–80) and a devout Neoclassicist; later sections were completed by Baldassare Longhena (1598–1682), Venice's other great architect, who belonged firmly to the Baroque tradition.

When Napoléon (1769–1821) entered Venice with his troops in 1797, he called Piazza San Marco "the world's most beautiful drawing room"—and promptly gave orders to redecorate it. His architects demolished an old church that stood behind you, at the end of the square farthest from the basilica, and put up the **Ala Napoleonica** (Napoleonic Wing), or Fabbrica Nuova (New Building), to unite the two 16th-century buildings on either side.

NEED A
BREAK?

On the Procuratie Vecchie side of Piazza San Marco is the historic **Caffè Quadri** (☎ 041/5289299), shunned by Venetians during the 19th century when the occupying Austrians made it their gathering place. **Caffè Florian** (☎ 041/5285338, Closed Wed.), on the Procuratie Nuove side, is where Casanova, Wagner, and Proust regularly visited.

Piazzetta San Marco. This square leads from Piazza San Marco down to the waters of the Bacino di San Marco (St. Mark's Basin). This landing stage, now crowded with excursion boats, was once the grand entrance to the Republic. Two tall columns rise here on the waterfront: One is topped by the winged lion, a traditional emblem of St. Mark that became by extension the symbol of Venice itself; the other bears aloft a statue of St. Theodore (the first patron saint of Venice) and his dragon.

Torre dell'Orologio. Erected in 1496, the Clock Tower has an enameled timepiece and animated figures of Moors that strike the hour (HORAS NON NUMERO NISI SERENAS says the inscription on the tower—"Only happy hours"). During Ascension Week (40 days after Easter) and on Epiphany (Jan. 6), an angel and three wise men go in and out of the doors and bow to the Virgin. It is closed for restoration until at least 2000. ⊠ *Northern side of Piazza San Marco.*

Along the Grand Canal

Venetians call it the Canalazzo, but to the rest of the world it's the Grand Canal, the city's main thoroughfare. A 3-km-long (2-mi-long), 40- to 76-yard-wide ribbon of water, wending its way from San Marco to the Stazione Ferroviaria Santa Lucia like an inverted letter *S*, it was, and to some extent still is, the Fifth Avenue of Venice. It was here, from the 14th to 18th centuries, that the city's richest families lived, building for themselves a series of magnificent Venetian Gothic and Renaissance palaces—200 at last count—remarkable even by the city's standards. Here, the combination of being surrounded by water and the most opulent, luxurious, and fantastic efforts of a people obsessed with opulence, luxury, and fantasy has created a seemingly endless unfolding panorama of unique architectural richness. It makes sense to attempt little more at first than to sample, to breathe in, the unparalleled magnificence of the Grand Canal, letting it wash over you—only metaphorically, of course; it may not be deep (average depth is 9 ft) but it's very dirty. To begin your exploration, catch Vaporetto 1 at the San Marco landing stage. Don't forget to return for a gondola ride an hour or so before sunset; this is the most romantic way to see Venice. However, for an overall sightseeing tour of the canal, you get a better, more extensive view from a vaporetto—which is both higher in the water and much less expensive. Try to get one of the coveted seats in the prow, where you have a clear view. Once off the vaporetto, keep in mind the two-man traghetti that allow you—at many points along the Canalazzo—to ferry across from one bank to the other for only 700 lire.

A Good Boat Trip

As you leave Piazza San Marco on the vaporetto, **Chiesa di Santa Maria della Salute** ⑥, the huge, white, domed 17th-century Baroque church designed by Longhena, is on the left. Not far from this stop is the small **Collezione Peggy Guggenheim** ⑦, filled with engaging 20th-century works, a nice departure from the cinquecento. Across the canal you can see the imposing terraced front of the **Gritti Palace** hotel (☞ Lodging, *below*), which occupies the former Palazzo Pisani. A few minutes farther on (after passing the Galleria dell'Accademia, ☞ *below*), on the left bank at the Ca' Rezzonico stop is Longhera's Baroque **Ca' Rezzonico** ⑧. Be sure to visit the Museo del Settecento Veneziano, housed here in gilded salons.

The canal narrows and boat traffic increases as you approach the **Ponte di Rialto** ⑨, arched high over the canal. The Ca' d'Oro landing on the right, just beyond the Rialto, marks the lovely Venetian Gothic palace of **Ca' d'Oro** ⑩. Across the canal from the Ca' d'Oro, you'll see the classical facade, with loggias on two stories, of the **Palazzo Corner della Regina** ⑪. Just beyond the Corner della Regina you can't miss the imposing bulk of the grand Baroque **Ca' Pesaro** ⑫, designed by Longhena, and unfortunately closed for restoration.

Not far beyond, on the left, another white church is adorned with Baroque statues; this is the Chiesa di San Stae, and the landing here is a gateway to an untrammeled San Stae neighborhood, with its narrow canals and airy squares. Back on the right bank, the Renaissance **Palazzo Vendramin-Calergi** ⑬ is now the winter home of Venice's glamorous Casino (☞ Nightlife and the Arts, *below*). Continuing along the Grand Canal, winding toward the railway station, you will see on your right the 16th-century Ponte delle Guglie, famed for its spires and adjacent to the elegant facade of **Palazzo Labia** ⑭.

TIMING

All these sights can be comfortably visited in one day. Jumping on and off the vaporetto is easy, although you may be tempted just to take the ride and view the sights from the canal.

Sights to See

⑩ Ca' d'Oro. This lovely Venetian Gothic palace is adorned with marble traceries and ornaments once embellished with pure gold. Today it houses the **Galleria Franchetti**, a fine collection of tapestries, sculptures, and paintings. ⊠ *Calle della Ca' d'Oro, 3933 Cannaregio,* ☏ *041/5238790.* 🎫 *4,000 lire.* 🕙 *Daily 9–2.*

⑫ Ca' Pesaro. Designed by Longhena in grand Baroque style, the palace is now home to two rather dull art collections, the **Museo Orientale** (Oriental Art Museum) and the **Galleria d'Arte Moderna** (Modern Art Gallery), containing mostly 19th-century and some 20th-century works. ⊠ *San Stae, S. Croce,* ☏ *041/5241173.* 🕙 *Museo Orientale: Tues.– Sun. 9–2; Galleria d'Arte Moderna closed for restoration until 1999.* 🎫 *4,000 lire.*

★ ⑧ Ca' Rezzonico. In this huge Baroque mansion you'll find Venice's most magnificent ballroom—site of Venice's greatest costume ball, the last of which was held in the 1960s to honor Elizabeth Taylor and Richard Burton. Longhena began work on it in the 1660s, and it was completed by architect Giorgio Massari in the 1740s. This was the English poet Robert Browning's (1812–89) last home, where he died. Be sure to visit the **Museo del Settecento Veneziano** (Museum of 18th-Century Venice), housed in gilded salons. Pictures by the 18th-century Venetian painters Francesco (1712–93) and Gianantonio (1699–1760) Guardi and Pietro Longhi (1702–85), and a fine series of frescoes by their younger contemporary Giandomenico Tiepolo (1727–1804) at the back of the palace, really open a window onto that charming and delightfully frivolous social era. Note that the second floor was closed for restoration at press time. ⊠ *Fondamenta Pedrocco, 3136 Dorsoduro,* ☏ *041/2410100.* 🎫 *12,000 lire.* 🕙 *Sat.–Thurs. 10–4.*

⑥ Chiesa di Santa Maria della Salute. Longhena designed this huge, white, domed 17th-century Baroque church. ⊠ *Punta della Dogana, Dorsoduro.* ☏ *041/731268.* 🕙 *Daily 10–noon and 4–6.*

⑦ Collezione Peggy Guggenheim. Visit and delight in this small but choice gallery of 20th-century painting and sculpture in the heiress's lavish former apartments in the Palazzo Venier dei Leoni. Through wealth and social connections, Guggenheim (1898–1979) became a serious patron of art—she was once married to the painter Max Ernst—and her holdings include several works by Picasso, Kandinsky, Ernst, Pollock, and Motherwell. ⊠ *Entrance on Calle San Cristoforo, 701 Dorsoduro,* ☏ *041/5206288.* 🎫 *12,000 lire.* 🕙 *Wed.–Mon. 11–6.*

⑪ Palazzo Corner della Regina. Now housing the Biennale's library, this palace is among the most beautiful in Venice. It was built in 1724 and named after the *regina* (queen) of Cyprus, Caterina Cornaro, who was born in an older palace on this site. On the second floor is a *portego*— a hall running the length of a palace, a feature typical of Venetian palazzi. ⊠ *Calle della Regina, San Stae,* ☏ *041/5218701.* 🎫 *Free. Closed for restoration until 2000.*

⑭ Palazzo Labia. Once the palatial stamping grounds of Venice's showiest 18th-century family, the palace today is the Venetian headquarters of RAI, the Italian radio and television giant. It is hard to imagine a broadcasting company in any other country establishing itself among such opulent splendor, however apt in Italy. The **Tiepolo Room,** a gorgeous ballroom in the palazzo, exhibits the final flowering of Venetian painting: Giambattista Tiepolo's (1696–1770) illusionistic frescoes of Antony and Cleopatra, teeming with dwarfs, Barbary pirates, and toy dogs. The artist's true sense of pleasure is evident. ⊠ *Campo San Geremia, Cannaregio,* ☎ *041/5242812.* 🖼 *Ballroom free. Guided tour of ballroom and other rooms (available in English) 12,000 lire.* ☉ *Tours (reservations essential) Wed. and Fri. 3–4.*

⑬ Palazzo Vendramin-Calergi. In 1883 the great German composer Wagner (1813–83) died in this Renaissance palazzo designed by Mauro Coducci (1440–1504) in white stone with red marble medallions and an imposing carved frieze. It is now the winter home of Venice's glamorous **Casino** (☞ *Nightlife and the Arts, below*).

★ ⑨ Ponte di Rialto (Rialto Bridge). The canal narrows and boat traffic increases as you approach this bridge arched high over the canal. The windows are those of the shops inside. The surrounding area is a commercial hub, with open-air vegetable, fruit, and fish markets and an upscale shopping district.

Castello and San Pietro

The city's eastern districts and some of its most beautiful churches are along the path of the Mercerie, one of Venice's busiest streets. It's actually a five-part series of streets (Merceria dell'Orologio, Merceria di San Zulian, Merceria del Capitello, Merceria di San Salvador, and Merceria 2 Aprile) leading more or less directly from Piazza San Marco to the Rialto Bridge.

A Good Walk

Head out of Piazza San Marco under the clock tower onto the Mercerie. At Campo San Zulian and the church of San Giuliano, turn right onto Calle Guerra and Calle delle Bande to reach the white marble **Chiesa di Santa Maria Formosa** ⑮. Follow Calle Borgoloco into Campo San Marina, where you turn right, cross the little canal, and take Calle Castelli to the **Chiesa di Santa Maria dei Miracoli** ⑯. Behind the church, bear right to Calle Larga Giacinto Gallina, which leads to **Campo dei Santi Giovanni e Paolo** ⑰, site of the massive Dominican Chiesa dei Santi Giovanni e Paolo, or San Zanipolo. The powerful equestrian monument of Bartolomeo Colleoni, by Florentine sculptor Andrea del Verrocchio (1435–88), stands in the square.

Behind the east end of San Zanipolo, on Barbaria del le Tole, is the church of Santa Maria dei Derelitti, with its over-the-top Baroque facade by Longhena, and the attached **Ospedaletto** ⑱. Continue beyond the Ospedaletto to another large church, **Chiesa di San Francesco della Vigna** ⑲, with its stern classical Palladian facade.

Go left as you leave the church to begin the 500-yard walk to the **Campo dell'Arsenale** ⑳, the main entrance to the immense arsenal dockyard. The **Museo Storico Navale** ㉑ on nearby Campo San Biagio has four floors of scale boat models. If you still have time and energy, go east to the island and the **Chiesa di San Pietro di Castello** ㉒; two footbridges lead to this island. About midway between the Arsenal and Piazza San Marco, on your way back from the eastern district, is the **Scuola di San Giorgio degli Schiavoni** ㉓.

TIMING

An exploration of this neighborhood and as far east as the island of San Pietro should take four to five hours. Try to avoid walking around this mostly open neighborhood during the hottest hours of the day if you plan to travel in summer. Allow some time to browse through the Merceria district.

Sights to See

★ ⑰ **Campo dei Santi Giovanni e Paolo.** This large square has the massive Dominican **Chiesa dei Santi Giovanni e Paolo**—or San Zanipolo as it's known in Venetian dialect—on one side, and the powerful equestrian **Monumento di Bartolomeo Colleoni** by Florentine sculptor Andrea del Verrocchio on the other. Colleoni had served Venice well as a *condottiere*, or mercenary commander (the Venetians preferred to pay others to fight for them on land). When he died in 1475, he left his fortune to the city on the condition that a statue be erected in his honor "in the piazza before St. Mark's." The republic's shrewd administrators coveted Colleoni's ducats but had no intention of honoring anyone, no matter how valorous, with a statue in Piazza San Marco. So they commissioned the statue and put it up before the Scuola di San Marco, which is off to the side and the headquarters of a charitable confraternity, enabling them to collect the loot. San Zanipolo contains tombs of several doges, as well as a wealth of art. Don't miss the Cappella del Rosario (Rosary Chapel), off the left transept; with its Veronese ceiling paintings, it's a sumptuous study in decoration, built in the 16th century to commemorate the victory of Lepanto in western Greece in 1571, when Venice and a combined European fleet succeeded in destroying the Turkish navy. ⊠ *Campo dei San Giovanni e Paolo.* ☉ *Mon.– Sat. 8–12:30 and 3–6, Sun. 3–6.*

⑳ **Campo dell'Arsenale.** The immense **Arsenale** (Arsenal) dockyard was founded in 1104 to build and equip the fleet of the Venetian republic. It was augmented continually through the 16th century. For a republic founded on sea might, having a huge state-of-the-art shipyard was of paramount importance, and this one was renowned for its size and skill. All subsequent dockyards were named after it (the name comes from the Arabic *d'arsina*, meaning workshop). No wonder it has such a grandiose entrance, with four stone lions from ancient Greece guarding the great Renaissance gateway. ⊠ *Arsenale, Castello.*

⑲ **Chiesa di San Francesco della Vigna** (St. Francis of the Vineyard). This large and austere classical Palladian church was built by Sansovino in 1534. A pretty cloister opens out from the severely simple and unadorned gray-and-white interior, its works of art minor and not particularly interesting. ⊠ *Campo di San Francesco della Vigna, Castello,* ☎ *041/ 5206102.* 🎟 *Free.* ☉ *Mon.–Sat. 8–noon and 3–7, Sun. 3–7.*

㉒ **Chiesa di San Pietro di Castello.** On the island of San Pietro, connected to the mainland by two footbridges, this church served as Venice's cathedral for centuries. It now presides over a picturesque workaday neighborhood, and its tipsy bell tower leans over a grassy square. ⊠ *Campo San Pietro Apostolo, Castello,* ☎ *041/5238950.* 🎟 *2,000 lire.* ☉ *Mon.–Sat. 10–5, Sun. 3–5.*

⑯ **Chiesa di Santa Maria dei Miracoli.** Perfectly proportioned and sheathed in marble, this church is an early Renaissance gem, decorated inside with exquisite marble reliefs. Notice how the architect, Pietro Lombardo, made the church look bigger with various optical illusions: varying the color of the exterior marble to create the effect of distance; using extra pilasters to make the building's canal side look longer; slightly offsetting the arcade windows to make the arches look deeper. The church was built in the 1480s to house an image of the Virgin that is said to perform miracles—look for this icon on the high altar. At press time the church was scheduled to reopen in fall 1998, after a three-year restoration to slow down the effects of saltwater erosion (☞ Close-Up: Save

La Serenissima, *below*). ✉ *Calle delle Erbe, Castello,* ☎ *041/5235293.* 🎫 *2,000 lire.* ⊙ *Mon.–Sat. 10–5, Sun. 3–5.*

⓯ **Chiesa di Santa Maria Formosa.** This graceful white marble church was inspired by a vision of *una Madonna formosa* (a buxom Madonna) that appeared to Saint Magno in the 7th century. The matronly Madonna told him to follow a small white cloud and build a church wherever it settled. The present building, built by Coducci in 1492, was grafted on to the foundations of an earlier 11th-century church that replaced Magno's original. The church's interior is a unique architectural blend, merging a welter of Renaissance decoration with Coducci's ersatz collection of Byzantine cupolas, barrel vaults, and narrow-columned screens. Of interest are two fine paintings, Bartolomeo Vivarini's *Madonna of the Misericordia* and Palma Vecchio's *Santa Barbara*. Outside there is a lively square with a few sidewalk cafés and a small vegetable market on weekday mornings. ✉ *Campo Santa Maria Formosa, Castello,* ☎ *041/5234645.* 🎫 *2,000 lire.* ⊙ *Mon.–Sat. 10–5, Sun. 3–5.*

🄲 ㉑ **Museo Storico Navale** (Museum of Naval History). Four floors of scale boat models and an annex containing actual boats—from gondolas to doges' ceremonial boats—are guaranteed to fascinate children and boat lovers. ✉ *Campo San Biagio, Arsenale, Castello,* ☎ *041/ 5200276.* 🎫 *2,000 lire.* ⊙ *Mon.–Fri. 8:45–1:30, Sat. 8:45–1.*

⓲ **Ospedaletto.** Literally little hospital, this was founded in the 16th century and was one of Venice's four foundling hospitals. The church of **Santa Maria dei Derelitti** (St. Mary of the Destitute) is next to the Ospedaletto. Each hospital had an orchestra and choir of little orphans (one of which was presided over by Antonio Vivaldi). Note the large gallery above the Derelitti's altar, built to accommodate the young musicians. The orphanage is now an old people's home, but the beautiful 18th-century **Sala della Musica** (Music Room), where rehearsals took place and patrons and honored guests were received—the only one of its kind to survive—has been magnificently restored and can be visited (enter through the church). On the Music Room's end wall is a lovely fresco by Jacopo Guarana, depicting Apollo, the God of Music, surrounded by the orphan musicians conducted by their music master, Pasquale Anfossi. ✉ *Calle Barbaria de le Tole, Castello.* 🎫 *Free; donations appreciated.* ⊙ *Church and Music Room: Apr.–Sept., Thurs.–Sat. 4–7; Oct.–Mar., Thurs.–Sat. 3–6.*

㉓ **Scuola di San Giorgio degli Schiavoni.** This is one of numerous *scuole* built during the time of the Republic. These weren't schools, as the present-day Italian word would imply, but confraternities devoted to charitable works. Many scuole were decorated lavishly, both in the private chapels and in the meeting halls. The confraternity features works by Vittore Carpaccio (circa 1465–1525), a local artist who often filled his otherwise devotional paintings with acutely observed details of Venetian life. Study the exuberance of his *St. George* as he slays the dragon or the vivid colors and details in *The Funeral of St. Jerome* and *St. Augustine in His Study.* ✉ *3259 Castello, near Ponte dei Greci,* ☎ *041/ 5228828.* 🎫 *7,000 lire.* ⊙ *Tues.–Sat. 10–12:30 and 3–6 (6:30 Apr.– Sept.), Sun. 10–12:30 (9:30–12:30 Apr.–Sept.).*

Dorsoduro, San Polo, and Santa Croce

If churches, further ramblings along dreamy canals, and masterpieces by great Venetian artists such as Titian and Tintoretto capture your interest, head out of Piazza San Marco under the arcades of the Fabbrica Nuova at the far end of the square.

A Good Walk

Leave Piazza San Marco via the Calle Bocca di Piazza. Next take Calle Larga XXII Marzo (or "wide street"), to **Campo San Stefano** ㉔, dominated by the 14th-century church of San Stefano. Join the stream of pedestrians crossing the Grand Canal on the Ponte dell'Accademia to the district Dorsoduro (literally, "hard back" for its strong clay foundation). The bridge leads you directly to the **Galleria dell'Accademia** ㉕, displaying an unparalleled collection of Venetian art.

Continue toward Campo Santa Margherita, passing Mondonovo, one of Venice's best mask shops (☞ Shopping, *below*). At Campo Santa Margherita, a busy neighborhood shopping square, stop in to see Giambattista Tiepolo's ceiling paintings in the **Scuola dei Carmini** ㉖. Tiepolo was strongly influenced by Paolo Veronese, some of whose finest works can be seen if you take a short and rewarding canal-side detour along Fondamenta del Soccorso, making a sharp left turn along Fondamenta de San Sebastiano, and crossing the second bridge on the right, which leads to the **Chiesa di San Sebastiano** ㉗.

Retracing your steps, continue from Campo Santa Margherita (via Calle San Pantalon to Calle dei Preti to Calle della Scuola) to the Franciscan **Chiesa dei Frari** ㉘. To the left of the Frari is the **Scuola Grande di San Rocco** ㉙, filled with dark, dramatic canvases by Mannerist Tintoretto. In the area around San Rocco, narrow alleys and streets give way to small canals and lead to little squares, where posters advertising political parties and sports events might seem to be the only signs of life. From the Frari, head back to Campo San Toma', to Calle di Nomboli, to Calle dei Saoneri to Salizzade San Polo to **Campo di San Polo** ㉚, one of Venice's largest squares. From here you take Calle della Madonetta, Calle dell'Olio, Rugheta del Ravano, and Ruga Vecchia San Giovanni to the Rialto shopping district, where you can cross the Grand Canal for the shortcut back to San Marco. Alternatively, you can go north from Campo di San Polo by way of Calle Bernardo, Calle dello Scaleter, Rio Terrà Parrucchetta, and Calle del Tintor to **Campo San Giacomo dall'Orio** ㉛, where the 13th-century church of San Giacomo stands in an enchanting square. Here you're not far from the San Stae vaporetto landing, so you can take the boat back along the Grand Canal to the heart of the city.

TIMING

Not including time spent in the Galleria dell'Accademia and time to get totally lost (as always, arm yourself with a good map), walking this route will take approximately three to four hours. There are fewer people out and about in the early afternoon, which makes it easier to get around, but keep in mind that many of the shops and some churches are also closed at that time. Also remember: only three bridges span the Grand Canal—the Ponte degli Scalzi, Ponte di Rialto, and the Ponte dell'Accademia—so be sure to be near one of them when you're ready to call it a day. If you're not, you may have to backtrack.

Sights to See

㉚ Campo di San Polo. One of Venice's largest squares and a favorite playground for neighborhood children, this *campo* has a church of the same name, **Chiesa di San Polo,** open to the public.

㉔ Campo San Stefano. One of the nicest campi in all of Venice, this neighborhood square, until 1802, was used for bullfights, during which bulls (or oxen) were tied to a stake and baited by dogs. For years the square was grassy, all except for a stone avenue known as the *liston.* This became such a popular place to stroll that it led to a Venetian expression, *andare al liston,* which means "go for a walk." Check out the

14th-century **Chiesa di San Stefano** and its bell tower—the tipsiest in all Venice—and stop in to see the ship's-keel roof, a type found in several of Venice's older churches and the work of its master shipbuilders. *Church:* ✉ *Campo San Stefano,* ☎ *041/5225061.* ⛩ *Free; sacristy 2,000 lire.* ☉ *Mon.–Sat. 10–5, Sun. 3–5.*

㉛ Campo San Giacomo dall'Orio. The 13th-century **Chiesa di San Giacomo dall'Orio** stands on this square, near a number of reasonably priced pizzerias. ⛩ *2,000 lire.* ☉ *Mon.–Sat. 10–5, Sun. 3–5.*

NEED A
BREAK?

Caffè Paolin (✉ 3464 Campo San Stefano, ☎ 041/5220710, Closed Tues.) makes some of the best gelato in Venice and is pleasant for watching the passing parade.

★ **㉘ Chiesa dei Frari** (Church of the Friars). This immense Gothic church, with its russet-color brick, was built in the 14th century for the Franciscans. I Frari, as it is known locally, is deliberately austere and plain, befitting the simplicity of the Franciscans' lives, in which spirituality and poverty were key tenets. Paradoxically, however, the Frari also contains a number of the most sumptuous and brilliant pictures in any Venetian church. Chief among them are the magnificent **Titian altarpieces**, arguably the most dazzling works that the prolific artist produced. For its mellow luminosity, first check out Giovanni Bellini's *Madonna and Four Saints* in the sacristy, painted in 1488 for precisely this spot. The contrast with the heroic energy of Titian's large *Assumption* over the main altar—painted little more than 30 years later—is startling, and clearly illustrates the immense and rapid development of Venetian Renaissance painting. This work caused a sensation when unveiled in 1519 and was immediately acclaimed for its winning combination of Venetian color—especially the glowing reds—and classical Roman figure style.

The *Pesaro Madonna* over the first altar on the left nave near the main altar is also by Titian; his wife, who died shortly afterward in childbirth, posed for the figure of Mary. The Madonna was radical for its time because the main figure was not placed squarely in the center of the painting, creating a dynamic result. On the same side of the church, look at the spooky pyramid-shape monument to the sculptor Antonio Canova (1757–1822) containing his heart. Across the nave is a neoclassical 19th-century monument to Titian, executed by two of Canova's pupils. ✉ *Campo dei Frari, San Polo,* ☎ *041/5222637.* ⛩ *3,000 lire.* ☉ *Mon.–Sat. 9–noon and 3–6, Sun. 3–6.*

㉗ Chiesa di San Sebastiano. Veronese established his reputation with the frescoes he painted at this church when still in his twenties, after leaving his native Verona. He continued to embellish the interior for over a decade with amazing perspective and trompe l'oeil scenes. In 1588 he was buried here. ✉ *Campo San Sebastiano, Dorsoduro,* ☎ *041/5282487.* ⛩ *2,000 lire.* ☉ *Mon.–Sat. 10–5, Sun. 3–5.*

★ **㉕ Galleria dell'Accademia** (Accademia Gallery). Housed in this magnificent museum is unquestionably the most extraordinary collection of Venetian art. Highlights include Giovanni Bellini's altarpiece from the church of San Giobbe (notice how he carried the church's architectural details right into the frame of the painting) and his moving *Madonna with St. Catherine and the Magdalen;* a fine *St. George* by Andrea Mantegna, Bellini's brother-in-law from Padua; and Veronese's monumental canvas, *Feast in the House of Levi.* Here is the Venetian High Renaissance in all its richness, even glamour. The painting was commissioned as a Last Supper, but the Inquisition took issue with Veronese's inclusion of jesters and German soldiers in the painting. Veronese avoided the charge of profanity by changing the title, and the picture was then supposed to depict the bawdy, but still biblical, feast of Levi. A room preserved from the Scuola della Carità—which previously occupied the museum's site—holds on one wall its original masterpiece, Titian's *Presentation of the Virgin.*

Don't miss the room containing various views of 15th- and 16th-century Venice by Vittore Carpaccio and Giovanni Bellini's brother Gentile—study them to see how little the city has changed since then. Room V holds one of the gallery's most famous paintings, the *Tempest,* by Giorgione (1477–1510), a work that has consistently baffled art historians as to its meaning, while charming all with its magical painterly qualities and exquisite landscape. The work is nothing if not ambiguous—what exactly is going on between this impassive young soldier and naked woman suckling a child?—but possesses a brooding sense of threat created by the gathering summer storm in the background. For the first time in art, the atmosphere of a painting became as important as the figures. The top floor displays paintings by Cima di Conegliano, Veronese, and Mansueti and hosts special exhibitions. ⊠ *Campo della Carità, Accademia, Dorsoduro,* ☎ *041/5222247.* 🎟 *12,000 lire.* ⊙ *Mon.–Sat. 9–10, Sun. 9–6.*

㉖ Scuola dei Carmini. This *scuola* is home to Giambattista Tiepolo's ceiling paintings, which were commissioned to honor the Carmelite order by depicting prominent Carmelites in conversation with saints and angels. Of the three great Venetian painters whose names start with *T* (Titian, Tintoretto, and Tiepolo), Tiepolo came last chronologically (he painted in the 18th century, the others in the 16th-century) and achieved the greatest international fame in his own time. An underlying melancholy in his ethereal, brightly colored paintings betrays a man of sober piety. Tiepolo's vivid techniques transformed some unpromising religious themes into flamboyant displays of color and movement. Mirrors on the benches make it easier to see the ceilings. ⊠ *Campo dei Carmini, Dorsoduro,* ☎ *041/5289420.* 🎟 *7,000 lire.* ⊙ *Mon.–Sat. 9–noon and 3–6. Closed Sun.*

㉙ Scuola Grande di San Rocco. This workshop is famed for its many dark, dramatic canvases by Tintoretto. Born some 30 years after Titian, Jacopo Robusti—called Tintoretto because his father was a dyer—was more mystical and devout than the sophisticated Titian. Though his colors are equally brilliant, he carried Titian's love of motion and odd composition to almost surreal effects, in the same Mannerist vein as El Greco (who was at one time a pupil of Titian's). In 1564, Tintoretto beat other painters competing for the commission to decorate this building by submitting not a sketch but a finished work, which he additionally offered gratis. The series of more than 50 paintings he ultimately created took a total of 23 years to complete. These works, depicting Old and New Testament themes, were restored in the 1970s, and Tintoretto's inventive use of light has once more been revealed. ⊠ *Campo San Rocco, Frari,* ☎ *041/5234864.* 🎟 *8,000 lire.* ⊙ *Nov.– Mar., Mon.–Fri. 10–1, weekends 10–4; Apr.–Oct., daily 9–5:30.*

Islands of the Lagoon

The perfect vacation from your Venetian vacation is an escape to the magical islands of the city's lagoon—Murano, Burano, and Torcello—which can provide a welcome relief after the brooding, enclosed charms of Venice itself. Far from the madding crowd, Torcello is the actual birthplace of Venice, today visited for its haunting melancholy, its great Byzantine-era church, and that famous outpost of elegance, the Locanda Cipriani. The island is also perfect for picnics, but bring food from Venice. Burano is a toy town of little houses all painted in a riot of color—

blue, yellow, pink, ocher, and dark red; here, visitors love to shop for the best in Venetian lace. Murano is known the world over for its glass—but guided tours usually involve high-pressure attempts to make you buy, with little time left for anything else. It's worth the extra effort to make your own way around the islands, using the good vaporetto connections.

There are several options in getting to these islands: lines 12 and 14 to Murano, Burano, and Torcello from the landing stage at Fondamente Nuove, almost due north of San Marco; on the opposite coast of the island and Line 52, which you can pick up in town (☞ Getting Around in Venice A to Z, below), to Fondamente Nuove, San Michele, and Murano, where you would then change to Line 14 to continue to Torcello and Santa Maria Elisabetta on the Lido.

Numbers in the text correspond to numbers in the margin and on the Venice and Venetian Lagoon maps.

A Good Boat Trip

Take Line 52 from Piazza San Marco to the Fondamente Nuove stop. There, in the Campo dei Gesuiti, is the **Chiesa dei Gesuiti** ㉜. It's only a five-minute ride from there to **San Michele** ㉝, the cemetery island home to the church of San Michele in Isola. Another five minutes on Line 52 takes you to **Murano** ㉞. Cross the Ponte Vivarini and turn right onto Fondamenta Cavour. Follow the Fondamenta Cavour around the corner to the Museo Vetrario, one of the most famous glass factories in the world.

Make your way back along the same route to the landing stage, and take Line 12 to **Burano** ㉟, where you can see traditional lace making at the Scuola di Merletti di Burano. Line 12 continues from the Burano landing stage to the sleepy green island of **Torcello** ㊱, about 10 minutes farther. A brick-paved lane leads up from the landing stage and follows the curve of the canal toward the center of the island. You pass the Locanda Cipriani, one of Hemingway's haunts. Just beyond is the grassy square that holds the island's only surviving monuments. Next to it is the cathedral of Santa Maria Assunta, also built in the 11th century.

TIMING

Boats leave every hour and the trip takes about 50 minutes each way. Stopping on every island and visiting the various sights will take a full day. If, however, you limit yourself to Torcello, Burano, and Murano, a full morning or a full afternoon will suffice.

Sights to See

★ ㉟ **Burano.** Dotting this fishing village are houses painted in cheerful colors and a raffishly raked bell tower on the main square, about 100 yards from the landing stage. Lace is to Burano what glass is to Murano, but be prepared to pay a lot for the real thing. Stalls line the way from the landing stage to Piazza Galuppi, the main square; the vendors, many of them fishermen's wives, are generally good-natured and blessedly unfamiliar with the techniques of the hard sell.

The **Scuola di Merletti di Burano** (Lace Museum) is the best place to learn the intricacies of the lace-making traditions of Burano, plus the nature of the skills needed to make the more expensive lace. ☒ *Piazza Galuppi,* ☎ *041/730034.* ☞ *5,000 lire.* ☉ *Apr.–Oct., Wed.–Mon. 9–5; Nov.–Mar., Wed.–Mon. 10–4.*

㉜ **Chiesa dei Gesuiti.** This 18th-century church dominating the Campo dei Gesuiti is extravagantly Baroque in style; the classical arches and straight lines of the Renaissance have been abandoned in favor of

Venetian Lagoon

flowing, twisting forms. The marble of the gray-and-white interior is used like brocade, carved into swags and drapes. Titian's *Martyrdom of St. Lawrence,* over the first altar on the left, is a dramatic example of the great artist's feel for light and movement. ⊠ *Campo dei Gesuiti,* ☎ *041/5231610.* ☞ *Free.* ⊙ *Daily 10–noon and 5–7.*

★ ㉞ **Murano.** Like Venice, Murano is made up of a number of smaller islands linked by bridges. It is known for its glassworks, which you can visit to see how glass is made. Many of these line the **Fondamenta dei Vetrai,** the canal-side walkway leading away from the Colonna landing stage. The houses along this walk are simpler than many of their Venetian counterparts; traditionally they were workmen's cottages. Just before the junction with Murano's Grand Canal—250 yards up from the landing stage—is the **Chiesa di San Pietro Martire.** This 16th-century reconstruction of an earlier Gothic church has several works by Venetian masters: notably, the *Madonna and Child* by Giovanni Bellini, and *St. Jerome* by Veronese.

The Venetian glass at the **Museo Vetrario** (Glass Museum) ranges from priceless antique to only slightly less-expensive modern. The museum details authentic Venetian styles and patterns and the history of Murano's glassworks, moved here from Venice in the 13th century because they were a fire hazard. ⊠ *Murano,* ☎ *041/739586.* ☞ *8,000 lire.* ⊙ *Apr.–Oct., Thurs.–Tues. 10–5; Nov.–Mar., Thurs.–Tues. 10–4.*

㉝ **San Michele.** Venice's cypress-lined cemetery island is home to the pretty Renaissance church of **San Michele in Isola,** designed by Coducci in 1478, and Venice's **cemetery.** It is a unique experience to walk among the gravestones with the sound of lapping water on all sides. The American poet Ezra Pound (1885–1972), the great Russian impresario and art critic Sergey Diaghilev (1872–1929), and the composer Igor Stravinsky (1882–1971) are buried here. For most Venetians, however, the stay here is short-lived, as the cemetery has a policy of transferring those interred more than 10 years to another, less grandiose cemetery, making room for more recent burials.

★ ㊱ **Torcello.** This is where the first Venetians landed in their flight from the barbarians 1,500 years ago. Even after many settlers left to found the city of Venice on the island of Rivo Alto (Rialto), Torcello continued to grow and prosper until its main source of income, wool manufacturing, was priced out of the marketplace. It's hard to believe now, looking at this almost deserted island, that in the 16th century it had 20,000 inhabitants and 10 churches.

The island's cathedral, **Santa Maria Assunta,** dates from the 11th century. The ornate Byzantine mosaics are testimony to the importance and wealth of an island that could attract the best artists and craftsmen of its day. The vast mosaic on the inside of the facade depicts the *Last Judgment* as artists of the 11th and 12th centuries imagined it: Figures writhe in vividly depicted contortions of pain. Facing it, as if in mitigation, is the calm mosaic figure of the Madonna, alone in a field of gold above the staunch array of Apostles. ⊠ *Torcello,* ☎ *041/ 730084.* 🎫 *3,000 lire.* ⊙ *June–Sept., daily 2–6:30; Oct.–May, daily 10–12:30 and 2–5.*

NEED A **Locanda Cipriani** (⊠ Torcello, ☎ 041/730150. ⊙ Jan.–Carnival.
BREAK? Closed Tues.) is an inn famous for its good food and the patronage of Ernest Hemingway, who often came to Torcello for the solitude. These days Locanda Cipriani—not to be confused by the Cipriani hotel on Giudecca—is about the busiest spot on the island, as well-heeled customers arrive on high-speed powerboats for lunch.

San Giorgio Maggiore and the Giudecca

Beckoning all travelers across the St. Mark's Basin like some sort of Venetian Bali Hai is the island of San Giorgio Maggiore, separated by a small channel from the Giudecca. A tall brick campanile on that distant bank perfectly complements the Campanile of San Marco. Behind it looms the stately dome of one of Venice's greatest churches, San Giorgio Maggiore. The island of Giudecca, a crescent cupped around the southern shore of Venice, is one of the most mysterious neighborhoods in all of Venice, with an obscure history and a somber feel.

Numbers in the text correspond to numbers in the margin and on the Venice map.

A Good Boat Trip

Take Line 82 from San Zaccaria near San Marco to head south for the island of San Giorgio Maggiore, across the lagoon. Here you should visit Palladio's **Chiesa di San Giorgio Maggiore** ㊲. Return to the pier and proceed by vaporetto (still Line 82) to the island of **Giudecca** ㊳. Explore the neighborhood and visit the Chiesa del Redentore, also by Palladio. Continue on the vaporetto to the next stop, Zattere, opposite the Giudecca. The promenade here is enchanting; you can eat in one of the many pizzerias that line the promenade, taking in the lively atmosphere.

TIMING
A half day should give you plenty of time to enjoy the sights. Allow at least an hour to visit each of the churches, and another hour to two hours to visit the Giudecca neighborhood and the Zattere promenade.

Sights to See

③⑦ **Chiesa di San Giorgio Maggiore.** A church has been on this island since the late 8th century, with a Benedictine monastery added in the 10th century. The present church, San Giorgio Maggiore, was begun in 1566 by Palladio, the greatest architect of his time. Two of Palladio's hallmarks are mathematical harmony and architectural elements borrowed from classical antiquity, both demonstrated in this superbly proportioned neoclassical church of red brick and white marble. Inside, the church is refreshingly airy and simply decorated. Two important late Tintoretto paintings hang on either side of the chancel: *The Last Supper* and *The Gathering of Manna*. Over the first altar on the right-hand side of the nave is an *Adoration of the Shepherds* by Jacopo Bassano (1517–92), a painter from Bassano del Grappa on the mainland who possessed considerable originality and was especially adept at portraying nature and country life. The campanile is so high that it was struck by a lightning bolt in 1993.

The **Monastero di San Giorgio Maggiore** (Monastery of San Giorgio Maggiore), where the conclave that elected Pope Pius VII took place in 1800, later a barracks for the occupying Austrians, now houses an artistic and cultural foundation where conferences are often held. Palladio designed the monastery's first cloister, and Longhena was the architect for the grand Baroque library. It's usually closed to the public. ⊠ *San Giorgio Maggiore,* ☎ *041/5289900.* ⊡ *Free.* ☉ *June–Sept., daily 9–12:30 and 2:30–6:30; Oct.–May, daily 10–12:30 and 3–5.*

③⑧ **Giudecca.** The island's name is something of a mystery; according to some, it derives from the possible settlement of Jews here in the 14th century, others believe it was so called because in the 9th century nobles condemned to exile (*giudicato* means judged or sentenced) were sent here. It became a pleasure garden for wealthy Venetians during the long and luxurious decline of the Republic. In one regard it is still the province of the wealthy: The exclusive Cipriani hotel (☞ Lodging, *below*) lies secluded on its eastern tip.

Palladio's **Chiesa del Redentore** is a tranquil, stately facade, actually a series of superimposed temple fronts topped by a dome and a pair of slim, almost minaret-like, bell towers. The interior, like San Giorgio Maggiore's (☞ *above*), is perfectly proportioned and airy, in contrast to the dusky Byzantine mystery of the Basilica di San Marco. ⊠ *Fondamenta San Giacomo, Giudecca,* ☎ *041/5231415.* ⊡ *2,000 lire.* ☉ *Mon.–Sat. 10–5, Sun. 3–5.*

DINING

Venetian cuisine is based on seafood—*granseola* (crab), *moeche* (small, soft-shelled crabs), and *seppie* or *seppioline* (cuttlefish). It can be very expensive, usually priced by the *etto* (100 grams, or about ¼ pound). Antipasti may take the form of a seafood salad, *prosciutto di San Daniele* (cured ham of the Veneto region), or pickled vegetables. As a first course Venetians favor risotto, the creamy rice dish, prepared here with vegetables or shellfish. Pasta, too, is paired with seafood sauces— Venice is *not* the place to order spaghetti with tomato sauce. *Pasticcio di pesce* is pasta baked with fish, usually *baccalà* (salt cod). A classic first course here and elsewhere in the Veneto is *pasta e fagioli* (thick bean soup with pasta). *Bigoli* is strictly a local pasta shaped like short, fat spaghetti, usually served with *nero di seppia* (squid ink sauce). Polenta, made of cornmeal, is another pillar of regional cooking. It's often served as an accompaniment to *fegato alla veneziana* (liver with onions).

SAVE LA SERENISSIMA

ON NOVEMBER 4, 1966, the Adriactic surrounding Venice swelled, barometric pressure dropped, and winds whipped the city. The watermark reached an unprecedented high of 1 meter, 94 centimeters, and holes were punctured in the *murazzi,* artifical stone sea walls erected in the 18th century. Flood damage to the historic center alone was estimated at 13 billion lire, and it was in the storm's aftermath that a rethinking of the delicate relationship between the city, lagoon, and sea was born. Venice and her artistic treasures were in jeopardy.

Venice is built on some 118 islands in a 200-square-mile lagoon. Rising from the lagoon are Byzantine, Gothic, and Renaissance buildings, aglitter with dazzling light, gold mosaics, and medieval works of art. Construction began slowly: in the 9th century thousands of wood pilings, sandwiched together, were driven into the land, mud banks, and ooze underneath the water to create the foundation for the first buildings, usually built of wood. After a devasting fire in the 12th century, brick and stone became the primary building materials.

Nature could claim some responsibility for the flood of '66; however, much of the damage wrought upon Venice is man-made. More and more today, Piazza San Marco finds itself knee-deep in the murky acque alte. A rise in the sea level, due to the creation of canals in the 1960s, as well as the deepening of channels throughout the 20th century, has rid the city of tidal flow–off areas. The city's ancient infrastructure is sinking, making flood conditions worse. Industrial development on the terra firma has virtually killed the ecological balance in the lagoon. Besides dioxins, there's algae, farm waste, and the threat of oil spills from tankers.

Works of art have always suffered through the passage of time, natural catastrophes such as earthquakes, floods, and fires notwithstanding. One of the biggest problems is the pervading damp: the water seeping into the masonry brings with it salt and other impurities, which cause paintings to chip and flake, stones to crumble, and buildings to become unstable. Church paintings have blackened from centuries' worth of candle smoke, and the faulty work of well-intentioned restorers has also had a hand in the damage.

Saving Venice boils down to a few primary issues. To safeguard against flooding, the government and various environmental groups are moving to restore the lagoon to its original condition (this means putting a halt to further industrial development, among other things). The coastal defense system of sandbanks needs to be strengthened, and the flow of rivers must be regulated to counteract the continuous rise in sea level. The precious works of art and the buildings in which they stand must also be restored.

One of the latest efforts has been the painstaking 10-year restoration of Santa Maria dei Miracoli, its colorful marble interior and exterior built 1481–1489 to the design by Pietro Lombardo (circa 1435–1515). The amounts of salt and moisture were measured, and the marbles were examined for cracks. The marbles were then removed from the brick and soaked in deionized water for a month to remove the salt, then reattached with metal hooks. (During a 19th-century refurbishment, the marbles had been detached and then reattached with cement.)

Who pays for these costly restorations? The Italian government cannot possibly pay for it all. Private organizations have come to La Serenissima's aid: at present, 23 in Italy and abroad defray costs through assiduous fund-raising. Perhaps the two most famous are **Save Venice** (✉ 15 E. 74th St., New York, NY 10021, ☎ 212/737–3141) and **Venice in Peril Fund** (✉ 314–322 Regent St., London W1R 5AB, ☎ 0171/636–6138).

Though it originated on the mainland, tiramisu is Venice's favorite dessert, a heavenly concoction of mascarpone (a rich, soft double-cream cheese), espresso, chocolate, and *savoiardi* (ladyfingers). Local wines are the dry white Tocai and Pinot from the Friuli region and bubbly white Prosecco, a naturally fermented sparkling wine that is a shade less dry. The best Prosecco comes from the Valdobbiadene; Cartizze, which is similar, is considered superior by some but is expensive. Popular red wines include merlot, cabernet, Raboso, and Refosco. You can sample all of these and more in Venice's many bacari (local osterie), where wine is served by the glass (known as an *ombra* in Venetian dialect) and accompanied by cicchetti (assorted tidbits), often substantial enough for a light meal.

It's always a good idea to reserve your table or have your hotel *portiere* (concierge) do it for you. Dining hours are short, starting at 12:30 or 1 for lunch and ending at 2:30 or 3, when restaurants close for the afternoon, opening up again to start serving at about 8 and closing again at 11 or midnight. Most close one day a week and are also likely to close without notice for vacation or renovation. Few have signs on the outside, so when the metal blinds are shut tight, you can't tell a closed restaurant from a closed TV-repair shop.

CATEGORY	COST*
$$$$	over 120,000 lire
$$$	80,000–120,000 lire
$$	50,000–80,000 lire
$	under 50,000 lire

Prices are per person, including house wine, service, and tax.

Cannaregio

$$$ ✕ **Fiaschetteria Toscana.** This warm restaurant in a former Tuscan wine and oil storehouse merits a jaunt from terra firma to Cannaregio for its cheerful, courteous service, fine cucina, and rose-hue walls. Gastronomic highlights include a delicate *tagliolini* (noodles), perhaps prepared *alla buranella* (with shrimp), the zabaglione, and the wine list. In warm weather, the best tables are in the arbor on the square. ✉ *Campo San Giovanni Crisostomo 5719, Cannaregio, ☎ 041/ 5285281. AE, DC, MC, V. Closed Tues. and 4 wks in July–Aug.*

$$ ✕ **Vini da Gigio.** A quaint, friendly, family-run trattoria on the quay
★ side of a canal just off the Strada Nuova, da Gigio is very popular with Venetians and visiting Italians, who appreciate the affable service; excellently cooked homemade pasta, fish, and meat dishes; and imaginative and varied cellar and good-quality draft wine. It's good, too, for a cheap, simple lunch at tables in the barroom. ✉ *Fondamenta de la Chiesa 3628/a, Cannaregio, ☎ 041/5285140. AE, DC, MC, V. Closed Mon., 2 wks in Jan., and 2 wks in Aug. No dinner Sun.*

Castello

$$$ ✕ **Al Covo.** This small and charming osteria changes its menu according to the day's bounty—mostly local seafood caught just hours before and specialties from other European waters. Cesare Benelli and his American wife, Diane, insist on only the freshest ingredients and claim to not use butter or animal fats. Try the *zuppa di pesce* (fish broth) followed by the fish of the day either grilled, baked, or steamed. Diane will guide you through some of her homemade desserts and the extensive wine selection. ✉ *Campiello della Pescaria 3968, Castello, ☎ 041/5223812. No credit cards. Closed Wed. and Thurs., 1 wk in Aug., and 1 month between Dec. and Jan.*

$$ ✕ **Al Mondo Novo.** In this fish restaurant you can get grilled *cape sante* (scallops) and *cape longhe* (razor clams), risottos and pastas, and the best of the day's catch. Meat dishes are also available. ⊠ *Salizzada San Lio 5409, Castello,* ☎ *041/5200698. AE, MC, V.*

$$ ✕ **Da Remigio.** This very popular local trattoria near San Giorgio dei Greci turns out reliable and tasty fish and meat dishes. ⊠ *Salizzada dei Greci 3416, Castello,* ☎ *041/5230089. Reservations essential. AE, DC, MC, V. Closed Tues., 2 wks. July–Aug. and 4 wks in Jan. No dinner Mon.*

$ ✕ **Al Mascaron.** The convivial, crowded Al Mascaron, with its paper tablecloths and very informal atmosphere, is a regular stop for Venetians who drop in to gossip, drink, play cards, and eat cicchetti at the bar. You can bet on delicious seafood, pastas, risottos, and seafood salads. So popular has Mascaron become that the owners, Gigi and Momi, have opened an offshoot called Mascareta a few doors down the calle (at No. 5183), where you can enjoy a glass of wine and cold snacks. ⊠ *Calle Lunga Santa Maria Formosa 5225, Castello,* ☎ *041/5225995. No credit cards. Closed Sun. and end of Dec.–mid-Jan.*

Dorsoduro

$$ ✕ **Cantinone Storico.** On a quiet canal near the Accademia, this comfortable trattoria serves excellently prepared specialties such as risotto *terra mare* (with seafood, vegetables, and porcini mushrooms) and tagliolini alla granseola. The house wines are good. ⊠ *Fondamenta di Ca' Bragadin 660/1, Dorsoduro,* ☎ *041/5239577. AE, MC, V. Closed Sun., last wk July–1st wk Aug., and Jan. 19–26.*

$$ ✕ **Locanda Montin.** Peggy Guggenheim used to take many of the leading artists of the day—including Jackson Pollock and Mark Rothko—to this archetypal Venetian inn, not far from her Palazzo Venier dei Leoni, in Dorsoduro. The walls are still covered with modern art, but it's far from the haute bohemian hangout it used to be, except for when the Biennale crowd takes charge. Outside, you can dine under an elongated arbor and enjoy such specialties as rigatoni *ai quattro formaggi* (with four cheeses), spaghetti *Adriatica* (with fish sauce), and antipasto *Montin* (seafood antipasto). ⊠ *Fondamenta di Borgo 1147, Dorsoduro,* ☎ *041/5227151. AE, DC, MC, V. Closed Wed., Jan. 7–26, and 15 days in Aug. No dinner Tues.*

$ ✕ **L'Incontro.** This trattoria has a faithful clientele of Venetians and vis-
★ itors, attracted by flavorsome food, friendly service, and reasonable prices. Menu choices include freshly made Sardinian pastas, juicy steaks, wild duck, boar, and (with advance notice) roast suckling pig. You'll find it between San Barnaba and Campo Santa Margherita. ⊠ *Rio Terrà Canal 3062/a, Dorsoduro,* ☎ *041/5222404. MC, V. Closed Mon., 2 wks in Jan. and 2 wks in Aug.*

$ ✕ **San Trovaso.** A wide choice of Venetian dishes and pizzas, reliable house wines, and economical fixed-price menus make this busy tavern, near the Accademia Gallery, a good value. ⊠ *Fondamenta Priuli 1016, Dorsoduro,* ☎ *041/5203703. AE, MC, V. Closed Mon.*

San Marco

$$$$ ✕ **Grand Canal.** The Grand Canal restaurant at the Hotel Monaco and
★ Grand Canal is a favorite with Venetians, who enjoy eating in summer on the lovely canal-side terrace looking across the mouth of the Grand Canal to San Giorgio Maggiore, and in the cozy dining room in winter. All the pasta is made fresh daily on the premises, and the smoked and marinated salmon are also prepared on-site. Chef Fulvio De Santa's traditional Venetian dishes are topflight; you'll marvel over savory meat and fish dishes such as *scampi alla Ca' d'Oro* (shrimp in

Venice Dining and Lodging

Dining ●

Al Covo, **43**
Al Mascaron, **27**
Al Mondo Novo, **28**
Cantinone Storico, **14**
Da Arturo, **15**
Da Ignazio, **6**
Da Remigio, **41**
Fiaschetteria
Toscana, **24**
Grand Canal, **34**
Harry's Bar, **36**
L'Incontro, **7**
La Caravella, **21**
Le Bistrot, **32**
Locanda Montin, **9**

Osteria Da Fiore, **5**
Quadri, **33**
San Trovaso, **10**
Vini da Gigio, **2**
Vino Vino, **16**

Lodging ○

Accademia, **11**
Ala, **19**
American, **13**
Bernardi
Semenzato, **3**
Bucintoro, **44**
Cipriani, **45**
Concordia, **31**
Danieli, **37**
Flora, **22**
Gritti Palace, **23**
Hesperia, **1**
Hotel Pausania, **8**
Istituto
San Giuseppe, **29**

La Calcina, **12**
Locanda Fiorita, **8**
Londra Palace, **39**
Luna Baglioni, **35**
Metropole, **42**
Paganelli, **38**
Quattro Fontane, **46**
Riva, **30**
San Samuele, **17**
Santa Marina, **25**
Saturnia
Internazionale, **20**
Scandinavia, **26**
Sturion, **4**
Wildner, **40**

Sacca della Misericordia

Canale delle Navi

Cimitero San Michele

0   440 yards
0   400 meters

Racchetta

Fondamenta

FOND. NUOVE

C. Racchetta

Rio S. Caterina

R.d. Cesuti Nuove

C. d. Squeria

C. d. Festa

Rio della Panada

R. dei Mendicanti

Campo Santi Giovanni e Paolo

OSPEDALE CIVILE

R. d. S. Giustina

R. d. S.

CELESTIA

3

Rio d' Santi Apostoli

mpo d. cheria

24

Rio d. S. Murina

25

R. Barbaria delle Tole

Campo di S. Maria Formosa

26 **27**

R. d. S. Severo

R.d S. Lorenzo

R. d. S. Francesco

R. d. S.

Canale d. Galeazze

Darsena Grande

Rio d. Vergini

Carbon

R. d. Fava

Sol. di S.

28

C. d. Bande

29 **30**

San Zaccaria

C. Lion

C. d. Furlani

R. d. Pieta

R. d. Greci

C. d. Pestrin

R. d. Scudi

R. d. Gorne

di S. Pietro

R. d. S. Daniele

C. d. Specchieri

32

31

R. d. Palazzo

Fond. Osmarin

40

41

42

Castello

43

R. d. Arsenale

33

37 **38** **39**

Riva degli

Schiavoni

Rio della Tana

Piazza San Marco

Molo

S. ZACCARIA

RIVA DEGLI SCHIAVONI

44

35

34 **36**

S. MARCO GIARDINETTI

ARSENALE

V. Garibaldi

Riva dei Sette Martiri

Rio d. S. Anna

Cam.

S. MARCO VALLARESSA

UTE

R. d. S. Giuseppe

Canale di S. Marco

S. GIORGIO

Isola di S. Giorgio Maggiore

Riva dei partigiani

Rio dei Giardini

ZITELLE

Fond. delle Zitelle

ci

Calle Michelangelo

45

▲ Boat stop

46

a cognac sauce). ⊠ *Hotel Monaco and Grand Canal, Calle Vallaresso 1325, San Marco,* ☎ *041/5200211. Jacket required. AE, DC, MC, V.*

$$$$ ✕ **Harry's Bar.** The humble door of this very less-than-humble watering hole leads to the legendary Venetian hangout of such notables as Hemingway, Maugham, and Onassis, not to mention Barbara Hutton, Peggy Guggenheim, and Orson Welles. Such company doesn't come cheap, but Harry's is still known for the best and driest martinis in town, the most heavenly Bellinis (fresh peach juice and Prosecco), and for its kitchen's fine *cucina veneta.* The decor is boring beige-on-beige, but the "pictures" on the walls upstairs—windows that look out on spectacular Chiesa di Santa Maria della Salute—easily compete with the finest Canaletto *vedute* (scenic paintings). ⊠ *Calle Vallaresso 1323, San Marco,* ☎ *041/5285777. Reservations essential. AE, DC, MC, V.*

$$$$ ✕ **La Caravella.** Affixing your gaze on the chateaubriand, bouillabaisse, and calves' kidneys' *au trois moutardes* (with three mustards), you might think you had wandered into a temple of French haute cuisine. Continue reading the very extensive menu to discover some of the best Venetian specialties in town, such as *taglierini alla granseola* (delicate pasta with crab sauce) and fillets of local sea bass and sole. The front room of this old favorite—long admired for its fine wine list and cordial, gracious service—is like the dining saloon of an old Venetian sailing ship. The pretty garden courtyard is open from May to September. ⊠ *Calle Larga XXII Marzo 2397, Saturnia Internazionale hotel (☞ below), San Marco,* ☎ *041/5208901. Reservations essential. AE, DC, MC, V.*

$$$$ ✕ **Quadri.** In the 19th century, princes, dukes, and countesses dined here, and you'll feel like one when you walk into the gilded salons of Venice's most beautiful restaurant. The decor is stunning—Quadri's second-floor aerie gives you a pigeon's-eye view of Piazza San Marco—and the four-star truffles-on-everything kitchen is also a major draw. Come September, when the Venice Film Festival is in session, the sequins-and-sunglasses set takes over. ⊠ *Piazza San Marco 120–124, San Marco,* ☎ *041/5289299. Reservations essential. AE, DC, MC, V. Closed Mon. No lunch Tues. or in July and Aug.*

$$$ ✕ **Da Arturo.** On the Calle degli Assassini—a name common to several Venetian streets and a reminder of the centuries gone by when violence and betrayal were everyday occurrences—this tiny restaurant can offer a most peaceful and enjoyable evening. It has the distinction (in Venice) of *not* serving seafood. Instead you'll choose from among fresh vegetable and salad dishes; tasty, tender, and generous meat courses, including the delicately pungent *braciola alla veneziana* (pork chop schnitzel with vinegar); and an authentic creamy homemade tiramisu to finish. ⊠ *Calle degli Assassini 3656, San Marco,* ☎ *041/ 5286974. Reservations essential. No credit cards. Closed Sun. and 4 wks in Aug.*

$ ✕ **Le Bistrot.** Live music, poetry readings, and art exhibits attract the younger crowd to this café-brasserie. Centrally located, it's open all day (until 1 AM) and features 16th-century Venetian cuisine, such as *l'ambrosino* (spiced chicken with nuts and raisins) and *biancomangiare* (soup with rice flour, almonds, pomegranates, and chicken). ⊠ *Calle dei Fabbri 4685, San Marco,* ☎ *041/5236651. MC, V.*

$ ✕ **Vino Vino.** The annex of the extremely expensive Antico Martini restaurant is a highly informal wine bar where you can sample Italian vintages and munch on a limited selection of (microwaved) dishes from the kitchens of its upscale big sister next door. ⊠ *Calle delle Veste 2007/a, near Campo San Fantin, San Marco,* ☎ *041/5237027. Reservations not accepted. AE, DC, MC, V. Closed Tues.*

San Polo

$$$ ✕ **Osteria Da Fiore.** Tucked away in a little calle off the top of Campo
★ di San Polo, Da Fiore is always packed. It's imperative to reserve for
a superlative seafood lunch or dinner, which might include delicate hors
d'oeuvres of moeche, scallops, and tiny octopus, followed by a suc-
culent risotto or tagliolini *con scampi e zucchine* (with shrimp and zuc-
chini), and a perfectly cooked main course of *rombo* (turbot) or
branzino (sea bass). ✉ *Calle del Scaleter 2202/A, San Polo,* ☎ *041/
721308. Reservations essential. AE, DC, MC, V. Closed Sun.–Mon.,
Aug. 10–early Sept., and Dec. 25–Jan. 15.*

$$ ✕ **Da Ignazio.** Smallish, pleasant, and near Campo di San Polo, Ignazio
is reliable for good food at reasonable prices (except for the expensive
fish dishes). The cuisine is classic Venetian, from seafood risotto to fegato alla veneziana, but there are standard Italian items as well. ✉ *Calle
dei Saoneri 2749, San Polo,* ☎ *041/5234852. AE, DC, MC, V. Closed
Sat., 2 wks during Christmas and 2 wks in July–Aug.*

LODGING

Everyone loves Venice, so hotels here can cater to all tastes and price
ranges. Rates are a little higher than in Rome and Milan, but you can
save off-season (November–March, excluding Christmas and Carnevale).
Most rates include breakfast. It is *essential* to know how to get to your
hotel when you arrive, as transport can range from arriving in a water
taxi or gondola direct to the front door or wandering down curious
alleys and side streets—luggage in hand—with relapses of déjà vu.

The busiest times for hotels are spring and autumn; December 20–January 2; and the two-week Carnival period leading up to Ash Wednesday. Book well in advance. If you don't have reservations, you can almost
always get a room in any category by going to the **AVA** (Venetian
Hoteliers Association, ✉ Stazione Ferroviaria Santa Lucia; Aeroporto
Marco Polo; parking garage at Piazzale Roma, ☎ 1678/43006 toll-
free) booths.

CATEGORY	COST*
$$$$	over 500,000 lire
$$$	290,000–500,000 lire
$$	180,000–290,000 lire
$	120,000–180,000 lire

*Prices are for a standard double room, including service and tax.

Cannaregio

$$ 🏨 **Hesperia.** A quiet, friendly hotel with some rooms overlooking the
wide (and clean!) Canale di Cannaregio, the Hesperia is convenient walk-
ing distance from the train station and right across from the Jewish
Ghetto. The restaurant, Il Melograno, has tables outside come sum-
mertime. ✉ *459 Cannaregio, 30121,* ☎ *041/715251,* ℻ *041/715112.
15 rooms, 2 without bath. Restaurant. CP. AE, DC, MC, V.*

$ 🏨 **Bernardi Semenzato.** This is a particularly inviting little hotel just
★ off Strada Nuova, and near the Rialto. All rooms in the main hotel
maintain high standards, making the Bernardi better value than ever.
Prices are even lower in the nearby annex, with six rooms and a big
room with a lovely canal view. ✉ *Calle dell'Oca, 4366 Cannaregio,
30121,* ☎ *041/5211052,* ℻ *041/5222424. 24 rooms, 10 without
bath. CP. AE, MC, V. Closed 2 wks Nov.–Dec.and 2 wks before
Carnevale.*

Castello

$$$$ 🏨 **Danieli.** You'll feel like a doge in Venice's largest luxury hotel, a collage of newer buildings around a 15th-century palazzo, built for the Doge Dandolo—all oozing with sumptuous Venetian decor and atmosphere. Some suites are positively palatial, but some of the less attractive rooms are still overpriced. The four-story-high lobby is supreme, its chic salons and bar offering relaxation and celebrity sightings. The rooftop terrace restaurant is justly famous for top-notch cuisine and its heavenly view of San Giorgio Maggiore and St. Mark's Basin. Guests have access to a pool and tennis courts. ⊠ *Riva degli Schiavoni 4196, Castello, 30122,* ☎ *041/5226480,* 🗚 *041/5200208. 219 rooms, 11 suites. Restaurant, bar, air-conditioning. CP. AE, DC, MC, V.*

$$$ 🏨 **Londra Palace.** This grand hotel commands a fine view of San Giorgio and St. Mark's Basin and has a distinguished ambience. A neoclassical touch graces the rooms, with light pastel colors and plenty of marble. The Deux Lions restaurant offers fine Venetian and French cuisine, and the piano bar is open late. Perks include a complimentary Mercedes for one-day excursions, free entrance to the city Casino (☞ Nightlife, *below*), and the therapeutic solarium. ⊠ *Riva degli Schiavoni 4171, Castello, 30122,* ☎ *041/5200533,* 🗚 *041/5225032. 36 rooms, 17 suites. Restaurant, piano bar, air-conditioning. CP. AE, DC, MC, V.*

$$$ 🏨 **Metropole.** Only a few minutes' stroll from Piazza San Marco, the Metropole offers spacious rooms and sitting areas furnished with style and panache from the owner's impressive collection of antiques. Many rooms have a view of the lagoon, but the others overlooking a canal and peaceful gardens are also inviting. You can step from your water taxi or gondola directly into the hotel lobby. ⊠ *Riva degli Schiavoni 4149, Castello, 30122,* ☎ *041/5205044,* 🗚 *041/5223679. 67 rooms, 7 suites. Restaurant, bar, air-conditioning. CP. AE, DC, MC, V.*

$$$ 🏨 **Scandinavia.** Central but off the main tourist arteries, the Scandinavia is housed in a medieval building dating from the 11th century. Despite the name, the rooms are done in Venetian style with brocade tapestry and Murano chandeliers. Ask for a room with a view onto the cheerful campo below. The top suite has a beautiful, private covered veranda with a view of the nearby church. ⊠ *Campo Santa Maria Formosa, 5240 Castello, 30122,* ☎ *041/5223507,* 🗚 *041/5235232. 33 rooms, 1 suite. Breakfast room. CP. AE, MC, V.*

$$ 🏨 **Bucintoro.** Whistler once stayed here and, today, the Bucintoro is still favored by artists drawn by the lagoon views outside each room. Off the tourist track, this friendly, family-run hotel on the waterfront by the Arsenal has clean, simple rooms and prices that are unbeatable for such a spectacular location. ⊠ *Riva San Biagio 2135, Castello, 30122,* ☎ *041/5223240,* 🗚 *041/5235224. 28 rooms, 10 without bath. Breakfast room. CP. No credit cards. Closed Dec.–mid-Jan.*

$$ 🏨 **Istituto San Giuseppe.** This is one of several religious institutions in Venice run by nuns that caters to families visiting Venice—and it's in an excellent location. All rooms overlook an inner courtyard. Curfew is 11 PM, and no breakfast is served. ⊠ *5402 Castello, 30122,* ☎ *041/5225352,* 🗚 *041/5224891. 16 rooms. No credit cards.*

$$ 🏨 **Paganelli.** The lagoon views here so impressed Henry James that he wrote the Paganelli up in the preface to his *Portrait of a Lady.* This enchanting, small hotel on the waterfront near Piazza San Marco, with an annex on the quiet square of Campo San Zaccaria (three rooms overlook the lagoon, six face the square), is tastefully decorated in the Venetian style. ⊠ *Riva degli Schiavoni 4687, Castello, 30122,* ☎ *041/5224324,* 🗚 *041/5239267. 23 rooms, 3 without bath. Bar. Breakfast room. CP. AE, MC, V.*

$$ ⚏ **Santa Marina.** In the small neighborhood campo home to this hotel, five minutes from the Rialto Bridge, you will probably see more Venetians than tourists passing by. Immaculate rooms are outfitted in pastel colors and laquered Venetian style furniture. The staff is helpful and kind, and breakfast is served on the veranda in summer. ⊠ *Campo Santa Marina, 6068 Castello, 30122,* ☎ *041/5239202,* FAX *041/5200907. 20 rooms. Breakfast room. CP. AE, DC, MC, V.*

$$ ⚏ **Wildner.** Right between the super deluxe Danieli and Londra hotels, this pleasant family-run, unpretentious pensione enjoys the same views. The rooms are spread over four floors (no elevator), half with a view of San Giorgio, the quieter look out onto Campo San Zaccaria. ⊠ *Riva degli Schiavoni, 4161 Castello, 30122,* ☎ *041/5227463,* FAX *041/5265615. 16 rooms. Breakfast room. CP. AE, DC, MC, V.*

$ ⚏ **Riva.** This small hotel, close to San Marco, is at the junction of three canals much used by all manner of Venetian watercraft. Although they are endlessly fascinating to watch, the boats can seem a little noisy early in the morning. ⊠ *Ponte dell'Angelo 5310, Castello, 30122,* ☎ *041/ 5227034,* FAX *041/5285551. 12 rooms, 2 without bath. CP. No credit cards. Closed mid-Nov.–Jan., except 2 wks at Christmas.*

Dorsoduro

$$ ⚏ **Accademia.** Probably the most enchanting hotel in Venice, the Ac-
★ cademia is also one of the most popular, so early reservations are a must. Just beyond an iron gate, a secret garden awaits, complete with mini Palladian-style villa, canal parterre, and verdant trees—all rarities in Venice. Lounges, the bar, and a wood-paneled breakfast room are cheery, and breakfast outside on the garden terrace is a special treat. ⊠ *Fondamenta Bollani 1058, Dorsoduro, 30123,* ☎ *041/5210188,* FAX *041/5239152. 27 rooms. Bar, breakfast room, air-conditioning. CP. AE, DC, MC, V.*

$$ ⚏ **American.** One of the smartest hotels among its peers, the American is on a quiet canal near the Ponte dell'Accademia. Rooms are stylish and classic, with warm wood detail and period furniture. Beautiful terraces overlooking the canal teem with red geraniums. You breakfast on the main terrace, shaded by a lovely vine canopy. ⊠ *Rio San Vio, 628 Dorsoduro, 30123,* ☎ *041/5204733,* FAX *041/5204048. 29 rooms. Bar, breakfast room, air-conditioning. CP. AE, MC, V.*

$$ ⚏ **Hotel Pausania.** This 14th-century palazzo delivers all of the modern comforts with taste, from the moment you ascend the grand staircase rising above a fountain. Light-shaded rooms are spacious, with comfortable furniture and carpets with rugs thrown over them. Some rooms (which can be noisy at times) face the small and quiet canal in front of the hotel, others look out over the large garden courtyard. The hotel has a convenient car service (75,000 lire) to and from the airport. ⊠ *2824 Dorsoduro, 30123,* ☎ *041/5222083,* FAX *041/5222989. 26 rooms. Bar, breakfast room, air-conditioning. CP. AE, DC, MC, V.*

$$ ⚏ **La Calcina.** On a wonderful, if not particularly central, position on
★ the Zattere with an enviable view on the Giudecca canal, this hotel is a must for those with a love of the lagoon and seagulls. There's an *altana* (wooden roof terrace) on which to rest and sunbathe, and in good weather, breakfast is served on a floating platform in front of the hotel. The hotel annex nearby offers bargain rooms without a view. ⊠ *780 Dorsoduro, 30123,* ☎ *041/5206466,* FAX *041/5227045. 42 rooms. Breakfast room. CP. AE, DC, MC, V.*

Giudecca

$$$$ ⚏ **Cipriani.** It's impossible to feel stressed in this sybaritic oasis of stunning rooms and suites, some with garden patios. The hotel launch whisks you to Giudecca from San Marco and back at any hour; those just dining at the exceptional Ristorante Harry Cipriani can use it as well. Cooking courses and fitness programs are offered. The restored and subtly integrated 17th-century style Palazzo Vendramin, an annex of seven suites and three double rooms, is open all year. ⊠ *Giudecca 10, 30133,* ☎ *041/5207744,* FAX *041/5203930. 54 rooms, 50 suites. Restaurant, bar, air-conditioning, pool, tennis court. CP. AE, DC, MC, V. Closed Dec.–mid-Mar.*

Lido

$$$ 🏨 **Quattro Fontane.** This fine hotel in a well-maintained mansion run
★   by a Danish couple offers the serenity of the Lido, although you will be a walk or a 15-minute boat ride from the center. Well-decorated rooms overlook the surrounding garden. The library has books in many languages. ⊠ *Via delle Quattro Fontane 16, Lido, 30126,* ☎ *041/5260227,* FAX *041/5260726. 59 rooms. Library. CP. AE, DC, MC, V.*

San Marco

$$$$ 🏨 **Gritti Palace.** Queen Elizabeth, Greta Garbo, and Winston Churchill
★   made this their Venetian address. The feeling of being in an aristocratic private home pervades this legendary hotel, replete with fresh flowers, fine antiques, sumptuous appointments, and old-fashioned service. The dining terrace on the Grand Canal is best enjoyed in the evening when the boat traffic dies down. Guests have access to pool and tennis courts. ⊠ *Campo Santa Maria del Giglio 2467, San Marco, 30124,* ☎ *041/794611,* FAX *041/5200942. 87 rooms, 6 suites. Restaurant, bar, café, air-conditioning. CP. AE, DC, MC, V.*

$$$–$$$$ 🏨 **Luna Baglioni.** Two minutes from San Marco, this handsome hotel has elegant rooms, several with a view of the Grand Canal. Breakfast is served in a salon fit for a king, with frescoes by the school of Tiepolo, 18th-century furniture, and Venetian floors. Most suites feature fireplaces, Jacuzzis, and terraces. Restaurant Canova offers modern Venetian cuisine. ⊠ *1243 San Marco, 30124,* ☎ *041/5289840,* FAX *041/ 5287160. 111 rooms, 7 suites. Restaurant. CP. AE, DC, MC, V.*

$$$ 🏨 **Concordia.** Half of the rooms in this central, attractive, and well-run hotel overlook the basilica of San Marco, as does the spacious breakfast room-bar, where light meals and snacks are also available all day. The romantic *mansarda* (rooftop room) has a panoramic view over the Piazza San Marco. The management offers good price deals at off-peak times, so check when booking. ⊠ *Calle Larga San Marco 367, San Marco, 30124,* ☎ *041/5206866,* FAX *041/5206775. 54 rooms and 3 suites. Bar, breakfast room, air-conditioning. CP. AE, DC, MC, V.*

$$$ 🏨 **Saturnia Internazionale.** There's lots of patinated charm in this historic palace, near Piazza San Marco, but it's peaceful and tranquil. Its beamed ceilings, damask-hung walls, and authentic Venetian decor impart real character to the solid comfort of its rooms and salons. Many rooms are endowed with glamorous, large bathrooms. La Caravella restaurant (☞ Dining, *above*) is of special note. ⊠ *Calle Larga XXII Marzo 2398, San Marco, 30124,* ☎ *041/5208377,* FAX *041/5207131. 95 rooms. Restaurant, bar, air-conditioning. CP. AE, MC, V.*

$$ 🏨 **Ala.** The Ala is between San Marco and Santo Stefano, a few steps from the Santa Maria del Giglio vaporetto stop. Some rooms are large with coffered ceilings and old-style furnishings, others are smaller, with more modern decor. Breakfast is served overlooking a small canal. ⊠ *2494 San Marco, 30124,* ☎ *041/5208333,* FAX *041/5206390. 85 rooms. Breakfast room. CP. AE, DC, MC, V.*

$$ 🏨 **Flora.** This hotel has what many in this category lack: plenty of sitting rooms and a pretty courtyard. It's in a quiet but central spot near San Moisè and Piazza San Marco. Rooms have Venetian period decor

and are a bit dark for some; a handful are small, with tiny bathrooms. Ask for a room with a view of the courtyard or the garden. ⊠ *Calle Bergamaschi 2283 (off Calle Larga XXII Marzo), San Marco, 30124,* ☎ *041/5205844,* FAX *041/5228217. 44 rooms. Bar, air-conditioning. CP. AE, DC, MC, V.*

$ ★ 🗓 **Locanda Fiorita.** This welcoming small hotel is tucked away in a sunny little square (where breakfast is served in the summer), just off Campo San Stefano, near the Accademia Bridge, a good position for sightseeing. The rooms have beamed ceilings and are simply furnished. Eight of the rooms are in an annex on Campo Santo Stefano. ⊠ *Campiello Novo o dei Morti, 3457/A San Marco, 30124,* ☎ *041/5234754,* FAX *041/5228043. 18 rooms, 4 without bath. CP. AE, MC, V. Closed 2 wks mid-Jan.*

$ 🗓 **San Samuele.** Near the Grand Canal and Palazzo Grassi, this friendly hotel has clean, sunny rooms, in surprisingly good shape for the price. ⊠ *Salizzada San Samuele 3358, San Marco, 30124,* ☎ FAX *041/5228045. 10 rooms, 8 without bath. No credit cards.*

San Polo

$$ 🗓 **Sturion.** You might recognize the facade of the hotel in a painting by Carpaccio that hangs at the Galleria dell'Accademia. Once frequented by merchants who traded at the nearby Rialto market, this small family-run hotel has two rooms overlooking the Grand Canal and a small but pretty breakfast room. Some rooms reserved for nonsmokers. ⊠ *Calle del Sturion, 679 San Polo, 30125,* ☎ *041/5236243,* FAX *041/5228378. 11 rooms. Breakfast room. CP. AE, DC, MC, V.*

NIGHTLIFE AND THE ARTS

The Arts

You'll find a list of current and upcoming events in the *Guest in Venice* booklet, free at your hotel, or available from the **Assessorato al Turismo** (⊠ Ca' Giustinia, 2nd floor) and **Calle del Ridoto** (⊠ Close to Piazza San Marco).

Venice hosts important temporary exhibitions in the Doge's Palace, in Palazzo Grassi at San Samuele on the Grand Canal, and in other venues. The **Biennale,** a cultural institution, organizes many events throughout the year, including the film festival, which begins at the end of August. The big Biennale international art exhibition, usually held from mid-June to the end of September, has been held since 1993 on odd-numbered years at the **Giardini di Castello** (Castello Gardens).

Festivals

Carnevale takes place the 10 or more days leading up to Ash Wednesday. Crowds of revelers make the city almost impossible to visit, so unless you are intent on joining in, stay away. For information on Carnival, check with the main APT office (☞ *above*). On the third Sunday of July, the **Festa del Redentore** (the Redeemer) is celebrated with the building of a pontoon bridge over the channel to the Giudecca, commemorating the doge's annual visit to this church to offer thanks for the end of a 16th-century plague. Venetians take to the water in boats, as midnight fireworks explode over the lagoon.

Music

Regular concerts at the **Chiesa della Pietà** (⊠ Riva degli Schiavoni, San Zaccaria, Castello) have an emphasis on Vivaldi. Those in San Stae and surrounding churches tend to be high priced and the performance quality uneven. Concerts (sometimes free) are also performed in other churches by visiting choirs and musicians. For up-to-date information, ask at the APT office (⊠ Palazzetto Selva, off Piazza San Marco, ☎ 041/5226356 or 5298730). **Kele e Teo Agency** (⊠ Ponte dei Bareteri, 4930 San Marco, ☎ 041/5208722, FAX 041/5208913), closed weekends, handles tickets for many musical events.

Opera and Ballet

Teatro La Fenice (⊠ Campo San Fantin) is one of Italy's oldest opera houses, a pilgrimage shrine for opera lovers everywhere, and scene of many memorable operatic premieres, including, in 1853, the dismal first-night flop of Verdi's *La Traviata*. The great opera house was badly damaged by fire in January 1996 and although plans are being made to restore it, performances are not forecast to recommence until the year 2000.

Nightlife

Piazza San Marco in fair weather, when the cafés stay open late, is a meeting place, though young Venetians tend to gravitate toward Campi San Luca, San Salvador, and San Bartolomeo, near Rialto.

Bars

The **Martini Scala Club** (⊠ Calle del Cafetier, 1007 San Marco, ☎ 041/5224121), is an elegant piano bar with a restaurant. Tunes start at 10 and go until the wee hours. **Devil's Forest Pub** (⊠ Calle del Stagneri 5185, off Campo San Bartolomeo, ☎ 041/5200623), is a favored hangout of many young Venetians. **Fiddler's Elbow** (⊠ Strada Nuova, Cannaregio 3847, ☎ 041/5239930) offers all the typical trappings of an Irish pub: gab, grub, and frothy Guinness. A nightspot with food, drinks, and music, **Paradiso Perduto** (⊠ Fondamenta della Misericordia 2540, Cannaregio, ☎ 041/720581) serves up inexpensive fish dishes, plus live music usually on Sundays.

Casino

The city-run gambling **Casino** operates June–September in a modern building on the Lido (⊠ Lungomare Marconi 4, ☎ 041/5297111), open 4 PM–2:15 AM, and in the splendorous Palazzo Vendramin Calergi (⊠ Grand Canal, ☎ 041/5297111), open 3 PM–2:15AM the other months. Admission costs 18,000 lire, or 6,000 lire for the slot machines.

Nightclubs

For dancing try the **Disco Club Piccolo Mondo** (⊠ 1056/a Dorsoduro, near the Accademia, ☎ 041/5200371), next to the Galleria dell' Accademia Gallery. Outside Venice on nearby Lido is **Piazza Caffé** (⊠ Lungomare Marconi 22, Lido, ☎ 041/5260466), one of the more trendy, hip spots, with disco and live performances.

OUTDOOR ACTIVITIES AND SPORTS

Golf

The 18-hole **Golf Club Lido di Venezia** (⊠ Via del Forte, Alberoni, Lido, ☎ 041/731333), closed Monday, is on Lido island.

Horseback Riding

Circolo Ippico Veneziano (⊠ Ca' Bianca, the Lido, ☎ 041/5265162), closed Sunday afternoon and Monday, rents horses for riding trails on the Lido, and it can refer you to terra firma clubs around the Veneto.

Running

The best running route heads east from the Giardini Pubblici in the Castello district and over to the pine wood on Sant'Elena; it allows a magnificent view of the city as you run back toward the center.

Swimming

Venice's only public pool is the **Piscina Comunale** (⌧ Island of Sacca Fisola, far end of Giudecca, ☎ 041/5285430); take Line 82 to Sacca Fisola.The deluxe **Hotel des Bains** (⌧ Lungomare Marcone, Lido, ☎ 041/5265921) opens its small pool to nonguests for a substantial fee (85,000–130,000 lire per day).

Tennis

The **Hotel des Bains** (☞ Swimming, *above*) rents tennis courts to nonguests. The exclusive **Sea Gull Club** of the Cipriani hotel (☞ Lodging, *above*) will also let nonguests play for a fee. There are several tennis clubs on the Lido, including **Lido Tennis Club** (⌧ Via Sandro Gallo 163, ☎ 041/5260954). The Lido's **Club Ca' del Moro** (⌧ Via F. Parri 6, ☎ 041/770965) has tennis and an outdoor pool in summer.

SHOPPING

You're sure to find plenty of pleasant shops and boutiques as you explore Venice. It's always a good idea to mark the location of a shop that interests you on your map; otherwise you may not be able to find it again in the maze of tiny streets. Regular store opening hours are usually 9–12:30 and 3:30 or 4–7:30 PM. Food shops are open 8–1 and 5–7:30, and are closed all day Sunday and on Wednesday afternoon (and sometimes on Monday morning). However, many tourist-oriented shops are open all day, every day. Some shops close for both a summer and a winter vacation.

Markets

The morning open-air fruit and vegetable market at **Rialto** offers animated local color and commerce. Another small market is near the train station. On Tuesday through Saturday mornings, the adjacent **fish market** teaches an impressive lesson in ichthyology, with species you've probably never seen before. In the Castello district is **Via Garibaldi**, the scene of another lively food market on weekday mornings.

Shopping Districts

The San Marco area is full of shops and couture boutiques such as Armani, Missoni, Valentino, Fendi, and Versace. Le Mercerie, along with the Frezzeria and Calle dei Fabbri, leading from Piazza San Marco, are some of Venice's busiest streets. Other good shopping areas surround Calle del Teatro and Campi San Salvador, Manin, San Fantin, and San Bartolomeo. Less expensive shops are between the Rialto Bridge and San Polo.

Specialty Stores

Embroidered Fabrics

Venice's top name is **Jesurum** (⌧ Piazza San Marco 60–61, ☎ 041/5229864). It is one of the few stores in Venice whose lace *is* made in and around the city. Go to **Lorenzo Rubelli** (⌧ Campo San Gallo 1089, just off Piazza San Marco, ☎ 041/5236110) for the same sumptuous brocades, damasks, and cut velvets used by the world's most prestigious decorators.

Much of the lace and embroidered linen sold in Venice and on Burano is really made in China or Taiwan. At **Norelene** (⌧ Calle de la Chiesa 727, ☎ 041/5237605) you'll find wonderful hand-printed fabrics. **Venetia Studium** (⌧ Calle Larga XXII Marzo 2403, San Marco, ☎ 041/5229281) has beautiful Fortuny-inspired lamps, furnishings, clothes, and accessories.

Glassware

Glass, most of it made in **Murano,** is Venice's number-one product, and you'll be confronted by mind-boggling displays of traditional and contemporary glassware, often kitsch. Take your time and be selective. You will probably find that prices in Venice's shops and the showrooms of Murano's factories are pretty much the same. However, because of competition, shops in Venice with wares from various glassworks may charge slightly lower prices.

Galleria San Nicolò (⊠ Calle del Traghetto 2793, Dorsoduro, by the Ca' Rezzonico vaporetto stop, ☎ 041/5221535) is owned by the American glass expert Louise Berndt. It shows the best of contemporary glass, including superb work by Yoichi Ohira, a Japanese designer long resident in Venice. **Domus** (⊠ Fondamenta dei Vetrai, Murano, ☎ 041/739215) has a selection of smaller objects and jewelry from the best glassworks. For chic, contemporary glassware designs, Carlo Moretti is a good choice; his signature designs are on display at **L'Isola** (⊠ Campo San Moisè 1468, near Piazza San Marco, ☎ 041/5285263).

Marina Barovier's gallery (⊠ Calle delle Botteghe 3172, San Marco, just off Campo San Stefano, ☎ 041/5236748) has an excellent selection of collectors' 20th-century glass. Go to Michel Paciello's **Paropàmiso** (⊠ Frezzeria 1701, near Piazza San Marco, ☎ 041/5227120) for stunning Venetian glass beads and traditional jewelry from all over the world. **Pauly** (⊠ Piazza San Marco 73–77, ☎ 041/5209899) is central, with a wide array of glassware.

In a category all his own is **Gianfranco Penzo** (⊠ Campo del Ghetto Nuovo 2895, ☎ no phone), who decorates Jewish ritual vessels in glass and makes commemorative plates; he takes special orders. **Salviati** (⊠ Piazza San Marco 79B, ☎ 041/5207075) is a reliable and respected firm. **Venini** (⊠ Piazzetta dei Leoncini 314, ☎ 041/5224048) has been an institution since the 1930s, attracting some of the foremost names in glass design. **Vetri d'Arte** (⊠ Piazza San Marco 140, ☎ 041/5200205) offers moderately priced glass jewelry.

Masks

The prices of wholesaler **Emilio Massaro** (⊠ Calle Vitturi 2934, San Marco, ☎ 041/5228635) tend to be cheaper than anywhere else; you can watch the masks being created. **Mondonovo** (⊠ Rio Terrà Canal, ☎ 041/5287344) is a cut above most other mask stores here. **Laboratorio Artigiano Maschere** (⊠ Barbaria delle Tole, near Campo dei Santi Giovanni e Paolo, ☎ 041/5223110) is home to Giorgio Clanetti, credited with starting the current revival in mask-making.

VENICE A TO Z

Arriving and Departing

By Bus

Buses connect the **bus terminal** (⊠ Piazzale Roma, across the Grand Canal from the train station, near the vaporetto stop of that name) to Mestre, the Brenta Riviera, Padua, and other destinations in the region.

By Car

Venice is on the east–west **A4** autostrada, which connects with Padua, Verona, Brescia, Milan, and Turin. If you bring a car to Venice, you will have to pay for a garage or parking space. Warning: Do not be waylaid by illegal touts—often wearing fake uniforms, and whose activities have in recent years become a scandal in a city generally remarkably free of con men and criminals—who may try to flag you down and offer to arrange parking and hotels; ignore them and continue on until you reach the automatic ticket machines.

Parking at **Autorimessa Comunale** (⊠ Piazzale Roma, end of S11 road) costs between 15,000 and 25,000 lire for 24 hours. The private **Garage San Marco** (⊠ Piazzale Roma, end of S11 road) costs between 34,000 and 46,000 lire per 24 hours, depending on the size of the car.

To reach the privately run **Tronchetto** parking area, follow the signs to turn right before Piazzale Roma. Parking costs 25,000 lire per 24 hours. The AVA (☞ Lodging, *above*) has arranged a discount of around 5,000 lire per day for hotel guests who use the Tronchetto facility. Ask for a voucher upon checking into your hotel and present it at Tronchetto when you pay. Line 82 runs from Tronchetto to Piazzale Roma and Piazza San Marco and also goes on to the Lido in summer. (When there is thick fog or extreme tides, a bus runs to Piazzale Roma instead.) Avoid private boats—they are a rip-off.

Do not leave valuables in the car. There is a left-luggage office, open daily 8 AM–8 PM, next to the Pullman Bar on the ground floor of the municipal garage at Piazzale Roma. You can take your car to the Lido; the car ferry (Line 17) makes the half-hour trip about every 50 minutes from a landing at Tronchetto, but in summer there can be long queues. It costs 12,000 to 30,000 lire, depending on the size of the car.

By Plane
Aeroporto Marco Polo (⊠ Tessera, about 10 km/6 mi north of the city on the mainland, ☎ 041/2609260 information) is served by domestic and international flights, including connections from London, Amsterdam, Brussels, Frankfurt, Munich, Paris, Vienna, and Zurich.

BETWEEN THE AIRPORT AND DOWNTOWN
By Boat. This may be the best way to get to Venice from the airport. The most direct way is by the **Cooperativa San Marco** launch, with regular scheduled service until midnight; it takes about an hour to get to the landing (just off Piazza San Marco), stopping at the Lido on the way, and the fare is 17,000 lire per person, including bags. A **water taxi** (☎ 041/5415084), a sleek, modern motorboat known as a *motoscafo,* from the airport costs about 130,000 lire, but it is always essential to agree on a water-taxi fare before boarding.

By Bus. Blue **ATVO** buses make the 25-minute nonstop trip from the airport to Piazzale Roma, where the road ends and the entrance to Venice; from Piazzale Roma you can get a vaporetto to the landing nearest your hotel. The ATVO fare is 5,000 lire. The local **ACTV** bus (Line 5) runs from the airport to Piazzale Roma, but you need a ticket (1,400 lire) before boarding, which can only be purchased at the airport tobacconist-newsstand, open daily 6:30 AM–9 PM. Luggage can be a hassle on the bus, which is usually crowded with local commuters.

By Taxi. A yellow taxi from the airport to Piazzale Roma costs about 60,000 lire.

By Train
Venice has rail connections with every major city in Italy and Europe. Some trains do not terminate at **Stazione Ferroviaria Santa Lucia** (⊠ On the Grand Canal in the northwest corner of the city, ☎ 147/8880880 toll free). Instead, they stop only at the **Stazione Ferroviaria Venezia-Mestre** (⊠ On the mainland, ☎ 1478/880880 toll free). All trains traveling to and from Santa Lucia stop at Mestre; to get from Venezia-Mestre to Santa Lucia, or vice versa (a 10-minute trip), take the first available train, remembering there is a *supplemento* (extra charge) for traveling on Intercity and Eurocity and Eurostar trains, and that if you do not

purchase it at the station booth and validate it in the machine on the platform before boarding, you are liable for a hefty fine.

Getting Around

First-time visitors find that getting around Venice presents some unusual problems: The layout is complex; the waterborne transportation can be bewildering; the house-numbering system is baffling; many street names in the *sestieri* (six districts) of San Marco, Cannaregio, Castello, Dorsoduro, Santa Croce, and San Polo, are duplicated; and often you must walk, whether you want to or not. It's essential to have a good map showing all street names and vaporetto routes; buy one at a newsstand. Signs are posted on many corners pointing you in the right direction for the nearest major landmark—San Marco, Rialto, Accademia, etc.—but don't count on finding such signs once you're deep into residential neighborhoods.

Venice's municipal Youth Department runs a special program to help young visitors: **"Rolling Venice"** (⊠ Assessorato alla Gioventù, Corte Contarini 1529, behind Piazza San Marco post office, ☎ 041/2707650, open weekdays 9:30–1, plus Tuesday and Thursday 3–5; ⊠ Campo della Lana, ☎ 041/5240232; ⊠ Calle Castelforte, near San Rocco, ☎ 041/5204414, open July–September only), is open to everyone ages 14–29, and costs 5,000 lire. You must show your passport to qualify. Benefits include handy guidebooks to the city, a good discount on ACTV vaporetto passes, and (sometimes substantial) discounts in some hotels, restaurants, and shops.

By Gondola

If you simply can't leave Venice without a gondola ride, the best time is in the late afternoon or early evening hours, when the Grand Canal isn't so heavily trafficked, and definitely not at low tide, when the foul odors of the canals are at their worst. It's best to start from a station on the Grand Canal because the lagoon is usually choppy. Make it clear that you want to see the smaller canals, and come to terms on the cost and duration of the ride before you start. Gondoliers are supposed to charge a fixed minimum of about 120,000 lire for up to six passengers for 50 minutes. After 8 PM and up to 8 AM the rate increases to approximately 150,000 lire. Bargaining may get you a better price.

By Motoscafo

These stylish powerboat water taxis are extremely expensive, and the fare system is as complex as Venice's layout. Plan on spending at least 130,000 lire. Always agree on the fare before starting out, and beware of other additions such as hand luggage and late or early hours. Call 041/5415084.

By Traghetto

Few tourists know about the two-man gondolas that ferry people across the Grand Canal at various fixed points. They are the cheapest and shortest gondola ride in Venice and can save a lot of walking. The fare is 700 lire, which you hand to the gondolier when you get on. Look for TRAGHETTO signs.

By Vaporetto

ACTV water buses (☎ 041/5287886 information), open daily 7:30 AM–8 PM), run the length of the Grand Canal and circle the city. There are several lines, some of which connect Venice with the major and minor islands in the lagoon.The fare is 4,500 lire on all lines. A 24-hour tourist ticket costs 15,000 lire, a three-day ticket 30,000 lire, and a seven-day ticket 55,000 lire; these are especially worthwhile if you are planning to visit the islands. Free timetables are available at the ticket office at

Piazzale Roma. Timetables are also posted at every landing stage, and there is a ticket booth at each stop. After 9 PM, tickets are available on the boats, but you must immediately inform the controller that you need a ticket. For this reason, it may be useful to buy a *blocchetto* (book of tickets) in advance. Be sure to validate tickets in the time-stamp machines before getting on board, or you could be subject to a fine.

Landing stages are clearly marked with name and line number, but check before boarding, particularly with the 52 and 82, to make sure the boat is going in your direction. **Line 1** is the Grand Canal local, calling at every stop, and continuing via San Marco to the Lido. (The trip takes about 45 minutes from the station to San Marco.) **Line 52** runs from the railway station to San Zaccaria via Piazzale Roma and Zattere, and continues to the Lido. **Line 52/** (note the difference) goes along the same route, but makes stops along the Giudecca instead of Zattere, and continues to Fondamenta Nuove (where boats leave for the islands of the northern Lagoon) and Murano (you can cut out the Murano loop by changing boats at Fondamenta Nuove, using the same ticket). **Line 82** runs in a loop from San Zaccaria to Giudecca, Zattere, Piazzale Roma, the train station, Rialto (with fewer stops along the Grand Canal than Line 1), and back to San Zaccaria (and out to the Lido in the afternoon).

Contacts and Resources

Car Rentals
Europcar (⊠ Piazzale Roma, ☎ 041/5289551). **Avis** (⊠ Piazzale Roma, ☎ 041/5225825; ⊠ Aeroporto Marco Polo, ☎ 041/5415030. **Hertz** (⊠ Piazzale Roma ☎ 041/5284091; ⊠ Aeroporto Marco Polo ☎ 041/5416075.

Consulates
U.K. (⊠ Campo della Carità 1051, Dorsoduro, ☎ 041/5227207). There is no U.S. or Canadian consular service.

Doctors and Dentists
The U.K. Consulate (☞ *above*) can recommend doctors and dentists. Your hotel or any pharmacy should also be able to offer advice.

Emergencies
General Emergencies ☎ 113. **Carabinieri** ☎ 112. **Ambulance** ☎ 118. **Venice Hospital First Aid** ☎ 041/5230000.

English-Language Bookstores
Fantoni (⊠ On Salizzada San Luca, ☎ 041/5220700). **Emiliana Editrice** (⊠ Calle Goldoni, between Piazza San Marco and Campo San Luca, ☎ 041/5220793). **Studium** (⊠ Calle de la Canonica, off Piazzetta dei Leoncini, ☎ 041/5222382). **Libreria Editrice Filippi** (⊠ On Casseleria, between Ponte de l'Anzolo, take the last left off Calle de la Canonica, ☎ 041/5236916) **Enrico Dori's** newspaper shop (⊠ Frezzaria shopping street, to the right of San Marco post office, ☎ no phone).

Guided Tours
EXCURSION TOURS
Islands of the Lagoon. The **Cooperativa San Marco** (⊠ Just off San Marco, ☎ 041/5222303) organizes tours of the islands of Murano, Burano, and Torcello. The 3½-hour tours depart daily at 9:30 and 2:30 from the landing stage in front of the Giardini Reali, just off Piazza San Marco; they cost about 25,000 lire. Tours tend to be annoyingly commercial and emphasize glass-factory showrooms, pressuring you to buy, sometimes at higher prices than normal.

Veneto. American Express (⊠ Salizzada San Moisè 1471, San Marco, ☎ 041/5200844, FAX 041/5229937) runs a day trip to Padova by boat along the Brenta River, with stops at three Palladian villas. The tours run three days a week from March to November and cost about 120,000 lire per person; bookings need to be made the day before.

Excursions aboard the **Burchiello** motor launch, from Venice to Padua along the Brenta River, are expensive (about 170,000 lire) and not necessarily the best way to see the famous villas, since so much time is spent on the boat. Tours run from April through October on Tuesday, Thursday, and Saturday.

ORIENTATION TOURS

Two-hour walking tours of the San Marco area can be booked through **American Express** (⊠ Salizzada San Moisè 1471, San Marco, ☎ 041/5200844, FAX 041/5229937). It's "Jewels of the Venetian Republic" tour (about 36,000 lire) ends with a glassblowing demonstration. From April 25 to November 15, American Express also offers an afternoon walking tour that ends with a gondola ride (about 40,000 lire).

PERSONAL GUIDES

APT tourist office (⊠ Palazzetto Selva, off Piazza San Marco, ☎ 041/5236356). **Guides' Association** (⊠ Calle San Antonio 5448/A, Castello, ☎ 041/5239902, FAX 041/5232012). **American Express** (⊠ Salizzada San Moisè 1471, San Marco, ☎ 041/5200844, FAX 041/5229937).

SPECIAL-INTEREST TOURS

Basilica di San Marco. From June through August, free guided tours (some in English) of the Basilica di San Marco are offered by the Procuratoria (☎ 041/5225205); information is available in the atrium of the church; no tours Sunday.

Gondola. American Express (⊠ Salizzada San Moisè 1471, San Marco, ☎ 041/5200844, FAX 041/5229937) offers group gondola rides with serenades, from May through October nightly (about 40,000 lire), and other tours that include dinner, followed by cabaret entertainment and a visit to the Casino (about 120,000 lire, drinks not included).

Late-Night Pharmacies

The nearest pharmacy is never far, and they take turns opening nights, Saturday afternoons and Sundays; the weekly list of after-hours pharmacies is posted on the front of every pharmacy.

Travel Agencies

American Express (⊠ Salizzada San Moisè 1471, San Marco, ☎ 041/5200844, FAX 041/5229937). **Sattis Viaggi** (⊠ Calle Larga dell'Ascensione 1261, ☎ 041/5285101/2/3). **Wagons-Lits/Turismo** (⊠ Piazzetta dei Leoncini 289, ☎ 041/5223405).

Visitor Information

APT (⊠ Palazzetto Selva, off Piazza San Marco, 30124, ☎ 041/5226356 or 5298730, FAX 041/5230399). **Information booths** (⊠ Santa Lucia train station, ☎ 041/5298727); in summer at the Lido; (⊠ Gran Viale S. Maria Elisabetta 6A, ☎ 041/5265721, FAX 041/5298720).

6 Venetian Arc

*Padua, Verona, Vicenza,
and Palladio Country*

*The art and architecture of every city in
the Venetian Arc—Verona, Vicenza,
Padua, Treviso—echo in some way
the graces and refinements of Venice.
Here you'll find Asolo—the City of a
Hundred Horizons; Padua, ennobled
by Giotto's frescoes; Verona's romantic
Romeo and Juliet settings; and the villas
of Andrea Palladio, where 16th-century
aristocrats led the privileged life.*

Updated by
Carla Lionello
and Jon Eldan

AS ROME PRESIDES OVER LAZIO, the arc to the north of Venice that stretches from Verona east to Trieste falls under the historical and spiritual influence of its namesake city. No lagoons, perhaps, but the region's architecture, paintings, and way of life all bask in the reflected splendor of La Serenissima.

Much of the pleasure of exploring this area comes from discovering the individual variations on the overall Venetian theme that confer special charm on each of the towns you'll visit. Some, such as Verona, Treviso, and Udine, have a solid medieval look; Asolo has an idyllic setting; Bassano combines a bit of both. If you are a confirmed or fledgling oenophile, you'll enjoy tasting local wines within view of the vineyards that produce some of the best-known Italian vintages—among them, Soave, Valpolicella, Bardolino, and Prosecco. But most of all, you'll find artistic jewels everywhere, from the great Venetian masters in Verona to Veronese's lighthearted frescoes in Villa Barbaro at Maser.

Pleasures and Pastimes

Concerts and Opera

The love of Italian culture need not stop at Venice. Verona, Trieste, and Vicenza offer some of the most spectacular opportunities for indulging in the passions of open-air operas and concerts.

Dining

In the main cities of the Veneto region, restaurants are in the middle to upper ranges of each price category, but in smaller towns and in the countryside you can find some real bargains. At the eastern end of the Arc, in less-trafficked Friuli–Venezia Giulia, prices are generally lower. Seafood is the specialty along the coast, of course, but inland the cuisine varies from the delicate risotto, radicchio, and asparagus of the Veneto to the more decisively flavored cooking of the Trieste area, heavily influenced by Austria. San Daniele del Friuli, near Udine, is famous for its delicious prosciutto. Polenta, made of cornmeal, is a staple throughout the area; it is served with thick, rich sauces or grilled as an accompaniment to meat dishes. Trieste's position near the Austrian and Slovenian borders has fostered a varied—and somewhat heavier—cuisine reflecting the tastes of those countries.

The best local wines are Soave, Tocai, Prosecco, Riesling, and pinot—all white; and reds Bardolino, Valpolicella, merlot, cabernet, and pinot nero. The Collio designation indicates wines from vineyards in the eastern part of Friuli, up against the Slovenian border. One of the best known and rarest wines produced here is the sauternelike Picolit, made in very limited quantities. The Veneto and Friuli regions are renowned for their grappas. Justifiably popular are those made by the families Nardini, in Bassano, and Nonino, at Udine. Trieste is the home of the famous Stock liqueur.

CATEGORY	COST*
$$$$	over 100,000 lire
$$$	80,000–100,000 lire
$$	40,000–80,000 lire
$	under 40,000 lire

Prices are per person, including house wine, service, and tax.

Lodging

The area around Venice has been playing host to visitors for centuries, and the result is a range of comfortable accommodations at every price. As with dining, common sense should tell you that the slightly out-of-the-way small hotel will cost you less than its counterpart in a stylish Adriatic resort. Expect to pay more as you approach Venice, since many of the mainland towns absorb the overflow during the times when Venice becomes most crowded, such as Carnevale (Carnival, the two weeks preceding Lent) and throughout the summer.

CATEGORY	COST*
$$$$	over 250,000 lire
$$$	180,000–250,000 lire
$$	90,000–180,000 lire
$	under 90,000 lire

Prices are for a standard double room for two, including service and tax.

Shopping

Many of the goods associated with Venice are actually produced in the surrounding areas of the Venetian Arc—which means that with a bit of diligence or luck you can pick up a bargain from the source. Mountain towns and villages such as Bassano del Grappa have the strongest handicraft tradition, and you can find a wide range of goods in artisans' shops on the side streets. The main towns on the coastal plain are often associated with one or two specialties, either because of traditional skills or because of ancient trading rights that set a pattern of importing specific items from other parts of the Mediterranean.

Villas and Palazzi

Countless villas and palaces are sprinkled throughout the Venetian hinterland. These gracious country homes give insight into the way wealthy Venetians used to—and still do—spend leisure time. Many of the villas are privately owned but are open to the public at certain times or by special request. Local tourist offices can be helpful in providing information on visiting these jewels.

Exploring the Venetian Arc

The Venetian Arc comprises principally the coastal crescent and the inland plain that stretches from the mouths of the Po and Adige rivers southwest of Venice. In addition, the cities of Trieste and Udine lie east of Venice, and close to the Slovenian border. They bridge two Italian regions—the Veneto and Friuli–Venezia Giulia—a landscape of flat green farmland spotted with low hills that swells and rises steeply inland in a succession of plateaus and high meadows to the snow-tipped Alps.

Numbers in the text correspond to numbers in the margin and on the Venetian Arc and Verona maps.

Great Itineraries

Hard as it may seem to leave the unique beauty of Venice behind, the Venetian Arc is the perfect last course to round off your stay. The towns are all beautiful, mixing grandiose architecture and medieval aristocracy flawlessly. One of these towns, Verona, also unknowingly produced the most tragic of all *storie d'amore* (love stories)—*Romeo and Juliet*. The sorrow that this tale inspires can be drowned in the delights of some of the best-known Italian wines.

Many towns can be seen on one- or two-day excursions from Venice itself. A three-day itinerary will exclude Trieste and restrict you to the other principal sights. A five-day exploration will give you plenty to remember and even savor, but you will have to discipline yourself to keep up a swift pace. A seven-day trip will give you the time to fully experience the architecture, history, and culture of this beautiful region.

Begin your drive at **Villa Pisani** ①, the most splendid of all Veneto villas. Move on to **Padua** ②, taking in the Cappella degli Scrovegni. Continue toward ⑆ **Verona** ③–⑯, the city of *Romeo and Juliet*. The following day see some of Palladio's works in **Vicenza** ⑰ and head for **Marostica** ⑱, ⑆ **Bassano del Grappa** ⑲, and **Asolo** ⑳. Save the last day for **Treviso** ㉒, **Conegliano** ㉓, and stop for a tour of **Udine** ㉔. Return to Venice along the A4, leaving out **Trieste** ㉗.

Follow the itinerary described above until Asolo. Instead of moving on directly to Treviso, travel toward **Villa Barbaro** ㉑ in Maser and then on to **Treviso** ㉒. Visit **Conegliano** ㉓ and ⑆ **Udine** ㉔, where you can overnight. The next day head for **Cividale** ㉕ and down then to ⑆ **Trieste** ㉗. Spend a day in this border city and then move on to **Castello di Miramare** ㉖ before taking the A4 back to Venice.

Follow the itinerary described above, but in **Bassano del Grappa** ⑲ take in a visit to the famous Nardini distillery on the edge of town. From ⑆ **Treviso** ㉒, head to Oderzo on the magnificent Red Wine Road, which winds through the cabernet and merlot country along the Piave River.

When to Tour the Venetian Arc

There is no particular good or bad time to see the sights around the Venetian Arc. Most of the year, the area is relatively free from very heavy traffic and congestion. If, however, you want to get the most out of your stay, come during the late spring and early summer months (May, June, July) or in early September. The region tends to welcome foggy conditions from November through March. Opera and theater buffs should come in spring and summer, when the outdoor performances are held.

ON THE ROAD FROM PADUA TO VERONA

Foremost among the treasures of the Veneto region are the beautiful villas of Andrea Palladio (1508–80) built to render la vita all the more dolce for 16th-century aristocrats. Other important sights include Giotto's 14th-century frescoes in Padua's Cappella degli Scrovegni and many of Donatello's greatest statues.

Villa Pisani

❶ *10 km (6 mi) southeast of Padua.*

This extraordinary house, also called Villa Nazionale, in **Stra** is the most spectacular of all the villas in the region. Through the 16th to 18th centuries, wealthy Venetians sought to enjoy *villeggiatura*—a vacation and escape from harried city life—by building stately residences on their country estates throughout Venetia. Many of them were constructed on the Brenta River, the main waterway used by Venetians to go inland. Villa Pisani may remind you more of Versailles, for it's an imposing 18th-century edifice that once belonged to Napoléon, who appreciated its similarities to Versailles. See the grandiose frescoes by Giambattista Tiepolo (1696–1770) on the ceiling of the ballroom. If you have youngsters surfeited with the old masters in tow, explore the gorgeous **park** and the **maze** (open only in the summer). ⊠ *Stra,* ☎ *0423/923004.* ⊡ *8,000 lire.* ☉ *Villa: Apr.–Sept., Tues.–Sun. 9–6; Oct.–Mar., Tues.–Sun. 9–1. Grounds: Apr.–Sept., Tues.–Sun. 9–6; Oct.–Mar. Tues.–Sun. 9–4.*

Venetian Arc

Verona 3–16

Villa Pisani 1
Padua 2
Vicenza 17
Bassano del Grappa 18
Marostica 19
Asolo 20
Villa Barbaro 21
Montebelluna
Treviso 22
Conegliano 23
Udine 24
Cividale 25
Castello di Miramare 26
Trieste 27

N

0 20 miles
0 30 km

Adriatic Sea

Golfo di Trieste
Golfo di Venezia

TO SPLIT, DUBROVNIK
AND ISTANBUL

SLOVENIA
CROATIA

ITALY

Padua

❷ *37 km (23 mi) west of Venice, 92 km (57 mi) east of Verona.*

Bustling Padua (Padova in Italian), has long been one of the major cultural centers in northern Italy. It's home to the peninsula's second-oldest university, founded in 1222, which attracted the likes of Dante (1265–1321), Petrarch (1304–74), and Galileo Galilei (1564–1642). Three great artists—Giotto (1266–1337), Donatello (circa 1386–1466), and Mantegna (1431–1506)—left great works here; if you will be visiting many of the local sites, plan on getting the Padua Biglietto Unico, a cumulative ticket.

★ The **Cappella degli Scrovegni** (Scrovegni Chapel) was erected in the 13th century by a wealthy Paduan, Enrico Scrovegno, to honor his deceased father. Scrovegni called on Giotto to decorate its interior, a task that occupied the great artist and his helpers from 1303 to 1305. They created a magnificent fresco cycle, arranged in typical medieval comic-strip fashion, illustrating the lives of Mary and Christ. The realism in these frescoes—which include the first blue skies in Western painting—was revolutionary. ✉ *Piazza Eremitani 8,* ☎ *049/8204550.* 🎟 *10,000 lire (includes admission to Museo Civico,* ☞ *below).* ☉ *Feb.–Oct., daily 9–7; Nov.–Jan., daily 9–6.*

The 13th-century **Chiesa dei Eremitani** contains some fragments of frescoes—most, however, were destroyed by the Allied bombing of 1944—by Andrea Mantegna, the brilliant locally born artist, some of whose masterpieces are in nearby Mantua. The **Museo Civico di Padova** (Civic Museum of Padua), housed in what used to be the monastery of the church, has its quota of works by Venetian masters, as well as a fine collection of ancient relics. ✉ *Piazza Eremitani 10,* ☎ *049/ 8204550.* 🎟 *Church free; Museo Civico 10,000 lire (includes admission to Cappella degli Scrovegni,* ☞ *above).* ☉ *Feb.–Oct., daily 9–7; Nov.–Jan., daily 9–6.*

The 16th-century **Palazzo del Bo'** houses the **Università di Padova,** founded in 1222. The building, which now features an 18th-century facade, is named after the Osteria del Bo' (Ox), an inn which once stood on the site. This is worth a visit to see the exquisite and perfectly proportioned anatomy theater and a hall with a lectern used by Galileo. ✉ *Via VIII Febbraio,* ☎ *049/8209711.* 🎟 *5,000 lire.* ☉ *Guided visits only; call for tour times.*

Palazzo della Ragione, also called Il Salone, was built in the Middle Ages as the seat of Padua's parliament. Today its street-level arcades shelter shops and cafés. In the frescoed **Salone** (Salon) on the upper level is an enormous wooden horse, a 15th-century replica of the bronze steed in Donatello's equestrian statue of Gattamelata. ✉ *Piazza della Ragione,* ☎ *049/8205006.* 🎟 *7,000 lire.* ☉ *Feb.–Oct., Tues.–Sun. 9–7; Nov.–Jan., Tues.–Sun. 9–6.*

The huge **Basilica di Sant'Antonio** is a cluster of Byzantine domes and slender, minaretlike towers that gives the church an Asian-inspired style, reminiscent of San Marco in Venice. The interior is sumptuous, too, with marble reliefs by Tullio Lombardo, the greatest in a talented family of marble carvers who decorated many churches in the area—among them, Santa Maria dei Miracoli in Venice. The artistic highlights here, however, all bear Donatello's name; the 15th-century Florentine master did the remarkable series of bronze reliefs illustrating the life of St. Anthony—whose feast day, June 13, draws pilgrims from all over Europe—as well as the bronze statues of the Madonna and saints on the high altar. ✉ *Piazza del Santo.* ☉ *Daily 7–7.*

To mark the 800th anniversary of the birth of St. Anthony in 1195, a new museum, the **Museo Antoniano,** with 300 exhibits relating to the image of the saint and of the basilica, was opened in 1995 on the first floor of the church cloister building. Standing in front of the church is Donatello's powerful statue of the *condottiere* (mercenary general) Gattamelata, which was cast in bronze—a monumental technical achievement—in 1453 and was to have an enormous influence on the development of Italian Renaissance sculpture. ⊠ *Piazza del Santo. Church:* ☎ *Free.* ☉ *Daily 7–7. Museum:* ☎ *5,000 lire.* ☉ *Jan.–Oct., Tues.–Sat. 9–1 and 2:30–6; Nov.–Dec., Tues.–Sun. 10–1 and 2–5.*

The **Orto Botanico** (Botanic Garden) was founded in 1545 by order of the Venetian Republic to supply the university with medicinal plants. The garden is in front of Sant'Antonio. ⊠ *Via Donatello,* ☎ *049/656614.* ☎ *5,000 lire.* ☉ *Apr.–Sept., daily 9–noon and 3–6; Oct.–Mar., Mon.–Sat. 9–1.*

Piazza dei Signori exhibits some fine examples of 15th- and 16th-century buildings. The cathedral **Santa Magdalena** is just a few steps from Piazza dei Signori.

Laid out in 1775, **Prato della Valle** is an unusual and attractive piazza with a central wooded oval park, surrounded by a canal. A market is featured here weekends (☞ Shopping, *below*). At the southeast end of this immense square is the **Chiesa di Santa Giustina,** with finely inlaid choir stalls and Veronese's (1528–88) colossal altarpiece, *The Martyrdom of St. Justine.* ⊠ *Prato della Valle.* ☉ *Daily 8–noon and 3–6.*

OFF THE BEATEN PATH

ABANO TERME AND MONTEGROTTO TERME – These two spas, about 12 km (7 mi) south of Padua, are set in the dreamy landscape of the Euganean Hills. Colorful gardens and fresh summer breezes make them havens if you are looking for a respite from city life.

PRAGLIA – You can tour the evocative 15th-century halls and cloisters of this Benedictine monastery hidden in the hills. Wine and honey produced by the monks are for sale. Head 12 km (7 mi) southwest of Padua, following signs for ABANO TERME on the south side of the city. ☎ 049/9900010. ☎ Free; donations appreciated. ☉ Tours Apr.–Oct., Tues.–Sun. (except major religious holidays) every ½ hr 3:30–5:30; Nov.–Mar., Tues.–Sun. every ½ hr 2:30–4:30.

MONTAGNANA – The surrounding walls of this medieval city 50 km (30 mi) southwest of Padua are remarkably well preserved, and there are 24 towers, a moat, and four city gates. Its former rivals, Este and Monselice, are only 20 km (12 mi) east on the same road.

Dining and Lodging

Hotels in nearby Vicenza, in Bassano del Grappa, along the Brenta, and in Venice are better in terms of variety and quality than in Padua itself, which caters primarily to business travelers.

$$$ ✕ **Belle Parti.** Angelo Rasi's sophisticated Belle Parti is the best restaurant in town. Adventurous, Venetian-accented seasonal specialties might include risotto *al fior d'arancio con gamberi di fiume* (with oranges and river prawns) and *quaglia tartufata in crosta* (truffled quails in pastry). The wine list offers a fine selection of the area's best bottles. ⊠ *Via Belle Parti 11,* ☎ *049/8751822. AE, DC, MC, V. Closed Sun. and 1st 3 wks in Aug.*

$$ ✕ **Cavalca.** A family-run establishment with a long tradition, Cavalca is just off Piazza dei Signori in the heart of Padua. Classic decor and simple but courteous service are hallmarks here. The specialties are *pasta e fagioli* (pasta and bean soup), *capretto arrosto* (roast kid), or a plat-

ter of *arrosti misti* (assorted roast meats). ⊠ *Via Manin 8,* ☎ *049/ 8760061. Reservations essential. AE, DC, MC, V. Closed Wed., 2 wks in Jan., and 3 wks in July. No dinner Tues.*

$ ✕ **Fagiano.** Near the Sant'Antonio, Fagiano is a popular trattoria with locals and tourists. The specialties are hearty standbys: pasta e fagioli and *fagiano farcito* (stuffed pheasant). ⊠ *Via Locatelli 45,* ☎ *049/ 8750073. MC, V. Closed Mon. and 2 wks in July. No dinner Sun.*

$$$ 🏨 **Donatello.** Directly opposite the basilica Sant'Antonio, Donatello has rooms with a view of the square and church, but it can be noisy. Rooms are contemporary, with color TVs. ⊠ *Via del Santo 102, 35100,* ☎ *049/8750634,* FAX *049/8750829. 49 rooms. Restaurant. AE, DC, MC, V. Closed mid-Dec.–mid-Jan.*

$$$ 🏨 **Villa Ducale.** Set in its own statuesque gardens, one of the country residences built along the Brenta River by Venetian noblemen has been turned into a stylish hotel with stuccoed walls and ceilings, Murano glass chandeliers and mirrors, and Venetian-style marble flooring. This is not in Padua but in Dolo, halfway between Venice and Padua, and is connected to both by a regular local train service. ⊠ *Riviera Martiri della Libertà 75, 30031 Dolo,* ☎ *041/5608020,* FAX *041/5608004. 11 rooms. Restaurant. AE, DC, MC, V.*

Nightlife and the Arts

CAFFÈ

The ever-popular **Caffè Pedrocchi** (⊠ Corso Garibaldi, ☎ 049/8752020), in a monumental 19th-century neoclassical coffeehouse that looks like a cross between a museum and a stage set, serves up an impressive cappuccino. The upstairs rooms, with their frescoed ceilings, often feature art shows. It's closed Monday.

JAZZ

A university crowd flocks to the **Video Club Sisma** (⊠ Via Chiesanuova 106, Padua, ☎ 049/8716577) for its art and film exhibitions mixed with music.

NIGHTCLUBS

Big Club (⊠ Via Armistizio, ☎ 049/680934). **Wag** (⊠ Via Savonarola 149, ☎ 049/8721530). **Le Petit Palais** (⊠ Via Vecellio 1, ☎ 049/ 600134). **Limbo** (⊠ Via San Fermo 44, ☎ 049/656882) has a pool table, a game room upstairs, and live music downstairs.

Outdoor Activities and Sports

GOLF

The 18-hole **Golf Club Padova** (⊠ Via Noiera 57, Valsanzibio di Galzignano, ☎ 049/9130078, FAX 049/9131193) is 18 km (11 mi) south of Padua.

Shopping

Padua's Saturday market in **Prato della Valle** has a wide range of goods; an antiques market is held the third Sunday of every month.

VERONA

On the banks of the fast-flowing Adige River, enchanting Verona lays claim to classical and medieval monuments, a picturesque town center where bright geraniums bloom in window boxes, and a romantic reputation, thanks to being the setting of Shakespeare's *Romeo and Juliet*. It is one of Italy's most alluring cities, despite extensive industrialization and urban development in its newer sections. Inevitably, with its lively Venetian air, proximity to Lake Garda, and renowned summer opera season, it attracts hordes of tourists, especially vacationing Germans and Austrians, who drive over the Brenner Pass to the north.

Verona grew to power and prosperity within the Roman Empire as a result of its key commercial and military position in northern Italy. After the fall of the Empire, the city continued to flourish under the guidance of Barbarian kings such as Theodoric, Alboin, Pepin, and Berenger I, reaching its cultural and artistic peak in the 13th and 14th centuries, under the della Scala dynasty. (You'll see the *scala*, or ladder, emblem all over town.) In 1404, however, Verona traded its independence for security and placed itself under the control of Venice. (The other recurring architectural motif is the lion of St. Mark, symbol of Venetian rule.) Verona remained under Venetian protection until 1797, when Napoléon invaded. In 1814 the entire Veneto region was won by the Austrians, and it was finally united with the rest of Italy in 1866.

Exploring Verona

Please note that the Duomo and churches in Verona enforce a strict dress code: no tanks, sleeveless shirts, shorts, or short skirts.

A Good Walk

Start at the **Arena di Verona** ③ in Piazza Brà, the vast and airy square at the center of the city. Built by the Romans in the 1st century AD, the arena is one of the largest and best-preserved Roman amphitheaters anywhere. Take Via Mazzini, the main shopping street in town, to **Piazza delle Erbe** ④, a busy square with an open-air market. The **Casa di Giulietta** ⑤, with the most famous balcony in Italy, is a block down Via del Cappello. Return and take a few moments to stroll around **Piazza dei Signori** ⑥, and admire the **Palazzo della Ragione** ⑦, **Loggia del Consiglio** ⑧, and **Palazzo degli Scaglieri** ⑨. It's a short walk through Piazza Indipendenza to Ponte Nuova and across the river toward the **Chiesa di Santa Maria in Organo** ⑩ and the **Giardino Giusti** ⑪. Follow Via Santa Maria in Organo up to the Teatro Romano and **Museo Archeologico** ⑫. The Romanesque **Duomo** ⑬ is just over Ponte Pietra. From there either walk down Via Doumo to Via Forti and the **Galleria d'Arte Moderna** ⑭, or turn toward the riverbank and stroll (or alternately take Bus 76) down to the 14th-century **Castelvecchio** ⑮, looking like a fairy-tale castle guarding the bridge reaching over the Adige. The stunning Romanesque **Chiesa di San Zeno Maggiore** ⑯ is another few minutes' walk downriver.

TIMING

It takes about 40 minutes to walk the route and three hours to see the sites en route.

Sights to See

★ ☾ ❸ **Arena di Verona.** Only four arches remain of the outer rings of the arena, but the main structure is so complete that it takes little imagination to picture it as the site of the cruel deaths of countless gladiators, wild beasts, and Christians. Today it hosts Verona's summer opera, famous for spectacular productions and audiences of as many as 16,000. The best operas to see here are the big splashy ones that demand huge choruses, Cinerama sets, lots of color and movement, and, if possible, camels, horses, and/or elephants. The music can be excellent, and the acoustics are fine, too. If you go, be sure to take or rent a cushion—four hours on 2,000-year-old marble can be an ordeal. ⊠ *Arena di Verona, Piazza Brà,* ☎ *045/8003204.* 🎟 *8,000 lire; free 1st Sun. of month.* ☉ *Tues.–Sun. 8–6:30 (8–1:30 during opera season, July–Aug.).*

❺ **Casa di Giulietta** (Juliet's House). The balcony in the small courtyard will help to bring Shakespeare's play to life, even if it was built this century. Historians now believe that the couple had no real-life counterparts, but this hasn't discouraged anyone from imagining that they

Verona

300 meters
300 yards

N

Arena di Verona, **3**
Casa di Giulietta, **5**
Castelvecchio, **15**
Chiesa di San Zeno
Maggiore, **16**
Chiesa di Santa
Maria in Organo, **10**
Duomo, **13**

Galleria d'Arte
Moderna, **14**
Giardino Giusti, **11**
Loggia del
Consiglio, **8**
Museo
Archeologico, **12**
Piazza dei Signori, **6**

Palazzo degli
Scaglieri, **9**
Palazzo della
Ragione, **7**
Piazza delle Erbe, **4**

did. After all, historians are not as renowned for their storytelling as Shakespeare is. ⊠ *Via Cappello 23,* ☎ *045/8034303.* ☞ *6,000 lire.* ⊘ *Tues.–Sun. 8–6:30.*

OFF THE
BEATEN PATH

TOMBA DI GIULIETTA – Romantic souls may want to see the pretty spot claimed to be Juliet's Tomb. Authentic or not, it is still popular with lovesick Italian teenagers, who leave notes for the tragic lover. ⊠ *Via del Pontiere,* ☎ *045/8000361.* ☞ *5,000 lire; free 1st Sun. of month.* ⊘ *Tues.–Sun. 9–7.*

GIARDINI DI VILLA ARVEDI – Recently opened to the public, these formal gardens surrounding a 17th-century villa 8 km (5 mi) northeast of town are worth a visit. ⊠ *Statale per Grezzana,* ☎ *045/907045.* ☞ *10,000 lire.* ⊘ *By appointment; minimum 10 people.*

⑮ **Castelvecchio** (Old Castle). This crenellated, russet brick building with massive walls, towers, turrets, and a vast courtyard was built for Cangrande II della Scala in 1354. It presides over a street lined with attractive old buildings and palaces of the nobility. Inside, the **Museo di Castelvecchio** gives you a good look at the castle's vaulted halls and the treasures of Venetian painting and sculpture that they contain. ⊠ *Corso Cavour,* ☎ *045/594734.* ☞ *6,000 lire; free 1st Sun. of month.* ⊘ *Tues.–Sun. 9–6:30; hrs and admission may change during special exhibitions.*

⑯ **Chiesa di San Zeno Maggiore.** What is possibly the finest example of a Romanesque church in Italy, with a 13th-century rose window and 12th-century portal, is set between two medieval bell towers. The light-gray– and white-brick color scheme—typical of Italy's Romanesque churches—is especially impressive here. Inside, look for Mantegna's *Madonna* over the main altar; there's a peaceful cloister off the left nave. ⊠ *Piazza San Zeno,* ☎ *045/8006120.* ☞ *4,000 lire.* ⊘ *Daily 8–noon and 4–6:30.*

⑩ **Chiesa di Santa Maria in Organo.** The choir and sacristy of this medieval church are decorated with inlaid-wood masterpieces by the 15th-century monk Fra Giovanni. A series of panels depicts varied scenes—local buildings, an idealized Renaissance town, wildlife, and fruit—that radiate a love of life and reveal the artist's eye for detail. ⊠ *Via Giardino Giusti,* ☎ *045/591440.* ⊘ *Daily 7:30–11 AM.*

⑬ **Duomo.** The ornate Romanesque Duomo has not only architectural characteristics typical of the Venetian style, but also some Byzantine attributes. A strict dress code is enforced (no tanks, sleeveless shirts, shorts, or short skirts). ⊠ *Via Duomo.* ☞ *4,000 lire.* ⊘ *Apr.–Oct., daily 8:30– 6:30; Nov.–Mar., Mon.–Sat. 10–4, Sun. 1:30–5.*

⑭ **Galleria d'Arte Moderna** (Gallery of Modern Art). In addition to a small collection of modern art, this museum in the handsome Palazzo Forti (where Napoléon once stayed) frequently hosts visting exhibitions of well-known artists such as Marcel Duchamp (1887–1968) and Andy Warhol (1928–87). ⊠ *Via Forti 1,* ☎ *045/8001903.* ☞ *5,000 lire.* ⊘ *Tues.–Sun. 9–7.*

⑪ **Giardino Giusti.** The formal Giusti Gardens, laid out on several levels around a 16th-century villa, is a symbol of things long past. There's a fine view of the city from the terrace, from which the German poet and dramatist Johann von Goethe (1749–1832) recorded his inspiration. At the southern end of the gardens is the Gothic church of **Sant'Anastasia.** ⊠ *Via Giardino Giusti,* ☎ *045/8034029.* ☞ *7,000 lire.* ⊘ *Gardens: Apr.–Sept., daily 9–8; Oct.–Mar., daily 9–sunset.*

⑧ **Loggia del Consiglio.** The graceful structure was built in the 12th century to house city council meetings, and still serves as the seat of the provincial government. ☒ *Piazza dei Signori.* ☉ *Closed to the public.*

⑫ **Museo Archeologico.** The museum is housed in an old monastery above the **Teatro Romano** that was built in the same era as the Arena di Verona. The Roman Theater is sometimes used for dramatic productions. From here there are good views over the entire city. ☒ *Rigaste del Redentore,* ☏ *045/8000360.* ☒ *5,000 lire; free 1st Sun. of month.* ☉ *Tues.– Sun. 9–3.*

⑥ **Piazza dei Signori.** Verona's great piazza has been at the center of things for over a thousand years, but the impressive facades and arched entrances surrounding it date from the early Renaissance.

⑨ **Palazzo degli Scaglieri.** This was the medieval stronghold from which the della Scalas ruled Verona with an iron fist. ☒ *Piazza dei Signori.* ☉ *Closed to the public.*

⑦ **Palazzo della Ragione.** The 12th-century palace has a somber courtyard, Gothic staircase, and medieval tower overlooking the piazza. ☒ *Piazza dei Signori.* ☉ *Closed to the public.*

④ **Piazza delle Erbe** (Vegetable Market Square). This square is the site of an ancient Roman forum and today a colorful morning market, with huge rectangular umbrellas raised to shade the neat ranks of fruits and vegetables.

Dining and Lodging

$$$$ ✕ **Dodici Apostoli.** Vaulted ceilings, frescoed walls, and a medieval ambience make this an exceptional place to enjoy classic local and regional dishes. Near Piazza delle Erbe, it stands on the foundations of a Roman temple. Specialties include *zuppa scaligera* (soup of meat stock with vegetables and bread) and *vitello Lessinia* (veal with mushrooms, cheese, and truffles). ☒ *Vicolo Corticella San Marco 3,* ☏ *045/596999. AE, DC, MC, V. Closed Mon., Jan. 1–7, and June 15–July 7. No dinner Sun.*

$$$$ ✕ **Le Arche.** True to its name, this elegant restaurant is in a medieval building a step away from the della Scala tombs. The art-nouveau dining room features candlelight and flowers, imparting turn-of-the-century air. Only seafood is served, absolutely fresh and superlatively prepared in the Venetian tradition. Try the ravioli *di branzino con vongole* (stuffed with sea bass with clam sauce) and *scorfano con olive nere* (baked sea scorpion with black olives). ☒ *Via Arche Scaligere 6,* ☏ *045/8007415. AE, DC, MC, V. Closed Sun. and 1st 2 wks of Jan. No lunch Mon.*

$$–$$$ ✕ **Osteria All'Oste Scuro.** This trusty, family-run trattoria varies its selection of traditional Veronese dishes, such as pasta e fagioli, polenta *con lardo* (with bacon), and *pastisada de caval* (horse-meat stew). From September to May, once- or twice-weekly special fixed-price dinners feature an Italian regional menu paired with regional wines. ☒ *Vicolo San Silvestro 10,* ☏ *045/592650. Reservations essential. MC, V. Closed Sun. No dinner Sat.*

$$ ✕ **Al Calmiere.** This congenial trattoria on the lovely piazza in front of San Zeno Maggiore is the ideal place to enjoy Veronese specialties of tagliatelle *con fegatini di pollo* (with chicken-liver sauce), various types of pasta in *brodo* (broth), meats, and local wines (there are some 20 different Valpolicellas alone available) at reasonable prices. The interior, with an enormous open fireplace used for cooking, is especially cozy in winter. ☒ *Piazza San Zeno 10,* ☏ *045/8030765. AE, DC, MC, V. Closed Thurs. and July. No dinner Wed.*

$$ ✕ **Antico Caffè Dante.** This historic coffeehouse is run by Guido Morari, the proprietor of the upscale Nuovo Marconi restaurant next door. It is now a brasserie-style café-restaurant, its stuccoed interior with portraits of Italian national heroes. The short but varied menu offers a delicious asparagus risotto (in season), fresh *papparedelle* (thick ribbons of pasta) with scampi, and *stinco di maiale* (roast pork shin served with polenta). Tempting homemade cakes and pastries are served all day. ✉ *Piazza dei Signori 2,* ☎ *045/595249. AE, DC, MC, V. Closed Mon. in winter.*

$$ ✕ **La Greppia.** The classic decor with vaulted ceilings sets the tone in this bustling restaurant off Via Mazzini between the Arena and Piazza delle Erbe. The kitchen produces fine versions of local and regional dishes, especially *tortelli di zucca* (pasta filled with squash) and *bolliti* (assorted boiled meats served with a choice of sauces). Service is courteous and efficient. ✉ *Vicolo Samaritana 3,* ☎ *045/8004577. AE, DC, MC, V. Closed Mon., 2nd wk of Jan., last 2 wks in June.*

$ ✕ **Pizzeria Vesuvio.** Between Castelvecchio and San Zeno Maggiore, this authentic Neapolitan pizzeria has tables on the riverbank in summer, with a lovely breezy view of the Adige. ✉ *Via Rigaste 41,* ☎ *045/595634. No credit cards. Closed Mon.*

$$$$ 🏨 **Colomba d'Oro.** This attractive four-star hotel right by the Arena occupies a building that dates from the 14th century. It has retained its clubby atmosphere and European charm while providing up-to-date comfort. ✉ *Via Cattaneo 10, 37121,* ☎ *045/595300,* ℻ *045/594974. 41 rooms, 10 suites. Parking (fee). AE, DC, MC, V.*

$$$$ 🏨 **Gabbia d'Oro.** Set in a historic building off Piazza delle Erbe in the
★   ancient heart of Verona, this hotel is a tasteful fantasia of romantic ornamentation, lavish trimmings, exquisite fabrics, and gorgeous period pieces. Rooms—each one different and more attractive than the next—have frescoes, beamed ceilings, pretty wallpaper, antique prints and furnishings, canopy beds, and some are festooned with flying cupids and peaceful cherubs. You can relax outdoors in the medieval courtyard, in the comfortable orangerie, or on the roof terrace. The breakfast spread is to die for. ✉ *Corso Porta Borsari 4/a, 37121,* ☎ *045/8003060,* ℻ *045/590293. 19 rooms, 8 suites. Restaurant. AE, DC, MC, V.*

$$$$ 🏨 **Villa del Quar.** This tranquil 16th-century villa is surrounded by gar-
★   dens and vineyards in the Valpolicella country, 10 minutes by taxi from the city. Architect Leopoldo Montresor and his wife, Evelina, who live here with their children, converted part of the villa into a stylish and sophisticated hotel. No expense has been spared: All rooms have marble bathrooms (some with Jacuzzi) and European antiques. ✉ *Via del Quar 12, Pedemonte, 5 km (3 mi) north of Verona, 37020,* ☎ *045/ 6800681,* ℻ *045/6800604. 18 rooms, 4 suites. Restaurant, pool. AE, DC, MC, V.*

$$ 🏨 **Torcolo.** The warm welcome extended by the owners, Signoras
★   Diana and Silvia, the pleasant rooms decorated unfussily, and the central location on a peaceful street close to Piazza Brà and the Arena make the Torcolo outstanding value in its class. Breakfast is served outside on the terrace in front of the hotel in summer. ✉ *Vicolo Listone 3, 37121,* ☎ *045/8007512,* ℻ *045/8004058. 19 rooms. AE, MC, V.*

Nightlife and the Arts

The Arts

OPERA

Of all the venues for enjoying opera in the region, pride of place must go to the summer opera season in the **Arena di Verona.** The season runs from July through August, and the 16,000 in the audience sit on the original stone terraces that date from the time when gladiators fought to the death. The opera stage is huge and best suited to grand operas such as *Aïda,* but the experience is memorable no matter what is being performed. Sometimes, while sipping a drink in a café at **Piazza Brà,** you can overhear the opera. A 15% advance-sale fee is added to the price of a ticket for bookings made more than 24 hours before performance. *Contact: Ente Lirico Arena di Verona,* ⊠ *Piazza Brà 28, Verona, 37121, Box office:* ⊠ *Via Dietro Anfiteatro 6B,* ☎ *045/ 8005151,* FAX *045/8015593.* ☉ *Daily 9–noon and 3–5:45; performance days 10–9.*

Nightlife

DISCOS

Alter Ego (⊠ Via Torricelle 9, ☎ 045/915130) packs a twentysomething crowd that might call itself alternative. **Berfi's** (⊠ Via Lussemborgo 1, ☎ 045/508024) is a popular and expensive spot. **Excalibur** (⊠ Via Provolo 24, ☎ 045/594295) attracts a young crowd.

Outdoor Activities and Sports

Golf

The 18-hole **Golf Club Verona** (⊠ Ca' del Sale 15, Sommacampagna, ☎ 045/510060, FAX 045/510242), closed Tuesday, is 16 km (10 mi) west of Verona, and 2 km (1 mi) from the Sommacampagna exit on the A4 autoroute.

Tennis

There are public courts at **Via Colonnello Galliano** (☎ 045/592828).

Shopping

Market

Verona's **Piazza delle Erbe** daily market, open Monday–Saturday 8–1 and 3:30–sundown, has a selection of food, wine, clothing, antiques, and even pets.

Specialty Stores

ANTIQUES AND HOUSEWARES

The area around the Gothic church of Sant'Anastasia is full of antiques shops, most of them catering to serious collectors. Picnic on the Piazza dei Signori in the cool breeze after a strenuous day of antiques hunting. The perfect place for a modern gift or imaginative decorative piece is the diminutive boutique **Fornasetti** (⊠ Via Rosa 8/d, ☎ 045/8000064), with the dreamy, geometric black-and-white designs of the namesake artist imparted onto everything from ties, umbrellas, pillowcases, lacquer furniture, and plates.

Vicenza

🄱 *60 km (37 mi) east of Verona, 32 km (19 mi) west of Padua.*

Vicenza bears the distinctive signature of the 16th-century architect Andrea Palladio and was designated by UNESCO in 1994 as a preeminent site of world cultural heritage. The architect, whose name is the root of the style referred to as "Palladian," gracefully incorporated elements of classical architecture—columns, porticoes, and domes—into a style that reflected the Renaissance celebration of order and harmony. His elegant villas and palaces were influential in propagating classical architecture in Europe, especially Britain, and later in America—most notably, at Thomas Jefferson's Monticello.

In the mid-16th century Palladio was given the opportunity to rebuild much of Vicenza, which had suffered great damage during the bloody wars waged against Venice by the League of Cambrai, an alliance of the Papacy, France, the Holy Roman Empire, and several neighboring city-states. He imposed upon the city a number of his grand Roman-style buildings—rather an overstatement, considering the town's status. With the basilica, begun in 1549 in the very heart of Vicenza, he ensured his reputation and embarked on a series of lordly buildings, all of which proclaim the same rigorous classicism.

The Gothic **Duomo** contains a gleaming altarpiece by Lorenzo Veneziano, a 14th-century Venetian painter. The cathedral itself was partly destroyed in World War II, but nearly all the damaged areas have been restored. ⊠ *Piazza Duomo.* ☒ *Free.* ⊘ *Daily 10:30–12 and 3:30–7.*

The avenue **Corso Palladio** is lined with a succession of imposing palaces and churches that run the gamut from Venetian Gothic to Baroque. Many of these palaces were designed by Palladio. The church of **Santa Corona** holds an exceptionally fine *Baptism of Christ* (1500) by Giovanni Bellini (1430–1516) over the altar on the left, just in front of the transept. ⊠ *Contrà S. Corona.* ⊘ *Daily 8:30–noon and 2:30–6.*

The exquisite and unmistakably Palladian **Palazzo Chiericati** houses the city municipal art gallery, with a representative collection of Venetian paintings. ⊠ *Piazza Matteotti,* ☎ *0444/321348.* ☒ *5,000 lire.* ⊘ *Apr.–Sept., Tues.–Sat. 9:30–noon and 3–6, Sun. 9:30–noon and 2–7; Oct.–Mar., Tues.–Sat. 9:30–12:30 and 2:15–5, Sun. 9–12:30.*

★ The **Teatro Olimpico** is Palladio's last, and perhaps most exciting, work. Based closely on the model of the ancient Roman theater, it represents an important development in theater and stage design and is noteworthy for its acoustics and the cunningly devised false perspective of a classical street in the permanent backdrop. The anterooms are all frescoed with important figures in Venetian history. ⊠ *Piazza Matteotti,* ☎ *0444/323781.* ☒ *5,000 lire.* ⊘ *Tues.–Sat. 9:30–12:30 and 2:15–5, Sun. 9:30–12:30 (Apr.–Sept., also Sun. 2–7).*

At the heart of Vicenza is **Piazza dei Signori,** also the site of Palladio's "basilica," a confusing way to refer to it, since it is not a church but a courthouse and public meeting hall, the **Palazzo della Ragione.** An early Palladian masterpiece, it was actually a medieval building that the architect modernized, and the skill with which he wedded the graceful two-story exterior loggias to the existing Gothic structure is remarkable. Also note the **Loggia del Capitaniato,** opposite, which Palladio designed, but never completed. ⊠ *Piazza dei Signori,* ☎ *0444/ 323681.* ⊘ *Tues.–Sat. 9:30–noon and 2:30–5, Sun. 9:30–noon (Apr.–Sept., also Sun. 2–7) .*

OFF THE
BEATEN PATH

VILLA LA ROTONDA – This is the most famous Palladian villa of all. In truth, it can hardly be called a villa, since Palladio was inspired by ancient Roman temples. Serene and symmetrical, it was the model for Jefferson's Monticello. Take the time to admire it from all sides, and you'll see that it was the inspiration not just for Monticello, but for nearly every state capitol in the United States. The interior is typical of Palladio's grand style, with a unique juxtaposition of solids and voids. You can walk 3 km (2 mi) along the Riviera Berica from Vicenza, or take Bus 8 from Viale Roma and ask the driver to let you off at the Villa. Note that the interior is only open Wednesday. ⊠ *Via della Rotonda 29,* ☎ *0444/321793.* ☒ *10,000 lire (grounds only 5,000 lire).* ⊘ *Grounds: Mar. 15–Nov. 4, Tues.–Thurs. 10–noon and 3–6. Interior: Mid-Mar.–Nov. 4, Wed. only 10–noon and 3–6.*

VILLA VALMARANA AI NANI –A short walk from Villa La Rotonda, this 18th-century country house is decorated with a series of marvelous frescoes by Giambattista Tiepolo: These are fantastic visions of a mythological world, including one of his most stunning works, the *Sacrifice of Iphegenia*. The neighboring Foresteria, or guest house, holds more frescoes, showing vignettes of 18th-century Veneto life at its most charming, executed by Tiepolo's son, Giandomenico (1727–1804). ✉ *Via dei Nani 2/8,* ☎ *0444/321803.* 🎫 *8,000 lire.* ☉ *Mar.–Apr., Tues.–Sat. 2:30–5:30; May–Sept., Tues.–Sat. 3–6; Oct.–Nov., Tues.–Sat. 2–5.*

Dining and Lodging

$$ ✕ **Da Remo.** About a kilometer or so outside town, Da Remo is worth the taxi ride simply because it is one of Vicenza's best restaurants. In an attractive country-house setting, with light, airy dining rooms and a garden terrace, you can enjoy a relaxing meal of Venetian specialties, among them *faraona* (guinea hen) with radicchio, and risotto with seasonal vegetables. ✉ *Via Ca'Impenta 14,* ☎ *0444/911007. AE, DC, MC, V. Closed Mon., last wk in July, and 1st 3 wks in Aug. No dinner Sun.*

$$ ✕ **Scudo di Francia.** A Gothic palace in the heart of town houses the
★ white vaulted dining rooms of Scudo di Francia. The regional cuisine features specialties such as *bignè caldi al prosciutto e tartufo* (hot pastry puffs with ham and truffles), pasta e fagioli, and *baccalà alla vicentina* (cod with a creamy sauce). ✉ *Contrà Piancoli 4,* ☎ *0444/ 323322. AE, DC, MC, V. Closed Mon. and Aug. No dinner Sun.*

$–$$ ✕ **Al Paradiso.** This pizzeria-trattoria just off the Piazza dei Signori is one of a pair right next door to each other, owned by two brothers; the other is Vecchia Guardia (✉ *Via Vecchia Guardia 15,* ☎ *0444/ 321231*), closed Thursday. It's particularly attractive in summer, when you can sit at tables outside. The pizzas and other dishes are tasty and very reasonably priced. ✉ *Via Pescherie Vecchie 5,* ☎ *0444/322320. AE, DC, MC, V. Closed Mon.*

$$ 🏨 **Due Mori.** In the heart of Vicenza just off Piazza dei Signori, this small hotel is a favorite with regular visitors. ✉ *Contrá Do Rode 26, 36100,* ☎ *0444/321886,* 📠 *0444/326127. 26 rooms. AE, MC, V.*

Nightlife and the Arts

MUSIC AND THEATER

Vicenza's **Teatro Olimpico** has a concert season in May and June, as well as a classical drama season in September. Even if your Italian is dismal, it's particularly thrilling to see a performance in Palladio's magnificent theater. For details, contact the Teatro Olimpico (☞ *above*).

Shopping

JEWELRY

Vicenza is one of Italy's leading centers for the production and sale of jewelry. Each year, in January, June, and September, it hosts an international trade fair for goldsmiths. For details, inquire at the local tourist office (☞ Contacts and Resources *in* Venetian Arc A to Z, *below*).

VILLA BARBARO, TREVISO, AND THE HILLSIDE TOWNS

Northern Arc

In this area directly north of Venice, market towns cling to the steep foothills of the Alps and the Dolomites alongside streams that rage down from the mountains. Villa Barbaro, Palladio's most beautiful creation, is here, as are the arcaded streets of Treviso and the graceful Venetian Gothic styles of the smaller hill towns.

Marostica

18   *7 km (4½ mi) west of Bassano del Grappa, 26 km (16 mi) northeast of Vicenza.*

The first and most evident feature of Marostica is its Castello Superiore, perched on the hillside overlooking the surrounding countryside. But the most famous site in town is Piazza Castello, the main square, paved in checkerboard fashion.

Outdoor Activities and Sports

A game of **human-scale chess** is acted out here by players in medieval costume on the second weekend in September in even-numbered years (tickets go on sale in April); for information, call 0424/72127 or fax 0424/72800.

Bassano del Grappa

19   *7 km (4½ mi) east of Marostica, 37 km (23 mi) north of Venice.*

Beautifully positioned directly above the swift-flowing waters of the Brenta River at the foot of the Mt. Grappa massif (5,880 ft), Bassano has old streets lined with low-slung buildings flanked by wooden balconies and pretty flowerpots. Bright ceramic wares produced here and in nearby Nove are displayed in shops along byways that curve uphill toward a centuries-old square, and, even higher, to a belvedere with a good view of Mt. Grappa and the beginning of the Valsugana Valley.

Bassano's most famous landmark is the **covered bridge** that has spanned the Brenta since the 13th century. Rebuilt countless times (floods are frequent), the present-day bridge is a postwar reconstruction using Andrea Palladio's 16th-century design. The great architect astutely chose to use wood as his medium, knowing that it could be replaced quickly and cheaply. Almost as famous is the liquor shop **Nardini,** where grappa has been distilled for more than a century. Stop in for a sniff or a snifter.

Dining and Lodging

$$ ✕ **Da Renzo.** This popular, family-run restaurant has a view of the hills and olive groves of Bassano and a pleasant terrace used year-round. Seafood antipasto and grilled fish fresh from the Adriatic are the specialty. You can also enjoy regional dishes made with fresh seasonal ingredients.⊠ *Via Santissima Trinitá 9,* ☎ *0424/503055. AE, D, MC, V. Closed Tues. and 2 wks in Aug. No lunch Wed.*

$–$$ ✕ **Ristorante Birreria Ottone.** This old-world restaurant in town center is a favorite with the locals, who tout the excellent cuisine, draft wine and beer, and the friendly Wipflinger family, headed by Otto, whose Austrian forebear founded this beer hall about 100 years ago. Equally good for a simple lunch or a more elaborate dinner, Ottone's specialties include a delicious goulash cooked with cumin. ⊠ *Via Matteoti 47/50,* ☎ *0424/522206. AE, D, MC, V. Closed Tues., 1st 3 wks in Aug., and last 2 wks in June. No dinner Mon.*

$$$–$$$$ 🏠 **Villa Palma.** This gracefully refurbished 18th-century country villa, only a short drive from Asolo (10 km/6 mi) and Bassano (5 km/3 mi), combines modern comforts and conveniences—including Jacuzzi baths or sauna showers, and fax and computer facilities—with rural calm and old-fashioned style and charm—wooden beams, vaulted brick ceilings, and tasteful furnishings. In summer, meals are served on the terrace, overlooking the splendid garden. ⊠ *Via Chemin Palma 30, Mussolente, 36061,* ☎ *0424/577407,* 𝖥𝖠𝖷 *0424/87687. 16 rooms, 9 suites. Restaurant. AE, DC, MC, V.*

$$$ ⊞ **Belvedere.** This historic hotel has richly decorated public rooms with
  ★   period furnishings and Oriental rugs. A fireplace and piano music in the
         lounge and an excellent restaurant with a garden make for a very pleas-
         ant stay. The rooms are decorated in traditional Venetian or chic con-
         temporary style. ⊠ *Piazzale G. Giardino 14, 36061,* ☎ *0424/529845,*
         ℻ *0424/529849. 81 rooms, 6 suites. Restaurant. AE, DC, MC, V.*

$$ ⊞ **Al Castello.** In a restored town house at the foot of the medieval Torre
         Civica (Civic Tower), the Cattapan family's Castello is a reasonable,
         attractive proposition. Rooms are well equipped and furnished sim-
         ply. ⊠ *Piazza Terraglio 19, 36061,* ☎ *0424/523462,* ℻ *0424/228665.*
         11 rooms. Café. AE, MC, V.

Shopping

Bassano del Grappa and nearby Nove are the best bets for ceramic items.
A large number of shops in town feature wrought-iron and copper utensils, many of them made on the premises.

Asolo

★ ⑳   *18 km (11 mi) east of Marostica, 11 km (7 mi) east of Bassano del
        Grappa, 33 km (20½ mi) northwest of Treviso.*

The romantic, charming hillside hamlet of Asolo was the consolation
prize of an exiled queen. At the end of the 15th century, Venetian-born
Caterina Cornaro was sent here by Venice's doges to keep her from
interfering with their administration of her former kingdom of Cyprus,
which she had inherited. To soothe the pain of exile, she established a
lively and brilliant court in Asolo. Over the centuries, Venetian aristocrats continued to build gracious villas on the hillside, and in the 19th
century Asolo once again became the idyllic haunt of musicians, poets,
and painters. From the outside, you can explore villas once inhabited
by Robert Browning and the actress Eleanora Duse. Be warned that
Asolo's dreamy old-world atmosphere vaporizes on holiday weekends
when the crowds pour in.

In town center is **Piazza Maggiore,** with its Renaissance palaces and
turn-of-the-century cafés. Uphill from the piazza, past Caterina's ruined castle and some Gothic-style houses, is **La Rocca,** the fortress
standing on the summit.

Dining

$$ ✕ **Hosteria Ca'Derton.** Right on the main square, Ca'Derton has a pleas-
        ant, old-fashioned ambience, with early photos of Asolo and bou-
        quets of dried flowers. The friendly proprietor takes pride in the
        homemade pasta and desserts and offers a good selection of both local
        and international dishes. ⊠ *Piazza D'Annunzio 11,* ☎ *0423/952730.*
        *AE, DC, MC, V. Closed Tues., mid–late Feb., and mid–late Aug. No
        dinner Mon.*

Shopping

Asolo center hosts an antiques market on the second Sunday of the
month (except July and August).

Villa Barbaro

⑳   *7 km (4½ mi) northeast of Asolo, 33 km (20½ mi) northwest of
     Treviso.*

Villa Barbaro is one of the most gracious Renaissance creations of Pal-
ladio. The fully furnished villa just outside the town of Maser is still in-
habited by its owners, who make you slip heavy felt scuffs over your
shoes to protect the highly polished floors. The elaborate stuccos and
opulent frescoes by Paolo Veronese bring the 16th century to life. After

La Rotonda, this is Palladio's greatest villa and is definitely worth going out of your way to see (before making the trip, note restricted hours, *below*). ✉ *Via Cornuda 2,* ☎ *0423/923004.* 🎟 *10,000 lire.* ☉ *Apr.–Sept., Tues. and weekends 3–6; Oct.–Mar., weekends 2:30–5.*

Dining and Lodging

$$ ✕ **Agnoletti.** In the town of Giavera del Montello near Maser, Agnoletti
★ is an 18th-century inn of a bygone era with a lovely summer garden. The kitchen can produce an all-mushroom menu; but if you order something else, at least try the mushroom zuppa or *crostata di funghi* (mushroom tart). ✉ *Giavera del Montello, Via della Vittoria 190,* ☎ *0422/776009. No credit cards. Closed Mon. and Tues. and 3 wks in Jan.*

$$ ✕ **Da Bastian.** A good place to stop for lunch before visiting the Villa Barbaro, this contemporary place has a pleasant garden for outdoor dining. Varied antipasto of pâtés, homemade vegetarian ravioli, and broiled meat with tasty sauces top the menu. ✉ *Via Cornuda,* ☎ *0423/565400. No credit cards. Closed Thurs. and Aug. No dinner Wed.*

$$$$ 🏨 **Villa Cipriani.** This historic villa is set in a romantic garden on the hillside and surrounded by other gracious country homes. Tastefully furnished with 19th-century antiques, it offers oldfangled atmosphere, creature comforts, and attentive service. The superb restaurant has a terrace overlooking the garden. ✉ *Via Canova 298, 31011,* ☎ *0423/952166,* 🖷 *0423/952095. 31 rooms. Restaurant. AE, DC, MC, V.*

Treviso

㉒ *30 km (19 mi) north of Venice.*

The arcaded streets, frescoed houses, and channeled streams that run through the center of Treviso date mostly from the 15th century. The most important church in Treviso is **San Nicolò,** an impressive Gothic building with an ornate vaulted ceiling. San Nicolò has frescoes of the saints by 14th-century artist Tommaso da Modena on the columns. But the best is the remarkable series of 40 portraits of Dominican friars by the same artist in the seminary next door. They are astoundingly realistic, considering that some were painted as early as 1352, and include one of the earliest-known portraits of a subject wearing glasses. ✉ *Capitolo dei Domenicani, Seminario Vescovile, Via San Nicolò,* ☎ *0422/3247.* ☉ *Daily 8–6:30. To enter, ring at custodian's desk at seminary entrance.*

Inside the **Duomo,** on the altar of one of the chapels to the right, is an *Annunciation* by Titian (circa 1488–1576). ✉ *Piazza del Duomo.* ☉ *10:30–12:30.*

Piazza dei Signori is the heart of medieval Treviso and still the town's social center, with outdoor cafés and some impressive public buildings. One of these, the **Palazzo dei Trecento,** has a small alley leading behind it. Follow the alley for about 200 yards to the **pescheria** (fish market), on an island in one of the small rivers that flow through town.

Dining and Lodging

$$$ ✕ **Da Alfredo.** This restaurant belongs to the El Toulà group, a small
★ chain of well-known, high-class restaurants in Italy and abroad. This is your chance to enjoy the art nouveau decor and classic international cuisine for which it became famous. Among regional dishes are risotto *con funghi* (with mushrooms) or asparagus in season. For cooking, ambience, and service, it's one of the region's best. ✉ *Via Collalto 26,* ☎ *0422/540275. AE, DC, MC, V. Closed Mon. and Aug. No dinner Sun.*

$$ ✕ **Beccherie.** In a town known for good eating, this rustic inn is a fa-
★ vorite. It's in the heart of old Treviso, behind the main square, and there are tables outside for fair-weather dining under the portico. Special-

ties vary with the season. In winter, look for *crespelle al radicchi* (crepes with radicchio) and *faraona in salsa peverada* (guinea hen with a peppery sauce); spring heralds risotto with spring vegetables, *stinco di vitello* (veal shin), and *pasticcio di melanzane* (eggplant casserole). ⊠ *Piazza Ancilotto 10,* ☎ *0422/56601. AE, DC, MC, V. Closed Mon. and 2 wks in July. No dinner Sun.*

$$$$ 🏨 **Continental.** You'll find this hotel within the old city walls, between the train station and the sights. It is a traditional four-star hotel offering solid comfort. Rich fabrics and Oriental rugs lend an air of opulence. ⊠ *Via Roma 16, 31100,* ☎ *0422/411216,* 🖷 *0422/55054. 80 rooms. AE, DC, MC, V.*

$$ 🏨 **Al Fogher.** On the outskirts, Al Fogher is handy if you're traveling by car. This part of the Best Western chain has a bright contemporary look, with lots of modern art and room decor about equally divided between classic and modern. ⊠ *Viale della Repubblica 10, 31100,* ☎ *0422/432950,* 🖷 *0422/430391. 54 rooms, 1 suite. AE, DC, MC, V.*

Outdoor Activities and Sports

HORSEBACK RIDING

Lancenigo (⊠ 6 km/4 mi north of Treviso, ☎ 0422/63357) provides riding and lessons for riding and jumping.

Shopping

Shops in Treviso feature wrought-iron and copper utensils.

Conegliano

㉓ *23 km (14 mi) north of Treviso, 71 km (44 mi) west of Udine.*

Conegliano is in the heart of wine-producing country. The town itself is attractive, with Venetian-style villas and frescoed houses, but the real draw is the wine.

Lodging

$$ 🏨 **Canon d'Oro.** The town's oldest inn, the Canon d'Oro is in a 15th-century building in a central location near the train station. The restaurant's tranquil decor lets you concentrate on the good food, mainly regional specialties such as risotto, Canon d'Oro gnocchi (gnocchi with a rich meat sauce), baccalà alla vicentina, and *fegato alla veneziana* (liver with onions). ⊠ *Via XX Settembre 129, 31015,* ☎ *0438/34246,* 🖷 *0438/34246. 25 rooms. Restaurant. AE, MC, V.*

En Route Well marked and leading southeast from Conegliano, the **Strada del Vino Rosso** (Red Wine Road) wends its way through cabernet and merlot country along the Piave River, and there are dozens of places to stop, sample, and buy the red—and some rosé—wines. The road ends at Oderzo.

UDINE AND TRIESTE
Eastern Arc

Italy's northeastern corner is an ethnically jumbled cocktail of Italian, Slavic, and central European cultures. A peripheral position usually puts this potentially fascinating area beyond the range of most visitors. The old Hungarian port of Trieste—a symbol of Italian nationalist aspirations for so long—and the medieval city of Udine are perfect bases for local excursions.

Udine

㉔ *71 km (44 mi) east of Conegliano, 64 km (40 mi) north of Trieste, 100 km (62 mi) east of Venice.*

Udine, in Italy's Friuli–Venezia Giulia region, commands a view of the surrounding plain and the Alpine foothills; according to legend, it stands on a mound erected by Attila the Hun so he could watch the burning of the important Roman center of Aquileia to the south. Udine flourished in the Middle Ages, thanks to its good location for trade and the rights it gained from the local patriarch to hold regular markets. There is a distinct Venetian feel to the city, noticeable in the architecture of Piazza della Libertà, under the stern gaze of the lion of St. Mark, symbol of Venetian power.

The **Galleria d'Arte Antica** is the best place to trace the history of the area and the importance of Cividale and Udine in the formative period following the collapse of the Roman Empire. A large collection of Lombard artifacts includes weapons, jewelry, and domestic wares from this warrior race, which swept into what is now Italy in the 6th century. ⊠ *Castello,* ☎ *0432/700700.* 🎟 *5,000 lire.* ⊙ *Tues.–Sat. 9:30–12:30 and 3–6, Sun. 9:30–1.*

Dining and Lodging

$$ ✕ **Alla Buona Vite.** This traditional restaurant in town center specializes in seafood. *Tagliolini dello chef* (noodles with a creamy scampi sauce) and *rombo al limone e capperi* (turbot with lemon and capers) are among the many choices here. ⊠ *Via Treppo 10,* ☎ *0432/21053. AE, DC, MC, V. Closed Mon. and Aug. No dinner Sun.*

$$ ✕ **Antica Maddalena.** Just a few steps from Udine's pretty Piazza del-
★ l'Unità is where you'll find this elegant eating place, defined by its owner as a deluxe trattoria. Lots of warm wood tones, fresh flowers, and stained glass complement a menu of regional and Italian specialties, among them *zuppa di funghi porcini* (porcini mushroom soup) and gnocchi *con zucca e ricotta* (with squash and ricotta cheese). ⊠ *Via Pelliccerie 4,* ☎ *0432/25111. AE, DC, MC, V. Closed Sun. and 2 wks in Aug. No lunch Mon.*

$$ ✕ **Trattoria al Lepre.** A characteristic *focolare* (hearth) in one of the dining rooms is a symbol of traditional local cooking, and that's what you'll enjoy in this simple establishment. The specialties include tagliatelle con funghi and stinco di maiale. ⊠ *Via Poscolle 27,* ☎ *0432/295798. AE, DC, MC, V. Closed Sun. and 10 days in Aug.*

$$$ 🏨 **Astoria Hotel Italia.** Centrally located, the Italia offers soundproofed rooms furnished in traditional style. Public rooms have Venetian glass chandeliers and comfortable armchairs. ⊠ *Piazza XX Settembre 24, 33100,* ☎ *0432/505091,* 🗏 *0432/509070. 80 rooms. Restaurant, minibars. AE, DC, MC, V.*

En Route From Udine, the road eastward follows the coast under the shadow of the huge geological formation called the Carso, a large, barren expanse of limestone that forms a giant ledge, most of which is across the border in Slovenia. Italian territory goes only a few kilometers inland in this strip, and Italy's small Slovenian minority ekes out an agricultural existence in the region, which has changed hands countless times since the final days of Imperial Rome.

Cividale

㉕ *17 km (11 mi) east of Udine.*

Cividale dates from the time of Julius Caesar. It is popularly supposed (particularly by locals) that it was built by Caesar when he was commander of Roman legions in the area. The city straddles the River Natisone and contains many examples of Venetian Gothic buildings, particularly the **Duomo** and the **Palazzo Comunale.** Duomo: ⊠ *Piazza Duomo,* ☎ *0432/731144.* ⊙ *Apr.–Sept., Mon.–Sat. 9:30–noon and*

3–7, Sun. 3–6:45; Oct.–Mar., Mon.–Sat. 9:30–noon and 3–6, Sun. 3–5:45.

Castello di Miramare

★ **㉖** *7 km (4½ mi) north of Trieste, 78 km (48 mi) south of Udine, 156 km (97 mi) east of Venice.*

This seafront castle in Miramare is a 19th-century extravaganza in white stone, built for the Archduke Maximilian of Hapsburg (brother of Emperor Franz Josef). Maximilian spent a brief, happy time here until Napoléon III of France took Trieste from the Hapsburgs and sent the poor archduke packing. He was given the title of Emperor of Mexico in 1864 as a compensation, but met his death before a Mexican firing squad in 1867. You can visit the lush grounds and admire the memorable views over the Adriatic. ⊠ *Miramare,* ☎ *040/224143.* 🎟 *Grounds free; castle 8,000 lire, plus 3,000 lire for guided visit.* ☉ *Grounds: daily, 9:30–1 hr before sunset; castle: Mon.–Sat. 9:30–1, Sun. 9:30–12:30; call for afternoon hrs June–July.*

Trieste

㉗ *64 km (40 mi) southeast of Udine, 163 km (101 mi) east of Venice.*

Surrounded by rugged countryside and beautiful coastline, Trieste is built on a hillside above what was once the chief port of the Austro-Hungarian Hapsburg Empire. Typical of Trieste are its turn-of-the-century cafés (☞ *Caffè, below*). Like Vienna's coffeehouses, these are social and cultural centers of the city, and much-beloved refuges from the city's prevailing northeast wind, the "*bora.*"

The sidewalk cafés on the vast seaside **Piazza dell'Unità d'Italia** are popular meeting places in the summer months. The square is similar to Piazzetta San Marco in Venice; both are focal points of architectural interest that command the best views of the sea. Behind **Palazzo Comunale** (Town Hall) (⊠ At the end of Piazza dell'Unità d'Italia), going away from the sea, steps lead uphill, following the city's pattern of upward expansion from its roots as a coastal fishing port in Roman times.

Civico Museo Revoltella e Galleria d'Arte Moderna was founded in 1872 when the Venetian Baron Revoltella left the city his palazzo, library, and art collection. The gallery has one of the most important collections of 19th- and 20th-century art in Italy, with Italian artists particularly well represented. ⊠ *Via Diaz 27,* ☎ *040/311361.* 🎟 *5,000 lire.* ☉ *Mon. and Wed.–Sat. 10–1 and 3–8, Sun. 10–1.*

The solid Romanesque construction of **San Silvestro** church (⊠ Via S. Silvestro), open Monday–Saturday 10–1, dates from the 11th century. Just beyond it is the Baroque extravagance of **Santa Maria Maggiore**, which backs onto a network of alleys closed to traffic.

The 14th-century **Cattedrale di San Giusto** incorporates two much-older churches, one dating from as far back as the 5th century. The exterior adds even more to the jumble of styles involved by using fragments of Roman tombs and temples: You can see these most clearly on the pillars of the main doorway. The highlights of the interior are the 13th-century mosaics and frescoes. ⊠ *Piazza Cattedrale.* ☉ *Apr.–Sept., Mon.–Sat. 8–noon and 3:30–7:30, Sun. 8–1 and 3:30–8; Oct.–Mar., Mon.–Sat. 8–noon and 2:30–6:30, Sun. 8–1 and 3:30–8.*

From the hilltop **Castello di San Giusto** you can take in some of the best views of the area. In the 15th century this castle was built by the Venetians, who always had an eye for the best vantage point in the cities they conquered or controlled. The Hapsburgs, subsequent rulers of Trieste, enlarged it to its present size. Some of the best exhibits in the **Museo Civico del Castello di San Giusto** are the displays of weaponry and armor. ⊠ *Piazza Cattedrale,* ☎ *040/313636.* ▦ *Museum 3,000 lire.* ☼ *Grounds: daily 9–sunset; museum: daily 9–7.*

Piazza della Borsa is the square containing Trieste's original stock exchange, the **Borsa Vecchia,** a neoclassical building now serving as the chamber of commerce. The **statue of Leopold I** is at one end of the square.

OFF THE BEATEN PATH	**GROTTA GIGANTE** – This is the largest cave in the world open to tourists. It is more than 300 ft high, 900 ft long, and 200 ft wide, with spectacular stalactites and stalagmites. Reserve 45 minutes for the tour. It is not far from Trieste, about 15 km (9 mi) north of the city (take Tram 2 from Piazza Oberdan). ☎ *040/327312.* ▦ *13,000 lire.* ☼ *Tours Mar.–Oct., hourly 9–noon and 2–5; Nov.–Feb., hourly 10–noon and 2:30–4:30.*

Caffè

Trieste being one of the most famous coffee towns in the world, perhaps it is no coincidence that its mayor is Riccardo Illy, of the city's best-known roasting family. You will have plenty of choices and setting in which to savor a good cup, but you should know that in Trieste your cappuccino will come in an espresso cup, with only half as much frothy milk as elsewhere in Italy, and topped with a dollop of whipped cream. The elegant civility of Trieste plays out beautifully in a caffè culture that rivals Vienna. Many caffès are part of a *torrefazione* (roasting shop), so you can sample the beans before you buy.

Few caffès in Trieste, in Italy, or in the world, can rival **Caffè San Marco** (⊠ Via Cesare Battisti 18, ☎ 040/369333) for its glimmering art deco style and old-world atmosphere. Occasionally, there is live music. **Cremecaffè** (⊠ Piazza Goldoni 10, ☎ 040/636555; closed Sun.) may not be the place to sit down and read the paper, but it's nonetheless one of the most frequented caffès in town, with 20 different blends to choose from.

One of the city's finest roasting shops, **Caffè La Colombiana** (⊠ Via Carducci 12, ☎ 040/370855; closed Sun.) has stood here since the 1940s. There is no better location in town than at **Caffè Piazza Grande** (⊠ Piazza dell'Unità d'Italia 5, ☎ 040/369878; closed Sun.), with a great view of the great piazza. **Il Gran Bar Malabar** (⊠ Piazza San Giovanni 6, ☎ 040/370855, Closed Sun.) is yet another wonderful stop for a coffee or aperitif, with an excellent wine list as well, and tastings every Friday.

Dining and Lodging

$$
✕ **Suban.** Though in the hills on the edge of town, this historic trattoria is worth the taxi ride. The rustic decor is rich in dark wood, stone, and wrought iron, and you'll find typical regional fare with imaginative variations. Among the specialties are *jota carsolina* (typical local minestrone made of cabbage, potatoes, and beans) and duck breast in Tokay sauce. ⊠ *Via Emilio Comici 2,* ☎ *040/54368. AE, DC, MC, V. Closed Tues., 2 wks in Aug., and 1 wk in Jan. No lunch Mon.*

$$$–$$$$ ▥ **Duchi d'Aosta.** On the spacious Piazza dell'Unità d'Italia, this hotel is beautifully furnished in lavish Venetian-Renaissance style. Its restaurant, Harry's Grill, is one of the city's most elegant. ⊠ *Piazza dell'Unità d'Italia 2, 34121,* ☎ *040/7600011,* ℻ *040/366092. 50 rooms, 2 suites. Restaurant, bar. AE, DC, MC, V.*

$$–$$$ ▥ **Colombia.** Unpretentious but adequate, this small hotel caters mainly to a business clientele. There is no restaurant, but there's a typical beer cellar restaurant close by. ⊠ *Via della Geppa 18, 34121,* ☎ *040/ 369333,* ℻ *040/369644. 40 rooms. AE, DC, MC, V.*

Nightlife and the Arts

The opera season in Trieste runs from October through May, with a brief operetta festival in July and August. Contact the **tourist information office** (⊠ Stazione Centrale, ☎ 040/420182) for further details on events.

Outdoor Activities and Sports

GOLF

Nine-hole **Golf Club Trieste** (⊠ Padriciano 80, ☎ 040/226159), closed Tuesday, is 6 km/4 mi from town center.

Shopping

Trieste's busy shopping street, **Corso Italia,** is reached from Piazza della Borsa. There are antiques markets on the streets of the city's old center on the third Sunday of each month. Trieste has some 60 antiques dealers, jewelers, and secondhand shops, and a large antiques fair is held in the city at the end of October.

VENETIAN ARC A TO Z

Arriving and Departing

By Car

The main access roads to the Venetian Arc from southern Italy are both linked to the **A1** (Autostrada del Sole), which connects Bologna, Florence, and Rome. They are the **A13,** which culminates in Padua, and the **A22,** which passes through Verona in a north–south direction. The road linking the region from east to west is the **A4,** the primary route from Milan to as far as Trieste.

By Plane

The main airport serving the Venetian Arc is **Aeroporto Marco Polo** (☎ 041/2609260) 10 km/6 mi north of Venice (☞ Venice A to Z *in* Chapter 5), which handles international and domestic flights to the region. A few European airlines schedule flights to **Aeroporto di Villafranca** (⊠ 11 km/7 mi southwest of Verona, ☎ 045/8095666), also served by a number of charter flights. A regular bus service connects Villafranca with Verona's Porta Nuova railway station.

Treviso's **Aeroporto San Giuseppe** (⊠ 5 km/3 mi southeast of Treviso, 32 km/19 mi north of Venice, ☎ 0422/22667) is also served by charter flights. Flights to Treviso usually include transportation from the airport to Venice or other destinations; otherwise there is a local bus service to Treviso every half hour during the day, or a taxi will come from Treviso, only 6 km (4 mi) away, to pick you up.

There are domestic flights to **Aeroporto Ronchi dei Legionari** (⊠ 35 km/22 mi northwest of Trieste, ☎ 0481/773224), linked with Via Miramare in town center by a regular bus service.

By Train

The most important train routes arriving from the south will stop almost every hour in either Verona, Padua, or Venice. From northern Italy and the rest of Europe, trains usually enter via Milan to the west or through Porta Nuova station in Verona. Call (☎ 147/888088) for train information.

Getting Around

By Bus

There are interurban and interregional connections throughout the Veneto and Friuli. Local tourist offices may be able to provide details of timetables and routes; otherwise contact the local bus station, or in some cases the individual bus companies operating from the station.

Bus stations: Bassano (⊠ Piazzale Trento, ☎ 0424/30850). **Padua** (⊠ Piazzale Boschetti, ☎ 049/8206811). **Treviso** (⊠ Via Lungosile Mattei, ☎ 0422/412222). **Trieste** (⊠ Piazza Libertà, ☎ 040/425001). **Venice** (⊠ Piazzale Roma, ☎ 041/5287886 for buses to Brenta Riviera, Padova, and Treviso, 041/5205530 for buses to Conegliano and Udine and for buses covering the Conegliano–Vittorio Veneto–Cortina route). **Verona** (⊠ Porta Nuova, ☎ 045/8004129). **Vicenza** (⊠ Viale Milano 138, ☎ 0444/544333).

By Car

The main highway in the region is **A4,** which connects Verona, Padua, and Venice with Trieste. The distance from Verona, in the west, to Trieste is 263 km (163 mi). Branches link A4 with Treviso (**A27**), Pordenone (**A28**), and Udine (**A23**).

By Train

To the west of Venice, on the main line running across the north of Italy, are Padua (20 mins), Vicenza (1 hr), and Verona (1½ hrs); to the east is Trieste (2 hrs). Local trains link Venice to Bassano del Grappa (1 hr), Padua to Bassano del Grappa (1 hr), Vicenza to Treviso (1 hr), and Udine to Trieste (1 hr). Treviso and Udine both lie on the main line from Venice to Treviso, on which Eurocity trains continue to Vienna and Prague. Call for train information (☎ 147/888088).

Contacts and Resources

Car Rentals

PADUA

Avis (⊠ Piazza Stazione 1, ☎ 049/664198). **Hertz** (⊠ Piazza Stazione 5, ☎ 049/657877).

TRIESTE

Avis (⊠ Piazza della Libertà, c/o Silos, ☎ 040/421521; ⊠ Aeroporto Ronchi dei Legionari, ☎ 0481/777085). **Hertz** (⊠ Piazza della Libertà, c/o Silos, ☎ 040/422122; ⊠ Aeroporto Ronchi dei Legionari, ☎ 0481/777025).

UDINE

Avis (⊠ Viale Leopardi 5/a, ☎ 0432/501149). **Hertz** (⊠ Via Crispi 19, ☎ 0432/609160).

VERONA

Avis (⊠ Stazione FS, ☎ 045/26636). **Hertz** (⊠ Stazione FS, ☎ 045/ 25832).

VICENZA

Avis (⊠ Viale Milano 88, ☎ 0444/321622). **Hertz** (⊠ Viale Europa 50, ☎ 0444/321313).

Emergencies

Police, Ambulance, Fire (☎ 113). For first aid, ask for *"pronto soccorso,"* and be prepared to give your address. **Doctors** and Dentists (☎ 112). **Ospedale Civile e Policlinico dell'Università** (⊠ Padua, ☎ 049/ 8211111). **Late-Night Pharmacies** take turns staying open late and on Sunday. Call for information on which one is open (☎ 192).

Guided Tours

Many of the best tours begin and end in Venice because so much of the region is accessible from there (☞ Venice A to Z *in* Chapter 5). The **Burchiello excursion boat** makes an all-day villa tour along the Brenta Canal, but the trip is expensive and not necessarily the best way to see the villas, since so much time is spent on the boat. For those who prefer to go it alone, **American Express** (☞ Travel Agencies, *below*) suggests itineraries that can be followed by car, with or without a hired driver. **Robe Vicentine** (☎ FAX 0444/585168) offers tours around the Vicenza area, such as guided visits to Palladian villas with Renaissance lunches and dinners. Local tourist offices will be able to put you in contact with the Tourist Guides Association or provide you with a list of authorized guides, for whom there is an official tariff rate.

Trieste and Vicenza offer special weekend package deals ("T for you" and "Vicenza Weekend") that include discounts in hotels and restaurants, free or reduced-price entrance to a selection of the cities' main tourist attractions, and some guided tours. Contact the Trieste and Vicenza tourist offices (☞ *below*).

Travel Agencies

For agencies in Venice, *see* Venice A to Z *in* Chapter 5.

Padua (✉ Tiarè Viaggi/American Express, Via Risorgimento 20, ☎ 049/666133). **Trieste** (✉ Paterniti Viaggi/American Express, Corso Cavour 7, ☎ 040/366161, FAX 040/368888). **Verona** (✉ Fabretto Viaggi/American Express, Corso Porta Nuova 11, ☎ 045/8009040, FAX 045/8009045).

Visitor Information

Veneto Regional Tourist Office (✉ Palazzo Sceriman, 168 Lista di Spagna, Cannareggio, Venice, 30121, ☎ 041/2792644).

Padua (✉ Stazione Ferroviaria, 35100, ☎ 049/8752077; ✉ Museo Civico Eremitani, ☎ 049/8751153; ✉ Prato delle Valle, ☎ 049/8753087). **Treviso** (✉ Via Toniolo 41, 31100, ☎ 0422/547632, FAX 0422/541397). **Trieste** (✉ Stazione Centrale, 34100, ☎ 040/420182). **Udine** (✉ Piazza Primo Maggio 7, 33100, ☎ 0432/295972). **Verona** (✉ Via Leoncino 61, 37100, ☎ 045/8068680; ✉ Piazza delle Erbe 42, ☎ 045/8030086; ✉ Stazione FS, ☎ 045/8000861). **Vicenza** (✉ Piazza Matteotti 12, 36100, ☎ 0444/320854; ✉ Conzorsio di Promozione Turistica "Vicenza è," ☎ 0444/327141).

7 Italian Riviera

Genoa, Portofino, and Cinque Terre

It was the Italians who perfected il dolce far niente—the sweet art of idleness—and all signs show they did it in Liguria. Flanking Genoa, an art-filled city of understated splendor, the twin rivieras bask in the sun, dotted with seaside resorts and quaint villages. Rapallo, Portovenere, and the Cinque Terre glisten like pearls on a string, but Portofino still wins the beauty contest, as it has since the days of Bogie and Bacall.

Updated by
Valerie
Hamilton

LIKE THE FAMILY JEWELS THAT BEDECK ITS HABITUAL visitors, the Italian Riviera is glamorous, but in the old-fashioned way. The resort towns and tiny coastal villages that stake intermittent claims on the rocky shores of the Ligurian Sea have much more in common than their analogues in other, newer, or more overbuilt seaside paradises. Here, the grandest palazzi share space with frescoed, turn-of-the-century apartment buildings, and brand-name glitz seems as foreign as the Maine lobster some of the region's tiniest restaurants, incongruously, fly in for dinner. The rustic and elegant, the provincial and smart set, the cosmopolitan and the small-town are blended together here in a sun-drenched pastiche that makes up this, the "other" Riviera.

The serpentine arc of Liguria's coastline, sweeping serenely from Ventimiglia to La Spezia, is the defining mark of the region's identity. Although it technically extends inland to the tops of the Ligurian Alps, Liguria is Italy's seaside region, and its greatest charms are those of the sea. For centuries, the region has inspired poets and artists. For this is where a captivated Percy Shelley praised the "soft blue Spezian bay"; here is where daredevil English poet Lord Byron swam from Portovenere to Lerici. Today, travelers escaping the conceits of civilization still head for the Italian Riviera for a cure. Mellowed by the balmy breezes blowing off the sea, they bask in the sun and explore the tiny coastal towns whose greatest treasures—peace, quiet, and dramatic natural beauty—remain for the most part undiscovered.

Liguria's narrow strip of mountain-protected coastline varies considerably between the two rivieras. The western Riviera di Ponente, which reaches from the French border to Genoa, has protected bays and wide sandy beaches, and is generally more developed and commercialized than its counterpart to the east, the Riviera di Levante. Beginning at the French border, the Ponente is home to the glamorous seaside resorts of San Remo and Bordighera, similar to their glittery francophone cousins to the west in their unabashed civic dedication to the pursuit of pleasure. Much of the eastward sweep of the Ponente coastline has been developed for the packs of sun worshipers who descend upon it in the summer. The minuscule bays and inlets spanning the coastline from Genoa to Portovenere become steeper, sculpted by nature into rocky cliffs.

If this coastline is a necklace, hung with jewels, the most dazzling pendant is the Portofino promontory. This must be the most photographed village in the world, and one look is enough to tell you why—if you pull up to the port by boat, chances are you'll shoot all your film before you disembark. Smooth-faced, brightly painted houses frame the port in a burst of color that becomes sheer enchantment at sunset, when the houses are reflected in the dancing waters of the harbor. Despite what all the shops and restaurants worldwide named "Portofino" would have you believe, however, once you've landed, there's not much to see or do in Portofino. The people here are the real attractions—it was, after all, Bogie and Bacall and Taylor and Burton who put the place on the map.

Farther along the coast is a second peninsula; here the road weaves inland, leaving the visitor to hike or take a train or boat to explore the Cinque Terre, a collective community of five fishing villages perched on bluffs above the sea. Here are some of Liguria's most uncrowded beaches, most picturesque village squares, and certainly its best views; from the hiking trails that link the Cinque Terre, the tiny villages seem like colorful blooms of flowers on hulking black mountains plunging into the sea. Their very inaccessibility is what preserves the Cinque Terre from the touristic exploitation that looms over every place of extraordinary natural beauty. This is the Italian Riviera at its unbuttoned best.

Set in the heart of the region is Genoa, Italy's largest commercial port, where magnificent Renaissance palaces wearing the dusty patina of time attest to the wealth of the city's seafaring past. Every schoolchild knows Genoa as the birthplace of Christopher Columbus, and many would become wide-eyed in knowing it's the home of Europe's largest aquarium. Despite the city's considerable charms, most visitors to Liguria are more interested in the less-historic waters found along the coast—not surprising, given the relaxed, easy lifestyle found alongside them.

Pleasures and Pastimes

Dining

Liguria's cooking might surprise you. It employs all sorts of seafood—especially anchovies, sea bass, squid, and octopus—but it makes even wider use of vegetables and the aromatic herbs that grow wild on the hillsides, together with liberal amounts of olive oil and garlic. Pesto is Liguria's classic pasta sauce; it's made from pine nuts, garlic, oil, cheese, and basil that grows only along the coastal hills. You will also find *pansoti* (ravioli) and *trofie* (a chewy, short pasta, sometimes made with chestnut flour) with *salsa di noci*, a delicate sauce of garlic, walnuts, and cream that, like pesto, is pounded with a mortar and pestle. *Vitello* (veal) is the most popular meat; *cima alla Genovese,* breast of veal stuffed with a mixture of eggs and vegetables, is served as a cold cut. You should also try the succulent *agnello* (lamb) and fresh wild mushrooms picked in the hills.

When not snacking on pizza sold by the slice or by weight, the Genovese and other Ligurians eat *torta pasqualina* (vegetable pie), or focaccia, the salty and oily pizzalike bread with various toppings that goes well with a glass of wine. Local vineyards produce mostly light and refreshing whites such as Pigato, Vermentino Ligure, and Cinque Terre. Reds called Rossese and Dolceacqua actually resemble whites in their light, crisp flavor; they go well with the lighter meat dishes of the region. Sweets are less rich than those in other parts of Italy; *panna cotta* (a cooked milk custard) and gelato are favorites for dessert, while *canestralli* (light almond cookies with powdered sugar) and various *frittelle* (crispy fried sweet dough cookies) are perfect with a *caffè* (espresso).

CATEGORY	COST*
$$$$	over 85,000 lire
$$$	65,000–85,000 lire
$$	35,000–65,000 lire
$	under 35,000 lire

Prices are per person, including house wine, service, and tax.

Hiking and Walking

Liguria's hilly terrain makes walking strenuous but rewarding, with stunning views of the sea and little villages dotting the coast. Portofino invites walking, whether you opt for the classic and relatively easy walk from Portofino to the Abbazia di San Fruttuoso or the more challenging hike from Ruta to the top of Monte Portofino. One of the best treks is along the five Cinque Terre fishing towns, all the while thumbing your nose at the tourists on the sightseeing boats. Everywhere in Liguria, roads, mule paths, or footpaths lead into the hills, where you can discover the region at its unspoiled best.

Lodging

If urban artistic and historic treasures are your passion but you also want some seaside relief, stay in Genoa and make it your base for exploring the rest of the region on day trips. But when choosing a hotel in Genoa, you should know that this is one of Italy's noisiest cities; make sure your windows are double-glazed (*doppi vetri*). Genoa has relatively few hotels, and they tend to be geared more to the needs of business travelers than to tourists. For a more relaxed approach, sea views, and recreation facilities, settle into a resort and make your day trips, including one to Genoa, from there. Reserve ahead year-round for Genoa, and during peak Easter and summer seasons for resorts. The best bargains and the warmest welcomes can be found in the less-visited inland areas; there are few hotels in this part of Liguria, but many of them are family-run and special because of it. Note many hotels and resorts in the area close for a number of weeks each year, usually late fall and early winter, and some in summer; it's best to call ahead.

CATEGORY	COST*
$$$$	over 300,000 lire
$$$	170,000–300,000 lire
$$	110,000–170,000 lire
$	under 110,000 lire

Prices are for a standard double room, including service and tax.

Sailing

With so much coastline—350 km (217 mi)—and so many pretty little harbors, it's no wonder that the Riviera attracts pleasure craft of all shapes and sizes, from rowboats to megayachts. San Remo, Rapallo, Santa Margherita Ligure, Chiavari, Finale Ligure, and Sestri Levante have large, well-equipped marinas, and nearly every town has a harbor and at least one marine shop. Every October Genoa hosts a mammoth international boat show.

Exploring the Italian Riviera

Liguria's cities, towns, and resorts dot the elongated coastal strip and are connected by a highway stretching 260 km (161 mi) from Ventimiglia on the French border to La Spezia and Sarzana. At the center, Genoa separates the western (Ponente) from the eastern (Levante) Riviera, forming two distinct geographic areas to explore (three, including Genoa itself). The hilly and mountainous hinterland, very different in scenery and character from the Riviera, can easily be explored from towns along the coast. From the sea, a series of narrow valleys extend inland, giving access to the sparsely settled interior.

Getting around the Riviera is an expedient affair, though the pace here is leisurely. Public transportation in the region is excellent, with every sight of interest reachable by train (along the coast) and/or bus (for areas inland); it takes two hours for a fast train to cover the entire coast. With the freedom of a car, you could drive from one end of the Riviera to the other on the autostrada in less than three hours. The A10 and A12 autostrade on either side of Genoa skirt the coast, avoiding local traffic on the old Via Aurelia, laid out by the ancient Romans. The Via Aurelia, now known as national highway S1, connects practically all the towns along the coast.

Numbers in the text correspond to numbers in the margin and on the Italian Riviera and Genoa maps.

Great Itineraries

In seven days you can visit the prettiest resorts and fishing villages, spend a day or two in Genoa, and perhaps make an excursion inland. Five days would allow you to see the highlights, but you will probably want to see Genoa in a day so that you can visit more of the smaller towns. In three days you will be able to see Genoa and perhaps two major resorts and two or three of the smaller, more picturesque towns.

IF YOU HAVE 3 DAYS

Tour time is limited, and you should concentrate on select towns. On your first day begin on the eastern Riviera di Levante. Stop at the delightful fishing villages of **Portovenere** ㊼ and **Camogli** ㊲, detouring for a look at romantic **Portofino** ㊵. For a more cosmopolitan resort atmosphere, opt instead for **Rapallo** ㊳ or ⚏ **Santa Margherita Ligure** ㊴. On the second day see ⚏ **Genoa** ⑭–㉟, exploring the historic center, old harbor, and **Acquario** ㉟. The western Riviera should be the focus of the third day; head for glitzy **San Remo** ④ or the more sedate **Bordighera** ③, but allow about half a day along the way to visit the medieval centers of **Albenga** ⑧, **Cervo** ⑦, and **Taggia** ⑤. Naturally, you should follow this itinerary in the opposite direction if you are arriving in the region from the west.

IF YOU HAVE 5 DAYS

In five days you can go from one end of the Riviera to the other, or start in Genoa and head east or west from there. If you make Genoa your base you can alternate excursions along the coast and into the interior with city sightseeing. On your first day explore ⚏ **Genoa** ⑭–㉟. If the day is a clear one, take the **Granarolo funicular** ⑭ to the top for an aerial view of the city. On the second day head west, making a detour to Spotorno, and proceed to Noli, one of the best-preserved medieval towns on the entire Riviera. Then see the medieval delights of Cervo before going on to sophisticated ⚏ **San Remo** ④ and palm-studded ⚏ **Bordighera** ③ for the night. Bask in the sun on the third day or venture inland to the well-preserved medieval villages of Dolcedo and Valloria instead. On the fourth and fifth days explore the eastern Riviera, starting with stately **Nervi** ㊱, near Genoa. Among the many allurements on the Portofino promontory, explore the fishing village of **Camogli** ㊲ and chichi **Portofino** ㊵; don't miss the hamlets of San Rocco, San Niccolò, and Punta Chiappa, accessible by foot from Camogli. You can overnight in a stylish resort such as ⚏ **Santa Margherita Ligure** ㊴ or ⚏ **Rapallo** ㊳; or you can go for lower-key **Sestri Levante** ㊷, an industrial town with a charming medieval center, or the secluded town of ⚏ **Levanto** ㊹, closer to the Cinque Terre. If you have time on your fifth day, a daylong excursion by train or boat to the five rock-perched coastal villages of the ⚏ **Cinque Terre** ㊺ is highly recommended. If you don't go to Cinque Terre, proceed to ⚏ **Portovenere** ㊼. Then, bypass industrialized La Spezia and wind up in the pretty port village of **Lerici** ㊽.

IF YOU HAVE 7 DAYS

If you begin your visit of the region in ⚏ **Genoa** ⑭–㉟, spend two days there; take the **Granarolo funicular** ⑭ and a boat tour of the port. You will have time for an excursion to **Nervi** ㊱. On the third day head west from Genoa, either working your way gradually to Ventimiglia or going directly to Ventimiglia and then heading back to Genoa. On the western Riviera, see the extraordinary cactus collection in the **Giardino Hanbury** ① near **Ventimiglia** ②, then turn inland to medieval Dolceacqua, only 10 km (6 mi) away. If it strikes your fancy, stop for tea in genteel **Bordighera** ③ before continuing on to the much busier and more commercial resort of ⚏ **San Remo** ④; stay overnight in San Remo or **Finale Ligure** ⑨. On the fourth day, if you're driving, take the coast road (S1) from Finale Ligure to Noli and Spotorno. If you don't have a car, a bus from Spotorno takes you to Noli, where time has practically stood still since the Middle Ages. With the exception of **Albisola Marina** ⑪ and **Pegli** ⑬, you can skip the industrialized coast between **Savona** ⑩ and Genoa.

On the fifth day, head east from Genoa on the A12 autostrada or on the slower S1 highway to the Riviera di Levante to see the offhand charm of **Camogli** ㊲. Take the turnoff for **Rapallo** ㊳ and **Santa Margherita Ligure** ㊴ and, if the traffic isn't heavy, head for ☷ **Portofino** ㊵. At the height of the season an excursion boat to Portofino from Camogli, Santa Margherita Ligure, or Rapallo may avoid the traffic jams on the narrow access road—and parking problems once you arrive. You may want to consider staying in **Chiavari** ㊶, a good hub for forays into the mountains on your sixth day, or even in ☷ **Levanto** ㊹, where you can make a detour to the ☷ **Cinque Terre** ㊺. On the seventh day head east to **La Spezia** ㊻ and look for signs to **Portovenere** ㊼. Doubling back to La Spezia, take the coast road to charming **Lerici** ㊽. The La Spezia turnoff on the A12 and S1 highways is only about 15 km (9 mi) from the border of Tuscany.

When to Tour the Italian Riviera

Though shops, cafés, clubs, and restaurants stay open late in resorts during high season (at Easter and during the summer), during the rest of the year they close early. Many hotels and restaurants in resort towns close from November through March. Avoid driving through Ventimiglia on Friday, the busy market day.

RIVIERA DI PONENTE

The Riviera di Ponente stretches from Ventimiglia on the French border to Genoa. For the most part it is an unbroken chain of popular beach resorts sheltered from the north by the Ligurian and Maritime Alps, mountain walls that guarantee mild winters and a long growing season—resulting in its other nickname, the Riviera dei Fiori (Riviera of Flowers). Actually, the name is prettier than the sight of once-verdant hillsides now swathed in plastic to form massive greenhouses. Many towns on the western Riviera have suffered from an epidemic of overdevelopment, but most have preserved their historic cores, usually their most interesting features. In major resorts large new marinas cater to the pleasure-craft crowd. The Riviera di Ponente has both sandy and pebbly beaches with some quiet bays. Varazze, with a wide, sandy beach and many tall palm trees, is perhaps the last pleasant beach resort on the Riviera di Ponente to resist the encroachment of greater Genoa's industrial influence and the unwelcome effects of the tourist boom.

Giardino Hanbury

★ ❶ *6 km (4 mi) east of Ventimiglia, 165 km (102 mi) southwest of Genoa, 23 km (14 mi) west of San Remo.*

Mortola Inferiore, only 2 km (1 mi) from the French border, is site of the world-famous Giardino Hanbury (Hanbury Garden), one of the largest botanical gardens in Italy. Planned and planted by a wealthy English merchant, Sir Thomas Hanbury, and his botanist brother, Daniel, in 1867, the terraced gardens contain a variety of species from five continents, including many palms and succulents (plants of the cactus group). There are panoramic views of the sea from the gardens, which descend right down to the beach. ⊠ *Giardino Hanbury, Mortola Inferiore,* ☎ *0184/229507.* 🎟 *8,500 lire.* ☉ *Mar.–mid-June, daily 10–6; mid-June–Sept., daily 9–7; Oct.–Mar., Thurs.–Tues. 10–5. Ticket office closes 1 hr before garden.*

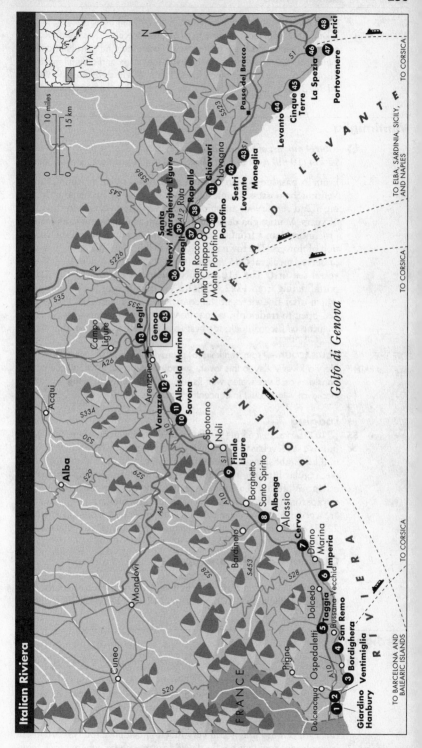

Italian Riviera

OFF THE
BEATEN PATH

BALZI ROSSI – At the French border, 7 km (4½ mi) from Ventimiglia and 2 km (1 mi) from the Giardino Hanbury, are the Balzi Rossi (Red Rocks), caves carved in the sheer rock in which prehistoric humans left traces of their lives and magic rites. You can visit the caves and a small museum displaying some of the objects found there. ⊠ *Via Balzi Rossi 9,* ☎ *0184/38113.* ⊠ *4,000 lire.* ☉ *Tues.–Sun. 9–1 hr before sunset.*

Ventimiglia

❷ *6 km (4 mi) east of Mortola Inferiore, 159 km (98 mi) southwest of Genoa, 17 km (10 mi) west of San Remo, 40 km (25 mi) northeast of Nice.*

From its past life as a pre-Roman settlement known as Albintimilium, Ventimiglia possesses some important archaeological remains, including a 2nd-century AD amphitheater. A vital trade center for hundreds of years, Ventimiglia declined in prestige as Genoa grew, and is now little more than a frontier town that lives on tourism and the cultivation of flowers. The town is divided in two by the Roia River. The well-preserved medieval **Città Vecchia** (Old City) on the western bank is what you'll see first. The 11th-century **Duomo** (Cathedral) has a Gothic portal dating from 1222. Walk up Via del Capo to the **ancient walls,** which offer fine views of the coast. On Friday the large flower market, open to trade only, is chaotic with bargain hunters from France, creating traffic gridlock; it's best to avoid Ventimiglia on that day.

OFF THE
BEATEN PATH

DOLCEACQUA – From Ventimiglia, a provincial road swings up the Nervia River valley to this lovely sounding medieval town, whose name translates as Sweetwater, with its ruined castle. Beyond is **Pigna,** another medieval village built in concentric circles on a hilltop.

Lodging

$$ ⊞ **La Riserva.** Just 5 km (3 mi) west of Ventimiglia, but more than 1,100
★ ft above sea level, is the village of Castel d'Appio, where you'll find this innlike establishment. The staff is very helpful, providing, for example, regular lifts into town for those without cars. Apart from its excellent restaurant, La Riserva offers numerous activities and a lovely terrace for drinks or sunbathing or candlelight dinners. Full-board rates are a good deal. ⊠ *Castel d'Appio, 18039,* ☎ *0184/229533,* ⅨX *0184/ 229712. 25 rooms. Restaurant, bar, pool. AE, DC, MC, V. Closed Sept. 30–Easter (except Dec. 22–Jan. 6).*

Outdoor Activities and Sports
BIKING

The Riviera's hilly terrain is a challenge for cyclists; contact the **Ventimiglia Cycling Club** (⊠ Corso Genoa 112, ☎ 0184/352879) for group rides.

Bordighera

❸ *5 km (3 mi) east of Ventimiglia, 12 km (7 mi) west of San Remo, 115 km (71 mi) southwest of Genoa.*

Bordighera, on a lushly vegetated, large promontory, wears its genteel past as a famous winter resort with unstudied ease. A large English colony, attracted by the mild climate, settled here in the second half of the 19th century and is still very much in evidence today. Bordighera is an elegant town with a fin-de-siècle atmosphere, where you'll regularly find people taking afternoon tea in the cafés. This garden spot was the first town in Europe to grow date palms, and its citizens still have the exclusive right to provide the Vatican with palm fronds for

Easter celebrations. Walk along the **Lungomare Argentina,** the magnificent mile-long seafront promenade beginning at the western end of the town, for a good view westward to the French Côte d'Azur. Thanks partly to its year-round English residents, Bordighera does not close down entirely in the winter like many Riviera resorts. With plenty of fine hotels and restaurants, it makes a good base for excursions and is quieter and less commercial than San Remo.

Dining and Lodging

$$–$$$ ✕ **La Reserve Restaurant.** This traditional and informal trattoria has access to the beach and excellent views of the sea from the dining room. There are even changing rooms for anyone who wants a post-lunch dip. Concentrate on the seafood here: Specialties are seafood ravioli *al finocchio selvatico* (with wild fennel) and assorted grilled seafood. ⊠ *Via Arziglia 20,* ☎ *0184/261322. AE, DC, MC, V. Closed Mon. (except July–Aug.) and Nov.*

$$–$$$ ✕ **Le Chaudron.** The charming rustic interior, with ancient Roman arches, has the look of restaurants across the French border in Provence. Ligurian specialties are featured on the predominantly seafood menu of this centrally located restaurant: Try the cheese pansoti (ravioli) with walnut sauce and *branzino* (sea bass) with artichokes or mushrooms. A café annex serves a daily lunch special. ⊠ *Piazza Bengasi 2,* ☎ *0184/263592. Reservations essential. DC, MC, V. Closed Mon., Feb., and July 1–15.*

$$ ✕ **Piemontese.** Only a block from the seaside and five minutes from the train station, this simple restaurant features the typical cooking of the neighboring Piedmont region, including *risotto al Barolo* (rice cooked with Barolo wine, sausage, and porcini mushrooms) and *bagna cauda* (raw vegetables with a garlic and oil sauce). Ligurian dishes and seafood are also prepared. ⊠ *Via Roseto 8, off Via Vittorio Veneto,* ☎ *0184/ 261651. AE, MC, V. Closed Tues., June 1–15, and Nov. 20–Dec. 20.*

$$$–$$$$ ▥ **Grand Hotel del Mare.** This elegant hotel at the top of a steep hill rising from the beach lives up to its name, with impeccable service and facilities. The large rooms have panoramic views of the coastline; ask for one facing the water. One floor is filled with beautiful antique furnishings. ⊠ *Via Portico della Punta 34, 18012,* ☎ *0184/262201,* Ⓕ *0184/262394. 104 rooms, 3 suites. Restaurant, piano bar, saltwater pool, beauty salon, mineral baths, tennis court, exercise room, beach. AE, DC, MC, V. Closed Nov. 1–Dec. 20.*

$$$ ▥ **Grand Hotel Capo Ampelio.** This hotel occupies a converted villa on a hill overlooking the town and the coastline. Traditional architectural details in the reception rooms and staircases are paired with convenient modern features in the rooms, all with balconies. The hotel is somewhat outside the town center, so the rooms are quiet. ⊠ *Via Virgilio 5, 18012,* ☎ *0184/264333,* Ⓕ *0184/264244. 104 rooms. Restaurant, bar, pool. AE, DC, MC, V. Closed Oct. 10–Dec. 22.*

San Remo

★ ❹ *12 km (7 mi) east of Bordighera, 146 km (90 mi) southwest of Genoa, 60 km (37 mi) east of Nice.*

The self-styled capital of the Riviera di Ponente is San Remo, also the area's largest resort, lined with elegant world-class hotels, exotic gardens, and seaside promenades. Renowned for its royal visitors, its famous casino, and its romantic setting, San Remo still maintains some of the glamour of its heyday from the late 19th century to World War II. Among the rich and famous who flocked to San Remo, drawn by the mild climate and pleasant countryside, were Alfred Nobel, who built a summer house here, and Russian Empress Maria Alexandrovna, wife of Czar Alexander II.

The onion-domed Russian Orthodox church of **San Basilio** stands at one end of the Corso dell'Imperatrice and, like this imposing seafront promenade, is a legacy of the empress. San Remo is famous for the **Mercato dei Fiori,** Italy's most important wholesale flower market, held in a market hall between Piazza Colombo and Corso Garibaldi and open to dealers only. More than 20,000 tons of carnations, roses, mimosa, and innumerable other cut flowers are dispatched from here each year.

In the old part of San Remo, **La Pigna,** or pinecone, explore the warren of alleyways that climb upward to Piazza Castello, with a splendid view of the town. The newer parts of San Remo suffer from the same epidemic of overbuilding that changed so many towns on the western Riviera for the worse. And as the center of northern Italy's flower-growing industry, the resort is surrounded by hills where once-verdant terraces are now blanketed with plastic to form immense greenhouses.

The Art Nouveau **San Remo Casino** is reminiscent of the turn of the century, with a restaurant, nightclub, and theater that hosts such concerts as the San Remo Music Festival. ⊠ *Corso Inglese, San Remo.* ☉ *Daily 2:30 PM–3 AM.*

OFF THE BEATEN PATH **BUSSANA VECCHIA** – About 8 km (5 mi) east of San Remo, in the hills where flowers are cultivated for export, is Bussana Vecchia, a self-consciously picturesque ghost town largely destroyed by an earthquake in 1877. The inhabitants packed up and left en masse after the quake, and for almost a century, the houses, church, and crumbling bell tower were empty shells, overgrown by weeds and wildflowers. Since the 1960s, an artist's colony has evolved among the ruins. Painters, sculptors, artisans, and bric-a-brac dealers have restored dwellings for themselves and sell their wares to visitors.

Dining and Lodging

$ ★ ✕ **Nuovo Piccolo Mondo.** This small, central trattoria has plenty of charm and a homey atmosphere, found in such details at the old wooden chairs dating from the 1920s, when the place opened. Family-run, it has a faithful clientele, so get there early to grab a table and order Ligurian specialties such as spaghetti with artichokes and *polpo e patate* (stewed octopus with potatoes). ⊠ *Via Piave 7,* ☎ *0184/509012. No credit cards. Closed Sun. and 1st 3 wks in July. No dinner Wed.*

$$$$ 🏨 **Royal.** It would take a dedicated hedonist to determine whether this deluxe hotel or the Splendido in Portofino (☞ Dining and Lodging *in* Portofino, *below*) is the most luxurious in Liguria. One major difference is the location: Only a few paces from the casino and the train station, the Royal is definitely part of San Remo, unlike the Splendido, which is set above Portofino. Rooms here have a mixture of modern equipment and antique furnishings. The heated seawater swimming pool, open April–September, is dug into a subtropical garden. On the terrace, candlelight dining and music get underway each night under the stars in season. ⊠ *Corso Imperatrice 80, 18038,* ☎ *0184/5391,* 🖷 *0184/661445. 136 rooms, 6 suites. Restaurant, bar, saltwater pool, miniature golf, 2 tennis courts. AE, DC, MC, V. Closed Oct. 6–Dec. 21.*

$$ 🏨 **Paradiso.** This small central hotel is adjacent to a lush public park near the Royal (☞ *above*). A quiet, palm-fringed garden gives it an air of seclusion, a plus in this sometimes hectic city. Rooms are modern and bright, and many have a little terrace. The hotel restaurant has a good fixed-price menu. ⊠ *Via Roccasterone 12, 18038,* ☎ *0184/571211,* 🖷 *0184/578176. 41 rooms. Restaurant, bar. AE, DC, MC, V.*

Outdoor Activities and Sports

GOLF

The 18-hole **San Remo Golf Club** (✉ Via Campo Golf, ☎ 0184/557093, Closed Tues.) is 5 km (3 mi) north of the town.

Taggia

❺ *10 km (6 mi) northeast of San Remo, 20 km (12 mi) west of Imperia.*

The town of Taggia has a medieval core and one of the most imposing medieval stone bridges in the area. The church of **San Domenico,** on a rise south of Taggia, was part of a monastery founded in the 15th century, and was a beacon of faith and learning in western Liguria for 300 years. An antiques market is held here on the fourth weekend of the month.

Imperia

❻ *23 km (14 mi) east of Taggia, 116 km (71 mi) southwest of Genoa.*

Imperia actually consists of two towns: **Porto Maurizio,** a medieval town built on a promontory, and **Oneglia,** now an industrial center for oil refining and pharmaceuticals. Obviously, Oneglia can be skipped entirely. Porto Maurizio has a virtually intact medieval center, the Parasio quarter, an intricate spiral of narrow streets and stone portals, and some imposing 17th- and 18th-century palaces.

OFF THE BEATEN PATH

MUSEO DELLE OLIVE – The story of the olive—its cultivation and the manufacture of olive oil—is the theme of this small museum in Imperia set up by the Carli olive oil company. Displays of farm implements, types of presses, and utensils demonstrate how olive oil has been made in many countries throughout history. ✉ *Museo dell'Ulivo, Via Garessio 11, Imperia,* ☎ *0183/720000.* 💲 *Free.* 🕐 *Mon. and Wed.–Sat. 9–noon and 3–6.*

Dining

$ ★ ✕ **Candidollo.** This charming and good-value restaurant is worth a detour to the village of Diano Borello, on the valley road a couple of miles north of Diano Marina, 6 km (4 mi) east of Imperia. In his rustic country inn, with checked tablecloths and worn terra-cotta floors, host Bruno Ardissone depends upon locally grown ingredients and seasonal traditional recipes. The menu usually includes *coniglio al timo* (rabbit with thyme and other herbs) and *lumache all'agliata* (grilled snails in piquant sauce). ✉ *Diano Borello,* ☎ *0183/43025. No credit cards. Closed Tues. and Nov.–Mar. No lunch Mon.*

Cervo

❼ *10 km (6 mi) northeast of Imperia, 106 km (65 mi) southwest of Genoa, 35 km (22 mi) east of San Remo.*

Cervo is the quintessential Ligurian coastal village, nicely polished for the tourists who come to explore its narrow byways and street staircases. It is a remarkably well-preserved medieval town, crowned with a big Baroque church.

Nightlife and the Arts

In July and August the square in front of the church is the setting for **chamber music** concerts.

Albenga

❽ *23 km (14 mi) north of Cervo, 90 km (55 mi) southwest of Genoa, 57 km (35 mi) northeast of San Remo.*

Albenga has a medieval core, with narrow streets laid out by the ancient Romans. A network of alleys is punctuated by centuries-old towers, surrounding the **cathedral** and **baptistery** dating back to the 5th century AD.

OFF THE
BEATEN PATH

BARDINETO – For a look at some of the Riviera's mountain scenery, make an excursion by car to this attractive village in the middle of an area rich in mushrooms, chestnuts, and raspberries, as well as local cheese. A ruined castle stands high above the village. From Borghetto Santo Spirito (between Albenga and Finale Ligure), drive inland 25 km (15 mi).

Finale Ligure

9 *20 km (12 mi) northwest of Albenga, 72 km (44 mi) southwest of Genoa, 52 km (32 mi) northeast of Imperia.*

Finale Ligure is made up of three villages: Finalborgo, Finalmarina, and Finalpia. The latter two have fine sandy beaches and modern resort amenities. The most attractive village is **Finalborgo,** a medieval settlement, planned to a rigid blueprint, with 15th-century walls. The village is crowned by the impressive ruins of the huge **Castel Gavone.** The Baroque church of **San Biagio** houses many works of art. The 14th- to 15th-century Dominican convent of **Santa Caterina** can be visited for the shade of the courtyard or to see the museum of paleontology and natural history, which houses prehistoric remains found in the area. ⊠ *Museo Civico,* ☎ *019/690020.* 🎫 *Free.* ☉ *May–Sept., Tues.–Fri. 10–noon and 3–6, weekends 9–noon; Oct.–Apr., Tues.–Fri. 9–noon and 2:30–4:30.*

The countryside around Finale Ligure is pierced by deep, narrow valleys and caves; the limestone outcroppings provide the warm pinkish stone found in many buildings in Genoa. Here lurk rare reptiles and exotic flora.

Dining

$$–$$$ ✕ **Ai Torchi.** You could easily become a homemade pesto snob at this restaurant in the center of Finalborgo. ⊠ *Via dell'Annunziata 12,* ☎ *019/690531. AE, DC, MC, V. Closed Tues. (except in Aug.) and Mon. (Oct.–May), and Jan. 7–mid-Feb.*

OFF THE
BEATEN PATH

NOLI – Just 9 km (5½ mi) northeast of Finale Ligure, picturesque ruins of a castle loom benevolently over the tiny medieval gem Noli. It is hard to imagine this charming village was—like Genoa, Venice, Pisa, and Amalfi—a prosperous maritime republic in the Middle Ages. If you don't have a car, you can get a bus for Noli at Spotorno, where local trains stop.

Savona

10 *11½ km (7 mi) east of Spotorno, 48 km (29 mi) southwest of Genoa.*

Savona is the fifth-largest seaport in Italy and handles vast oil and coal cargoes, as well as car and truck ferries. Much of the town is modern and not very interesting, although a small, austere older quarter near the harbor contains some fine homes of the town's merchant class. The large **Palazzo della Rovere** (⊠ Via Pia) was designed for Pope Julius II by the Florentine Giuliano da Sangallo in 1495. Other medieval monuments include the 14th-century **Palazzo degli Anziani,** and three 12th-century towers. Every other year (next in 2000) on Good Friday, antique wooden carvings depicting the Passion of Christ are carried in procession.

Shopping

Watch for shops selling crystallized fruit, a local specialty. In Millesimo, a town 4 km (2½ mi) west and 36 km (18 mi) inland of Savona, little rum chocolates known as *millesimi* are produced. Look for bargains, too, in wrought-iron work, relief work on copper plate, and pieces in local sandstone.

Albisola Marina

⑪ *4½ km (3 mi) northwest of Savona, 43 km (26 mi) east of Genoa.*

Albisola Marina has preserved its centuries-old tradition of ceramic making. Numerous shops here sell these distinctive wares, and even a whole sidewalk, **Lungomare degli Artisti,** has been transformed by the colorful ceramic works of well-known artists. It runs along the beachfront. The 18th-century **Villa Faraggiana** has interesting antique ceramics and exhibits on the history of the craft. ⊠ *Near the parish church on Via dell'Oratorio.* ☜ *Free.* ⊙ *Apr.–Sept., Wed.–Mon. 3–7.*

Shopping

Ceramiche San Giorgio (⊠ Corso Matteotti 5, ☎ 019/482747) has been producing ceramics since the 17th century and is known for both classic and modern designs. **Mazzotti** (⊠ Corso Matteotti 25, ☎ 019/481626) has an exclusive selection and a small in-house museum. In Albisola Superiore, **Ernan** (⊠ Corso Mazzini 77, ☎ 019/489916) features the classic blue-and-white Old Savona patterns typical of the 18th century.

Varazze

⑫ *7 km (4½ mi) northeast of Albisola, 36 km (22 mi) west of Genoa.*

Varazze, known for its fine sandy beach, is a good place to stop for some sea and sun. The town also has well-preserved ancient ramparts, with a 10th-century church facade built into one of the rampart walls.

Pegli

⑬ *23 km (14 mi) northwest of Varazze, 13 km (8 mi) west of Genoa.*

Once a popular summer home for many patrician Genovese families, Pegli has museums, parks, and some elegant old villas with well-tended gardens. This residential suburb manages to maintain its dignity despite encroaching industry and the proximity of airport and port facilities. Two lovely villas make it worth an excursion. Pegli can be reached conveniently by commuter train from Stazione Porta Principe in Genoa.

☺ **Villa Doria,** near the Pegli train station, has a large park. The villa itself, built in the 16th century by the Doria family, has been converted into a naval museum. ⊠ *Villa Doria, Piazza Bonavino 7, Pegli,* ☎ *010/6969885.* ☜ *Villa: 6,000 lire.* ⊙ *Tues.–Thurs. 9–1, Fri.–Sat. 9–7, 1st and 3rd Sun. of month 9–1.* ☜ *Park: Free.* ⊙ *Daily 10–noon and 2–6.*

Villa Durazzo Pallavicini is set in 19th-century gardens with temples and artificial lakes. The villa has an archaeological museum. ⊠ *Via Pallavicini 11, Pegli,* ☎ *010/6981048.* ☜ *7,000 lire.* ⊙ *Apr.–Sept., Tues.–Thurs. 9–7, Fri.–Sat. 9–1, 2nd and 4th Sun. of month 9–1; Oct.–Mar., Tues.–Thurs. 9–5, Fri.–Sat. 9–1, 2nd and 4th Sun. of month 9–1.*

GENOA

501 km (310 mi) northwest of Rome, 236 km (146 mi) northwest of Florence, 142 km (88 mi) south of Milan, 170 km (105 mi) southeast of Turin, and 194 km (120 mi) northeast of Nice.

Ligurian beach bums beware: Genoa (Genova in Italian) is a busy, sprawling, and cosmopolitan city, apt to break the spell of the coastal towns in a hurry. This isn't necessarily bad news, though; with 700 years of history under its belt, magnificent palaces and art, an intact medieval center, and all the modern conveniences, Genoa may be just the dose of culture you were looking for. This is the birthplace of Columbus—a historical tidbit of which you'll be reminded at every turn, due to the citywide sprucing-up that took place in 1992 for the Columbus Quincentennial celebrations—but the city's proud history of trade and navigation predates Columbus by several hundred years.

Known as *La Superba* (The Proud), Genoa was from the 13th century a great maritime center rivaling Venice and Pisa in power and splendor. Modern container ships unload at docks that centuries before served galleons and vessels bound for the spice routes. By the 3rd century BC, when the Romans conquered Liguria, Genoa was already an important trading station. The Middle Ages and the Renaissance saw the rise of Genoa as a great seaport and city. As a jumping-off place for the Crusaders, a commercial center of tremendous wealth and prestige, and a strategic bone of international contention, it was of key importance to Europe. Its bankers, merchants, and princes adorned the city with palaces and churches and amassed impressive art collections. By the 18th century, however, Genoa had declined as a sea power. Although it brims with historical curiosities and buildings (its lively medieval center is Europe's largest), it is also a thoroughly modern city struggling with problems of traffic, noise, and air pollution as well as a growing immigrant population. Its port is being equipped to keep up with new technologies; the city is also advanced in communications, electronics, and general commerce.

Europe's biggest boat show, the annual Salone Nautico Internazionale, takes place here, as does the Euroflora flower show (held every five years—next in 2001). Classical dance and music are richly represented; the Teatro Carlo Felice is the local opera venue (☞ Nightlife and the Arts, *below*). The internationally renowned annual Niccolò Paganini Violin Contest also takes place in Genoa.

The historic harbor area was given a face-lift for the Columbus celebrations in 1992, and some of the fair installations, such as the Bigo elevator ride with harbor view, have become a permanent part of the city scene. The Acquario di Genova (Aquarium), the largest in Europe and second largest in the world, is one of Genoa's more recent attractions.

Medieval and Renaissance Genoa

A Good Walk

The best way to start your exploration of Genoa is to see it from above. From Piazza Principe, behind Stazione Principe, take the **Granarolo funicular** ⑭ and return to the piazza to start your walk along Via Balbi, which runs southeast from Stazione Principe toward the medieval town. On Via Balbi you pass Palazzo Balbi Durazzo, also known as **Palazzo Reale** ⑮, and **Palazzo dell'Università** ⑯. Continue straight ahead, crossing Piazza della Nunziata past **Santissima Annunziata** ⑰ to Via P. Bensa and continue southeast on Via Cairoli to reach Via Garibaldi, where you can pause to see the collections in the museums of **Palazzo Rosso** ⑱ and **Palazzo Bianco** ⑲. Stop in at **Palazzo Tursi** ⑳, Genoa's town hall, and ask the guard at the door if it happens to be open to visitors that day; if it is you can see one of Paganini's violins. At the end of Via Garibaldi go left and left again to Piazza del Portello, where you can take the **Castelletto** ㉑ elevator for another view of the city. Returning to Piazza Fontane Marose at the end of Via Garibaldi, turn southwest, taking Via Luccoli into the medieval Caruggi District. Beyond Piazza Soziglia, detour to the left, taking Via Campetto to Piazza San Matteo, flanked by the well-preserved houses of the Dorias and the church of **San Matteo** ㉒. Follow Salita Arcivescovado and turn right on Via Reggio to the cathedral of **San Lorenzo** ㉓, medieval Genoa's religious heart. North of the cathedral is Vico degli Indoratori, onto which you turn northwest. Follow it to Via degli Orefici, on which you turn left to reach the **Loggia dei Mercanti** ㉔. Head north on Via San Luca to the **Galleria Nazionale** ㉕. At the northern end of Via San Luca is the church of **San Siro** ㉖.

TIMING

Allow a full day for this walk. Note that the Galleria Nazionale is open until 7 every day except Monday, when it closes at 1 PM.

Sights to See

Caruggi District. The winding, picturesque alleys—known as *caruggi*—that make up the popular side of medieval Genoa are the city's heart and soul. Wealthy Genovese built their homes in this quarter in the 16th century, and prosperous guilds, such as the goldsmiths for whom Vico dei Indoratori and Via Orefici were named, set up shop here. In this warren of narrow, cobbled streets, extending north from Piazza Caricamento, you'll find the city's oldest churches punctuating unbroken blocks of 500-year-old apartment buildings, and tiny shops selling antique furniture, coffee, rifles, cheese, wine, gilt picture frames, camping gear, even live fish. When exploring, however, do bear in mind that this quarter is also the city's most disreputable. Don't come here at night, or on holidays, when shops are closed and the alleys deserted, unless you're willing to part with your valuables.

㉑ **Castelletto.** One of Genoa's handy municipal elevators whisks you skyward from Piazza Portello, at the end of Via Garibaldi, for a good view of the old city. 🎫 *600 lire 1-way.* ☉ *Continuous service 6:40 AM–midnight.*

OFF THE
BEATEN PATH

MUSEO D'ARTE ORIENTALE CHIOSSONE – In the Villetta di Negro park on the hillside above Piazza Portello, the Chiossone Oriental Art Museum has one of Europe's most extensive and noteworthy collections of Japanese, Chinese, and Thai objects. You can get a fine view of the city from the museum's terrace. ✉ *Piazzale Mazzini (Piazza Corvetto),* ☎ *010/542285.* 🎫 *6,000 lire.* ☉ *Tues. and Thurs.–Sat. 9–1; 1st and 3rd Sun. of month, 9–1.*

㉕ **Galleria Nazionale** (National Gallery). This collection, housed in the richly adorned **Palazzo Spinola** north of Piazza Soziglia, contains masterpieces by Luca Giordano and Guido Reni. The *Ecce Homo,* by Antonello da Messina, is a hauntingly beautiful painting and is also of historical interest because it was the Sicilian da Messina who first brought Flemish oil paints and techniques to Italy from his voyages in the Low Countries. ✉ *Piazza Pellicceria 1,* ☎ *010/2477061.* 🎫 *8,000 lire.* ☉ *Mon. 9–1, Tues.–Sat. 9–7, Sun. 2–10.*

⑭ **Granarolo funicular.** Actually a cog railway, this tram takes you up the steeply rising terrain from the downtown area to one of the fortified gates in the 17th-century city walls. Dotted around the circumference

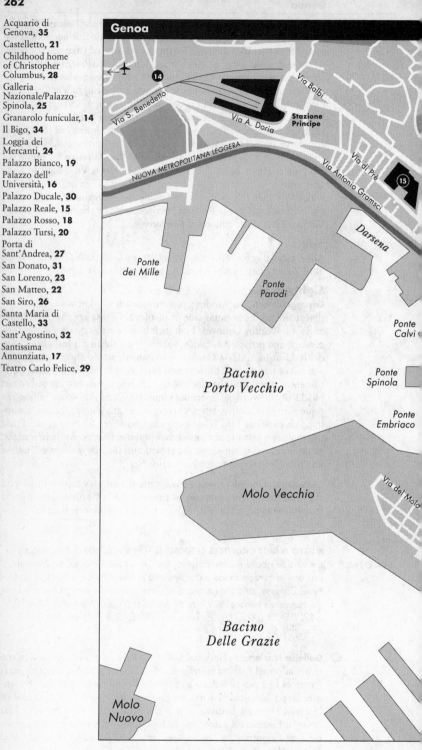

Genoa

Via Balbi

Via S. Benedetto

Via A. Doria

Stazione Principe

Via di Pre

Via Antonio Gramsci

NUOVA METROPOLITANA LEGGERA

Darsena

Ponte dei Mille

Ponte Parodi

Ponte Calvi

Ponte Spinola

Bacino Porto Vecchio

Ponte Embriaco

Molo Vecchio

Via del Molo

Bacino Delle Grazie

Molo Nuovo

Corso Dogali

Piazza E. Brignole

Corso Firenze

Corso Firenze

Corso Carbonara

Corso Firenze

Corso Paganini

Corso Paganini

V. Brig. de Ferrari

Parco Villa Gruber

0   300 Meters

0   300 yards

N

16

Via Balbi

17

Piazza d. Nunziata

V. delle Fontane

Via P. Bensa

Via del Campo

Lomellini

Via Cairoli

Gal. Garibaldi

Via Caffaro

Salita S. Maria di Sanità

Via G. Mameli

Via Palestro

21

Piazza del Portello

Battistine

Piazzale Mazzini

Via M. Piaggio

26

19

20

Via Garibaldi

18

Via de la Maddalena

Piazza Fontane Marose

25

Via S. Luca

35

Piazza Caricamento

24

Via degli Orefici

Via Luccoli

Piazza Corvetto

Piazza Soziglia

Vico degli Indoratori

Via Chiossone

Via David

Via Luccoli

Via Roma

Via Ceba

CARUGGI

Via Campetto

Piazza San Matteo

Via 25 Aprile

22

34

Via F. Turati

Via S. Lorenzo

23

29

30

Via XII Ottobre

Via di Cannelo 'l Curto

Via dei Giustiniani

Piazza G. Matteotti

Piazza De Ferrari

E. Vernazza

Stazione Brignole →

Via S. Bernardo

Salita Pollaiuoli

V. Pta. Soprana

Via Dante

Via XX Settembre

Piazza Embriaci

31

V. S. Donato

28

Piazza Dante

Via Fieschi

33

Via di Santa Croce

Stradone di S. Agostino

Via S.M. di Castello

Piazza Negri

32

27

Porta di Sant' Andrea

Gall. C. Colombo

Corso M. Quadrio

NUOVA METROPOLITANA LEGGERA

Piazza Sarzano

Via Ravasco

Via Fieschi

S. Leonardo Mura S. Chiara

Via Corsica

Piazza Carignano

Via Alessi

Viale IV Novembre

of the city are a number of huge fortresses, and this gate was part of the city's system of defenses. It takes 15 minutes to hoist you from Piazza del Principe, behind Stazione Principe on Piazza Acquaverde, to **Porta Granarolo**, 1,000 ft above, where the sweeping view gives you a sense of Genoa's size. ✉ *1,500 lire; bus tickets valid.* ⊙ *Departs on the ¼ hr, 6 AM–11:45 PM.*

㉔ Loggia dei Mercanti This merchants' row dating from the 16th century is lined with shops selling local foods and gifts as well as raincoats, rubber boots, and fishing line. ✉ *Piazza Banchi.*

⑲ Palazzo Bianco. Originally white, as its name suggests, this palace has become considerably darkened from age and grime. It has a fine art collection, with the Spanish and Flemish schools well represented. ✉ *Via Garibaldi 11,* ☎ *010/2476377.* ✉ *6,000 lire, or 10,000 lire in combination with Palazzo Rosso (☞ below).* ⊙ *Tues., Thurs.–Fri. 9–1, Wed. and Sat. 9–7, Sun. 10–6.*

⑯ Palazzo dell'Università. Built in the 1630s as a Jesuit college, this institution has been Genoa's university since 1803. Climb the stairway flanked by lions to visit the elegant courtyard, with its portico of double Doric columns. ✉ *Via Balbi 5.*

★ ⑮ Palazzo Reale. In a city where conspicuous consumption was a hobby of high society, this sumptuous 17th-century palace—also known as Palazzo Balbi Durazzo—contains lavish, frivolous Rococo rooms displaying paintings, sculptures, tapestries, and Oriental ceramics. The former royal digs were inhabited by Italy's rulers, then bought by the Royal House of Savoy in the early 19th century. The gallery of mirrors and the ballroom on the upper floor are particularly decadent. You'll also find works by Sir Anthony Van Dyck, who lived in Genoa for six years, from 1621, and painted many fine portraits of the Genovese nobility. ✉ *Via Balbi 10,* ☎ *010/27101.* ✉ *8,000 lire.* ⊙ *Sun.–Tues. 9–1:45, Wed.–Sat. 9–7.*

⑱ Palazzo Rosso (Red Palace). The 17th-century Baroque palace was named for the red stone used in its construction. It now contains, apart from a number of lavishly frescoed suites, works by Titian, Veronese, Reni, and Van Dyck. ✉ *Via Garibaldi 18,* ☎ *010/282641.* ✉ *6,000 lire, or 10,000 lire in combination with Palazzo Bianco (☞ above).* ⊙ *Tues., Thurs.–Fri. 9–1, Wed. and Sat. 9–7, Sun. 10–6.*

⑳ Palazzo Tursi. Wealthy Nicolò Grimaldi had this palace built in the 16th century of pink stone quarried in the region. It's been reincarnated as Genoa's Palazzo Municipale (Municipal Building), and so most of the goings-on inside are the stuff of local politics and quickie weddings. When the rooms aren't in use by Genovese officialdom, however, you are welcome to view the richly decorated rooms and the famous Guarnerius violin that belonged to Niccolò Paganini (1782–1840) and is played once a year on Columbus Day (October 12). ✉ *Via Garibaldi 9,* ☎ *010/20982223.* ✉ *Free.* ⊙ *Weekdays; call for hrs.*

㉓ San Lorenzo. This cathedral, at the heart of medieval Genoa's political and religious center, is embellished inside and out with the contrasting black slate and white marble so common in Liguria. It was consecrated in 1118 to St. Lawrence, who passed through the city on his way to Rome in the 3rd century; the last campanile dates from the early 16th century. For hundreds of years the building was used for state and religious purposes such as civic elections, court rulings, and religious ceremonies and festivals. Note the lively 13th-century Gothic portal and the 15th- to 17th-century frescoes inside. The **Museo del Tesoro di San Lorenzo** (San Lorenzo Treasury Museum) has some stunning pieces from medieval goldsmiths and silversmiths, for which medieval Genoa was renowned. ⊠ *Piazza San Lorenzo,* ☏ *010/311269. Museum:* 🖃 *8,000 lire.* ⊗ *Mon.–Sat. 9–noon and 3–6; guided visits every ½ hr (last visits at 11:30 and 5:30).*

㉒ San Matteo. This typically Genovese, black-and-white-striped church dates from the 12th century; its crypt contains the tomb of Andrea Doria (1466–1560), the Genovese admiral and statesman who maintained the independence of his native city. ⊠ *Piazza San Matteo.*

㉖ San Siro. Genoa's oldest church served as the city's cathedral from the 4th to the 9th centuries. It was rebuilt in the 16th and 17th centuries. ⊠ *Via San Luca.*

⑰ Santissima Annunziata. The 16th- to 17th-century church has exuberantly frescoed vaults and is an excellent example of Genovese Baroque architecture. ⊠ *Piazza della Nunziata.*

★ Via Garibaldi. Thirteen palaces were built along what was once known as the Via Aurea (Golden Street) in just 10 years. Genoa's leading patrician families built their residences here from 1554 onward to escape the cramped conditions of the medieval section. It is one of the most impressive streets in Italy, and the palace-museums house some of the finest art collections in the country. Most of the other palaces without museums on Via Garibaldi can be visited only by special application, but many have courtyards that are open to the public. ⊠ *West from Piazza Fontane Marose.*

The Southern Districts and the Aquarium

A Good Walk

Start at **Porta di Sant'Andrea** ㉗ and pay homage to the purported **childhood home of Christopher Columbus** ㉘ on the square. Then follow Via Dante into Piazza de Ferrari to **Teatro Carlo Felice** ㉙. On the west side of the piazza stands the **Palazzo Ducale** ㉚, with its imposing neoclassic facade on Piazza Matteotti. Leading uphill from Piazza Matteotti, Salita Pollaiuoli takes you to **San Donato** ㉛. On the west side of the church is Stradone Sant'Agostino, which leads to Piazza Negri and **Sant'Agostino** ㉜. At the top of Stradone Sant'Agostino, from the west end of elongated Piazza Sarzano, take Via Santa Croce and turn right and then left onto Via Santa Maria di Castello, climbing up to the church of **Santa Maria di Castello** ㉝ atop the hill. From Piazza Embriaci turn west and follow the little streets downhill to Via Canneto il Curto, turning downhill on Via San Lorenzo to reach Piazza Caricamento and the old Port, where you can take a ride in the panoramic **Il Bigo** ㉞ elevator and visit the **Acquario di Genova** ㉟.

TIMING

This walk will take from two to three hours, with stops at churches and the museum at Sant'Agostino; add an hour or two if you are stopping at the Acquario di Genova.

Sights to See

㊳ ㉟ Acquario di Genova. Europe's biggest aquarium, second in the world only to the Osaka aquarium in Japan, is the third-most-visited museum in Italy and a must for children. Fifty tanks of marine species, including sea turtles, dolphins, seals, eels, penguins, and sharks, share space with educational displays and re-creations of marine ecosystems, including a new tank for live corals from the Red Sea. An annexed ecosimulation of Madagascar was a recent exhibit. ⊠ *Ponte Spinola,* ☏ *010/2481205.* 🖃 *14,000 lire.* ⊗ *Tues.–Fri. 9:30–6:30 (April–mid-Sept. also open Mon., same hrs), weekends 9:30–8; ticket office closes 1 hr before museum.*

28 **Childhood home of Christopher Columbus.** The ivy-covered ruins of this fabled medieval house stand in the gardens adjacent to the Porta di Sant'Andrea. ⊠ *Piazza Dante.*

Harbor. A boat tour gives you a good perspective on the layout of the harbor, which dates to Roman times. The Genoa inlet, the largest along the Italian Riviera, was also used by the Phoenicians and Greeks as a harbor and a vantage point from which they could penetrate inland to form settlements and to trade. The **Lanterna,** a lighthouse more than 360 ft high, was built in 1544 at the height of Andrea Doria's career; it is one of Italy's oldest lighthouses and a traditional emblem of Genoa.

34 **Il Bigo.** The view from the Ascensore Panoramico Bigo elevator at the top of this mast, erected as a symbol of the 1992 Columbus Quincentennial events, takes in the harbor, city, and sea. ⊠ *Ponte Spinola, next to Acquario.* 🎫 *5,000 lire, 4,000 lire with Acquario ticket.* 🕙 *Mar.– Aug., Tues.–Sat. 11–1 and 3–6, Sun. 11–1 and 2:30–6:30; Sept.–Feb., Tues.–Fri. 11–1 and 2:30–4, Sun. 11–1 and 2:30–5.*

30 **Palazzo Ducale.** This palace was built in the 16th century over a medieval hall, and its facade was rebuilt in the late 18th century and later restored. It now houses temporary exhibitions. ⊠ *Piazza Matteotti and Piazza de Ferrari.*

Piazza San Matteo. The excellently preserved medieval square was, for 500 years, the seat of the Doria family, who ruled Genoa and much of Liguria from the 16th to the 18th century. The square is bounded by 13th- to 15th-century houses decorated with portals and loggias. ⊠ *South of Piazza Soziglia.*

27 **Porta di Sant'Andrea.** The twin-towered, 12th-century edifice also known as Porta Soprana stands at the old gateway to the Roman road that led through Genoa. ⊠ *Piazza Dante.*

31 **San Donato.** The 12th-century Romanesque church with its original portal and octagonal campanile is slightly north of Sant'Agostino. ⊠ *Piazza San Donato.*

32 **Sant'Agostino.** This 13th-century Gothic church was damaged during World War II, but it still has a fine campanile and two well-preserved cloisters, which now house an excellent sculpture museum. ⊠ *Piazza Sarzano 35/r,* ☎ *010/265949.* 🎫 *6,000 lire, Sun. free.* 🕙 *Tues.–Sat. 9–7, Sun. 9–12:30.*

33 **Santa Maria di Castello.** One of Genoa's greatest religious buildings, an early Christian church, was rebuilt in the 12th century and finally completed in 1513. You can visit the adjacent cloisters and see the fine artwork contained in the museum. Call ahead to book a visit. ⊠ *Salita di Santa Maria di Castello 15,* ☎ *010/2549511.* 🎫 *Free.* 🕙 *Mon.– Sat. 9–noon and 3:30–6, Sun. 3:30–6; call ahead.*

29 **Teatro Carlo Felice.** The World War II–ravaged opera house in Genoa's modern center, **Piazza de Ferrari,** was rebuilt and reopened in 1991; its massive tower has been the subject of much criticism. It stands next to the **Accademia delle Belle Arti** (Academy of Fine Arts) which contains a collection of Ligurian paintings from the 13th to the 19th centuries. *Theater:* ⊠ *Passo al Teatro 4,* ☎ *010/53811. Academy:*⊠ *Largo Pertini 4,* ☎ *010/581957.* 🎫 *Free.* 🕙 *Mon.–Sat. 9–1.*

Dining and Lodging

$$$–$$$$ ✕ **Gran Gotto.** Innovative classic regional dishes are served in this elegant, spacious restaurant festooned with contemporary paintings.

The service is quick and helpful. Try *filetti di triglia* (red mullet fillets with rosemary, celery, and balsamic vinegar) and the sumptuous *flan di cioccolato* (dark chocolate flan with white chocolate sauce), one of the many excellent homemade desserts. It's near Stazione Brignole in the modern part of town. ⊠ *Viale Brigata Bisagno 69/r,* ☎ *010/ 564344. Jacket and tie. AE, DC, MC, V. Closed Sun. and Aug. 10– 31. No lunch Sat.*

$$$–$$$$ ✕ **Zeffirino.** The five Belloni brothers share the chef's duties at this re-
★ markable restaurant, which is full of odd combinations. The decor is a mixture of styles and materials, ranging from rustic wood to modern metallic. Try the *passutelli* (ravioli stuffed with ricotta cheese and fruit) or any of the homemade pasta dishes. ⊠ *Via XX Settembre 20,* ☎ *010/591990. Jacket and tie. AE, DC, MC, V. Closed Wed.*

$$–$$$ ✕ **Sette Nasi.** The historic Quarto dei Mille district is the setting for this large establishment, with accents of gray slate and pink marble. The chef, Fausto Nasi, specializes in a wide range of Ligurian seafood dishes and makes some mean homemade desserts. Top off a lovely day spent at the annexed pool and beach club with a dinner of ravioli *di pesce* (seafood) or lasagna with pesto. ⊠ *Via Quarto 16,* ☎ *010/ 3731344. AE, DC, MC, V. Closed Tues. and Nov.*

$$ ✕ **Da Genio.** At the top of a pedestrian stairway near Piazza Dante in old Genoa, this classic trattoria serves equally classic Genovese dishes, including *trenette al pesto* (pasta with pesto sauce) and minestrone, also laced with a dollop of pesto. ⊠ *Salita San Leonardo 61/r,* ☎ *010/588463. AE, MC, V. Closed Sun. and Aug.*

$ ✕ **Trattoria Walter.** This casual family-run restaurant is in the city heart, with nice touches of vaulted ceilings and classical music. The owners pride themselves on courteous service and Genovese specialties such as *stoccafisso in umido con patate* (dried codfish stew with potatoes). ⊠ *Vico Colalanza 2, corner of Via San Luca,* ☎ *010/ 290524. No credit cards. Closed Sun. and Aug. 13–Sept. 3. No dinner Thurs.*

$$$$ ▥ **Bristol Palace.** This grand hotel, on a fashionable downtown shopping street, was built in the last century and maintains the old-fashioned traditions of courtesy and discretion. The rooms are large, with high ceilings; paintings decorate the large reception rooms. There's no restaurant, but you're in the heart of the downtown area. ⊠ *Via XX Settembre 35, 16121,* ☎ *010/592541,* ℻ *010/561756. 133 rooms. Bar, café, snack bar, meeting rooms. AE, DC, MC, V.*

$$$ ▥ **Novotel.** Built in 1994, this hotel is a good choice for tourists who value modern comfort over atmosphere. It is in a semicentral area just beyond one end of the harbor; you can take a bus or taxi to the heart of town. ⊠ *Via Cantore 8/c, 16126,* ☎ *010/64841,* ℻ *010/6484844. 223 rooms. Restaurant, bar, pool, free parking. AE, DC, MC, V.*

$$ ▥ **Agnello d'Oro.** In Genoa's old quarter, about 100 yards from
★ Stazione Principe and next to the Palazzo Reale, this hotel has simple and modern rooms, and several have a balcony with a view. The friendly owner does double duty as a travel agent and is happy to help guests with plane reservations and travel plans. ⊠ *Vico delle Monachette 6, 16126,* ☎ *010/2462084,* ℻ *010/2462327. 30 rooms. Bar. AE, DC, MC, V.*

$$ ▥ **Cairoli.** This family-run, central hotel is on a historic street near Stazione Principe and the Aquarium. It is neatly furnished and has a roof terrace. Happily, the rooms have been soundproofed so you'll get a good night's sleep—not always the easiest thing to do in this noisy city. ⊠ *Via Cairoli 14, 16124,* ☎ *010/206531,* ℻ *010/280041. 14 rooms, 12 with bath. Free parking. AE, DC, MC, V.*

Nightlife and the Arts

Opera

The opera season (October–May) at **Teatro Carlo Felice** (⊠ Passo al Teatro 4, ☎ 010/53811, 010/591697 box office) attracts many lavish productions and occasionally sees the debut of a new work.

Shopping

Liguria is famous for its fine laces, its silver and gold filigree work, and its ceramics. Look also for bargains in velvet, macramé, olive wood, and marble. Genoa is the best spot to find all these specialties. In the heart of the medieval quarter, **Via Soziglia** is lined with shops selling handicrafts and tempting foods. **Via XX Settembre** is famous for its wide range of small, exclusive shops. Fine shops also line **Via Luccoli.**

Chocolates

Judge for yourself whether the handmade chocolates at **Pietro Romanengo fu Stefano** (⊠ Via Soziglia 74, ☎ 010/297869) are the best in Genoa (the management says they are).

Jewelry, Perfumes, and Clothing

The well-established **Codevilla** (⊠ Via Orefici 53, ☎ 010/206567) is one of the best jewelers on a street devoted to goldsmiths. At the elegant **Pescetto** (⊠ Via Scurreria 8, ☎ 010/206633), you'll find designer clothes, perfumes, and gift ideas.

Wines

Vinoteca Sola (⊠ Piazza Colombo 13, near Stazione Brignole, ☎ 010/561329) stocks a good selection of Italian and Ligurian wines.

Side Trip from Genoa

Nervi

36 *11 km (7 mi) east of Genoa, 23 km (14 mi) northwest of Chiavari.*

The true identity of this elegant turn-of-the-century resort, famous for its mile-long Anita Garibaldi seaside promenade, palm-lined roads, and 300 acres of parks rich in orange trees and exotics, is given away only by the sign on the sleepy train station in the center of town: It's technically part of the city of Genoa. Nervi's secret is an easy one to keep, though: Its attractions are peace and quiet, the natural beauty of its lush gardens, and the dramatic black cliffs that drop into the sea, as different from Genoa's hustle and bustle as Nervi's clear blue water is from Genoa's crowded port. Despite the contrast, it's easy to visit this remarkable part of the city for a stroll along the water or a day at the beach. Frequent trains take 15 minutes from Stazione Principe (buy a ticket for Genova–Nervi). Alternatively, a taxi from town center will run about 25,000 lire one-way. From the Nervi train station, walk along the seaside promenade east to reach beach stations, a cliff-hanging restaurant, and the 2,000 varieties of roses in the **Parco Villa Grimaldi,** all the while enjoying one of the most breathtaking views on the Riviera.

DINING AND LODGING

$$ ✕ **Marinella.** This restaurant is perched on seaside shoals a few minutes outside Genoa. Competing for attention are an impressive wrought-iron chandelier and great sea views from windows and terrace. (There's an inexpensive hotel annex, too.) Try *zuppa di pesce* (fish soup); main dishes change according to the fishermen's catch. ⊠ *Passeggiata Anita Garibaldi 18,* ☎ *010/3728343. MC, V. Closed Mon. and Nov.*

$$$ ▥ **Romantik Hotel Villa Pagoda.** This small, top-quality hotel in sea-★   side Nervi is an elegant choice that offers the best of both worlds— luxurious peace and quiet, with the city's attractions just 15 minutes

away. Housed in a gated 19th-century merchant's mansion designed after a Chinese pagoda, the hotel boasts a private park, private access to Nervi's famed cliff-top seawalk, and magnificent sea views. Request a tower room if one's available. ✉ *Via Capolungo 15, 16167* , ☎ *010/3726161,* FAX *010/321218. 14 rooms, 4 suites. Restaurant, piano bar, in-room safes, minibars, meeting rooms. AE, DC, MC, V.*

NIGHTLIFE AND THE ARTS

An **International Ballet Festival** is held every July in the Villa Gropallo park, drawing performers and audiences from all over the world. Contact the Genoa APT office (☎ 010/2467658) for ticket and schedule information.

RIVIERA DI LEVANTE
On the Road to Portofino

Of the two Ligurian Rivieras, the Riviera di Levante east of Genoa, is overall the wilder and more rugged, yet here you will also find towns like Portofino and Rapallo, world-famous for their classic, elegant style. Around every turn of this area's twisting roads, the hills plummet sharply to the sea, forming deep, hidden bays and inlets. Beaches on this coast are rocky, backed by spectacular sheer cliffs. The Portofino promontory has one sandy beach, on the east side, at Paraggi. From Chiavari to Cavi di Lavagna, the coast becomes a bit gentler, with a few sandy areas.

Sailing conditions along the rugged coast from Sestri Levante down to Portovenere are good. Waterskiing, tennis, and golf are also popular. You may want to choose a base and take short day trips or explore the area by boat from the larger towns. You can anchor your boat in the relatively calm waters of small *ciazze* (coves) found all along the coast.

Camogli

★ ㊲ *20 km (12 mi) southwest of Genoa, 23 km (14 mi) northwest of Chiavari.*

Camogli, at the edge of the large promontory and nature reserve known as the Portofino peninsula, has always been a town of sailors. By the 19th century this small village was leasing its ships throughout the Continent. Today multicolor houses and the massive 17th-century seawall mark this harbor community. The **Castello Dragone,** built onto the sheer rock face near the harbor, is home to the **Acquario** (Aquarium), which has display tanks of local marine life actually built into the ramparts. ✎ *4,000 lire.* ☉ *May–Sept., daily 10–noon and 3–7; Oct.–Apr., Fri.–Sun. 10–noon and 2:30–6, Tues.–Thurs. 10–noon.*

OFF THE
BEATEN PATH

SAN ROCCO, SAN NICCOLÒ, AND PUNTA CHIAPPA – By foot or boat from Camogli, you can reach these hamlets along the western coast of the peninsula; they are more natural and less fashionable than those facing south on the eastern coast. In the small Romanesque church at San Nicolò, sailors who survived dangerous voyages came to offer thanks.

ABBAZIA DI SAN FRUTTUOSO – On the sea at the foot of Monte Portofino, 30 minutes by boat from Camogli (20 minutes by boat from Portofino) the medieval Abbey of San Fruttuoso—built by the Benedictines of Monte Cassino—protects a minuscule fishing village and can be reached only on foot or by boat from Camogli, Portofino, Santa Margherita Ligure, or Rapallo. The restored abbey is now property of a national conservation fund (FAI). The church holds the tombs of some illustrious members of the Doria family. The historic abbey and its grounds are a delightful place to spend a few hours, perhaps lunching at one of the modest beach trattorias nearby. But boatloads of visitors can make it very crowded very fast; you'll appreciate it most off-season. ☎ 0185/ 772703. ☎ 5,000 lire. ⊘ Mar.–Apr., Tues.–Sun. 10–1 and 2–4; May– Oct., Tues.–Sun. 10–1 and 2–6; Nov.–Jan., weekends 10–1 and 2–4.

Dining and Lodging

$$$　✕ **Vento Ariel.** This tiny, friendly restaurant is right on the port, and it has informal but elegant decor and place settings. It serves seafood only and regularly runs out of items because it relies on the day's catch. Try the spaghetti *alle vongole* (with clams) or the grilled mixed fish. ⊠ Calata Porto, ☎ 0185/771080. AE, DC, MC, V. Closed Wed. and Jan.

$$$–$$$$　🏨 **Cenobio dei Dogi.** Although this hilltop villa perched over the town
★　was once the summer home of Genoa's doges, it now has a modern look. Guests can relax in the well-kept park affording outstanding views of the Portofino peninsula, or they can enjoy numerous sporting activities. ⊠ Via Cuneo 34, 16032, ☎ 0185/7241, 🖷 0185/772796. 107 rooms. Restaurant, bar, pool, tennis courts, beach. AE, MC, V.

Nightlife and the Arts

During the festival of San Fortunato, held on the second Sunday of May each year, is the **Sagra del Pesce,** a crowded, festive, and free-to-the-public—yes, that includes you—feast of freshly caught fish, cooked outside at the port in a frying pan 12 ft wide.

Ruta

4 km (2½ mi) east of Camogli.

The footpaths that leave from Ruta up to and around Monte Portofino thread through rugged terrain, home to a wide variety of plant species. Weary hikers will be sustained by stunning views of the Riviera di Levante from the various vantage points along the way.

Rapallo

③⑧　*10 km (6 mi) east of Camogli, 37 km (23 mi) west of Genoa, 79 km (49 mi) east of La Spezia.*

Rapallo was once one of Europe's most fashionable resorts, but it passed its heyday before World War II and has suffered from the building boom brought on by tourism. Ezra Pound and D. H. Lawrence lived here, and many other writers, poets, and artists have been drawn to it. Today, the town's harbor is filled with yachts. A single-span bridge on the eastern side of the bay is named after Hannibal, who is said to have passed through the area after crossing the Alps. Two ancient buildings are highlights in town center: the cathedral of **Santi Gervasio** and **Protasio,** at the western end of Via Mazzini, founded in the 6th century. Across the road is the Leper House of **San Lorenzo,** which still retains parts of its original medieval frescoes on its exterior walls.

The **Museo del Pizzo a Tombolo,** in a 19th-century mansion, has a collection of antique lace for which Rapallo was renowned. ⊠ Villa Tigullio. ☎ Free. ⊘ Oct.–Aug., Tues.–Wed., Fri.–Sat. 3–6, Thurs. 10–12:30.

Dining and Lodging

$$　✕ **Da Ardito.** This lively trattoria is in the village of San Pietro di Novella, just north of Rapallo. If you love wine, you'll appreciate the attention given to the wine list. For a change from seafood, try the pan-

soti alla salsa di noci. ⊠ *Via Canale 9, San Pietro di Novella,* ☎ *0185/ 51551. Reservations essential. MC, V. Closed Mon. and Feb.*

$$$$ 🏨 **Grand Hotel Bristol.** This large Victorian showcase is in an elevated position overlooking road and sea outside Rapallo, and is set in lush gardens with a huge seawater pool. Spacious rooms, many with balcony and sea view, are decorated in soft colors in a smart, contemporary style and have extra-large beds. Dinner is served on the roof terrace. ⊠ *Via Aurelia Orientale 369, 16035,* ☎ *0185/273313,* ℻ *0185/ 55800. 90 rooms. Restaurant, bar, pool, 18-hole golf course, tennis court, horseback riding, meeting rooms. AE, MC, V. Closed Jan.–Feb.*

$$ 🏨 **Giulio Cesare.** Only a block from the sea, this old town house was transformed into a hotel that offers rooms with modern furnishings and sea views. Many rooms have balconies, but noise may be a problem, since the hotel is on a main street. ⊠ *Corso Colombo 52, 16035,* ☎ *0185/50685,* ℻ *0185/60896. 33 rooms. AE, MC, V. Closed Nov.– mid-Dec.*

Outdoor Activities and Sports

GOLF

The **Rapallo Golf Club** (☎ 0185/261777) has a lush 18-hole course about 2 km (1 mi) northwest of town center.

HORSEBACK RIDING

The **Rapallo Riding Club** (⊠ Via Santa Maria del Campo 196, ☎ 0185/50462) is near the golf club, about 2 km (1 mi) northwest of town.

Shopping

The attractive coastal village of **Zoagli** (⊠ On S1, 4 km/2½ mi east of Rapallo) has been famous for silk, velvet, and damask since the Middle Ages.

The traditional, light—they weigh only 3 pounds—*campanine* chairs made of olive wood or walnut are still produced in **Chiavari** (⊠ On S1, 12 km/7 mi east of Rapallo) by a few craftsmen. Macramé lace can also be found here.

Santa Margherita Ligure

❸❾ *3 km (2 mi) south of Rapallo, 40 km (25 mi) southeast of Genoa, 82 km (51 mi) northwest of La Spezia.*

A pretty resort favored by well-to-do Italians, Santa Margherita Ligure has everything a Riviera playground should have—plenty of palm trees and attractive hotels, cafés, and a marina packed with yachts. Some of the older buildings here are still decorated on the outside with the trompe l'oeil frescoes typical of this part of the Riviera. This is a pleasant and convenient base for excursions by land and by sea.

Dining and Lodging

$$$ ✕ **La Paranza.** As befits a spot just off of Santa Margherita's port, the specialty here is fresh seafood in every shape and form, from the piles of tiny *bianchetti* (whitebait) in oil and lemon in the *antipasto di mare* to a simple, perfectly grilled whole sole. In between you'll find mussels, clams, octopus, salmon, and whatever else is fresh that day. Locals say this is the town's best restaurant (make reservations), but if you're looking for a stylish evening out, look elsewhere—La Paranza is about food, not fashion. ⊠ *Via Jacopo Ruffini 46,* ☎ *0185/283686. AE, DC, MC, V. Closed Thurs. and Nov.*

$$ ✕ **Il Frantoio.** The large, hand-carved wooden screws that turned the olive press for which this rather elegant little restaurant is named stand at the entrance. And here you not only select from the wine list, you can also choose from the olive oil list for just the right piquancy or mellowness. Quality is a keynote in the food, too, as in the specialties: spaghetti with shellfish cooked in a pastry crust, and either rabbit or seafood with pomegranate sauce. ☒ *Via del Giunchetto 23/a,* ☎ *0185/ 286667. AE, DC, MC, V. Closed Tues. and Nov. 7–30.*

$$$$ 🏨 **Grand Hotel Miramare.** Take the shore road south from town to reach
★ this palatial turn-of-the-century hotel overlooking the bay. It has a lush garden and swimming pool, and a private swimming area on the sea. The bright and airy rooms are furnished with antique furniture and marble bathrooms. ☒ *Lungomare Milite Ignoto 30, 16038,* ☎ *0185/ 287013,* 🅵🅰🆇 *0185/284651. 75 rooms, 9 suites. 2 restaurants, bar, in-room safes, minibars, pool, beach, waterskiing, meeting rooms. AE, DC, MC, V.*

$$$$ 🏨 **Imperial Palace.** Via Pagana climbs north out of Santa Margherita Ligure on its way toward Rapallo; just outside town it passes this Old-World–style luxury hotel, set in an extensive park. The rooms are furnished with antiques; many overlook the shore drive to the sea. The reception rooms are elegantly decorated with tall windows, plush chairs, and potted plants. ☒ *Via Pagana 19, 16038,* ☎ *0185/288991,* 🅵🅰🆇 *0185/284223. 102 rooms. Restaurant, bar, pool. AE, DC, MC, V. Closed Nov. 1–Mar. 27.*

$$$ 🏨 **Continental.** This stately seaside mansion with a columned portico was built in the early 1900s and set in a lush garden shaded by tall palms and pine trees. The decor is a blend of traditional furnishings, mostly in 19th-century style, with some more functional pieces. There is also a modern wing. The hotel's own cabanas and swimming area are at the bottom of the garden. ☒ *Via Pagana 8, 16038,* ☎ *0185/286512,* 🅵🅰🆇 *0185/ 284463. 76 rooms. Restaurant, bar. AE, DC, MC, V. Closed Nov.*

$ 🏨 **Fasce.** An extremely good value, this small, modern hotel is on one
★ of the town's main thoroughfares, but from its pleasant roof garden you have views of the sea and surrounding hills. The Italian owner and his English wife take cordial interest in their guests' well-being and comfort, providing free bus passes and bicycles. Rooms are attractive, with satellite TVs. ☒ *Via Bozzo 3, 16038,* ☎ *0185/286435,* 🅵🅰🆇 *0185/ 283580. 16 rooms. Restaurant. AE, DC, MC, V.*

Portofino

★ ⓐ *5 km (3 mi) south of Santa Margherita Ligure, 38 km (23 mi) southeast of Genoa, 87 km (54 mi) northwest of La Spezia.*

One of the most picturesque villages along the coast, with a decidedly romantic and affluent aura, is also precious, in the true sense of the word. Unless you are traveling on a deluxe level and can keep up with the Agnellis and Berlusconis, you should probably choose a hotel in Rapallo or Santa Margherita Ligure rather than one of Portofino's few and very expensive hotels, restaurants, and cafés. Some of Europe's wealthiest lay anchor here, but they stay out of sight by day, appearing in the evening after buses and boats have carried off the day-trippers. If you have had to sit out a traffic jam to get here, you may wonder why you bothered; there's little to do in Portofino, other than stroll around the wee harbor, walk to Punta del Capo, and look at the pricey boutiques. Trying to reach Portofino by bus or car on the single narrow road can be a nightmare in the summer and on holiday weekends. An alternative is to take a boat from Santa Margherita.

From the harbor, follow the signs for the climb to the **Castello di San Giorgio,** with its medieval relics and sweeping views. 🎫 *4,000 lire.* ☉ *Apr.–Sept., Wed.–Mon. 10–6; Oct.–Mar., Wed.–Mon. 10–4.*

Sitting on a ridge above the harbor is the church of **San Giorgio,** which is supposed to contain the saint's relics, brought back from the Holy

Land by the Crusaders. Portofino enthusiastically celebrates St. George's Day every April 23. Other pristine views can be seen from the lighthouse at **Punta del Capo,** a 15-minute walk along a marked path from the village.

Dining and Lodging

$$$$ ✕ **Il Pitosforo.** A chic, tan clientele, many with luxury yachts in the harbor, gives this waterfront restaurant a glamorous atmosphere augmented by outlandish prices. Spaghetti *ai frutti di mare* (with seafood) is recommended; adventurous diners might want to try *lo stocco accomodou* (dried cod in a savory sauce of tomatoes, raisins, and pine nuts). ✉ *Molo Umberto I, 9,* ☎ *0185/269020. Reservations essential. AE, DC, MC, V. Closed Mon.–Tues. and Jan.–mid-Feb. No lunch June–Sept.*

$$$$ ▦ **Splendido.** Most people resort to superlatives when trying to describe this luxury hotel, built in the '20s on a hill overlooking the sea. The abiding theme is color, from the coordinated fabrics and furnishings of the rooms to the fresh flowers in the reception rooms and on the large terrace. It's like a Jazz Age film set, and you almost expect to see a Bugatti or Daimler roll up the winding drive from Portofino below. Even more grand than the hotel are its prices (think three times the lower limit of this price range), making this a place for very special occasions indeed. ✉ *Viale Baratta 13, 16034,* ☎ *0185/269551,* FAX *0185/ 269614. 64 rooms. Restaurant, 2 bars, pool, tennis court. AE, DC, MC, V. Closed Jan.–mid-Mar.*

Outdoor Activities and Sports

HIKING

If you have the stamina, you can hike to the Abbazia di San Fruttuoso (☞ Off the Beaten Path *in* Camogli, *above*) from Portofino. It's a steep climb at first, and the walk takes about 2½ hours one-way. By boat, the trip takes about 20 minutes.

Chiavari

41 *22 km (13 mi) southeast of Portofino, 38 km (23 mi) southeast of Genoa, 69 km (43 mi) northwest of La Spezia.*

Chiavari is a fishing town, rather than village, and it has considerable character, with narrow, twisting streets and a good harbor. Chiavari's citizens were intrepid explorers, and many emigrated to South America in the 19th century. The town boomed, thanks to the wealth of the returning voyagers, but Chiavari still retains many medieval traces in its buildings.

There is an interesting **Museo Archeologico** (Archaeological Museum) in the center of town. Here you can see finds from an 8th-century BC necropolis, or ancient cemetery (literally, city of the dead), excavated nearby. ✉ *Palazzo Rocca, Piazza Matteotti.* ▦ *Free.* ☉ *Tues.–Thurs. 9–1, Fri.–Sun. 2–7.*

Outdoor Activities and Sports

HORSEBACK RIDING

Riding is a rewarding way to explore the wooded hills framing Chiavari. **Rivarola Carasco** (✉ Via Veneto 212, ☎ 0185/382204) provides mounts.

Sestri Levante

42 *8 km (5 mi) southeast of Chiavari, 50 km (31 mi) southeast of Genoa, 59 km (36 mi) northwest of La Spezia.*

Though industrialized, with steelworks and shipyards, Sestri Levante has good views and an interesting medieval district surrounding what is known as the Baia del Silenzio (Bay of Silence), the small harbor just behind Piazza Matteotti. Walk up one of the alleyways to see some of the worked slate doorways of the older houses.

En Route From Sestri, S1 turns inland past the spectacular Passo del Bracco and does not reach the coast again until the large port of La Spezia, more than 60 km (37 mi) southeast. The Cinque Terre, five towns that lie on the less accessible coastal strip between Levanto and Portovenere (near La Spezia) could be reached only by boat or on foot until about 50 years ago.

Moneglia

43 *12 km (7 mi) southeast of Sestri Levante, 58 km (36 mi) northwest of La Spezia, 58 km (36 mi) southeast of Genoa.*

The town of Moneglia, sheltered by the wooded hills of a nature preserve, faces a little bay guarded by ruined castles. An out-of-the-way alternative to fussier resorts, it's a quiet base for walks and excursions by boat, car, or train to Portofino and the Cinque Terre towns. A classical guitar festival is held here in September.

Lodging

$$ 🏨 **Villa Edera.** Ingeniously merging an older building on a verdant hillside with a smart contemporary stone and glass wing, the family that owns this small hotel offers guests their personal and caring attention. Terraces, a garden, luminous bedrooms, and lounges with stylish wicker armchairs are among the comforts. Mamma Ida's cooking is special, too. ⊠ *Via Venino 12, 16030,* ☎ *0185/49291,* 🅵🅰🆇 *0185/ 49470. 11 rooms. Restaurant. AE, MC, V. Closed Nov. 6–Mar.*

Levanto

44 *25 km (15 mi) southeast of Sestri Levante, 32 km (20 mi) northwest of La Spezia, 83 km (51 mi) southwest of Genoa.*

Secluded Levanto has good beaches and a few graceful buildings dating from the 13th century. Take a closer look at the buildings; some are adorned with clever trompe l'oeil frescoes that give the impression that real town folk are looking at you from their windows.

Dining and Lodging

$$–$$$ ✕ **Araldo.** Arches and frescoes add to the atmosphere of this elegant
★ little restaurant. Ambience, food, and service are outstanding. Seasonal, creative Mediterranean cuisine is complimented by more than 100 wines. Try *pesce con patate alla ligure* (fillets of fish baked with potatoes in wine with olives and fresh thyme), or put your faith in the chef and order the tasting menu, a good deal and a real treat. ⊠ *Via Jacopo 24,* ☎ *0187/807253. AE, DC, MC, V. Closed Tues. (except July–Aug.) and Nov.*

$$$ 🏨 **Stella Maris.** In Levanto center and only a 10-minute walk from the
★ beach, this is a real find. It takes up one floor of a 19th-century palazzo (the ground floor houses a bank). Seven rooms are decorated with original frescoes and 19th-century furniture, and seven are modern; the couple who run the hotel have an infectious enthusiasm for the building's history and decoration. A half-board plan is included in the price, but that's no sacrifice because the home cooking features Ligurian seafood specialties; you can have your homemade gelato in the sunny garden. ⊠ *Via Marconi 4, 19015,* ☎ *0187/808258,* 🅵🅰🆇 *0187/807351. 14 rooms. Restaurant. AE, DC, MC, V. Closed Nov.*

Cinque Terre

★ ㊺ *94 km (58 mi) southeast of Genoa.*

The aura of isolation that has surrounded five almost inaccessible coastal villages known as Cinque Terre, together with their dramatic coastal scenery, has made them one of the eastern Riviera's premier attractions. Clinging haphazardly to steep cliffs, they are linked by footpaths, by train, and now by narrow, unasphalted and rather tortuous roads, a fairly recent development. The local train on the Genoa–La Spezia line stops at each town between Levanto and Riomaggiore. The westernmost village is Monterosso, but the easiest to reach by car is Riomaggiore, easternmost of the villages and closest to La Spezia and the A12 autostrada.

All five of the Cinque Terre and the sanctuaries and tiny mountain settlements that are linked to them are connected by well-established hiking footpaths—for much of their history, these were the only way to get from town to town on land. Although today the train, and to a certain extent the road, have surpassed the footpaths, they're still well kept and showcase breathtaking ocean views as well as access to rugged, secluded beaches and grottoes that will never have a train station. The most famous and easiest of these trails is the **Via dell'Amore** (Lover's Lane), which—going west to east—links Riomaggiore with Manarola (2 km/1 mi, 30 min) with a flat path cut into the cliff side. The same trail continues to Corniglia (3 km/2 mi, 1 hr), then becomes more difficult between Corniglia and Vernazza (3 km/2 mi, 1½ hrs) and more so still from Vernazza to Monterosso (2 km/1 mi, 1½ hrs). Additionally, trails lead from Monterosso up the mountainside and back down to Vernazza, and into the mountains from Corniglia, Manarola, and Riomaggiore, with historic churches and great views along the way. Trail maps are available at the Monterosso tourist office. Be sure to wear sturdy shoes and a hat, and bring a water bottle, as there is little shade.

Monterosso al Mare

12 km (7 mi) east of Levanto.

Monterosso is the largest and most developed of the five fishing towns, with the Cinque Terre's only real hotels and most of its restaurants. The narrow alleys and colorful houses of the historic center are clustered on a hilltop above the port and its seaside promenade. Stone stairways link the two areas of town, affording lovely views of the mountains that tumble down onto a wide, sandy beach below. In the historic center, the 12th-century **church** (⊠ Piazza Garibaldi) is striped black and white in the Ligurian Gothic fashion. On Thursday morning the town comes alive with its weekly **market**, where you can pick up local anchovies and lemons. If you are traveling in summer, note that due to Monterosso's relative accessibility and the increasing popularity of the Cinque Terre, you'll have this town less to yourself than you might have five years ago. The little effort it takes to visit the other, smaller towns will be amply rewarded. The **Pro Loco** tourist office (⊠ Via Fegina 38, below train station, ☎ 0187/817506) can help with trail maps and boat schedules.

DINING AND LODGING

$$ ✕ **Il Gigante.** A good introduction to Ligurian seafood is the zuppa di pesce served at this traditional trattoria in Monterosso. This soup is usually served as a first course, but is filling enough to be an entrée. Daily specials might include risotto di frutti di mare and spaghetti with an octopus sauce. ⊠ *Monterosso al Mare,* ☎ *0187/817401. AE, DC, MC, V. Closed Tues.*

$$ ✕ **Il Pirata.** Bright and rustic, this trattoria near the port should be the
★   first stop for lunchtime visitors, especially those who make it in time
to grab a seat at the long tables on the front porch outside. Specialties
are those of the region, with a few surprising gourmet touches, like
the Maine lobster and French wines lining the shelves. ✉ *Via Molinelli
6/8,* ☎ *0187/817536. Reservations essential weekends. MC, V. Closed
Wed. and mid-Jan.–mid.-Feb.*

$$$ 🏨 **Porto Roca.** In a panoramic position above the sea, Porta Roca is
★   set slightly apart, blessedly removed from the crowds who visit espe-
cially on weekends. It has the look of a well-kept villa; its interiors have
authentic antique pieces and there are ample terraces. The rooms are
bright and airy, with sea breezes. Porto Roca is on a network of not-
too-demanding hill walks and has a faithful American clientele. ✉ *Via
Corone 1, 19016,* ☎ *0187/817502,* 🖷 *0187/817692. 43 rooms.
Restaurant, bar. AE, MC, V. Closed Nov. 4–Mar. 23.*

Vernazza
3½ km (2 mi) east of Monterosso.

A few kilometers to the east of Monterosso is Vernazza, with the
largest and best-equipped port of the Cinque Terre towns. The town's
pink, slate-roofed houses and picturesque squares contrast strangely
with remains of a medieval fort and castle. The castle's tower was struck
by lightning in 1896; it's been rebuilt and today offers some of the best
views in Cinque Terre. Summertime in Vernazza brings smart-set Italians to the town's cafés and restaurants. Stay in town and delve right
in, or escape on one of the many footpaths leading up through the hillsides' terraced vineyards.

DINING

$$$ ✕ **Gambero Rosso.** On Vernazza's main square, looking out at the
church, this fine trattoria serves refined treats like shrimp salads, veg-
etable tortes, and squid-ink risotto; for dessert don't miss the Cinque
Terre's own *schiacchetrà,* a dessert wine served with hard, semisweet
biscotti (hard cookies). Don't drink it out of the glass—dip the biscotti
in the wine and eat them instead. ✉ *Piazza Marconi 7,* ☎ *0187/
812265. AE, MC, V. Closed Mon. (Oct.–Mar.) and first 3 wks of Nov.*

Corniglia
3 km (2 mi) east of Vernazza.

Tiny, isolated Corniglia is unquestionably the most difficult of the
Cinque Terre to visit: It has no port and no (usable) access road for
automobiles, so you will have to arrive by local train or on foot, using
the difficult trail from Vernazza or the easy one from Manarola. The
town is strung back from a hilltop overlooking the sea to the moun-
tainside behind it; within you'll find pretty pastel squares and the
14th-century **San Pietro church.** The rose window of marble imported
from Carrara is particularly impressive considering the work it must
have taken merely to get it to Corniglia.

Manarola
3 km (2 mi) east of Corniglia.

Manarola is the most photogenic of the Cinque Terre; here multicolor
houses spill down a dark hillside to town squares that hang over the
port like balconies overlooking the tiny turquoise harbor. This is also
the center of the Cinque Terre's wine making, and you can taste the
fruits of local labor in a number of *cantine,* as well as the **Cooperativa
Agricoltura di Riomaggiore, Manarola, Corniglia, Vernazza e Monterosso**
(Groppo, 0187/920435), just outside town.

Riomaggiore

1½ km (1 mi) east of Manarola, 10 km (6 mi) west of La Spezia.

Civilization and all that goes with it begins to resurface in Riomaggiore, where you'll find the same sorts of picturesque little squares that bedeck the town's four siblings, interspersed with modern stucco houses and a sense that the population is less isolated here. This may be because Riomaggiore is comparatively convenient to La Spezia; get here via car, following signs from La Spezia's port.

La Spezia

46 *8 km (5 mi) north of Portovenere, 103 km (64 mi) southeast of Genoa, 144 km (89 mi) northwest of Florence.*

La Spezia is a large industrialized naval port on routes to the Cinque Terre and to Portovenere. La Spezia lacks the charm of the smaller towns, but it does have the remains of the massive 13th-century **Castel San Giorgio** (⊠ Via XX Settembre).

Outdoor Activities and Sports

WATERSKIING

La Spezia Motorboat Club (⊠ Via della Marina 224, ☎ 0187/50401) will get you up and skiing.

Portovenere

★ **47** *24 km (15 mi) east of Riomaggiore, 114 km (70 mi) southeast of Genoa.*

Portovenere's small colorful houses, some dating from the 12th century, were once all connected to the 12th- to 16th-century citadel, so that in times of attack the villagers could reach the safety of the battlements. The town commands a strategic position at the end of a peninsula that extends southeast from the Cinque Terre and forms the western border of the Gulf of La Spezia. Lord Byron (1788–1824) is said to have written *Childe Harold* here. Near the entrance to the huge, strange **Grotto Arpaia** at the base of the sea-swept cliff is a plaque recounting the poet's strength and courage as he swam across the gulf to the village of San Terenzo, near Lerici, to visit his friend Percy Shelley (1792–1822); the feat is commemorated as well by the name of the stretch of water, "Golfo dei Poeti," or Poets' Gulf. Above the grotto, on a formidable solid mass of rock, is **San Pietro**, a 13th-century Gothic church built on the site of an ancient pagan shrine. With its black-and-white-stripe exterior, it is a landmark recognizable from far out at sea.

Dining and Lodging

$$ ✕ **Da Iseo.** Try to get one of the tables outside at this waterfront restaurant, with bistro accents and paintings of Portovenere. Seafood is the only choice, and it's fresh and plentiful. Pasta courses are inventive; try spaghetti *alla Giuseppe* (with shellfish and fresh tomato) or spaghetti *alla Iseo* (with a seafood curry sauce). ⊠ *Waterfront,* ☎ *0187/790610. AE, DC, MC, V. Closed Wed. and Jan. 2–Feb. 15.*

$ ✕ **Antica Osteria del Carrugio.** Near the castle built to defend the coast from Pisan incursions is this 100-year-old tavern with maritime decor. The menu features seafood, which varies with the catch of the day. Specialties include *mescina* (soup of beans, chickpeas, and wheat) and *polpo in insalata* (octopus salad). ⊠ *Via Cappellini 66,* ☎ *0187/ 900617. Reservations not accepted. No credit cards. Closed Thurs. and mid-Nov.–mid-Dec.*

$$$ 🏨 **Royal Sporting.** Appearances are deceptive at this modern hotel on ★ the beach about a 10-minute walk from the village. From the outside,

the stone construction seems austere and unwelcoming, but the court-yards and interior—with fresh flowers, potted plants, and cool, airy rooms—are colorful and vibrant. The sports facilities are among the best in the area. ⊠ *Via dell'Olivo 345, 19025,* ☎ *0187/790326,* FAX *0187/529060. 62 rooms. Restaurant, bar, saltwater pool, tennis court, beach. AE, DC, MC, V. Closed mid-Oct.–Apr. (except Easter wk).*

Lerici

48   *11 km (7 mi) east of La Spezia, 65 km (40 mi) northeast of Pisa.*

Lerici, near Liguria's border with Tuscany, is set on a magnificent coastline of gray cliffs and pine forests. The town once belonged to Tuscan Pisa, and the 13th-century Pisan **Castello Doria** standing above the splendid bay has attracted lovers of nature for centuries. Shelley was one of Lerici's best-known visitors and spent some of the happiest months of his life in the lovely white village of **San Terenzo**, 2 km (1 mi) away. The **Villa Magni,** where he lived, has a collection devoted to him. After Shelley drowned at sea here in 1822, the bay was renamed Golfo dei Poeti, in honor of him and Byron.

Dining and Lodging

$$$ ✕▥ **Miranda.** Perched amid the clustered old houses in the seaside hamlet of Tellaro, 4 km (2½ mi) southeast of Lerici, this small family-run inn has become a pricey gourmet's destination because of chef Angelo Cabani's imaginative way with Ligurian cooking. His unusual dishes include *insalata di gamberoni e aragosta con finocchio* (shrimp and lobster salad with fennel) and *involtino di branzino farcito di cozze* (fish roulade stuffed with mussels). If you stay in one of the seven comfortable rooms with bath, you can take half board for 300,000. ⊠ *Via Fiascherino 92,* ☎ *0187/964012. 7 rooms. Restaurant, bar. Reservations essential. AE, DC, MC, V. Closed Mon. and mid-Jan.–mid-Feb.*

$$ ▥ **Florida.** This seafront family-run establishment has bright rooms with all the extras you would expect in a higher category, including soundproofing and a balcony with a sea view. For an even better view, loll in one of the deck chairs on the roof terrace. The Florida overlooks a small beach area and is close to tennis courts and a golf course. ⊠ *Lungomare Biaggini 35, 19032,* ☎ *0187/967332,* FAX *0187/967344. 37 rooms. AE, DC, MC, V. Closed Jan. 7–Mar. 15.*

ITALIAN RIVIERA A TO Z

Arriving and Departing

By Boat

Genoa is Italy's largest port and can be reached from the United States as well as other parts of Liguria and Italy (Sardinia, La Spezia, and Savona). Ships berth in the heart of Genoa, including cruise ships of the Genoa-based **Costa Cruise Line** (⊠ Via Gabriele D'Annunzio 2, ☎ 010/54831). Ferries to various ports around the Mediterranean are operated by **Tirrenia Navigazione** (⊠ Stazione Marittima, ☎ 010/2758041).

By Bus

The main bus station in Genoa is at Piazza Principe. Several bus lines, including PESCI, provide connections along the Ligurian coast and link Genoa with other parts of Italy, with the French Riviera, and with other cities in Europe. Bus tickets, reservations, and information in Genoa are handled by **PESCI** (⊠ Piazza della Vittoria 94/r, Genoa, ☎ 010/564936), **Geotravels** (⊠ Piazza della Vittoria 302/r, Genoa, ☎ 010/587181), and **Guimar Tours** (⊠ Via Balbi 192, Genoa, ☎ 010/256337).

By Car

Autostrada **A12** southeast from Genoa links up with the autostrada and superstrada network for all northern and southern destinations; Rome is a six-hour drive from Genoa. The 150-km (93-mi) trip north to Milan on **A7** takes two hours. Nice is 2½ hours west on **A10.**

By Plane

Aeroporto Internazionale Cristoforo Colombo (⊠ Sestri Ponente, ☎ 010/ 60151) is only 6 km (4 mi) from the center of Genoa. It has regular service to all main European cities. The nearest airports for U.S. flights are Nice, in France, about 2½ hours west of Genoa, and Milan's Linate and Malpensa, about 2 hours northeast.

BETWEEN THE AIRPORT AND DOWNTOWN

Volabus services (☎ 010/5997414) from Cristoforo Colombo connect with Genoa's Stazione Brignole, stopping also at Piazza Acquaverde (Stazione Principe).

By Train

Frequent and fast train service connects Liguria with the rest of Italy. Genoa is 1½ hours fromMilan and five hours from Rome. Many services from France (in particular, the French Riviera) pass along the Ligurian Coast on the way to all parts of Italy.

Getting Around

By Boat

This is the most pleasant—and, in some cases, the only—way to get from place to place within Liguria. A busy network of local services connects many of the resorts. For general information about availability of services in Liguria, contact **Servizio Marittimo del Tigullio** (⊠ Via Palestro 8/1b, Santa Margherita Ligure, ☎ 0185/284670). Another source is **Alimar** (⊠ Calata Zingari, Genoa, ☎ 010/256775). Or contact **Servizio Marittimo Camogli–San Fruttuoso** (⊠ Società Golfo Paradiso, Via Scalo 2, Camogli, ☎ 0185/772091), which runs between Camogli and San Fruttuoso (on the Portofino promontory), as well as between Recco and Punta Chiappa, two towns close to Camogli. **Navigazione Golfo dei Poeti** (⊠ Viale Mazzini 21, La Spezia, ☎ 0187/967676 or 0336/258037) runs frequent ferry-shuttle services between Portofino, Portovenere, and the Cinque Terre.

By Bus

PESCI (⊠ Piazza della Vittoria 94/r, Genoa, ☎ 010/564936) buses run the length of the Ligurian Coast in both directions. Local buses serve the steep valleys that run to some of the towns along the western coast. Tickets may be bought at local bus stations, or at newsstands for local buses. Buy your ticket before you board the bus.

By Car

Two good roads run parallel to each other along the coast of Liguria. Closer to shore and passing through all the towns and villages is **S1,** which has excellent views at almost every turn but which gets crowded in July and August. More direct and higher up than S1 is the autostrada **A10** west of Genoa and **A12** to the east. This route saves a lot of time on weekends, in summer, and on days when festivals slow traffic in some resorts to a standstill.

By Train

Regular service, connecting all parts of Liguria, operates from Genoa's two stations, **Stazione Principe** (points west, ⊠ Piazza Principe, ☎ 1478/ 88088 toll free) and **Stazione Brignole** (points east, ⊠ Piazza Giuseppe Verdi, ☎ 147/888088 toll free). All the coastal resorts are on this line, and many international trains stop along the coast west of Genoa on their way from Paris to Milan or Rome.

Contacts and Resources

Car Rentals

GENOA

Avis (⊠ Piazza Acquaverde, ☎ 010/564412, 06/4780150 reservations). **Budget** (⊠ Aeroporto Internazionale Cristoforo Colombo, ☎ 010/6503822). **Hertz** (⊠ Via delle Casacce 3, ☎ 010/564412).

LA SPEZIA

Avis (⊠ Via Fratelli Rosselli 86/88, ☎ 0187/33345). **Hertz** (⊠ Via Casaregis 76/r, ☎ 010/592101).

SAN REMO

Avis (⊠ Corso Imperatrice 96, ☎ 0184/73897). **Hertz** (⊠ Via XX Settembre 17, ☎ 0184/85618).

Emergencies

Police, Doctor (☎ 113). **Genoa municipal police** (☎ 010/53631). **Ambulance** (☎ 010/595951). **Ospedale Generale Regionale San Martino** (⊠ Viale Benedetto XV, Genoa, ☎ 010/516748).

Guided Tours

ORIENTATION TOURS

Informal harbor cruises or excursion cruises among coastal towns are scheduled and operated by the main ferry lines (☞ Getting Around by Boat, *above*), but you can have as much fun—if not more—negotiating a price with a boat owner at one of the smaller ports. You're likely to get a boat operator who commands rudimentary English at best.

Boat Tours: You can also take a boat tour of Genoa harbor. The tour lasts about an hour and includes a visit to the breakwater outside the harbor, the Bacino delle Grazie, and the Molo Vecchio (Old Port). You can see extensive views of the city throughout the tour. For information, contact the **Cooperativa Battellieri** (⊠ Stazione Marittima, Ponte dei Mille, Genoa, ☎ 010/265712).

Bus Tours: A three-hour bus tour of Genoa with an English-speaking guide is the best way to see the city and its panoramic upper reaches. A coach with a multilingual guide aboard leaves every day at 9 AM from the **AMT** (municipal bus company) office (⊠ Piazza della Vittoria, ☎ 010/5997414), stopping to pick up passengers at several points in the center of town; the last pickup point is Piazza Acquaverde, at the Stazione Principe, at 9:25 AM. Tickets (about 20,000 lire) can be purchased on the bus, but seats should be reserved at **Cooptur Liguria** (☎ 010/592658), or AMT. The tour includes an optional one-hour walking tour of the historic center and an optional 15-minute walk through the fishing enclave of Boccadasse.

Late-Night Pharmacies

Genoa: Europa (⊠ Corso Europa 676, ☎ 010/380239). **Ghersi** (⊠ Corte Lambruschini, Tower A, ☎ 010/541661).

Visitor Information

Genoa: Main **APT** (⊠ Palazzina Santa Maria, Old Port, ☎ 010/24871, FAX 010/2467658). Additional offices: (⊠ Stazione Principe, ☎ 010/2462633; ⊠ Aeroporto Internazionale Cristoforo Colombo, ☎ 010/2415247).

Local tourist offices are IAT and Pro Loco: **Alassio** (⊠ Palazzo Hanbury, Via Gibb 26, 17021, ☎ 0182/640346, FAX 0182/644690). **Albenga** (⊠ Via B. Ricci, corner of Piazza San Michele, 17031, ☎ 0182/554752,

In case you want to be welcomed there.

We're here to see that you're always welcomed at establishments everywhere. That's why millions of people carry the American Express® Card — for peace of mind, confidence, and security, around the world or just around the corner.

do more

Cards

In case you're running low.

We're here to help with more than 118,000 Express Cash locations around the world. In order to enroll, just call American Express before you start your vacation.

do more

Express Cash

And just in case.

We're here with American Express® Travelers Cheques and Cheques *for Two*.® They're the safest way to carry money on your vacation and the surest way to get a refund, practically anywhere, anytime.

Another way we help you...

do more ®

Travelers Cheques

FAX 0182/51325). **Bordighera** (✉ Via Roberto 1, 18012, ☎ 0184/262322, FAX 0184/264455). **Camogli** (✉ Via XX Settembre 33/r, 16032, ☎ 0185/771066). **Imperia** (✉ Via Matteotti 54/a, 18100, ☎ 0183/24947, FAX 0183/24950). **La Spezia** (✉ Via Mazzini 47, 19100, ☎ 0187/770900, FAX 0187/770908). **Lerici** (✉ Via Gerini 40, 19032, ☎ 0187/967346). **Levanto** (✉ Piazza Cavour 12, 19015, ☎ 0187/808125, FAX 0187/808125). **Monterosso** (✉ Via Fegina 38, 19016, ☎ 0187/817506). **Rapallo** (✉ Via A. Diaz 9, 16035, ☎ 0185/230346, FAX 0185/63051). **San Remo** (✉ Corso Nuvoloni, 18038, ☎ 0184/571571, FAX 0184/507649). **Varazze** (✉ Viale Nazioni Unite, 17019, ☎ 019/934609, FAX 019/97298). **Ventimiglia** (✉ Via Cavour 61, 18039, ☎ 0184/351183).

8 Piedmont/ Valle d'Aosta

From Turin to the Alps and Across the Po Plain

Italy's windows on France and Switzerland are delightful surprises even in a land of natural beauty. Snowcapped Monte Bianco and Monte Cervino climb to the highest heights in Europe, and below them, Alpine valleys cradle storybook castles. From here come Alba's truffles, Barolo's wine, and the FIATs, Borsalino hats, and Asti Spumante of Turin, sparkling at the center of it all.

Updated by
Valerie
Hamilton

FROM ALPINE VALLEYS hemming the highest mountains in Europe to the mist-shrouded lowlands skirting the Po River, from pulsating industrial centers turning out the best of Italian design to tiny stone villages isolated above the clouds, and from hearty peasant cooking in farmhouse kitchens to French-accented delicacies *accompagné* by some of Italy's finest wines, Piedmont and the spectacular Valle d'Aosta promise the traveler a store of historical, cultural, and natural riches.

The Valle d'Aosta's Italian Alps afford excellent skiing and climbing at renowned resort towns such as Courmayeur and Breuil-Cervinia. In the Piedmontese lowlands, Turin, the regional capital, is a historical center that today also serves as the heart of Italy's booming auto industry. Don't be put off by Turin's industrial reputation—it's also home to churches, elegant piazzas, and worthwhile museums. Nearby are Alba, home of fragrant Italian white truffles, seasonal delicacies that sell for more than $1,000 per pound; Asti, Barolo, and Barbaresco, the famous wine centers; and the modern business hubs Ivrea, Novara, and Alessandria.

Tucked away at the foot of the Pennine, Graian, Cottian, and Maritime Alps (Piemonte, in Italian, means "foot of the mountains"), Piedmont and the autonomous region of Valle d'Aosta just north of it seem more akin to neighboring France and Switzerland. Well-dressed women in the refined cafés of Turin are addressed more often as *madama* than *signora,* and French is often used in the more remote mountain hamlets.

Piedmont was originally inhabited by Celtic tribes who were absorbed by the conquering Romans. As allies of Rome, the Celts held off Hannibal when he came down through the Alpine passes with his elephants but were eventually defeated, and their capital—Taurasia, the present Turin—was destroyed. The Romans rebuilt the city, giving its streets the grid pattern that survives today. Roman ruins can be found throughout both regions and are particularly conspicuous in the town of Aosta.

With the fall of the Roman empire, Piedmont suffered the fate of the rest of Italy and was successively occupied and ravaged by barbarians from the east and the north. In the 11th century, a feudal French family named Savoy ruled Turin briefly; toward the end of the 13th century they returned to the area, where they would remain, almost continuously, for 500 years. In 1798 the French Republican armies invaded Italy, but when Napoléon's empire fell, the House of Savoy returned to power.

Beginning in 1848, Piedmont was one of the principal centers of the Risorgimento, the movement for Italian unity. In 1861 the Chamber of Deputies of Turin declared Italy a united kingdom. Rome became the capital in 1870, marking the end of Piedmont's importance in the political sphere. Nevertheless, the architectural splendors of Turin, together with some unheralded but excellent museums, continue to draw travelers.

Piedmont became one of the first industrialized regions in Italy, and the automotive giant FIAT—the Fabbrica Italiana Automobili Torino—was established here in 1899. Today the region is the center of Italy's automobile, metalworking, chemical, and candy industries, having attracted thousands of workers from Italy's impoverished south.

The Valle d'Aosta, to the north, is famous for its impressive fortified castles and splendid Alpine beauty. It was settled in the 3rd millennium BC by people from the Mediterranean and later by a Celtic tribe known as the Salassi, who eventually fell to the Romans. The Saracens were here in the 10th century; by the 12th century, the Savoy family had established itself, and the region's feudal nobles moved into the country, building the massive castles that still stand. Valle d'Aosta enjoyed relative autonomy as part of the Savoy kingdom and was briefly ruled by the French four separate times. The region is still officially bilingual, so you will hear both Italian and French.

Pleasures and Pastimes

Dining

These two regions offer rustic specialties, from farmhouse hearths to fine cuisine with a French accent—and everything in between. The favorite form of pasta is *agnolotti,* similar to ravioli and filled with meat, spinach, or ricotta cheese, often served in a delectably simple coating of melted butter and shaved truffles. Another regional specialty is *fonduta,* a local version of fondue, made with melted Fontina (a cheese from the Valle d'Aosta), eggs, and sometimes grated truffles. Alba is the home of *tartufi bianchi* (white truffles), much rarer and more expensive than black ones and considered the tastiest by connoisseurs. They sell for at least $1,000 a pound wholesale. Another local dish is *bagna cauda,* a heated sauce (*bagna cauda* means hot bath) made from butter, oil, anchovies, cream, and shredded garlic; it is served with *cardi* (edible thistles) or other raw vegetables for dipping.

Although as a rule desserts here are less sweet than in some other Italian regions, treats like *panna cotta,* a cooked milk custard, and *torta di nocciole* (hazelnut torte) still delight. Turin is renowned for its delicate pastries and fine chocolates, especially for the hazelnut *gianduiotti.* Valle d'Aosta is famous for a variety of schnappslike brandies made from fruits or herbs.

Piedmont is one of Italy's most important wine-producing regions. Most of the wines are full-bodied reds, such as Barolo, Nebbiolo, Freisa, Barbera, and Barbaresco. Asti Spumante, a sparkling wine, comes from the region, as does vermouth, which was developed in Piedmont by A. B. Carpano in 1786. Many prefer dry (brut) Spumante to the sweet Asti varietal.

CATEGORY	COST*
$$$$	over 90,000 lire
$$$	60,000–90,000 lire
$$	35,000–60,000 lire
$	under 35,000 lire

Prices are per person, including house wine, service, and tax.

Lodging

There is a high standard of old-world opulence in Turin's better hotels, and it is translated into the Alpine idiom in the top resort hotels in the mountains. Less-expensive hotels in cities and towns are generally geared to business travelers. You can usually count on a measure of charm at resorts and the Italian version of gemütlichkeit even in more modest resort hotels. Summer and winter occupancy rates and prices are usually quite high at resorts, with summer vacationers and skiers, respectively, monopolizing available accommodations. Hotels in mountain resorts may offer attractive half-board or off-season rates that can sometimes reduce the cost by a full price category. Many mountain resort hotels cater primarily to half- or full-board guests only, for stays of at least a week. It's a good idea to take a package deal on a ski vacation; it may give you a break on the price of lift tickets.

CATEGORY	COST*
$$$$	over 300,000 lire
$$$	220,000–300,000 lire
$$	150,000–220,000 lire
$	under 150,000 lire

Prices are for a standard double room, including service and tax.

Skiing

This is the major sport in both Piedmont and the Valle d'Aosta. Resorts with excellent facilities abound near the highest mountains in Europe—Monte Bianco (Mont Blanc), Monte Rosa, Monte Cervino (the Matterhorn), and the Gran Paradiso. Lift tickets, running around 45,000 lire for a day's pass, are significantly less expensive than at major U.S. resorts.

Exploring Piedmont/Valle d'Aosta

The vast Po Plain that stretches eastward in a wide belt across the top of the Italian peninsula begins in Piedmont, where the River Po has its source in the Coolidge Glacier on 11,000-ft-high Monviso. But Piedmont is primarily a mountainous region. The Maritime Alps lie to the south of Turin, and the rolling hills of the Monferrato and Langhe districts fold the landscape southeast of Turin. High Alpine crests of the Valle d'Aosta rise to the north and west of the plain. As you wind your way northeast into the Valle d'Aosta, you are in the Italian Loire, where solid, imposing castles sit in the shadow of Europe's most impressive peaks, Mont Blanc and the Matterhorn. Nature has endowed Piedmont and the Valle d'Aosta with some of the most striking scenery in Italy.

Like any rugged, mountainous region, the Alps of Piemonte and the Valle d'Aosta can be tricky to navigate. Roads that look like superhighways on the map can be narrow and twisting, with steep slopes and cliffside drops. Generally, roads are well maintained, but the sheer distance covered by all of those curves tends to take longer than you might have anticipated, and so it's best to figure in extra time for getting around. This is especially true in winter, when weather conditions can cause slow traffic and road closings. Be sure to check with local tourist offices and police before venturing off the beaten path, and find out whether you may need tire chains for snowy and icy roads.

Numbers in the text correspond to numbers in the margin and on the Piedmont/Valle d'Aosta and Turin maps.

Great Itineraries

With the exception of the mountain resorts, which may be packed at the height of the season, much of Piedmont and Valle d'Aosta is off the beaten track for tourists. These regions of Italy offer the pleasures of discovery: uncrowded, unhurried samplings of scenery, art, food, and some of Italy's finest wines.

The amount of time you choose to spend here depends on your interests. If you want to admire the highest mountains in the Alps from the pistes or the deck of a chalet, sneak up on the chamois in the Parco Nazionale del Gran Paradiso, and still have time to devote to Turin and the wine country, a total of seven days should be ideal. Five days would give you a chance to visit Turin's attractions, make an excursion into the mountains, and discover some of the smaller cities. In three days you can see Turin and then head to Aosta for a look at some impressive Roman ruins and a quick trip into the mountains. If you budget your time carefully, you can spend half a day in Asti.

Piedmont/Valle d'Aosta

SWITZERLAND

Monte Cervino
(Matterhorn)

Breuil-
Cervinia **26**

Monte Bianco **30**

Monte Rosa

Courmayeur **29**

Great St. Bernard
Pass

S406 Valtournenche

Gressoney-
la-Trinité

S27

Dora

S26

Baltéa

VALLE D' AOSTA

Aosta **28**

Nus Châtillon

Saint **25**
Vincent

S26

Castello Fénis **27**

Little St. Bernard
Pass

Verrès

S505

Cogne **31**

Bard **24**

Pont St. Martin

Parco Nazionale
de Gran Paradiso

S26

Ceresole Reale

Ivrea

FRANCE

S460

Orco

Forno Alpi Gràie

Dora

Cuorgnè

Baltéa

Balme

A5

Céres

S26

S24

Chivasso

Susa

S25

Bardonecchia **23**

A4

Sacra di San Michele

Abbazia di Sant'Antonio
di Ranverso

20

19

Avigliana

18

17

Sestriere

Rivoli

Turin

22
TO
CLAVIERE

S23

1 — **15**

S10

Stupinigi

16

S589

A21

N

S20

S23

Pinerolo

Carignano

A6

0   10 miles

0   15 km

Saluzzo
21

TO
BRÀ

TO
ALBA

S29

ITALY

IF YOU HAVE 3 DAYS

Visitors with limited time should concentrate first on ☷ **Turin** ①–⑮ and its main sites, including the **Duomo di San Giovanni** ①, where the famous shroud is housed; the 17th-century **Palazzo Reale** ②, former residence of the Savoy royal family; and the churches of **San Carlo** ⑤ and **Santa Cristina** ⑥, which flank the impressive **Piazza San Carlo** ⑦, considered by many to be Italy's finest square. Take time to enjoy one or more of the city's authentic old-world cafés and the view from the striking **Mole Antonelliana** ⑩, an odd structure that was once the world's tallest building. On the second day, head northeast along the A5 motorway to **Aosta** ㉘ to see its large and well-preserved Roman ruins before continuing on to ☷ **Courmayeur** ㉙ for magnificent views of **Monte Bianco** ㉚. You have several choices for the third day: You can stay in the mountains, heading for ☷ **Breuil-Cervinia** ㉖ for a look at the Matterhorn, or you can double back from Aosta to **Cogne** ㉛, where you can make a foray into the Parco Nazionale Gran Paradiso. Another alternative is to return to Turin and head southeast into the vineyard-blanketed hills around medieval **Asti** ㉜.

IF YOU HAVE 5 DAYS

Spend two days in ☷ **Turin** ①–⑮, then head for the Roman city of **Aosta** ㉘, perhaps stopping on the way to see the fairy-tale **Castello Fénis** ㉗. On the third day, you can drink in the views of the **Monte Bianco** ㉚ from ☷ **Courmayeur** ㉙, see the Matterhorn from ☷ **Breuil-Cervinia** ㉖, or follow the trails from **Cogne** ㉛ into the Parco Nazionale Gran Paradiso. On the fourth day double back to Turin and make an excursion to **Saluzzo** ㉑, an old town steeped in 15th-century atmosphere. On the fifth day continue southeast to **Asti** ㉜, exploring the rolling hills where great wines and good food make this a gourmet's paradise.

IF YOU HAVE 7 DAYS

Make ☷ **Turin** ①–⑮ your base for three days, from which you can explore the city and the outlying towns, including **Saluzzo** ㉑, with its picturesque hilltop center and castles. Another second-day excursion from Turin takes you to the castle at **Rivoli** ⑰, a sanctuary of contemporary art, and then over a pilgrim's route to two medieval abbeys, **Sant'Antonio di Ranverso** ⑱ and the **Sacra di San Michele** ⑳. Alternatively, travel westward to Piedmont's high mountains and see the resorts of **Sestriere** ㉒ and ☷ **Bardonecchia** ㉓ close to the French border. On the third day head for the mountains of the Valle d'Aosta; visit the **Castello Fénis** ㉗ on the way to ☷ **Aosta** ㉘, a good base for excursions into the mountains that will keep you moving on the fourth and fifth days between ☷ **Courmayeur** ㉙, ☷ **Breuil-Cervinia** ㉖, and **Cogne** ㉛. Head south on the sixth day, doubling back past Turin and continuing southeast to **Asti** ㉜. Follow the provincial roads through the vineyards of the hilly Monferrato and Langhe districts of south-central Piedmont, delving into their culinary and enological delights. On the seventh day head east across the fertile Po Plain toward the rice-growing capital of **Vercelli** ㉞, making sure you see the Duomo, the final resting place of several Savoy rulers. The easternmost city of Piedmont is ☷ **Novara** ㉟, of little interest, but a rest stop on the way to Milan, only 32 km (20 mi) away.

When to Tour Piedmont/Valle d'Aosta

Unless you are dead set on skiing, the region can be visited in either summer or winter (and for that matter, there's summer skiing at Monte Cervino). In winter, road conditions can be treacherous, especially higher up in the mountains, requiring the use of snow tires or chains. The ski resorts of the Valle d'Aosta are popular with Italians and non-Italians alike, so book your accommodations in advance. If you are visiting in summer, try to avoid coming in August, the holiday month for the vast majority of Italians, many of whom will come here for an Alpine holiday of walking, hiking, and relaxation.

TURIN

176 km (105 mi) northwest of Genoa, 97 km (59 mi) southeast of Milan.

Turin—in Italian, Torino—is roughly in the center of Piedmont/Valle d'Aosta; it is on the Fiume Po River, on the edge of the Po plain that stretches eastward all the way to the Adriatic. Apart from its role as northwest Italy's major industrial, cultural, and administrative hub, Turin is a center of education, science, and the arts. It also has a reputation as Italy's capital of black magic and the supernatural. This distinction is enhanced by the presence of Turin's most famous, controversial, and unsettling relic, the Sacra Sindone (Holy Shroud), still believed by many Catholics to be the cloth in which Christ's body was wrapped when he was taken down from the cross.

Downtown Turin

Many of Turin's major sights are clustered around Piazza Castello, and others are on or just off the porticoed Via Roma, one of the city's main thoroughfares, which leads 1 km (½ mi) from Piazza Castello south to Piazza Carlo Felice, a landscaped park with a fountain in front of the train station. First opened in 1615, Via Roma was largely rebuilt in the 1930s, during the time of Premier Benito Mussolini.

A Good Walk

Start on Piazza San Giovanni at the **Duomo di San Giovanni** ①, the hushed and shadowy repository of a controversial relic. Step into the **Palazzo Reale** ②, adjacent to the Duomo, to see the sumptuous interiors and, in a separate wing also on Piazza Castello, the **Armeria Reale**. The massive building occupying an entire block at the center of Piazza Castello is **Palazzo Madama** ③; step inside for a look at the **Museo Civico d'Arte Antica**. In the northwest corner of the same square, take time to observe Guarini's lively architectural vision in the church of **San Lorenzo** ④. Go southwest on Via Roma, a street rebuilt with arcades in the 1930s, during the time of Premier Benito Mussolini. Continuing a few blocks down Via Roma, you come to **Piazza San Carlo** ⑦, with its twin churches of **San Carlo** ⑤ and **Santa Cristina** ⑥. Just off the northeast end of Piazza San Carlo is the imposing **Palazzo dell'Accademia delle Scienze** ⑧, where you may devote upward of an hour or two to the collections in the Museo Egizio and Galleria Sabauda. To the east, across the street is the graceful **Palazzo Carignano** ⑨, not only historic but also an example of Piedmontese Baroque. The east facade of the palace faces Piazza Carlo Alberto, where you turn into Via Po, heading east to Via Montebello, where you turn left to reach the **Mole Antonelliana** ⑩, Turin's oddest and most conspicuous building.

TIMING

This walk takes the better part of a day if you allow plenty of time for the museums. Since it includes the most important of Turin's sights, it can constitute a satisfactory, albeit speedy, visit.

Sights to See

① **Duomo di San Giovanni.** The most impressive piece in Turin's 15th-century cathedral is the shadowy, black marble–walled **Cappella della Sacra Sindone** (Chapel of the Holy Shroud), where the Holy Shroud was housed before a severe fire in 1997. The chapel was designed by the priest and architect Guarino Guarini (1604–1683), a genius of the Baroque style who was official engineer and mathematician to the court

290

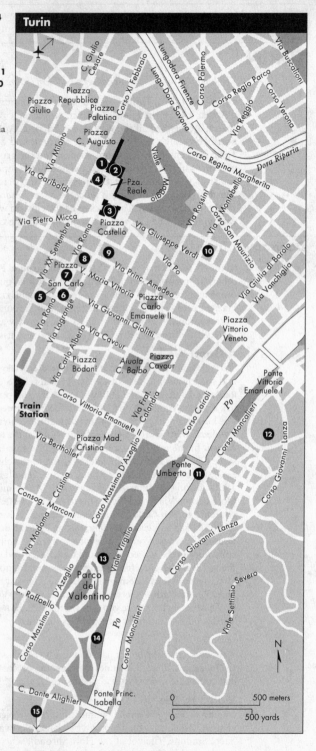

of Duke Carlo Emanuele II of Savoy. The fire was a major setback to ongoing restorations; the chapel is expected to remain closed for many years as a result of the damage.

The **shroud** is a 4-yard-long sheet of linen, unremarkable except for the fact that it contains an imprint of what the faithful claim is an image of the crucified Christ. It first made an appearance around the middle of the 15th century, when it was presented to Ludovico of Savoy in Chambéry. In 1578 it was brought to Turin by another member of the Savoy royal family, Duke Emanuele Filiberto. It is only in the last few years that the Catholic Church has allowed rigorous scientific study of the shroud. The results have come in on both sides of the argument. On the one hand, three separate university teams—in Italy, Britain, and the United States—have concluded, as a result of carbon-14 dating, that the cloth is a forgery dating from between 1260 and 1390. On the other hand, they are unable to explain how the shroud's image, which is like a photographic negative, could have been created, and the shroud continues to be revered as a holy relic. It will be exhibited again in 2000 to mark the beginning of the third millennium. ⊠ *Piazza San Giovanni,* ☎ *011/4361540.* ⊘ *Daily 7–noon and 3–7.*

★ ❿ **Mole Antonelliana.** You won't miss the unusual square dome and thin, elaborate spire tower of this Turin landmark above the city's rooftops. This odd structure, built between 1863 and 1897, was originally intended to be a synagogue, but costs escalated and eventually it was bought by the city of Turin. In its time it was the tallest building in the world. There is an excellent view of the city, the plain surrounding it, and the Alps beyond from a terrace at the top of the dome. Take the elevator to the top. ⊠ *Via Montebello 20,* ☎ *011/8170496.* ☒ *5,000 lire.* ⊘ *Tues.–Fri. 10–4, weekends 9–7.*

❾ **Palazzo Carignano.** Another one of Guarini's Baroque triumphs, this redbrick palace was built from 1679 to 1685 and is one of Turin's and Italy's most historic buildings. Kings of Savoy, Carlo Alberto (1798–1849) and Vittorio Emanuele II (1820–1878), were born within its walls. Italy's first parliament met here from 1860 to 1865. ⊠ *Piazza Carignano.*⊘ *Tues.–Sun. 9–6:30*

❽ **Palazzo dell'Accademia delle Scienze** (Palace of the Academy of Sciences). Guarini's large Baroque tour de force, prefiguring the 18th century's preoccupation with logic and science, houses two of Turin's most famous museums, the Museo Egizio and the Galleria Sabauda.

The **Museo Egizio** (Egyptian Museum) is considered to be one of the finest outside Cairo. Its superb collection includes statues of pharaohs and mummies, and entire frescoes taken from royal tombs. Equally fascinating are the papyrus, art objects, and day-to-day utensils taken from the tombs of less noble ancient Egyptians. Look for the papyrus *Book of the Dead* and the 13th-century BC statue of Ramses II, which still glistens in its original colors. ⊠ *Via Accademia delle Scienze 6,* ☎ *011/ 5617776.* ☒ *12,000 lire.* ⊘ *Tues.–Sat. 9–10, Sun. 9–6.*

The **Galleria Sabauda** houses the collections of the house of Savoy. It is particularly rich in 16th- and 17th-century Dutch and Flemish paintings: note Jan Van Eyck's *St. Francis with Stigmata,* with the saint receiving the marks of Christ's wounds while a companion cringes beside him as if feeling it all himself. Other Dutch masterpieces include paintings by Anthony Van Dyck and Rembrandt. Piero del Pollaiuolo's *Tobias and the Angel* is showcased, and other Italian artists featured include Fra Angelico, Andrea Mantegna, and Paolo Veronese. ⊠ *Via Accademia delle Scienze 6,* ☎ *011/547440.* ☒ *8,000 lire.* ⊘ *Tues., Thurs., Sat., and Sun. 9–10; Wed. and Fri. 2:30–7:30.*

➌ Palazzo Madama. In the center of Piazza Castello, this castle was named for the French queen Maria Cristina, who made it her home in the 17th century. The castle incorporates the remains of a Roman gate, as well as medieval and Renaissance additions. The architect Filippo Juvarra (1678–1736) designed the castle's elaborate Baroque facade in the early 18th century: He was intent on dispelling the idea that Italy's importance as a producer of contemporary art and architecture was in decline. Juvarra's bold use of the Baroque is also evident in the interior of the castle, where the huge marble staircase heralds his patron's wealth and prestige. The large assembly hall was the scene of the first Italian senate meetings in the mid-19th century. ⊠ *Piazza Castello.* ⊙ *Tues.–Sat. 9–7, Sun. 10–1 and 2–7.*

➋ Palazzo Reale (Royal Palace). This 17th-century palace is the former Savoy royal residence. It is an imposing work of brick, stone, and marble that stands on the site of Turin's ancient Roman city gates. In contrast to its austere exterior, the palace's interior is swathed in luxurious, mostly Rococo, trappings, including tapestries, gilded ceilings, and sumptuous 17th- to 19th-century furniture. ⊠ *Piazza Castello,* ☎ *011/ 4361455.* ☜ *8,000 lire.* ⊙ *Groups of 15 allowed every 40 mins Tues.– Sun. 9–7.*

The **Armeria Reale** (Royal Armory), in a wing of the Royal Palace, holds one of Europe's most extensive collections of arms and armor. It is a must-see for connoisseurs. ⊠ *Entrance on Piazza Castello,* ☎ *011/ 543889.* ☜ *8,000 lire.* ⊙ *Tues. and Thurs. 2:30–7:30, Wed., Fri. (groups only), and Sat. 9–2.*

➐ Piazza San Carlo. While standing in the stately, formal expanse, you too may proclaim this to be the grandest square in Italy. In the center stands a **statue of Duke Emanuele Filiberto of Savoy,** victor, in 1557, of the battle of San Quintino. The melee heralded the peaceful resurgence of Turin under the Savoys, after years of bloody dynastic fighting. The fine bronze statue, erected in the 19th century, is one of Turin's symbols.

NEED A BREAK?	The historic **Café San Carlo** (⊠ Piazza San Carlo) is usually lively with locals, gathered at the marble-top tables under the huge crystal chandelier. On the opposite side of the square is **Stratta,** one of Turin's best-known, and most decadent, chocolate shops.

➎ San Carlo. The ornate Baroque facade of this 17th-century church was enhanced in the latter part of the 19th century to harmonize with the facade of Santa Cristina. ⊠ *Piazza San Carlo, entrance to the southern end of the square.*

➍ San Lorenzo. The cupola and vividly painted interior of this church are standouts. Guarino Guarini was in his mid-sixties when he began work on the church in 1668, but the sprightly collection of domes, columns, and florid Baroque features seems more the work of a younger architect cutting his teeth with a daring display of mathematical invention. ⊠ *Piazza Castello.*

NEED A BREAK?	**Baratti e Milano** (⊠ Just to the east of Piazza Castello), in the glass-roofed gallery between Via Lagrange and Via Po, is another one of Turin's charming old-world cafés. It's famous for its chocolates, so you can indulge your sweet tooth here or buy some gianduiotti or candied chestnuts to take home to friends.

➏ Santa Cristina. Built in the mid-17th century, this church received a Baroque-style face-lift by Juvarra in 1715. ⊠ *Piazza San Carlo.*

Along the Po

The River Po is narrow and unprepossessing here in Turin, only a hint of the broad and mighty watercourse that it becomes as it flows eastward toward the Adriatic. It is flanked, however, by formidable edifices, a park, and a lovely pedestrian path.

A Good Tour

Start at the east end of Piazza Vittorio Veneto, at the end of Via Po. Cross the river on Ponte Vittorio Emanuele I, the bridge leading to the church of **Gran Madre di Dio** ⑪, a replica of Rome's Pantheon. To reach the church of **Santa Maria del Monte** ⑫, follow Corso Moncalieri south and then wend your way upward to the top of the hill. Then return to Corso Moncalieri and cross the next bridge downstream, Ponte Umberto I, to the **Parco del Valentino,** opened in 1856. One of the city's many pretty pedestrian paths, **Viale Virgilio** runs parallel to the river and leads to the **Castello del Valentino** ⑬, reminiscent of castles on the Loire. Go south on Viale Virgilio to the **Borgo Medioevale** ⑭, replica of a medieval hamlet and castle. From the park, catch a bus or taxi or just keep on walking south on Corso Massimo d'Azeglio to the **Museo dell'Automobile** ⑮, a low modern building that sweeps you into a world of nostalgia for the sleek, glamorous cars of yesteryear.

TIMING

Three hours should be enough to allow you to cover the ground with ease, but if you are an automobile buff, allow well over an hour for the Museo dell'Automobile.

Sights to See

⑭ **Borgo Medioevale** (Medieval Village). This was a veritable forerunner of today's theme parks. The village, a faithful reproduction of medieval Piedmontese buildings, was created for the Turin Exposition of 1884. A visit here is like stepping back into the Middle Ages, with craftsmen's shops, houses, churches, and stores clustered along narrow streets and lanes. ⊠ *By the riverside, southern edge of the Parco del Valentino.* 🔄 *Free.* ☉ *Daily 9–7.*

⑬ **Castello del Valentino.** The design of this 17th-century castle, built more for appearance than for defense, is based on models of 16th-century French châteaux. It stands on the left bank of the Po, in the pretty **Parco del Valentino**, laid out in 1856. The interior is elaborate, with frescoed walls and rich decoration, but the real attraction of the castle is its riverside setting amid the greenery of the park. ⊠ *Parco del Valentino.* ☉ *Tues.–Sat. 9:30–4, Sun. 10:30–4.*

⑪ **Gran Madre di Dio** (Great Mother of God). This 19th-century church was built in a neoclassical style based on the Pantheon in Rome. ⊠ *East bank of the Po, west of Piazza Castello.*

⑮ **Museo dell'Automobile** (Car Museum). No visit to car-manufacturing Turin would be complete without a pilgrimage to see perfectly conserved Bugattis, Ferraris, and Isotta Fraschinis. Here you'll get an idea of the importance of FIAT—and automobiles in general—to Turin's economy. There's a collection of antique cars dating from 1893, and displays show how the city has changed over the years as a result of its premier industry. ⊠ *Corso Unita d'Italia 40,* 🕾 *011/677666.* 🔄 *8,000 lire.* ☉ *Tues.–Sun. 9–12:30 and 3–7.*

⑫ **Santa Maria del Monte.** The church and convent standing on top of 150-ft Monte dei Cappuccini date from 1583. Don't be surprised if you find yourself in the middle of a wedding party: Local couples often come here to have their pictures taken.

Dining and Lodging

$$$–$$$$ ✕ **Del Cambio.** The setting and atmosphere of this town center restau-
    ★   rant in a palace dating from 1757 is nearly unmatched. It is probably
              one of Europe's most beautiful and historic restaurants, with decora-
              tive moldings, mirrors, and hanging lamps that look just as they did
              when Italian national hero Cavour dined here more than a century ago.
              The cuisine draws heavily on Piedmontese tradition and is paired with
              a wide array of fine Piedmontese wines. Great pastas might include ag-
              nolotti in an *arrosto* (roast veal) sauce; the veal carbonada is another
              savory treat. ⊠ *Piazza Carignano 2,* ☎ *011/546690. Reservations es-
              sential. Jacket and tie. AE, DC, MC, V. Closed Sun. and Aug.*

$$$–$$$$ ✕ **Vecchia Lanterna.** Sumptuously decorated with brocades, old paint-
              ings, and rich carpets, this elegant, intimate restaurant in town center
              serves classic food, made from age-old regional recipes. For a first course,
              try *fagottino di verza con fegato d'oca* (cabbage tart with goose liver),
              and for a second course, *supreme di anatra allo scalogno* (glazed duck).
              A set menu of local fare is offered at a special price. ⊠ *Corso Re Um-
              berto 21,* ☎ *011/537047. Reservations essential. Jacket and tie. DC,
              MC, V. Closed Sun. and Aug. No lunch Sat.*

$$$ ✕ **Due Lampioni.** Join the stylish clientele of this elegant Baroque-
              style restaurant in a 17th-century palace in the heart of the city for fine
              classic cuisine and an excellent selection of French and Italian wines.
              Try the artichoke flan *Vecchio Piemonte* (with meat sauce) and *agnello
              ai funghi con marsala* (boned leg of lamb with mushrooms in a marsala
              wine sauce). ⊠ *Via Carlo Alberto 45,* ☎ *011/8179380. Jacket and tie.
              AE, DC, MC, V. Closed Sun. and Aug.*

$$$ ✕ **La Prima Smarrita.** Intimate and elegant, this restaurant is widely
    ★   recognized by critics as one of Turin's best. It is on the fringes of the
              Lingotto neighborhood, a short taxi ride from the city center. Host
              Moreno Grossi's light, innovative versions of Mediterranean dishes are
              a departure from the usual Piedmontese fare. Try *tortelli di borragine*
              (fresh pasta filled with borage and served with fresh tomato sauce) or
              sea bass with artichokes, potatoes, and olives. And for dessert try the
              gianduia (hazelnut chocolate) mousse. Wine lovers will revel in this
              restaurant's cellar—one of the best in town. ⊠ *Corso Unione Soviet-
              ica 244,* ☎ *011/3179657. Reservations essential. Jacket and tie. AE,
              DC, MC, V. Closed Mon. and Aug.*

$$–$$$ ✕ **Taverna delle Rose.** The cooking of the Piedmont and Veneto regions,
              with some creative touches, dominates in this characterful restaurant
              near the train station. One dining room has walls covered with paint-
              ings; the other is done in old bricks and candlelight. Specialties include
              faraona farcita di carciofi (guinea fowl stuffed with artichokes) and roast
              venison with raspberry sauce. From the Veneto comes *bigoli con ragù
              d'anatra* (whole-wheat pasta with duck sauce). ⊠ *Via Massena 24,* ☎
              011/538345. AE, DC, MC, V. Closed Sun. and Aug. No lunch Sat.

$$ ✕ **Da Mauro.** Try the Tuscan dishes in this lively, popular family-run
              trattoria. Specialties include cannelloni *alla Mirella* (baked with moz-
              zarella cheese, prosciutto, and tomato), *involtini di Gorgonzola* (veal
              roulades with Gorgonzola cheese and a sauce of peppers and olives),
              and famous grilled Florentine beef. ⊠ *Via Maria Vittoria 21,* ☎ *011/
              8170604. Reservations not accepted. No credit cards. Closed Mon. and
              July.*

$$ ✕ **Ostu Bacu.** You'll find this small wood-paneled restaurant, in the
              same family for three generations, on the edge of town near the au-
              tostrada to Milan. Regional Piedmontese dishes are the draw, such as
              agnolotti and *fritto misto di carne* (a typical Piedmontese specialty of
              fried mixed meats, vegetables, and sweet morsels). ⊠ *Corso Vercelli
              226,* ☎ *011/2464579. AE, DC, MC, V. Closed Sun. and Aug.*

$$ ✕ **Tre Galline.** Set in a portion of the ancient Roman wall only a few blocks northwest of Piazza Castello, this trattoria has a long history of serving good Piedmontese cooking. The menu changes regularly, but whatever's available will be flavorfully prepared. The *insalata di gallina* (chicken salad) has the tang of mustard, and the *stinco di vitello* (veal shin) is redolent of thyme. ⊠ *Via Bellezia 37,* ☎ *011/4366553. AE, DC, MC, V. Closed Sun. and Aug. No lunch Mon.*

$–$$ ✕ **Porto di Savona.** Look for this centuries-old tavern under the arcades of vast Piazza Vittorio Veneto, where it once served as a terminal for the Turin–Savona stagecoach line. The small street-level and upstairs dining rooms have a decidedly old-fashioned air; the marble stairs are well worn and the walls are decked with period photos of Old Turin. Customers sit at long wooden tables to eat home-style Piedmontese cooking, including gnocchi with the owner's handmade Gorgonzola and *bollito misto* (mixed boiled meats). The Barbera house wine is good. ⊠ *Piazza Vittorio Veneto 2,* ☎ *011/8173500. MC, V. Closed Mon. and 2 wks Aug. No lunch Tues.*

$$$$ ▥ **Jolly Hotel Principi di Piemonte.** Over a half century old, the central Principi is one of the best hotels in town and often caters to a famous clientele. The rooms, elegantly furnished in antique style, are spacious and light, with high ceilings. ⊠ *Via Gobetti 15, 10123,* ☎ *011/5629693,* FAX *011/5620270. 99 rooms, 8 suites. Restaurant, bar, minibars. AE, DC, MC, V.*

$$$ ▥ **Turin Palace.** You're right across from the train station at this century-old building in the center of town. Quiet, spacious, and well-furnished rooms have high ceilings and feature either leather-and-wood classic modern style or Imperial Louis XV furnishings. ⊠ *Via Sacchi 8, 10128,* ☎ *011/5625511,* FAX *011/5612187. 123 rooms. Restaurant, bar, minibars. AE, DC, MC, V.*

$$$ ▥ **Victoria.** Uncommon style and comfort are the hallmarks of this bou-
★ tique hotel, personally decorated and supervised by the caring management to create the atmosphere of a refined town house. The newer wing has a grand marble staircase and rooms individually decorated according to a theme, from romantic to clubby. The same attention to detail is given to the older rooms and to the attractive sitting room and breakfast room overlooking a small park. ⊠ *Via Nino Costa 4, 10123,* ☎ *011/5611909,* FAX *011/5611806. 90 rooms. Bar, breakfast room. AE, DC, MC, V.*

$$ ▥ **Genio.** This 120-year-old building is done in a smart, modern style. The rooms are large and bright, with big, comfortable beds. There's no restaurant, but you're in the hub of town center. ⊠ *Corso Vittorio Emanuele 47, 10125,* ☎ *011/6505771,* FAX *011/6508264. 100 rooms, 3 suites. Bar, minibars, meeting room. AE, DC, MC, V.*

$$ ▥ **Liberty.** Liberty is the Italian term that refers to the Art Nouveau style, and this small, conveniently located hotel maintains that style in turn-of-the-century furnishings and an old-world atmosphere, enhanced by the Anfossi family's attentive courtesy. The hotel is a favorite of academics, artists, and others who appreciate its solid, old-fashioned comfort. ⊠ *Via Pietro Micca 15, 10121,* ☎ *011/5628801,* FAX *011/ 5628163. 35 rooms. Restaurant, bar. AE, DC, MC, V.*

Nightlife and the Arts

Music

Classical music concerts are held in the famous **Conservatorio Giuseppe Verdi** (⊠ Via Mazzini 11, ☎ 011/832632) throughout the year, but mainly in the winter months. The **Salone della Musica Torino** music festival (September 3–24) also highlights classical music; call the organizers (☎ 011/4424715) for specifics. Sacred music and some modern religious pieces are performed in the **Duomo** (☞ Sights to See, *above*) on Sunday evening; these are usually advertised in the vestibule or in the local edition of Turin's nationally distributed daily, *La Stampa*.

Nightclubs

A plush after-hours venue for Turin's smart set, **Hennessy** (⊠ Strada Traforo del Pino 23, ☎ 011/8998522) is in the upscale Superga residential district; it's open Thursday, Friday, and Saturday nights until late. The aptly named **Big Club** (⊠ Corso Brescia 28, ☎ 011/2485656) is a large disco that also hosts rock concerts. Hot Latin music, often live, is dished up with gusto every day but Monday at **Sabor Latino** (⊠ Via Stradella 10, ☎ 011/852327). **Pick Up** (⊠ Via Barge 8, ☎ 011/4472204) caters to a mixed crowd of young Turinese, university students, and visitors; it, too, closes Monday.

Opera

The **Teatro Regio** (☎ 011/88151, FAX 011/88105214), one of Italy's leading opera houses, begins its season in December. You can buy tickets for most performances (premieres are sold out well in advance) at the box office.

Outdoor Activities and Sports

Boating

Turin makes good use of the Po's recreational potential for boating. The **Lega Navale di Torino** (Turin Boating League, ⊠ Corso Unione Sovietica 316, ☎ 011/530979) organizes courses and special races throughout the summer.

Golf

There are several courses in the Turin area. Three 18-hole courses are northwest of the city, one at **La Mandria,** 18 km (11 mi) northwest (☎ 011/9235719), and two at **Fiano Torinese,** 20 km (12 mi) northwest (☎ 011/9235440).

Soccer

Turin's two professional soccer clubs, Juventus and Torino, play their games in the **Stadio delle Alpi** (⊠ 6 km/4 mi northwest of city), a stadium that was used during the World Cup of 1990. Juventus is one of Italy's best teams, and there is fierce rivalry among its supporters and those of visiting clubs, especially with Milan's Inter and AC Milan teams. Home matches are usually played on Sunday afternoons during the season, which runs from late August to mid-May. The **tourist office** (⊠ Via Roma 226, ☎ 011/535901) can provide information on where to find tickets, which are difficult to come by.

Shopping

Antiques

Piazza San Carlo, Via Po, and Via Maria Vittoria are lined with antiques shops, some—but not all—specializing in 18th-century furniture and domestic items.

Boutiques

Most people know that Turin produces more than 75% of Italy's cars, but they are often unaware that it is also a clothing manufacturing city. Top-quality boutiques stocking local, national, and international lines are clustered along Via Roma and Via Garibaldi.

Food and Flea Markets

Go to the famous **Balon Flea Market** (⊠ Piazza Repubblica) on a Saturday morning for some excellent bargains in secondhand books and clothing and some stalls selling local specialties such as gianduiotti. The second Sunday of every month, a special **antiques market** sets us shop in Piazza Repubblica.

WEST FROM TURIN

Stupinigi

⑯ *8 km (5 mi) southwest of Turin.*

The **Palazzina di Caccia** in the town of Stupinigi is an elaborate building built by Juvarra in 1729 as a hunting lodge for the House of Savoy. It is more like a royal villa, with its many wings, landscaped gardens, and surrounding forests. This regal aspect was not lost on Napoléon, who lived here before claiming the crown of Italy. The castle interior is sumptuously decorated and today houses a collection of art and furniture in the matter-of-factly named **Museo d'Arte e Ammobiliamento** (Museum of Art and Furniture). Take Bus 41 from Stazione Porta Nuova. ☎ *011/3581220.* ✑ *10,000 lire.* ◷ *Tues.–Sun. 9–11:50 and 2–4:20.*

Rivoli

⑰ *13 km (8 mi) west of Turin.*

The Savoy court was based in Rivoli in the Middle Ages. The 14th- to 15th-century **Casa del Conte Verde,** right in the center of town, is a good example of medieval architecture of the transitional period, when its defensive function was giving way to the decorative. To get to Rivoli, take Tram 1 from downtown Turin, then Bus 36.

The 18th-century Savoy castle, built in the Baroque style under the direction of Juvarra, now houses the **Museo d'Arte Moderna** (Modern Art Museum), which contains many examples of 20th-century Italian art. The Futurist movement is particularly well represented. ✉ *Piazza del Castello,* ☎ *011/9581547.* ✑ *10,000 lire.* ◷ *Tues.–Fri. 10–5, weekends 10–7, 1st and 3rd Thurs. of month 10–10.*

Abbazia di Sant'Antonio di Ranverso

⑱ *23 km (14 mi) west of Turin, 10 km (6 mi) west of Rivoli.*

The abbey was originally an abbey hospital, founded in the 12th century by the Hospitalers of St. Anthony to care for victims of St. Anthony's Fire, a crippling disease contracted by eating contaminated grains. Pilgrims came here over the centuries for cures or, sometimes, to offer thanks for a miraculous recovery. The 15th-century fresco decorations, with their lifelike depictions of pilgrims and saints, retain their original colors. ✉ *Battigliera Alta, Avigliana exit off autostrada and Battigliera Alta exit off S25,* ☎ *011/9367450.* ✑ *5,000 lire.* ◷ *Tues.– Sun. 9–12:30 and 2–5.*

Avigliana

⑲ *29 km (18 mi) west of Turin, 6 km (4 mi) west of the Abbazia di Sant'Antonio di Ranverso.*

Perhaps due to its attractive setting, medieval Avigliana was a favorite of the Savoys up until the mid-15th century. Medieval houses still line the twisting and narrow streets.

Casa della Porta Ferrata, on the street of the same name, is a well-preserved example of Piedmont Gothic domestic architecture: Notice how the fascination with narrow, pointed arches is carried through even to private houses.

Outdoor Activities and Sports

GOLF

Avigliana has a well-laid-out 18-hole golf course, **Le Fronde** (☎ 011/935083), closed January and February.

Sacra di San Michele

★ **⑳** *43 km (27 mi) west of Turin, 14 km (8½ mi) west of Avigliana.*

A car is essential for an excursion to the Abbey of St. Michael. San Michele was built on Monte Pirchiriano in the 11th century to stand out: It is the most prominent location for miles around. When monks came to enlarge the abbey, they had to build part of the structure on supports more than 90 ft high—an engineering feat that was famous in medieval Europe and still impressive today. By the 12th century, this important abbey controlled 176 churches in Italy, France, and Spain, and one of the abbeys under its influence was Mont Saint-Michel in France. Because of the abbey's strategic position, it came under numerous attacks over the next five centuries, and it was eventually abandoned in 1622. It was restored in the late 19th and early 20th centuries.

From **Porta dello Zodiaco,** a splendid Romanesque doorway decorated with the signs of the zodiac, you climb 150 steps, past 12th-century sculptures, to reach the church. On the left side of the interior 16th-century frescoes are religious subjects representing New Testament themes; on the right are stories depicting the founding of the church. Go down to the crypt to see the 9th- to 12th-century chapels. ✉ *Donation requested.* ☉ *Apr.–Sept., daily 9–noon and 2–7; Oct.–Mar., daily 9–noon and 2–dusk.*

Saluzzo

㉑ *58 km (36 mi) southwest of Turin.*

The older and more interesting part of Saluzzo hugs a hilltop in the Po Valley and is crowned by a castle. This town of time-worn russet brick was once a flourishing medieval center and was seat of a ducal court during the Renaissance. The narrow, winding streets and frescoed houses, the Gothic cathedral and the church of **San Giovanni,** and the 15th-century **Casa Cavassa,** a richly decorated palace that now houses a museum, take you back in time to the age of chivalry.

Knights and damsels of old, heroes and heroines of an allegorical poem written by Marquis Tommaso III of Saluzzo, humanist lord of the castle, parade in full costume in the 15th-century frescoes in the **Sala del Barone** (Baron's Hall) of the **Castello di Manta** (Castle of Manta), only 4 km (2½ mi) south of Saluzzo. The castle's exterior is austere, but inside are frescoes and other interior decorations. ✉ *Via al Castello, Manta,* ☎ *0175/87822.* ✉ *5,000 lire.* ☉ *Tues.–Sun. 10–1 and 2–6. Closed last 2 wks in Dec. and Jan.*

Sestriere

㉒ *93 km (58 mi) west of Turin, 32 km (20 mi) east of Briançon.*

In the early 1930s, before skiing became a sport for the commoners, the patriarch of the FIAT automobile dynasty had this resort built, with two distinctive tower hotels and ski facilities that have been developed into some of the best in the Alps. The resort lacks the charm of other, older Alpine centers, overdevelopment added some eyesores, and the mountains don't have the striking beauty of those in the Valle d'Aosta. But skiers have an excellent choice of trails, some of them crossing the border into France.

Lodging

$$$$ 🏨 **Principi di Piemonte.** Large and elegant, this luxurious hotel is on the slopes above the town, near the lifts and golf course. Its secluded location heightens the sense of exclusivity, a quality appreciated by a very stylish clientele. The restaurant and a cozy bar invite après-ski relaxation. ✉ *Via Sauze, 10058,* ☎ *0122/7941,* FAX *0122/755411. 94 rooms. Restaurant, bar. AE, DC, MC, V. Closed Easter–June and Sept.–Dec. 21.*

$$ 🏨 **Miramonti.** Nearly every room has a terrace at this pleasant, central modern chalet. The ample, comfortable rooms are done in traditional mountain style, featuring lots of wood paneling and coordinated floral-print fabrics. ✉ *Via Cesana 3, 10058,* ☎ *0122/755333,* FAX *0122/755375. 30 rooms. Restaurant, bar. DC, MC, V.*

Outdoor Activities and Sports

GOLF

Sestriere's 18-hole golf course (☎ 0122/755170) is open from mid-June to mid-September.

SKIING

At 6,670 ft, this resort was built in the late 1920s under the auspices of Turin's Agnelli clan. Although it's near the French border, it is just 93 km (58 mi) west of Turin. The slopes get good snow from November through May. A quaint village with slate-roof houses, **Claviere** (✉ 17 km/11 mi west of Sestriere) is one of Italy's oldest ski resorts. Its slopes overlap with those of the French resort of Montgenèvre.

Bardonecchia

㉓ *36 km (22 mi) northwest of Sestriere, 89 km (55 mi) west of Turin, 20 km (12 mi) south of Modane.*

This sunny town is one of Italy's oldest winter ski resorts, attracting hardy sports enthusiasts from Turin ever since the 1920s. It is near the entrance to the Fréjus train and automobile tunnels.

Lodging

$$ 🏨 **Asplenia.** Skiers love this small, modern version of a mountain
★ chalet, near the town center and the ski lifts. The ample rooms are comfortably furnished, with a small entryway and a balcony affording beautiful views. ✉ *Viale della Vittoria 31, 10052,* ☎ *0122/999870,* FAX *0122/ 96192. 19 rooms, 4 suites. MC, V. Closed Easter–May and Sept.–Nov.*

$$ 🏨 **Des Geneys-Splendid.** One of the best hotels in the area is in a private park near the town center. Its 1930s style is evident in the arched windows on the ground floor, the stucco walls, and the long wrought-iron balconies. The public rooms are spacious and comfortable, and there's a playroom for children. ✉ *Via Einaudi 21, 10052,* ☎ *0122/ 99001,* FAX *0122/999295. 57 rooms. Restaurant, bar. DC, MC, V. Closed mid-Apr.–mid-June and mid-Sept.–mid-Dec.*

$$ 🏨 **Riky.** This central, modern hotel has lots to offer: good service, comfy and spacious rooms, a good restaurant, and pleasant public rooms, including a children's playroom equipped with video games. There's a solarium and a piano bar with a cozy fireplace. It caters mainly to longer stays at half-board rates, and offers excellent low-season rates (nearly half price) for people staying at least a week. ✉ *Via della Vittoria 22, 10052,* ☎ *0122/999353. 76 rooms. Restaurant, bar. AE, DC, V. Closed Apr.–June and Sept.–mid-Dec.*

VALLE D'AOSTA, THE MATTERHORN, AND MONT BLANC

The unspoiled beauty of the highest peaks in the Alps competes with the magnificent scenery of Italy's oldest national park in the Valle d'Aosta, a semiautonomous, French-speaking region tucked away at the border with France and Switzerland. Luckily, you don't have to choose—the region is small, and so you can fit ski, après-ski, and wild ibex into one memorable trip. The main Aosta Valley, largely on an east–west axis, is hemmed in by high mountains where glaciers have gouged out 14 tributary valleys, six to the north and eight to the south. A car is very helpful here, but take care: Distances here are relative, short horizontally, as the crow flies, and much longer vertically, on steep slopes over tortuous roads.

En Route   Coming up from Turin, beyond Ivrea, the road takes you through countryside that becomes hillier and hillier, passing through steep ravines guarded by brooding, romantic castles. Pont St. Martin, about 18 km (11 mi) north of Ivrea, is the beginning of French-speaking territory.

Bard

㉔ *3 km (2 mi) beyond Pont St. Martin.*

A few minutes beyond the French-speaking village of Pont St. Martin, you pass through the narrow Gorge de Bard and reach the **Forte di Bard** (closed to the public), a 19th-century reconstruction of a fort that stood for eight centuries, serving the Savoys for six of them. In 1800 Napoléon entered Italy through this valley and used the cover of darkness to get his artillery units past the castle unnoticed. Ten years later he remembered this inconvenience and had the fortress destroyed.

Saint Vincent

㉕ *88 km (55 mi) north of Turin, 46 km (29 mi) north of Ivrea, 97 km (60 mi) northwest of Vercelli.*

The town of Saint Vincent has been a popular spa resort since the late 18th century. Its main game these days is the **Casinò de la Vallée,** one of Europe's largest gambling casinos. Remember to pack your black tie—and plenty of lire.

Dining and Lodging

$$$$ **✕ Batezar.** With only eight tables, this restaurant is considered by some
★   to be one of Italy's best. The ambience is rustic yet elegant, with arches and beamed ceilings enhanced by local antiques and fine crystal and silver place settings. The menu is seasonal, and the chef prepares set menus if you have trouble choosing. For a starter, try the *tazzarella* (a small pizza with porcini mushrooms, mozzarella, and truffles) or fettuccine with herbs, artichokes, and fillet of rabbit. Book well in advance. ⊠ *Via Marconi 1, steps from casino,* ☎ *0166/513164. Reservations essential. Jacket and tie. AE, DC, MC, V. Closed Wed., June 10–30, and Nov. 15–30. No lunch weekdays.*

$$$$ **⌂ Billia.** A luxury belle-epoque hotel with pseudo-Gothic touches, the Billia is in a park in the middle of town and connected directly to the casino by a passageway. Half the rooms are done in modern and half in period decor, replete with all creature comforts. The hotel has extensive facilities, including a conference center and a private fishing reserve on a nearby mountain stream. ⊠ *Viale Piemonte 72, 11027,* ☎ *0166/5231,* FAX *0166/523799. 250 rooms. 3 restaurants, bar, pool, sauna, tennis courts, health club, fishing, billiards, casino, nightclub. AE, DC, MC, V.*

$–$$ ⊞ **Elena.** The central location is the selling point of this hotel near the casino. The spacious rooms, some with balconies and/or king-size beds, are decorated with color-coordinated fabrics in a comfortable modern style and have air-conditioning. ⊠ *Via Biavaz 2 (Piazza Zerbion), 11027,* ☎ *0166/512140,* ℻ *0166/537459. 48 rooms. Restaurant, bar. AE, DC, MC, V. Closed Nov.–Feb.*

Breuil-Cervinia

㉖ *30 km (18 mi) north of Saint Vincent, 27 km (17 mi) north of Châtillon.*

Breuil-Cervinia is a village at the base of the Matterhorn (Monte Cervino, in Italian; Mont Cervin in French). Like the village, the famous peak straddles the border between Italy and Switzerland, and all sightseeing and skiing facilities are operated jointly. Splendid views of the peak can be seen from **Plateau Rosa** and the **Cresta del Furggen**, both of which can be reached by cable car from the center of Breuil-Cervinia. While many locals complain that the tourist facilities and the condominiums in the village have changed the face of their beloved Breuil, most would agree that the cable car has given them access to climbing and off-trail skiing in ridges that were once inaccessible.

Lodging

$$$$ ⊞ **Hermitage.** A marble relief of St. Theodolus at the entrance reminds
★   guests that this was the site of the saint's hermitage. But asceticism has given way to sybaritic comfort and elegance in what is now one of the most exclusive hotels in this Alpine region. A Relais & Châteaux property, it has the look and atmosphere of a relaxed but posh family chalet, with a fire always glowing in the enormous hearth and a romantic, candlelit dining room. The decor includes rustic antiques, petit-point upholstery, and the Neyroz family's collection of paintings of the Matterhorn. The bright bedrooms have balconies; suites have antique fireplaces and 18th-century furnishings. ⊠ *Strada Cristallo, 11021,* ☎ *0166/948998,* ℻ *0166/949032. 36 rooms. Restaurant, bar, indoor pool, sauna, health club, meeting rooms. AE, DC, MC, V. Closed May–June and Sept. 10–Nov.*

$$$–$$$$ ⊞ **Bucaneve.** This small, central hotel, catering to longer stays, is decorated in typical mountain style, with lots of wood paneling throughout, cheery floral upholstery in spacious lounges, and terraces dripping with geraniums. Après-ski, there's a restaurant (with half board) and a cozy bar with a big fireplace and pianist in the evening. ⊠ *Piazza Jumeaux 10, 11021,* ☎ *0166/949119,* ℻ *0166/948308. 26 rooms. Restaurant, bar, piano bar, sauna, exercise room. AE, MC, V. Closed May–July and Sept.–Oct.*

$$$–$$$$ ⊞ **Gran Hotel Cristallo.** An elegantly modern hotel high above town, the Cristallo has spectacular views. You can try local specialties like fonduta at the two restaurants and relax poolside year-round in this place noted for its feeling of pampered comfort. ⊠ *Via Piolet 6, 11021,* ☎ *0166/943411,* ℻ *0166/948377. 102 rooms. 2 restaurants, bar, indoor and outdoor pools, 2 tennis courts, exercise room, meeting room. AE, DC, MC, V. Closed May–June and Sept.–Nov.*

$$$ ⊞ **Chalet Valdotain.** About a mile outside the town on the road from Châtillon, this Alpine chalet has wooden balconies and snug rooms with terrific views of the Matterhorn. It is known for good food and a friendly atmosphere. ⊠ *Località Lago Bleu 2, 11021,* ☎ *0166/949428,* ℻ *0166/ 948874. 35 rooms. Restaurant, bar, pool, health club, sauna. AE, MC, V. Closed May and Oct.–Nov.*

$$–$$$ ⊞ **Les Neiges D'Antan.** In a pine wood at Perrères, just outside Cervinia,
★   this small, rustic family-run inn is quiet and cozy, with lots of wood, three big fireplaces, and a nice view of the Matterhorn. There are no

TVs in the rooms: "It disturbs the atmosphere," says one of the proprietors. There's an excellent restaurant serving local specialties, such as fonduta, *zuppa Valpellinentze* (a peasant soup of bread, cabbage, and Fontina cheese), and an opulent antipasto (local salami, country pâté, and tomino cheese). ⊠ *Località Perrères, 3½ km (2 mi) outside Cervinia, 11021,* ☎ *0166/948775,* 🖷 *0166/948852. 28 rooms. Restaurant, bar. AE, MC, V. Closed May 15–June 25 and Sept. 8–Dec. 5.*

Outdoor Activities and Sports

CLIMBING

Serious climbers can make the ascent of the Matterhorn from Breuil-Cervinia after registering with the local mountaineering officials at the tourist office (☞ Visitor Information *in* Piedmont/Valle d'Aosta A to Z, *below*). This climb is for skilled and experienced climbers only.

SKIING

Because its slopes border the Cervino glacier, this resort at the foot of the Matterhorn offers year-round skiing.

Castello Fénis

★ ㉗ *17 km (11 mi) west of Saint Vincent.*

The best-preserved fortress in the Valle d'Aosta, the many-turreted castle of Castello Fénis was built in the mid-14th century by Aimone di Challant, a member of a prolific family that was related to the Savoys. This castle is the sort imagined by schoolchildren, with pointed turrets, portcullises, and spiral staircases. The 15th-century courtyard has a stairway leading to a loggia (open walkway) with wooden balconies. Inside you can see the medieval kitchen, with much of the original cooking equipment, and a collection of weapons in the armory. If you have time to visit only one castle in the Valle d'Aosta, this should be it, even though parts of it may be closed for restoration. ☎ *0165/764263.* 🖷 *4,000 lire.* ☉ *Apr.–Sept., Wed.–Mon. 9:30–6 (group tour every ½ hr); Oct.–Mar., Wed.–Mon. 10–5 (group tour every hr).*

En Route The highway continues climbing through the Valle d'Aosta to the town of Aosta itself. The road at this point is heading almost due west, with rivulets from the wilderness reserve Parco Nazionale del Gran Paradiso streaming down from the left to join the Dora Baltea River, one of the major tributaries of the Po. Be careful driving here in late spring, when melting snow can turn some of these streams into torrents.

Aosta

㉘ *12 km (7 mi) west of Castello Fénis, 30 km (18 mi) west of Saint Vincent.*

Aosta stands at the junction of two important trade routes from France to Italy—from the valleys of the Rhône and the Isère. Its significance as a trading post was recognized by the Romans, who built a garrison here in the 1st century BC. The present-day layout of streets in this small city, tucked away in the Alps more than 644 km (400 mi) from Rome, is the clearest example of Roman street planning in Italy. Well-preserved Roman walls form a perfect rectangle around the center of Aosta, and the regular pattern of streets reflects its role as a military stronghold. St. Anselm was born in Aosta, and later became archbishop of Canterbury in England.

At the eastern entrance to town, in the Piazza Arco d'Augusto commanding a fine view over Aosta and the mountains, is the **Arco di Augusto** (Arch of Augustus), built in 25 BC to mark Rome's victory over the Celtic Salassi tribe. The sloping roof, quite clearly, is not original—

an early effort at preservation of the site, it was added in 1716 in an attempt to keep rain from seeping between the stones.

The **Collegiata di Sant'Orso** (Collegiate Church of St. Orso) is the sort of church that has layers of history in its architecture. Originally there was a 6th-century chapel on this site, founded by the Archdeacon Orso, a local saint. Most of this structure was destroyed or hidden when an 11th-century church was erected over it. This church, in turn, was encrusted with Gothic, and later Baroque, features, leaving the church a jigsaw puzzle of styles, but, surprisingly, not a chaotic jumble. The 11th-century features are almost untouched in the crypt, and if you go up the stairs on the left from the main church you can see the 11th-century frescoes (ask the sacristan for entrance). These restored frescoes depict the life of Christ and the Apostles: Although only the tops are visible, you can see the expressions on the faces of the disciples. Take the doorway by the entrance to the crypt to see the crowning glory of Sant'Orso, the 12th-century **cloister**. Next to the church, it is enclosed by some 40 stone columns with masterfully carved capitals representing Old and New Testament themes and scenes from the life of St. Orso. ⊠ *Via Sant'Orso,* ☎ *0165/362026.* ⊙ *Wed. 9:30–noon and 2–5:30, Sat. 9–7.*

The huge **Roman Porta Pretoria** is a remarkable relic of the Roman era. The area between the inner and outer gates was used as a mini–parade ground for the changing of the guard. ⊠ *Western end of Via Sant' Anselmo.*

The 72-ft-high ruin of the facade of the **Teatro Romano** (Roman Theater) guards the ruins of the 1st-century BC **amphitheater**, which once held 20,000 spectators. Only seven of the amphitheater's original 60 arches remain, and these are built onto the facade of the adjacent convent of the sisters of San Giuseppe. The convent usually allows visitors in to see these arches (ask at the entrance or call 0165/362149 to set up in advance). ⊠ *Via de Baillage.*

Aosta's **Duomo** dates from the 10th century, but all that remains from that period are the campaniles. The decoration inside is mainly Gothic, but the main attraction of the cathedral predates that era by 1,000 years: A carved ivory diptych (devotional work with two images) showing the Roman Emperor Honorius and dating from AD 406 is among the many ornate objects housed in the **treasury**. ⊠ *Via Monsignor de Sales,* ☎ *0165/40251.* ⊙ *Treasury Mon.–Sat. 10–noon and 3–6, Sun. 3–5:45.*

Dining and Lodging

$$ ★ ✗ **Piemonte.** A small restaurant in the center of town, the Piemonte has a welcoming atmosphere and rustic decor. Heartwarming dishes might include *crespelle alla valdostana* (crepes with cheese) and *camoscio* (chamois) with polenta. ⊠ *Via Porta Pretoria 13,* ☎ *0165/40111. MC, V. Closed Sun.*

$$ ✗ **Vecchio Ristoro.** The chef-proprietor of this central converted mill furnished with antiques and a large ceramic stove takes pride in creative versions of regional favorites. Among them may be *petto di faraona in crosta* (breast of guinea hen in a crisp potato crust) and *pizzoccheri* (buckwheat pasta), a specialty of his native Lombardy. ⊠ *Via Tourneuve 4,* ☎ *0165/33238. AE, DC, MC, V. Closed Sun. No lunch Mon.*

$ ✗ **La Brasserie du Commerce.** Small, lively, and informal, this place is in the heart of Aosta, near central Piazza E. Chanoux. On a sunny summer day try to get a table on the terrace. Typical valley dishes, such as fonduta, are on the menu, together with a wide range of vegetable dishes and salads. ⊠ *Via de Tillier 10,* ☎ *0165/35613. Reservations not accepted. MC, V. Closed Sun.*

$ ✕ **Taverna Nando.** A wine cellar with wooden floors and vaulted ceilings, this family-run tavern is in the center of Aosta, and it has a terrace for outdoor dining. Try regional specialties such as fonduta, *carbonada* (veal stew), and *cervo* (venison) with mushrooms. ⊠ *Via de Tillier 41,* ☎ *0165/44455. AE, DC, MC, V. Closed Thurs. and June.*

$$$ ▦ **Holiday Inn Aosta.** This modern, comfortable, and highly regarded hotel has the advantages of a central location and rooms with the chain's predictable amenities. There's local color, however, in the attractive Provençal fabrics and the views of the mountains. There are rooms equipped for people with disabilities. ⊠ *Corso Battaglione Aosta 30, 11100,* ☎ *0165/236356,* ℻ *0165/236337. 50 rooms. Restaurant, bar. AE, DC, MC, V.*

$$ ▦ **Milleluci.** A small, cozy, family-run hotel, Milleluci is set in its own
★ garden on a hillside overlooking Aosta, next to Castello Jocteau and with good views of the city and mountains. A huge brick hearth and rustic wooden beams highlight the lounge. Bedrooms are bright, with prints *de Provence* and attractive wood fittings. The hotel provides breakfast only. ⊠ *Località Roppoz 15, 11100,* ☎ *0165/235278,* ℻ *0165/ 235284. 15 rooms. Bar, tennis court. AE, MC, V. CP.*

$ ▦ **Rayon de Soleil.** Saraillon, a residential district in the hills above Aosta, is the setting for this traditional redbrick mountain hotel in a park. There are excellent views from the rooms, which are large, bright, and quiet. Furnishings in mellow oak are solid and comfortable. There are rooms equipped for guests with disabilities. ⊠ *Via Bernardo, Saraillon, 11100,* ☎ *0165/262247,* ℻ *0165/236085. 45 rooms. Restaurant, bar, pool. AE, DC, MC, V. Closed Nov. and Jan.*

Nightlife and the Arts

Each summer a series of **concerts** is held in different venues around the city. Organ recitals in July and August attract performers of world renown. Call the tourist board (⊠ Piazza E. Chanoux 8, ☎ 0165/ 236627) for information.

Shopping

Aosta and the surrounding countryside are famous for wood carvings and wrought-iron work. There is a permanent **crafts exhibition** in the arcades of Piazza E. Chanoux, in the heart of Aosta; it's a good place to pick up a bargain. Each year, on the last two days of January, the whole town turns out for the **Sant'Orso Fair,** when all sorts of crafts are on sale, including handmade lace from nearby Cogne, carved wood and stonework, and brightly colored woolens.

Courmayeur

★ ㉙ *35 km (21 mi) northwest of Aosta, 24 km (15 mi) from Chamonix.*

The main attraction of Courmayeur is a knock-'em-dead view of Europe's tallest peak, Monte Bianco, better known as Mont Blanc. The jet-set celebrities who flock here are following a tradition that dates from the late 17th century, when Courmayeur's natural springs first began to draw visitors. The scenic spectacle of the Alps gradually surpassed the springs as the biggest drawing point (the Alpine letters of the English poet Shelley were almost advertisements for the region), but the biggest change in the history of Courmayeur came in 1965, when the Mont Blanc tunnel opened. Now Courmayeur stands on one of the main routes from France into Italy, although the planners have managed to maintain some restrictions on wholesale development within the town.

Dining and Lodging

$$ ✕ **Cadran Solaire.** This charming restaurant in town center, in what was the oldest tavern in Courmayeur, has been renovated by the Garin family, owners of the Maison de Filippo (☞ Monte Bianco, *below*), to highlight the 17th-century stone vault, old wooden floor, and huge fireplace. The menu offers seasonal specialties and innovative interpretations of regional dishes, such as gnocchi *gratinati* (potato and ricotta dumplings) and *filetto di trota alle nocciole* (fillet of trout with hazelnuts). ⊠ *Via Roma 122,* ☎ *0165/844609. AE, MC, V. Closed Tues., May, and Oct.*

$$$$ 🏨 **Royal.** A classic mountain hotel in town center, the Royal is decorated with terraces, flowers, and wood paneling. Informal but elegant, it has modern rooms, a restaurant, and an evening piano bar. The hotel caters to longer stays with half- or full-board service. ⊠ *Via Roma 87, 11013,* ☎ *0165/846787,* ℻ *0165/842093. 92 rooms. Restaurant, bar, piano bar, minibars, pool, sauna, health club. AE, DC, MC, V. Closed wk after Easter–mid-June and mid-Sept.–Dec. 1. FAP, MAP.*

$$$–$$$$ 🏨 **Pavillon.** This is an elegant modern version of rustic chalet architecture, complete with warm golden-toned wood paneling, stylish furnishings, a clubby bar, and some stunning contemporary stained glass in the public areas and in the well-equipped health center. Full-board rates are good value. ⊠ *Strada Regionale 62, 11013,* ☎ *0165/846120,* ℻ *0165/846122. 50 rooms. Restaurant, bar, indoor pool, sauna, health club, meeting room. AE, DC, MC, V. Closed May–June 15 and Oct. 8–Nov. FAP.*

$$$ 🏨 **Palace Bron.** Set in a lovely pinewood above the town, this posh,
★ comfortable hotel is an ideal spot to relax. Guest rooms are bright and pretty, furnished with period pieces and local designs. The sitting room has picture windows with magnificent views of Mont Blanc, and for chilly winter nights, the recommended restaurant offers a cozy fireplace. There's a free shuttle between the hotel, town center, and ski lifts. ⊠ *Via Plan Gorret 14, 11013,* ☎ *0165/846742,* ℻ *0165/844015. 27 rooms. Restaurant, bar, piano bar, minibars, meeting room. AE, DC, MC, V. Closed May–June and Oct.–Nov.*

$$ 🏨 **Cresta et Duc.** A bright, modern Alpine hotel in town center, the Cresta features plenty of wooden terraces, flowers, and wooden furnishings. For fun and relaxation there's a billiards room and lounges. The rooms are large and warm, and the hotel offers good full- and half-board rates. ⊠ *Via Circonvallazione 7, 11013,* ☎ *0165/842585,* ℻ *0165/842591. 39 rooms . Restaurant, bar, minibars, billiards. AE, DC, MC, V. Closed Easter–June and mid-Sept.–mid-Dec.*

$$ 🏨 **Croux.** This bright, comfortable hotel is near the town center on the road leading to Mont Blanc. Half the rooms have balconies, the other half have great views of Mont Blanc. ⊠ *Via Circonvallazione 94, 11013,* ☎ *0165/846735,* ℻ *0165/845180. 33 rooms. Bar. AE, DC, MC, V. Closed mid-Apr.–June and Sept. 15–Dec. 20.*

Monte Bianco (Mont Blanc)

㉚ *3 km (2 mi) north of Courmayeur.*

At La Palud you can catch the cable car up to the top of Monte Bianco. In the summertime, if you get the inclination, once up top you can switch cable cars and descend into France. The Funivie La Palud whisks you up to the viewing platform at **Punta Helbronner** (more than 11,000 ft), which is also the border post with France. Mont Blanc's attraction is not so much its shape (much less distinctive than the Matterhorn) as its expanse and the vistas from the top. The next stage, as you pass into French territory, is particularly impressive: you dangle over a huge glacial snowfield (more than 2,000 ft below) and make your way

slowly to the viewing station above Chamonix. From this point you're
looking down into France, and if you change cable cars, you can make
your way down to Chamonix itself. The return trip covers the same
route, and the total time should be 90 minutes, weather permitting.
⊠ *Funivie La Palud*, ☎ *0165/89925*. ☒ *44,000 lire round-trip to Punta
Helbronner; 280 francs from Punta Helbronner to Chamonix.* ☉
*Hours change throughout year: daily from 7:20 to 8:50 AM–4:30 to
5:50 PM (Aug. 24–July 24, closed 12:40–2). Closed Nov. 2–Dec. 10.*

Dining

$$ ✕ **Maison de Filippo.** Here you'll find country-style home cooking in
a picturesque mountain house furnished with antiques. Reserve in ad-
vance, for it's one of the most popular restaurants in the Valle d'Aosta.
There is a set menu only, featuring a daily selection of specialties in-
cluding a wide choice of antipasti and pasta dishes, such as agnolotti
in various sauces and spaghetti *affumicata* (with salami and bacon).
⊠ *Entreves*, ☎ *0165/869797*, ℻ *0165/869719. Reservations essen-
tial. V. Closed Tues., June–July 6, and Nov.–mid-Dec.*

Outdoor Activities and Sports

SKIING

The famous **Courmayeur,** for the well-heeled, is well equipped and easy
to reach, just outside the Italian end of the Mont Blanc tunnel. The
skiing around Mont Blanc is particularly good, and the off-piste op-
tions are among the best in Europe.

Cogne and the Parco Nazionale del Gran Paradiso

③① *52 km (32 mi) southeast of Courmayeur, 27 km (17 mi) south of
Aosta.*

Cogne is the gateway to the Parco Nazionale del Gran Paradiso. This
huge park, once the domain of King Vittorio Emanuele II and bequeathed
to the nation after World War I, is one of Europe's most rugged and
unspoiled wilderness areas, with wildlife and many plant species pro-
tected by law. Try to visit in May, when spring flowers are in bloom
and most of the meadows are clear of snow. This is one of the few places
in Europe where you can see the ibex (a mountain goat with horns up
to 3 ft long) or the chamois, a small soft-skin antelope nearly driven
to extinction.

Outdoor Activities and Sports

HIKING

There's wonderful hiking to be done here, both on daylong excursions
and longer journeys with overnight stops in the park's mountain
refuges. The Cogne tourist office (☞ Visitor Information *in* Pied-
mont/Valle d'Aosta, *below*) has a wealth of information and trail maps
to help.

FORTIFIED CITIES OF THE PO PLAIN

Southeast of Turin, in the hilly wooded area around Asti known as the
Monferrato and in another, similar area around Alba known as the
Langhe, farther south, the rolling landscape is a patchwork of vine-
yards spotted with dark woods and dotted with little hill towns and
castles. This is wine country, producing Italy's most famous reds and
sparkling whites. And hidden away in the woods are the secret places
where hunters and their dogs unearth the precious, aromatic truffles
worth their weight in gold at Alba's truffle fair. To the north of these
hills, across the Po, are the cities of the plain. Beyond them lies Lago
Maggiore and eastward, across the Ticino River, is Milan.

Asti

32 *60 km (37 mi) southeast of Turin, 116 km (72 mi) northwest of Genoa, 127 km (78 mi) southwest of Milan.*

Asti is best known to Americans for its wines—excellent reds as well as the famous sparkling white Spumante—but its strategic position on trade routes between Turin, Milan, and Genoa has given it a broad economic base. In the 12th century, Asti began to develop as a republic, at a time when other Italian cities were also flexing their economic and military muscles. It flourished in the following century, when the inhabitants began erecting lofty towers for its defense, giving rise to the medieval nickname "city of 100 towers." In the center of Asti, some of these remain, among them the 13th-century **Torre Cometini** and the well-preserved **Torre Troyana,** a tall, slender tower attached to the **Palazzo Troya.**

Corso Vittorio Alfieri is Asti's main thoroughfare, running west–east across the city. This road, known in medieval times as Contrada Maestra, was built by the Romans. The 18th-century church of **Santa Caterina** (⊠ Western end of Corso Vittorio Alfieri) has incorporated one of the medieval towers, the **Torre Romana** (itself built on an ancient Roman base), as its bell tower.

The **Duomo** is an object lesson in the evolution of the Gothic architectural style. The cathedral, built in the early 14th century, is decorated mainly in a Gothic style that emphasizes geometry and verticality: Pointed arches and narrow vaults are counterbalanced by the earlier, Romanesque attention to balance and symmetry. The porch, on the south side of the cathedral facing the square, was built in 1470 and represents Gothic at its most florid and excessive. ☉ *Daily 8–noon and 3–7.*

The Gothic church of **San Secondo** (⊠ South of Corso Alfieri) is dedicated to Asti's patron saint, reputedly decapitated on the spot where the church now stands. Secondo is also patron of the city's favorite folklore and sporting event, the annual **Palio,** the colorful medieval-style horse race, held each year on the third Sunday of September in the vast Campo del Palio to the south of the church.

OFF THE BEATEN PATH	**ALBA –** Thirty kilometers (18 miles) southwest of Asti, this small town has a compact core studded with medieval towers and Gothic buildings, and a gracious old-world atmosphere. The town is the wine and truffle capital of the area. Visit in October for the National Truffle Fair, the Cento Torri Joust, and the Palio degli Asini (donkey races), held the first Sunday in October.

BAROLO – Some of Italy's finest wines are made within a radius of about 16 km (10 mi) of Alba. The zone is dotted with castles, and every town has a wineshop where you can sample the local vino. The Castello di Barolo houses a wineshop and a museum of wine making. ☉ *Fri.– Wed. 10–12:30 and 3–6:30. Closed Jan. and part of Feb.*

Dining and Lodging

$$$$ ✕ **Gener Neuv.** Family-run and one of Italy's top restaurants, the
★   Gener Neuv offers a sumptuous menu of regional specialties in a warm, welcoming atmosphere of rustic-style elegance, highlighted by excellent service, fine linen, silver, and crystal. The setting in a park on the bank of the Tanaro River is splendid, although it resulted in severe flood damage in 1994; the restaurant had to be rebuilt. Your choices may include agnolotti *ai tre stufati* (with a filling of ground rabbit, veal, and pork) and *faraona farcita alle erbe* (guinea fowl with herbs). The prix-fixe menu is good value ($$$) but does not include beverages. ⊠

Lungo Tanaro 4, ☎ *0141/557270,* 🖷 *0141/436723. AE, MC, V. Closed Mon. and Aug. No dinner Sun.*

$$$ ✕ **Falcon Vecchio.** There's been a restaurant in this ancient house in the historic center of Asti since the year 1670. Today, in intimate surroundings, the Falcon Vecchio serves rich local dishes that vary with the season. In fall and winter there are mushroom, truffle, and game dishes. Otherwise, there's a big selection of antipasti, grilled vegetables, and bollito misto (seven types of boiled meat, served with various sauces, and heaped on a steaming tray). ✉ *Via San Secondo 8,* ☎ *0141/593106. Reservations essential. AE, DC, MC, V. Closed Mon., 20 days in Aug., 10 days in Jan. No dinner Sun.*

$$$ 🏨 **Palio.** The hotel is in the historic heart of Asti and, though in an ultramodern building, it also has considerable character in individually decorated rooms featuring authentic antiques. Bathrooms in the mini-suites have whirlpool baths. ✉ *Via Cavour 106, 14100,* ☎ *0141/ 34371,* 🖷 *0141/34373. 29 rooms. AE, MC, V. Closed Aug. 10–25 and Dec. 23–Jan. 3.*

$–$$ 🏨 **Rainero.** An older hotel in the town center, near the station, Rainero has been under the same family management for three generations. It's fitted with cheerful modern furnishings, but has no restaurant. ✉ *Via Cavour 85, 14100,* ☎ *0141/353866,* 🖷 *0141/594985. 55 rooms. AE, DC, MC, V. Closed Jan. 1–8.*

Nightlife and the Arts
September is a month of fairs and celebrations in this famous wine city, and the **Asti Competition** in the middle of the month brings musicians, who perform in churches and concert halls. For 10 days in September, Asti is host to the **Douja d'Or National Wine Festival**—an opportunity to see Asti and celebrate the product that made it famous.

Shopping
The **Enoteca** on Piazza Alfieri, a square adjacent to Campo del Palio, is a wine center and shop, open Monday–Saturday 9–4:30, where you can try the range of Asti vintages, buy some as souvenirs or picnic ingredients, and even have a light snack.

En Route   From Alba double back to Asti to pick up the A21 autostrada. The road east from Asti to Alessandria is straight, skirting the southern edge of the Po plain, but for the first half of the drive you see to the south the green hillsides covered with vineyards. If you find yourself driving along this road during a thunderstorm (quite common on late summer afternoons), don't be surprised by the sound of explosions. Wine growers will often let off cannons loaded with blanks to persuade heavy clouds to rain, rather than build up and develop destructive hailstones.

Casale Monferrato

③③   *42 km (26 mi) northeast of Asti, 31 km (19 mi) north of Alessandria, 75 km (46½ mi) southwest of Milan.*

Casale Monferrato, strategically situated on the southern banks of the Po, was held by the Gonzagas, rulers of Mantua, before falling into the hands of the Savoys. The 16th-century **Torre Civica,** marking the heart of Casale Monferrato in Piazza Mazzini, commanded extensive views up and down the Po. From March 19 through March 29, the **Festa di San Giuseppe feast** brings artisans, musicians, and vendors of traditional sweets to the central Piazza del Castello.

Casale's most enlightening sight is the **Museo Israelitico** (Jewish Museum) in the women's section of the synagogue. Inside is a collection of documents and sacred art of a community that was vital to the prosperity of this mercantile city. The synagogue dates from the late 16th century, and neighboring buildings on the same street formed the Jewish ghetto of that period. ✉ *Vicolo Olper 44, south of the Torre Civica,* ☎ *0142/71807.* 🎫 *7,000 lire.* ⊙ *Feb.–Dec., Sun. 10–noon and 3:30–5:30; at other times by appointment only (with extra charge of 10,000 lire per person). Closed Sat.*

Vercelli

34 *23 km (14 mi) north of Casale Monferrato, 80 km (50 mi) northeast of Turin, 74 km (46 mi) southwest of Milan.*

Vercelli is the rice capital of Italy and of Europe itself. Northern Italy's mainstay, risotto, owes its existence to the crop that was introduced to this fertile area in the late Middle Ages. **Piazza Cavour** is the heart of the medieval city and former market square. It was to this small square that merchants across northern Italy came in the 15th century to buy bags of the novelty grain from the East. Rising above the low rooftops around the square is the **Torre dell'Angelo** (Tower of the Angel), whose forbidding military appearance reflects its origins as a watchtower. ✉ *Piazza Cavour.*

The **Duomo,** a mainly late 16th-century construction on the site of what was a 5th-century church, contains tombs of several Savoy rulers in an octagonal chapel along the south (right) wall. The cathedral's **Biblioteca** (chapter library; for entrance, see cathedral office) contains the "Gospel of St. Eusebius," a 4th-century document, and the *Codex Vercellensis,* an 11th-century book of Anglo-Saxon poetry. ✉ *Piazza Sant' Eusebio.*

The **Basilica di Sant'Andrea,** a Cistercian abbey church built in the early 13th century with funds from another Abbey of St. Andrew (in England), witnessed the growing influence of northern Europe on Italy. Sant'Andrea is one of Italy's earliest examples of Gothic architecture, which spread from the north but ran out of steam before getting much farther south than the Po plain. The church interior is a soaring flight of Gothic imagination, with slender columns rising up to the ribbed vaults of the high ceiling. Tombs along the side aisle continue the preoccupation with stylized decoration and relief work. The gardens on the north side (Corso de Gasperi side) of the basilica hold the remains of the abbey itself and some of the secondary buildings. It is only here that the unadulterated Gothic style is interrupted. The buildings surround a cloister in which you can see the pointed Gothic arches resting on the severe and more solid 12th-century Romanesque column bases. ✉ *Piazza G. Bicheri.* ⊙ *Daily 8–noon and 3–6:30.*

The **Città Vecchia** is a collection of narrow streets and alleys. Many of the houses are five centuries old, and you can see partly hidden gardens and courtyards beyond the wrought-iron gates.

OFF THE
BEATEN PATH

BORSA MERCI – You can take an unusual guided tour of the commodities market (✉ Via Zumaglini 4, ☎ 0161/5981), where rice has been traded for centuries. Call first to check on tour times.

Novara

35 *23 km (14 mi) northeast of Vercelli, 95 km (59 mi) northeast of Turin, 51 km (31 mi) west of Milan.*

Novara is the easternmost city in Piedmont, only about 10 km (6 mi) west of the Ticino River, forming the border with Lombardy. Milan is only 32 km (20 mi) beyond the border, and over the centuries the opposing attractions of this neighboring giant and of the regional capital, Turin, have given Novara a bit of an identity crisis. In the Middle Ages, Novara's pivotal position actually made it a battlefield. A major engagement took place as recently as 1849, when the Austrian forces from the east defeated the Piedmontese armies.

Much of the present city dates from the late 19th and early 20th centuries, although there are interesting buildings from earlier periods scattered around Novara. Novara's most famous landmark is the tall, slender cupola of **San Gaudenzio.** The church itself, built between 1577 and 1690, conforms to a Baroque design, with twisted columns and sumptuous statues. The main attraction for most people, though, is the **cupola,** built from 1840 to 1888 and soaring to a height of just under 400 ft. This spire is visible from everywhere in the city and the surrounding countryside, and has become as much a symbol of Novara as the Mole Antonelliana is of Turin.

The **Broletto,** a cluster of well-preserved late-medieval buildings, is next to the **Duomo,** of medieval origins but reconstructed in neoclassical style. The **Battistero** (Baptistery), just outside the entrance to the cathedral, shows its august age in a much more evident manner. This rotunda-shape building dates from the 5th century, although it was substantially enlarged in the 10th and 11th centuries. Recent restoration work has uncovered pre-Romanesque frescoes, more than 1,000 years old, decorating the inside walls. Their flat, two-dimensional style reflects the influence of Byzantine icons, and their restored colors add a frightening feel to the apocalyptic scenes depicted.

Lodging

$$ ▦ **Italia.** This modern hotel in the center of the city offers comfortable rooms and efficient service; the facilities cater mainly to businesspeople. There is a restaurant, and some rooms have extensive views of the town. ✉ *Via Solaroli 8, 28100,* ☎ *0321/399316,* ℻ *0321/ 399310. 55 rooms. Restaurant, bar. AE, DC, MC, V.*

PIEDMONT/VALLE D'AOSTA A TO Z

Arriving and Departing

By Bus

Turin's main **bus station** is on the corner of Corso Inghilterra and Corso Vittorio Emanuele. The Turin-based **SADEM** line (✉ Via della Repubblica 14, 10095 Grugliasco, Turin, ☎ 011/3111616) services the autostrada network to Milan and other, more distant destinations in Italy. The Turin-based **SAPAV** line (✉ Corso Torino 396, 10064 Pinerolo, Turin, ☎ 0121/322032) services the same area. **SITA** buses, part of the nationwide system, also connect Turin with the rest of Italy.

By Car

Italy's autostrada network links the region with the rest of Italy and neighboring France. Aosta, Turin, and Alessandria all have autostrada connections, with the **A4** heading east to Milan and the **A6** heading south to the Ligurian coast and Genoa. If you drive in from France or Switzerland, you pass through either the Mont Blanc or Grand Saint Bernard tunnels: These are two of the most scenically dramatic entrances to Italy.

For travel between the French and Italy borders, only a few passes are usable year-round in Piedmont/Valle d'Aosta: the Colle del Gran San Bernardo/Col du Grand St. Bernard (Martigny to Aosta on Swiss Highway E27 to Italian Highway S27, with 6-km/4-mi tunnel); the Mont

Blanc Tunnel (Chamonix to Courmayeur on French Highway 205 and Italian Highway 26D, with 12-km/7-mi tunnel); and the Traforo del Fréjus, which follows the Italian S335 west through a 13-km (8-mi) tunnel. There are plenty of other passes, but they are not reliable from at least November through April. Bear in mind this is very rough country, so no matter what time of year and what route, you are always advised to check with the tourist office or, in a pinch, with the police, to make sure roads are passable and safe.

By Plane

The region's only international airport, **Aeroporto Caselle** (☎ 011/5676361 information), is 18 km (11 mi) north of Turin. The airport is notoriously foggy in winter, and many flights are diverted to Genoa, on the coast, with bus connections provided to Turin.

BETWEEN THE AIRPORT AND DOWNTOWN
From Aeroporto Caselle, local buses to Turin arrive at the bus station on Corso Inghilterra in the city center.

By Train

Turin is on the main Paris–Rome express line and is also connected with Milan, only 90 minutes away on the fast train. The fastest trains cover the 667-km (400-mi) trip to Rome in about six hours, but most take about nine.

Getting Around

By Bus

SADEM and SAPAV (☞ Arriving and Departing by Bus, *above*) are the specialists in bus transportation in Piedmont and the Valle d'Aosta. **SAVDA** (⊠ Strada Ponte Suaz 6, 11100 Aosta, ☎ 0165/361244) specializes in mountain service, providing frequent links between Aosta, Turin, and Courmayeur.

By Car

Turin is the hub of all the transportation systems in Piedmont, with autostrada connections to the north, south, and east. Well-paved secondary roads (superstrade) run through the rest of the region, following the course of mountain valleys in many places. Sudden winter storms can close off some of the mountain stretches; contact local tourist offices (☞ Visitor Information, *below*) for up-to-date road information before you set out.

By Train

Services to the larger cities east of Turin are part of the extensive and reliable train network serving the Lombard Plain. West of the region's capital, however, the train services soon peter out in the steep mountain valleys. Continuing connections by bus serve these valleys, and information about train-bus mountain services can be obtained from train stations and tourist information offices.

Contacts and Resources

Car Rentals

TURIN
Avis (⊠ Corso Turati 15, ☎ 011/500852; ⊠ Aeroporto Caselle, ☎ 011/4701528). **Hertz** (⊠ Via Magellano 12, ☎ 011/502080; ⊠ Caselle Airport, ☎ 011/5678166).

Emergencies

Emergencies (☎ 113). **Police** (☎ 112).

Guided Tours

Turin's group and personally guided tours are organized by the city's tourist office (☞ Visitor Information, *below*).

ALPINE GUIDES

Alpine guides are not only recommended, they're essential if you're planning to traverse some of the dramatic ranges outside Saint Vincent, Courmayeur, or Breuil-Cervinia. Before embarking on an excursion (however short) into the mountains in these areas, contact the representative of the **CAI** (Club Alpinisti Italiani; ⊠ Piazza E. Chanoux 8, Aosta, ☎ 0165/40194) about the risks involved and the availability of an experienced guide. CAI information is also available at each tourist information office (☞ Visitor Information, *below*).

Late-Night Pharmacies

Pharmacies throughout the region take turns staying open late and on Sunday. Call ☎ 192 for the latest information, in Italian, on which are open.

Aosta Farmacia Centrale (⊠ Piazza E. Chanoux 35, Turin, ☎ 0165/262205). **Turin Farmacia Internazionale** (⊠ Via Carlo Alberto 24, Turin, ☎ 011/535144).

Visitor Information

Alba (⊠ Piazza Medford, 12051, ☎ 0173/35833, FAX 0173/363878). **Aosta** (⊠ Piazza E. Chanoux 8, 11100, ☎ 0165/236627, FAX 0165/34657). **Asti** (⊠ Piazza Alfieri 34, 14100, ☎ 0141/530357, FAX 0141/538200). **Bardonecchia** (⊠ Viale Vittoria 44, 10052, ☎ 0122/99032, FAX 0122/980612). **Breuil-Cervinia** (⊠ Via Carrel 29, 11201, ☎ 0166/949136, FAX 0166/949731). **Cogne** (⊠ Piazza E. Chanoux, 11012, ☎ 0165/74040, FAX 0165/749125). **Courmayeur** (⊠ Piazzale Monte Bianco 13, 11013, ☎ 0165/842060, FAX 0165/842072). **Novara** (⊠ Via Dominioni 4, 28100, ☎ 0321/623398, FAX 0321/39329). **Saluzzo** (⊠ Via Griselda 6, 12037, ☎ 0175/46710, FAX 0175/46718). **Turin** (⊠ Via Roma 226, 10141, ☎ 011/535901, FAX 011/530070; ⊠ Stazione Porta Nuova, 10121, ☎ 011/531327). **Vercelli** (⊠ Viale Garibaldi 90, 13100, ☎ 0161/64631, FAX 0161/64632).

BONUS MILES MAKE GREAT SOUVENIRS.

Earn Miles With Your MCI Card.

Take the MCI Card along on this trip and start earning miles for the next one. You'll earn frequent flyer miles on all your calls and save with the low rates you've come to expect from MCI. Before you know it, you'll be on your way to some other international destination.

Sign up for MCI by calling
1-800-FLY-FREE

Earn Frequent Flyer Miles.

Is this a great time, or what? :-)

Easy To Call Home.

1. To use your MCI Card, just dial the WorldPhone access number of the country you're calling from.
2. Dial or give the operator your MCI Card number.
3. Dial or give the number you're calling.

# Austria (CC)♦	022-903-012
# Belarus (CC)	
From Brest, Vitebsk, Grodno, Minsk	8-800-103
From Gomel and Mogilev regions	8-10-800-103
# Belgium (CC)♦	0800-10012
# Bulgaria	00800-0001
# Croatia (CC)★	0800-22-0112
# Czech Republic (CC)♦	00-42-000112
# Denmark (CC)♦	8001-0022
# Finland (CC)♦	08001-102-80
# France (CC)♦	0-800-99-0019
# Germany (CC)	0800-888-8000
# Greece (CC)♦	00-800-1211
# Hungary (CC)♦	00▼800-01411
# Iceland (CC)♦	800-9002
# Ireland (CC)	1-800-55-1001
# Italy (CC)♦	172-1022
# Kazakhstan (CC)	8-800-131-4321
# Liechtenstein (CC)♦	0800-89-0222
# Luxembourg	0800-0112
# Monaco (CC)♦	800-90-019
# Netherlands (CC)♦	0800-022-9122
# Norway (CC)♦	800-19912
# Poland (CC)∻	00-800-111-21-22
# Portugal (CC)∻	05-017-1234
Romania (CC)∻	01-800-1800
# Russia (CC)∻ ♦	
To call using ROSTELCOM ■	747-3322
For a Russian-speaking operator	747-3320
To call using SOVINTEL ■	960-2222
# San Marino (CC)♦	172-1022
# Slovak Republic (CC)	00-421-00112
# Slovenia	080-8808
# Spain (CC)	900-99-0014
# Sweden (CC)♦	020-795-922
# Switzerland (CC)♦	0800-89-0222
# Turkey (CC)♦	00-8001-1177
# Ukraine (CC)∻	8▼10-013
# United Kingdom (CC)	
To call using BT ■	0800-89-0222
To call using C&W ■	0500-89-0222
# Vatican City (CC)	172-1022

9 Milan, Lombardy, and the Lakes

Old and new are often unexpectedly fused in Italy, and in Lombardy, they marry magnificently. The 19th-century Lakes Como, Maggiore, and Garda— of opulent villas, exotic gardens, and Alpine vistas—remain the perfect escapes from Milan, Italy's business hub and crucible of chic. Pavia, Cremona, and Mantua, once proud medieval fortress towns dictating the fortunes of northern Italy, are today bustling centers of industry and commerce, still playing a key role in Italy's richest region.

Updated by
Fionn
Davenport

ONE IS TEMPTED TO DESCRIBE LOMBARDY as a place with something for everyone—Milan, capital of all that is new in Italy; the great Renaissance cities of the Po plain, Pavia, Cremona, and Mantua, where even the height of summer can be comparatively peaceful; and the lakes, where glacial waters framed by the Alps have been praised as the closest thing to Paradise by writers as varied as Virgil, Tennyson, and Hemingway.

"Nothing in the world," wrote Stendhal in 1817, "can be compared to the fascination of those burning summer days passed on the Milanese lakes, in the middle of those chestnut groves so green that they immerse their branches in the waves . . ." Millions of travelers have since agreed that, for sheer beauty, the lakes of Northern Italy—Como, Maggiore, Garda, and Orta—have few equals. Where else can you find magnificent 18th- and 19th-century villas on the shores of lakes bordered by toy villages and nestled under the foothills of mountains of almost Scandinavian grandeur? From Pliny to d'Annunzio, visitors have found this region—to quote Stendhal—"elegant, picturesque, and voluptuous."

The truth, of course, is more complicated. The lakes, home to dozens of resorts that were once Italy's—and Europe's—most fashionable, have preserved an astonishingly unspoiled beauty, often enhanced by sumptuous summer palaces and exotic formal gardens. Still, one cannot imagine Catullus returning to his "jewel" Sirmione, on Lago di Garda (Lake Garda), without being a little daunted by its development as a lively resort town. Milan can be disappointingly modern—rather too like the place you have come here to escape—but it is also the perfect blend of old and new, with historic buildings and art collections rivaling those in Florence and Rome.

More than 3,000 years ago—the date and the details are lost in the mysteries of Etruscan inscriptions—explorers from the highly civilized realm of Etruria in central Italy wandered northward beyond the River Po. The Etruscans extended their dominance into this region for hundreds of years but left little of their culture. They were succeeded by the Cenomanic Gauls, who, in turn, were conquered by the legions of Rome in the latter days of the Republic. The region became known as Cisalpine Gaul, and under the rule of Augustus it became a Roman province. Its warlike, independent people became citizens of Rome. Virgil, Catullus, and both the Plinys were born in the region during this relatively tranquil era.

The decline of the Roman Empire was followed by the invasions of the Huns and the Goths. Attila and Theodoric, in turn, gave way to the Lombards, who ceded their iron crown to Charlemagne as the emblem of his vast but unstable empire. Even before the fragile bonds that held this empire together had begun to snap, the cities of Lombardy were erecting walls in defense against the Hungarians and against each other. These communes did, however, form the Lombard League, which, in the 12th century, finally defeated Frederick Barbarossa.

Once the invaders had been defeated, new and even bloodier strife began. In each city the Guelphs (bourgeois supporters of the popes) and the Ghibellines (noble adherents to the so-called emperors) clashed with each other. The communes declined, and each fell under the yoke of powerful local rulers. The Republic of Venice dominated Brescia and Bergamo. Mantua was ruled by the Gonzaga, and the Visconti and Sforza families took over Como, Cremona, Milan, and Pavia.

The Battle of Pavia in 1525, when the generals of Charles V defeated the French (and gave Francis I the chance to coin the famous phrase "All is lost save honor"), brought on 200 years of Spanish occupation. The Spaniards were, on the whole, less cruel than the local tyrants and were hardly resisted by the Lombards. The War of the Spanish Succession, in the early years of the 18th century, threw out the Spaniards and brought in the Austrians instead, whose dominion was "neither liked nor loathed" during the nearly 100 years of its existence.

Napoléon and his generals routed the Austrians. The Treaty of Campoformio resulted in the proclamation of the Cisalpine Republic, which quickly became the Republic of Italy and, just as rapidly, the Kingdom of Italy, which lasted only until Napoléon's defeat brought back the Austrians. But Milan, as the capital of Napoléon's republic and of the Kingdom of Italy, had a taste of glory, and the city's inherently independent citizens, along with those of the other Lombardian cities, were not slow to resent and combat the loss of "national" pride.

From 1820 on, the Lombards joined the Piedmontese and the House of Savoy in a long struggle against the Hapsburgs and, in 1859, finally defeated Austria and brought about the re-creation of the Kingdom of Italy two years later.

Milan and other cities of Lombardy have not lost their independence and their hatred of domination. Nowhere in Italy was the partisan insurrection against Mussolini—to whom they first gave power—and the German regime better organized or more successful. Milan was liberated from the Germans by its own partisan organization before the entrance of Allied troops; escaping Allied prisoners could find sanctuary there when fighting was still going on far to the south. Today, the Milanesi independent spirit is demonstrated through the increasingly popular separatist movement known collectively as the Lega Nord (Northern League), whose aims are to divide the northern regions from the rest of Italy and create a new state called Padania, with Milan as its capital. Although it seems unlikely that secession will occur, the movement maintains a strong voice of protest against the government in Rome, whom it accuses of squandering revenue from the prosperous north on ill-fated projects in the poorer south.

Pleasures and Pastimes

Car Racing

Though the fortunes of Italy's beloved Ferrari have waned in recent years, passion for the sport is undiminished here. A Formula 1 race is held in Monza, 15 km (9 mi) from Milan, every September. The track was built in 1922 in the Parco di Monza, where there is also a hippodrome, golf course, and other facilities.

Dining

Unlike most Italian regions, Lombardy exhibits a northern European preference for butter rather than oil as its cooking medium, which imparts a rich and distinctive flavor to the cuisine. *Alla milanese*–style cooking means the food is usually dipped in egg and bread crumbs mixed with grated Parmesan, then sautéed in clarified butter. One of the most popular specialties here, osso buco, is almost always paired with risotto—its alla milanese preparation enriching it with chicken broth and saffron, imparting a rich flavor and yellow hue. The lakes are a good source of fish, particularly trout and pike.

Gorgonzola, a strong, creamy, veined cheese, and panettone, a sweet yeast bread with raisins, citron, and anise, both hail from the Milan area and can be enjoyed throughout Lombardy. Although most of the wines in Lombardy can be paired well with the cuisine, try in particular to have the red Grumello or Sangue di Giuda (blood of Judas) wines or the delicious light sparkling whites from the Franciacorta area.

CATEGORY	MILAN*	OTHER AREAS*
$$$$	over 120,000 lire	over 90,000 lire
$$$	80,000–120,000 lire	60,000–90,000 lire
$$	45,000–80,000 lire	35,000–60,000 lire
$	under 45,000 lire	under 35,000 lire

Prices are per person, including house wine, service, and tax.

Golf

Golf is a recent addition to Italy's sporting roster, and the success of Italy's most famous professional golfer, Constantino Rocca, has added to the sport's popularity among Italians. Facilities have improved dramatically over the last decade, resulting in a proliferation of courses groomed into northern Italy's landscape. Five courses are convenient to Milan, and seven courses are near Lago di Como (Lake Como).

Lodging

Lombardy is one of Italy's most prosperous regions, and hotels cater to a clientele of high standards, willing to pay for extra comfort. Most of the famous lake resorts are expensive, although more basic—and reasonably priced—accommodations can be found in the smaller towns and villages. Milan may seem to have fewer tourists than other large Italian cities, but there is always competition for rooms, generated by the nearly year-round trade fairs and other business-related bookings. It is best—and almost essential in spring and summer—to make reservations. Many Lombardy hotels are converted from handsome old villas with well-landscaped grounds. Try to visit one or two, even if they are out of your price range as accommodations.

CATEGORY	COST*
$$$$	over 400,000 lire
$$$	200,000–400,000 lire
$$	125,000–200,000 lire
$	under 125,000 lire

Prices are for standard double room, including service and tax.

Soccer

Like the rest of Italy, the region is soccer-mad, with fans from all over Italy exhibiting fierce support for Milan's soccer teams, AC Milan and Inter Milan, two of the most successful in Europe. Matches are usually played on Sunday, with both teams sharing the San Siro soccer stadium in Milan for home matches. On match day, close to 85,000 fans pile into the San Siro to watch, cheer, and boo the performances of each team. For the rest of the week, Sunday's performance is debated and scrutinized in bars, cafés, and restaurants (not to mention the home, workplace, barbershop . . .). Match tickets are difficult but not impossible to get; information is available from the city tourist offices.

Water Sports

Schools for sailing, scuba diving, waterskiing, and windsurfing are in Riva del Garda, on Lake Garda. Torbole, 5 km (3 mi) east of Riva del Garda on S240, is a prime spot for windsurfing. At Lake Como, there are well-equipped sailing and windsurfing schools as well as waterskiing.

Exploring Milan, Lombardy, and the Lakes

This area of northern Italy is dominated by the region of Lombardy and especially by Milan, which lies at its heart. Many of the region's most important cities—Pavia, Cremona, and Mantua—are to the south and southeast of Milan. These cities all have in common flat geo-graphical surroundings bordered by the Po River, hence they are cat-egorized here as cities of the plain. "The lakes" actually denotes a vast region spread over the middle third of the northern border region. The roads that connect major cities are excellent and are supported by sev-eral major highways (autostrade) as well as by secondary routes.

From the north to the east of Milan lie all of the region's lakes. Some border Switzerland; others are at the foot of the Dolomites, Italy's fore-most mountain range. The best way to see the lake country is to rent a car in fall or spring and thread a path, at as leisurely a pace as pos-sible, along the small mountain roads that link the lakes' least-spoiled northern tips. This is splendid mountain-driving country, with some of the most beautiful and challenging roads in the world. Without a car, however, it is still possible to see many of the region's sights, thanks to extensive bus routes and the many vaporetti that ferry the lakes. The throngs that descend upon the lakes in July and August, week-ends particularly, make reservations absolutely necessary—especially so at Lake Como, the quintessential Italian lake resort.

Numbers in the text correspond to numbers in the margin and on the Milan and Lombardy and the Lakes maps.

Great Itineraries

Traveling by car is usually the best way to get around and to fully ap-preciate the beauty of the landscape. Allow plenty of time to travel the windy lake roads at leisure, as photo opportunities abound. A week is enough to see the area thoroughly, and although five days will not exclude any sights, you have to keep on the move. Three days will give you a taste of the major sights in the area, but time will be precious and morning starts will have to be early.

IF YOU HAVE 3 DAYS

Begin in ⊠ **Milan** ①–⑭, taking in the city's major sights, before head-ing south on the A7 autostrada to the cities of **Pavia** ⑮ and **Cre-mona** ⑯, home to Stradivari, violin maker extraordinaire. End your day in ⊠ **Mantua** ⑱. The next day head north on the A22 as far as **Riva del Garda** ㉒ and make your way back through **Gargnano** ㉓, **Gar-done Riviera** ㉔, and down into the jewel of Lake Garda's crown, **Sirmione** ㉕. Overnight in ⊠ **Bergamo** ㉗. The next day go as far as **Madonna del Ghisallo** ㉘ and ⊠ **Bellagio** ㉙ on Lake Como. Finally, move on to Lake Maggiore via **Cernobbio** ㉜, taking time out to cruise the lake on one of the steamers.

IF YOU HAVE 5 DAYS

Travel south along the A7 to **Pavia** ⑮ and **Cremona** ⑯, and then move on to the star-shape fortress city of **Sabbioneta** ⑰, ending your day in ⊠ **Mantua** ⑱, where you can enjoy Mantegna's masterpieces. The next day head north to Lake Garda through the lakefront towns of **Punta di San Vigilio** ⑳, **Malcesine** ㉑, and, at the top of the lake, the pretty town of **Riva del Garda** ㉒. Head down the western side of the lake through **Gargnano** ㉓ and **Gardone Riviera** ㉔, where you should visit Gabriele d'Annunzio's former home, Il Vittoriale, before reach-ing ⊠ **Sirmione** ㉕. The next day pass through the wealthy city of **Bres-cia** ㉖ and on to **Bergamo** ㉗. From here head via **Madonna del Ghisallo** ㉘ to ⊠ **Bellagio** ㉙ on Lake Como, said to be the prettiest town in Eu-rope. Take time in the afternoon to explore the lake towns of **Varen-na** ㉚ and **Tremezzo** ㉛, where you'll find the magnificent Villa Carlotta. If you can manage an early start the following morning, head for **Cer-nobbio** ㉜ and then west to **Orto San Giulio** ㉞ on Lake Orto. It's only a short hop to Lake Maggiore. You can explore the area from here by

Lombardy and the Lakes

SWITZERLAND

Locarno
Ascona
Brissago

Cannobio

Cannero Riv.

Verbania Pallanza **36**

Lago Maggiore

S34

S36

S33

Moltarone
Stresa **35**
Laveno
Gignese
Omegna
Armeno
Belgirate
Orta San Giulio **34**

Lago di Orta

Arona

Angera

Lugano

Lago di Lugano

Menaggio
Cadenabbia
Tremezzo **31**

Bellano
Varenna **30**

Lago di Como

Bellagio **29**

Madonna del Ghisallo **28**

Cernobbio **32**
Como **33**

Lecco

Lago Varese

Varese

S394

S342

S340

S342

S36

S35

S233

A8

A8

A9

S38

S42

Bergamo **27**

Capriate San Gervasio

A4

Aeroporto Malpensa ✈

Milan
1 **14**

Aeroporto Milano Linate ✈

Cassano d'Add.

Treviglio

TO TURIN
Novara

S11

S11

S211

Abbiategrasso

S494

Vigevano

Ticino

A7

Certosa di Pavia

Pavia **15**

Lodi

Adda

A4

Cre

S415

S235

S234

A1

N

Po

A21

A7

S10

A26

A21

A7

S35

ITALY

| 0 | | 20 miles |
| 0 | | 30 km |

steamer, traveling north to ▨ **Stresa** ㉟ on the western side of the lake. From here it's a short excursion to the town of **Verbania Pallanza** ㊱, across the bay of the same name. That afternoon or the following day (alternately staying in Stresa) head for ▨ **Milan** ①–⑭ to see the main sights. Alternatively, you could visit Milan first before setting off on your tour of the rest of the region.

IF YOU HAVE 7 DAYS

If you have the luxury of seven days to tour the area, make sure you linger in some of the lake towns, especially **Riva del Garda** ㉒ and ▨ **Sirmione** ㉕, ▨ **Bellagio** ㉙ on Lake Como, and Lake Maggioire's **Verbania Pallanza** ㊱, where you can explore the magnificent botanical gardens of Villa Taranto. Take an extra day to visit ▨ **Milan** ①–⑭, which may appear to be yet another industrialized city at first glance but reveals artistic and architectural treasures once you scratch its surface.

When to Tour Milan, Lombardy, and the Lakes

In summer months, particularly July and August, lake roads can become congested, especially on evenings and weekends. Fewer people visit in fall, winter, and spring, so many of the lakeside towns are deserted and some restaurants and hotels close. Note that many of the ferry and steamer boat services stop running in October and recommence in May. Early summer, late summer, and early fall are the best times to see the area, but October can be a tad chilly for swimming.

MILAN

93 km (60 mi) northwest of Cremona, 38 km (24 mi) north of Pavia.

Milan's history as a capital city goes back at least 2,500 years. Its fortunes ever since—both as a great commercial trading center and as the object of regular conquest and occupation—are readily explained by its strategic position at the center of the Lombard plain. Directly south of the central passes across the Alps, Milan is bordered by three highly navigable rivers—the Po, Ticino, and Adda—for centuries the main arteries of an ingenious network of canals crisscrossing all Lombardy (and ultimately reaching most of northern Italy).

Virtually every invader in European history—Gaul, Roman, Goth, Longobard, and Frank—as well as every ruler of France, Spain, and Austria, has taken a turn at ruling the city and the region. Milan's glorious heyday of self-rule proved comparatively brief, from 1277 until 1500, when it was ruled by its two great family dynasties, the Visconti and subsequently the Sforza. These families were known, justly or not, for a peculiarly aristocratic mixture of refinement, classical learning, and cruelty, and much of the surviving grandeur of Gothic and Renaissance art and architecture is their doing. Be on the lookout in your wanderings for the Visconti family emblem—a viper, its jaws straining wide, devouring a child.

If you are wondering why so little seems to have survived from Milan's antiquity, the answer is simple—war. Three times in the city's history, partial or total destruction has followed conflict—in AD 539, 1157, and 1944.

Exploring Milan

The subway system, known as the Metropolitana, is a good way to get around, but staying above ground in the trolley cars or buses gives a better view.

A Good Walk

Start at the **Duomo** ① and visit its roof, **museum,** and the **Battistero Paleocristiano** ②. Then move on to **Galleria Vittorio Emanuele** ③, just beyond the northern tip of the cathedral's facade. Continue across the transepts of the Galleria and head north to **Teatro alla Scala** ④, where Verdi attained his fame. Head northeast on Via Manzoni, which leads to the **Giardini Pubblici** (great for kids); on the eastern side of the park is the **Museo Civico di Storia Naturale** ⑤. Via Manzoni and the southwestern corner of the park lead to Via Fatebenefratelli; follow it west to Via Pontaccio and then to Via Brera to the **Pinacoteca di Brera** ⑥, home to stellar masterpieces. Next, a brisk walk west along Via Pontaccio will bring you to the imposing **Castello Sforzesco** ⑦. A few blocks southwest of the Castello, on Corso Magenta is **Santa Maria delle Grazie** ⑧, home to the renowned *Last Supper.* Go east on Corso Magenta, across Via Carducci, to visit the city's **Museo Civico Archeologico** ⑨. Next to the Museo Civico Archeologico, Via Sant'Agnese leads to the church of **Sant'Ambrogio** ⑩. Across from the church's main doors, turn left on Via San Vittore to see the **Museo Nazionale della Scienza e Tecnica** ⑪. From the museum, take a right and walk down Via Edmondo de Amicis, then take a left on Corso Porta Ticinese to reach the church of **San Lorenzo Maggiore** ⑫. From here (down Corso Porta Ticinese) you can explore the laid-back **Navigli district** ⑬. From San Lorenzo Maggiore, take Corso Porta Ticinese north to Via Torino, where, after a few blocks, you'll find **San Satiro** ⑭, yet another of Bramante's Renaissance masterpieces.

TIMING

To visit each sight in Milan will take a couple of days, but the most important sights can be seen in one day. Note that some sites are closed Monday, including Santa Maria delle Grazie (*The Last Supper*). Expect long lines waiting to see *The Last Supper,* even in the early morning.

Sights to See

❷ **Battistero Paleocristiano.** This subterranean ruin of the baptistery dating from the 4th century is beneath the Duomo's piazza. Although opinion remains divided, it is widely believed that this may have been where Ambrose, Milan's first bishop and patron saint, baptized Augustine. ⊠ *Enter through Duomo, Piazza Duomo.* ☐ *Free.* ⏱ *Tues.–Sun. 10–noon and 3–5.*

❼ **Castello Sforzesco.** For the serious student of Renaissance military engineering, the imposing Castello must be something of a travesty, so often has it been remodeled or rebuilt since it was begun in 1450 by the *condottiere* (hired mercenary) who founded the city's second dynastic family, Francesco Sforza, fourth duke of Milan.

Though today the word "mercenary" has a strongly pejorative ring, during the Renaissance all Italy's great soldier-heroes were professionals hired by the cities and principalities that they served. Of them— and there were thousands—Francesco Sforza is considered to have been one of the greatest and most honest. It is said he could remember not only the names of all his men, but of their horses, as well. And it is with his era, and the building of the Castello, that we know we have entered the enlightened age of the Renaissance. It took barely half a century before it and the city were under foreign rule.

Today, the Castello houses municipal museums devoted variously to Egyptian and other antiquities, musical instruments, paintings, and sculpture. Highlights are the **Salle delle Asse,** a frescoed room still sometimes attributed to Leonardo da Vinci, and Michelangelo's unfinished *Rondanini Pietà,* believed to be his last work—an astounding achieve-

Milan

0 ____ 440 yards

0 ____ 400 meters

Battistero
Paleocristiano, **2**

Castello Sforzesco, **7**

Duomo, **1**

Galleria Vittorio
Emanuele, **3**

Museo Civico
Archeologico, **9**

Museo Civico di
Storia Naturale, **5**

Museo Nazionale
della Scienza e
Tecnica, **11**

Navigli district, **13**

Pinacoteca di Brera, **6**

San Lorenzo
Maggiore, **12**

San Satiro, **14**

Sant'Ambrogio, **10**

Santa Maria delle
Grazie, **8**

Teatro alla Scala, **4**

ment for a man nearly 90 and a moving coda to his life. ✉ *Piazza Castello,* ☎ *02/62083191.* 🎫 *Free.* 🕐 *Tues.–Sun. 9:30–5:30.*

NEED A BREAK? **Viel** (✉ Largo Cairoli), just across the road from Castello Sforzesco, is said to be the best *gelateria* in northern Italy.

★ ❶ **Duomo.** This intricate Gothic structure—Italy's largest—has been fascinating and exasperating visitors and conquerors alike since it was begun by Galeazzo Visconti III (1351–1402), first duke of Milan, in 1386. Consecrated in 1577, it was not wholly completed until 1897.

Whether you concur with travel writer H. V. Morton, writing some 25 years ago, that the cathedral is "one of the mightiest Gothic buildings ever created," or regard it as a spiny pastiche of centuries, there is no denying that for sheer size and complexity it is unequaled; its very size and appearance suggest Gotham rather than Milan. Its capacity—though it is hard to imagine the church filled—is reckoned to be 40,000. Usually it is empty, a perfect sanctuary from the frenetic pace of life outside and the perfect place for solitary contemplation. The poet Shelley swore by it—claiming it was the only place to read Dante.

The building is adorned with 135 marble spires and 2,245 marble statues. The oldest part is the **apse** (the end of the cruciform opposite the portals). Its three colossal bays of curving and counter-curved tracery, especially the bay adorning the exterior of the stained-glass windows, should not be missed. Step inside and walk down the right aisle to the southern transept, to the **tomb of Gian Giacomo Medici.** The tomb owes something to Michelangelo, but is generally considered its sculptor's (Leone Leoni's) masterpiece; it dates from the 1560s.

Directly ahead is the Duomo's most famous sculpture, the rather gruesome but anatomically instructive figure of **San Bartolomeo** (St. Bartholomew), whose glorious martyrdom consisted of being flayed alive. It is usually said the saint stands "holding" his skin, but this is not quite accurate. It would appear more that he is luxuriating in it, much as a 1950s matron might have shown off a new fur stole.

As you enter the apse to admire those splendid windows, glance at the **sacristy doors** to the right and left of the altar. The lunette on the right dates from 1393 and was decorated by Hans von Fernach. That on the left also dates from the 14th century and is ascribed jointly to Giacomo da Campione and Giovanni dei Grassi.

Don't miss the view from the Duomo's **roof;** walk out the left (north) transept to the stairs and elevator. Sadly, late 20th-century air pollution, on all but the rarest days, drastically reduces the view. As you stand among the forest of marble pinnacles, remember that virtually every inch of this gargantuan edifice, including the roof itself, is decorated with precious white marble. ✉ *Piazza del Duomo.* 🎫 *Stairs 7,000 lire, elevator 10,000 lire.* 🕐 *Mar.–Oct., daily 9–5:30; Nov.–Feb., daily 9–4:30.*

Exhibits at the **Museo del Duomo** shed more light on the cathedral's history and include some of the treasures removed for safety from the exterior. ✉ *Piazza del Duomo 14,* ☎ *02/860358.* 🎫 *8,000 lire.* 🕐 *Tues.–Sun. 9:30–12:30 and 3–6.*

NEED A BREAK? The best alternative to a conventional restaurant is **Peck** (✉ Via Spadari 9, ☎ 02/860842), one of Italy's, if not the world's, most irresistible food emporiums. In the Duomo area, it is something better than a shop—it's six shops. **Peck Rosticceria** (✉ Via Cantù 3, ☎ 02/8693017; closed Mon.) offers grilled takeout. Best for a quick stand-up lunch is **Bottega del Vino** (✉ Via Victor Hugo 4, ☎ 02/861040), which pours almost 200 wines by the glass. For a relaxed lunch, try **Il Restaurant** (⊠ Via Victor Hugo 4, ☎ 02/876774; closed Sun.). For do-it-yourself, try the **Delicatessen** (⊠ Via Spadari 11, ☎ 02/86461158).

★ ❸ **Galleria Vittorio Emanuele.** Anyone who has grown up on the periphery of a contemporary American city should recognize this spectacularly extravagant late 19th-century glass-topped, barrel-vaulted tunnel for what it is—one of the planet's earliest and most select of shopping malls. It may be rivaled perhaps only by GUM, off Red Square in Moscow, for sheer belle epoque splendor. Its architect, Giuseppe Mengoni, accidently lost his footing while on the roof and tumbled to his death on the floor of his own creation, just days before its opening.

Like its suburban American cousins, the Galleria fulfills a variety of social functions vastly more important than its ostensible commercial purpose. This is the city's heart, midway between the cathedral and La Scala opera house, and it is sometimes called *Il Salotto* (the Living Room). It teems with life, inviting people-watching from the tables that spill from the Galleria's bars and restaurants, where you can enjoy a ridiculously overpriced coffee.

Like the cathedral, the Galleria is a cruciform. The space at the crossing, however, forms an octagon. If this is where you're standing, don't be afraid to look up and gawk. Even in poor weather, the great glass dome makes for a splendid sight. And the mosaics, usually unnoticed, are a vastly underrated source of pleasure, even if they are not to be taken too seriously. They represent Europe, Asia, Africa, and America; those at the entrance arch are devoted to science, industry, art, and agriculture.

Books, clothing, food, wine, pens, jewelry, and myriad other goods are all for sale in the Galleria, and one of Milan's most traditional restaurants, Savini, is here (☞ Dining and Lodging, *below*). There is, in addition, one of those curious Italian institutions, an *albergo diurno* (daytime hotel), where you can take an hour's nap or a bath, get a haircut or a pedicure, and have your suit pressed or a button replaced. Most of its patrons are Italian, but it is hard to think of a better oasis for a vacationer worn out from sightseeing. ⊠ *Piazza del Duomo, beyond northern tip of cathedral's facade.*

❾ **Museo Civico Archeologico** (Civic Archaeological Museum). Housed in a former monastery, this museum has some enlightening relics from Milan's Roman past—from everyday utensils and jewelry to several fine examples of mosaic pavement. ⊠ *Corso Magenta 15,* ☎ *02/86450011.* 🎟 *Free.* ☉ *Tues.–Sun. 9:30–5:30.*

�ястре ❺ **Museo Civico di Storia Naturale** (Civic Natural History Museum). Exhibits here appeal to animal and nature lovers. Just behind the museum is the **Giardini Pubblici** (Public Gardens), a refuge for active young children. ⊠ *Corso Venezia 55,* ☎ *02/62085405.* 🎟 *Free.* ☉ *Tues.–Fri. 9:30–5:30, weekends 9:30–6:30.*

☺ ⓫ **Museo Nazionale della Scienza e Tecnica** (National Museum of Science and Technology). Models based on technical projects by Leonardo da Vinci and collections of locomotives, planes, and cars hold your attention. ⊠ *Via San Vittore 21, near Sant'Ambrogio,* ☎ *02/485551.* 🎟 *10,000 lire.* ☉ *Tues.–Fri. 9:30–5, weekends 9:30–6.*

⓭ **Navigli district.** This romantic, bohemian neighborhood in the southern part of the city was, in medieval times, a network of navigable canals, called *navigli,* crisscrossing Milan. Almost all have been covered over, except for two long canals, Naviglio Grande and Naviglio Pavese, and part of a third, Darsena. The canals are lined with quaint shops, art galleries, cafés, restaurants, and clubs. ⊠ *Corso Porta Ticinese.*

★ ⑥ **Pinacoteca di Brera** (Brera Gallery). The picture collection in this art gallery is star studded, even by Italian standards. Start with the best, while you're still fresh, and leave the charming minor masterpieces for afterward. In Room 22, note that Raphael painted *Betrothal of the Virgin* when he was 22. The other painting, Piero della Francesca's *Madonna with Saints and Angels,* is just as lovely, much aided by its skillful restoration and cleaning.

The somber, beautiful, and moving *Dead Christ* by Mantegna, in Room 6, is by far the smallest painting in the room, but it dominates, with its sparse palette of gray and terra-cotta, and especially for its original perspective. Mantegna's shocking, almost surgical, precision—in the rendering of Christ's wounds, the face propped up on a pillow, the day's growth of beard—tells of an all-too-human agony. It is one of Renaissance painting's most quietly wondrous achievements, finding an unsuspected middle ground between the excesses of conventional gore and beauty in representing the Passion's saddest moment. On your way out, pause a moment to view the fine paintings by Carlo Carrà— especially *La Musa Metafisica,* or *Metaphysical Muse*—suggesting Italy's confident and stylish response to the likes of Picasso and Max Ernst and to the schools of Cubism and Surrealism. ⊠ *Via Brera 28,* ☎ *02/722631.* ☞ *10,000 lire.* ☉ *Tues.–Sat. 9–5:30, Sun. 9–12:45.*

OFF THE
BEATEN PATH

LATIN QUARTER – Take time to wander around the lively quarter surrounding the Pinacoteca di Brera. The narrow streets, lined with boutiques, crafts shops, cafés, restaurants, and music clubs, comprise what is often referred to as Milan's Greenwich Village. A longtime haunt of artists and musicians, it has a number of clubs and cafés offering live music until late at night.

MINITALIA PARK – Between Milan and Bergamo, this theme park has a 1:500-scale relief model of Italy, with about 200 replicas of the country's most important monuments. ⊠ *A4 autostrada toward Bergamo, Capriate San Gervasio, 35 km (22 mi) east of Milan,* ☎ *02/9091341.* ☞ *17,000 lire.* ☉ *Mar.–Oct., daily 9–dusk.*

PARCO DELLA PREISTORIA – Kids of all ages marvel at the 70-ft-long brontosaurus, the fierce tyrannosaurus, and the 4-km (2½-mi) path with 20 more full-size replicas of prehistoric animals. There is a picnic area and, for the adults, two cafés. ⊠ *25 km (16 mi) east of Milan on S11 near Cassano d'Adda,* ☎ *0363/78184.* ☞ *11,000 lire.* ☉ *Mar.–Nov., daily 9–dusk; ticket office closes at 6.*

⑫ **San Lorenzo Maggiore.** Sixteen ancient Roman columns line the front of this sanctuary; 4th-century mosaics still survive in the Cappella di Sant'Aquilino (Chapel of St. Aquilinus). ⊠ *Corso di Porta Ticinese.*

⑭ **San Satiro.** This church is another architectural gem in which Bramante's perfect command of proportion and perspective, keynotes of Renaissance architecture, makes a small interior seem extraordinarily spacious and airy. ⊠ *Via Torino.*

⑩ **Sant'Ambrogio** (St. Ambrose). Noted for its medieval architecture, the church was consecrated by St. Ambrose in AD 387, and is the model for all Lombard Romanesque churches. Ancient pieces inside include a remarkable 9th-century altar in precious metals and enamels and some 5th-century mosaics. ⊠ *Piazza Sant'Ambrogio.*

★ ⑧ **Santa Maria delle Grazie.** H. V. Morton once noted that Milan might well be the only city on earth where you could give a taxi driver the title of a painting as your destination. If this appeals to you, flag one down and say, *"L'Ultima Cena,"* since this is how **The Last Supper** is known here.

The Last Supper, housed in the church and former Dominican monastery of Santa Maria delle Grazie, has had an almost unbelievable history of bad luck and neglect—its near destruction in an American bombing raid in August 1943 was only the latest chapter in a series of misadventures, including, if one 19th-century source is to be believed, being whitewashed by the monks. Well-meant but disastrous attempts at restoration have done little to rectify the problem of the work's placement: It was executed on a wall unusually vulnerable to climatic dampness. Yet the artist chose to work slowly and patiently in oil pigments—which demand dry plaster—instead of proceeding hastily on wet plaster according to the conventional fresco technique. Novelist and critic Aldous Huxley (1894–1963) called it "the saddest work of art in the world." After years beneath a scaffold, with restorers patiently shifting from one square centimeter to another, Leonardo's famous masterpiece remains in a sad state, and studies in further methods to preserve this great fresco continue.

Despite Leonardo's carefully preserved preparatory sketches in which the apostles are clearly labeled by name, there still remains some small debate about a few identities in the final arrangement. But there can be no mistaking Judas, small and dark, his hand calmly reaching forward toward the bread, isolated from the terrible confusion that has taken the hearts of the others. One critic, Professor Frederick Hartt, offers an elegantly terse explanation for why the composition works: It combines "dramatic confusion" with "mathematical order." Certainly, the amazingly skillful and unobtrusive repetition of threes, when first you see it—in the windows, in the grouping of the figures, and in their placement—adds a mystical aspect to what at first seems simply the perfect observation of spontaneous human gesture.

Santa Maria delle Grazie is the **Cenacolo Vinciano** (Vincian Refectory), which used to be the order's refectory. Take at least a moment to visit Santa Maria delle Grazie itself. It's a handsome church, with a fine dome by Bramante, which was added along with a cloister about the time that Leonardo was commissioned to paint *The Last Supper.* If you're wondering how two such giants came to be employed decorating and remodeling the refectory and church of a comparatively modest religious order, and not, say, the Duomo, the answer lies in the ambitious but largely unrealized plan to turn Santa Maria delle Grazie into a magnificent Sforza family mausoleum. Though Ludovico il Moro Sforza (1452–1508), seventh duke of Milan, was but one generation away from the founding of the Sforza dynasty, he was its last ruler. Two years after Leonardo finished *The Last Supper,* Ludovico was defeated and was imprisoned in a French dungeon for the remaining eight years of his life. ✉ *Corso Magenta, Cenacolo Vinciano,* ☎ *02/4987588.* 🎫 *12,000 lire.* ⊘ *Tues.–Sun. 8–10; hrs may vary.*

NEED A BREAK? For those who don't scream for ice cream, a venerable neighborhood institution, the **Bar Magenta** (✉ Via Carducci 13 at Corso Magenta) provides an excellent alternative en route. Beyond lunch, beer, or coffee, the real attraction is its casual but civilized, quintessentially Milanese ambience.

❹ Teatro alla Scala. You need know nothing of opera to sense that, like Carnegie Hall, La Scala is something rather more than an auditorium—here Verdi established his reputation and Maria Callas sang her way into opera lore. It looms as a symbol—both for the performer who dreams one day of singing here and for the buff who knows every note of *Rigoletto* by heart. Audiences here can be notoriously fickle, and have been known to jeer performers who do not do appropriate justice to their beloved *opera lirica,* as it is known in Italian. The opera house was completely renovated after its destruction by Allied bombs in 1943 and reopened at a performance led by the great Arturo Toscanini in 1946.

If you are lucky enough to be here during the opera season, which runs for approximately six months beginning each December 7, St. Ambrose Day, do whatever is necessary to attend—even if it requires perching among the rafters in one of the dreaded gallery seats. Hearing a Verdi or Puccini opera sung in Italian by Italians in Italy is a magical experience. Rumors abound about an eventual closing of the opera house for a full-scale renovation, but political machinations and intrigue have conspired to create a cloud of doubt over whether the closure will occur in late 1998 or later, after the millennium. At press time (spring 1998), La Scala was officially open and planned to remain so for the forseeable future. During a quick stroll through the theater's small **Museo Teatrale alla Scala,** you will get a peek at the gilded grandeur of the boxes and admire the excellent collection of original, hand-painted Art Nouveau posters. ✉ *Piazza della Scala,* ☎ *02/8053418.* ✉ *5,000 lire.* ◷ *Mon.–Sat. 9–noon and 2–6; plus May–Oct., Sun. 9:30–noon and 2:30–5 (except during rehearsals).*

Dining and Lodging

$$$$ ✕ **L'Antica Osteria del Ponte.** Rich, imaginative seasonal cuisine at the
★ whim of chef Ezio Santin is reason enough to make your way 20 km (12 mi) southwest of Milan to one of Italy's finest (and most expensive) restaurants. It is set in a traditional country inn, its interior a cozy combination of wooden ceiling beams with a blazing fire in chilly weather. The Naviglio Grande (Grand Canal) flows nearby; it was built to carry the area's produce to Milan. Inventive recipes include ravioli *di aragosta* (filled with lobster meat) in summer and, in the fall, a range of heartwarming specialties, many using the prized wild porcini mushrooms. ✉ *Cassinetta di Lugagnano, 3 km (2 mi) north of Abbiategrasso,* ☎ *02/9420034. Reservations essential. Jacket and tie. AE, DC, MC, V. Closed Sun.–Mon., Dec. 25–Jan. 15, and Aug.*

$$$$ ✕ **Savini.** Red carpets and glass chandeliers characterize the classy Savini, in the Galleria Vittorio Emanuele. It's a typical old-fashioned Milanese restaurant, with dining rooms on three floors, including a "winter garden," with views of the Galleria. Try the Milanese specialty risotto *al salto* (cooked as a sort of pancake, flipped in the pan) or *costoletta di vitello* (veal cutlets). ✉ *Galleria Vittorio Emanuele,* ☎ *02/72003433. AE, DC, MC, V. Closed Aug. 10–20, Jan. 1–Jan. 6, and Sun.*

$$$$ ✕ **Scaletta.** The restaurant's name means "little stairway" in Italian, perhaps inspired by its own stairway ascending to culinary paradise. This tiny restaurant could be the dining room of a gracious home, with cool pastels, book-lined walls, and a superb collection of blown glass. Host-sommelier Aldo Bellini and genius cook Mamma Pina in the kitchen treat you with cordiality and take time to discuss wines and menus, if you like. Pina's cooking is a light, personalized version of traditional Italian cuisine. ✉ *Piazzale Stazione Porta Genova 3,* ☎ *02/ 58100290. AE, DC, MC, V. Closed Sun. and Aug. No lunch Mon.*

$$$–$$$$ **× Boeucc.** Milan's oldest restaurant (pronounced "birch") is in the same
★ square as novelist Alessandro Manzoni's house, not far from La Scala.
Subtly lit, with cream-color fluted columns, chandeliers, thick carpets,
and a garden for warm-weather dining, it has come a long way from
the time when it was simply a basement "hole" (*boeucc* is old Milanese
for *buco,* or hole). Typical Milanese and Italian dishes served include
penne *al branzino e zucchini* (with sea bass and zucchini sauce) and
gelato *di castagne con zabaglione caldo* (chestnut ice cream with hot
zabaglione). ⊠ *Piazza Belgioioso 2,* ☎ *02/76020224. Reservations es-
sential. AE. Closed Sat. and Aug. No lunch Sun.*

$$–$$$ **× Antica Trattoria della Pesa.** Turn-of-the-century decor, dark wood
paneling, and old-fashioned lamps re-create the atmosphere of this restau-
rant at its opening more than 100 years ago. This is authentic Old Milan,
as the menu confirms, offering risotto, minestrone, and osso buco. ⊠
Viale Pasubio 10, ☎ *02/6555741. AE, DC, MC, V. Closed Sun., 2 wks
in Aug., and Dec. 23–Jan. 6.*

$$ **× Al Cantinone.** Opera enthusiasts still come here for an after-theater
drink, just as they did a century ago. The decor is classic Milanese, the
service is fast, and the food is homey and reliable. Try the homemade
pappardelle (thick, flat noodles) or Tuscan ravioli with meat sauce. There's
a wide selection of grilled meats and a staggering choice of wines. ⊠
Via Agnello 19, entrance on Via Ragazzi del 99, ☎ *02/86461338. AE,
DC, MC, V. Closed Sun., Aug., and Dec. 24–Jan. 5. No lunch Sat.*

$$ **× La Capanna.** Signora cooks and her husband pours wine and sees
that everything goes smoothly in this popular trattoria near the Piola
Metro stop (and the university). The food is predominantly Tuscan—
Tuscan salami, pappardelle, fish, and steak—but some Milanese spe-
cialties are also on the menu. ⊠ *Via Donatello 9,* ☎ *02/29400884.
AE, DC, MC, V. Closed Sat. and Aug.*

$$ **× La Libera.** Although this establishment in the heart of Brera bills itself as a *birreria con cucina* (beer cellar with kitchen), its young clien-
tele comes here for the excellent food and convivial atmosphere. A soft
current of jazz soothes the ripple of conversation, amid restful dark
green decor. Sample the creative cooking, including the *insalata esot-
ica* (avocado, chicken, rice, and papaya salad) or *rognone di vitello con
broccoletti e ginepro* (veal kidneys with broccoli and juniper berries).
⊠ *Via Palermo 21,* ☎ *02/8053603. Reservations not accepted. No credit
cards. Closed Sat., Aug., and Dec. 22–Jan. 1. No lunch Sun.*

$$ **× Nabucco.** This smart, tasteful restaurant in the Brera offers such de-
lights as risotto *con porcini,* an excellent range of salads, and home-
made pastries and desserts. It serves good fixed-price lunches ($). ⊠
Via Fiori Chiari 10, ☎ *02/860663. AE, DC, MC, V. Closed Tues.*

$$ **× Trattoria Milanese.** Between the Duomo and the Basilica of San-
t'Ambrogio, this small, popular trattoria has been run by the same fam-
ily for more than 60 years and is crowded with businesspeople lunch
and with regulars, and the occasional Milanese celeb at dinner. Food
is authentic regional, with risotto and *costoletta alla milanese* (milanese-
style breaded veal cutlet) good choices. ⊠ *Via Santa Marta 11,* ☎ *02/
86451991. DC, MC, V. Closed Tues. and Aug.*

$–$$ **× Bistrot di Gualtiero Marchesi/Brunch.** Atop the Rinascente depart-
ment store off Piazza del Duomo, this brunch eatery, bar, and bistro
is supervised by the well-known chef Gualtiero Marchesi and offers a
variety of menus with a full range of prices. A bonus is a great view
of the Duomo's spires. ⊠ *La Rinascente, Piazza Duomo,* ☎ *02/
877120. AE, DC, MC, V. Closed Sun. No lunch Mon.*

$–$$ **× La Bruschetta.** You'll find this tiny, busy pizzeria off Corso Vittorio
Emanuele, behind the Duomo; it is run by a partnership of Tuscans
and Neapolitans. The woodstove is in full view, so you can see your
pizza cooking in front of you, although there are plenty of nonpizza

dishes available, too, such as spaghetti *alle cozze e vongole* (with clam and mussel sauce). ☒ *Piazza Beccaria 12,* ☎ *02/8692494. MC, V. Closed Mon., 3 wks in Aug., and 1st wk in Jan.*

$ ✕ **La Giara.** The quality of the food from the limited menu in this simple Pugliese restaurant is a revelation. Here you eat tavern style, at wooden tables and benches, often sharing a table with other diners. Start with the antipasto *sott'olio* (eggplant, artichoke, mushroom, and tomato preserved in olive oil), and try one of the grilled-meat courses, cooked on a range at the front of the restaurant. ☒ *Viale Monza 10,* ☎ *02/26143835. No credit cards. Closed Wed.*

$ ✕ **San Tomaso.** The informality of a beer hall, a trendy young clientele, and a self-service counter here add up to pleasant, easy eating. Very busy at lunch, it's usually quieter at night. ☒ *Via San Tomaso 5,* ☎ *02/874510. No credit cards. Closed Sun.*

$ ✕ **Taverna Moriggi.** Near the stock exchange, this is a dusky, wood-paneled wine bar serving a fixed-price lunch for about 30,000 lire, or cold cuts and cheeses in the evening. ☒ *Via Moriggi 8,* ☎ *02/86450880. Reservations essential. DC, MC, V. Closed Sun. No lunch Sat.*

$$$$ 🏨 **Carlton-Senato.** This hotel is the ideal choice for visitors who intend to spend time shopping—or window shopping—in the nearby high-fashion streets, Via della Spiga, Via Sant'Andrea, and Via Monte Napoleone. The hotel is very light and airy, with double-thick windows, a garage with direct access to the hotel, and lots of little touches—*gratis* chocolates and liqueurs—to make up for the rather functional rooms. Some have terraces large enough for a table, chair, and potted shrubs. ☒ *Via Senato 5, 20124,* ☎ *02/77077,* ℻ *02/783300. 79 rooms. Restaurant, bar, parking (fee). AE, DC, MC, V.*

$$$$ 🏨 **Duomo.** Guests' comfort is the important thing at this spacious, modern hotel: Celebrities have been turned away when it was thought they would attract noisy fans and paparazzi. This is the obvious choice if a central location is also your priority: You're only 20 yards from the cathedral itself, yet within a quiet pedestrian-only zone. Air-conditioned rooms and duplex suites are swankily done in golds, creams, and browns. If in a room on the second, fourth, or fifth floor, you'll be eye to eye with the Gothic gargoyles and pinnacles of the Duomo. ☒ *Via San Raffaele 1, 20121,* ☎ *02/8833,* ℻ *02/86462027. 153 rooms. Restaurant, bar, parking (fee). AE, DC, MC, V.*

$$$$ 🏨 **Four Seasons.** The renaissance of a 14th-century monastery on an exclusive shopping street in the center of Milan has produced a precious gem, for which you'll pay dearly. The hotel blends European sophistication with American comfort. Individually decorated rooms have opulent marble bathrooms; most rooms face the quiet courtyard. Downstairs is the hotel's well-regarded Il Teatro restaurant. ☒ *Via Gesù 8, 20121,* ☎ *02/77088,* ℻ *02/7708500. 98 rooms. 2 restaurants, bar, business services, meeting rooms. AE, DC, MC, V.*

$$$$ 🏨 **Palace.** The rather unprepossessing 1950s Milanese exterior is no ★ indication of what lies within, a truly superior hotel, with personalized service. Beyond the sumptuous Renaissance and postmodern lobby, rooms reveal precious Empire-style antiques; exquisite bathrooms are done in Portugal pink and Issoire green marble. It's aim is to be Milan's premier business hotel, with Internet and modem connections in every room, and more. Mediterranean cuisine is served in the Casanova Grill. You can putt on the computer-simulated golf centeror avail yourself of lessons on the putting green and driving range at the City Golf Center. ☒ *Piazza della Repubblica 20, 20124,* ☎ *02/6336,* ℻ *02/654485. 216 rooms. Restaurant, bar, breakfast room, in-room modem lines, in-room safes, minibars, laundry service, business services, meeting rooms, parking (fee). AE, DC, MC, V.*

$$$$ ⊞ Pierre. No expense was spared to furnish each room of this luxury hotel in a different style with the lavish color-coordinated fabrics and a variety of modern and antique furniture. Everything is electronic: You can open the curtains, turn off the lights, get personal messages on your TV screen—all with the touch of a button. It's on the inner beltway, near the medieval church of Sant'Ambrogio. ⊠ *Via De Amicis 32, 20123,* ☎ *02/72000581,* ℻ *02/8052157. 49 rooms. Restaurant, bar, in-room safes, minibars, parking (fee). AE, DC, MC, V.*

$$$$ ⊞ Principe di Savoia. Of the three deluxe ITT-Sheraton Luxury Col-
★   lection hotels here, this is the most posh. Opened in 1923, it has set and borne the standards for European hotels. Behind the Liberty-style facade, the decor is in 19th-century Lombard style, with lavish mir-rors, drapes, and carpets. The understated, gracious bedrooms are de-signed to reflect the eclectic architectural styles of the fin de siècle. If you want to spoil yourself in full Roman-emperor style, book the Pres-idential Suite, complete with private marbled pool. The hotel isn't cheap, but if you stay here you're in good company: This is the favorite Milanese destination of such notables as the Sultan of Brunei, George Bush, Demi Moore, and Woody Allen. You can dine alfresco in the re-fined Galleria restaurant. ⊠ *Piazza della Repubblica 17, 20124,* ☎ *02/ 62301,* ℻ *02/6595838. 299 rooms. Restaurant, bar, health club, dry cleaning, laundry service, business services, convention center, meet-ing rooms. AE, DC, MC, V.*

$$$ ⊞ Canada. This friendly small hotel is close to Piazza del Duomo on the edge of a district full of shops and restaurants. It offers good value in rooms that are furnished in a nondescript fashion but have the usual modern trappings. ⊠ *Via Santa Sofia 16, 20122,* ☎ *02/58304844,* ℻ *02/58300282. 35 rooms. Bar. AE, DC, MC, V.*

$$$ ⊞ Casa Svizzera. A faithful clientele considers this one of Milan's best small hotels in its price category, so it's advisable to reserve early. Ad-jacent to the Duomo and a few yards from the Galleria, it's central and handy to Metro and bus lines. The hotel is soundproofed; air-condi-tioned rooms have refrigerator-bars and cheery floral-print fabric. ⊠ *Via San Raffaele 3, 20121,* ☎ *02/8692246,* ℻ *02/72004690. 45 rooms. Bar, minibars. AE, DC, MC, V. Closed Aug. and Dec. 24–Jan. 6.*

$$$ ⊞ Gritti. The Picassos, Matisses, and van Goghs in the lobby here are originals—so the manager will tell you—except that they were painted quite recently "in the spirit." The Gritti is a bright hotel with a cheer-ful atmosphere, adequate rooms, and good views (from the inside upper floors) of tiled roofs and the gold Madonnina statue on top of the Duomo, only a few hundred yards away. ⊠ *Piazza Santa Maria Beltrade 4, north end of Via Torino, 20123,* ☎ *02/801056,* ℻ *02/ 89010999. 48 rooms. Bar, breakfast room. AE, DC, MC, V.*

$$$ ⊞ Hotel Vittoria. This family-owned hotel is in a quiet residential street only minutes from the Galleria Vittorio Emmanuele and the Duomo. The guest rooms are tiny, but in pristine condition. The staff are courteous and extremely friendly, eager to do whatever they can to ensure their guests' comfort and satisfaction. In summer, breakfast is served in the small garden at the back. ⊠ *Via Pietro Calvi 32, 20129,* ☎ *02/5456520,* ℻ *02/55190246. 20 rooms. Breakfast room, in-room safes, minibars. AE, DC, MC, V.*

$$–$$$ ⊞ London. Close to the Duomo, the London has clean, spacious rooms
★   and a staff unfailing in their politeness and efficiency, attending to their guests' every need. ⊠ *Via Rovello 3, 20121,* ☎ *02/72020166,* ℻ *02/ 8057037. 29 rooms. Bar. MC, V. Closed Dec. 23–Jan. 3 and Aug.*

$$ ⊞ Hotel Garda. This modern hotel can claim the best location in Milan: It's a two-minute walk from the main train station, three sub-way lines, and a multistory parking lot. Although the lobby looks spar-tan, rooms beyond are well furnished, comfortable, and clean. Most rooms overlook the busy center streets, thankfully quieter at night. ✉ *Via Napo Torriani 21, 20124,* ☎ *02/66982626,* FAX *02/66982576. 55 rooms. Bar, breakfast room. AE, DC, MC, V.*

$$ ⊞ **San Francisco.** Near Metro stations on two lines (Loreto, Piola, or Pasteur stops) and not far from the Central Station, this modern hotel has a functional, flag-bedecked lobby, simply furnished rooms, and a small garden. ✉ *Viale Lombardia 55, 20131,* ☎ *02/2361009,* FAX *02/ 26680377. 31 rooms. AE, DC, MC, V.*

Nightlife and the Arts

The Arts

MUSIC
Teatro alla Scala opera house (☞ Exploring, *above,* and Opera, *below*) features a two-month season of **classical concerts** in October and November.

OPERA
The season at Milan's famous **Teatro alla Scala** opera house runs from December 7 (St. Ambrose Day) through May or later. Seats are usually sold out well in advance, but if you are prepared to pay the desk clerk at your hotel, you will probably be able to get hold of a pair of tickets. For information on schedules, ticket availability, and how to buy tickets, there is an **Infotel Scala Service** (with English-speaking staff) at the ticket office (✉ Teatro alla Scala, Ufficio Biglietteria, Via Filodrammatici 2, ☎ 02/72003744), open daily noon–6. Telephone bookings are not accepted. From abroad you can book in advance, within a short specified period for each presentation (the dates are published at the beginning of the season; these tickets are allocated on a first-come, first-served basis), by applying for a reservation by mail or fax (transmitted 9–6 local time, with time and date of transmission, and sender's fax number indicated on the fax, to FAX 02/8607787 or 02/861778), or at CIT or other travel agencies (at agencies, no more than 10 days before performance). Consult the listings in the informative monthly *Milano Mese,* free at APT (tourist board) offices, or the weekly *Viva Milano.*

THEATER
Milan's **Piccolo Teatro** (✉ Via Rovello 2, ☎ 02/877663) is noted for its excellent productions, given in Italian, of course. **Teatro Manzoni** (✉ Via Manzoni 40, ☎ 02/790543) is equally renowned.

Nightlife

BARS
El Brellin (✉ Vicolo Lavandai at Alzaia Naviglio Grande, ☎ 02/ 58101351) is one of the many bars in the Navigli district. It is closed Sunday. In the Brera quarter, **Momus** (✉ Via Fiori Chiari 8, ☎ 02/ 8056227) is upscale and intimate; it is closed on Monday.

NIGHTCLUBS
Head to the hot spot of late, **Le Scimmie** (✉ Via Ascanio Sforza 49, ☎ 02/89402874), for cool jazz and relaxed atmosphere. It's closed Tuesday.

Milan clubs are good bets for an evening of dinner and dancing, but don't expect to get them for a song. Club kids with plenty of money crowd **Stage** (✉ Galleria Manzoni off Via Monte Napoleone, ☎ 02/ 76021071; closed Sun.). **Hollywood** (✉ Via Como 15/c, ☎ 02/6598996) is the in place for the fashion set.

Lizard (✉ Largo La Foppa, ☎ 02/6590890; closed Sun.–Tues.) is trendy, loud, and expensive—a formula that doesn't deter the young Milanese crowd. **Nepentha** (✉ Piazza Diaz 1, ☎ 02/804837; closed Sun.) is also a popular spot.

Outdoor Activities and Sports

Golf

The **Parco di Monza** (⊠ 15 km/9 mi from Milan) has 18- and nine-hole courses. Contact the **Golf Club Milano** (☎ 039/303081). For information and bookings for other golf clubs in the Milan area, contact **City Golf Club** (⊠ Hotel Palace, Piazza della Repubblica 20, ☎ 02/29030075).

Health Club

The best-equipped of Milan's many sport centers is the **Centro Saini** (⊠ Via Corelli 136, ☎ 02/7380841), in the vast Parco Forlanini. Much like a municipal gym, it offers squash and volleyball facilities and weight rooms. It's outside the city center; take Bus 38.

Shopping

Milan's fortissimo occurs twice a year, in the end of February and October (for women) and June and January (for men), when the world's fashion elite descend upon the city for the famous ready-to-wear designer shows that invariably set next season's international styles (☞ Close Up: Clothes Make the City, *below).*

Department Stores

La Rinascente (⊠ Piazza del Duomo) is one of the bigger department stores in Milan. **Coin** (⊠ Piazza Loreto) is smaller but stylish.

Markets

Markets selling food and a vast array of items, new and old, are displayed in open-air stalls all over Milan. In many markets, bargaining is no longer the custom. You can try to haggle, but if you fear getting ripped off, go to the stalls where prices are clearly marked. On Saturday there is the huge **Mercato Papiniano** (⊠ Viale Papiniano, and the Fiera di Senigallia, on Via Calatafimi) with old and new bargains. If you collect coins or stamps, go on Sunday morning to the specialized market at **Via Armorari** (⊠ Near Piazza Cordusio). The best antiques markets are held on the last Sunday of each month along the Navigli and the third Saturday of each month on **Via Fiori Chiari** (⊠ Near Via Brera).

Shopping Districts

At the northern end of Piazza della Scala, Via Manzoni leads straight into the heart of Milan's most luxurious shopping district, perhaps the most luxurious shopping district in all of Italy. Right here, in a few small streets laid out like a game of hopscotch—Via Monte Napoleone, Via Sant'Andrea, Via della Spiga—exist the shops of the great Italian designers, such as Armani, Versace, and Gianfranco Ferré. Don't come here looking for affordable fashion—that has been relegated to the other side of the Duomo. Shops are usually open 9–1 (except Monday morning) and 4–7:30; many are closed in August. A good locator map (posted on a pole) of the best boutiques in the area can be found at the corner of Via della Spiga and Via Borgospesso.

Brera is a Milanese neighborhood with many unique shops. Walk along Via Brera, Via Solferino, Corso Garibaldi, and Via Paolo Sarpi. **Corso Buenos Aires** is a wide avenue with a variety of shops, several offering moderately priced items. **Corso Vittorio Emanuele** has clothing, leather goods, and shoe shops, some with items at reasonable prices. **Via Monte Napoleone** has 10 top-notch jewelers and a profusion of antiques stores and designer fashion boutiques, as well.

CLOTHES MAKE THE CITY

WHEN DESIGNER Mariuccia Mandelli decided in 1954 to stamp her collection with the name "Krizia," she anticipated fashion-mad 1990s Milan with an uncanny foresight. The name adopted by the former teacher is derived from a character in one of Plato's dialogues who spends all of his money on clothes and jewelry for fatuous and vain women; while this may be a designer's dream consumer, the name remains an ironic reminder of the fashion world's constant clash of art and commerce. Nowhere do the two come together as tumultuously as in Milan's Golden Triangle, the half-mile area spanning Via della Spiga, Via Montenapoleone, and Via Sant'Andrea that is home to most of Italy's high-fashion houses and the source of several billion dollars of revenue each year. It's here that top designers like Donatella Versace, Gianfranco Ferré, and Giorgio Armani have their workshops, and here that the fashion world's attention is focused four weeks a year for the men's and women's summer and winter collection shows. The city has grown out of its long-standing rivalry with Florence, home to Gucci and Salvatore Ferragamo, over the title of Italy's fashion capital, and in the 1990s has become a rival to Paris and New York for the presentation of top-quality, top-price *alta moda*.

Milan's designers, Mandelli among them, are known for a subversive attitude toward the conventions of fashion. Legends abound: Missoni's famous 1967 show in which the black silk dresses of braless models became transparent on the catwalk; Moschino's 1980s-era anti-fashion Minnie Mouse dresses and fried-egg buttons; the late Gianni Versace's "rock and roll" aesthetic that put chains and leather on the catwalk. Italian style is still Italian style, however; one notable exception to this revolutionary fervor is Giorgio Armani, the former medical student whose fluid, elegant designs have made him not only one of the world's leading stylists but also a top Hollywood designer, for films including *American Gigolo* (1980), *True Romance* (1993), *Rising Sun* (1993), and *Prêt-à-Porter* (1994), the Robert Altman fashion world spoof that, coincidentally, featured another Milanese designer, Nicola Trussardi.

Unfortunately, it's all but impossible for the general public to get in to watch fashion history being made at the collections, held mid-January (Men's Spring-Summer), at the end of February (Women's Spring-Summer), at the beginning of October (Women's Fall-Winter) and the end of June (Men's Fall-Winter). Houses hold their own lavish, celebrity-studded presentations, and admission is by jealously guarded invitation only. The national trade organization, the Camera Nazionale della Moda Italiana (✉ Largo Domodossola 1, ☎ 02/48008286) suggests giving it a go anyway. If you contact design houses in Milan directly before the shows, you may be able to wheedle your way in among the glitterati. Missoni (✉ Via T. Salvini 1, 20122, ☎ 02/76001479), Dolce & Gabbana (✉ Via Santa Cecilia 7, 20122, ☎ 02/54108152), Trussardi (✉ Piazza Duse 4, 20122, ☎ 02/760641), Gianfranco Ferré (✉ Via San Andrea 18, 20121, ☎ 02/784460), Prada (✉ Via A. Maffei, 20122, ☎ 02/546701), Krizia (✉ Palazzo Melzi d'Eril, Viale Manin 19, 20121, ☎ 02/6596415), Moschino (✉ Via Ceradini 11/a, 20129, ☎ 02/7610200), Giorgio Armani (✉ Via Borgonuovo 21, 20121, ☎ 02/290931), Gianni Versace (✉ Via Gesu 12, 20121, ☎ 02/760931).

Specialty Stores
CLOTHING AND ACCESSORIES
For the constant redefinition of cut, design, and style, **Giorgio Armani** (⊠ Via Sant'Andrea 9, ☎ 02/76003234) is the fashion temple. Hip, sleek, less formal Armani wear is sold at **Emporio Armani** (⊠ Via Durini 24, ☎ 02/76003030), at less formal prices. **Cerruti 1881** (⊠ Via della Spiga 20, ☎ 02/76009777) has elegant, classic styles for men and women. Head to **Prada** (⊠ Via della Spiga 1, ☎ 02/76002019) for Miucca's bewitching, chic spartan design found on everything from celebrities to runways these days, smart leather goods, and a look at the famous series of turn-of-the-century murals with a travel theme. **Gianfranco Ferré** (⊠ Via Sant'Andrea 19, ☎ 02/782212) concentrates on swank, ready-to-wear apparel. Daring design and color on the cutting edge is the fashion at **Gianni Versace** (⊠ Via Monte Napoleone 20, ☎ 02/76001982, 02/76008529). **Moschino** (⊠ Via Sant'Andrea 7, ☎ 02/76000832 or 02/76009404) counters the conventional.

HOUSEWARES
L'Utile e il Dilettevole (⊠ Via della Spiga) sells enchanting Italian country-style items for the home.

SHOES
Beltrami (⊠ Via Monte Napoleone 16, ☎ 02/76006660; ⊠ Piazza San Babila 4/a) *scarpe*(shoes) enjoy the fashion limelight, with assurance of good quality. For top-quality, classic design in the finest of hides, choose **Ferragamo** (⊠ Via Monte Napoleone 3, ☎ 02/76000054). For a taste of the audacious mixed with tradition, head to **Fratelli Rossetti** (⊠ Corso Matteotti 9, ☎ 02/76021650). Shoe addicts would be hard pressed not to find a gorgeous pair from **Lario 1898** (⊠ Via Monte Napoleone 21, ☎ 02/76002641) in their closets.

PAVIA, CREMONA, AND MANTUA
Cities of the Po Plain

Great Lombard cities of the Po River plain south of Milan are worthy of discovery. Pavia is celebrated for its Certosa, the Carthusian monastery. In Cremona, history's great violin makers lived and worked. A diminutive utopian Renaissance city, Sabbioneta was the fruit of one man's lifelong obsession. Mantua was home for almost 300 years of the fantastically wealthy Gonzaga dynasty.

Pavia

⑮ *38 km (24 mi) south of Milan (on E62), 57 km (35 mi) west of Cremona.*

Pavia was once Milan's chief local rival. The city dates at least from the Roman era and was the capital of the Lombard kings for two centuries (572–774). Pavia came to be known as "the city of a hundred towers" (of which only a handful have survived). Its prestigious university was founded in 1361 on the site of a 10th-century law school but has claims dating from antiquity.

The 14th-century **Castello Visconteo** now houses the local **Museo Civico** (Civic Museum), with an interesting archaeological collection and a picture gallery featuring works by Correggio. ⊠ *Viale 11 Febbraio, near Piazza Castello,* ☎ *0382/33853.* ☜ *5,000 lire.* ☉ *Tues.– Sun. 9–1:30.*

In the Romanesque church of **San Pietro in Ciel d'Oro,** you can visit the tomb of Christianity's most celebrated convert, St. Augustine, housed in a Gothic marble ark on the high altar. ⊠ *Via Matteotti.* 🖾 *Free.* ☉ *Mon.–Sat. 9–5, Sun. mass.*

The main reason for stopping in Pavia is **Certosa** (the Carthusian monastery) 8 km (5 mi) north of Pavia city center. Its facade is stupendous, with much the same relish as the Duomo in Milan, the delightful first commandment of Victorian architecture: Always decorate the decoration.

The Certosa's extravagant grandeur was due, in part, to the plan to have it house the tombs of the family of the first duke of Milan, Galeazzo Visconti III (he died during a plague, at age 49, in 1402). And extravagant it was—almost unimaginably so in an age before modern roads and transport. Only the very best marble was used in construction, transported, undoubtedly by barge, from the legendary quarries of Carrara, roughly 240 km (150 mi) away. Though the ground plan may be Gothic—a cruciform planned in a series of squares—the gorgeous fabric that rises above it is triumphantly Renaissance. On the facade, in the lower frieze, are medallions of Roman emperors and Eastern monarchs; above them are low reliefs of the life of Christ, as well as that of Galeazzo Visconti III.

The first duke was the only Visconti to be interred here, and then only some 75 years after his death, in a tomb designed by Gian Cristoforo Romano. Look for it in the right transept. In the left transept is a tomb of greater human appeal—that of a rather stern middle-aged man and a beautiful young woman. The man is Ludovico il Moro Sforza, seventh duke of Milan, who commissioned Leonardo da Vinci to paint *The Last Supper.* The woman is his wife, one of the most celebrated women of her day, Beatrice d'Este (1475–1497), the embodiment of brains, culture, birth, and beauty. Married when he was 40 and she was 16, they had enjoyed six happy years of marriage when she died suddenly, while giving birth to a stillborn child. Ludovico commissioned the sculptor Cristoforo Solari to design a joint tomb for the high altar of Santa Maria delle Grazie in Milan. Originally much larger, the tomb for some years occupied the honored place in Santa Maria delle Grazie as planned. Then, for reasons that are still mysterious, the Dominican monks, who seemed to care no more for their former patron than they did for their faded Leonardo fresco, sold the tomb to their Carthusian brothers to the south. Sadly, part of the tomb, and its remains, were lost. ⊠ *Certosa, 8 km (5 mi) north of Pavia,* ☎ *0382/925613.* 🖾 *Free; donation requested.* ☉ *Oct.–Mar., Tues.–Sat. 9–11:30 and 2:30– 4:30; Apr. and Sept., Tues.–Sun. 9–11:30 and 2:30–5:30; May–Aug., Tues.–Sun. 9:30–11:30 and 2:30–6.*

Dining

$$$ ✕ **Locanda Vecchia Pavia.** At this sophisticated, art-nouveau style
★ restaurant, you'll find creative versions of traditional regional cuisine, including *rane* (frogs), the local specialty, in risotto or on a spit. *Casoncelli* (stuffed pasta), *petto d'anatra* (breast of duck), and veal cutlet alla milanese are done with style, as are more imaginative seafood dishes. For dessert, choco-addicts will relish the hot chocolate pudding with white chocolate sauce. It's next to the Duomo. ⊠ *Via Cardinale Riboldi 2,* ☎ *0382/304132. Reservations essential. AE, DC, MC, V. Closed Mon., Jan. 1–9, and Aug. No lunch Wed.*

Nightlife and the Arts

During the first half of September, Pavia's **Settembre Pavese** festival presents street processions, displays, and concerts.

Cremona

⑯ *86 km (53 mi) east of Pavia, 67 km (42 mi) west of Mantua, 93 km (60 mi) southeast of Milan.*

If there is only one place in Italy to buy a violin, it's Cremona—as true today as when Andrea Amati (1510–80) opened up shop here in the middle of the 16th century. Though cognoscenti continue to revere the Amati name, it was the apprentice of Amati's nephew, Nicolo (1596–1684), for whom the fates had reserved a wide and lasting international fame. In a career that spanned an incredible 68 years, Antonio Stradivari (1644–1737) made more than 1,200 instruments—including violas, cellos, harps, guitars, and mandolins, in addition to his fabled violins. Labeled simply with a small printed slip, "Antonius Stradivarius Cremonensis. Faciebat anno . . ." (the date added in a neat italic hand), they remain the best, most coveted, and most expensive stringed instruments in the world.

Cremona's Romanesque **Duomo** was consecrated in 1190 and his home to the beautiful *Storia della Vergine e della Passione di Cristo* (Story of the Virgin Mary and the Passion of Christ), the central fresco of an extraordinary cycle commissioned in 1514 and featuring the work of primarily local artists, including Boccacio Boccancino, Giovan Francesco Bembo, and Altobello Melone. ⊠ *Piazza del Comune.* ☉ *Mon.–Sat. 7:30–noon and 3:30–7, Sun. 7:30–1 and 3:30–7.*

If you would like to see the original Stradivarius instruments, go to the second floor of **Palazzo del Comune** (City Hall), where five masterpieces by Cremonese *liutai* (violin makers), dating from the 16th to the 18th centuries, are on view. ⊠ *Piazza del Comune,* ☎ *0372/4071.* ☞ *6,000 lire, valid for all other Cremona museums, including the Museo Stradivariano (☞ below).* ☉ *Tues.–Sat. 8:30–6, Sun. 9:15–12:15 and 3–6.*

Piazza del Comune, with its Duomo (☞ *above*), campanile, baptistery, and city hall, is particularly distinctive and harmonious. The combination of old brick, rose- and cream-color marble, terra-cotta, and old copper roofs brings Romanesque, Gothic, and Renaissance together with unusual success.

The large campanile that dominates the square is the **Torrazzo** (Big Tower), perhaps the tallest bell tower in the country, visible for a considerable distance across the Po plain. Its height, however, was the source of tragedy in 1997, as three people committed suicide by throwing themselves from the top; consequently, the tower was closed for renovation, at press time due to reopen summer 1998. Italy, however, is the land of the overdue project, so check with the tourist authority for its eventual reopening. ⊠ *Piazza del Comune.* ☞ *6,000 lire.* ☉ *Apr.–Oct., Mon.–Sat. 10:30–noon and 3–6, Sun. 10:30–12:30 and 3–6:30.*

At No. 1 **Piazza Roma**, Antonio Stradivari lived, worked, and died. It's a lovely square of gardens, trees, and lawns. It is said that in addition to knowing all there was to know about woods, varnish, and the subtleties of assembling the 70-odd component parts that make up a violin, Stradivari liked to keep each new instrument in his bedroom for a month before varnishing it. This way, he claimed, by virtue of some mysterious somnolent transmigration, he gave a soul to each of his creations. In the center of the park is **Stradivari's grave,** marked by a simple tombstone.

The small **Museo Stradivariano** (Stradivarius Museum) has an informative display of Stradivari's plans and models, and violins made by Cremona's more modern masters. ⊠ *Via Palestro 17,* ☎ *0372/461886.* ☞ *6,000 lire valid for Palazzo del Comune (☞ above).* ☉ *Tues.–Sat. 8:30–6, Sun. 9:15–12:15 and 3–6.*

Strolling about town, you may notice that violin making continues to flourish here. There are, in fact, more than 50 *liutai* (violin makers), many of them graduates of the **Scuola Internazionale di Liuteria** (International School of Violin Making), who continue to work by traditional methods in small shops scattered throughout Cremona. You are usually welcome to these ateliers, especially if contemplating the acquisition of their own ready-made or custom-built Cremonese violin. You can always drop in on any shop, otherwise the local tourist office can arrange appointments.

Dining

$$$$
★
✕ **Ceresole.** This unobtrusive restaurant just off the Piazza del Comune is Cremona's best—and most expensive—establishment. It offers a variety of elegant international dishes but concentrates on local delights: *cotecchino* (a rich boiled sausage) and risotto, to name a couple. ⊠ *Via Ceresole 4,* ☎ *0372/30099. AE, DC, MC, V. Closed Mon. No dinner Sun.*

$$–$$$
★
✕ **Centrale.** Close to the cathedral, this is a favorite among the locals for traditional Cremonese fare, such as cotecchino *con mostarda* (with mustard-hot crystallized fruit), at moderate prices. ⊠ *Vicolo Pertusio 4,* ☎ *0372/28701. AE, DC, MC, V. Closed Thurs. and July.*

Shopping

Cremona is famous throughout Europe as the home of nougat, known here as *torrone*. If the thought of sweet, tooth-crunching nougat is too much to resist, go to **Spellari** (⊠ Via Solferino 26), home of *the* best nougat in the world. The store also sells all kinds of mostarda.

Sabbioneta

❶ *53 km (33 mi) southeast of Cremona, 34 km (21 mi) southwest of Mantua.*

Vespasiano Gonzaga (1531–1591), Sabbioneta's lord, founder, and chief architect, was not a particularly sympathetic man. The glory of his attainments in a life of public service is said to have been excelled only by the ignominy of his treatment of three wives and his only son. Upon retiring from military life at 47, he resolved to turn an old castle and a few squalid cottages into the Perfect City—a tiny, urbane metropolis where the most gifted artists and greatest writers would live in perfect harmony with a perfect patron. After some five years of planning and another five of work, the village was transformed into an elegant, star-shape, walled fortress, with a rational grid of streets, two palaces, two squares, two churches, an exquisite theater (said to be the first in Europe with a roof) by Vincenzo Scamozzi, and a noble Gallery of Antiquities (a forerunner of today's art galleries). Gonzaga died four years later, survived only by the last of his wives.

When Aldous Huxley and his wife visited Sabbioneta in 1924, the town had reached an appalling state of neglect and decay. The Huxleys were given a tour (still the only way of seeing the interiors of most of Sabbioneta's buildings) much like the tour you take today. Apply at the Ufficio Turistico (Tourist Office; ⊠ Via Vespasiano Gonzaga 31, ☎ 0375/52039). *Tours:* ⊠ *Piazza Ducale.* ☎ *Tour 10,000 lire.* ☉ *Apr.– Sept., Tues.–Sun. 9–noon and 2:30–7; Oct.–Mar., Tues.–Sat. 9– noon and 2:30–5, Sun. 9–noon and 2:30–5:30.*

In the majestic **Palazzo Ducale** (Ducal Palace) are four fine equestrian figures of Vespasiano and his Gonzaga forebears. They were led through what had once been the Cabinet of Diana, the ducal saloon, and other rooms, only to discover that the rooms had been converted to serve the structure's new function as the town hall. They were shown the little **theater** (an adaption of Palladio's, at Vicenza, by the man who helped him build it), but it lacked its stage, and its frescoes were covered with whitewash. Today you will find the theater restored and its frescoes uncovered. The third building on the tour, the **Palazzo del Giardino,** has a dusty but impressive gallery of antique sculptures. Tours (☞ *above*) begin whenever enough interested people have assembled.

The **synagogue** is now a shuttered and derelict building, the sole surviving trace of Sabbioneta's prosperous 16th-century Jewish community. You'll have to ask someone to point it out. ⊠ *Town center.*

Mantua

⓲ *67 km (42 mi) east of Cremona, 64 km (40 mi) south of Bardolino, 160 km (102 mi) southeast of Milan.*

Mantua (Mantova) is known as the seat of the Gonzagas, who, like the Viscontis and Sforzas of Milan (with whom they intermarried), lived with the regal pomp and circumstance befitting one of Italy's richest family dynasties. Their reign, first as marquesses, and later as dukes, was a long one—stretching from the first half of the 14th century into the beginning of the 18th.

Even if you've had enough of old palaces, you may still wish to come to Mantua. First, Virgil was born near here. Second, Mantegna (painter of the poignant *Dead Christ* in Milan's Brera) was the Gonzaga court painter for 50 years, and his best-known and only large surviving fresco cycle can be seen here. In addition, there are two fine churches by Leon Battista Alberti (1404–72). Much like Mantegna's work here, both proved highly influential and were widely emulated by lesser architectural lights later in the Renaissance.

A home to the Gonzagas for centuries, the 500-room **Palazzo Ducale** gives one the sense that the palace took centuries to build. From a distance, the group of buildings dominates the skyline, and the effect is fascinating. The **Appartamento dei Nani** (Dwarfs' Apartments) were literally that, dwarf collecting being one of the more amusing occupations of Renaissance princes. According to historians, the dwarfs were not mistreated but were considered to be something between members of the family and celebrity comics. The apartments were built both for the dwarfs' enjoyment and for that of the court.

The **Appartamento del Paradiso** is praised for its view but is somewhat more interesting for its decorator and first resident, Isabella d'Este (1474–1539). Not only was she married at 16, like her younger sister Beatrice (the beautiful young woman of the tomb in the Certosa at Pavia; ☞ *above*), she was apparently also Ludovico il Moro Sforza's first choice for a wife—until he learned she was already affianced to a Gonzaga rival. Isabella, too, was one of the great patrons of the Renaissance. She survived her sister by more than 40 years, and the archives of her correspondence, totaling more than 2,000 letters, are considered some of the most valuable records of the era.

The high point of all 500 rooms, if not of the city, is the **Camera degli Sposi** (literally, "Chamber of the Wedded Couple," because Duke Ludovico and his wife are the focus of attention; it was actually an audience chamber). It was painted by Mantegna over a nine-year period, when he was at the height of his power, and finished when he was 44. Here, Mantegna made a startling advance in painting by organizing the picture's plane of representation in a way that systematically mimics the experience of human vision. Even now, more than five centuries later, you can almost sense the excitement of a mature artist, fully aware of his painting's great importance, expressing his vision with a masterly, joyous confidence. The interiors of Mantua's Palazzo Ducale may be seen today only on a rigorous guided tour normally conducted in Italian by the museum. However, if you wish to be accompanied by an English-speaking guide, call the Tourist Guide Association (☎ 0376/368917) or the APT (tourist board) (⊠ Piazza A. Mantegna 6, ☎ 0376/328253). ⊠ *Piazza Sordello,* ☎ *0376/320283.* ☜ *12,000 lire.* ☉ *Tues.–Sat. 9–1 and 2:30–6, Sun.–Mon. 9–1.*

The most serious Mantegna aficionado will want to visit the **Casa di Andrea Mantegna,** designed by the artist himself and built around an intriguing circular courtyard, usually open to view (the interior can only be seen by appointment or occasional art exhibitions). ⊠ *Via Acerbi 47,* ☎ *0376/360506.* ☜ *Free.* ☉ *Daily 9–12:30 and 3–6.*

The artist's tomb is in the first chapel on the left in another church, **Sant'Andrea** (1471, some sections earlier or later) a masterwork of the architect Alberti, which itself is considered Mantua's most important Renaissance creation. ⊠ *Piazza delle Erbe, south of Piazza Sordello.* ☉ *Daily 8–12:30 and 3–6.*

Palazzo Tè is one of the greatest of all Renaissance palaces, built by Isabella d'Este's son, Federigo II Gonzaga (1500–40), between 1525 and 1535, for his mistress. It is the singular Mannerist creation of artist-architect Giulio Romano, decorated with mythological trompe l'oeil paintings not to every visitor's taste. Nevertheless, as the magnificently frescoed **Sala dei Giganti** (Room of Giants) proves, the palace does not skimp on pictorial drama. ⊠ *Viale Tè, south of town walls,* ☎ *0376/365886.* ☜ *12,000 lire.* ☉ *Mon. 1–6, Tues.–Sun. 9–6.*

Dining and Lodging

$$$$ ✕ **Al Bersagliere.** One of Lombardy's best restaurants can be found
★ in this rustic four-room inn, in the tiny riverside hamlet of Goito, some 16 km (10 mi) northwest of Mantua on Route 236 (the main Mantua–Brescia road). It has been run by a single family for more than 150 years. The fish in particular is excellent, as is a Mantuan classic, frog soup. ⊠ *Via Goitese 258, Goito,* ☎ *0376/60007. Reservations essential. AE, DC, MC, V. Closed Mon., 15 days in Jan., and 15 days in Aug. No lunch Tues.*

$$$ ✕ **L'Aquila Nigra.** Down a small side street opposite the Palazzo Ducale, this popular restaurant is set in a former medieval convent. Frescoes look down from the walls on diners making their way through local dishes, such as *frittata di zucchine* (zucchini frittata) and *faraona al pepe verde* (guinea fowl with green pepper). ⊠ *Vicolo Bonacolsi 4,* ☎ *0376/327180. Reservations essential. AE, DC, MC, V. Closed Sun.–Mon., 3 wks in Aug., and Dec. 24–Jan. 5.*

$$–$$$ ✕ **Trattoria dei Martini–Il Cigno.** In a romantic 16th-century palazzo featuring some period frescoes, this restaurant scores well with atmosphere. The menu features local specialties such as *tortelli di zucca* (pasta stuffed with squash), *insalata di cappone* (capon salad), and local variations on the Lombard favorite, risotto. ⊠ *Piazza Carlo d'Arco 1,* ☎ *0376/327101. Reservations essential. AE, DC, MC, V. Closed Mon.– Tues., 1 wk in Jan., 3 wks in Aug.*

$–$$ ✕ **Cento Rampini.** In a square in the heart of medieval Mantua, this friendly, family-run trattoria is a local favorite. Among the tasty traditional dishes are risotto, *agnoli* (meat-filled pasta dumplings, and *costoletta d'agnello al timo* (lamb cutlet with thyme). ⊠ *Piazza Erbe 11,* ☎ *0376/366349. AE, DC, MC, V. Closed Mon., 1 wk in late Jan., and Aug. 1–15. No dinner Sun.*

$$$ ☷ **San Lorenzo.** Rooms in this center city hotel are large, with authentic early-19th-century decor. Although there is no restaurant, you're within easy walking distance of many. Some people may find the rooms in the front a little noisy at night, when locals perform their ritualistic *passeggiata*, or social stroll. The San Lorenzo has a rooftop terrace and exudes comfort and individual attention. ⊠ *Piazza Concordia 14, 46100, ☎ 0376/220500, ℻ 0376/327194. 32 rooms. Minibars, parking (fee). AE, DC, MC, V.*

Nightlife and the Arts

Each year on the feast of the Assumption (August 15), a contest is held in Mantua to determine who is the best *madonnaro* (street artist). Some of the painters can re-create masterpieces in a matter of minutes.

LAKE GARDA, BRESCIA, BERGAMO

Of all the curious things to be noted about Lake Garda, one is its perennial attraction for writers. Even the 16th-century essayist Michel de Montaigne (1533–92), whose 15 months of travel journals contain not a single other reference to nature, paused to admire the view down the lake from Torbole, which he called "boundless."

Lake Garda is 50 km (31 mi) long, ranges from roughly 1–16 km (½–10 mi) wide, and is as much as 1,135 ft deep. The terrain is flat at the lake's southern base, and mountainous at its northern tip. As a consequence, the standard descriptions of it vary from stormy inland sea to crystalline Nordic fjord. It is the biggest lake in the region and by most accounts the cleanest. If you are traveling by car, you should be particularly careful when driving in and out of the hairpin turns on the lake road, as there have been several fatal accidents in recent years, caused mostly by local youths driving at high speeds.

Bardolino

⑲ *64 km (40 mi) north of Mantua, 6 km (4 mi) south of Punta di San Vigilio, 34 km (21 mi) south of Malcesine.*

Bardolino, which makes unremarkable but famous red wine, is one of the biggest summer resorts on the lake. It stands on the eastern shore at the widest end of the lake. Here there are two handsome Romanesque churches: **San Severo,** from the 11th century, and **San Zeno,** from the 9th. Both are in the center of the small town. Bardolino is very lively at night, especially compared to other towns on the lake.

Punta di San Vigilio

⑳ *70 km (44 mi) north of Mantua, 6 km (4 mi) north of Bardolino, 28 km (17 mi) south of Malcesine.*

Punta di San Vigilio, which just about everyone agrees is the prettiest spot on Garda's eastern shore, is full of cypresses from the gardens of the 15th-century **Villa Guarienti di Brenzone.**

Nightlife and the Arts

Bardolino is host to several festivals, but the best one is the **Cura del Grappolo** (Grape Cure Festival), a great excuse to indulge in some of the local vino, since the idea is that the more you drink the better the cure will be. Bring aspirin, just in case.

Malcesine

㉑ *34 km (21 mi) north of Bardolino, 19 km (12 mi) south of Riva del Garda.*

One of the loveliest areas along the upper eastern shore of Lake Garda, Malcesine is principally known as a summer resort with sailing and windsurfing schools. The 13 campsites and tourist villages do tend to make the town a little crowded in summer. There are however, some nice walks from the town toward the mountains behind. Dominating the town is the 13th- to 14th-century **Castello Scaligero,** built by the Della Scalas.

OFF THE
BEATEN PATH
MONTE BALDO – You're in the Veneto now, and if you are fond of cable cars, take the 15-minute *funivia* (funicular) ride to the top of Monte Baldo (5,791 ft) for a great view of the whole lake in summer, or possibly a short ski run in winter.

Outdoor Activities and Sports

SKIING

Malcesine (☎ 045/7400555) is a well-equipped resort with six lifts and more than 11 km (7 mi) of runs of varying degrees of difficulty.

Riva del Garda

㉒ *21 km (13 mi) north of Malcesine, 27 km (17 mi) north of Gargnano.*

One of the biggest towns on the northern tip of the lake, Riva del Garda is large and prosperous, and if you're there in summer, you may want to lodge there if the towns farther south seem too crowded. Many of the town's public buildings date from the 15th century, when it was a strategic outpost of the Venetian Republic. The heart of town, the lakeside **Piazza 3 Novembre,** is surrounded by medieval *palazzi*. The newly cleaned **Torre Apponale,** predating the Venetian period by three centuries, looms above the medieval residences of Riva del Garda's main square: Its crenellations recall its defensive purpose. Standing in the piazza and looking out onto the lake, you can understand Riva del Garda's importance as a windsurfing center. Mountain air currents ensure good breezes on even the sultriest midsummer days.

OFF THE
BEATEN PATH
TORBOLE – Take the 10-minute boat ride from Riva del Garda to Torbole (5 km/3 mi east), with a slightly less-resorty feel, quaint waterfront, and colorful windsurfers as far as the eye can see. For lovely Italian-made items such as unique costume jewelry and decorative fixtures, find your way to the little store called Pescicoltura (⊠ Piazza Alpini 16, ☎ 0335/283858), great for gifts.

CASCATA DEL VARONE – This waterfall, some 295 ft high, is 4 km (2½ mi) north of town on the road to Tenno. You can walk up to an observation platform and look up at the water plummeting down the cavity it has carved over time; bring a waterproof jacket.

CASTEL TOBLINO – A lovely stop for a lakeside drink or a romantic dinner is this castle, right on a lake in Sarche, about 20 km (12 mi) north of Riva towards Trento. The compound is fabled to be a prehistoric, then Roman village, and then later associated with the Church of Trento. Bernardo Clesio had it rebuilt in the 16th century in the Renaissance style. It is now a sanctuary of fine food, serving such dishes as *garganelli alla salsa di carciofi* (grooved tubular-shape pasta with artichoke sauce) and *filetto di cavalli ai finferli* (horse meat fillet with wild mushrooms). ⊠ *Via Caffaro 1, Sarche,* ☎ *0461/864036. MC, V. Closed Tues. No dinner Mon.*

Lodging

$ ⊡ **Hotel Sole.** Occupying a restored 15th-century palazzo, this understated, lovely hotel offers comfortable, well-appointed rooms at affordable rates, which these days is a rare combination for the ever-popular Lake Garda. The terraced rooms in front have breathtaking views of the lake, mountains, and the medieval rooftops of the town. In summer, sun worshipers who despair of the often-crowded beaches can sun themselves in the secluded privacy of the roof terrace. ⊠ *Piazza 3 Novembre, 38066,* ☎ *0464/552686,* FAX *0464/552811. 49 rooms, 3 suites. Restaurant, bar, in-room safes, refrigerators, room service, sauna, steam room. AE, DC, MC, V.*

Outdoor Activities and Sports

WINDSURFING

Contact **Circolo Surf Torbole** (⊠ Colonia Pavese, ☎ 0464/505385) for news on windsurfing in the area.

En Route   After passing the town of Limone—where it is said the first lemon trees in Europe were planted—take the fork to the right about 5 km (3 mi) north of Gargnano and head to Tignale. The view from the **Madonna di Monte Castello** church, some 2,000 ft above the lake, is spectacular. Adventurous travelers will want to follow this pretty inland mountain road to Tremosine; the road winds its way up the mountain through hairpin turns and blind corners that can test even the most experienced drivers.

Gargnano

㉓   *27 km (17 mi) south of Riva del Garda, 12 km (7 mi) north of Gardone Riviera.*

This small port town was an important Franciscan center in the 13th century. One of the two houses owned and lived in by Mussolini is now a language school; the other, **Villa Feltrinelli,** has not yet been opened to the public, but plans are being made for a museum to open some time in 1999. An Austrian flotilla bombarded the town in 1866 and some of the houses still bear signs of cannon fire. The town comes alive in the summer months when mostly German tourists, many of whom have villas here, invade the small pebble beach.

Dining and Lodging

$$$–$$$$ ✕ **La Tortuga.** This highly acclaimed restaurant may have the appearance of a rustic trattoria, but the decor belies the sophisticated, nouvelle-style twists on local dishes. The six-course meals are divine: Begin with the *petto d'anitra all'aceto balsamico a caponata di verdure* (breast of duck in balsamic vinegar on shredded vegetables), followed by the *pasta fresca gamberi e radicchio Trevisano* (fresh pasta with shrimp and radicchio from Treviso). The main course is the *branzino e lenticchio* (sea bass covered in marinated lentils) followed by a thyme and rosemary rack of lamb, between which you can enjoy the palate-cleansing passion-fruit sorbet. Tempting desserts include hot chocolate soufflé smothered in white-and-dark chocolate sauce. Wines surface from the owner's extensive cellar; try the local white Lugana. ⊠ *Via XXIV Maggio, Gargnano,* ☎ *0365/71251. AE, MC, V. Closed Tues. and Jan.–Feb. No dinner Mon. Oct.–May.*

$ 🏨 **Hotel Bartabel.** This cozy hotel on the main street offers comfortable, basic accommodations at a reasonable price. The restaurant has an elegant terrace overlooking the lake. ⊠ *Via Roma 39,* ☎ *0365/71330,* FAX *0365/790009. 10 rooms. Restaurant. AE, DC, MC, V.*

Outdoor Activities and Sports

HIKING

Tremosine, some 17 km (11 mi) north of Gargnano, is known as the "Garda Terrace," and is a mountain forest area that is an ideal place for nature hikes. For more information, write or call the **Ufficio Comunale** (⊠ Via Papa Giovanni XXIII, ☎ 0365/953185).

En Route Going from Gargnano to Gardone you pass the small town of **Toscolano-Maderno,** which has a delightful lakefront piazza and one of the oldest paper recycling factories in Italy. The town itself hails from Etruscan times but there are also remnants of Roman influence.

Gardone Riviera

㉔ *12 km (7 mi) south of Gargnano, 32 km (19 mi) north of Sirmione.*

Gardone Riviera is a once-fashionable turn-of-the-century resort, now delightfully faded, and the former home of the flamboyant Gabriele d'Annunzio (1863–1938), one of Italy's greatest modern poets.

D'Annunzio's estate, **Il Vittoriale,** perched on the hills above the town, is an elaborate memorial to himself, clogged with the trappings of conquests in art, love, and war (of which the largest is a ship's prow in the garden), and complete with a mausoleum. ⊠ *Gardone Riviera,* ☎ *0365/20130.* ⊡ *16,000 lire, including tour of house.* ☉ *Oct.–Mar., Tues.–Sun. 9–12:30 and 2–5:30; Apr.–Sept., Tues.–Sun. 8:30–8.*

OFF THE **SALÒ MARKET** – 4 km (2½ mi) south of Gardone Riviera is the pretty
BEATEN PATH lakeside town of Salò, which history buffs may recognize as the capital of the ill-fated Social Republic, set up in 1943 by the Germans after they liberated Mussolini from the Gran Sasso. Every Saturday morning, in the Piazza dei Martiri della Libertà, an enormous market is held, with great bargains on everything from household items to clothing to foodstuffs. In August or September, a lone vendor often sells locally unearthed *tartufi neri* (black truffles) at affordable prices.

Dining and Lodging

$$$–$$$$ ✕⊞ **Villa Fiordaliso.** The pink-and-white lakeside Villa Fiordaliso—
★ once home to Claretta Petacci, given to her by her lover Benito Mussolini—is a high-quality restaurant, but it also has seven tastefully furnished rooms, some overlooking the lake. The art-nouveau style restaurant (no lunch Tues.) features seasonal ingredients like zucchini flowers or porcini mushrooms, paramount in salads and soups. ⊠ *Via Zanardelli 132, 25083,* ☎ *0365/20158,* ℻ *0365/290011. 7 rooms. Restaurant. AE, DC, MC, V. Closed Mon. and Jan.–Feb.*

$$$–$$$$ ⊞ **Villa del Sogno.** A small, winding road takes you from the village
★ to this imposing villa, which surveys the valley and the lake below it. The large hotel terrace and the quiet surrounding grounds add to the feeling of getting away from it all, and you'll probably think twice about a busy sightseeing itinerary once you've settled into position in the sun, cool drink in hand. ⊠ *Corso Zanardelli 107, 25083,* ☎ *0365/290181,* ℻ *0365/290230. 34 rooms. Restaurant, pool, tennis court. AE, DC, MC, V. Closed mid-Oct.–Easter.*

$$$ ⊞ **Grand Hotel Fasano.** A former 19th-century hunting lodge on the lakefront, the Fasano has matured into a seasonal hotel of a high standard. The staff is friendly, as are most of the guests, who seem to be keen on making the most use of the water sports at their disposal. It's worth paying a bit extra to get one of the larger rooms with a lake view and balcony. ⊠ *Corso Zanardelli 160, 25083,* ☎ *0365/290220,* ℻ *0365/290221. 75 rooms. Restaurant, bar, pool, beach, windsurfing, waterskiing. MC, V. Closed Nov.–mid-May.*

Nightlife and the Arts

MUSIC
Il Vittoriale (☎ 0365/20130, ☞ *above*) holds a series of concerts in its outdoor theater during July and August.

Sirmione

★ ㉕ *32 km (19 mi) south of Gardone Riviera, 41 km (25 mi) east of Brescia.*

The ruins at this enchanting town on an isthmus at the southwestern shore of Lake Garda, complete with narrow, cobbled streets that wind their way through medieval arches, are a reminder that Garda has been a holiday resort for the leisurely well-to-do since the height of the Roman era. Most of the historic town, which stretches the length of the spit, is inaccessible to cars, so you must park the car at the bottom of the historic center and walk the rest of the way. The locals will almost certainly tell you that the so-called **Grotte di Catullo** (Grottoes of Catullus) were once the site of the villa of Catullus, one of the greatest pleasure-seeking poets of all time. Present archaeological wisdom, however, does not concur, and there is some consensus that this was the site of two villas of slightly different periods, dating from about the 1st century AD. But never mind—the view through the cypresses and olive trees is lovely, and even if Catullus didn't have a villa here, he is closely associated with the area and undoubtedly did have a villa somewhere nearby. The ruins are at the top of the isthmus and are badly signposted: walk through the historic center and past the various villas to the top of the spit; the grottoes are on the right. ✉ *Grotte di Catullo, Sirmione,* ☎ *030/916157.* 🎫 *8,000 lire.* ☉ *Mar.–Sept., Tues.–Sun. 8:30–6; Oct.–Feb., Tues.–Sat. 8:30–4:30, Sun. 9–4:30.*

The **Rocca Scaligera** castle was built, along with almost all the other castles on the lake, by the Della Scala family. As hereditary rulers of Verona for more than a century before control of the city was seized by the Visconti in 1402, they counted Garda among their possessions. You may wish to go inside, since there is a nice view of the lake from the tower. Or you may want to go for a swim at the nearby beach before continuing on. Entry to the old part of town is gained through the castle's gates, over what was originally a drawbridge. ✉ *Rocca Scaligera, Sirmione,* ☎ *030/916468.* 🎫 *7,000 lire.* ☉ *June–Sept., Tues.–Sat. 9–6 , Sun. 9–1; Oct.–Apr., Mon.–Sat. 9–1.*

OFF THE BEATEN PATH

GARDALAND AMUSEMENT PARK – This park has more than 40 different rides and water slides and is one of Italy's biggest amusement parks to thrill your children. It is 16 km (10 mi) east of Sirmione. ✉ *Castelnuovo del Garda,* ☎ *045/6449777.* 🎫 *27,000 lire.* ☉ *July–mid-Sept., daily 9 am–midnight; Apr.–June, daily 9–6 (some days until 7 or 8); mid- to late Mar. and Oct., weekends 9–6.*

Dining and Lodging

$$$ ✗ **Vecchia Lugana.** At the base of the peninsula and outside the town,
★ this restaurant is considered one of Italy's best. Fish from the lake, grilled trout, and fillet of perch with artichokes are especially good. There's also an elegant garden. ✉ *Piazzale Vecchia Lugana 1, Lugana di Sirmione,* ☎ *030/919012. AE, DC, MC, V. No dinner Mon. Closed Tues. and Jan.*

$$ ✗ **Ristorante Al Pescatore.** The specialty of this simple rustic looking, but very popular restaurant is lake fish. Try grilled trout with a bottle of local white wine and finish your meal with a walk in the nearby public park. ✉ *Via Piana 20,* ☎ *030/916216. DC, MC, V. Closed Jan.–Feb. and Wed. Oct.–May.*

$$$$ 🏨 **Villa Cortine Palace.** A formidably decorative former private villa in a secluded park, Villa Cortine is in danger of being just plain ostentatious. It dominates a low hill, and the grounds—a colorful mixture of lawns, trees, statues, and fountains—go down to the lake. The

villa itself dates from the early part of the 19th century, although a wing (1952) was added: The trade-off is between the more charming old-world decor in the older rooms and the better lake views from the newer ones. ✉ *Via Grotte 6, 25019,* ☎ *030/9905890,* 🖷 *030/916390. 57 rooms. Restaurant, bar, pool, tennis court, beach. AE, DC, MC, V. Closed Oct.–Apr. 10.*

$$–$$$ 🏨 **Continental.** On the lakefront, right next to a spa, the Continental operates on a half-pension basis only. This works to keep the cost in check, and the hotel has the amenities and feel of a much more expensive establishment. Most rooms have balconies, but ask specifically for a lake view. ✉ *Via Punta Staffalo 7, 25019,* ☎ *030/9905711,* 🖷 *030/916278. 51 rooms. Pool, beach. AE, DC, MC, V. Closed Dec.–Mar. MAP.*

$$ 🏨 **Hotel Sirmione.** Just inside the city walls, near the Castello, this hotel
★ and spa sits amid lakeside gardens and terraces. Some rooms display superb execution, with comfortable Scandinavian slat beds, matching floral draperies and wall coverings, and built-in white furniture. Many guests have been returning for years, largely due to the homespun feel and the attentiveness of its staff. Full and half pension are offered. ✉ *Piazza Castello 19, 25019,* ☎ *030/916331,* 🖷 *030/916558. 76 rooms. Restaurant, bar, pool, spa, meeting rooms. AE, DC, MC, V.*

Brescia

㉖ *19 km (12 mi) west of Lake Garda, 49 km (30 mi) east of Bergamo, 50 km (31 mi) east of Milan.*

The ruins of the **Capitolino,** a Capitoline temple built by the Emperor Vespasian in AD 73, testify to Brescia's Roman origin. Outstanding among the sculptures in the adjoining **Museo Romano** is the famed 1st-century bronze *Winged Victory.* ✉ *Via dei Musei 57/a,* ☎ *030/46031.* 🎟 *5,000 lire.* ☉ *Apr.–Oct. 14, Mon.–Sat. 10–5, Sun. 9–1 and 2:30–7; Oct. 15–Mar., Mon.–Sat. 8:30–4:30, Sun. 9–4:30.*

In addition to the Brescia School, the **Pinacoteca Civica Tosio-Martinengo** houses paintings by Raphael, Tintoretto, Tiepolo, and Clouet. ✉ *Piazza Moretto,* ☎ *030/3774999.* 🎟 *5,000 lire.* ☉ *June–Sept., Tues.–Sun. 10:30–7; Oct.–May, Tues.–Sun. 9–1 and 2:30–5.*

Palladio and Sansovino contributed to the splendid **Palazzo della Loggia,** the Lombard-Venetian palace of marble overlooking the Piazza della Loggia. The **Torre dell'Orologio** (Clock Tower; ✉ Piazza della Loggia) dates from the 16th century and is modeled on the campanile in Venice's Piazza San Marco. In the church of **Madonna del Carmine** are a flight of stairs that climb to the ramparts of the Venetian **Castello,** high enough to give a panoramic view over the town and across the plain to the distant Alps. ✉ *Piazza del Duomo. Closed Mon. and Wed.*

Dining and Lodging

$$$$ ✕ **Gualtiero Marchesi.** Never afraid to try something new, owner-chef
★ Gualtiero Marchesi is celebrated as the founder of *la cucina nuova* (nouvelle cuisine). Since 1993 the kitchen in this deluxe hotel villa has been revered for its spectacular flights of fantasy grounded with classic Lombardian finesse. Tiny lake fish are served within white paper, folded origami fashion, soups are garnished with caviar, and ravioli are served *aperto* (open and unsealed at the edges) or *fazzoletto,* handkerchief-style. You can easily become Romeo to Marchesi's dazzling Juliet—*a rombo in crosta di sale* (turbot in salt crust). The desserts—and prices—are stellar. ✉ *Via Vittorio Emanuele 11, Erbusco, part of the Albereta Hotel,* ☎ *030/7760562. Reservations essential. Jacket and tie. AE, DC, MC, V. Closed Mon. and Jan. 12–Feb. 12. No dinner Sun.*

$$$ ✕ **La Sosta.** Just south of Brescia's cathedral, La Sosta occupies a 17th-century building. The cuisine and service suggest a more expensive establishment. A Brescian specialty is *casonsei* (large meat-filled ravioli). *Capretto alla bresciana* (roast kid with polenta) is an outstanding main course, but make sure you have room for it. ⊠ *Via San Martino della Battaglia 20,* ☎ *030/295603,* ℻ *030/292589. AE, DC, MC, V. Closed Mon., 1st wk in Dec., and 3 wks in Aug. No dinner Sun.*

$$$ ☲ **Vittoria.** Centrally located among 16th-century buildings, Vittoria has more than its share of atmosphere. Erected in 1933, the hotel is in the Venetian style, with a hint of Byzantium and the Spice Routes in its pointed arches and windows. Many of the rooms are adorned with antiques. ⊠ *Via delle X Giornate 20, 25019,* ☎ *030/280061,* ℻ *030/280065. 66 rooms. Restaurant, bar, meeting rooms. AE, DC, MC, V.*

Nightlife and the Arts

Brescia's **Teatro Grande** (☎ 030/3750459) has a series of classical music concerts from May to November.

Bergamo

➋ *49 km (30 mi) west of Brescia, 58 km (36 mi) southeast of Bellagio.*

Bergamo is two cities—**Bergamo Bassa** (Lower Bergamo) and **Bergamo Alta** (Upper Bergamo), connected by a funicular railway. High up on the hillside, walled in by the ruins of ancient Venetian fortifications, surmounted by a fortress, is Bergamo Alta. The old city of Bergamo, one of northern Italy's most charming medieval centers, lies at the foot of the Bergamese Alps.

The massive **Torre Civica** offers a great view of the two cities, the lower and upper. ⊠ *Piazza Vecchia,* ☎ *035/262566.* ☉ *Apr.–Sept., Mon.–Thurs. and Sun. 9–noon and 2–8, Fri.–Sat. 9–noon and 2–11; Oct., weekends 10–noon and 2–6; Nov.–Feb., weekends 10–noon and 2–4; Mar., Mon.–Sun. 10–noon and 2–6.*

The **Duomo** of Bergamo and the **Battistero** are the most notable buildings in Piazza Vecchia. But the most impressive is the **Cappella Colleoni,** which has been cleaned, and its elaborate marble decoration is resplendent. ⊠ *Piazza Vecchia,* ☎ *035/217317.* ☉ *Cappella Colleoni weekdays 7:30–noon and 3–6:30. Baptistery visits by arrangement with Duomo parish priest.*

★ In the **Accademia Carrara** you will find one of Italy's greatest and most important art collections. Many of the Venetian masters are represented—Mantegna, Carpaccio, Tiepolo, Guardi, Canaletto—and there are some magnificent Bellinis and Botticellis as well. ⊠ *Bergamo Bassa, Piazza Carrara,* ☎ *035/399426.* ☲ *5,000 lire; Sun. free.* ☉ *Wed.–Mon. 9:30–noon and 2:30–5:30.*

Dining and Lodging

$$$$ ✕ **Dell'Angelo–Taverna del Colleoni.** Angelo Cornaro has closed the
★ celebrated Antico Ristorante dell'Angelo to concentrate all his attention on the Taverna del Colleoni, on the 15th-century Piazza Vecchia, right behind the Duomo, where he continues to serve a wide and imaginative range of fish and meat dishes, all expertly prepared. ⊠ *Piazza Vecchia 7,* ☎ *035/232596. AE, DC, MC, V. Closed Mon., 1 wk in Jan., and 2 wks in Aug.*

$$ ✕ **Agnello d'Oro.** A 17th-century tavern on a main street in Upper Bergamo, with wooden booths and walls hung with copper utensils and ceramic plates, Agnello d'Oro is a good place to imbibe the atmosphere as well as the good local wine. Specialties are typical Bergamasque risotto and varieties of polenta served with game and mushrooms. The same

establishment also has 20 modestly priced rooms. ⊠ *Via Gombito 22,* ☎ *035/249883. AE, DC, MC, V. Closed Mon. and Jan. No dinner Sun.*

$$ ✕ **Da Ornella.** On the main street in the upper town, this trattoria is well attended, so reservations are a must. Vaulted ceilings, wooden beams, and antique ceramic ware on the walls enhance the old worldliness. Ornella herself is in the kitchen, turning out casonsei in butter and sage and platters of assorted roast meats. ⊠ *Via Gombito 15,* ☎ *035/232736. Reservations essential. AE, DC, MC, V. Closed Thurs. and July. No lunch Fri.*

$$ ✕ **La Trattoria del Teatro.** Traditional regional food tops the bill at this good-value restaurant in the Upper Town. The polenta is heart rending, and game is recommended in season. Fettuccine *con funghi* (with mushrooms) is a deceptively simple but rich and memorable specialty. ⊠ *Piazza Mascheroni 3,* ☎ *035/238862. No credit cards. Closed Mon. and July 15–30.*

$–$$ ✕ **Bernabò.** From the funicular it's worth heading straight ahead, past Piazza Vecchia to the old military fortress and this corner trattoria. It has two simple rooms with vaulted ceilings, wrought-iron lamps, and wood-paneled walls. The clientele is a mix of locals and economy-minded tourists. All are treated cordially. Specialties are casonsei served with butter and sage, and veal scallopini or game with polenta. Pizza is also served. ⊠ *Via Colleoni 31,* ☎ *035/237692. MC, V. Closed Thurs. and July 15–Aug. 15.*

$$$ 🏨 **Cristallo Palace.** On the periphery of town, the Cristallo Palace offers the amenities of a modern, efficient hotel, plus the bonus of being on the *tangenziale* (the road that bypasses the center). The rooms are large and well equipped, and the service is polished and prompt. The hotel's restaurant, L'Antica Perosa, is very good. A shuttle runs into town in the mornings and late afternoon. ⊠ *Via Betty Ambiveri 35, 24126,* ☎ *035/311211,* FAX *035/312031. 90 rooms. Restaurant, bar. AE, DC, MC, V.*

$$$ 🏨 **Excelsior San Marco.** The most comfortable hotel in the lower part of Bergamo, the Excelsior San Marco is only a short walk from the walls of the Upper Town. The rooms are surprisingly quiet, considering the central location of the hotel. Its restaurant, Tino Fontana, has a rooftop terrace. ⊠ *Piazza della Repubblica 6, 24126,* ☎ *035/366111,* FAX *035/223201. 162 rooms. Restaurant, bar. AE, DC, MC, V.*

Nightlife and the Arts

A **Festival Internazionale del Pianoforte** (International Piano Festival), an event of more than 30 years' standing, is held in **Bergamo's Teatro Donizetti** (⊠ Piazza Cavour 14, ☎ 035/249631) in summer.

LAKE COMO

For those whose idea of heaven is palatial villas, rose-laden belvederes, operetta towns, hanging gardens of wisteria and bougainvillea, flickering lanterns casting a glow over lakeshore restaurants, and dreamy alpine vistas, heaven exists at Lake Como. Virgil liked Como at least as much as Garda, calling it simply our "greatest" lake. Stendhal described it as an "enchanting spot, unequaled on earth for loveliness," in his *Charterhouse of Parma*. Though summer crowds do their best to vanquish the lake's dreamy mystery and civilized, slightly faded, millionaire's-row gentility, they fail. Como remains a place of consummate partnership between the beauties of nature and those of humanity. Like so many of Italy's most beautiful villa gardens, those of Como owe their beauty to the landscape architecture of two eras: Renaissance Italian, with its taste for order; and 19th-century English, with its fondness for illusions of natural wildness. The two are often framed by vast areas of the most picturesque farmland—notably olive groves, fruit trees, and vineyards.

Lake Como is some 47 km (30 mi) long north to south, and it is also Europe's deepest lake (almost 1,350 ft). Rarely out of sight to visitors, it looks like a burnished mirror—until a breeze ruffles its incandescence. Here, in the *centro di lago* (center region of the lake), travelers have long headed for Bellagio. This alluring town is known as the "punta di Bellagio" because it's at the point that divides Lake Como into three branches. It's an enchanting location, one that inspired Gabriel Faure to call Bellagio "a diamond contrasting brilliantly with the sapphires of the three lakes in which it is set." After just a few days on Lake Como, you'll understand why Verdi chose to compose *La Traviata* in Cadenabbia (across the lake from Bellagio). Today, for Milanese weekend-trippers, countless honeymooners, and visitors from around the world, going to Lake Como is not so much escape, as return; not so much getting away from it all, but returning to that *douceur de vie,* that sweetness of life rarely encountered today.

If you're not going by car, you arrive at the lake by pulling into the railway station at Como, a leading textile center, famous for its silks. Most visitors hasten to the vaporetti (water taxis) waiting to take them to the centro di lago, the most beautiful part of the lake. Art lovers, however, should note that 15 or so blocks south of the station is one of the greatest Italian Romanesque churches, Sant'Abbondio—a detour they will consider well worth making once they've seen its awe-inspiring, gigantic nave interior. Although you can take a bus up either shoreline, most people take a ferry to Bellagio, the key town of the centro di lago; be sure to take an express ferry, as the local vaporetti can turn a half-hour ride into a three-hour ordeal. Once at Bellagio, vaporetti and car-ferries traverse the lake, making it easy for travelers to get to the other main towns, Cernobbio, Cadenabbia, and Varenna.

Madonna del Ghisallo

28 *48 km (30 mi) northwest of Bergamo, 18 km (11 mi) north of Cernobbio.*

The **Chiesa della Madonna del Ghisallo** (Church of the Patroness of Bicyclists) is not far from the shores of Lake Como, arriving from Bergamo, and offers a fine view. You will often see cyclists parked outside taking a breather after their uphill struggle, but many come just as a homage to this unique Madonna. From Bergamo you pass it on the road to Bellagio. ⊠ *Magreglio.* 🎫 *Free.* ☉ *Mar.–Nov.*

Bellagio

★ **29** *58 km (36 mi) northwest of Bergamo, 28 km (17 mi) north of Cernobbio.*

Sometimes called the prettiest town in Europe, Bellagio also has ferry services to most towns on the lake. Here, buildings always seem to be flag bedecked, geraniums rustle from every window, and bougainvillea veils the staircases, or *montées,* that thread through the town. At dusk, Bellagio's nightspots—including the wharf where an orchestra serenades dancers under the stars—beckon vacationers to come and make merry.

★ **Villa Serbelloni,** a property of the Rockefeller Foundation, can also be visited for its celebrated gardens, on the site of Pliny the Elder's villa, overlooking Bellagio. As there are only two guided visits per day restricted to 30 people, and these tend to be commandeered by group bookings especially during May, you'd do well to book far in advance with the Bellagio tourist office (✉ Piazza della Chiesa 14, ☎ 031/950204). ☑ *5,000 lire.* ☉ *Guided visits mid-Apr.–mid-Oct., Tues.–Sun. at 10:30 and 4.*

The famous gardens of the **Villa Melzi** are open to the public and were once a favorite picnic spot for Franz Lizst, who advised author Louis de Ronchaud in 1837: "When you write the story of two happy lovers, place them on the shores of Lake Como. I do not know of any land so conspicuously blessed by heaven." High praise, indeed. Although you can't get into the 19th-century villa, don't miss the lavish Empire-style family chapel. The Melzi were Napoléon's greatest allies in Italy (the family has passed down the name of Josephine to the present); directly across the lake is the Villa Carlotta (☞ Tremezzo, *below*), once residence of Count Sommariva, Napoléon's worst Italian enemy. ✉ *3 km (2 mi) outside Bellagio,* ☎ *031/950318.* ☑ *5,000 lire.* ☉ *Late Mar.–early Nov., daily 9–6:30.*

OFF THE BEATEN PATH	**VILLA BALBIANELLO –** This may be the most magical house in all of Italy. It sits on its own little promontory, Il Dosso d'Avedo—separating the bays of Venus and Diana—around the bend from the tiny fishing village of Ossuccio. Relentlessly picturesque, the villa is comprised of loggias, terraces, and *palazzetini* (tiny palaces), all of which spill down verdant slopes to the lakeshore where an old Franciscan church, magnificent stone staircase, and statue of San Carlo Borromeo blessing the waters welcome visitors (the only access to the villa is by launch, which leaves Ossuccio three times a week). Designed in 1596 by Pellegrino Pelligrini, it was enlarged by Count Lambertenghi (who insisted on calling all his guests "Count," but refused the title himself). In 1974 it was sold to Count Monzino, who graciously willed it to the Fondo Ambiente Italiano, which has opened it to the public. Check with the Bellagio the tourist office (✉ Piazza della Chiesa 14, ☎ 031/950204) for the hours of launch tours. ✉ *Il Dosso d'Avedo.* ☑ *5,500 lire.* ☉ *Tues. and weekends 10–12:30 and 4–6:30.*

Dining and Lodging

$$ ✕ **Silvio.** At the edge of town, this family-owned trattoria with a terrace on the lakeshore is for those who love fresh lake fish. Served cooked or marinated, with risotto or as a ravioli stuffing, the fish is caught by Silvio's family. This is local cooking at its best. There are also 17 modestly priced rooms. ✉ *Lòppia di Bellagio, Via Carcano 12,* ☎ *031/950322. MC, V. Closed Jan.*

$–$$ ✕ **La Pergola.** In Pescallo, about 1 km (½ mi) from Bellagio, on the other side of the peninsula, La Pergola is a popular lakeside restaurant. Of course, try to reserve a table on the lakeside terrace and order the daily special of freshly caught lake fish. You can also stay in one of the inn's 13 rooms, all of which have baths. ✉ *Pescallo,* ☎ *031/950263. AE, DC, MC, V. Closed Tues. and Nov.–Feb.*

$$$$ ★ 🏨 **Grand Hotel Villa Serbelloni.** They used to say that those who drove Rolls-Royces stayed at the Villa d'Este hotel in Cernobbio and those who drove Bentleys came here. Once designed to cradle dukes and duchesses in high luxury, this hotel is now a refined haven for the discreetly wealthy. Just down the road from the punta di Bellagio, the hotel is set within a pretty park. Inside, the atmosphere is one of 19th-century luxury that has not so much faded as mellowed: The rooms are immaculate and plush. The public rooms are a mix of gilt, marble, and thick, colorful carpets. Service is unobtrusive, and the staff is particularly good about arranging transportation across and around the lake. The best rooms—in which Churchill and Kennedy have stayed—face

the lake and the Tremezzina, a group of towns on the shores opposite Bellagio. ⊠ *Lungolago Bellagio, Via Roma 1, 22021,* ☎ *031/950216,* FAX *031/951529. 95 rooms. Restaurant, pool, beauty salon, tennis court, health club. AE, DC, MC, V. Closed end Oct.–early Apr.*

$$ ⊞ **Du Lac.** In the center of Bellagio, by the Lake Como landing dock, Du Lac is a comfortable medium-size hotel owned by an Anglo-Italian family who set a relaxed and congenial tone. Most rooms have views of the lake and mountains, and there is a rooftop terrace garden for drinks or just unwinding. ⊠ *Piazza Mazzini 32, 22021,* ☎ *031/ 950320,* FAX *031/951624. 48 rooms. Restaurant, bar. MC, V. Closed late Oct.–late Mar.*

$$ ⊞ **Excelsior-Splendide.** Chances are you'll be lulled to sleep at night here by the lilting sounds of an orchestra directly under your window—this hotel is opposite Bellagio's enchanting quay, where live music beckons one and all on summer nights. It's in town center, handy to restaurants, and just a five-minute walk from the stunning gardens of Villa Melzi. ⊠ *Lungo Lalio Mazzoni, 22021,* ☎ *031/950225,* FAX *031/951224. 47 rooms. Restaurant, pool. AE, DC, MC, V. Closed Oct. 21–May 1.*

Varenna

㉚ *10 km (6 mi) north of Bellagio.*

Using the ferry boat services in Bellagio, make your way to the town of Varenna. The principal sight here is the spellbindingly beautiful garden of the **Villa Monastero,** which, as its name suggests, was a monastery before it was a villa. Now it's an international science center. ⊠ *Varenna.* ☎ *4,000 lire.* ☉ *Apr.–Oct., daily 9–noon and 2–5.*

Tremezzo

㉛ *34 km (21 mi) north of Cernobbio.*

If you are lucky enough to visit this small lakeside town late spring or very early summer, you will find the magnificent **Villa Carlotta** a riotous blaze of color, with more than 14 acres of azaleas and dozens of varieties of rhododendron in full bloom. The villa itself was built between 1690 and 1743 for the luxury-loving Marquis Giorgio Clerici. The range of the garden's collection is remarkable, particularly when you consider the difficulties of transporting delicate, exotic vegetation before the age of aircraft. Palms, banana trees, cactus, eucalyptus, a sequoia, orchids, and camellias are only the beginning of a list that includes more than 500 species.

According to local lore, one motive for the Villa Carlotta's magnificence was a keeping-up-with-the-Joneses sort of rivalry between the marquis's ambitious, self-made son-in-law, who inherited the estate, and the son-in-law's arch rival, who built *his* summer palace directly across the lake. Whenever either added to his villa and garden, it was tantamount to taunting the other in public. Eventually the son-in-law's insatiable taste for self-aggrandizement prevailed. The villa's last (and final) owners were Prussian royalty (including the "Carlotta" of the villa's name), and the property was confiscated during World War I.

The villa's interior is worth a visit, particularly if you have a taste for Antonio Canova's most romantic sculptures. The best known is his *Cupid and Psyche,* which depicts the lovers locked in an odd but graceful and passionate embrace, with the young god above and behind, his wings extended, while Psyche, her lips willing, waits for a kiss that will never come. Check with the Bellagio tourist office (⊠ *Piazza della Chiesa 14,* ☎ *031/950204*) for the hours of launch tours. ⊠ *Tremezzo,* ☎ *0344/40405.* ☎ *Villa and gardens 8,000 lire.* ☉ *Apr.–Sept., daily 9– 6; mid- to late Mar. and Oct.–early Nov., daily 9–11:30 and 2–4:30.*

Cernobbio

32 *28 km (17 mi) south of Bellagio, 34 km (21 mi) south of Tremezzo, 50 km (31 mi) east of Lake Maggiore.*

Cernobbio is the first town you come to as you head north from the town of Como. Although many of the villas of the southwest branch—the lake's most overbuilt district—remain private and closed to the public, they can be enjoyed from a boat. If you're planning to say "budget be damned" in only one place, the **Villa d'Este** could be it. If you can't stay at this legendary lakeside resort hotel, call ahead and ask to see the grounds or enjoy a wonderful meal in the hotel's restaurant (☞ Lodging, *below*).

Originally built for Cardinal Tolomeo Gallio (who began life humbly as a fisherman) over the course of approximately 45 years (it was completed in 1615), the Villa d'Este has had a colorful and somewhat checkered history, swinging wildly between extremes of grandeur and dereliction. Its tenants have included the Jesuits, two generals, a ballerina, the disgraced and estranged wife of a future king of England (Caroline of Brunswick and George IV, respectively), a family of ordinary Italian nobles, and, finally, a czarina of Russia. Its life as a private summer residence ended in 1873, when it was turned into the fashionable hotel it has remained ever since.

Though the gardens are not as grand as they are reputed to have been during the villa's best days as a private residence and though they have suffered some modification in the course of the hotel's building of tennis courts and swimming pools, they still possess an aura of stately, monumental dignity. The alley of cypresses is a fine example of a proudly repeated Italian garden theme. The fanciful pavilions, temples, miniature forts, and mock ruins make for an afternoon's walk of quietly whimsical surprises.

Lodging

$$$$ 🏨 **Villa d'Este.** From Napoléon to the Duchess of Windsor, this grand
★ establishment has welcomed the rich and famous of several centuries. One of the most luxurious hotels in Italy, the 16th-century Villa d'Este provides just about every conceivable comfort, even a nightclub. The sparkling chandeliers in the vast lobby cast their light on the broad, marble staircases that lead to the guest rooms. Indeed, they are so regal that one could be forgiven for ascending them as Napoléon surely did, one hand on the banister, the other placed inside the coat. The rooms are furnished in the manner of wealthy Italians, Empire-style: walnut paneling, sofas striped in silk, and plenty of gorgeous antiques. A broad veranda sweeps out to the lakefront, where a large swimming pool juts out above the water. Across the lake blue, snowcapped mountains gradually blend into the deep green of the slopes that lead down to the shore. The restaurant may possibly be the sole imperfection in an otherwise perfect Villa d'Este. ⊠ *Via Regina 40,* ☎ *031/3481,* 📠 *031/348844. 158 rooms. Restaurant, bar, indoor and outdoor pools, sauna, 8 tennis courts, squash, nightclub. AE, DC, MC, V. Closed Nov.–Feb.*

Como

33 *34 km (21 mi) south of Bellagio, 40 km (25 mi) south of Tremezzo, 56 km (33 mi) east of Lake Maggiore.*

Como, on the shores of the eponymous lake, is part elegant resort, with cobbled pedestrian streets that wind their way elegantly past parks and bustling cafés and away from the lakefront. The other part is industrial town, renowned throughout the world for its production of silk.

If you're traveling by car leave it outside town center, as traffic can be mayhem and streets are often closed.

The splendid 15th-century Renaissance-Gothic **Duomo** was begun in 1396, the facade was added in 1455, and the transepts completed in the mid-18th century. The dome was designed in 1744 by Filippo Juvara, who was the chief architect of many of the sumptuous palaces of Italy's royal family, the Savoys (☞ Chapter 8). On the facade there are statues of two of Como's most famous sons, Pliny the Elder and Pliny the Younger, whose chronicles are some of the most important documents of antiquity. Inside, the works of art include Luini's *Holy Conversation,* a fresco cycle by Morazzone, and the *Wedding of the Virgin Mary* by Ferrari. ⊠ *Piazza del Duomo.* ☉ *Daily 9–6.*

At the heart of Como's medieval quarter, the city's first cathedral, **San Fedele,** is also worth a peek, if only for the fact that it is one of the oldest churches in the region. ⊠ *Piazza San Fedele.*

If you can brave Como's industrial quarter, you will find the beautiful church of **Sant'Abbondio,** a gem of Romanesque architecture begun by Benedictine monks in 1013 and consecrated by Pope Urban II in 1095. Inside, the five aisles of the church converge on a presbytery with a semicircular apse decorated with a cycle of 14th-century frescoes—all of which have been restored to their original magnificence—by Lombard artists heavily influenced by the Sienese school. In the nave, the cubical capitals supporting the pillars are the first example of this style in all of Italy. ⊠ *Via Sant'Abbondio.* ☉ *Daily 9–6.*

OFF THE BEATEN PATH

CASTIGLIONE OLANA – Just 18 km (11 mi) west of Como is a Gothic Collegiata and baptistery, with superlative frescoes by Giotto's pupil Masolino da Panicale.

Dining and Lodging

$$$ 🏨 **Barchetta Excelsior.** Despite its rather unprepossessing exterior, this central, modern hotel is comfortable, with many rooms looking directly across Piazza Cavour over to Lake Como. The rooms are airy and spacious, with those on the upper floors commanding the best views. Ask for a lake view because not all rooms have one, although the noise of the piazza can be a distraction. ⊠ *Piazza Cavour 1, 22021,* ☎ *031/3221,* 📠 *031/302622. 85 rooms. Restaurant, bar, breakfast room, minibars. AE, DC, MC, V.*

$$$ ✕ **Da Angela.** Reservations are a must at this small and intimate restaurant serving Piedmontese specialties. Owner Angela and her staff are attentive, and the waiters will help you select from a menu that includes various homemade pasta dishes and tasty *coniglio alle olive e alloro* (rabbit with olives and bay leaves). ⊠ *Via Ugo Foscolo 16,* ☎ *031/304656. Reservations essential. AE, DC, MC, V. Closed Mon. and Aug.*

$$$ ✕ **La Locanda dell'Isola.** Isola Comacina, Lake Como's only island, five minutes by regular boat from Sala Comacina, is rustic and restful, but at times crowded. The same could be said for the Locanda. Forget any notions of choosing from a menu, because here the deal is a set price for a set meal, with drinks included. The good news is that the food is delicious, the service friendly, and the setting magnificent. You'll have to pace yourself through a mixed antipasto, salmon, trout, chicken, salad, cheese, coffee, and dessert. ⊠ *Isola Comacina, Sala Comacina,* ☎ *0344/55083. No credit cards. Closed Nov.–Feb. and Tues. Sept.–May.*

$$$ 🏨 **Palace.** This well-run, refurbished grand 19th-century hotel on the waterfront has fine lake views and the advantage of being set back in its own gardens, where there is an outside bar in summer. The rooms,

however, are a little disappointing: The simple, almost plain, furnishings do little justice to the magnificent exterior. ⊠ *Lungo Lario Trieste 16, 22100,* ☎ *031/303303,* FAX *031/303170. 100 rooms. Restaurant, bar, meeting rooms, travel services. AE, DC, MC, V.*

\$\$–\$\$\$
★
🏨 **Terminus.** Commanding a panoramic view over Lake Como, this turn-of-the-century, Liberty-style building is perhaps the city's finest hotel. The public spaces have a quiet, understated elegance, with plenty of marble and high ceilings. The guest rooms are done in floral patterns and are tastefully furnished with large, walnut wardrobes and silk-covered sofas. The best room in the hotel is Room 500, in a small tower: The split-level room is divided by a thin spiral staircase and the three-sided view from the bedroom is magnificent. In summer, the garden terrace is perfect for relaxing over a drink. ⊠ *Lungo Lario Trieste 13, 22100,* ☎ *031/329111,* FAX *031/302550. 41 rooms. Restaurant, bar, breakfast room, in-room modem lines, in-room safes, minibars, no-smoking rooms, massage, sauna, meeting rooms. AE, DC, MC, V.*

\$\$
🏨 **Tre Re.** This clean, spacious, and welcoming hotel is just a few steps west of the cathedral and convenient to the lake. Although the exterior gives away the age of this 16th-century former convent, the rooms inside are airy, comfortable, and modern. The moderately priced restaurant shares an ample terrace with the hotel. ⊠ *Via Boldoni 20, 22021,* ☎ *031/265374,* FAX *031/241349. 34 rooms, 30 with bath or shower. Restaurant, bar. MC, V. Closed Dec. 10–Jan. 15.*

Outdoor Activities and Sports

SEAPLANES

The school at the **Seaplane Club Como** (⊠ Viale Masia 44, ☎ 031/574495) gives lessons to would-be pilots.

SKIING

In the province of Como, fine snow-skiing facilities abound: Valsassina, Val Lesina, Valvarrone, Valcavargna, and Val d'Intelvi (**Provincial Tourist Board, Como,** ⊠ Via Borgovico 148, ☎ 031/230329 or 031/230111).

WATERSKIING

Various facilities for waterskiing and all water sports can be found on the lake; contact the Provincial Tourist Board (☞ *above*).

Shopping

MARKET

Every Saturday (except the first Saturday of every month), Piazza San Fedele holds a **crafts market** from 9 to 7, featuring local crafts.

SILK

Como is renowned for its production of high-quality silk. **Mantera** (⊠ Via Volta) sells a wide range of locally made silks. **In Seta** (⊠ Piazza Cavour) offers the latest in silk fashions for both men and women. **Binda** (⊠ Viale Geno) is a silk wholesale store, with great prices on a variety of items, including shirts, ties, and scarves.

LAKE MAGGIORE AND LAKE ORTA

Magnificently scenic, Lake Maggiore has its less mountainous eastern shore in Lombardy, its higher western shore in Piedmont, and its northern tip in Switzerland. Never more than 5 km (3 mi) wide, the lake is almost 50 km (30 mi) long. The better-known resorts are on the Piedmontese shore, particularly Stresa, a well-established tourist town that partly provided the setting for Hemingway's *A Farewell to Arms.*

A mountainous strip of land separates Lake Maggiore from Lago di Orta (Lake Orta), its smaller neighbor to the west, in Piedmont. Orta attracts fewer visitors than the three larger lakes, and consequently a tour around this lake can be a pleasant alternative in the summer. Stresa is the main town on Lake Maggiore, and Orta San Giulio is the largest center on Lake Orta; all points of interest on the two lakes are reached from these towns, respectively.

Orta San Giulio

34 *15 km (9 mi) west of Stresa, 76 km (47 mi) northwest of Milan.*

Orta San Giulio is at the end of a small peninsula that juts out into Lake Orta about a third of the way up its eastern shore. Intricate wrought-iron balustrades and balconies adorn the 18th-century buildings of this small and charming town. The shady main square looks out across the lake to the small island of San Giulio. There are few more relaxing experiences than sipping a drink at one of the piazza cafés and looking out at the languid waters being stirred by a mountain breeze, with sailboats busily making their way to nowhere in particular.

OFF THE
BEATEN PATH
SACRO MONTE – Rising up behind Orta and looking down on the lake, Sacred Mountain offers an enjoyable and interesting hike up from Orta. Pass the church of the Assumption, and just ahead you see a gateway marked SACRO MONTE. This leads to the path up the hill, a comfortable climb that takes about 40 minutes for the round-trip. As you approach the top, you pass no fewer than 20 17th-century chapels, all devoted to St. Francis of Assisi. They are decorated with frescoes and striking, life-size terra-cotta statue groups (a total of almost 400 figures) that illustrate incidents in the saint's life. You can climb the campanile of the last chapel for a panoramic view over the whole lake and the town, about 350 ft below.

The island of **San Giulio,** just offshore, is accessible by hiring a boatman. The lake is no more than 2 km (1 mi) wide, and most charge about 10,000 lire for up to four people to make the round-trip. The island takes its name from the 4th-century St. Julius, who—like St. Patrick in Ireland—is said to have banished snakes from the island. Julius is also said to have founded the Basilica in AD 390, although the present building shows more signs of its renovations in the 10th and 15th centuries. Inside, there is a black marble pulpit (12th century) with elaborate carvings, and downstairs you'll find the crypt containing relics of the saint. In the sacristy of the church is a large bone said to be from one of the beasts destroyed by the saint, but on closer examination it seems to be a whalebone.

It only takes a few minutes to walk around the parts of the island that are open to the public: Much of the area is taken up by the grounds of private villas. The view back across the lake to Orta, with Sacro Monte behind it, is memorable, particularly in the late afternoon, when the light picks up the glint of the wrought-iron traceries.

Lodging

$$$ ☑ **Hotel San Rocco.** Half of the rooms in this converted 17th-century convent in a lakeside garden on the edge of town have views of the lake, garden, and surrounding mountains. Many have balconies and are furnished in modern style. The restaurant features international cuisine and beautiful views of the lake. Among the specialties is *pesce persico* (perch). ☒ *Via Gippini da Verona 11, 28016,* ☎ *0322/905632,* 𝖥𝖠𝖷 *0322/905635. 74 rooms. Restaurant, bar, pool, health club. AE, DC, MC, V.*

En Route   Follow the shore drive from Orta San Giulio north to Omegna, at the head of Lake Orta. A couple of kilometers west of Omegna, in the village of Quarna Sotto, there's a musical instrument factory that's worth a stop. The shore drive continues around the rest of the lake, and at the southern end you can pick up S229, which will take you back to the A4 autostrada.

If you're going to Stresa from Lake Orta, take the twisting mountain road past Mottarone, the tallest peak between the lakes, to Gignese, where you'll be about 2,300 ft above sea level and can take in a last dramatic view of Maggiore. Follow the road up to Lake Orta, through the town of Armeno, shaded first by forests of evergreens, then oaks. In the late summer and early fall, you're likely to see whole families out in these woods, crouched down in their hunt for wild mushrooms, or—if they're particularly lucky—truffles.

Stresa

③⑤ *70 km (43 mi) west of Cernobbio, 16 km (10 mi) east of Orta San Giulio.*

Stresa, which has capitalized on its central lakeside position and its good connections to the Isole Borromee (Borromean Islands) in Lake Maggiore, has to some extent become a victim of its own success. The luxurious elegance that distinguished it in its heyday has grown somewhat faded; the grand hotels are still grand but their surrounding parks and gardens are now encroached by traffic. Even the undeniable loveliness of the lakeshore drive has been threatened by the roar of diesel trucks and BMW traffic. One way to escape is to head for the Isole Borromee just off Stresa.

As you wander around the grounds of **Villa Pallavicino,** with their palms and semitropical shrubs, don't be surprised if you're followed by a peacock or even an ostrich: They're part of the zoological garden, and they are allowed to roam almost at will. From the top of the hill on which the villa stands, you can see the gentle hills of the Lombardy shore of Lake Maggiore and, nearer and to the left, the jewel-like Borromean Islands. As well as a bar and restaurant on the grounds, there are also picnicking spots. ⊠ *Via Sempione Sund 8,* ☎ *0323/31533.* ⊡ *11,500 lire.* ☉ *Mid-Mar.–Oct. 30, daily 9–6.*

Boats to the **Borromean Islands** leave every 15–30 minutes from the dock at Stresa's Piazza Marconi. Although you can hire a boatman to take you, it's cheaper and just as convenient to use the regular service. Make sure you buy a ticket allowing you to visit all the islands—Bella, Dei Pescatori, and Madre.

The islands take their name from the Borromeo family, which has owned them since the 12th century. **Isola Bella** (Beautiful Island) is the most famous of the three, and the first that you'll visit. Its name is actually a shortened form of Isabella, wife of the 16th-century Count Carlo III Borromeo (1538–84) who built the palace and terraced gardens for her. Few wedding presents anywhere have been more romantic. Wander up the 10 terraces of the gardens, where peacocks roam among the scented shrubs, statues, and fountains. The view of the lake is splendid from the top terrace. Before Count Carlo began his project, the island was rocky and almost devoid of vegetation, and the soil for the garden had to be transported from the mainland. Visit the **palazzo** to see the rooms where famous guests—including Napoléon and Mussolini—stayed in 18th-century splendor. ☎ *0323/30556.* ⊡ *Garden and palazzo 10,000 lire.* ☉ *Apr.–Oct., daily 9–noon and 1:30–5:30.*

Stop for a while at the tiny **Isola dei Pescatori** (Island of the Fishermen), less than 100 yards wide and only about ½ km (¼ mi) long. Of the three islands, this is the one that has remained closest to the way they all were before the Borromeos began their building projects. The island's little lanes, strung with fishing nets and dotted with shrines to the Madonna, are so picturesque they practically drip off the canvas. Little wonder that this tiny fishing village is crowded with postcard stands in high season.

Isola Madre (Mother Island) is the largest of the three and, like Isola Bella, has a large botanical garden. Even dedicated nongardeners should stop to appreciate the profusion of exotic trees and shrubs running down to the shore in every direction. Two special times to visit are April (for the camellias) and May (when azaleas and rhododendrons are in bloom). Also on the island is a 16th-century palazzo, where an antique puppet theater is on display, complete with string puppets, prompt books, and elaborate scenery designed by Alessandro Sanquirico, who was a scenographer at La Scala in Milan. ⊠ *12,000 lire.* ☉ *Apr.–Oct., daily 8:30–noon and 2–5:30.*

For more information about the islands and how to get there, contact the local tourist office in Stresa (⊠ Via Principe Tomaso 70, ☎ 0323/30150) or ask at the landing stages. ⊠ *Landing stage in Piazza Matteotti, look for* NAVIGAZIONE LAGO MAGGIORE *signs.* ☉ *Mid-Mar.–Oct.*

Lodging

$$$$ 🏨 **Grand Hotel des Iles Borromees.** A palatial old-world hotel, this princely establishment has catered to a demanding European clientele since 1863. And though it still has the spacious salons and lavish decor of the turn of the century, it has also been discreetly modernized; rooms have luxurious bathrooms, and there is an exercise room. ⊠ *Lungolago Umberto I 67, 28049 Stresa, ☎ 0323/30431, ℻ 0323/32405. 172 rooms. Restaurant, bar, indoor pool, spa, golf privileges, tennis courts, exercise room, convention center. AE, DC, MC, V.*

$–$$ 🏨 **Primavera.** In a plain 1950s building in the heart of Stresa, Primavera has balconies embellished with flower boxes. It has the advantage of a location in a quiet pedestrian zone only three minutes from the lake and embarcadero. Rooms are compact and simply furnished. ⊠ *Via Cavour 39, Stresa, 28049, ☎ 0323/31286, ℻ 0323/33458. 32 rooms. AE, MC, V. Closed Jan.–Feb. and mid-Nov.–mid-Dec.*

Verbania Pallanza

③⑥   *16 km (10 mi) north of Stresa.*

Verbania Pallanza lies across the Gulf of Pallanza from Stresa. It's known for the **Villa Taranto,** which has magnificent botanical gardens containing some 20,000 species. Created by an enthusiastic Scotsman, Captain Neil McEachern, these gardens rank among Europe's finest. ⊠ *Verbania Pallanza, ☎ ℻ 0323/404555.* ⊠ *8,000 lire.* ☉ *Apr.–Oct., daily 8:30–7:30.*

Dining

$$$–$$$$ ✕ **Ristorante del Sole.** Chef Carlo Brovelli presides over this lakeside
★   inn with a cheerfulness that is infectious. The lake figures into the menu, in the form of carpaccio made of fine slices of trout and perch. The seasonal menu suggests various interpretations of artichokes in spring, eggplant in summer. Squab caramelized in honey might also top the menu. There are also nine sizable apartments. ⊠ *Piazza Venezia 5, Ranco, near Angera, ☎ 0331/976507, ℻ 0331/976620. Reservations essential. AE, DC, MC, V. Closed Tues. and Jan.–mid-Feb. No dinner Mon. mid-Feb.–mid-Mar.*

$$ ✕ **Monferrato.** Off Piazza Cadorna and close to the embarcadero, this hotel restaurant serves tasty risotto *con filetti di persico* (with perch fillets) and typical Piedmontese meat dishes, such as beef braised in Barolo

wine. ⊠ *Via Mazzini 14,* ☎ *0323/31386. AE, DC, MC, V. Closed Tues. and mid-Dec.–late Feb.*

MILAN, LOMBARDY, AND THE LAKES A TO Z

Arriving and Departing

By Bus

Italian bus service is best avoided on intercity routes, since it is neither faster, cheaper, nor more convenient than the railways. Most bus companies use Piazza Castello as a terminus, because Milan has no central bus terminal. For bus information, call **Autostradale** (☎ 166/845010). You can also try **Zani Viaggi** (☎ 02/867131).

By Car

Two major autostrada routes cross at Milan: the **A1,** which leads south to Bologna, Florence, and Rome, and the **A4,** which runs west–east from Turin to Venice. **A7** angles southwest down to Genoa from Milan. Milan is ringed by a bypass road (the Tangenziale). The **A9** leads north past Como to Chiasso and the Saint Gottard Pass into Switzerland.

By Plane

Aeroporto Malpensa (⊠ About 50 km/31 mi northwest of Milan, ☎ 02/40099110) handles all intercontinental air traffic. **Aeroporto Milano Linate** (⊠ Less than 10 km/6 mi east of Milan, ☎ 02/7561372) handles international and domestic air traffic. For **air-traffic information** for both airports and information on connections with Milan, call 02/74851. **Air Pullman** (☎ 02/40099260 information) coaches run twice daily in the morning between Malpensa and Linate airports. The fare is 18,000 lire, and the trip takes about 75 minutes.

BETWEEN THE AIRPORT AND DOWNTOWN

By Bus. There is bus service from **Malpensa** to the bus station at Stazione Centrale. Air Pullman (☎ 02/40099260 information) shuttle buses usually leave Malpensa every half hour on the half hour from 7 AM to 5 PM (excluding a bus at 1:30) and hourly 5–9 PM, the last bus leaving at 10:15 PM. Buy your ticket inside the airport before embarking. Buses leave the bus terminal every half hour on the half hour 5:30 AM–5:30 PM (excluding a bus at 3) and hourly on the half hour 5:30–10:30 PM. A trip either way costs 13,000 lire and takes about one hour. Buses leave **Linate** every 20 minutes for Milan's Stazione Centrale. The trip takes about 20 minutes; the cost is 5,000 lire. You can also take ATM municipal Bus 73 to Piazza San Babila (every 15 minutes); the cost is 1,500 lire. Alternatively, there is a bus-service link between the airport and an airport terminal at **Lumpagnano** (☎ 02/74851 information). The trip costs 10,000 lire. Lumpagnano is on the subway route to the city center.

By Car. From **Malpensa** take Route **S336** east to the **A8** autostrada southeast toward Milan. The drive takes about 40 minutes, depending on traffic and destination. From **Linate,** take what was once the Old Brescia Road west into the central downtown area.

By Taxi. A taxi stand is directly outside the arrivals building doors at **Malpensa.** Approximate fare is 130,000 lire; the trip takes 40 minutes. From **Linate,** the approximate fare is 30,000 lire; the trip takes less than 20 minutes.

By Train

Although Milan claims a bewildering number of railway stations, only one is of concern, **Milano Stazione Centrale** (✉ About 5 km/3 mi northwest of the Duomo and Galleria, ☎ 147/888088 for toll-free information, 02/72524370 for APT office), unless you travel on local routes at peculiar hours—in which case service can begin or terminate in suburban stations (most notably **Milano Lambrate** for Bergamo, and **Stazione Nord** for Como). Premium international (EC) service and premium (IC) domestic service connect Milano Centrale with major European cities. Metro line 3 links Milano Centrale with Piazza de Duomo.

Getting Around

By Bicycle

As part of its campaign to ban cars from Milan's center, the city government has begun to set up a network of one-way bicycle rental stations. At first, rentals were free; now there is a small charge. Though the bicycles are clearly intended for residents who would otherwise use cars, current opinion is that tourists may use them, too (although individual proprietors of stands may arbitrarily decide to disagree, especially if you are unable to explain your rights in Italian). Look for yellow stands filled with yellow bicycles.

By Boat

There is frequent daily ferry and hydrofoil service between towns on the lakes, and a range of round-trip excursions, with a dining service (optional) aboard. For all lakes call **Navigazione Laghi** (✉ Via Ariosto 21, Milan, ☎ 02/4676101). Call locally: **Navigazione Lago di Garda** (✉ Piazza Matteotti 2, Desenzano, ☎ 030/9149511). **Navigazione Lago di Como** (✉ Via Per Cernobbio 8, Tavernola, near Como, ☎ 031/579211). **Navigazione Lago Maggiore** (✉ Viale Baracca 1, Arona, ☎ 0322/46651).

By Bus

Trains are generally better than buses for getting around the cities of the plain. There is regular bus service between the small towns on the lakes, and it tends to be a cheaper way of getting around than ferry or hydrofoil service. The bus service around Lake Garda serves mostly towns on the western coast. Call **SIA** (☎ 0365/3774237) for information.

MILAN

Milan has an excellent system of public transport (for information, call ATM, ☎ 02/48032403) consisting of trolley cars, buses, and a subway system, the **Metropolitana,** which runs on three lines. Tickets for each must be purchased before you board and must be canceled by machines at underground station entrances and mounted on poles inside trolleys and buses. Tickets cost 1,500 lire and can be purchased from news vendors, tobacconists, and machines at larger stops. Buy several at once—they remain valid until canceled. One ticket is valid for 75 minutes on all surface lines, or for one subway trip. A 24-hour ticket valid on all public transport lines costs 5,000 lire, and one ticket valid for 48 hours costs 9,000 lire; they are sold at **Duomo Metro** and **Stazione Centrale Metro** stations.

By Car

The **A4** autostrada is the main east–west highway for this region. The **A22** is a major north–south highway running just east of Lake Garda. Although these major highways will allow you to make good time between the cities of the plain, you'll have to follow secondary roads—often of great beauty—around the lakes. **S572** goes along the southern and western shores of Lake Garda, **S45b** is along the northernmost section of the western shore, and **S249** along the eastern shore. Around Lake Como, follow **S340** along the western shore, **S36** on the eastern coast, and **S583** on the lower arms. **S33** and **S34** trace the western shore of Lake Maggiore.

MILAN

Serious pollution is responsible for a rigorously enforced effort to control excessive traffic in and out of the city's center. Cars lacking a special resident's permit will be stopped and ticketed. Parking in city center is possible 7 AM–8 PM for a fee. For **taxi service,** call ☎ 02/6767, 02/8585, or 02/8388. For **limousine service,** call **Autonoleggio Pini** (☎ 02/29400555, FAX 02/204748). If age or infirmity entitle you to special dispensation, ask your rental agency or hotel concierge about car permits for special cases.

By Taxi

Taxi fares in Milan seem expensive compared with those in American cities, but drivers are honest (to an extreme, compared with those in some cities). A short downtown hop averages 15,000 lire. Taxis wait at stands or can be called (☎ 02/6767, 02/8585, or 02/8388). It is not unknown to travel by taxi throughout the region, but the prices are prohibitive, making train or bus travel the better option.

By Train

From Milan, there is frequent **direct service** to Cremona, Bergamo, Pavia, Brescia, Mantua, Desenzano del Garda–Sirmione, and Como. Call ☎ 147/888088 for toll-free information.

Contacts and Resources

Car Rental

MILAN

Avis (✉ Via Carlo D'Adda 19, ☎ 02/58101748; ✉ Aeroporto Milano Linate, ☎ 02/717214; ✉ Aeroporto Malpensa, ☎ 02/400099375). **Hertz** (✉ Via Novegro 49, ☎ 02/70200258; ✉ Aeroporto Milano Linate, ☎ 02/70200256; ✉ Aeroporto Malpensa, ☎ 02/40099022). **Europcar** (✉ Via Galbani 12, ☎ 02/66710491; ✉ Aeroporto Milano Linate, ☎ 02/76110277; ✉ Aeroporto Malpensa, ☎ 02/40099351).

Consulates

Australia (✉ Via Borgogna 2, Milan, ☎ 02/777041). **Canada** (✉ Via Pisani 19, Milan, ☎ 02/67581). **U.K.** (✉ Via San Paolo 7, Milan, ☎ 02/723001). **U.S.** (✉ Via Principe Amedeo 2, Milan, ☎ 02/290351).

Emergencies

Carabinieri (☎ 112); English-speaking officers are available 24 hours a day to deal with every kind of emergency. **Police, Ambulance** (☎ 113). You can dial this number wherever you are and it will connect you to the nearest local police emergency service. For first aid, ask for *"pronto soccorso,"* and be prepared to give your address.

English-Language Bookstores

MILAN

American Bookshop (✉ Largo Cairoli at Via Camperio, ☎ 02/878920). **English Bookshop** (✉ Via Ariosto at Mascheroni, ☎ 02/4694468). **Feltrinelli Bookstore** (✉ Via Manzoni 12, ☎ 02/76000386). **Hoepli** (✉ Via Hoepli 5, ☎ 02/864871).

Guided Tours

For tours in Milan, contact the tourist office (✉ Via Marconi 1, ☎ 02/72524301). Lake tours can often be arranged by private launches at lakeside hotels. Also, *see* Getting Around, By Boat, *above.*

Late-Night Pharmacies

There are a number of pharmacies open 24 hours a day, including one on the upper level of **Stazione Centrale** (☎ 02/6690735). The **Cooperativa Farmaceutica** (✉ Piazza Duomo, ☎ 02/86460408) is also open 24 hours. Others take turns staying open late and on weekends; to find the nearest one, check the roster outside any chemist, or the list published in the *Corriere della Sera*.

Travel Agencies

Milan: Compagnia Italiana Turismo (✉ CIT, Galleria Vittorio Emanuele, ☎ 02/863701). **American Express Travel Agency** (✉ Via Brera 3, ☎ 02/809645).

Visitor Information

Bellagio (✉ Piazza della Chiesa 14, ☎ 031/950204). **Bergamo** (✉ Vicolo Aquila Nera at Piazza Vecchia, Upper Bergamo, ☎ 035/232730; ✉ Viale Papa Giovanni 106, Bergamo Bassa, ☎ 035/213185). **Brescia** (✉ Corso Zanardelli 34, ☎ 030/43418). **Como** (✉ Piazza Cavour 16, ☎ 031/3300111; ✉ Train station, ☎ 031/267214; Provincial Tourist Board, ✉ Via Borgovico 148, Como, ☎ 031/230329 or 031/230111). **Cremona** (✉ Piazza del Comune 8, ☎ 0372/23233). **Malcesine** (✉ Via Capitanato del Porto 6, ☎ 045/7400555). **Mantua** (✉ Piazza A. Mantegna 6, ☎ 0376/328253). **Milan** (✉ Via Marconi 1, ☎ 02/72524301; ✉ Stazione Centrale, ☎ 02/72524370; ✉ Municipal Information Office, Galleria Vittorio Emanuele, Piazza della Scala, ☎ 02/8690734). **Pavia** (✉ Via Fabio Filzi 2, ☎ 0382/22156). **Riva del Garda** (✉ Giardini di Porta Orientale 8, ☎ 0464/554444). **Sabbioneta** (✉ Via Vespasiano Gonzaga 31, ☎ 0375/52039). **Sirmione** (✉ Viale Marconi 2, ☎ 030/916245 or 030/916114). **Stresa** (✉ Via Principe Tomaso 70, ☎ 0323/30150).

10 The Dolomites: Trentino–Alto Adige

Trento, Rovereto, Bolzano, and Cortina d'Ampezzo

Little wonder Leonardo da Vinci depicted the Dolomites behind his Mona Lisa. Nature's skyscrapers, they are hemmed in by stupefying cliffs, emerald-green meadows, and crystal-clear lakes. Dramatic rose-color peaks take on a purple hue at summer's sunset; in winter, the lure is the see-and-be-seen ski resort Cortina d'Ampezzo. In the valleys bustle the history-rich cities of Trento, Rovereto, and Bolzano.

Updated by
Fionn
Davenport

UNLIKE OTHER FAMOUS ALPINE RANGES, this vast mountainous domain in northeast Italy has remained relatively undeveloped. The virginal landscape is the ultimate playground for the family or traveler on a quest for an original adventure. Ski fanatics travel across the world to dare some of the steep slopes that test Olympic champions. Mountaineers risk the climb up sheer rock faces. For calmer souls the seduction of a landscape painted from a palette of extreme colors prevails. The lowland valleys are laced with rivers spanned by awkward bridges and are dotted with secluded villages, picture-book castles, and unexpected historic sites.

The Dolomites, sprawling over the Trentino–Alto Adige region and into parts of Lombardy by the Swiss border and the Veneto along the Austrian border, became known to Americans as a winter sports center after Cortina d'Ampezzo catapulted to fame by hosting the Winter Olympics of 1956. Today, scores of funiculars, chairlifts, and ski lifts provide access to 1,200 km (750 mi) of ski runs, as well as ski jumps and bobsled runs.

Then there are the "untouchable" zones—inaccessible by means of chairlift or ski lift. These are the famous plateaus topping some of the highest mountains, from which you can see Italy on one side and Austria or Switzerland on the other. To enjoy such a rare spectacle, you must spend arduous hours climbing beyond where the lifts leave you, and when you reach the top, you will probably see cows casually grazing on the grass. It can make you dizzy just thinking of how they got there, but contradictions are common in the Dolomites.

Called "the most beautiful work of architecture ever seen" by Le Corbusier, this expansive land of rocks and valleys has long attracted Italians and other Europeans seeking a diverse natural environment. What they—and you—find is a profusion of brilliant colors, architectural styles, and languages. A meander through the valleys becomes a botanical escapade, with rare plant species abounding; high above you on the cliffs are castles, protected by their size and position. The serious climber will get a closer view of these remote fortresses. There, on the higher levels, are some rarely seen animals: bears, deer, mountain goats, and birds of prey. It's perhaps not surprising that Reinhold Messer, the first man to climb Everest without oxygen, lives in the Dolomites.

Straddling the Brenner Pass—the main access point to Italy from central Europe—the Dolomites play host to a mixture of cultures and languages. The people of the Alto Adige are predominantly German speaking, and their crafts and food have an Austrian accent (until World War I, the area was Austria's South Tyrol). The Trentino, on the other hand, is Italian speaking. Reflecting this diversity, the area, since 1948, has enjoyed special status as the Autonomous Region of Trentino–Alto Adige, made up of the independent provinces of Trento and Bolzano. But there is still another language to be heard in the area: Ladin, an offshoot of Latin still spoken by a small Ladin community, can credit centuries of isolation in mountain strongholds for its survival.

Signs throughout much of the Dolomites are bilingual. Place-names are given in Italian with German equivalents, where useful, in parentheses below.

Pleasures and Pastimes

Cross-Country Skiing

The Dolomites are an ideal place to learn or improve your *sci di fondo* (cross-country skiing). The major Alpine resorts, and even many out-of-the-way villages, have prepared trails (usually loops marked off by km) appropriate for differing degrees of ability. Two of the best are at Ortisei and Dobbiaco. You can have a lot of fun blazing new trails across virgin snowfields; you can usually get permission by asking at the nearest farmhouse or by inquiring at local tourist offices.

Dining

Encompassing the Germanic Alto Adige province and the Italian Trentino province, the Dolomites region combines Italian cuisine with local Tyrolean specialties, which are much like the dishes of Austria and central Europe. Local *alimentari* (food shops) stock a bounty of regional cheeses, pickles, salami, and smoked meats, while local bakeries turn out a wide selection of crusty dark rolls, caraway rye bread, and the like—perfect for picnics. Local dishes vary from one isolated mountain valley to the next. Don't miss *speck,* the local smoked ham. Other specialties include *canederli,* or *knoedel,* a type of dumpling with many variations, served either in broth or with a sauce; hot sauerkraut; ravioli made from rye flour, stuffed with spinach, and fried; and apple or pear strudel. And—as befits a wine-producing region—the local vintages (and fruit brandies) are delicious. In the fall in the South Tyrol, when autumn colors beautify the mountains, it's a tradition to make a tour of the cozy country wine taverns to drink the new wine and eat hot roasted chestnuts.

CATEGORY	COST*
$$$$	over 85,000 lire
$$$	60,000 lire–85,000 lire
$$	30,000 lire–60,000 lire
$	under 30,000 lire

Prices are per person, including house wine, service, and tax.

Downhill Skiing

The Dolomites command some of the best downhill skiing environments and facilities in Europe, with some centers equipped for summer skiing. Generally the ski season runs from late November to April, by which time some people prefer to ski in shirtsleeves. The most comprehensive centers are Cortina d'Ampezzo, in the heart of the Dolomites to the east of Bolzano, and Madonna di Campiglio, west of Trento. These resorts are unabashedly upscale, but you get the extras you expect from world-class centers: miles of interconnecting runs linked by cable cars and lifts, plus skating rinks, heated indoor pools, and lively après-ski. Less-expensive adventures can be had at Badia Valley, south from Brunico, and Ortesei, a modern, popular resort.

Folk Festivals

Essentially rural in character, the Dolomites offer a rich selection of folk festivals, harvest fairs, and religious celebrations. Chief among these is Trento's weeklong festival of San Vigilio (the last week of June), when marching bands and costumed choirs perform in the streets and squares of the heart of the city. The other major towns have similar festivals, but equally enjoyable are the more informal and low-key celebrations in the villages of the many valleys, sometimes amounting to nothing more than excuses for hardworking mountain farmers to get together for some local wine and song.

Hiking and Climbing

The Dolomites have a well-maintained network of trails for hiking and rock climbing, with *rifugi* (huts) in both hiking terrain and near the most difficult ascents. At these spartan accommodations you can just refuel with a meal or stay overnight in a dormitory-type room. Routes are designated by grades of difficulty (T, tourist path; H, hiking path; EE for expert hikers; EEA, for equipped expert hikers). It is important to follow safety procedures, have the necessary equipment, and obtain the latest information on trails and conditions. For information, call the Club Alpino Italiano (⊠ Piazza delle Erbe 46, Bolzano, ☎ 0471/978172; ⊠ C. Libertà 188, Merano, ☎ 0473/448944).

Lodging

Accommodations in the Dolomites range from restored castles to spick-and-span chalet guest houses, from stately 19th-century hotels to chic modern ski resorts. Even a small village may have scores of lodging places, many of them very inexpensive. Hotel information offices at train stations and tourist offices can help you avoid the language problem if you arrive without reservations: Bolzano train station has a 24-hour hotel service, and tourist offices will give you a list of all the hotels in the area, arranged by location and price. We've tried to mention here a few hotels in towns that make good bases for travel, as well as some notable hotels found along the road. Remember that many hotels in ski resorts cater primarily to longer stays at full or half board: it's wiser to book ski vacations as a package in advance. A word of warning: Although spring and fall are wonderful times to travel in the region, many mountain hotels are closed for a month or two after Easter and for about six weeks before Christmas.

CATEGORY	COST*
$$$$	over 300,000 lire
$$$	200,000 lire–300,000 lire
$$	80,000 lire–200,000 lire
$	under 80,000 lire

Prices are for a standard double room, including tax and service.

Shopping

Shopping is an event in the Dolomites, where larger towns, such as Bolzano, Bressanone, and Brunico have shops clustered in arcaded shopping streets designed to keep shoppers dry on rainy or snowy days. The ethnic mixture, with its strong Tyrolean influence, makes for local products and crafts that are quite different from those elsewhere in Italy. Tyrolean clothing—loden goods, lederhosen, dirndls, and linen suits with horn buttons—is a good buy and costs less than in neighboring Austria. Local crafts, such as embroidered goods, wood carvings, figures for nativity scenes, pottery, and handcrafted copper and iron objects, make good gifts.

Exploring the Dolomites

The best—and only—way to get around in this mountainous region is by following the course of the valleys that find their way to the heart of the massifs that compose the Dolomites. Two of the most important valleys are those formed by the Isarco and Adige rivers. The Isarco River begins at the Brenner Pass and runs due south to Bolzano where it joins the Adige River. The Adige itself originates near the Swiss border and also runs south through Bolzano. Italy's main road and rail connections to north central Europe follow the same rivers northward en route to the Brenner Pass.

Numbers in the text correspond to numbers in the margin and on the Dolomites: Trentino–Alto Adige and Bolzano maps.

Great Itineraries

The area of the Dolomites is a vast expanse of valleys, mountain roads, and hillside towns. Unfortunately, most roads, although of excellent quality, can be hazardous, especially during the winter months. Instead of rushing to get all the sights into your travels, try to be discerning and stick to the areas you would most like to see. A further note of caution involves the closure of some roads during the winter season, which can begin as early as November and continue until May, in particular the high mountain passes such as Passo di Gavia and Passo dello Stelvio in the east.

IF YOU HAVE 3 DAYS

Start in **Trento** ① and head south to **Rovereto** ② and **Riva** on the tip of Lake Garda (☞ Chapter 9), then on to the quaint towns of **Pinzolo** ③ and **Madonna di Campiglio** ④ for a bird's-eye view of the Dolomites, ending your day via Dimaro in ⚅ **Bolzano** ⑨–⑮. The next day head for the lovely town of **Bressanone** ⑱ and on via **Brunico** ⑲ to the exclusive resort of ⚅ **Cortina d'Ampezzo** ㉑. The last day take the Great Dolomites road passing **Lake Carezza** ㉖ and return to Trento.

IF YOU HAVE 5 DAYS

Follow the three-day itinerary above as far as Dimaro, but instead of going directly to Bolzano, swing east and head for the dizzily high Passo di Gavia and down then to the small town of ⚅ **Bormio** ⑤. The next day proceed to the breathtaking **Passo dello Stelvio** ⑥ and on down to **Naturno** ⑦ before stopping in one of the pearls of the Alto Adige region, **Merano** ⑧. Continue on to ⚅ **Bolzano** ⑨–⑮, the principal city in this region. The next day head for **Cornedo** ⑯, **Chiusa** ⑰, and **Bressanone** ⑱. Move on to Brunico and ⚅ **Cortina d'Ampezzo** ㉑. The next day head to **Canazei** ㉒ via the breathtaking Passo di Sella and on down into **Ortisei** ㉓ in the heart of the Val Gardena. Return to Trento via **Fiè** ㉔ and **Caldaro** ㉕.

IF YOU HAVE 8 DAYS

Follow the five-day itinerary as far as Brunico. The following day stroll through **Dobbiaco** ⑳ before moving on to ⚅ **Cortina d'Ampezzo** ㉑. From here follow the Great Dolomites Road through the Passo di Falzarego and slightly north through the Passo di Sella and into the Val Gardena and ⚅ **Ortisei** ㉓. On the last day, drive to **Fiè** ㉔ and south on the A22. Just south of Cornedo, turn left onto the S241 to get to **Lake Carezza** ㉖. Continue along the road until you reach Vigo di Fassa, veering south onto the S48, passing through the small towns of Predazzo, Cavalese, and Ora, until you rejoin the A22 and continue south back to Trento.

When to Tour the Dolomites

If you are here for the skiing, most resorts open from mid-December to April. With the exception of the main bargain period known to Italians as *settimane bianche* (white weeks), ski-package weeks usually running from January to February, the slopes are relatively crowd free. Booking well in advance of your ski holiday is highly recommended, as lack of snow in the early part of the season can sometimes cause overcrowding later on. During the rest of the year accommodations are easier to find, but booking is still recommended. Note that nearly all hotels and guest houses outside the main urban centers close from early November to mid- or late December.

The Dolomites: Trentino–Alto Adige

SWITZ.

AUSTRIA

AUSTRIA

Brenner Pass

PUSTERIA

L. Misurina

Cortina d'Ampezzo **21**

Pieve di Cadore

Dobbiaco **20**

Brunico **19**

S49

S51

S51

S49

S244

Passo di Falzarego

Arabba

S48

S203

Bressanone **18**

Ortisei **23**

Passo di Sella

Canazei **22**

Résia

S40

Glorenza

PARCO NAZIONALE DELLO STELVIO

VAL VENOSTA

S44

Tirolo

Merano **8**

S38

Naturno **7**

Lana

Silandro

Adige

Gargazzone

VAL GARDENA

Chiusa **17**

S242

Fiè **24**

S12

Isarco

16

Laives

Cornedo

Caldaro

25

Vigo di Fassa

Lake Carezza **26**

S241

S48

Predazzo

San Martino

S50

Cavalese

Ora

S48

S12

A22

Adige

S43

Bolzano **9 — 15**

Passo dello Stelvio

S38

Bormio **5**

6

Dimaro

Passo di Gavia

S42

Madonna di Campiglio **4**

Pinzolo **3**

S300

S239

S300

WESTERN TRENTINO

The areas east and west of Trento are collectively known as Trentino, a region shaped roughly like a butterfly. The west side includes the peaks of the Brenta Massif, the Stelvio Pass, and the Venosta Valley. Some of the passes in this region close during the winter months, so if you are traveling during this period you will not be able to follow the entire itinerary. Towns are given in order as you come upon them by road.

Trento

❶ *51 km (32 mi) south of Bolzano, 24 km (15 mi) north of Rovereto.*

Capital of the autonomous Trentino province, Trento has somehow escaped the ravages of commercialization and retains its architectural charm, artistic attractions, and historic importance. It was here, from 1545 to 1563, that the structure of the Catholic Church was redefined, at the famous Council of Trent. This was the starting point of the Counter-Reformation, which brought half of Europe back to Catholicism. Until 1803, Trento itself was ruled by prince-bishops. You'll see the word *consiglio* (council) everywhere in Trento—in hotel, restaurant, and street names, and even on wine labels.

In Piazza del Duomo is a Baroque **Fontana di Nettuno**; the massive, low, Romanesque **Duomo** forms the southern edge of the square. Locals refer to the piazza as the city's *salotto,* or sitting room, as in fine weather it is always filled with students and residents drinking coffee, enjoying an aperitif, or reading the newspaper. Before entering the cathedral, pause to savor the view of the mountaintops ranged majestically around the city in every direction when skies are clear.

Step inside to see the unusual arcaded stone stairways on either side of the austere nave. Ahead of you is the *baldacchino* (altar canopy), a clear copy of Bernini's masterpiece in St. Peter's in Rome. In the small Chapel of the Crucifix to the right is a mournful 15th-century Crucifixion, with Mary and the Apostle John. This crucifix, built by German artist Sixtus Frei, was a focal point of the Council of Trent: Each decree agreed on during the two decades of deliberations was solemnly read out in front of it. Outside, walk around to the back of the cathedral to see an exquisite display of 14th-century stonemasons' art, from the small porch to the intriguing knotted columns on the graceful apse. Within the Duomo grounds is an **archaeological area,** displaying ancient ruins including a gate dating from the 9th century. ⊠ *Piazza del Duomo.* 🎟 *Archaeological area 2,000 lire.* ⊙ *Weekdays 10–noon and 2–6, Sat. 10–noon.*

The crenellated **Palazzo Pretorio,** which seems to be a wing of the cathedral, was built in the 13th century as the prudently fortified residence of the prince-bishops. Endowed with considerable power and autonomy, these clerics enjoyed a unique position in the medieval hierarchy. The Palazzo Pretorio now houses the **Museo Diocesano Tridentino,** where you can see paintings showing the seating plan of the prelates during the Council of Trent; early 16th-century tapestries by Pieter van Aelst, the Belgian artist who carried out Raphael's (1483–1520) designs for the Vatican tapestries; carved wood altars and statues; and an 11th-century sacramentary, or book of services. These and other precious objects all come from the cathedral's treasury. ⊠ *Piazza del Duomo 18,* ☎ *0461/234419.* 🎟 *6,000 lire includes Duomo archaeological area.* ⊙ *Mid-Feb.–mid-Nov., Mon.–Sat. 9:30–12:30 and 2:30–6.*

Off the northwest side of the Piazza del Duomo, about 650 ft down Via Cavour, is the Renaissance church of **Santa Maria Maggiore,** where many sessions of the Council of Trent were held. The only light in the church comes from a beautifully simple rose window over the main door, so you'll have to strain to see the magnificent ceiling, an intricate combination of stucco and frescoes. ⊠ *Via Cavour.*

Locals refer to **Via Belenzani** as Trento's outdoor gallery because of the frescoed facades of the hallmark Renaissance palazzi. It's an easy 50-yard walk up the lane behind the church of Santa Maria Maggiore. The climb up **Via Manci** is pleasant, past 200 yards of souvenir shops and glassware outlets.

Castello del Buonconsiglio (Castle of Good Counsel), at the end of Via Manci, was once the stronghold of the prince-bishops; its position and size made it easier to defend than the Palazzo Pretorio. As you stand facing it, you can see the evolution of architectural styles, starting with the medieval fortifications of the Castelvecchio section on the far left, down to the more decorative Renaissance **Magno Palazzo,** built three centuries later in 1530. The Castello now houses the **Museo Provinciale d'Arte** (Provincial Art Museum), where permanent and visiting exhibits of art and archaeology are displayed in Renaissance frescoed medieval halls or under Renaissance coffered ceilings. The 13th-century **Torre dell'Aquila** (Eagle's Tower) holds the highlight of the museum, a medieval fresco cycle of the months of the year. It is full of charming and informatively detailed scenes of 15th-century life in both court and countryside. ⊠ *Via B. Clesio 5,* ☎ *0461/233770.* 🖸 *10,000 lire July–Oct., 7,000 lire Nov.–June.* ☉ *May–Sept., Tues.–Sun. 9–6; Oct.–Apr., Tues.–Sun. 9–12:15 and 2–5:15. Admission and hrs vary when exhibitions are held.*

The emphasis of the **Museo Storico di Trento** (Trento Historical Museum), housed in the former joiner's shop inside the castle walls, is on modern Trentino history, with displays, dioramas, and the occasional exhibition on the region from the unification of Italy in 1861 up to and including World War II. ⊠ *Via B. Clesio 3,* ☎ *0461/230482.* 🖸 *7,000 lire, 10,000 during an exhibition.* ☉ *Apr.–Sept., Tues.–Sun. 9–noon and 2–6; Oct.–Mar., Tues.–Sun. 9–noon and 2–5.*

The **Torre Verde,** or Green Tower (⊠ Piazza Raffaello Sanzio), is part of Trento's 13th-century fortifications standing alongside other fragments of the city walls. The **Torre Vanga** (⊠ Via Torre Vanga) is another 13th-century fortification, this time guarding the medieval bridge across the Adige, Ponte San Lorenzo.

The progressive, modern works in the **Museo d'Arte Moderna e Contemporanea di Trento** collection are installed in a Renaissance villa, Palazzo delle Albere, next to the Adige river. Permanent works date from the 19th and 20th centuries; a recent exhibition titled "Trash" featured, you guessed it, artwork created from garbage. ⊠ *Palazzo delle Albere, Via R. da Sanseverino 45,* ☎ *0461/234860.* 🖸 *4,000–10,000 lire.* ☉ *Tues.–Sun. 10–6.*

OFF THE BEATEN PATH **BELVEDERE DI SARDAGNA –** Take the cable car from the station at the Ponte San Lorenzo bridge to this scenic spot, a vantage point 1,200 ft above Trento.

LEVICO TERME – About 20 km (13 mi) east of Trento City and just east of Lago di Caldonazzo, the Lago di Levico is the undiscovered Levico Terme, a medieval *terme* (thermal bath) town nestled in the Valsugana Valley; the valley was inhabited by the Celts and then conquered by the Romans, and today the Latin-derived Ladin is still spoken by remote peoples in a valley enclave. Today, settle into a hotel here for a spa treatment, summer sports, and relaxation. For cosseting, spa treatment, and modern comforts, the gracious Imperial Grand Hotel Terme (⊠ Via Silva Domini 1, 38056, Levico Terme, ☎ 0461/706104, FAX 0261/706350) is in a lordly restored Austrian noble estate, with a beautiful indoor pool, garden, and a fine Tuscan restaurant.

Dining and Lodging

$$$ ✕ **Chiesa.** Near the castle in a building that dates from about 1400 is this light and nicely lit restaurant with a mix of antiques and modern detail, and power lunchers. Bright red chairs with black trim, apple prints, and even risotto *alle mele* (with apples) celebrate the local produce. The food is traditional: *maccheroncini con salsiccia e verze* (short, narrow pasta tubes with sausage and cabbage) and *tonco de Pontesel* (a stew of mixed meat served with polenta and made according to a 15th-century recipe). ⊠ *Via San Marco 64,* ☎ *0461/238766. AE, DC, MC, V. Closed Sun.*

$$$ ✕ **Le Due Spade.** Near the Duomo, small and cozy, with wood panel-
★ ing and chairs and an antique stove, this typical Tyrolean tavern has an atmosphere of warmth and comfort, able service, and superb locally inspired food. You can sample heartwarming, traditional *gnocchetti di ricotta* (ricotta cheese dumplings) and polenta *con funghi* (with mushroom sauce) and such savory *secondi* (second courses) as *tagliata di Angus alla griglia* (thin slivers of beef, grilled) and served with an aromatic herb sauce. Given its deserved popularity with locals and limited seating, reservations are a must. ⊠ *Via Don Arcangelo Rizzi 11,* ☎ *0461/234343. Reservations essential. AE, DC, MC, V. Closed Sun. No lunch Sun. or Mon.*

$ ✕ **Trattoria Pizzeria Laste.** Owner Guido Rizzi invented pizza Calabrese, a white pizza with garlic, mozzarella, and hot red pepper flakes. He's also a national pizza champion. Well, the proof is in the pudding. Each of his 35 pies—including the *sedano* (mozzarella, celery root, *grana* cheese, oregano)—is delectable. Save room for dessert: pizza *dolce,* with bananas, strawberries, kiwi, and caramel. The trattoria is housed in a pleasant villa in the hills above city center. ⊠ *Via alle Laste 39, Cognola,* ☎ *0461/231570. MC, V. Closed Tues.*

$$ ✕⊞ **Castel Pergine.** On a hilltop outside of town toward Levico looms this castle, which in the 13th century was transformed into a fort, and in the 16th century was occupied by the prince-bishop Bernardo Clesio. Today, the involved Swiss Schneider-Neffs manage it. In the labyrinth of brooding stone and brick chambers, prisons, and chapels are sparse, rustic rooms with carved wood trim, lace curtains, and heavy wooden beds, some canopied. The grounds often have brightly colored modern-art installations—an interesting juxtaposition. The candlelit restaurant, which serves age-old seasonal recipes from Trento in lighter guises, is a favorite of locals and visitors alike. Lodging rates are happily at the bottom of this category. ⊠ *38057 Pergine Valsugana, about 10 km (6 mi) east of Trento* ☎ *0461/531158,* FAX *0461/531329. 21 rooms, 7 without bath. Restaurant, horseback riding, library. AE, MC, V. Closed Nov. 2–Thurs. before Easter.*

$$$ ⊞ **Accademia.** This friendly character-filled hotel occupies an ancient house in the historic center of Trento, close to Piazza del Duomo. The public rooms retain the ancient vaulting, but the bedrooms are modern and comfortably equipped. There's a good but expensive restaurant and a courtyard garden. ⊠ *Vicolo Colico 4/6, 38100,* ☎ *0461/233600,* FAX *0461/ 230174. 42 rooms. Restaurant, wine bar. AE, DC, MC, V.*

$$$ ⊞ **Grand Hotel Trento.** Its contemporary facade amid ancient palaces makes this hotel on Piazza Dante an anomaly. Inside it's lush with modern appointments, from the marble and woodwork in the lobby and lounges to the Clesio restaurant's rich drapery. Rooms are ample and have thick carpets in blues and creams with clubby, wood-trim match-

ing furniture and remote controls. ⊠ *Via Alfieri 1/3, 38100,* ☎ *0461/ 271000,* FAX *0461/271001. 136 rooms. Restaurant, bar, meeting rooms, parking (fee). AE, DC, MC, V. Closed Dec. 24–Jan. 6.*

$$ 🖭 **Aquila d'Oro.** This small hotel offers comfort, efficiency, and a prime location in the historic town center. Most rooms have modern furniture in somber colors. The hotel serves breakfast, and the owner is more then willing to pitch in names of places for lunch and dinner. ⊠ *Via Belenzani 76, 38100,* ☎ FAX *0461/986282. 20 rooms. Bar, breakfast room. AE, DC, MC, V. Closed Dec. 24–Jan. 6.*

Nightlife and the Arts

FESTIVALS

From late June to late September a regional **Superfestival** highlights historic castles as venues for performances and evocations of fact and legend. Trains taking passengers on excursions to the castles are part of it, as are music, costumes, and banquets. The **Festivale di Musica Sacra** (Sacred Music Festival)—a monthlong series of concerts held in the churches of Trento and the Trentino—is held in May and June; for information, call 0462/983880.

A summer bonus is the weeklong **Festive Vigiliane,** a spectacular pageant in the Piazza del Duomo, culminating on June 26, when townspeople don medieval clothing in honor of their patron saint. For more than 60 years the May wine festival **Mostra dei Vini** has attracted every Bacchus, from farmers of surrounding hillside towns to sommeliers from all over Italy. The weeklong festival includes tastings, sommelier tours, and prizes; for information, call 0461/983880.

MARKETS

The small morning **Mercato di Piazza Lodron** is now held in Piazza Allessandro Vittoria, where you can pick up meats, cheeses, produce, and local truffles and porcini mushrooms. On **Piazza Arogno** is a flea market held the third Sunday of every month; there is also a crafts market every Friday and Saturday, but the big shopping day is Thursday, when the weekly market spreads out around this piazza and winds down next to the cathedral.

WOODEN CRAFTS AND CERAMICS

Il Pozzo (⊠ Piazza Pasi 14/L) sells excellent handcrafted wooden objects. **Il Laboratorio** (⊠ Via Roma 12) specializes in terra-cotta pieces molded by local artists.

Rovereto

❷ *24 km (15 mi) south of Trento and 75 km (47 mi) south of Bolzano.*

The 15th-century **Castello di Rovereto** looks down on the medieval town of Rovereto, on the main north–south valley of the Adige. Some of the fiercest fighting of World War I took place in the wooded hills around Rovereto, with Italian and Austrian troops bogged down in prolonged and costly conflict. Every evening at nightfall you're reminded of the thousands who fell by the ringing of the Campana dei Caduti (Bell of the Fallen). Today, it's a noble, peaceful city filled with baby carriages and bright geraniums. Crumbling pastel-color medieval villas inhabit long-shadowed piazzas and winding streets.

Among the city's brooding history, a Futurist vision explodes at the **Museo Depero.** This small installment of native Fortunato Depero's (1892–1960) dynamic works, from 1914–50, includes his hectic New York impressions. ⊠ *Via della Terra 53,* ☎ *0464/434393.* 🖭 *5,000.* ☉ *Tues.–Sun. 9–12:30 and 2:30–6.*

Dining

$$–$$$ ✗ **Ristorante Novecento.** Owner Marco Zani can't for the life of him persuade his grandmother, Wanda, to stop cooking. But after a superb dinner in this airy, candlelit restaurant, you'll be happy she still reigns in the kitchen. Heartwarming dishes, paired with local wines, include *tortelli con fonduta di formaggi* (pasta squares with spinach and ricotta bathed in a butter sauce) and *petto di faraona con finferli su fonduta di porri* (guinea fowl with wild mushrooms and leek puree). ⊠ *Corso Rosmini 82/d,* ☏ *0464/435222. AE, D, MC, V. Closed Sun.*

$–$$ ✗ **La Lanterna.** Up the stairs from the sprawling piazza is this homey, simple, wood-trim trattoria, perfect for a hearty meal among locals. You can start with plates of polenta, *crostini* (grilled bread with toppings) and *trippe en brodo* (tripe in broth), and move on to the rich pastas and meats. ⊠ *Piazza Malfatti 12,* ☏ *0464/436612. AE, MC, V. Closed Thurs. No dinner Wed.*

Nightlife and the Arts

The **Rovereto Festival** (☏ 0464/452159) in early September celebrates modern dance and art exhibitions. Late September welcomes the **Festival Internazionale W. A. Mozart** (☏ 0464/452159), with classical performances at **Teatro Zadonai** (⊠ Corso Bettini 82, ☏ 0464/452159).

En Route   Traveling south from Rovereto, head west on S240, passing the lovely lakeside town of Riva del Garda (☞ Chapter 9), and then north on S45bis to Comano, a small but locally renowned spa. The road continues to Tione, a small farming community. From here head north on S239 to reach Pinzolo.

Pinzolo

❸   *75 km (47 mi) northwest of Rovereto, 14 km (9 mi) south of Madonna di Campiglio.*

In this quaint mountain village you can see a remarkable 16th-century fresco on the side of a small church. Follow the signs for the church of **San Vigilio,** which you'll come to after a short walk through the pines. On an exterior wall, a vivid fresco painted in 1539 by the artist Simone Baschenis describes the Dance of Death, with 40 ghoulish figures offering a stern rebuke to potential sinners. Unfortunately, the church is usually closed to the public.

Madonna di Campiglio

★ ❹   *14 km (9 mi) north of Pinzolo, 92 km (57 mi) southeast of Bormio, 88 km (55 mi) southwest of Bolzano.*

The chichi winter resort Madonna di Campiglio grooms more than 130 km (80 mi) of ski runs and operates some 39 lifts. The resort itself is at a 5,000-ft altitude, and some of the ski runs, summer hiking paths, and mountain biking routes venture onto the surrounding peaks, including Pietra Grande, more than 9,700 ft up. An excursion to the Spinale Peak on the year-round chairlift affords magnificent views of the Brenta Dolomites.

Lodging

$$$$ 🏨 **Golf.** You'll have to make your way up to Campo Carlo Magno, the
★   famous pass just north of town, to reach this grand hotel, the former summer residence of Hapsburg Emperor Franz Joseph. A modern wing has been added to the more-than-a-century-old structure, but old-world charm remains: Rooms 114 and 214 are still lavished in the old imperial style. Replete with verandas, Persian rugs, and bay windows, it's practically on the fairway of a golf course that draws a tony summer crowd.

A shuttle bus makes runs into town. ⊠ *Campo Carlo Magno, 38084,* ☎ *0465/441003,* FAX *0465/440294. 124 rooms. Restaurant, bar, 9-hole golf course. AE, DC, MC, V. Closed mid-Apr.–June, mid-Sept.–mid-Dec.*

$$$$ 🏨 **Savoia Palace.** One of the more traditional hotels at the resort is full of mountain-style furnishings with lots of carved wood and an intimate atmosphere. Two fireplaces blaze away in the bar, where guests recall the day's exploits on the ski slopes. The elegant restaurant serves a mixture of local specialties and hearty dishes drawing on Italian and Austrian influences. Guests stay on full- or half-board terms only. ⊠ *Via Dolomiti di Brenta, 38084,* ☎ *0465/441004,* FAX *0465/440549. 55 rooms. Restaurant, bar. AE, DC, MC, V. Closed mid-Apr.–June, mid-Sept.–Nov.*

$$$ 🏨 **Grifone.** A comfortable hotel that catches the sun, the Grifone has distinctive wood paneling on the outside, flower-decorated balconies, and rooms with views of the forested slopes. The restaurant serves home cooking as well as international dishes. ⊠ *Via Vallesinella 7, 38084,* ☎ *0465/442002,* FAX *0465/440540. 40 rooms. Restaurant, bar. AE, DC, MC, V. Closed mid-Apr.–June, mid-Sept.–Nov.*

Outdoor Activities and Sports

GOLF

On **Campo Carlo Magno** (☎ 0465/41003) is a nine-hole course, set in the mountains near Madonna di Campiglio, open from July through mid-September.

HIKING

The local **tourist office** (⊠ Via Pradalago 4, ☎ 0465/442000, FAX 0465/440404) supplies maps of the dozen or so treks for walking amid waterfalls, lakes, and stupendous views.

SKIING

This quaint resort is one of the better-skied resorts in the Dolomites, with miles of interconnecting runs linked by cable cars and lifts. The popularity of this town is due to the well-organized lodging, skiing, and trekking facilities it provides.

En Route Just a few kilometers north of Madonna di Campiglio is one of the highest points in the Dolomites, the **Campo Carlo Magno** pass. This is where Charlemagne is said to have stopped in AD 800 on his way to Rome to be crowned emperor. Stop here to glance over the whole of northern Italy. Resume your descent with caution (in the space of a couple of kilometers, you descend more than 2,000 ft via hairpin turns and switchbacks). The strange, rocky pinnacles of the Dolomites, which jut straight up like chimneys and look at times more like Utah's Monument Valley than any European ranges, loom over scattered mountain lakes.

Turn left at Dimaro, and continue 37 km (23 mi) east to Ponte di Legno through another high pass, **Passo del Tonale** (5,600 ft).

Here turn right on S300 and, passing the so-called Black Lake on your left, head for Bormio, the famous Lombard skiing center, through the **Passo di Gavia,** which also must be approached carefully and attentively when open to traffic.

Bormio

❺ *20 km (12 mi) south of Passo dello Stelvio, 100 km (60 mi) southwest of Merano.*

At the foot of the Stelvio Pass, in the Valtellina Valley, Bormio is one of the most famous ski resorts on the western side of the Dolomites, with 38 km (24 mi) of pistes. It differs greatly from Madonna di

Campiglio in that it is both a town and a summer resort. With an altitude of close to 4,000 ft, Bormio has clean, fresh air that in summer draws Italians escaping the humidity of the cities. There are plenty of shops, restaurants, and hotels throughout the town. Bormio has also been known for the therapeutic qualities of its waters since the Roman era. You'll find spas throughout the town.

Bormio is the place to enter the Alps' biggest national park, the **Parco Nazionale dello Stelvio,** spread over 520 square mi and four provinces. Opened in 1935 with the express intent to preserve flora and protect fauna, today it thrives with over 1,200 types of plants—not to mention 600 different mushrooms—and over 160 species of animals, including the chamois, ibex, and roe deer. ⊠ *Visitor center: Via Monte Braulio 56,* ☎ *0342/901582.* 🖃 *Free.*

Lodging

$$$ 🏨 **Posta.** Ostelli della Posta hotels, staging inns of days gone by, are a time-honored tradition in northern Italy. The warm reception and atmosphere of this town center hotel will temper the cold, with its warm wood detail in the low-vaulted areas. The rooms are cozy and comfortable, with heavy drapery and bed linens. Perks include a small health center with a pool, sauna, gym, and Turkish bath and a slopes shuttle bus. ⊠ *Via Roma 66, 23032,* ☎ *0342/904753,* ᴵᴬˣ *0342/904484. 50 rooms. Restaurant, pub, indoor pool, sauna, Turkish bath, health club. AE, DC, MC, V. Closed Oct.–Dec. 19.*

$$ 🏨 **Nazionale.** Bordering the Stelvio National Park, this central hotel caters to the winter and summer crowd. Rooms are small but well equipped, with TVs and safes. The exterior is, for the most part, wood, with balconies on nearly all floors except the top. The hotel operates a shuttle bus to and from the cable cars. ⊠ *Via al Forte 28, 23032,* ☎ *0342/903361,* ᴵᴬˣ *0342/905294. 48 rooms. 2 restaurants, bar, sauna, shops, recreation room. AE, DC, MC, V. Closed Oct.–Dec.*

Passo dello Stelvio

★ ⑥   *20 km (12 mi) north of Bormio, 61 km (38 mi) west of Naturno, 80 km (48 mi) west of Merano.*

At just over 9,000 ft, the Passo dello Stelvio (Stelvio Pass) is the second-highest pass in Europe. The view from the top is worth the effort because the pass connects the Venosta Valley with the Valtellina in neighboring Lombardy. Just to the left as you enter the pass is Switzerland. Stelvio is a year-round skiing center, with summer skiing on many of its runs.

En Route   Between the Stelvio Pass and Spondigna is 30 km (19 mi) of picturesque, winding road, with 48 hairpin turns. This section of road can be a bit hair-raising for anyone who doesn't like mountain driving. In Spondigna keep to the right for the road to Naturno.

ALTO ADIGE AND CORTINA

Alto Adige (Südtirol), the northern half of the region, was ceded to Italy at the end of World War I, hitherto having been part of the Austro-Hungarian Empire. As a result, everything here has more than a tinge of the Teutonic, which is none more apparent than in the fact that the majority of the inhabitants speak German. Ethnic differences have led to inevitable tensions (including, alas, acts of terrorism), though a large measure of autonomy has, for the most part, kept the lid on nationalist ambitions. Towns are listed in order as you come upon them by road.

Naturno

❼ *61 km (38 mi) east of Passo dello Stelvio, 14 km (9 mi) west of Merano, 44 km (27 mi) northwest of Bolzano.*

Naturno is a large horticultural center, with streets lined with colorful houses that display painted murals on their walls. Art lovers will appreciate the church of **San Procolo,** which is frescoed inside and out, and has wall paintings that are the oldest in the German-speaking world, dating from the 8th century. It is usually open only on Sunday.

Above the town, a short distance away, is the 13th-century **Castello Juval,** since 1983 the home of the South Tyrolese climber and polar adventurer Reinhold Messner—the first man to conquer Everest solo, and the first to scale all 14 of the world's highest peaks without oxygen. Since 1995, part of the castle has been a museum, showing Messner's collection of Tibetan art, mountaineering illustrations, and masks from around the world. ☎ *0473/221852.* ☑ *12,000 lire.* ☉ *Mid-Apr.–June and Sept.–mid-Nov., daily 10–5.*

Dining

$$ ✕ **Juval Inn.** Just below Juval Castle, Reinhold Messner's Juval Inn is an old-style hostelry in a restored farmhouse, serving traditional local dishes and wines provisioned from his own farm. ⊠ *Schlosswirt-Juval,* ☎ *0473/668238. No credit cards. Closed Wed., July, and mid-Nov.–Easter.*

Merano

★ ❽ *24 km (15 mi) north of Bolzano, 100 km (62 mi) northeast of Bormio.*

The second-largest town in the Alto Adige, Merano has been famous as a spa town for 150 years due to its therapeutic thermal waters. It is also renowned for its grape cure. Sheltered by mountains, Merano has an unusually mild climate, with summer temperatures rarely exceeding 80°F and winters that usually stay above freezing, despite the skiing that is within easy reach. Chairlifts and cable cars connect Merano with the high Alpine slopes of Avelengo and San Vigilio. Along the narrow streets of Merano's old town, houses have little towers and huge wooden doors, and the pointed arches of the Gothic cathedral sit with harmony next to neoclassical and art nouveau–style buildings.

In the heart of the old town, **Piazza del Duomo** is the 14th-century Gothic **cathedral,** with a crenellated facade and an ornate campanile. The **Cappella di Santa Barbara,** just behind the cathedral, is an octagonal church containing a 15th-century Pietà.

The **terme** (thermal baths) is a huge complex and nerve center for spa facilities; although some hotels have their own, these are unique. Technicians are trained to treat you with mud packs, massages, and inhalation and sauna routines, or just with the thermal waters, which are said to be especially good for coronary and circulatory problems. Other cures include the famous grape cure at harvest time in the fall, when a two-week diet of fresh grapes has, since Roman times, been reputed to tone up digestive, liver, and urinary tract functions. ⊠ *Close to the Ponte del Teatro.*

Dining and Lodging

$$$$ ✕ **Andrea.** This relaxed but elegant showcase for fine cuisine and service is just off Via dei Portici and right by a cable-car station. Surrounded by wood paneling and lots of green plants, you can dine on local and international cuisine, such as risotto *alle erbe* (with herbs) and *filetto di vitello con salsa di alloro* (veal fillet with bay leaf sauce). A set menu (about 100,000 lire) offers a complete five-course dinner, including su-

perb wine. ☒ *Via Galilei 44,* ☎ *0473/237400. Reservations essential. Jacket and tie. AE, DC, MC, V. Closed Mon. and 2 wks in Feb. No dinner Sun. Nov.–Mar.*

$$$ ✕ **Flora.** There's room for only about 20 diners in this intimate candlelit restaurant under the historic arched arcades of Merano's ancient center. Chef Louis Oberstolz describes his cooking as "fresh, spontaneous, and natural, using only the finest ingredients." He offers a seven-course set menu. Among the specialties are *quaglia ripiena con fegato d'oca grasso* (boned quail stuffed with foie gras), and *schlutzkrapfen* (fresh pasta ravioli with various fillings). ☒ *Via dei Portici 75,* ☎ *0473/231484. Reservations essential. AE, DC, MC, V. Closed Sun. and mid-Jan.–mid-Feb. No lunch Mon.*

$$$ ✕ **Schloss Maur.** Stained-glass lamps and wood paneling create a warm
★ art nouveau effect in this restaurant in the Hotel Palace (☞ *below*). Schloss Maur is the height of elegance, with huge marble columns, high ceilings, and crystal chandeliers. Italian and international dishes include the signature spaghetti with a sauce of zucchini, sage, and green pepper or roast saddle of lamb and lobster. ☒ *Hotel Palace, Via Cavour 2/4,* ☎ *0473/211300. Reservations essential. AE, DC, MC, V.*

$–$$ ✕ **Terlaner Weinstube Putz.** This local favorite is an old rustic *stube* (Tyrolean-style drinking hall) in Merano's old town. The seasonal menu focuses on Tyrolean specialties. Try *zuppa al vino bianco* (soup with white wine) and the various risottos, including one with asparagus in the spring, and with Barolo in chillier months. ☒ *Via dei Portici 231,* ☎ *0473/235571. No credit cards. Closed Wed. Feb.–Mar., and July.*

$$$–$$$$ 🏨 **Hotel Palace.** Merano's grandest hotel is an opulent turn-of-the-cen-
★ tury institution set in an extensive garden. Rooms are spacious, decorated in a stately modern classic design. The public rooms are attractive and comfortable with art-nouveau touches, Tiffany glass, marble pillars, and high ceilings. The impressive spa features various baths, massages, mud treatments, and other cures. A lovely fountain gurgles with thermal Merano water. ☒ *Via Cavour 2/4, 39012,* ☎ *0473/211300,* FAX *0473/234181. 136 rooms. 2 restaurants, bar, indoor-outdoor pool, spa. AE, DC, MC, V.*

$$$ 🏨 **Castel Labers.** On a hilltop amid forested slopes about 3 km (2 mi) east of Merano's center, this castle hotel with red-tile gables, towers, and turrets is unmistakably Tyrolean in style. Ceiling beams, painted fresco decorations, and crossed halberds on the walls complete the look. The hospitable Stapf-Neubert family owns the hotel and takes an active part in its management. ☒ *Via Labers 25, 39012,* ☎ *0473/234484,* FAX *0473/234146. 32 rooms. Restaurant, pool, tennis court. AE, DC, MC, V. Closed Nov.–Mar.*

Nightlife and the Arts

The Bristol hotel has a **disco** that's popular with locals as well as with visitors. The **Grape Festival** on the second Sunday of October has parades and wine tastings in Piazza del Duomo.

Outdoor Activities and Sports

Farmers test their horses in the highly charged **horse race** that is the highlight of Easter Monday. **Tennis Merano** (☒ Tennis Club Merano, Via Piave 46, ☎ 0473/236550) maintains nine clay courts (four indoor) and two hard courts, which are open to the public. Lessons are given at the tennis university.

Shopping

Merano's main shopping street, the narrow, arcaded **Via dei Portici** (Laubengasse) runs west from the cathedral. It features most of the best regional products: wood carvings, Tyrolean-style clothing, embroidery, cheeses, salami, and fruit schnapps. From the end of November until Christmas Eve, Merano holds a traditional *Christkindlmarkt* (Christmas market) in the main square.

Bolzano

32 km (19 mi) south of Merano, 110 km (68 mi) west of Cortina d'Ampezzo, 50 km (31 mi) north of Trento.

Bolzano (Bozen) is the capital of the autonomous province of Alto Adige. It is protected by the mountains to the north and the east and is on the main north–south artery between northern Europe and Italy. This quiet city at the confluence of the Isarco (Eisack) and Talvera rivers has retained a provincial appeal, with no high-rises. With the highest per capita earnings of any city in Italy and a standard of living that is second to none, Bolzano was voted the best place to live in Italy in a 1996 poll conducted by *L'Espresso* magazine.

9 Bolzano's heart is pedestrians-only **Piazza Walther**, named after the 12th-century German wandering minstrel Walther von der Vogelweide, whose songs lampooned the papacy and praised the Holy Roman Emperor. The square serves as an open-air living room where locals and tourists alike can be found at all hours sipping a drink (perhaps a glass of chilled Riesling) at the café tables.

10 The city's Gothic **Duomo** was built between the 12th and 14th centuries; its lacy spire looks down on the mosaiclike tiles covering its pitched roof. Inside the church are 14th- and 15th-century frescoes and an intricately carved stone pulpit dating from 1514. ⊠ *Piazza Walther.* ☉ *Weekdays 9:30–6, Sat. 9:30–noon.*

11 The 13th-century **Dominican church** in Piazza Domenicani is renowned as Bolzano's main repository for paintings, especially frescoes. In the adjoining **Cappella di San Giovanni** you can see frescoes of the Giotto school, one of which is the *Triumph of Death* (circa 1340). Despite its macabre title, this fresco shows the birth of a pre-Renaissance sense of depth and individuality. ⊠ *Piazza Domenicani.* ☉ *Church and chapel: Mon.–Sat. 9–6:30, Sun. mass.*

12 In **Piazza delle Erbe,** a bronze statue of Neptune presides over a bountiful fruit and vegetable market. The stalls spill over with colorful displays of local produce; bakeries and grocery stores showcase hot breads, pastries, cheeses, and delicatessen meats—a complete range of picnic supplies. Try the speck and the Tyrolean-style apple strudel. The market is at the beginning of Bolzano's best-known shopping street, **Via dei Portici** (Laubengasse).

13 The **Museo Civico** (Civic Museum) houses a rich collection of traditional costumes, wood carvings, and archaeological exhibits. The mixture of styles is a reflection of the region's cultural cross-fertilization. ⊠ *Via Cassa di Risparmio 14,* ☎ *0471/974625.* ☞ *7,000 lire.* ☉ *June–Sept., Tues.–Sat. 9–12:30 and 2:30–5:30, Sun. 10–1; Nov.–May, Tues.–Sat. 9–noon and 2–5.*

14 The **Parrocchiale** (parish church) of Gries is worth a visit, if only for the elaborately carved 15th-century wooden Altar of Michael Pacher, considered a masterpiece of the Gothic style. The 11th-century wooden Romanesque crucifix was probably brought here from France, and is also considered important. ⊠ *Corso Libertà.* ☉ *Apr. 21–Oct., weekdays 10:30–noon and 2–4, Sun. mass.*

Passeggiata del Guncina (⊠ Quartiere di Gries) is an 8-km-long (5-mi-long) botanical promenade, dating from 1892, that culminates in a panoramic view of Bolzano.

Bolzano

N

400 yards
400 meters

Via S. Osvaldo
Via Brénnero
Via Renon
Via Crispi
Via Garibaldi
Via A. Hofer
Via Piave
Via Weggenstein
Via Laurin
Viale Stazione
Via Castel Róncolo
V. Francescani
Via Portici
Via d. Mostra
Pza. Walther
Via Alto Adige
Via Isarco
Via Roggia
V. Cappuccini
Via L. da Vinci
Pza. Domenicani
Via Museo
Via Dante
V. Castel Mareccio
Via Marconi
Lungotalvera Bolzano
Via Cassa di Risparmio
Talvera
Ponte Talvera
Lungotalvera S. Quirino
Ponte Druso
Via L. Cadorna
Viale Venézia
Pza. IV Novembre
Via S. Quirino
Libertà
Via Orazio
Viale Druso
Corso
Via Amonio Diaz
Via Cesare Battisti
Corso Italia
Via Orazio
Viale Druso
Viale Duca d' Aosta
Via della Mendola
Via Penegal

Castel Mareccio, **15**
Dominican
Church, **11**
Duomo, **10**
Museo Cívico, **13**
Parrocchiale, **14**
Piazza delle Erbe, **12**
Piazza Walther, **9**

⑮ **Castel Mareccio** (Schloss Maretsch) dates from the 13th century and is nestled under mountains and surrounded by vineyards. The castle is now a well-equipped conference center with a restaurant and bar, all open to the public. ⊠ *Lungotalvera Promenade,* ☎ *0471/976615.* ⊘ *Closed Tues.*

OFF THE
BEATEN PATH
RENON (RITTEN) PLATEAU – The Earth Pyramids of Renon Plateau make up a bizarre geological formation where erosion has left a forest of tall, thin, needlelike spires of rock, each topped with a boulder. The Soprabolzano funicular leaves from Via Renon, about 300 yards left of Bolzano train station. At the top, an electric train takes you to the site, which is at Collalbo, just above Bolzano.

Dining and Lodging

$$–$$$ ✕ **Abramo.** Although outside Bolzano's attractive old center, this restaurant is the best in town. Chef Abramo Pantezi offers an Italian variation of nouvelle cuisine in an attractive, modern Renaissance setting. At tables set with crystal and silver, you'll choose among seafood dishes such as *salmone allo champagne* (salmon in champagne sauce). There's a vegetarian antipasto selection. The extensive wine cellar features top-quality California vintages, among others. ⊠ *Piazza Gries 16,* ☎ *0471/280141. AE, DC, MC, V. Closed Sun. and Aug. 1–25.*

$$ ✕ **Alexander.** Typical Tyrolean dishes are served up in a convivial atmosphere at this city-center restaurant. The venison ham and the lamb cutlets *al timo con salsa all'aglio* (with thyme and garlic sauce) are particularly delicious, but make sure to leave room for the rich chocolate cake. ⊠ *Via Aosta 37,* ☎ *0471/918608. AE, DC, MC, V. Closed Sat.*

$$ ✕ **Gostner Flora's Bistrot.** In a medieval tower on Bolzano's market square, this tiny tavern has been around for centuries, and it has been lovingly restored. There is no menu; you choose from a limited number of typical homey Tyrolean specialties, different every day. They may include canederli or *schlutzkrapfen* (ravioli). The desserts are homemade, too. The young owner takes pride in a selection of good wines. ⊠ *Piazza delle Erbe 17,* ☎ *0471/974086. No credit cards. Closed Sun. No dinner Sat.*

$ ✕ **Batzenhausl.** A medieval building in the center of town houses this crowded stube. It's a popular hangout for the local intellectual set, who hold long, animated conversations over glasses of local wine and tasty local South Tyrolean specialties, such as *herrngröstl* (beef on a bed of boiled potatoes) and apple pancakes with ice cream. Try the fried Camembert. ⊠ *Via Andreas Hofer 30,* ☎ *0471/976183. No credit cards. Closed Tues. and 3 wks in June–July. No lunch.*

$$$–$$$$ 🏨 **Park Hotel Laurin.** This turn-of-the-century hotel, an exercise in art-
★ nouveau opulence, is set in a large park in the middle of town. Its history is speckled with visits from Europe's grand nobility, including the Archduke Franz Ferdinand (whose murder in Sarajevo sparked World War I), King Leopold of Belgium, and Field Marshall Montgomery. Some rooms carry through the Belle Epoque decor; others are classic modern; all have original paintings by artists including Oskar Kokoschka, Max Klinger, and Ernst Nepo. The popular Belle Epoque restaurant prides itself on its use of fresh seasonal ingredients. ⊠ *Via Laurin 4, 39100,* ☎ *0471/980500,* 📠 *0471/970953. 96 rooms. Restaurant, bar, no-smoking rooms, pool, convention center . AE, DC, MC, V.*

$$$ 🏨 **Schloss Korb.** It's worth the 5-km (3-mi) drive west from Bolzano
★ to reach this hotel. It's set in a romantic 13th-century castle with a crenellated roof and a massive central tower, perched in a park amid vine-covered hills. Much of the ancient decor is preserved, and the public rooms are filled with Tyrolean antiques, elaborate wood carvings, old paintings, and attractive plants. The rooms are comfortably furnished—some tower rooms have the old Romanesque arched windows. ⊠

Missiano, Strada Castel d'Appiano 5, 39056, ☎ 0471/636000, FAX 0471/636033. 56 rooms. Indoor pool, sauna, tennis courts. No credit cards. Closed Nov.–Easter.

$$–$$$ 🏨 **Luna/Mondschein.** This central yet secluded hotel was built in 1798. Set in a lovely garden, it washes a tranquil, friendly calm over its guests. The rooms are comfortable, with classic style using wood paneling throughout. Some rooms overlooking the garden have balconies, but even the rooms overlooking the garage have good views of the mountains. The two restaurants include a typical Tyrolean weinstube that serves inexpensive local specialties in a cozy, convivial setting. ⊠ *Via Piave 15, 39100,* ☎ *0471/975642,* FAX *0471/975577. 85 rooms. Restaurant, weinstube. AE, DC, MC, V.*

$$ 🏨 **Città.** This palazzo hotel in town center has modern decor, but still retains the charm of the building's original style. Rooms are well appointed, often with spacious bathrooms and excellent views out over the piazza. The restaurant serves local dishes at decent prices. ⊠ *Piazza Walther 21, 39100,* ☎ *0471/975221,* FAX *0471/976688. 98 rooms. Restaurant, bar, parking (fee). AE, DC, MC, V.*

Nightlife and the Arts

Spring is heralded each May with large flower markets and events, including concerts and folklore and art exhibits. On August 24 is the **Bartolomeo Horse Fair,** on Renon Mountain just northeast of the town. Hundreds of farmers converge for a day of serious trading and frivolous merriment.

Outdoor Activities and Sports

HIKING

Club Alpino Italiano (⊠ Piazza delle Erbe 46, ☎ 0471/978172) is a helpful organization that provides information for hiking and rock climbing. It is important to follow safety procedures and to have all the latest information on trails and conditions.

TENNIS

Courts can be found in Bolzano at **Circolo Tennis Bolzano** (⊠ Via M. Knoller 8, ☎ 0471/280587).

Shopping

LOCAL CRAFTS

The long, narrow arcades of **Via dei Portici** house shops that specialize in Tyrolean crafts and clothing—lederhosen, loden goods, linen suits, and dirndls. The best store for locally made handcrafted goods is **Artigiani Atesini** (⊠ Via Portici 39).

MARKETS

From the end of November until Christmas Eve there are traditional **Christkindlmarkt** in the main square of Bolzano with stalls selling all kinds of Christmas decorations and local handcrafted goods. The outdoor fruit and vegetable market is held in the central **Piazza delle Erbe** (☞ *above*) Monday through Saturday 8–1. The big weekly flea market takes place Saturday morning in **Piazza della Vittoria.**

Cornedo

⓰   *6 km (4 mi) east of Bolzano and 24 km (15 mi) southwest of Chiusa.*

At the mouth of the Ega Valley (Eggental), Cornedo is a place to savor the view of the Catinaccio Mountains. Craggy peaks seem to be props for a lighting display, as pink and purple reflections dance over huge rocks. Their creation is the subject of a local German legend that tells of King Laurin, who lived in a vast palace on the Catinaccio, at a time when the mountain was covered with roses. King Laurin became infatuated with the daughter of a neighboring king, Similde, and kidnapped her, but Similde, searching for his daughter, recognized her place of imprisonment by the red roses that grew there. Laurin freed the girl and was made Similde's prisoner. When Laurin finally escaped he decreed that the betraying roses should be turned to rocks, so that they could be seen neither by day nor by night. Today, the spectacular pinkish-red display is at its best at dawn and at sunset.

Chiusa

⑰ *30 km (19 mi) northeast of Bolzano, 14 km (9 mi) south of Bressanone.*

Beautiful narrow streets lined with houses built in the 15th and 16th centuries best characterize Chiusa (Klausen). Geraniums and begonias fill window boxes beneath the carved wooden shutters.

Above the town of Chiusa is the Benedictine monastery of **Saviona** (Saeben), built as a castle in the 10th century but occupying a site that was fortified in Roman times. The monastery buildings date from the late Middle Ages and are a mixture of Romanesque and Gothic architecture, surrounded by walls and turrets. Guided visits are organized by the Tourist Association in Chiusa; contact the local tourist office (✉ Piazza Tinne 6, ☎ 0472/847424, ℻ 0472/847244). Churches are open daily 9–5.

Bressanone

⑱ *14 km (9 mi) north of Chiusa, 40 km (25 mi) northeast of Bolzano, 100 km (62 mi) northwest of Cortina d'Ampezzo.*

Bressanone (Brixen) is an important artistic center of the Alto Adige and for centuries was the seat of prince-bishops. Like their counterparts in Trento, these medieval administrators had the delicate task of serving two opposing masters—the pope (the ultimate spiritual supervisor) and the Holy Roman Emperor (the civil and military leader). Since the papacy and the Holy Roman Empire were virtually at war throughout the Middle Ages, Bressanone's prince-bishops became experts at tact and diplomacy in order to survive. As you arrive from Brunico, you enter the town on Via Mercato Vecchio, a broad road leading to the imposing **Duomo.** It was built in the 13th century but acquired a Baroque facade 500 years later, and its 14th-century cloister is decorated with medieval frescoes.

The Bishop's Palace, which now houses the **Museo Diocesano** (Diocesan Museum), is a treasure trove of local medieval art, particularly Gothic wood carving. The wooden statues and liturgical objects were all collected from the cathedral treasury. During the Christmas season, the curators highlight displays of the museum's large collection of antique nativity scenes: Look for the shepherds wearing Tyrolean hats. ✉ *Palazzo Vescovile,* ☎ *0472/830505.* ☞ *7,000 lire (3,000 lire for nativity scenes exhibition only).* ☉ *Mid-Mar.–Oct., Mon.–Sat. 10–5; nativity scenes Dec. 15–Feb. 10, Mon.–Sat. 2–5.*

Dining and Lodging

$$ ✕ **Fink.** This restaurant under the arcades in the pedestrians-only town
★ center has a friendly staff and offers an affordable daily set menu. It has a rustic ambience upstairs with lots of wood paneling, and serves international as well as hearty Tyrolean specialties. Try the *carré di maiale gratinato* (pork roasted with cheese and served with cabbage and potatoes) or the *castrato alla paesana* (a kind of lamb stew). ✉ *Via Portici Minori 4,* ☎ *0472/834883. AE, DC, MC, V. Closed Wed. and July. No dinner Tues. Oct.–June.*

$$–$$$ ⊞ **Elefante.** This cozy inn, one of the area's best hotels, is in a historic
★ 15th-century building. The hotel takes its name from an incident in
1550, when King John of Portugal stopped here for a few days while
leading an elephant over the Alps as a present for Austria's Emperor
Ferdinand. Each room is different, many with antiques and paintings.
Housed on the park property is the separate Villa Marzari, with 14
rooms. The hotel restaurant is known as one of the region's best. ⊠
Via Rio Bianco 4, 39042, ☎ *0472/832750,* FAX *0472/836579. 44
rooms. Restaurant, pool. DC, MC, V. Closed Nov. 15–Dec. 25 and
Jan. 10–Feb. 28.*

$$ ⊞ **Croce d'Oro** (Goldenes Kreuz). A five-centuries-old tradition of
hospitality is still practiced by staff at this centrally placed hotel. Shops
line the ground floor of the pink building, with styles inside ranging
from the more modern, tasteful reception area to the tavern-style bar.
The rooms are spacious with sturdy wood appointments. ⊠ *Bastioni
Minori 8, 30042,* ☎ *0472/836155,* FAX *0472/834255. 72 rooms. Restau-
rant, bar. No credit cards.*

Outdoor Activities and Sports

Tennis can be played at **Club Bressanone** (⊠ Via Von Kemter 1, ☎ 0472/
834792).

Shopping

From the end of November until Christmas Eve there are traditional
Christkindlmarkt (Christmas markets) in the main square of Bres-
sanone, with stalls selling all kinds of Christmas decorations and local
handcrafted goods.

Brunico

★ ⑲ *33 km (20 mi) east of Bressanone, 65 km (40 mi) north of Cortina
d'Ampezzo.*

With its medieval quarter nestling below the 13th-century bishop's cas-
tle, Brunico (Bruneck) is within the heart of the Pusteria Valley. This
picturesque little town, often noted for its quiet and relaxing qualities,
is divided by the Rienza River with the old quarter on one side and
the modern quarter on the other.

The **Museo degli Usi e Costumi della Provincia di Bolzano** (Bolzano
Province Customs and Costumes Museum, or Ethnographic Museum)
re-creates a typical local village, and is built around an authentic 300-
year-old mansion. It examines the functions and significance of tradi-
tional architecture. The wood-carving displays are particularly interesting.
It's in the district of Teodone, just outside the town. ⊠ *Via Duca
Teodone 24,* ☎ *0474/550781.* ⊠ *6,000 lire.* ☉ *Mid-Apr.–Oct., Tues.–
Sat. 9:30–5:30, Sun. 2–6.*

Lodging

$–$$ ⊞ **Andreas Hofer.** There's a Tyrolean feel to this comfortable hotel set
in a large garden outside the center of town. Rooms are modern, with
chalet-style balconies overlooking the Pusteria Valley. ⊠ *Via Campo Tures
1, 39031,* ☎ *0474/551469,* FAX *0474/551284. 54 rooms. Restaurant,
weinstube, sauna. MC, V. Closed Apr.–May and mid-Nov.–mid-Dec.*

$–$$ ⊞ **Post.** Locals recommend this traditional, homey hotel for its friendly
rates and restaurant, café, and pastry shop. It has its own parking, which
is important because of the pedestrians-only rules in effect throughout much of the central area. ⊠ *Via Bastioni 9, 39031,* ☎ *0474/
555127,* FAX *0474/551603. 54 rooms, 45 with bath. Restaurant, café,
weinstube, free parking. MC, V. Closed Nov.*

Outdoor Activities and Sports

On January 22 locals turn up for the **dogsled race,** and there seems nary a soul without a flask of hot mulled wine to back their favorites. A comparatively inexpensive ski area is at **Badia Valley,** reached by heading south on S244 from Brunico.

Dobbiaco

㉑ *25 km (16 mi) east of Brunico, 34 km (21 mi) north of Cortina d'Ampezzo.*

In Dobbiaco (Toblach), just 12 km (7 mi) to the east along the Drau Valley, Austria's influence intensifies. Italian is spoken grudgingly here, Austrian money is accepted at most shops and restaurants, and the locals appear more blond and blue-eyed than the average Italian. It is not surprising that Gustav Mahler (1860–1911), the great Austrian composer, would have come here often for inspiration.

Lodging

$–$$ ✿ **Alpino Monte Rota/Alpengasthof Ratsberg.** To reach this hotel,
★ you take the 10-minute cable-car ride to Monte Rota. It is in traditional style, with the timeless look of local chalets. Front rooms have stunning mountain views from balconies, while those in the back look out over the dense mountain forest. You needn't take the cable car back down for sustenance: The Alpino has a good restauran, a bar, and a Tyrolean-style stube. ⊠ *Monte Rota 10, 39034,* ☎ *0474/972916,* ℻ *0474/972213. 30 rooms. Restaurant, bar, pool, sauna. No credit cards. Closed Easter–May and Oct. 20–mid-Dec.*

$–$$ ✿ **Cristallo.** Wood beams and paneling lend an Old Tyrolean tone to this small hotel set in a garden just outside town. The architecture and furnishings reflect the local preference for combining traditional chalet design with functional, but comfortable, modern furniture. You can relax in the cozy and informal stube. ⊠ *Viale S. Giovanni 37, 39034,* ☎ *0474/972138,* ℻ *0474/972755. 30 rooms. Restaurant, bar, indoor pool. AE, MC, V. Closed mid-Apr.–mid-May and mid-Oct.–mid-Dec.*

Outdoor Activities and Sports

SKIING

Prepared trails for cross-country skiing (usually loops marked off by km) accommodate differing degrees of ability. One of the best of this kind can be found at **Dobbiaco.** Inquire at the local tourist office. Downhill skiing can be found at **Monte Rota** slopes, accessible from Dobbiaco. These offer considerably lower rates than in many of the more exclusive resorts.

Cortina d'Ampezzo

★ **㉑** *65 km (40 mi) south of Brunico, 140 km (87 mi) east of Bolzano.*

"The Pearl of the Dolomites" is set in a lush meadow 4,000 ft above sea level. Dense forests adjoin the town, and mountains encircle the whole valley. The town sprawls on the slopes along a fast-moving stream; a public park extends along one bank. Luxury hotels and the villas of the rich are conspicuously scattered over the slopes above the town— identifiable by their attempts to hide behind stands of firs and spruces.

The bustling center of Cortina d'Ampezzo has little nostalgia for old-time atmosphere, despite its Alpine appearance. The tone is set by elegant shops and stylish cafés, as opulent as their well-dressed patrons, whose corduroy knickerbockers may well have been tailored by Armani. Cortina is the place to go for a whiff of the heady aroma of wealth and sophistication; if you want authentic Tyrolean gemütlichkeit, pass through Cortina and stop at one of the resorts later on the tour.

Dining and Lodging

$$$ ✕ **De la Poste.** The exclusive restaurants of the hotel on Cortina's main square have a casually chic clientele and a lively atmosphere. There's an elegant, high-ceilinged main dining room with three big chandeliers where you can dine on soufflés and nouvelle cuisine dishes (every Friday fresh fish is served). There's also a more informal grill room with wood paneling and the family pewter collection. ⌧ *Piazza Roma 14,* ☎ *0436/4271. Reservations essential. Jacket and tie. AE, DC, MC, V.*

$$–$$$ ✕ **Tavernetta.** Near the Olympic ice-skating rink, this popular restaurant has an authentic Tyrolean ambience, with wood-paneled dining rooms and a local clientele. Here you can try Cortina specialties such as *zuppa di porcini* (porcini mushroom soup), ravioli *di cervo* (stuffed with venison), and game. ⌧ *Via dello Stadio 27/a,* ☎ *0436/867494. AE, DC, MC, V. Closed mid-June–mid-July, Nov., and Wed. No lunch Thurs. May and Sept.*

$$$$ 🏨 **Miramonti Majestic.** This imposing and luxurious hotel, nearly a century old, has a magnificent mountain valley location about a km (½ mi) south of town. A touch of old-world formality accompanies the imperial Austrian design, and the interior reflects the period style throughout. There's always a roaring fire in the cozy bar. ⌧ *Località Peziè 103, 32043,* ☎ *0436/4201,* 𝔽𝔸𝕏 *0436/867019. 128 rooms. Restaurant, pool, sauna, golf course, tennis courts, exercise room. AE, DC, MC, V. Closed Easter–June and Sept. 15–Dec. 20.*

$$$ 🏨 **De la Poste.** Skiers who want to be seen keep returning to this lively hotel on the main square in a pedestrian zone. It's been under the same family management since 1826, and the furnishings feature antiques in characteristic Dolomite style. Almost all rooms have wooden balconies. One of Cortina's social centers, the hotel's main terrace bar is always crowded. ⌧ *Piazza Roma 62, 32043,* ☎ *0436/4271,* 𝔽𝔸𝕏 *0436/ 868435. 83 rooms. Restaurant, bar. AE, DC, MC, V. Closed mid-Apr.– mid-June and mid-Oct.–mid-Dec.*

Nightlife and the Arts

At **Europa** hotel (⌧ Corso Italia 207, ☎ 0436/3221) you can expect to mingle with the couture set at the VIP disco; nonguests are welcome, but don't expect to spend less than 50,000 lire.

Outdoor Activities and Sports

In Cortina d'Ampezzo's several accessible mountain ranges you will be challenged by slopes of all degrees of difficulty. Public courts can be used at **Via Sopiazes** (☎ 0436/2937).

En Route   As you enter the Crepa Tunnel along the S48 from Cortina d'Ampezzo, the ascent for the Passo di Falzarego begins. The **Passo Pordoi** will lead to the so-called heart of the Dolomites. The roads around this region of the Sella mountains are deemed to be among the most spectacular in Europe and many consider their rugged beauty to be unparalleled. A fork in the road farther ahead will lead left to Canazei and right into Val Gardena.

HEART OF THE DOLOMITES

The area between Cortina d'Ampezzo and east to Bolzano is dominated by two major valleys, the Val di Fassa and the famous Val Gardena. Both share the spectacular panorama of the Sella mountain range, known because of its circular shape as the Heart of the Dolomites. Val di Fassa is made up primarily of the Grande Strada delle Dolomiti (Great Dolomites Road), which runs from the mountain resort of Cortina d'Ampezzo as far as Bolzano. The route, opened in 1909, now comprises 110 km (68 mi) of easy grades and smooth driving between the two cities.

With some of the best views of the Dolomites, Val Gardena is famous as a ski resort, dotted with well-equipped picturesque towns overlooked by the oblong Sasso Lungo (Long Rock), which is more than 10,000 ft above sea level. It is also home of the Ladins, descendants of soldiers sent by the Roman Emperor Tiberius to conquer the Celtic population of the area in the 1st century AD. Forgotten in the narrow cul-de-sacs of isolated mountain valleys, the Ladins have developed their own folk traditions and speak an ancient dialect that is derived from Latin and is similar to Romansch, which is spoken in some high valleys in Switzerland.

Canazei

㉒ *60 km (37 mi) west of Cortina d'Ampezzo, 23 km (14 mi) east of Lake Carezza, 52 km (32 mi) east of Bolzano.*

Of the towns in the Fassa Valley, Canazei is the most popular ski resort as well as a summer haven. The area around this small town is full of mountain trails and ski slopes, surrounded by large pockets of conifers.

OFF THE BEATEN PATH
COL RODELLA – An excursion from Campitello di Fassa to the vantage point at Col Rodella is a must. The cable car rises some 3,000 ft up the mountain to this most panoramic of vistas. From the balcony at the top you can see full circle around the region, including the Sasso Lungo and the rest of the Sella range.

En Route **Passo di Sella** is one of the most famous mountain passes in the Dolomites. It can be approached from the S48 and continues into Val Gardena among the most panoramic mountain scenery in Europe. The road descends to Ortisei, passing the small ski resort of Santa Cristina.

Lodging

$$$ ☷ **Alla Rosa.** Facilities are modern, and good for a big family. Centrally located, the hotel has a modest restaurant with a choice of either local or international cuisine, and a cozy bar. The three-story building has balconies in half of all rooms, and large reception areas. The bedrooms are well laid out with a pleasant rustic and modern mix, but the real attraction is the view over the imposing Dolomites. ⊠ *Via Dolomite 142, 39046,* ☎ *0462/601107. 37 rooms. Restaurant, bar, recreation room. MC, V. Closed Oct.*

Ortisei

㉓ *80 km (50 mi) west of Cortina d'Ampezzo, 28 km (17 mi) north of Canazei, 35 km (22 mi) northeast of Bolzano.*

Ortisei (St. Ulrich), the jewel in the crown of Val Gardena's ski resorts, is a hub of activity both in summer and, especially, in winter. There are hundreds of miles of hiking trails as well as several hundred miles of accessible ski slopes, including the Siusi slopes to the south. Hotels are everywhere and facilities are excellent, with swimming pools, ice rinks, health spas, tennis courts, and bowling. Most impressive of all is the location, a valley surrounded by formidable views in all directions. For further information on activities in Val Gardena, contact the main tourist office in Ortisei (☞ Visitor Information *in* The Dolomites: Trentino–Alto Adige A to Z, *below*).

For centuries Ortisei has also been famous for the expertise of its
wood-carvers and there are still numerous workshops here. Apart
from making religious sculptures—particularly the wayside Calvaries
you come upon everywhere in the Dolomites—Ortisei's carvers were
long famous for producing wooden dolls, horses, and other toys. As
itinerant peddlers, every spring they traveled by foot with their loaded
packs as far as Paris, London, and St. Petersburg to sell their wares.
Fine historic and contemporary examples of all kinds of locally carved
wooden sculptures and artifacts can be seen at the **Museo della Val Gardena** at Cesa di Ladins. ⊠ *Via Rezia 83, Ortisei,* ☎ *0471/797554.* 🖭
5,000 lire. ☉ *July–Aug., daily 10–noon and 3–7; June, Sept., Dec.
28–30, Jan. 4–7, and Feb. 8–Mar., Tues.–Fri. 3–6:30.*

Lodging

$$$ 🏨 **Adler.** Since 1810, this hotel, one of the best in the valley, has been
under the same family management. Set in a large park, the original
building has been enlarged several times in the intervening years, yield-
ing spacious guest rooms, but it retains a lot of the old turreted-castle
appeal. The Tyrolean character is carried through in special parties held
once a week for guests. ⊠ *Via Rezia 7, 39046,* ☎ *0471/796203,* 🖬
*0471/796210. 94 rooms, most with bath. Restaurant, bar, pool, beauty
salon, sauna, tennis courts, health club. AE, DC, MC, V. Closed mid-
Apr.–mid-May and mid-Oct.–mid-Dec.*

$$–$$$ 🏨 **Posta Cavallino Bianco.** In town center and a five-minute walk from
the main ski facilities, this hotel looks more like a gigantic dollhouse,
with delicate wooden balconies and an eye-catching wooden gable. In-
side, the decor is full of deep colors and ornate carpets and drapery.
Wood is incorporated throughout the interior, most notable in the cozy
hotel bar with a large handcrafted fireplace. The rooms are a good size
with all amenities. ⊠ *Via Rezia 22, 39046,* ☎ *0471/796392,* 🖬 *0471/
797517. 99 rooms. Restaurant, bar, coffee shop, dance club. MC, V.
Closed mid-Apr.–mid-May and mid-Oct.–mid-Dec.*

Outdoor Activities and Sports

The Val Gardena comes alive with a parade of **horse-drawn sleighs**
on January 1. With almost 600 km (370 mi) of accessible downhill slopes,
Ortisei is one of the most popular **skiing** resorts in the Dolomites. Prices
are good and facilities are among the most modern. There are more
than 90 km (56 mi) of cross-country skiing lanes. **Tennis courts** can be
found in Roncadizza (☎ 0471/797275).

Fiè

㉔   *26 km (16 mi) southwest of Ortisei, 18 km (11 mi) east of Bolzano.*

Fiè (Voels) is set in a valley with the Renon mountains on one side and
the Siusi on the other. The town is surrounded by acres of green conif-
erous forests. In the town is the parish church of **Santa Maria Assunta**
in the late Gothic style, built in the 16th century. The church is being
perpetually restored, and is closed to the public.

Lodging

$$$ 🏨 **Turm.** The *turm* (tower) that houses this welcoming hotel on the edge
★   of the Sciliar National Park dates from the 13th century and has been
used as a courthouse, prison, and tavern. Now owned and run by the
Pramstrahler family, it's furnished with their charming collection of paintings and antiques. The picturesque hostelry also has an excellent restaurant. ⊠ *Piazza della Chiesa 9, Fiè allo Sciliar (Voels am Schlern),
39040,* ☎ *0471/725014,* 🖬 *0471/725474. 26 rooms. Restaurant, indoor and outdoor pools, sauna. MC, V. Closed early Nov.–Dec. 19.*

Outdoor Activities and Sports

The **Oswald von Wolkenstein Cavalcade,** named after the medieval South Tyrolese knight and troubadour, is held every year over the first or second weekend of June. After a colorful procession, teams of local horsemen and -women compete in fast-paced events.

Caldaro

㉕ *35 km (22 mi) west of Lake Carezza, 15 km (9 mi) south of Bolzano.*

Caldaro is a vineyard village with clear views of castles high up on the surrounding mountains, a backdrop that reflects the centuries of division that forged the unique character of the area. Caldaro architecture is famous for the way it blends Italian Renaissance elements of balance and harmony with the soaring windows and peaked arches of the local Gothic tradition. The church of **Santa Caterina,** on the main square, is a good example.

Close to the main square is the **South Tyrolean Museum of Wine,** illustrating the history of wine production in this region. ⊠ *Via dell'Oro 1,* ☎ *0471/963168.* 🎟 *5,000 lire.* ☉ *Easter–Oct., Tues.–Sat. 9:30–noon and 2–6, Sun. 10–noon.*

Lake Carezza

㉖ *23 km (14 mi) west of Canazei, 29 km (18 mi) east of Bolzano.*

A lake of icy cold glacial waters, **Lago di Carezza** is some 5,000 ft above sea level. The azure blue of the waters can at times change to magical greens and purples, reflections of the surrounding forest and rosy peaks of the Dolomites.

THE DOLOMITES: TRENTINO– ALTO ADIGE A TO Z

Arriving and Departing

By Car

The most important route in the region, **A22,** is the main north–south autostrada linking Italy with northern Europe via the Brenner Pass. It links Bressanone, Bolzano, Trento, and Rovereto, and at Verona joins the **A4,** running east–west across northern Italy from Trieste to Turin.

By Plane

The nearest airports are Verona's **Aeroporto Villafranca** (⊠ 11 km/7 mi southwest of Verona, ☎ 045/8095666) in Italy and Munich's **Franz Josef Strauss (FJS) Airport** in Germany, both well connected by road and rail with the Dolomite area.

By Train

The express train line that links the towns of Bolzano, Trento, and Rovereto connects with other main lines at Verona, just south of the region. Eurocity trains on the Dortmund–Venice and Munich–Rome routes also stop at these stations. Call ☎ 147/888088 for toll-free information.

Getting Around

By Bus

Local buses connect the train stations at Trento, Bolzano, and Merano with the mountain resorts. The service is fairly frequent between most main towns during the day. Though some parts of the region remain out of the reach of public transportation, it is possible to visit even the remotest villages without a car if you are equipped with the local bus timetables, available from regional and local tourist offices (☞ Visitor Information *in* Contacts and Resources, *below*).

By Car

Autostrada **A22** connects Bressanone, Bolzano, Trento, and Rovereto. Roads in the broad mountain valleys are usually wide two-lane routes, but the roads up into the highest passes can be narrow and subject to sudden closure, even in the months when they are open to drivers. A Bolzano number (☎ 0471/993810 or 0471/978577) provides information on weather-related closures.

By Train

An express train line follows the course of the Adige Valley from the Brenner Pass southward past Bolzano, Trento, and Rovereto. Branch lines from Trento and Bolzano go to some of the smaller valleys, but most of the mountain attractions described above are beyond the reach of trains. Call 147/888088 for toll-free information.

Contacts and Resources

Car Rentals

BOLZANO

Avis (⊠ Piazza Verdi 18, Bolzano, ☎ 0471/971467). **Hertz** (⊠ Via Garibaldi 34, Bolzano, ☎ 0471/981411).

Emergencies

Carabinieri (☎ 112). English-speaking officers are available 24 hours a day to deal with any kind of emergency. **Police, Ambulance** (☎ 113). For first aid, ask for "Pronto Soccorso," and be prepared to give your address.

Guided Tours

If you are without a car or if you don't care to drive over mountain roads, guided tours from Bolzano or Trento can show you the Dolomites the easy way. However, the sudden and frequent snowfalls mean that tours are offered in summer only.

SIGHTSEEING TOURS

In Bolzano, city sightseeing and local excursions are organized by the **SAD** bus company (⊠ Via Conciapelli 60, near the train station, ☎ 167/846047). In July and August, full-day mountain tours include a **Great Dolomites Tour** from Bolzano to Cortina and a tour of the **Venosta Valley** that climbs over the Stelvio Pass into Switzerland. A tour of the **Val Gardena** and the Siusi Alps is available from April to October.

In Trento, city sightseeing can be arranged through the city **APT** office (☞ Visitor Information, *below*). From June through September, the **Calderari e Moggioli** travel agency (⊠ Via Manci 46, ☎ 0461/980275) offers a full-day guided bus tour of the **Brenta Dolomites** and the **Great Dolomites Tour**, a full-day drive over the Pordoi and Falzarego passes to Cortina d'Ampezzo and Lake Misurina.

The Trentino regional **APT** (☞ Visitor Information, *below*) organizes guided tours and excursions by train to castles in the region.

Hiking and Climbing

A helpful organization is the **Società degli Alpinisti Tridentini** (⊠ Via Manci 57, 38100 Trento, ☎ 0461/981871, FAX 0461/986462). **Club Alpino Italiano** (⊠ Piazza delle Erbe 46, Bolzano, ☎ 0471/978172; ⊠ C. Libertà 188, Merano, ☎ 0473/448944). Local tourist offices can provide information on less-demanding trails (☞ Visitor Information, *below*). For rifugi information in Trentino: **Associazione Rifugi del Trentino** (✉ Piazza Centa 13/7, 38100 Trento, ☎ FAX 0461/826066).

Late-Night Pharmacies

Pharmacies take turns staying open late or on Sunday; for the latest information, consult the current list posted on the front door of each pharmacy or ask at the local tourist office (☞ Visitor Information, *below*).

Visitor Information

Alto Adige province (✉ Piazza Parrocchia 11–12, Bolzano, ☎ 0471/993808, FAX 0471/975448). **Trentino Tourist Board** (✉ Via Alfieri 4, Trento, ☎ 0461/983880, FAX 984508).

Bolzano (✉ Piazza Walther 8, ☎ 0471/975656, FAX 0471/980300). **Bormio** (✉ Via Roma 131/B, ☎ 0342/903300, FAX 0342/904696). **Bressanone** (✉ Viale Stazione 9, ☎ 0472/836401, FAX 0472/836067). **Chiusa** (✉ Piazza Tinne 6, ☎ 0472/847424, FAX 0472/847244). **Cortina d'Ampezzo** (✉ Piazzetta San Francesco 8, ☎ 0436/3231, FAX 0436/3235). **Dobbiaco** (✉ Via Dolomiti 3, ☎ 0474/972132, FAX 0474/972730). **Madonna di Campiglio** (✉ Via Pradalago 4, ☎ 0465/442000, FAX 0465/440404). **Merano** (✉ Corso della Libertà 45, ☎ 0473/212404, FAX 0473/235524). **Naturno** (✉ Via Municipio 1, ☎ 0473/666077, FAX 0473/666369). **Ortisei** (✉ Str. Rezia 1, ☎ 0471/796328, FAX 0471/796749). **Riva del Garda** (✉ Giardini di Porta Orientale 8, ☎ 0464/554444). **Rovereto** (✉ Via Dante 63, ☎ 0464/430363). **Trento** (✉ Via Alri 4, ☎ 0461/983880).

11 Emilia-Romagna

Parma, Bologna, Rimini, and Ravenna

Gourmets the world over claim that Emilia-Romagna's greatest contribution to humankind has been gastronomic. Birthplace of fettuccine, tortellini, and lasagna, Bologna offers a bevy of great restaurants. But there are also many cultural riches here: Parma's Correggio paintings, Verdi's villa at Sant'Agata, the Renaissance splendors of Ferrara, and the Byzantine beauty of mosaic-rich Ravenna—glittering today as brightly as it did 1,500 years ago.

Updated by
Valerie
Hamilton

EMILIA-ROMAGNA OWES ITS BEGINNINGS to a road. In 187 BC the Romans laid out the Via Aemelia, a long highway running straight northwest from the Adriatic port of Rimini to the central garrison town of Piacenza, and it was along this central spine that the primary towns of the region developed. The old Roman road is called Via Emilia (S9) today, and the autostrada (A1 and A14) runs parallel to it.

Despite the unifying factor of the Via Emilia, the region has had a fragmented history. The eastern portion of the region, roughly the area from the city of Faenza to the coast, known as Romagna, has looked first to the east and then to Rome for art, political power, and, some say, national character. The western portion, Emilia, from Bologna to Piacenza, had a more northern, rather dour sense of self-government and dissent. Italians say that in Romagna a stranger will be offered a glass of wine; in Emilia, a glass of water—if anything at all.

The principal city of the region is Bologna. It was founded by the Etruscans but eventually came under the influence of the Roman Empire. The Romans established a garrison there, renaming the old Etruscan settlement Bononia, the Bologna of today.

It was after the fall of Rome that the region began its fragmentation. Romagna, centered in Ravenna, was ruled from Constantinople. Ravenna eventually became capital of the empire in the West in the 5th century, passing to papal rule in the 8th century. The city today, however, is still filled with reminders of two centuries of Byzantine rule.

The other cities of the region, from the Middle Ages on, became the fiefs of important noble families—the Este in Ferrara and Modena, the Pallavicini in Piacenza, the Bentivoglio in Bologna, and the Malatesta in Rimini. Today all of these cities bear the marks of their noble patrons. When in the 16th century the papacy managed to exert its power over the entire region, some of these cities were divided among the families of the reigning popes—hence the stamp of the Farnese family on Parma, Piacenza, and Ferrara.

In the 19th century, the region was one of the first to join the fight for a unified Italy, pledging itself to the king of Italy and the forces of Garibaldi in the 1840s. Loyalty to the crown did not last long, however. The Italian socialist movement was born in the region, and throughout Italy Emilia-Romagna has been known for rebellion and dissent. Benito Mussolini was born here, although in keeping with the political atmosphere of his home state, he was a firebrand socialist during the early part of his career. Despite being the birthplace of Il Duce, Emilia-Romagna did not take to fascism: It was in this region that the antifascist resistance was born, and during World War II the region suffered terribly at the hands of the Fascists and the Nazis.

Despite a long history of bloodletting, turmoil, and rebellion, the arts—both decorative and culinary—have always flourished in Emilia-Romagna. The great families financed painters, sculptors, and writers (Dante found a haven in Ravenna after being expelled from his native Florence). In modern times, Emilia-Romagna has given to the arts such famous sons as painter Giorgio Morandi, author Giorgio Bassani (author of *The Garden of the Finzi-Continis*), filmmaker Federico Fellini, and tenor Luciano Pavarotti.

Bologna is the acknowledged leading city of Italian cuisine, and the rest of the region follows—eating is a seminal part of any Emilia-Romagnan experience. The area's history is replete with culinary chronicles that raise food to the level of legend: the original tortellino, modeled on the shape of Venus's navel; the original *tagliolini* (long, thin egg pasta) served at the wedding banquet of Annibale Bentivoglio and Lucrezia d'Este; and Bologna's centuries-old, anything-but-pejorative nickname, "The Fat." It's impossible to eat badly here, and everything is worth trying. Parma's famed prosciutto and Parmigiano-Reggiano cheese, Modena's *zampone* (pig's feet stuffed with minced meat) and jet-black, sweet balsamic vinegar, Bologna's tortellini, fettucine, mortadella, and *ragù* (meat sauce) are served throughout the region, along with *tortelli alla zucca* (dumpling- or ravioli-shape pasta stuffed with squash), fresh fruits and vegetables, ancient Roman *piadina* (chewy, flat griddle bread), and a number of fine, robust wines.

Pleasures and Pastimes

Dining

Emilia-Romagna's reputation as Italy's gourmet region is well deserved, ever more so as the spreading of its reputation spurs the region's chefs onto even greater heights of gastronomic achievement. For you, this means a virtual moral obligation to eat lots and eat well: A trip through Emilia-Romagna wouldn't be complete without sampling what the region does best.

Emilia-Romagnan *cucina* is not without its drawbacks, however. What the region does best, for example, does not include preparing light meals—in Emilia-Romagna, eating light means leaving half of your *tortellini con noci e panna* (tortellini with nuts and cream) on your plate. Ravioli stuffed with spinach and ricotta cheese, tortelli and *cappellacci* (triangular pasta dumplings) stuffed with squash, tortellini stuffed with minced pork and beef all have in common one key word—and you'll inevitably be stuffed, too.

This is not to say that the uninitiated should be wary of the culinary delights of Bologna the Fat and its sister cities. The specialties are nothing new in name, they're just better here, where they were born: Parma's crumbly Parmigiano-Reggiano cheese and world-famous Parma ham (look for prosciutto di Parma); Bologna's pasta *al ragù*, a heavenly, slow-cooked mix of onions, carrots, minced pork and beef, and fresh tomatoes that in no way resembles the bolognese sauce served worldwide; likewise the rich, soft, peppery mortadella sausage that has been reincarnated elsewhere to its detriment as "baloney." Although most local specialties are served throughout the region, traditionalists will have their zampone and *aceto balsamico* (sweet, black-herb balsamic vinegar) in Modena, their risotto *in padella* (with fresh herbs and tomatoes) in Piacenza, their *brodetto* (tangy seafood stew) in Rimini, their *cappellacci di zucca* in Ferrara, and everything else in Bologna.

Emilia-Romagna's wines, fittingly, are meant to accompany the region's fine food rather than vie with it for attention and accolades. The best-known wine of the region is Lambrusco, a sparkling red that has some admirers and many detractors. Some praise it for its tartness; others condemn it for the same quality. A lesser-known wine is Vino del Bosco, also a sparkling red, which comes from the region around Ferrara.

CATEGORY	COST*
$$$$	over 90,000 lire
$$$	60,000–90,000 lire
$$	30,000–60,000 lire
$	under 30,000 lire

Prices are per person, including house wine, service, and tax.

Lodging

In Italy, the region of Emilia-Romagna has a reputation for an efficiency uncommon in most of the rest of the country. Consequently, even the smallest hotels are well run, with high levels of service and quality. Bologna is very much a businessperson's city, and most of the hotels cater to travelers of this type. There are, of course, smaller, more intimate hotels that cater to the tourist.

The business of Rimini, on the other hand, is tourism. There are hundreds of hotels, grand ones with all sorts of luxury facilities and modest boardinghouses with only a few rooms. Many offer full- or half-board plans—an economical alternative to eating in Rimini's many, but not particularly distinguished, restaurants. Despite the abundance of lodging, however, you should not go to Rimini during tourist season without confirmed hotel reservations: In July and August the city is filled to overflowing. Hotels in Rimini are closed off-season.

CATEGORY	COST*
$$$$	over 300,000 lire
$$$	160,000–300,000 lire
$$	100,000–160,000 lire
$	under 100,000 lire

Prices are for a standard double room, including service and tax.

Exploring Emilia-Romagna

A tour through Emilia-Romagna has something for everyone: great art, stirring history, fabulous food—even a day at the beach at the seaside resort of Rimini. The best way to see the region is to begin your tour in the west, in Piacenza, and to proceed east along the Via Emilia (S9) to the sea. The major towns are either on that route or just off it, the longest detours being no more than 48–65 km (30–40 mi) off the main road.

Numbers in the text correspond to numbers in the margin and on the Emilia-Romagna and Bologna maps.

Great Itineraries

Although Emilia-Romagna has a geographical logic—following the Via Emilia through the Po Valley and Romagna plain—it is not a compact area, making it hard to cover much of it in a short time. If you are traveling straight through, then you will have to confine your stops to places along the main north–west artery. Alternatively, you could base yourself in the regional capital, Bologna, and make forays from this hub. From Bologna there are three choices of itineraries: Head north on A13 to Ferrara and then southeast on S16 to Ravenna, or continue east or west along the Via Emilia (S9), stopping for short visits at some of the smaller towns en route northwest to Piacenza or southeast to Rimini and the sea.

IF YOU HAVE 3 DAYS

Given three days, you should set aside two nights to see ▨ **Bologna** ⑤–⑭ and its environs, including **Dozza** ⑮. The city itself has enough to fill much more than this, but while you are there, make a point of seeing the sights in and around Piazza Maggiore, including the **Basilica di San Petronio** ⑤, the **Palazzo Comunale** ⑥, and the nearby two towers. On day two, take a train or drive the short distance to ▨ **Ferrara** ⑲, a calm, unspoiled Renaissance city. Where you spend your third day will depend on your route out of Emilia-Romagna. If you are going to Milan or Turin, make a stop after less than 100 km (62 mi) from Bologna at **Parma** ③, where you could cover the major sights in two or three hours. If you are heading toward the Adriatic coast, ▨ **Ravenna** ⑱ should be your priority stop. Of course, if you are heading north toward Venice, you should see Ferrara on this leg of the trip and see Parma and Ravenna on the other days.

IF YOU HAVE 5 DAYS

Spend the first day in ⊞ **Rimini** ⑰ and see its cathedral and sample some of its fish restaurants. If the resort scene and its concomitant chaos doesn't appeal, skip it altogether or quickly move on to ⊞ **Ravenna** ⑱, being sure to see Sant'Apollinare in Classe, outside the city proper but well worth the excursion. On your way to Bologna on day two, drop in on a factory in the ceramic center of **Faenza** ⑯, famed for its faience pottery. Stay two nights in ⊞ **Bologna** ⑤–⑭ itself, savoring meals and taking in the sites. From Bologna, take a day trip to (or spend night four in) ⊞ **Ferrara** ⑲, enjoying the pleasures ambling around its turreted and towered medieval streets. Spend the last night or two sampling the fine food and wine in ⊞ **Parma** ③, stopping in **Modena** ④, another culinary capital, along the way. Northwest of Parma, make a slight detour from the autostrada or Via Emilia to see the cluster of places associated with the composer Verdi, centered on the village of **Busseto** ②. Still heading northwest, spend your last morning or afternoon in **Piacenza** ①, its elegance and harmony typical of Emilia-Romagna's centers of culture, and a fitting exit or entrance to the region. From here, it's a mere 66 km (41 mi) to Milan.

When to Tour Emilia-Romagna

You would never visit Emilia-Romagna for the weather. In this predominantly flat landscape, the winters are gray and cold, and summers are airless and hot, though sea breezes on the coast offer some respite. If you are here in summer, get up early and do as much as you can in the morning. Ideally, mid-afternoons in summer should be left unplanned; the hours after five are best for sightseeing and traveling. In winter, make sure you are equipped for the frequent rain and damp, penetrating cold. Fog is common throughout the low-lying areas of the region and can be starkly beautiful, but it can also be very hazardous when driving. No matter what the season, make sure you reserve ahead for rooms: The cities are often awash with commercial conventions and business conferences. Note that restaurants and hotels in Rimini are usually closed up tight during the off-season.

ON THE ROAD TO PARMA AND MODENA

The Via Aemelia runs through Emilia's heart in a straight shot from medieval Piacenza to thoroughly modern Modena. On the way from the past to the present you'll pass through the homes of many of Italy's famous cultural riches—from the culinary and artistic treasures of Parma to the opera country around Bussetto, birthplace and home of Giuseppe Verdi. It may be tempting to emulate Modena's Ferraris and zoom over the short (113-km/70-mi) stretch of highway spanning the region, but if you take the time to detour into the countryside or stop for a taste of prosciutto di Parma, you will be richly rewarded.

Piacenza

❶ *66 km (41 mi) southeast of Milan, 182 km (114 mi) east of Turin, 40 km (25 mi) west of Cremona, 62 km (39 mi) northwest of Parma, 150 km (94 mi) northwest of Bologna.*

The city of Piacenza has always been associated with industry and commerce. Its position on the River Po has made it an important inland port

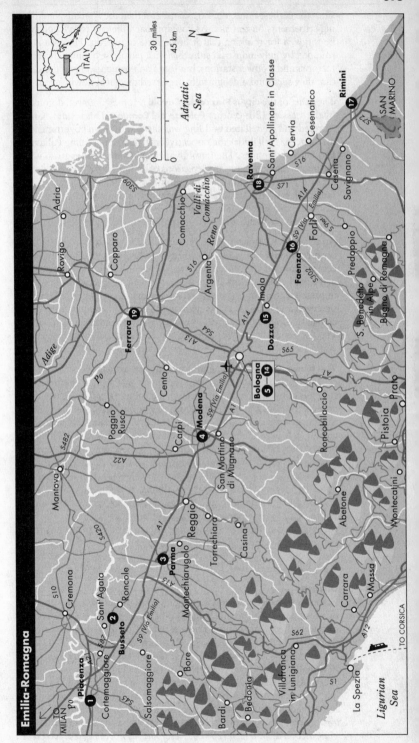

Emilia-Romagna

Adriatic Sea

30 miles
45 km

N

ITALY

TO MILAN

Po

① Piacenza

Cremona

S10

Sant'Agata

Busseto

② Roncole

Cortemaggiore

S62

S7

A21

Salsomaggiore

S45

Bore

Bedonia

Bardi

Villafranca in Lunigiana

S62

Mantova

S420

S482

Poggio Rusco

Carpi

A22

③ Parma

Reggio

Montechiarugolo

Torrechiara

Casina

S9 (Via Emilia)

A1

A15

④ Modena

San Martino di Mugnano

S9 (Via Emilia)

A1

Cento

Po

Adige

Rovigo

Adria

S309

Copparo

⑲ Ferrara

A13

S64

Argenta

Comacchio

Valli di Comacchio

Reno

S16

A14

Imola

⑮ Dozza

S65

⑤ ⑭ Bologna

A1

Roncobilaccio

Pistoia

Prato

Abetone

Montecatini

Carrara

Massa

La Spezia

Ligurian Sea

TO CORSICA

A12

S1

S62

Ravenna ⑱

Sant'Apollinare in Classe

Cervia

Cesenatico

S16

S71

Forlì ⑯

S9 (Via Emilia)

Faenza

S302

S9 bis

Predappio

S. Benedetto in Alpe

Bagno di Romagna

Cesena

Savignano

A14

S71

S72

Rimini ⑰

SAN MARINO

A1

since the earliest times; the Etruscans, and then the Romans, had thriving settlements on this site. As you approach the city today, you could be forgiven for thinking that it holds little of interest. Piacenza is surrounded by ugly industrial suburbs (with particularly unlovely cement factories and a power station), but forge on through and you'll discover that they surround a delightfully preserved medieval downtown.

The heart of the city is **Piazza dei Cavalli** (Horses' Square), dominated by the massive 13th-century **Palazzo del Comune.** This severely Gothic turreted and crenellated building was the seat of town government before Piacenza fell under the respective iron fists of the ruling Pallavicini and Farnese families. The flamboyant **equestrian statues** from which the piazza takes its name are depictions of members of the last and greatest of the Farnese: On the right is Ranuccio Farnese; on the left is his father, Alessandro. Alessandro was a beloved ruler, enlightened and fair; Ranuccio, his successor, was less successful. Both statues are the work of Francesco Mochi, a master sculptor of the Baroque period.

Attached like a sinister balcony to the bell tower of Piacenza's 12th-century **Duomo** is a *gabbia* (iron cage), where miscreants were incarcerated naked and subjected to the scorn (and missiles) of the crowd in the marketplace below. Inside the cathedral, a less-evocative but equally impressive array of fine medieval stonework decorates the pillars and the crypt, and there are extravagant frescoes by 17th-century artist Guercino in the dome of the cupola. The Duomo can be reached by following Via XX Settembre down from Piazza dei Cavalli. ⊠ *Piazza Duomo,* ☎ *0523/335154.* ⊙ *Daily 7:30–noon and 4–7.*

The **Museo Civico** (Civic Museum), the city-owned collection of Piacenzan art and antiquities, is housed in the vast **Palazzo Farnese.** The ruling family originally commissioned a monumental palace, but the construction, begun in 1558, was never completed. The highlight of this rather eclectic exhibit is the 2nd century BC *Etruscan Fegato di Piacenza,* a bronze tablet in the shape of a *fegato* (liver), with the symbols of the gods of good and ill fortune marked on it. By comparing this master "liver" with one taken from the body of a freshly slaughtered sacrifice, the priests could predict the future. On a more humanistic note, the collection also contains a painting by Botticelli, the *Madonna with St. John the Baptist,* and a series of Roman bronzes and mosaics. There is also a collection of carriages, arms and armor, and other paraphernalia owned by the Farnese, which give life to the history of that powerful family. ⊠ *Piazza Cittadella,* ☎ *0523/330567.* ⊠ *4,500 lire.* ⊙ *Tues.–Wed. and Fri. 9–12:30, Thurs. 9–12:30 and 3:30–5:30, Sat. 9–12:30 and 3–6, Sun. 9:30–noon and 3:30–6:30.*

Dining

$$$ ✕ **Antica Osteria del Teatro.** Set on a lovely piazza in the center of town,
★ this restaurant is generally touted to be the best in Piacenza. Try the tortelli stuffed with ricotta, the roast duck, or the steamed sea bass. ⊠ *Via Verdi 16,* ☎ *0523/323777. Reservations essential. AE, DC, MC, V. Closed Mon. and Aug. 1–25 and Jan. 1–10. No dinner Sun.*

$ ✕ **Agnello.** Central (on the corner of Piazza dei Cavalli), simple, and cheap, Agnello is an excellent place to sit down and enjoy a lunchtime snack. Try the tortelli *alla Piacentina* (stuffed with ricotta and spinach and served in a butter and Parmigiano sauce) or *coniglio alla Cacciatora* (rabbit in a sauce of greens, tomato, white wine, and garlic). ⊠ *Via Calzolai 2,* ☎ *0523/320874. Reservations not accepted. No credit cards. Closed Mon. and Aug. 1–Sept. 1.*

En Route   If you are driving from Piacenza, take S10 northeast for Cremona (☞ *Chapter 9*), but turn off it just a few miles out of Piacenza and follow the signs for S587 to the town of Cortemaggiore. From Cortemaggiore, turn right onto a smaller rural road (not numbered) and follow the signs for Busseto, some 10 km (6 mi) away. If you plan to visit all the area's Verdi sights, invest in an 8,000-lire ticket valid for Villa Pallavicino, Palazzo Orlandi, Teatro Verdi, and Verdi's birthplace (but not Villa Sant'Agata).

Busseto

❷ *30 km (19 mi) southeast of Piacenza, 15 km (9 mi) south of Cremona, 40 km (25 mi) northwest of Parma.*

Busseto's main claim to fame is the **Villa Pallavicino,** where Giuseppe Verdi (1813–1901), Italian opera composer of *Aïda, Rigoletto, La Traviata,* and *Otello,* worked and reportedly lived with his mistress (and later wife), Giuseppina Strepponi. The small **Verdi museum** here displays such relics of the maestro as his piano, scores, composition books, walking sticks, and other bits of memorabilia. 🎫 *4,000 lire.* ⊘ *Apr.–Sept., Tues.–Sun. 9:30–12:30 and 3–7; Oct.–Nov., Tues.–Sun. 9:30–noon and 2:30–5.*

Palazzo Orlandi, owned for the past century by the Orlandi family, was Verdi's home for a few years from 1845. Only a few of its stately rooms are open to the public. 🎫 *4,000 lire.* ⊘ *Apr.–Sept., Tues.–Sun. 9:30–12:30 and 3–7; Oct.–Nov., Tues.–Sun. 9:30–noon and 2:30–5.*

In the center of Busseto is the lovely **Teatro Verdi,** dedicated, as one may expect, to the works of the hamlet's famous son. It is a well-preserved 19th-century-style theater, and it's worth a look to get a feel for the place where Verdi worked. After a lengthy restoration (that's not quite finished), the theater opened up in spring 1998 for a few performances; it is expected to be open in full swing by mid-1998. 🎫 *4,000 lire.* ⊘ *Apr.–Sept., Tues.–Sun. 9:30–12:30 and 3–7; Oct.–Mar., Tues.–Sun. 9:30–noon and 2:30–5.*

OFF THE
BEATEN PATH

VILLA SANT'AGATA – Five kilometers (3 miles) north of Busseto, Villa Sant'Agata is the grand country home Verdi built for himself in 1849, where some of his greatest works were composed. For Verdi lovers, Sant'Agata is a veritable shrine. ✉ *3 km (2 mi) north of Busseto on the Fidenza-Cremona (S588) toward Cremona.* 🎫 *8,000 lire.* ⊘ *Apr.–Oct., Tues.–Sun. 9–11:40 and 3–6:40.*

RONCOLE – Giuseppe Verdi was born in a simple farmhouse on the edge of the town of Roncole, 3 km (2 mi) southeast of Busseto. Equally modest is the church in which he took some of his earliest steps in a musical career; he was the church organist here when still in his teens. ✉ *5 km (3 mi) east of Busseto on local road to Soragna (follow signs).* 🎫 *Verdi's birthplace: 3,000 lire.* ⊘ *June–Sept., Tues.–Sun. 9–12:30 and 2:30–7; Oct.–Nov., Tues.–Sun. 9:30–noon and 2:30–5; Dec., weekends 10–noon and 2:30–7:30.*

Parma

❸ *28 km (17½ mi) southeast of Roncole (S588 and A1 or Via Emilia, 62 km (39 mi) southeast of Piacenza, 97 km (61 mi) northwest of Bologna.*

Dignified, delightful Parma stands on the banks of a tributary of the River Po. Much of the historic center has been untouched by modern times, despite heavy damage during World War II, and thanks to the efforts being made by the city fathers to control traffic, strolling Parma's cobbled streets is a charming experience. The traffic regulations, although a boon to pedestrians, are a nightmare for motorists. Every obstacle is put in the way of motor traffic—one-way streets, no-turning zones, and the like—so it is best to leave your car outside the center and see the town on foot.

Almost every major European power has had a hand in ruling Parma at one time or another. The Romans founded the city—it was little more than a garrison on the Via Emilia—and then a succession of feudal lords held sway here. In the 16th century came the ever-avaricious Farnese family (who are still the dukes of Parma) and then, in fast succession, the Spanish, French, and Austrians, with the Austrians taking over following the upheavals in central Europe after the fall of Napóleon. The French influence is strong. The French novelist Stendhal (1783–1842) lived in the city for several years and set his classic novel *The Charterhouse of Parma* here.

★ The **Piazza del Duomo,** site of the cathedral, the baptistery, the church of San Giovanni, and the palaces of the bishop and other notables, is the heart of the city. This square and its buildings make up one of the most harmonious, tranquil city centers in Italy.

The focal point of the piazza is the magnificent 12th-century **Duomo,** with its two vigilant stone lions standing guard beside the main door. The arch of the entrance is decorated with a delicate frieze of figures representing the months of the year, a motif repeated inside the baptistery on the right-hand side of the square. Some of the original artwork still exists in the church, notably the simple yet evocative *Descent from the Cross,* a carving in the right transept, by Benedetto Antelami (1150–1230), a sculptor and architect whose masterwork is this cathedral's Baptistery (☞ *below*).

It is odd to turn from this austere work of the 12th century to the exuberant fresco in the dome, the *Assumption of the Virgin,* by the 16th-century painter Antonio Correggio (1494–1534). The fresco was not well received when it was unveiled in 1530. "A mess of frogs' legs," the bishop of Parma is said to have called it. In contrast to the rather dark, somber interior of the cathedral, though, the beauty and light of the painting in the dome are a welcome relief. Today, of course, Correggio is acclaimed as one of the leading masters of Baroque painting; his many works on view in Parma now constitute one of the greatest draws of the city. ✉ *Piazza del Duomo,* ☎ *0521/235886.* ☉ *Daily 9–12:30 and 3–7.*

The **Baptistery** is a solemn, simple Romanesque building on the exterior and an uplifting Gothic building within. The doors of the Baptistery are richly decorated with figures, animals, and flowers, and the interior is adorned with figures carved by Antelami, showing the months and seasons. ✉ *Piazza del Duomo,* ☎ *0521/235592.* ▣ *4,000 lire.* ☉ *Daily 9–12:30 and 3–6.*

Once beyond the elaborate Baroque facade of **San Giovanni Evangelista,** the Renaissance interior reveals several works by Correggio; his *St. John the Evangelist* (left transept) is considered the finest of them. Also in this church (in the second and fourth chapels on the left) are works by Girolamo Parmigianino—a contemporary of Correggio's and the spearhead of the astonishing Mannerist art movement. Once seen, Parmigianino's anorexic and swan-necked Madonnas are never forgotten: They pose with all the precious élan of today's high-fashion models. ✉ *Piazzale San Giovanni.* ☉ *Daily 6:30–noon and 3:30–8.*

Next door to the church of San Giovanni Evangelista, in the adjoining monastery, is the **Spezieria di San Giovanni**—once a pharmacy where Benedictine monks used to mix medicines and herbals. The 16th-century decorations still survive, although the potions, which people of

Parma swore would cure almost every malady, are, alas, gone—the pharmacy stopped production in 1881. ⊠ *Borgo Pipa 1, off Piazzale San Giovanni.* ☎ *4,000 lire.* ☉ *Daily 9–1:45.*

★ Works by Parma's own Correggio and Parmigianino as well as Leonardo da Vinci, El Greco, and Il Bronzino are the highlights of the **Galleria Nazionale,** housed in the vast but rather grim-looking **Palazzo della Pilotta,** on the banks of the river. The palace was built about 1600 and is so big that from the air it is Parma's most recognizable sight—hence, the destruction done to it when it was bombed by Allied forces in 1944. Much of the building has been restored, but not all. The palazzo takes its name from the ball game *pilotta,* a sort of handball played within the palace precincts in the 17th century.

To enter the Galleria Nazionale, on the ground floor of the palace, you pass through the magnificent and elaborately Baroque **Teatro Farnese,** built in 1628 and based on Palladio's theater in the northern Italian town of Vicenza. Built entirely of wood, the theater was burned badly during Allied bombing but has been flawlessly restored. ⊠ *Palazzo della Pilotta, Piazza Pilotta,* ☎ *0521/233309.* ☎ *12,000 lire.* ☉ *Daily 9–1:45.*

The **Camera di San Paolo** is the former dining room of the abbess of the Convent of St. Paul. It was extensively frescoed by Correggio, and despite the religious character of the building, the decorations are entirely secular, with ravishingly beautiful (and very worldly) depictions of mythological scenes—the *Triumphs of the Goddess Diana,* the *Three Graces,* and the *Three Fates.* It is near the Palazzo della Pilotta, off Strada Garibaldi. ⊠ *Via Melloni.* ☎ *4,000 lire.* ☉ *Daily 9–1:45.*

Near the central Piazza Garibaldi is **Madonna della Steccata,** a delightful 16th-century domed church famous for a wonderful fresco cycle by Parmigianino. The painter took so long to complete it that his exasperated patrons imprisoned him briefly for breach of contract before releasing him to complete the work. ⊠ *Via Dante,* ☎ *0521/234937.* ☉ *Daily 9–noon and 3–6.*

Dining and Lodging

$$$ ✕ **La Greppia.** The most elegant and most talked-about restaurant in
★ the city is also the best. Taste from whence come the plaudits with innovative treats like the *tortino vegetale di melanzane* (eggplant and vegetable tartlet) and the *fegato di vitello ore due* (two-hour veal liver), taken from a recipe of the Farnese kitchen. ⊠ *Via Garibaldi 39,* ☎ *0521/233686. Reservations essential. AE, DC, MC, V. Closed Mon.–Tues., July, and Dec. 25.*

$$ ✕ **Croce di Malta.** The premises of this appealing turn-of-the-century style restaurant once housed a convent, then an inn. Traditional local fare includes light, delicate homemade pasta—try the tortelli with squash filling or tagliatelle in any fashion. Second courses are well-prepared, filling versions of classic veal and cheese dishes. ⊠ *Borgo Palmia 8,* ☎ *0521/235643. Reservations essential. AE, MC, V.*

$$ ✕ **Parma Rotta.** An old inn about 2 km (1 mi) from downtown Parma,
★ the Parma Rotta remains an informal neighborhood trattoria serving hearty dishes like spit-roasted lamb and roast pork, topped off with a wide array of homemade desserts. ⊠ *Via Langhirano 158,* ☎ *0521/ 966738. AE, DC, MC, V. Closed Sun. June–Aug., Mon. Sept.–May.*

$-$$ ✕ **Sant'Ambrogio.** This is an ideal spot for informal dining in the cen-
★ ter of town. Duck and quail are the best bets, but don't overlook the *crauti spinaci* (boiled pork sausage with pickled cabbage or spinach). ⊠ *Vicolo Cinque Piaghe 1/a,* ☎ *0521/234482. AE, DC, MC, V. Closed Mon.*

$$$$ 🏨 **Palace Hotel Maria Luigia.** A top-quality hotel convenient to old Parma and the train station, the Maria Luigia has large, well-furnished rooms and is popular with business travelers. ⊠ *Viale Mentana 140, 43100,* ☎ *0521/281032,* FAX *0521/231126. 92 rooms, 9 suites. Restaurant, bar, minibars, meeting rooms. AE, DC, MC, V.*

$$$ 🏨 **Hotel Torino.** A warm reception and pleasant, relaxed surroundings are the best reasons for staying in this former convent, tucked away in a quiet pedestrian zone in the heart of town. It has modern, small-ish rooms with Correggio reproductions on the walls. ⊠ *Via Mazza 7, 43100,* ☎ *0521/281046,* FAX *0521/230725. 33 rooms. Bar. AE, DC, MC, V. Closed Aug. 1–20.*

$$$ 🏨 **Park Hotel Stendhal.** The Stendhal is again one of the best hotels in Parma. It is on the edge of the historic center of town and convenient for the tourist and business traveler alike. Rooms are thickly carpeted and spacious, some with chandeliers and period furniture. Some rooms have views of the Palazzo della Pilotta. ⊠ *Via Bodoni 3, 43100,* ☎ *0521/208057,* FAX *0521/285655. 60 rooms. Restaurant, bar, meeting rooms. AE, DC, MC, V.*

Nightlife and the Arts

Parma is the region's opera center, with performances held at the **Teatro Regio** (⊠ Via Garibaldi, ☎ 0521/218910). Opera here is taken just as seriously as in Milan, although tickets are a little easier to come by. Playwright Dario Fo, the recipient of the 1997 Nobel Prize in Literature, helped found the **Teatro Due** (⊠ Viale Basetti 12, ☎ 0521/230242), a theater whose productions still maintain a mixture of comedy and politics—though your understanding of the themes will be limited without a knowledge of Italian.

Modena

❹ *56 km (35 mi) southeast of Parma along Route A1, 38 km (23 mi) north-west of Bologna.*

Old town Modena has today gained recognition for being home to three very contemporary names. The luxury high-performance cars Maserati and Ferrari come from Modena, and so does the world-famous opera star Luciano Pavarotti. The modern town that encircles the historic center is extensive, and although the old quarter is small, it is filled with an old-world atmosphere, narrow medieval streets, and pleasant piazzas.

The 12th-century **Duomo** is one of the finest examples of Romanesque architecture in the country. As in Parma, the exterior is decorated with medieval sculptures depicting scenes from the life of San Geminiano—the patron saint of Modena—and fantastic beasts, as well as a realistic-looking scene of the sacking of a city by barbarian hordes, a reminder to the faithful to be ever vigilant in defense of the church. The bell tower is made of white marble and is known as **La Ghirlandina** (The Little Garland) because of its distinctive garland-shape weather vane on the summit.

The somber church interior is divided by an elaborately decorated gallery carved with scenes of the Passion of Christ. The carvings took 50 years to complete and are by an anonymous Modenese master of the 12th century. The tomb of San Geminiano is in the crypt. ⊠ *Piazza Grande,* ☎ *059/216078.* ⏾ *Daily 6:30–12:30 (closes noon July–Aug.) and 3:30–7.*

The principal museum of the town is housed in the **Palazzo dei Musei,** a short walk from the Duomo. The collection was assembled in the mid-17th century by Francesco d'Este, Duke of Modena, and the gallery **Galleria Estense** is named in his honor. In the first room, there is a portrait bust of him by Bernini. The duke was a man of many interests, as you can see from the collection of objets d'art—ivories, coins, medals, and bronzes, as well as fine art dating from the Renaissance to the Baroque. There are works here by Correggio and by masters from other parts of Italy, such as the Venetians Tintoretto and Veronese, the Bolognese Reni and the Carracci brothers, and the Neapolitan Salvator Rosa.

The gallery also houses the duke's **Biblioteca Estense**, a huge collection of illuminated books, of which the best known is the beautifully illustrated bible of the 15th century, the *Bible of Borso d'Este*. A map, dated 1501, was one of the first in the world to show Columbus's discovery of America. Follow Via Emilia, the old Roman road runs through the heart of the town, to Via di Sant'Agostino. ⊠ *Piazza Sant' Agostino,* ☎ *059/222145.* ▨ *8,000 lire.* ☉ *Tues. and Fri.–Sat. 9–7, Wed.–Thurs. 9–2, Sun. 9–1.*

The huge Baroque **Palazzo Ducale** of the dukes of Modena now houses a military academy; once the province of the dukes only, it is still off-limits, except to flocks of cadets in elaborate uniforms. Behind the academy are Modena's large **Giardini Pubblici** (Public Gardens). ⊠ *Piazza degli Estensi.*

Dining and Lodging

$$$ ✕ **Borso d'Este.** One of the city's most highly regarded restaurants—
★ particularly with the *crema* of the region's monied set—offers some delicious variations on old themes, like ravioli stuffed with game and Parmesan. In season don't miss the truffle specialties: ricotta- and spinach-stuffed *tortelloni* (pasta squares) in a truffle-mushroom sauce, and the mushroom tart laced with the perfumy tubers. ⊠ *Piazza Roma 5,* ☎ *059/214114. Reservations essential. AE, DC, MC, V. Closed Sun. and Aug. No lunch Sat.*

$$$ ✕ **Fini.** A Modena institution, elegant, modern Fini is widely held to be the best restaurant the city has to offer. It's Pavarotti's favorite—and you could easily gain a Pavarottiesque figure by making a habit of the excellent local wines, *gran bollito misto,* a groaning board of boiled meats in a *salsa verde* (vegetable sauce), and homemade desserts. ⊠ *Piazzale San Francesco,* ☎ *059/223314. Reservations essential. AE, DC, MC, V. Closed Mon.–Tues., July 20–Aug. 20, and last wk in Dec.*

$$ ✕ **Da Enzo.** This cheerful, well-patronized trattoria is in the old town's pedestrian zone, close by the synagogue and a few steps from Piazza Mazzini. All the classic Modenese specialties are here, including zampone and *cotechino* (animal bladders stuffed with pork). For starters, try the tortelloni *di ricotta e spinaci* (stuffed with ricotta and spinach). ⊠ *Via Coltellini 17,* ☎ *059/225177. Reservations essential weekends. AE, DC, MC, V. Closed Mon. and Aug.*

$$$ ▦ **Canal Grande.** Once a ducal palace, the Canal Grande offers large, airy, well-equipped rooms with minibars. The hotel's restaurant, La Secchia Rapita (closed Wednesday and August), gets rave reviews. ⊠ *Corso Canalgrande 6, 41100,* ☎ *059/217160,* ₣₳₸ *059/221674. 72 rooms, 3 suites. Restaurant, bar, in-room safes, minibars. AE, DC, MC, V.*

$$ ▦ **La Torre.** Not particularly exciting, La Torre is nonetheless the best hotel choice in the low end of this price category, thanks to its being in town center just off the Via Emilia. The somewhat stuffy rooms are functional, comfortable, and well equipped. ⊠ *Via Cervetta 5, 41100,* ☎ *059/222615,* ₣₳₸ *059/216316. 26 rooms. Bar. AE, DC, MC, V.*

BOLOGNA

38 km (23 mi) southeast of Modena, 210 km (131 mi) southeast of Milan, 154 km (96 mi) southwest of Venice.

Through its long history, first as an Etruscan city, then a Roman one, then as an independent city-state in the Middle Ages, Bologna—106 km (66 mi) north of Florence—has always been a power in the north of Italy. Over the centuries, the city has acquired a number of nicknames: Bologna the Learned, in honor of its ancient (the oldest in the world) university; Bologna the Red, for its rosy rooftops and political leanings; Bologna the Turreted, recalling the forest of medieval towers that once rose from the city center (two remarkable examples still exist); and Bologna the Fat, a tribute to its preeminent position in the world of cuisine.

Centuries of wars, sackings, rebellions, and aerial bombing that have left such dramatic evidence in other cities of the region seem not to have taken their toll on the old city center: The narrow cobblestone streets remain as they were hundreds of years ago, as do the ancient churches, massive palaces, medieval towers, and famous porticoed arcades lining many of the main thoroughfares.

Bologna's vibrancy is due in large part to its student population. The university was founded in about the year 1088 and by the 13th century already had more than 10,000 students. It was a center for the teaching of law and theology, and it was ahead of its time in that many of the professors were women. Today the university has one of the most prominent business schools in Italy and has the finest faculty of medicine in the country. Guglielmo Marconi, the inventor of the wireless telegraph, first formulated his groundbreaking theories in the physics labs of the university.

Exploring Bologna

Piazza Maggiore and the adjacent Piazza del Nettuno make up the heart of the city. Arranged around these two squares are the imposing Basilica di San Petronio, the massive Palazzo Comunale, the Palazzo del Podestà, the Palazzo di Re Enzo, and the fountain of Neptune—one of the most visually harmonious groupings of public buildings in the entire country. From here, sights that aren't on one of the piazzas are but a short walk away, along delightful narrow cobbled streets or under the ubiquitous porticoes that double as municipal umbrellas in case of rain.

A Good Walk

Start at the southern end of sprawling Piazza Maggiore at the 14th-century **Basilica di San Petronio** ⑤, peeking into its museum to see the church's original designs, some never realized. On the west side of Piazza Maggiore is the **Palazzo Comunale** ⑥, especially great if you like the work of modern artist Giorgio Morandi. Next, on to the **Palazzo del Podestà** ⑦ and its Torre dell'Arengo, at the north end of Piazza Maggiore in the adjoining Piazza Nettuno, where stands the Fontana del Nettuno, a.k.a. Il Gigante. To the left (west) is **Palazzo di Re Enzo** ⑧ with its dark medieval associations. The busy, chic Via Rizzoli runs east from Piazza Nettuno directly into the medieval section of the city to Piazza di Porta Ravegnana, where you can climb the slightly off-kilter **Torre degli Asinelli** ⑨, next to the smaller **Torre Garisenda**. From Piazza di Porta Ravegnana, you have two choices of routes if you want a shorter walk: Head south and southwest to two churches (bullets ⑩ and ⑪), or continue northeast along Via Zamboni for the last three important sites (bullets ⑫–⑭). If you want a long walk, explore all five sites. From the piazza, walk five minutes southeast down Via Santo Stefano to the church of **Santo Stefano** ⑩, actually several churches in one. From there, head west on Via Farini and take a left on Via Garibaldi; a few blocks down take a left to reach Piazza San Domenico and **San Domenico** ⑪, containing the saint's tomb and a minor work by Michelangelo. Retrace your steps back to Piazza di Porta Ravegnana, and walk northeast on Via Zamboni a few blocks to **San Giacomo Maggiore** ⑫, haunt of the Bentivoglio. Continue up Via Zamboni to Via delle Belle Arti and the **Pinacoteca Nazionale** ⑬, with works of Raphael, Giotto, Parmigianino, and Bolognese masters. Stroll north to the **Università di Bologna** ⑭ district for a *caffè* and snack.

TIMING

You'll want at least a full day to explore Bologna; it's compact, but it lends itself to easy exploration. This walk, allowing a little time to explore each site, should take at least four hours, not including the hour you should devote to the Pinacoteca Nazionale, a half hour to climb the Torre degli Asinelli, and a lunch break for a sampling of Bologna's culinary bounty. Note that the Pinacoteca closes at 1 or 2 PM, so plan your exploration accordingly.

Sights to See

❺ **Basilica di San Petronio.** Construction on this cathedral began in the 14th century, and work was still in progress on this vast building some 300 years later. It is still not finished, as you can see: The wings of the transept are missing and the facade is only partially decorated, lacking most of the marble face the architects planned several hundred years ago. The main doorway was carved by the great Sienese master of the Renaissance, Jacopo della Quercia. Above the center of the door is a Madonna and Child, flanked by Saints Ambrose and Petronius, patrons of the city.

The interior of the basilica is huge and echoing, 432 ft long, 185 ft wide, and 144 ft high. It is so vast that it's sobering to note that originally the Bolognans had planned an even bigger church—you can still see the columns erected to support the larger church outside the east end—but had to tone down construction when the University seat was established next door in 1561. The **Museo di San Petronio** contains models to show how the original church was intended to have looked. The most important artworks in the church are in the left aisle, frescoes by Giovanni da Modena dating from the first years of the 1400s. Also in the left aisle, laid out in the pavement of the church, is a huge sundial, placed there in 1655, showing the time, date, and month. ⊠ *Piazza Maggiore.* ☉ *Basilica: Apr.–Sept., daily 7:15–1:30 and 2:30–6:45; Oct.–Mar., daily 7:15–1 and 2:30–6:30. Museo di San Petronio: Mon., Wed., Fri.–Sun. 10–12:30.*

Fontana del Nettuno. Sculptor Giambologna's elaborate 1566 Baroque monument to Neptune in stone occupying Piazza Nettuno has been aptly nicknamed Il Gigante (The Giant). Its exuberantly sensual mermaids and undraped God of the Sea drew fire when it was constructed, but not enough, apparently, to dissuade the populace from using the fountain as a public washing stall for centuries. ⊠ *Piazza Nettuno, next to the Palazzo di Re Enzo.*

❻ **Palazzo Comunale.** A mélange of building styles and constant modifications characterize this palace, dating from the 13th to 15th centuries. When Bologna was an independent city-state, this huge palace was the seat of government, a function it still serves today. Over the door is a statue of Bologna-born Pope Gregory XIII, most famous for his reorganization of the calendar. The "Gregorian" system remains in use today. ⊠ *Piazza Maggiore.*

The **Collezioni Comunali d'Arte** exhibits paintings from the Middle Ages as well as some Renaissance works by Luca Signorelli and Tintoretto. On the same floor, a separate **Museo Morandi** is dedicated to the 20th-century still-life artist Giorgio Morandi; in addition to his paintings, you'll see a re-creation of his studio and living space. An equally good reason to come is to get a look at the views of the piazza from the upper stories of the palace. ⊠ *Piazza Maggiore, west side,* ☎ *051/ 203629, Collezioni Comunali, 051/203646, Museo Morandi.* ☞ *8,000 lire each, 10,000 lire both .* ☉ *Tues.–Sun. 10–6.*

⑦ Palazzo del Podestà. This classic Renaissance palace facing the Basilica di San Petronio was erected in 1484, and attached to it is the soaring **Torre dell'Arengo.** The bells in the tower have rung since 1453, whenever the city has celebrated, mourned, or called its citizens to arms. ⊠ *Piazza Nettuno,* ☎ *051/224500.*

⑧ Palazzo di Re Enzo. King Enzo of Sardinia was imprisoned in this 13th-century medieval palace for 23 years until his death in 1272. He had been unwise enough to wage war on Bologna and was captured after the fierce battle of Fossalta in 1249. The palace has other macabre associations: Common criminals received the last rites of the church in the tiny chapel in the courtyard before being taken out to be executed in Piazza Maggiore. ⊠ *Piazza Nettuno, next to the Palazzo del Podestà,* ☎ *051/224500.*

⑬ Pinacoteca Nazionale. Bologna's principal art gallery—housing one of the most important collections in Italy— contains many works by the immortals of Italian painting, including Raphael's famous *Ecstasy of St. Cecilia.* There is also a beautiful multipaneled painting by Giotto and a

Parmigianino *Madonna and Saints*. The centerpieces of the collection, however, are the many rooms devoted to the two most important late 16th-century Bolognese masters, painters Guido Reni and Annibale Carracci. Some of the most interesting works, from a historical point of view, are by Giuseppe Crespi, a Bolognese painter of the 18th century who avoided grand religious or historical themes, preferring instead to paint scenes of daily life in his native city. These small canvases convey marvelously the boisterous, earthy life of Old Bologna. ⊠ *Via delle Belle Arti 56,* ☎ *051/243222.* ☞ *8,000 lire.* ☉ *Tues.–Sat. 9–2, Sun. 9–1.*

⓫ **San Domenico.** The tomb of Saint Dominic, who died here in 1221, is called the Arca di San Domenico and found in the sixth chapel on the right. Many artists participated in the decoration, notably Niccolò di Bari, who was so proud of his contribution that he changed his name to Niccolò dell'Arca to recall this famous work. The young Michelangelo carved the angel on the right. In the right transept of the church is a tablet marking the last resting place of the hapless King Enzo, whose prison you saw in Piazza Maggiore (☞ Palazzo di Re Enzo, *above*). In the square in front of San Domenico are two curious tombs raised above the ground on pillars, commemorating two famous 14th-century lawyers. ⊠ *Piazza San Domenico 13, off Via Garibaldi,* ☎ *051/640-0411.* ☉ *Apr.–Sept., daily 7–1 and 2–7; Oct.–Mar., daily 7–1 and 3–7.*

⓬ **San Giacomo Maggiore.** Inside this church is the burial chamber of the Bentivoglio family, the leading family in Bologna in the Middle Ages. The crypt is connected by underground passage to the Teatro Comunale, across the street—a rather odd feature, until you realize that the family palazzo of the Bentivoglio used to stand on that spot. The most notable tomb is that of Antonio Bentivoglio, carved by Jacopo della Quercia in 1435. You can tell his profession—lecturer in law—from the group of students carved on the base, all listening intently to their professor. ⊠ *Piazza Rossini, off Via Zamboni,* ☎ *051/225970.* ☉ *Daily 6–noon and 3:30–6.*

⓾ **Santo Stefano.** The oldest of the four churches contained in this basilica is **Santi Vitale e Agricola**, which dates from the 8th century and contains a 14th-century nativity scene much loved by Bologna's children, who come at Christmastime to pay their respects to the baby Jesus. The church of **San Sepolcro** (12th century) contains the **Cortile di Pilato** (Courtyard of Pontius Pilate), so named for the basin in the center of the court that's said to be the basin in which Pilate washed his hands after condemning Christ. Also in the building is a **museum** displaying various medieval religious works you can buy sundry items made by the monks, such as honey, shampoo, and jam. ⊠ *Via Santo Stefano 24, Piazza Santo Stefano,* ☎ *051/223256.* ☞ *Free.* ☉ *Daily 9–noon and 3:30–6:30.*

⓽ **Torre degli Asinelli/Torre Garisenda.** The taller (320 ft high) of the twin towers in the compact Piazza di Porta Ravegnana, Torre degli Asinelli, leans an alarming 7½ ft out of the perpendicular. The Torre Garisenda, now tilting 10 ft, was shortened to 165 ft for safety in the 1500s. The towers were built at the same time (1488) and are mentioned by Dante in *The Inferno*. They are two of the only 60 towers that remain of the more than 200 that once graced the city: Every family of any importance had a tower as a symbol of its prestige and power, and as a fortified retreat when that prestige and power were threatened. For a fine view of Bologna's rooftops, climb up the 500 steep stairs of Torre degli Asinelli. ⊠ *Piazza di Porta Ravegnana.* ☞ *3,000 lire tower.* ☉ *Apr.–Sept., daily 9–6; Oct.–Mar., daily 9–5.*

⑭ Università di Bologna. Take a stroll through the adjoining streets in the university district, a jumble of buildings, some dating as far back as the 15th century and most to the 17th and 18th centuries. This neighborhood, like neighborhoods in most college towns, is full of bookshops, coffee bars, and cheap restaurants. None of them is particularly distinguished, but they're all characteristic of student life in the city. Political slogans and sentiments are scrawled on walls all around the university and tend, for the most part, to be ferociously leftist. ✉ *Via Zamboni.*

Dining and Lodging

$$$ ✕ **Al Pappagallo.** Almost directly beneath Bologna's famous Asinelli and Garisenda towers, the Pappagallo, facing stiff competition today, retains enough of its reputation and quality cuisine to merit at least one feast, served in a stylish, semiformal atmosphere. Try the first-course specialty, lasagna *del Pappagallo,* made with veal, sirloin of pork, and porcini mushrooms. The *filetto di tacchino al Pappagallo* (turkey stuffed with truffles, ham, and Parmesan cheese) is decadently rich. ✉ *Piazza della Mercanzia 3/c,* ☎ *051/232807. Reservations essential. AE, DC, MC, V. Closed Sun., Dec. 25–Jan. 5, and Aug. 7–Sept. 15.*

$$$ ✕ **I Carracci.** Classic, old-world elegance reaches its artistic height here, at meticulously laid tables under a magnificent ceiling frescoed in the 16th century with scenes of the four seasons. That the restaurant takes its name from the family of artists who decorated it invites a critical eye to its cuisine; some question whether the kitchen is on a par with the decor. Food or no food, this is the most exquisite room in the city. ✉ *Grand Hotel Baglioni (☞ below), Via dell'Indipendenza 8 (hotel guests) or Via Manzoni 2,* ☎ *051/225445. Reservations essential. AE, DC, MC, V.*

$$$ ✕ **Nuovi Notai.** If you get the time just right, you'll hear the Angelus ring from the cathedral at this spot, just off beautiful Piazza Maggiore. The building is 14th-century, the decor 19th-century, and the food a rich, complex blend of classic regional specialties and imaginative uses of seasonal ingredients. The *tortino tiepido* (warm tartlet) of porcini mushrooms makes a good starter. ✉ *Via de' Pignattari 1,* ☎ *051/228694. Reservations essential. AE, DC, MC, V. Closed Sun.*

$$$ ✕ **Rosteria Luciano.** A changing list of daily specials at this art-deco style restaurant augments what is already one of Bologna's most varied menus. Some of the best offerings are grilled lamb and beef, breast of duck, and excellent guinea fowl. Among the desserts, the *ricottina al forno* (charcoal-flavored oven-baked ricotta) is worth the splurge. ✉ *Via Nazario Sauro 19,* ☎ *051/231249. Reservations essential. AE, DC, MC, V. Closed Wed., Aug., Dec. 23–Jan. 2.*

$$ ✕ **Bertino.** Happy, gregarious diners don't seem to mind the crammed quarters in the large, bustling room here. Maybe it's because popularity hasn't spoiled this traditional neighborhood trattoria and its simple, home-style dishes. Tried-and-true highlights are the *paglia e fieno* (yellow and green pasta) with sausage and the choices on the steaming tray of bollito misto. ✉ *Via delle Lame 55,* ☎ *051/522230. AE, DC, MC, V. Closed Sun. and Aug. No dinner Mon.*

$$ ✕ **Da Carlo.** Dining on the medieval terrace in summer is a treat in this attractive restaurant, so be sure to reserve a table outside. The delicate game dishes, such as braised pigeon with artichokes, are favorites. ✉ *Via Marchesana 6,* ☎ *051/233227. Reservations essential. AE, DC, MC, V. Closed Sun., Tues., Jan. 1–22, Aug. 23–Sept. 3.*

$$ ✕ **Da Cesari.** Wine made by the owner's family, famous Bolognese dishes such as *gramigna alla salsiccia* (pasta with a sauce of sausage and tomato), and entrées such as duck with rosemary make this one of the best restau-

rants in Bologna in its price category. ⊠ *Via de' Carbonesi 8,* ☎ *051/ 237710. Reservations essential. AE, DC, MC, V. Closed Sun. and Aug.*

$$ ✕ **Osteria Du Madon.** Young chef Lorenzo Boni, formerly of San
★ Domenico in Imola (☞ Dining *in* Dozza, *below*) and New York, brought this country *osteria*—its interior undistinguished and clientele academic—to the University district and is now quietly turning out some of the city's most sophisticated food. Dishes are cosmopolitan takes on traditional ingredients, with a light touch and an emphasis on truffles (in season) and mushrooms. Not so light but equally gratifying is a *semifreddo* (soft ice cream) with pine nuts and honey in an apricot sauce— don't miss it if it's available. ⊠ *Via San Vitale 73/d,* ☎ *051/226221. AE, DC, MC, V. Closed Sun. and 1st 3 wks in Aug. No lunch Sat.*

$$ ✕ **Rostaria Antico Brunetti.** Housed next door to a Romanesque tower steps away from Piazza Maggiore, this wood-paneled restaurant was founded in 1873 and is known as Bologna's oldest. Specialties here range from "Mama's tortellini" to veal in a white-wine sauce, but most diners opt for the pizzas or simple pastas with seafood sauces. Dining is on two floors, but even then the restaurant fills quickly. ⊠ *Via Caduti di Cefalonia 5,* ☎ *051/234441. AE, DC, MC, V. Closed Wed.*

$$ ✕ **Victoria.** It is not unusual for this unpretentious and charming trat-
★ toria-pizzeria off Via dell'Indipendenza to have lines, so reserve ahead. Although locals come for the wide choice of cheap pizzas, the rest of the menu is not to be overlooked, particularly the *tortellini con noci e speck,* a ridiculously rich treatment of Bologna's classic pasta in a sauce of cream, ground walnuts, and cured ham. The back room has a lovely 17th-century painted wooden ceiling. ⊠ *Via Augusto Righi 9/c,* ☎ *051/ 233548. Reservations essential. AE, DC, MC, V. Closed Thurs.*

$$$$ ⊞ **Corona d'Oro.** A medieval printing house in a former life, this hotel
★ has delightful, lyrical art-nouveau decor in its public space, an atrium, and enough flowers for a wedding. Guest rooms make opulent use of original 15th- and 16th-century decorations, like painted wood ceilings and Gothic-vault windows; don't miss the morning breakfast buffet. ⊠ *Via Oberdan 12, 40126,* ☎ *051/236456,* ℻ *051/262679. 35 rooms. Bar, breakfast room, in-room safes, minibars, meeting room. AE, DC, MC, V. Closed 1st 3 wks in Aug.*

$$$$ ⊞ **Dei Commercianti.** Designed on the original building plan of the 11th-
★ century palace and tower occupied by the hotel, rooms here are cozy and unique, with original wood beams built into the walls. Tower rooms and suites have balconies with magnificent views of the church; all rooms are stylishly furnished with, among other things, Carrara marble desks custom-built on a 15th-century design. ⊠ *Via dei Pignattari 11, 40124,* ☎ *051/233052,* ℻ *051/224733. 32 rooms, 3 suites. Bar, breakfast room, in-room safes, minibars. AE, DC, MC, V.*

$$$$ ⊞ **Grand Hotel Baglioni.** Sixteenth-century paintings and frescoes by
★ the Bolognese Carracci brothers are rarely seen outside a museum or church, but here they provide the stunning backdrop for the public rooms and restaurant (☞ I Carracci, *above*) of one of Italy's most glamorous hotels. Lady Di slept here, and you'll feel no less royal in an elegant room with antique furniture and brocaded walls. ⊠ *Via dell'Indipendenza 8, 40121,* ☎ *051/225445,* ℻ *051/234840. 131 rooms. Restaurant, bar, breakfast room, in-room safes, minibars, no-smoking rooms, meeting rooms, parking (fee). AE, DC, MC, V.*

$$$ ⊞ **Orologio.** Under the same management as the Corona d'Oro and the Dei Commercianti (☞ *above*), the Orologio is in a quiet pedestrian zone off Piazza Grande and is in an ideal sightseeing location. Top-floor rooms have good views of Bologna's skyline. ⊠ *Via IV Novembre 10, 40123,* ☎ *051/231253,* ℻ *051/260552. 35 rooms. Bar, minibars. AE, DC, MC, V.*

$$ \text{\$\$}\quad \boxed{\text{T}}\ \textbf{Accademia.}$$ This small hotel is right in the middle of the university quarter, a comfortable base for exploring the area. The rooms are adequate, the staff friendly. ⊠ *Via delle Belle Arti 6, 40126,* ☎ *051/232318,* FAX *051/263590. 28 rooms. Bar. No credit cards. Closed 10 days in Aug.*

$$ \text{\$\$}\quad \boxed{\text{T}}\ \textbf{San Vitale.}$$ Modern furnishings and a garden distinguish this modest hostelry, a five-minute walk from the center of town. The service is courteous, and rooms are clean and bright. Rates come into the bottom end of the price category. ⊠ *Via San Vitale 94, 40125,* ☎ *051/225966,* FAX *051/239396. 17 rooms. No credit cards.*

Nightlife and the Arts

The city hosts a wide selection of orchestral and chamber music concerts as well as an acclaimed opera season. The winter season at the newly renamed **Europa Auditorium** (⊠ Piazza Costituzione, ☎ 051/372540) features shows from comedy to cabaret, and an occasional pop concert thrown in for good measure.

Ballet

Ballet can be enjoyed at the historic **Arena del Sole** (⊠ Via Indipendenza 44, ☎ 051/270790).

Music

The 18th-century **Teatro Comunale** (⊠ Largo Respighi 1, ☎ 051/529999) presents concerts by Italian and international orchestras throughout the year. Check concert schedules for the **Sala Bossi** (⊠ Piazza Rossini 2, ☎ 051/236346) and the **Sala Mozart** in the Accademia Filarmonica (⊠ Via Guerazzi 13, ☎ 051/222997), the principal music school of the city.

Opera

Opera dominates the **Teatro Comunale** (☞ *above*) in winter season. All events sell out quickly, so be sure to reserve seats well in advance.

Theater

A wide range of theatrical productions are staged throughout the winter at the **Teatro Duse** (⊠ Via Cartoleria 42, ☎ 051/231836). Theater productions are staged at the **Arena del Sole** (☞ *above*). **Teatro delle Moline** (⊠ Via delle Moline 1, ☎ 051/235288) is just one of the many small venues where contemporary drama, dance, and comedy productions are performed. Children learning Italian may enjoy the kids' productions at the **Teatro Testoni** (⊠ Via Matteotti 16, ☎ 051/377968).

Outdoor Activities and Sports

Swimming

There is a public indoor swimming pool (⊠ Via Costa 174, ☎ 051/6152520) open June–September, daily 10:30–7, and October–May, weekdays noon–3, Saturday 10:30–1:30, and Sunday 9–12:30; admission is 9,000 lire.

RIMINI, RAVENNA, AND FERRARA

Byzantine Splendors and Simple Pleasures

After taking the Via Emilia (S9) to Dozza, Faenza, and Savignano, the road leads to the next three important destinations: Rimini, Ravenna, and Ferrara, hooking back northwest along the S16.

Dozza

⑮ *31 km (19 mi) southeast of Bologna, 15 km (9 mi) west of Imola.*

As you head southeast out of Bologna, the first port of call is the little hamlet of Dozza, just off the Via Emilia (S9). It is a small village on a hill crowned with a splendid restored medieval castle, the **Rocca di Dozza.** Artists from all over the world flock to the town in September of odd years to take part in the mural competition that has left virtually every square foot of the town covered with colorful scenes executed with varying degrees of skill. The castle is home to the **Enoteca Regionale,** the wine "library" for the region. Here you can sample the different vintages that come from the surrounding countryside, particularly Dozza's own Albana, a white wine that comes dry or sweet. ☎ *0542/678240, Rocca di Dozza, 0542/678089, Enoteca Regionale.* ⊠ *Rocca di Dozza 6,000 lire.* ☉ *Apr.–Sept., Tues.–Sat. 10–noon and 3–6, Sun. 10–noon and 3–7; Oct.–Mar., Tues.–Sat. 10–noon and 2–5, Sun. 10–noon and 2–6.*

Dining

$$$$ ✕ **San Domenico.** Despite a recent cooling of reviews, leading food crit-
★ ics still count San Domenico among Italy's top 10 restaurants, and so dedicated gourmands will want to make the trip from Bologna (about 33 km/20 mi away) to this luxe spot in the town of Imola. Majestic decor reflects the truly royal prices you'll pay for homemade pâté with white truffles, a delicious breast of duck in a sauce of black olives, and hand-stuffed tortellini. With more than 3,000 wines, the wine list is the second-most-extensive in Europe, after the Tour d'Argent in Paris. Make reservations well in advance. ⊠ *Imola, Via Sacchi 1,* ☎ *0542/ 29000. Reservations essential. AE, DC, MC, V. Closed Mon. June– Aug. No dinner Sun.*

Faenza

⑯ *49 km (30 mi) southeast of Bologna, 23 km (14 mi) southeast of Dozza, 14 km (9 mi) northwest of Forlì.*

Renowned faience pottery has been produced in Faenza, on the Via Emilia, since the 12th century. In the central **Piazza del Popolo** are dozens of shops selling the native wares. Faenza is unsurprisingly home to the **Museo delle Ceramiche** (Museum of Ceramics), one of the largest of its kind in the world, covering the potter's art in all phases of history the world over. ⊠ *Viale Baccarini 19,* ☎ *0546/21240.* ⊠ *10,000 lire.* ☉ *Apr.–Oct., Tues.–Sat. 9–7, Sun. 9:30–1; Nov.–Mar., Tues.–Fri. 9–1:30, Sat. 9–1:30 and 3–6, Sun. 9:30–1.*

OFF THE **PREDAPPIO** – From Faenza continue on S9 to the town of Forlì, 14 km
BEATEN PATH (9 mi) away, and turn off onto the rural Route 9ter (in Italian travel parlance, the abbreviation "ter" means a third, variant highway). This leads you through hilly country to the small town of Predappio, the birthplace of Benito Mussolini and Il Duce's final resting place. The cemetery on the outskirts of town contains the crypt of the Mussolini family, with the former dictator himself in the place of honor. A spotlighted bust glowers at visitors, and glass cases contain some of his decorations and medals. It is a chilling place and has become the object of pilgrimage for followers of fascism (young and old), who write repugnant political slogans in the visitors' book. ⊠ *Cimitero Municipale.* ☉ *Daily 8 AM–sunset.*

SAVIGNANO – On S9 beyond Forlì, you pass through the modern towns of Forlimpopoli, Cesena, and Savignano. At this last town, there is a reminder that no matter how new the towns might look, you are still traveling in a place of great history—just outside the town is a small stream, the Rubicone. Cross it and you, too, have crossed the Rubicon, the river made famous by Julius Caesar when, in 49 BC, he defied the Senate of Rome by bringing his army across the river and plunging the country into civil war.

Rimini

⑰ *121 km (76 mi) southeast of Bologna, 54 km (34 mi) southeast of Forlì, 52 km (32 mi) southeast of Ravenna.*

Rimini is the principal summer resort on the Adriatic Coast and one of the most popular holiday destinations in Italy. Every summer, beginning in June, the city is flooded with vacationers, not just from Italy, but from France, Austria, Germany, Scandinavia, and Great Britain, as well. Be warned: The city is given over almost exclusively to tourism, with hundreds of hotels, grand and modest, and restaurants catering to virtually every national palate: you are just as likely to find a *bierkeller* (beer cellar) or an English tea shop as you are an Italian restaurant. The waterfront is lined with beach clubs that rent a patch of sand, a deck chair, and an umbrella by the day, week, month, or the entire season. Hotels along the beachfront have staked out their own private turf, so the chance of swimming (or even seeing the sea close up) without paying for the privilege is slim.

In the off-season (October–March), Rimini is a ghost town. Some hotels and restaurants are open, but the majority are closed tight, hibernating until the return of the spendthrifty tourists. Summers are so crowded here that it is most unwise to go to Rimini without confirmed hotel reservations.

The **new town** has just about swallowed the **old town,** but there are signs here and there that tell of Rimini's long and turbulent history. Rimini stands at the junction of two great Roman consular roads: the Via Aemelia, or Via Emilia as it is known now, and the Via Flaminia. In addition, in Roman times, it was an important port, making it a strategic and commercial center. From the 13th century onward, the city was controlled by the Malatesta family, an unpredictable group capable of grand gestures and savage deeds. The famous lovers in Dante's *Inferno,* Paolo and Francesca, were Malatestas. Paolo was the brother of Gianciotto Malatesta; Francesca, Gianciotto's wife. Gianciotto murdered them both for having betrayed him. Sigismondo Malatesta, lord of the city in the middle of the 15th century, was considered a learned man of great wit and culture. He also banished his first wife, strangled his second, and poisoned his third. He lived with his beautiful mistress, Isotta, until her death. He was so grief-stricken that he raised a mag-

★ nificent monument in her honor, the **Tempio Malatestiano** (⊠ Via IV Novembre), the principal sight in the town.

Despite the irregular—from the church's point of view—nature of Sigismondo's relationship with Isotta, Sigismondo's memorial to his great love is today the cathedral of Rimini. The building was in fact originally a Franciscan church before Sigismondo took it over to make it into a monument to his beloved. The Renaissance facade by Leon Battista Alberti is in the shape of a Roman triumphal arch and is considered to be one of Alberti's masterpieces.

The interior is light and spacious and contains the tombs of both the lovers. The intertwined *I,* for Isotta, and *S,* for Sigismondo, are dotted about everywhere and look rather like dollar signs. The carvings of elephants and roses recall the coat of arms of the Malatesta family. Sigismondo's tomb, on the right of the entrance door, is some distance from Isotta's in the second chapel on the right. (Her tomb is on the left wall of the chapel; the original inscription in marble had a pagan twist and was covered with another in bronze.) To the right of the entrance, in what is now the Tempio's book and gift shop, is a wonderful but badly damaged fresco by Piero della Francesca showing Sigismondo paying homage to his patron saint. When the shop is closed, one of the cathedral's staff will be glad to unlock the room containing the fresco. Over the main altar of the church is a crucifix attributed to Giotto; the painted feet are all but worn off from years when it was hung low enough for curious visitors to touch. ⊠ *Via Quattro Novembre,* ☎ *0541/51130.* ☉ *Daily 7–noon and 3:30–7.*

Rimini's oldest monument is the **Arco d'Augusto** (Arch of Augustus), now stranded in the middle of a square just inside the city ramparts. It was erected in 27 BC, making it the oldest Roman arch in existence, and it marks the meeting of the Via Aemelia and the Via Flaminia. To reach the Arch of Augustus from the Tempio Malatestiano, walk up Via Quattro Novembre to Piazza Tre Martiri (where, legend says, the mule carrying Saint Anthony suddenly stopped and knelt in honor of the Holy Sacrament that was being carried past at the time) and turn left onto Corso d'Augusto. ⊠ *Largo Giulio Cesare.*

Dining and Lodging

$$ ✕ **Picnic.** Take a break from Rimini's seaside crowds in the leafy garden of this casual restaurant in the city center, near Tempio Malatestiano. The menu is varied, with choices such as *pappardelle al sugo di carciofi* (pasta with artichoke sauce), *faraona ripiena alla castagna* (guinea hen with chestnut stuffing), or in the evenings, even just a simple pizza. ⊠ *Via Tempio Malatestiano 30,* ☎ *0541/21916. AE, DC, MC, V. Closed Mon.*

$$ ✕ **Taverna degli Artisti.** The row of stylish glass-and-wood doors that
★ enclose this restaurant give it the air of a French bistro, but once in the door, the atmosphere is abundantly Italian. A local clientele of resort types and expatriates chat table-to-table over such specialties as *crudaiola* (spaghetti with fresh tomatoes, basil, tuna, olives, anchovies, oil, hot pepper, and Parmigiano) or the Chianina steaks. An enormous wood oven and marble pizza-making counter provide a centerpiece to the sunny dining room. ⊠ *Viale Vespucci 1,* ☎ *0541/28519. AE, DC, MC, V. Closed Wed.*

$$ ✕ **Zio.** Nothing but seafood is served here, and all of it is good value
★ for the money. Two small rooms are unpretentiously furnished, one with antiques. Recommended treats are the *brodetto dell'Adriatica* (deliciously tangy shellfish broth), tortellini *al salmone* (in a salmon sauce), and simple grilled sole. ⊠ *Vicolo Santa Chiara 16,* ☎ *0541/786160. Reservations essential weekends and July–Aug. AE, DC, MC, V. Closed Wed. and mid-July–mid-Aug.*

$$$$ ⌆ **Grand Hotel.** This turn-of-the-century extravaganza, immortalized
★ by Fellini in his *Amarcord,* is grander than ever. The hyper-luxe atmosphere begged by enormous crystal chandeliers in the lobby and inlaid wood in the rooms seems playful, rather than formal; with bright pink hallways, potted trees, and spotless adjacent beach, the Grand is a beach resort above all else. While entourages and steamer trunks will never be out of place here, neither would it be any surprise to see a greyhound loping through the restaurant on her way to the pool. ⊠ *Parco Federico Fellini, 47037,* ☎ *0541/56000,* FAX *0541/56866. 115 rooms, 6 suites. 2 restaurants, 2 bars, minibars, 2 pools, beauty salon, sauna, tennis court, beach, nightclub, meeting rooms. AE, DC, MC, V.*

$$$ ⌆ **Club House Hotel.** The Club House is a bit of a double-edged sword: For some, the suburban office building architecture may be off-putting; however, thanks to the design, all rooms have balconies, an asset right

on the sea. Likewise with the hotel's location (for some, right on the main commercial strip and next door to McDonald's is a good thing). The hotel's rooms and facilities invite less debate: Lovely, clean, airy rooms with green-and-white striped ticking and across-the-street private beach access will spell summer vacation to all. ⊠ *Viale Vespucci 52, 47037,* ☎ *0541/391460,* ℻ *0541/391442. 28 rooms. Restaurant, bar, minibars, pool, beach. AE, DC, MC, V.*

$ 🏠 **Annarita.** Set back on a residential road leading off the main Viale Vespucci, this is small but comfortable, with a loyal clientele (availability may consequently be limited). Facilities are rudimentary, rooms are basic (though all have TVs), but the main benefits here are its closeness to the beach promenade and the friendly price. ⊠ *Viale Misurata 24, 47037,* ☎ *0541/391044. 14 rooms. Restaurant, bar. No credit cards.*

En Route   There are two routes from Rimini to Ravenna. The coast road, S16, clings to the shoreline as far as Cervia before edging inland. Although its distance, 52 km (32 mi), is not great, the scenic route is slower by nature. The coast north of Rimini is lined with dozens of small resort towns, only one having any charm, the seaport of Cesenatico; the others are mini-Riminis, and during summer the narrow road is hopelessly clogged with traffic. A faster route is to head inland on A14 and then turn off onto the inland S71, which leads directly into Ravenna; the distance is 64 km (39 mi).

Ravenna

⑱   *76 km (47½ mi) east of Bologna, 52 km (32 mi) northwest of Rimini, 74 km (46 mi) southeast of Ferrara.*

Ravenna is a small, quiet city of brick palaces and cobbled streets, whose magnificent monuments are the only indicators of its storied past. Indeed, the city's greatest assets are its oldest; the art treasures for which it is known outshine anything the last thousand years have brought. The high point in Ravenna's history was 1,500 long years ago, when the city became the capital of the Roman Empire. The honor was short-lived—the city was taken by the barbarian Ostrogoths in the 5th century; then, in the 6th, it was conquered by the Byzantines, who ruled the city from Constantinople.

Because Ravenna spent much of its history looking to the East, its greatest art treasures show much Byzantine influence: Above all, Ravenna is a city of mosaics, the finest in Western art. A single combination 10,000-lire ticket (available at ticket offices of all included sights) will admit you to six of Ravenna's most important monuments: the Tomb of Galla Placidia, the Basilica di San Vitale, the Battistero Neoniano, and the church of Sant'Apollinare Nuovo (☞ *below*), as well as the church of Spirito Santo and the Museo Arcivescovile e Cappella Sant'Andrea.

★   The **Tomb of Galla Placidia** and the **Basilica di San Vitale** are decorated with the best-known, and most elaborate, mosaics in the city. The little tomb and the great church stand side by side, but the tomb predates the church by at least a hundred years. Galla Placidia was the sister of the last emperor of Rome, Honorius, the man who moved the imperial capital to Ravenna in AD 402. She is said to have been beautiful and strong-willed, and to have taken an active part in the governing of the crumbling empire. One of the most active Christians of her day, she endowed churches and supported priests and their congregations throughout the realm. This tomb, constructed in the mid-5th century, is her memorial.

Outside, the tomb is a small, unassuming building of red brick, whose seeming poverty of charm only serves to enhance the richness of the interior mosaics, in deep midnight blue and glittering gold. The tiny, low central dome is decorated with symbols of Christ and the evangelists, and over the door is a depiction of the Good Shepherd. Eight of the Apostles are represented in groups of two on the four inner walls of the dome; the other four appear singly on the walls of the two transepts. Notice the small doves at their feet, drinking from the water of faith. Also in the tiny transepts are some delightful pairs of deer (which represent souls), drinking from the fountain of resurrection. There are three sarcophagi in the tomb, and, it is thought, not one contains the remains of Galla Placidia. She died in Rome in AD 450, and there is no record of her body having been transported back to the place where she wished to lie.

The mosaics of the Galla Placidia tomb are simple works that do not yet show the full impact of Byzantine influence. Quite the opposite is the case of the mosaics in the church of San Vitale, next door. The octagonal church was built in AD 547, after the Byzantines conquered the city, and its interior style shows a strong Byzantine influence. In the area behind the altar are the most famous works in the church, accurate portraits of the emperor of the East, Justinian, attended by his court and the bishop of Ravenna, Maximian. Facing him, across the chancel, is the emperor's wife, Theodora, with her entourage, holding a chalice containing the communion wine. The elaborate headdresses and heavy cloaks of the emperor and empress convey a marvelous sense of the grandeur of the imperial court, and of the mastery of the artisans responsible for the depictions. Presiding over the royal couple from the apse is Christ the King with San Vitale (the saint for whom the church was named) and the founder of the church, Bishop Ecclesio, who holds a model of the building. Unfortunately, these mosaics will undergo a lengthy restoration planned to start in the summer of 1998 and expected to continue until the year 2000, and may be covered for most of that time. ⊠ *Via San Vitale off Via Salara, near Piazza del Popolo.* ⚏ *6,000 lire tomb and basilica, 5,000 lire for ticketholders for adjacent Museo Nazionale, 10,000 combination ticket (☞ above).* ⊙ *Apr.– Sept., daily 9–7.*

Next to the Church of San Vitale, the **Museo Nazionale** of Ravenna contains artifacts of ancient Rome, Byzantine fabrics and carvings, and other pieces of early Christian art. The collection is housed in a former monastery but is well displayed and artfully lit. ⊠ *Piazza Fiandrini,* ☎ *0544/34424.* ⚏ *8,000 lire, 10,000 lire combination ticket.* ⊙ *Tues.–Sat. 8:30–7, Sun. 8:30–10. Ticket office closes ½ hr before museum.*

Next door to Ravenna's 18th-century cathedral, the **Battistero Neoniano** is one of the town's most important mosaic sites. In keeping with the purpose of the building, the great mosaic in the dome shows the baptism of Christ, and beneath that scene are the apostles. The lowest band of mosaics contains Christian symbols, the Throne of God and the Cross. ⊠ *Via Battistero.* ⚏ *5,000 lire (includes Museo Arcivescovile and Cappella Sant'Andrea), 10,000 lire combination ticket.* ⊙ *Apr.–Sept., daily 9–7; Oct.–Mar., daily 9:30–4:30.*

The **Mausoleo di Dante** (tomb of Dante) is in a small neoclassical building next door to the large church of St. Francis. Exiled from his native Florence, the great poet, author of *The Divine Comedy,* died here in 1321. The Florentines have been trying to reclaim their famous son for hundreds of years, but the Ravennans refuse to give him up, arguing that Florence did not welcome Dante in life, so it doesn't deserve him in death. Next door in the church courtyard, note the site that served as temporary, less-grand quarters for the poet's distinguished bones: A plaque identifies the mound of earth under which the Franciscan brothers put Dante's remains for safekeeping from March 1944 to December 1945. A small **museum** is also on the site. ⊠ *Via Dante Alighieri 9,* ☎ *0544/30252. Tomb:* 🎟 *Free.* ☉ *Apr.–Sept., daily 9–7; Oct.–Mar., daily 9–noon and 2–5. Museum:* 🎟 *3,000 lire; free on Sun. and holidays, 10,000 lire combination ticket.* ☉ *Apr.–Sept., Tues.–Sun. 9–noon and 3:30–6; Oct.–Mar., Tues.–Sun. 9–noon.*

The last great mosaic site in the city proper is the church of **Sant' Apollinare Nuovo.** Since the left side of the church was reserved for women, it is only fitting that the mosaic decoration on that side is a scene of 22 virgins offering crowns to the Virgin Mary. On the right wall are 26 men carrying the crowns of martyrdom. They are approaching Christ, who is surrounded by angels. The mosaics in Sant' Apollinare Nuovo date from the early 6th century and are slightly older than the works in San Vitale. ⊠ *Via Roma, at intersection of Via Guaccimanni.* 🎟 *5,000 lire (includes church of Spirito Santo), 10,000 lire combination ticket.* ☉ *Summer, daily 9–7; winter, daily 9:30–4:30.*

OFF THE BEATEN PATH

SANT'APOLLINARE IN CLASSE – This church, about 5 km (3 mi) southeast of Ravenna, is landlocked now, but when it was built, it stood in the center of the busy shipping port of Classis. The arch above and the area around the high altar are rich in mosaics. Those on the arch, older than those behind it, are considered superior to the rest. They show Christ in judgment and the 12 lambs of Christianity leaving the cities of Jerusalem and Bethlehem. In the apse is the figure of Sant'Apollinare himself, a bishop of Ravenna, and above him is a magnificent Transfiguration decorated with flowers, trees, and little birds. ⊠ *Classe,* ☎ *0544/527004.* ☉ *Apr.–Sept., daily 8:50–noon and 2–6; Oct.–Mar., daily 8:50–noon and 2–5:30.*

Dining and Lodging

$$–$$$ ✕ **Bella Venezia.** Graceful low archways lead into this elegant restaurant's two small dining rooms. Try the owner's special risotto *Bazzani* (with butter, Parmigiano, cured ham, mushrooms, and peas) and, for the entrée, *bistecca all'ortolana* (veal in cream sauce with cured ham and zucchini). A good-value tourist menu is available. ⊠ *Via IV Novembre 16,* ☎ *0544/212746. Reservations essential weekends. AE, DC, MC, V. Closed Sun.*

$ ✕ **Ca' de Ven.** A vaulted wine cellar in the heart of the old city, the Ca' de Ven is great for a hearty lunch or dinner. You sit at long tables with the other diners and feast on platters of delicious cold cuts; *piadine* (griddle breads); and cold, heady white wine. If you're here in chilly weather, try the *pasta e fagioli* (pasta and bean soup). ⊠ *Via C. Ricci 24,* ☎ *0544/30163. Reservations not accepted. MC, V. Closed Mon.*

$$$ 🏨 **Hotel Bisanzio.** Just steps from San Vitale and the tomb of Galla Placidia, this is the most convenient lodging for mosaic enthusiasts. Rooms are comfortable and modern, and the lobby's Florentine lamps add a touch of style. Ask for a room on the top floor and you may get a view of the basilica. ⊠ *Via Salara 30, 48100,* ☎ *0544/217111,* FAX *0544/32539. 36 rooms. Bar, breakfast room, in-room safes, minibars, meeting rooms. AE, MC, V.*

$$ 🏨 **Hotel Centrale Byron.** In the heart of Ravenna's old town, this is an old-fashioned, well-managed hotel, its rooms spotless if uninspiring. Because it's in a pedestrian zone, tranquillity is assured, though you will have to leave your car in one of the nearby garages. ⊠ *Via IV Novembre 14, 48100,* ☎ *0544/33479,* FAX *0544/34114. 54 rooms. Bar, in-room safes, minibars. AE, DC, MC, V. Closed Dec. 20–Jan. 5.*

$ 🏨 **Hotel Ravenna.** A functional stopover near the train station but still only a few minutes' walk from the center of town, this modern hotel offers smallish rooms with TVs and telephones. ⊠ *Viale Maroncelli 12, 48100,* ☎ *0544/212204,* ℻ *0544/212077. 25 rooms. Bar. AE, MC, V.*

Ferrara

⑲ *47 km (29 mi) northeast of Bologna, 74 km (46 mi) northwest of Ravenna along S16.*

Ferrara is a city of turrets, towers, and marvelous pleasure palaces, all presided over by a mighty castle protected by a deep moat. Although the site was settled before Christ and was once ruled by Ravenna, the history of Ferrara begins in the 13th century, with the coming of the Este family. From 1259 until 1598 the dukes of the Este family reigned in Ferrara, and in those 3½ centuries the city was stamped indelibly with their mark.

It was during the Renaissance that the court of the Este came into full flower. In keeping with their time, the dukes could be politically ruthless—brother killed brother, son fought father—but they were avid scholars and enthusiastic patrons of the arts. The cultivated Duke Niccolò III murdered his wife and her lover. The greatest of all the dukes, Ercole I, tried to poison the nephew who challenged his power, and when that didn't work, Ercole I beheaded him, but it is to this pitiless man that Ferrara owes its great beauty. One of the most celebrated villains in Italian history, Lucrezia Borgia, married into the Este family—and unlike that of her in-laws, it seems that her infamous reputation is not at all deserved. Beloved by the Ferrarese people and mourned greatly when she died, she is buried in the church of Corpus Domini in the city.

★ Naturally enough, the building that was the seat of Este power dominates the town: It is the massive **Castello Estense,** placed square in the center of the city in Piazza Castello. It is a suitable symbol for the Este family: cold and menacing on the outside, lavishly decorated within. The public rooms are grand, but deep in the bowels of the fortress are chilling dungeons where enemies of the state were held in wretched conditions—a function these quarters served as recently as 1943, when antifascist prisoners were detained there.

The castle was established as a fortress in 1385, but work on its luxurious ducal quarters continued into the 16th century. Representative of the Este grandeur are the Sala dei Giochi (the Games Room), extravagantly painted with pagan athletic scenes, and the Sala dell'Aurora, decorated to show the times of the day. From the terraces of the castle and from the hanging garden, reserved for the private use of the duchesses, are fine views of the town and surrounding countryside. ⊠ *Piazza Castello,* ☎ *0532/299279.* ▨ *6,000 lire.* ◷ *Tues.–Sun. 9:30–5 (open Mon. holidays).*

A few steps from the castle is the magnificent Gothic **Duomo,** with its facade of three tiers of arches and beautiful carvings over the central door. It was begun in 1135 and took more than a hundred years to complete. The interior was completely remodeled in the 17th century, and very little of the original decoration remains in place, much of it residing instead in the **cathedral museum** above the church (entrance inside the church). Displayed here are some of the lifelike carvings, dating from the 13th century and showing the months of the year, taken from the cathedral doors. Also in the museum are a statue of the Madonna by the Sienese master Jacopo della Quercia and two masterpieces by the Ferrarese painter Cosimo Tura, an *Annunciation* and *St. George Slaying the Dragon.* ⊠ *Piazza Cattedrale,* ☎ *0544/207449.* ◷ *Duomo: Mon.–Sat. 7:30–noon and 3–6:30, Sun. 7:30–1 and 4–*

7:30; museum: Tues.–Sat. 10–noon and 3–5, Sun. 10–noon and 4–6. ☞ Museum free, but donation appreciated.

The area behind the Duomo, the southern part of the city stretching between the Corso Giovecca and the ramparts of the city above the river, is the oldest and most characteristic part of Ferrara. In this part of the old town various members of the Este family built themselves pleasure palaces, the most famous of which is the **Palazzo Schifanoia** (*schifanoia* means carefree, or literally, "fleeing boredom"). Begun in the 14th century, the palace was remodeled in 1466 and is the first Renaissance palazzo in the city. The interior is lavishly decorated, particularly the **Salone dei Mesi,** with an extravagant series of frescoes showing the months of the year and their mythological attributes. The **Museo Civico** has a collection of coins, statuary, and paintings. ✉ *Via Scandiana 23,* ☏ *0544/64178.* ☞ *6,000 lire, free 2nd Mon. of each month, 8,000 lire in combination with Palazzina Marfisa d'Este.* ☉ *Daily 9–7.*

The grand but unfinished courtyard is the most interesting part of the luxurious **Palazzo di Ludovico il Moro,** a magnificent 15th-century palace built for Ludovico Sforza, husband of Beatrice d'Este. Reopened in 1997 after 13 years of restoration, the palazzo also houses the region's **Museo Archeologico,** a repository of the relics of early man, the Etruscans, and Romans, found in the country surrounding the city. ✉ *Near the Palazzo Schifanoia, on Via XX Settembre,* ☏ *0544/66299.* ☞ *8,000 lire.* ☉ *Tues.–Fri. 9–2, weekends 9–6.*

The courtyard of the peaceful palace called the **Palazzo del Paradiso** contains the tomb of the great writer Ariosto, author of the most popular work of literature of the Renaissance, the poem "Orlando Furioso." The building now houses the **city library.** ✉ *Via Scienze,* ☏ *0544/ 206977.* ☞ *Free.* ☉ *Weekdays 9–7, Sat. 9–1:30.*

The Estes were patrons of the poet Ariosto, and he passed a good deal of his life in Ferrara. The interior of **Casa Ariosto** (✉ Via Ariosto 67) has been converted into an office building and is not open to the public. One of the best preserved of the Renaissance palaces scattered along Ferrara's old streets is the charming **Casa Romei.** Downstairs are rooms with 15th-century frescoes and several sculptures collected from churches that have been destroyed. The house lies not far from the **Palazzo del Paradiso,** in the area behind Ferrara's castello. ✉ *Via Savonarola 30,* ☏ *0544/240341.* ☞ *4,000 lire.* ☉ *Tues.–Sat. 8:30– 7, Sun.–Mon. 8:30–2.*

On the busy Corso Giovecca is the **Palazzina di Marfisa d'Este,** an elegant 16th-century home that belonged to Marfisa d'Este, a great patron of the arts. The house has painted ceilings, fine 16th-century furniture, and a garden containing a grotto and an outdoor theater. ✉ *Corso Giovecca 170,* ☏ *0544/64178.* ☞ *3,000 lire, free 2nd Mon. of month, 8,000 lire in combination with Palazzo Schifanoia.* ☉ *Apr.– Sept., daily 9–12:30 and 3–6; Oct.–Mar., daily 9–12:30 and 2–5.*

The collection of ornate religious objects in the **Museo Ebraico** (Jewish Museum) bears witness to the long and dramatic history of the city's Jewish community. This history had its high points—Ercole I d'Este's 1492 invitation to Sephardic Jews exiled from Spain to come settle in Ferrara—and its lows, notably the papal government's 1624 closure of the **ghetto,** which was reopened only with the advent of a united Italy in 1859. The triangular warren of narrow, cobbled streets that made up the ghetto originally extended as far as Corso Giovecca (from Corso Giudecca, or Ghetto Street); with the closure, the neighborhood was restricted to the area between Via Scienze, Via Contrari, and Via di San Romano. The museum, in the center of the ghetto, is also home to Ferrara's **synagogue**. ⊠ *Via Mazzini 95*, ☎ *0532/210228.* ▨ *7,000 lire.* ⊙ *Hour-long guided tours only, Sun.–Thurs. at 10, 11, and 12.*

The **Palazzo dei Diamanti** (Palace of Diamonds) is so called for the 12,600 blocks of diamond-shape stone that stud the facade. The palace was built in the 15th and 16th centuries and today contains an extensive art gallery devoted primarily to the painters of Ferrara. ⊠ *Corso Ercole I d'Este 21.* ▨ *10,000 lire.* ⊙ *Tues.–Sat. 9–2, Sun. 9–1.*

Dining and Lodging

$$–$$$ ✕ **La Provvidenza.** One of the best-known restaurants in Ferrara, Provvidenza is a pleasant country-style inn with a lovely garden for summertime alfresco dining. The local specialties—fish grilled over charcoal (Thursday and Friday) and the bollito misto (weekends in winter)—are the best. ⊠ *Corso Ercole d'Este 92*, ☎ *0532/205187. Reservations essential. AE, DC, MC, V. Closed Mon. and 10 days in mid-Aug.*

$$ ✕ **Trattoria La Romantica.** The former stables of a 17th-century mer-
★ chant's house have been transformed into this casually elegant, welcoming restaurant that is the unanimous choice among well-fed locals. While the decor (warm light and wood-beam ceilings marred by incongruous prints and a piano) seems to be in a perpetual transitional stage, the haute-rustic food is fully realized: Ferrarese specialties like cappellacci di zucca in a cream-tomato-walnut-Parmesan sauce are served side-by-side with Texan beef and French oysters. Reservations are recommended. ⊠ *Via Ripagrande 36*, ☎ *0532/765975. AE, DC, MC, V. Closed Wed., Jan. 7–18, and July 1–17.*

$–$$ ✕ **Guido Ristorante.** Down a long cobbled street in an atmospheric part of the old Jewish ghetto, this restaurant is a leading choice of locals. The menu is made up of all the Ferrarese specialties, plus some inventive dishes you won't find anywhere else. To wit: gnocchi with black olives and zucchini in curry sauce. ⊠ *Via Vignatagliata 61*, ☎ *0532/761052. Reservations essential. AE, DC, MC, V. Closed Tues.*

$$$$ 🏨 **Duchessa Isabella.** Live out your Marie Antoinette fantasies, if you have them, at this converted 16th-century mansion near Piazza Ariostea. The exceptionally elegant dining rooms and entryway are sumptuously decorated in authentic style; the lacy, satiny rooms, however, teeter on the border between royal and ridiculous. Some may find the formality wearying and the tone somewhat bogus; others will find a stay here marvelous. A horse and carriage are available for those who feel so inclined. ⊠ *Via Palestro 70, 44100*, ☎ *0532/202121*, 🆑 *0532/202638. 22 rooms, 6 suites. Restaurant, bar, in-room safes, minibars, meeting rooms. AE, MC, V.*

$$$ 🏨 **Hotel Ripagrande.** The courtyards, vaulted brick lobby, and break-
★ fast room of this 15th-century noble palazzo retain much of their lordly pre-Renaissance flavor, but rooms are decidedly more down-to-earth. Standard doubles as well as the many bi- and tri-level suites have faux-Persian rugs, tapestries, and cozy period-style furniture; top-floor rooms and suites with terraces are like a Colorado ski lodge. Unlike in many hotels, the Ripagrande's suites are a good deal and remain in this price category. ⊠ *Via Ripagrande 21, 44100*, ☎ *0532/765250*, 🆑 *0532/764377. 20 rooms, 20 suites. Restaurant, bar, breakfast room, in-room safes, minibars, meeting rooms. AE, DC, MC, V.*

$$ 🏨 **Locanda Borgonuovo.** This lovely B&B opened in 1994 in a 17th-century monastery on a quiet but central pedestrian-only street, and since then has been booking up months in advance, partly due to the musicians and actors from the local theater who make this their home away from home. Individually named rooms are furnished with antiques, and one room has its own kitchen available for longer stays. Summer breakfasts are taken in the leafy courtyard. ⊠ *Via Cairoli 29,*

44100, ☎ *0532/211100*, FAX *0532/248000. 4 rooms. Breakfast room, in-room safes, minibars. AE, MC, V.*

$–$$ ⊞ **Hotel San Paolo.** On the edge of the old city, San Paolo is the best inexpensive choice in town. The 10-minute walk from the heart of Ferrara's medieval quarter is effortless in a town so amenable to strolling, and there are some good restaurants in the vicinity. The rooms are institutional—modern, with TVs and telephones. ⊠ *Via Baluardi 9, 44100,* ☎ *0532/762040,* FAX *0532/762040. 32 rooms. No credit cards.*

EMILIA-ROMAGNA A TO Z

Arriving and Departing

By Bus
Thanks to the autostrada bisecting the region and Emilia-Romagnan efficiency, bus travel in the region is easy—although the train, blessed with the same benefits but no traffic, is still easier.

By Car
Bologna is on the autostrada network, allowing direct and quick driving from cities.

By Plane
Bologna is an important business and convention center and is therefore served by air routes that link it with other Italian cities, as well as by direct flights to European capitals. The airport, **Guglielmo Marconi** (⊠ Viale dell'Aeroporto, ☎ 051/6479615) is 10 km (6 mi) northwest of town.

BETWEEN THE AIRPORT AND DOWNTOWN
Half-hourly bus service (6,000 lire) connects Guglielmo Marconi with a downtown air terminal at Bologna's central train station.

By Train
Bologna is an important rail hub for the entire northern part of Italy and has frequent, fast train service to Rome, Milan, Florence, and Venice. For information about train departures, call ☎ 1478/88088 (toll-free).

Getting Around

By Bus
Private bus service links all the cities of Emilia-Romagna, with Bologna being the central hub. The *autostazione* (bus terminal, ⊠ In Piazza XX Settembre, ☎ 051/350172 information), is at the top of Via dell'Indipendenza. City-run bus routes connect major towns with smaller villages and hamlets in the district, but routes are roundabout, and schedules vary from place to place.

By Car
The Via Emilia (**S9**) runs through the heart of the region. It is a straight, low-lying modern road, the length of which can be traveled in a few hours. Ferrara and Ravenna are joined to it by good modern highways. Although less scenic, the **A14** autostrada, which runs parallel to the S9, will get you where you're going even more quickly.

By Train
The railway follows the Via Emilia (S9), and all the cities covered can be reached by train. Call ☎ 147/888088 toll-free for train information.

Contacts and Resources

Car Rentals

BOLOGNA

Avis (⊠ Via del Triumvirato 84, ☎ 051/6472032). **Eurodollar** (⊠ Viale Mazzini 4/3, ☎ 051/255546). **Europcar** (⊠ Via Amendola 12/f, ☎ 051/247101).

PARMA

Avis (⊠ Viale Frati 24, ☎ 0521/772418). **Eurodollar** (⊠ Hotel Baglioni, Viale Piacenza 12, ☎ 0521/995226). **Europcar** (⊠ Viale Piacenza 51/ c, ☎ 0521/293035).

RIMINI

Avis (⊠ Aeroporto di Rimini, ☎ 0541/370721). **Europcar** (⊠ Via Giovanni XXIII 126, ☎ 0541/54746).

Emergencies

Police (☎ 112). **Ambulance** (☎ 113). **Doctors and Dentists** (☎ 113). **Late-Night Pharmacies** (☎ 051/192 information).

Travel Agencies

Bologna: Marconi Tours (⊠ Via Marconi 47, ☎ 051/235783). **Rimini:** Viaggi Urbinati (⊠ Viale Vespucci 127, ☎ 0541/391660 or 390720).

Visitor Information

Bologna (⊠ Aeroporto Gugliemo Marconi, ☎ 051/6472036; ⊠ Stazione Centrale, 40121, ☎ 051/246541; ⊠ Piazza Maggiore 6, 40124, ☎ 051/239660). **Busseto** (⊠ Comune, Piazza Giuseppe Verdi 10, 43011, ☎ 0524/91841). **Dozza** (⊠ Via XX Settembre, 40050, ☎ 0542/678052). **Faenza** (⊠ Piazza del Popolo 1, 48018, ☎ 0546/ 25232). **Ferrara** (⊠ Corso Giovecca 21, 44022, ☎ 0532/209370). **Modena** (⊠ Piazza Grande 17, 41100, ☎ 059/206660). **Parma** (⊠ Via Melloni 1/b, 43100, ☎ 0521/234735). **Piacenza** (⊠ Piazzetta Mercanti 7, 29100, ☎ 0523/329324). **Ravenna** (⊠ Via Salara 8, 48100, ☎ 0544/ 35404). **Rimini** (⊠ Via Dante 86, near train station, 47037, ☎ 0541/ 51331; ⊠ Piazzale Fellini 3, waterfront, 47037, ☎ 0541/56902).

12 Umbria and the Marches

Perugia, Urbino, Spoleto, Assisi, and Orvieto

Legends linger in smiling Umbria, ethereal birthplace of the saints. Here await Gothic treasures—Assisi's Basilica di San Francesco and Orvieto's awe-inspiring cathedral— and the more urbane pleasures of Spoleto's Festival dei Due Mondi and timeless, Renaissance-stamped Urbino. Above serpentine hills toward the Adriatic are Le Marche and its noble Urbino.

BIRTHPLACE OF SAINTS AND CONDOTTIERI, Umbria has remained true to its name: "land of shadows." The hills, olive groves, and terraced vineyards of this mystic province are often wrapped in a bluish haze that gives its landscape an ethereal painted look—a landscape often recognized in the frescoes of its celebrated local artists, even when they were decorating churches far from their native soil. Blessed with steep, austere hills, deep valleys, and fast-flowing rivers, the region—roughly halfway between Florence and Rome—has not yet been swamped by tourism and has escaped the unplanned industrial expansion that afflicts much of central Italy. No town in Umbria boasts the extravagant wealth of art and architecture of Florence, Rome, or Venice, but this works in your favor. Cities can be experienced whole, rather than as a series of museums and churches, forced marches through 2,000 years of Western culture; in Umbria the visitor comes to know the towns as people live in them today.

Updated by Jon Eldan and Carla Lionello

This is not to suggest that the cultural cupboard is bare—far from it. Perugia, the capital of the region, and Assisi, Umbria's most prominent city, are rich in art and architecture, as are Orvieto, Todi, and Spoleto. Virtually every small town in the region has a castle, church, or museum worth a stop.

The earliest inhabitants of Umbria, the Umbri, were thought by the Romans to be the most ancient inhabitants of Italy. Little is known about them, since with the coming of Etruscan culture, the tribe fled into the mountains in the eastern portion of the region. The Etruscans, who founded some of the great cities of Umbria, were in turn supplanted by the Romans. Unlike Tuscany and other regions of central Italy, Umbria had few powerful medieval families to exert control over the cities in the Middle Ages—its proximity to Rome ensured that Umbria would always be more or less under papal domination.

The relative political stability of the region did not mean that Umbria was left in peace. Located in the center of the country, it has for much of its history been a battlefield where armies from north and south clashed. Hannibal destroyed a Roman army on the shores of Lago Trasimeno, and the full and bloody course of the interminable Guelph-Ghibelline conflict of the Middle Ages was played out in Umbria. Dante considered it the most violent place in Italy. Trophies of war still decorate the facade of the Palazzo dei Priori in Perugia, and the little town of Gubbio continues a warlike rivalry begun in the Middle Ages—every year it challenges the Tuscan town of Sansepolcro to a crossbow tournament. Today, of course, the bowmen shoot at targets, but neither side has forgotten that 500 years ago its ancestors shot at each other.

In spite of—or perhaps because of—this bloodshed, Umbria has produced more than its share of Christian saints. The most famous is St. Francis, the decidedly unmartial saint whose life shaped the Church and the history of his time. His great shrine at Assisi is visited by hundreds of thousands of pilgrims each year. St. Clare, his devoted follower, was Umbria-born, as were St. Benedict, St. Rita of Cascia, and, ironically, the patron saint of lovers, St. Valentine.

East of Umbria, the Marches (Le Marche to Italians) stretch between the hills of the southern Apennines down to the Adriatic sea. It is a scenic region of mountains and valleys, with great turreted castles standing on high peaks defending passes and roads—silent testament to the region's bellicose past. The Marches have passed through numerous hands. First the Romans supplanted the native civilizations; then Charlemagne supplanted the Romans (and gave the region its name—it was divided into "marks," or provinces, under the rule of the Holy Roman Emperor); then began the seemingly never-ending struggle between popes and local lords. Cesare Borgia (circa 1475–1507) succeeded in wresting control of the Marches from the local suzerains, annexing the region to the papacy of his father, Alexander VI.

Despite all this martial tussling, it was in the lonely mountain town of Urbino that the Renaissance came to its fullest flower; that small town became a haven of culture and learning that rivaled the greater, richer, and more powerful city of Florence, and even Rome itself.

Pleasures and Pastimes

Dining

Umbria is mountainous, and its food is hearty and straightforward, with a stick-to-the-ribs quality that sees hardworking farmers and artisans through a long day's work and helps them make the steep climb home at night. The region has made several important contributions to Italian cuisine. Particularly prized are *tartufi neri* (black truffles) from the area around Spoleto (signs warning against unlicensed truffle hunting are posted at the base of the grand Ponte delle Torri) and from the hills around the tiny town of Norcia. The local pasta specialty—thick, handmade *ciriole* (roughly shaped, fat spaghetti) or *strangozzi* (pasta like ciriole, *above,* but with holes in the middles)—is even better *al tartufo,* enriched with excellent local olive oil and truffles. Norcia's pork products—especially sausages, salami, and *arista* (roast loin perfumed with rosemary)—are so famous that pork butchers throughout Italy are called *norcini,* no matter where they hail from, and pork butcher shops are called *norcinerie.*

In the coastal Marches, fish in various forms is the thing to look for. One of the characteristic dishes in Ancona is *brodetto,* a rich fish chowder containing as many as nine types of Adriatic saltwater fish. Ascoli Piceno, inland, is known for two dishes: *olive ascolane* (olives stuffed, rolled in batter, and deep fried) and *vincisgrassi* (lasagna with innards to enrich the sauce, sometimes with black truffles, and more sauce than usual), far richer than you're likely to find elsewhere in Italy. Ascoli Piceno is also the home of the licorice-flavored liqueur anisette.

CATEGORY	COST*
$$$$	over 85,000 lire
$$$	60,000–85,000 lire
$$	25,000–60,000 lire
$	under 25,000 lire

Prices are per person, including house wine, service, and tax.

Hiking

Magnificent scenery makes Umbria excellent hiking and mountaineering country. The area around Spoleto is particularly good, and the tourist office supplies itineraries of walks and climbs to suit all ages and levels of ability.

Lodging

Virtually every historic town in Umbria has some kind of hotel, no matter how small the place may be. A popular trend is the conversion of old villas and monasteries into first-class hotels. These tend to be outside the towns, in the countryside, and the splendor of the settings often outweighs the problem of getting into town. In all cases, these country hotels are comfortable, often luxurious, and offer a mixture of old-world charm and modern convenience. Reservations at any hotel are recommended, and traveling in high season to Perugia, Assisi, Spoleto, or Orvieto without advance bookings is a chancy proposition.

CATEGORY	COST*
$$$$	over 300,000 lire
$$$	160,000–300,000 lire
$$	100,000–160,000 lire
$	under 100,000 lire

Prices are for a standard double room for two, including service and tax.

Shopping

Pottery and wine are the two most celebrated Umbrian exports, and examples of both commodities are excellent and unique to the region. Torgiano, south of Perugia, is one of the best-known centers of wine making, where you can watch the process and buy the product; you can find some of the best ceramics at Gubbio, Perugia, and Assisi. Those with the most flair are found in Deruta, south of Torgiano on S3bis. The red glazes of Gubbio pottery have been renowned since medieval times. The secret of the original glaze died with its inventor some 500 years ago, but some contemporary potters produce a fair facsimile.

Exploring Umbria and the Marches

The steep hills and deep valleys that make Umbria and the Marches so picturesque also make them difficult to explore. Driving routes must be chosen carefully to avoid tortuous mountain roads; major towns are not necessarily linked to each other by train, bus, or highway. A convenient base for exploring the region is Perugia, the largest city in Umbria, but to see the region properly you would still need to stay overnight in other towns along the way.

Numbers in the text correspond to numbers in the margin and on the Umbria and the Marches, Perugia, Spoleto, and Assisi maps.

Great Itineraries

The region of Umbria is particularly suited to touring in a limited time. Basing yourself in Perugia, you can see all the major sights in the regional capital in the equivalent of a day, making easy excursions to the hill villages on your other days without feeling stressed out by constant travel. East of Perugia, the Marches invite leisurely exploring, but expect some lengthy rides in between the main points of interest.

IF YOU HAVE 3 DAYS

In ⊞ **Perugia** ①–④, your main stops will be the refurbished Galleria Nazionale and the Collegio del Cambio, both contained in the atmospheric **Palazzo dei Priori** ②; much of the rest of your time will be spent alternately ambling along Corso Vannucci and toiling up and down the steep lanes on either side. Devote your second day to ⊞ **Assisi** ⑲–㉒, where the spiritual and the material are fused in a place that remains in essence a small medieval Umbrian town. The choice for a third excursion is a tough one, and you won't be disappointed by whichever place you opt for. Consider **Spoleto** ⑫–⑱: a tight-knit hill town whose narrow streets abound with evocative views and delightful surprises.

IF YOU HAVE 5 DAYS

Given five days, you will be able to spend a couple of them exploring the neighboring region of Le Marche. How you enter these rather inaccessible parts will depend on your mode of transport. In any case, start your tour in ⊞ **Perugia** ①–④, and follow the itinerary above for your first two days. If you are traveling by public transportation, spend your third night in ⊞ **Spoleto** ⑫–⑱, from which you can jump on a train bound for ⊞ **Ancona** ⑨, where you can board a bus or a train for Pésaro and ⊞ **Urbino** ⑧. This hilltop gem retains its proud, self-contained character, almost untouched by 20th-century construction. Plan for at least half a day for reaching Urbino from Spoleto, and it's not much shorter by car, crossing the Marches border from ▦ **Gubbio** ⑦, where you might spend your third day appreciating the views, shops, and choice hotels and restaurants.

IF YOU HAVE 7 DAYS

Reserve four days for Umbria and three for the Marches. With greater flexibility you can choose how many nights you want to spend in Umbria's capital, ▦ **Perugia** ①–④, and how many in the region's smaller centers. More time in Perugia will allow you to explore the city thoroughly, including the archaeological museum, and you might take in the easy excursion to the wine village of **Torgiano** ⑤ or the ceramics town of **Deruta** ⑥. ▦ **Spoleto** ⑫–⑱ and ▦ **Assisi** ⑲–㉒ are essential stops farther afield, where you might stay for a night in each. ▦ **Gubbio** ⑦ is also worth overnighting in. From Spoleto, you can explore the quintessential hill town of **Todi** ㉓, unspoiled **Narni** ㉔, and the wine mecca **Orvieto** ㉙; they can also be seen on your way to or from Rome, only about 90 minutes away. ▦ **Urbino** ⑧ is the premier destination in the Marches. The region's biggest city, ▦ **Ancona** ⑨ has little of interest, but good facilities—sleep here if you must; otherwise head south for the infinitely preferable inland town of ▦ **Ascoli Piceno** ⑪. There is little in the way of hotels, galleries, or sophisticated shops here, but the atmosphere is marvelously quaint. On the way, or en route back, drop in at the holy sanctuary of **Loreto** ⑩, nestled in the mountains 24 km (15 mi) south of Ancona.

When to Tour Umbria and the Marches

The forested hills of Umbria and the Marches ensure beguiling colors in the fall and an explosion of greenery in spring—and fewer crowds. From a culinary standpoint, winter is best: January–April heralds the Norcia and Spoleto truffle season; October–December brings a bounty of fresh local mushrooms.

Book accommodations far in advance if you are planning to visit in June and July, when the Spoleto Festival dei Due Mondi and the Jazz Festival of Perugia take place. Sightseers and pilgrims throng the streets of Assisi year-round; the religious festivals of Christmas, Easter, the feast of St. Francis (October 4), and the Calendimaggio Festival (May 1) draw even more visitors.

PERUGIA TO GUBBIO

Umbrian Heights

Perugia is the capital of a region rich in history, art, tradition, and beautiful landscapes—those depicted by Perugino in his paintings: hills with a few sparse trees, flat land, lakes. On your way to or from Perugia, stop by Lago di Trasimeno for fresh fish. Nearby Gubbio climbs straight up a mountain, filling the bottom half with its houses and churches. Costumed runners, outsize pillars in hand, climb the rest of the way, up to the church of San Ubaldo, during Gubbio's bizarre Festa dei Ceri.

Perugia

180 km (112 mi) north of Rome, 153 km (96 mi) southeast of Florence, 455 km (284 mi) southeast of Milan.

Perugia, the largest and richest of Umbria's cities, has retained its air of elegance and venerable character. Despite rather grim fringe modern suburbs, Perugia's location on a series of hills high above the suburban plain has ensured that the medieval city remains almost completely intact. Perugia is the best well-preserved hill town of its size, and few other places in Italy illustrate better the concept of the self-contained city-state that so shaped the course of Italian history.

The best approach to the city is by train—the station is in the unlovely suburbs, but frequent buses run directly to Piazza d'Italia, the heart of the old town. If you are driving to Perugia, it is best to leave your car in one of the parking lots near the station and then take the bus or the escalator, which passes through fascinating subterranean excavations of the Roman foundations of the city, to town center.

The nerve center of the city is the broad, stately **Corso Vannucci,** a pedestrian street that runs from Piazza d'Italia to Piazza IV Novembre. As evening falls, Corso Vannucci is filled with Perugians out for their evening *passeggiata,* a pleasant predinner stroll that may include a pause for an aperitif at one of the many bars that line the street.

❶ The **Duomo** is a large and rather plain building dating from the Middle Ages but with many additions from the 15th and 16th centuries. The interior is vast and echoing, with little in the way of decoration. There are some elaborately carved choir stalls, executed by Giovanni Battista Bastone in 1520. The great relic of the church—the wedding ring of the Virgin Mary that the Perugians stole from the nearby town of Chiusi—is kept in a chapel in the left aisle. The ring is the size of a large bangle and is kept under lock (15 locks, actually) and key every day of the year except July 30, when it is exposed to view. ⊠ *Piazza IV Novembre.* ☉ *Daily 8–noon and 4–7:30.*

A large array of precious objects associated with the cathedral are on display at the **Museo del Duomo,** including vestments, vessels, manuscripts, and gold work. An early masterpiece by Luca Signorelli (circa 1450– 1523) is the altarpiece showing the Madonna with St. John the Baptist, St. Onophrius, and St. Lawrence (1484). At press time, the museum was closed for restoration. ⊠ *Piazza IV Novembre.* ▣ *2,000 lire.* ☉ *Wed.–Fri. 9–noon, Sat. 9–noon and 3:30–5:30, Sun. 3:30–5:30.*

★ ❷ The imposing **Palazzo dei Priori,** begun in the 13th century, has an unusual staircase that fans out into Piazza IV Novembre. The facade is decorated with symbols of Perugia's pride and past power: The griffin is the city's symbol; the lion denotes Perugia's allegiance to the Guelph (or papal) cause. Both figures support the heavy chains of the gates of Siena, which fell to Perugian forces in 1358.

The fourth floor of the Palazzo dei Priori contains the region's most comprehensive art gallery, the **Galleria Nazionale d'Umbria.** Enhanced by skillfully lit displays and computers allowing you to focus on details of the works and background information on them, the collection in 33 rooms includes work by native artists—most outstandingly Pinturicchio (1454–1513) and Perugino (1450–1523)—and others of the Umbrian and Tuscan schools, including Gentile da Fabriano (1370–1427), Duccio (circa 1255–1318), Fra Angelico (1387–1455), Fiorenzo di Lorenzo (1445–1525), and Piero della Francesca (1420–92). In addition to paintings, the gallery has frescoes, sculptures, and some superb examples of crucifixes from the 13th and 14th centuries; other rooms are dedicated to the city of Perugia itself, showing how the medieval city evolved. ⊠ *Corso Vannucci 19, Piazza IV Novembre.* ▣ *8,000 lire.* ☉ *Mon.–Sat. 9–7, Sun. 9–10. Closed 1st Mon. of each month.*

★ ❸ The series of elaborate rooms of **Collegio del Cambio** housed the meeting hall and chapel of the guild of bankers and money changers. The walls were frescoed from 1496 to 1500 by the most important Perugian painter of the Renaissance, Pietro Vannucci, better known as Pe-

Umbria and the Marches

Adriatic Sea

ITALY

Pesaro

Fano

Marotta

Senigallia

Numana

Ancona **9**

10 Loreto

Recanati

Macerata

Potenza

Jesi

S76

Misa

Cesano

A14

SA24

Metauro

E78

S3

Fossombrone

Pergola

LE MARCHE

Fabriano

S16

SA23

S72

SAN MARINO

Urbino **8**

E78/S73bis

S3

S1b

S3

Gubbio **7**

S298

UMBRIA

S258

S71

S73

Città di Castello

S3bis

Umbertide

Sansepolcro

S73

Tevere

S75

Lago di

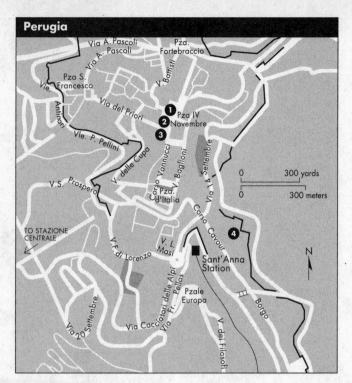

rugino. The iconography prevalent in the works includes common religious themes, like the Nativity and the Transfiguration (on the end walls),
but also figures intended to inspire the businessmen who congregated
here. On the left wall are female figures representing the virtues, beneath
them the heroes and sages of antiquity. On the right wall are the
prophets and sibyls—said to have been painted in part by Perugino's
most famous pupil, Raphael (1483–1520), whose hand, the experts say,
is most apparent in the figure of Fortitude. On one of the pilasters is a
remarkably honest self-portrait of Perugino, surmounted by a Latin inscription and contained in a faux frame. The Collegio is attached to Pal-
lazzo dei Priori, but entered via Corso Vannucci. ⊠ *Corso Vannucci
25.* ✉ *5,000 lire.* ⊗ *Mar.–Oct., Mon.–Sat. 9–12:30 and 2:30–5:30,
Sun. 9–12:30; Nov.–Feb., Tues.–Sat. 8–2, Sun. 9–12:30. During
Christmas season (Dec. 20–Jan. 6) museum follows summer timetable.*

➍ A 10-minute walk south of the center along Corso Cavour leads to the
Museo Archeologico Nazionale, containing an excellent collection of
Etruscan artifacts from throughout the region. Perugia was a flourishing
Etruscan site long before it fell under Roman domination in 310 BC.
(Other than this collection, little remains of Perugia's mysterious an-
cestors, although the **Arco di Augusto** (Arch of Augustus), in Piazza
Fortebraccio, the northern entrance to the city, is of Etruscan origin.)
⊠ *Piazza Giordano Bruno.* ✉ *4,000 lire.* ⊗ *Mon.–Sat. 9–1:30 and
2:30–7, Sun. 9–1.*

🝔 Umbria's only attraction aimed directly at the younger set is **La Città
della Domenica,** a Disney-style playground in the town of Montepulito,
just west of Perugia on the secondary road that leads to Corciano. The
500 acres of parkland contain a variety of buildings based on familiar fairy-tale themes—Snow White's House, the Witches' Wood—as
well as a reptile house, a medieval museum, an exhibit of shells from

all over the world, game rooms, and a choice of restaurants. ✉ *Località Montepulito, 8 km (5 mi) west of Perugia,* ☎ *075/5054941.* 🖃 *16,500 lire (17,500 lire Sun. and holidays).* ◷ *Apr.–mid-Sept., daily 10–7; mid-Sept.–Oct., weekends and holidays only 10–7; Nov.–mid-Mar. (aquarium and reptile house only), Sat. 2–7, Sun. 10–7.*

Dining and Lodging

\$\$ ✕ **Il Falchetto.** Here you'll find exceptional food at reasonable prices, making this Perugia's best restaurant bargain. The service is smart but relaxed in the two medieval dining rooms, with the kitchen and chef on view. The house specialty is *falchetti* (homemade gnocchi with spinach and ricotta cheese). ✉ *Via Bartolo 20,* ☎ *075/5731775. Reservations essential. AE, DC, MC, V. Closed Mon.*

\$\$ ✕ **La Rosetta.** This restaurant, in the hotel of the same name, is a peaceful, elegant spot. In the winter you dine inside under medieval vaults; in summer, in the cool courtyard. The cuisine is simple but reliable and flawlessly served. ✉ *Piazza d'Italia 19,* ☎ *075/5720841. Reservations essential. AE, DC, MC, V.*

\$\$ ✕ **La Taverna.** Medieval steps lead to this rustic restaurant on two levels, where lots of wine bottles and artful clutter heighten the tavern atmosphere. The menu features regional specialties and better-known Italian dishes. Good choices include *chitarrini* (extra-thick spaghetti), with either *funghi* (mushrooms) or tartufi (truffles), and grilled meats. ✉ *Via delle Streghe 8, next to the Teatro Pavone, off Corso Vannucci,* ☎ *075/ 5724128. Dinner reservations essential. AE, DC, MC, V. Closed Mon.*

\$\$\$\$ 🏨 **Brufani Hotel.** The two hotels (this one and the Palace Hotel Bellavista) in this 19th-century palazzo were once one. The Brufani's public rooms and first-floor guest rooms have high ceilings and are done in the grand belle epoque style. The second-floor rooms are more modern, and many on both floors have a marvelous view of the Umbrian countryside or the city. ✉ *Piazza d'Italia 12, 06121,* ☎ *075/5732541,* 𝔽𝔸𝕏 *075/ 5720210. 24 rooms. Restaurant, bar, meeting rooms. AE, DC, MC, V.*

\$\$\$ 🏨 **Locanda della Posta.** This luxuriously decorated small hotel in the
  ★ center of Perugia's historic district is a delight to behold, from its fauxmarble moldings, paneled doors, and tile bouquets in the baths to the suede-upholstered elevator and fabric-covered walls. Architectural details of the 18th-century palazzo are beautiful, and views of city rooftops from windows and balconies are soothing. Breakfast is included here. ✉ *Corso Vannucci 97, 06121,* ☎ *075/5728925,* 𝔽𝔸𝕏 *075/5732562. 39 rooms. Breakfast room, lobby lounge. AE, DC, MC, V.*

\$\$ 🏨 **Priori.** On an alley leading off the main Corso Vannucci, this unpretentious but elegant hotel has spacious and cheerful rooms with modern furnishings. There is a panoramic terrace where breakfast (included in the price) is served in summer. The hotel is difficult to find if you're driving, and a car is an encumbrance wherever you are in Perugia's historic center—but, there is a garage you can pay extra for. ✉ *Via Vermiglioli 3, 06123,* ☎ *075/5723378,* 𝔽𝔸𝕏 *075/5723213. 50 rooms. Bar, parking (fee). V.*

\$ 🏨 **Rosalba.** This is a bright and friendly choice on the fringes of Perugia's historic center. Basic rooms are scrupulously clean, and the ones at the back enjoy a view. Although somewhat out of the way, the hotel is only a matter of minutes from Corso Vannucci by virtue of the nearby escalator stop, saving a good deal of legwork. Parking is easy, too. ✉ *Via del Circo 7, 06121,* ☎ *075/5728285. 11 rooms. No credit cards.*

Nightlife and the Arts

Summer sees two music festivals in Perugia: the **Jazz Festival of Umbria** (July) and the **Festival of Sacred Music** (September). Event and ticket information for both festivals can be obtained, year-round, from the Perugia Tourist Office (✉ Piazza IV Novembre 3, ☎ 075/5736458).

A true devotee of Umbrian music should consider the lengthy trek to the **Chamber Music Festival of Umbria,** which is held every August and September in the town of Città di Castello, about 80 km (49½ mi) north of Perugia on the S3bis. For information, contact the tourist office (⌧ Via R. di Cesare 2/b, ☎ 075/8554817).

Shopping

Perugia is a well-to-do town, and judging by the array of expensive shops on **Corso Vannucci,** the Perugians are not afraid to part with their money. The main streets of the town are lined with clothing shops selling the best-known Italian designers, in luxurious shops such as Gucci, Ferragamo, Armani, and Fendi.

The best and most typical thing to buy in Perugia is, of course, some of the famous and delicious **Perugina chocolate.** *Cioccolato al latte* (milk chocolate) and *fondente* (dark chocolate) set in tiny jewel-like boxes or in giant gift boxes the size of serving trays are sold all over town. The best-known chocolates made by Perugina are the round chocolate- and hazelnut-filled candies called Baci (kisses), which come wrapped in silver paper and, like fortune cookies, contain romantic sentiments or sayings.

Torgiano

❺ *15 km (9 mi) southeast of Perugia.*

Wine aficionados are certain to want to visit this home to the winery **Cantina Lungarotti,** best known for delicious Rubesco Lungarotti, San Giorgio, and chardonnay. ⌧ *Torgiano 06089,* ☎ *075/9880348.* ☉ *Tours Mon.–Fri., by appointment only.*

The fascinating **Museo del Vino** (Wine Museum) has a large collection of ancient wine vessels, presses, documents, and tools that tell the story of viticulture in Umbria and beyond. The museum traces the history of wine in all its uses—for drinking at the table, as medicine, and in mythology. At the **Osteria del Museo** (☎ ℻ 075/9880069), you can taste and buy Lungarotti's award-winning reds or whites. ⌧ *Corso Vittorio Emanuele 11,* ☎ *075/9880200.* 🗐 *5,000 lire.* ☉ *Apr.–Sept., daily 9–1 and 3–7; Oct.–Mar., daily 9–1 and 3–6.*

Deruta

❻ *7 km (4 mi) south of Torgiano, 20 km (12 mi) southeast of Perugia.*

Deruta has been distinguished since the 16th century for its ceramics. Notable in the medieval hill town are the 14th century **Church of San Francesco** and the **Palazzo Comunale**—but its main attraction is the magnificent ceramics collection in the **Museo delle Ceramiche.** ⌧ *Piazza dei Consoli 1,* ☎ *075/9711000.* 🗐 *5,000 lire.* ☉ *July–Sept., Tues.–Sun. 10–1 and 4–7; Mar. 15–June and Oct. 1–15, Tues.–Sun. 10–1 and 3–6.*

Lodging

$$$ 🏨 **Nel Castello.** This little turretted castle, which the owner says dates from the 5th century, has nine guest rooms and a good Umbrian restaurant. Atop a hill 5 km (3 mi) outside Deruta, it is surrounded by grass and trees, and is a quiet, peaceful place to stay. The restaurant serves local specialties like boar meat and dishes with truffles. ⌧ *Castelleone, Deruta, 06503,* ☎ *075/9711302. 9 rooms. Restaurant, pool. AE, DC, MC, V.*

Shopping

CERAMICS

There are about 70 ceramics workshops and shops in and around this small town. Start your browsing in the central Piazza dei Consoli, where you can find a nice selection at **Maioliche Cintia** (⌧ Piazza dei Consoli, ☎ 075/9711255), specializing in reproductions of antique Deruta ceramics, **Maioliche Fanny** (✉ Piazza dei Consoli, ☎ 075/9711064), **Ceramiche Michela Cavallini** (✉ Piazza dei Consoli 2, ☎ 075/9711772), **Ceramiche El Frate** (✉ Piazza dei Consoli 29, and ☎ 075/9711435). If you want to visit a workshop, try **Fabbrica Maioliche Tradizionali** (✉ Via Tiberina Nord 37, ☎ 075/9711220), or ask for a suggestion at the tourist information office in Piazza dei Consoli 4.

Gubbio

❼ *40 km (25 mi) northeast of Perugia.*

There is something otherworldly about this small jewel of a medieval town tucked away in a rugged, mountainous corner of Umbria. Even at the height of summer, the cool serenity of the City of Silence's streets remain intact. The town is perched on the slopes of Monte Ingino, and the streets are dramatically steep. Parking in the central Piazza dei Quaranta Martiri, named for 40 hostages murdered by the Nazis in 1944, is easy and secure, and it is wise to leave your car there and explore the narrow streets on foot.

★ The striking Piazza Grande is dominated by the **Palazzo dei Consoli** (Palace of the Consuls), the 14th-century meeting place of the parliament of Gubbio. The palace is attributed to a local architect known as Gattapone, a man still much admired by today's residents—every other hotel, restaurant, and bar has been named after him—though studies have suggested that the palazzo was in fact the work of another architect, Angelo da Orvieto.

The Palazzo dei Consoli houses a small museum, famous chiefly for the **Tavole Eugubine** (Gubbio Tablets), seven bronze tablets written in the ancient Umbrian language, employing Etruscan and Latin characters, and providing the best key to understanding this obscure tongue. Also in the museum are a captivating miscellany of coins, medieval arms, paintings, and majolica and earthenware pots, not to mention the exhilarating views over Gubbio's roofscape and beyond from the lofty loggia. For a few days at the beginning of May, the palace also displays the famous *ceri,* the ceremonial pillars at the center of Gubbio's annual festivities (☞ Nightlife and the Arts, *below*). ✉ *Piazza Grande.* ᠊ *5,000 lire.* ◷ *Apr.–July and Sept., daily 10–1:30 and 3–6; Aug., daily 10–1:30 and 3–7; Oct.–Mar., daily 10–1 and 2–5.*

The **Duomo,** on a narrow street on the highest tier of the town, dates from the 13th century, with some Baroque additions—in particular, a lavishly decorated bishop's chapel. ✉ *Via Ducale.* ◷ *Daily 8–12:45 and 3–7:30.*

The **Palazzo Ducale** (Ducal Palace) is a scaled-down copy of the Palazzo Ducale in Urbino (Gubbio was once the possession of that city's ruling family, the Montefeltro). Gubbio's palazzo contains a small **museum** and a **courtyard.** There are magnificent views from some of the public rooms. ✉ *Via Ducale.* ᠊ *4,000 lire.* ◷ *Mon.–Sat. 9–1:30 and 2:30–7, Sun. 9–1:30.*

Just outside the city walls at the eastern end of town (follow Corso Garibaldi or Via XX Settembre to the end), is a **funicular** that provides a bracing ride to the top of Monte Ingino. Aside from the spectacular views, the mountain has the basilica of **Sant'Ubaldo,** repository of Gubbio's famous ceri, three 16-ft-high poles crowned with statues of Sts. Ubaldo, George, and Anthony. The pillars are transported to the Palazzo dei Consoli on the first Sunday of May to honor the Festival of the Ceri (☞ Nightlife and the Arts, *below*). ✉ *Top of Monte Ingino.*

Dining and Lodging

$$$ ✕ **Taverna del Lupo.** The "Tavern of the Wolf" is one of the city's best, and one of the largest—it seats 200 people and can still get a bit hectic during the high season. Lasagna made in the Gubbian fashion, with ham and truffles, is the best pasta. You'll also find excellent desserts and an extensive wine list. ✉ *Via G. Ansidei 21,* ☎ *075/9274368. Reservations essential. AE, DC, MC, V. Closed Mon. Oct.–July.*

$$ ✕ **Bosone Garden.** This restaurant is in the former stables (note the stone arches inside) below the palace that houses the Hotel Bosone (☞ *below*), and has a summer garden that seats 200. It features dishes laced with truffles in season: two-mushroom salad with truffles and risotto *alla porcina*(with porcini mushrooms, sausage, and truffles). Another savory treat is the leg of pork. ✉ *Via XX Settembre 22,* ☎ *075/ 9220688. AE, DC, MC, V. Closed Jan.*

$$ ✕ **Grotta dell'Angelo.** This rustic trattoria is in the lower part of the old town, near the main square and tourist information office. The menu features simple local specialties, including *capocollo* (type of salami), strangozzi pasta, and lasagna *tartufate* (with truffles). A few tables welcome outdoor dining. Inexpensive guest rooms are also available. ✉ *Via Gioia 47,* ☎ *075/9273438. Reservations essential. AE, DC, MC, V. Closed Tues. and Jan. 7–Feb. 7.*

$$ 🏨 **Hotel Bosone.** Occupying the old central Palazzo Raffaelli, this hotel in a former palace has preserved many original frescoes in the guest rooms. The suites furnished with period detail are particularly lavish. ✉ *Via XX Settembre 22, 06024,* ☎ *075/9220688,* FAX *075/ 9220552. 30 rooms. Bar. AE, DC, MC, V. Closed Jan.*

$$ 🏨 **Hotel Gattapone.** Right in town center is this hotel with wonderful views of the sea of rooftops. It is casual and family run, with good-size, modern, comfortable rooms, some with well-preserved timber-raftered ceilings. ✉ *Via Ansidei 6, 06024,* ☎ *075/9272489,* FAX *075/ 9271269. 18 rooms. AE, DC, MC, V. Closed Jan.*

Nightlife and the Arts

Every May 15, teams of Gubbio's young men dressed in medieval costumes race up the steep slopes to the basilica of Sant'Ubaldo carrying its heavy, fabled pillars to celebrate the **Festa dei Ceri.** This festival, enacted faithfully every year since 1151, is to thank the town's patron saints for their assistance in a miraculous Gubbian victory over a league of 11 other towns.

Outdoor Activities and Sports

☙ Among the region's other historical pageants, Gubbio's costumed **Palio della Balestra** (crossbow tournament) takes place on the last Sunday in May; contact the Gubbio tourist office (✉ Piazza Oderisi 6, ☎ 075/ 9220693) for details.

THE MARCHES

Mirror to the Renaissance

An excursion from Umbria into the region of the Marches is recommended if you want to get off the beaten track and see a part of Italy rarely visited by foreigners. Not as wealthy as Tuscany or Umbria, the Marches has a diverse landscape of mountains and beaches, and marvelous views. Like its neighbors to the west, Le Marche's patchwork of rolling hills is stitched with grapevines and olive trees, bearing delicious wine and olive oil.

Traveling in the Marches is not as easy as in Umbria or Tuscany. Beyond the narrow coastal plain and away from major towns, the roads are steep and twisting. There's an efficient bus service from the coastal town of Pésaro to Urbino, the other principal tourist city of the region. Train travel in the region is slow, and stops are limited, although you can reach Ascoli Piceno by rail.

Urbino

8 *170 km (106 mi) northeast of Perugia, 190 km (119 mi) east of Florence, 30 km (19 mi) southwest of Pésaro.*

Majestic Urbino, atop a steep hill with a skyline of towers and domes, is something of a surprise to come upon—it's oddly remote—and it is even stranger to reflect that it was once a center of learning and culture almost without rival in western Europe. The town looks much as it did in the glory days of the 15th century, a cluster of warm brick and pale stone buildings, all topped with russet-color tiled roofs. The focal point is the immense and beautiful Palazzo Ducale.

The tradition of learning in Urbino continues to this day. The city is the home of a small but prestigious Università di Urbino—one of the oldest in the world—and during school term the streets are filled with lively students. It is very much a college town, with the usual array of bookshops, record stores, bars, and coffeehouses. During the summer, the Italian student population is replaced by foreigners who come to study Italian language and arts at several prestigious private fine-arts academies.

Urbino's fame rests on the reputation of three of its native sons: Duke Federigo da Montefeltro (1422–82), the enlightened warrior-patron who built the Palazzo Ducale; Raphael, one of the most influential painters in history and an embodiment of the spirit of the Renaissance; and the architect Donato Bramante (1444–1514), who translated the philosophy of the Renaissance into buildings of grace and beauty. Why three of the greatest men of the age should have been born within a generation of one another in this remote town has never been explained. Oddly enough, there is little work by either Bramante or Raphael in the city, but the duke's influence can still be felt strongly, even now, some 500 years after his death.

★ The **Palazzo Ducale** holds the place of honor in the city, and in no other palace of its era are the principles of the Renaissance stated quite so clearly. If the Renaissance was, in ideal form, a celebration of the nobility of man and his works, of the light and purity of the soul, then there is no place in Italy, the birthplace of the Renaissance, where these tenets are better illustrated. From the moment you enter the peaceful courtyard, you know that you are in a place of grace and beauty, the harmony of the building reflecting the high ideals of the artists who built it.

Today the palace houses the **Galleria Nazionale delle Marche** (National Museum of the Marches), with a superb collection of paintings, sculpture, and other objets d'art, well arranged and properly lit. Some works were originally the possessions of the Montefeltro family, others brought to the museum from churches and palaces throughout the region. Perhaps the most famous is Piero della Francesca's enigmatic work, long known as *The Flagellation of Christ*. Much has been written about this painting, and few experts agree on its meaning. Legend had it that the three figures in the foreground represented a murdered member of the Montefeltro family (the barefoot young man) and his two murderers. Others claimed the painting was a heavily veiled criticism of certain parts of Christian Europe—the iconography is obscure and the history extremely complicated. However, Sir John Pope-Hennessy—the preeminent scholar of Italian Renaissance art—has proved that it represents the arcane subject of the Vision of St. Lawrence. All the experts have always agreed that the painting is one of Piero della Francesca's masterpieces. Piero himself thought so. It is one of the few works he signed (on the lowest step supporting the throne).

Other masterworks in the collection are Paolo Uccello's *Profanation of the Host,* Piero della Francesca's *Madonna of Senigallia,* and Titian's *Resurrection* and *Last Supper.* Duke Federigo's study is an astonishingly elaborate but tiny room decorated with inlaid wood, said to be the work of Botticelli. ⊠ *Piazza Duca Federico,* ☎ *0722/2760.* 🎫 *8,000 lire.* ⊙ *Mon.–Sat. 9–7, Sun. 9–1.*

The **Casa di Raffaello** (House of Raphael) really is the house in which he was born and where he took his first steps in painting, under the direction of his artist father. There is some debate about the fresco of the Madonna here; some say it is by Raphael, others attribute it to the father—with Raphael's mother and the young painter himself standing in as models for the Madonna and Child. ⊠ *Via Raffaello,* ☎ *0722/ 320105.* 🎫 *5,000 lire.* ⊙ *Mar.–Sept., Mon.–Sat. 9–1 and 3–7, Sun. 9–1; Oct.–Jan., Thurs.–Sat. and Mon.–Tues. 9–2, Sun. 10–10.*

Dining and Lodging

$$ ✕ **La Vecchia Fornarina.** These two small rooms just down from Urbino's central Piazza della Repubblica are often filled to capacity. The trattoria specializes in meaty country fare, such as rabbit and *vitello alle noci* (veal cooked with walnuts) or *ai porcini* (with mushrooms). There is also a good range of pasta dishes. ⊠ *Via Mazzini 14,* ☎ *0722/ 320007. Reservations essential. AE, DC, MC, V.*

$ 🏨 **Hotel San Giovanni.** This hotel is in the old town and is housed in a renovated medieval building. The rooms are basic, clean, and comfortable—with a wonderful view from Nos. 18–21 and 24–31—and there is a handy restaurant-pizzeria below. ⊠ *Via Barocci 13, 61029,* ☎ *0722/2827. 33 rooms, 21 with shower. No credit cards. Closed July and Christmas wk.*

Ancona

❾ *87 km (54 mi) southeast of Urbino, 139 km (87 mi) northeast of Perugia, 262 km (164 mi) east of Florence.*

Ancona was probably once a lovely city. It is set on an elbow-shape bluff (hence its name; *ankon* is Greek for "elbow") that juts out into the Adriatic. But Ancona was the object of serious aerial bombing during World War II—it was, and is, an important port city—and was reduced to rubble. The city has been rebuilt in the unfortunate postwar poured-concrete style, practical and inexpensive but not aesthetically pleasing. Unless you are taking a ferry to Venice, there is little reason to visit the city—with a few exceptions. Once in a while, glimpses of old architectural detail are redeeming, as seen in the **Duomo San Ciriaco** and the **Loggia dei Mercanti.** In addition, Ancona can be the base for an excursion to Loreto or to Ascoli Piceno, farther south along the Adriatic coast.

Dining and Lodging

$$ ✕ **La Moretta.** This family-run trattoria is on the central Piazza del Plebiscito. In summer there is dining outside in the square, which has a fine view of the Baroque church of San Domenico. Among the specialties here are *stoccafisso all'Anconetana* (stockfish baked with capers, anchovies, potatoes, and tomatoes) and the famous brodetto fish stew. ⊠ *Piazza del Plebiscito 52,* ☎ *071/202317. Reservations essential. AE, DC, MC, V. Closed Sun.*

$$$ ⊞ **Grand Hotel Palace.** In town center, near the entrance to the port of Ancona, and widely held to be the best in town, this is an old-fashioned place well run by a courteous staff. ⊠ *Lungomare Vanvitelli 24, 60100,* ☎ *071/201813,* ℻ *071/2074832. 41 rooms. Bar, free parking. AE, DC, MC, V.*

Loreto

⑩ *31 km (19 mi) south of Ancona.*

★ Loreto is famous for one of the best-loved shrines in the world, that of the **Santuario della Santa Casa** (House of the Virgin Mary), within the **Basilica**. The legend is that angels moved the house from Nazareth, where the Virgin was living at the time of the Annunciation, to this hilltop in 1295. The reason for this sudden and divinely inspired move was that Nazareth had fallen into the hands of Muslim invaders, not suitable landlords, the angelic hosts felt. More recently, following archaeological excavations made at the behest of the Church, evidence has come to light proving that the house did once stand elsewhere and was brought to the hilltop by human means around the time the angels are said to have done the job.

The house itself consists of three rough stone walls contained within an elaborate marble tabernacle; built around this centerpiece is the giant basilica of the Holy House, which dominates the town. Millions of visitors come to the site every year (particularly at Easter and on the Feast of the Holy House, December 10), and the little town of Loreto can become uncomfortably crowded with pilgrims. Many great Italian architects, including Bramante, Antonio Giamberti da Sangallo (the Younger, 1483–1546), Giuliano da Sangallo (circa 1445–1516), and Sansovino (1467–1529), contributed to the design of the basilica. The basilica was begun in Gothic style in 1468 and continued in Renaissance style through the late Renaissance. The bell tower is by Luigi Vanvitelli (1700–73). Inside the church are a great many mediocre 19th- and 20th-century paintings but also some fine works by Renaissance masters such as Luca Signorelli and Melozzo da Forlì. ⊠ *Piazza della Maddona.* ☉ *June–Sept., daily 8–8; Oct.–May, daily 6 AM–7 PM.*

If you're a nervous air traveler you can take comfort in the fact that the Holy Virgin of Loreto is the patroness of air travelers and that Pope John Paul II has composed a prayer for a safe flight—available in the church in a half dozen languages.

Ascoli Piceno

⑪ *105 km (65 mi) south of Ancona.*

Ascoli Piceno is not a hill town; rather, it sits in a valley ringed by steep hills and cut by the fast-racing Tronto River. The town is almost unique in Italy, in that it seems to have its traffic problems—in the historic center, at any rate—pretty much under control; you can drive *around* the picturesque part of the city, but driving *through* it is most difficult. This feature makes Ascoli Piceno one of the most pleasant large towns in the country for exploring on foot. True, there is traffic, but you are not constantly assaulted by jams, noise, and exhaust fumes the way you are in other Italian cities.

★ The heart of the town is the majestic **Piazza del Popolo,** dominated by the Gothic church of **San Francesco** and the **Palazzo del Popolo,** a 13th-century town hall that contains a graceful Renaissance courtyard. The square itself functions as the living room of the entire city. At dusk each evening the piazza is packed with people strolling and exchanging news and gossip—the sweetly antiquated ritual called the passeggiata, done all over the country.

☾ Ascoli Piceno's **Giostra della Quintana** (Joust of the Quintana) takes place on the first Sunday in August. Children should love this medieval-style joust and the richly caparisoned processions that wind through the streets of the old town. Contact Ascoli's tourist office (⊠ Piazza del Popolo, ☎ 0736/257288) for details.

Dining and Lodging

$$ ✕ **Ristorante Tornasacco.** In this family-run restaurant with modern
★   decor, you can sample Ascoli's specialties, like olives ascolane (here, stuffed with minced meat), as well as *maccheroncini alla contadina* (a homemade pasta in a thick meat sauce). ⊠ *Piazza del Popolo 36,* ☎ *0736/254151. AE, DC, MC, V. Closed Fri. and July 1–15.*

$ ☷ **Piceno.** This modest hostelry is one of the few lodgings in the historic center. It offers clean, basic amenities—no frills at all here. The staff is helpful and courteous, and the setting is perfect. ⊠ *Via Minucia 10,* ☎ *0736/252553. 32 rooms, 14 without bath. No credit cards. Closed Jan.*

En Route The 175-km (108-mi) drive from Ascoli Piceno to Spoleto takes you out of the Marches and back into Umbria. The route—S4 southwest to Rieti, then S79 north to Terni, then S3 into Spoleto—is roundabout but vastly preferable to a series of winding mountain roads that connect Ascoli Piceno with Umbria.

SPOLETO

"Quaint" may be an overused term, but it is the most appropriate word to describe this city 50 km (30 mi) south of Perugia, still enclosed by stout medieval walls. From the churches set among silvery olive groves on the outskirts of town to the imposing fortress at it's peak, Spoleto radiates grandeur and hushed charm. You can simply delight in the enchanting mazes of twisting streets and cobbled stairways, and wonderful peace and quiet.

Quiet, that is, except when Spoleto is hosting the Festival dei Due Mondi (Festival of Two Worlds) (☞ Nightlife and the Arts, *below*), an arts festival held every year from mid-June to mid-July. During that month the sleepy town is swamped with visitors who come to see world-class plays and operas, to hear concerts, and to see extensive exhibitions of paintings and sculpture. It is unwise to arrive during this period without confirmed hotel reservations.

Exploring Spoleto

Like most towns made up of narrow, winding streets, Spoleto is best explored on foot. Several pedestrian walkways cut down the hill, crossing the Corso Mazzini, which turns up the hill. Parking in Spoleto is always difficult; park outside the walls in Piazza della Vittoria.

A Good Walk

Spoleto is small, and its noteworthy sites are clustered in the upper part of town; allow a full day for a thorough exploration. Begin at Piazza del Duomo, and visit the **Duomo** ⑫, which stands against a backdrop of hill and sky with La Rocca towering overhead. Cross the piazza and go up the stairs to Via Saffi and the church of **Sant'Eufemia** ⑬ and its museum. If you are short on time, skip Sant'Eufemia and head straight up to **La Rocca** ⑭ and **Ponte delle Torri** ⑮. Retrace your steps back to the picturesque Via Fontesecca (Sant'Eufemia), with its tempting shops selling local pottery and other handicrafts; it descends to the **Pinacoteca** ⑯ and **Casa Romana.** Have a visit or continue on to Piazza del Mercato, built on the site of the Roman Forum and home to Spoleto's open-air produce market, open daily Monday–Saturday 8–1:30. At the narrow end of Piazza del Mercato is the **Arco di Druso** ⑰. Turn right on Via Brignone and cross Piazza della Libertà to Via Sant'Agata, which leads to the **Teatro Romano** ⑱ and **Museo Archeologico.**

TIMING

Spoleto is not the most demanding town in terms of sites. A day will allow you to see all of the highlights, leaving time for leisurely strolls and a walk to the Ponte delle Torri.

Sights to See

⑰ **Arco di Druso** (Arch of Drusus). This structure was built in the 1st century AD by the Senate of Spoleto to honor the Roman general Drusus (circa 13 BC–AD 23), son of the emperor Tiberius. It once marked the entrance to the Foro Romano (Roman Forum). ⊠ *Piazza del Mercato.*

⑫ **Duomo.** The church's rather dour 12th-century Romanesque facade is lightened up by the addition of a Renaissance loggia and eight rose windows. The contrast demonstrates the difference in style and philosophy of the two eras: The earlier was strong and ungiving, the later, human and open-minded.

The Duomo's interior holds the best art in town, most notably the immaculately restored frescoes in the apse by Fra Filippo Lippi (1406–69), showing the *Annunciation,* the *Nativity,* and the *Death of Mary,* with a marvelous *Coronation of the Virgin* adorning the dome; be ready with a 500-lire coin to illuminate the masterpiece. The Florentine artist died shortly after completing the work, and his tomb—designed by his son, Filippino Lippi (1457–1504)—lies in the church's right transept. Another fresco cycle, including work by Pinturicchio, can be seen in the **Cappella Eroli** off the right aisle. ⊠ *Piazza Duomo.* ⊙ *Mar.–Oct., daily 8–1 and 3–6:30; Nov.–Feb., 3–5:30.*

⑭ **La Rocca.** Built in 1359–63 by the Gubbio-born architect Gattapone, the fortress dominates Spoleto. Until recently it served as a high-security prison, but at press time it was undergoing restoration and was to open in 1999 as a museum about medieval Spoleto, art restoration center, and exhibition space. Until it opens, you can admire the formidable exterior from the road that circles around it. ⊠ *Take Via Saffi (off Piazza del Duomo) to Via del Ponte.*

⑯ **Pinacoteca.** The town picture gallery has a small collection of works from the 12th to the 18th centuries. Admission to the 1st-century-AD Casa Romana, around the corner, is included on the same ticket. *Pinacoteca:* ⊠ *Palazzo del Municipio, Via Aurelio Saffi. Casa Romana:* ⊠ *Palazzo del Municipio, Via Visiale 9. Both:* ☎ *0743/2181.* ⌑ *5,000 lire.* ⊙ *Tues.–Sun. 10–1 and 3–6.*

⑮ **Ponte delle Torri.** La Rocca was built to protect the town's most famous monument, the massive Bridge of the Towers. It was built in the 14th century by Gattapone over the foundations of a Roman-era aqueduct, and stands 262 ft above the gorge at its highest point—taller than the dome of St. Peter's in Rome. The bridge is open to pedestrians, and a walk over it affords marvelous views. ⊠ *Via del Ponte.*

⑬ **Sant'Eufemia.** Set in the courtyard of the archbishop's palace, this ancient, austere church dates from the 11th century. Its most interesting feature is the gallery above the nave where female worshipers were required to sit—a holdover from the Eastern Church—one of the few such galleries in this part of Italy. There is also a **Museo Diocesano** attached to the church containing some important paintings, including a Madonna by Fra Filippo Lippi. ✉ *Via Saffi, between Piazza del Duomo and Piazza del Mercato.* 🎫 *Church 3,000 lire; museum 4,000 lire; both 5,000 lire.* ☉ *Apr.–Oct., daily 10–12:30 and 3:30–7; Nov.–Mar., daily 2:30–6.*

⑱ **Teatro Romano.** The small but well-preserved Roman Theater is used in summer for performances of Spoleto's arts festival. It was the site of one of the town's most macabre incidents. During the Middle Ages, Spoleto took the side of the Holy Roman Emperor in the interminable struggle between Guelph (papal) and Ghibelline (imperial) factions over the question of who would control central and northern Italy. Four hundred of the pope's supporters were massacred in the theater, and their bodies were burned in an enormous pyre. The Guelphs were triumphant in the end and Spoleto was incorporated into the states of the Church in 1354. Through a door in the west portico, the **Museo Archeologico** displays assorted artifacts and the *Lex Spoletina* (Spoleto Law) tablets dating from 315 BC. This ancient legal document prohibited the destruction of the Bosco Sacro (Sacred Forest), just south of town on Monteluce, a pagan prayer site later frequented by St. Francis. ✉ *At the southern end of Corso Mazzini,* ☎ *0743/223277.* 🎫 *4,000 lire.* ☉ *Mon.–Sat. 9–1:30 and 2:30–7, Sun 9–1.*

OFF THE
BEATEN PATH

SAN SALVATORE – You may already have seen a lot of old churches in Italy, but few are as old as this one. It needed renovation in the 9th century—by that time it was already 500 years old. Nestled under cypresses and surrounded by Spoleto's cemetery, it's quiet, cool, and peaceful. The church was built by Eastern monks in the 4th century, and little has been added (or removed) since its renovation. San Salvatore has an air of timelessness and antiquity rarely found in churches so close to major towns. ✉ *Via della Basilica di San Salvatore, just out of town on the Via Flaminia.* ☉ *Nov.–Feb., daily 7–5; Mar.–Apr. and Sept.–Oct., daily 7–6; May–Aug., daily 7–7.*

Dining and Lodging

$$ ✕ **Il Pentagramma.** Just off the central Piazza della Libertà, this modern restaurant features such local dishes as fresh ravioli *alle noci* (walnut-stuffed ravioli with butter and sage) and lamb in a truffle sauce. ⊠ *Via Martani 4,* ☎ *0743/223141. Reservations essential during the festival and on weekends. DC, MC, V. Closed Mon.*

$$ ✕ **Il Tartufo.** Spoleto's most famous restaurant has a smart modern dining room on the second floor and a rustic dining room downstairs—both of which incorporate the ruins of a Roman villa. The traditional cooking is spiced up in summer to appeal to the cosmopolitan crowd that is attending (or performing in) the Festival dei Due Mondi. As its name indicates, the restaurant specializes in dishes prepared with truffles, though there is a second menu from which you can choose items not perfumed with this expensive delicacy. ⊠ *Piazza Garibaldi 24,* ☎ *0743/40236. Reservations essential. AE, DC, MC, V. Closed Wed. and mid-July–1st wk in Aug.*

$$ ✕ **Trattoria Panciolle.** In the heart of Spoleto's medieval quarter, this restaurant has one of the most romantic settings you could wish for. Dining outside in summer is a welcome respite, in a small piazza filled with lemon trees. Specialties include strangozzi pasta with mushroom sauce and *agnello scottadito* (grilled lamb chops). Seven guest rooms are also available here. ⊠ *Via del Duomo 3,* ☎ *0743/45598. Reservations essential. AE, MC, V. Closed Wed.*

$$$ 🏨 **Dei Duchi.** This excellent, well-run hotel is a favorite among performers in the Festival dei Due Mondi. It's in town center, near the Roman amphitheater. Some rooms have fine views of the city. ⊠ *Viale Matteotti 4, 06049,* ☎ *0743/44541, FAX 0743/44543. 49 rooms. Restaurant, bar, meeting rooms, free parking. AE, DC, MC, V.*

$$$ 🏨 **Hotel Gattapone.** The tiny four-star Hotel Gattapone at the top of the old town, near the Ponte delle Torri, has wonderful views of the ancient bridge and the wooded slopes of Monteluco. The rooms are modern and tastefully decorated. ⊠ *Via del Ponte 6, 06049,* ☎ *0743/223447, FAX 0743/223448. 16 rooms. Bar. AE, DC, MC, V.*

$$ 🏨 **Nuovo Clitunno.** A renovated 18th-century building houses this pleasant hotel, a five-minute walk from the town center. Bedrooms and public rooms, some with lovely timber-beamed ceilings, have a mixture of period as well as less characterful modern furniture. ⊠ *Piazza Sordini 6, 06049,* ☎ *0743/223340, FAX 0743/222663. 38 rooms. Restaurant, bar. AE, DC, MC, V.*

Nightlife and the Arts

The **Festival dei Due Mondi** (Festival of Two Worlds) in Spoleto (mid-June–mid-July) features accomplished artists in all branches of the arts—particularly music, opera, and theater—and draws thousands of visitors from all over the world. Tickets for all performances should be ordered in advance from the festival's box office (⊠ Piazza Duomo 9, ☎ 0743/44325), which has full program information starting in April.

OFF THE **VALNERINA –** This is the name of the area southeast of Spoleto, and it is
BEATEN PATH the most beautiful of central Italy's many well-kept secrets. The roads that
serve the rugged landscape are poor, but a drive through the region,
even with all those time-consuming twists and turns, will be worth it to
see forgotten medieval villages and dramatic mountain scenery.

CASCATA DEL MARMORE – The first stop should be these waterfalls, said
to be the highest in Europe. You'll find them a few kilometers east of
Terni, on the road to Lake Piediluco and Rieti. The waters are diverted
on weekdays to provide hydroelectric power for the town of Terni, so

check with the tourist office (✉ Viale C. Battisti 7/a, ☎ 0744/423047) in Terni before heading there. On summer evenings, when the falls are in full spate, the cascading water is floodlit.

SAN PIETRO IN VALLE – Close to the picturesque town of Ferentillo (northeast of Terni on S209) is the outstanding 8th-century abbey of San Pietro, with fine frescoes in the church nave and a peaceful cloister. As a bonus, one of the abbey outbuildings houses a fine restaurant with moderate prices.

NORCIA – East of Spoleto in the Valnerina is this town, most famous for Umbrian food specialties. It is also the birthplace of St. Benedict. Norcia exports truffles to France and hosts a truffle festival, Mostra Internazionale del Tartufo Nero di Norcia, every November.

ASSISI

The legacy of St. Francis, founder of the Franciscan monastic order, pervades the rose-color hills of Assisi, 47 km (30 mi) north of Spoleto and 25 km (16 mi) east of Perugia. Each year, several million pilgrims come here to pay homage to the man who made God accessible to commoners. But not even the steadily massive flow of visitors to this town with just 3,000 residents can spoil the singular beauty of Italy's most significant religious center. The hill on which Assisi sits rises dramatically from the flat plain, and the town is dominated at the top of the mount by a medieval castle; on the lower slopes of the hill is the massive Basilica di San Francesco, rising majestically on graceful arched supports. From a distance, St. Francis's birthplace looks—to use an evocative phrase of travel essayist James Reynolds—"calm, white, pure as the fresh-washed wool from the Pascal Lamb."

A series of severe earthquakes in late September and October 1997 centered in nearby Foligno did devastating damage to Assisi and many towns in Umbria and the Marche. Particularly hard hit was the Basilica di San Francesco; frescoes by Giotto (1266–1337), widely held to be masterpieces of Western art, were destroyed when the vault of the upper basilica collapsed. Since then Assisi has risen again. With the exception of the upper basilica, at press time the other sites in town have been reopened.

St. Francis was born here in 1181, the son of a well-to-do merchant. After a sinful youth, he gave up the pleasures of the flesh and adopted a life of austerity. His mystical approach to poverty, asceticism, and the beauty of man and nature struck a responsive chord in the medieval mind, and he quickly attracted a vast number of followers. The compassion and humility of this humble and unassuming man brought him great love and veneration in his own lifetime. Without actively seeking power, as did many clerics of his day, he amassed great influence and political power, changing the history of the Catholic Church. He was the first person to receive the stigmata (wounds in his hands, feet, and side corresponding to the torments of Christ on the cross), injuries that caused him great pain and suffering, which he bore with characteristic patience. Today the Franciscans are the largest of all the Catholic orders. And among the mass of clergy at Assisi, you can identify the saint's followers by their simple, coarse brown habits bound by sashes of knotted rope.

Exploring Assisi

The train station is 4 km (2½ mi) from town, with bus service about every half hour. The walled town is closed to outside traffic, so cars must be left in the parking lots at Porta San Pietro, near Porta Nuova or beneath Piazza Matteotti. Frequent city buses run between the parking lots and the center of town. For up-to-date details about what is closed due to earthquake damage, call the tourist office (☞ Visitor Information *in* Umbria and the Marches A to Z, *below*).

A Good Walk

Much of your visit to Assisi will likely be spent in churches and walking through the quiet streets. You'll want to set aside a good portion of your time for the **Basilica di San Francesco** ⑲, even if only the lower basilica is open. Via San Francesco leads back to Piazza del Comune and its Pinacoteca, Museo Civico, and the **Tempio di Minerva** ⑳. From the piazza, Via di San Rufino leads to **San Rufino** ㉑, which serves as Assisi's Duomo. Double back to the piazza and take Corso Mazzini to **Santa Chiara** ㉒, then continue through the Porta Nuova to the church of **San Damiano,** a 1-km (½-mi) walk a few minutes outside the walls. Also of interest outside the walls are the **Eremo delle Carceri,** east of the center along Via Santuario delle Carceri, and the church of **Santa Maria degli Angeli,** near the train station.

TIMING

Devote a half day or good part of the day for this walk. After seeing the Basilica di San Francesco, you can stroll along the length of town, stopping in at churches and shops.

Sights to See

★ ⑲ **Basilica di San Francesco.** Begun just a few years after the death of St. Francis, one wonders what he would have made of a church of such size, wealth, and grandeur—the opposite of all he preached and believed. His coffin, unearthed from its secret hiding place in 1818, is on display in the crypt below the lower church and is a place of piety. The basilica is not one church but two huge structures built one over the other. The lower church is dim and full of candlelit shadows, whereas the upper church is bright and airy. Both are magnificently decorated artistic treasure houses, however, the upper basilica suffered extensively damage in the wake of the 1997 earthquakes. Only the lower basilica is open to the public.

The first chapel in the **lower church** on the left of the nave was decorated by the Sienese master Simone Martini (1284–1344). Frescoed in 1322–26, the paintings show the life of St. Martin—the sharing of his cloak with the poor man, the saint's knighthood, and his death. There is some dispute about the paintings in the third chapel on the right. Experts have argued for years as to their authorship, with many saying that they were done by Giotto. The paintings depict the life of St. Mary Magdalen. There is a similar dispute about the works above the high altar—some say they are by Giotto; others claim them for an anonymous pupil. They depict the marriage of St. Francis to poverty, chastity, and obedience.

In the right transept are frescoes by Cimabue (circa 1240–1302), a Madonna and saints, one of them St. Francis himself. In the left transept are some of the best-known works of the Sienese painter Pietro Lorenzetti (circa 1280–1348). They depict the Madonna with Sts. John and Francis, a crucifixion, and a Descent from the Cross.

It is quite a contrast to climb the steps next to the altar and emerge into the bright sunlight and airy grace of the double-arched Renaissance **Chiostro dei Morti** (Cloister of the Dead). A door to the right leads to the treasury of the church and contains relics of St. Francis and other holy objects associated with the order.

Assisi

Basilica di
San Francesco, **19**
San Rufino, **21**
Santa Chiara, **22**
Tempio di
Minerva, **20**

At press time, the cloister (☞ *above*), Tesoro (Treasury), and **upper church** were closed because of earthquake damage and were due to be open by late 1999. The basilica is dominated by Giotto's 28 frescoes (some damaged or obliterated from the earthquake), each portraying incidents in the life of St. Francis. Although the artist was only in his twenties when he painted this cycle, the frescoes show that Giotto was the pivotal artist in the development of Western painting, breaking away from the stiff, unnatural styles of earlier generations and moving toward a realism and grace that reached their peak in the Renaissance. The paintings are viewed left to right, starting in the transept. The most beloved of all the scenes is probably *St. Francis Preaching to the Birds*, a touching painting that seems to sum up the gentle spirit of the saint. It stands in marked contrast to the scene of the dream of Innocent III. The pope dreams of a humble monk who will steady the church. Sure enough, in the panel next to the sleeping pope, you see a strong Francis supporting a church that seems to be—bitterly ironic today—on the verge of tumbling down. ⊠ *Piazza di San Francesco.* ☎ *Treasury 3,000 lire.* ☉ *Lower church: Easter–Oct., daily 7–7; Nov.–Easter, daily 7–12:30 and 2–6. Upper church: closed through 1999 for restoration.*

㉑ San Rufino. St. Francis and St. Clare were among those baptized in Assisi's Duomo, the principal church in town until the 12th century. The baptismal font has since been redecorated, but it is possible to see the **crypt** of San Rufino, the martyred 3rd-century bishop who brought Christianity to Assisi. Admission to the crypt includes a look at the small **Museo Capitolare,** which features detached frescoes and artifacts. This site is closed due to earthquake damage. ⊠ *Piazza San Rufino,* ☎ *075/ 812534 (tourist office).* ☎ *Museo Capitolare 2,500 lire; crypt 2,500 lire; both 4,000 lire.* ☉ *Closed indefinitely for restoration.*

㉒ Santa Chiara. This 13th-century church is dedicated to St. Clare, one of the earliest and most fervent of St. Francis's followers and the founder of the order of the Poor Ladies, or Poor Clares, in imitation of the Franciscans. The church contains the body of the saint, and in the **Cappella del Crocifisso** (Chapel of the Crucifix) is the cross that spoke to St. Francis and led him to a life of piety. A heavily veiled member of St. Clare's order is stationed before the cross in perpetual adoration of the image. ⊠ *Piazza Santa Chiara.* ☉ *Daily 8–noon and 2:30–sunset.*

㉒ Tempio di Minerva (Temple of Minerva). Bits and pieces of a Roman temple dating from the time of Augustus (63 BC–AD 14) make up this sanctuary dedicated to the Roman goddess of wisdom. The expectations raised by the perfect classical facade are not met by the interior, subjected to a thorough Baroque assault in the 17th century. ⊠ *Piazza del Comune.* ☉ *Daily 7–noon and 2:30–sunset.*

OFF THE BEATEN PATH

EREMO DELLE CARCERI – Just 4 km (2½ mi) east of Assisi is this monastery set in dense woodlands on the side of Monte Subasio. In the caves on the slope of the mountain, Francis and his followers established their first home, to which he returned often during his lifetime to pray and meditate. The church and monastery retain the tranquil contemplative air St. Francis so prized. From a vantage point within the monastery visitors can take in one of the most beautiful vistas over the Umbrian countryside. True to their Franciscan heritage, the friars here are entirely dependent on alms from visitors. ⊠ *Via Santuario delle Carceri.* ☎ *Donations accepted.* ☉ *Dawn–dusk.*

SANTA MARIA DEGLI ANGELI – On the outskirts of the town, near the train station, this Baroque church was built over the **Porziuncola**, a little chapel restored by St. Francis. The shrine is much venerated because it was here, in the **Cappella del Transito,** then a humble cell, that St. Francis died (1226). ⊠ *Località Santa Maria degli Angeli.* 🎫 *Free.* ☉ *Daily 9–12:30 and 2:30–sunset.*

CANNARA – A pleasant excursion from Assisi leads to this tiny town; a half-hour walk outside the town are the fields of Pian d'Arca, which legend identifies as the site of St. Francis's sermon to the birds.

Dining and Lodging

$$ ✕ **Buca di San Francesco.** This central restaurant is Assisi's busiest—it's no wonder for the setting is lovely no matter what the season. In summer you dine outside in a cool green garden; in winter, in the cozy cellars of the restaurant. The food is first rate, and the *filetto al rubesco* (fillet steak cooked in a heady red wine) is the specialty of the house. ⊠ *Via Brizi 1,* ☎ *075/812204. Reservations essential. AE, DC, MC, V. Closed Mon. and July.*

$$ ✕ **La Fortezza.** Parts of the walls of this modern, family-run restaurant were built by the Romans. The service is personable and the kitchen reliable. A particular standout is *anatra al finocchio selvatico* (duck cooked with wild fennel). La Fortezza also has seven simple but clean guest rooms available. ⊠ *Vicolo della Fortezza 19/b,* ☎ *075/812418. Reservations essential. AE, DC, MC, V. Closed Thurs. and Feb.*

$ ✕ **La Stalla.** A kilometer or two outside the town proper, this onetime stable has been turned into a simple and rustic restaurant. In summer, lunch and dinner are served outside under a trellis shaded with vines and flowers. In keeping with the decor, the kitchen turns out hearty country fare. ⊠ *Via Santuario delle Carceri 8,* ☎ *075/812317. No credit cards. Closed Mon. Oct.–June.*

$$$ 🏨 **Hotel Subasio.** This hotel, close to the Basilica of St. Francis, has counted Marlene Dietrich and Charlie Chaplin among its guests. It is housed in a converted monastery and has plenty of atmosphere. Some of the rooms remain a little monastic, but the views, comfortable old-fashioned sitting rooms, flowered terraces, and a lovely garden more than make up for the simplicity. Ask for a room with a view of the valley. ⊠ *Via Frate Elia 2, 06081,* ☎ *075/812206,* 📠 *075/816691. 61 rooms. Restaurant, bar. AE, DC, MC, V.*

$$ 🏨 **Hotel Umbra.** A 16th-century town house is home to this hotel, which
★ is in a tranquil part of the city, an area closed to traffic, near Piazza del Commune. The rooms are arranged as small apartments, each with a tiny living room and terrace. The restaurant does not serve lunch Tuesday or Wednesday. ⊠ *Via degli Archi 6, 06081,* ☎ *075/812240,* 📠 *075/813653. 25 rooms. Restaurant, bar. AE, DC, MC, V. Closed mid-Jan.–mid-Mar. and Dec. 1–20.*

$$ 🏨 **San Francesco.** This is a central hotel in a renovated 16th-century building. Some of the rooms have a view of the basilica or the valley. ⊠ *Via di San Francesco 48, 06082,* ☎ *075/812281,* 📠 *075/816237. 44 rooms. Restaurant, bar. AE, DC, MC, V.*

SOUTHERN UMBRIA

Save room for Orvieto, built on a tufa mount, with one of Italy's greatest cathedrals and most compelling fresco cycles. Nearby Narni and Todi are two pleasant medieval hill towns. The former stands firm over a steep gorge, its Roman pedigree evident in the dark alleyways and winding streets; the latter a fairy-tale town with incomparable Umbrian views and one of Italy's most perfect piazzas.

Todi

㉓ *39 km (24 mi) east of Orvieto, 60 km (37 mi) southwest of Assisi, 45 km (28 mi) south of Perugia.*

Standing on **Piazza del Popolo,** it's easy to see why Todi is often described as Umbria's prettiest hill town. The square is a model of spatial harmony with stunning views onto the surrounding countryside. On one end is the 12th-century Romanesque-Gothic **Duomo,** with a famous choir stall. Its simple square facade is echoed by the solid Palazzo dei Priori across the way. Narrow cobblestone streets go winding around the hill, every so often finishing in a tiny, quiet piazza. Quite unexpected is the Renaissance church of **Santa Maria della Consolazione,** with an elegant white dome, on the outskirts of town.

Dining

$$ ✕ **Ristorante Umbria.** Todi's most popular restaurant for over four decades, Umbria is reliable for sturdy country food, plus a wonderful view from the terrace. There's always a hearty soup simmering away, as well as homemade pasta with truffles, game, and the specialty of the house, *palombaccio alla ghiotta* (roasted squab). ⊠ *Via San Bonaventura 13,* ☎ *075/8942390. AE, D, MC, V. Closed Tues. and in July.*

Narni

㉔ *35 km (22 mi) south of Todi, 84 km (46 mi) southeast of Perugia.*

At the edge of a steep gorge, Narni—like so many other towns in Umbria—is a medieval city of Roman origins. Below its finely paved streets and pretty Romanesque churches, excavations have revealed parts of its fascinating past. The **Lacus,** under Piazza Garibaldi, is a large cistern with remnants of a Roman floor that was in use until the late Middle Ages. Two more cisterns and Roman fragments are visible in the crypt of the 12th-century church of **Santa Maria in Pensole** (⊠ Via Mazzini; ♥ Daily 9:30–noon and 4–6:30). More interesting are the rooms under the ex-church of **San Domenico,** where the prisoners of the Inquisition engraved mysterious symbols and dates. The best day to visit is Sunday, when the excavated sites are open and tours are given in English. ⊠ *Via Mazzini,* ☎ *0744/747203.* ♥ *Library: Mon.–Fri. 9–12:30; Excavations: Sun. and holidays 11–1 and 3–5.*

Dining

$ ✕ **Il Cavallino.** Run by the third generation of the Bussetti family, Il Cavallino is a first-rate trattoria about 2 km (1 mi) outside Narni. There are always several pastas to choose from, but it's the meat that makes this a worthy detour. Stuffed rabbit roasted like pork and juicy grilled T-bone steaks are house favorites. The wine list features the best of what's local. ⊠ *Via Flamina Romana 220,* ☎ *0744/722683. AE, D, MC, V. Tues. and in July.*

Orvieto

㉕ *112 km (70 mi) southwest of Assisi, 86 km (53 mi) south of Perugia, 96 km (60 mi) northwest of Rome, 37 km (23 mi) west of Todi, off A1.*

Sitting atop an enormous plateau of volcanic rock high above the valley below, Orvieto's natural defenses eliminated the need for high walls. The Etruscans were the first to take advantage of this and settled here, carving a network of 1,200 wells and storage caves out of the soft stone. The Romans attacked, sacked, and destroyed the city in 283 BC. From that time, Orvieto has had close ties with Rome. It was solidly Guelph in the Middle Ages, and for several hundred years popes sought refuge in the city, at times needing protection from their enemies, at times fleeing from the summer heat of Rome.

Orvieto is known for its white wines. Some of the region's finest wines are produced here (Signorelli, when painting the Duomo, asked that part of his contract be paid in wine), and the rock on which the town sits is honeycombed with caves used to ferment the Trebbiano grapes that are used in making Orvieto wines.

★ Orvieto's **Duomo** is one of the most dazzling in all of Italy, a triumph of Romanesque-Gothic architecture. Legend has it that a priest in the nearby town of Bolsena suddenly found himself assailed by doubts about the transubstantiation—he could not bring himself to believe that the body of Christ was contained in the consecrated communion host. His doubts were put to rest, however, when a wafer he had just blessed suddenly started to drip blood. Drops of blood fell onto the linen covering the altar, and this cloth and the host itself are the principal relics of the miracle. The pope seized the opportunity to proclaim a new religious holiday— the Feast of Corpus Christi—and the duomo was built to celebrate the miracle and house the stained altar cloth. The stunning facade is the work of some of Italy's finest artists and took 300 years to complete. The bas-reliefs on the lower parts of the pillars were carved by Maitani, one of the original architects of the building, and show scenes from the Old Testament and some particularly gruesome renderings of the Last Judgment and Hell, as well as a more tranquil Paradise. (They have been covered with Plexiglas following some vandalizing in the 1960s.)

The major works inside are the two chapels in the transepts. To the left is the **Cappella del Corporale,** where the famous altar cloth is kept in a golden reliquary modeled on the cathedral, inlaid with enamel images of the miracle. The cloth is removed for public viewing on Easter and on Corpus Christi (the ninth Sunday after Easter). A trio of local artists executed frescoes depicting the miracle on the chapel walls. The **Cappella Nuova** (a.k.a. Cappella della Madonna di San Brizio), in the right transept, is the artistic jewel of Orvieto. It contains Luca Signorelli's fresco cycle *Stories of the Antichrist,* among the most delightfully gruesome works in Italy. As the damned fall to hell, demons with green buttocks bite off ears, step on heads, and spirit away young girls. Dante would surely have approved; in the chapel, his portrait accompanies *Scenes from Purgatorio.* Signorelli and Fra Angelico, who also worked on the chapel, witness the gory scene. ⊠ *Piazza del Duomo.* ☎ *Cappella Nuova: 3,000 lire (buy tickets at tourist office across the piazza).* ⊙ *Daily 7–1 and 2:30–sunset.*

Next door, the **Museo dell'Opera del Duomo** (⊠ Piazza del Duomo, ☎ 0763/342477), closed for restoration, contains original and later plans for the cathedral, as well as some paintings and sculptures. Right across the piazza, the **Museo Claudio Faina** (⊠ Palazzo Faina, ☎ 0763/ 341511) holds Etruscan and Roman artifacts; the museum is designed in a way that makes its Roman coins, bronze pieces, and sarcophagi accessible and interesting. On Piazza Cahen, the **Fortezza,** built in the mid-14th century, encloses a public park with grass, benches, shade and an incredible view. The nearby **Pozzo di San Patrizio** (⊠ Via Sangallo, off Piazza Cahen, ☎ 0763/343768), or Well of St. Patrick, was commissioned by Pope Clement VII in 1527 to ensure a plentiful water supply. Descend into the well via a pair of zigzagging mule paths, designed to avoid animal traffic jams.

Dining and Lodging

$$ ✕ **Le Grotte del Funaro.** This restaurant has an extraordinary spot, deep
★ in a series of caves within the volcanic rock beneath Orvieto. Once you

have negotiated the steep steps, typical Umbrian specialties like tagliatelle *al vino rosso* (with red wine sauce) and grilled beef with truffles, await. Sample the fine Orvieto wines, either the whites or the lesser-known reds. ⊠ *Via Ripa Serancia 41,* ☎ *0763/343276. Reservations essential. AE, DC, MC, V. Closed Mon.*

$$ ✕ **Maurizio.** In the heart of Orvieto, just opposite the cathedral, this
★ warm and welcoming restaurant gets its share of tourists and has a local clientele as well. The decor is unusual, with wood sculptures by Orvieto craftsman Michelangeli. The menu offers hearty soups and homemade pastas such as *tronchetti* (a pasta roll with spinach and ricotta filling). ⊠ *Via del Duomo 78,* ☎ *0763/341114. Reservations essential in summer. AE, MC, V. Closed Tues.*

$$$ ⊞ **Hotel La Badia.** This is one of the best-known country hotels in Umbria. The 700-year-old building, a former monastery, is set in rolling parkland that provides wonderful views of the valley and the town of Orvieto in the distance. The rooms are well appointed. ⊠ *Località La Badia, 4 km (2½ mi) south of Orvieto, 05018,* ☎ *0763/90359,* ℻ *0763/ 92796. 26 rooms. Restaurant, bar, pool, 2 tennis courts, meeting rooms. AE, MC, V. Closed Jan.–Feb.*

$$–$$$ ⊞ **Grand Hotel Reale.** This hotel is in the center of Orvieto, across a square that hosts a lively market. Facing the impressive Gothic-Romanesque Palazzo del Popolo, rooms are spacious and adequately furnished, with a traditional accent. ⊠ *Piazza del Popolo 25, 05018,* ☎ *0763/341247,* ℻ *0763/341247. 32 rooms. Bar. MC, V.*

$$–$$$ ⊞ **Villa Bellago.** Outside Orvieto, in a tranquil setting on a spit of land overlooking Lake Corbara, three farmhouses have been completely overhauled. The result is welcome: The hotel now includes well-lighted and spacious guest rooms, generous facilities, and a fine restaurant (closed Tuesday) specializing in imaginatively prepared Umbrian and Tuscan dishes. Fresh fish is always on the menu. ⊠ *Outside the village of Baschi, 7½ km (4½ mi) south of Orvieto on S448, 05018,* ☎ *0744/950521,* ℻ *0744/950524. 12 rooms. Restaurant, bar, pool, tennis court, exercise room. AE, DC, MC, V. Closed 4 wks Jan.–Feb.*

$$ ⊞ **Virgilio.** The modest Hotel Virgilio is right in Piazza del Duomo, and the views of the cathedral are wonderful. The rooms are small but nicely furnished. ⊠ *Piazza del Duomo 5, 05018,* ☎ *0763/341882,* ℻ *0763/343797. 13 rooms. Bar. MC, V. Closed Feb.*

Shopping

EMBROIDERY AND LACE

Minor arts, such as embroidery and lace making, flourish in Orvieto. One of the best shops for *merletto* (lace) is **Duranti** (⊠ Corso Cavour 107).

WINES

Excellent Orvieto wines are justly prized throughout Italy and in foreign countries. The whites pressed from the region's Trebbiano grapes are fruity, with a tart finish. Orvieto also produces its own version of the Tuscan dessert wine *vin santo*. It is darker than its Tuscan cousin and is aged five years before bottling. You may stop for a glass of *vino* (wine) at the **wine cellar** (⊠ No. 2, Piazza del Duomo), where there's also a good selection of sandwiches and snacks and vin santo is on sale.

WOODWORKING

Orvieto is a center of woodworking, particularly fine inlays and veneers. The Corso Cavour has a number of artisan shops specializing in woodwork, the best known being the **Michelangeli family studio** (⊠ Corso Cavour), crammed with a variety of imaginatively designed objects ranging in size from a giant *armadio* (wardrobe) to a simple wooden spoon.

UMBRIA AND THE MARCHES A TO Z

Arriving and Departing

By Bus

Perugia and Orvieto are served by the Sulga Line (☎ 075/5009641) with daily departures from Rome's Stazione Tiburtina and Aeroporto Fiumicino, and from Piazza Adua in Florence.

By Car

On the western edge of the region is the Umbrian section of the Autostrada del Sole (**A1**), the principal north–south highway in Italy. It links Florence and Rome with the important Umbrian town of Orvieto and passes near Todi and Terni. The **S3** intersects with A1 and leads on to Assisi and Urbino. The Adriatica superhighway (**A14**) runs north–south along the coast, linking the Marches to Bologna and Venice.

By Plane

The closest airports are Rome's **Fiumicino** (☎ 06/65953640), Pisa's **Aeroporto Galileo Galilei** (☎ 050/500707), and Florence's **Peretola** (☎ 055/333498).

By Train

Assisi lies on the Terontola–Foligno rail line, with almost hourly connections to Perugia, and direct trains to Rome and Florence several times per day. The main rail line from Rome to Ancona passes through Narni, Terni, Spoleto, and Foligno. Travel time from Rome to Spoleto is a little less than 90 minutes on intercity trains. The main Rome–Florence line stops at Orvieto. With a change of trains at the small town of Terontola, one can travel by rail from Rome or Florence to Perugia and Assisi. For train information, dial ☎ 147/888088 toll-free.

Getting Around

By Bus

There is good local bus service between all the major and minor towns of Umbria. Some of the routes in rural areas, especially in the Marches, are designed to serve as many destinations as possible and are, therefore, quite roundabout and slow. Schedules often change, so consult with local tourist offices before setting out.

By Car

Umbria has an excellent and modern road network. Central Umbria is served by a major highway, **S75bis** ("bis" means alternative highway), which passes along the shore of Lake Trasimeno and ends in Perugia. Assisi is well served by the modern highway **S75,** which connects to **S3** and **3bis,** which cover the heart of the region. Major inland routes connect coastal **A14** to large towns in the Marches, including Urbino, Jesi, Macerata, and Ascoli Piceno, but inland secondary roads in mountain areas can be tortuous and narrow.

By Train

Branch lines link the central rail hub, Ancona, with the inland towns of Fabriano and Ascoli Piceno. Dial 147/888088 for toll-free train information. In Umbria, a small, privately owned railway, run by Ferrovia Centrale Umbra (FCU), runs from Città di Castello in the north to Terni in the south via Perugia.

Updated by
Robert
Andrews

IT'S A PITY THAT MOST TOURISTS see Apulia (called Puglia by the Italians—English-speakers are really using the Latin term) as merely a blur outside their car or train windows as they hurtle toward Bari or Brindisi for ferry connections to Greece.

This ancient land, the heel and spur of Italy's boot, possesses some of the country's most unspoiled scenery, interesting artistic and historical sites, and finest beaches. What's more, beyond the increasingly popular seaside resorts and the few major sites lies sunbaked countryside where expanses of silvery olive trees and giant prickly-pear cacti fight their way through the rocky soil, as if in defiance of the relentless summer heat. Local buildings, too, do their best to dispel the effects of the sun: Whitewashed ports stand coolly over the turquoise Mediterranean; the landscape is studded with the odd stone trulli, used as farmhouses and storage bins.

The trulli date from the Middle Ages, but Apulia had long before then been inhabited, conquered, and visited. The Greeks and later the Romans were quick to recognize the importance of this strategic peninsula, and among the nations later to raid or colonize Apulia were the Normans, Moors, and Spaniards, each leaving their mark. Romanesque churches and the powerful castles built by 13th-century Holy Roman Emperor Frederick II of Swabia (part of present-day Bavaria), king of Sicily and Jerusalem, are among the most impressive of buildings in the region. Frederick II, dubbed Wonder of the World for his wide-ranging interests in literature, science, mathematics, and nature, was an outstanding personality in the Middle Ages.

The last 50 years have seen a huge economic revival after the centuries of neglect that followed Apulia's golden age under the Normans and Swabians. Having benefited from EU and state subsidies for irrigation and incentive programs, Apulia is now Italy's biggest producer of wine, with most of the rest of the land devoted to olives, citrus fruits, and vegetables. The main ports of Bari, Brindisi, and Taranto are lively and economically thriving centers, though there remain serious problems of unemployment and poverty. However, the much publicized arrival of thousands of asylum-seekers from Albania has not significantly destabilized these cities, as had been feared, and the economic and political refugees have been dispersed throughout Italy. Enjoying good communications networks for road and rail travelers, Apulia is blessed with plenty of quality restaurants testifying to the region's comparative prosperity, though don't expect to find the same abundance of accommodation facilities outside the business circuit.

Apulia's inexpensive, hearty cuisine employs local seafood and produce and has evolved from more than 2,000 years of foreign influences. In colorful markets around the region, you can get a closer look at these ingredients, plus the local crafts, ranging from lace, wood carvings, and baskets to ceramic pots and painted clay whistles. Hundreds of miles of beaches and an extensive cave complex punctuating the region let you explore, bask in the sun and sea, or just stay cool.

Pleasures and Pastimes

Beaches

Italians and the region's other visitors return each summer for the draw of the sea, one of the major attractions of Apulia. Though no longer "undiscovered," the beaches along the Gargano Promontory, to the northwest of the region, offer safe swimming and sandy beaches. The whole coastline between Bari and Brindisi is well served with beach facilities. In even the smallest villages you'll find beaches where there are changing rooms and—essential in the blazing Apulian sun—beach umbrellas. If you don't mind venturing farther afield, Gallipoli, on the south coast of the heel, is exceptional.

Dining

Anyone who likes to eat will love Apulia. Southern cuisine is hearty and healthy, based around homemade pastas and cheeses, fresh vegetables, seafood, and local olive oil. Open-air markets and delicatessens burst with local fruits, vegetables, pastries, sausages, smoked meats, and cheeses. Here you will find dishes unavailable elsewhere in Italy, such as *'ncapriata,* also called *favi e fogghi* (a first course fava-bean puree with bitter chicory or other cooked vegetables). Focaccia *barese* (stuffed with fried onions, black olives, anchovies, and ricotta) makes a great snack or lunch.

Apulia's pasta specialties include *orecchiette* (ear-shape pasta), *troccoli* (homemade noodles cut with a special ridged rolling pin), and *strascenate* (rectangles of pasta with one rough side and one smooth side). Among the many typical sauces is *salsa alla Sangiovanniello* (sauce of olive oil, capers, anchovies, parsley, and hot peppers) from Brindisi. Don't miss the dairy products, such as ricotta and buttery *burrata* cheese. Sample Apulia's wealth of excellent local wines, ranging from the strong white wine of Martina Franca to the sweet white Moscaro di Trani and the rich dry red Castel del Monte to the sweet red Aleatico di Puglia.

CATEGORY	COST*
$$$$	over 85,000 lire
$$$	60,000–85,000 lire
$$	25,000–60,000 lire
$	under 25,000 lire

Prices are per person, including house wine, service, and tax.

Festivals

In keeping with the provincial nature of Apulia, the arts take on a folk flavor, with processions on religious occasions more prevalent than performing arts in theaters or opera houses. Still, there are some good festivals and pageants to help broaden your experience of life in Italy's deep south. The best newspaper for listings is the daily *Gazzetta del Mezzogiorno,* which covers the entire region.

Lodging

Along the miles of sandy beaches on the Gargano spur and elsewhere on the coast, big white Mediterranean-style beach hotels have sprung up in profusion. Most are similar in design, price, and quality. In summer, many cater only to guests paying full board (lodging plus three meals per day) or half board (lodging plus breakfast and one other meal) for longer stays. If you are traveling to the Gargano Promontory in summer, you should reserve through a travel agent to avoid complications with limited lodging and public transportation. During Easter, rooms in the Alberobello area may be at a premium.

In some cases, such as visiting Bari during the annual Trade Fair in September, you must make reservations. Outside the big cities, hotel accommodations are limited and modest—both in amenities and price—though this may be more than compensated for by friendly service. Throughout the region, hotels are often booked up with commercial travelers, so reserve well in advance. Many establishments, particularly the beach resorts, close during the winter months. And remember that in a region like this—blazing hot in summer and bitter cold in winter—air-conditioning and central heating are important.

CATEGORY	COST*
$$$$	over 300,000 lire
$$$	160,000–300,000 lire
$$	100,000–160,000 lire
$	under 100,000 lire

Prices are for a standard double room, including service and tax.

Shopping

Apulia is rich in folk art, reflecting the influences of the many nations that have passed through the region or ruled it. Don't expect boutiques; instead, snatch up handmade goods, such as pottery with traditional designs, and baskets, textiles, and carved wood figures. These are on sale in shops and in open markets, where some bargaining can enter into the purchase.

Exploring Apulia

If you are mainly interested in spending time at the beach, the promontory of Gargano in the north harbors some of Apulia's best coastline, although there are pleasant beach resorts within easy reach of most of the region's attractions. Convenient travel bases include Alberobello or Martina Franca in the trulli country; Lecce, near the tip of the heel; and the small ports of Barletta, Molfetta, and Trani, up the coast from Bari.

Bari and Brindisi are notorious for purse-snatchings, car thefts, and break-ins. If you are driving in these cities, try not to leave valuables in the car or lock everything inside the trunk, and find a guarded parking space if possible.

Numbers in the text correspond to numbers in the margin and on the Apulia and Bari maps.

Great Itineraries

Apulia's attractions are so varied and scattered that you may want to take a full week or more to explore it at a leisurely pace, selecting two or three bases in different parts of the region and taking day trips to nearby sights.

IF YOU HAVE 3 DAYS

With three days in Apulia, you will need to focus on one stop per day, starting in ⊞ **Bari** ①–③ for a morning stroll in the old town. After lunch, head south as far as ⊞ **Lecce** ㉔, spending the next day in this Baroque town. On the morning of the third day, retrace your steps northwest to **Brindisi** ㉓, stopping at the famous column marking the end of the Via Appia. Veer west along the Via Appia (S7) and head to ⊞ **Taranto** ㉒ for your last night, to take in the Museo Nazionale. If you are heading back to Bari, drive on the S172 through the **trulli district** ⑰–㉑ to get an impression of the dwellings.

IF YOU HAVE 5 DAYS

Spend a couple of days exploring the forested ⊞ **Gargano Promontory** ⑧–⑯, northwest of ⊞ **Bari** ①–③, where you'll need about two hours to absorb the flavor of this old center. Take the coastal road (S16) from the city northwest toward **Molfetta** ④, **Trani** ⑤, and **Barletta** ⑥, with old ports reminiscent of Venetian ports such as Dubrovnik, across the Adriatic Sea in Croatia. The seaside fishing villages–cum–resorts of ⊞ **Vieste** ⑪, ⊞ **Peschici** ⑫, and ⊞ **Rodi Garganico** ⑬ offer the best choice of accommodations, although ⊞ **Foggia** ⑧ or ⊞ **Manfredonia** ⑨ make good bases. Aim to spend your fourth night in ⊞ **Alberobello** ⑰, the capital of trulli country—touristy but engaging—or in whitewashed ⊞ **Ostuni** ⑳. From Alberobello, it's a short run to **Taranto** ㉒ to whip around the archaeological museum. Break your journey for an hour or

Apulia

Adriatic Sea

Golfo di Taranto

PROMONTORIO DEL GARGANO

ITALY

50 miles

75 km

Leuca

Otranto

Maglie

Nardò

Lecce **24**

Gallipoli **25**

Brindisi **23**

Campi

Mesagne

Manduria

Ostuni **20**

Grottaglie

Martina Franca **21**

Fasano

19

Locorotondo **17**

Alberobello **18**

Grotte di Castellana

Gioia del Colle

Taranto **22**

Mare Piccolo

Mare Grande

Massafra

Castellaneta Marina

Lido di Metaponto

Scanzano

Bari **1 3**

Molfetta

Trani **4**

Barletta **5**

6

Andria

Corato

Castel del Monte **7**

Spinazzola

Gravina in Puglia

Altamura

Matera

Santeramo in Colle

Polenza

Potenza

BASILICATA

S. Angelo dei Lombardi

Auletta

Battipaglia

TO SALERNO

Melfi

S. Angelo

Cerignola

Zapponeta

Foggia **8**

Lucera

San Severo

L'Annunziata

Manfredonia **9**

Golfo di Manfredonia

Mattinata **10**

Vieste **11**

Peschici **12**

Foresta Umbra **14**

Rodi Garganico **13**

Monte Sant'Angelo **15**

San Giovanni Rotondo **16**

Lago di Varano

Isole Tremiti

TO TERMOLI

two in **Brindisi** ㉓, but save your last night for ▓ **Lecce** ㉔, a treat that will generate some of your most abiding memories of Apulia.

IF YOU HAVE 7 DAYS
If your base is ▓ **Bari** ①–③, devote about a half day to the city before venturing to the **Gargano Promontory** ⑧–⑯. A car is indispensable since transport connections are tortuous and slow, but be prepared to abandon it for a half-day ramble through the **Foresta Umbra** ⑭ and **Monte Sant'Angelo** ⑮, dominated by a large Norman castle that was once host to Crusaders setting off for the East, and **San Giovanni Rotondo** ⑯. Proceed down the Adriatic Coast back toward Bari, landing at the pretty fishing villages of **Barletta** ⑥, **Trani** ⑤, and **Molfetta** ④, and making an inland detour to view the fascinatingly geometrical **Castel del Monte** ⑦. Head southeast toward trulli country, spending a night in ▓ **Alberobello** ⑰ or ▓ **Martina Franca** ㉑. At some point take a trip underground at the **Grotte di Castellana** ⑱, a soothing respite from the summer heat. The bustling cities of **Taranto** ㉒ and **Brindisi** ㉓ are worth stopping in for their archaeological relics. Spend your last two nights in the heel of Italy, dividing your time between the Baroque pleasures of ▓ **Lecce** ㉔ and the seaside village of ▓ **Gallipoli** ㉕.

When to Tour Apulia

Summers are torrid this far south, and even the otherwise perfect villages of the interior are too dazzlingly white for easy comfort between the months of July and early September. So unless you are planning to be thoroughly idle—always an alluring prospect in Apulia—avoid the hot season. Of course, if you're on the Gargano Promontory, which has Apulia's only elevation of any significance, you'll be able to appreciate the forested interior during these months. The Gargano and Bari to Brindisi littorals, however, are strictly summer-holiday zones.

Wintertime in Apulia can see heavy bursts of rain, often lasting several days at a time. However, the temperatures rarely fall to freezing. In spring, days are usually warm and the light crystal clear; you can generally find water warm enough for comfortable bathing into October. Note that lodging availability can be limited off-season.

BARI AND THE COAST

The coast has a strong flavor of the Norman presence in the south, embodied in the distinctive Apulian-Romanesque churches, the most graceful contribution of the Normans. Bari is a busy, commercial port, with charm in its compact, labyrinthine old quarter abutting the sea. Molfetta and Barletta are small fishing ports. Make an excursion inland to the imposing Castel del Monte, an enigmatic, 13th-century octagonal structure of unknown origin.

Bari

260 km (162 mi) southeast of Naples, 450 km (281 mi) southeast of Rome.

Bari is a big, hectic, rough-and-tumble port and a transit point for travelers catching ferries across the Adriatic to Greece. Most of the city is set out in a logical 19th-century grid pattern, following the designs of Joachim Murat, Napoléon's brother-in-law and "King of the Two Sicilies." The heart of the modern town is Piazza della Libertà, but just beyond it, across Corso Vittorio Emanuele, is the *Città Vecchia* (Old Town), a maze of narrow, crooked streets on the promontory that juts out between Bari's old and new ports. Here, overlooking the sea and ❶ just off Via Venezia, is the **Basilica di San Nicola,** built in the 11th century to house the bones of Saint Nicholas, better known to us as Saint Nick, or Santa Claus. His remains, buried in the crypt, are said to have been stolen by Bari sailors from Myra, in what is now Turkey. The basilica, of solid and powerful construction, was the only building to survive the otherwise wholesale destruction of Bari by the Normans in 1152. ⊠ *Piazza San Nicola.* ⊘ *Daily 9–noon and 5–7.*

➋ A century younger than the basilica, the **Cattedrale** is the seat of the local bishop and was the scene of many significant political marriages between important families in the Middle Ages. The cathedral's solid architecture reflects the Romanesque style favored by the Normans of that period. ⊠ *Piazza dell'Odegitria.* ⊘ *Daily 9–noon and 5–7.*

➌ The huge **Castello** looms behind the cathedral. The current building dates from the time of Holy Roman Emperor Frederick II, who rebuilt an existing Norman-Byzantine castle to his own exacting specifications. Designed more for power than beauty, it looks out beyond the cathedral to the small Porto Vecchio (Old Port). Inside is a collection of medieval Apulian art. ⊠ *Piazza Federico II di Svevia.* ☺ *4,000 lire.* ⊘ *Tues.–Sat. 8:30–1 and 3:30–7, Sun. 8:30–1, Mon. 3:30–7 (times may change).*

Dining and Lodging

$$ ✕ **Ristorante al Pescatore.** This is one of Bari's best fish restaurants, in the old town opposite the castle and just around the corner from the cathedral. Summer cooking is done outside, where you can sit amid a cheerful clamor of quaffing and dining. Try the *céfalo* (mullet) if it is available, accompanied by crisp salad and a carafe of invigorating local wine. ⊠ *Piazza Federico II di Svevia,* ☎ *080/5237039. Reservations essential in high season. AE, DC, MC, V. Closed Mon.*

$$$$ 🏨 **Sheraton Nicolaus.** This large, modern hotel on the edge of the city is easily reached by car from Highway S16, which skirts the congested town center. It caters mainly to businesspeople and is well equipped for meetings, conferences, and banquets. Rooms are spacious and comfortable, with the usual Sheraton amenities. There's even an indoor pool and a sauna. ⊠ *Via Agostino Ciasca 9, 70124,* ☎ *080/5042626,* FAX *080/5042058. 170 rooms. Restaurant, bar, indoor pool, sauna, convention center, meeting rooms. AE, DC, MC, V.*

$$ 🏨 **Adria.** In a city sadly short of inexpensive hotels, this two-star's main virtue is its convenience to the train station. Facilities are adequate if undistinguished (rooms have showers only, not baths, for instance), but this is primarily a one-night stopover. Guest rooms are comfortable enough—avoid those facing inward, if you can. Turn right out of the station to find it. ⊠ *Via L. Zuppetta 10, 70121,* ☎ *080/5246699,* FAX *080/5213207. 35 rooms. Restaurant, bar. AE, DC, MC, V.*

Nightlife and the Arts

Bari's famous **Teatro Petruzzelli** (⊠ Corso Cavour, ☎ 080/5241761) features performances of drama, opera, and ballet. The theater is still being restored after a devastating fire in 1991.

Outdoor Activities and Sports

BIKING

G. S. De Bendictus (⊠ Via Nitti 23, ☎ 080/5744345) rents bikes and mountain bikes, a great way to explore the flat roads winding through the trulli region.

FISHING

For information on approved spots and license applications, contact **Federazione Italiana Pesca Sportiva** (⊠ Molo Pizzoli, Bari, ☎ 080/5247070).

Basilica di
San Nicola, **1**
Castello, **3**
Cattedrale, **2**

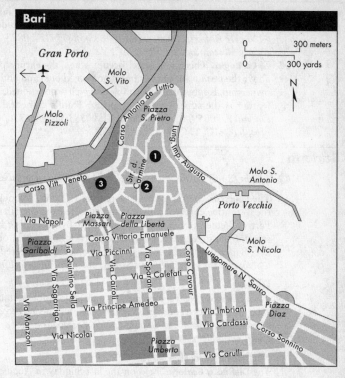

Bari

Molfetta

4 *25 km (16 mi) northwest of Bari.*

Molfetta has an unusual 12th-century cathedral with distinct Byzantine features, such as the pyramid-shape covers to the three main
domes. If you are in the area around Easter, don't miss Molfetta's colorful Holy Week processions, a surefire hit for young and old alike.

Trani

5 *18 km (11 mi) northwest of Molfetta, 43 km (27 mi) northwest of Bari.*

Smaller than the other ports along this coast, Trani has a quaint old
town with polished stone streets and buildings, medieval churches, and
a harbor filled with fishing boats. The 11th-century **Duomo,** considered one of the finest in Apulia, is built on a spit of land jutting into
the sea. The Jewish community flourished here in medieval times, and
on Via Sinagoga (Synagogue Street) two of the four synagogues still
exist: the 13th-century **Santa Maria Scolanova** and **Santa Anna,** which
still bears a Hebrew inscription.

Dining and Lodging

$$ ✕ **La Regia.** Just in front of the cathedral, on a swath of land jutting
★ out into the sea, La Regia has an antique feel, with stonework, vaulted
ceilings, and terra-cotta tile floors. Regional specialties are presented
imaginatively: Try the baked crepes (similar to cannelloni); risotto
made with salmon, crab, and cream; lobster; or grilled fish. ✉ *Piazza
Archivio 2,* ☎ *0883/586568. Reservations essential for Sun. lunch and
dinner on summer weekends. MC, V. Closed Mon. and Nov 1–17.*

$$$ 🏨 **Royal.** This is an unpretentious and modern four-star hotel near the train station. Furnishings are comfortable, and rates include breakfast. ⊠ *Via De Robertis 29, 70059,* ☎ *0883/588777,* 𝕱𝕬𝕏 *0883/582224. 40 rooms. Restaurant. AE, DC, MC, V.*

$ 🏨 **La Regia.** This small hotel occupies a 17th-century palazzo; it's above the restaurant of the same name (☞ *above*) and under the same ownership. Rooms are comfortable and well proportioned, but the best feature is the superb setting opposite Trani's cathedral. ⊠ *Piazza Duomo 2, 70059,* ☎ *0883/584527,* 𝕱𝕬𝕏 *0883/553798. 9 rooms. Restaurant, bar. MC, V. Closed Nov. 1–17.*

Barletta

❻ *13 km (8 mi) northwest of Trani, 56 km (35 mi) northwest of Bari.*

The **Colossus,** a bronze statue more than 15 ft tall, is thought to be of the Byzantine emperor Valentinian and date from the 5th century AD. Part of Venice's booty after the sack of Byzantium's capital, Constantinople, in the 1200s, the Colossus was abandoned on the beach near Barletta when the ship carrying it to Venice foundered in a storm. ⊠ *Next to the church of San Sepolcro, Corso Vittorio Emanuele.*

Dining

$$ ✕ **La Casaccia.** Near a picturesque castle, this simple restaurant serves such local dishes as homemade orecchiette and penne *piccanti* (spicy). ⊠ *Corso Cavour 40,* ☎ *0883/533719. Reservations not accepted. No credit cards. Closed Mon.*

Nightlife and the Arts

The **Disfida a Barletta,** held on the last Sunday in August, is a reenactment of an event of the same name, which took place in 1503. Every Italian child is taught in school that the *disfida* (challenge) was issued by 13 Italian officers to 13 French officers, after one of the French insulted the Italians by stating that Italy would always be under foreign domination. The Italians taught the rash Frenchman and his compatriots a lesson.

Castel del Monte

★ ❼ *30 km (19 mi) south of Barletta, 56 km (35 mi) west of Bari.*

Built on an isolated hill in the first half of the 13th century by Frederick II, Castel del Monte is a huge, bare, octagonal castle with eight towers. Very little is known about the structure, since virtually no records exist. It has none of the usual defense features associated with medieval castles, so it probably had little military significance. Some theories suggest it might have been built as a hunting lodge or may have served as an astronomical observatory or a stop for pilgrims on their quest for the Holy Grail. ⊠ *On signposted minor road 18 km (11 mi) south of Andria.* 🎫 *4,000 lire.* ☉ *Apr.–Sept., Mon.–Sat. 8:30–7, Sun. 9–1; Oct.–Mar., Mon.–Sat. 8:30–2, Sun. 9–1.*

Dining

$$ ✕ **Ostello di Federico.** This large, beautifully positioned restaurant, at the foot of the hill on which the celebrated Castel del Monte rises, has a terrace overlooking splendid scenery, plus a bar, and a pizzeria with a wood oven. The restaurant serves local dishes, including orecchiette *a rape* (with bitter greens), and local cheeses, such as ricotta and creamy burrata. ⊠ *Castel del Monte,* ☎ *0883/569877. Reservations essential. AE, DC, MC, V. Closed Mon., 2 wks in mid-Nov., and last 2 wks in Jan.*

Shopping

In Andria, between Castel del Monte and Barletta, **copper** objects and containers are made by local craftsmen.

GARGANO PROMONTORY

Lining the spur of Italy's boot—the Gargano Promontory (Promontorio del Gargano)—are the region's most beautiful and popular beaches. Until a few years ago, this rocky peninsula of whitewashed coastal towns, wide sandy beaches, and craggy limestone cliffs topped by deep-green scrub pine was practically unknown, and some parts of the interior are still well off the usual tourist track. The resort business here has boomed in the past decade, though, and beaches can become crowded in midsummer. For the kids, the beaches and forests of the Gargano Promontory are great places for letting off steam, and many towns stage puppet shows in their public gardens.

Foggia

8 *95 km (60 mi) west of Bari, 39 km (24 mi) southwest of Manfredonia.*

Foggia, the chief city in Apulia's northernmost province is not the most inspiring destination, though it makes a useful overnight stop for visitors to the Gargano. On the main line from Rome and Naples, and easily accessible from the autostrada, Foggia has all the amenities one might expect from a major commercial center, the venue for numerous fairs and conventions throughout the year. This means that while it enjoys a decent selection of lodgings and restaurants, you'll need to reserve to make sure of accommodations. This is the place to get or exchange cash or rent a car for excursions to the Gargano.

Dining and Lodging

$$ **✕ Mangiatoia.** In an old farmhouse, this rustic restaurant has lovely
★ arches, white walls, and wood-beamed ceilings. You can dine outdoors in a large garden, where tables made from wagon wheels surround an old well. Seafood is the specialty; fish and shellfish are displayed live in tanks. The chef will supply recipes for dishes, such as spaghetti *ai datteri di mare al cartoccio* (with razor clams in bags), and fettuccine in a creamy scampi sauce. It's on the main road to Bari, near the Foggia Agricultural Fairgrounds. ✉ *Via Virgilio 2,* ☎ *0881/634457. Reservations essential on weekends. MC, V. Closed Mon.*

$$$ **🏨 Cicolella.** This 1920s hotel near the station has modern amenities and tastefully decorated rooms, a few of which have balconies. There are also some suites that are particularly recommended, though these fall into the $$$$ category. The restaurant (closed weekends) specializes in international dishes and well-prepared local dishes. ✉ *Via Ventiquattro Maggio 60, 71100,* ☎ *0881/688890,* 🆋 *0881/678984. 106 rooms. Restaurant, meeting rooms. AE, DC, MC, V.*

Manfredonia

9 *60 km (37 mi) northwest of Barletta, 39 km (24 mi) northeast of Foggia.*

This lazy resort town on the southern lip of the promontory was once a flourishing port ferrying Crusaders across the Adriatic to Greece and beyond. It now makes an excellent starting point for expeditions into the peninsula. There is a small **museum** in the Angevin castle located on the seafront, containing relics of the Daunian people who once inhabited the Gargano. Apart from some adequate hotels and a buzz of the evening *passeggiata*—the most Mediterranean of pageants when locals stroll through the streets—there is little else.

Lodging

$$-$$$ 🏨 **Gargano.** The functional, rather boxy rooms in this typical, white beach hotel are decorated in blue and white and have terraces. The public rooms are open-plan, the dining area overlooks the pool and the sea, and the dance club–bar keeps it lively on summer evenings. ⊠ *Viale Beccarini 2, 71043,* ☎ *0884/587621,* FAX *0884/586021. 46 rooms. Restaurant, bar, pool, dance club. MC, V. Closed 2 wks in Jan. or Feb.*

Outdoor Activities and Sports

BIKING

There are no bike trails here per se, but the forest and interior is exciting biking terrain. Bicycles can be serviced at **G. S. Cicli Castriotta** (⊠ Viale Beccarini 7, ☎ 0884/583424).

En Route From Manfredonia, take the winding coastal road (S89), which threads through miles of silvery olive groves interspersed with almond trees and prickly-pear cacti. Along the way you'll come across many local craftsmen's stalls, selling homemade preserves, baskets, and carved olive-wood bowls and utensils.

Mattinata

❿ *15 km (9 mi) northeast of Manfredonia.*

Just inland of a fine sandy beach, where you'll find most of the campsites and hotels, this is a generally quiet village that comes into its own in the summer season.

Lodging

$$$ 🏨 **Baia delle Zagare.** On the shore road around the Gargano Promontory, north of Mattinata, Baia delle Zagare is a secluded, modern group of cottages overlooking an inlet. An elevator takes you down to a private beach, and the hotel restaurant is good enough to warrant staying on the premises all day. (You're expected to take full board in August.) ⊠ *Strada Litoranea (17 km/10 mi northeast), 71030,* ☎ *0884/550155,* FAX *0884/550884. 144 rooms. Restaurant, pool, tennis court, beach. MC, V. Closed Oct.–May.*

$$-$$ 🏨 **Alba del Gargano.** Although it's in the town center, the modern Alba provides a restful atmosphere. Large balconies overlook a quiet courtyard garden, and a frequent (and free) bus service connects with a private beach, where you can use the hotel's beach chairs and umbrellas. Rooms are comfortably furnished, and there is a good restaurant. ⊠ *Corso Matino 102, 71030,* ☎ *0884/550771,* FAX *0884/550772. 40 rooms, 3 suites. Restaurant, bar, beach. MC, V.*

Vieste

⓫ *50 km (30 mi) northeast of Manfredonia.*

This large town on the tip of the spur is the Gargano's main commercial center and an attractive place to wander around. Make for the **castle,** not open to the public but offering good views from its high position overlooking the beaches and town. The resort attracts legions of tourists in summer, some bound for the **Isole Tremiti** (☞ Off the Beaten Path, *below*), a tiny archipelago connected to Vieste by regular ferries.

Lodging

$$$$ 🏨 **Pizzomunno.** Probably the most luxurious resort on the Gargano,
★ Pizzomunno is right on the beach and is surrounded by a large park. It is large, white, modern, air-conditioned, and well equipped. The rooms

are ample and comfortable, all with terraces. Here you can unwind, or try your hand at tennis or archery. ⊠ *Lungomare E. Mattei, 71019,* ☎ *0884/708741,* ℻ *0884/707325. 183 rooms. Restaurant, air-conditioning, pool, sauna, health club, cinema, dance club, children's programs. AE, DC, MC, V. Closed Oct.–Mar.*

Peschici

⑫ *22 km (14 mi) northwest of Vieste.*

You may want to make this pleasant resort on Gargano's north shore your base for spending a few days exploring the surrounding beaches and coast. Development has not wreaked too much havoc on this whitewashed town, and the mazelike center retains its characteristic low houses topped with little domes.

Rodi Garganico

⑬ *20 km (12 mi) west of Peschici, 40 km (25 mi) west of Vieste.*

This fishing village squeezed between the hills and the sea takes its name from the island of Rhodes, recalling its former Greek population. Ringed by pine woods and citrus groves, Rodi is linked by hydrofoils with the Isole Tremiti, and things can get pretty hectic in high summer.

OFF THE BEATEN PATH

ISOLE TREMITI – A ferry service from Termoli, west of the Gargano (1 hr, 40 mins), and hydrofoil service from Vieste, Peschici, Rodi Garganico, and Manfredonia (40 mins to 1 hr, 40 mins) connect the mainland with these three small islands north of the Gargano. Although somewhat crowded with Italian tourists in summer, they are famed for their sea caves, pine forests, and craggy limestone formations. Interesting medieval churches and fortifications dot the islands.

Dining

$$ ✕ **Gabbiano.** Admire the view facing the sea in Rodi Garganico at this cheerful restaurant while savoring freshly caught seafood. ⊠ *Via Trieste 14,* ☎ *0884/965283. MC, V. Closed Thurs.*

Foresta Umbra

★ **⑭** *30 km (19 mi) southwest of Vieste, 25 km (16 mi) south of Rodi Garganico.*

In the middle of the peninsula is the majestic Foresta Umbra (Shady Forest), a dense growth of beech, maple, sycamore, and oak generally found in more northerly climates, thriving here because of the altitude—3,200 ft above sea level. Between the trees are occasional dramatic vistas opening out over the Golfo di Manfredonia. From the north coast, take S528 (midway between Peschici and Rodi Garganico) south to head through the interior of the Gargano, where you'll discover a different world.

Monte Sant'Angelo

★ **⑮** *60 km (19 mi) southwest of Vieste, 16 km (10 mi) north of Manfredonia.*

Perched amid olive groves on the rugged white limestone cliffs overlooking the gulf is the town of Monte Sant'Angelo. Pilgrims have flocked here for nearly 1,500 years—among them, St. Francis of Assisi and the Crusaders setting off for the Holy Land from the then-flourishing port of Manfredonia. The town is centered on the **Santuario di San Michele** (Sanctuary of San Michele), built over the grotto where the archangel Michael is believed to have appeared before shepherds in the year 490. Walk down a long series of steps to get to the grotto itself—on the walls you can see the hand tracings left by pilgrims as votive symbols.

Steps lead left from the sanctuary down to the **Tomba di Rotari** (Tomb of Rotari), believed to have been a medieval baptistery, with some remarkable 12th-century reliefs. More steep steps lead up to the large, ruined **Castello Normano** (Norman Castle) that dominates the town, with a view of the intricate pattern of the streets and steps winding their way up the side of the valley. The town's medieval quarter, the **Rione Junno,** is a maze of little white houses squeezed into a corner of the narrow valley.

Lodging

$–$$ 🏨 **Hotel Rotary.** This simple but welcoming modern hotel is set amid olive and almond groves just outside town. Most rooms have terraces with a good view of the Golfo di Manfredonia. ✉ *Via per Pulsano, 71037,* 🖷 *0884/562146. 24 rooms. Restaurant. AE, DC, MC, V.*

Shopping

Most food shops in the Junno sell a local specialty called *ostia piena* (filled host), a pastry made with candied almonds and wafers of the type similar to communion hosts. The best place to get—or munch—them is at the southern end of the Junno, by the Villa Comunale. Shoemaker **Domenico Palena** displays his unique leather sculptures at his tiny shop in the Junno quarter. Local wood craftsmen make and sell wooden utensils, furniture, and wrought-iron goods.

San Giovanni Rotondo

⑯   *25 km (16 mi) west of Monte Sant'Angelo.*

The ancient village of San Giovanni Rotondo, on the winding S272, has gained importance in recent years as a center of religious pilgrimage. Devotees have flocked here to pay their respects to the shrine and **Tomba di Padre Pio** (1887–1968), a monk revered for his pious life, for miraculous intercessions, and for his having received the stigmata, the signs of Christ's wounds. The **Casa Sollievo della Sofferenza** (Foundation for the Mitigation of Suffering), supported through contributions from around the world, is a testament to the enduring appeal of this holy man.

En Route   A short ride south on S273, and then east (left) at L'Annunziata, will take you back to Manfredonia, where you can link up with the coastal road to return to Bari.

TRULLI DISTRICT
Alberobello, Locorotondo, Ostuni, and Martina Franca

The inland area to the southeast of Bari is one of Italy's oddest enclaves, a flat land devoted to olive cultivation and dotted with the idiosyncratic habitations that have lent their name to the district. The origins of the igloo-shape trulli go back to the 13th century and maybe further. The trulli are built of local limestone, without mortar, and with a hole in the top for escaping smoke. Some are painted with mystical or religious symbols; some are isolated, and others are joined together with roofs on various levels. The center of trulli country is Alberobello, hosting the greatest concentration of the buildings, though you will spot scores of them all over this region, some in states of disrepair but always adding a quirky charm to the landscape.

Alberobello

★ ⑰ *59 km (37 mi) southeast of Bari on S100 south and east on S172, 45 km (28 mi) north of Taranto.*

The trulli zone of Alberobello, where more than 1,000 trulli huddle together along steep, narrow streets, is a national monument. It is also one of the most popular tourist destinations in Apulia and a gold mine if you like picking up local crafts (☞ Shopping, *below*).

Dining and Lodging

$$–$$$ ✕ **Il Poeta Contadino.** Proprietor Marco Leonardo serves "creative regional cooking" in this rustic-style restaurant. In the heart of the attractive trulli zone, it features candlelit tables and a refined, understated ambience. Specialties to look for are fish platters and antipasti. ⊠ *Via Indipendenza 21,* ☎ *080/4321917. Reservations essential. AE, DC, MC, V. Closed Mon. (Oct.–June), Jan. 7–22, and 10 days June–July. No dinner Sun. (Oct.–June).*

$$ ✕ **Trullo d'Oro.** This welcoming, rustic restaurant set in five trulli
★ houses has dark wood beams, whitewashed walls, and an open hearth. Local country cooking includes dishes using lamb and veal, vegetable and cheese antipasti, pasta dishes with crisp raw vegetables on the side, and almond pastries. Among the specialties are roast lamb with *lampasciuni* (a type of wild onion) and spaghetti *al trullo,* made with tomatoes, garlic, olive oil, *rughetta* (arugula), and four cheeses. ⊠ *Via F. Cavallotti 27,* ☎ *080/4321820. Reservations essential. AE, DC, MC, V. Closed Mon. and Jan. 6–Feb. 2.*

$$$ ▦ **Dei Trulli.** Trulli-style cottages in a pine wood near the trulli zone make this a pleasant hotel, decorated with rustic furnishings and folk-art rugs. The modestly priced restaurant serves local specialties. You're expected to take half or full board in high season. ⊠ *Via Cadore 28, 70011,* ☎ *080/9323555,* 𝔽𝔸𝕏 *080/9323560. 33 rooms. Restaurant, pool. AE, MC, V. FAP, MAP.*

Shopping

In the trulli zone, you'll find small shops selling hand-painted clay figurines. Rugs and fabrics are the best bets here, but there is also a good deal of shoddy merchandise.

Grotte di Castellana

⑱ *20 km (12 mi) northwest of Alberobello.*

The Grotte di Castellana are a huge network of caves discovered in 1938. You can take one of the hourly guided tours through the grottoes, filled with fantastically shaped stalagmites and stalactites. The grottoes constitute the largest network of caves on the Italian mainland. ☎ *080/4965511.* ◪ *15,000 lire (1-hr tour), 20,000 lire (2-hr tour).* ☉ *Apr.–Oct., daily 8:30–12:30 and 2:30–6:30; Nov.–Mar., daily 8:30–12:30.*

Dining

$$ ✕ **Al Parco Chiancafredda.** The refined ambience and cuisine of this restaurant, set apart from the tourist haunts, make it pricier than its neighbors. But the food and service are worth it: try such regional dishes as *sformato di verdura* (vegetable stew) and *agnello alla castellanese* (local lamb). ⊠ *Via Chiancafredda 12,* ☎ *080/4968710. Reservations essential. MC, V. Closed Tues. and Nov.*

\$\$ ✕ **Taverna degli Artisti.** Near the caves, this rustic tavern-style restaurant with a big garden specializes in local home cooking, such as roast
lamb, homemade orecchiette, and dishes with ominous names like
timballo fine del mondo (end-of-the-world timbale) and *involtini al purgatorio* (purgatory roulades). ⊠ *Via Vito Matarrese 27,* ☎ *080/
4968234. AE, DC, MC, V. Closed Thurs. (Oct.–June) and Dec.*

Locorotondo

🔟 *9 km (5½ mi) southeast of Alberobello, 40 km (25 mi) north of Taranto.*

Still inside the trulli district, Locorotondo is an attractive hillside town
in the Itria Valley (take S172 from Alberobello). The *rotondo* in the
town's name refers to the circular pattern of the houses, apparent
from any vantage point at the top of the town.

Ostuni

🔟 *50 km (30 mi) west of Brindisi, 40 km (25 mi) northeast of Locorotondo.*

This sun-bleached, picturesque medieval town lies on three hills a
short distance from the coast. The **old center,** on the highest of the hills,
has steep cobbled lanes and stupendous views out over the coast and
the surrounding plain.

Dining and Lodging

\$\$ ✕ **Chez Elio.** Enjoy local dishes and a memorable view of the coastline
★   from the terrace of this modern restaurant, set amid green hills outside town. White walls and table linens contrast with plants and bright
flowers, creating a light, fresh atmosphere. Specialties include orecchiette
with tomato sauce and tagliatelle with blueberries. ⊠ *Via dei Colli Selva
67,* ☎ *0831/308726. Reservations essential. AE, MC, V. Closed Mon.
and Nov.–Mar.*

\$\$ 🏨 **Incanto.** At this modest yet modern hotel outside the old town, you
can admire the countryside and the sea in the distance from many of
its rooms. It makes a basic, but adequate, overnight base for seeing the
area. ⊠ *Via dei Colli, 72017,* ☎ *0831/301781,* 𝔽𝔸𝕏 *0831/338302. 70
rooms. 2 restaurants, 2 bars. AE, DC, MC, V.*

Martina Franca

🔟 *6 km (4 mi) south of Locorotondo, 36 km (22 mi) north of Taranto.*

Martina Franca is an appealing town with a dazzling mixture of medieval and Baroque architecture in the light-color local stone. Ornate
balconies hang above the twisting, narrow streets, with little alleys leading off into the surrounding hills. Martina Franca was developed as a
military stronghold in the 14th century, when a surrounding wall with
24 towers was built, but now all that remains of that role are the four
gates that had been the only entrances to the town. Each July and August Martina Franca holds a music festival.

Dining and Lodging

\$\$ ✕ **La Tavernetta.** This small restaurant with a vaulted ceiling in the old
town center serves large portions of good home cooking, starting with
a pottery bowl full of local olives, and excellent house wine. Specialties include favi e fogghi and, in summer, orecchiette with *cocomero*
(a vegetable that looks like a miniature round watermelon but tastes
like a cross between a cucumber and a honeydew melon). Main courses
include mixed grilled lamb, liver, and spicy local sausage. ⊠ *Corso Vittorio Emanuele 30,* ☎ *080/4306323. MC, V. Closed Mon. (Oct.–June).*

$$–$$$ ☷ **Park Hotel San Michele.** This garden hotel makes a pleasant base in the warm months, thanks to its pool. The two categories of rooms have a small price difference; opt for the higher-priced ones. All are spacious, some embellished with handsome furniture and bowls of fruit. ✉ *Viale Carella 9, 74015,* ☎ *080/4807053,* ⅋ *080/4808895. 86 rooms. Restaurant, bar, pool. AE, DC, MC, V.*

Nightlife and the Arts

Martina Franca concentrates on music in its annual **Festa della Valle Itria** (Festival of the Itria Valley) each July and August.

ACROSS THE HEEL AND SOUTH TO LECCE

Taranto, Brindisi, Lecce, Gallipoli

This far south, the mountains run out of steam and the land is uniformly flat although agriculturally quite important. The monotonous landscape, however, is redeemed by some of the region's best sandy coastline and a handful of alluring small towns. Taranto and Brindisi don't quite fit this description: Both are big ports where historical importance is obscured by unsightly heavy industry. Nonetheless, Taranto has its special attractions, not the least its archaeological museum; Brindisi's marks the end of the Via Appia. Farther south, in Il Salentino (Salentine peninsula), Lecce is an unexpected oasis of grace and sophistication, and its swirling architecture will melt even the most uncompromising critic of the Baroque.

Taranto

㉒ *100 km (62 mi) southeast of Bari, 40 km (25 mi) south of Martina Franca.*

Taranto—the stress is on the first syllable—was an important port even in Roman times. It lies toward the back of the instep of the boot on the broad Mare Grande bay, which is connected to a small internal Mare Piccolo basin by two narrow channels, one artificial and one natural. The old town is on an island between the larger and smaller bodies of water; the modern city stretches inward along the mainland. Little remains of Taranto's past except the 14th-century church of **San Domenico,** at one end of the island, and the city's maritime heritage: Taranto is the home of a famous naval academy.

A shining beacon to shed light on the millennia of local history is the ★ **Museo Nazionale,** whose large collection of prehistoric, Greek, and Roman artifacts came mainly from the immediate vicinity. The museum is just over the bridge from the old town on the promontory. Some of the prehistoric items from Apulian tombs date from before 1000 BC, but more plentiful are the examples of intricate craftsmanship in the Grecian jewelry dating from around 500 BC. The museum is a testament to the importance of this ancient port, which has always taken full advantage of its unique trading position at the end of the Italian peninsula. ✉ *Corso Umberto 41,* ☎ *099/4532112.* ☞ *8,000 lire.* ☉ *Mon.–Sat. 9–2, Sun. 10–10.*

OFF THE BEATEN PATH **MATERA** – Sixty kilometers (37 miles) inland west of Taranto, over the border with Basilicata, the region of stark beauty lacking a successful tourism infrastructure thus far, lies one of the south's most curious towns. Matera has some elegant Baroque churches, broad piazzas (filled to bursting during the evening passeggiata), and fine restaurants, but what really sets this town apart is its *sassi,* rock-hewn dwellings piled chaotically on top of each other and straggling along the sides of a steep ravine. Until relatively recently, these troglodytic abodes presented a Dante-esque vision of squalor and poverty, graphically described in Carlo Levi's *Christ Stopped at Eboli*, but today they have been cleaned up and emptied of their inhabitants (now largely consigned to the ugly blocks you saw on your way into town), and a Strada Panoramica leads you safely through this desolate region. The eerie atmosphere still lingers.

There are two areas of sassi, the Sasso Caveoso and the Sasso Barisano, and both can be viewed from vantage points in the upper town. To get the full picture, however, follow the Strada Panoramica, and feel free to ramble and clamber among the strange structures, which include abandoned churches, and in the words of H. V. Morton, in his *Traveler in Southern Italy*, "resemble the work of termites rather than of man." When you've had your fill, Matera has a good museum, the Museo Ridola, illustrating the human and geological history of the area. ⊠ *Take the S7 west from Matera.*

Dining and Lodging

$ ✕ **Da Basile.** Here's an ideal spot just a couple of blocks from the museum for a quick lunch or a good, straightforward (and cheap!) evening meal. You'll be sharing the four small rooms with a motley crew—families, crowds of youths, solitary businessmen, and groups of women—and you may have to wait for a table. Pizzas with fresh vegetables, no-frills pasta dishes, fish and meat, and delicious homemade gelato round out the menu. Service is fast and attentive. ⊠ *Via Pitagora 76,* ☎ *099/4526240. MC, V. Closed Sat.*

$$$ 🏨 **Golf Hotel.** Less than an hour's drive along the coast from Taranto, this hotel, as its name implies, caters to golf enthusiasts, but its modern amenities and proximity to the sea make it a good refuge for beach fans, too. Guests are required to take half or full board in high season. ⊠ *Località Riva dei Tessali, Castellaneta Marina, 74011,* ☎ *099/8439251,* ‖AX *099/8439255. 70 rooms. Dining room, bar, pool, tennis court. AE, DC, MC, V. Closed Dec.–Jan. FAP, MAP.*

$$$ 🏨 **Grand Hotel Delfino.** This big, modern, well-equipped hotel downtown caters to business clients. Airy rooms have balconies. The restaurant features regional seafood. Rates fall into the bottom of this price category. ⊠ *Viale Virgilio 66, 74100,* ☎ *099/7323232,* ‖AX *099/7304654. 198 rooms. Restaurant, minibars, pool. AE, DC, MC, V.*

Nightlife and the Arts

Taranto has Easter processions on Holy Thursday and Good Friday, the Processione dei Misteri (Procession of the Mysteries) and the Processione dell'Addolorata.

Outdoor Activities and Sports

GOLF

Apulia's only 18-hole golf course is the **Riva dei Tessali** (⊠ Marina di Castellaneta, 40 km/25 mi west of Taranto along the coast road, ☎ 099/8431844).

SAILING

Sailors should contact the **Lega Navale** (⊠ Lungomare Vittorio Emanuele II, ☎ 099/4593801); you can also rent boats and take lessons here.

Brindisi

❷❸ *114 km (71 mi) southeast of Bari, 72 km (45 mi) east of Taranto.*

Occupying the head of a deep inlet on the eastern Adriatic coast, Brindisi (stress placed on first syllable) has long been one of Italy's most important ports, and today most people think of the town only as a terminus for the ferry crossing that links Italy with Greece. Although this impression fails to give credit to the broader importance of the city (it has a population of nearly 100,000), it is a present-day reminder of the role Brindisi has always played as gateway to the eastern Mediterranean and beyond. Brindisi has seen a constant flow of naval and mercantile traffic over the centuries, and in the Middle Ages it was an important departure point for several Crusades to the Holy Land.

The core of the city is at the head of a deep channel, which branches into two harbors with the city between them. Look for the steeple of the cathedral to get your bearings, but go beyond it and down the steps to the water's edge. Just to the left is a tall **Roman column** and the base of another one next to it. These were built in the 2nd century AD and marked the end of the **Via Appia** (Appian Way), the Imperial Roman road that led from the capital to this important southern seaport. ⊠ *Viale Regina Margherita.*

A short walk from the column, the mosaic floor in the apse of the **Duomo** is worth stopping to have a look at; the floor dates from the 12th century, although much of the rest of the cathedral was rebuilt in the 18th. ⊠ *Piazza Duomo.*

The **Castello Svevo,** another of the defense fortifications built by the illustrious Frederick II in the 13th century, guards the larger of Brindisi's two inner harbors, though it is inaccessible to the public. ⊠ *Piazza Castello.*

Lodging

$$$ ⊞ **Majestic.** A modern hotel across from the train station and near the port, the Majestic is fully air-conditioned and furnished in a comfortable, though uninspired, style. The hotel is somewhat overpriced for what it offers, but breakfast is included. ⊠ *Corso Umberto 151, 72100,* ☎ *0831/222941,* 𝐅𝐀𝐗 *0831/524071. 68 rooms. Restaurant. AE, DC, MC, V. CP.*

$$$ ⊞ **Mediterraneo.** Comfort and a convenient central location are the advantages of this modern, air-conditioned hotel—though it is less accessible from the port than the Majestic. Most rooms have balconies. ⊠ *Viale Aldo Moro 70, 72100,* ☎ *0831/582811,* 𝐅𝐀𝐗 *0831/587858. 65 rooms. Restaurant. AE, DC, MC, V.*

Nightlife and the Arts

The **Festa della Città di Brindisi** (City of Brindisi Festival), July–September, is a citywide display of art and folklore; contact the tourist office (⊠ Piazza Dionisi, ☎ 0831/521944).

Outdoor Activities and Sports

SAILING

Contact Brindisi's **Lega Navale** (⊠ Via Vespucci, ☎ 0831/418824).

Lecce

➁ *40 km (25 mi) southeast of Brindisi, 87 km (54 mi) east of Taranto.*

Although Lecce, the crowning jewel on the tour of Apulia, was founded before the time of the ancient Greeks, it is almost always associated with the term Lecce Baroque. This is because of a citywide impulse in the 17th century to redo the town in the Baroque fashion. But this was Baroque with a difference. Although Baroque architecture is often heavy and monumental, here it took on a lighter, more fanciful tone.

★ Just look at the **Basilica di Santa Croce,** with the **Palazzo della Prefettura** abutting it. Although every column, window, pediment, and balcony is given a curling Baroque touch—and then an extra one for good measure—the overall effect is lighthearted. The scale of the buildings is unintimidating and the local stone is a glowing honey color: it couldn't look menacing if it tried. ⊠ *Via Umberto I.*

In the middle of **Piazza Sant'Oronzo** is a **Roman column** of the same era and style as the one in Brindisi. Next to the column the shallow rows of seats in the **Anfiteatro Romano** suggest a small-scale Roman Colosseum or Verona's arena.

Dining and Lodging

$$ ✕ **Plaza.** Tucked away behind Lecce's castle, this high-quality restaurant has been keeping the city's gourmets happy for 30 years. Regional dishes reveal a personal touch. Try the *tubettini alle cozze* (pasta with clams) and the antipasti, worth dipping into. ⊠ *Via 140 Fanteria 12,* ☎ *0832/305093. AE, MC, V. Closed Sun. and Aug.*

$$–$$$ ▦ **Risorgimento.** An old-fashioned hotel in a converted palace in the heart of the Baroque old town, the Risorgimento combines historic charm with modern comfort. The roof garden has great town views. ⊠ *Via Augusto Imperatore 19, 73100,* ☎ *0832/242125,* ℻ *0832/245571. 57 rooms. Restaurant, lounge, meeting rooms. AE, DC, MC, V.*

$ ▦ **Cappello.** This popular hotel is close to the train station but outside the old city walls, about a 10-minute walk from the town center. Rooms are small but clean and comfortable, and fully equipped with TV, telephone, and air-conditioning. Those at the back can get noisy from the nearby railroad. Reservations are advised. ⊠ *Via Montegrappa 4, 73100,* ☎ *0832/308881,* ℻ *0832/301535. 32 rooms. Bar. AE, MC, V.*

Nightlife and the Arts

In July, the public gardens are venues for productions of drama and, sometimes, opera. A **Baroque music festival** in September is held in churches throughout the city.

Shopping

Wrought-iron work is the local specialty. Also look for works in papier-mâché, especially nativity scenes.

Gallipoli

㉕ *37 km (23 mi) south of Lecce.*

The modern section of the town of Gallipoli, on the Golfo di Taranto, lies on the mainland; turn right on the main street at the end of the central square and cross a 17th-century bridge to the old town, crowded onto its own small island in the gulf. The Greeks called it Kallipolis, the Romans Anxa. Like the famous Turkish town of the same name on the Dardanelles, the Italian Gallipoli occupies a strategic location and thus was repeatedly attacked through the centuries—by the Normans in 1071, the Venetians in 1484, the British in 1809. The historic quarter, a mesh of narrow alleys and squares, is guarded by a formidable **Castello Aragonese,** a massive fortification that grew out of an earlier Byzantine fortress that you can still see at the southeast corner. Notable churches in town are the Baroque **Duomo** and the church of **La Purissima,** with a stuccoed interior as elaborate as a wedding cake (note especially the tiled floor).

Dining and Lodging

$$ ✕ **Marechiaro.** You have to cross a little bridge to this simple port-side
★ restaurant, actually not far from the town's historic center. It's built out onto the sea, replete with wood paneling, flowers, and terraces with panoramic coastal views. Try the renowned *zuppa di pesce alla gallipolina* (fish stew made without tomatoes), succulent shellfish, and linguine with seafood. ⊠ *Lungomare Marconi,* ☎ *0833/266143. Reservations essential weekends. AE, DC, MC, V. Closed Tues. (Oct.–May).*

$$$ ⊡ **Costa Brada.** The rooms all have terraces with sea views at this modern white beach hotel of classic Mediterranean design. The interiors are comfortable and tasteful; Rooms 110–114 are particularly spacious and overlook the beach. The hotel accepts only half-board or full-board guests in the high season. ⊠ *At Baia Verde beach, Litoranea Santa Maria di Leuca, 73014,* ☎ *0833/202551,* FAX *0833/202555. 80 rooms. Restaurant, snack bar, indoor and outdoor pools, sauna, tennis court, exercise room. AE, DC, MC, V. FAP, MAP.*

$$–$$$ ⊡ **Le Sirenuse.** There is a private beach and pine forest at this gleaming white Mediterranean-style beach hotel complex. Its comfortable rooms are air-conditioned with terraces. Half- or full-board is required in high season. ⊠ *At Baia Verde beach, 73014,* ☎ *0833/202536,* FAX *0833/202539. 119 rooms. Pool, tennis court, beach. MC, V. Closed Nov.–Apr. FAP, MAP.*

Outdoor Activities and Sports

BEACHES

Ample swimming, clean, fine sand, and water sports make Gallipoli a good choice for families.

APULIA A TO Z

Arriving and Departing

By Boat

Ferries ply the waters from Bari and Brindisi to Greece (Corfu, Igoumenitsa, Patras, and Kephalonia), Turkey, Albania, even Egypt and Croatia. Contact **Adriatica di Navigazione** (Ditta A. Galli e Figlio, ⊠ Corso Manfredi 4, 71043 Manfredonia, ☎ 0884/582520; Intercontinental Viaggi, ⊠ Corso Umberto 93, 86039 Termoli, ☎ 0875/705341); Ditta Cafiero Emilio, ⊠ Via Degli Abbati 10, 71040 Tremiti, ☎ 0882/663008; Gargano Viaggi, ⊠ Piazza Roma 7, 71019 Vieste, ☎ 0884/708501). **European Seaways** (⊠ Corso Garibaldi 97, 72100 Brindisi, ☎ 0831/527684).

By Plane

Alitalia flies regularly from other Italian cities to Bari and Brindisi. **Aeroporto Palese** (☎ 080/5382370) is 8 km (5 mi) west of Bari. **Aeroporto Papola Casale** (☎ 0831/418805) is 5 km (3 mi) north of Brindisi.

BETWEEN THE AIRPORT AND DOWNTOWN

Regular bus service connects the two airports with the cities. Alitalia buses provide service from the cites to arrivals and departures at both airports.

By Train

Bari is a transit hub for train connections with northern Italy.

Getting Around

By Boat

☞ **Adriatica di Navigazione** *in* Arriving and Departing, *above.*

By Bus

Direct, if not always frequent, connections operate between most destinations in Apulia. In many cases the bus service is actually the backup to the train service (☞ *below*).

By Car

Driving is the best way to get around Apulia and the only way to see remote sights. Apulia is linked with the Italian autostrada system, making it just a four- or five-hour drive from Rome to the Gargano Promontory or Bari. Roads are good, and major cities are linked by fast autostrade. Secondary roads (superstrade) connect the whole region; more direct—but sometimes less scenic—routes provide a convenient link between Bari, Brindisi, and Lecce. Don't plan on any night driving in the countryside, because the roads can become confusing without the aid of landmarks or large towns.

By Train

Good train service, operated by **FS** (Italian State Railways), links Bari to Brindisi, Lecce, and Taranto, but smaller destinations can often be reached only by completing the trip on a connecting bus operated by the railroad. The private **Ferrovie Sud-Est** (FSE) line connects the trulli area and Martina Franca with Bari and Taranto, and the fishing port of Gallipoli with Lecce.

Contacts and Resources

Car Rentals

BARI

Avis (⊠ Via Zuppetta 5/a, ☎ 080/5247154). **Hertz** (⊠ Piazza Moro 47, ☎ 080/5242250; ⊠ Aeroporto Palese, ☎ 080/373666).

BRINDISI

Avis (⊠ Via del Mare 50, ☎ 0831/526407). **Hertz** (⊠ c/o Silver Travel, Corso Garibaldi 95, ☎ 0831/528333).

FOGGIA

Avis (⊠ Train station, ☎ 0881/778912). **Hertz** (⊠ Via Monfalcone 39, ☎ 0881/608400).

TARANTO

Avis (⊠ Corso Umberto 61, ☎ 099/4532278). **Hertz** (⊠ Corso Umberto 49, ☎ 099/4533763).

Emergencies

Police, Ambulance, Fire, First-Aid ("Pronto Soccoroso") (☎ 113).

Guided Tours

The **CIT** office in Bari (☞ Visitor Information, *below*) is the best connection for guided tours in Apulia, otherwise poorly served by tour operators. The CIT office can put you in touch with one of a number of local operators that offer everything from chauffeur-driven cars to a quick regional primer as part of a longer excursion.

Late-Night Pharmacies

Pharmacies take turns remaining open late and on Sunday. A list of hours is posted on each *farmacia* (pharmacy).

Travel Agencies

BARI

CIT (⊠ Via Abate Gimma 150, ☎ 080/5213552). **Wagon-Lits** (⊠ Thomas Cook, Via Cardassi 85, ☎ 080/5540580).

BRINDISI

Silver Viaggi (⊠ Corso Garibaldi 95, 72100, ☎ 0831/528333). **Utac Viaggi** (⊠ Via Cesare Braico 8, 72100, ☎ 0831/560780, FAX 0831/529040).

Visitor Information

Bari (⊠ Piazza Moro 32a, 70122, ☎ 080/5242244). **Brindisi** (⊠ Piazza Dionisi, 72100, ☎ 0831/521944). **Foggia** (⊠ Via Perrone 17, 71100, ☎ 0881/723141). **Foresta Umbra** (⊠ Piazza Europa 104, San Giovanni Rotondo, 71013, ☎ 0882/456240). **Lecce** (⊠ Via Vittorio Emanuele 24, 73100, ☎ 0832/248092). **Taranto** (⊠ Corso Umberto 113, 74100, ☎ 099/4532392). **Trani** (⊠ Via Cavour 140, 70059, ☎ 0883/588830; ⊠ Kiosk in Piazza della Repubblica, summer only, ☎ 0883/43295). **Vieste** (⊠ Piazza Kennedy, 71019, ☎ 0884/708806).

15 Sicily

On this fabled island, you can ski down a snow-muffled volcano, wander through palm and orange groves, and swim within sight of majestic ruins. It has a stubborn personality: cynical yet passionate, languorous yet industrious. But the ethereal subtleties of this seemingly far-off kingdom reveal themselves in panoramic Taormina, the Valley of the Temples, and the unforgettable rose-tinted moon rising over Mt. Etna.

Updated by
Robert
Andrews

EN ROUTE SOUTH TO SICILY, you realize you are entering a world apart from the north. Ample, succulent lemons whirl by the hurtling train's windows, while cacti wave their prickly appendages and balmy air wafts gently about. Women look up from clotheslines, a sunglassed *ragazzo* (teenage boy) on a Vespa pauses at a stoplight just below. Once arrived, you may be surprised to see a profusion of blond hair and blue eyes and to learn that two of the most popular man's names are Ruggero (Roger) and Guglielmo (William).

Lying in a strategic position between Europe and Africa, Sicily at one time hosted two of the most advanced and enlightened capitals of Europe—a Greek one in Siracusa and an Arab-Norman one in Palermo. (The Normans are responsible for the blond-haired Rogers and blue-eyed Williams.) Sicily was one of the great melting pots of the ancient world and home to every great civilization that existed in the Mediterranean: Greek and Roman; then Arab and Norman; and, finally, French, Spanish, and Italian. Something of all of these peoples was absorbed into the island's artistic heritage, a rich tapestry of art and architecture that includes massive Romanesque cathedrals, two of the best-preserved Greek temples in the world, Roman amphitheaters, and delightful Baroque palaces and churches.

Modern Sicily is still a land of surprising contrasts. The traditional graciousness and nobility of the Sicilian people exist side by side with the atrocities and destructive influences of the Mafia, although recent events suggest that the Mafia's grip on the island is being slowly loosened. Alongside some of the most exquisite architecture in the world are the shabby products of some of the worst speculation imaginable. In recent years, Sicily, like much of the Mediterranean coast, has experienced a boom in tourism and a surge in condominium development that has only now begun to be checked. The chic boutiques purveying lace and linen in jet-set resort towns like Taormina give no clue to the poverty in which their wares are produced.

In Homer's *Odyssey,* Sicily represented the unknown end of the world, yet the region eventually became the center of the known world under the Normans, who recognized a paradise in its deep blue skies and temperate climate, its lush vegetation, and rich marine life. Much of this paradise does still exist today. Add to it Sicily's unique cuisine—another harmony of elements—which mingles Arab and Greek spices with Spanish and French dishes, using some of the world's tastiest seafood, and you can understand why those who arrived here were often reluctant to leave.

You do not have to be paranoid about safety in Sicily, but you do have to be careful: Do not flaunt jewelry, and keep your handbag securely strapped across your chest. Leaving valuables visible in your car while you go sightseeing is inviting trouble. Be careful; then enjoy the company of the Sicilians. You will find them to be friendly and often willing to go out of their way to help tourists. It is not uncommon in small towns for visitors to receive invitations to a local's house for dinner. It doesn't matter if you don't speak Italian or speak only a little: they aren't usually offended if your pronunciation isn't perfect. One of the reasons for this, no doubt, is the fact that many Sicilians or their close relatives have themselves been strangers in foreign lands, and empathy goes a long way.

Pleasures and Pastimes

Beaches

There is a surfeit of beaches in Sicily, but many of them are too rocky, too crowded, or too dirty to be enjoyed for long. Among the exceptions are Mondello, near Palermo, a popular sandy beach on a tiny peninsula jutting out into the Mediterranean; Sant'Alessio and Santa Teresa, north of Taormina (the beaches just below Taormina itself are disappointing); and Capo San Vito, on the northern coast, near Erice, a sandy beach on a promontory overlooking a bay in the Gulf of Castellammare.

Camping

Sicily has excellent camping facilities on both the main island and its satellite islands. The two best are El Bahira, in San Vito Lo Capo, and Bazia, in Furnari Marina, west of Milazzo. Both have restaurants and showers, as well as swimming pools, tennis courts, and discos.

Dining

Sicilian cooking reflects the various Mediterranean influences that have left their mark on the island. Fish, vegetables, and grains are used in imaginative combinations, sometimes served with Italian pastas or Arab or North African ingredients, such as couscous. Sweet and sour tastes are deftly mingled, and cooks have distinctive touches, so that *caponata* (an antipasto of eggplant, capers, olives, and, in eastern Sicily, peppers) is different at every restaurant.

Sicily has always been one of Italy's poorest areas, so meat is not the centerpiece on menus. It is usually prepared *alla brace* (skewered) or in *falso magro* (a thin slice of meat rolled around sausage, onion, bacon, bits of egg, and cheese). In Sicily, naturally, you'll enjoy the freshest seafood in all of Italy, and you'll also find the most variety. *Tonno* (tuna) is a staple in many coastal areas, and *pesce spada* (swordfish) is equally common, if more expensive. Try *ricci* (sea urchins), a specialty of Mondello, near Palermo. Fish sauces are often tossed on pasta: Pasta *con le sarde* is made with fresh sardines, olive oil, anchovies, raisins, and pine nuts, and has the distinctive flavor of wild fennel. In Catania, spaghetti *alla Norma,* named for the heroine in the opera by local composer Vincenzo Bellini, is prepared with a sauce of tomato and fried eggplant.

Desserts from Sicily are famous. The traditional Easter cake is the *cassata siciliana,* a rich sponge cake with candied fruit, marzipan, and icing. From behind bakery windows and glass cases all over beam tiny marzipan sweets, fashioned into bright-color apples, cherries, corncobs, hamburgers, and more. Local gelato is excellent and is usually homemade, as are brilliant *granite* (granitas) in flavors such as lemon. Gooey cakes and very sweet desserts such as chestnut ice cream covered with hot zabaglione provide a sugar fix. The sweet dessert wine, Marsala, is Sicily's most famous, but there is a range of other local wines, from the dark red Faro to the sparkling dry Regaleali, excellent with fish.

CATEGORY	COST*
$$$	60,000–85,000 lire
$$	25,000–60,000 lire
$	under 25,000 lire

Prices are per person, including house wine, service, and tax.

Kids' Stuff

Almost every major city in Sicily has a theater giving performances of the world-famous Sicilian *pupi* (marionettes). The most popular are in Palermo, Acireale, and Taormina. Stories center on heroes from the Norman fables, distressed damsels, and Saracen invaders. Even if you can't understand Italian, the action is fast and furious, so it's easy to figure out what's going on. Palermo has an International Museum dedicated to these and other types of marionettes. If you are in Sicily at Carnival time (the week before Ash Wednesday, about 45 days before Easter), Acireale has one of Italy's best celebrations, when dozens of colorful torch-lit floats, papier-mâché characters aboard, are pulled through the streets by costumed revelers.

Lodging

Though Sicily is Italy's largest region, it has some of the most remote countryside and only a limited number of good-quality hotels. The major cities and resorts of Palermo, Taormina, and Agrigento are the only spots with a real range of accommodations. There are, of course, some superb establishments, such as converted villas with sea views and well-equipped modern hotels, but it is best not to expect to come across some enchanting oasis in the middle of nowhere. If you want to get away from the major centers, make reservations well in advance.

Hotels in the $$$$ category provide comfort and services to match those in other Italian regions; they are usually the older, more established hotels. In the $$–$$$ range, you'll find newer hotels built to cater to the increased tourist trade of the past 20 years. Chains, such as Jolly Hotels, are predictable but reliable. Inexpensive establishments are usually family-run and offer a basic level of comfort: Although the bathroom will be clean, it will probably also be down the hall.

CATEGORY	COST*
$$$$	over 300,000 lire
$$$	160,000–300,000 lire
$$	100,000–160,000 lire
$	under 100,000 lire

Prices are for a standard double room, including service and tax.

Scuba Diving

The island of Ustica, north of Palermo, is an international center for scuba diving and snorkeling. Its rugged coast is dotted with grottoes that are washed by crystal-clear waters and filled with an incredible variety of interesting marine life. In July Ustica hosts an International Meeting of Marine Fishing that attracts sportsmen as well as marine biologists from all over the world.

Shopping

Sicily is one of the leaders in the Italian ceramics industry, with important factories at Caltagirone, in the interior, and Santo Stefano di Camastra, along the northern coast between Messina and Cefalù. Colorful Sicilian folk pottery can still be bought at bargain prices. Place mats, tablecloths, napkins, and clothing decorated with fine petit point are good buys in Cefalù, Taormina, and Erice, but they are not cheap. Make sure that any linen you buy is produced in Sicily and not on another continent.

Collectors have been combing Sicily for years for pieces of the colorful *carretti siciliani* (Sicilian carts). Before the automobile, these were the major form of transportation in Sicily, and they were decorated in bright primary colors and in primitive styles, with scenes from the Norman troubadour tales. The axles of these carts were ornamented with open filigree work, which was also brightly painted.

Skiing

Skiing is fast becoming a popular sport in Sicily. Ski areas can be found on the slopes on the north side of Mt. Etna. The most popular is at Linguaglossa, in a magnificent pine forest about 45 km (27 mi) from

Catania. The other area for skiing in Sicily is in the Le Madonie mountains, south of Cefalù.

Exploring Sicily

Sicily is about 180 km (112 mi) north to south and 270 km (168 mi) across. For exploration purposes, the country can be divided into four distinct areas of interest: historic Palermo and its environs; the western coast to Agrigento, the Greek temple belt; Eastern Sicily, of untrammeled inland villages and coastal towns such as Siracusa; and the northeastern Isole Eolie, an archipelago of seven volcanic islands.

Sicily is so dense with places of interest that not even a week is sufficient to explore the island in depth, though with a car at your disposal you will be able to cover all the most important sites. The best way to visit it is to travel counterclockwise along the coast by car, bus, or train, making occasional detours inland.

You needn't visit all seven of the Isole Eolie individually. In summer, hydrofoils and ferries connect all seven, so one or two of them can be admired from the sea. Lipari is the most equipped of the islands for tourism, though all of the islands except Stromboli offer some kind of accommodation, from small, family-run guest houses to beds in private homes.

Numbers in the text correspond to numbers in the margin and on the Sicily, Palermo, and Agrigento maps.

Great Itineraries

In nine days, you can do a thorough loop around the island, which starts in Palermo, moves west and south to the stunning Greek cities of Selinunte and Agrigento, then dips inland and continues southeast to Siracusa, and finally heads north to picturesque Taormina and the Isole Eolie. Smaller explorations concentrated around Palermo and environs can be done in three or five days.

IF YOU HAVE 3 DAYS

A three-day sojourn on the island should not necessitate renting a car if you base yourself in Sicily's capital, ⊞ **Palermo** ①–⑪. In this hub of Norman Sicily, the highlights include the **Palazzo dei Normanni** ① and the **Museo Archeologico Regionale** ⑩, as well as a handful of characteristic churches. Head out to **Monreale** ⑫ to admire the splendid cathedral, and compare it with the slightly earlier mosaic-laden monument at **Cefalù** ⑬. Spend your last day exploring this seaside resort.

IF YOU HAVE 5 DAYS

A longer time on the island will allow you to add choice excursions to the three-day itinerary. From **Cefalù** ⑬ proceed westward along the northwestern coast to panoramic ⊞ **Erice** ⑮, a good spot to overnight. Just up the road is **Trapani** ⑯, a port-city that has little to offer the visitor. Heading east through the interior, drop in on the imposing half-finished temple of **Segesta** ⑭, then swing south to the ruins of **Selinunte** ⑲, with remarkable metopes you will have seen in Palermo's archaeological museum. Following the coast down, aim for the Greek temple site at ⊞ **Agrigento** ⑳–㉗. Allow a full day to explore Agrigento before heading north on the S189, back to Palermo.

IF YOU HAVE 9 DAYS

This itinerary is an extension of the five-day itinerary, *above.* From Agrigento, head inland toward **Enna** ㉘, worth a quick whirl around, then make a lunch stop at **Piazza Armerina** ㉙ before viewing the exuberant mosaics of the Roman villa at **Casale** ㉚. If you have time, stop off to see the Museo della Ceramica at **Caltagirone** ㉛ before continuing on the S124 to ⊞ **Siracusa** ㉝ for a full day. Head north up the coast—

TO NAPLES

Stromboli 43

Panarea 42

Alicudi 44 **Filicudi** 45 **Salina** 41 **Lipari** 39 **Vulcano** 40 **Liparo**

ISOLE EOLIE

Golfo di Gióia

TO NAPLES

Mortelle

Milazzo

Capo d'Orlando

Patti

Messina 38

Reggio di Calabria

Cefalù 13 Caldura

Santo Stefano di Camastra

S113

S113

A20

S117

Castelmola

A18

Taormina 37

Bronte

Mt. Etna 36

Adrano

Biancavilla

Acireale

Paterno

S192

A19

Enna 28

issetta

Catania 35

Golfo di Catania

Piazza Armerina 29

Casale 30

S288

Ionian Sea

Athenian Sea

Caltagirone 31

S124

Gela

Palazzolo Acreide 32

Euryalus

Siracusa 33

Comiso

S114

Ragusa

Noto 34

Avola

Golfo di Gela

Modica

S115

Golfo di Noto

Capo Passero

TO MALTA

a visit to **Catania** ㉟ is of limited interest—and keep going until you can see the silhouette of **Mt. Etna** ㊱ (most fog-free in the morning), an essential stop on any Sicilian tour. Spend the night in ☷ **Taormina** ㊲. A couple of hours are enough for a drive up to the village of **Castelmola,** above Taormina; otherwise, go directly to **Messina** ㊳. If you can, see the Museo Regionale here for your last blast of Sicilian art, before crossing the Straits to the seven islands of the Aeolian archipelago: **Lipari** ㊴, the biggest and most developed island, with a superb Museo Archeologico, **Vulcano** ㊵, **Salina** ㊶, **Panarea** ㊷, **Stromboli** ㊸, **Alicudi** ㊹, and **Filicudi** ㊺. Then, it's back to reality and the mainland.

When to Tour Sicily

Sicily comes into its own in the spring, but you're not alone in knowing this. Taormina and Erice attract a flood of visitors around Easter, and any visit scheduled for this time should be backed up by solid advance bookings. Many sites, such as inland Segesta, are at their best in the clear spring light, and are far enough off the beaten track to ensure a fairly hassle-free time. August, on the other hand, is hellish wherever you choose to roam—not just for the presence of fellow travelers, but for the extreme, uncomfortably hot temperatures. Cities should be avoided. Beaches don't necessarily offer refuge from the sizzling temperatures; they can get pretty clogged with Italian and foreign vacationers. Come in September or October, and you'll find acres of beach space. Cefalù, like Taormina, sees year-round tourism, though some of the luxury hotels close down for the winter. As with Easter, Christmas and New Year's draw visitors to the island, and reservations should always be made as early as possible. Other festivals, such as Agrigento's almond festival in February, can also mean a dearth of vacancies.

PALERMO

The heritage of the past encompasses all ages, but Palermo's most unique aspect is its Arab-Norman identity, an improbable marriage that, mixed in with Byzantine and Jewish elements, created some unforgettable and resplendent works of art. These are most notable in the churches, small jewels such as San Giovanni degli Eremiti or larger-scale works such as the cathedral.

Once the intellectual capital of southern Europe, Palermo has always been at the crossroads of civilization. Favorably situated on a crescent-shape bay at the foot of Monte Pellegrino, it has attracted almost every people and culture touching the Mediterranean world. To Palermo's credit, it has absorbed these diverse cultures into a unique personality that is at once Arab and Christian, Byzantine and Roman, Norman and Italian.

Palermo was first colonized by Phoenician traders in the 6th century BC, but it was their descendants, the Carthaginians, who built the important fortress here that caught the covetous eye of the Romans. After the First Punic War, the Romans took control of the city, in the 3rd century BC. After several invasions by the Vandals, Sicily was settled by Arabs, who made the country an emirate and made Palermo a showpiece capital that rivaled both Cordoba and Cairo in Asian splendor. Nestled in the fertile Conca d'Oro (Golden Conch) plain; full of orange, lemon, and carob groves; and enclosed by limestone hills, Palermo became a magical world of palaces and mosques, minarets and palm trees.

It was so attractive and sophisticated a city that the Norman ruler Roger de Hauteville (1031–1101) decided to conquer it and make it his capital (1072). The Norman occupation of Sicily resulted in the Golden

Age of Palermo (from 1072 to 1194), a remarkable period of enlightenment and learning in which the arts flourished. The city of Palermo, which in the 11th century counted more than 300,000 inhabitants, became the center of the Norman court in all Europe and one of the most important ports of trade between East and West.

Eventually the Normans were replaced by the Swabian ruler Frederick II, the Holy Roman Emperor, and incorporated into the Kingdom of the Two Sicilies. You will also see evidence in Palermo of the Baroque art and architecture of the Spanish viceroys, who came to power after the bloody Sicilian Vespers uprising of 1282, in which the French Angevin dynasty was overthrown. The Aragonese viceroys also brought the Inquisition to Palermo, which some historians believe helped foster the protective secret societies that eventually evolved into today's Mafia.

Exploring Palermo

The Sicilian capital is a multilayered, vigorous metropolis, packed with interest. Approach the city with an open mind, and you'll find it an enriching and enjoyable place to explore, with a strong historical profile. Regulate your pace, don't attempt to see too much too quickly, and keep your head. If you have a car, park it in a garage as soon as you can, and don't take it out until you are ready to depart.

Palermo is easily explored on foot, though you may choose to spend a morning taking a city bus tour to help you get oriented. The Quattro Canti, or Four Corners, is the hub that separates the four sections of the city: La Kalsa is southeast; southwest is Albergheria; Capo is the northwest quadrant; and Vucciria is northeast. Each of these is a tumult of activity during the day, though at night the narrow alleys empty out and are best avoided altogether, in favor of the more animated avenues of the new city, north of Piazza Castelnuovo. Sights you will want to see by day are scattered along three major streets: Corso Vittorio Emanuele, Via Maqueda, and Via Roma. The tourist information office in Piazza Castelnuovo will give you a map and a valuable handout that lists opening and closing times, which sometimes change with the seasons.

A Good Walk

Start at the **Palazzo dei Normanni** ①, at the far west end of Corso Vittorio Emanuele, to see the mosaics in the Cappella Palatina and the royal apartments. Walk down Via dei Benedettini, following the five pink domes of **San Giovanni degli Eremiti** ②. Back east on the Corso stands Palermo's **Duomo** ③, a cacophony of Arab, Norman, and Gothic influences. Farther east is Piazza Vigliena, better known as **Quattro Canti** ④, the intersection of Via Maqueda and Corso Vittoria Emanuele. Just east off Quattro Canti is **Piazza Pretoria.** Just south is Piazza Bellini, holding a trio of eminent churches: the Baroque **Santa Caterina** ⑤, and up the stairs, **San Cataldo** ⑥ and **La Martorana** ⑦ form a delightful Norman complex. Walk northeast along Via Alloro to **Palazzo Abatellis** ⑧ and its Galleria Regionale. If you like puppets, take Via Alloro east and go northwest (left) in Via Butera to the **Museo delle Marionette** ⑨. Then, either take Bus 104 or 105 (to 101) or take a 40-minute walk: cross Corso Vittorio Emanuele to reach Via Cala, follow this busy road around the old port, which becomes Via Barilai, turning left at Piazza XIII Vittime onto Via Cavour. Follow this as far as Via Roma, where you turn left, walking south 50 meters to the **Museo Archeologico Regionale** ⑩. (If you're more adventurous and want a short cut, you can turn left off the noisy Via Cala, though you need a good sense of direction to negotiate the labyrinth of the Vucciria.) Cut through Via Bara all'Olivella to Piazza Verdi and the **Teatro Massimo** ⑪.

Palermo

Porto

Faro Italico

Villa Giulia

Orto Botanica

Cala

Via Barilai

VUCCIRIA

Giardini Garibaldi

Pza. Marina

Via Alloro

LA KALSA

Via Garibaldi

Corso Via dei Mille

Corso Via Lincoln

Train Station

Via Roma

Piazza San Domenico

Via Roma

Pza. Corso Vittorio Emanuele

Pretoria

Via Maqueda

Corso Tuköry

Teatro Massimo

Via Maqueda

Via Candelai

Via Verdi

Quattro Canti

Pza. Pza.

Via Volturno

Pza. Vitt. Emanuele Orlando

Via Papireto

Villa Bonanno

Pza. d. Parlamento

V. Benedettini

C. Re Ruggero

ALBERGHERIA

Via Mongitore

Via Albergheria

Corso Alberto Amadeo

Corso Finocchiaro Aprile

Via d'Ossuna

Via G. Mosca

Colonna Rotta

CAPO

Via

Pza. Indipendenza

V. G. il Buono

Via Zisa

Via C. Lascaria

Via Cipressi

Piazza Danisinni

Via Cappuccini

Corso Vittorio Emanuele

C. dei Pisani

N

0   300 yards
0   300 meters

KEY

i Tourist Information

Duomo, 3
La Martorana, 7
Museo Archeologico Regionale, 10
Museo delle Marionette, 9
Palazzo Abatellis, 8

Palazzo dei Normanni, 1
Quattro Canti, 4
San Cataldo, 6
San Giovanni degli Eremiti, 2
Santa Caterina, 5
Teatro Massimo, 11

Allow the best part of a day for this walk, with lunch around the Quattro Canti. Check first with the tourist office if all the sights on your itinerary are open, as they tend to close at short notice, national holidays, renovations, or staff shortages usually being the causes.

Sights to See

❸ Duomo. A lesson in Palermitan eclecticism—originally Norman (1182), then Catalan Gothic (14th–15th century) and Baroque and Neoclassical interior (18th century)—sums up this church: Turrets, towers, dome, and arches come together in the kind of meeting of diverse elements that King Roger II (1095–1154), whose tomb is inside along with that of Frederick II, fostered during his reign. Be sure to walk outside and look at the back of the apse, which is gracefully decorated with interlacing Arab arches, inlaid with limestone and black volcanic tufa. ⊠ *Corso Vittorio Emanuele.* ⊘ *Daily 7–noon and 4–6.*

❼ La Martorana. Distinguished by an elegant campanile, this church was erected in 1143 but had its interior altered considerably during the Baroque period. High along the western wall, however, is some of the oldest mosaic artwork of the Norman period. Near the entrance is an interesting mosaic of Roger being crowned by Christ. In it, Roger is dressed in a bejeweled Byzantine stole, reflecting the Norman court's penchant for all things Byzantine. Archangels along the ceiling wear the same stole, wrapped around their shoulders and arms. Like the archangels, the Norman monarchs liked to think of themselves as emissaries from heaven, engaged in defending Christianity by ridding the island of infidel invaders. ⊠ *Piazza Bellini.* ⊘ *Apr.–Sept., Mon.–Sat. 9:30–1 and 3:30–6:30; Oct.–Mar., Mon–Sat. 9:30–1 and 3:30–5:30.*

❿ Museo Archeologico Regionale. Especially interesting pieces in this small but excellent collection are the examples of prehistoric cave drawings and a marvelously reconstructed Doric frieze from the Greek Temple at Selinunte that gives you a good idea of the high level of artistic culture attained by the Greek colonists in Sicily some 2,500 years ago. ⊠ *Piazza Olivella 24, Via Roma,* ☎ *091/6116805.* ▦ *8,000 lire.* ⊘ *Tues.–Fri. 9–1:45 and 3–7:30, Sat.–Mon. 9–1:45.*

⊙ ❾ Museo delle Marionette (Museum of Marionettes). The traditional Sicilian pupi, with their glittering armor and fierce expressions, have become a symbol of Norman Sicily. Plots center on the chivalric legends of the troubadours, who, before the puppet theater, kept alive tales of Norman heroes in Sicily, such as Orlando Furioso and William the Bad. ⊠ *Via Butera 1,* ☎ *091/328060.* ▦ *5,000 lire.* ⊘ *Weekdays 9–1 and 4–7, Sat. 9–1.*

❽ Palazzo Abatellis. Housed in this late 15th-century Catalan Gothic palace with Renaissance elements is the **Galleria Regionale**. Among its treasures is an Annunciation (1474) by Sicily's prominent Renaissance master, Antonello da Messina (1430–79), and an arresting fresco by an unknown painter, titled *The Triumph of Death*, a macabre depiction of the plague years. ⊠ *Via Alloro 4,* ☎ *091/6164317.* ▦ *8,000 lire.* ⊘ *Mon.–Sat. 9–1:30 (Tues. and Thurs. also 3–7:30), Sun. 9–12:30.*

★ ❶ Palazzo dei Normanni (Norman Royal Palace). The seat of the Sicilian Parliament was, unfortunately, closed to the public for security reasons in 1992, but the **Cappella Palatina** (Palatine Chapel) inside, one of Italy's greatest art treasures, remains open. Built by Roger II (1095–1154) in 1132, this is a dazzling example of the unique harmony of artistic elements that came together under the Normans. In it, the skill of French and Sicilian masons was brought to bear on the decorative purity of Arab ornamentation and the splendor of Greek Byzantine mosaics. The interior is covered with glittering mosaics and capped by a splendid Arab honeycomb stalactite wooden ceiling. Biblical stories blend happily with scenes of Arab life—look for one showing a picnic in a harem—and Norman court pageantry. Stylized Moorish palm branches run along the walls below the mosaics and recall the battlements on Norman castles—each one a different mosaic composition.

Upstairs are the royal apartments, including the **Sala di Ruggero** (King Roger's Hall), decorated with medieval murals of hunting scenes. Tour guides escort you around these halls, which once hosted one of the most splendid courts in Europe. French, Latin, and Arabic were spoken here, and Arab astronomers and poets exchanged ideas with Latin and Greek scholars in what must have been one of the most unique marriages of culture in the Western world. ⊠ *Piazza Indipendenza,* ☎ *091/ 7054317.* ☒ *Free.* ☉ *Weekdays 9–noon and 3–5, Sat. 9–noon, Sun. 9–10 and noon–1. Tours must be arranged in advance. Closed during religious services and for weddings.*

Piazza Pretoria. The square's centerpiece, a lavishly decorated fountain, was originally intended for a Florentine villa. Its abundance of nude figures so shocked some Palermitans when it was unveiled in 1575 that it got the nickname the "Fountain of Shame." It is even more of a sight at night, when illuminated. ⊠ *Just east of Piazza Pretoria.*

❹ **Quattro Canti.** The Four Corners is the converging point of Corso Vittorio Emanuele and Via Maqueda. Four rather traffic-blackened Baroque palaces from the Spanish rule meet at concave corners, each with its own fountain and representations of a Spanish ruler, patron saint, and one of the four seasons.

❻ **San Cataldo.** Orange-red domes mark this church, built in 1160. Its spare but intense interior, punctuated by antique Greek columns, retains much of its original medieval simplicity. If the church is closed, the custodian at La Martorana (☞ *above*) will let you in during public hours. ⊠ *Piazza Bellini.* ☉ *Apr.–Sept., Mon.–Sat. 8–1 and 3:30– 6:30, Sun. 8–1; Oct.–Mar., Mon.–Sat. 9:30–1 and 3:30–5:30, Sun. 9:30–1.*

❷ **San Giovanni degli Eremiti.** Distinguished by its five pink domes, this 12th-century church was built by the Normans on the site of an earlier mosque—one of 200 that once stood in Palermo. The emirs ruled Palermo for almost two centuries and brought to it their passion for lush gardens and fountains. One is reminded of this while sitting in San Giovanni's delightful cloister of twin half-columns, surrounded by palm trees, jasmine, oleander, and citrus trees. ⊠ *Via dei Benedettini.* ☉ *Daily 9–12:30, Mon. and Thurs. also 3–6.*

❺ **Santa Caterina.** The walls of this splendid Baroque church (1596) in Piazza Bellini are covered in decorative 17th-century inlays of precious marble. ⊠ *Piazza Bellini.* ☉ *Daily 9–noon and 3–6.*

⓫ **Teatro Massimo.** Construction of this formidable neoclassical theater was started in 1875 by Giovanni Battista Basile and completed by his son, Ernesto, in 1897. Claimed to be Italy's largest, the theater was featured in scenes in *The Godfather Part III,* under Francis Ford Coppola's direction. ⊠ *Piazza Verdi, at the top of Via Maqueda,* ☎ *091/ 6053315.*

Vucciria outdoor market. "Vucciria," in dialect, means "voices" or "hubbub," and it's easy to see why. In the maze of side streets around Piazza San Domenico, hawkers everywhere deliver their unceasing chants from behind stands brimming with mounds of olives, blood oranges, wild fennel, and long-stemmed artichokes. One of them goes at the trunk of a swordfish with a cleaver, while across the way another holds up a giant squid or dangles an octopus. It may be Palermo, but this is really the Casbah. ⊠ *Around Piazza San Domenico.*

Dining and Lodging

If you're a street-food fanatic, Vucciria is your Eden. Stalls around the neighborhood sell everything from *calzoni* (deep-fried meat- or cheese-filled pockets of dough) to *panelle* (chickpea-flour fritters). If you're feeling adventurous for something typically Palermitan, look for a stall with a big cast-iron pot selling delicious *guasteddi* (fresh buns filled with thin strips of calf's spleen, ricotta cheese, and a delicious hot sauce).

$$$ ✕ **Charleston.** You'll feel pampered by the discreet service and elegant
★ surroundings in this famous Palermo restaurant. Impeccably outfitted waiters coast effortlessly through the high-ceiling rooms, producing a range of Sicilian and international dishes, with an emphasis on seafood. Try the delicious spaghetti *all'aragosta,* (with lobster sauce), or the pesce spada *arrosto* (roasted), but leave room for the house dessert, *semifreddo alle mandorle*(a soft ice cream made with almonds). The whole restaurant operation moves 8 km (5 mi) north to Mondello in summer, where it sets up shop in a pavilion on the sea. ⊠ *Piazza Ungheria 30,* ☎ *091/321366. Mondello:* ⊠ *Charleston le Terrazze, Viale Regina Elena,* ☎ *091/450171. Reservations essential. Jacket and tie. AE, DC, MC, V. Closed Sun.*

$$$ ✕ **Da Renato.** The view from this top-quality restaurant on the sea road
★ toward Cefalù is enough out of the way to make it the insider's choice. And the well-heeled locals know their way around a good seafood and grills menu. *Frutti di mare* (mixed seafood) makes a good antipasto, and the *zuppa di mare* (fish soup) is hearty enough to be a meal in itself. ⊠ *Via Messina Marina 224,* ☎ *091/6302881. AE, DC, MC, V. Closed Mon. and Aug. 10–25.*

$$$ ✕ **Gourmand's.** A chic clientele frequents this modern restaurant, with its high-tech decor (lots of metal and primary colors) and nouvelle cuisine–influenced menu. Pesce spada *affumicato* (smoked) goes well with a bottle of local Regaleali. It's in the northern end of Palermo, near Piazza Castelnuovo. ⊠ *Via della Libertà 37/e,* ☎ *091/323431. AE, DC, MC, V. Closed Sun. (except Dec.) and Aug. 10–25.*

$$ ✕ **Strascinu.** The specialty in this informal and busy restaurant is pasta con le sarde, the famous Arab-Sicilian blend of pasta, fresh sardines, wild fennel fronds, sultanas, and pine nuts. ⊠ *Viale Regione Siciliana 2286,* ☎ *091/401292. AE, DC, MC, V. Closed 2 wks in Aug.*

$ ✕ **Antica Focacceria San Francesco.** This place in Palermo's heart is an institution, as you can see from the turn-of-the-century wooden cabinets and fixtures of what is still a neighborhood bakery. It bakes and fries the snacks that locals love—and from which you can make an inexpensive meal. You can sit at marble-topped tables or take food out. The good gelateria in the piazza is under the same management. ⊠ *Via Paternostro 58,* ☎ *091/320264. Reservations not accepted. No credit cards.*

$ ✕ **Pizzeria Bellini.** The pizzas are good, the pastas are better, but the best reason to eat in this former theater is the location, overlooking the churches of San Cataldo and La Martorana in the heart of old Palermo. Get a seat next to the window—or better still, in summer, eat alfresco. Trade is brisk, and so is the service, which can be offhand. ⊠ *Piazza Bellini 6,* ☎ *091/6165691. AE, MC, V. Closed Wed.*

$ ✕ **Shangai.** There is nothing Chinese about this Palermo institution in the busy Vucciria market. It's on a terrace above the market (the source of all the ingredients): Look down and order your fish from the displays below, and it will be hoisted up in a wicker basket. The atmosphere can get jovial and frantic, with lots of teasing and shouting. Although the fare here has become quite mediocre in recent years, the calamari *al forno* (baked in the oven) is always a good bet. ⊠ *Vicolo Mezzani 34,* ☎ *091/589702. No credit cards. Closed Sun.*

$$$$ 🏨 **Villa Igea.** A short taxi ride through some rough-looking districts of
★ Palermo takes you to this oasis of luxury and comfort, in its own tropical garden at the edge of the bay. A meander through the grounds reveals such relics as an ancient Greek temple at the water's edge. Large rooms are furnished individually, the nicest with an Italian art-nouveau flavor. Spacious lobbies and public rooms unfold onto a terrace and restaurant. Sports facilities help make this elegant villa a self-contained enclave in frenetic Palermo. ⊠ *Salita Belmonte 43, Aquasanta, 3 km/2 mi north of Palermo, 90142,* ☎ *091/543744,* 𝔽𝔸𝕏 *091/547654. 111 rooms, 6 suites. Restaurant, bar, pool, tennis court. AE, DC, MC, V.*

$$$ 🏨 **Grande Albergo e delle Palme.** There is a faded charm about this grande dame, whose public rooms suggest the elegant life of Palermo society before World War I, when tea dances and balls were held here. Guest rooms are uneven—some are charming period pieces stuffed with antiques and heavy fabrics, others are dark and cramped. There is an American-style cocktail bar and a rooftop terrace. ⊠ *Via Roma 396, 90139,* ☎ *091/583933,* 𝔽𝔸𝕏 *091/331545. 187 rooms, 5 suites. Restaurant, bar, parking (fee). AE, DC, MC, V.*

$$$ 🏨 **Mondello Palace.** This is the leading hotel at the Mondello resort,
★ making the best use of its location near the beach. The private beach has cabins and changing rooms for the use of Mondello Palace guests, as well as sailing and windsurfing facilities and an exercise room. The rooms are well equipped and large, and most have balconies. In summer you can choose between the hotel's own restaurant or the beachside venue of Palermo's excellent Charleston (☞ *above*)—just across the road. ⊠ *Viale Principe di Scalea, Mondello Lido, just north of Palermo, 90139,* ☎ *091/450001,* 𝔽𝔸𝕏 *091/450657. 82 rooms, 9 suites. Restaurant, bar, pool, exercise room, beach, windsurfing, boating. AE, DC, MC, V.*

$ 🏨 **Principe di Belmonte.** This is a tasteful choice among Palermo's cheaper hotels. It is family-run, friendly, and central—a convenient walk both from the port and Piazza Castelnuovo—but is on a relatively quiet street. Rooms are smallish. Advance reservations are advised. ⊠ *Via Principe di Belmonte 25, 90139,* ☎ *091/331065,* 𝔽𝔸𝕏 *091/6113424. 17 rooms, 3 without bath. Bar. AE, MC, V.*

Nightlife and the Arts

The Arts

FESTIVALS

Palermo stages a **street fair** July 11–15 in honor of its patron saint, Santa Rosalia. There are fireworks displays in the evenings. **Epiphany** (January 6) is celebrated with Byzantine rites and a procession of townspeople in local costume through the streets of Piana degli Albanesi, near Palermo. The village, 24 km (15 mi) south of the island's capital, is named for the Albanian immigrants who first settled there, bringing with them the Byzantine Catholic rites.

MUSIC AND OPERA

Teatro Massimo (⊠ Piazza Verdi, at the top of Via Maqueda, ☎ 091/6053315) finally reopened in summer 1997, after 23 years of restoration. A program of concerts and operas is presented throughout the year. The grandiose **Politeama Garibaldi** (⊠ Piazza Ruggero Settimo, ☎ 091/6053315) auditorium stages a winter season of opera and orchestral works. Choral and chamber recitals are performed at the **Teatro Golden** (⊠ Via Terrasanta, ☎ 091/300745).

PUPPET SHOW
Bring children to the **Opera dei Pupi** (⊠ Via Bara all'Olivella 95, ☎ 091/323400). Check with the tourist office for details.

THEATER
Palermo's **Teatro Biondo** (⊠ Via Roma, ☎ 091/582364) is Sicily's foremost theater, featuring a winter season of plays from November to May.

Nightlife
Apart from some trendy bars lining Via Principe del Belmonte, intersecting with Via Roma and Via Ruggiero Settimo (a northern extension of Via Maqueda), nightlife is concentrated in the nightclubs and discotheques scattered around the northern, newer end of town, a taxi-ride away. Check out **Il Cerchio** (⊠ Viale Strasburgo 312, ☎ 091/6885421) and **Paramatta** (⊠ Viale Lazio 51, ☎ 091/513621). In summer, the scene shifts to Mondello, Palermo's seaside satellite on the other side of Monte Pellegrino.

Shopping

Markets
Looking to pick up antique marionettes of the Norman cavaliers or brilliantly colored pieces from the carretti siciliani? Head to the flea market, behind Palermo's Duomo, on Via Papireto, held daily. Don't miss the raucous outdoor market around Vucciria's Piazza San Domenico, every day but Sunday.

Specialty Stores
ANTIQUES
The area behind the Duomo, in the midst of the flea market on Via Papireto and spreading to the next street, Corso Amedeo, is also the antiques-store neighborhood.

CERAMICS
De Simone has a wide selection of ceramics decorated in a modern style that remind many of Picasso. You can browse through the workshop (⊠ Piazza Leoni 2) or get a glimpse of what's on offer at a more central retail outlet (⊠ Via Daita 136, near Piazza Ruggero Settimo).

AROUND PALERMO

Palermo's Arab-Norman theme is continued in the cathedral at nearby Monreale and in Cefalù, a viable alternative to staying in the capital itself.

Monreale

⑫ *10 km (6 mi) southwest of Palermo.*

Don't miss the splendid **Duomo,** lavishly executed with mosaics depicting events from the Old and New Testaments. One hundred thirty pictures cover 6,000 square yards. Be sure to see the rear exterior and the graceful Romanesque **cloister** to the left, laced with intricate arches, mosaic-inlaid twin columns, and capitals that represent one of the richest collections of Sicilian medieval sculpture. In a corner by the stylized palm-tree fountain, look for a capital showing William II offering the cathedral to the Virgin. Bring 500-lire coins to illuminate the mosaics. ⊠ *Piazza Duomo,* ☎ *091/6404413.* ⊙ *Daily 8–12:10 and 3:30–6:30. Cloister:* ☎ *091/6404403.* 🎟 *4,000 lire.* ⊙ *Mon.–Sat. 9–1, Sun. 9–12:30; Mon.–Tues. and Thurs. also 3–6.*

Dining

$$ ✕ **La Botte.** It's worth the short drive or inexpensive taxi fare to reach this good-value restaurant, which features local specialties. Dine alfresco on daily specials, such as *pennette agli odori* (little penne with chopped tomato, garlic, and fresh herbs, including parsley, basil, mint, and oregano), or regular favorites, such as *involtini* (meat or fish roulades). Local wines are a good bet. ⊠ *Contrada Lenzitti 20, S186,* ☎ *091/ 414051. AE, DC, MC, V. Closed Mon.–Thurs. and Aug.*

Cefalù

★ ⓭ *70 km (42 mi) east of Palermo.*

Cefalù is a charming town built on a spur jutting out into the sea and dominated by a massive 12th-century Romanesque **Duomo,** one of the finest Norman cathedrals in Italy. King Roger began it in 1131 as a thanks offering for having been saved here from a shipwreck. Its mosaics rival those of Monreale. Both cathedrals are dominated by colossal mosaic figures of the Byzantine Pantocratic Christ, high in the bowl of their apses. The Monreale figure is an austere and powerful image, emphasizing the divinity of Christ, while the Cefalù Christ, softer and more compassionate, seems to stress his humanity. The traffic going in and out of Cefalù town can be heavy in summer; you may want to take the 50-minute train ride or 40-minute bus ride from Palermo instead of driving. ⊠ *Piazza Duomo,* ☎ *0921/722021.* ☉ *Daily 8–noon and 3–7. No shorts or beachwear.*

Dining and Lodging

$$ ✕ **Gabbiano.** "Seagull" is an appropriate name for a harborside seafood restaurant with a nautical theme. House specialties are involtini di pesce spada and spaghetti marinara. ⊠ *Via Lungomare Giardina 17,* ☎ *0921/421495. AE, DC, MC, V. Closed Wed.*

$$ ✕ **La Brace.** This bistro-style restaurant near the cathedral has been serving upchoice dishes and a lively atmosphere for 22 years. Graceful ceiling arches and rustic walls lend an informal air. Stick to the excellent grills, and save room for the homemade cassata siciliana. ⊠ *Via Venticinque Novembre 10,* ☎ *0921/423570. AE, DC, MC, V. Closed Mon. and mid-Dec.–mid-Jan.*

$$$ 🏨 **Baia del Capitano.** The peaceful district of Mazzaforno, about 5 km
★ (3 mi) outside town, sets the stage for this handsome hotel with great amenities. The building is less than 30 years old, but it blends in with the traditional homes nearby. The colorful gardens, extending to the surrounding olive groves, are ideal for quiet reading or an afternoon siesta in the shade. A good sandy beach is an easy walk away. The rooms are large and quiet. You must pay half board in high season. ⊠ *Contrada Mazzaforno, 90015 Mazzaforno,* ☎ *0921/420005,* 📠 *0921/ 420163. 39 rooms. Restaurant, bar, pool, tennis court. AE, MC, V. Closed Nov.–Feb.*

$$$ 🏨 **Kalura.** Caldura, 3 km/2 mi east along the coast, is the setting for
★ this modern hotel on a small promontory that is hard to reach without a car. Taxis from Cefalù take only a few minutes, though. Sports facilities keep you from getting too sedentary, and the private beach is ideal for swimming. Rooms are bright and cheerful. Rates are low in this category. ⊠ *Via V. Cavallaro 13, 90015 Contrada Caldura,* ☎ *0921/ 421354,* 📠 *0921/423122. 65 rooms. Restaurant, bar, pool, tennis court, beach. AE, DC, MC, V.*

WESTERN COAST TO AGRIGENTO
Land of Temples

Western Sicily has a remote air, less developed than the eastern coast, and bearing traces of the North African culture that for centuries exerted a strong influence on this end of the island. Influences are most tangible in the coastal towns of Trapani and Marsala, and the outlying island of Pantelleria, nearer to the Tunisian coast than the Sicilian. In contrast, the cobbled streets of the hilltop town of Erice, outside Trapani, retain a strong medieval complexion, giving the town the air of a last outpost gazing out over the Mediterranean. The Greek presence is still strong, however, in the splendidly isolated site of Segesta, and the cluster of ruined temples at Selinunte. But the crowning glory of this tour is the concentration of Greek temples at Agrigento, occupying a fabulous position on a height between the modern city and the sea.

Segesta

⑭ *85 km (53 mi) southwest of Palermo, 30 km (19 mi) east of Trapani.*

Segesta is the site of one of the most impressive **Greek temples,** constructed on the side of a windswept barren hill overlooking a valley of wild fennel. Virtually intact today, the temple is considered by some to be finer, in its proportions and setting, than any other Doric temple left standing. The Greeks started the temple in the 5th century BC but never finished it. The walls and roof never materialized, and the columns were never fluted. Just over 1 km (½ mi) away, near the top of the hill, are the remains of a fine **Greek theater,** with impressive views, especially at sunset, of nearby Monte Erice and the sea.

Erice

⑮ *35 km (22 mi) west of Segesta, 112 km (70 mi) west of Palermo.*

Erice perches 2,450 ft above sea level, an enchanting medieval mountaintop aerie of castles and palaces, fountains and cobblestone streets. Erice was the ancient Eryx and was dedicated to a fertility goddess, whom the Phoenicians called Astarte; the Greeks, Aphrodite; and the Romans, Venus. According to Virgil, Aeneas built a temple to the goddess here, but it was destroyed when the Arabs took over and renamed the place Mohammed's Mountain. When the Normans arrived, they built a castle where today you'll find a public park with benches and belvederes, from which there are striking views of Trapani, the Egadi Islands, and, on a *very* clear day, Cape Bon and the Tunisian coast.

Dining and Lodging

$$ ✕ **La Taverna di Re Aceste.** This popular restaurant is named for Acestus, the first king of Erice, and the house specialty, couscous Aceste (a spicy Arab-influenced couscous with seafood) is made in his honor, as are the murals along the walls. The chef also has a special pesto dish made with wild herbs. Try the grilled fish, but ask for the price, since you'll be paying by weight, not per order. ⊠ *Viale Conte Pepoli,* ☎ *0923/869084. AE, DC, MC, V. Closed Nov. and Wed. mid-Sept.–mid-June. No dinner Tues.*

$$$ ▥ **Moderno.** Local craft work and some antiques decorate the gracious rooms of this intimate and well-run hotel on the cobblestone streets of the medieval town. Some rooms are in the modern annex. The main building has a fire blazing in the lounge in winter. The restaurant serves seafood pasta and homemade desserts. ⊠ *Via Vittorio Emanuele*

63, 91016, ☎ 0923/869300, 🖷 0923/869139. 40 rooms. Restaurant, bar. AE, DC, MC, V.

$$ 🏨 **Ermione.** Spectacular views and cool breezes are the rewards of a visit to Erice, and this 1960s hotel overlooking the Tyrrhenian Sea is in a position to offer both. Nearly every room has a good view, although some would say that the terrace bar has the most panoramic vista. The hotel restaurant is popular locally, with fish couscous a standout. Breakfast is included. ⊠ Via Pineta Comunale 43, 91016, ☎ 0923/869138, 🖷 0923/869587. 46 rooms. Restaurant, bar, pool. AE, DC, MC, V.

Trapani

⑯ 30 km (18 mi) west of Segesta, 107 km (67 mi) west of Palermo.

The modern town of Trapani, below Erice, is the departure point for ferries to the Egadi Islands and the island of Pantelleria, near the African coast. The lanes near Corso Italia hold a handful of churches worth wandering into. **Santa Maria di Gesù,** on Via San Pietro, has Renaissance and Gothic doors and a Madonna by Andrea della Robbia (1435–1525), and **Sant'Agostino,** on Piazzetta Saturno, behind the town hall, with a 14th-century rose window. This rugged western end of Sicily is reminiscent of the terrain in American westerns—as it well should be, for many spaghetti westerns were filmed here. If you fancy North African couscous, Trapani is the place to try the Sicilian version, made with fish instead of meat. The result is a kind of fish stew with semolina, laced with cinnamon, saffron, and black pepper.

Dining

$$ ✕ **P&G.** Couscous is a specialty of this small, popular restaurant on a
★ quiet street between the train station and the Villa Margherita public gardens. The couscous features fish in summer (Friday only) and meat in winter. A mixed grill of meats in a zesty orange sauce will revive any appetite suffering from fish fatigue. Wash it all down with a bottle of Donnafugata, a good white from the Rallo vineyards at Marsala. ⊠ Via Spalti 1, ☎ 0923/547701. Reservations essential. AE, DC, MC, V. Closed Sun. and Aug.

Pantelleria

⑰ 100 km (62 mi) southwest of Sicily.

Pantelleria, near the Tunisian coast, is one of Sicily's most evocative islands, although many find its starkness unappealing. Its volcanic formations, scant patches of forest, prehistoric tombs, and dramatic seascapes constitute an otherworldly landscape. From its grapes—the zibibbo—the locals make an amber-color dessert wine and a strong, sweet wine called Tanit. Daily ferries and hydrofoils connect the island with Trapani.

Marsala

⑱ 30 km (18 mi) south of Trapani, 140 km (87 mi) southwest of Palermo.

The quiet seaside town of Marsala was once the main Carthaginian base in Sicily, from which Carthage fought for supremacy of the island against Greece and Rome. Some of the flavor of those times is recaptured by the well-preserved **Punic warship** displayed in the town's **Museo Archeologico Baglio Anselmi,** along with some of the amphoras and other artifacts recovered from the wreck. The vessel, which was probably sunk during the great sea battle that ended the First Punic War in 241 BC, was dredged up from the mud near the Egadi Islands in the 1970s, and is now installed under a climate-controlled plastic

tent. ✉ *Via Boeo 30,* ☎ *0923/952535.* 🎫 *4,000 lire.* ☉ *May–Sept.,
daily 9–2, also Wed., Sat., and Sun. 3–7; Oct.–Apr., daily 9–1, also
Wed. and Sat. 4–6.*

Nowadays, Marsala is more readily associated with the world-famous,
rich-color, sweet-tasting wine named after the town. In 1773 a British
merchant named John Woodhouse happened upon Marsala and discovered that the wine there was as good as the port the British had
long imported from Portugal. Two other wine merchants, Whitaker
and Ingram, rushed in, and by 1800 Marsala was exporting its wine
all over the British Empire.

Selinunte

⑲ *88 km (55 mi) southeast of Marsala, 15 km (9 mi) south of Castelvetrano.*

Near the town of Castelvetrano, an overwhelming array of ruined **Greek
temples** is perched on a plateau overlooking the Mediterranean at Selinunte. The city was one of the most superb colonies of ancient Greece.
The original complex held seven temples scattered over two sites separated by a harbor. Of the seven, only one—reconstructed in 1958—
stands. Founded in the 7th century BC, Selinunte became the rich and
prosperous rival of Segesta, which in 409 BC turned to the Carthaginians for help. The Carthaginians sent an army commanded by Hannibal to destroy the city. The temples were demolished, the city was razed,
and 16,000 of Selinunte's inhabitants were slaughtered. The beautiful
metopes preserved in Palermo's Museo Archeologico Regionale come
from the frieze of Temple E here. A small **museum** on the site contains
other excavated pieces. Selinunte is named after a local variety of wild
celery that in spring still grows in profusion among the ruined columns
and overturned capitals. ☎ *0924/46251.* 🎫 *4,000 lire.* ☉ *Daily 8:30–
1 hr before sunset.*

Agrigento

⑳ *100 km (60 mi) southeast of Selinunte, 126 km (79 mi) south of
Palermo.*

Look out for the golden temples of Agrigento on a rise above the highway, a short distance inland from the sea. Agrigento, or Akragas as
the Greeks called it, was settled by the Greeks in 580 BC and grew
wealthy through trade with Carthage, just across the Mediterranean.
Despite attacks from the Carthaginians at the end of the 5th century
BC, the city survived through the Roman era, the Middle Ages (when
it came under Arab and Norman rule), and into the modern age, and
structures from all these eras sit side by side in Agrigento today. The
birthplace of both the ancient Greek philosopher Empedocles (circa
490–430 BC) and the modern Italian playwright Luigi Pirandello, Agrigento is a study in contrasts, but its chief attraction, the Valley of the
Temples, remains one of the most impressive classical sites in all of
Italy.

★ Coming upon the **Valle di Templi** (Valley of the Temples) for the first
time is a memorable moment—whether in the sunshine of spring,
when the temples are surrounded by blossoming almond trees, or at
night, when they are floodlit. Even in winter, when the vegetation is
limited—perfectly limited—to agaves and gnarled gray olive trees, it
is easy to understand why Pindar called Agrigento "the most beautiful city built by mortal men." Exiting from the highway, walk down
from the parking lot on Via dei Templi and turn left.

㉑ The first temple you encounter as you enter the complex is the **Tempio di Ercole** (Temple of Hercules)—eight pillars of the oldest temple in Agrigento, built during the 5th century BC. Up the hill from the Tem-
㉒ ple of Hercules is the **Tempio di Concordia** (Concord), one of the best-preserved Doric temples in the world and certainly the most impressive in Sicily. In the late afternoon, as the sun descends below the horizon, the temple's sandstone begins to change from honey-gold to pink russet, and the vertical lines of the fluted columns and their triangular pediment sharpen against the fading skyline. The columns were probably once covered by brightly painted stucco.

㉓ Follow up the Via Sacra to reach the **Tempio di Giunone** (Juno), which commands an exquisite view of the valley, especially at sunset. If you look carefully, you can see red fire marks on some of the columns—the result of the Carthaginian attack in 406 BC that destroyed the city. From the parking lot in the Piazzale dei Templi (where there is a bar selling drinks and ice cream), cross to the opposite side of the road,
㉔ where some of the most impressive ruins lie. The **Tempio di Giove** (Jupiter) is the largest temple ever planned in Sicily. Though never completed, it was considered the eighth wonder of the world. The nearby sleeping giant is a copy of one of the 38 colossal Atlas figures, or telamones, that supported the temple's immense roof. Note that the Temple of Jupiter usually closes at 5.

The four columns supporting part of an entablature of the much-pho-
㉕ tographed **Tempio di Castore e Polluce** (Castor and Pollux) have become a symbol of Agrigento, even though they were reconstructed in 1836, and probably from diverse buildings.

At the end of Via dei Templi, where it turns left and becomes Via Pe-
★ **㉖** trarca, stands the **Museo Archeologico Nazionale,** which contains one of the original telamones, an impressive collection of Greek vases dating from the 7th century BC, and models of what the temples once looked like. ⊠ *Contrada San Nicola,* ☎ *0922/401565.* 🎫 *8,000 lire.* ⊙ *Sun.– Tues. 9–1, Wed.–Sat. 9–1 and 2:30–5:30.*

On the opposite side of the road from the archaeological museum is
㉗ the **Hellenistic and Roman Quarter,** which consists of four parallel streets, running north and south, that have been uncovered, along with the foundations of some houses from the Roman settlement (2nd century BC). Some of these streets still have their original mosaic pavements.

There is little reason to go up the hill to the rather dreary modern city of Agrigento, where industrial speculation threatens to encroach upon the Valley of the Temples below—except to ring the doorbell at the **Convento di Santo Spirito** on the Salita di Santo Spirito off Via Porcello and try the *kus-kus* (sweet cake) made of pistachio nuts and chocolate, that the nuns there prepare.

....

OFF THE   **CASA PIRANDELLO** – One of Agrigento's native sons was the distin-
BEATEN PATH   guished dramatist Luigi Pirandello (1867–1936), whose plays, such as
                 Six Characters in Search of an Author, express the fundamental ambigu-
                 ity of life. Pirandello is buried under a pine tree behind the house where
                 he was born, in Piazzale Caos, a few kilometers west of town. His
                 house has been made into a museum of Pirandello memorabilia. Every
                 year, a festival of Pirandello's plays is held in Agrigento from late July to
                 early August. ☎ *0922/511102.* 🎫 *4,000 lire.* ⊙ *Daily 8:30–7.*

....

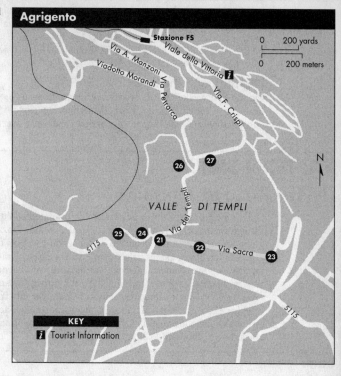

Dining and Lodging

$$ ✕ **Caprice.** The specialty of this popular restaurant in the temple area is meat prepared alla brace (skewered), although there is also a good selection of seafood, particularly pesce spada. The waiters—when they are not rushed—are proud to explain some of the less-familiar entries on the wine list, which is relatively extensive. ✉ *Via Panoramica dei Templi 51,* ☎ *0922/26469. AE, DC, MC, V. Closed Fri. and July 1–15.*

$$ ✕ **Taverna Mosè.** This restaurant can get busy in the early evening, when it becomes too dark for temple exploring. The atmosphere bustles with waiters shouting orders at each other and at the kitchen. The house specialties are homemade sausages and grilled fish, and the wine list is varietal, so to speak. ✉ *Contrada San Biagio 6,* ☎ *0922/26778. AE. Closed Mon. and Aug.*

$$ ✕ **Vigneto.** Unless you make reservations at this popular restaurant, it's best to arrive early to snag one of the good tables on the terrace, which has a memorable view of the temples. Seasonal daily specials and the fish market's freshest top the changing menu. *Arrosti* (roast meats) are always a good bet. ✉ *Via Cavaleri Magazzeni 11,* ☎ *0922/414319. Reservations essential. No credit cards. Closed Tues.*

$$$ 🏨 **Jolly dei Templi.** Guests travel 8 km (5 mi) southeast of town to Villaggio Mosè to stay in this Jolly hotel. Rooms are large, bright, and airy, and if there's a sense of having seen it all before, you probably have—in one of the other Jolly hotels or in any well-equipped U.S. motel. That is the price to pay for what are always comfortable, hassle-free accommodations. The Pirandello restaurant here is excellent. ✉ *Parco Angeli, 92100 Villagio Mosè,* ☎ *0922/606144,* 🆑 *0922/606685. 144 rooms. Restaurant, bar, pool. AE, DC, MC, V.*

$$$ 🏨 **Villa Athena.** There is much demand for this well-furnished former
★ villa right in the midst of the archaeological zone, so make reservations as early as possible. Many rooms—they're all different—have terraces

looking out on the large gardens and the swimming pool. The temples are an easy walk from the hotel, and there is a convivial atmosphere in the bar, where a multinational crowd swaps stories. ✉ *Via dei Templi 33, 92100,* ☎ *0922/596288,* FAX *0922/402180. 40 rooms. Restaurant, bar, pool. AE, DC, MC, V.*

Nightlife and the Arts

On the first weekend in February, Agrigento hosts a **Festa delle Mandorle,** or Almond Blossom Festival, with international folk dances, a costumed parade, and the sale of marzipan and other sweets made from almonds.

EASTERN SICILY

On the Road to Taormina

Sicily's interior is for the most part underpopulated and untrammeled, though the Imperial Roman Villa at Casale, outside Piazza Armerina, gives precious evidence from an epoch gone by. Don't miss Caltagirone, a ceramics center of renown. On the coast, Siracusa offers a fascinating mix of ancient Greek, Renaissance, and Baroque architecture with some excellent museums. To the north, Catania packs the vivacity of Palermo, if not the artistic wealth; the city makes a good base for exploring lofty Mt. Etna, as does Taormina. Messina's scant attractions include unparalleled position opposite the mountains of Calabria, one of the island's best museum collections.

Enna

28 *105 km (63 mi) northeast of Agrigento, 136 km (85 mi) southeast of Palermo, 85 km (53 mi) west of Catania.*

Deep in Sicily's interior, the fortress city of Enna commands exceptional views of the surrounding rolling plains, and, in the distance, Mt. Etna. The narrow winding streets are dominated at one end by the impressive castle built by Frederick II, easily visible as you approach the town.

Lodging

$$ 🏨 **Grande Albergo Sicilia.** Sicily's interior has a dearth of decent accommodations, so it's a relief to find Enna's only hotel a reliable and comfortable choice. In the heart of town (don't be put off by the unsightly facade), the Sicilia has bright, clean rooms, some with excellent views, and all equipped with TV and telephone. ✉ *Piazza Colaianni 5, 94100,* ☎ *0935/500850,* FAX *0935/500488. 70 rooms. Bar, parking (fee). AE, DC, MC, V.*

Piazza Armerina

29 *40 km (25 mi) south of Enna, 110 km (69 mi) west of Catania.*

Reached through pine and eucalyptus woods and low farmland, Piazza Armerina is a tiny Baroque town noted mainly for the sumptuous emperor's Imperial Roman Villa country house in nearby Casale (☞ *below*).

Dining

$$ ✕ **Centrale da Totò.** At this reliable trattoria, the emphasis is on a family clientele, rather than intimate or expense-account dining, and the portions reflect this *mangia, mangia* outlook. Try the *pappardelle alla Centrale* (wide pasta with a rich tomato sauce and fresh vegetables), or the *bocca di lupo* (literally "wolf's mouth": veal stuffed with eggplant, ham, and Parmesan). ✉ *Via Mazzini 29,* ☎ *0935/680153. AE, DC, MC, V. Closed Mon. Oct.–Mar.*

Nightlife and the Arts

The **Palio dei Normanni,** a medieval tournament with participants dressed in 14th-century fashion, takes place on August 13.

Casale

③⓪ *6 km (4 mi) southwest of Piazza Armerina.*

The exceptionally well-preserved **Imperial Roman Villa** here is thought to have been a hunting lodge of the Emperor Maximianus Heraclius (4th century AD). The excavations were not begun until 1950, and the wall decorations and vaulting have been lost. However, some of the best mosaics of the Roman world cover more than 12,000 square ft under a shelter that hints at the layout of the original buildings. The mosaics were probably made by Carthaginian artisans, because they are similar to those in the Tunis Bardo Museum. The entrance was through a triumphal arch that led into an atrium surrounded by a portico of columns. Through this, the *thermae,* or bathhouse, is reached. It is colorfully decorated with mosaic nymphs, a Neptune, and slaves massaging bathers. The peristyle leads to the main villa, where in the Salone del Circo you look down on mosaics that illustrate Roman circus sports. Another apartment shows hunting scenes of tigers, elephants, and ostriches; the gym shows girls exercising; the private apartments are covered with scenes from Greek and Roman mythology; and Room 38 even reveals a touch of eroticism. ⊠ *Imperial Roman Villa, Casale,* ☎ *0935/680036.* ☞ *4,000 lire.* ☉ *Daily 9–1 and 3–1 hr before sunset.*

Caltagirone

③① *30 km (18 mi) southeast of Piazza Armerina, 60 km (37 mi) southwest of Catania.*

Built over three hills, the charming Baroque town of Caltagirone is a leader in the Sicilian ceramics industry. Here you will find majolica balustrades, tile-decorated windowsills, and a monumental **tile staircase** of 142 steps—each decorated with a different pattern—leading up to the neglected **Santa Maria del Monte.** On the feast of San Giacomo (July 24), the staircase is illuminated with candles that form a tapestry design over the steps. It is the result of months of work preparing the 4,000 *coppi,* or cylinders of colored paper that hold oil lamps. At 9:30 PM on July 24, a squad of hundreds of boys springs into action to light the lamps, so that the staircase flares up all at once. There is an interesting **Museo della Ceramica** (Ceramics Museum) in the public gardens, which were designed by Basile, the master of Sicilian art nouveau. The exhibits in the museum trace the history of the craft from specimens excavated from the earliest settlements, through the influential Arab period, to the present. ⊠ *Museo della Ceramica, Giardino Pubblico,* ☎ *0933/21680.* ☞ *8,000 lire.* ☉ *Daily 9–6.*

Shopping

CERAMICS

The ceramic creations of De Simone, whose Picasso-like faces on plates and pitchers are popular abroad, can be seen at the shop, **Akatos** (⊠ Via Romeo 14).

Palazzolo Acreide

③② *60 km (40 mi) east of Caltagirone, 40 km (25 mi) west of Trapani.*

This small inland town is best known for its archaeological zone, the old Greek *Akrai,* containing the foundations of a temple dedicated to Aphrodite, and a well-preserved theater.

Dining

$ ✕ **Da Alfredo.** This one-man show (Alfredo is the owner-chef) is on one of the most attractive streets of this Baroque town between Caltagirone and Siracusa. Specialties depend on the season and the whims of Alfredo himself. Homemade pasta, such as penne and cheese-filled ravioli, are specialties, and the sauces are hearty and spicy. ⊠ *Via Duca d'Aosta 27,* ☎ *0931/883266. AE. Closed Wed.*

Siracusa

㉝ *100 km (60 mi) east of Caltagirone, 60 km (37 mi) south of Catania.*

Greek Sicily began along the Ionian coast, and some of the finest examples of Baroque art and architecture were also created here, particularly in Siracusa. The city was founded in 734 BC by Greek colonists from Corinth and soon grew to rival, and even surpass, Athens in splendor and power. Siracusa became the largest, wealthiest city-state in Magna Graecia and the bulwark of Greek civilization. Although it suffered from tyrannical rule, kings such as Dionysius filled their courts in the 5th century BC with Greeks of the highest artistic stature—among them, Pindar, Aeschylus, and Archimedes. The Athenians did not welcome the rise of Siracusa and sent a fleet to destroy the rival city, but the natives outsmarted them in what was one of the greatest naval battles of ancient history (413 BC). Siracusa continued to prosper until it was conquered two centuries later by the Romans.

There are essentially two areas to explore in Siracusa—the Parco Archeologico, on the mainland, and the island of Ortygia, the ancient city first inhabited by the Greeks, which juts out into the Ionian sea and is connected to the mainland by two small bridges.

The **Parco Archeologico** (Archaeological Park) at the western edge of town, contains the ruins of a fine **Anfiteatro Romano** (Roman Amphitheater) and the most complete **Teatro Greco** (Greek Theater) existing from antiquity. A comparison of these two structures reveals much about the differences between the Greek and Roman personalities. The Greek theater, in which the plays of Aeschylus premiered, was hewn out of the hillside rock in the 5th century BC. All the seats converge upon a single point—the stage—which had the natural scenery and the sky as its background. Drama as a kind of religious ritual was the intention here. In the Roman amphitheater, however, the emphasis was on the spectacle of combative sports and the circus. The arena is one of the largest of its kind and was built around the 2nd century AD. The corridor where gladiators and beasts entered the ring is still intact, and the seats, some of which still bear the occupants' names, were hauled in and constructed on the site from huge slabs of limestone. A crowd-pleasing show, and not the elevation of men's minds, was the intention here. Climb to the top of the seating area in the Greek theater, which could accommodate 15,000, for a fine view. In May and June of even-numbered years, Greek tragedies are performed here. If the Archaeological Park is closed, go up Viale G. Rizzo from Viale Teracati, to the belvedere overlooking the ruins, which are floodlit at night.

Near the entrance to the park is the gigantic **Ara di Lerone** (Altar of Hieron), which was once used by the Greeks for spectacular sacrifices involving hundreds of animals. Just beyond the ticket office you will come upon a lush tropical garden full of palm and citrus trees. This is the **Latomie del Paradiso**, a series of quarries that served as prisons for the defeated Athenians, who were enslaved; the quarries once rang with the sound of their chisels and hammers. At one end is the Orecchio di Dionisio, with an ear-shape entrance and unusual acoustics inside, as you'll discover if you clap your hands. The legend is that Dionysius used to listen in at the top of the quarry to hear what the slaves were plotting below. ⊠ *Viale Augusto,* ☎ *0931/66206.* 🖅 *4,000 lire.* ☉ *Daily 9–1 hr before sunset (last tickets sold 2 hrs before sunset).*

Not far from the Archaeological Park, off Viale Teocrito, are the **catacombs** of San Giovanni, one of the earliest-known Christian sites in the city. Inside the crypt of San Marciano is an altar where St. Paul preached on his way through Sicily to Rome. The frescoes in this small chapel are still bright and fresh, though some dating from the 4th century AD show their age. ⊠ *Piazza San Giovanni.* 🖅 *4,000 lire.* ☉ *Mid-Mar.–mid-Nov., Wed–Mon. 9–noon and 2:30–6; mid-Nov.–mid-Mar., Wed–Mon. 9–1 and 3–5 (hrs subject to change).*

The impressive collection contained in Siracusa's splendid **Museo Archeologico** is arranged by region around a central atrium and ranges from neolithic pottery to fine Greek statues and vases. You will want to compare the Landolina Venus—a headless, stout goddess of love who rises out of the sea in measured modesty (she is a 1st-century-AD Roman copy of the Greek original)—with the much earlier (300 BC) elegant Greek statue of Hercules in Section C. Of a completely different style is a marvelous fanged Gorgon, its tongue sticking out, that once adorned the cornice of the temple of Athena to ward off evildoers. One exhibit depicts the Temple of Apollo, the oldest Doric temple in Sicily, on the island of Ortygia. ⊠ *Viale Teocrito,* ☎ *0931/464022.* 🖅 *8,000 lire.* ☉ *Tues.–Sun. 9–1; closed 1st and 3rd Sun. of the month.*

Close to Siracusa's Museo Archeologico, the **Museo del Papiro** (Papyrus Museum) demonstrates how papyruses are prepared from reeds and then painted—an ancient tradition in the city. Siracusa, it seems, has the only climate outside the Nile Valley in which the papyrus plant—from which we get our word "paper"—thrives. ⊠ *Viale Teocrito 66,* ☎ *0931/61616.* 🖅 *Free.* ☉ *Tues.–Sun. 9–1.*

The central part of Siracusa is a modern city, with Corso Gelone its main shopping street. At its southern end, Corso Umberto leads to the **Ortygia Island** bridge, which crosses a pretty harbor lined with fish restaurants. In the piazza on the other side of the bridge, you'll find a model of the ruins of the **Tempio di Apollo** in the Museo Archeologico. In fact, little of this noble Doric temple still remains today, except for some crumbled walls and shattered columns, along with a fragment (the window in the south wall) of a Norman church that was built much later on the same spot. ⊠ *Piazza Pancali.*

Apart from the Temple of Apollo, Ortygia is composed almost entirely of warm, restrained Baroque buildings. This uniformity is the result of an earthquake in 1693 that necessitated major rebuilding at a time when the Baroque was de rigueur. Wander into the backstreets—especially along Via della Maestranza or Via Veneto—and notice the bulbous wrought-iron balconies (said to have been invented to accommodate ladies' billowing skirts), the window surrounds and cornices of buildings decorated with mermaids and gargoyles, and the stucco decoration on Palazzo Lantieri on Via Roma.

Ortygia's main piazzas are **Piazza Archimede,** with its Baroque fountain festooned with fainting sea nymphs and dancing jets of water, and ★ **Piazza del Duomo,** one of Italy's most beautiful piazzas. The **Duomo** is an archive of island history, beginning with the bottommost excavations that have unearthed remnants of Sicily's distant past, when the Siculi inhabitants worshiped their deities here. During the 5th century BC, the Greeks built a temple to Athena over it, and in the 7th century, Siracusa's first Christian cathedral was built on top of the Greek structure. The elegant columns of the original temple were incorporated into the present structure and are clearly visible, embedded in the exterior wall along Via Minerva. The Greek columns were also used to dramatic advantage inside, where on one side they form chapels connected by elegant wrought-iron gates. The Baroque facade, added in 1700, displays a harmonious rhythm of concaves and convexes. In front, the piazza is encircled by pink and white oleanders and elegant buildings ornamented with filigree grillwork. ⊠ *Piazza del Duomo.*

In the right corner of Piazza del Duomo is the elegant **Palazzo Beneventano del Bosco,** with an impressive interior courtyard ending in a grand winding staircase. At one end of Piazza del Duomo stands the Baroque church of **Santa Lucia alla Badia,** with an engaging wrought-iron balcony and pleasant facade. Siracusa's **Museo Regionale** is housed inside Palazzo Bellomo, a lovely Catalan-Gothic building with mullioned windows and an elegant exterior staircase. Among the select group of paintings and sculptures inside is a Santa Lucia by Caravaggio (1573–1610) and a damaged, but still brilliant, *Annunciation* by Antonello da Messina. ⊠ *Via Capodieci 14,* ☎ *0931/69617.* ⊠ *8,000 lire.* ☉ *Mon.–Sat. 9–2, Sun. 9–1.*

Just off the promenade along the harbor, you'll find the **Fonte Aretusa** (Fountain of Arethusa), a freshwater spring next to the sea. This anomaly is explained by a Greek legend that tells how the nymph Arethusa was changed into a fountain by the goddess Artemis (Diana) when she tried to escape the advances of the river god Alpheus. She fled from Greece, into the sea, with Alpheus in close pursuit, and emerged in Sicily at this spring. Supposedly even today, if you throw a cup into the River Alpheus in Greece, it will emerge here at this fountain, which at present is home to a few tired ducks and some dull-color carp—but no cups. Steps lead to the tree-lined promenade along the harbor front. The southern tip of Ortygia island is occupied by the **Castello Maniace,** now an army barracks but once a castle of Frederick II, from which there are fine views of the sea.

North of the city, on the highlands that overlook the sea, the **Castello Eurialo** (Euryalus Castle) was created by Dionysius, with the help of Archimedes, for protection against the Carthaginians. This astonishing boat-shape structure once covered 15,000 square yards. The intricate maze of tunnels is fascinating, and the view from the heights is superb. ⊠ *Belvedere, 8 km (5 mi) northwest of Siracusa.* ⊠ *Free.* ☉ *Daily 9–1 hr before sunset.*

Dining and Lodging

$$–$$$ ✕ **Ionico.** Enjoy seaside dining in the coastal Santa Lucia district. The
   ★   Ionico boasts a terrace and veranda for alfresco meals, and the interior is plastered with diverse historical relics and has a cheerful open hearth for the winter. Chef-proprietor Roberto Giudice cooks meals to order or will suggest a specialty from a selection of market-fresh ingredients. Try the *pasta con acciughe e il pan grattato* (pasta in an anchovy sauce). ⊠ *Riviera Dionisio il Grande 194,* ☎ *0931/65540. AE, DC, MC, V. Closed Tues.*

$$ ✕ **Archimede.** The *antipasto misto* (mixed antipasto) should whet your appetite for the predominantly seafood menu of this small establishment in the *città vecchia* (old town), Ortygia. Risotto di mare and pesce spada are specialties, but the menu veers away from seafood when game is in season. Otherwise, sample the *involtini all'Archimede* (roulades stuffed with cheese and ham with bread crumbs). ⊠ *Via Gemmellaro 8,* ☎ *0931/69701. AE, DC, MC, V. No dinner Sun.*

$$ ✕ **Arlecchino.** A bustling bohemian atmosphere pervades this restaurant, found midway between the archaeological zone and the old town. It's popular with artists and students, always a sign of good value. The Palermo-born proprietor serves specialties from his hometown, such as risotto *ai ricci* (with sea urchins) and homemade cassata for dessert. ⊠ *Via dei Tolomei 5,* ☎ *0931/66386. AE, DC, MC, V. Closed Mon. (May–Sept.) or Sun. (Oct.–Apr.).*

$$ ✕ **Minosse.** You'll find this small, old-fashioned restaurant in the heart of Siracusa's old town. Fish is the specialty, and it comes broiled, baked, stuffed, and skewered. For an introduction to the local seafood, try the antipasto misto di frutti di mare. Ask for the daily special as your main course, or try the pesce spada alla brace. The zuppa di pesce is a local favorite. ⊠ *Via Mirabella 6,* ☎ *0931/66366. AE, MC, V. No dinner Mon. (Oct.–Mar.).*

$$$ ✕ **Grand Hotel.** One of only two hotels on Ortygia island, the Grand is a venerable institution, enjoying a prime position overlooking the Porto Grande, as it has done since 1898. It has modernized its facilities without sacrificing its innate style. Despite the location, only six bedrooms have a sea view, though there is a magnificent view from the third-floor restaurant. All guest rooms are furnished with period trappings, which, together with the sumptuous public rooms, make this Siracusa's best choice. ⊠ *Viale Mazzini 12, 96100,* ☎ *0931/464600,* FAX *0931/464611. 39 rooms, 19 suites. Restaurant, bar, minibars, free parking. AE, DC, MC, V.*

$$$ ☷ **Jolly Hotel.** The rooms are uniformly comfortable in this member of the Jolly hotel chain, Italy's answer to Holiday Inns. The big advantage, apart from knowing that the plugs work and the rooms are soundproofed, is the location. The hotel is ½ km (¼ mi) from the train station and within easy walking distance of the archaeological zone. ⊠ *Corso Gelone 45, 96100,* ☎ *0931/461111,* FAX *0931/461126. 100 rooms. Restaurant, bar. AE, DC, MC, V.*

Nightlife and the Arts

The feast of the city's patroness, Santa Lucia (St. Lucy), is held on December 13 at **Santa Lucia alla Badia** (⊠ Piazza del Duomo). A splendid silver statue of the saint is carried from the cathedral to the church on the site of her martyrdom, near the Catacombs of San Giovanni. A torchlight procession and band music accompany the bearers.

In May and June of even-numbered years only (next 2000), Siracusa's impressive **Teatro Greco** (⊠ Parco Archeologico, ☎ 0931/67710) is the setting for performances of classical drama and comedy.

Noto

④ *32 km (19 mi) southwest of Siracusa.*

Modeled on a hierarchical plan following the destruction of the old town during the great earthquake of 1693, Noto presents a pleasing ensemble of honey-color Baroque architecture, strikingly uniform in style, but never dull. Its centerpiece is the majestic Duomo, completed in 1776, atop a broad flight of steps.

Dining

$ ✕ **Il Giglio.** Seafood dishes with a Spanish touch are the specialty at this pleasant trattoria in the center of town run by Maria Luz Corruchaga and her husband, Corrado. Particularly recommended are pasta *al nero di seppia* (with cuttlefish), ravioli *di ricotta* (ricotta-stuffed ravioli with fresh tomato and basil), and *zuppa di vongole e cozze* (clam and mussel soup). ⊠ *Piazza Municipio,* ☎ *0931/838640. MC, V. No lunch Sat.*

Catania

35 *60 km (37 mi) north of Siracusa, 94 km (59 mi) south of Messina.*

The chief wonder of Catania, Sicily's second city, is that it is there at all. Its successive populations were deported by one Greek tyrant, sold into slavery by another, and driven out by the Carthaginians. Every time the city got back on its feet, it was struck by a new calamity: Plague decimated the population in the Middle Ages, a kilometer-wide stream of lava from Mt. Etna swallowed most of the city in 1669, and 25 years later a disastrous earthquake forced the Catanese to begin again. Today the city needs considerable renovation. Traffic flows in ever-increasing volume and adds to the smog from the industrial zone between Catania and Siracusa, but the views of Mt. Etna from Catania are superb. To Mt. Etna, Catania also owes a fertile surrounding plain and its site on nine successive layers of lava. Many of Catania's buildings are constructed from solidified lava, and the black lava stone has given the city a singular appearance. As a result, Catania is known as the city of lava and oranges. Catania's greatest native son is the composer Vincenzo Bellini (1801–35), whose operas have thrilled audiences since their premieres about 170 years ago. His home, now the **Museo Bellini,** in Piazza San Francesco, preserves memorabilia of the man and his work. ⊠ *Piazza San Francesco 3,* ☎ *095/7150535.* ⊡ *Free.* ☉ *Mon.–Sat. 9–1:30, Sun. 9–12:30.*

The **Villa Bellini** (⊠ To the north, just off Via Etnea), Catania's public gardens, on clear days has lovely views of snowcapped Mt. Etna. The **Duomo** (⊠ At the bottom end of Via Etnea), is a fine work by Vaccarini (1736), as is the obelisk-balancing elephant carved out of lava stone in the piazza in front. Bellini is buried inside the cathedral. Also inside is the sumptuous Cappella di Sant'Agata, Catania's patron saint, who is credited with having held off, more than once, the fiery flows of lava that threatened the city. During her feast (February 3–5), huge 16-ft-tall, highly ornate carved wooden *cannelore* (large bundles of candles) are paraded through the streets at night.

OFF THE
BEATEN PATH

ACIREALE – Sixteen kilometers (10 miles) up the coast from Catania, Acireale sits amid a clutter of rocky pinnacles and lush lemon groves. The craggy coast is known as the Riviera dei Ciclopi, after the legend narrated in the *Odyssey,* in which the blinded cyclops, Polyphemus, hurled boulders at the retreating Ulysses, creating the spires of rock, or *faraglioni.* The richly Baroque town comes into its own during its Carnival celebrations, when the streets are jammed with thousands of fancy-dressed revelers and floats dripping with flowers and gaudy papier-mâché models. Acireale is also known for its puppet theater, a Sicilian tradition that has all but died out in other parts (call the tourist office, ⊠ Corso Umberto 177, ☎ 095/604521).

Dining and Lodging

If you haven't had cannoli in Sicily yet, the pastry shops along Via Etnea are good places to try one of these wafer tubes filled with silky smooth ricotta cheese. If you're in need of something more substantial, duck into one of the trattorias along this street and order a dish of pasta *alla Norma.* It's named after one of Bellini's most famous operas and consists of short pasta with a rich eggplant-and-tomato sauce, garnished with basil leaves and grated ricotta cheese, really a typical Sicilian pasta dish.

$$$ ✕ **Costa Azzurra.** At this seafood restaurant in the Ognina district, re-
  ★   serve a table on the veranda by the edge of the sea with good views of the harbor. The fritto misto can be ordered as an antipasto or a main course, and the pesce spada steak is a simple classic, served grilled with

a large slice of lemon. ⊠ *Via De Cristofaro 4, Ognina (just north of the center, on the way to the Taormina road)*, ☎ *095/494920. Jacket and tie. AE, DC, MC, V. Closed Mon.*

$$ ✕ **Pagano.** This restaurant, behind the Hotel Excelsior, has been around since the 1950s and remains a favorite with locals for genuine Catanese cooking. Seafood is the specialty, but it's the unpretentious kind that won't jettison the check into the stratosphere. Try *insalata di polipo* (octopus salad) as a starter and then sarde or *acciughe* (anchovies) in a variety of sauces. Like the sober, rather dated decor, the service is formal. ⊠ *Via De Roberto 37*, ☎ *095/537045. AE, DC, MC, V. Closed 1 wk in mid-Aug. No lunch Sat.*

$$$ 🏨 **Excelsior.** Ask for a room facing Piazza Verga, a neat tree-lined square in this quiet but central district of Catania. The Excelsior has air-conditioning and sound-insulated windows in all rooms. The rooftop garden is one of Catania's most chic meeting places, and the American Bar should provide solace to anyone waxing nostalgic for a Manhattan. ⊠ *Piazza Verga 39, 95129*, ☎ *095/537071*, 𝖥𝖠𝖷 *095/537015. 150 rooms. Restaurant, bar, air-conditioning, parking (fee). AE, DC, MC, V.*

$$ 🏨 **Savona.** The Savona is an efficiently run and well-maintained hotel a shot put's throw from Piazza del Duomo. The rooms are spacious and comfortable, solidly furnished, and equipped with TV and telephones. Prices include Continental breakfast. Reception can help with parking suggestions. ⊠ *Via Vittorio Emanuele 210, 95124*, ☎ *095/326982*, 𝖥𝖠𝖷 *095/7158169. 25 rooms, 10 without bath. Bar. No credit cards.*

Nightlife and the Arts

The opera season at **Teatro Bellini** (⊠ Piazza Bellini, Catania, ☎ 095/7306111), October to mid-June, attracts top singers and productions to the birthplace of the great operatic composer Vincenzo Bellini.

Mt. Etna

★ ㊱ *30 km (19 mi) north of Catania, 60 km (37 mi) south of Messina.*

Mt. Etna is one of the world's major active volcanoes and is the largest and highest in Europe—the cone of the crater rising to 10,958 ft above sea level. It has erupted 10 times in the past three decades, most spectacularly in 1971 and 1983, when rivers of molten lava destroyed the two highest stations of the cable car that rises from the town of Sapienza. Travel in the proximity of the crater depends on Mt. Etna's temperament, but you can walk up and down the enormous lava dunes and wander over its moonlike surface of dead craters. The rings of vegetation change markedly as you rise, with vineyards and pine trees gradually giving way to growths of broom and lichen. Catania is the departure point for excursions around—but not always to the top of—Mt. Etna. Buses leave from Catania's train station in the early morning, or you can take the Circumetnea railroad around the volcano's base.

Taormina

★ ㊲ *43 km (27 mi) southwest of Messina, 50 km (31 mi) north of Catania.*

The natural beauty of the medieval mountaintop town of Taormina is so great that even the considerable overdevelopment that it has suffered in the past 50 years has not spoiled its grandeur. The view of the sea and Mt. Etna from its jagged cactus-covered cliffs is as close to perfection as a panorama can get, especially on clear days when the snow-capped volcano's white puffs of smoke are etched against the blue sky. Writers have extolled Taormina's beauty almost since its founding in the 6th century BC by Greeks from Naples. Goethe and D. H. Lawrence were among its enthusiasts. The Greeks put a lofty premium on finding impressive locations to stage their dramas, and Taormina's **Teatro Greco** occupies one of the finest sites of any such theater. It was built during the 3rd century BC and rebuilt by the Romans during the 2nd century AD. Its acoustics are exceptional: Even today a stage whisper can be heard in the last rows. In summer, Taormina hosts an arts festival of music, film, and dance events, many of which are held in the Teatro Greco (☞ *below*). ⊠ *Via Teatro Greco.* 🎟 *4,000 lire.* ☉ *Daily 9–2 hrs before sunset.*

Taormina's many 14th- and 15th-century palaces have been carefully preserved. Especially beautiful is the **Palazzo Corvaja** (⊠ Palazzo Corvaja, Largo Santa Caterina, ☎ 0942/23243), with characteristic black-lava and white-limestone inlays. Today it houses the tourist office. The medieval **Castello Saraceno** (⊠ Monte Tauro), enticingly perched on an adjoining cliff above the town, can be reached by footpath or car.

NEED A BREAK?	If a marzipan devotee, you should not leave Taormina without trying one of the gooey sweets—maybe in the guise of the ubiquitous *fico d'India* (prickly pear)—at **Bar Mocambo** (⊠ Piazza 9 Aprile).

Dining and Lodging

$$ ✕ **Granduca.** There's an antiques shop in the entrance, and the antique theme continues within this tastefully decorated restaurant, where cane chairs and luxurious plants jostle for space among the objets d'art. Your attention, however, will be principally occupied with the riveting views from the glassed-in terrace, when it's not focused on such well-executed dishes as *pappardelle al Granduca* (wide-ribbon pasta with a creamy nut sauce) or *polpettine alla Siciliana*, grilled meatballs wrapped in lemon leaves. There's also a wood-fired oven for pizzas. ⊠ *Corso Umberto 172,* ☎ *0942/24983. AE, DC, MC, V. Closed Tues.*

$$ ✕ **Luraleo.** You can dine indoors by candlelight or in the vine-covered garden in summer. It's touristy, but the food is of a high standard, with the accent on fish—delight in the different risotto with salmon and pistachios, a house specialty. There is a rich selection of antipasti. Service can be slow. ⊠ *Via Bagnoli Croci 27,* ☎ *0942/24279. DC, MC, V. Closed Wed. Oct.–June.*

$$$$ 🏨 **San Domenico Palace.** Sweeping views from this converted 15th-
★ century convent will linger in your mind long after you're gone. Luxury and comfort are bywords in this deluxe hotel, which has managed to sneak a number of unobtrusive 20th-century comforts in (such as wheelchair access and climate control). The essential Renaissance flavor is preserved, however, with the cloisters and the chapel, now a bar. Rooms are brimming with antiques and fresh flowers. ⊠ *Piazza San Domenico 5, 98039,* ☎ *0942/23701,* 𝖥𝖠𝖷 *0942/625506. 101 rooms. 2 restaurants, 2 bars, pool. AE, DC, MC, V.*

$$$–$$$$ 🏨 **Villa Diodoro.** High on a cliff near the Greek amphitheater, this hotel commands superlative views. One of its most attractive features is the relaxing, sprightly garden, where you can have a drink and watch the play of light over the sea. ⊠ *Via Bagnoli Croce 75, 98039,* ☎ *0942/23312,* 𝖥𝖠𝖷 *0942/23391. 103 rooms. Restaurant, bar, pool. AE, DC, MC, V.*

$$$ 🏨 **Villa Fiorita.** This converted private home near the Greek amphitheater has excellent northerly coastal views from nearly every room. Rooms vary in size and furnishings, but most are bright, breezy, and colorful, with large windows and balconies (do ask). Prices are reasonable considering the compact swimming pool and garden. The elevator is at the top of 65 steps. ⊠ *Via Pirandello 39, 98039,* ☎ *0942/ 24122,* 𝖥𝖠𝖷 *0942/625967. 24 rooms. Pool, sauna. AE, MC, V.*

Nightlife and the Arts

FESTIVALS

The Greek Theater and the Palazzo dei Congressi, near the entrance to the theater, are the main venues for the summer festival dubbed **Taormina Arte,** held each year from May to September and embracing classical music, ballet, theater performances, and also the famous **film festival** in July and August. For information, call ☎ 0942/21142, or check with the tourist office.

MUSIC

Free classical music concerts take place in the Duomo and some of Taormina's other churches between November and January, in **Natale a Taormina** (Christmas in Taormina), an initiative sponsored by the tourist office. Performances usually start at around 7 PM and last about an hour.

Shopping

ANTIQUES

Pieces of carretti siciliani sometimes surface at **Chez le Français** (⊠ Piazza San Domenico 6).

Castelmola

5 km (3 mi) west of Taormina.

If your passion for heights hasn't been quelled, visit Castelmola, the tiny town above Taormina, where local bars make their own refreshing almond wine—the perfect complement to the spectacular 360-degree panorama.

En Route The 50-km (30-mi) stretch of road between Taormina and Messina is flanked by lush vegetation and seascapes. Inlets punctuated by gigantic oddly shaped rocks distract from the road. It was along this coast, legend says, that the giant one-eyed cyclopes hurled their boulders down on Ulysses and his terrified men as they fled to the sea and on to their next adventure in Homer's *Odyssey.*

Messina

③ *43 km (27 mi) northeast of Taormina, 94 km (59 mi) northeast of Catania.*

Messina's ancient history tells of series of disasters, but the city nevertheless managed to develop a fine university and a thriving cultural environment. But at 5 o'clock in the morning on December 28, 1908, Messina changed from a flourishing metropolis of 120,000 to a heap of rubble, shaken to pieces by an earthquake that turned into a tidal wave and left 80,000 dead and the city almost completely leveled. As you approach the sickle-shape bay, through which ferries connect Sicily to the mainland, you see nothing of relatively recent disaster, except for the modern countenance of a 3,000-year-old city. The somewhat flat look is a precaution of seismic planning: Tall buildings are not permitted.

The reconstruction of Messina's Norman and Romanesque **Duomo,** originally constructed by the Norman King Roger II in 1197, has retained much of the original plan, including a handsome crown of Norman battlements, an enormous apse, and a splendid wood-beam ceiling. The adjoining **bell tower**—of a much later date—is one of the city's principal attractions. It contains one of the largest and most complex mechanical clocks in the world, constructed in 1933 with a host of gilded automatons—a roaring lion, a crowing rooster, and numerous biblical figures—that spring into action every day at the stroke of noon. ⊠ *Piazza del Duomo.*

NEED A
BREAK?   **Billé** (✉ Corner of Piazza Cairoli and Via Cannizzaro) proffers good
lunchtime snacks, if you don't mind standing up. You can sample (or
take away) such typical Sicilian snacks as *arancini* (deep-fried, breaded
rice balls stuffed with cheese or meat sauce), mozzarella in *carrozza*
(deep-fried bread pockets), and *piddoni* (savory parcels of mozzarella
or vegetables).

Messina is the birthplace of the great Renaissance painter Antonello da
Messina, whose *Polyptych of the Rosary* (1473) can be viewed along
with two large Caravaggios in the **Museo Regionale,** along the sea in the
northern outskirts of the city. ✉ *Viale della Libertà,* ☎ 090/361292. ⊡
8,000 lire. ⊙ *Mon., Wed., Fri. 9–1:30; Tues., Thurs., Sat. 9–1:30 and
4–6:30 (3–5:30 in winter), also 8–10:30 July–Sept.; Sun. 9–12:30.*

OFF THE
BEATEN PATH   **REGGIO DI CALABRIA** – From Messina, a hydrofoil will speed you across
the strait to this city on the toe of the boot, where two larger-than-life-size
5th-century Greek bronze statues are exhibited in the excellent **Museo
Nazionale della Magna Grecia.** The statues, known as the Riace bronzes,
were found by accident by an amateur deep-sea diver off the coast of
Calabria in 1972 and are worth going out of your way to see. ✉ *Piazza de Nava, Corso Garibaldi,* ☎ *0965/812255.* ⊡ *8,000 lire.* ⊙
*Mon.–Sat. 9–1:30 and 2:30–6:30; Sun. 9–1:30 and 2:30–10. Closed
1st and 3rd Mon. of the month Oct.–Mar.*

Dining and Lodging

$$$ ✕ **Alberto Sporting.** Transferred from the center of town to Mortelle,
★   Messina's seaside satellite 10 km (6 mi) up the coast, this deluxe
restaurant still brings in plenty of business. If you're adventurous and
feeling flush, have the waiter order for you: You'll get a succession of
seafood courses. À la carte items are delicious, particularly the spaghetti
con frutti di mare *al cartoccio* (cooked in silver foil) and the involtini
di pesce spada. Vintage Marsala sipped with one of the rich homemade
desserts makes for a grand finale. ✉ *Via Nazionale, Mortelle,* ☎ *090/
321009. AE, DC, MC, V. Closed Mon. and Jan.*

$$$ ▦ **Royal Palace.** Amid a surprising lack of quality accommodation in
downtown Messina, the Royal Palace stands out like a beacon. Oc-
cupying a modern six-story block just steps away from the station and
Piazza Cairoli, the hotel offers a welcome hush from the bustle of the
surrounding streets. Public rooms are grand and the bedrooms comfortably equipped, though the overall impression leans towards the
anonymous (i.e., don't expect much character). ✉ *Via T. Cannizzaro
224, 98123,* ☎ *090/6503,* ℻ *090/2921075. 106 rooms. Restaurant,
bar. AE, DC, MC, V.*

Nightlife and the Arts

Messina stages a folklore parade of huge traditional effigies, called **Giganti,** each year on August 13 and 14.

THE AEOLIAN ISLANDS

Just off Sicily's northeast coast lies an archipelago of seven spectacular islands of volcanic origin. The Isole Eolie (Aeolian Islands), also
known as the Isole Lipari (Lipari Islands), were named after Aeolus,
the Greek god of the winds, who is said to keep all the Earth's winds
stuffed in a bag in his cave here. The Aeolians are a fascinating world
of grottoes and clear-water caves carved by waves through the centuries.
Superb snorkeling or scuba diving abounds in the clearest and cleanest of Italy's waters. Of course, the beautiful people of high society discovered the archipelago years ago—since Roberto Rossellini courted

his star Ingrid Bergman, prior to marrying her, in 1950—and you should not expect complete isolation, at least on the main islands. August, in particular, can get unpleasantly overcrowded, and lodging and travel should always be booked as early as possible.

Lipari provides the best range of accommodations and is a good jumping-off point for day trips to the other islands. Most exclusive are Vulcano and Panarea, the former noted for its black sands and stupendous sunsets (and prices), as well as the acrid smell of its sulphur emissions, while the latter is, according to some, the prettiest. Most spectacular is Stromboli (pronounced with the accent on the first syllable) with its constant eruptions, and remotest are Filicudi and Alicudi, where electricity has only recently been introduced. Access to the islands is gained via ferry and hydrofoil from Sicily or Naples (☞ Arriving and Departing *in* Sicily A to Z, *below*)

The bars in the Aeolian Islands, and especially those on Lipari, are known for their granite of fresh strawberries, melon, peaches, and other fruits. Many Sicilians, especially Aeolians and in Messina, Taormina, and Catania, begin the hot summer days with a *granita di caffè* (a coffee ice topped with whipped cream), into which they dunk their breakfast rolls. You can get one any time of day.

Lipari

39 *37 km (23 mi) north of Milazzo.*

The largest and most developed of the Aeolians, Lipari welcomes you with distinctive pastel-color houses. Fields of spiky agaves dot the northernmost tip of the island, **Acquacalda,** indented with pumice and obsidian quarries. In the west is **San Calogero,** where you can explore hot springs and mud baths. From the red lava base of the island rises a plateau crowned with a 16th-century castle and a 17th-century **cathedral.** Next door is the **Museo Archeologico,** one of the best in Europe, with an intelligently arranged collection of prehistoric finds—some dating as far back as 4000 BC—from various sites in the archipelago. ✉ *Via Castello,* ☎ *090/9880174.* 🎟 *Free.* ☉ *Mon.–Sat. 9–1:30 and 3–7 (3–6 in winter), Sun. 9–12:30 and 3–7 (3–6 in winter).*

Dining and Lodging

In slower periods, you may be greeted at the dock by people offering hotels and *affittacamere* (rooms in private homes).

$$$ ✕ **Il Filippino.** The views from the flower-strewn outdoor terrace of this restaurant in the upper town are a fitting complement to the superb fare on offer. Founded in 1910, the restaurant is rated one of the archipelago's best, and on the whole lives up to expectations. Top choice is seafood, especially the zuppa di pesce, and the smoked pesce spada is a must, in season. Just leave some room for the local version of cassata, accompanied by sweet Malvasia wine from Salina. ✉ *Piazza Muncipio,* ☎ *090/9811002. AE, DC, MC, V. Closed Nov. 10–Dec. 20 and Mon. Oct.–May.*

$$$$ 🏨 **Gattopardo Park Hotel.** Bright bougainvillea and fiery tiger lilies set
★ the tone in this grand villa, whose restaurant enjoys sweeping views out to sea. Guest quarters are in the 19th-century main building, or in whitewashed bungalows in the surrounding tranquil parkland. Public rooms have wood-beamed ceilings and rustic-style furnishings. A minibus shuttles between the hotel and Spiagge Bianche. There are also trips round the island, boat excursions, and folk evenings. Half board in required in summer. ✉ *Via Diana, 98055,* ☎ *090/9811035,* 🆑 *090/9880207. 53 rooms. Restaurant, bar, garden. AE, DC, MC, V.*

$$$ ⊞ **Villa Augusto.** Tucked away off a side-street in the center of Lipari's
old town, this is a peaceful enclave, where a simple homey spirit pre-
vails, with friendly service and a discreet attention to detail. In addi-
tion to a palm-shaded garden, there is a roof-garden offering good views.
The rooms are bright and spacious, and fully equipped. ⊠ *Vico Au-
sonia, 98055,* ☎ *090/9811232,* ℻ *090/9812233. 35 rooms. Piano bar,
free parking. MC, V. Closed Oct.–Easter.*

Vulcano

40 *55 km (34 mi) northwest of Milazzo, 18 km (11 mi) northwest of
Lipari.*

True to its name, Vulcano has a profusion of fumaroles sending up jets
of hot vapor, but the volcano here has long been dormant. Many come
to soak in the strong-smelling sulfur baths, whose odors will greet you,
with the wind in the right direction, long before you disembark. The
island has some of the archipelago's best beaches, though the volcanic
black sand can be offputting at first. You can ascend to the crater (1,266
ft above sea level) on muleback for a wonderful view, or take boat rides
into the grottoes around the base. From **Capo Grillo** there is a view of
all the Aeolians.

Salina

41 *15 km (9 mi) north of Lipari, 52 km (38 mi) northwest of Milazzo.*

The second-largest island, Salina is also the most fertile—which accounts
for its good wine, the golden Malvasia. Excursions go up Mt. Fossa
delle Felci, which rises to over 3,000 ft. It is also the highest of the is-
lands, and the vineyards and fishing villages along its slopes add to its
allure. Malvasia wine here is locally produced, unlike that found on
other islands. Salina has a good range of reasonably priced accom-
modations and restaurants—and fewer crowds.

Panarea

42 *55 km (33 mi) north of Milazzo, 18 km (11 mi) north of Lipari.*

Panarea has some of the most dramatic scenery of the islands: wild caves
carved out of the rock and dazzling flora. The exceptionally clear
water and the richness of life on the seabed make Panarea especially
suitable for underwater exploration, though there is little in the way
of beaches. The outlying rocks and islets make a stirring sight, and you
can enjoy the panorama on an easy excursion to the small Bronze Age
village at **Capo Milazzese.**

Stromboli

43 *63 km (40 mi) north of Milazzo, 40 km (25 mi) north of Lipari.*

This northernmost Aeolian (also accessible from Naples) consists en-
tirely of the cone of an active volcano. The view from the sea—espe-
cially at night, as an endless stream of glowing red-hot lava flows into
the water—is unforgettable. Stromboli is in a constant state of mild
dissatisfaction, and every now and then its anger flares up, so authorities
insist that you climb to the top (about 3,031 ft above sea level) only
with a guide. The return climb, pause, and descent, usually starting at
around 6 PM, take about four hours. You will find a small selection of
reasonably priced hotels and restaurants in the main town, and a
choice of lively clubs and cafés for the younger set. In addition to the
round-island tour, excursions include boat trips around the naturally
battlemented isle of **Strombolicchio.**

Alicudi

44 *65 km (40 mi) west of Lipari, 102 km (68 mi) northwest of Milazzo.*

The farthest outpost of the Aeolians remains sparsely inhabited, wild, and at peace. Here and on Filicudi there is a tiny selection of accommodations, but you can rent rooms cheaply. There is about one eatery on both islands.

Filicudi

45 *30 km (16 mi) west of Salina, 82 km (54 mi) northwest of Milazzo.*

Just a dot in the sea, Filicudi is famous for its unusual volcanic rock formations and the enchanting **Grotta del Bue Marino** (Grotto of the Sea Ox). At Capo Graziano is a prehistoric village. The island has a hotel, and some local families put up guests.

SICILY A TO Z

Arriving and Departing

By Boat

Frequent car ferries cross the strait between Villa San Giovanni in Calabria and Messina on the island. The crossing usually takes about a half hour, but during the summer months there can be considerable delays. From Naples, overnight car ferries (**Tirrenia,** ☎ 081/7201111) operate daily to Palermo. Passenger-only *aliscafi* (hydrofoils) also cross the strait from Reggio di Calabria in about 15 minutes.

By Plane

Sicily can be reached from all major cities via Rome, Milan, or Naples. Planes land at **Aeroporto Punta Raisi** (⊠ 32 km/19 mi west of Palermo, ☎ 091/591698). Catania's **Aeroporto Fontanarossa** (⊠ 5 km/3 mi south of city center, ☎ 095/7306266) also services flights. During the high season, there are also direct charter flights to Sicily from New York, London, and Paris.

BETWEEN THE AIRPORT AND DOWNTOWN
Hourly **Prestia & Comandè** (☎ 091/580457; tickets 5,000 lire) buses ply between Palermo's Punta Raisi airport and the city center (Piazza Castelnuovo and the central station). Taxis charge around 70,000 lire for the same 45-minute trip. Catania's Fontanarossa airport is served by **Alibus** (☎ 095/7360450; tickets 1,500 lire), which leaves about every half-hour from the airport and the central train station, with a stop at Piazza Stesicoro, on Via Etnea. The journey takes around 25 minutes. Taxis cost around 50,000 lire.

By Train

There are direct express trains from Milan and Rome to Palermo, Catania, and Siracusa. The Rome–Palermo and Rome–Siracusa trips take at least 11 hours. After Naples, the run is mostly along the coast, so try to book a window seat on the right if you're not on an overnight train. At Villa San Giovanni, in Calabria, the train is separated and loaded onto a ferryboat to cross the strait to Messina.

Getting Around

Renting a car is definitely the best way to get around Sicily. The trains are unreliable and slow, and the buses, though faster and air-conditioned in summer, can be subject to delays and strikes.

By Boat
The Aeolian Islands are reachable by hydrofoil from Naples, Messina, Palermo, and Milazzo. From Messina you can get ferry service to the islands. Call **Siremar** (☎ 081/5800340) and **SNAV** ☎ (081/7612348).

By Bus and Train
Air-conditioned coaches connect major and minor cities and are often faster and more convenient than local trains but slightly more expensive. Call ☎ 147/888088 for toll-free train information.

By Car
This is the ideal mode of Sicilian exploration. Modern highways circle and bisect the island, making all main cities easily reachable. **A20** (supplemented by S113 at points) connects Messina and Palermo; Messina and Catania are linked by **A18**; running through the interior, from Catania to west of Cefalù, is **A19**; threading west from Palermo, **A29** runs to Trapani and the airport, with a leg stretching down to Mazara del Vallo. The superstrada **S115** runs along the southern coast, and connecting superstrade lace the island. Cars can be rented at airports and downtown locations in every major city (☞ Car Rentals, *below*).

By Train
Main lines connect Messina, Taormina, Siracusa, and Palermo. Secondary lines are generally very slow and unreliable. The Messina–Palermo run, along the northern coast, is especially scenic. Call 147/888088 for toll-free information.

Contacts and Resources

Car Rentals
Cars can be rented at airports and downtown locations in every major city.

CATANIA
Avis (✉ Aeroporto Fontanarossa, ☎ 095/340500; ✉ Via Federico De Roberto 10, ☎ 095/536470). **Hertz** (✉ Aeroporto Fontanarossa, ☎ 095/341595; ✉ Via Toselli 16/c, ☎ 095/322560). **Maggiore** (✉ Aeroporto Fontanarossa, ☎ 095/340594; ✉ Piazza Verga 48, ☎ 095/538109).

PALERMO
Avis (✉ Aeroporto Punta Raisi, ☎ 091/591684; ✉ Via Principe Scordia 28, ☎ 091/586940). **Hertz** (✉ Aeroporto Punta Raisi, ☎ 091/591682; ✉ Via Messina 7/e, ☎ 091/331668). **Maggiore** (✉ Punta Raisi airport, ☎ 091/591681; ✉ Via De Gasperi 179, ☎ 091/513172).

Emergencies
Police, Ambulance, Fire (☎ 113). **Hospital:** Palermo (☎ 091/6662207); Catania (☎ 095/322216).

Guided Tours
Saturday-morning tours of Palermo and Monreale are provided by the Italian tour operator **CST** (✉ Via E. Amari 124, Palermo, ☎ 091/582294; ✉ Corso Umberto 101, Taormina, ☎ 0942/23301), leaving at 9 AM from outside the Politeama Hotel. CST also arranges complete seven-day tours of Sicily's major sights in a comfortable air-conditioned coach with an English-speaking guide. Departures are once a week from either Palermo and Catania, and the cost includes all meals and accommodations in three- or four-star hotels.

Visitor Information

Acireale (⊠ Corso Umberto 177, ☎ 095/604521). **Aeolian Islands** (⊠ Corso Vittorio Emanuele 202, Lipari 98055, ☎ 090/9880095). **Agrigento** (⊠ Viale della Vittoria 255, 92100, ☎ 0922/401352; ⊠ Via Cesare Battisti 15, ☎ 0922/20454). **Caltagirone** (⊠ Palazzo Libertini, 95041, ☎ 0933/53809). **Caltanisetta** (⊠ Corso Vittorio Emanuele 109, 93100, ☎ 0934/530411). **Catania** (⊠ Largo Paisiello 5, 95124, ☎ 095/7306233; ⊠ Stazione Centrale, 95129, ☎ 095/7306255; ⊠ Aeroporto Fontanarossa, 95121, ☎ 095/7306266). **Cefalù** (⊠ Corso Ruggero 77, ☎ 0921/21050 and 0921/21458). **Enna** (⊠ Via Roma 413, 94100, ☎ 0935/528228; ⊠ Piazza Napoleone Colajanni 6, ☎ 0935/26119). **Erice** (⊠ Via Conte Pepoli 11, 91016, ☎ 0923/869388). **Marsala** (⊠ Via XI Maggio 100, 91025, ☎ 0923/714097). **Messina** (⊠ Piazza della Repubblica, 98122, ☎ 090/672944; ⊠ Via Calabria 301/b, ☎ 090/674236; ⊠ Piazza Cairoli 45, ☎ 090/2936294). **Monreale** (⊠ Piazza Duomo, 90046, ☎ 091/6564570). **Palermo** (⊠ Piazza Castelnuovo 35, 90141, ☎ 091/583847; ⊠ Aeroporto Punta Raisi, 90045, ☎ 091/591698). **Piazza Armerina** (⊠ Via Cavour 1, 94015, ☎ 0935/680201). **Siracusa** (⊠ Via San Sebastiano 43, 96100, ☎ 0931/67710; ⊠ Via Maestranza 33, ☎ 0931/464255. **Taormina** (⊠ Palazzo Corvaja, Largo Santa Caterina, 98039, ☎ 0942/23243). **Trapani** (⊠ Piazza Saturno, 91100, ☎ 0923/29000; ⊠ Via Francesco d'Assisi 25, ☎ 0923/545511).

16 Sardinia

An uncut jewel of an island, Sardinia remains unique and enigmatic. Too distant from Rome to be influenced by the character of the mainland, this island is as fascinating as its prehistoric stone structures, the nuraghi. *Modern luxury can also be found here: just follow the jet-setters who sail their yachts to the Costa Smeralda. Beautiful in its severity, Sardinia is a prime destination if you're seeking a getaway.*

THE SECOND-LARGEST ISLAND in the Mediterranean—just smaller than Sicily—Sardinia is about 180 km (112 mi) from mainland Italy and very much off the beaten track. A Phoenician stronghold in ancient times and later a Spanish dominion, Sardinia doesn't seem typically "Italian" in its color and flavor. It lies just a bit too far from the mainland—from imperial and papal Rome and from the palaces of the Savoy dynasty—to have been transformed by the events that forged a national character. Yet Giuseppe Garibaldi, the charismatic national hero who led his troops in fervid campaigns to unify Italy in the mid-19th century, chose to spend his last years in relative isolation on the small island of Caprera, just off the coast of Sardinia.

Updated by
Robert
Andrews

Although Sardinia (Sardegna in Italian) is less than an hour by air and only several hours by boat from mainland Italy, it is removed from the mainstream of tourism except for July and August, when Italians take its beautiful coasts and clean waters by storm. The interior is *never* crowded; Italian tourists in Sardinia come for the sea, less for the rugged and deserted mountain scenery.

Sardinia closely resembles Corsica, the French island across the 16-km-wide (10-mi-wide) windswept Strait of Bonifacio to the north. A dense bush, or *macchia,* barely penetrable in some districts, covers large areas. The terrain is rough, like the short, sturdy shepherds you see in the highlands—impassive figures engaged in one of the few gainful occupations that the stony land allows. Shaggy flocks of sheep and goats are familiar features in the Sardinian landscape, just as their meat and cheese are staples of the island's cuisine. The main highway linking Cagliari with Sassari was begun in 1820 by the Savoy ruler Carlo Felice; designated S131, but still referred to as the Strada Carlo Felice by the islanders, it heads northwest through the fertile Campidano Plain for 216 km (134 mi) to Sassari.

Aside from the chic opulence of the Costa Smeralda, there's little sophistication in Sardinia, but the cost of living on the island is typically higher than on the mainland. The sprawling cities of Cagliari and Sassari have a distinctly provincial air. Newer hotels may seem a little old-fashioned, and hotels—of any vintage—are hard to find inland. There's little traffic on the roads, and trains, buses, and people in general move at a gentle pace. In hamlets, women swathed in black shawls and long, full skirts look with suspicion upon strangers passing through. Sardinians are courteous but remote, perhaps because of their innate dignity.

Like mainland Italians, the Sardinians are of varied origin. On the northwest coast, fine traceries of ironwork around a balcony underscore the Spanish influence. In the northeast, the inhabitants boast Genoese or Pisan ancestry, and the headlands display the ruined fortresses of the ancient duchy of Malaspina on the Italian mainland. As you explore the southern coast, you'll come upon the physiognomies, customs, dialects, place-names, and holy buildings of the Turks, Moors, Phoenicians, Austrians, and the mainland Italians. If there are any pure Sardinians—or Sards—left, perhaps they can be found in the south-central mountains, south of Nuoro, under the 6,000-ft crests of the Gennargentu Massif, in the rugged country still ironically called Barbagia, "Land of Strangers."

Pleasures and Pastimes

Beaches

For their fine sand and lack of crowds, Sardinia's beaches are among the best in the Mediterranean; its waters are among the cleanest, with the exception of those in the immediate vicinity of Cagliari, Arbatax, and Porto Torres. The beach resorts of the Costa Smeralda are exclusive and expensive, but elsewhere on the island you can find a wide range of beaches.

Many agree that the most beautiful beaches on the island are those of Cala di Luna and Cala Sisine, hidden among the rocky cliffs between Baunei and Dorgali, on the eastern coast; these remote strands can be reached only by boat from Cala Gonone or Arbatax. For more accessible beaches with more amenities, go to Santa Margherita di Pula, near Cagliari, where you'll find several hotels; to Villasimius and the Costa Rei, on the southeastern coast; or to the sandy coves sheltered by wind-carved granite boulders on the northern coast in the Gallura district and the archipelago of La Maddalena. There are also beaches around Olbia, Alghero, and on the Costa Paradiso, near Castelsardo.

Dining

In the island's restaurants you'll find that Sardinian regional cuisine is basically Italian, with interesting local variations. Meat dishes are usually veal, lamb, or *porcheddu* (roast suckling pig). On the coast, seafood is king and is served in great variety. Langouste or *aragosta* (lobster) is a specialty of the northern coast; it can be expensive. Foreign conquerors left legacies of bouillabaisse (known here as *zimino*), couscous, and paella, but there are native pastas: *malloreddus* (small shells of bran pasta sometimes flavored with saffron) and *culingiones* (the Sardinian version of ravioli). Sharp pecorino cheese made from sheep's milk, and thin crispy bread called *carta di musica* are typical island fare. Try the *sebadas* (fried cheese-filled ravioli doused with honey) for dessert. The red wines are sturdy and strong, the whites tend toward a light and delicate quality. Amber-color Vernaccia is dry and heady.

CATEGORY	COST*
$$$$	over 85,000 lire
$$$	60,000–85,000 lire
$$	35,000–60,000 lire
$	under 35,000 lire

Prices are per person, including house wine, service, and tax.

Festivals

As one of Italy's most—perhaps *the* most—remote regions, Sardinia is not really a prime spot for sophisticated visual or performing arts. This same remoteness, however, can prove fruitful for sampling some of the culture here, sometimes natively inspired, sometimes drawing on the influences of the traders and invaders who have left their mark on the islands over the millennia. Sardinia's own brand of Catholicism—occasionally bordering on the grotesque—can be witnessed in the local *feste*, or festivals. Ostensibly, the festivals celebrate a saintly or religious occasion, but often they are imbued with an almost pagan feel.

The main festivals are at Cagliari (Festa di Sant'Efisio, May 1), Sassari (Ascension Day, the 40th day after Easter, and August 14), and Nuoro (penultimate Sunday in August). There are smaller festivals throughout the year, some of the best in the scattered mountain villages of the interior, such as the celebrations in local costume during the Festa di San Giovanni, June 24, at Fonni, in the heart of the Barbagio; these festivities are not just expressions of religious devotion but also an explicit statement of community identity.

Fishing

Check locally for regulations on deep-sea fishing. Underwater fishing is restricted to the daylight hours, and no more than 5 kilos (11 pounds) of fish and shellfish may be taken. No oxygen tanks or nets may be used for underwater fishing. Freshwater fishing is good along the Flumendosa, Tirso, Rio Mannu, and other rivers rising in the mountainous interior and in the artificial basins of Flumendosa and Omodeo.

Golf

Sardinia has two world-class golf courses, including the Pevero Golf Club on the Costa Smeralda, which was designed by Robert Trent Jones; and the Is Molas 18-hole course at Santa Margherita di Pula. Four more courses are planned for the Costa Smeralda.

Horseback Riding

Spaghetti westerns were once filmed in Sardinia, and it's easy to imagine why: The rugged, mountainous terrain of the inland is the perfect frontier setting for an adventure on horseback. On the barren hilltops of the Barbagio you may even catch a glimpse of the wild dwarf horse that is native to these parts, though numbers have dwindled over the years. If you prefer a more sedate way of seeing the island on horseback, you can stick to the coast, where the riding is easier but the scenery is still magnificent. Group itineraries and horse rentals can be arranged (☞ Contacts and Resources *in* Sardinia A to Z, *below*).

Kids' Stuff

Sardinia is a vast playground where children can explore and swim in season. There's nothing like a long hike along deserted beaches or through herb-perfumed hills to send them to bed early. Let them clamber over the nuraghi and poke into the countless *domus de janas* (witches' houses) and *tombe di giganti* (giants' tombs), fancifully named grottoes hewn in the rock by the island's prehistoric inhabitants. Near Sassari, at Anghelu Ruhu, and near Dorgali, they served as burial places, but with a little imagination you can make up some fanciful fairy tales.

Lodging

The island's most luxurious hotels are on the Costa Smeralda. They have magnificent facilities but close from fall to spring; many are too out of the way to be good touring bases. Other, equally attractive coastal areas have seen a spate of resort hotels and villa colonies sprouting up; they, too, close from October through April, which narrows the choice of hotels considerably during the other months. In the cities suggested as touring bases, you can expect to find standards of comfort slightly below those on the mainland. The best accommodations may be available at commercial hotels, which can mean little atmosphere. In smaller towns throughout the island, you'll find modest hotels offering basic accommodations, restrained but genuine hospitality, and low rates.

CATEGORY	COST*
$$$$	over 300,000 lire
$$$	160,000–300,000 lire
$$	100,000–160,000 lire
$	under 100,000 lire

Prices are for a standard double room, including service and tax.

Nightlife

Be prepared to part with a cool sum if you visit the Costa, but if that doesn't deter you, go to the complex at the Cervo for a selection of high-class bars, restaurants, and discos. Nightlife elsewhere on Sardinia means a quiet drink before turning in early, tired out from the day's outdoor activity. But as if to make up for the sleepy atmosphere of most of the island, the Costa Smeralda sparkles most nights in the summer.

Sailing

Sailing enthusiasts tack for Sardinia in droves by virtue of its craggy coast, full of wildly beautiful inlets only accessible by sea. You can witness the very rich engage in one of their favorite sports—yachting—at the posh resorts of Costa Smeralda each August, when a number of regattas are held.

Shopping

Sardinia is crafts heaven. Locally produced goods include bright woolen shawls and rugs, hand-carved wooden objects, gold filigree jewelry in traditional designs, coral jewelry, and, above all, handwoven baskets in all shapes and sizes. The best places to go for crafts are the various government-sponsored ISOLA centers in Cagliari, Olbia, Castelsardo, and Sant'Antioco.

Exploring Sardinia

The entire island is about 260 km (162 mi) from north to south, and roughly 120 km (75 mi) across. Driving is the best way to see the island's most interesting sights. Sardinia's mountainous terrain can make driving rigorous and slow. Local transportation is not geared to the needs of visitors, so you can cover more ground in less time if you have a car. If you are not traveling with a car, establish yourself in one of the larger towns and make excursions to as many attractions as time and schedules allow. There are bus and train connections to most places, except some areas of the Costa Smeralda and Su Nuraxi nuraghe.

Numbers in the text correspond to numbers in the margin and on the Sardinia and Cagliari maps.

Great Itineraries

Three days in Sardinia will only give you enough time to see one corner of the island. In five days, you will be able to venture out to some of the attractions in the north of the island. A fairly comprehensive tour taking in the coastline and interior can be accomplished in seven days.

IF YOU HAVE 3 DAYS

You would do well to confine your visit to 🖭 **Cagliari** ①–⑥ and its environs. In Sardinia's capital, you'll find Italianate architecture, churches of all styles, and the Museo Archeologico, with the island's best antiquity collection. If you do not have your own transport, you can make use of taxis or buses to make easy day trips from Cagliari. Your priority should be the **Su Nuraxi** ⑪, the island's best preserved nuraghic monument. On your third day (or second day, staying the night here), head out to the small coastal village of 🖭 **Pula** ⑧; great beaches are here and just outside is Nora, a Carthaginian and Roman archaeological site.

IF YOU HAVE 5 DAYS

Stay in 🖭 **Cagliari** ①–⑥ two days, still leaving enough time for a visit to 🖭 **Pula** ⑧. Spend your third night in 🖭 **Alghero** ⑰, an appealing walled town on the northwest coast with a distinctly Spanish flavor, perhaps stopping for lunch en route at **Oristano** ⑬. For your last two nights, you have a choice: You could spend them in the lap of luxury in one of the hotels in and outside 🖭 **Porto Cervo** ㉒; if you are on a limited budget and/or prefer adventure, make 🖭 **Nuoro** ⑮ your base from which to explore the rugged interior of the island; spend as little time as possible exploring the provincial capital before veering south into the mountainous **Barbagio** region, the island's most primitive district.

IF YOU HAVE 7 DAYS

Spend your first two days exploring ⊞ **Cagliari** ①–⑥. On the third day, you could hit the beaches at **Villasimius** ⑦ on the southeastern tip of the island. Alternatively, go southwest from Cagliari, taking in the remains of antiquity outside of **Pula** ⑧, and moving up along the western coast on the Strada Carlo Felice as far as the sleepy village of **Sant'Antioco** ⑨. Here, you can catch a ferry over to the small island of ⊞ **San Pietro** ⑩ for the night, a favorite weekend retreat of wealthy Cagliarans, with delightful picnic and swimming spots. Continue up toward Oristano, making an inland detour to the fascinating nuraghe of **Su Nuraxi** ⑪, off the main road outside the quiet town of Barumini. Wildlife enthusiasts may want to take another jaunt north of Barumini to the **Giara di Gesturi** ⑫, a basalt plateau with the island's more exotic wildlife. On your fourth night, stay in ⊞ **Oristano** ⑬, which saw its heyday in the Middle Ages, but it now merits a cursory walk through town and glimpse of the Carthaginian ruins at **Tharros** ⑭, just outside the city. Head northeast for **Nuoro** ⑮, a town of little interest, and strike south into the **Barbagia** region: Tortuous roads wind and loop their way over a wild and primitive terrain that seems impervious to the 20th century. If you prefer coastal attractions to the inland ones, spend no more than half a day exploring the region and then head west from Nuoro on road 129 to Bosa, where you turn right into hilly and arid scrub country that eventually brings you to ⊞ **Alghero** ⑰, on the northwest coast, where you should consider spending your fifth night. While heading northeast across an area fringed with low cliffs, inlets, and small bays, don't be distracted by **Sassari** ⑱, but stop to appreciate the exquisite nature of the seaside resorts, including **Castelsardo** ⑲, a walled citadel that is a delight for basket lovers, and to the relaxed fishing village of **Santa Teresa di Gallura** ⑳. If you have a night or two left and love the resort life, plan to pamper yourself on the sun-kissed beaches of one of Europe's premier summer holiday meccas, the **Costa Smeralda,** its most exclusive address ⊞ **Porto Cervo** ㉒.

When to Tour Sardinia

If you can help it, avoid Sardinia in steamy August, when not only is the island swamped by tourists from the mainland, but the Sards, too, take their annual break. A combination of unbearable heat, crowded beaches, accommodation shortage, and shuttered shops and offices can be a hair-raising experience. May and September, on the other hand, are much quieter and still temperate. Sudden storms can be a hazard, but these quickly blow over. The sea remains warm enough for swimming well into October. In winter, rain and clouds are common over high ground—and most of Sardinia is mountainous—and it snows most years in the Barbagia region. In the south, the weather rarely turns cold, but winter is not beach weather. The mountainous interior is probably at its best in the spring, when the woods and valleys are alive with color and burgeoning growth. For the gradations of color, the fall is also a good time.

Try to coincide your visit to Sardinia with one of the famous annual festivals (☞ Festivals *in* Pleasures and Pastimes, *above*). They are mega affairs, with accommodation and restaurant space at a premium, so plan well ahead.

CAGLIARI AND THE SOUTHERN COAST

Cagliari

30 km (19 mi) northeast of Pula, 50 km (31 mi) west of Villasimius, 212 km (132 mi) south of Sassari.

The island's capital reveals impressive Italianate 7architecture and churches in a variety of styles; it's clear that medieval Spanish conquerors from Aragon were here, as well as Austrians and Italians. Sardinia's largest city, Cagliari—the stress is on the first syllable—is characterized by its busy commercial center and waterfront with broad avenues, as well as by the typically narrow streets of the old town on a hill. Explorations from town can include the ancient site of Nora and the popular picnic islands of Sant'Antioco and San Pietro (☞ *below*).

❶ Begin your visit at the **Museo Archeologico,** within the walls of the castle that the Pisans erected in the early 1300s to ward off attacks by the Aragonese and Catalans, from what is now Spain. Among the intriguing artifacts from Nuraghic, Carthaginian, and Roman times are bronze statuettes from the tombs and dwellings of Sardinia's earliest inhabitants, who remain a prehistorical enigma. These aboriginal people left scant clues to their origins. Ancient writers called them the nuraghic people, from the name of their stone dwellings, the nuraghi. The structures' features are unique to Sardinia, just as the Aztec pyramids' are to Mexico. Archaeologists date the nuraghi from about 1300–1200 BC, a time when the ancient Israelites were establishing themselves in Canaan; when the Greeks were besieging Troy; when the Minoan civilization collapsed in Crete; when the Ramses pharaohs reigned in Egypt; and when many migrations were taking place along the shores and water routes of the Mediterranean. During the next 1,000 years, the nuraghic people gradually withdrew to the island's highland fastnesses to avoid more disciplined and better-armed invaders. (Their only weapons, say the chroniclers, were stones and boulders hurled down from the hilltops.) They eventually succumbed when the Romans, following on the heels of Carthaginian invaders, conquered the island in the 3rd century BC. ⊠ *Cittadella dei Musei, Piazza Arsenale,* ☎ *070/ 655911.* ⊡ *4,000 lire.* ⊙ *Apr.–Sept., Tues.–Sun. 9–2 and 3–8; Oct.– Mar., Tues.–Sun. 9–7.*

❷ The medieval **Torre di San Pancrazio** (Tower of San Pancrazio) (⊙ Sun. 9–1), part of the imposing Pisan defenses, is just outside the archaeo-
❸ logical museum. The **Torre dell'Elefante** (Tower of the Elephant), twin to that of San Pancrazio, is at the seaward end of the bastions. **Piazza**
❹ **Palazzo,** at the top of Via Martini, is where you'll find the **Duomo,** which has been extensively rebuilt and restored. The tiers of columns on the facade echo those of medieval Pisan churches, but only the central portal is an authentic relic of that era. All around the church are the narrow streets of the **Spanish quarter,** where humble dwellings still open directly onto the sidewalk and the wash is hung out to dry on elaborate wrought-iron balconies.

❺ The Bastion of St. Remy, better known as the **Terrazza Umberto I,** is a monumental neoclassic staircase and arcade. It was added in the 19th century to the bastion built by the Spaniards 400 years earlier.

❻ Below the Museo Archeologico are the **Anfiteatro Romano,** some very old churches, and a few good restaurants near the waterfront. The amphitheater, which dates from the second century AD, is a well-preserved arena complete with underground passages and beasts' pit, and evidence of the importance of this Roman outpost. ⊠ *Viale Fra Ignazio,* ☎ *070/652130.* ⊡ *Free.* ⊙ *Apr.–Sept., Tues.–Sun. 9–1 and 5–8; Oct.– Mar., Tues.–Sun. 8:30–5:30.*

Dining and Lodging

$$$ ✕ **Dal Corsaro.** This formal restaurant near the port is one of the island's most commended eating places, so make reservations. The decor is refined, the welcome cordial. The menu features seafood and meat

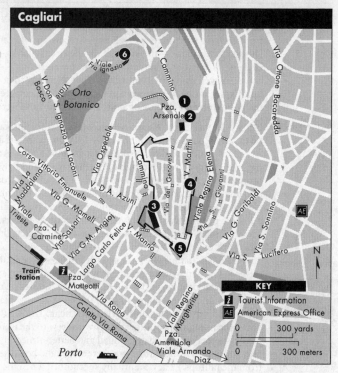

specialties, such as seafood antipasto and porcheddu. ⊠ *Viale Regina Margherita 28,* ☎ *070/664318. Reservations essential. AE, DC, MC, V. Closed Sun., Aug., and 1 wk at Christmas.*

$$ ✕ **Il Gatto.** "The Cat," near the train station and the central Piazza del Carmine, is popular with locals. Follow their lead and make sure you have reservations because the restaurant can fill up quickly. It serves some of the best Sardinian seafood, such as the risotto with shellfish, but for a change of pace try the zesty *insalata di funghi, rucola, e grana padano* (salad of mushrooms, rocket, and a young Parmesan cheese). ⊠ *Viale Trieste 15,* ☎ *070/663596. Reservations essential weekends. AE, DC, MC, V. No lunch weekends*

$$$ 🏨 **Panorama.** With its unprepossessing exterior, this useful hotel in downtown Cagliari is geared toward the business class. Rooms are functional, spacious, and comfortable. Try to reserve one on the upper of the nine floors and enjoy the view over the harbor and bay. Rates are low in the category. ⊠ *Viale Armando Diaz 231, 09100,* ☎ *070/307691,* ℻ *070/305413. 97 rooms. Restaurant, bar, pool, meeting rooms. AE, DC, MC, V.*

$$–$$$ 🏨 **Quattro Mori.** A sure bet, this hotel is convenient to the train station and town center. Rooms are clean and homey, with wood and wicker. The name—"four moors"— refers to Sardinia's emblem of four blindfolded Moorish heads in profile. ⊠ *Via G. M. Angioj 27, 09124,* ☎ *070/668535,* ℻ *070/666087. 40 rooms. Bar. AE, DC, MC, V.*

Nightlife and the Arts

FESTIVAL

Sardinia's greatest annual festival, the **Festa di Sant'Efisio** on May 1 involves a procession between Cagliari and Pula (☞ *below*), a good chance to take part in the centuries-old folklore.

MUSIC

Cagliari's **university** (⊠ Via Università) holds concerts throughout the academic year.

Outdoor Activities and Sports

FISHING

For information on obtaining a fishing license, contact the **Assessorato Regionale alla Difesa dell'Ambiente** (⊠ Via Biasi 7/9, Cagliari, 09100, ☎ 070/6066620).

SAILING

Berthing and provisions facilities are available on all coasts, though concentrated in the area around the Costa Smeralda and La Maddalena areas in the northeast. Altogether, there are 15 nautical schools, nearly half of these in the northeast. The harbor master, or *capitano di porto*, can issue permits for anchorage. The **Lega Navale Italiana** at Marina Piccola in Cagliari (☎ 070/303794) will furnish information on the island's facilities.

Shopping

The best place for crafts is **ISOLA** (⊠ Via Bacaredda 176, ☎ 070/400707), a government-sponsored exhibition of artisanal crafts where most of the work is for sale.

OFF THE BEATEN PATH	**SAN SPERATE** – Practically every wall in this town 20 km (12 mi) north of Cagliari has been brightened with *murales* (mural paintings) by local artists and some well-known Italian painters, transforming the entire town into an open-air art gallery.

Villasimius

❼ *50 km (31 mi) east of Cagliari.*

The eastern route takes you through some dismal industrial suburbs on the road that leads to the scenic coast and beaches of Capo Boi and Capo Carbonara; Villasimius ranks as the chief resort here.

Pula

❽ *30 km (19 mi) south of Cagliari.*

The area southwest of the capital has its share of fine scenery and good beaches—resort villages sprawl along the coast, and the **Is Molas** championship golf course near Pula has won tributes from Tom Watson, Jack Nicklaus, and other professionals of the sport. On the marshy shoreline between Cagliari's Aeroporto di Elmas and Pula, huge flocks of flamingos are a common sight.

Visit the small **Museo Archeologico Comunale** (archaeological museum), with finds from the Nora site. ⊠ *Corso Vittorio Emanuele 67,* ☎ *070/9209610.* ▨ *4,000 lire.* ☉ *Apr.–Sept., daily 9–8; Oct.–Mar., daily 9–6.*

★ For the real thing, head to the narrow promontory less than 3 km (2 mi) outside the town of Pula called **Nora,** the site of a Phoenician, then Carthaginian and, later, Roman settlement. Extensive excavations here have shed light on life in this ancient city from the 8th century BC onward. Many of the exhibits in Cagliari's archaeological museum were found here. An old Roman road passes the moss-covered ruins of temples, an amphitheater, and a small Roman theater. You can make out the channels through which hot air rose to warm the Roman baths; watch for the difference between the simple mosaic pavements laid by the Carthaginians and the more elaborate designs of the Romans. Taking in the views from Nora, you can see why the Phoenicians chose the site for settlement. They always scouted for locations with good harbors, cliffs to shelter their craft from the wind, and a position such as a promontory, from which they could defend themselves from attack. If the sea is calm, look under the clear waters along the shore for more **ruins** of the ancient city, submerged by earthquakes, rough seas, and erosion. ⌦ *Free.* ☉ *Excavations Apr.–Sept., daily 9–8; Oct.–Mar., daily 9–6; guided tours hourly.*

Sant'Efisio, the little Romanesque church at the base of the Nora promontory, plays a part in one of the island's most colorful annual events. Efisio, the patron saint of Sardinia, was a 3rd-century Roman soldier who converted to Christianity. A procession in early May accompanies a statue of the saint all the way from Cagliari and back again. The processional round-trip takes four days, with festive stops along the way, and culminates in a huge parade down Cagliari's main avenue. If you're in Sardinia from May 1 to May 4, don't miss it.

Lodging

The hotels and beaches that cater to the summer hotel trade around Pula and Nora are concentrated a couple of miles south, in a conglomeration of hotels that is the town of Santa Margherita di Pula.

$$$$ 🏨 **Is Morus.** A luxurious enclave, the Is Morus is on a sandy cove and
★ offers all the amenities of a fine beach resort, with low, attractive buildings shaded by pinewoods, plus the option (for guests taking half or full board) of golfing at the fine Is Molas course, about 11 km (7 mi) away. ✉ *Santa Margherita di Pula, 09010,* ☎ *070/921171,* 🖷 *070/ 921596. 85 rooms. Restaurant, bar, pool, miniature golf, tennis court, beach. AE, DC, MC, V. Closed Jan.–mid-Apr. FAP, MAP.*

$$$ 🏨 **Flamingo.** Also directly on the beach and in a shady setting, this resort hotel features a main building and several two-story cottages nestled among eucalyptus trees. ✉ *Santa Margherita di Pula, 09010,* ☎ *070/9208361,* 🖷 *070/9208359. 134 rooms. Restaurant, piano bar, pool, miniature golf, tennis court, dance club. AE. Closed mid-Oct.–Apr.*

Outdoor Activities and Sports

GOLF

Guests at any of the hotels in Santa Margherita di Pula can avail of the international-standard 18-hole **Is Molas** course (☎ 070/9209165); the adjacent **Is Molas Golf Hotel** (☎ 070/9241006) offers special golfing vacations.

Sant'Antioco

⑨ *92 km (57 mi) west of Cagliari.*

Off the southwest coast is Sant'Antioco, one of two islands that is a popular picnic spot with good beaches. You drive over a causeway to get on the island, where the most hectic activity seems to be the silent repairing of nets by local fishermen who have already pulled in their daily catch.

Shopping

You can stock up on local crafts at **ISOLA** (✉ Lungomare Vespucci).

....

OFF THE   **CARBONIA AND IGLESIAS –** If your curiosity prods you to explore more es-
BEATEN PATH   oteric places, you could go just inland of Sant'Antioco to explore the rugged, once-booming mining country around Carbonia (14 km/9 mi northeast), a town built by Mussolini in 1938 to serve as an administrative center for the coal miners and their families. With its overpowering

fascist architecture, it has been called an urban UFO set down in the Sardinian landscape. Nearby Iglesias (30 km/19 mi northeast of Sant'Antioco) is an authentic Sardinian town, with a medieval cathedral; traveling east past Domusnovas on the Cagliari–Iglesias highway, you can detour and drive right through an immense cave, the Grotta di San Giovanni.

San Pietro

⑩ *5 km (3 mi) northwest of Sant'Antioco.*

A ferry at the small northern port of Calasetta connects Sant'Antioco with the smaller island of San Pietro. This is a favorite of wealthy Cagliarians, many of whom have built weekend cottages here.

Lodging

$$$ ☎ **Hieracon.** This three-star hotel in Carloforte, the main town on San Pietro, is well-equipped for short stays or longer sojourns. The central location means that the views aren't great, and the hubbub of promenaders can be loud, but rooms are comfortable and the service friendly. Half-board is required in summer. ✉ *Corso Cavour 63, 09014,* ☎ FAX *0781/854028. 17 rooms. Restaurant, bar. MC, V.*

FROM BARUMINI TO THE COSTA SMERALDA

The Bare and the Beautiful

A more traditional—and wild—Sardinia awaits the traveler who ventures into the mountainous inland of the island. The Italian film directors, the Taviani brothers, made the hinterland of the Barbagia region, where traditional Sardinian customs are carried out in remote hilltop villages, the subject of an extraordinary portrait of rural life among the sheepherders of the area, *Padre Padrone.* Inland Sardinians are hardy souls, used to living in a climate that is as unforgiving in winter as it is intolerable in summer. Old traditions, including the vendetta, are firmly rooted in the social fabric of this mountainous land that is both barren and beautiful. Here, rare species of wildlife share the rocky uplands with sturdy medieval churches and mysterious nuraghi—ancient stone citadels left by prehistoric people. You may want to make your base Oristano, on the west coast and the medieval center of Sardinian nationalism.

As you move northward the timeless beauty of the landscape begins to show greater sign of 20th-century development. The sunny resort of Alghero, the Spanish-influenced port on the west coast, is the preferred vacationing spot of wealthy Sardinians. In the '60s and '70s, the Costa Smeralda, the luxury resort complex developed by the Aga Khan on the northeast corner of Sardinia, was *the* place to summer, along with the Côte d'Azur.

Su Nuraxi

★ ⑪ *60 km (37 mi) north of Cagliari.*

It is worth making a detour to the fascinating **nuraghe** of Su Nuraxi, off the main road outside the quiet little town of Barumini. You could spend hours clambering over this extraordinary structure of concentric rings of stone walls, chambers, passages, wells, and beehive tower. This nuraghe is probably about half its original height, and some of the smaller towers around the main one have been reduced by pillaging and erosion to mere circles of stones on the ground.

The nuraghi were fortified villages, prehistoric versions of medieval walled towns and the forts of the American West. Though this particular type of construction is unique to Sardinia, similar buildings dating from the same era are found in other parts of the Mediterranean, such as Cyprus and the Balearic islands off Spain. Of the 7,000 nuraghi on Sardinia, Su Nuraxi is the most impressive, with those of Sant'Antine and Losa, both near Macomer, close runners-up. It's a good idea to take a flashlight along. ⊠ *1 km (½ mi) west of Barumini.* 🎫 *4,000 lire.* ☉ *Daily 9–1 and 4–sunset.*

Giara di Gesturi

⑫ *8 km (5 mi) north of Barumini, 68 km (42 mi) north of Cagliari.*

On the basalt plateau of Giara di Gesturi roam some of the island's more exotic wildlife, including a species of wild dwarf horse. Another rare species in the Giara is the mouflon, a wild sheep distinguishable from its domesticated counterpart by its long curving horns and skittishness. Long hunted for their decorative horns, the mouflon are now an endangered species, with only a few surviving on Sardinia and Corsica.

Oristano

⑬ *93 km (58 mi) northwest of Cagliari, 89 km (56 mi) southwest of Nuoro, 120 km (75 mi) south of Sassari.*

Oristano, on the west coast, shone in the Middle Ages when it was capital of the Giudicato of Arborea, an independent duchy led by Sardinia's own Joan-of-Arc-type heroine, Eleanora di Arborea. In the 14th century, Eleanora inherited the difficult task of defending the duchy's freedom, constantly undermined by the superior military might of the Spanish troops from Aragon. Although the duchy eventually reverted to Aragonese rule, Eleanora made a lasting contribution to Sardinia by implementing a code of law that was adopted throughout the island and remained in effect until Sardinia's unification with Italy in 1847. Now an important but slow-paced agricultural center, Oristano is the scene of livestock fairs and a rousing series of horse races, called Sa Sartiglia, marking the end of the February's Carnival.

OFF THE   **CABRAS –** Ten kilometers (6 miles) northwest of Oristano, you can see
BEATEN PATH   the extensive marshlands where fishermen pole round-bottomed rush
               boats through shallow ponds teeming with eel and crayfish.

Dining and Lodging

$$$ ✕ **Il Faro.** Locals and visiting foodies consider this elegant seafood restau-
★   rant to be one of the best in the area, as it offers authentic and well-prepared seasonal dishes. There's *capretto allo spiedo* (spit-roasted goat) in the winter and an aromatic *zuppa di fave* (fava bean soup) with bacon and fennel in the spring. ⊠ *Via Bellini 25,* ☎ *0783/70002. AE, DC, MC, V. Closed Jan. 1–15 and July 1–15. No dinner Sun.*

$$ ✕ **Salvatore.** In this classic seafood restaurant near the church of Santa Giusta, just outside Oristano, you can sample seafood from the tidal ponds of Cabras and Santa Giusta. Specialties are spaghetti *alla bottarga* (with smoked fish roe) and grilled *anguilla* (eel). ⊠ *Via Carbonia 1,* ☎ *0783/357134. DC, MC, V. Closed Sun.*

$ 🏨 **Cama.** Near the train station, this hotel is also within walking distance of Oristano's interesting old town center. Rooms are air-conditioned, but otherwise undistinguished. A parking lot and garage make it convenient for drivers. ⊠ *Via Vittorio Veneto 119, 09170,* ☎ *0783/74374,* 📠 *0783/74375. 54 rooms. Restaurant, bar, parking (fee). AE, DC, MC, V. Closed Dec. 20–Jan. 10.*

Nightlife and the Arts

The **Sartiglia** festival, on the last Sunday of Carnival season, includes rich costumes and a ritual joust. Each summer, the town holds an **arts and crafts exhibition,** with local foods and wines given prominence. Contact the tourist office (✉ Via Cagliari 278, ☎ 0783/74191) for information.

Tharros

⑭ *10 km (6 mi) west of Cabras, 20 km (12 mi) west of Oristano.*

The ruins of this Carthaginian city are along the road marked San Giovanni di Sinis; its position afforded it a strategic view over scenic Sinis peninsula. Like Nora to the south, the site was chosen because it commanded the best views of the harbor and could provide an easy escape route if inland tribes threatened.

On your way to Tharros, you'll pass the ghost town of **San Salvatore,** revived briefly in the 1960s as a locale for spaghetti westerns and since abandoned. The saloon of the movie set still stands. Farther along, among the dunes, are large **rush huts** formerly used by fishermen and now much in demand as back-to-nature vacation homes. The 5th-century church of **San Giovanni di Sinis,** also on the peninsula, is the oldest Christian church in Sardinia.

Nuoro

⑮ *89 km (56 mi) northeast of Oristano, 181 km (113 mi) north of Cagliari.*

The somewhat shabby provincial capital of Nuoro is on the edge of a gorge in the harsh mountainous area that culminates in **Gennargentu,** the island's highest massif (6,000 ft). The only things likely to interest you in Nuoro are the views from the park on Sant'Onofrio hill and the exhibits in the **Museo della Vita e delle Tradizioni Popolari Sarde** (Museum of Sardinian Life and Folklore), where you can see local costumes, domestic and agricultural implements, and traditional jewelry. ✉ *Via Mereu 56, ☎ 0784/31426. ☎ 3,000 lire. ☉ May–Sept., daily 9–7; Oct.–Apr., daily 9–1 and 3–7.*

Make an excursion about 3 km (2 mi) east to **Mt. Ortobene** (2,900 ft) for some dizzying views over the gulch below Nuoro. Here you can also see up close the imposing statue of Christ the Redeemer overlooking the city. Picnic tables make this a handy spot for an alfresco lunch stop.

OFF THE BEATEN PATH | **ORGOSOLO** – This old center of banditry halfway between Nuoro and Fonni is still a poor and largely depopulated village, but the houses have been daubed with *murales* (mural paintings) by local artists and some well-known Italian painters, transforming the town into an open-air art gallery.

Dining and Lodging

$$$ **✕🏨 Su Gologone.** Despite attracting tourists in droves, this bustling
★ country inn still manages a friendly atmosphere. The restaurant alone is worth a detour for an authentic Sardinian meal. Island specialties include *maccarones de busa* (thick homemade pasta), culingiones, porcheddu, and sebadas. Wash it all down with the local Vernaccia. The hotel organizes riding and trekking expeditions. ✉ *Località Su Gologone, 08025, ☎ 0784/287512, 𝔽𝔸𝕏 0784/287668. 65 rooms. Restaurant, bar, pool, miniature golf, 3 tennis courts. AE, DC, MC, V. Closed Nov.–Mar.*

Nightlife and the Arts

The **Festa del Redentore** (Feast of the Redeemer) is held on the next-to-last Sunday in August.

Shopping

Crafted for local festivals, wooden masks are available at local shops and make unusual and festive souvenirs.

Fonni

🔟 *30 km (19 mi) south of Nuoro.*

In the heart of the Barbagia region, Fonni is the highest town on the island and a good base for excursions by car to all sites of interest in this mountainous district that is Sardinia's most primitive, as well as the Monte Spada and the Bruncu Spina refuge on the Gennargentu Massif. Life in some villages seems not to have changed much since the Middle Ages. Here a rigidly patriarchal society perpetuates the unrelenting practice of vendetta, and strangers are advised to mind their own business. Tortuous roads wind and loop their way through the landscape; towns are small and undistinguished, their social fabric seemingly impervious to the 20th century. On feast days elaborate regional costumes are taken out of mothballs and worn as an explicit statement of community identity.

OFF THE
BEATEN PATH

ARBATAX – If you have the stamina, take the rickety old train on a leg of the journey that runs on a single-gauge track between Cagliari and Arbatax, midway up the east coast. If all goes well, it takes about nine hours to cover the approximately 250 km (155 mi) of track, guaranteeing you a look at a Sardinia few tourists ever see. With daily, early-morning departures, the train rattles up into the Barbagia district through some breathtaking mountain scenery, then eases down into the desert landscape inland of Arbatax, where the trip ends on the dock next to the fishing boats. The train is run by the Ferrovie Complementari (☎ 070/491304), and the ticket costs less than 12,000 lire. In Tortoli, just outside Arbatax, **Dolce Casa** (✉ Via Scarcidano 3, ☎ 0782/624235, 🖷 0782/623484) is a modest, one-star hotel, scrupulously clean, run by an English-speaking couple.

Nightlife and the Arts

You can see one of the most characteristic of the Barbagia's celebrations in local costume in Fonni on the **Festa di San Giovanni,** June 24.

Shopping

Special candies are made from honey and nougat and sold in hilltop Tonara, southwest of Fonni. In the mountain village of Aritzo, about 3½ km (2 mi) south of Fonni, high up in the Barbagia, you'll find handcrafted wooden utensils and furniture.

En Route   From Nuoro, take 129 west about 65 km (40 mi) to coastal Bosa, where you turn right into hilly and arid scrub country, with its abundance of cactus and juniper. Pines and olive trees shelter low buildings from the steady winds that make these parts ideal for sailing. About the only cash crop here is cork from the cork trees dotting the landscape. Yet in the low valleys and along the riverbeds, masses of oleander bloom in the summer, creating avenues of color.

Alghero

⑰ *40 km (25 mi) north of Bosa, 34 km (21 mi) southwest of Sassari.*

Among the larger centers on the northwest coast is Alghero, an appealing walled resort town with a distinctly Spanish flavor. It was built and inhabited in the 14th century by the Aragonese and Catalans, who constructed seaside ramparts and sturdy towers encompassing an inviting nucleus of narrow, winding streets. Rich, wrought-iron scrollwork decorates balconies and screened windows; Spanish motifs appear in stone portals and in bell towers. The dialect spoken here is a version of Catalan, not Italian: Locals would find it easier to converse in Barcelona than in Rome.

Nearby are broad sandy beaches and the spectacular heights of **Capo Caccia,** an imposing limestone headland to the west. At the base of the sheer cliff, the pounding sea has carved an entrance to the vast **Grotta di Nettuno,** a fantastic cavern, which you must visit with a guide. By land, you reach the entrance at the base of the cliff by descending the more than 600 steps of the aptly named *escala del cabirol* (mountain goat's stairway), a dizzying enterprise—and the ascent is just as daunting. The excursion by sea is much less fatiguing, but is not possible in winter or when seas are rough. Boats leave the port of Alghero four times daily, or every hour or so in peak season, and the trip takes 2½ hours. *Grotto:* ☎ *12,000 lire (includes mandatory tour).* ☉ *Apr.–Sept., daily 9–7; Oct., daily 10–5; Nov.–Mar., daily 9–2; tours on the hr. Boat tour:* ☒ *Navisarda,* ☎ *079/975599.* ☎ *15,000 lire excluding ticket for grotto.* ☉ *Apr.–Oct., daily.*

Dining and Lodging

$$ ✕ **Da Pietro.** On a narrow street in the picturesque old town near Largo San Francesco, this seafood restaurant has vaulted ceilings and a bustling atmosphere. The menu features *bucatini all'algherese* (pasta with a sauce of clams, capers, tomatoes, and olives) and baked fish with white wine sauce. ☒ *Via Ambrogio Machin 18,* ☎ *079/979645. AE, DC, MC, V. Closed Wed. Oct.–May and 2 wks at Christmas.*

$$ ✕ **La Lepanto.** A covered veranda by the seafront marks out Alghero's top seafood restaurant, usually thronged with locals. The specialty is aragosta cooked in a variety of ways, including *alla catalana* (with tomato and onions). For starters, try risotto *nero di seppia* (with cuttlefish ink). ☒ *Via Carlo Alberto 133,* ☎ *079/979116. AE, DC, MC, V. Closed Mon. Oct.–May.*

$$$–$$$$ 🏨 **Villa Las Tronas.** The villa is a former royal mansion on a rocky bluff
   ★ above the sea but still near town center. The gardens sheltering the hotel from the road impart a regal sense of seclusion, and there are great views across the water to the old town. Inside, the turn-of-the-century atmosphere is complemented by modern comforts and good en-suite facilities. The restaurant is open in summer only. ☒ *Lungomare Valencia 1, 07041,* ☎ *079/981818,* ℻ *079/981044. 29 rooms. Restaurant, pool, exercise room, beach. AE, DC, MC, V.*

$$$ 🏨 **Carlos V (Carlos Quinto).** On the shore boulevard about 1 km (½ mi) from the center of town, this hillside hotel is modern but attractive, with porticoes and terraces, one of which has a swimming pool. Smallish but bright rooms all have a balcony, many with a sea view. Low season rates are a bargain. ☒ *Lungomare Valencia 24, 07041,* ☎ *079/979501,* ℻ *079/980298. 110 rooms. Restaurant, pool, 2 tennis courts. AE, MC, V.*

$ 🏨 **San Francesco.** Centrally located in Alghero's Spanish quarter, this hotel occupies the convent that was once attached to the church of San Francesco. The rooms are grouped around the 14th-century cloister and, though somewhat cramped, are modern and quiet. Breakfast is included in the price. ⊠ *Via Machin 2, 07041,* ☎ FAX *079/980330. 21 rooms. Bar, meeting rooms. MC, V. Closed Nov. CP.*

Shopping

Coral, still harvested in the bay, and gold jewelry are displayed in many specialist shops as well as more touristy outlets throughout Alghero's old quarter.

Sassari

⑱   *34 km (21 mi) northeast of Alghero, 212 km (132 mi) north of Cagliari.*

Inland Sassari is an important university town and administrative center, notable for its historic, ornate cathedral and a good archaeological museum. Sassari is the hub of several highways and secondary roads leading to various scenic coastal resorts, among them Stintino and Castelsardo (☞ *below*).

Castelsardo

⑲   *32 km (20 mi) northeast of Sassari.*

The walled seaside citadel of Castelsardo is a delight for basket lovers. Roadside stands and shops in the old town sell tons of island crafts: rugs, wrought iron, and baskets—in myriad shapes and colors. Take the children to see the **Elephant Rock** on the road into Castelsardo; hollowed out by primitive man to become a domus de janas, it resembles an elephant, trunk and all.

Shopping

There is an **ISOLA** workshop on Lungomare Colombo, where local handicrafts can be bought. The local specialty is a brightly colored basket made of dwarf palms.

Santa Teresa di Gallura

⑳   *68 km (42 mi) northeast of Castelsardo, 65 km (41 mi) northwest of Olbia.*

At the northern tip of Sardinia, Santa Teresa di Gallura retains the relaxed, carefree air of an authentic fishing village turned resort.

Dining and Lodging

$$ ✕🏨 **Canne al Vento.** This cheerful, family-run hotel and restaurant on
★   the edge of town is a popular choice. The restaurant specializes in authentic island cuisine, for example *zuppa cuata* (bread, cheese, and tomato soup), porcheddu, or seafood. The guest rooms fall into the inexpensive ($) category. ⊠ *Via Nazionale 23, 07028,* ☎ *0789/754219,* FAX *0789/754948. 22 rooms. Restaurant. MC, V. Closed Mon. and Oct.– Easter.*

$$$–$$$$ 🏨 **Grand Hotel Corallaro.** This hotel offers luxury accommodations in a panoramic spot overlooking the sea, not far from town center. Half or full board is required in peak season. ⊠ *Località Rena Bianca, 07028,* ☎ *0789/755475,* FAX *0789/755431. 81 rooms. Restaurant, pool, Turkish bath, exercise room. MC, V. Closed mid-Oct.–Easter.*

La Maddalena

㉑   *30 km (19 mi) east of Santa Teresa di Gallura, 45 km (20 mi) northwest of Olbia.*

From the port of Palau you can visit the archipelago of La Maddalena, seven granite islands embellished with lush green scrub and wind-bent pines. Pilgrims pay homage to Garibaldi's tomb on the grounds of his hideaway on Caprera, one of the islands.

Porto Cervo

★ ㉒ *30 km (19 mi) north of Olbia.*

Sardinia's northeastern coast is fringed with low cliffs, inlets, and small bays. This has become an upscale vacationland, with glossy resorts, such as Baia Sardinia and Porto Rotondo, just outside the confines of the famed Costa Smeralda, developed by the Aga Khan, who accidentally discovered its charms—and potential—in 1965, when his yacht took shelter here from a storm. The Costa Smeralda is still dominated by his personality; its attractions remain geared to those who can measure themselves by the yardstick of his fabled riches. Sardinia's most expensive hotels are here, and the world's most magnificent yachts anchor in the waters of Porto Cervo. The trend has been to keep this enclave of the really rich an exclusive haven by encouraging more multimillionaires to build discreetly luxurious villas, and planning four more golf courses for their leisure.

All along the coast, carefully tended lush vegetation surrounds vacation villages and elaborate villa colonies that have sprung up over the past decade in a range of spurious architectural styles best described as bogus Mediterranean.

Lodging

$$$$ 🏨 **Cala di Volpe.** Long a magnet for the beautiful people, this luxury five-star establishment was built to resemble an ancient Sardinian village. The hotel's decor is rustic-elegant, with beamed ceilings, Sardinian arts and crafts, and porticoes overlooking the sea. The presidential suite in the highest tower has a private pool. ⊠ *Cala di Volpe, 07020,* ☎ *0789/976111,* FAX *0789/976617. 121 rooms and 12 suites. Restaurant, bar, air-conditioning, pool, 3 tennis courts, beach. AE, DC, MC, V. Closed mid-Oct.–Mar.*

$$$–$$$$ 🏨 **Cervo.** Low Mediterranean buildings surround a large pool and garden in the heart of the Costa Smeralda's Porto Cervo. This complex is next to the marina and *piazzetta* (small piazza), a popular spot to see and be seen. The rooms are large and most have a terrace. Guests have access to five good tennis courts in summer. ⊠ *Porto Cervo, 07020,* ☎ *0789/931111,* FAX *0789/931613. 111 rooms. Restaurant, piano bar, air-conditioning, pool, 5 tennis courts, exercise room, squash, beach. AE, DC, MC, V.*

$$$ 🏨 **Nibaru.** Pinkish-red brick buildings with tiled roofs stand in a secluded inlet set in lush gardens—not bad for a hotel that enjoys all the best features of the Costa Smeralda at comparatively low rates. Guests are just a few yards from the sea and some superb swimming spots and also within easy access to the Pevero Golf Club and the tennis courts of Porto Cervo. ⊠ *Località Cala di Volpe, 07020,* ☎ *0789/96038,* FAX *0789/96474. 45 rooms. Restaurant, bar, pool. AE, DC, MC, V. Closed Oct.–Apr.*

Outdoor Activities and Sports

GOLF

An 18-hole, world-class **Pevero Golf Course** (☎ 0789/96210), designed by Robert Trent Jones, is on the Bay of Pevero, near Porto Cervo.

SAILING

The **Yacht Club Costa Smeralda** (☎ 0789/91332) at Porto Cervo offers temporary memberships.

Shopping

Contemporary pottery displaying traditional motifs is a hot item, snatched up at whim along the Costa Smeralda.

Olbia

㉓ *30 km (19 mi) south of Costa Smeralda, 106 km (66 mi) north of Nuoro.*

Set amid the resorts of Sardinia's northeastern coast, Olbia is a lively little seaport, not heavily industrialized, at the head of a long, wide bay.

Lodging

$$–$$$ ⊡ **De Plam.** Though aesthetically unimpressive, this seafront hotel a walk from town can at least claim the best views in Olbia. The rooms are furnished in a motel style that is functional if not particularly memorable. It's convenient to the port (though still a taxi ride away). ⊠ *Via de Filippi 33, 07026,* ☎ *0789/25777,* ℻ *0789/22648. 60 rooms. Restaurant, bar, air-conditioning, meeting rooms. AE, DC, MC, V.*

Shopping

The local **ISOLA** (⊠ Corso Umberto 28) has works for sale.

Golfo Aranci

㉔ *19 km (12 mi) northeast of Oristano.*

At the mouth of the Gulf of Olbia, Golfo Aranci is a blossoming resort and debarkation point for FS ferries from the mainland.

SARDINIA A TO Z

Arriving and Departing

By Boat

Large modern ferries run by Tirrenia Lines, Navarma Lines, and the FS (Italian State Railways) connect the island (ports at Porto Torres, Olbia, Arbatax, and Cagliari) with the mainland. **Tirrenia** (☎ 06/4742041 or 06/4742242 in Rome, 010/2758041 in Genoa, 081/7201111 in Naples) sails to several ports in Sardinia from Genoa, La Spezia, Civitavecchia, Naples, Palermo, and Trapani. **Navarma** (☎ 0565/9361) transports passengers and cars between Livorno and Olbia. **FS** ferries (☎ 0766/23273 on the mainland, 0789/46800 in Golfo Aranci) carry trains as well as passengers and cars; they sail from Civitavecchia to Golfo Aranci, near Olbia. The Civitavecchia–Olbia/Golfo Aranci run takes about eight hours and there are overnight sailings. Depending on the season, the service is scheduled two or three times a week; reservations are essential in the summer.

By Plane

Alitalia and Meridiana connect Rome, Milan, Pisa, and other cities on the mainland and in southern Europe with Sardinia. Flying is by far the fastest and easiest way to get to the island. The Rome–Cagliari flight takes about an hour. Sardinia's major airports are at Cagliari and Alghero, with another, smaller one, at Olbia, providing access to the Costa Smeralda.

Cagliari's **Aeroporto di Elmas** (☎ 070/240079) at Elmas is about 6 km (4 mi) west of town center, and there is a regular bus service from the airport to Piazza Matteotti, in front of the train station. Alghero's **Aeroporto Fertilia** (☎ 079/935282) is 13 km (8 mi) from the city. A bus links the airport with the air terminal on Corso Vittorio Emanuele II. **Aeroporto Costa Smeralda** (☎ 0789/52600) is 4 km (2½ mi) southeast of Olbia.

Getting Around

By Bus

Cagliari is linked with the other towns of Sardinia by a network of buses. Local destinations are served by **ARST** (☎ 070/4098324). Major cities, excluding Olbia, are served by **PANI** (☎ 070/652326). The heart of the Sardinian bus system is the **Stazione Autolinee** (✉ Piazza Matteotti, across the square from the main tourist office) in Cagliari. City buses in Cagliari and Sassari operate on the same system as those on the mainland: Buy your ticket first, at a tobacco shop or machine, and cancel it by punching it in the machine on the bus. Fares are about 1,500 lire per ride or 3,500 lire all day.

By Car

The best way to get around Sardinia is to drive. The roads are generally in good condition, but bear in mind that such roadside conveniences as gas stations and refreshment stands are infrequent on some routes, especially in the east. Cars may be taken on board most of the ferry lines connecting Sardinia with the mainland. The north–south S131 (Strada Carlo Felice) connects Cagliari, Oristano, Sassari, and Porto Torres. The S131 Dir and S129 connects the Carlo Felice Highway with Nuoro and the Barbagia. The S597 connects Sassari and Olbia.

By Train

The Stazione Centrale (☎ 147/888088 toll-free) in Cagliari is west of Piazza Matteotti, on Via Roma. There are fairly good connections between Olbia, Cagliari, Sassari, and Oristano. You can reach Nuoro via Macomer; Alghero is reached via Sassari. Service on the few other local lines is infrequent and slow. The fastest train between Olbia and Cagliari takes more than four hours. A local train connects Golfo Aranci, the FS port for the train ferry, with Olbia and takes 20 minutes.

Contacts and Resources

Car Rentals

ALGHERO

Maggiore (✉ Via Sassari 87, ☎ 079/979375).

CAGLIARI

Avis (✉ Stazione Centrale , ☎ 070/668128; ✉ Aeroporto di Elmas, ☎ 070/240081). **Hertz** (✉ Piazza Matteotti 8, ☎ 070/668105; ✉ Aeroporto di Elmas, ☎ 070/240037). **Maggiore** (✉ Viale Monastir 116, ☎ 070/273692).

OLBIA

Avis (✉ Via Genova 67, ☎ 0789/22420; ✉ Aeroporto Costa Smeralda). **Hertz** (✉ Via Regina Elena 34, ☎ 0789/21733; ✉ Aeroporto Costa Smeralda, ☎ 0789/66024).

SASSARI

Avis (✉ Via Mazzini 2, ☎ 079/235547). **Hertz** (✉ Corso Francesco Vico, ☎ 079/232184). **Maggiore** (✉ Piazza Santa Maria 6, ☎ 079/235507).

Emergencies

Police (☎ 112 or 113). **Hospital** (✉ Via Peretti, Cagliari, ☎ 070/543266). **Ambulance** (✉ Cagliari, ☎ 070/4092901).

Guided Tours

HORSEBACK RIDING

The **Associazione Nazionale di Turismo Equestre** (✉ Via Carso 35a, Sassari, ☎ 079/299889) can provide information on renting mounts and joining riding parties with itineraries along the coast or into the heart of the island. The **Centro Vacanze Alabirdi** (✉ Arborea, near Oristano, ☎ 0783/800512) organizes horseback riding vacations. The **Centro Vacanze Su Gologone** (✉ Oliena, ☎ 0784/287512) also offers riding vacations.

ORIENTATION

Guided tours are good introductions to Sardinia. Travel from the Italian mainland is included, as are travel and accommodations on Sardinia. They should be booked through a travel agent.

To book a tour, contact a travel agent such as **Viaggi Orru** (✉ Via Roma 95, ☎ 070/659858). **Chiariva** offers two group tours of Sardinia by bus with guide. A nine-day tour leaves from Genoa; an eight-day tour departs from Rome. Both operate from April–September. **Aviatour** has a similar eight-day tour leaving from either Milan or Rome. The tour also runs from April–September only. **Appian Line** can arrange a fly-drive package on the Costa Smeralda; transportation is by air, the rental car is picked up at the airport at Olbia. Accommodations are in good, but not outlandishly expensive, hotels on this famous coastline for the rich.

Late-Night Pharmacies

Late-night pharmacies are open on a rotating basis; information on current schedules is pinned up on any pharmacy door or can be obtained by calling (☎ 192).

Travel Agency

Cagliari (Viaggi Orru; ✉ Via Roma 95, ☎ 070/659858).

Visitor Information

Alghero (✉ Piazza Porta Terra 9, 07041, ☎ 079/979054). **Cagliari** (✉ Piazza Matteotti, 09100, ☎ 070/669255; ✉ Piazza Deffenu 9, 09100, ☎ 070/654811 or 167/013153 toll-free; ✉ Aeroporto di Elmas, ☎ 070/240200). **Nuoro** (✉ Piazza Italia 19, 08025, ☎ 0784/30083). **Olbia** (✉ Via Catello Piro, 07026, ☎ 0789/21453; ✉ City Hall, Golfo Aranci, 07026, ☎ 0789/21672 June–Aug. only; ✉ Aeroporto Costa Smeralda, ☎ 0789/21453). **Oristano** (✉ Via Cagliari 278, 09170, ☎ 0783/74191). **Sassari** (✉ Viale Umberto 72, ☎ 079/233534).

17 Portraits of Italy

Italy at a Glance: A Chronology

The Artless Art of Italian Cooking

The Passionate Eye: Italian Art Through the Ages

Books and Videos

ITALY AT A GLANCE: A CHRONOLOGY

ca. 1000 BC Etruscans arrive in central Italy.

ca. 800 Rise of Etruscan city-states.

753 Traditional date for the founding of Rome.

750 Greek city-states begin to colonize Sicily and southern Italy.

600 Latin language becomes dominant in Etruscan League; Rome becomes established urban center.

510 Foundation of the Roman republic; expulsion of Etruscans from Roman territory.

410 Rome adopts the 12 Tables of Law, based on Greek models.

343 Roman conquest of Greek colonies in Campania.

312 Completion of Via Appia (Appian Way) to the south of Rome; an extensive Roman road system begins to develop.

264–241 First Punic War (with Carthage): increased naval power helps Rome gain control of southern Italy and then Sicily.

218–200 Second Punic War: Hannibal's attempted conquest of Italy, using elephants, is eventually crushed.

176 Roman Forum begins to take shape as the principal civic center in Italy.

146 Third Punic War: Rome razes city of Carthage and emerges as the dominant Mediterranean force.

133 Rome rules entire Mediterranean Basin except Egypt.

49 Julius Caesar conquers Gaul.

45 Civil War leaves Julius Caesar as sole ruler; Caesar's Forum is established.

44 Julius Caesar is assassinated.

31 The Battle of Actium resolves the power struggle that continued after Caesar's death; Octavian becomes sole ruler.

27 Rome's Imperial Age begins; Octavian (now named Augustus) becomes the first emperor and is later deified. The Augustan Age is celebrated in the works of Virgil (70 BC–AD 19), Ovid (43 BC–AD 17), Livy (59 BC–AD 17), and Horace (65 BC–AD 27).

14 AD Augustus dies.

29 Jesus is crucified in the Roman colony of Judea.

43 Rome invades Britain.

50 Rome is the largest city in the world, with a population of a million.

65 Emperor Nero begins the persecution of Christians in the empire; Saints Peter and Paul are executed.

70–80 Vespasian builds the Colosseum.

98–117 Trajan's military successes are celebrated with his Baths (98), Forum (110), and Column (113); the Roman Empire reaches its apogee.

165 A smallpox epidemic ravages the Empire.

ca. 150–200 Christianity gains a foothold within the Empire, with the theological writings of Clement, Tertullian, and Origen.

212 Roman citizenship is conferred on all nonslaves in the Empire.

238 The first wave of Germanic invasions penetrates Italy.

293 Diocletian reorganizes the Empire into West and East.

313 The Edict of Milan grants toleration of Christianity within the Empire.

330 Constantine founds a new Imperial capital (Constantinople) in the East.

410 Rome is sacked by Visigoths.

476 The last Roman Emperor, Romulus Augustus, is deposed. The Empire of Rome falls.

552 Eastern Emperor Justinian (527–565) recovers control of Italy.

570 Lombards gain control of much of Italy, including Rome.

590 Papal power expands under Gregory the Great.

610 Heraldius revives the Eastern Empire, thereafter known as the Byzantine Empire.

774 Frankish ruler Charlemagne (742–814) invades Italy under papal authority and is crowned Holy Roman Emperor by Pope Leo III (800).

ca. 800–900 The breakup of Charlemagne's (Carolingian) realm leads to the rise of Italian city-states.

811 Venice is founded by mainlanders escaping Barbarian invasions.

1054 The Schism develops between Greek (Orthodox) and Latin churches.

ca. 1060 Europe's first university is founded in Bologna.

1077 Pope Gregory VII leads the Holy See into conflict with the Germanic Holy Roman Empire.

1152–90 Frederick I (Barbarossa) is crowned Holy Roman Emperor (1155); punitive expeditions by his forces (Ghibellines) are countered by the Guelphs, creators of the powerful Papal States in central Italy. Guelph–Ghibelline conflict becomes a feature of medieval life.

1204 Crusaders, led by Venetian doge Dandolo, capture Constantinople.

1257 The first of four wars is declared between Genoa and Venice; at stake is the maritime control of the eastern Mediterranean.

1262 Florentine bankers issue Europe's first bills of exchange.

1264 Charles I of Anjou invades Italy, intervening in the continuing Guelph–Ghibelline conflict.

1275 Marco Polo (1254–1324) reaches the Orient.

1290–1375 Tuscan literary giants Dante Alighieri (1265–1321), Francesco Petrarch (1304–74), and Giovanni Boccaccio (1313–75) give written imprimatur to modern Italian language.

1309 The pope moves to Avignon in France, under the protection of French kings.

1355 Venetian doge Marino Falier is executed for treason.

1376   The pope returns to Rome, but rival Avignonese popes stand in opposition, creating the Great Schism until 1417.

1380   Venice finally disposes of the Genovese threat in the Battle of Chioggia.

1402   The last German intervention into Italy is repulsed by the Lombards.

1443   Brunelleschi's (1377–1446) cupola is completed on Florence's Duomo.

1447   Nicholas V founds the Vatican Library. This begins an era of nepotistic popes who devalue the status of the papacy but greatly enrich the artistic and architectural patronage of the Holy City.

1469–92   Lorenzo "Il Magnifico" (1449–92), the Medici patron of the arts, rules in Florence.

1498   Girolamo Savonarola (1452–98), the austere Dominican friar, is executed for heresy after leading Florence into a drive for moral purification, typified by his burning of books and decorations in the "Bonfire of Vanities."

1499   Leonardo da Vinci's (1452–1519) *Last Supper* is completed in Milan.

1508   Michelangelo (1475–1564) begins work on the Cappella Sistina.

1509   Raphael (1483–1520) begins work on his *Stanze* in the Vatican.

1513   Machiavelli's (1469–1527) *The Prince* is published.

1521   The Pope excommunicates Martin Luther (1483–1546) of Germany, precipitating the Protestant Reformation.

1545–63   The Council of Trent formulates the Catholic response to the Reformation.

1546   Andrea Palladio (1508–80), architectural genius, wins his first commission in Vicenza.

1571   The combined navies of Venice, Spain, and the Papacy defeat the Turks in the Battle of Lepanto.

1626   The Basilica di San Pietro is completed in Rome.

1633   Galileo Galilei (1564–1642) faces the Inquisition.

1652   Sant'Agnese in Agone church, Borromini's (1599–1667) Baroque masterpiece, is completed in Rome.

1667   The Piazza di San Pietro, designed by Bernini (1598–1680), is completed.

ca. 1700   Opera develops as an art form in Italy.

1720–90   The Great Age of the Grand Tour: Northern Europeans visit Italy and start the vogue for classical studies. Among the famous visitors are Edward Gibbon (1758), Jacques-Louis David (1775), and Johann Wolfgang von Goethe (1786).

1778   Teatro alla Scala is completed in Milan.

1796   Napoléon begins his Italian campaigns, annexing Rome and imprisoning Pope Pius VI four years later.

1815   Austria controls much of Italy after Napoléon's downfall.

1848 Revolutionary troops under Risorgimento (Unification) leader. Giuseppe Mazzini (1805–72) and Giuseppe Garibaldi (1807–8. establish a republic in Rome.

1849 French troops crush rebellion and restore Pope Pius IX.

1860 Garibaldi and his "Thousand" defeat the Bourbon rulers in Sicily and Naples.

1870 Rome is finally captured by Risorgimento troops and is declared capital of Italy by King Vittorio Emanuele II.

1900 King Umberto I is assassinated by an anarchist; he is succeeded by King Vittorio Emanuele III.

1915 Italy enters World War I on the side of the Allies.

1922 Fascist "black shirts" under Benito Mussolini (1883–1945) march on Rome; Mussolini becomes prime minister and later "Il Duce" (head of Italy).

1929 The Lateran Treaty: Mussolini recognizes Vatican City as a sovereign state, and the Church recognizes Rome as the capital of Italy.

1940–44 In World War II, Italy fights with the Axis powers until its capitulation (1943), when Mussolini flees Rome. Italian partisans and Allied troops from the landings at Anzio (January 1944) win victory at Cassino (March 1944) and force the eventual withdrawal of German troops from Italy.

1957 The Treaty of Rome is signed, and Italy becomes a founding member of the European Economic Community.

1966 November flood damages many of Florence's artistic treasures.

1968–79 The growth of left-wing activities leads to the formation of the Red Brigades and provokes right-wing reactions. Bombings and kidnappings culminate in the abduction and murder of Prime Minister Aldo Moro (1916–1978).

1980 Southern Italy is hit by a severe earthquake.

1991 Waves of refugees from neighboring Albania flood southern ports on the Adriatic. Mt. Etna erupts, spewing forth a lava stream that threatens the Sicilian town of Zafferana.

1992 The Christian Democrat Party, in power throughout the postwar period, loses its hold on a relative majority in Parliament.

1993 Italians vote for sweeping reforms after the Tangentopoli (Bribe City) scandal exposes widespread political corruption, including politicians' collusion with organized crime. A bomb outside the Galleria degli Uffizi in Florence kills five, but spares the museum's most precious artwork; authorities blame the Cosa Nostra, flexing its muscles in the face of a crackdown.

1994 A center-right coalition wins in spring elections, and media magnate Silvio Berlusconi becomes premier—only to be deposed within a year. Italian politics seem to be evolving into the equivalent of a two-party system.

1995 Newly appointed Lamberto Dini takes hold of the government's rudder and, as president of the Council of Ministers, institutes major reforms and replaces old-line politicians.

1996 A league of center-left parties wins national elections and puts together a government coalition that sees the Democratic Party of the Left (PDS), the former Communist party, into power for the first time ever in Italy. Thousands of Romans gathered in Piazza del Campidoglio to bid farewell to the late beloved actor Marcello Mastroianni, revered for his portraits of the consummate Italian charmer in films such as *La Dolce Vita, 8½*—both Federico Fellini films—and *Divorce Italian Style.*

1997 Political stability and an austerity program put Italy on track toward the European Monetary Union and adoption of the single Euro currency. Though only a copy, the statue of Roman emperor Marcus Aurelius is returned to its pedestal on the Campidoglio as a symbol of Rome's historic grandeur. A series of earthquakes hit the mountainous interior of central Italy, severely damaging villages and some historic towns. In Assisi, portions of the vault of the Basilica di San Francesco crumble, destroying frescoes by Cimabue.

1998 The secessionist Northern League continues to threaten to disrupt Italy's national unity, achieved little more than 100 years ago. The protest revolves around the disparity between the highly prosperous, industrialized North and the underdeveloped South, as proposals for a new federalist system of government founder on political shoals. In Rome, public works projects designed to take some of the snarls out of Jubilee Year traffic in the year 2000 get under way. In Turin's Duomo, the relic of the Sacra Sindone (Holy Shroud) was on display from late April to mid-June of 1998, a rare occurrence that will be repeated in 2000.

THE ARTLESS ART OF ITALIAN COOKING

You are staying with friends in their villa in a windswept olive orchard above Florence. After a day in town—a morning at the Palazzo Pitti, afternoon in the Brancacci Chapel—you have returned to rest. In the garden, you find your hostess lifting heavy tomatoes into a basket, the acrid smell of their skins wafting up in the gentle September heat. You pick basil and tug figs from a tree that warms its back against the 14th-century kitchen wall. Inside, you watch while your hostess rinses the greens in the quarried stone sink. The tomatoes are still sun-warm when she scoops them, chopped, into a blender with the basil and a stream of olive oil; she pours the mixture into a faience bowl over steaming pasta. You eat at the kitchen table, pour wine from a crockery pitcher, and wipe your bowl with torn chunks of flour-flecked bread. Over the greens your hostess drizzles more olive oil and a bit of rock salt pinched from an open bowl. The figs melt in your mouth like chocolate. A scalding syrup of Arabic coffee streams from the *macchinetta,* and you're ready for a midnight survey of the olive groves.

SIMPLE, EARTHY, at once wholesome and sensual, as sophisticated in its purity as the most complex cuisine, as inspired in its aesthetics as the art and architecture of its culture, Italian cooking strikes a chord that resonates today as it did in the Medici courts. Its enduring appeal can be traced to an ancient principle: respect for the essence of the thing itself—nothing more, nothing less. Like Michelangelo freeing the prisoners that dwelt within the stone—innate, organic—an Italian chef seems intuitively to seek out the crux of the thing he is about to cook and flatter it, subtly, with the purest of compliments. To lay a translucent sheet of prosciutto—earthy, gamey, faintly redolent of brine—across the juicy pulchritude of a melon wedge is a stroke of insight into the nature of two ingredients as profound as the imaginings of Galileo.

Considering the pizzas, lasagnas, and red-drenched spaghetti that still pass for Italian food abroad (despite a wave of enlightenment that revived "Northern" techniques in the 1980s), it's no surprise that visitors to Italy are often struck by the austerity of the true Italian dishes put before them. The pasta is only lightly accented, not drowning in an industrial ladle-full of strong, soupy sauce. And while there may have been a parade of vegetable *antipasti,* the salad itself bears no resemblance to the smorgasbord of Anglo-American salad bars—it's a simple mix of greens, a drizzle of oil, a spritz, perhaps, of red-wine vinegar. If you've just come from Germanic countries, you'll notice a lack of Maggi, the bottled brown "flavor enhancer" that singes the tongue with monosodium glutamate, on the table. If you've come from Belgium, you'll miss the sauceboat of Hollandaise. And if you've come from France, you may shrug dismissively at the isolated ingredients you're served, saying as other Frenchmen before you, "But this is not really a true *cuisine . . .*"

Ah, but it is. Shunning the complexities of heavy French sauces and avoiding the elaborate farce, Italian cuisine—having unloaded the aspirations of *alta cucina* onto its northern neighbors when Catherine de' Medici moved (chefs and all) to Paris—stands alone, proud, purist, unaffected.

The Italians' pride comes in part from a confidence in their raw ingredients, an earthiness that informs the appreciation of every citizen-connoisseur, from the roughest peasant in workers' blue to the vintner in shoulder-tied cashmere: they are in touch with land and sea. In the country, your host can tell you the source of every ingredient on the table, from the neighbor's potted goose to the porcini gathered in the beech grove yesterday. In the city, the market replaces the country network, and aggressive shopping will trace the genealogy of every mushroom, every artichoke, every wooden scoop of olives. And in balconies overhanging the seashore, the squid floating in their rich, blue-black ink were bought from a fisherman on the beach at dawn.

The spectrum of Italian regional cooking is as broadly varied as Italy's terrain, and cuisine and countryside are intimately allied. Emerging into sunlight from the Great St. Bernard pass into the Valle d'Aosta, the Piedmont, the hills of Lombardy, you'll find wood-lined alpine trattorias offering rib-sticking gnocchi and air-dried beef, bubbling pots of *bagna cauda,* slabs of polenta, hearty walnut *torta.* The pearl-spotted rice of Arborio, in the Po Valley, fuels an extraordinary array of risottos in Milan, where chefs shun olive oil in favor of the region's rich butter. Descend to Alba and savor the earthy perfume of truffles, the muscular Barolo wines. Cross over into Liguria and the cuisine changes as abruptly as the landscape: wild herbs, greens, and ground nuts flavor a panoply of sauces (consider the famous pesto, flavored with a "riviera" basil rarely found elsewhere), served as condiments to meat as often as over pasta. The succulent pink pork of a Parma ham, the golden butterfat in a Reggiano cheese were nurtured on the same fertile soil of Emilia-Romagna, both the culinary and agricultural heart of Italy, while the *bistecca* of Tuscany comes from Chianina beef, pampered on local prairie grass and slaughtered at a tender age. Head south for sun-plumped eggplant, and quasi-tropical artichokes—in Rome, fried in delicate batter; in Calabria, stuffed with meat and sharp Pecorino from its hillside sheep herds. The chickpeas in Sicilian dishes remind you you're nearly in North Africa. And, of course, on this slender leg of land you are never far from the sea, and the harvest of its *frutti di mare* graces nearly every region—but none more than the islands and tide-washed shores of the south.

Careening in your rental car down the western coast, clinging to the waterfront through sea-shanty villages that cantilever over the roaring surf, you feel a morning lag: your breakfast of *latte macchiato* and sugary *cornetto* has worn away. A real espresso would hit the spot; you hurtle down a web of switchbacks and pull into a seaside inn. You sip aromatic coffee and watch the waves. An hour passes in reverie—an aperitif, perhaps? Another hour over the Martini rosso, and you give in to the impulse, adjourning to the dining room. The odor of wood smoke drifts from the kitchen. A nutty risotto with a blush of tomato precedes a vast platter—austere, unembellished—of smoke-grilled fish, still sizzling, lightly brushed with oil, and glittering with rock salt. At the table

beside yours, when the platter arrives, the woman rises and fillets the fish dextrously, serving her husband and sons.

THERE'S A WHOLESOMENESS in the way Italians eat that is charming and contagious. If American foodies pick and kvetch and French gastronomes worship, Italians plunge into their meal with frank joy, earnest appreciation, and ebullient conversation. Yet they do not overindulge: portions are light, the drinking gentle, late suppers spartan with concern for digestion uppermost. It's as if the voice of Mamma still whispers moderation in their ear. They may, on the other hand, take disproportionate pleasure in watching guests eat, in surrounding them with congenial company, in pouncing on the bill. (This wholesome spirit even carries into the very bars: unlike the dark, louche atmosphere of Anglo lounges and pubs, in Italy you'll drink your *amaro* in a fluorescent-lit coffee bar without a whiff of sin in the air.)

Yet for all their straightforwardness, Italians are utterly at ease with their heritage, steeped from birth in the art and architecture that surrounds them. Without a hint of the grandiose, they'll construct a still life of figs and Bosc pears worthy of Caravaggio; a butcher will drape iridescent pheasants and quail, heads dangling, with the panache of a couturier. Consider the artless beauty of ruby-raw beef on an emerald bed of arugula, named for the preferred colors of the Venetian painter Carpaccio; pure white porcelain on damask; a mosaic of olives and pimientos in blown glass; a flash of folkloric pottery on a polished plank of oak.

In fact, it must be said: a large part of the pleasure of Italian dining is dining in Italy. We have all eaten in Italian restaurants elsewhere. The food can be superb, the ingredients authentic, the pottery and linens imported by hand. Yet who can conjure the blood-red ocher crumbling to gold on a Roman wall, the indigo and pastel hues of fishing boats rocking in a marina, the snow flurry of sugar papers on a café floor? These impart the essence that—as much as the basil on your *bruschetta*—flavors your Italian dining experience.

Inside the great walls of Lucca, you are lunching—slowly, copiously, and at length—in the shade of a vaulted portico. Strips of roasted eggplant and pepper steeped in garlic and oil; tortelloni stuffed with squab in a pool of butter and sage; roasted veal laced with green peppercorns; blackberries in thick cream. The bottle of Brunello di Montalcino, alas, is drained. It has been a perfect morning, walking the ramparts, and you have found the perfect restaurant: a Raphaelesque perspective of arcades and archways, pillars, porches, and loges spreads before you. The shadows and lines are strong in the afternoon sun; you admire from your seat in the cross breeze. It's only slowly that you realize that this Merchant/Ivory moment has a sound track, so organic to the scene you hadn't noticed—but now you feel goosebumps rising on your neck. It is Puccini: a young woman is singing, beautifully, from a groined arcade across the square, accompanied by a portable tape player.

". . . Ma quando vien lo sgelo . . . il primo sole è mio . . ."

Your coffee goes cold, untouched until the song, the moment, are over—and, in all its multifaceted magnificence, your Italian meal as well.

— Nancy Coons

THE PASSIONATE EYE: ITALIAN ART THROUGH THE AGES

ITALIAN ART FLOWS as naturally as its wine, its sunshine, and its amore, and it has been springing from the Italian spirit for nearly as long. Perhaps nowhere in the world has such a vital creative impulse flourished so bountifully within the noble sweep of the classical tradition. Perhaps no other country's cultural life has been so inextricably interwoven with its history.

And yet, Italy lives comfortably in the midst of all her accumulated treasures. She accepts them casually and affectionately, as she does her children and her flowers. True, some of her precious store has been gathered into world-famous museums, but Italians know best and love most intimately the art that surrounds their daily activity. They go to church among thousand-year-old mosaics, buy their groceries in a shop open since the time of Columbus, picnic on the steps of a temple that was old when Christ was born, and attend the opera in the same theaters where Rossini and Verdi saw their works premiered. Italy wears the raiment of her heritage with a light and touching grace. She must: it is the very fabric of her life. For travelers from other countries, however, Italian art remains unique, extraordinary, worthy of worship. Here we offer a short history, focusing on Italy's greatest artistic achievement, the Renaissance—often called the nursery of Western art. The discoveries of 14th- and 15th-century Italian artists making it possible to render a realistic image of a person or an object determined the course of Western art right up until the late 19th century. Following the essay is a glossary of art and architectural terms that will prove useful in understanding the artistic treasures of Italy.

Art in the Middle Ages

The eastern half of the Roman Empire, based in Constantinople (Byzantium) was powerful long after the fall of Rome in AD 476: Italy remained influenced—and at times ruled—by the Byzantines. The artistic revolution began when artists started to rebel against the Byzantine ethic, which dictated that art be exclusively Christian and that its aim be to arouse a sensation of mystical awe and reverence in the onlooker. This ethic forbade frivolous pagan portraits, bacchanalian orgy scenes, or delicate landscapes with maidens gathering flowers, as painted and sculpted by the Romans. Instead, biblical stories were depicted in richly colored mosaics—rows of figures against a gold background. (You can see some of the finest examples of this art at Ravenna, once the Western capital of the Empire, on the Adriatic coast.) Even altarpieces, painted on wood, followed the same model—stiff figures surrounded by gold, with no attempt made at an illusion of reality.

In the 13th century, the era of St. Francis and of a new humanitarian approach to Christianity, artists in Tuscany began to portray real people in real settings. Cimabue was the first to feel his way in this direction, but it was Giotto who broke decisively with the Byzantine style. Even if his sense of perspective is nowhere near correct and his figures still had typically Byzantine slanting eyes, he painted palpably solid people who, presumably, experienced real emotions.

By the end of the 14th century, the International Gothic Style (which had arrived in Italy from France) had made further progress toward realism, but more with depictions of plants, animals, and clothes than with the human figure. And, as you can see from Gentile da Fabriano's *Adoration of the Magi,* housed in the Galleria degli Uffizi in Florence, it was mainly a decorative art, still very much like a Byzantine mosaic.

Italian architecture during the Middle Ages followed a number of different trends. In the south, the solid Norman Romanesque style was dominant; towns such as Siena and Pisa in central Italy had their own Romanesque style, more graceful than its northern European counterparts. Like northern Romanesque, it was dominated by simple geometric forms, but buildings were covered with decorative toylike patterns done in multicolored marble. In northern Italy, building was in a more solemn red brick.

In Tuscany, the region around Florence, the 13th century was a time of great political and economic growth, and there was a desire to celebrate the new wealth and power in the region's buildings. This is why such civic centers as the Palazzo Vecchio in Florence are so big and fortresslike. Florence's cathedral, the Duomo, was built on a colossal scale mainly in order to outdo the Pisans and the Sienese, Florence's rivals. All these Tuscan cathedrals are in the Italian version of Gothic, a style that originated in France and found its expression there in tall, soaring, light-and-airy verticality, intended to elevate the soul. The spiritual aspect of Gothic never really caught on in Italy, where the top priority for a church (as representative of a city) was to be grander and more imposing than the neighboring cities' churches.

Art in the Renaissance

The Renaissance, or "rebirth," did not evolve simply from a set of newfound artistic skills; the movement represented a revolution in attitudes whereby each individual was thought to play a specific role in the divine scheme of things. By fulfilling this role, it was believed the individual gained a new dignity. It was no coincidence that this revolution took place in Florence, which in the 15th century was an influential, wealthy, highly evolved city-state. Artists here had the leisure, prestige, and self-confidence to develop their talent and produce works that would reflect this new dignity and strength as well as their own prowess.

The sculptor Donatello, for example, wanted to astound, rather than please, the spectator with his defiant warts-and-all likenesses and their intense, heroic gazes. In painting, Masaccio's figures have a similarly assured air.

Art had changed gears in the early Renaissance: the Classical Age was now the model for a noble, moving, and realistic art. Artists studied ancient Roman ruins for what they could learn about proportion and balance. They evolved the new science of perspective and took it to its limits with sometimes bizarre results, as in Uccello's dizzily receding *Deluge* (in Florence's church Santa Maria Novella) or his carousel-like *Battle of San Romano* (in the Uffizi in Florence). One of the most frequently used perspective techniques was that of fore-shortening, or making an object seem smaller and more contracted, to create the illusion of distance. From this technique emerged the *sotto in su* effect—literally, "from below upwards," meaning that the action in the picture takes place above you, with figures, buildings, and landscapes correspondingly foreshortened. It's a clever visual trick that must have delighted visitors who walked into, for example, Mantegna's Camera degli Sposi in Mantua and saw what appeared to be people curiously looking down at them through a gap in the ceiling.

The concept of the universal man was epitomized by the artist who was at home with an array of disciplines, including the science of perspective, Greek, Latin, anatomy, sculpture, poetry, architecture, philosophy—even engineering, as in the case of Leonardo da Vinci, the universal man par excellence. Not surprisingly, there was a change in attitude toward artists: whereas previously they had been considered merely anonymous workmen trained to carry out commissions, now they were seen as giant personalities, immensely skillful and with highly individual styles.

The new skills and realistic effects of Florentine painting rapidly found a sympathetic response among Venetian painters. Gentile Bellini and Antonio Carpaccio, just two of the many whose work fills the Accademia, took to covering their canvases with crowd scenes, buildings, canals, processions, dogs, ships, parrots, and chimneys. These were generally narrative paintings, telling the story of a saint's life or simply depicting everyday scenes.

It was the emphasis on color, though, that made Venetian art Venetian, and it was the 15th-century masters of color, preeminently Giovanni Bellini and Giorgione, who began to use it no longer as decoration but as a means to create a particular atmosphere. How different the effect of Giorgione's *Tempest* (in the Accademia) would be with a sunny blue sky instead of the ominous grays and dark greens that fill the background! For the first time, the atmosphere not the figures became the central focus of painting.

In architecture the Gothic excesses of the 13th century were toned down in the 14th, while the 15th ushered in a completely new approach. The humanist ideal was expressed through classical Roman design.

In Florence, Brunelleschi used Roman columns for the basilica of San Lorenzo; Roman-style rustication (massive exterior blocks) for the Pitti Palace; and Roman round arches—as opposed to pointed Gothic ones—for his Ospedale degli Innocenti (Foundling Hospital), which is generally considered the first truly classical building of the Renaissance. Leon Battista Alberti's treatise on ideal proportion was even more influential as a manifesto of the Renaissance movement. Suddenly, architects had become erudite scholars and architecture far more earnest.

High Renaissance and Mannerism

Florence in the late 15th century and Rome in the early 16th (following its sacking in 1527) underwent a traumatic political and religious upheaval that naturally came to be reflected in art. Classical proportion and realism no longer seemed enough. The heroic style suddenly looked hollow and outdated. Tuscan artists such as Pontormo and Rosso Fiorentino found expression for their unease in discordant colors, elongated forms, tortured looks in staring eyes. Giambologna carved his *Hercules and the Centaur* (in Florence's Museo del Bargello) at the most agonizing moment of their battle, when Hercules bends the Centaur's back to the point where it is about to snap. This is Mannerism, a style in which optimism and self-confidence are gone. What remains is a self-conscious, stylized show of virtuosity, the effect of which is neither to please (like Gothic) nor to impress (like Renaissance art), but to disquiet. Even Bronzino's portraits are cold, unsmiling, and far removed from the relaxed mood of the Renaissance portrait. By the 1530s an artistic exodus from Florence had taken place; Michelangelo had left for Rome, and Florence's golden age was over.

Venice, meanwhile, was following its own path. Titian's painting was a more virtuoso version of Bellini's and Giorgione's poetic style, but Titian later shifted the emphasis back to figures, rather than atmosphere, as the central focus of his paintings. Titian's younger contemporaries in Venice—Veronese, Tintoretto, and Bassano—wanted to make names for themselves. They started working on huge canvases—which gave them more freedom of movement—playing all sorts of visual games: juggling with viewpoints and perspective and using dazzlingly bright colors. This visual trickery suggests a natural parallel with the self-conscious artifice of Florentine painting of the same period, but the exuberance of these Venetian painters, and the increasingly emotional quality of their work remained significantly more vital than the arid and ever more sterile works of central Italy toward the end of the 16th century.

Mannerism found a fairly precise equivalent in architecture. In Florence the rebellious younger generation (Michelangelo, Ammanati, Vasari) used the same architectural vocabulary as the Renaissance architects, but distorted it deliberately and bizarrely in a way that would have made Alberti's hair stand on end. Michelangelo's staircase at the Biblioteca Laurenziana in Florence, for example, spills down like a gush of stone water, filling almost the entire floor space of the vestibule. Likewise, the inside walls are treated as if they were facades, though with columns and niches disproportionately large for the size of the room.

Andrea del Palladio, whose theories and elegant palaces were to be immensely influential on architecture elsewhere in Europe and as far north as England, was one of the greatest architects of the period.

The 17th and 18th Centuries

In the second half of the 16th century, Italy was caught up in the Counter-Reformation. This movement was a reaction against the Protestant Reformation of the Christian church that was sweeping through Europe. The Counter-Reformation enlisted art as a weapon, an instrument for the diffusion of the Catholic faith. Artists were discouraged from expressing themselves as freely as they had been before and from creating anything that was not of a religious nature. But within this religious framework they were able to evolve a style that appealed to the senses.

The Baroque—an emotional and heroic style that lasted through most of the 17th century—was propaganda art, designed to overwhelm the masses through its visual illusion, dramatic lighting, strong colors, and violent movement. There was an element of seduction in this propaganda: the repressive religiosity of the Counter-Reformation went hand in hand with a barely disguised eroticism. The best-known example of this ambiguity is Bernini's sculpture of the *Ecstasy of Santa Teresa* in Rome, in which the saint sinks back in what could be a swoon of either pain or pleasure, while a smiling angel stands over her holding an arrow. Both the painting and architecture of this period make extensive use of sensuous curves.

The cradle of the Baroque was Rome, where Pietro da Cortona and Bernini channeled their genius into spectacular theatrical frescoes, sculptures, palaces, and churches. Rome had become the artistic center of Italy. Florence was politically and artistically dead by this time, and Venice was producing only hack imitations of Titian's and Tintoretto's paintings.

In the 18th century, Venice came back into its own and Rome was practically finished as an artistic center. Venetian artists adopted the soft, overripe version of Baroque—known as Rococo—that had originated in France. Free from the spiritual ideals that motivated the Baroque style, Rococo celebrated sensuousness (and sensuality) for its own sake. Although Venice was nearing the last stages of its political decline, there was still immense wealth in the city, mostly in the hands of families who wished to make the world know about it—and what better way than through vast, dazzling Rococo canvases, reassuringly stylized and removed from reality? The revival began with Sebastiano Ricci and was expertly elaborated on by Tiepolo. But it could never have taken place had there not been a return to the city's great artistic traditions. Late-16th-century color technique and expertise were drawn on and fused with what had been learned from the Baroque to create the breathtaking, magical, decadent world of the Venetian Rococo.

This was the final flowering of Venetian painting. The death of Francesco Guardi in 1793, compounded by the fall of the Republic of Venice in 1797, marked the effective end of the city's artistic life. Neoclassicism found no champion here, except for the sculptor Canova, who, in any case, did his finest work after he left Venice.

Today, the great tradition of Italian art is widely diffused, perhaps diluted, but it is certainly too early to write its obituary. That has been done periodically over the past 20 centuries, inevitably to the chagrin of the mistaken commentator. In the midst of the burgeoning vitality, which charms and occasionally maddens the visitor, the arts are not long to be neglected. Italians live the tradition too deeply.

— Sheila Brownlee

BOOKS AND VIDEOS

Books

The Italians, by Luigi Barzini, is a comprehensive, lively analysis of the Italian national character, still worthy reading although published in 1964 (Atheneum). More recent musings on Italian life include *Italian Days,* by Barbara Grizzuti Harrison (Ticknor & Fields), and *That Fine Italian Hand,* by Paul Hofmann (Henry Holt), for many years *New York Times* bureau chief in Rome. Matthew Spender's *Within Tuscany* (Viking) and Tim Parks's *Italian Neighbors* (Grove) are accounts of life in rural Tuscany and Verona by British expatriates.

Classics of the travel essay genre include James Morris's *World of Venice* (Harcourt Brace Jovanovich), Mary McCarthy's *Venice Observed* and *The Stones of Florence* (both HBJ also), Lawrence Durrell's *Sicilian Carousel* (out of print), Elizabeth Bowen's *A Time in Rome* (Penguin), and James Lees-Milne's *Roman Mornings* and *Venetian Mornings* (New Amsterdam). To some observers, the most beautiful book about the most beautiful city in the world is Richard de Combray's *Venice, Frail Barrier* (Doubleday). Historic musings about Italy are offered in Henry James's perceptive *Italian Hours* (offered in many editions, including *Traveling in Italy with Henry James: Essays,* William Morrow), Edith Wharton's *Italian Backgrounds* and *Italian Villas and their Gardens* (Ecco Press), and Axel Munthe's *Story of San Michele* (Carroll and Graf) about his celebrated villa on Capri.

For historical background, Edward Gibbon's *Decline and Fall of the Roman Empire* is available in three volumes (Modern Library). Consult Giorgio Vasari's *Lives of the Artists* and *The Autobiography of Benvenuto Cellini,* and Machiavelli's *The Prince* (all available in Penguin Classics) for eyewitness accounts of the 16th century. Otherwise, *The Civilization of the Renaissance in Italy,* by 19th-century Swiss historian Jacob Burckhardt (Modern Library), offers a classic foundation. Christopher Hibbert's *House of Medici* (Quill/William Morrow) details the family's rise and fall.

A comprehensive introduction to Italian art is Frederick Hartt's *History of Italian Renaissance Art* (Abrams). For aficionados of Rome's artistic treasures, Georgina Masson's *Companion Guide to Rome* (Penguin) is a must. Eloquent writing as well as important scholarship is found in the works of such celebrated art historians as Richard Krautheimer, John Pope-Hennessy, John Shearman, Irving Lavin, Charles de Tolnay, and André Chastel. Palladio's architecture is beautifully distilled in James Ackerman's *Palladio* (Penguin).

For lively historical fiction, pick up Irving Stone's *Agony and the Ecstasy* (New American Library) based on the life of Michelangelo. Susan Sontag's *Volcano Lover* (Farrar Straus Giroux), set in 18th-century Naples, is about Sir William Hamilton, his wife Emma, and Lord Nelson. *The Leopard,* by Giuseppe di Lampedusa (Pantheon), is a compelling portrait of Sicily during the political upheavals of the 1860s. Historical fiction set in World War II includes *History: A Novel,* by Elsa Morante (Vintage Aventura), about the fate of inhabitants of wartime Rome, and *Bread and Wine* by Ignazio Silone (Signet Classics), about Italian peasants under the control of the Fascists. Anne Cornelison's nonfiction *Women of the Shadows* portrays the life of peasant women in early–World War I southern Italy (Vintage). More recently, mysteries set in Italy have found great popularity, including the Urbino Macintyre series of Edward Sklepowich and the Lovejoy series of Jonathan Gash. Florence is the setting for two of Magdalen Nabb's entertaining thrillers: *Death in Autumn* and *Death of a Dutchman.*

To catch glimpses of the Tuscan landscape, pick up Harold Acton's *Great Houses of Tuscany: The Tuscan Villas* (Viking) or Carey More's *Views from a Tuscan Vineyard* (Pavillion). For a recent look at Umbrian life, try Lisa St. Aubin de Terán's *A Valley in Italy: The Many Seasons of a Villa in Umbria* (HarperCollins). The glories of historic Italian gardens are caught in the ravishing photographs of three recent volumes: Judith Chatfield's *Gardens of the Italian Lakes* (Rizzoli), Ethne Clark's

Gardens of Tuscany (Weidenfeld & Nicolson), and Nicolas Saphiena's *Gardens of Naples* (Scala Books). Waverley Root's *Food of Italy* (Vintage), published in 1977, is not a cookbook but an unsurpassed region-by-region exploration of the subject. Marcella Hazan's *Essentials of Classic Italian Cooking* (Knopf)—with modern sensibilities and low-fat diets in mind—is an update of her earlier cookbooks. It goes well with *Italian Wine* (Knopf), by her husband, Victor Hazan, or with *Vino,* by Burton Anderson (Little Brown). *Made in Italy,* a shopper's guide by Annie Brody and Patricia Schultz (Workman) is unrevised but still valuable for its knowledge of Italian products and producers.

Magazines

A magazine for Italophiles, *Italy Italy,* published in Italy in English, is available in the United States (Italian American Multimedia Corporation: ✉ 138 Wooster St., New York, NY 10012, ☎ 212/674–4132, FAX 212/674–4933; $30 for six issues). Italian travel magazines, such as *Bell'Italia, Dove,* and *Gulliver,* often give pointers to new, exotic, and overlooked destinations.

Videos

The delightful *Roman Holiday* (1953), in which a young princess plays hooky from her royal entourage to go "slumming" with Gregory Peck, won Audrey Hepburn an Oscar. In *Summertime* (1955), a visiting American (Katharine Hepburn) falls in love with Venice and a handsome Venetian shopkeeper (Rossano Brazzi). Federico Fellini's *La Dolce Vita* (1961), with Marcello Mastroianni discovering the decadence of high society in Rome, gave its name to an era. *Fellini's Roma* (1972) is the director's paean to the city; *Amarcord* (1974), his paean to the small Adriatic town of his childhood. Merchant/Ivory's *Room with a View* (1986), a period piece based on the E. M. Forster novel of the same name, is good cinema with good views of Florence.

ITALIAN VOCABULARY

	English	Italian	Pronunciation
Basics			
	Yes/no	Sí/No	see/no
	Please	Per favore	pear fa-**vo**-ray
	Yes, please	Sí grazie	see **grah**-tsee-ay
	Thank you	Grazie	**grah**-tsee-ay
	You're welcome	Prego	**pray**-go
	Excuse me, sorry	Scusi	**skoo**-zee
	Sorry!	Mi dispiace!	mee dis-spee-**ah**-chay
	Good morning/ afternoon	Buon giorno	bwohn **jor**-no
	Good evening	Buona sera	**bwoh**-na **say**-ra
	Good bye	Arrivederci	a-ree-vah-**dare**-chee
	Mr. (Sir)	Signore	see-**nyo**-ray
	Mrs. (Ma'am)	Signora	see-**nyo**-ra
	Miss	Signorina	see-nyo-**ree**-na
	Pleased to meet you	Piacere	pee-ah-**chair**-ray
	How are you?	Come sta?	**ko**-may **stah**
	Very well, thanks	Bene, grazie	**ben**-ay **grah**-tsee-ay
	And you?	E lei?	ay **lay**-ee
	Hello (phone)	Pronto?	**proan**-to

Numbers

	English	Italian	Pronunciation
	one	uno	**oo**-no
	two	due	**doo**-ay
	three	tre	tray
	four	quattro	**kwah**-tro
	five	cinque	**cheen**-kway
	six	sei	say
	seven	sette	**set**-ay
	eight	otto	**oh**-to
	nine	nove	**no**-vay
	ten	dieci	dee-**eh**-chee
	eleven	undici	**oon**-dee-chee
	twelve	dodici	**doe**-dee-chee
	thirteen	tredici	**tray**-dee-chee
	fourteen	quattordici	kwa-**tore**-dee-chee
	fifteen	quindici	**kwin**-dee-chee
	sixteen	sedici	**say**-dee-chee
	seventeen	diciassette	dee-cha-**set**-ay
	eighteen	diciotto	dee-**cho**-to
	nineteen	diciannove	dee-cha-**no**-vay
	twenty	venti	**vain**-tee
	twenty-one	ventuno	vain-**too**-no
	twenty-two	ventidue	vayn-tee-**doo**-ay
	thirty	trenta	**train**-ta

forty	quaranta	kwa-**rahn**-ta
fifty	cinquanta	cheen-**kwahn**-ta
sixty	sessanta	seh-**sahn**-ta
seventy	settanta	seh-**tahn**-ta
eighty	ottanta	o-**tahn**-ta
ninety	novanta	no-**vahn**-ta
one hundred	cento	**chen**-to
ten thousand	diecimila	dee-eh-chee-**mee**-la
one hundred thousand	centomila	chen-to-**mee**-la

Useful Phrases

Do you speak English?	Parla inglese?	**par**-la een-**glay**-zay
I don't speak Italian	Non parlo italiano	non **par**-lo ee-tal-**yah**-no
I don't understand	Non capisco	non ka-**peess**-ko
Can you please repeat?	Può ripetere?	pwo ree-**pet**-ay-ray
Slowly!	Lentamente!	**len**-ta-men-tay
I don't know	Non lo so	noan lo **so**
I'm American/ British	Sono americano(a)	**so**-no a-may-ree-**kah**-no(a)
	Sono inglese	**so**-no een-**glay**-zay
What's your name?	Come si chiama?	**ko**-may see kee-**ah**-ma
My name is . . .	Mi chiamo . . .	mee kee-**ah**-mo
What time is it?	Che ore sono?	kay **o**-ray **so**-no
How?	Come?	**ko**-may
When?	Quando?	**kwan**-doe
Yesterday/today/ tomorrow	Ieri/oggi/domani	**yer**-ee/**o**-jee/ do-**mah**-nee
This morning/ afternoon	Stamattina/Oggi pomeriggio	sta-ma-**tee**-na/**o**-jee po-mer-**ee**-jo
Tonight	Stasera	sta-**ser**-a
What?	Che cosa?	kay **ko**-za
What is it?	Che cos'è?	kay ko-**zay**
Why?	Perché?	pear-**kay**
Who?	Chi?	kee
Where is . . .	Dov'è . . .	doe-**veh**
the bus stop?	la fermata dell'autobus?	la fer-**mah**-ta del ow-toe-**booss**
the train station?	la stazione?	la sta-tsee-**oh**-nay
the subway station?	la metropolitana?	la may-tro-po-lee-**tah**-na
the terminal?	il terminal?	eel ter-mee-**nahl**
the post office?	l'ufficio postale?	loo-**fee**-cho po-**stah**-lay
the bank?	la banca?	la **bahn**-ka
the . . . hotel?	l'hotel . . .?	lo-**tel**
the store?	il negozio?	ell nay-**go**-tsee-o
the cashier?	la cassa?	la **kah**-sa
the . . . museum?	il museo . . .?	eel moo-**zay**-o

the hospital?	l'ospedale?	lo-spay-**dah**-lay
the first aid station?	il pronto soccorso?	eel **pron**-to so-**kor**-so
the elevator?	l'ascensore?	la-shen-**so**-ray
a telephone?	un telefono?	oon tay-**lay**-fo-no
Where are the restrooms?	Dov'è il bagno?	doe-**vay** eel **bahn**-yo
Here/there	Qui/là	kwee/la
Left/right	A sinistra/a destra	a see-**neess**-tra/ a **des**-tra
Straight ahead	Avanti dritto	a-**vahn**-tee **dree**-to
Is it near/far?	È vicino/lontano?	ay vee-**chee**-no/ lon-**tah**-no
I'd like . . .	Vorrei . . .	vo-**ray**
a room	una camera	**oo**-na **kah**-may-ra
the key	la chiave	la kee-**ah**-vay
a newspaper	un giornale	oon jor-**nah**-lay
a stamp	un francobollo	oon frahn-ko-**bo**-lo
I'd like to buy . . .	Vorrei comprare . . .	vo-**ray** kom-**prah**-ray
a cigar	un sigaro	oon see-**gah**-ro
cigarettes	delle sigarette	day-lay see-ga-**ret**-ay
some matches	dei fiammiferi	day-ee fee-ah-**mee**-fer-ee
some soap	una saponetta	**oo**-na sa-po-**net**-a
a city plan	una pianta della città	**oo**-na **pyahn**-ta day-la chee-**tah**
a road map of . . .	una carta stradale di . . .	**oo**-na **cart**-a stra-**dah**-lay dee
a country map	una carta geografica	**oo**-na **cart**-a jay-o-**grah**-fee-ka
a magazine	una rivista	**oo**-na ree-**veess**-ta
envelopes	delle buste	**day**-lay **booss**-tay
writing paper	della carta da lettere	**day**-la **cart**-a da **let**-air-ay
a postcard	una cartolina	**oo**-na car-toe-**lee**-na
a guidebook	una guida turistica	**oo**-na **gwee**-da too-**reess**-tee-ka
How much is it?	Quanto costa?	**kwahn**-toe **coast**-a
It's expensive/ cheap	È caro/economico	ay **car**-o/ay-ko-no-mee-ko
A little/a lot	Poco/tanto	**po**-ko/**tahn**-to
More/less	Più/meno	pee-**oo**/**may**-no
Enough/too (much)	Abbastanza/troppo	a-bas-**tahn**-sa/**tro**-po
I am sick	Sto male	sto **mah**-lay
Please call a doctor	Chiami un dottore	kee-**ah**-mee oon doe-**toe**-ray
Help!	Aiuto!	a-**yoo**-toe
Stop!	Alt!	ahlt
Fire!	Al fuoco!	ahl **fwo**-ko
Caution/Look out!	Attenzione!	a-ten-**syon**-ay

Dining Out

A bottle of . . .	Una bottiglia di . . .	**oo**-na bo-**tee**-lee-ah dee
A cup of . . .	Una tazza di . . .	**oo**-na **tah**-tsa dee
A glass of . . .	Un bicchiere di . . .	oon bee-key-**air**-ay dee
Bill/check	Il conto	eel **cone**-toe
Bread	Il pane	eel **pah**-nay
Breakfast	La prima colazione	la **pree**-ma ko-la-**tsee**-oh-nay
Cocktail/aperitif	L'aperitivo	la-pay-ree-**tee**-vo
Dinner	La cena	la **chen**-a
Fixed-price menu	Menù a prezzo fisso	may-**noo** a **pret**-so **fee**-so
Fork	La forchetta	la for-**ket**-a
I am diabetic	Ho il diabete	o eel dee-a-**bay**-tay
I am vegetarian	Sono vegetariano/a	**so**-no vay-jay-ta-ree-**ah**-no/a
I'd like . . .	Vorrei . . .	vo-**ray**
I'd like to order	Vorrei ordinare	vo-**ray** or-dee-**nah**-ray
Is service included?	Il servizio è incluso?	eel ser-**vee**-tzee-o ay een-**kloo**-zo
It's good/bad	È buono/cattivo	ay **bwo**-no/ka-tee-vo
It's hot/cold	È caldo/freddo	ay **kahl**-doe/**fred**-o
Knife	Il coltello	eel kol-**tel**-o
Lunch	Il pranzo	eel **prahnt**-so
Menu	Il menù	eel may-**noo**
Napkin	Il tovagliolo	eel toe-va-lee-**oh**-lo
Please give me . . .	Mi dia . . .	mee **dee**-a
Salt	Il sale	eel **sah**-lay
Spoon	Il cucchiaio	eel koo-kee-**ah**-yo
Sugar	Lo zucchero	lo **tsoo**-ker-o
Waiter/Waitress	Cameriere/ cameriera	ka-mare-**yer**-ay/ ka-mare-**yer**-a
Wine list	La lista dei vini	la **lee**-sta **day**-ee **vee**-nee

MENU GUIDE

English	Italian
Set menu	Menù a prezzo fisso
Dish of the day	Piatto del giorno
Specialty of the house	Specialità della casa
Local specialties	Specialità locali
In season	Di stagione
Cover charge/Service charge	Coperto/Servizio
Tasting menu	Menù degustazione
Tourist menu	Menù turistico
First course	Primo piatto
Second course	Piatto secondo

Breakfast

Butter	Burro
Croissant	Cornetto
Eggs	Uova
Honey	Miele
Jam/Marmalade	Marmellata
Roll	Panino
Toast	Pane tostato

Starters

Assorted cold cuts	Affettati misti
Assorted seafood	Antipasto di pesce
Assorted appetizers	Antipasto misto
Toasted rounds of bread, fried or toasted in oil	Crostini/Crostoni
Diced-potato and vegetable salad with mayonnaise	Insalata russa
Eggplant parmigiana	Melanzane alla parmigiana
Fried mozzarella sandwich	Mozzarella in carrozza
Ham and melon	Prosciutto e melone
Cooked sausages and cured meats	Salumi cotti
Filled pastry shells	Vol-au-vents

Soups

"Angel hair," thin noodle soup	Capelli d'angelo
Cream of . . .	Crema di . . .
Pasta-and-bean soup	Pasta e fagioli
Egg-drop and Parmesan cheese soup	Stracciatella

Pasta, Rice, and Pizza

Filled pasta	Agnolotti/ravioli/tortellini
Potato dumplings	Gnocchi
Semolina dumplings	Gnocchi alla romana
Pasta	Pasta
with four cheeses	*ai quattro formaggi*
with basil/cheese/pine nuts/ garlic sauce	*al pesto*
with tomato-based meat sauce	*al ragù*
with tomato sauce	*al sugo/al pomodoro*
with butter	*in bianco/al burro*

with egg, Parmesan cheese, and pepper	*alla carbonara*
green (spinach-based) pasta	*verde*
Rice	Riso
Rice dish	Risotto
with mushrooms	*ai funghi*
with saffron	*alla milanese*
Noodles	Tagliatelle
Pizza	Pizza
Pizza with seafood, cheese, artichokes, and ham in four different sections	Pizza quattro stagioni
Pizza with tomato, basil, and mozzarella	Pizza margherita
Pizza with tomatoes, oil, garlic, and oregano	Pizza marinara

Fish and Seafood

Anchovies	Acciughe
Bass	Persico
Carp	Carpa
Clams	Vongole
Cod	Merluzzo
Crab	Granchio
Eel	Anguilla
Lobster	Aragosta
Mackerel	Sgombro
Mullet	Triglia
Mussels	Cozze
Octopus	Polpo
Oysters	Ostriche
Pike	Luccio
Prawns	Gamberoni
Salmon	Salmone
Shrimp	Scampi
Shrimps	Gamberetti
Sole	Sogliola
Squid	Calamari
Swordfish	Pescespada
Trout	Trota
Tuna	Tonno

Methods of Preparation

Baked	Al forno
Cold, with vinegar sauce	In carpione
Fish stew	Zuppa di pesce
Fried	Fritto
Grilled (usually charcoal)	Alla griglia
Seafood salad	In insalata
Smoked	Affumicato
Stuffed	Ripieno

Meat

Boar	Cinghiale
Brain	Cervella

Braised meat with wine	Brasato
Chop	Costoletta
Duck	Anatra
Lamb	Agnello
Baby lamb	Abbacchio
Liver	Fegato
Pheasant	Fagiano
Pork roast	Arista
Rabbit	Coniglio
Steak	Bistecca
Sliced raw steak with sauce	Carpaccio
Mixed boiled meat	Bollito misto

Methods of Preparation

Battered with eggs and bread crumbs and fried	. . . alla milanese
Grilled	. . . ai ferri
Grilled (usually charcoal)	. . . alla griglia
Raw, with lemon egg sauce	. . . alla tartara
Roasted	. . . arrosto
Very rare	. . . al sangue
Well done	. . . ben cotta
With ham and cheese	. . . alla valdostana
With parmesan cheese and tomatoes	. . . alla parmigiana

Vegetables

Artichokes	Carciofi
Asparagus	Asparagi
Beans	Fagioli
Brussels sprouts	Cavolini di Bruxelles
Cabbage	Cavolo
Carrots	Carote
Cauliflower	Cavolfiore
Cucumber	Cetriolo
Eggplants	Melanzane
Green beans	Fagiolini
Leeks	Porri
Lentils	Lenticchie
Lettuce	Lattuga
Mushrooms	Funghi
Onions	Cipolle
Peas	Piselli
Peppers	Peperoni
Potatoes	Patate
Roasted potatoes	*Patate arroste*
Boiled potatoes	*Patate bollite*
Fried potatoes	*Patate fritte*
Small, roasted potatoes	*Patatine novelle*
Mashed potatoes	*Purè di patate*
Radishes	Rapanelli
Salad	Insalata
vegetable	*mista*
green	*verde*

Spinach	Spinaci
Tomatoes	Pomodori
Zucchini	Zucchini

Sauces, Herbs, and Spices

Basil	Basilico
Bay leaf	Lauro
Chervil	Cerfoglio
Dill	Aneto
Garlic	Aglio
Hot dip with anchovies (for vegetables)	Bagna cauda
Marjoram	Maggiorana
Mayonnaise	Maionese
Mustard	Mostarda/senape
Oil	Olio
Parsley-based sauce	Salsa verde
Pepper	Pepe
Rosemary	Rosmarino
Tartar sauce	Salsa tartara
Vinegar	Aceto
White sauce	Besciamella

Cheeses

Fresh:	Caprino fresco
	Mascarpone
	Mozzarella
	Ricotta
Mild:	Caciotta
	Caprino
	Fontina
	Grana
	Provola
	Provolone dolce
	Robiola
	Scamorza
Sharp:	Asiago
	Gorgonzola
	Groviera
	Pecorino
	Provolone piccante
	Taleggio
	Toma

Fruits and Nuts

Almonds	Mandorle
Apple	Mela
Apricot	Albicocca
Banana	Banana
Blackberries	More
Black currant	Ribes nero
Blueberries	Mirtilli
Cherries	Ciliege
Chestnuts	Castagne

Coconut	Noce di cocco
Dates	Datteri
Figs	Fichi
Green grapes	Uva bianca
Black grapes	Uva nera
Grapefruit	Pompelmo
Hazelnuts	Nocciole
Lemon	Limone
Melon	Melone
Nectarine	Nocepesca
Orange	Arancia
Pear	Pera
Peach	Pesca
Pineapple	Ananas
Plum	Prugna/Susina
Prune	Prugna secca
Raisins	Uva passa
Raspberries	Lamponi
Red currant	Ribes
Strawberries	Fragole
Tangerine	Mandarino
Walnuts	Noci
Watermelon	Anguria/Cocomero
Dried fruit	Frutta secca
Fresh fruit	Frutta fresca
Fruit salad	Macedonia di frutta

Desserts

Custard filled pastry, with candied fruit	Cannoli
Ricotta filled pastry shells with sugar glaze	Cannoli alla siciliana
Ice cream with candied fruit	Cassata
Ricotta filled cake with sugar glaze	Cassata siciliana
Chocolate	Cioccolato
Cup of ice cream	Coppa gelato
Caramel custard	Crème caramel
Pie	Crostata
Fruit pie	Crostata di frutta
Ice cream	Gelato
Flaked pastry	Millefoglie
Chestnuts and whipped-cream cake	Montebianco
Whipped cream	Panna montata
Pastries	Paste
Sherbet	Sorbetto
Chocolate coated ice cream	Tartufo
Fruit tart	Torta di frutta
Apple tart	Torta di mele
Ice-cream cake	Torta gelata
Vanilla	Vaniglia
Egg-based cream with sugar and Marsala wine	Zabaione
Ice-cream filled cake	Zuccotto

Alcoholic Drinks

On the rocks	Con ghiaccio
Straight	Liscio
With soda	Con seltz
Beer	Birra
light/dark	*chiara/scura*
Bitter cordial	Amaro
Brandy	Cognac
Cordial	Liquore
Aniseed cordial	Sambuca
Martini	Cocktail Martini
Port	Porto
Vermouth	Vermut/Martini
Wine	Vino
blush	*rosé*
dry	*secco*
full-bodied	*corposo*
light	*leggero*
red	*rosso*
sparkling	*spumante*
sweet	*dolce*
very dry	*brut*
white	*bianco*
Light wine	Vinello
Bottle	Bottiglia
Carafe	Caraffa
Flask	Fiasco

Nonalcoholic Drinks

Mineral water	Acqua minerale
carbonated	*gassata*
still	*non gassata*
Tap water	Acqua naturale
Tonic water	Acqua tonica
Coffee with steamed milk	Cappuccino
Espresso	Caffè espresso
with milk	*macchiato*
decaffeinated	*decaffeinato*
lighter espresso	*lungo*
with cordial	*corretto*
Fruit juice	Succo di frutta
Hot chocolate	Cioccolata calda
Lemonade	Limonata
Milk	Latte
Orangeade	Aranciata
Tea	Tè
with milk/lemon	*col latte/col limone*
iced	*freddo*

INDEX

NOTES

NOTES

NOTES

Fodor's Travel Publications

Available at bookstores everywhere. For descriptions of all our titles, a key to Fodor's guidebook series, and on-line ordering, visit http://www.fodors.com/books/

Gold Guides

U.S.

Alaska

Arizona

Boston

California

Cape Cod, Martha's Vineyard, Nantucket

The Carolinas & Georgia

Chicago

Colorado

Florida

Hawai'i

Las Vegas, Reno, Tahoe

Los Angeles

Maine, Vermont, New Hampshire

Maui & Lāna'i

Miami & the Keys

New England

New Orleans

New York City

Oregon

Pacific North Coast

Philadelphia & the Pennsylvania Dutch Country

The Rockies

San Diego

San Francisco

Santa Fe, Taos, Albuquerque

Seattle & Vancouver

The South

U.S. & British Virgin Islands

USA

Virginia & Maryland

Washington, D.C.

Foreign

Australia

Austria

The Bahamas

Belize & Guatemala

Bermuda

Canada

Cancún, Cozumel, Yucatán Peninsula

Caribbean

China

Costa Rica

Cuba

The Czech Republic & Slovakia

Denmark

Eastern & Central Europe

Europe

Florence, Tuscany & Umbria

France

Germany

Great Britain

Greece

Hong Kong

India

Ireland

Israel

Italy

Japan

London

Madrid & Barcelona

Mexico

Montréal & Québec City

Moscow, St. Petersburg, Kiev

The Netherlands, Belgium & Luxembourg

New Zealand

Norway

Nova Scotia, New Brunswick, Prince Edward Island

Paris

Portugal

Provence & the Riviera

Scandinavia

Scotland

Singapore

South Africa

South America

Southeast Asia

Spain

Sweden

Switzerland

Thailand

Toronto

Turkey

Vienna & the Danube Valley

Vietnam

Special-Interest Guides

Adventures to Imagine

Alaska Ports of Call

Ballpark Vacations

The Best Cruises

Caribbean Ports of Call

The Complete Guide to America's National Parks

Europe Ports of Call

Family Adventures

Fodor's Gay Guide to the USA

Fodor's How to Pack

Great American Learning Vacations

Great American Sports & Adventure Vacations

Great American Vacations

Great American Vacations for Travelers with Disabilities

Halliday's New Orleans Food Explorer

Healthy Escapes

Kodak Guide to Shooting Great Travel Pictures

National Parks and Seashores of the East

National Parks of the West

Nights to Imagine

Orlando Like a Pro

Rock & Roll Traveler Great Britain and Ireland

Rock & Roll Traveler USA

Sunday in San Francisco

Walt Disney World for Adults

Weekends in New York

Wendy Perrin's Secrets Every Smart Traveler Should Know

Worlds to Imagine

Fodor's Special Series

Fodor's Best Bed & Breakfasts
America
California
The Mid-Atlantic
New England
The Pacific Northwest
The South
The Southwest
The Upper Great Lakes

Compass American Guides
Alaska
Arizona
Boston
Chicago
Coastal California
Colorado
Florida
Hawai'i
Hollywood
Idaho
Las Vegas
Maine
Manhattan
Minnesota
Montana
New Mexico
New Orleans
Oregon
Pacific Northwest
San Francisco
Santa Fe
South Carolina
South Dakota
Southwest
Texas
Underwater Wonders of the National Parks
Utah
Virginia
Washington
Wine Country
Wisconsin
Wyoming

Citypacks
Amsterdam
Atlanta
Berlin
Boston
Chicago
Florence
Hong Kong
London
Los Angeles
Miami
Montréal
New York City
Paris

Prague
Rome
San Francisco
Sydney
Tokyo
Toronto
Venice
Washington, D.C.

Exploring Guides
Australia
Boston & New England
Britain
California
Canada
Caribbean
China
Costa Rica
Cuba
Egypt
Florence & Tuscany
Florida
France
Germany
Greek Islands
Hawai'i
India
Ireland
Israel
Italy
Japan
London
Mexico
Moscow & St. Petersburg
New York City
Paris
Portugal
Prague
Provence
Rome
San Francisco
Scotland
Singapore & Malaysia
South Africa
Spain
Thailand
Turkey
Venice
Vietnam

Flashmaps
Boston
New York
San Francisco
Washington, D.C.

Fodor's Cityguides
Boston
New York
San Francisco

Fodor's Gay Guides
Amsterdam
Los Angeles & Southern California
New York City
Pacific Northwest
San Francisco and the Bay Area
South Florida
USA

Karen Brown Guides
Austria
California
England B&Bs
England, Wales & Scotland
France B&Bs
France Inns
Germany
Ireland
Italy B&Bs
Italy Inns
Portugal
Spain
Switzerland

Pocket Guides
Acapulco
Aruba
Atlanta
Barbados
Beijing
Berlin
Budapest
Dublin
Honolulu
Jamaica
London
Mexico City
New York City
Paris
Prague
Puerto Rico
Rome
San Francisco
Savannah & Charleston
Shanghai
Sydney
Washington, D.C.

Languages for Travelers (Cassette & Phrasebook)
French
German
Italian
Spanish

Mobil Travel Guides
America's Best Hotels & Restaurants
Arizona

California and the West
Florida
Great Lakes
Major Cities
Mid-Atlantic
Northeast
Northwest and Great Plains
Southeast
Southern California
Southwest and South Central

Rivages Guides
Bed and Breakfasts of Character and Charm in France
Hotels and Country Inns of Character and Charm in France
Hotels and Country Inns of Character and Charm in Italy
Hotels and Country Inns of Character and Charm in Paris
Hotels and Country Inns of Character and Charm in Portugal
Hotels and Country Inns of Character and Charm in Spain
Wines & Vineyards of Character and Charm in France

Short Escapes
Britain
France
Near New York City
New England

Fodor's Sports
Golf Digest's Places to Play (USA)
Golf Digest's Places to Play in the Southeast
Golf Digest's Places to Play in the Southwest
Skiing USA
USA Today The Complete Four Sport Stadium Guide

Fodor's upCLOSE Guides
California
Europe
France
Great Britain
Ireland
Italy
London
Los Angeles
Mexico
New York City
Paris
San Francisco

Looking for a different kind of vacation?

Fodor's makes it easy with a full line of international guidebooks to suit a variety of interests—from adventure to romance to language help.

At bookstores everywhere.
www.fodors.com

You've read the book. Now book the trip.

For all the best deals on flights, hotels, rental cars, and vacation packages, book them online at www.previewtravel.com. Then click on our Destination Guides featuring content from Fodor's and more. You'll find hotels, restaurants, attractions, and things to do around the globe. There are even interactive maps, videos, and weather forecasts. You'll have everything you need to make your vacation exactly what you want it to be. All it takes is a trip online.

Travel on Your Terms™
www.previewtravel.com
aol keyword: previewtravel

preview travel℠

WHEREVER YOU TRAVEL, *H*ELP IS NEVER FAR AWAY.

From planning your trip to

providing travel assistance along

the way, American Express®

Travel Service Offices are

always there to help

you do more.

American Express Travel Service
Offices are found in central locations
throughout Italy.

Travel

http://www.americanexpress.com/travel